HANDBOOK OF
NARRATIVE
INQUIRY

Editor
D. JEAN CLANDININ
University of Alberta

HANDBOOK OF
NARRATIVE
INQUIRY
Mapping a Methodology

SAGE Publications
Thousand Oaks ▪ London ▪ New Delhi

Clandinin and Connelly (2000) quotes throughout the book are from *Narrative inquiry: Experience and story in qualitative research* by Clandinin, D. J. & Connelly, F. M., copyright © 2000. Reprinted with permission of John Wiley & Sons, Inc.

For information:

Sage Publications, Inc.
2455 Teller Road
Thousand Oaks, California 91320
E-mail: order@sagepub.com

Sage Publications Ltd.
1 Oliver's Yard
55 City Road
London EC1Y 1SP
United Kingdom

Sage Publications India Pvt. Ltd.
B-42, Panchsheel Enclave
Post Box 4109
New Delhi 110 017 India

Printed in the United States of America.

Library of Congress Cataloging-in-Publication Data

Handbook of narrative inquiry: mapping a methodology / edited by D. Jean Clandinin.
   p. cm.
Includes bibliographical references and index.
ISBN 1-4129-1562-7 or 978-1-4129-1562-5 (cloth)
   1. Narrative inquiry (Research method) 2. Social sciences—Research—Methodology.
I. Clandinin, D. Jean.
H61.295.H36 2007
001.4'2—dc22

                                              2006020694

This book is printed on acid-free paper.

06 07 08 09 10   10 9 8 7 6 5 4 3 2 1

Acquisitions Editor:	Lisa Cuevas Shaw
Editorial Assistant:	Karen Greene
Project Editor:	Tracy Alpern
Typesetter:	C&M Digitals (P) Ltd.
Proofreader:	Dorothy Hoffman
Indexer:	Molly Hall
Cover Designer:	Edgar Abarca

Contents

International Advisory Board Members   viii

Preface   ix

Acknowledgments   xviii

PART I: SITUATING NARRATIVE INQUIRY   **1**

1. Locating Narrative Inquiry Historically:
   Thematics in the Turn to Narrative   3

   Stefinee Pinnegar and J. Gary Daynes

2. Mapping a Landscape of Narrative Inquiry:
   Borderland Spaces and Tensions   35
   D. Jean Clandinin and Jerry Rosiek

PART II: STARTING WITH TELLING STORIES   **77**

3. Narrative Inquiry in Archival Work   81
   Barbara Morgan-Fleming, Sandra Riegle, and Wesley Fryer

4. The Unsayable, Lacanian Psychoanalysis, and
   the Art of Narrative Interviewing   99
   Annie G. Rogers

5. Autobiographical Understanding and Narrative Inquiry   120
   Mark Freeman

6. Talking to Learn: The Critical Role of
   Conversation in Narrative Inquiry   146
   Sandra Hollingsworth and Mary Dybdahl

7. Charting the Life Story's Path:
   Narrative Identity Across the Life Span   177
   Jenna Baddeley and Jefferson A. Singer

8. The Language of Arts in a Narrative Inquiry Landscape   203
   Dilma Maria de Mello

9. The Life Story Interview as a Bridge in Narrative Inquiry   224
   Robert Atkinson

PART III: STARTING WITH LIVING STORIES   247

10. Relational Reverberations: Shaping and
    Reshaping Narrative Inquiries in the
    Midst of Storied Lives and Contexts   251
    Cheryl J. Craig and Janice Huber

11. Composing a Visual Narrative Inquiry   280
    Hedy Bach

12. My Story Is My Living Educational Theory   308
    Jean McNiff

13. From Wilda to Disney: Living Stories in
    Family and Organization Research   330
    David M. Boje

PART IV: NARRATIVE INQUIRY IN THE PROFESSIONS   355

14. Studying Teachers' Lives and Experience:
    Narrative Inquiry Into K–12 Teaching   357
    Freema Elbaz-Luwisch

15. Narrative Inquiry in and About Organizations   383
    Barbara Czarniawska

16. Acted Narratives: From Storytelling to Emergent Dramas   405
    Cheryl F. Mattingly

17. Narrative Inquiry in the Psychotherapy Professions:
    A Critical Review   426
    Catherine Kohler Riessman and Jane Speedy

PART V: COMPLEXITIES IN NARRATIVE INQUIRY   457

18. Understanding Young Children's Personal Narratives:
    What I Have Learned From Young Children's Sharing Time
    Narratives in a Taiwanese Kindergarten Classroom   461
    Min-Ling Tsai

19. Exploring Cross-Cultural Boundaries   489
    Molly Andrews

20. Mo'ōlelo: On Culturally Relevant Story Making
    From an Indigenous Perspective   512
    Maenette K. P. Benham

**PART VI: NARRATING PERSISTING ISSUES IN
NARRATIVE INQUIRY**   **535**

21. The Ethical Attitude in Narrative Research:
    Principles and Practicalities   537
    Ruthellen Josselson

22. In-Forming Re-Presentations   567
    Margot Ely

PART VII: FUTURE POSSIBILITIES   **599**

23. Narrative Inquiry: What Possible Future
    Influence on Policy or Practice?   600
    Nona Lyons

24. Looking Ahead: Conversations With Elliot Mishler,
    Don Polkinghorne, and Amia Lieblich   632
    D. Jean Clandinin and M. Shaun Murphy

Author Index   651

Subject Index   665

About the Editor   685

About the Contributors   686

International Advisory Board Members

Maria Antonieta Celani, Pontificia Universidade Catolica de São Paulo, Brazil

Barbara Czarniawska, Goteborg University

Jane Elliott, Institute of Education, University of London

Mark Freeman, College of the Holy Cross

Ruthellen Josselson, Towson State University

Geert Kelchtermans, University of Leuven, Leuven, Belgium

Amia Lieblich, Hebrew University, Israel

Elliot Mishler, Harvard University Medical School

Donald Polkinghorne, University of Southern California

Michael Samuel, Deputy Dean of the Faculty of KwaZulu-Natal, South Africa

Working Editorial Group

Dilma de Mello, Federal University of Uberlândia/CAPES-Brazil

Janice Huber, St. Francis Xavier University, Canada

Barbara Morgan-Fleming, Texas Tech

Stefinee Pinnegar, Brigham Young University

Guming Zhao, University of Alberta

Preface

Looking back over the more than 2 years of editing the *Handbook of Narrative Inquiry*, I find it hard to recollect those feelings of surprise and uncertainty I had when Lisa Cuevas Shaw from Sage Publications first approached me about undertaking the task. I realized, in the moment of her asking, that her request was a timely one for the field of narrative inquiry. While composing a handbook was not something I had considered, I knew there was a veritable explosion of narrative inquiry across disciplines, in professional schools, and around the world. I also knew there was no one resource that those new to the field or those trying to stay connected to the wide range of work that was ongoing under the heading of narrative inquiry could turn to. Lisa's suggestion that Sage publish such a handbook would be a much-needed first for the field.

In that moment, however, I knew that the task would not be an easy one. So much work is being undertaken under the broad heading of narrative research and narrative inquiry that conceptualizing such a handbook would be difficult. Lisa convinced me that my position in a professional school in a Canadian university would allow for rich multidisciplinary and international perspectives. Looking back, while I tried for that, I am not sure I was able to include all the richness of voices from the range of contexts across boundaries, both of disciplines and of nations.

Defining a Handbook

Lisa shared Sage's guidelines for a handbook. Overall, in their terms, a handbook is designed to be a review, account, or audit of a discipline or a subdiscipline. A handbook is designed to answer the following questions: What is the state of the art? Where is the discipline going? What are the key debates/issues that pertain to the discipline? Academics, researchers, practitioners, and advanced postgraduate students are the intended audience. Handbooks have a pedagogic function in that they should address how a discipline is understood and, therefore, taught. The key dynamic of a handbook is a retrospective and prospective overview of the discipline—a rich, critical assessment of past and present theory that also looks to the future. A handbook should emphasize theoretical diversity within the discipline by examining the integrity and intellectual coherence of the discipline while also looking at resonances with and between key components and other disciplines. A handbook should be a map of the discipline: What defines the present, what signs and indications are there for new directions? Overall, a handbook should recognize the changing social and political context of the discipline, consolidate and develop theoretical frameworks, discuss the core substantive issues, and offer a critical review of issues that are both central and not yet central to the discipline. The key defining principles for each contribution should then be breadth, depth, and multiplicity, illuminating the themes and also identifying, critically, some of the problems inherent in these themes.

Composing an Editorial Team

As I thought about Lisa's offer and considered these guidelines, I realized I would need help. This was not something I could do alone. I would need to create response and discussion groups to ensure that the handbook would be a useful resource.

I first put together a small working editorial group composed of both people with diverse interests in narrative and those who brought diverse backgrounds to their work in narrative inquiry. I valued their opinions and knew we would have provocative and substantive conversations. I also liked them and enjoyed talking with them. I invited Stefinee Pinnegar of Brigham Young University to join. Stefinee has a rich background in English, a fascination with narrative, and a complex understanding of narrative structure and representation from her language education background. I also invited Barbara Morgan-Fleming from Texas Tech University, with her background in folklore and performance as well as a strong interest in using archival materials in narrative inquiry, to join. Janice Huber from St. Francis Xavier University was the third member. Janice is steeped in issues of cultural diversity and curriculum theorizing, and she sees herself as a narrative inquirer into the lives of children, teachers, and parents. The four of us, with my interests in narrative inquiry in studies of curriculum and teacher education, made a strong team, but I realized that we also needed non–North American voices. I invited two doctoral students to join us. Dilma de Mello, a doctoral student from Brazil and a visitor to the Centre for Research for Teacher Education and Development, where I work, is a linguist, a native speaker of Portuguese, an English-as-a-foreign-language teacher, and someone with a passionate interest in the arts and narrative inquiry. Dilma and Guming Zhao, a doctoral student from China and also a teacher of English as a foreign language with an interest in narrative inquiries into the experiences of immigrant children and families, joined the small working editorial team. With this small but diverse group, I hoped we could imagine a handbook that would serve the overall purposes that Sage envisioned and become an important conceptual resource in the burgeoning field of narrative inquiry.

I also carefully considered possible members for an international advisory board. Working with the small editorial group, we suggested names of people who seemed not only to come from diverse groups across the international community but also to be key resources in the narrative inquiry literature. Everyone who was invited accepted the invitation, many of them noting the importance and timeliness of such a handbook. Members of the international advisory board, both as a group and through individual responses, offered ongoing advice and help with major conceptual problems, with identifying appropriate authors and consulting editors, and with trivial technical problems. They were alongside throughout the process. With these two groups, one close and intimate and one more dispersed and somewhat more distant from the day-to-day development of the handbook in place, I began work on an overall framework.

Structuring the Handbook

The seven-part structure of the handbook evolved through discussions, reading, and reflecting on the field. Part I, two chapters, is designed to provide something of a historical overview and a delineation of the tensions, boundary conditions, and borderlands among narrative inquiry and other research methodologies. These two chapters set a frame for the handbook, although some other chapter authors eventually wrote short pieces in their chapters that outlined their particular takes on the history of the field and the tensions they identify from their contextual standpoints.

The next two parts, Parts II and III, were organized around a simple distinction that Michael Connelly and I developed for a chapter in the *Handbook of Complementary Methods* (Connelly & Clandinin, 2006). The distinction was between narrative methodologies that begin with the telling of stories—that is, in the told stories of participants—and those that begin with living alongside participants— that is, in the living out of stories. In some, perhaps most, narrative inquiry methodologies, participants are asked to tell their stories. For example, Kramp (2004) writes that narrative inquiry is both a process (in which the narrator tells) and a product (the story told). In most narrative inquiry focused on "telling," where the interest is in stories told or in interpretations and meanings generated, the working methods are interviews, conversations, autobiographical writings, and so on. In other narrative inquiries, the inquiry begins with the "living" of stories. In these studies, the beginning point is in living in relation with participants. The research ground for such studies is the ongoing life of participants. Of course, there are also tellings involved in such studies, but living is the main focus. The difference between *telling* and *living* is often a difference between life as lived in the past (telling) and life as it unfolds (living). The chapters in Part II were commissioned to focus on research methods that began with the telling of stories, while the chapters in Part III focused on methods where the initial starting point was in action or in the lives being lived.

In choosing chapter topics for Parts II and III, we did a kind of reflexive "back and forthing" as we thought about the topics as well as about influential researchers known for each particular method. The working editorial group read widely about each particular method, and we talked often, eventually selecting potential authors based on our reading and talking. We selected seven chapter topics for Part II and four chapter topics for Part III.

We realized there was a great range of narrative inquiry in many professions. Part IV, focused on narrative inquiry in the professions, is composed of four chapters from the professional fields where the most narrative research is going on—that is, teaching, organizational studies, therapy in health fields, and social work, counseling, and psychotherapy. While narrative inquiry is also found in nursing, medicine, and law, we did not commission separate chapters in those fields, although several chapters make reference to narrative inquiry in those fields.

As these sections were designed, we decided to ask authors not only to review literature in the broad area of their topic, paying attention to breadth, depth, and multiplicity to illuminate themes, but also to describe and use their own research as an exemplar in which to ground the discussion of issues and concerns. In this way, we hoped the chapters would offer readers more developed examples of the ways a particular method was being engaged.

We designed Part V as a separate section to highlight narrative inquiry in areas that we felt warranted special attention. Narrative inquiry in cross-cultural situations seems to generate a unique set of concerns, as does narrative inquiry with children. I wanted to attend closely to the particular issues in engaging in narrative inquiry with indigenous peoples. Because ethical issues and representational issues emerge again and again in narrative inquiry, we designed Part VI to draw attention to them as well as to highlight their importance as topics in narrative inquiry.

Finally, Part VII was designed to provide a forward-looking overview of narrative inquiry. By looking to policy and practice as well as by looking backward and forward, we hoped to offer something of a future-oriented map for narrative inquiry. By asking key scholars for their views, we hoped not only to define the present but also to highlight future directions. At this moment in time, narrative inquiry is alive with a rich explosion of ideas. However, this is also a time of retrenchment and backlash as policy makers try to exercise control over what counts as research and what research counts. In these final chapters, we hope to offer insights into the current debates as well as to offer openings for continuing narrative inquiry as a vibrant, scholarly area.

Working With the Authors

Once the design of the handbook was in place and invitations to potential authors proffered and accepted, the working editorial group asked each chapter author(s) to develop a chapter outline, which was read and responded to by the working editorial group. Authors then wrote chapter drafts, and we invited two consulting editors to work with each chapter draft. We asked authors and editorial board members to suggest names of potential consulting editors and made the decision to have the process be an open one where chapter authors would know the names of reviewers and reviewers would know the names of authors. We wanted the review process to be a respectful and helpful process in which reviewer comments would be taken seriously by authors. We were amazed by the intellectual, scholarly responses of the consulting editors. They all took particular care with the chapters. I read each chapter and all reviewer comments and asked authors to further develop their chapters.

By spring (2006), complete chapters were received from all authors, and again I read each chapter. Janice Huber, Stefinee Pinnegar, and Barbara Morgan-Fleming each took responsibility for reviewing final chapters and writing introductory pieces to handbook parts. We agreed to use a structure to read across the chapters in each part, and after some discussion, we framed the introduction around terms, tools, and tensions that resonated across the chapters. Lauren Starko worked with authors on technical and stylistic matters.

Deciding What Was in and What Was Out

One difficulty in designing this first *Handbook of Narrative Inquiry* was that it is the first one. I could not check back on earlier versions of handbooks in the field to see how the field was defined, where the boundaries were located, and what might serve as a useful structure. Trying to figure out what was in and what was out was a challenge. As we tried to delimit the boundaries for what we included in the handbook, we began with reading the work of those who stated they were using narrative inquiry or narrative research methodologies. If someone defined his or her work as using narrative research methodologies, we took that person seriously as offering something to the field and, possibly, to the handbook. We decided against including work that was seen as narrative therapy, although we do include narrative research on therapy, including narrative therapy. We also decided against inviting authors who named their methodology other names such as *ethnography, phenomenology,* or an inclusive name such as *interpretive inquiry.* Sometimes, we recognized a particular methodology as narrative inquiry, but if the researchers were claiming a different name for their work, we did not include them as potential chapter authors or include their work in the overall framework for the handbook.

Problems Not Foreseen

When the working editorial team and I began work on the handbook structure, contents, and authors, we assumed there was a commonly used and accepted distinction between the terms *narrative research* and *narrative inquiry.* We assumed that narrative research was a broad catchall term that included the range of work that Pinnegar and Daynes planned to review in their chapter on the history of narrative research. Narrative inquiry was a more specialized term that referred to the more relational forms of narrative inquiry. We were, however, surprised when we learned the terms are used almost interchangeably in the literature. Given that, we, too, began to use the terms interchangeably. While we do note the substantive and substantial differences in what counts as narrative inquiry or narrative research (see Chapters 1 and 2), the terms narrative research and narrative inquiry are not used to signify these differences.

Pressing Debates

Phenomenon Under Study

As noted in several chapters, most particularly Chapters 1 (Pinnegar & Daynes) and 2 (Clandinin & Rosiek) as well as Chapter 17 (Riessman & Speedy), many ways of conceptualizing narrative inquiry suggest that while all narrative inquirers agree that narrative inquiry is the study of experience, there are differences in what narrative inquirers see themselves as studying. Some, particularly those with a more post-structuralist set of assumptions, argue that narrative inquirers do not "study lived experience; rather, we examine lived textuality" (Denzin, 1995, p. 9). Elbaz-Luwisch summarized Denzin's position in the following way:

> We are already in the midst of language and narrative form; our lives and experiences in society have been written, formulated, theorized, analyzed, categorized, presented, and represented in the various media, print and electronic; they have been verbalized and represented visually to the point where we apparently can no longer have a "pure" experience that has not already been textualized for us. For Denzin, experience is a mystery, a "labyrinth, with no fixed origins, no firm center, structure, or set of recurring meanings." (2005, p. 35)

Elbaz-Luwisch argued, however, that "textuality can be seen as an important feature of experience rather than something set against it" (2005, p. 36), and in so doing, she created an opening to support the idea that experience can be studied as a storied, lived phenomenon as well as studied in the stories that one tells about the living.

What we see as we examine the literature on various forms of narrative research in the social sciences is a broad range of epistemological, ideological, and ontological understandings of the phenomenon under study. This theoretical debate about the phenomenon that narrative inquirers are studying is an important one. The debate highlights a distinction within narrative inquiry—that is, that we are studying either lived experience as a storied phenomenon or the stories people tell about their experiences, such as those who study only language texts would argue. This underscores the distinction between beginning with telling stories (Part II) and beginning with living stories (Part III). Reading the chapters and reconsidering the distinctions, it may be possible to reimagine experience as more complex and, in so doing, to compose a view of experience such as one Stone-Mediatore (2000) offers. She suggests an understanding of experience that "consists of tensions between experience and language, tensions that are endured subjectively as contradictions within experience—contradictions between ideologically constituted perceptions of the world and reactions to these images endured on multiple psychological and bodily levels" (p. 122). This creates a more complex view of experience with space for understanding the phenomenon that narrative inquirers study as both the living of storied experience and the stories one tells of their lived experience. Evidence of the complexity and differences in understandings about the phenomenon under study in narrative inquiry is woven throughout the handbook and partially accounts for the diversity of strands within narrative inquiry. However, it is not the intention of this handbook to point to one or the other as the preferable one but, rather, to encourage researchers to continue the debate and to continue to locate themselves as to their underlying epistemological and ontological assumptions.

Narrative Analysis/Narrative Interpretation

Other pressing debates occur around the place of analysis in narrative inquiry. At first, narrative analysis was going to be a separate chapter in the handbook. A chapter on narrative analysis could have, for example, picked up on Polkinghorne's (1995) distinction between narrative analysis and analysis of narrative. In one form of analysis, experiential data are collected and the research aim is to organize the data to create a narrative with a plot that unifies the data. The created story is a narrative explanation of the phenomenon being studied. In the second form of narrative analysis, data (stories) are collected from research participants or subjects and the narrative data is analyzed for common themes, metaphors, plotlines, and so on to identify general themes or concepts. Work such as that of Lieblich, Tuval-Mashiach, and Zilber (1998) in which they create a four-cell matrix to categorize four different kinds of narrative inquiries—whole content, whole form, categorical content, and categorical form—could have been discussed. In the handbook, there are chapters that reference narrative analysis to work such as Labov's (1982; see Hollingsworth & Dybdahl, Chapter 6; Riessman & Speedy, Chapter 17; Tsai, Chapter 18) and Gee's (2000; Tsai, Chapter 18) ways of approaching analysis in narrative inquiry. Hollingsworth and Dybdahl (Chapter 6) reference McCormack's (2004) process of storying stories, Craig and Huber (Chapter 10) reference Clandinin and Connelly's (2000) three-dimensional narrative inquiry space as an interpretive frame, and Mattingly (Chapter 16) draws on an analysis dependent on the notion of dramatic or narrative time.

In the end, as we considered the possibility of one chapter, we realized that there are multiple ways of engaging in narrative analysis and narrative interpretation and that it would be better to allow each chapter author to treat the question of analysis and interpretation within their specific field and with careful attention to context.

Intervention or Description

Another pressing debate in the field is whether narrative inquiry/narrative research is descriptive or interventionist; that is, does narrative inquiry set out to change the world as people engage in the processes of narrative inquiry with their participants, or is it a more descriptive kind of inquiry. Again we realized that narrative inquirers locate themselves differently in relation to this question. The handbook does lay out the possibilities here; again, however, it is important not to close the debate but to suggest that narrative inquirers locate themselves in relation to this debate. That some narrative inquirers see their work as involving questions of social justice, locating oneself in relation to this debate seems particularly important.

Ethical Complications in Narrative Inquiry

As shown throughout the handbook, narrative inquiry is a profoundly relational form of inquiry. Therefore, ethics plays a central role throughout and beyond the research process. As narrative inquirers, we and our participants are always in the midst of living and telling our stories. We are also situated in the midst of larger cultural, social, and institutional narratives. Because so many of the chapters make it clear that ethics permeates narrative inquiry from puzzle setting and question posing to living in the field to composing field texts and research texts as well as to the ways that research texts follow or haunt participants and researchers, attending to ethical matters is an ongoing and always present part of narrative inquiry. These questions of what it means to work relationally with participants in narrative inquiry takes on added importance as we consider the place of institutional research boards, as we think about the ways participants and researchers are situated in relation to each other in dominant cultural and institutional narratives, and as we think about the ways that engaging in narrative inquiries can shift the stories of both participants and researchers. Questions of ethics in narrative inquiry are beginning to be explored, and as many chapter authors make clear, we have much to continue to consider. The handbook chapters begin a conversation that will, we hope, be ongoing.

The Thorny Topics of Memory and Imagination

Memory and imagination are both central concepts in narrative inquiry work, and I planned a chapter to address these important topics. I invited Ted Sarbin and Jerry Ginsberg to write a chapter that would draw forward some of the important ideas Sarbin (2004) discussed in his chapter in the Daiute and Lightfoot book.
In that chapter, Ted linked imagination to

> stories read or told, that imaginings are instances of attenuated role-taking, that attenuated role-taking requires motoric actions that produce kinesthetic cues and other embodiments, and that embodiments become a part of the total context from which persons decide how to live their lives. (p. 17)

I hoped Ted and Jerry would have taken these ideas of imagination and emplotted narratives and worked to make links with memory, particularly embodied memory. Ted and Jerry were making good progress on their chapter when Ted fell ill in the summer of 2005. Unfortunately, the chapter was not completed, and Ted's death makes the handbook less rich in what would have been an important discussion of memory and imagination.

Bounded by the English Language

Narrative inquiry is published in languages other than English. However, the handbook draws on work that is published in English. Working with my colleagues whose work is published in languages other than English, I know there are rich sources of narrative inquiry work that we English speakers do not know. In the future, I hope we find ways to bring their voices to the discussion of narrative inquiry.

References

Clandinin, D. J., & Connelly, F. M. (2000). *Narrative inquiry: Experience and story in qualitative research.* San Francisco: Jossey-Bass.

Connelly, F. M., & Clandinin, D. J. (2006). Narrative inquiry. In J. Green, G. Camilli, & P. Elmore (Eds.), *Handbook of complementary methods in education research* (pp. 375–385). Mahwah, NJ: Lawrence Erlbaum.

Denzin, N. (1995). The experiential text and the limits of visual understanding. *Educational Theory, 45*(1), 7–18.

Elbaz-Luwisch, F. (2005). *Teachers' voices: Storytelling and possibility.* Greenwich, CT: Information Age.

Gee, J. P. (2000). *Discourse analysis: Theory and method.* New York: Routledge.

Kramp, M. K. (2004). Exploring life and experience through narrative inquiry. In K. de Marrais & S. D. Lapan (Eds.), *Foundations for research: Methods of inquiry in education and the social sciences* (pp. 103–122). Mahwah, NJ: Erlbaum.

Labov, W. (1982). Speech actions and reactions in personal narrative. In D. Tannen (Ed.), *Analyzing discourse: Text and talk* (pp. 219–247). Washington, DC: Georgetown University Press.

Lieblich, A., Tuval-Mashiach, R., & Zilber, T. (1998). *Narrative research: Reading, analysis and interpretation.* Thousand Oaks, CA: Sage.

McCormack, C. (2004). Storying stories: A narrative approach to in-depth interview conversations. *International Journal of Social Research Methodology, 7*(3), 219–236.

Polkinghorne, D. (1995). Narrative configuration in qualitative analysis. In A. J. H. Hatch & R. Wisniewski (Eds.), *Life history and narrative* (pp. 5–23). London: Falmer Press.

Sarbin, T. R. (2004). The role of imagination in narrative construction. In C. Daiute & C. Lightfoot (Eds.), *Narrative analysis. Studying the development of individuals in society* (pp. 5–20). Thousand Oaks, CA: Sage.

Stone-Mediatore, S. (2000). Chandra Mohanty and the revaluing of "experience." In U. Narayan & S. Harding (Eds.), *Decentering the center. Philosophy for a multicultural, post-colonial, and feminist world* (pp. 110–127). Bloomington: Indiana University Press.

Acknowledgments

E diting this handbook was not something I undertook alone. Over the more than 2-year period, many people came alongside and worked to make the handbook come alive. Many colleagues, some familiar and some I came to know through their published work, have been companions on the journey.

My most sincere thanks goes to the members of the working editorial group, Janice Huber, Stefinee Pinnegar, Barbara Morgan-Fleming, Dilma de Mello, and Guming Zhao. Thank you for your guidance, wisdom, and hard work throughout the process. Thank you for being there all along the way.

Thanks are also due to members of the international advisory board, with special thanks to Mark Freeman, Elliot Mishler, Amia Lieblich, and Ruthellen Josselson. Their questions helped me clarify my ideas, their suggestions were invaluable, and their wise advice was always appreciated. They always answered my frantic e-mails for help and advice. Thank you all. A special thanks also to Elliot Mishler and Amia Lieblich, who, along with Don Polkinghorne, agreed to engage in the conversations that form the basis for the final chapter in the handbook. Their thoughtful responses will continue to generate new dialogues.

I am fortunate to work in the wonderful Centre for Research for Teacher Education and Development at the University of Alberta, Canada, where each week, graduate students and faculty from around the campus and from other places gather at our table for what is known as Research Issues. This gathering place, and the conversations with so many over the years of this journey, has enriched the handbook. Several colleagues from the table, Joy Ruth Mickelson, Pam Steeves, and Shaun Murphy, did extra editorial work with the chapter authors, and for this, too, I am grateful.

This handbook would not have happened without the involvement of Lisa Cuevas Shaw at Sage. She nurtured the handbook and me throughout the process. Without her constant support, encouragement, and good ideas, this handbook may have remained just "a good idea." I also thank Karen Greene and Tracy Alpern at Sage for their help in the final production days.

I had a strong technical support group here, at the Centre for Research for Teacher Education and Development. Angela Gauthier, a former doctoral student, and Cherie Geering both worked to handle the many versions of chapters, reviewer comments, editorial letters, and so on. Without their support, I do believe there would have been chaos on many days. Lauren Starko came alongside as final manuscripts were sent in and helped authors with style and formatting. She, too, helped bring the handbook together.

The consulting editors who worked with each chapter were remarkable. They are acknowledged for their work with each chapter. They kept to strict timelines but gave detailed and helpful advice in their responses. Thank you all so much.

Finally, of course, I want to thank the chapter authors, who worked hard to compose compelling chapters that, I hope, will encourage the development of the field of narrative inquiry. Thank you for all that you have done that made this handbook possible.

—D. Jean Clandinin
University of Alberta

PART I

Situating Narrative Inquiry

In Part I there are two chapters. The first, by Stefinee Pinnegar and Gary Daynes, gives us a particular historical read of the movement to narrative inquiry, showing how, through a series of narrative turns, there are key moves toward narrative inquiry. The four turns are a change in the relationship between the researcher and the researched; a move from the use of number toward the use of words as data; a change from a focus on the general and universal toward the local and specific; and a widening in acceptance of alternative epistemologies or ways of knowing. The four turns offer readers a set of terms with which to read the field historically, to read current work being published, and to consider their own genealogy and development as a narrative inquirer. Pinnegar and Daynes highlight the tensions that ensue from the significant epistemological and ontological differences between the ways in which narrative researchers continue to undertake their work. The terms Pinnegar and Daynes offer will both help narrative researchers locate themselves in relation to the four turns and help readers of narrative research understand the different ways researchers position their work within the overall field. In their chapter, they outline a challenge to narrative inquirers that is echoed throughout the handbook: "To enter conversations with the rest of our communities to develop a method—a way of talking and asking and answering and making sense—that will allow narrative to flourish in this congenial moment for stories."

In Chapter 2, Jerry Rosiek and I offer a particular map of the field of narrative inquiry. While we realize that "any attempt to organize these divergent views into a summary representation inevitably risks short-changing one view in favor of the priorities of another," we highlight "real differences of opinion on the epistemological, ideological, and ontological commitments of narrative inquirers as well as real differences with those who do not identify as narrative inquirers." We argue that these differences "require careful attention and discussion if the field of narrative inquiry is to realize its potential for making a contribution to the study of human experience and lives." Our chapter offers one

> representation of the field of narrative inquiry that holds one aspect of narrative inquiry constant, and uses this as a point of reference from which to examine the internal and external boundaries of this area of scholarship. The map we construct, with its borders and borderlands, allows researchers to locate themselves on the landscape of narrative inquiry methodologies.

We take as the point of constancy "the observation that narrative inquirers study experience" but note

> there are many philosophical treatments of the word "experience," from Aristotle's dualistic metaphysics in which knowledge of particulars and universals were considered separately, to early empiricist atomistic conceptions of experience, Marxist conceptions of experience distorted by ideology, behaviorist notions of stimulus and response, and post-structuralist assertions that state our experience is the product of discursive practices.

However, the view of experience that serves as "the cornerstone" of our analysis has its roots in John Dewey's (1938) pragmatic philosophy. By doing this we "work toward clarifying differences and affinities narrative inquiry has with other areas of scholarship" with an intent

> to sharpen distinctions both between narrative inquiry and other scholarly traditions as well as to sharpen distinctions within the field of narrative inquiry. Through highlighting the tensions at the boundaries with other areas of scholarship, we bring into sharper relief the differences with other areas of scholarship.

—D. Jean Clandinin

CHAPTER 1

Locating Narrative Inquiry Historically

Thematics in the Turn to Narrative

Stefinee Pinnegar and J. Gary Daynes

In attempting to locate narrative inquiry historically, we begin by marking off the territory of this methodology. Ultimately this chapter is not a history of the emergence of narrative. Instead, we provide a description of how the academy opened up in a way that made space for narrative inquiry. Put another way, we are describing the creation of an environment in which narrative inquiry can flourish. Most of these changes did not come about because of pressure from narrative practitioners. Nor are they the result of competition between narrative and nonnarrative ways of inquiry, with narrative gaining the upper hand. To this day, most academic work is nonnarrative, and in many disciplines the most prominent theories, methods, and practitioners continue to do work that is based on quantitative data and positivist assumptions about cause, effect, and proof.

In this chapter, we begin by defining qualitative research and narrative inquiry. These definitions provide the reader with markers from which they can identify where they stand in relationship to narrative inquiry. Next we describe the ways in which situating oneself within a particular history of the move to narrative has been part of the structure of the presentation of narrative inquiry reports. From an analysis of examples of this phenomenon, we consider four turns researchers complete as they turn to narrative inquiry. Finally, we explicate the four turns: the attention to relationships among participants, the move to words as data, the focus on the particular, and the recognition of blurred genres of knowing.

Marking the Territory

In providing these definitions, we are marking the territory of narrative inquiry not at its boundaries (which was done by Clandinin & Connelly, 2000) but at its intersections. Narrative inquiry is not simply another in a cadre of qualitative research strategies. In this section, we provide not complex definitions of any of these traditions but instead highlight the relationships and distinctions that mark the territory of narrative inquiry. We do this by considering qualitative research and narrative inquiry.

Qualitative Research

The first marking is the distinction between qualitative and quantitative research. Denzin and Lincoln (1994) begin their first *Handbook of Qualitative Research* with the following definition:

> Qualitative research is multimethod in focus, involving an interpretive naturalistic approach to its subject matter . . . qualitative researchers study things in their natural settings attempting to make sense of, or interpret, phenomena in terms of the meanings people bring to them. Qualitative research involves the studied use of and collection of a variety of empirical materials . . . that describe routine and problematic moments and meaning in individuals' lives. (p. 2)

As this definition reveals, the distinction between the two research paradigms rests not on the decision to use numbers or not, since researchers from either of these paradigms might employ numbers. Instead, the assumptions underlying the research distinguish one from the other (although in terms of practice the boundary is porous, particularly in terms of specific methods). Quantitative research rests exclusively in positivistic and post-positivistic assumptions. In contrast, qualitative research forms around assumptions about interpretation and human action. Another difference is the purpose of the research. Qualitative researchers are interested not in prediction and control but in understanding.

Narrative Inquiry

Qualitative researchers often use words in their analysis, and they often collect or construct stories about those they are studying. But there are territorial markings that distinguish narrative researchers. These boundaries do not, necessarily, match up with a distinction between the two research paradigms.

What narrative researchers hold in common is the study of stories or narratives or descriptions of a series of events. These researchers usually embrace the assumption that the story is one if not the fundamental unit that accounts for human experience. But what counts as stories, the kinds of stories they choose to study, or the methods they use for study vary. Within the framework of narrative research, researchers use a number of research approaches, strategies, and methods (Lieblich, Mashiach-Tuval, & Zilber, 1998).

Some researchers use the metaphor of story to articulate learning from research generally. From this perspective, metanarrative, historiography, and critical analysis can be seen as potential methods. Some narrative researchers employ sociolinguistic analytic tools to analyze qualitative data collected as field notes or interviews and either piece together or develop a generic narrative of experience that generalizes as a "typical" narrative such as learning or everyday experience within a culture (Josselson, 1996; Polanyi, 1989). Others use conceptions from narrative such as *plotline, characterization, theme, role*, and other literary terms to analyze and make general sense of experience. Other researchers explore narrative as fundamental to cognition (Schank, 1990). Narrative researchers might also study the impact of particular narratives on experience. Again, these researchers may use surveys or measurement strategies to calculate and represent the impact of narratives (Green, Strange, & Brock, 2002). Other narrative researchers may code narratives, translate the codes to numbers, and use statistical analysis, or they may analyze the factors involved during a storytelling event as a predictor of some phenomenon of interest (Pasupathi, 2003).

Narrative researchers use narrative in some way in their research. Narrative inquiry embraces narrative as both the method and phenomena of study. Through the attention to methods for analyzing and understanding stories lived and told, it can be connected and placed under the label of qualitative research methodology. Narrative inquiry begins in experience as expressed in lived and told stories. The method and the inquiry always have experiential starting points that are informed by and intertwined with theoretical literature that informs either the methodology or an understanding of the experiences with which the inquirer began (Clandinin & Connelly, 2000). In essence, narrative inquiry involves the reconstruction of a person's experience in relationship both to the other and to a social milieu (Clandinin & Connelly, 2000).

Conceptions of the Historical Emergence of Narrative Inquiry

Through an exploration of the emergence of narrative inquiry, we found comprehensive outlines of this development existing already. However, within these histories we identified four themes that are clear indicators of movement toward narrative inquiry both in the research lives of individuals and in the disciplines. Thus, in this section we outline our exploration of the history, the identification of the four themes, and finally a careful consideration of each theme.

The original direction of this chapter was a historical charting of the emergence of narrative inquiry within and across the various disciplines of the human sciences. As we read this literature (Bruner, 1986; Clandinin & Connelly, 2000; Martin, 1986; Polkinghorne, 1988; Sarbin, 1986), it became apparent that there already existed several historic accounts. Polkinghorne (1988) provides a careful, scholarly, detailed analysis and theoretical defense of narrative knowing. Bruner (1986), using a broad-brush stroke, argues for two ways of knowing in the human sciences—narrative and traditional positivistic social science research (paradigmatic knowing)—and in doing so articulates the historical basis for the credibility of narrative knowing. Geertz (1983) provides a more metaphoric account of this same process. *Narrative Psychology* (Sarbin, 1986) provides a series of chapters that define the field, but in defining the field they outline the history behind narrative in psychology and a defense of the method's emergence and viability. Martin (1986), from the perspective of the literary critic, articulates how Barthes and others used social science strategies for understanding narrative in literature.

In the process of tracing the history of narrative theories in literary criticism, Martin brings the reader to see how the approaches of the literary critics, such as Joseph Campbell, Northrop Frye, Wayne Booth, Roland Barthes, and Mikhail Bahktin, came to be tools for narrative research. He also articulates the historical contribution of these literary critics to the development of the use of narrative in human science research.

In contrast with these other historical plotlines, Clandinin and Connelly's (2000) tracing of their development as narrative inquirers is more intimate and personal. Yet it is also a stronger theoretical account of how, in the moment of their own development as researchers, narrative inquiry emerged as the most compelling and appropriate way to study human interaction.

Emergence of Themes in Historical Accounts

When we then turned to examinations of research studies or projects (Clandinin, Davies, Hogan, & Kennard, 1993; Josselson, Lieblich, & McAdams, 2003; Witherell & Noddings, 1991), we began to notice that providing a historically based defense of narrative as the method or phenomenon for study was almost a convention for accounts of narrative research. Narrative researchers routinely and consistently situated themselves and their methods historically in the accounts they provided of their work.

What intrigued us, and gave direction for this chapter, were thematic commonalities in these accounts. The themes highlighted changes in the thinking and action of individual researchers and research movements within disciplines. They provided a way of tracing the process by which one becomes a narrative researcher and ultimately a narrative inquirer or just four definitional points in the stance that narrative inquirers embrace in their research. We realized these themes could be conceptualized as the individual and collective historical bases for the turn toward narrative inquiry, the bases on which a space for this kind of inquiry opened. These themes involved changes in the relationships of researchers and research participants, kinds of data collected for a study, the focus of the study, and kinds of knowing embraced by the researcher.

Four Themes in the Turn Toward Narrative Inquiry

As we read the literature that has emerged from various narrative research projects (Bruner, 1986; Clandinin & Connelly, 2000; McAdams, 1993; Polkinghorne, 1988) and the critiques of postitivism (Faulconer & Williams, 1990; Geertz, 1983; Thayer-Bacon, 2003), post-modernism and post-structuralism (Sarup, 1993), the accounts of research groups in various disciplines that have embraced narrative or asserted narrative as a way of knowing the world, we identified some common themes in the movement toward narrative inquiry. From our study, we came to realize that as an individual, discipline, or group of researchers moves toward a narrative inquiry approach to research, there are four turns in their thinking and action that occur. By *turn*, we mean a change in direction from one way of thinking or being toward another. We do not argue that these turns occur in a particular order; they evolve based on the experiences of a particular researcher in the process of designing, studying, and engaging in inquiries. We also do not assert that researchers either ought to or must make these turns if they are to be considered "researchers." We recognize that there are indeed multiple ways of knowing and studying the world and the interactions of people. However, we become narrative inquirers only when we recognize and embrace the interactive quality of the researcher-researched relationship, primarily use stories as data and analysis, and understand the way in which what we know is embedded in a particular context, and finally that narrative knowing is essential to our inquiry.

We use the term *turn* strategically because we want to emphasize the movement from one way of thinking to another and highlight the fact that such changes can occur rapidly or slowly, depending on the experience of the researchers and their experiences when doing research.

How fully the researcher embraces narrative inquiry is indicated by how far he or she turns in her or his thinking and action across what we call here the four turns toward narrative. The four include the following: (1) a change in the relationship between the person conducting the research and the person participating as the subject (the relationship between the researcher and the researched), (2) a move from the use of number toward the use of words as data, (3) a change from a focus on the general and universal toward the local and specific, and finally (4) a widening in acceptance of alternative epistemologies or ways of knowing. Those who most fully embrace narrative inquiry are those who, like Clandinin and Connelly (2000), simultaneously embrace narrative as a method for research and narrative as the phenomenon of study. For narrative inquirers both the stories and the humans are continuously visible in the study.

In the movement toward narrative inquiry, researchers, research communities, and research disciplines in particular forge their own idiosyncratic journey. In other words, while we have chosen to list these four turns in a particular order, we do not suggest that every researcher who becomes a narrative inquirer negotiates the turns in any particular order. Instead, we recognize that researchers, research groups, or disciplines of inquiry begin at different points. For example, narrative or story has long played a central role in anthropology and word data, and its analysis was always part of this discipline. However, part of anthropology's growth as a discipline involved marking a distinction between anthropological studies and travelogs, personal narratives, and memoirs. Thus, what can prompt a move toward narrative inquiry on the part of an anthropologist is not so much a turn from numbers as data but a turn toward a new understanding of the authority of the anthropologist and the relationship of the anthropologist and those they are studying (Pratt, 1986). A recognition that capturing the particular and local rather than insisting on the development and validity of a "grand narrative" of a culture is a worthy goal (Geertz, 1983). Thus, anthropologists who become narrative inquirers, like historians, may have begun from a position of embracing words rather than numbers as data.

Indeed, the turn to narrative occurs in ways that suggest the image of water that Foucault (1976) uses to discuss negotiations of power. Water flows move differently across different landscapes with different seasons, feeder streams, or impediments. In turning toward narrative inquiry, different researchers begin at different places. Some researchers take the turns slowly and more gently, just as some flows meander slowly, with deep turns that become almost switchbacks. The switchbacks may periodically erode through a loop. This straightens the water's path, and former meanders are abandoned, and new streambeds are cut. The path for others may be more constrained, and because of their socialization into research and the kinds of publications available, they may be less able to freely turn toward one or another research methodology. Indeed, some water flows are cemented in place, such as the Rio Grande at the U.S. border with Mexico. The path of the water is restricted and held in place, with others maintaining authority, power, and control. In such settings, the turns may appear in the currents and eddies or in pools created by barriers.

Having grown up in the dry desert Southwest, we have experienced flash floods where the roaring water coalesces and separate streams flow together forcefully, being stalled by dams that emerge from the flotsam their action creates. The stream may suddenly divide into new flows because of impediments in the path, abandoning old streambeds and destroying homes and buildings that no one thought were even in the way. For many, this is the path toward narrative inquiry. Concern with humans, experience, recognizing the power in understanding the particular, and broader conceptions of knowing coalesce in flashes of insight, and old ways of researching and strategies for research seem inadequate to the task of understanding humans and human interaction.

We know that water flows and creates the streambed we see at a particular moment in time based in a particular landscape because of the interaction of water, landscape, humans, animals, climate, and so on. In the same way, inquiry stance and identity as a researcher emerge in a particular place, with particular people, around particular questions, and based on desires to understand humans and human interaction in particular ways. What we present here are four of the common turns in the stream that direct the flow of inquiry into a narrative channel.

Because we are narrative inquirers, we have of course made these turns and embraced these ways of studying and understanding the phenomenon we care about. For us, of course, other ways of inquiry are less appealing and appropriate.

However, we do not assert that other ways are invalid or that those who employ them are less qualified as researchers.

In the rest of the chapter we begin by exploring the turns. We focus first on the change in the relationship between researcher and researched, and then we discuss the characteristics of the move from using numbers toward using words as data. Next, we consider the movement from a focus on the general and universal toward the local and particular. Finally, we explore the turn in acceptance of a wider range of ways of knowing and the blurring of epistemologies in research.

Narrative Turn 1: Relationship of Researcher and Researched

In the turn toward narrative inquiry, no change in direction is more important than the change in an understanding of the relationship of the researcher to the researched. In the move toward narrative inquiry, the turn is characterized as a movement away from a position of objectivity defined from the positivistic, realist perspective toward a research perspective focused on interpretation and the understanding of meaning. In turning, narrative inquirers recognize that the researcher and the researched in a particular study are in relationship with each other and that both parties will learn and change in the encounter.

An important movement in the social sciences occurred in the late 19th century. At that time Comte, Mill, Durkheim (Smith, 1983), and others convinced social scientists that they could use the methodology of the physical sciences to study human learning and interaction. An essential feature of this stance is the sense that things being studied are real and that they exist independently and are not brought into existence by the act of studying. In taking this step, social scientists would then be able to identify "facts" and use them to develop social laws that, like physical laws, would articulate invariant relationships among social objects. On the basis of such laws, social scientists could control causation in social relations and thus assert control over and make accurate predictions about the social world (Smith, 1983). Martin (1986), in his exploration of narrative theories and literary criticism, charts the development of the current narrative theories in literary study. In his discussion, he reminds us that just as the social sciences sought to embrace a rationalist approach to the study of human sciences, scholarly work in the humanities flowed into a similar approach in the use of theories of literary criticism.

Asserting the realist perspective in the social sciences allowed researchers to treat social facts as things. In this way, the objects of study in the social sciences (human relationships, interactions, dispositions, and culture) could be treated as if they were physical things. This would allow social scientists to "stand apart from their subjects and think of [them] as having an independent, object-like existence with no intrinsic meaning" (Smith, 1983, p. 7). From this perspective, research into the social world could be constituted as a neutral activity. Researchers could proceed with their work as though the person and phenomenon that were being researched could be bounded, that they were atemporal and static, and that findings from such a study are not context bound but are generalizable under certain conditions. Researchers base this stance on an assumption that they can be objective in doing research. In other words, they can wholly distance themselves from the researched. As human scientists, they can consider themselves bounded, static, and atemporal particularly in regard to their relationship with the researched. As a result, the observations they make are considered systematic, reliable, and unbiased.

By labeling the researcher or researched as *bounded*, we mean that the knowledge of the researcher and the knowledge of the researched are separate and distinct from each other and even when they interact the distance between them can be maintained and guaranteed. Most importantly, under objective conditions, they are almost completely knowable, or at the very least, the things under study (culture, humans, human interaction, human traits or dispositions) can be explained. As a result, true beliefs about the social world can become valid and sure knowledge. In other words, social "things" are knowable in a foundational sense, and researchers have a secure base from which, with surety, they can assert knowledge about that thing. Through careful, systematic, and structured observations guided by uniform instrumentation that has high reliability and validity, coupled with skilled manipulation of potentially intervening variables, randomization, and controlled treatment settings, researchers can insert sufficient distance between themselves and their subjects to make formal knowledge claims on the basis of the scientific method.

Another condition of the researcher-researched relationship is atemporality. This is a state whereby the findings of research are considered outside time, and time itself is a neutral and controllable entity. Even when the research projects involve a longitudinal, developmental study, the process of change being studied is treated as if it exists independent of time. Piagetian research (Gruber & Vonèche, 1977) is an example of this, whereby child development researchers, even when they are dissatisfied with the age range labels or quibble with conceptions of the study, still work from the developmental stages outlined and the time sequence proposed either in opposing or developing further support. From a position of atemporality, the phenomenon studied or the process studied can be asserted to exist even generations since those original findings. Such a stance assumes that time is real and static rather than constructed or influenced by culture or individual human interaction (Slife, 1993).

The participants and interactions studied are considered static when the scientist acts as though the thing under study can be held still or that the action entailed in observation will not influence what is being studied. Furthermore, researchers who take this stance proceed as if they can hold themselves at a particular point in their thinking about a phenomenon as they engage in systematic observation of it. Even if the phenomenon is expected to evolve or progress or change during the observation, researchers assume that they can control this process or distance themselves from it enough so that they can objectively observe what is being studied in such a way that they themselves as researchers will remain unchanged. They act as though even if their thinking about the thing studied changes it will not be affected by changes in the phenomenon brought about because of their observation or changes in their own feelings and emotions or fundamental understanding. During the research process, both the researcher and researched will be suspended in a static state, each uninfluenced by the other.

Within this perspective, researchers act on the premise that context can be controlled in ways that result in decontextualized research findings. As a result, others can then apply the findings to contexts and settings beyond the group being studied. In the case of anthropology, it allows researchers to treat findings about a culture as a monolithic capturing of the essence of the culture (Clifford, 1986; Geertz, 1983). Psychology provides another example. Research in learning sought basic learning principles that could be applied to any learning setting regardless of the age, the environment, or the dispositions of the learner. When such characteristics (age, environment, or disposition) might intervene, then the results of the research would provide clear directions about how to avoid or control for the potential interference from those variables. Indeed, one of the powers of this kind of research, and the controlled relationship between researcher and researched, is the ability to assert valid and reliable and, therefore, generalizable findings.

The move away from an acceptance of the researcher-researched relationship as an objective one toward a more relational view involves a reconceptualization of the status of the researched in the relationship. Researchers acknowledge that their subjects are not bound, static, atemporal, and decontextualized. However, researchers may continue to view themselves as capable of preserving the distance between themselves as researchers and the subjects they are researching. They continue to assume that in their interaction with the researched they can maintain a distance (particularly during the processes of analysis and interpretation of data) between themselves and their subjects.

Ironically, when researchers make the turn from an objective stance in the researcher-researched relationship, it is their view of the other rather than the self that changes. Researchers admit that the humans and human interaction they study exist in a context and that the context will influence the interactions and the humans involved. They recognize the researched is not atemporal but exists in time and that time is itself a socially constructed concept (Slife, 1993). Furthermore, they recognize that humans and human interactions are seldom, if ever, static. Researchers acknowledge that since context matters, human interaction and humans are embedded in context, and people, cultures, and events have histories that affect the present, findings from one setting cannot be effectively decontextualized. Researchers need to provide accurate descriptions of these characteristics of the research experience for without them it becomes impossible to understand and use findings from the project.

So while researchers have new respect for the human in the subjects they study, they continue to perceive themselves as capable of being objective. Researchers outlining their movement from a positivistic discourse to a discourse of self-study describe and characterize their stance in the role of the researcher in ways that articulate and catalog the position of narrative inquirers as they move away from an objective conception of the researcher-researched relationship (Guilfoyle, Hamilton, Pinnegar, & Placier, 2004):

> In this discourse, as researchers we continued to act in our role as researchers as if we were capable of remaining in some way intellectually and objectively separate from what we were studying—we did not remove the boundaries we had drawn around ourselves as researchers. We felt that in our role as researchers the self was unchangeable. (p. 1136)

Thus in this turn toward narrative, objectivity becomes a property of the researcher, almost a role the researcher puts on as he or she engages in the research process. The researcher puts energy into maintaining an objective stance and distancing himself or herself from the relationship with the researched; he or she uses strategies such as member checks, triangulation, and audit trails to assure accuracy, consistency, and trustworthiness (Lincoln & Guba, 1985; Miles & Huberman, 1984). What is important at this point in the turn toward narrative inquiry is that the researchers still maintain a belief that in the interpretive process they can relate to the research in such a way that they can provide "valid" and "generalizable" interpretations in their research projects.

In the late 1960s through the 1980s many changes occurred in research in the social sciences, resulting in researchers turning away from this objective conception of the relationship of the researcher and the researched. One of these changes grew out of the disenchantment of the social scientists with behaviorism. After the infusion of funding for social science research in the 1960s, researchers saw little of value in the results of the studies conducted. They lost faith that research in the human sciences, at least research based in current social science methodologies, would help solve human social problems even though increasing numbers of individual people looked to psychotherapists for help. Thus, the generalizable findings from social science research appeared unhelpful, while the local knowledge of particular social scientists investigating and responding to the individual problems of humans seemed increasingly more productive (Polkinghorne, 1988). Clandinin and Connelly (2000) provide a personal example of this disenchantment in articulating Clandinin's dissatisfaction with her thesis study and Connelly's dissatisfaction with an international group of educational researchers regarding their conception of assessment and curriculum.

Researchers studying human learning and interaction began to look beyond "behavior" alone to account for what they observed. For example, through speech-act theory studies, researchers began to treat speech as action (Hymes, 1955). As researchers moved to include human thinking in research on learning, healing, and other human interaction, they also began to recognize the value of the particular, the role of culture, and the value of the case. In studying human thinking, researchers had to rely on language as a vehicle for expressing cognition. As a result, researchers required new tools for collecting data and making sense of it. For example, graduate students in nursing were often engaged in collecting interview data with terminally ill patients. In this process, the patients or their family would confide in the researchers, telling personal, often intimate, stories about their experiences in relationship to the question prompts on the questionnaires being filled out. These nursing graduate students, who were tape recording the questionnaire process and taking notes of patient responses, were suddenly inundated with data that were not easily translatable into Likert scales. The word *data* raised questions about the constructs represented by the questionnaires and provided insights into human interactions and the healing process. The graduate students and their professors began seeking ways of making sense of the narratives they collected in addition to the quantitative instruments they were marking (Lauren Clark, personal communication, May 1986). Like Clandinin (Clandinin & Connelly, 2000) in her thesis work, researchers became interested in what their subjects were saying. Relationships developed.

Rychlak (1994) critiqued studies based in behaviorism. When he conducted new studies, they revealed that in behavioristic experiments much of the noise or variance of response emerged because subjects' behavior was not so much "shaped" by the process, but the subjects learned what response the researchers desired and willfully chose to act oppositionally. Those subjects who, according to the data, were not "shaped" by the treatment actually intentionally responded in the direction opposite to that shaped by the researcher. In other words, attention to the meaning of subjects' responses led to an understanding different from the one the researchers claimed. Bateson's (1984) response to the debate about the criticism of her mother's (Margaret Mead) fieldwork in Samoa was not a defense of Mead's work but an assertion of the ways in which different researchers, because of their personality, interaction skills, and access to particular community members, have a different experience in their fieldwork.

These kinds of experiences led and lead researchers to reconsider their relationship with the research subject. As researchers begin to collect verbal data, they seek to make sense of it (Josselson, 1996). If the words of participants represent the thinking, and in some cases stand as a proxy for behavior, then researchers need to engage in more responsive and interactive ways with the research participants. They also become more concerned with a different sets of issues—things such as the articulateness of subjects, the integrity or honesty of the accounts, and the role of tacit knowledge in a research subject's ability to reveal his or her thought or belief. Of course, this raises new issues about and discussion of validity in social science research. But just as importantly, in a turn toward narrative inquiry, new ways of collecting and analyzing data also raised issues about the appropriate relationship between the researcher and the researched. Pratt (1986) articulates the problematics in such relationships in her discussion of Shostak's study of the !Kung. In *Nisa: The Life and Words of a !Kung Woman*, Shostak, as a neophyte researcher, comes to explore and understand the !Kung through her interaction with Nisa, a native !Kung woman. Nisa meets Shostak the evening of her arrival to do work among the !Kung. Nisa seeks Shostak out because Nisa has been a participant in an earlier study of the !Kung and she is not only personally but economically curious about this new set of anthropologists. As a result, not only does Shostak name her study for Nisa, but she also acknowledges Nisa's growth and change in the study and the role Nisa plays in helping Shostak come to understand the life of !Kung women.

Part of this movement in the relationship of the researcher and the researched is represented by Bruner's (1986) assertion of two paradigms of knowing, one narrative and the other paradigmatic, and Geertz's (1983) insistence that research increasingly involved blurred genres. The emergence of post-modernism, post-structualism, neopositivism, and cultural studies called into question the authority of the researcher for knowing or asserting knowledge (Denzin & Lincoln, 1994). This is captured well in *Writing Culture* (Clifford & Marcus, 1986), where the various authors explore the impact of writing on the authority, interpretations, and findings of anthropologists. Denzin and Lincoln's (1994) discussion of Stoller's struggle with his work in representing his findings from his research among the Songhay of Niger is an example. In this instance, Stoller finally creates a memoir as his research account. In this memoir, Stoller, rather than the Songhay, becomes the central character as he presents an analysis of his own struggle to reconcile his worldview with the sorcery of the Songhay. As researchers begin to embrace those they research as humans rather than as objects of study and as they struggle to make sense of the narratives that such interactions produce, they begin to embrace other ideas about how to make data interpretable and how to provide interpretations of data that are coherent, that resonate with the data, and that are true to them.

Coles's (1989) *The Call of Stories* captures a researcher enmeshed in the process of moving away from a conception of the objective researcher toward a relational view of researcher-researched interaction. Not that *Call* is a research study, but contrast it with *Women of Crisis* (Coles, 1978), in which Coles continues to use a more objective research stance. We see the difference in stance as Coles begins to articulate the ways in which engagement with narratives, whether fiction, anecdotal evidence, or nonfiction reports, causes learning and growth. Bateson's (1990) *Composing a Life* presents a similar view in focusing on the lives of five women researchers. She raises conceptions such as "unfolding stories," "improvisations," and "rethinking achievement" and articulates how looking back across those lives and their research and professional activities, one sees the ways in which the women composed their lives. This is a stance considerably different from the one in which the researcher constructs theories and then designs studies that measure subjects, manipulate data, and validate constructs, thus instantiating the accuracy of the researcher's theoretical construction. This movement is further articulated and captured even move clearly in Clandinin and Connelly's (2000) descriptions of their work in research conducted at Bay School. They tell us that building relationships allowed them to support the development of the school, deepen their understanding of educating children in diverse settings, and carry out their research.

Thus, in this turn toward narrative inquiry, the researcher not only understands that there is a relationship between the humans involved in the inquiry but also who the researcher is and what is researched emerge in the interaction. In this view, the researched and the researcher are seen to exist in time and in a particular context. They bring with them a history and worldview. They are not static but dynamic, and growth and learning are part of the research process. Both researcher and researched will learn.

Many researchers who engage in narrative research move in this direction and may even recognize the accuracy of this account of the relationship of the researcher and the researched, but they may still covet being able to assert that they have a basis for turning their "true belief" into knowledge. While they value meaning and understanding as goals of research, they may still want to assert knowing and stand in a position of objectivity whereby what they come to "understand" is generalizable. This is the final aspect of this turn, when researchers recognize the implausibility of being able to truly distance themselves from what they come to know and understand and yet continue to act in integrity and demonstrate trustworthiness, virtuosity, and rigor (Bullough & Pinnegar, 2001) in their scholarship. For those who, no matter how much they value and embrace narrative knowing, continue to harbor remnants of the positivistic dream of control, prediction, objectivity, and generalizability, letting these glittering stars go is not easy. Some researchers may draw back from this turn. While they continue to work with narratives and interpret narratives, they simply value their own sense of objectivity whereby their interpretations can be termed objective and valid—they hold tight to the image of themselves as having foundational criteria that allow true beliefs to become formal knowledge (Fenstermacher, 1994).

What this section attempts to capture is the first turn that researchers make in becoming narrative inquirers. To use narrative as methodology and explore narrative as the phenomenon of interest, they must come to embrace a relational understanding of the roles and interactions of the researcher and the researched.

Narrative Turn 2: From Numbers to Words as Data

The next turn toward narrative inquiry is the turn from number to word data. In the historical development of narrative inquiry and the personal development of narrative inquirers, what is labeled here as the second turn toward narrative flows from and is intertwined with the other turns. The turns are discussed in the order presented because of the relationship of the turns to each other and to the philosophical development of narrative inquiry and inquirers—but in actual experience any of these turns can proceed to any other, and indeed we may pause in one turn as we begin another or we may take two or three or even four turns simultaneously.

The turn from numbers to words as data is not a general rejection of numbers but a recognition that in translating experience to numeric codes researchers lose the nuances of experience and relationship in a particular setting that are of interest to those examining human experience. An important positivistic assumption underlying the use of numbers relates to reliability. Quantitative researchers, who base their research in modernist and post-positivist views of the appropriate way of conducting studies of the social sciences, have concerns about reliability. They want to be able to assert that anyone experiencing a phenomenon would label it with a similar, hopefully identical, number or in the same way. Numbering a phenomenon and then correlating the consistency of ratings allows researchers to assert a level of reliability upon which validity can then be asserted.

The movement of research in the human sciences from number to word data is clearly articulated by Lincoln and Guba (1985), Polkinghorne (1988), and Reason (1988) and more recently by Denzin and Lincoln (1994). These accounts articulate the problems of using numbers to capture experience. In this section of the chapter we begin by articulating two general paths that lead toward the landscape of narrative inquiry. We then discuss qualities of number data that contribute to that development. First we discuss the sterile and deadening quality of the linguistic aspects of the discourse of human inquiry when there is an insistence that data ultimately be represented as numbers. Next, we present an understanding of the linguistic qualities of numbers. Third, we explore a recognition that numbers provide limited ways of representing findings, and finally, we consider the trustworthiness of numbers.

Paths Toward the Landscape of Narrative Inquiry

As researchers are confronted with verbal accounts and personal descriptions and explanations regarding the phenomenon under study, their response to the veracity, value, and vigor of word data in contrast to number data either nudges them toward a more relational stance with the researched (Turn 1), a greater concern with the particular (Turn 3), or a valuing of different ways of knowing (Turn 4). Researchers, who ultimately became (or become) narrative inquirers, found (or find) the use of numbers as the exclusive way of representing data increasingly dissatisfying.

If this is the first turn a researcher makes toward narrative, the path is a deceptively simple one. Researchers begin to question the ability of numbers, particularly numbers collected in standardized ways, to reveal deep understandings about human interaction. One pathway away from the exclusive insistence on numbers begins when researchers become intrigued with the nonnumeric responses of their research subjects and with what those responses begin to teach them or cause them to question about positivistic research in the social sciences. The apocryphal story of Piaget (Darrell Sabers, personal communication, September 1983) intrigues beginning social science researchers. In that story, Piaget was administering the Stanford-Binet intelligence test to norm it (provide a way of standardizing its administration and provide a framework for interpretation of test scores). In this process, he became interested in the wrong answers of his students. As Piaget turned away from interest in norming a test and toward understanding what the answers meant, he focused not on numbering the answers but on the children's explanations (words) about their understanding of particular events.

Piaget did not turn completely toward narrative inquiry in that he developed standardized tasks and ratings for students' answers to interpret their stories. Indeed, this is a common stopping point on the path toward narrative inquiry that modern researchers who begin to move toward narrative take when confronted with the problem of making sense of the stories they elicit from their research participants. Often, these researchers, in a sense, turn back from narrative inquiry because they desire to create "grand theories" in the human sciences, and they embrace the efficiency that numbers provide for convincing other social scientists of the fundamental accuracy and reliability of their findings. They recognize that without standardizing the process of data collection they open themselves to charges of unreliability and lack of accuracy in their final representations of their findings (Franzosi, 2004).

A second way a researcher might move away from numbers and through the landscape that leads to narrative inquiry begins with researchers questioning whether or not the survey questions asked, the test scores recorded, and the relationships discovered through causal modeling or multiple regression are an adequate account of the experiences they represent. Researchers may begin to be interested in the noise, the other fit, the other model that gets submerged when significant findings emerge from a study. For example, they may begin to explore parenting and the impact on children's development. They wonder when authoritative parenting begins to feel like authoritarian parenting and what difference the child's experience of the parent-child relationship makes in that assessment. They wonder about the blurred areas on the demandingness-responsiveness table, wondering when authoritativeness begins to be more like indulgence and when it fades off into authoritarian or indifferent parenting (Maccoby & Martin, 1983). They may wonder what their own parenting reveals about what they know about parenting and what stories of parenting or parent-child interaction collected from the parent or the child reveal about the relationship of parenting to development and growth. They decide to ask parents or children to tell stories of that experience. Again, some researchers may stop on the path, simply using the stories to develop a new or different survey that attempts to capture the experience of parenting that can be administered to scores of parents and the numeric findings can be used to develop a new, numerically based empirical and scientifically accurate account of parenting.

Of course, there are other paths through the landscape of human science research that lead from positivistic research conceptions to narrative inquiry, and there are also many points for stopping on the path or turning back toward the reassuring use of numbers as anchors for the research and as strategies for making sense of linguistic data.

Numbers as Sterile Discourse

A strong reason why narrative inquirers may turn from numbers to words as data is the sterility of numbers as discourse as well as the sterility of the discourse surrounding the presentations of number data. As Foucault (1976) explains, when attempts are made to restrict or reduce particular kinds of discourse or discourse about a particular topic, the inhibition results in an increase rather than decrease in discourse. In the same way, an insistence on number rather than word data in the human sciences results not in the disappearance of words or a substitution of numbers for words but an escalation in language. First of course is the defense of numbers, and the justification for the value of changing word to number data (Franzosi, 2004). Essential to this discussion is the explanation of how, when, and where numbers can reliably, consistently, and accurately replace words.

Kirk and Miller (1985), in discussing quality in qualitative research, argue that validity is the ability to count to one. They articulate this strategy as a way of proposing the potential validity of claims of qualitative researchers. However, implicit in their assertion is the idea that if a researcher can establish that the phenomenon being labeled can be defined so that it can be identified with a one, then it can be counted. If a phenomenon can be counted, its occurrence or absence, its repetition, and its regularity can be chronicled. When numbers become involved, then further statistical analysis can be conducted.

In the process of counting to one, language plays an important role, for to count one of something, the thing to be counted must be defined and specified. The distinction between this one and that must be clearly articulated. Kuhn (1970) argues that language attached to numbers results in the limited, flat, and sterile language of science. When numbers replace the phenomenon under study, the exact nature of the phenomenon or construct must be specified. The definition must establish clear boundaries between more general uses of the label of the phenomenon and the specified scientific boundaries for the term. Furthermore, in establishing definitions for a term, there are often long discussions about the meaning, not only of the phenomenon but also of each term used in the definition. The consistency with which other scientists can agreeably use the definition to number the phenomenon must also be established numerically. Reaching agreement about the count, the degree of likeness, or amount of phenomenon visible results in lengthy and ongoing discourse and negotiation about the definition produced. As a result, researchers in the human sciences may spend exponentially more time trying to constrict and control the words used to describe when, how, and where to number than they do in numbering, and the tone of their discourse can be experienced as tedious, mundane, and tangential to understanding.

The rules that govern counting highlight the limits of numbers in accounting for the particular, local, and contextual in human relationships. When children learn to count a set of things, they learn that each item must be counted separately and counting must proceed in an invariant sequence. This rule points out the fragmentation and the sense of control that the use of numbers can impose. In addition, when counting, the child can begin with any object and continue until each item has been numbered once. The process of counting highlights the characteristics of number data that are so satisfying in positivistic research. Each occurrence is independent of any other, each occurrence is interchangeable, and each occurrence is equal to every other occurrence. Furthermore, these properties of counting highlight the static, atemporal, knowable, and controllable aspects of things so valued by positivistic researchers. Attending to these qualities, Bruner (1986) labels the findings of paradigmatic knowing *actual*, in contrast to the findings of narrative knowing, which he labels *possible*.

Bruner (1986), in fact, argues that positivistic research begins in wild metaphor. He asserts that it is through the wild metaphors and their interconnections that researchers arrive at a level of abstraction where meaning can be made of the phenomenon of interest. According to Bruner, at that point in time, researchers working from a base of paradigmatic knowing then define the phenomenon and develop instruments that provide numbers for accounting for the relationships that emerged metaphorically. They continue to use a restricted and confined language, as free of metaphor as possible to account for the facts they observe and the laws they develop. As a result, since metaphor is a tool for opening and deepening understanding, the opportunity for insight and meaning making is flattened. As researchers became less content with labeling numerically the level of kindness or the degree of hope, they may become more interested in understanding the stories of kindness and hopefulness. They begin to wonder about the stories, words, and other linguistic accounts their research masks. In taking this step, they may begin to turn toward narrative inquiry. When researchers become interested in the nuances of meaning, then reducing what was originally word data to numbers is viewed as restricting opportunities for meaning making and understanding.

Numbers as Language

One reason for a turn from the insistence on the use of numbers rather than words in quantitative social science research emerges from certain kinds of understandings about the characteristics of numbers and formulas. The insistence on numbers for use in positivistic human science research allows researchers to make justifiable claims about the reality they are studying. Numbers, scientists sometimes assert, are less ambiguous than language, and thus their interpretation is more straightforward. Such reasoning ignores certain properties of numbers.

While numbers, through probability and norm curves, provide the bedrock for turning true beliefs into knowledge and have the potential for allowing social scientists to believe they can predict and control human relationships and interactions in the same way scientists can assert control and prediction over the physical world, they remain a language. Numbers are often nouns and formulas, sentences that represent stories about the relationship of one essence to another. However, while a story invites participants into the research, formulas can intimidate and exclude them.

Indeed, numbers are linguistic entities and have certain linguistic properties that are often overlooked when numbers are asserted as valuable because of their concreteness, specificity, and consistency. Each number or letter in a formula is symbolic of quantities and relationships. Thus, letters in formulas are symbolic entities and have the properties of such entities. Meaning in a formula never resides exclusively in the number but is established through the ways in which the numbers and symbols are held in relationship to each other. In addition, a letter in a formula is merely a placeholder for a number, and since any number might replace each letter in the formula, the letter represents infinity. As a result, formulas are less sterile and controllable than might be imagined. Furthermore, infinity constantly emerges in any consideration of a number line or scale since it exists between one number and the next.

In any discussion, numbers are labeled with words, and as words, numbers introduce all the metaphoric qualities of language—possibly not as unfettered but still present. When a number is inserted into a discussion, it enters discourse, becomes embedded in sentences, and through the interconnection of the meaning of the number in relationship to the other entities in the sentence, has meaning beyond itself or even the immediate relationship specified in the formula.

Numbers as Limited, Untrustworthy Representations

Social science researchers may turn from numbers to words as data because they provide limited representations of what is studied and rely more heavily on the researcher constructing a narrative to account for the numbers and their relationships with each other. Numbers, through formulas, charts, graphs, and tables, provide limited ways of representing the understandings that emerge in inquiry involving humans and human interaction. When the audience of research is presented with numeric findings, the reader must provide a narrative to explain and capture the relationships presented with statistical values. In addition, numbers also impose a limit on the ways in which participants in the research can present what they know or understand.

Plotlines, character, setting, and action (Bal, 1997) provide ways of holding meaning together in more complex, relational, and therefore more nuanced ways than flowcharts or number tables. For example, using the interpretive lens of the three-dimensional narrative space articulated by Clandinin and Connelly (2000) allows researchers to both present and interrogate findings and allows the narrative inquirer to represent the contingent, nuanced, and symbolic aspects of the findings.

Sometimes narrative inquirers begin to turn away from numbers because they become suspicious of their trustworthiness in providing an authentic research account. Indeed, numbers are purported to hold out great promises of validity for human science researchers, but the sterility of their representation and the imposition of meaning on the participants leads to questions about the validity of the data when questions about their trustworthiness emerge. Since numbers alone represent findings from each subject, the researcher has no way of exploring the coherence of the reports or the consistency of expression or the nuances of language that suggest integrity. Participants in research that elicits only numeric responses are given little space to provide their own understanding of concepts being studied. Audiences of the research and the researcher themselves must rely on the adequacy and appropriateness of definitions and the ways in which those definitions have been operationalized. The limiting of the opportunity for participants to express meaning by circling a number or building a score provides participants with few ways of expanding the meaning. Numbers as findings, even with descriptions of the sample, the treatment, definitions, and significance levels, reduce the context for exploring or establishing the integrity of findings. While researchers who use numbers will, of course, follow the assumptions and guidance of the standards of statistical research, researchers may begin to feel that there is not sufficient data or explanation to determine the data's authenticity or integrity.

According to Lincoln and Guba (1985), the fact that the researcher constructed or selected the instrument to explore her or his understanding of the concepts and their interrelationships raises problems regarding the trustworthiness of the research findings. Indeed, there is little textual evidence that allows the audience to determine whether the research was simply designed to impose the worldview of the researcher on what was researched.

Researchers who desire a deeper opportunity to establish the authenticity and trustworthiness of their findings may move toward formats of research that allow research findings to be presented in the words of the participants in ways that represent the experience of the researchers and the researched and allow evidence of the quality of the interaction and relationship to emerge in the research report (Kirk & Miller, 1985).

Narrative inquiry, in both the collection and presentation of the data, allows a clear arena for addressing questions of the trustworthiness of the data and their interpretations. The three-dimensional narrative inquiry space described by Clandinin and Connelly (2000) prompts researchers to both question explanations and meanings constructed and provide the audience with accounts that uncover and reveal such questions of meaning, value, and integrity.

There are common themes in researcher accounts of their move toward use of word data. These themes include the sterility of numbers in representing the complexity of human interaction, the arbitrary and impositional nature of the assignment of numbers to observations or accounts, the increasing desire of researchers to understand better the meaning of human interaction for the humans involved in the action, and, finally, a hesitancy about the integrity and trustworthiness of data where only a number is recoverable.

Narrative Turn 3: From the General to the Particular

When researchers make the turn toward a focus on the particular, it signals their understanding of the value of a particular experience, in a particular setting, involving particular people. Coles (1978) captures the power of the particular in his book *Women of Crisis*. His earlier books focused on accounts and analysis of the experience of impoverished groups of Americans. In this retrospective, he revisits and explicates the story of one child from the earlier study. In capturing the life story of these children, he instantiates the difficulties emerging from poverty and the resiliency of the human spirit in such circumstances. The accounts resonate and provide readers a potentially deeper and more valuable understanding of the impact of poverty on children's lives. In a similar way, Bullough's (2001) *Uncertain Lives* provides educators with a deeper and more complex understanding of the lives of children enmeshed in poverty and the potential value of teachers and schools.

To understand this turn, we begin with a discussion of this turn as a move from generalizability. We then capture the strength and value of this turn through a consideration of particular evidence of this turn in the discipline of history.

Generalizability and the Power of the Particular

One of the powers that quantitative research holds out for researchers is the potential for generalizability. Indeed, it may be this tantalizing prospect that stalls researchers in a move to narrative inquiry. According to this paradigm for knowing, if the researcher can remove the impact of the particular, then the findings of a research study can be generalized beyond that setting.

This concern with generalizability and the capturing of the universal is an ethos that occupied all branches of the human sciences. The anthropologist, historian, psychologist, medical practitioner, and educator (for example) were interested in constructing grand narratives: theories of the world that could be applied universally, regardless of particular circumstances. The basis for the grand narrative is the careful study and accumulation of facts from which laws are determined. Such laws, based as they are on irrefutable facts, allow social scientists to predict and control human life.

Geertz (1983), in his discussion of the relationship of law to fact in four different cultural settings, demonstrates clearly that law and fact do not necessarily interact in these ways. His analysis of the relationship of fact and law in four particular cultures raises doubts about the possibility of using facts as the basis for developing laws since, just as fact might be seen to determine law, law can actually bring facts into existence. For many researchers, it is this unease about the actual relationship of fact and law that turns them from a study of the general to a study of the particular. The other chapters in this handbook, through the authors' reporting of their own particular work to capture and explain the overarching themes, provide clear examples of the power that a focus on the particular brings narrative inquirers. The emergence of narrative therapy is an especially powerful example. White and Epston (1990) and their colleagues became interested in embracing the particular stories and experiences of particular clients and using the value of narrative rather than grand theories of psychology as a way of helping clients reimagine and reshape their lives.

Geertz (1983) turned social scientists in this direction. One step was his use of the narrative of the Balinese cockfight as a particular case for understanding the Balinese culture. Kitchen (2005) provides a recent example of the power of focusing on the particular for understanding teacher development. Through his careful narrative of the experience of his work with one teacher who transforms his teaching, we come to better understand the value of relationships in bringing about profound changes. His textured, layered focus on this narrative and his careful description of the particular setting and people involved provide a secure anchor for using what is learned in this narrative inquiry in our work in other settings.

History as an Example

In exploring this turn from the general to the particular, we would be wrong to say that the social sciences focused solely on general issues by the close of World War II. Social scientists, after all, carried out case studies and gathered local data. But in the decades that followed the war, key social science texts attended to abstractions, using particular facts to make broad points about the society under examination. In the United States, works such as Gunnar Myrdal's (1944) *An American Dilemma* or David Potter's (1954) *People of Plenty* sought to describe an

American character, a set of traits or beliefs that could be used to understand contemporary American society as a whole. In both instances, a single topic—race relations for Myrdal and the middle class for Potter—served as a lens through which to understand the entire nation. In Europe, structuralists such as Claude Levi-Strauss and historians of the Annales School worked at the same level of abstraction. Levi-Strauss's (1969) key ideas, that societies were hot or cold, raw or cooked, gave other social scientists a frame through which they could see things whole. Annales historians used a different tack—casting their eyes on a place over such an extended period (*la longue durée*) that the particularities of personalities and events fell away under the persistent forces of time (Braudel, 1949/1972).

These works were responding to trends in the social sciences, most particularly to the postwar embrace of positivist science and the availability of large amounts of data. Positivism made it possible for social scientists to think that their results would be generalizable across time and space if only their methods were replicated. And longitudinal, or panel, data made it possible for social scientists to generalize about the characteristics of a large number of people. Of course, positivism continues to frame the assumptions of most social scientists, and the stores of data are even richer and more complete. If positivism and data were all it took to turn social scientists to the general, there would be no room for narrative today. But in the postwar world, cultural forces were as important as academic ones, and preeminent among those cultural trends was the contest between the United States and the Soviet Union for global predominance.

In some cases, the Cold War was the explicit context in which social scientists worked. Some sought to find national traits that could be used to distinguish between one superpower and the other. This is the goal of George Kennan's (1947) "long telegram," which described the Soviet character for American policy makers and birthed a huge social science enterprise dedicated to laying out the grounds for containing the Soviet Union. In other instances, the Cold War was the implicit context, presenting issues in an either-or format—freedom or totalitarianism, individualism or conformity—which themselves became the terms of debate for social scientists (Arendt, 1951; Chambers, 1952). Finally, the ideologies of the superpowers themselves formed the basis for academic social science. Both Marxist academics and their modernization theory adversaries saw the world in general terms, a home for social systems best understood according to the assumptions of Marx or the assumptions of capitalism (Lerner, 1958; Williams, 1959).

In form, the Cold War continued until the collapse of the Soviet Union in the late 1980s. But the dualism behind it came under question much earlier. In global politics, the challenge came from the movement of nonaligned nations, which carved out some space between the United States and its allies, and the Soviet Union and its supporters. But the more profound challenge came from liberation movements around the globe that sought to replace Cold War orthodoxy with a worldview that was at once more nuanced and narrower. While these movements were primarily focused on political and social change, they created their own social science, one that by giving attention to the experience of minorities created space in which narrative could flourish.

In the United States, the women's movement and the movement for black civil rights both brought the nation's self-definition into question. By pointing out that the nation failed to live up to its promise of equality for all citizens, these movements created a space in which to question both Cold War orthodoxy and social science. Both movements used positivist evidence to point out American inequalities—quantitative studies of salary inequity by gender or of the absence of African Americans on voting roles—and certainly pointed out the gap between theory and reality in the United States. But perhaps more powerful than the quantitative evidence was a more particular, personal body of evidence, amassed and shared in both movements.

In women's consciousness-raising groups, and in black churches across the South, personal stories became the rhetorical basis for grassroots movements. These stories played at least four roles. They united members of the movements by making public the experiences that, when hidden, were reminders of their oppression. They made it possible for people without "expertise" to contribute to the intellectual work of the movement. They created a repository of stories upon which movement leaders could theorize and plan. And they provided powerful, authentic evidence of the need for political and social change, evidence that had more persuasive power than positivist social science.

The women's and civil rights movements, along with other, less well-known movements, influenced the social sciences in key ways. By the early years of the 1970s, each movement had an academic cognate—women's studies, black studies, Chicano studies, gay and lesbian studies—that did scholarly work on the questions raised by social movements. In many instances, the academic leaders of these disciplines were former (or current) movement activists who brought their own experiences to bear on their research. And those experiences influenced the methodologies of these disciplines, both explicitly in those works that drew social scientific conclusions from the scholar's autobiography and implicitly in those works that drew on storytelling and stories for some or all their evidence.

In many instances, personal stories added richness to social scientific works that otherwise fell comfortably into the positivist mainstream. But in others, narratives became the basis for innovation in theory and presentation of social science. Sara Evans's (1979) *Personal Politics* used her own experience as a civil rights activist and that of dozens of her colleagues to argue for a new understanding of politics. In it, issues that had once been considered private or personal—sexuality, child care, reproductive rights, mental health, abuse—became central public concerns, sources of political agitation, and the subject of legislation and litigation. Mary Belenky's (Belenky, Clinchy, Goldberger, & Tarule, 1986) *Women's Ways of Knowing* went a step further, arguing that narrative and storytelling constituted part of a gendered epistemology with as much explanatory power as any other. And, more quietly, dozens of autobiographies, biographies, and memoirs made a simpler point—that the particular deserves as much attention as the general among social scientists. Thus, as researchers, narrative inquirers embrace the power of the particular for understanding experience and using findings from research to inform themselves in specific places at specific times.

Narrative Turn 4: Blurring Knowing

The final turn we explore here is the turn from one way of knowing the world to an understanding that there are multiple ways of knowing and understanding human experience. In many ways, this understanding of the variety of ways of knowing leads researchers away from a secure base. In explicating this turn, we begin with an exploration of validity and a renewed understanding of it as a basis for this turn. We then explore the reemergence of narrative knowing as a valid and important tool for knowing in the human sciences.

Blurred Knowing and Validity

Social science has traditionally been anchored in numbers and focused on a concern with proving facts that lead to the development of law and theory to have a secure basis for asserting a specific view of the ways things are. Reliance on the assumptions of positivistic and post-positivistic science allows researchers to assert that their findings are valid. A turn toward acceptance of multiple ways of knowing the world is a turn toward establishing findings through authenticity, resonance, or trustworthiness (Clandinin & Connelly, 2000; Denzin & Lincoln, 1994). For some researchers, an understanding of the limits of validity within a quantitative paradigm precipitated a move toward narrative inquiry. The acceptance of the relational and interactive nature of human science research, the use of the story, and a focus on a careful accounting of the particular are hallmarks of knowing in narrative inquiry. Narrative inquirers recognize that embracing and executing the methodology of narrative inquiry, rather than an exclusive reliance on the assumptions of a positivistic paradigm, provides authentic and resonant findings. In making this turn, narrative inquirers recognize the tentative and variable nature of knowledge. They accept and value the way in which narrative inquiry allows wondering, tentativeness, and alternative views to exist as part of the research account.

Knowing in the Human Sciences

If this chapter were simply about the history of narrative, then this section, on the turn away from positivist ways of knowing in the academy, would be unnecessary. Outside the academic disciplines, there seems to be little question about the ability of narrative to convey information. Television and film, fiction and journalism, and video games all contain strong, complex narrative strands (Johnson, 2005). Readers and listeners are sophisticated consumers of narrative, actively determining which stories to trust and which to doubt, even in the face of "official" interpretations offered by government and the academy (McGlaughlin, 1996; Turner, 1994).

But inside the university, narrative ways of knowing fell from favor early in the 20th century and have only in the past 30 years begun to reemerge as a legitimate field of study, means of communication, and orientation toward truth. Their reemergence is due to several key trends—a mounting critique of the enlightenment philosophies that underlie positivist epistemologies, close studies of scientific practice and its relationship to scientific rhetoric, growing attention to the histories of the social sciences, and a more robust debate about who owns the stories that have traditionally been the raw material of social science research. Together, these trends have opened space for narrative inquiry. The size and shape of that space depends, at least in part, on the narrative forms traditionally associated with particular disciplines—as in history, where biography flourishes while post-modern narratives have had a narrower appeal. (Compare, for example, the response to Simon Schama's, 1988, traditional narrative *The Embarrassment of Riches* and his experimental *Dead Certainties: Unwarranted Speculations;* Schama, 1992.)

Of the social sciences, only sociology was born as a positivist discipline. By the time that Karl Marx, Max Weber, and Émile Durkheim gave the discipline its academic shape, sociologists had already embraced key components of positivism— that social structure, not individual behavior, was central to understanding human life, that social structure could be best understood through number data, that there were "laws" that governed human societies, and that those societies should be described in analytical, not narrative, terms (Stark, 2004).

Other disciplines that are now part of the social sciences had their birth in narrative. History, in its ancient or 19th-century guise, told stories, often relying on the record of individual actors to carry the narrative along (Higham, 1990). Anthropology grew in part out of travelogs, and psychology's first preferred genre was the case study (Freud, 1913; Pratt, 1986). But as these disciplines became professionalized, narrative practitioners fell to the side. Particularly instructive is the case of history, where "amateur" historians without a graduate education in history continued to practice narrative, while their "professional" credentialed colleagues wrote analytical, positivist history and slowly excluded amateurs from disciplinary organizations (Appleby, Hunt, & Jacob, 1994; Higham, 1990; Novick, 1990). By the 1930s, these disciplines were as devoted to the rhetoric of objectivity and science as sociology.

The resurgence of narrative in the social sciences is due, in part, to the unraveling of the certainties that upheld positivistic social science. The "unravelers" are pulling from a number of different, and sometimes contradictory, directions. They should not be seen as united or as having a monolithic perspective on truth or knowledge. Nor are they all partisans of narrative. But their efforts have made room for narrative inquiry and writing in the social sciences.

The philosophical basis of positivistic knowing faces challenges from at least two directions. The first, growing out of the work of the moral philosopher Alisdair MacIntyre, casts doubt on key elements of the Enlightenment. MacIntyre is particularly skeptical of two Enlightenment commitments—the encyclopedia and the search for social scientific law. For MacIntyre (1990), the encyclopedia is the model of rational, radically decontextualized knowledge. The organizing structure of the encyclopedia means that things must appear to be rational on their own since they are not meaningfully connected to the things that surround them. (Thus, at www.encyclopedia.com, the term *enlightenment* is preceded by *Enkoping*, an industrial center in Sweden, and followed by *Enlil*, the ancient Sumerian earth god.)

MacIntyre doubts that things are rational on their faces. Instead, he argues that people trust things that claim to be rational because they trust the institution or the person responsible for those particular things. Part of the enlightenment, then, must be to create a type of organization that can provide credence for decontextualized things. MacIntyre argues that that organization is the bureaucracy and that one of the key roles within the bureaucracy is the social scientist. The social scientist's task is to provide generalizations about the way things are and to assert that these generalizations are predictive. By doing so, they lend authority to bureaucracies—corporations and universities among them—who in turn buttress the moral claims of enlightenment rationality (MacIntyre, 1984, especially chap. 8).

The Christian ethicist Stanley Hauerwas has played out the implications of MacIntyre's work for narrative. If encyclopedic knowing lacks any rational basis, then there must be some other source for trusting information. Hauerwas and MacIntyre both identify embodied tradition as the way of knowing that provides the soundest basis for truth. Embodied traditions share important characteristics. First, knowledge is not decontextualized. Instead, it exists in the context of a narrative that gives it meaning, nuance, and application. Second, that narrative is shared by members of a community who provide support to those who wish to live in accordance with the narrative. Together, the narrative (or narratives) and community provide a rich context in which claims about the world can be evaluated (Hauerwas, 1995/2001a, 1980/2001b, 1981/2001c).

Hauerwas's attention to embodied narratives lived in community connects moral philosophy's critique of the enlightenment with the second major intellectual trend undermining the scientific certainty of positivism—neopragmatism. Neopragmatism is a sprawling philosophic movement, much of which is beyond the scope of this essay. But the work of Richard Rorty, and in particular his 1986 article "Science as Solidarity," is particularly apropos. In it he, like MacIntyre and Hauerwas, seeks to show that "rationality" need not be the sole domain of positivists. But while MacIntyre is predominantly concerned with social scientists, Rorty's attention focuses on natural scientists. He argues that in the West the scientist has replaced the priest at the top of the cultural hierarchy. As a result, humanists find themselves in the position of borrowing the rhetoric of the sciences, particularly claims to objectivity and rationality, to bolster their cultural position. For Rorty, this mimicry is troubling for two reasons. First, it turns the humanities away from their role of supporting the civilization of society. Second, it misunderstands the work of scientists by assuming that their work is always cold, rational, objective, and clear. Rorty argues that the practice of science (in contrast with its rhetoric) in fact grows out of the values of a particular culture—that is, it is a sign of solidarity (or "ethnocentrism") among scientists. As such, the practice of science differs little from the practice of the humanities, where interpretation and argument grow out of particular cultural contexts as well.

While it is Rorty's hope that seeing science as solidarity might place the work of humanists on an equal footing with scientists, his work, together with the work of the sociologist Bruno Latour (1979; and others doing social studies of science), has had another effect, weakening the hold that the natural sciences have over some social sciences. In its simplest form, Latour's work shows that scientists' laboratory work is influenced both by personal history and the culture of their particular laboratories and research specialties.

This insight has borne rich theoretical insights into the work of science, but its greatest contribution to narrative inquiry has been in its opening a space where scientists and social scientists from outside the mainstream of science culture have been able to question that culture. The questioning has drawn scientists and social scientists to investigate the history of the disciplines, both scientific and social scientific. Both investigations have been useful for narrative inquiry. In the hard sciences, Sandra Harding (1991) and others have shown the gendered (and more recently, race-d and class-ed) nature of science. Perforce some of that demonstration has been narrative, as women scientists have described their own difficult paths to professional success and historians of science have uncovered the stories of earlier generations of women who practiced science in the shadow of their male colleagues (e.g., Sheffield, 2001). In the social sciences, historians and anthropologists have uncovered the narrative pasts of their disciplines, in some cases turning them to theoretical ends (e.g. Clifford & Marcus, 1986; White, 1987), in others using narratives to do academic work that could not be done by other means, whether that means describing culture through multiple frames or uncovering voices that would otherwise be hidden in the social sciences (Glassie, 1995; Marcus, 2005; White, 1998).

To this point, we have perhaps implied that the move away from scientific objectivity and toward narrative has happened largely within the academy. That is only partly true, for while the academy has moved down certain paths toward narrative, the larger culture has done the same. The past 20 years have hosted a flowering of narrative in the broader culture—memoir and creative nonfiction have been among the most successful genres in popular publishing; museums have embraced the stories of individuals as a way of making connections with the public (Handler & Gable, 1997); new confessional and "reality" shows populate television; and blogs, Web pages, and podcasts have granted individuals both the audience and the freedom to narrate. In essence, then, social science and public culture are converging on stories. The blurred nature of knowing provides narrative inquirers space and tools for exploring these concerns.

Conclusion

This chapter does not argue for an academy-wide move to narrative. Nor, in contrast to positivist social science, does it assume that there should be unanimity among narrative practitioners on key points of philosophy, method, or argument. This is both a strength and weakness of the movement toward narrative—a strength because multiple views make for closer attention to a wider variety of human experience; a weakness because it seems unlikely that narrative will ever come to dominate the academy in the way that positivism has done since the beginning of the 20th century. While narrative is still in its infancy, narrative practitioners will eventually have to come to grips with this problem, either to rethink the political and social impact of their work or to accept the place of narrative on the margins of academic work.

In the movement toward narrative inquiry, each of the turns represents a philosophical turn from four important assumptions that underlie what Bruner calls paradigmatic knowing.

The first of these assumptions, intertwined with the second, is the assumption of reliability. Anchored in the use of numbers as data, the assumption of reliability is founded on the realist conception that what we choose to study can be thought of as having an "independent, objectlike existence with no intrinsic meaning" (Smith, 1983, p. 7). When social facts, like rocks, can be treated as "thinglike," then researchers can measure them and number them, believing that they can create a number trail that allows the measurement of feeling, thinking, and caring to be consistent, accurate, and metaphor free. The language of numbers is basic to the use of statistical inference and probability, which ultimately provide foundational criteria for knowing. What distinguishes narrative inquiry is the understanding that all research is based on language whether in the language of numbers or the discourse of researchers and those being researched. Rather than imposing the antiseptic, narrow, and confining definition of scientific discourse heralded as necessary for "normal" social science (Kuhn, 1970), narrative inquirers embrace the metaphoric quality of language and the connectedness and coherence of the extended discourse of the story entwined with exposition, argumentation, and description.

The second assumption is objectivity—what has been expanded to be "scientific" objectivity and characterizes the basic relationship between the researcher and what is being researched. The assumption is made that what is being studied has the properties of a "thing," with an existence that is separate from and not connected to the researcher. Indeed, research is a neutral activity. Such a position denies human connectedness and growth. It fails to take into account the fact that researchers choose to study one thing rather than another and that just the facts of choice, curiosity, and interest without considering passion, caring, or insight connect the researcher in a nonneutral way to what is being studied. In denying the nonneutrality of curiosity and interest, a stance of objectivity ignores as well what Bruner (1986) identifies as the scientist's use of "wild metaphors" to climb the mountain of abstraction that is most often the foundation of the conceptualization of scientific inquiry and their subsequent "forgetfulness" regarding the metaphoric basis for an embracing of a logical reworking of the insight gained through insight and metaphor. What fundamentally distinguishes the narrative turn from "scientific" objectivity is understanding that knowing other people and their interactions is always a relational process that ultimately involves caring for, curiosity, interest, passion, and change.

The third assumption that narrative inquirers turn from is generalizability. This assumption dismisses the value of the local and particular in favor of the power of prediction and control provided by the universal. Social scientists embraced positivistic research processes because of the seductive quality of generalizability.

Researchers in the social sciences wanted to be able to discover universal laws that could be used in any context to account for and guide prediction about and thus help control humans and human interaction. Behaviorism—the search for a single mechanism to account for learning—is the most severe and extreme example of this desire. Through controlled treatments and manipulation of variables and randomization, researchers determined that they could account for and remove the power of context in human relationship and interaction. What distinguishes narrative inquirers is their understanding that understanding the complexity of the individual, local, and particular provides a surer basis for our relationships and interactions with other humans. Schank and Abelson's (1977) work on schemata demonstrated that humans appear to build up from particular experiences ways of acting in their world. Expert-novice research reveals the ways in which a deep understanding of the particular forms the basis for valuable and insightful action in virtually all settings (Bereiter & Scardamalia, 1993). Geertz (1983) argues convincingly that local knowledge forms the most important basis for understanding human culture and personal interaction.

The final assumption that narrative inquirers turn from is a positivistic conception of validity. Validity and insistence on the necessity of particular kinds of evidence for epistemology narrow the arena of epistemology from broader conceptions of knowing, the properties of knowledge, and the ways of knowing to one of a rigidified insistence on one way of moving "true belief" to knowledge, which is anchored in an objective relationship of researcher and researched, based on the use of reliable and numeric measurements such that settings can be controlled or manipulated so that generalizable research findings can be applied. The insistence on this particular conception of validity, which relies on statistics, denies the variety of ways of knowing and questioning of what counts as knowledge and insists on a single kind of truth, indeed denying what Lincoln and Guba (1985) label *Truth 1*—the metaphysical beliefs, the true beliefs that form the basis from which positivistic researchers design their research studies. What distinguishes narrative inquirers is their desire to understand rather than control and predict the human world.

The convergence between social science and the public is undoubtedly good for narrative. It grants stories both popularity and credence. But it also raises a set of questions, about power (Who owns a story? Who can tell it? Who can change it?), about authority (Whose version of a story is convincing? What happens when narratives compete?), and about community (What do stories do among us?). These are questions about philosophy, but even more, they are questions about method. Academic narrative inquirers have developed a set of methods that give narrative credibility on campus. The challenge now is to enter conversations with the rest of our communities to develop a method—a way of talking and asking and answering and making sense—that will allow narrative to flourish in this congenial moment for stories.

Consulting Editors: Donald Polkinghorne, Margaret Olson, and Robert Bullough, Jr.

References

Appleby, J., Hunt, L., & Jacob, M. (1994). *Telling the truth about history*. New York: W. W. Norton.

Arendt, H. (1951). *The origins of totalitarianism*. New York: Harcourt, Brace.

Bal, M. (1997). *On narratology: Introduction to the theory of narrative* (2nd ed.). Toronto, Canada: University of Toronto Press.

Bateson, M. C. (1984). *With a daughter's eye: A memoir of Margaret Mead and Gregory Bateson*. New York: William Morrow.

Bateson, M. C. (1990). *Composing a life*. New York: Atlantic Monthly Press.

Belenky, M., Clinchy, B., Goldberger, N., & Tarule, J. (1986). *Women's ways of knowing: The development of self, voice, and mind*. New York: Basic Books.

Bereiter, C., & Scardamalia, M. (1993). *Surpassing ourselves: An inquiry into the nature and implications of expertise*. Chicago: Open Court.

Braudel, F. (1972). *The Mediterranean and Mediterranean world in the age of Phillip II* (S. Reynolds, Trans.). New York: Harper & Row. (Original work published 1949)

Bruner, J. (1986). *Actual minds, possible worlds*. Cambridge, MA: Harvard University Press.

Bullough, R. V., Jr. (2001). *Uncertain lives: Children of hope, teachers of promise*. New York: Teachers College Press.

Bullough, R. V., Jr., & Pinnegar, S. (2001). Guidelines for quality in autobiographical forms of self-study research. *Educational Researcher, 30*(3), 13–22.

Chambers, W. (1952). *Witness*. New York: Random House.

Clandinin, D. J., & Connelly, M. (2000). *Narrative inquiry: Experience and story in qualitative research*. San Francisco: Jossey-Bass.

Clandinin, D. J., Davies, A., Hogan, P., & Kennard, B. (Eds.). (1993). *Learning to teach, teaching to learn: Stories of collaboration in teacher education*. New York: Teachers' College Press.

Clifford, J. (1986). Introduction. In J. Clifford & G. E. Marcos (Eds.), *Writing culture: The poetics and politics of ethnography* (pp. 1–26). Berkeley: University of California Press.

Clifford, J., & Marcus, G. E. (Eds.). (1986). *Writing culture: The poetics and politics of ethnography*. Berkeley: University of California Press.

Coles, R. (1978). *Women of crisis: Lives of struggle and hope*. New York: Delacorte Press.

Coles, R. (1989). *The call of stories: Teaching and the moral imagination*. Boston: Houghton Mifflin.

Denzin, N. K., & Lincoln, Y. S. (1994). *Handbook of qualitative research*. Thousand Oaks, CA: Sage.

Dewey, John. (1938). *Experience and education*. New York: Collier Books.

Evans, S. (1979). *Personal politics: The roots of women's liberation in the civil rights movement and the new left*. New York: Knopf.

Faulconer, J. E., & Williams, R. N. (1990). Reconsidering psychology. In J. E. Faulconer & R. N. Williams (Eds.), *Reconsidering psychology: Perspectives from contemporary continental philosophy* (pp. 9–60). Pittsburgh, PA: Duquesne University Press.

Fenstermacher, G. D. (1994). The knower and the known: The nature of knowledge in research on teaching. *Review of Research in Education, 20*, 3–56.

Foucault, M. (1976). *History of sexuality: Vol. I. An introduction*. New York: Pantheon.

Franzosi, R. (2004). *From words to numbers: Narrative, data, and social science*. Cambridge, UK: Cambridge University Press.

Freud, S. (1913). *The interpretation of dreams*. New York: Macmillan.

Geertz, C. (1983). *Local knowledge: Further essays in interpretive anthropology*. New York: Basic Books.

Glassie, H. (1995). *Passing the time in Ballymenone: Culture and history of an Ulster community.* Bloomington: Indiana University Press.

Green, M. C., Strange, J. J., & Brock, T. C. (2002). *Narrative impact: Social cognitive foundations.* Mahwah, NJ: Lawrence Erlbaum.

Gruber, H. E., & Vonèche, J. J. (Eds.). (1977). *The essential Piaget: An interpretive reference guide.* New York: Basic Books.

Guilfoyle, K., Hamilton, M. L., Pinnegar, S., & Placier, P. (2004). The epistemological dimensions and dynamics of professional dialogue in self-study. In J. J. Loughran, M. L. Hamilton, V. K. LaBoskey, & T. Russell (Eds.), *International handbook of self-study of teaching and teacher education practices* (Vol. 1, pp. 1109–1168). Dordrecht, Netherlands: Kluwer Academic.

Handler, R., & Gable, E. (1997). *The new history in an old museum.* Durham, NC: Duke University Press.

Harding, S. (1991). *Whose science, whose knowledge: Thinking from women's lives.* Ithaca, NY: Cornell University Press.

Hauerwas, S. (2001a). Casuistry in context: The need for tradition. In J. Berkman & M. Cartwright (Eds.), *The Hauerwas reader* (pp. 267–284). Durham, NC: Duke University Press. (Original work published 1995)

Hauerwas, S. (2001b). Character, narrative, and growth in the Christian life. In J. Berkman & M. Cartwright (Eds.), *The Hauerwas reader* (pp. 221–254). Durham, NC: Duke University Press. (Original work published 1980)

Hauerwas, S. (2001c). A story-formed community: Reflections on *Watership Down.* In J. Berkman & M. Cartwright (Eds.), *The Hauerwas reader* (pp. 171–199). Durham, NC: Duke University Press. (Original work published 1981)

Higham, J. (1990). *History: Professional scholarship in America.* Baltimore: Johns Hopkins University Press.

Hymes, D. (1955). Toward ethnographies of communication. *American Anthropologist, 66,* 1–34.

Johnson, S. (2005). *Everything bad is good for you: How today's popular culture is actually making us smarter.* New York: Riverhead.

Josselson, R. (1996). *Revising herself.* Oxford, UK: Oxford University Press.

Josselson, R., Lieblich, A., & McAdams, D. (2003). *Up close and personal: The teaching and learning of narrative research.* Washington, DC: American Psychological Association.

Kennan, G. (1947, July). The sources of Soviet conduct. *Foreign Affairs,* pp. 566–582.

Kirk, J., & Miller, M. L. (1985). *Reliability and validity in qualitative research.* Beverly Hills, CA: Sage.

Kitchen, J. D. (2005). *Relational teacher development: A quest for meaning in the garden of teaching experience.* Unpublished master's thesis, University of Toronto, Canada.

Kuhn, T. S. (1970). *The structure of scientific revolutions.* Chicago: University of Chicago Press.

Latour, B. (1979). *Laboratory life: The social construction of scientific facts.* Beverly Hills, CA: Sage.

Lerner, D. (1958). *The passing of traditional society: Modernity in the Middle East.* Glencoe, IL: Free Press.

Levi-Strauss, C. (1969). *The raw and the cooked.* New York: Harper & Row.

Lieblich, A., Mashiach-Tuval, R., & Zilber, T. (1998). *Narrative research: Reading, analysis and interpretation.* Thousand Oaks, CA: Sage.

Lincoln, Y. S., & Guba, E. G. (1985). *Naturalistic inquiry.* Beverly Hills, CA: Sage.

MacIntyre, A. (1984). *After virtue: A study in moral theory* (2nd ed.). Notre Dame, IN: Notre Dame University Press.

MacIntyre, A. (1990). *Three rival versions of moral enquiry: Encyclopaedia, genealogy, and tradition.* Notre Dame, IN: Notre Dame University Press.

Maccoby, E., & Martin, J. (1983). Socialization in the context of the family: Parent-child interactions. In E. M. Heatherington (Ed.), *Handbook of child psychology: Socialization, personality, and social development* (pp. 1–101). New York: Wiley.

Marcus, G. (2005). *Ocasiao: The Marquis and the anthropologist: A collaboration.* Walnut Creek, CA: AltaMira Press.

Martin, W. (1986). *Recent theories of narrative.* Ithaca, NY: Cornell University Press.

McAdams, D. (1993). *The stories we live by: Personal myths and the making of self.* New York: Guilford Press.

McGlaughlin, T. (1996). *Street smarts and critical theory: Listening to the vernacular.* Madison: University of Wisconsin Press.

Miles, M. B., & Huberman, A. M. (1984). *Qualitative data analysis: An expanded sourcebook.* Beverly Hills, CA: Sage.

Myrdal, G. (1944). *An American dilemma: The negro problem and modern democracy.* New York: Harper.

Novick, P. (1990). *That noble dream: The "objectivity question" and the American historical profession.* New York: Cambridge University Press.

Pasupathi, M. (2003). Emotion regulation during social remembering: Differences between emotions elicited during an event and emotions elicited when talking about it. *Memory, 11*(2), 151–164.

Polanyi, L. (1989). *Telling the American story: A structural and cultural analysis of conversational storytelling.* Cambridge: MIT Press.

Polkinghorne, D. (1988). *Narrative knowing in the human sciences.* Albany: State University of New York Press.

Potter, D. (1954). *People of plenty: Economic abundance and the American character.* Chicago: University of Chicago Press.

Pratt, M. L. (1986). Fieldwork in common places. In J. Clifford & G. E. Marcos (Eds.), *Writing culture: The poetics and politics of ethnography* (pp. 27–50). Berkeley: University of California Press.

Reason, P. (Ed.). (1988). *Human inquiry in action: Developments in new paradigm research.* London: Sage.

Rorty, R. (1986). Science as solidarity. In J. Nelson, A. Megill, & D. McCloskey (Eds.), *The rhetoric of the human sciences* (pp. 38–52). Madison: University of Wisconsin Press.

Rychlak, J. F. (1994). *Logical learning theory: A human teleology and its empirical support.* Lincoln: University of Nebraska Press.

Sarbin, T. R. (Ed.). (1986). *Narrative psychology: The storied nature of human conduct.* New York: Praeger.

Sarup, M. (1993). *An introductory guide to post-structuralism and postmodernism* (2nd ed.). Athens: University of Georgia.

Schama, S. (1988). *The embarrassment of riches.* Berkeley: University of California Press.

Schama, S. (1992). *Dead certainties: Unwarranted speculations.* New York: Knopf.

Schank, R. C. (1990). *Tell me a story: A new look at real and artificial memory.* New York: Scribner.

Schank, R., & Abelson, R. (1977). *Scripts, plans, goals, and understanding.* Hillsdale, NJ: Lawrence Erlbaum.

Sheffield, S. (2001). *Revealing new worlds: Three Victorian women naturalists.* New York: Routledge.

Slife, B. D. (1993). *Time and psychological explanation.* Albany: State University of New York Press.

Smith, J. K. (1983). Quantitative versus qualitative research: An attempt to clarify the issue. *Educational Researcher, 12*(3), 6–13.

Stark, R. (2004). *Sociology* (9th ed.). Belmont, CA: Wadsworth.

Thayer-Bacon, B. J. (2003). *Relational "(e)pistemologies."* New York: Peter Lang.

Turner, P. (1994). *I heard it through the grapevine: Rumor in African-American culture.* Berkeley: University of California Press.

White, H. (1987). *The content of the form: Narrative discourse and historical representation.* Baltimore: Johns Hopkins University Press.

White, M., & Epston, D. (1990). *Narrative means to therapeutic ends.* New York: W. W. Norton.

White, R. (1998). *Remembering Ahanagran: Storytelling in a family's past.* New York: Farrar, Straus and Giroux.

Williams, W. (1959). *The tragedy of American diplomacy.* Cleveland, OH: World Publishing.

Witherell, C., & Noddings, N. (1991). *Stories lives tell: Narrative and dialogue in education.* New York: Teachers College Press.

CHAPTER 2

Mapping a Landscape of Narrative Inquiry

Borderland Spaces and Tensions

D. Jean Clandinin and Jerry Rosiek

Epistemic agents may no longer claim merely to find the world and so thereby shirk responsibility not only for what they find, but also for the nature of what is found. These objects, these substances of the world, are so often not just epistemic constructions but rather ontological artifacts of our own making and doing . . . practices of representation are peculiarly situated in this process, for representation is itself a mode of intervention.

—Kory Sorrell (2004, pp. 74–75)

The only thing that keeps us from floating off with the wind is our stories. They give us a name and put us in a place, allow us to keep on touching.

—Tom Spanbauer (1992, p. 190)

Narrative inquiry is an old practice that may feel new to us for a variety of reasons. Human beings have lived out and told stories about that living for as long as we could talk. And then we have talked about the stories we tell for almost as long. These lived and told stories and the talk about the stories are one of the ways that we fill our world with meaning and enlist one another's assistance in building lives and communities. What feels new is the emergence of narrative methodologies in the field of social science research. With this emergence has come intensified talk about our stories, their function in our lives, and their place in composing our collective affairs. This development has required greater philosophical precision in our use of the terms *narrative* and *narrative inquiry*, classification schemes that respectfully acknowledge the diversity of lived and told stories and story talk, and an examination of the boundaries with other traditions of research.

As seen in Chapter 1, each of the various approaches to the use of narrative inquiry has a history, a history that is itself becoming a topic of scholarly discussion. Lieblich, Tuval-Mashiach, and Zilber (1998, p. 1) referred to a "narrative revolution" that was made possible by the decline of an exclusively positivist paradigm for social science research. Also commenting on this revolution some years earlier, Connelly and Clandinin (1990) wrote that although the idea of narrative inquiry as research methodology is new to the social sciences, it has intellectual roots in the humanities and other fields under the broad heading of narratology. Hurwitz, Greenhalgh, and Skultans (2004) trace the emergence of narrative research in the field of medicine as a response to ethical scandals in medical research of the 20th century and the adversarial relationship it precipitated between patients and doctors. Narrative inquiry, they argue, can help heal that relationship. Writing in the field of women's studies, Vaz (1997) locates the inspiration for the use of oral narrative research in a history of Africana women struggling against patriarchy and colonialism.

What becomes apparent in this brief historical tracing is how interwoven narrative ways of thinking about phenomena are with the ways that narrative methodologies are emerging. For example, we hear Bruner speaking of narrative ways of knowing when he says, "Telling stories is an astonishing thing. We are a species whose main purpose is to tell each other about the expected and the surprises that upset the expected, and we do that through the stories we tell" (Bruner, cited in Charon, 2002, p. 8). While Bruner points us toward narrative as a mode of knowing, Lieblich et al. (1998) point us toward the need for narrative inquiry as a methodological response to the positivist paradigms. Connelly and Clandinin (1990) link the research methodological turn to the alternative ways of thinking about experience. The need for both narrative ways of thinking about experience and new narrative methodologies becomes apparent in the works of Hurwitz et al. (2004) and Vaz (1997). It is this interweaving of narrative views of phenomena and narrative inquiry that marks the emerging field and that draws attention to the need for careful uses and distinctions of terms. The ways that scholars in many fields have taken this narrative turn both in thinking about the phenomenon of experience and in thinking about research methodologies makes the situation even more complex.

Reissman and Speedy (this volume) hint at this complexity when they note,

> Beginning in the late 1960s and continuing at a hectic pace, the idea of narrative has penetrated almost every discipline and school. No longer the sole province of literary scholarship, narrative study is now cross-disciplinary, not fitting within the boundaries of any single scholarly field.

Furthermore, they note that while "narrative inquiry in the human sciences is a 20th-century development, the field has 'realist,' 'modernist,' 'post-modern,' and 'constructionist' strands, and scholars disagree on origins and precise definition" (Reissman and Speedy, this volume). Sconiers and Rosiek (2000) note similar divergences within the field, citing phenomenological, post-modern, and performative approaches to narrative research. From these different standpoints, we want to draw attention to the narrative turn, a turn that is remarkable in the intensity and enthusiasm with which it has shifted research methodological undertakings.

Any attempt to organize these divergent views into a summary representation inevitably risks shortchanging one view in favor of the priorities of another. There are, however, real differences of opinion on the epistemological, ideological, and ontological commitments of narrative inquirers as well as real differences with those who do not identify as narrative inquirers. These differences, we believe, require careful attention and discussion if the field of narrative inquiry is to realize its potential for making a contribution to the study of human experience and lives. It is the project of this chapter to help clarify these discussions by mapping some of those differences.

Our approach to this conceptual cartography will not be naively objectivist. We do not assume we have access to a stance outside of the history of the field, from which to impartially document all its parts. We are, after all, among those whose work is part of what is being mapped. Leslie Marmon Silko (1997) describes the problem with the metaphor of mapping:

"A portion of territory the eye can comprehend in a single view" does not correctly describe the relationship between the human being and his or her surroundings. This assumes the viewer is somehow outside or separate from the territory she or he surveys. Viewers are as much a part of the landscape as the boulders they stand on. (p. 27)

Following Piles and Thrift (1995), authors of *Mapping the Subject,* we therefore employ the metaphor of mapping with a cognizance that all representations are partial and involve trade-offs between distortions and instrumental ends.[1] We will offer a representation of the field of narrative inquiry that holds one aspect of narrative inquiry constant and uses this as a point of reference from which to examine the internal and external borders of this area of scholarship. The map we construct, with its borders and borderlands, allows researchers to locate themselves on the landscape of narrative inquiry methodologies.

The point of constancy we take as our point of departure is the observation that narrative inquirers study experience. Connelly and Clandinin (1990, 2006) observed that arguments for the development and use of narrative inquiry are inspired by a view of human experience in which humans, individually and socially, lead storied lives:

People shape their daily lives by stories of who they and others are and as they interpret their past in terms of these stories. Story, in the current idiom, is a portal through which a person enters the world and by which their experience of the world is interpreted and made personally meaningful. Narrative inquiry, the study of experience as story, then, is first and foremost a way of thinking about experience. Narrative inquiry as a methodology entails a view of the phenomenon. To use narrative inquiry methodology is to adopt a particular view of experience as phenomenon under study. (Connelly & Clandinin, 2006, p. 375)

There are many philosophical treatments of the word *experience*, from Aristotle's dualistic metaphysics in which knowledge of particulars and universals were considered separately, to early empiricist atomistic conceptions of experience, Marxist conceptions of experience distorted by ideology, behaviorist notions of stimulus and response, and post-structuralist assertions that state our experience is the product of discursive practices. The view of experience to which Clandinin and Connelly refer, and which will serve as the cornerstone of our analysis, has its roots in John Dewey's (1938) pragmatic philosophy.

By situating the philosophical foundation of narrative inquiry within a Deweyan theory of experience, we intend to work toward clarifying differences and affinities narrative inquiry has with other areas of scholarship. Our intent in claiming a Deweyan theory of experience as central to the epistemology and ontology of narrative inquiry allows us to sharpen distinctions between both narrative inquiry and other scholarly traditions as well as to sharpen distinctions within the field of narrative inquiry. Through highlighting the tensions at the borders with other areas of scholarship, we bring into sharper relief the differences with other areas of scholarship. However, as we bring into sharper relief the distinctions, we also highlight the affinities among narrative inquiry and other forms of scholarship.

Deweyan Theory of Experience[2]

For the purposes of our discussion, there are two particularly salient features of Dewey's (1976) conception of experience. The first is that experience is the fundamental ontological category from which all inquiry—narrative or otherwise—proceeds:

The importance attached to the word "experience," then . . . is to be understood as an invitation to employ thought and discriminative knowledge as a means of plunging into something which no argument and no term can express; or rather as an invitation to note the fact that no plunge is needed, since one's own thinking and explicit knowledge are already constituted by and within something which does not need to be expressed or made explicit. . . . The word "experience" is, I repeat, a notation of an inexpressible as that which decides the ultimate status of all which is expressed; inexpressible not because it is so remote and transcendent, but because it is so immediately engrossing and matter of course. (p. 325, footnote 1)

The last line here is important, because it points us to the aspect of pragmatism that makes it unique in the Western philosophical tradition as well as particularly germane to narrative inquiry. Dewey says experience is "a notation of an inexpressible." Other philosophers have made similar claims. Kant spoke of the ding an sich or "thing-in-itself," an idea necessary for a coherent theory of knowledge but fundamentally unrepresentable. The phenomenologists spoke of an infinite duree (Bergson, 1889/1960; Merleau-Ponty, 1962; Schutz, 1973), undifferentiated immediate experience that our reflection edits into. For Kant and the phenomenologists, there is something beyond the reach of our writing and reflection toward which our inquiries must nonetheless reach. The inexpressible reality of the ding an sich or the infinite duree thus serves as a regulative ideal for human inquiry while remaining untouched by the representations.

Dewey's (1981c) conception of experience differs from this. It does not refer to some precognitive, precultural ground on which our conceptions of the world rest. Instead, it is a changing stream that is characterized by continuous interaction of human thought with our personal, social, and material environment:

> Because every experience is constituted by interaction between "subject" and "object," between a self and its world, it is not itself either merely physical nor merely mental, no matter how much one factor or the other predominates. . . . [experiences] are the products of discrimination, and hence can be understood only as we take into account the total normal experience in which both inner and outer factors are so incorporated that each has lost its special character. In an experience, things and events belonging to the world, physical and social, are transformed through the human context they enter, while the live creature is changed and developed through its intercourse with things previously external to it. (p. 251)

In other words, Dewey's ontology is not transcendental, it is transactional. The epistemological implications of this view are nothing short of revolutionary.[3] It implies that the regulative ideal for inquiry is not to generate an exclusively faithful representation of a reality independent of the knower. The regulative ideal for inquiry is to generate a new relation between a human being and her environment—her life, community, world—one that "makes possible a new way of dealing with them, and thus eventually creates a new kind of experienced objects, not more real than those which preceded but more significant, and less overwhelming and oppressive" (Dewey, 1981b, p. 175) In this pragmatic view of knowledge, our representations arise from experience and must return to that experience for their validation.

There are several features of this ontology of experience that make it particularly well suited for framing narrative inquiry as we are discussing it here. First, the temporality of knowledge generation is emphasized. Experience, for the pragmatist, is always more than we can know and represent in a single statement, paragraph, or book. Every representation, therefore, no matter how faithful to that which it tries to depict, involves selective emphasis of our experience. Dewey (1958) warns against obscuring the selection process, thus naturalizing the objects of our inquiry and treating them as if they are given:

> Honest empirical method will state when and where and why the act of selection took place, and thus enable others to repeat it and test its worth. . . . Under all the captions that are called immediate knowledge, or self-sufficient certitude of belief, whether logical, esthetic, or epistemological, there is something selected for a purpose, and hence not simple, not self-evident, and not intrinsically eulogizable. State the purpose so that it may be re-experienced, and its value and the pertinency of selection undertaken in its behalf may be tested. (p. 271)

Another way of saying this is that an honest empirical method will present inquiry as a series of choices, inspired by purposes that are shaped by past experience, undertaken through time, and will trace the consequences of these choices in the whole of an individual or community's lived experience.

In our view, narratives are the form of representation that describes human experience as it unfolds through time. Therefore, narratives are, arguably, the most appropriate form to use when thinking about inquiry undertaken within a pragmatic framework. Although narrative forms of representation are often used in inquiries framed by other philosophical frameworks, they are, in those cases, almost always regarded as having a degraded epistemic status; if the reality we seek to describe is presumed to be independent of our representations of it, then there is no need to tell the story of how our representation of the world emerged within a stream of experience nor how it returned to that experience.[4]

Second, a pragmatic ontology of experience emphasizes continuity, that is,

> the idea that experiences grow out of other experiences, and experiences lead to further experiences. Wherever one positions oneself in that continuum— the imagined now, some imagined past, or some imagined future—each point has a past experiential base and leads to an experiential future. (Clandinin & Connelly, 2000, p. 2)

It is important to note that this continuity is not merely perceptual; it is ontological. Experiences do not simply appear to be connected through time; they are continuous.

This conception of continuity is required by the pragmatic promotion of a transactional ontology. Rejecting centuries of speculation about what transcendent reality (God, eternal forms, pure substance) is needed to hold the amazing variety of human experiences together, William James (1909) states the basic principle of ontology of experience:

> The generalized conclusion is that therefore the parts of experience hold together from next to next by relations that are themselves parts of experience. The directly apprehended universe needs, in short, no extraneous transempirical

connective support, but possesses in its own right a concatenated or continuous structure. (p. 195)

In other words, what you see (and hear, feel, think, love, taste, despise, fear, etc.) is what you get. That is all we ultimately have in which to ground our understanding. And that is all we need.

This continuity has important implications for the way we think about inquiry, narrative or otherwise. It reinforces the idea that inquiry is not a search "behind the veil" of appearances that ends in the identification of an unchanging transcendent reality. Instead, inquiry is an act within a stream of experience that generates new relations that then become a part of future experience. It also problematizes the boundaries of inquiry. If experience is continuous, then the initial parameters we set up for our inquiries are themselves a form of relation that can and should be questioned in the course of ongoing research. Dewey (1976) explains it as follows:

It intimates that while the results of reflection, because of the continuity of experience, may be of wider scope than the situation which calls out a particular inquiry and invention, reflection itself is always specific in origin and aim; it always has something special to cope with. For troubles are concretely specific. It intimates also that thinking and reflective knowledge are never an end-all, never their own purpose nor justification, but that they pass naturally into a more direct and vital type of experience, whether technological or appreciative or social. (pp. 332–333)

Referring to inevitable inferential spillover of our inquiries, Dewey describes experience as having something that "stretches." This stretch is almost "indefinitely elastic" and extends into realms of personal, aesthetic, and social meaning.

This brings us to a third feature of a pragmatic ontology of experience that makes it particularly well suited for framing narrative inquiries—its emphasis on the social dimension of our inquiries and understanding. Narrative inquiries explore the stories people live and tell. These stories are the result of a confluence of social influences on a person's inner life, social influences on their environment, and their unique personal history. These stories are often treated as the epiphenomenal to social inquiry—reflections of important social realities but not realities themselves. Dewey (1981a) warns against this prejudice that condescends to impoverishing experience as a source of knowledge:

The most serious indictment to be brought against non-empirical philosophies is that they have cast a cloud over the things of ordinary experience. They have not been content to rectify them. They have discredited them at large. In casting aspersions upon the things of everyday experience, the things of action and affection and social intercourse, they have done something far worse than fail to give these affairs intelligent direction. . . . To waste of time and energy, to disillusionment with life that attends every deviation from concrete experience must be added the tragic failure to realize the value that intelligent search could reveal among the things of ordinary experience. I cannot calculate how much of current cynicism, indifference, and pessimism is due to these causes and the deflection of intelligence they have brought about. (pp. 40–41)

It is stunning how well Dewey's warning here seems to describe the contemporary climate in many service professions—teaching, health professions, social work, urban planning, and so on. Narrow standards of effectiveness are imposed on an undertaking whose significance to those involved is both nuanced and manifold. And this imposition of procrustean standards of evidence threatens to drain the meaning of that service from both the service providers and those receiving services. In contrast, narrative inquiry is an approach to the study of human lives conceived as a way of honoring lived experience as a source of important knowledge and understanding:

Narrative inquiry is a way of understanding experience. It is collaboration between researcher and participants, over time, in a place or series of places, and in social interaction with milieus. An inquirer enters this matrix in the midst and progresses in the same spirit, concluding the inquiry still in the midst of living and telling, reliving and retelling, the stories of the experiences that make up people's lives, both individual and social. (Clandinin & Connelly, 2000, p. 20)

Beginning with a respect for ordinary lived experience, the focus of narrative inquiry is not only a valorizing of individuals' experience but also an exploration of the social, cultural, and institutional narratives within which individuals' experiences were constituted, shaped, expressed, and enacted—but in a way that begins and ends that inquiry in the storied lives of the people involved. Narrative inquirers study an individual's experience in the world and, through the study, seek ways of enriching and transforming that experience for themselves and others.

Viewed in this way, we can see that not only is a pragmatic ontology of experience a well-suited theoretical framework for narrative inquiries, narrative inquiry is an approach to research that enacts many if not all of the principles of a Deweyan theory of inquiry. In fact, we offer that narrative inquiry as we describe it is a quintessentially pragmatic methodology. What genealogy is to post-structuralist Foucauldian sociology, what critical ethnography is to critical theory, what experiments are to positivism, narrative inquiry is to Deweyan pragmatism.

Holding a Deweyan theory of experience as a constant, as we construct our map of narrative inquiry, allows us to see borders and borderlands between narrative inquiry and other forms of inquiry. It also allows us to see borderlands within the work of those of us engaged in narrative inquiry. A Deweyan view of experience allows for the study of experience that acknowledges the embodiment of the person living in the world (Johnson, 1987). Framed within this view of experience, the focus of narrative inquiry is not only on individuals' experiences but also on the social, cultural, and institutional narratives within which individuals' experiences are constituted, shaped, expressed, and enacted. Narrative inquirers study the individual's experience in the world, an experience that is storied both in the living and telling and that can be studied by listening, observing, living alongside another, and writing and interpreting texts.

This constant view of experience understood from a Deweyan perspective and of narrative inquiry as the study of experience understood in this way makes possible an understanding of borders and possible borderlands with other forms of research methodologies.

Border Conditions

It is often helpful in describing phenomena to explain both what it is and what it is not. Having located the conceptual roots of narrative inquiry in a Deweyan ontology of experience, we can now contrast this with the philosophical assumptions that underlie other forms of scholarship. This, in turn, will permit us to make sense of the kinds of questions asked and methods employed in narrative inquiry. In what follows, we explore the conceptual border between narrative inquiry and social science grounded in three other philosophical traditions: post-positivism, Marxism, and post-structuralism.

Post-Positivism

The contrast with post-positivism is perhaps the most frequently discussed in the literature on narrative inquiry. For example, Clandinin and Connelly (2000) described this conceptual border as the boundary between narrative inquiry and reductionist thinking. We realize that the literature on positivist and post-positivist epistemology and its implications for the social sciences is vast and beyond the scope of this chapter to summarize. Our modest goal here is to identify the most general features of this approach to social science inquiry and clarify its relation to narrative inquiry.

At the most general level, positivist philosophies begin with epistemological commitments and treat ontological commitments as secondary considerations. In other words, it begins with a theory of knowledge and, from there, ventures into claims about the nature of reality. This approach to philosophy was developed in the 19th century as a reaction to the proliferation of baroque and confusing metaphysical claims about natural and social phenomena. Whether it is notions of corpuscular ether that moves objects, the influence of God on human souls, or evidence that someone was practicing witchcraft, positivism rejected any claims about reality that could not be grounded in empirical observations of the facts of experience.

Over the last century, positivist philosophers moderated their ambitions. Whereas early positivists sought to produce verifiable descriptions of reality, later post-positivists concluded that descriptions cannot be verified in any final way; they can only be falsified. Thus, they are willing to admit into the category of knowledge only those statements that can be demonstrably falsified by procedures that can be made public but that—when tried—have not proven false. The conception of reality that underlies this theory of knowledge is called critical realism and is the subject of considerable debate. Adherents minimally maintain (1) that reality is independent of our minds and (2) that something is real if it can bring about observable consequences that permit for public testing of a claim about the world (Bhaskar, 1997; Phillips & Burbules, 2000).

It is important to note, here, that this is not a naive realism, the idea that we have direct knowledge of the world without any mediation by our senses, social influence, or the like.[5] The critical realist can in fact claim that "there is no conflict between seeing our scientific views as being about objectively given real worlds, and understanding our beliefs about them as subject to all kinds of historical and other determinations" (Norris, 1999, p. 39).

Rather than deny the various social and cultural influences on social science inquiry, the post-positivist seeks to identify methodological procedures that can help communities deal critically with the many mediations of our experience of the world in a way that permits an identification of a reality that we all share. The virtue of this epistemologically conservative stance is that it provides a very stable consensus about a knowledge base for social science inquiry. The drawback is that the price of this stability is that large regions of human experience that influence human affairs—personal meaning, love, hate, aesthetic considerations, religious experience, narrative coherence of individual lives—are often placed outside the bounds of that inquiry.

Narrative inquiry, by way of contrast, begins with an ontology of experience. From this conception of reality as relational, temporal, and continuous, it arrives at a conception of how that reality can be known. This ontology is fundamentally different from that of a critical realist. The critical realist can admit the existence of an infinite variety of private impressions, personal significances, and personal meanings. However, she reserves the term *reality* for something beyond our immediate experience that structures everyone's experience similarly. Following Dewey, the narrative inquirer takes the sphere of immediate human experience as the first and most fundamental reality we have. Building on Dewey, the narrative inquirer focuses on the way the relational, temporal, and continuous features of a pragmatic ontology of experience can manifest in narrative form, not just in retrospective representations of human experience but also in the lived immediacy of that experience.

Following from this ontology, the narrative inquirer arrives at a very different conception of knowledge than the post-positivist. Whereas post-positivists seek a description of a reality that stands outside human experience, the narrative inquirer seeks a knowledge of human experience that remains within the stream of human lives. In other words, narrative inquiry does not merely describe this or that feature of someone's experience. It is simultaneously a description of, and intervention into, human experience; it acknowledges that descriptions add meaning to experience, thus changing the content and quality of the experience. Dewey (1981a) describes this irreducible interplay of description and intervention as follows:

Knowledge or science, as a work of art, like any other work of art, confers upon things traits and potentialities which did not previously belong to them. [It] . . . is an act which confers upon non-cognitive material traits which did not belong to it. It marks a change by which physical events exhibiting properties of mechanical energy, connected by relations of push and pull, hitting, rebounding, splitting and consolidating, realize characters, meanings and relations of meaning hitherto not possessed by them. (p. 126)

Such recursive knowledge effects might be regarded as a design flaw in a post-positivist inquiry on human meaning, one that creates feedback loops that distort the data and undermine the researchers' ability to identify falsifiable claims. For the narrative inquirer, the fact that the inquiry is altering the phenomena under study is not regarded as a methodological problem to be overcome. It is the purpose of the research.

These differences in a general conception of inquiry call for different styles and approaches to scholarship on human experience. Clandinin and Connelly (2000) described how a focus on the temporal nature of human experience requires a particular kind of thinking. To think as a narrative inquirer is to think of events as happening over time; each event or thing has a past, present as it appears to us, and implied future. This temporality has semiotic implications. In narrative inquiry, an action is

seen as a narrative sign . . . it is necessary to give a narrative interpretation of that sign before meaning can be attached to it. Without understanding the narrative history of the child [individual], the significance or meaning of the performance [action], the sign, remains unknown. (pp. 30–31)

This view of action can be contrasted to post-positivist research in which

an action is taken as directly evidential. There is an equation connecting action and meaning, connecting performance and cognitive level. In narrative thinking [inquiry], however, there is an interpretive pathway between action and meaning mapped out in terms of narrative histories. (p. 31)

Clandinin and Connelly (2000) also describe a difference between narrative inquiry and post-positivist research based on the treatment of the context of human meaning. In post-positivist research, while the influence of context is acknowledged, the purpose of research design is to limit attention to that context. The ideal is often considered an experiment in which all contextual influences can be controlled or at least accounted for. In narrative inquiry, multiple contexts beyond the researcher's control—such as spatial contexts, cultural contexts, social contexts, institutional contexts, place contexts, and people contexts—are always present. Narrative inquiry is, following this, a relational form of inquiry. Describing the way people go about making sense of their experience within these contexts, and contributing to that ongoing sensemaking, is the purpose of narrative inquiry.

There is a trade-off involved in embracing a robust engagement with the temporal and contextual nature of human experience. What narrative inquirers gain in the proximity to ordinary lived experience and the scope of their considerations, they, at times, sacrifice in certainty. Narrative inquirers work with an attitude of knowing that other possibilities, interpretations, and ways of explaining things are possible. This sense of uncertainty or tentativeness is one of the most visible and remarked on in the differences between narrative and post-positivist inquirers. It often inspires exchanges in which both forms of research are grossly misrepresented. Post-positivists can accuse narrative inquirers of being confused about the object they are describing, self-indulgent, and substituting opinion for knowledge. Narrative inquirers accuse post-positivists of being naive about the nature of human experience, inhumanly procrustean in their conception of knowledge, and politically complicit with government powers that want to silence whole regions of human experience.

Such hyperbolic exchanges are, in the opinion of these authors, unhelpful. It is better to look more closely at the practice of each type of research and critique specific commitments. For narrative inquirers, a sense of tentativeness in representing their own experiences or the experiences of others is the necessary condition for conceiving of a form of inquiry whose object is the transformation of lived human experience. In other words, narrative inquirers must think of any description of human meaning as tentative, if they are to keep alive the possibility that the description can change the quality of the experience being described.

The challenge for the narrative inquirer, therefore, is less one of achieving the highest possible grade of epistemic clarity and is instead how to integrate ethical and epistemic concerns—how to put knowledge in the service of enhancing human experience. The post-positivist conception of knowledge has a role to play in refining narrative inquiry. False or delusional representations of human experience are unlikely to enhance that experience in any sustainable way. But falsehoods are not the only risk about which narrative inquirers are concerned. They are also concerned with missing heretofore unrealized possibilities in human experience. As William James (1897) exclaimed in "The Will to Believe and Other Essays in Popular Philosophy,"

> Believe truth! Shun error!—these, we see, are two materially different laws; and by choosing between them we may end by coloring differently our whole intellectual life. . . . We must remember that these feelings of our duty to either truth or error are in any case only expressions of our passional life. Biologically considered, our minds are as ready to grind out falsehood as veracity, and he who says, "Better go without belief forever than believe a lie!" merely shows his own preponderant private horror of becoming a dupe. He may be critical of many of his desires and fears, but this fear he slavishly obeys. He cannot imagine anyone questioning its binding force. For my own part, I have also a horror of being duped; but I can believe that worse things than being duped may happen to a man in this world. . . . Our errors are surely not such awfully solemn things. In a world where we are so certain to incur them

in spite of all our caution, a certain lightness of heart seems healthier than this excessive nervousness on their behalf. At any rate, it seems the fittest thing for the empiricist philosopher. (p. 721)

Marxism and Critical Theory

Post-positivism is not the only philosophical neighbor with which narrative inquirers negotiate border conditions. Less frequently explored, but often more morally and politically charged, is the border between narrative inquiry and approaches to social analysis grounded in some form of Marxism, including but not limited to the work of Marxist sociologists, critical theorists, critical ethnographers, and post-Marxists.

Narrative inquirers and Marxist-influenced scholars working in the applied social sciences often share an interest in analyzing the way large institutions dehumanize, anesthetize, and alienate the people living and working within them. They also share an interest in resisting those effects by producing a scholarship that intervenes in this process by helping people develop a more robust sense of the reality around them and their agency within that reality. What is different between their approaches is their underlying conception of that reality.

As with post-positivism, the literature on Marxist, critical theory, and post-Marxist social theory is vast and beyond the scope of this chapter to summarize. Our modest goal here is to identify the most general features of these conceptions of social science inquiry and clarify its relation to narrative inquiry. If narrative inquiry traces its philosophical roots to Dewey's philosophy, then contemporary critical theory can be said to trace its philosophical roots to Marxist philosophy. Like Dewey and the pragmatists, Marxist philosophies begin with ontological commitments and treat epistemological commitments as important subsequent considerations. The differences between the two lie in the details of their ontological commitments.

For the Marxist, the fundamental motivation for their analysis is the observation that large-scale social arrangements conspire not only to physically disempower individuals and groups but also to epistemically disempower people. In other words, systems of oppression in modern capitalistic societies include the means by which the sources of that oppression are obscured. This process of deflecting attention from the real causes of oppression is no mere momentary distraction. It involves, according to Marxist theorists, sustained deflections of thought perpetrated by the most cherished and respected traditions of our cultures: religion, nationalism, and liberal humanism.

Marx's term for this deflection of attention from the real cause of oppression was *ideology*. Ideology has been such a generative idea in western social inquiry that it has acquired many definitions (Hawkes, 2003). For our purposes we will let ideology refer here to a system of thought and practice that gives rise to false consciousness in individuals and communities. False consciousness is a condition in which a person acquires a habit of thinking and feeling that prevents him or her from noticing and analyzing the real causes of his or her oppression.

It is the Marxist critique of humanism that is germane to our discussion. Humanism, according to this view, is an ideological system. The false consciousness it produces is an exclusive attention to individuals and individual human experience as a source of knowledge. The humanist idea that all knowledge must begin in the observations and content of individual consciousness leaves people trapped in their inherited ideologies. This is the charge that Marxist-influenced scholars most often bring to bear on the work of narrative inquirers. By focusing on individual experience as a source of insight, the larger social conditions that shape the narratives in which people live go unexamined. Marx and Engles warned that humanist ideologies simultaneously shape institutions that distort human experience and then point to that distortion as the fundamental condition of truth. The result is an inversion of reality and falsehood.

> Consciousness can never be anything else than conscious existence, and the existence of men is their actual life-process. If in all ideology men and their circumstances appear upside-down as in a camera obscura,[6] this phenomenon arises just as much from their historical life-process as the inversion of objects on the retina does from their physical life-process. . . . We set out from real, active men, and on the basis of their real life-process we demonstrate the development of the ideological reflexes and echoes of this life-process. The phantoms formed in the human brain are also, necessarily, sublimates of their material life-process, which is empirically verifiable and bound to material premises. (Marx, 1846/1972, p. 118)

Over the last century, this early formulation of "false consciousness" has been critiqued, refined, and elaborated by many social theorists (Adorno, 2000; Augoustinos, 1999; Horkheimer, 2005; Lukacs, 1972; Wetherell, 1999). These critiques have focused on the class-identity essentialism that underlies the juxtaposition of false consciousness and a proletariat consciousness that is free from the distortions of ideology (Laclau & Mouffe, 1987). They have also examined the limits of processes of representation to actually describe ideology (Jameson, 1992; Marcuse, 1964; Zizek, 1999). In most cases, however, some version of Marxist anti-humanism—the idea that ordinary individual experience is distorted by ideology and is, therefore, not a trustworthy source of insight about the social challenges we face—has remained a central analytical commitment of critical theory and post-Marxist scholarship.

This rejection of individual experience as a valid source of knowledge stands in clear contrast to the commitments of narrative inquiry as we have presented it. Precisely understanding that difference, however, requires a careful examination of the philosophical assumptions underlying each tradition. A casual read of the idea of "false" consciousness may give the impression that the first commitment of Marxist-influenced theorists is epistemological—an idea of how to discern truth from falsehood. It is, instead, an ontological principle that ultimately anchors their analysis—the assertion that the material conditions of society precipitate ideologies that shape and distort our ability to understand our world. These material conditions precede and influence epistemological fashions in ways that function to protect and reproduce a grotesquely unequal distribution of human wealth and social power. It is, therefore, in the fundamental reality of these material conditions that Marxist-influenced scholars seek explanation for social and psychological phenomena.

> In the social production which men carry on they enter into definite relations that are indispensable and independent of their will; these relations of production correspond to a definite stage of development of their material powers of production. The sum total of these relations of production constitutes the economic structure of society—the real foundation, on which rise legal and political superstructures and to which correspond definite forms of social consciousness. The mode of production in material life determines the general character of the social, political and spiritual processes of life. It is not the consciousness of men that determines their existence, but on the contrary, their social existence determines their consciousness. (Marx, 1964, p. 51)

Although it may seem extremely abstract, understanding the ontological as opposed to epistemological starting point of Marxist-influenced social theory is necessary for understanding the style and content of this scholarship as well as its relationship with narrative inquiry. A mode of inquiry founded in epistemological commitments—such as positivism—takes accurate description of the world as its primary objective. Epistemic principles, in this case, determine the way the accuracy of research conclusions will be assessed. A mode of inquiry founded in ontological commitments—such as Marxism or critical theory—takes transformation of those ontological conditions as its primary objective.[7] For the Marxist-influenced scholar, research and analysis is an intervention that seeks to change the material conditions that underlie oppressive social conditions.

As remarked on earlier, narrative inquiry shares with Marxism an explicit grounding in ontological commitments as well as the goal of generating scholarship that transforms the ontological conditions of living. The differences between these two traditions of inquiry are located in the specifics of those commitments and their conception of intervention. Scholarship grounded in Marxism privileges the macrosocial material conditions of life as the primary influence on human life and thinking. The relational texture of everyday life, including the personal, religious, historical, and cultural narratives that provide meaning to that life, are treated as derivative of the macrosocial conditions of life. Furthermore, these narratives are frequently considered obstacles to be overcome on the way to a more realistic understanding of the causes of human experience.

The narrative inquirer, by way of contrast, privileges individual lived experience as a source of insights useful not only to the person himself or herself but also to the wider field of social science scholarship generally.[8] As described in the comparison to post-positivism, this approach to analyzing human experience is grounded in a pragmatic relational ontology. It takes the immediacy of lived experiences, specifically its narrative qualities, as a fundamental reality to be examined and acted on. According to this view, all representations of experience—including representations of the macrosocial influences on that experience—ultimately arise from first-person lived experience and need to find their warrant in their influence on that experience. Dewey (1981a) is unequivocal on the latter point:

> Thus here is supplied, I think, a first rate test of the value of any philosophy which is offered us: Does it end in conclusions which, when they are referred back to ordinary life-experiences and their predicaments, render them more significant, more luminous to us, and make our dealings with them more fruitful? Or does it terminate in rendering the things of ordinary experience more opaque than they were before, and in depriving them of in "reality" even the significance they had previously seemed to have? (p. 18)

In privileging lived experience as the ultimate source of, and site of, validation for knowledge, the narrative inquirer does not exclude the possibility of analyzing the oppressive effects of macrosocial conditions. Many social theorists who ground their work in a pragmatic ontology examine the macrosocial conditions of oppression (de Lauretis, 1986; Hook, 1987; Sullivan, 2001, 2006; West, 1989), as do many narrative inquirers (Chang & Rosiek, 2004; Hadden, 2000; Henry & Tator, 2005; Laubscher & Powell, 2003; Maher & Ward, 2002; Sconiers & Rosiek, 2000). However, ultimately, narrative inquirers demur at the Marxist contention that individual lived experience needs to be approached first as the product of ideologies, meaning that the first step in social inquiry is the critique of ideologies. For the narrative inquirer, a person's experience must be listened to on its own terms first, without the presumption of deficit or flaw, and critique needs to be motivated by the problematic elements within that experience. Consequently, the intervention envisioned by the narrative inquirer focuses first on the qualities of lived experience; it is in collaboratively trans-forming the narratives within which people live that narrative inquiry seeks to lay the foundations for social change. Without such foundations rooted in the storied experiences of ordinary people, it is believed that efforts at social change are con-demned to either be ineffective or hollow exercises of externally imposed authority.

Herein lies the most important difference in the practice of inquiry of these two traditions of scholarship. For the Marxist-influenced scholar, the insistence on beginning inquiry in the lived experience of individuals can at best seem overly burdensome. For problems with a clearly macrosocial provenance, this would be like requiring an injured patient to describe their wounds at the cellular level before providing medical care—an unreasonable and dangerous delay of action. At worst, in the Marxist view, the narrative inquirer appears to be the willing dupe of humanist ideologies that function to deflect any attempt to analyze the real causes of oppression. They would say that narrative inquiry stays within the comfortable zone of private experience and provides no leverage for insisting that the mostly middle- and upper-class professionals who conduct and read the research examine their complicity with institutionalized oppression.

Narrative inquirers, on the other hand, often find scholarship grounded in Marxism at best condescending. It approaches people's experience with the presumption of deficits that only the Marxist academic can remedy. At its worst, the narrative inquirer can find scholarship grounded in Marxist theory to be imperialist and self-defeating. By preemptively dismissing the lived experience of persons as a possible source of insight, it simply replaces one totalizing source of external authority—be it church, state, or post-positivist social science—with another. The result is the continued disempowerment of exactly those persons the Marxist-influenced scholars seek to emancipate.

This dismissal of lived experience is particularly egregious when applied to communities who have been historically silenced by processes of colonialism, patriarchy, homophobia, and other forms of oppression. Stone-Mediatore (2003) describes this excess as follows:

> Worse still, when we treat experience-based narratives as mere ideological arti-facts, we reinforce the disempowerment of people who have been excluded from official knowledge production, for we deny epistemic value from a central means by which such people can take control over their own representation. (p. 2)

When reciprocal criticisms between different research paradigms reach the level of mutual recrimination and inspire an unwillingness to listen across disciplinary differences, they are not constructive. This need not be the outcome in this case. There is, in our opinion, much that narrative inquirers can gain from a continued dialogue with Marxist-influenced social theorists. Scholarship grounded in Marxist philosophy serves as a much-needed tonic for Pollyannaish liberal social policy that seeks a solution to all social problems through programs of individual self-improvement. It has also provided some of the most cogent challenges to liberal social science that cravenly ignores the possibility that large-scale socioeconomic conditions can explain both individual behavior and the way researchers choose the unit of analysis for their scholarship. There is nothing that makes such myopias a necessary feature of narrative inquiry. However, by taking the experience of the individual as the starting point and the site of validation for narrative inquiries, the risk of slipping into self-insulating habits of attention and analysis is high.

The question of whether narrative inquiry as a field can avoid this risk is ulti-mately an empirical question. The development of a narrative inquiry research community that can avoid simply reproducing narratives that support macrosocial systems of oppression, and can instead contribute to the amelioration of oppressive conditions, will depend on (1) educating narrative inquirers for whom the promo-tion of social justice is a central commitment, (2) the increased inclusion of voices examining experiences of oppression in the narrative inquiry literature, and (3) regular dialogue with scholars in other disciplines who can provide construc-tive political critique of narrative inquiry practices and texts.

Post-Structuralism

A third scholarly community with which narrative inquirers negotiate border conditions are post-structural social and cultural theorists. Post-structuralism and the more diffuse post-modern cultural developments to which it contributed are often considered the natural home to narrative inquiry. Post-structuralism focuses attention on the linguistic and narrative structure of knowledge. It raises fundamental and highly technical questions about the ways we represent the world and makes compelling arguments for encouraging epistemic and methodological diversity in the social sciences. Lyotard (1984), in his watershed work *The Postmodern Condition: A Report on Knowledge*, explained the narrative connection as follows:

> In the first place, scientific knowledge does not represent the totality of knowledge; it has always existed in addition to, and in competition and conflict with, another kind of knowledge, which I will call narrative in the interests of simplicity (its characteristics will be described later). I do not mean to say that narrative knowledge can prevail over science, but its model is related to ideas of internal equilibrium and conviviality next to which contemporary scientific knowledge cuts a poor figure. (p. 7)

There can be little question that narrative inquirers have benefited from the widespread influence of post-structuralist critiques of a narrowly and naively conceived scientism. These critiques have made audiences more receptive to the idea that there may be other ways of knowing that merit scholarly attention. However, narrative inquiry as we present it here cannot ultimately be grounded in post-structuralist theories about knowledge. To understand the reasons for this epistemic immiscibility, a brief review of the conceptual history of post-structuralism will be necessary.

Post-structuralism traces its roots to the linguistic structuralism of Ferdinand de Saussure (1959). Saussure challenged Aristotelian notions of an ideal one-to-one correspondence between a word and its object. Using the term *signifier* to denote a linguistic sign and *signified* to denote the object to which the sign referred, Saussure argued that, despite a few notable exceptions, the relation between words and their objects was essentially arbitrary. A signifier maintained a stable relationship to its signified, according to Saussure, through its embedded relationship with a whole system of signs, *la langue,* the language. (See graphic below.)

The full story of the development of contemporary post-structuralism from Saussurean linguistics is beyond the scope of this chapter. It would suffice to say

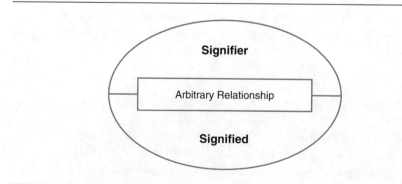

here that 20th-century anthropologists (e.g., Levi-Straus), psychoanalysts (e.g., Lacan), sociologists (e.g., Foucault, Buarillard), literary critics (e.g., Barthes, Spivak), philosophers (e.g., Derrida), and feminists (e.g., Kristeva, Butler) picked up Saussure's theories, elaborated on them, and extended their application to almost every area of study in the humanities and social sciences. For our purposes, the most important of these elaborations was the application of structuralism to the study of the academic disciplines themselves.

Academic disciplines are often thought to be defined by an object of study. The existence of the object and normative views about its ideal state are assumed to precede research on it. A scholar's method of study is chosen because it uniquely suits the object. For example, "mental illness" is assumed to have preexisted and inspired the development of the field of psychiatry. "Intelligence" is often assumed to exist in individuals and this fact is thought to justify the development of methods of measuring the characteristic. "Race" was long presumed to exist and the science of eugenics was presumed to be the study of the differences between human races. In each case, the object of study had clear normative binaries built in before inquiry began: illness/health, intelligent/unintelligent, white/non-white, and so on.

Post-structuralists used Saussure's theories to invert these assumptions. They took Saussure's argument about the arbitrary relationship between signifiers and signified and extended it to the relationship between an academic discipline and its object of study. (See graphic below.)

They argued that a close examination of the history and rhetoric of the human sciences revealed that objects of scholarly attention within disciplines often shift in ways that are unrelated to the accumulation of empirical evidence. What keeps a disciplinary community stable instead is its relationship to wider social and historical discourses, discourses that are shaped by and express a variety of competing interests that have little to do with the reality of the object of study. Just as words retain a somewhat stable meaning because they are embedded in a larger system of language, disciplinary discourses remain stable because they are embedded in a larger system of social discourses.

The result is an inversion of the traditional conception of an academic discipline. Instead of the object of study defining the process of inquiry, the process of inquiry creates the object that it examines. This social production of the object of

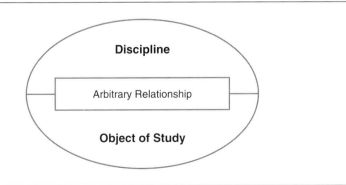

inquiry serves to legitimate the norms associated with that object. Foucault (1982) explains,

> I would like to show with precise examples that in analyzing discourses themselves, one sees the loosening of the embrace, apparently so tight, of words and things, and the emergence of a group of rules proper to discursive practice. These rules define not the dumb existence of a reality, nor the canonical use of a vocabulary, but the ordering of objects. . . . [This presents us with] a task that consists of not—of no longer treating discourses as groups of signs (signifying elements referring to contents or representations) but as practices that systematically form the objects of which they speak. (p. 176)

If it is not the objects, but instead various human interests expressed through social discourses, that ultimately shape academic disciplines, then the enlightenment project of establishing a knowledge base beyond politics becomes impossible. The norms that guide our inquiry become an effect of, not a refuge from, the operation of power:

> Power and knowledge directly imply one another. . . . There is no power relation without the correlative constitution of a field of knowledge that does not presuppose and constitute at the same time power relations. (Foucault, 1977, pp. 27–28)

What emerges from this analysis is a powerful argument for encouraging epistemic and methodological diversity in the social sciences. The interdependent relationship between knowledge and power implies that oppression operates, in part, by artificially narrowing the range of what counts as legitimate knowledge. Remarking on the relation between power and narrative forms of knowledge, Lyotard (1984) elaborates,

> In the West, narrative knowledge has been subjugated by scientific knowledge. The latter is "governed by the demand for legitimation" and, as a long history of imperialism from the dawn of Western civilization demonstrates, cannot accept anything that fails to conform to the rules (the requirement for proof or argumentation) of its own language game. (p. 27)

What also emerges from this analysis is a deep ambivalence about social science that seeks to intervene in the lives of those it studies. Post-structuralism provides analytic tools that help surface the way allegedly objective social science inquiry has served the function of legitimating arbitrary and hurtful social practices. Post-structuralism does not, however, make the development of alternative normative commitments part of its project. Just because our way of knowing the world is mediated by power and human interests it does not mean that there is an alternative way of knowing that escapes this condition. The gap between our descriptions of the world and the actual world is, for the post-structuralist, ultimately unbreachable.[9]

What we are left with is an infinite series of supplemental descriptions of the world, and descriptions of those descriptions, of which we need to remain suspicious. Post-structuralist social analysis self-consciously locates itself as one more of these redescriptions.[10]

Here, then, we can see both the similarities and the differences between post-structuralist social analysis and narrative inquiry. Narrative inquiry seeks to examine experience with an eye to identifying new possibilities within that experience. It maintains that knowledge gained from that experience has a linguistic structure; specifically, it maintains, with Lyotard, White, Jameson, and others, that some knowledge is narrative in form.

For the post-structuralist, however, our narrative knowledge has an entirely discursive provenance. Signs can only rely on other signs for their meaning, and thus inquiry does not deal with lived experience itself. Such experience may exist. But as soon as we speak or write about it, we have moved into the process of re-presentation. Representations depend on other representations and discursive systems for their meaning. Consequently, the post-structuralist researcher may listen to stories that individual persons tell her or him. But in so doing she or he will not be interpreting those experiences as immediate sources of knowledge and insight; instead, she or he will be listening through the person's story to hear the operation of broader social discourses shaping that person's story of their experience.

Narrative inquiry, by way of contrast, begins with a pragmatic ontology that treats lived experience as both the beginning and ending points of inquiry. Various social and cultural influences may come into play during the inquiry. As Clandinin and Connelly (2000) note,

> In narrative inquiry, people are looked at as embodiments of lived stories. Even when narrative inquirers study institutional narratives, such as stories of school, people are seen as composing lives that shape and are shaped by social and cultural narratives. (p. 43)

In a narrative inquiry, these social and cultural influences are not treated only as the occasions for critical exposure. They are treated as resources to be used in the pursuit of always tentative and partial ameliorations of experience. This is, of course, a normative project. The norms, for better or worse, must come from within the lived experience being studied. This translates into a collaborative ethic for inquiries, one in which researchers trained in the academy do not presume a transcendent perspective that explains away the stories they and their participants live as mere effects of preexisting social discourses. Clandinin and Connelly (2000) express a narrative inquirer's ambivalence about post-structuralism and post-modernism as follows:

> Because nothing is, as it seems, the only things worth noticing are the terms, the formal structures, by which things are perceived. One does not teach, one mindlessly reproduces a social structure; one does not have emotionally credited intentions, one has preset expectations; one does not have experiences

that are one's own, one merely moves forward by contextual design. . . . Persons, they argue, can never see themselves as they are because they are always something else; specifically, they are whatever social structure, ideology, theory or framework is at work in the inquiry. Because narrative inquiry entails a reconstruction of a person's experience in relation to others and to a social milieu, it is under suspicion as not representing the true context and the proper "postera" by formalists. (p. 39)

The use of the term *formalist* here may be confusing to some, because in the field of literary criticism, post-structuralism emerged as a critical alternative to a school of thought known as formalism.[11] In the above passage, Clandinin and Connelly use the term more generally. The point they make is that once our representations of experience are assumed to be unmoored from any genuine relation with that experience, then all that is left to analyze is the formal relationship between different discursive systems.

So why not accept the post-structural emphasis on formal symbolic relations, besides the fact that some might find it distasteful? A precise philosophical answer requires returning to the way post-structuralism is grounded in the application of Saussurean ideas about the operation of language to the whole of human experience. Rosiek and Atkinson (2005) explain the limitation of this view as follows:

At a logical level, the presumption that all signifiers have an arbitrary relationship with the things they signify is questionable at best. This view of semiotics, taken as an article of faith by most post-structuralists (Derrida, 1974; Sherriff, 1989), is based on an extrapolation of the characteristics of linguistic signs to all other signifying activity. . . . Without a sound defense of a general arbitrariness in the sign relation, the complete collapse of individual experience into social dynamics is not possible. (p. 12)

There are alternative semiotic theories that pay more attention to individual embodied experience as a source of meaning. For example, Charles Sanders Peirce (1991), arguably the founder of the pragmatic philosophical tradition, argued that meaning required a signifier, a signified, and an embodied interpreter of the sign. Peirce recognized that some meaning existed primarily at a linguistic level in the formal relations between signifiers. Other meaning, however, arises from more immediate less socialized experiences. Physical pain, visual stimulation, viscerally experienced affections, abrupt disconfirmations of one's expectations, and so forth are also sources of meaning. Additionally, according to Peirce, the encounter with any sign—linguistic or not—is mediated by embodied habits of interpretation, habits that have a history in the individual and his or her community. Thus, when a person loves, his or her love is not a floating signifier that simply acquires meaning because the object of affection fits the category of loveable. It is also a habit of relating to an individual with a unique history and for whom there is no substitute.

The existence of such alternative semiotic theories does not foreclose debates between post-structuralists and narrative inquirers. The post-structuralist scholar, like the Marxist-influenced scholar, can still accuse the narrative inquirer of being at best naive about the way social forces shape personal experience and the social construction of knowledge. At worst, they can accuse narrative inquirers of creating a program of research that, through its commitment to an ontology of experience, functions to silence forms of analysis that cannot be readily reconciled with those commitments. The narrative inquirer can respond that the post-structuralist's privileging of macrosocial discursive formations as an exclusive unit of analysis is excessive. Yet such macrosocial influences exist and must be considered. However, the claim that they are all that exists, and that therefore nothing is to be learned from a study of experience as lived, is at best condescending and unjustified. At worst, in its exclusive preoccupation with critique, post-structuralism can be accused of sacrificing real possibilities for amelioration and political engagement.

As we have stated before, divisiveness in interdisciplinary exchanges is not helpful. In our view, the differences between narrative inquiry and post-structuralist analysis are more a matter of emphasis. Each form of emphasis comes with its attendant risks. Narrative inquirers choose to take their risks with people and the stories they live and tell. Sometimes this means working within problematic social discourses longer than the post-structuralist would. In the following, Cornel West (1993) describes the kind of decision that ultimately must be made at this philosophical boundary:

> It takes us right to the center of a dialogue between various postmodern theorists, who would put forth a social constructivist thesis, and pragmatists, who themselves claim to endorse a social constructivist thesis, but do not render in their own writings a consciousness of the degree to which they are deploying terms which themselves are constructs.
>
> Now see, I would opt for the latter. . . . I would opt for the pragmatist who does in fact affirm social constructs from culture to culture, civilization to civilization. Why? Because it is so unavoidable, given the kind of socialization and acculturation human beings undergo in a given culture . . . we can accent the constructive character of the individual deed and what have you. Once we have done that, I am not sure we have done as much as the post-modern theorists think we have. (pp. 51–52)

Having identified some of the border conditions of what we are calling the field of narrative inquiry, we now turn to an exploration of the way those borders blur and run together—in other words, to an exploration of the borderlands of narrative inquiry.

Borderlands of Narrative Inquiry

Borders are abstractions. They exist as clear demarcations of territory only on maps but do not show up so clearly in the real world (Clandinin & Connelly, 1995). The preceding review of the philosophical territory in which narrative inquiry takes place highlighted the differences between four traditions of inquiry. In our effort to make these distinctions clear, we spoke in terms of epistemological and ontological differences. In the practice of research, however, such philosophical exactness is often a luxury. The actual business of interpreting human experience is messier. As researchers we find ourselves drifting, often profitably, from one paradigm of inquiry into another. We do not cross borders as much as we traverse borderlands.

Although we believe attention to the philosophical assumptions that distinguish narrative inquiry from other forms of research can be very useful to a narrative inquirer, experience has also taught us that some caution is in order. The temptation to reify borders, to think of them as real and necessary features of experience, is often strong, especially for academics. As some feminist philosophers warn,

> This tendency to dichotomize human experiences is persistent, powerful, and pernicious. Dualistic categories are such an organizing force because they provide a simple classification system that allows even the most complex and elusive qualities to be compared and contrasted in bold, clear terms. (Belenky, Bond, & Weinstock, 1997, p. 119)

To avoid this pitfall, it is important to respectfully examine, rather than conveniently ignore, the cases that don't fit our categorizations and dichotomies.

Fortunately, much work has already been done in this regard. Clandinin and Connelly (2000) have described the places where narrative inquiry intersects with other ways of thinking as "bumping places," conceptual spaces where different traditions of inquiry come together and where tensions become apparent. Clandinin and Connelly note that all inquirers come to their inquiries with their own views, attitudes, and ways of thinking. Our personal narratives of inquiry may

> coincide with or cross a boundary to varying degrees with the actual inquiries that we undertake. Almost all of us—it is almost unimaginable that we could not—come to narrative inquiries with various versions of formalistic and reductionistic histories of inquiry . . . we are forever struggling with personal tensions as we pursue narrative inquiry . . . narrative inquirers need to reconstruct their own narrative of inquiry histories and to be alert to possible tensions between those narrative histories and the narrative research they undertake. (p. 46)

Huber and Keats Whelan (in press) employ the language of "borders." Citing Gloria Anzaldúa's writing on mestiza consciousness, they write about "a struggle of borders, both interior and exterior." They draw our attention to the close connection between the struggles within each of us and our struggle with external forces as we locate ourselves in the landscape of narrative inquiry. These interior and exterior struggles, according to these authors, do not take the form of clear and distinct borders. Instead, they are better thought of as borderlands in which scholars situate themselves.

In what follows, we play with the idea of borderlands, those spaces that exist around borders where one lives within the possibility of multiple plotlines. This way of understanding the spaces around the philosophical borders we have described fits with a view of a landscape that does not have sharp divides that mark where one leaves one way of making sense for another. Anzaldúa (1987) writes of a borderland as a

> vague and undetermined place created by the emotional residue of an unnatural boundary . . . a constant state of transition. Los atravesados live here . . . those who cross over, pass over, or go through the confines of the "normal." (p. 3)

Although Anzaldúa is writing of individuals' experiences as they compose themselves in crossing cultural and national boundaries, the idea of a borderland is helpful for understanding the tensions that exist for those of us who work within the broad plotlines of narrative inquiry. Narrative inquirers frequently find themselves crossing cultural discourses, ideologies, and institutional boundaries. In this work they often encounter both deep similarities and profound differences between their own experience and those with whom they work, neither of which can be reduced to the other.

The result is less a harmonious single explanation of their world than it is an expanded understanding of the tensions and conflicted possibilities in the stories people live. Maria Lugones (1992) notes that Anzaldúa affirms this dissonance. She writes of a "mestiza consciousness [which] is characterized by the development of a tolerance for contradiction and ambiguity, by the transgression of rigid conceptual boundaries, and by the creative breaking of the new unitary aspect of new and old paradigms" (p. 34).

We need to be careful in appropriating Anzaldúa's words, so as not to engage in an imperialist whitewashing of her work. Narrative inquiry does not take as its primary focus the intersection of processes of colonization, patriarchal oppression, and racist exclusion that Anzaldúa made it her life's work to engage. All of these systemic injustices and their intersections, however, do find their way into narrative inquiries because they are a part of people's lives and lived stories. Furthermore, the institutional terrain in which narrative inquirers often struggle to locate themselves are similarly fraught with power struggles over whose voices are worth listening to. Therefore, as narrative inquirers locate themselves within the broad ideas of what it means to engage in narrative inquiry, they too seem to enter into a liminal space, where conceptual boundaries are still in the making and the possibilities for what we might do are diverse. Thus, although Anzaldúa was not originally writing about narrative inquiry, we think her ideas apply here.

What Anzaldúa teaches us is that borders are never clean and clear but are blurred as regions overlap and come together. A view of borderlands understood as Anzaldúa explicated them is a view that fits well with the borderland spaces inhabited by narrative inquiry as it bumps up against post-positivism, Marxism, and post-structuralism but it also fits with the borderland spaces that exist within the broad field of narrative inquiry.

Borderland Spaces With Post-Positivism

As we considered these borderland spaces, we began to see that there is no sharp divide; there are blurred borders and researchers are more or less clear about how they can engage their research questions and practices depending on their place on the landscape in relation to narrative inquiry and post-positivist forms of inquiry. Adopting a view of borderlands between narrative inquiry and post-positivism, we began to see that researchers, working from a post-positivist view and searching for ways to understand phenomena, sometimes design their research in ways that allow them to draw on practices similar to those narrative inquirers might use.

For example, post-positivist research that attempts to understand how contexts, understood temporally, influence, shape, and are shaped by people's actions shift researchers toward examining the context-dependent and temporal nature of human thinking generally. As they search for ways to study the shaping influence of context over time, they begin to engage in practices that might be seen as having an affinity with the practices of narrative inquirers who are also interested in studying how context shifts individuals' storied experiences over time. Narrative inquirers, in turn, often find this kind of post-positivist research affirming and illuminating of their own inquiry projects.

These affirmations and illuminations can lead narrative inquirers deeper into the borderlands, where the priorities of post-positivist research begin to replace the priorities of narrative inquiry. For example, some narrative inquirers search for ways to speak to a sense of "the universal case" (Clandinin & Connelly, 2000, p. 32). Some narrative inquirers, unable to live with the tension produced by constantly proliferating counter narratives, search for ways to ameliorate this tension by seeking universal themes in which the narrative tensions can be contained. In that search, they move into the borderlands with post-positivist research, which takes the identification of generalizable patterns in human experience as its primary goal (Clandinin & Connelly, 2000). This desire to speak to the universal comes, we think, from being immersed in an academic world that encourages us to speak to the universal. Thomas King (2003) describes this impulse as an attraction to

> dichotomy, the elemental structure of Western society. And cranky old Jacques Derrida notwithstanding, we do love our dichotomies. Rich/poor, white/black, strong/weak, right/wrong, culture/nature, male/female, written/oral, civilized/ barbaric, success/failure, individual/communal. We trust easy oppositions. We are suspicious of complexities, distrustful of contradictions, fearful of enigmas. (p. 25)

As narrative inquirers move further into this borderland, the desire to speak of general trends, of the context free, and to provide a stable knowledge base for social science inquiry stands in tension with a narrative inquiry view that knowledge of human experience begins and must return to the stream of particular human lives. This tension can be a source of new ideas and rich interdisciplinary dialogue. It can also become the cover for forms of academic violence.

Take, for example, the researcher who listens to people's stories, not as a prelude to collaboratively enhancing those persons' continuing experience but instead as a prelude to identifying common themes and universal narrative structures. On the one hand, important insights about narrative aspects of human experience might be revealed in such a study. On the other hand, from our Deweyan view, such a study severs the narratives from the relational, temporal, and continuous features of experience that give it meaning. The story is thus ripped from the personal history of the one living it and is treated as fixed data, much as one might treat numerical data. We use the word *ripped* deliberately, to highlight not only the decontextualization of the story but also the power and status differentials that are often involved when social scientists conduct research on, as opposed to with, people. (See a discussion of this point in Tsai's chapter in this volume.)

Tracking the lines of epistemic and ethical responsibility in this kind of research becomes more difficult in the borderlands, where paradigmatic standards become blurred. As a result, these borderland disputes within the broad field of narrative inquiry are frequently glossed over. We, however, see the importance of naming the struggle of living in the borderlands and acknowledging both the possibilities and the violence that accompany the emergence of subtly different but nonetheless conflicting ontological and epistemological stances.

Borderland Spaces With Marxism

As in the borderlands between narrative inquiry and post-positivism, we see researchers working from a Marxist-influenced view sometimes asking research questions and raising concerns that resemble narrative inquiry in many respects. Most frequently, this movement is inspired by a felt need to bring a Marxist-influenced critique of the macrosocial sources of oppression into practical relation with immediate experience. Critical ethnographer Barry Kanpol (1997) describes the questions he encountered in his travels along this borderland as follows:

> I have over the last few years or so begun to ask these problematic questions: To what end do critical educators theorize? Why is theory so devoid of personal narrative? What relationship has critical theory to the everyday life-world of those who work in the trenches, such as teachers, administrators, students and researchers? Why doesn't critical analysis and practice seriously find its way into public schools?

Once the importance of personal narratives to critical theoretic analysis is acknowledged, many political purposes are ascribed to narrative inquiry. Critical race theorist Richard Delgado (1989) made exactly this point in his widely cited article "Legal Storytelling: Storytelling for Oppositionists and Others: A Plea for Narrative," which highlights three ways that attention to people's stories can be an important way of responding to macrosocial forms of oppression. First, he argues, it serves a healing function:

So, stories—stories about oppression, about victimization, about one's own brutalization—far from deepening the despair of the oppressed, lead to healing, liberation, mental health. . . . Storytelling emboldens the hearer, who may have had the same thoughts and experiences the storyteller describes, but hesitated to give them voice. Having heard another express them, he or she realizes, I am not alone. (p. 2437)

Second, it can contribute to the transformation of oppressors. Silence is an essential part of processes of macrosocial oppression. Inequality and injustice are sustained, in part, by the ways in which privileged members of society insulate themselves from the suffering of others. Attending to the narratives of marginalized groups can disrupt this insularity.

Yet, stories help oppressed groups in a second way—through their effect on the oppressor. Most oppression, as was mentioned earlier, does not seem like oppression to those perpetrating it. It is rationalized causing few pangs of conscience. The dominant group justifies its privileged position by means of stories, stock explanations that construct reality in ways favorable to it. (Delgado, 1989, p. 2437)

Finally, Delgado (1989) argues that paying attention to people's stories opens up possibilities for generating new stories in which we can all live:

Listening to stories makes the adjustment to further stories easier; one acquires the ability to see the world through others' eyes. It can lead the way to new environments. . . . Listening to the stories of outgroups can avoid intellectual apartheid. Shared words can banish sameness, stiffness, and monochromaticity and reduce the felt terror of otherness when hearing new voices for the first time. . . . If we would deepen and humanize ourselves, we must seek out storytellers different from ourselves and afford them the audience they deserve. The benefit will be reciprocal. (p. 2439)

As we noted above, for the narrative inquirer, a person's experience needs to be listened to on its own terms first, without the presumption of deficit or flaw. Critique of that experience needs to be motivated by the problematic elements within that experience. For the critical scholar drawn into the borderland with narrative inquiry, such commitments do not come easily. It requires that they simultaneously acknowledge that an individual's experience is shaped by macrosocial processes of which she or he is often unaware and that the same individual's experience is more than the living out of a socially determined script. We see some of this struggle in Shari Stone-Mediatore's (2003) book *Reading Across Borders: Storytelling and Postcolonial Struggles*, in which she writes,

Feminist epistemologists, for instance, have warned that we cannot rely on experience to counter ideology because experience itself is formed through ideological processes. Furthermore, as feminists in the Marxist tradition emphasize, the "reality" that we encounter is a product of human history, but everyday experience tends to confront such historical reality as if it were mere fact. As Sandra Harding puts it, "our experience lies to us." (p. 99)

As she enters a borderland space between Marxist-influenced views and narrative inquiry, Stone-Mediatore does not want to lose track of the large-scale material conditions that shape human life, but she also wants to credit the force of the experiences of individuals who live in marginal positions in dominant narratives. As she searches for ways to study experience, she begins to engage in practices that might be seen as having an affinity with the practices of narrative inquirers who are also interested in studying individual's storied experiences as shaped by cultural, institutional, and social narratives. Citing the work of other transnational feminists in this methodological borderland, she observes that

> these critics explore concrete ways that the most disempowered people can use resources in their daily lives to challenge the discourses and institutions that keep them in subservient positions . . . they . . . investigate how we might transform lived experiences of discontent into critical knowledge and political consciousness. They recognize narration to be key in the transformation of experience into useful knowledge. (p. 126)

We see this struggle to reconcile respect for the experience of individuals with a concern about the way ideologies distort experience in critical ethnography informed by feminist scholarship, such as that done by Michelle Fine and Lois Weis (Fine, 1987; Fine & Weis, 2003). As early as her landmark work in New York schools in the 1980s, Fine wanted to hear the stories of experience of the high-school students even as she wanted to engage in a macrosocial analysis. Focusing on the silencing of voices that she defines as "the process by which contradictory evidence, ideologies, and experiences find themselves buried, camouflaged, and discredited" (Fine, 1987, p. 157), she attends to the voices of Deidre, Alicia, Monique, and Patrice. An example of the borderland struggle is evident when Fine writes that students' voices helped her see that, for her, "participation was encouraged, delighted in, and a measure of the 'good student.' For these adolescents, given their contexts of schooling, 'participation' signified poor discipline and rude classroom behavior" (Fine, 1987, p. 167). It was, it seems, as she listened first to the stories of the students' experiences that she began to attend differently to what she was hearing. In her later work with Weis, we continue to see her working in the borderland of contradictions between narrative inquiry and Marxist-influenced scholarship. It is in this borderland space between acknowledging the macrosocial dimensions of oppression and attending to the voices of youth, teachers, and others that Fine and Weis see the possibility for "facilitating individual and collective movements toward social change and social justice" (Fine & Weis, 2003, pp. 4–5).

Approaching from the other side of the border, the narrative inquirer drawn to the borderland with Marxist-influenced scholarship also faces struggle. These narrative inquirers often experience conflict as they recognize their own and others' complicity with institutionalized oppression and find it difficult to continue listening to the storied experience of participants. The more attention a researcher pays to macrosocial structural processes of oppression—be it patriarchy, white supremacist ideologies, institutionalized homophobia, or market economies commodifying every aspect of our lives—the less it may seem that individuals and their experiences make a difference. Focusing on the details of personal experience can feel like escapism.

The need to respond to the structural conditions of oppression is often most acutely felt by narrative inquirers who have previously done service in urban communities or remote rural communities where poverty rates are high and the maldistribution of wealth and resources is most felt. However, scholars who begin their analysis from a position of service to those among us who suffer most, often do so because they feel respect for members of these communities. Frequently, the researchers are members of the communities themselves. Consequently, they want to listen to the stories of the people they seek to serve. They prefer to conduct research with, not on, the people with whom they work.

It is this commitment to listening and collaboration, on the one hand, and an awareness that large-scale social systems set people up to perpetuate their own oppression, on the other hand, that can lead a researcher to the borderlands between narrative inquiry and critical-theoretic scholarship. We offer no easy resolution to this tension. Instead, we offer a caution. Ultimately, the narrative inquirer traveling in this borderland will find it necessary to steer between the Scylla of political naïveté and the Charybdis of collecting stories from participants only to treat them as examples of an oppressive social structure. The former can render narrative inquiries irrelevant to the most pressing social justice concerns. The latter can end up dismissing the lived experience of persons as a possible source of insight and thus simply replace one habit of silencing voices from the margins with another similar habit.

Borderland Spaces With Post-Structuralism

Perhaps the most highly trafficked theoretical and methodological borderland of the three we discuss here is the one between narrative inquiry and post-structuralism. As described in the preceding sections, narrative inquirers share a use of linguistic terms for describing human knowledge and experience with post-structuralists. Consequently, many scholars draw liberally from both traditions when conducting their research. Differences in the underlying ontological assumptions of these two theoretical frameworks, however, occasionally surface in this borderland, producing tensions, confusions, as well as new possibilities for analysis.

The tensions are similar to those found in the previous theoretical borderlands we have described. For example, post-structuralists share with post-positivists a primary focus on description of broad patterns in human activity as distinct from narrative inquirers' focus on individuals' experience. Despite the profound differences between these two theories, each has its way of minimizing what people learn struggling to live in the interstices of these broad patterns of human activity, be they behavioral or discursive, cognitive or cultural. Stone-Mediatore (2003) speaks to the borderland spaces created between post-positivism, post-structuralism, and narrative inquiry. Referring to post-positivist research paradigms broadly as "empiricist," she explains,

> Neither empiricist nor poststructuralist theories of experience can account for the subversive force of many marginal experience narratives . . . both schools presume that stories of experience are mere unreflective reports of spontaneous awareness. As a result, both obscure the capacity of writers to grapple with muted, contradictory, or even traumatized experience. Moreover, both overlook the capacity of readers to attend to phenomena that are only intimated by metaphors or tension within texts, phenomena that are not directly articulated because they defy our categories for representing experience. (p. 2)

Post-structuralists also share with critical theory scholars a concern that large-scale social processes can condition individual experience so thoroughly that individuals cannot recognize the operation of those processes. This only reinforces their skepticism about truth claims based on personal experience. The difference between post-structuralists and critical theory scholars, as described earlier, is that the post-structuralist sees no escape from discursive processes, no way to finally anchor even scholarly representations in an extradiscursive reality.

Consequently, post-structuralists who find themselves in the borderlands with narrative inquiry often arrive there less because they consider the people's stories sources of new knowledge about social reality and more because they are attracted to the productive power of stories. They are looking for a way to move beyond description of the formal qualities of social discourses to transformative intervention but need a mode of intervention that is not totalizing:

> What is sought is a reflexive process that focuses on our too easy use of taken-for-granted forms and that might lead us towards a science capable of continually demystifying the realities it serves to create. [I envisage] an altogether different approach to doing empirical inquiry which advocates the creation of a more hesitant and partial scholarship capable of helping us to tell a better story in a world marked by the elusiveness with which it greets our efforts to know it. (Lather, 1991, p. 15)

Scholars influenced by post-structuralist theory and attracted to the productive power of stories frequently focus on exploring the use of narrative representations in educational research. They frame the purpose of crafting narrative representations in different ways, sometimes emphasizing political and rhetorical value, at other times their aesthetic value, and at other times their ability to foster emotional and moral responses to a topic. Across these purposes, however, lies a sense that narratives can make things happen in ways that other forms of representation cannot. Sconiers and Rosiek (2000) explain this as follows:

When used in the postmodern sense, narrative research treats all representations of educational events—informant's as well as researcher's—as partially fictionalized (re)presentations whose meaning exists in a contested space between authors and their audiences (Hall, 1992; Kincheloe, 1997; Stake & Kerr, 1995). In this case, the researcher's project is not to escape the textual play of meaning by establishing privileged access to "one true account" of a classroom event, but to participate constructively in an intertextual dialogue about the meaning of these events (Denzin, 1997). When used in the arts-based, performative sense, narrative research can employ fictionalized accounts of events as a way of pointing to as yet unrealized possibilities within that experience (Eisner, 1995; Noddings, 1995; Stake & Kerr, 1995) or as a means of producing the conditions that make certain meanings possible (Butler, 1997; Conquergood, 1991; Lather, 1997). (p. 400)

The promise of this focus on using narrative modes of representation in social science research is that it may "open up an imaginative space for us to recognize alternative identities and ways of life" (Stone-Mediatore, 2000, p. 99) or "lift the veil of conventionality from my eyes as they subtly raise disturbing questions about the necessity and desirability of comfortable, familiar . . . discourses and practices" (Barone, in press). The danger is that the ambition to generate new and better versions of our world will presumptively erase or displace the stories people are already living. The goal of transformation inevitably involves hubris and raises the question "Whose transformation?" Where the motivation is more aesthetic than political, we see narrative inquirers occasionally becoming entranced by a particularly striking metaphor through which they choose to read their participants' stories. They become so caught up in the metaphor that they no longer attend to the stories of experience but, rather, attend to how the stories of experience fit within the entailments of the metaphor. The threat of colonialism and dehumanization looms large.

For those approaching this borderland from the other side, starting closer to narrative inquiry as we have described it, the attraction to post-structuralist theory is often similar to the attraction to critical theory. Concern about the way broad systems of social oppression obscure people's ability to see their own participation in those systems inspires a search for language that can express ambivalence about insights that arise from within stories as lived, without completely discounting first-person experience as a source of important knowledge.

For example, in a study of the experiences of four white teachers who taught in aboriginal schools, Kennedy (2001) struggled to attend to her participants' stories of experience while simultaneously attending to how theoretical constructions of race shaped the teachers' stories. The tension of the borderland was evident as she struggled to listen to the reconstruction of the teachers' experiences in relation to others and to a social milieu without being caught into attending only to the social structure of race. She wrote of trying to snag the race thread in individuals' experiences as it emerged rather than beginning with it preemptively. Within this borderland space, Kennedy frequently finds her work being read for the post-structuralist terms that apply:

A person is a member of a race, a class, a gender, and may be said to have varying degrees of power in any situation. Part of the tension for a narrative inquirer is to acknowledge these truths while holding to a different research agenda. (Clandinin & Connelly, 2000, p. 45)

This borderland tension and struggle is also evident in the work of Soreide (in press). In her paper titled "Narrative Construction of Teacher Identity: Positioning and Negotiation," Soreide explores how the discourse communities of five Norwegian elementary school teachers shape their teacher knowledge landscapes. She shows how the teachers draw from the available discourses to compose and to construct their teacher identities. Her struggle emerges when she wants to treat each individual's experience as a unique case, deserving respect and attention tailored to their situation and personal history, even as she wants to use their words to illustrate and illuminate how broader social discourses condition their experience. Soreide uses post-structuralist theory to analyze the stories teachers tell of themselves—that is, what Soreide calls their ontological narratives. Instead of presenting these narratives as derivative of the discourses, she attempts to show how the teachers' subject positions were used as a resource by the teachers in constructing their personal narratives of teacher identity. Soreide writes in the borderland between narrative inquiry and its attention to individual experience and the post-structuralist's privileging of macrosocial discursive formations as a unit of analysis. She turns uneasily in both directions, that is, to the individual's narratives of experience as source of identity and the macrosocial discursive formations to show how teacher identity is context dependent, negotiable and negotiated, shifting, multiple, and contradictory.

Another striking example of the struggles inherent in the borderland between narrative inquiry and post-structuralist research is found in Borland's (1991) description of her feminist oral history research with her grandmother. She described how her grandmother, Beatrice, recounted her life "in a highly structured and thoroughly entertaining narrative . . . to her folklorist-granddaughter, who recorded her words on a tape for later transcription and analysis" (p. 63). Beatrice and her granddaughter, however, did not interpret this narrative in the same way, and this later led to conflicts between the two. The grandmother wanted her stories of experience to be both the starting and ending points of the inquiry. Borland writes that her analysis of those stories was informed by "contemporary feminist conceptions of patriarchal structures, which my grandmother does not share" (p. 69). Borland found herself in the borderland between narrative inquiry and post-structuralism as she wanted to attend to her grandmother's experience but did not want to abandon her feminist theories. Borland speculates that some form of polyphonic representation may be needed to honor both these interpretations:

I am suggesting that we might open up the exchange of ideas so that we do not simply gather data on others to fit into our own paradigms once we are safely ensconced in our university libraries ready to do interpretation. By extending the conversation we initiate while collecting oral narratives to the later state of interpretation, we might more sensitively negotiate issues of interpretive authority in our research. . . . At the very least, it would allow us to discern more clearly when we speak in unison and when we disagree. Finally, it would restructure the traditionally unidirectional flow of information out from source to scholar to academic audience by identifying our field collaborators as an important first audience for our work. Lest we, as feminist scholars, unreflectively appropriate the words of our mothers for our own uses, we must attend to the multiple and sometimes conflicting meanings generated by our framing or contextualizing of their oral narratives in new ways. (p. 73)

As these examples illustrate, the narrative inquirer who lives in the borderland spaces with post-structuralist researchers lives in spaces that do not allow for easy oppositions. As narrative inquirers live in such spaces, we need to find ways to stay open to complexities, contradictions, and enigmas. As we do this, we acknowledge the richness and complexity as well as the possibility for tension, violence, and strong disagreement that make these borderland spaces.

Looking Back Across the Borderlands

We began this section by acknowledging that borders, philosophical or geographic, become less clear the closer you get to them. We offered, therefore, that it was better to speak of borderlands, regions of shared influence between different research traditions. Before we close, we should also acknowledge that these influences themselves lack clear edges. Even when a researcher's primary philosophical commitments are clear, other scholarly paradigms can shape their work with important findings, by posing pressing questions or by offering critique from outside. In other words, the influence of, say, positivism on narrative inquiry does not abruptly end as much as it tapers off depending on who you are talking to and what you are talking about.

Consequently, the influence of our philosophical neighbors can be seen even far from what we have described as borderlands. We can see what we might call borderlands *within* the community of narrative inquirers. Some narrative inquirers are more interested in the structure of professional identity narratives. Others are more interested in the difficulty some individuals have in addressing the big picture social justice issues in our world. Others are more interested in working with people to aesthetically craft new narrative representations of experience. Some find themselves working to combine these interests and others. Such differences of emphasis and interest, we offer, are not simply idiosyncratic. They can often be traced to the scholarly literature being read by a given narrative inquirer.

These borderlands within, just like the borderlands with other traditions, can create tensions and provoke strong disagreements. Ultimately, however, we see these multiple influences that overlap and shade into one another as contributing to the richness and complexity of narrative inquiry.

Shared Commitments: Commonplaces on the Narrative Inquiry Landscape

In this chapter, we laid out an understanding of narrative inquiry that emerges from Dewey's theory of experience. As we did this, we created a map that positioned narrative inquiry alongside, but distinct from, post-positivist, Marxist, and post-structuralist forms of inquiry. In doing so we suggested there were borderland spaces between these various forms of inquiry, borderlands in which these distinctions become blurred and difficult to identify. We attempted to show how these borderlands were spaces of tension and struggle and how these struggles and tensions become apparent within differing research practices and texts. We ended by saying these borderland struggles are echoed to some extent in the differences we see within and among narrative inquirers.

In this section, we want to affirm that amid the influence of our philosophical neighbors, there is something distinctive about narrative inquiry that marks it as narrative inquiry. There are affinities and commonplaces among those of us who engage in narrative inquiry. These multiple influences and tensions enhance the field of narrative inquiry rather than overwhelm it.

The most defining feature of narrative inquiry, as we have presented it, is the study of experience as it is lived. As noted throughout this chapter, experience is what is studied in narrative inquiry and we argued for a Deweyan view of experience. This shared commitment to the study of experience is central to narrative inquiry. Within this focus, there are additional shared commitments in narrative inquiry. Connelly and Clandinin (2006), based on their own work with narrative inquiry and based on a review of others' writing about narrative inquiry (Josselson, 1993; Lieblich, 1995; McAdams, 1996; Mishler, 2000; Polkinghorne, 1988), identified three further commonplaces of narrative inquiry—attention to temporality, sociality, and place—which specify dimensions of narrative inquiry spaces and mark out the landscape space of narrative inquiry.

The first commonplace, temporality, attends to Dewey's notion of continuity in experience—that is, that every experience both takes up something from the present moment and carries it into future experiences. Events, people, and objects under study are in temporal transition and narrative inquirers describe them with a past, a present, and a future.

The second commonplace, sociality, points toward the simultaneous concern with both personal and social conditions. This commonplace connects with Dewey's notion of interaction—that is, that people are always in interaction with their situations in any experience. By personal conditions Clandinin and Connelly (2000) mean the feelings, hopes, desires, aesthetic reactions, and moral dispositions of the person, whether inquirer or participant. By social conditions they mean the existential conditions, the environment, surrounding factors and forces, people and otherwise, that form the individual's context.

Another important dimension of the sociality commonplace is the relationship between participant and inquirer. Narrative inquirers are always in an inquiry relationship with participants' lives. They cannot subtract themselves from relationship.

Narrative inquirers, throughout each inquiry, are in relationship, negotiating purposes, next steps, outcomes, texts, and the other concerns that go into an inquiry relationship. Nor can they pretend to be free of contextual influences themselves. As Rosiek (2005) points out, practitioners and their academic collaborators both "face similar conflicts between the discourses of their professional training and the discourses of the non-academic communities in which they live and work" (p. 269). In narrative inquiry, research questions and texts are ones where inquirers give an account of who they are in the inquiry and who they are in relation to participants.

The third commonplace, place or sequences of places, draws attention to the centrality of place, that is, to the specific concrete, physical, and topological boundaries of place where the inquiry and events take place. This commonplace recognizes that all events occur in some place. It draws attention to borderland tensions because those who work from post-positivist, post-structuralist, or Marxist positions may wish to escape the limitations of place in the interests of generalizability. For narrative inquirers, the specificity of location is important. The qualities of place and the impact of places on lived and told experiences are crucial. As Basso (1996) writes,

> As places animate the ideas and feelings of persons who attend to these same ideas and feelings animate the places on which attention has been bestowed, and the movements of this process—inward toward facets of the self, outward toward aspects of the external world, alternately both together—cannot be known in advance. When places are actively sensed, the physical landscape becomes wedded to the landscape of the mind, to the roving imagination, and where the latter may lead is anybody's guess. (p. 107)

As an inquiry proceeds temporally, place may also change and narrative inquirers need to stay awake to how place shifts the unfolding stories of lives.

These commonplaces are ideas that hold us together. They are commonplaces or touchstones that allow narrative inquirers to understand their research as occupying a distinct place on the methodological landscape.

Concluding Thoughts

Not everyone who engages in narrative inquiry will be inclined to dwell on its underlying philosophy at length. However, given the explosion of research under the broad heading of narrative inquiry, we feel opening up the debate about the philosophical roots of narrative inquiry as a research methodology brings a helpful clarity to the field. More important, in our view, it helps us not to waste energy on conflicts born of confusion and serves as an important starting point for helping narrative inquirers to be good neighbors in the broader community of scholars. As we continue to develop the ideas of narrative inquiry, we hope it enables us to recognize the good neighbors in others, even if they speak different theoretical languages.

As we reflect on our conceptual cartography of narrative inquiry, we are struck by the energy generated by those interested in studying people's lives. This rush to narrative inquiry and the willingness to move into the borderlands with narrative inquiry suggests an eagerness to understand in more complex and nuanced ways the storied experiences of individuals as they compose storied lives on storied landscapes.

We are also struck by the enthusiasm for narrative ways of thinking, for narrative ways of understanding knowledge and identity that cuts across disciplines and professions. As Rita Charon (2006), a leader in bringing narrative practices to medicine, writes,

> We search the horizon—astronomers, oceanographers, artists, musicians, doctors, novelists, geneticists—seeking ways to recognize ourselves and those who surround us, yearning to place ourselves within space and time (and infinity), dramatizing our stubborn beliefs that life means something and that we ourselves matter. (p. 69)

What Charon draws our attention to is that stories matter and that, increasingly, we are interested in knowing the stories that all people live and tell. As we, and other narrative inquirers now know, inquiry, narrative inquiry, into those stories that people live and tell, also matters.

Consulting Editors: Becky Atkinson, Samford University, and Janice Huber, St. Francis Xavier University

Notes

1. For example, a Mercator map of the globe preserves relative shapes and permits a viewing of the entire globe but makes objects appear larger the farther they are from the equator. A globe preserves both shape and size, but all areas cannot be viewed simultaneously. However, what area is selected as a center for the map shifts what is seen as marginal. For example, a map with North America in the center makes other areas marginal. A map that moves Asia from the margin to the center shifts how North America and Asia are seen. Something similar happens when the North Pole is in the center of the map. Each projection serves a purpose but also involves limitations in usefulness and accuracy.

2. Quotes from *The Collected Works of John Dewey* are copyright © 1986 by the Board of Trustees, Southern Illinois University, reproduced by permission of the publisher.

3. In the opinion of the authors, while Dewey's views are revolutionary, the revolution in the human sciences that his philosophy points to is yet to occur.

4. More will be said about this comparison in later sections.

5. Many who are attracted to narrative inquiry can be tempted to oversimplify the positivist position as a prelude to rejecting it. This does not advance the cause of narrative inquiry nor does it make for sound foundations of scholarship. For an economical summary of positivist and post-positivist epistemologies, see Phillips and Burbules (2000) and Archer, Bhaskar, Collier, Lawson, and Norrie (1998).

6. A *camera obscura* was an instrument used by artists during the Middle Age to cast an image onto paper by means of mirrors. Because the image was inverted, a lens was needed to correct it.

7. Epistemic questions about the accuracy of an analysis will inevitably arise in the course of such inquiry; however, epistemic standards would be adopted as a means to onto-logical intervention.

8. This utility, it perhaps should be pointed out, would not simply be in the form of a case illustration of ideologically distorted false consciousness—although narrative inquiry could, in fact, provide such illustrations.

9. Derrida (1972/1982) called this gap *différance,* of which he said:

> In fact "Older" than Being itself, such a *différance* has no name in our language. But we "already know" that if it is unnamable, it is not provisionally so, not because our language has not yet found or received this name, or because we would have to seek it in another language, outside the finite system of our own. It is rather because there is no name for it at all, not even the name of essence or of Being, not even that of "differance," which is not a name, which is not a pure nominal unity, and unceasingly dislocates itself in a chain of differing and defer-ring substitutions (p. 26).

10. This emphasis on description may seem to move post-structuralism closer to posi-tivism. Such proximity, if it exists, would be limited at best. The premise underlying post-structuralism is that our representations of the world (signifiers) cannot, by their very nature, achieve some kind of uniquely faithful relationship to the things that describe (sig-nifieds). Given this assumption, the post-positivist ideal of assembling knowledge only from discrete falsifiable statements is both naive and nonsensical. Post-structuralists interpret post-positivism, like all epistemologies, as a discursive formation that functions primarily as a mode of social control masquerading as an ideal rationality.

11. These latter formalists approached the interpretation of literature with an eye to the formal qualities of the text alone, whereas the post-structuralists insisted on historicizing the meaning of the text and interpreting it in relation to the broader context of the entire social and cultural moment in which it was produced and read.

References

Adorno, T. (2000). *The Adorno reader* (B. O'Connor, Ed.). Boston: Blackwell.

Anzaldúa, G. (1987). *Borderlands/La Frontera: The new mestiza.* San Francisco: Aunt Lute Books.

Archer, M., Bhaskar, R., Collier, A., Lawson, T., & Norrie, A. (Eds.). (1998). *Critical realism: Essential readings.* New York: Routledge.

Augoustinos, M. (1999). Ideology, false consciousness and psychology. *Theory & Psychology, 9*(3), 295–312.

Barone, T. (in press). A return to the gold standard? Questioning the future of narrative construction as educational research. *Qualitative Inquiry.*

Basso, K. (1996). *Wisdom sits in places: Landscape and language among the Western Apache.* Albuquerque: University of New Mexico Press.

Belenky, M. F., Bond, L. A., & Weinstock, J. S. (1997). *A tradition that has no name.* New York: Basic Books.

Bergson, H. (1960). *Time and free will: An essay on the immediate data of consciousness* (F. L. Pogson, Trans.). New York: Harper & Brothers. (Original work published 1889)

Bhaskar, R. (1997). *A realist theory of science* (2nd ed.). New York: Verso.

Borland, K. (1991). "That's not what I said": Interpretive conflict in oral narrative research. In S. Gluck & D. Patai (Eds.), *Women's words: The feminist practice of oral history* (pp. 63–75). New York: Routledge.

Chang, P., & Rosiek J. (2003). Anti-colonial antinomies: A case of cultural conflict in the high school biology curriculum. *Curriculum Inquiry, 33*(3), 251–290.

Charon, R. (2002). Meaning and anticipation: The practice of narrative ethics. In R. Charon & M. Montello (Eds.), *Stories matter: The role of narrative in medical ethics.* London: Routledge.

Charon, R. (2006). *Narrative medicine. Honoring the stories of illness.* Oxford, UK: Oxford University Press.

Clandinin, D. J., & Connelly, F. M. (1995). *Teachers' professional knowledge landscapes.* New York: Teachers College Press.

Clandinin, D. J., & Connelly, F. M. (2000). *Narrative inquiry. Experience and story in qualitative research.* San Francisco: Jossey-Bass.

Connelly, F. M., & Clandinin, D. J. (1990). Stories of experience and narrative inquiry. *Educational Researcher, 19*(5), 2–14.

Connelly, F. M., & Clandinin, D. J. (2006). Narrative inquiry. In J. Green, G. Camilli, & P. Elmore (Eds.), *Handbook of complementary methods in education research* (pp. 375–385). Mahwah, NJ: Lawrence Erlbaum.

de Lauretis, T. (1986). Through the looking glass. In P. Rosen (Ed.), *Narrative, apparatus, ideology: A film theory reader* (pp. 360–372). New York: Columbia University Press.

Delgado, R. (1989). Storytelling for oppositionists and others: A plea for narrative. *Michigan Law Review, 87*(8), 2411–2441.

Derrida, J. (1982). *Margins of philosophy* (A. Bass, Trans.). Chicago: University of Chicago Press. (Original work published 1972)

de Saussure, F. (1959). *Course in general linguistics.* New York: McGraw-Hill.

Dewey, J. (1938). *Experience and education.* New York: Collier Books.

Dewey, J. (1958). *Experience and nature.* New York: Dover.

Dewey, J. (1976). *The middle works, 1899–1924: Vol. 10. Journal articles, essays, and miscellany published in the 1916–1917 period* (J. A. Boydston, Ed.). Carbondale: Southern Illinois University Press.

Dewey, J. (1981a). *The later works, 1925–1953: Vol. 1. Experience and nature* (J. A. Boydston, Ed.). Carbondale: Southern Illinois University Press.

Dewey, J. (1981b). *The later works, 1925–1953: Vol. 4. The quest for certainty: A study of the relation of knowledge and action* (J. A. Boydston, Ed.). Carbondale: Southern Illinois University Press.

Dewey, J. (1981c). *The later works, 1925–1953: Vol. 10. Art as experience* (J. A. Boydston, Ed.). Carbondale: Southern Illinois University Press.

Fine, M. (1987). Silencing in public schools. *Language Arts, 64*(2), 157–174.

Fine, M., & Weis, L. (2003). *Silenced voices and extraordinary conversations: Reimagining schools.* New York: Teachers College Press.

Foucault, M. (1977). *Discipline and punishment: The birth of the prison* (A. Sheridan, Trans.). New York: Pantheon.

Foucault, M. (1982). *The archaeology of knowledge.* London: Routledge.

Hadden, J. (2000). A charter to educate or a mandate to train: Conflicts in theory and practice. *Harvard Educational Review, 70*(4), 524–536.

Hawkes, D. (2003). *Ideology (the new critical idiom)*. New York: Routledge.

Henry, F., & Tator, C. (2005). *The colour of democracy: Racism in Canadian society*. Toronto, Canada: Nelson Thomson.

Hook, S. (1987). *Paradoxes of freedom*. Amherst, NY: Prometheus Books.

Horkheimer, M. (2005). *Eclipse of reason*. New York: Continuum International.

Huber, J., & Keats Whelan, K. (in press). Entangled lives: Enacting transient social identities. In S. Kouritzin, N. Piquemal, & R. Norman (Eds.), *Qualitative research: Challenging the orthodoxies*. Mahwah, NJ: Lawrence Erlbaum.

Hurwitz, B., Greenhalgh, T., & Skultans, V. (2004). *Narrative research in health and illness*. Oxford, UK: Blackwell.

James, W. (1897). *The will to believe: And other essays in popular philosophy*. New York: Longmans, Green.

James, W. (1909). *The meaning of truth*. New York: Longmans, Green.

Jameson, F. (1992). *Postmodernism, or, the cultural logic of late capitalism*. Durham, NC: Duke University Press.

Johnson, M. (1987). *The body in the mind: The bodily basis of meaning, imagination and reason*. Chicago: University of Chicago Press.

Josselson, R. (1993). A narrative introduction. In R. Josselson & A. Lieblich (Eds.), *The narrative study of lives* (pp. ix–xv). Newbury Park, CA: Sage.

Kanpol, B. (1997). Reflective critical inquiry on critical inquiry: A critical ethnographic dilemma continued. *Qualitative Report, 3*(4). Retrieved July 27, 2006, from www.nova.edu/ssss/QR/QR3-4/kanpol.html

Kennedy, M. (2001). *Race matters in the life/work of four, white female teachers*. Unpublished doctoral dissertation. University of Alberta, Edmonton, Canada.

King, T. (2003). *The truth about stories*. Toronto, Canada: House of Anansi Press.

Laclau, E., & Mouffe, C. (1987). Post-Marxism without apologies. *New Left Review, 66*, 77–106.

Lather, P. (1991). *Getting smart: Feminist research and pedagogy with/in the postmodern*. New York: Routledge.

Laubscher, L., & Powell, S. (2003). Skinning the drum: Teaching about diversity as "other." *Harvard Educational Review, 73*(2), 203–222.

Lieblich, A. (1995). *Seasons of captivity: The inner world of POWS*. New York: State University of New York Press.

Lieblich, A., Tuval-Mashiach, R., & Zilber, T. (1998). *Narrative research: Reading, analysis and interpretation*. Thousand Oaks, CA: Sage.

Lugones, M. (1992). On borderlands/La Frontera: An interpretive essay. *Hypatia, 7*(4), 31–37.

Lukacs, G. (1972). *History and class consciousness*. Boston: MIT Press.

Lyotard, F. (1984). *The postmodern condition: A report on knowledge* (G. Bennington & B. Massumi, Trans.). Minneapolis: University of Minnesota Press.

Maher, F., & Ward, J. (2002). Sexism in the classroom. In F. Maher & J. Ward (Eds.), *Gender and teaching* (pp. 1–18). Mahwah, NJ: Lawrence Erlbaum.

Marcuse, H. (1964). *One-dimensional man*. Boston: Beacon.

Marmon Silko, L. (1997). *Yellow woman and a beauty of the spirit*. New York: Touchstone.

Marx, K. (1964). *Selected writings in sociology and social philosophy* (T. B. Bottomore, Trans.). London: McGraw-Hill.

Marx, K. (1972). *The German ideology*. In R. C. Tucker (Ed.), *The Marx-Engels reader* (pp. 110–166). New York: W. W. Norton. (Original work published 1846)

McAdams, D. P. (1996). *The stories we live by*. New York: Guilford Press.

Merleau-Ponty, M. (1962). *Phenomenology of perception* (C. Smith, Trans.). London: Routledge & Kegan Paul.

Mishler, E. (2000). *Storylines: Craft artists' narratives of identity*. Harvard, MA: Harvard University Press.

Norris, C. (1999, Autumn). Bhaskar interview. *Philosophers' Magazine*, p. 34.

Peirce, C. S. (1991). *Peirce on signs: Writings on semiotic* (J. Hooper, Ed.). Chapel Hill: University of North Carolina Press.

Phillips, D., & Burbules, N. (2000). *Postpositivism and educational research*. Lanham, MD: Rowman & Littlefield.

Piles, S., & Thrift, N. J. (1995). *Mapping the subject: Geographies of cultural transformation*. London: Routledge.

Polkinghorne, D. E. (1988). *Narrative knowing and the human sciences*. Albany: State University of New York Press.

Rosiek, J. (2005). Toward teacher education that takes the study of culture as foundational: Building bridges between teacher knowledge research and educational ethnography. In G. Spindler (Ed.), *New horizons in the ethnography of education*. Mahwah, NJ: Lawrence Erlbaum.

Rosiek J., & Atkinson, B. (2005). Bridging the divides: The need for a pragmatic semiotics of teacher knowledge research. *Educational Theory, 55*(4), 231–266.

Schutz, A. (with Luckman, T.). (1973). *The structures of the life-world* (R. Zaner & H. T. Engelhardt, Jr., Trans.). Evanston, IL: Northwestern University.

Sconiers, Z. D., & Rosiek, J. L. (2000). Historical perspective as an important element of teachers' knowledge: A sonata-form case study of equity issues in a chemistry classroom. *Harvard Educational Review, 70*(3), 370–404.

Soreide, G. (in press). Narrative construction of teacher identity: Positioning and negotiation. *Teachers and Teaching: Theory and Practice, 12*(5).

Sorrell, K. (2004). *Representative practices: Peirce, pragmatism and feminist epistemology*. New York: Fordham University Press.

Spanbauer, T. (1992). *The man who fell in love with the moon*. New York: Grove Press.

Stone-Mediatore, S. (2003). *Reading across borders: Storytelling and knowledges of resistance*. New York: Palgrave Macmillan.

Sullivan, S. (2001). *Living across and through skins: Transactional bodies, pragmatism, and feminism*. Bloomington: Indiana University Press.

Sullivan, S. (2006). *Revealing whiteness: The unconscious habits of racial privilege*. Bloomington: Indiana University Press.

Vaz, K. (Ed.). (1997). *Oral narrative research with black women*. Thousand Oaks, CA: Sage.

West, C. (1989). *The American evasion of philosophy: A genealogy of pragmatism*. Madison: University of Wisconsin Press.

West, C. (1993). *Beyond eurocentrism and multiculturalism. Vol. I: Prophetic thought in postmodern times*. Monroe, ME: Common Courage Press.

Wetherell, M. (1999). Beyond binaries. *Theory & Psychology*, 9(3), 399–406.

Zizek, S. (1999). *The ticklish subject: The absent centre of political ontology*. New York: Verso.

PART II

Starting With
Telling Stories

In Part II, narrative inquirers of diverse life, professional, and theoretical backgrounds show how attending to narrative inquiry that begins with telling stories has informed not only their work but also the research undertaken and emerging in a variety of disciplines. Across this handbook section, intersections between narrative inquiry and historical/archival, interviewing, autobiographical, conversational, developmental psychology, art, and life story research are explored.

As the chapters unfold, readers glimpse some of the authors' past and present puzzles that emerged as they lived through, and wrote about, their engagements with storytelling as a way to understand people's experiences across times, places, and situations. These puzzles have, in turn, shaped lingering questions that the authors address: How might we understand the stories lived and told by everyday people as a way to expand hegemonic versions of history? How might we respect voices and silences of participants in interpreting the stories they tell? How might we develop deeper understandings of the human condition through autobiography? How might we engage in conversations and then interpret this talk to make educative meaning of our and others' lives and situations? How might we employ storytelling to understand identity as narratively constructed and reconstructed across the life span? How might we compose arts-based and/or arts-informed narrative inquiries? How might we situate the life story interview as a bridge between disciplines and between the temporal and fragmented aspects of lives and as beneficial to both researchers and participants?

In compelling ways, these puzzles and questions shape a language of narrative inquiry that begins with telling stories—terms such as "a symphony of lives," "ordinary people," "first hand, spontaneous accounts" (see Morgan-Fleming, Riegle, and Fryer's chapter); "talking to learn" (see Hollingsworth and Dybdahl), "developmental junctures" (see Baddeley and Singer), and "life-as-a-whole personal narrative" (see Atkinson), as well as narrative conceptualizations or processes such as "interpretive poetics" (see Rogers), "poetic science" (see Freeman), "conversational narrative inquiry" (see Hollingsworth and Dybdahl), "narrative identity" (see Baddeley and Singer), and "arts-based/informed narrative inquiry" (see de Mello).

Through tracing how these authors, alongside a range of narrative inquirers whose works are reviewed, understand both their living in the field with participants or coresearchers and their composition of field texts and research texts, readers are invited into a gripping conversation about the complexities, promise, and future directions of narrative inquiries that start with telling stories.

In their exploration of the potential of digital archives, Barbara Morgan-Fleming, Sandra Riegle, and Wesley Fryer show how the reconceptualization of historical research, in which narrative became valued, "symbolizes a recognition that historical actors constitute society and that their understandings of self and society shape the extent to which a particular society or perhaps more specifically its institutions are reproduced." By attending to "the crossroads of the institution and the individual," Morgan-Fleming, Riegle, and Fryer push readers to seek out the stories of individuals whose lives are inextricably shaped by past institutional policies and practices. The promise of this kind of narrative inquiry work is that as we attend to wider, more multidimensional, and complex stories of history, our understandings of the past, as well as the present and future, are increased: "Multiple voices of the past can help educate us about our history, inform our present, and (we hope) improve our future."

Experiencing contradictions around how the "self as narrator" has been understood within the field of narrative psychology, Annie G. Rogers became drawn toward an exploration of the "unsayable"—a language of the unconscious that she sees as ever-present when human beings story their experiences: "I kept hearing something in narratives I could not grasp: the presence of the unsayable *in* words, *in* language, which also fell *between* sentences, *between* words, rendering every elaboration of "meaning" in the interpretation of text inadequate." Rogers challenges narrative inquirers to listen to the unsayable both in hearing and responding to stories in the midst of an interview and, later, in interpreting field texts of the told stories.

It is particularly around issues related to the "truthfulness" of autobiographical understanding and writing that Mark Freeman is drawn, especially as they are entangled with dualistic questions of the scientific or artful nature of autobiography as narrative inquiry. For Freeman, "the challenge at hand is a *poetic* one, the foremost aim being not to reproduce reality but to actualize and explicate it, to bring meaning into being in such a way that the world is made visible." A complexity then is "to find a language that moves beyond . . . highly schematized, conventualized, even clichéd portraits" of lives by moving toward the telling and interpretation of stories in ways that increase knowledge and understanding of human experience while also attending to "the *ethical* aim of increasing sympathy and compassion." Freeman urges autobiographers and narrative inquirers not to "minimize the artful dimension and to maximize the dimension of scientificity, thereby leaving the aforementioned 'deep human stuff' to poets and philosophers."

As they explore the potential of "learning from conversation," Sandra Hollingsworth and Mary Dybdahl present the following eight key principles: (1) Develop trust. Listen nonjudgmentally. (2) Initially scaffold or structure conversations and set norms, if necessary. (3) Encourage talk about topics that are controversial and difficult. (4) Allow emergent purposes for the conversation to develop. (5) Value different discourse styles. (6) Specifically articulate the learning that occurs in conversation. (7) Examine assumptions. (8) Pay attention to issues of power-in-relationship. It is, Hollingsworth and Dybdahl argue, through the living out of these kinds of principles that conversational narrative inquiry has impacted policy and practice across the professional fields of education, medicine, social work, business, and law. Through their review of this literature, Hollingsworth and Dybdahl discuss how conversational practices are transforming: national- and school-level reform, the relationships between health- and social-care providers and clients, the power of criminals to engage in their own self-defense, as well as legal policy and the education of lawyers.

As the field of psychology continues to be shaped by the capacity "of narrative methods to demarcate the shifting contributions of self and society while charting identity across the human life span," seeing "narratives of self and identity as embedded in interpersonal contexts that are sensitive to both cultural and developmental influences" will, as outlined by Jenna Baddeley and Jefferson A. Singer, be at the forefront.

Dilma Maria de Mello sees arts-based and arts-informed narrative inquiry as "pushing boundaries in the qualitative research landscape." Working to illuminate the differences between arts-based and arts-informed narrative inquiry and between narrative inquiry and other forms of qualitative inquiries, de Mello highlights (a) creative field text gathering; (b) creative research text presentation; (c) empowering coresearchers or participants through the inquiry process; (d) inviting readers to make their own conclusions; (e) supporting the construction of personal knowledge; and (f) honoring multiple perspectives as opening "doors through which we realize that there are other contexts to be studied or at least other ways of looking at the world."

Working against using the life story interview as "a procedure for collecting and documenting a category of data" or as a process through which data are collected around specific research questions, Robert Atkinson illustrates how a definition of a life story that attends to the experience a person has lived and chooses to narrate draws attention to "keeping the story in the words and voice of the one telling it." Interconnected with these issues of the definition, processes, and

products of life story interviews are ethical and interpretive issues that urge readers to continue to keep in view questions of the truth of life stories, of the potential of relationships between the interviewee and the interviewer, and of ways in
which the life story interview might shape increased opportunities to more fully
enter into another person's "life, culture, and world."

—*Janice Huber*

CHAPTER 3

Narrative Inquiry in Archival Work

Barbara Morgan-Fleming, Sandra Riegle, and Wesley Fryer

Many chapters in this handbook have shown the importance of doing narrative inquiry into the multiple stories of the present. In this chapter, we explore ideas related to inquiries into the multiple stories of the past. According to Clandinin and Connelly (2000), the following characteristics are a part of narrative inquiry:

> Narrative inquiry is a way of understanding experience. It is a collaboration between researcher and participants, over time, in a place or series of places, and in social interaction with milieus. An inquirer enters this matrix in the midst and progresses in this same spirit, concluding the inquiry still in the midst of living and telling, reliving and retelling, the stories of the experiences that make up people's lives, both individual and social. Simply stated . . . narrative inquiry is stories lived and told. (p. 20)

The question becomes, How can this method be applied to stories told by those of a different time and recorded by another person distant in time and, often, place? In this chapter, we explore the role narrative inquiry can play in accessing and understanding archival documents such as oral histories, diaries, letters, and photographs. We ask the question, How can we come to understand stories lived and told in the past?

As context for this story, we must understand the essence of history. Emerson's (1941) work helps guide us in this endeavor:

> This human mind wrote history, and this must read it. The Sphinx must solve her own riddle. If the whole of history is in one man, it is all to be explained from individual experience. There is a relation between the hours of our life

and the centuries of time. As the air I breathe is drawn from the great repositories of nature, as the light on my book is yielded by a star a hundred millions
of miles distant, as the poise of my body depends on the equilibrium of centrifugal and centripetal forces, so the hours should be instructed by the ages
and the ages explained by the hours. (p. 1)

When studying the past, we must still ask the following questions: "Whose story
is it? Who authored this tale? Whose voices were included? Whose voices were
silenced? As our attention is called to one facet of an event, what aspects are nudged
into shadow?" As lives are synthesized, conclusions about what is important and
what is equivalent are made. The life of the author filters the experiences of the
other, leaving us with one hegemonic tale instead of a symphony of lives. Archived
data allow access to the differentiated particular, helping us to understand the complexities of the past. In Carr's (1986) words,

The shapes of time are determined by our ongoing experiences and actions in
which we project or protend the future and retain the past. But it is not simply
the past; one feature of this temporal structure is that it is always a particular past,
the past that forms part of the progress of this particular event I am following (a
movement, a game, the illness of a beloved) or of this particular action or project in which I am engaged (serving the tennis ball, doing the shopping, preparing a class, finishing this book). These story-lines may combine to make up larger
stories; or, unrelated, they may criss-cross and interrupt one another, sometimes
hindering and sometimes contributing to one another's progress. (pp. 97–98)

The field texts mentioned by Clandinin and Connelly (1994)—oral history,
annals and chronicles, family stories, research interviews, journals, autobiographical writing, letters, conversations, and field notes—all can be found in written,
audio, and visual media in archives. This allows the individual to write his or her
own story of the past—combining his or her own story with the stories represented
in the archives, creating, "a relation of staggered and overlapping narratives . . .
what we have been looking for all along; a pre-thematic role for the social past in
the individual's experience and action" (Carr, 1986, p. 113).

It is also important to investigate and articulate the stance of the researcher and
the context of the research. The positivist lens of research can be contrasted with
new views of what it means to study and come to understanding. The following
table illustrates some distinctions in the goals of inquiry:

Positivist Research	Narrative Inquiry
Generalization, distillation	Understand the particular
Findings	Meanings
Single voice	Multiple voices
Discard "outliers"	Maintain distinctions

This preservation of the particular is important if those reading the inquiry are to get a multifaceted, complex view of the past. We can think of it in terms of the story of the elephant in the dark, in which blindfolded individuals touching different parts of the elephant come to very different conclusions about the animal in the room with them. The story usually ends here, but one could extend it by including the audience. Hearing all the descriptions, an individual might be able to reconstruct the elephant. Hearing only a single story or a synthesis would make that reconstruction difficult or impossible. Understanding the past also requires access to multiple experiences and stories. Archival materials are one potential source for such stories.

As online sources become more available, we see the possibility of creating an anthology of the past. We are entering a time when individuals can have direct access to others' stories related to experience, enabling each of us to explore history inductively rather than simply accepting the deductions of others. In this way, pictures of the past can be constructed as mosaics rather than as a single painting.

In this chapter, we first explore the potential contributions of archival materials to history and other academic fields. Second, we will provide examples of stories that can be told by primary sources in archives.

Modernity and the Emergence of the Individual Self

The modern period, Appleby, Hunt, and Jacob (1994) argue, gave birth to a new understanding of the person, namely, the "autonomous individual" (p. 40). This individual, himself a product of Kant's challenge of "dare to know," was concerned primarily with issues about "personal authenticity and material progress;" he was an individual who questioned authority and its structures, and who did not feel wedded to societal traditions (p. 40). Seemingly implicit within this autonomous being, then, was an individual in search of an identity; without the previous feudal constraints of community-identification attached, the emergent being needed to locate himself within both his culture and himself—in short, he needed to authenticate himself.

It is precisely this modern issue of individualism and identity seeking with which narrative researchers might wrestle. According to Revel and Hunt (1995),

> History, like other disciplines, does not progress by producing ever-more precise accounts of the processes of the past. . . . Historical knowledge progresses not by totalization but . . . by zooming and refocusing. (p. 488)

Stone (1979/2000) points to the importance of narrative history because "its arrangement is descriptive rather than analytical and its focus is on man not circumstances. It therefore deals with the particular and specific rather than the collective and statistical" (p. 254).

Historical Considerations

In social theory, structural functionalism emerged in part as an effort to displace teleological paradigms from the social sciences to establish an objectively based methodological framework for understanding and explaining how societies are preserved and maintained. Concerns with the modern, industrial state also furthered its development as social scientists sought to identify a theory for the linear transformation of societies from traditional agrarian roots to the modern industrial complex. Within these efforts, the concept of "system" remained at the core, with the overarching systemic framework the entity that structure (i.e., the arrangement of roles and institutions such as education within the society) and functions (i.e., the activities and interactions of those structures) ultimately must preserve (Morrow & Torres, 1995).

In the historical discipline, structuralism, as documented in the *Annales*, addressed the issue of system (Revel & Hunt, 1995, pp. 191–307). For example, writers such as Althusser (1972/1995) argued that "broad structures and process, not individual actions" shaped history (p. 195). The group, in other words, was thought to be the level at which society best could be understood and subsequently the level at which historians should focus (Althusser, 1972/1995). The attempt, ultimately, was to understand how reality both was presented, and re-presented, to provide insight into structures that did not change over time.

In the social sciences, structural functionalists increasingly came under attack for their emphasis on the notion of system. Structural functionalists were criticized for advancing a theoretical framework that lacked a sense of agency for the individual (Morrow & Torres, 1995). The theory personified, in other words, the structures of society, apparently overstepping the actual persons who create and maintain those structures and who determine the extent to which those structures and functions themselves will be preserved and reproduced. The question of how best to look at the notion of collectivity, also a question in historical structuralism, was in the structural-functionalism of the social sciences, most particularly in the works of Talcott Parsons (1959). The emphasis on preservation of the system thus lacked full consideration of particular human input and construction of those systems and their components; moreover, this omission seemingly robbed the individual of a sense of agency in the reproduction of the very system and subsystems that he constructed (Morrow & Torres, 1995).

In the historical discipline, the emergence of a history of *mentalités* in *Annales* (Revel & Hunt, 1995), as well as the emergence of gender studies, the notion of people's history, and eventually post-modernism (Joyce, 1995/2000; Scott, 1991/2000) paralleled social scientists' criticisms of structural-functionalism. More specifically, the works of historians such as Aries (1962) and Burguiere (1971/1995) advanced a reconceptualization of history that looked at society from the bottom up. By considering the voices of those whom Aries referred to as the "ordinary people" (as cited in Hutton, 1998, p. 482), the group level of analysis was broadened to privilege more disparate opinions and attitudes.

Narrative research, then, provides a means for researchers to access these disparate voices. Indeed, whereas a macrolevel analysis emphasizes the structures and those who control them, narrative research and microlevel analyses potentially provide opportunities to glean how the ordinary people interpret and enact the imposed representations placed on them by those in power.

Theory, History, and a Reconsideration of Structuralism

Critics maintained that an emphasis on the system lost the individual in, and to, the framework. In this way, then, narrative research is relevant to issues of identity. By presenting how history was experienced and understood by those at the micro level, a sense of agency could be restored, giving voice to those ordinary people and reminding historians and other researchers of the disparate voices—and perspectives—that ultimately make up, and make, history.

Historians began to reconsider the level of analysis to include gradually the reconstruction of ideas and understandings of disparate groups such as those who had historically been marginalized. Here, the works of Philippe Aries (1962), for example, are illustrative in understanding how this reconsideration emerged and why. Aries considered how themes such as love and belonging, and mortality, were manifested in historical constructs such as family and death. While studies about these topics had been conducted by other historians, Aries redirected the approach, to consider the *mentalité* of the ordinary people to glean a different narrative about France's past (Hutton, 1998, p. 482). Aries's (1962) work on childhood, for example, provided an historical analysis of a structure (i.e., the family) that in fact had changed through time. By arguing that the modern family "satisfied a desire for privacy and also a craving for identity" (p. 413), he showed that the modern family was a particular historical construct wherein identity was a consideration. In this way, identity construction began to emerge as an issue in historical studies and could be conceptualized as something that occurred within a process rather than something that was largely determined. The history of *mentalités,* in short, provided an experiential framework, rather than a biological, teleological, or psychological one, for understanding issues of self.

As Tosh (2000) documents, this experiential framework for identity construction was taken to a different level of historical analysis by post-modern historians. For example, Joan Scott (1991/2000) addressed the problem inherent in attempting to construct a unified concept of "woman" (p. 284). Patrick Joyce (1995/2000) noted that "human subjectivity is itself a historical creation" (p. 275). In short, historical post-modernists, advancing the arguments of their predecessors, attacked the notion that identity is either static or determined. Instead, post-modern historians asserted that identity is a creative process in which the individual is influenced by forces from the political and social spheres.

More than this, the history of mentalities and post-modernism concurrently provide an understanding of history that is not characterized by static structures but rather by structures created by historical actors who themselves were influenced by forces from the political and social spheres. Indeed, as Philip Abrams (1982/2000) asserted, the agency question might be addressed best through both a historical and sociological lens; by doing so, researchers might better account for the interdependence of identity construction and societal reproduction. Identity and agency, in other words, are concerned with "a question of trying to build a sociology of process" (p. 228). In this way, the notion that identity is determined by institutions is disavowed; the interaction of historical forces shapes but need not necessarily determine one's sense of self. As Abrams (1982/2000) noted, the notion of individual action is thus preserved to provide individuals with a sense of ownership of historical and present time (p. 228). The shift in historiography specifically and the social sciences generally, from structuralism toward considerations of *mentalité* and ultimately narrative, then symbolizes a recognition that historical actors constitute society and that their understandings of self and society shape the extent to which a particular society or perhaps more specifically its institutions are reproduced.

By using narrative, the researcher is tacitly questioning the legitimate authority of macrolevel history. The researcher's skepticism of histories offered in macrolevel analysis underscores a certain power to question that which is said to be true; that inherited authority and power, the researcher suggests, is institutional. Narrative research thus addresses identity politics, at least insofar as it offers an account of individual(s) who in effect (and in part) fill the gap where the authority of macrolevel analysis had been. The researcher is able to document truth through these individualized accounts and, in effect, free herself or himself from dependence on top-down accounts. A historical, narrative framework through which to examine influences such as family, gender, childhood, and race as the *mentalités* that shaped the construction of societal institutions thus provides an opportunity to consider how and what forces and actors created the traditions we know today and, perhaps more importantly, those we wish to reproduce and those we seek to change or terminate.

The shift in historical methodology from structuralism toward *mentalités,* and eventually toward post-modernism, provides insight into the multiple frameworks through which historians have attempted to glean understandings of the traditions we inherit and how those traditions have been preserved. In social theory, these considerations first definitively emerged with the work of Émile Durkheim (1973), whose work sought to construct units of analysis that concurrently were outside the individual and controlled and shaped his behaviors (de Sousa, 1975; Rossides, 1968). Structuralist historians such as Althusser (1972/1995) and Burguiere (1971/1995), much like the social theorists, sought to provide a level of analysis that got underneath the shifting tides of historical time to locate something more fundamental in the human experience. Yet their framework, like that of social theorists, was criticized as too broad a level of analysis; the individual was lost in translation and, subsequently, so was an understanding of agency and the voices of the Other. The emergence of a history of *mentalités* that sought to explain the historical factors that shaped experience, as well as narrative, wherein individual voices are analyzed to understand historical memory at the micro level, represented a growing awareness that the reproduction of society is an interactive process between individuals and the traditions they inherit. This historical reconceptualization, later expanded by post-modernists, provided a lens through which to analyze society and its inherited traditions (whether those traditions are represented by ideas or structures).

Narrative accounts of history are useful for questioning the extent to which the social and human sciences can be compounded to provide understandings of identity and agency. More specifically, by examining personal correspondence and pictures or listening to oral histories individuals leave to posterity, researchers can continue to question the appropriate level of analysis as well as the extent to which a particular idea or structure has been accepted or shaped one's experience. They thus might gain insight into the ways in and through which we have historically explained our society, its institutions, and the reproduction of each. A critical reconsideration of the extent to which attempts at writing a total history (e.g., see Braudel, 1958/1995), as Revel and Hunt (1995) note, is essential "to enrich reality by including the widest possible range of social experience" (p. 497). In doing so, researchers might understand better the factors that have shaped identity construction and agentic perceptions in the past to understand better those factors that continue to wield influence today.

Digital Archival Research: Benefits and Limitations

As access to the Internet becomes more widespread, digital research is increasingly conducted by investigators of all ages. While the aesthetic value and benefit of in-person archival research experience will likely never be replicated in full with digital tools, the advantages of digital research are compelling, especially in terms of access to and preservation of historical materials. While the availability of digital archive materials is still limited in the early 21st century, the volume of materials is steadily increasing and is likely to grow exponentially in the years to come.

Digital archival research is defined as the analysis of digitized files, which may include images (photos, scanned graphics, or documents), full-text documents, audio files, video files, and stitched or composite VR (virtual reality) objects that can be manipulated to varying degrees by users. Digital archival resources may be available on the Internet's World Wide Web on static Web pages, dynamic, searchable Web pages supported by a database "back-end," or password-protected Web sites available over the Internet or only on a local network or on other media including CD-ROM or DVD.

Traditional archival research offers the distinct advantage of providing investigators direct access to primary source materials but has many limitations that make it time-consuming, costly, and often impractical. Digital archival research, on the other hand, can transcend many of these limitations and provide greater access to a larger number of potential researchers, less confined by limits of time and space. Additionally, digital archival research can offer instantaneous search capabilities to individual researchers that would otherwise require a large team of traditional investigators innumerable hours of work to replicate. Whether or not a researcher is technologically "savvy," the potential power and access options afforded by digital archival research deserve careful scrutiny and consideration.

In addition to these limitations, the materials in a physical archive may be subject to physical degradation and loss of quality, depending on the format of the materials and the storage method employed. Archivists typically exercise extreme care in ensuring optimal preservation of their materials and limit investigator access to and use of archived materials with the ideal of preservation in mind. However, even when extreme care is taken to preserve and care for materials, accidents can happen, and materials can decay in quality over time. An example is taped interviews. Some audio recordings available in archives may be stored on reel-to-reel magnetic tape media. These reels are subject not only to the gradual degradation of magnetically defined patterns on fragile and thin strips of plastic but also may jam in old tape players available in the archive and be irreparably damaged. Heat, extreme cold, and dust can also damage these materials over time.

When archived artifacts have been converted to full-text versions, digital research can afford time-saving efficiencies that were unimaginable before computer technology became a reality. Preservation of the quality and content of archived materials can also be perfected in digital formats. While digital media such as Web servers, CD-ROMs, and DVD media are subject to corrosion, fire loss, and so on, the ability to create perfect copies of these materials backed up in different locations can help ensure the quality and availability of materials to posterity in ways not possible with physical objects.

Online archives provide the opportunity for students to have access to a wide variety of personal stories about historical events. As archival sources become more readily available, one can imagine anthologies that reference individual diaries, pictures, and other primary sources of a particular time (for example, the Civil War), allowing students direct access to individuals' experience of that event.

Two digital archives housed at our institution (Texas Tech University) are offered here as examples of the possibilities of digital archival collections. Other digital archives are detailed in the appendix.

The Uysal-Walker Archive of Turkish Oral Narrative (U-W ATON)

The following description of the collection is available on the archive's Web site (www.aton.ttu.edu):

> The Uysal-Walker Archive of Turkish Oral Narrative (U-W ATON) is the world's largest well-organized, thoroughly indexed, and completely accessible collection of Turkish folktales and related forms. (www.aton.ttu.edu/descript.asp)
>
> The work towards an Archive began in 1961, culminating in the Uysal-Walker Archive of Turkish Oral Narrative we know today. During that year the three original Founders (Ahmet E. Uysal, Warren S. Walker, and Barbara K.

Walker) first began collecting materials from the field when they met in Ankara as a result of Warren Walker having been awarded a U.S. Fullbright Grant tenable in the Turkish Republic. After the first ten years of fieldwork, in many villages, the task of organization and the need for a permanent place began occupying their thoughts. With these concerns in the background, the original Founders eventually donated their holdings to Texas Tech University in 1980. (www.aton.ttu.edu/about.asp)

The term *oral narrative* as it is used here encompasses a wide range of forms and subjects. For purposes of order and convenience, U-W ATON holdings have been divided into eight major sections (the supernatural, perplexities and ingenious deductions, humor, moralizing, Romance—heroic and /or ama-tory, anticlerical satire, anecdotal wit and wisdom, miscellaneous). The divisions are by no means mutually exclusive—the reader will find some tales coded with two different division numbers—and anyone wishing to do so might well voice reservations about the taxonomy. The rubrics have, nevertheless, served users satisfactorily since this research facility opened its doors in 1971. (www.aton.ttu.edu/descript.asp)

The Vietnam Center

The Vietnam Center provides the following description of its purpose and holdings (www.vietnam.ttu.edu):

The Project
    The mission of the Vietnam Center at Texas Tech University is to support and encourage research and education regarding all aspects of the American Vietnam experience; promoting a greater understanding of this experience and the peoples and cultures of Southeast Asia.

(2 Feb 2006)—The Virtual Vietnam Archive 2005 Update
    The Virtual Vietnam Archive continues to grow at a remarkable rate. With more than 2.3 million pages and in excess of 300,000 individual records, it is the largest online archive of Vietnam War related materials in the world. We add approximately 30,000–35,000 pages of new material online each month making the Virtual Vietnam Archive a very dynamic electronic research resource. . . . Virtual Vietnam Archive researchers downloaded more than 934,000 documents, photos, and other online artifacts—a total of more than 1.12 Terabytes of material. (www.vietnam.ttu.edu)

The Southwest Collection

Although the advent of digital archives has provided increased access to archival materials, many excellent collections have yet to be digitized. One such example at our institution is the Southwest Collection. Many of the audiotapes used in this section were first transcribed by Sandra, and copies of the transcripts were shared with the archive. According to its Web site (www.swco.ttu.edu/Oral_History/oralhistory.asp),

> the Oral History collection of the Southwest Collection is one of the largest in Texas. More than 4,500 tapes, containing 2,800 interviews have been abstracted and indexed.... These interviews trace the development of West Texas from settlement to the present time when the area has become a major agribusiness and medical region. Subjects covered include, oil, ranching, community and economic development.

Further, according to its Web site (www.swco.ttu.edu/Oral_History/main.htm),

> since the 1930s when the narratives of former slaves were recorded, the taped interview has proven its worth as a means of acquiring the historical accounts of all people, including those unlikely to leave written records. Thus historical research has become more egalitarian, allowing historians the potential to record and express many viewpoints. Historians are constantly looking for new methods to peer into the past. Taped interviews provide an exciting way of doing just that. Researchers are able to hear first hand, spontaneous accounts in the eyewitness's own words.... While the Oral History Program specializes in collecting audio and videotaped interviews, it also actively collects photographs, videotapes, film footage, books, newspapers and periodicals, memorabilia, and a wide variety of manuscript items such as letters, business records, personal records, diaries, and memoirs.

It is precisely at the crossroads of the institution and the individual that archival research can provide opportunities to uncover—or recover—stories of those voices and accounts that might otherwise have been lost. For example, the Southwest Collection contains materials that could offer researchers chances to understand the complex history of race relations in the South Plains generally and Lubbock more specifically. Primary source materials such as meeting minutes and personal correspondence indicate the rationales of those in positions of local power not to close or pair schools as well as to limit boundary changes that would affect zoning.[1] While these documents do provide considerable historical detail from the individuals who determined such institutional policies, they lack the stories and experiences of individuals whose educational and professional opportunities were, essentially, established by those decisions.

Here, again, the materials available in archives prove invaluable for providing such information. Indeed, the Southwest Collection houses numerous oral histories that supply rich narratives about historical, institutional racism and the ways in which certain individuals were able to navigate boundaries to challenge the status quo. Such navigations certainly are illustrative of the agentic power the victims of racism recognized and employed. For example, George Scott's interview on January 14, 1980, offers details about his encounters with racism in the *Lubbock Avalanche-Journal,* Lubbock's local newspaper, and in the schools. Mr. Scott's interview presents researchers with specific glimpses into the institutional boundaries these structures created—and re-created—for African Americans in Lubbock in the early and mid-20th century. Furthermore, the interview suggests the ways in which Mr. Scott constructed his identity as an African American male experiencing such prejudice. Indeed, Mr. Scott's story reveals his considerable sense of agentic power, which he used to challenge culturally inherited notions of African American capabilities.

In addition to such narratives, the materials in the Southwest Collection offer researchers media accounts of race relations in the town. More specifically, files for Dunbar High School, a historically predominantly African American school in Lubbock, contain *Lubbock Avalanche-Journal* articles written in the late 20th century that provide some detail about both the history of the school and the battle for desegregation in the larger town.

Apart from primary source materials that provide insight into the exercise of individual agency to challenge institutional power, the Southwest Collection contains materials that potentially offer researchers opportunities to challenge metalevel narratives that have influenced and shaped the experiences of ordinary people. Indeed, papers such as those of M. L. Russell and Martin Homer could offer peeks into the realities of westward settlement, thereby presenting researchers means of understanding the limitations of Fredrick Jackson Turner's romantic, mythologized tales of westward expansion and life.

Archival research affords researchers opportunities to unearth the realities of the ordinary people as well as the local institutions that helped to shape their experiences. The materials at the Southwest Collection provide primary source material rich with detail from those who navigated the challenges of mezzo- and metalevel institutional structures to affect change. Indeed, narrative accounts and personal papers, as well as local institutional records, contain historical documentation that, when analyzed and synthesized contextually, can give a fuller account of our past.

The Story of Dunbar School: An Archival Example

One example of the multiple stories surrounding a particular place can be seen by looking at stories about Dunbar school. Newspaper articles, oral histories, and other archival sources tell the stories of Dunbar school from its beginning in 1922, through its attempted desegregation in 1970, at which time a 16-year-old white student shot a 15-year-old black student during class, causing rioting and a massive withdrawal of white and Mexican American students from Dunbar (Parks, 1999), and finally through its closure as a high school in 1993 despite community opposition.

The perspectives of a variety of educators and students of Dunbar can be found through archival collections of oral histories. The following people were interviewed, and the audiotapes are available at the Southwest Collection of the Texas Tech library:

Clarlandis Lane, who attended Dunbar from 1946 to 1956.

Mae Simmons, born 1911, who began teaching at Dunbar in 1943. She continued working as a teacher and principal in Lubbock until her retirement in 1972.

George Scott, Jr., born 1926, who served as head football coach at Dunbar from 1953 to 1964 and as principal of Dunbar from 1964 to 1969. In 1969, he was named Assistant Dean of Students at Texas Tech University.

George C. Woods came to Lubbock on May 20, 1928. He was unable to attend Dunbar because the school did not offer classes beyond the 10th grade. He returned to Temple, Texas, to finish high school. He was unable to attend Texas Tech because at that time the college did not allow African American students to attend.

E. C. Struggs came to Lubbock in 1930. He served as teacher and principal at Dunbar when it had approximately 100 students and three rooms. Two other teachers (Mrs. Iles and Mr. Wilson) worked at Dunbar at that time.

William R. Powell graduated from Dunbar in 1945 and returned as a teacher in 1958. He later served as Director of Student Activities and was principal of Dunbar from 1968 to 1970. During his second year as principal of Dunbar, court-ordered desegregation began.

Damon Hill, Sr. came to Dunbar in 1937 to teach industrial arts and coach all sports. He taught and coached in Lubbock for 37 years.

Stories of E. C. Struggs and William Powell

In the following section, we present excerpts from the transcribed interviews of two of these individuals. The full text of the interviews is available at the archive.

E. C. Struggs

This is an interview with Mr. E. C. Struggs, conducted by Lynn Musclewhite, on February 22, 1969.

I came here in 1930.

The Negro school was on 17th Street. It was just a three-room building, on 17th Street. At that particular time, that was the oldest school in this area. We had a little better than a hundred students, in all. I had two other teachers besides myself when

I came. . . . I was the teacher and principal. . . . Mrs. Iles was one, the one that Ella Iles School was named for . . . And the other teacher was named Mr. Wilson.

Well now, that building was moved in there . . . and worked it over . . . and made a school out of it. In fact, there was just two rooms in, when they moved it. And then added one more room onto it.

I had to get there early enough in the morning to start the fire . . . one of my other teachers had to be responsible for the fire in his room . . . we'd have to get there early enough to have the fire, and we'd get . . . the coal and stuff to get the fire started in the evening so we could get it ready for the kids—kiddos by morning.

Oh, it was crowded. You'd have 30, 35, 40 children, you know? . . . It was getting very crowded. We had to use the churches over there. They had the Presbyterian Church, right across the street . . . (we) taught in the church—in the Presbyterian Church. And then, it got so crowded over there, until they put another teacher on, why they had to use the Methodist Church.

During the, during the depression—it was, it was certainly harder. I'll tell you, we'd work a month, and we didn't know whether we was gonna get anything or not. . . . As a matter of fact, . . . we were paid with a check, and we had found that we'd have to take the check to the bank and have the check discounted so much for them to cash it. And along the way, they started cutting the checks up, so we if we could, if we'd get so much money, uh, the check would be cut up, into 25, and 50 dollars, like that. So they can just take that check on to the grocery store, and take they'd take the check at face value. Otherwise, you can take it to the bank, and discount it. And when the, the check wasn't too big, even at that (laughs).

What brought most of our people into this country was the harvesting period. They came out here to pick cotton. And after they got out here, and after they got through harvesting, why they came to town, and found jobs, and stayed here then.

I've seen, right here, people come from dugouts, they dug under the ground . . . made their homes under the ground. They just came out here on cotton picking. And nobody knew 'em, and they couldn't borrow their money, therefore they just, they'd bought a lot. And then they took that lot, and dug under the ground, and then they stayed there, until they were able to build a home.

William Powell

GP: *This is Gene Preuss interviewing William R. Powell in Lubbock, Texas, on July 7, 1995. We're at the all-class reunion of former Dunbar High School students.*

I was born in Williamson County, June the seventh, 1928. . . . I've been in education all my life. I finished high school here at Lubbock Dunbar in 1945, and graduated from college in 1950 . . . then I came back to Lubbock in 1958. Professor Struggs hired me to teach—initially, to teach junior high school math. And then just before the new school was built over Manhattan, I was moved into chemistry and physics, I was also director of student activities and then principal for two years, at Dunbar. And then I did a year in the central office, as the administrator, and left Lubbock in 1972.

My parents were both teachers, . . . that's how I ended up in attending Lubbock Dunbar. My father came to West Texas, from Central Texas, to teach in Slaton. And he taught there for two years. I went to school with him, in Slaton, for two years. And then when I was in the 11th grade, he went to Littlefield to teach, and I stopped off in Lubbock, and spent the 11th and 12th grades here, at Lubbock Dunbar.

I attended school at Slaton for two years, so when I came to Lubbock (chuckles), I thought I had reached the mountain top . . . because I was in a high school where they had a . . . number of teachers . . . and teachers were specialized in their fields, and . . . there were all kinds of sports, and other extra curricular activities going on, and . . . we probably had as many people in my senior class, as we did in, in two or three grades at Slaton, at that time. So I thought I had reached the mountaintop. Teachers were very good, very interested in teaching us. They were young, energetic; we all lived together in, in the same neighborhoods. . . . I found it to be a good healthy and wholesome atmosphere. And Prof. Struggs was an excellent man, in fact, he's a hero, to a lot of us. . . . He . . . was extremely student-oriented . . . if there was anything at all that he could do to, help a student, he would do it . . . even if that meant paddling them, or bending over backwards to see to it that he had clothes on his back, to wear to school, or money in his pocket for his lunch . . . and that was kind of, inspirational, to me, to kind of want to emulate him, in his orientation to, to students, and, and even to his community, because he was very active in his church, and in his community. Prof. also encouraged his teachers to be that way. He was active in the teacher's associations at that time, and encouraged his teachers to be likewise.

I hope that somehow or other, I had the same influence on some of my teachers . . . Prof. Struggs had a lot of young, high-spirited, energetic teachers . . . we just worked hard together; we were a community . . . we related very well to our students, and to our parents. . . . In fact, the community was entwined around the school . . . the school embraced the community, which meant that it was close, a close alliance between the school, the staff, students, and teachers . . . we taught school seven days a week, sort of. Because the students knew us, we knew their parents, so our teaching didn't end at four o'clock, it continued, because we socialized with their parents. We went to church together . . . so that kind of feeling toward our kids, in our community, at that time, prevailed, seven days a week, 24 hours a day. That's what I meant when I said that we taught everyday, because we had contact with parents all of the time, through our churches, and our civic organizations, and . . . we had a lot of community support from parents.

(Speaking of the integration of Dunbar) *Some of those folks across town that I thought was so supportive of Dunbar suddenly turned on us. I didn't realize the negative attitudes about Lubbock Dunbar were as strong as they were until we were forced into court-ordered desegregation. And the first year I was principal, we were desegregated. Our faculties have been desegregated for a number of years. Lubbock Classroom Teacher's Association has been desegregated, and I was serving as president of that association before court-ordered desegregation of the schools! And as a result, I had grown to, to accept a lot of people from across the community, regardless of their race or color, and it felt as though we were being accepted by them. But there was a great deal of hostility that surfaced on the day of the court decision, in which the government kept Dunbar open, and brought court-ordered bussing to the community. Much of that was done, because of the gerrymandering of school districts within the city, which kept all of the black people attending the same school regardless to where they lived.*

I served as principal in '68–'69, '69–'70. Those were the years. So the court-ordered desegregation occurred the second year, at the end of my first year term as principal . . . we had a lot of changes at the school system that year. And it . . . turned out to be volatile in both communities.

Initially it (the response of the black community) *was very good, because we had taught our students that this was coming, and you need to get ready for it. And I think the students were ready for it, the parents were ready for it. But the people from across town weren't ready to come, because I think the anticipation was that Lubbock Dunbar was going to close. And we would be scattered, you know, to the winds . . . but the court unexpectedly ruled otherwise. So now here we are the doors open, and, they had redrawn school district lines, and some school policies and all of that were rewritten in the court order. And we had less than 24 hours to get ready to open up. That decision was rendered on a Saturday afternoon, and school started Monday morning.*

We didn't have much time to get ready, we didn't have much time to, to readjust and change attitudes and, and prepare for it . . . we had support. Ed Irons— Mr. Irons—was a good superintendent, and he was a lot of support to Lubbock Dunbar. It's just that I think we got so much attention that first year, and certainly I didn't even know, I didn't know how to handle it. I—we got attention that you would not believe. And it came from everywhere . . . so much so, that sometimes . . . I would . . . almost say it was unwarranted. We needed to have been left alone, to a great degree, even in a, integrated setting, with a very stable faculty, so that we could continue to do the work that we had been, over the years, trained to under Prof. Struggs, and some of the others. But under court-ordered desegregation, we lost the strength of our faculty, and we ended up with a lot of young white people coming in, who were commuters. The faculty no longer lived in the community. And I think that made for a great difference in the relationship between parents and teachers.

Living Alongside Archival Documents

As we finish this chapter, we ask ourselves, how can we come to understand the stories of the past? How can we live alongside those from an earlier time? As we have interacted with these stories, we find overlap and distinction in the stories of our lives and the storied lives of those from Dunbar.

Barbara teaches her Language Arts methods course at Wheatley Elementary, which is located a few blocks from the current Dunbar school. Wheatley's principal, Margaret Randle, speaks of the history of the neighborhood, and Mr. Colvin, who was Wheatley's principal from the school's opening in 1955 until 1971, still lives across the street and keeps an eye on the school, calling Margaret if any teachers are late. Two projects completed at Wheatley help connect with the stories of Dunbar. As part of an integrated-methods block taught at Wheatley, Wes and Barbara worked with students from Wheatley and Texas Tech, studying Yellow

House Canyon, an area currently called Dunbar Lake, located behind the athletic field at Dunbar. We studied locations where Buffalo soldiers fought the Comanche, saw where the tornado came through in 1970 (see Parks, 1999), and collected water samples to test current pollution levels in the lake.

We respond to the stories of Professor Struggs and William Powell as educators and fellow residents of Lubbock, appreciating their courage, determination, and intelligence, hoping to introduce others to these individuals and their stories of schooling in Lubbock. Our roles here are alongside in location and occupation but distant in time and race. As Sandra transcribed the oral histories—some for the first time—and provided the transcripts to the archive and to fellow educators, we were motivated by the desire to reconnect with the multiple stories and experiences of the past. Just as "the present" differs for all those who experience it, so does "the past." Returning to Emerson (1941),

> We, as we read, must become Greeks, Romans, Turks, priest and king, martyr and executioner; must fasten these images to some reality in our secret experience, or we shall learn nothing rightly. . . . All history becomes subjective. . . . Every mind must know the whole lesson for itself—must go over the whole ground. What it does not see, what it does not live, it will not know. (pp. 2–3)

If we are able to see the past through multiple, particular lenses, our sense of history is widened and our potential understandings are increased. Multiple voices of the past can help educate us about our history, inform our present, and (we hope) improve our future.

Consulting Editors: Craig Kridel and Walter Doyle

Note

1. In a letter dated July 26, 1968, from then superintendent of the Lubbock Independent School District Nat Williams to Jerold Ward, then Executive Chief in Dallas, Mr. Williams argues that pairing or closing schools would prove too "prohibitive."

References

Abrams, P. (2000). Historical sociology. In J. Tosh (Ed.), *Historians on history* (pp. 224–229). New York: Pearson Education. (Original work published 1982)

Althusser, L. (1995). Reply to John Lewis. In J. Revel & L. Hunt (Eds.), *Histories: French constructions of the past* (pp. 195–201). New York: New Press. (Original work published 1972)

Appleby, J., Hunt, L., & Jacob, M. (1994). *Telling the truth about history.* New York: W. W. Norton.

Aries, P. (1962). *Centuries of childhood: A social history of family life.* New York: Alfred A. Knopf.

Braudel, F. (1995). History and the social sciences: The *longue durée*. In J. Revel & L. Hunt (Eds.), *Histories: French constructions of the past* (pp. 115–146). New York: New Press. (Original work published 1958)

Burguiere, A. (1995). History and structure. In J. Revel & L. Hunt (Eds.), *Histories: French constructions of the past* (pp. 231–240). New York: New Press. (Original work published 1971)

Carr, D. (1986). *Time, narrative, and history.* Bloomington: Indiana University Press.

Clandinin, D., & Connelly, F. (1994). *Personal experience methods.* In N. Denzin & Y. Lincoln (Eds.), *Handbook of qualitative research.* Thousand Oaks, CA: Sage.

Clandinin, D. J., & Connelly, F. (2000). *Narrative inquiry: Experience and story in qualitative research.* San Francisco: Jossey-Bass.

de Sousa, D. (1975). *Sociological formalism and structural-functional analysis: The nature of the 'social' reality sui generis form system.* Hicksville, NY: Exposition Press.

Durkheim, É. (1973). *Émile Durkheim: On morality and society* (R. Bellah, Ed.). Chicago: University of Chicago Press.

Emerson, R. W. (1941). *Essays of Ralph Waldo Emerson: Including essays, first and second series, English traits, nature and considerations by the way.* New York: A. S. Barnes.

Hutton, P. (1998). The politics of the young Philippe Aries. *French Historical Studies, 21*(3), 475–495.

Joyce, P. (2000). The end of social history? In J. Tosh (Ed.), *Historians on history* (pp. 274–281). New York: Pearson Education. (Original work published 1995)

Morrow, R. A., & Torres, C. A. (1995). *Social theory and education: A critique of theories of social and cultural reproduction.* New York: State University of New York Press.

Parks, K. (Ed.). (1999). *Remember when? A history of African Americans in Lubbock, Texas.* Lubbock, TX: Friends of the Library/Southwest Collection.

Parsons, T. (1959). The school class as a social system: Some of its functions in American society. *Harvard Educational Review, 29,* 297–318.

Revel, J., & Hunt, L. (1995). Let's try the experiment. In J. Revel & L. Hunt (Eds.), *Histories: French constructions of the past* (pp. 484–491). New York: New York Press.

Rossides, D. W. (1968). *Society as a functional process: An introduction to sociology.* New York: McGraw-Hill.

Scott, J. (2000). Women's history. In J. Tosh (Ed.), *Historians on history* (pp. 283–288). New York: Pearson Education. (Original work published 1991)

Stone, L. (2000). The revival of narrative: reflections on a new old history. In J. Tosh (Ed.), *Historians on history* (pp. 254–263). New York: Pearson Education. (Original work published 1979)

Tosh, J. (Ed.). (2000). *Historians on history.* New York: Pearson Education.

Appendix

- Presidential Libraries
    - Herbert Hoover Presidential Library and Museum: www.ecommcode .com/ hoover/hooveronline/
    - FDR Presidential Library and Online Documents: www.fdrlibrary.marist .edu/online14.html
    - Thomas Jefferson Digital Archive: http://etext.virginia.edu/jefferson/
    - Truman Presidential Archive: www.trumanlibrary.org/photos/av-photo.htm
- National Digital Information Infrastructure and Preservation Program: www .digitalpreservation.gov/
- U.S. Library of Congress: http://loc.gov/
- Smithsonian Institution Digital Library: www.sil.si.edu/digitalcollections/
- Digital National Security Archive Online: http://nsarchive.chadwyck.com/
- iBiblio: The Public's Library and Digital Archive: www.ibiblio.org/
- WorldGenWeb Project: www.worldgenweb.org/archives/
- Boston College Digital Archive of Art: www.bc.edu/bc_org/avp/cas/fnart/art/
- Boston College Digital Archive of Architecture: www.bc.edu/bc_org/avp/cas/ fnart/arch/
- Brown v. Board of Education Digital Archive: www.lib.umich.edu/exhibits/ brownarchive/
- U.S. State Archives
    - Pennsylvania State Archives: www.digitalarchives.state.pa.us/
    - University of Pennsylvania Digital Library Projects: http://digital.library .upenn.edu/
- Online Archive of California: www.oac.cdlib.org/
- United Kingdom
    - National Archives of the United Kingdom: www.nationalarchives.gov.uk/
    - UK National Archive of Datasets: http://ndad.ulcc.ac.uk/
- The September 11 Digital Archive: http://911digitalarchive.org/

The Open Content Alliance (OCA; www.opencontentalliance.org/) is a collaborative effort of organizations worldwide seeking to build "a digital archive of global content for universal access." The OCA is obtaining publisher permission for content digitization and Web distribution and is therefore able to provide full-text versions of text and media artifacts in its growing archive.

The Internet Archive (http://archive.org) is another organization digitizing vast quantities of resources but invites contributions from researchers, historians, scholars, and the general public. The Internet Archive provides free hosting for audio and video files, and free tools are available for uploading and opening licensing content (http://creativecommons.org/tools/ccpublisher).

CHAPTER 4

The Unsayable, Lacanian Psychoanalysis, and the Art of Narrative Interviewing

Annie G. Rogers

I t's a curious truth that even as we speak, we circle around what it's not possible to say, reading one another about what to elaborate, what to revise (and even try to erase), coming, almost inevitably, to what eludes any possibility of being heard. This is what I call the unsayable. It points simultaneously to a distinctive form of language in human interchange and to the elusive presence of the unconscious everywhere in speaking. In this paper, I review the field of narrative psychology and its practices of interviewing, argue that the idea that the "self" so central to narrative psychology is nothing less than a site of illusion, and introduce a method of listening to the unconscious as an alternative way to explore human subjectivity. In doing so, I show how the art of interviewing is shaped by conceptions of language, self, and subjectivity.

Narrative Psychology and Interviewing: History, Conceptions, and Contradictions

Narrative research in psychology is not new; in fact, it has a long history. William James (1901/1994) captured the spirit of narrative research in the fledgling field of psychology in terms of an effort to understand "the varieties of the human mind in living action." Clinical case studies were responsible for the founding insights of psychoanalysis (Breuer & Freud, 1885/1955), the description of psychosocial stages of human development (Erikson, 1958, 1963), and the conceptualization of developmental structures in childhood play and moral thought (Piaget, 1948). From the 1930s to the 1960s, a major catalyst to explore the psychology of individual lives came from the personology[1] of Henry Murray (1938) and his students such as Robert White (1952). Gordon Allport (1937) and his colleagues, similarly influential and productive during this time, were using idiographic methods and personal documents in their research. In the 1930s, John Dollard (1937) conducted narrative, field-based research on race relations in the South, and after World War II, Kurt Lewin (1948) studied group processes using qualitative methods. Muzafer and Caroline Sherif and their colleagues (Sherif, Harvey, White, Hood, & Sherif, 1961) explored the rivalries among boys in summer camp in the 1950s and 1960s using narrative methods of inquiry. In the 1970s and 1980s, psychology was challenged and influenced by narrative research on individual lives, social structures, psychobiographies, and group histories (Block, 1971; Elder, 1974; Fine, 1983; Gilligan, 1982/1993; Josselson, 1973, 1978; McAdams, 1988; Runyan, 1982). This kind of work has burgeoned so much during the 1990s and into the first decade of the 21st century that it is impossible to review even the major contributions (for a range of approaches, see Luttrell, 2003; Wertsch, 1991; Wetherell & Potter, 1992).

Literature conceptualizing the psychology of narrative has proliferated over the past several decades. It is worth considering some of the key ideas in this area to note how psychologists, in the main, have come to espouse different ideas about the nature of the self in narrative research and the implications for practices of interviewing.

In the field of narrative psychology it is impossible to overlook Jerome Bruner (1986), who authorized a narrative approach through what he called "narrative modes of knowing." He provided a crucial framework for the psychological study of autobiographies, stories, and life narratives. Narrative modes of knowing, Bruner argued, function as a central form of human thinking. What's more, they play a key role in the construction of self and identity. These ideas raised an epistemological challenge to the field as a whole, especially in America, where empiricism, experimental studies, and statistics were synonymous with psychology. Bruner gave us permission to explore human lives through narratives, particularly interviews, and to make such studies part of the discipline of psychology.

Elliot Mishler (1986) challenged us to reconsider the art of interviewing in an entirely new way. Psychological research, embedded in the legacies of behaviorism, reduced interviews to the idea of questions and answers as if these were no more than a stimulus-response exchange. Criticizing this approach because it suppressed discourse, Mishler argued that the interview is a type of discourse, a speech event that is a joint product that has been shaped and organized by asking and answering questions within a social context. He also noted that different interview practices had different effects on participants and showed us that the interviewer was far from objective. Furthermore, he advocated a deep respect for participants in research by inviting interviewees into a collaborative role in the research process.

But the respect and collaboration Mishler advocated was fraught, and nowhere was this more striking than in feminist approaches to narrative psychology. Katherine Borland's (1991) research was a prime example. Working with her grandmother's narrative of an event of attending a horse race in 1944, Borland described the young Beatrice Hanson as a woman choosing her own horse, a rogue horse at that, in conflict with her father (and by proxy, with the men of her time), who made bets for women. But when she asked her grandmother about this idea, her grandmother didn't agree with Borland's interpretation. Borland presented both points of view in some detail and commented, "While I have already stacked the deck in my favor by summarizing the story, reducing it through my subjective lens, my grandmother's comments powerfully challenge my assumption of exegetical authority over the text" (p. 65). Narrative researchers, refreshingly respectful of the voices of research participants, inevitably came to this difficult authorial problem.

Louise Kidder and Michelle Fine (1997) highlighted the merits of narrative approaches for understanding human beings fully and accurately yet introduced a paradox into that very project. In their research, they developed a critical psychology showing how race, class, and gender shape lived experience. Like other psychologists and sociologists (see, e.g., Ezzy, 1998), they argued that narrative interview research offers an opportunity to analyze "the nuanced strategies by which power operates though individual and collective psychologies" (Kidder & Fine, 1997, p. 37). In doing so, however, they challenged the assumption that participants speak for themselves in some uncritical way and suggested that narrative researchers assert authority over their data.

How is it possible to fully credit and respect the voices of participants in research while at the same time exerting interpretive authority over those voices? This question provides the launching point for a short discussion on discursive psychology. The traditional representational approach to language and interpretation proceeds from the idea that people use words to describe the world as it is, in contrast to understanding language as a means of constructing reality (Gergen, 1993). Discursive psychology is built on the premise that words, rather than simply serving a simple representational function, gain their meaning through the way they are used to construct the world in a linguistic community (Searle, 1969; Wittgenstein, 1963). Human beings use language to perform actions in relation to others—we make requests, blame, persuade, promise, challenge, take vows, guarantee a result, and so on. This approach embraced a dialogic conception of language (Bakhtin, 1986; Wertsch, 1991). Words were seen to represent relatively arbitrary meanings that had a history in social relations. Discourse analysis offered a range of methods for identifying patterns of meanings embedded in larger speech genres and patterns of communication that serve various social, ideological, and political interests (see, e.g., Harre & Streams, 1995; Wood & Kroger, 2000). If meanings were formed in a discursive activity between people, this included not only social groups but also researchers and participants. In this sense, discourse analysis emphasized "the active and subjective involvement of researchers in hearing, interpreting and representing . . . voices" (Alldred & Burman, 2005, p. 175). Discourse analysis relies on social construction, or the centrality of spoken or written language as a mediator of social activity and social meanings (De Rivera & Sarbin, 2000).

While many narrative researchers embrace the notion that the individual must be viewed within a social context, the idea that all social "reality" (and therefore the interview itself) can be understood through the effects of language is more alarming. Discourse analysis, with its emphasis on how language shapes us as social beings, moves away from the traditional Cartesian conceptualization of the individual as a fully autonomous agent. Some narrative researchers guard against the loss of that agency, which, after all, allows us to comment reflectively and authoritatively on "experience" in an interview. Diane Hogan (2005) comments,

> Recent movements, such as social constructionism, the social scientific wing of postmodernism, have played their part in undermining any claim that we can or should place experience at the centre of our interest. Where there is an attack on the notion of the unitary self, an attack on the notion of individual experience cannot be far behind. If there is no self, who is the experiencer? (p. 2)

Hogan is right; the questions posed by post-modernism threaten the very premises of narrative psychology as it is now conceived, and this includes, centrally, the idea of self.

Over the past several decades, psychologists have invoked distinctive and incompatible ideas about the self as narrator. Some researchers take a phenomenological approach, regarding narratives of life stories as expressions of lived experience. This approach assumes a unitary, rational narrator, a coherence of identity, and a transparency of meanings between interviewer and interviewee. Within this framework, it makes sense to ask questions about facts, events, and personal meanings without challenging the participant's point of view.

Researchers working from a social constructivist stance reject any "natural" account of the self but retain the idea of self as a social creation. This viewpoint assumes a self capable of generating meanings, but these meanings are necessarily conveyed through structures (logical, syntactical) that are social in nature. In brief, the narrator (and the narrative) cannot be separated from the social context. This stance blurs the traditional disciplinary boundaries among psychologists, anthropologists, and sociologists. These researchers view the narrator as self-reflective within a social context. In an interview analysis, then, it is possible to interpret relations between external (social) contingencies and internal (individual and self-reflective) experience. Often this includes an examination not only of the participant's social experience but also of multiple truths and shifting identity positions.

The linguistic turn in the social sciences, in particular post-structuralism (which theorizes how language works as a structure or system of signs and is sometimes subsumed under post-modernism), changes our narrator yet again. Whereas the socially constructed narrator has identities that shift with differing social contexts, the post-structuralist narrator *has been created* in and through social discourses. There is no fixed category (or categories) of identity. There is also no truth or identity behind discourse. Rather, the post-structuralist subject speaks a multiplicity of possible meanings, not all of them recognized by the speaker. What a researcher pursues in an interview depends on the understanding of that researcher. Here, the theorizing of the researcher gains ascendancy, but the nature of the theory takes into account the inherent ambiguities in language. The implication is that it is impossible to ascertain the meaning(s) of an interview narrative. The researcher is aware of social discourses and power relations but sees discourse itself as the place where power is seized.

Each of these three frames represents a particular understanding of language and of the narrator that in turn leads to a slightly different interviewing practice and interpretation. Because they are incompatible, it is not possible to aggregate them.

Returning to Mishler's (1986) point that different practices will have differing effects on the interviewee, I now introduce an interviewer speaking with a child. The interviewer is an adult woman, a graduate student at Harvard, who is interviewing for a study of children's relationships and memories.[2] While she was given a set of guiding questions, she was asked to pursue them entirely in her own way and to follow the child's lead. The interviewee is 9-year-old Sam, a Caucasian child in an urban school in Boston. This interview is recorded, and the audio player whirrs lightly in a small, quiet room, in the midst of his school day. Sam has just spoken about the divorce of his parents. The interviewer's voice is denoted in italics, and Sam's response appears underneath hers.

How often do you see your father?
Well, I usually see him around Christmas, and then there's [Vicion], France. Um, we go there every summer.

Your father lives in France?
No, he lives in New York, but he was born there and we have some relatives there.

Do you speak French?
Un peu. A little.

Do you speak French with your father?
Sometimes, now and then.

And what about with your mother?
My mother, not so much. But we still speak French sometimes.

Is your mother American or was she born in France?
Well, actually no, she was born in Hawaii.

Really?

We're from all over the place. Do you know that I'm part Japanese?

You are?

Yeah, just a bit. Very small though, but I am. Shocked me when I learned that.

When did you find that out?

Um, I think it was two years, three years, I'm not sure.

Do you still have relatives in Japan?

No, I don't know how I got it, but, um, I don't think any of us were born there, it's just somehow I, we're part Japanese. I think it's because we lived there for a bit of time. I remember living, I can remember a few things from Japan, from my childhood as well.

When you were little.

Yeah.

It sounds like you remember a lot from a long time ago.

Um, yeah, I remember much things. I even remember my super, soak, ugh, my super-soaker.

What's a super-soaker?

It's a water gun.

Oh. And you had that a long time ago?

Yeah but I lost it somehow when we were living back in Newton. My brother hid it and now I, I've never been able to find it.

So what's it like living in Boston now?

Well, after um about I think it was maybe five years I've . . . no. Ah, four years and a half I've been living here and I'm, I'm getting used to it much more every day.

The interviewer proceeds as though Sam is a transparent reporter of lived experience, and while she is surprised that he says he's partly Japanese, she does not question this assertion. From the point of view of phenomenology, a researcher may craft a story about Sam's experience of his French and Japanese ancestry, his understanding of the divorce, and his feelings about now living with his mother. It is possible then to view him as a boy who remembers his early life vividly and is still adjusting to the divorce and shifting family arrangements. Constructing stories and interpretations in this way from excerpts of an interview implies that the speaker in the interview is capable of conveying his experience as an individual and that his meanings are transparent enough to offer particular interpretations.

Shift the frame to a focus on the social construction of the interview, and everything changes. Now the interpreter sees that Sam changes his mind in this interview excerpt about what he can remember: "But, um, I don't think any of us were born there [in Japan], it's just somehow I, we're part Japanese. I think it's because we lived there for a bit of time." Sam then tries to assert that he is Japanese more strongly, but he doesn't know how that happened and guesses that it had to do with living there. He continues, as if this logic makes sense, "I remember living, I can remember a few things from Japan, from my childhood as well." "When you were little?" the interviewer asks, not pushing his logic at all. Sam goes along, "Yeah." The interviewer confirms his perspective then: "It sounds like you remember a lot from a long time ago." Sam responds awkwardly and changes the topic: "Um, yeah, I remember much things. I even remember my super, soak, ugh, my super-soaker." The interviewer focuses on the toy rather than questioning Sam's memory or account: "What's a super-soaker?" And Sam tells her, "It's a water gun."

Exploring this dialogic exchange, the social constructionist researcher might ask questions about other relationships in his life, which may, in turn, shed light on the stumbling answers in his narrative. Such an approach allows a researcher to examine how various versions of relationships, events, and memories are created and told in different social contexts and in distinctive relationships. Crucially, the researcher does not want to lose sight of either the individual or the social context in which stories are related.

From the third, post-structural and linguistic point of view, it is impossible to interpret a narrative in a singular way, even through an examination of a co-constructed, relational process. Sam's speaking has been created through shifting social discourses, and his voice is necessarily polyphonic, rendering a multiplicity of possible meanings. What becomes crucial now is the perspective of the researcher whose theorizing takes center stage. The danger is that the voice of the interviewee may be entirely subsumed.

To some extent, I have borrowed from each of these three approaches in narrative interviewing and the interpretation of texts (Rogers, 1993, 1998, 2000) and come to an impasse with all of them, though I am closest to the third perspective. In short, I kept hearing something in narratives I could not grasp: the presence of the unsayable *in* words, *in* language, which also fell *between* sentences, *between* words, rendering every elaboration of "meaning" in the interpretation of text inadequate. I'll return to the unsayable and how it changed my listening, provoked a new method of interpretation, and shaped a new way of interviewing. But, first, I must introduce the framework that caused me to question my ideas about the self as the narrator of a life and the nature of narrative interviewing.

Lacanian Psychoanalysis, the Subject, and the Illusion of Self

My listening has changed radically (at the root) since I've begun training in Lacanian psychoanalysis. In this section, I'll begin with some of Lacan's ideas about the subject and go on to discuss their implications for how we consider language, memory, and the narrator of an interview. It's impossible to introduce Lacan adequately or speak about his significance for psychoanalysis in this chapter. What I will do is provide a brief sketch of Lacan as a figure in psychoanalysis and then hone in on several ideas concerning language and the subject, ideas that are crucial to my argument.

Jacques Lacan (1901–1984) was a brilliant psychoanalyst, but relatively few people in America, including psychoanalysts, understand his work. He is far better known in Europe, Canada, and South America. This is due, in part, to the fact that he draws from French philosophical and cultural traditions, surrealist art, and post-structural linguistics, and he refers to all these ideas as though the reader is also familiar with them. Second, Lacan makes a return to Freud in his work, and most psychoanalysts, trained in ego psychology, object relations, or relational psychoanalysis, find this peculiar and antiquated. Finally, Lacan's seminars (drawn from oral presentations) play with language; include multiple references, puns, and word resonances; and are best appreciated in French. Until relatively recently, translations were few and acquired surreptitiously, only adding to the difficulty of accessing Lacan's thinking.

While I refer to Lacan's words directly (from official translations) in this chapter, I also rely on secondary sources to explain his ideas more clearly, particularly the commentary of Derek Sayer (2004) in his article "Incognito Ergo Sum: Language, Memory, and the Subject."

The most crucial Lacanian concept is not technical at all. It is simply that we are born into language (1977a). In fact, we're marked by language even before our birth because we arrive into a line of names, and then we are saturated in language before we begin to speak. We also create an illusion about a unified self before we begin to speak. These three things are part of the emergence of the subject, the one who will speak. What's more crucial is the point that as speaking subjects, we cannot know *anything* directly and wholly, least of all ourselves.

Lacan (1977a) challenges the Cartesian concept of "self" as a coherent, rational, self-reflective being and grounds his thinking in the post-modern idea of the subject. The difference between self and subject depends on this question: Is language a means used to describe and express the self, or does the self exist only by taking its particular form within and from language? Sayer (2004), discussing Lacan, asserts: "To say, then, that the subject is constituted in language is first of all to reject any notion of an essential human subject that exists prior to or outside of language, a subject for whom language serves merely as a vehicle of expression" (p. 67).

The implications are revolutionary. Outside of language there is no way to describe or refer to the self. Sayer (2004) quotes Lacan: "I identify myself in language, but only by losing myself in it like an object." He goes on to explain this enigmatic statement, "The subject is only created in this act of objectification—of 'losing oneself' in language. It is found(ed), we might say, in this original loss" (p. 68).

Intriguing as this is, Sayer assumes his readers understand what he means by language and loss, the self and the subject. The following schema of language helps to explain the difference between the Cartesian self and the post-modern subject:

$$\frac{\text{Signified: idea, concept}}{\text{Signifier: sound, image}}$$

Think of the word *dog*, a signifier for the signified concept of a quadruped, barking, furry animal. But the word for this quadruped, barking, furry animal in French is *chien*. Sausseur (1915/1977) asserted that signifiers and signifieds are linked arbitrarily in any language. What is this arbitrary link that joins the signifier and the signified? For Sausseur, it is the structure of their relation to one another through the sign, which we understand once we know a language. Furthermore, we understand the precise meaning of signs (signifier-signified pairs) though grammar, a system for generating and reading signs. So far, this does not disturb the Cartesian self as a unified, self-conscious entity for whom language functions as a toolbox of signs ordered by a society into various compartments via grammar. This self is still the master of language.

Lacan (1977a), following Freud's articulation of the unconscious, made a new relation between the signifier and the signified:

$$\frac{\text{Signifier}}{\text{Signified}}$$

Lacan (1977a) made the signifier, and not the signified, primary for human beings. Furthermore, we use acoustic images to say things that are barred, or separated, from what they signify. While the line between signifier and signified joins these two components for Sausseur, Lacan (1977a) makes a radical separation between them. Let's go back to our quadruped, barking, furry animal. *Dog* may actually refer to a poodle, a German shepherd, or a mutt—and we don't know which one. Let's say it's a poodle. Now we are on safe and steady ground. The woman who says "poodle" owns a particular dog she calls Claire. When she says "poodle," it's in a story about her boss who is "always pooh-poohing my ideas." His name is Mr. Adair, and she refers to him simply as "Adair." Now *poodle* resonates with the sound of dismissal (pooh-poohing), and also, the sound of the surname (Adair) works with the sound of the poodle's name, and none of this appears to be conscious. When the narrator gets angry, we see that she tends to say, "Shit," followed by "Whoops, I'm sorry; I didn't mean to say that." We can hear "shit" and its association though "whoops" with the sound of *poodle* (the *poo* as a sound byte in this word). We can notice the repetition of a dismissal too; "shit" is followed by another dismissal, a self-disavowal, "I didn't mean to say that." And this is just the beginning. Lacan (1977b) says, "A signifier is that which represents a subject for another signifier" (p. 207). Signifiers slide into one another, pointing beyond themselves in an endlessly moving chain, which Lacan denotes S, S, S . . . −1. I'll say more about −1 later, but this refers to what cannot be said. In other words, there is a place in the understanding of signifiers (words) for what cannot be represented.

From this discussion about language, there are two critical points. A signifier, as a word in language used to express a concept, "exceeds" the signified. Each word holds so many meanings that we can never say something and express only what we intend to say. We say more than we want to say and do not hear it in our own speech.

How does this understanding of language affect the subject? Sayer (2004) sums up Lacan's understanding eloquently:

> The materials in and out of which the subject is fashioned are labile, fluid, slippery and treacherous—shifting markers that are always deferring beyond the self, always pointing somewhere else, toward some otherness that perpetually threatens to undo who we (think we) are. (p. 69)

If this is true, if every word leads to a chain of meanings that goes beyond what was intended by the speaker, what does this mean for the idea of self?

For Lacan (1977a), the self is a misconception, a place of illusion. To explain this, I'll return to the point where Lacan wrote about the emergence of the self in relation to the subject. In 1936, Lacan developed his theory of the "mirror stage" and published a number of articles about its importance in the development of the subject. The mirror stage concerns the ability of an infant (6–18 months of age) to recognize her own image in a mirror before she is able to speak or have control over her motor skills. The infant must see the image as hers and, later, as a reflected image at the same time. To become a social being, the infant mistakenly locates herself first in the mirror and then re-creates herself as an imago, an imagined whole person, living in a cohesive body. This process marks the child's entry into language and the formation of ego, for both boys and girls. The emergence of the "I" is based on a decentering of the self from the body, a process that is denied, covered by the illusion of perfect wholeness. Although we construct the self, the "I," from this illusion, the subject, who we are, escapes us. This is the loss entailed in entering language.

From 1953 to 1963, Lacan concentrated on the role of the symbolic, which altered his ideas about language. He acknowledged that Freud understood human psychology as linguistically based but would have needed Saussure's theory and a structuralist concept of language as a system of differences to articulate this psychology. In *The Psychoses: Seminar III*, Lacan (1993) claimed that the unconscious is "structured like a language" and governed by the order of the signifier. He went on to argue that the symbolic order, the order of signification, is the place where the individual is formed as a subject.

In his essay "The Function and Field of Speech in Psychoanalysis" in *Ecrits*, Lacan (1977a) concentrates on the idea that although the subject is symbolically constituted, this is not the entirety of the subject. The *symbolic* order, one of three orders that constitute the subject in Lacanian psychoanalysis, is made up of the moral, cultural, and historical demands of a social being. The other two orders are the *imaginary* and the *real*. The imaginary is the register most connected to what we experience as subjectivity in relation to the visible world and is reminiscent of the mirror stage. In short, the imaginary is the place of necessary illusion in which we believe that we are whole and in control of our actions and speaking. At the level of the imaginary, the split of the human being into an unconscious subject is not acknowledged. The register of the real can be understood as that which is always "in its place," because only what is absent from its place can be symbolized. The symbolic is the substitute for what is missing from its place; language cannot be in the same place as its referent. The real is also what is transitory, fleeting, and impossible to represent. Furthermore, there is a defect in signification; something that resists representation remains, even in the symbolic.

Signifiers are formed out of all three registers. Recall that a signifier does not stand for a thing; it points to another signifier. The subject is created between these signifiers or resides in the signifying chain that goes on and on in an attempt to say what, in the end, can't be represented—the real. In other words, we use language to say what we mean, and language carries both more and less than we intended to say. Here is the takeaway message: The concept of the subject born within language means that the known and prized self (the Cartesian self at the center of much of narrative psychology) is a shade of a lost subject that is rarely acknowledged as lost.

An Interpretive Poetics: Listening to the Unconscious

In the course of learning about Lacanian psychoanalysis, my listening has changed over the past several years, especially with regard to interviewees as "subjects" in the post-modern sense of that term. As a researcher, I listen to interview participants outside the framework of psychoanalysis, of course. I want to clarify this point because psychoanalysis works as a constraint that produces particular effects in the unconscious. Yet the unconscious is at work everywhere in each of us as speaking subjects.

I've created a textual method called *interpretive poetics* (Rogers et al., 1999), a method that has changed over time (Rogers, 2004), to guide my listening and my responses in an interview situation.[3]

The interpretive poetics is composed of five interpretive readings or layers, each designed to investigate what is at play in the unconscious in a distinctive way: story threads, the divided "I," the address, languages of the unsayable, and signifiers of the unconscious. While the method was created as an analytic tool for reading texts, it informs how I interview. I form my questions in relation to how I read the subject addressing me, listening for *the limits of what can be said consciously* and responding to both *conscious and unconscious aspects of language*. The way this works in actual practice is that an interview analysis of the kind I present here (which can take weeks or even months) deeply affects how I listen to the *next* person I interview. In an actual interview, I do not know, and cannot pretend to know, the unconscious of the person I am sitting with. I am curious about markers of unconscious experiencing, and they direct my attention, but many decisions in the interview are unconscious on my part and are seen clearly only in retrospect.

Below I will introduce myself with an interviewee, explicating how each layer of the interpretive poetics method illuminates the experience of the unconscious. My writing this, and your reading it, will only show its effects if you find yourself listening differently as a result. If not, then this presentation was merely an intellectual exercise and, at least in my view, of little use to the field, since it had no effect.

Story Threads

Let me begin with the most basic aspect of my listening. We use language to communicate, but the price of each attempt to communicate is that it involves a repression—a repression that is necessary in order to be heard. This repression, inherent in the shaping of our speech (to be received by another), is an unconscious censorship. The stories people tell in an interview are marked unwittingly with this censorship. Listening for story threads is a little like listening for the melody of a song, rather than following the story's content and becoming attached to it as a narrative. A story thread might run through an entire interview, disappearing, reemerging, and leaving a trace in subtle ways. Furthermore, different story threads play against one another, creating particular effects through their associative positioning. Listening in this way, one begins to discern contradictions and specific ways of shaping a narrative though unconscious censorship.

The following passage is taken from the text of an interview with a 24-year-old woman, "Emily." I spoke with her several years ago about her experiences growing up—first in France and then in America.[4]

> I'd always been led to believe that my mother had a brain tumor and had just probably died, because in my family you don't talk about mental illness, um. Since then I've understood that schizophrenia is certainly not the diagnosis . . . I have her paintings and I have pictures and I have her letters . . . at the time it was just a label, a way of saying, "she's crazy," so they could commit her, lock her away from the world and from me. I was about 9 months old, but I only heard this explanation when I was 14.

Emily begins speaking by telling me about the deceit she became aware of when she was 14 years old—that her mother was not dead after all but was institutionalized because she was "crazy"—and schizophrenia was just a label the family used to lock her mother away. As Emily goes on, it becomes clear that there are things she knows and things she doesn't know about her own history: "I know, because I've been told, that I moved from Paris and to be with my grandmother in a teeny village in France until I was 4." Then she, her older brother, and her father came to New York, to live in America.

> I dream in a language I don't know, I dream in French a lot. I don't know how to speak it in my waking, so. So I know there's definitely something I'm not remembering. I've always known that I have very vivid memories of early childhood, but then up until 6 years ago, no memories . . . a gigantic gap, from about 4 years old to 14.

Dreaming in French becomes a clue to Emily that "there's definitely something I'm not remembering." This is a subtle level of construction: Not knowing is evidence of knowing something else—that she has virtually no memories of a large portion of her childhood. However, 6 years ago, Emily was 18, not 14. Furthermore, as we go on, I realize she does have memories of the time between 4 and 14. I ask about this, and she tells me her memories include horrific scenes of being abused by her older brother when she was 11. But Emily does not want to talk about these painful experiences (understandably). Instead, she wants to tell me about remembering her mother:

> When I started to write, I started to remember all sorts of things, like my mother holding my feet, it's a very important memory for me. You know, I have this rabbit that I sleep with, and I call her Lou, and I always hold her feet when I'm carrying her around . . . and I remembered through my writing, that's um, what my mother did. And then I have a photograph that I enlarged. A teeny little weenie photograph that when it was enlarged it was so grainy. But you could see her holding me up and holding my feet . . . and then I started to remember all sorts of things, not just these horrible images that were violating in themselves to remember in isolation, but you know, things that could help me to build a life.

Here, the memory of her mother holding her feet in a picture from her infancy (under 9 months) contrasts with other "horrible images that were violating in themselves," which Emily does not specify in this passage. The development of the brain makes it impossible for us to remember our lives much before we are 2 years old because the mylenization of the neurons is incomplete. This makes me wonder about Emily's memory. What she says she can remember is theoretically impossible, and what she can't remember (in the years from 4 to 14) she knows has happened but doesn't want to speak about it. Through her narrative, Emily creates an experience of memory. Whether or not it's factual doesn't interest me; how she creates it does.

I can now identify two major story threads in Emily's narrative. The first refers to knowing, saying, and writing, and the second moves in and out of the first and refers to not knowing, not saying, and denial or erasure. The conflict inherent between these two threads is not always unconscious. For example, asked directly about being torn between speaking and not speaking, Emily can elaborate. But the contradictions about what she can and can't remember remain unexplained and seem to be largely unconscious.

Lacan (1977b) reminds us, "Remembering always involves a limit" (p. 40); the story threads analysis is meant to show the limits of consciously told memories.

The Divided "I"

The second layer of the interpretive poetics analysis is also fundamental to my listening. The divided "I" acknowledges that the subject's discourse necessarily engages more than one voice, even when using the same pronoun construction. When the subject speaks, she must become divided in order to represent herself. She will try to romanticize herself and her life through stories in which she tries to re-create the whole and perfect imago of the mirror. But this evocation of an ideal self, this imaginary "I," is interrupted by involuntary faltering, slips of the tongue, and unconscious signifiers that imply unknown truths. In this way, the imaginary "I," who upholds the ideal self, is undermined by the voice of a faltering "i" linked to the real and characterized by momentary incoherence in the subject's narrative. These opposing voices define the divided "I."

Returning to Emily's interview transcript, I find the place where she tells a story about a therapist who was harmful to her (later, as if in counterpoint, she will also tell a story of a good therapist). At the start of each of these two powerful stories, Emily talks about her writing. She has just quit a graduate program in sociology to become a full-time fiction writer. She begins the story of her first therapist by referring to her writing:

> I quit [the graduate program] because it was ruining my writing. My writing, it has a sound to it, I can recognize it, that's where the real remembering comes, like the life, the me in there. That's something I could never have done with Dr. Stevens [the therapist], never.

"Why couldn't you experience that kind of writing with her?" I ask. Emily falters: "Because I, I mean she, she abused language, really, she abused power and she abused language [8-second pause] and I know that's a strong thing to say."

Here, Emily shifts from a story that justifies her choice to leave her graduate program and choose a life of writing, connecting writing with remembering and with "the life in me." This is the voice of the imaginary "I," who guides her conscious narrative. Suddenly, she is reminded of abuse. She wants to say that her therapist abused language, but she makes a slip of the tongue, saying, "I, I mean she." Who is this "I" who (also) abused language? I can't answer that question, but the faltering voice of "i" falls into the place between two lines of thought here: a story about writing a life that is, in Emily's terms, about "the life in me" and a story in which Emily experienced something terrible with her therapist.

The Address

The divided "I" is closely related to the concept of the address. This aspect of the method explores the other to whom the subject speaks in the narrative. It may seem obvious that Emily speaks to me, her interviewer, and this is certainly the case when she addresses me as someone she can read and understand, as a "you" in an imaginary "you-me relationship." But when her unconscious comes into play, when her voice falters in the narrative, she is no longer speaking to the constructed "other" of a "you-me" relationship but to what Lacan calls the "Other" of the unconscious. This symbolic Other refers to someone unrecognized in the discourse. I quote the dialogue with Emily as she continues to speak, to give a clear sense of how the address changes in the next part of the interview:

Emily: Dr. Stevens abused her power by not embodying it . . . she doesn't speak English, she doesn't, I guess that's kind of a mean thing to say . . .

Annie: What do you mean by not-embodying?

Emily: Do you know about how Cixous talks about writing from the body?

Annie: Uh, huh.

Emily: Dr. Stevens doesn't talk from a body, well a lot of people don't, but to sit in a room with me and talk about intensely bodily experiences, profoundly violent bodily experiences, and not to speak with words that come from a body? It's unthinkable. How do you do that?

Annie: I don't really know, but how could you tell that her words were not from within her body?

Emily: She never loved me. That's the truth. [8-second pause] I can't believe we've been sitting here for four years and you can't, you don't know me, you don't love me, you play peek-a-boo in my life, in my memory, but you don't know me, the person.

I quote this passage at length and my side of the conversation because toward its end, Emily shifts from speaking about her former therapist to speaking in the first person and addressing her therapist in the present tense. This is conscious, to some extent, and it vivifies her anger and sense of betrayal with Dr. Stevens. But Emily's choice of the phrase "peek-a-boo" resonates with an earlier time in her life, and "four years" also reminds us that Emily left her grandmother at this age to come to America. Curiously, although she remembers her grandmother, Emily does not mention her again in the entire interview. The address to the Other contains some-thing unspoken. She may also be speaking to me unconsciously as an Other, the Other of her own unconscious knowing.

Languages of the Unsayable

This brings me to the fourth layer of interpretive poetics, which attempts to foreground the unsayable in an interview. It is crucial to note that the unsayable is *in* speaking, though its references lie beyond speaking. Languages of the unsayable can be detected in negations, revisions, smokescreens (diverting attention to a safer place), and silences. Lacan (1977a) captures the essence of the unsayable in the following passage:

An enunciation that denounces itself, a statement that renounces itself, an ignorance that sweeps itself away, an opportunity that self-destructs—what remains here if not the trace of what really must be in order to fall away from being? (p. 288)

Verbal negations invoke their opposites, revisions show a subject at odds with her own thinking, smokescreens direct the listener away from something that leaves a trace, and silences evoke the real, the impossible to represent, in the stream of speaking.

Returning to Emily now, I wondered how she remembered her mother as she started to write with her new therapist. "Is there a difference in what you can remember, what you can write, now, with your current therapist?" I asked her.

In response, Emily begins a narrative about her new therapist, a person she's seen for just a few months: "Oh yes, with my current therapist, with, ah, what will I call her? I'll call her Bea, like be, 'to be or not to be,' but with an 'a.' With Bea it's completely different." Emily gives me a flavor of how different in the following story: "We sat together side-by-side on a Saturday afternoon, a double–session, putting together the fragments that have fallen away from my old photographs." Emily reads to me what she wrote to Bea:

> You searched for me in those photographs, and let out a little cry when you found me. We sat next to each other, side-by-side on the floor. Today you thought I might be overwhelmed by it, but I feel you touching me, holding me.

Emily then describes to me how her memories and writing have come to life in this relationship and how "in contrast to Dr. Stevens, Bea locates herself, again and again." I ask her to say what this means, how Bea does this, and Emily tells me,

> You know, she feels very bad about giving me the bill, and she says, she's always awkward [Emily laughs], "I can't do this, I don't want to talk about this, I just can't do this," and it's not that she's not going to bill me, it's that she brings it into the room, says she doesn't want to talk about it, that makes it allowable to actually talk about it, this as a professional relationship, me paying her. And, one time, she was going away on vacation, and I said, "You know, could you maybe, tell me where you'll be, but I won't have to, to know, but just in case." And she said, "Sweetheart, in this room with us, your knowing can be known. You will always know where I am in this, in this world." "Um," she said, "I could not have committed to work with you and put up that kind of restriction. You've never known where your mother is. How could I deprive you of knowing where I am?" I mean, she tells me that she loves me, she says it, she calls me sweetheart, she just takes enormous risks.

These are very moving passages, even as I revisit them now. But what is striking to me is the way they are built on negations. Emily quotes Bea as saying "I can't do this" and "I don't want to talk about this" (in relation to the bill for therapy), which Emily interprets as making room to talk: "[It] makes it allowable to actually talk about it, this as a professional relationship, me paying her." Emily does not wonder how she creates something "allowable" to speak out of a statement that her therapist makes about *not* wanting to speak about the bill. Emily also speaks about her response to Bea as her therapist heads off for a vacation: "You know, could you maybe, tell me where you'll be, but I won't have to, to know." And Bea responds, "Sweetheart, in this room with us, your knowing can be known. You will always know where I am in this, in this world." "'Um,' she said, 'I could not have committed to work with you and put up that kind of restriction. You've never known where your mother is. How could I deprive you of knowing where I am?'" Emily does not question the impossibility of "always" knowing where her therapist is, nor does she wonder about the role Bea is accepting and offering as she makes this promise.

What begins to emerge is a picture of Emily's imaginary (recall that the imaginary mistakes a construction for reality itself)—a world of maternal women who appear as idealized or destructive figures. In the next level of analysis, I return to these figures to search for signifiers—in order to find what is at stake in the unconscious, to discover something that *contradicts* what is consciously narrated.

Signifiers of the Unconscious

The final layer of interpretation explores the unconscious as it appears in discourse through signifiers. Signifiers of the unconscious repeat in discourse in ways the subject herself cannot hear. Listening to Emily's life narrative, I trace recurring words, sounds, and phrases to find meanings that she did not intend to create. Lacan argues that signifiers provide a direct path to the unconscious. Through their chaining, that is, their organization and interplay, it is possible to hear what is unconscious.

I return now to Emily's story about her former therapist. Here, Emily speaks about writing along the margins of one of her therapist's articles on trauma, in an attempt to "overwrite" her expertise. This time, I flag (in italics) repeating phrases, sounds, and words that begin in this story and repeat later in the interview:

> I wrote in magic marker all my complaints . . . big gigantic letters and I read it to her, I mean I wanted her to see that I hated it so much, that I overwrote her . . . and basically, please get this woman out of patients' lives, because it's like that Auden poem, you ask not to *be dropped* one more time, I mean, you get thrown into this room with this woman and you will *be dropped*, and if you're *dropped* enough, you shatter. . . . And she just said she was very *committed* to my recovery, and I said, "I don't need your *commitment* to an illness, my recovery from what you see as pathology, you're not hearing me. *Be committed* to my life, *be committed* to my memory, my writing, my voice, but not my fucking recovery." It was very frustrating.

I read this passage with admiration for this young woman's resistance to what felt to her like an authority imposed on her by her therapist, an acknowledged expert[5] on trauma. As I mark repeating words and phrases, I'm also listening to

Emily in a way that goes beyond my admiration, beyond what she consciously intends to say. "Be" repeats, not only in this passage but also in Emily's choice of a fictive name for her current therapist, Bea, and crucially in the story Emily tells about Bea leaving for her vacation.

Emily quotes her therapist, saying, "You know, could you maybe, tell me where you'll *be*, but I won't have to, to know." And *Bea* said, "Sweetheart, in this room with us, your knowing can be known. You will always know where I am in this, in this world." "'Um,' she said, 'I could not have *committed* to work with you and put up that kind of restriction. You've never known where your mother is. How could I deprive you of knowing where I am?'"

The word *committed* refers me back to the beginning of the interview, when Emily first spoke about her mother:

> I'd always been led to believe that my mother has a brain tumor and had just probably died. . . . Since then I've understood that schizophrenia is certainly not the diagnosis . . . at the time it was just a label, a way of saying, "she's crazy," so they could *commit* her, lock her away from the world and from me.

When I find repeating words or phrases that have shifting meanings, I consider these as potential signifiers. In the preceding passages, the words *be, commit*, and *dropped* all serve this function in Emily's discourse. To understand what is at play in the unconscious, I listen to these words as they cross several stories—with doubled, condensed, or substituted meanings that seem to lie beyond Emily's conscious hearing.

I begin with the signifier *commit* and its variant, *be committed*. This phrase works through condensed meanings; one meaning echoes with another when it is heard in a new context. *Committed* means being locked away; *be committed* means Dr. Stevens's dedication to the wrong thing (recovery from pathology), and *be committed* also means Bea's dedication to the right thing (Emily's knowing where she is). As I read this phrase across stories, however, as a signifier that can have several meanings *at once*, all these meanings carry from one story to another. Thus, I hear Emily hearing in Bea's voice, "I could not have committed," not only as meaning "I could not have committed" to working with you without your knowing where I am but also as meaning "I could not have committed [your mother]."

Bea's name (a name Emily chooses to disguise her therapist) also functions as a signifier. Bea resounds with be, as in "to be or not to be," to live or to die. These linkages may sound preposterous at first glance, but listen again. The very first time Emily says *to be*, it is near the start of the interview, when she says, "I moved from Paris and *to be* with my grandmother." Then it becomes *be committed* and *be dropped*, and finally *be* is associated with *Bea*. In other words, *be* builds in the narrative, adding new resonance to older meanings.

Dropped functions as a powerful metaphor that carries a dual meaning of falling and being shattered, and being left. But *dropped* can also be understood in relation to *be*. Emily says, "Please get this woman [Dr. Stevens] out of patients' lives, because it's like that Auden poem, you ask not to *be dropped* one more time, I mean, you get thrown into this room with this woman and you will *be dropped*." To be dropped is to be left and to be shattered, and Emily wants to believe that this can never happen with *Bea*, her new therapist. But from my point of view, the promises Bea makes to Emily about always being available, coupled with Bea's conflict about Emily paying her in a professional relationship, are signs of potential trouble. These statements, if accurate, point toward the possibility that both therapist and patient are caught up in an idealized relationship that cannot be sustained in reality—and Emily may know unconsciously that she may be dropped.

In this interpretation, I am listening for signifiers that modify and extend the plausible unconscious meanings in Emily's discourse, so that it is possible to hear her at the threshold of the unsayable. Emily does not consciously connect her mother in this interview with her two therapists, one so damaging and the other so ideal. But based on this interpretation, one could argue that Emily creates a composite surrogate mother of two, connecting her two therapists through signifiers of being, being dropped, and being committed, in her search for the lost mother of her infancy.

To the extent that her current therapist tries to take the position of Emily's lost mother as an actual surrogate, she prevents Emily from seeing her construction of her as an imago of the imaginary and from learning about her own unconscious at play in her speaking, actions, and fantasies. To me, this robs Emily of full subjectivity, full speech. To the extent that the discipline of narrative psychology makes the self and its imaginary constructions ideal and central, in theory, we make the same mistake of denying speaking subjects their very subjectivity.

But Jane Gallop (1985) argues, "Avoiding delusion altogether is not a possible alternative. There is no direct apprehension of the real, no possible liberation from imagoes, no unmediated reading of a text" (p. 70). My interpretive poetics method is itself flawed in this sense; there is always the danger of overinterpretation or of missing something quite crucial in the signifiers of subjectivity. Then, too, there's the real—something in the experience of sitting with Emily defies language and analysis, a sense of enormous mystery in her, and a respect for her because she cannot and will not be pinned down in my interpretive analysis. I end here because that's the whole point—that the subject is transitory, fleeting, lost already, yet always coming into being.

Consulting Editors: Ruthellen Josselson and Wendy Luttrell

Notes

---

1. Personology was an attempt to understand how particular personality traits were influenced by social values and personal history, using methods designed to explore personal narratives with instruments such as the Thematic Apperception Test.

2. This study, Telling All One's Heart, involved interviewing ordinary school children several times each year over 3 years. It was supported by grants from the Milton Fund at the Harvard Medical School, Spencer Foundation Research Apprenticeship Grants, and a series of faculty grants from the Harvard Graduate School of Education. The interview with Sam that follows is reprinted with permission of Annie Rogers.

3. The *interpretive poetics* was initially constructed around the analysis of languages of the unsayable, the presence of negativity and silence in all speech, in collaboration with a group of my graduate students at Harvard. Since its inception in 1999, the method has evolved and become a method of exploring the unconscious through the terms of Lacan's theory and my exploration in clinical work, as well as research.

4. Emily was originally part of my study of women remembering childhood sexual abuse, and the interview is published as "Exiled stories and cultural denial" by Rogers, A., in *Irish Journal of Women's Studies, IV*(1), 31–55, copyright © 2000. Reprinted with permission of Cork University Press.

5. Dr. Stevens is a pseudonym, as is Emily.

References

Alldred, P., & Burman, E. (2005). Analyzing children's accounts using discourse analysis. In S. Greene & D. Hogan (Eds.), *Researching children's experience: Approaches and methods* (pp. 175–198). London: Sage.

Allport, G. (1937). *Personality: A psychological interpretation.* New York: Holt.

Bakhtin, M. (1986). *Speech genres and other late essays.* Austin: University of Texas Press.

Block, J. (1971). *Lives through time.* Berkeley, CA: Bancroft Books.

Borland, K. (1991). "That's not what I said": Interpretive conflict in oral narrative research. In S. Gluck & D. Patai (Eds.), *Women's words: The feminist practice of oral history* (pp. 63–75). New York: Routledge.

Breuer, J., & Freud, S. (1955). *Studies on hysteria.* In J. Strachey (Ed. & Trans.), *Standard edition* (Vol. 2, pp. 19–305). London: Hogarth Press. (Original work published 1885)

Bruner, J. (1986). *Actual minds, possible worlds.* Cambridge, MA: Harvard University Press.

De Rivera, J., & Sarbin, T. (Eds.). (2000). *Believed-in imaginings: The narrative construction of reality.* Washington, DC: American Psychological Association.

Dollard, J. (1937). *Caste and class in a southern town.* Garden City, NY: Doubleday.

Elder, G. (1974). *Children of the Great Depression.* Chicago: University of Chicago Press.

Erikson, E. (1958). *Young man Luther.* New York: W. W. Norton.

Erikson, E. (1963). *Childhood and society* (2nd ed.). New York: W. W. Norton.

Ezzy, D. (1998). Theorizing narrative identity: Symbolic interactionism and hermeneutics. *Sociological Quarterly, 39,* 239–252.

Fine, M. (1983). Coping with rape: Critical perspectives on consciousness. *Imagination, Cognition and Personality: A Scientific Study of Consciousness, 3,* 249–264.

Gallop, J. (1985). *Reading Lacan.* Ithaca, NY: Cornell University Press.

Gergen, K. (1993). *The saturated self.* New York: Basic Books.

Gilligan, C. (1993). *In a different voice.* Cambridge, MA: Harvard University Press. (Original work published 1982)

Harre, R., & Streams, P. (Eds.). (1995). *Discursive psychology in practice.* London: Sage.

Hogan, D. (2005). Researching "the child" in developmental psychology. In S. Greene & D. Hogan (Eds.), *Researching children's experience: Approaches and methods* (pp. 22–41). London: Sage.

James, W. (1994). The varieties of religious experience: A study in human nature. New York: Modern Library. (Original work published 1901)

Josselson, R. (1973). Psychodynamic aspects of identity development in college women. *Journal of Youth and Adolescence, 2,* 3–52.

Josselson, R. (1978). *Finding herself: Pathways to identity development in women.* San Francisco: Jossey-Bass.

Kidder, L., & Fine, M. (1997). Qualitative inquiry in psychology: A radical tradition. In D. Fox & I. Prilleltensky (Eds.), *Critical psychology: An introduction* (pp. 34–50). Thousand Oaks, CA: Sage.

Lacan, J. (1977a). *Écrits: A selection* (A. Sheridan, Trans.). London: Tavistock.

Lacan, J. (1977b). *The four fundamental concepts of psychoanalysis* (A. Sheridan, Trans.; J.-A. Miller, Ed.). London: Hogarth Press.

Lacan, J. (1993). *The seminar of Jacques Lacan: Book III. The psychoses* (R. Grigg, Trans.; J.-A. Miller, Ed.). New York: W. W. Norton.

Lewin, K. (1948). *Resolving social conflicts: Selected papers on group dynamics.* New York: Harper & Row.

Luttrell, W. (2003). *Pregnant bodies, fertile minds: Gender, race, and the schooling of pregnant teens.* New York: Routledge.

McAdams, D. (1988). *Power, intimacy and the life story.* New York: Guilford.

Mishler, E. (1986). *Research interviewing: Context and narrative.* Cambridge, MA: Harvard University Press.

Murray, H. (1938). *Explorations in personality.* New York: Oxford University Press.

Piaget, J. (1948). *The moral judgment of the child* (M. Gabain, Trans.). Glencoe, IL: Free Press.

Rogers, A. (1993). Voice, play and a practice of ordinary courage in girls' and women's lives. *Harvard Educational Review, 63*(3), 265–295.

Rogers, A. (1998). In the "I" of madness: Shifting subjectivities in *The Yellow Wallpaper.* In J. Fisher & E. Silber (Eds.), *Analyzing the different voice: Feminist psychological theory and literary texts* (pp. 45–66). New York: Rowman & Littlefield.

Rogers, A. (2000). Exiled stories and cultural denial. *Irish Journal of Women's Studies, 4*(1), 31–55.

Rogers, A. (2004). *Reading the unsayable: An interpretive poetics.* Unpublished manuscript.

Rogers, A., Casey, M., Holland, J., Ekert, J., Nakkula, V., & Sheinberg, N. (1999). An interpretive poetics: Languages of the unsayable. In R. Josselson & A. Lieblich (Eds.), *The narrative study of lives* (pp. 77–106). Thousand Oaks, CA: Sage.

Runyan, M. (1982). In defense of the case study method. *American Journal of Orthopsychiatry, 52*, 440–446.

Sausseur, F. (1977). *Course in general linguistics.* (C. Balley & A. Sechehaye, Eds.). London: Fontana/Collins. (Original work published 1915)

Sayer, D. (2004). Incognito ergo sum: Language, memory, and the subject. *Theory, Culture & Society, 21*(6), 67–89.

Searle, J. (1969). *Speech acts.* Cambridge, MA: Cambridge University Press.

Sherif, M., Harvey, O., White, B., Hood, W., & Sherif, C. (1961). *Intergroup conflict and co-operation: The robbers' cave experiment.* Norman, OK: University Book Exchange.

Wertsch, J. (1991). *Voices of the mind: A sociocultural approach to mediated action.* Cambridge, MA: Harvard University Press.

Wetherell, M., & Potter, J. (1992). *Mapping the language of racism.* Hemel Hempstead, UK: Harvester Wheatsheaf.

White, R. (1952). *Lives in progress.* New York: Holt, Rinehart & Winston.

Wittgenstein, L. (1963). *Philosophical investigations.* New York: Macmillan.

Wood, L., & Kroger, R. (2000). *Doing discourse analysis: Methods for studying action in talk and text.* Thousand Oaks, CA: Sage.

CHAPTER 5

Autobiographical Understanding and Narrative Inquiry

Mark Freeman

Autobiography is the inroad par excellence into exploring the dynamic features—as well as the profound challenges—of narrative inquiry, or at least that portion of it that looks to the comprehensive study of lives as an important vehicle for understanding the human condition. This is so for one quite obvious reason: Autobiography is itself a fundamental form of narrative inquiry, and by examining what Georges Gusdorf has referred to as the "conditions and limits of autobiography" (1956/1980), there exists a valuable opportunity for examining the conditions and limits of narrative inquiry more generally. But there is another, perhaps less obvious, reason for seizing on autobiography and memoir as an inroad into exploring the dynamic features of narrative inquiry as applied to the study of lives. And that is that it can help show how and why narrative inquiry might lessen the distance between *science* and *art* and thereby open the way toward a more integrated, adequate, and humane vision for studying the human realm.

Before developing this line of argumentation, it will be necessary to consider the birth of autobiographical understanding and to chart the contours of its transformation in history. In doing so, I shall draw significantly on the seminal essay by Gusdorf (1956/1980)[1] referring exclusively to this essay in all references to Gusdorf in the pages to follow. It should be emphasized that there are numerous additional works on autobiography that might be drawn on in this context.[2] It should also be emphasized that Gusdorf's essay is but one account—indeed one kind of account, classically modernist in orientation, focused mainly on the West—of the emergence of autobiographical understanding and has been the subject of significant critique, especially by those who wish to tell a rather less individualistic, and perhaps less male-oriented, story (Benstock, 1988; Brodski & Schenck, 1988; Smith & Watson, 1992, 1998, 2001). This essay, however, provides a particularly informative, as well as provocative, treatment of the birth of autobiographical understanding as well as that of the elusive being we have come to call the *self*. For all its limits, therefore— some of which will be explored in what follows—it remains a useful takeoff point for exploring the matters at hand.

After considering the birth and development of autobiographical understanding, I will move on to consider in greater detail both the modern and "postmodern" self, focusing especially on the interrelationship of memory and autobiographical narrative. Finally, I will try to articulate some of the challenges attendant on exploring the role of autobiographical understanding in narrative inquiry. Of particular significance in this context is the challenge posed by what I have come to refer to as the *poetic* dimension of autobiographical understanding and writing and the associated question of whether autobiographical narratives may be deemed sufficiently *truthful* to earn a place in the pantheon of (valid, legitimate, important) scientific knowledge (Freeman, 2002a, 2002b, 2003a, 2004). According to some, this poetic dimension, insofar as it entails the artfulness generally ascribed to imaginative literature, cannot help but render suspect the value of autobiographical data for narrative inquiry, particularly if it aspires toward achieving some measure of scientificity. As shall be argued herein, however, it is this very dimension that can open the way toward a fuller conception of narrative inquiry and its promise in understanding the human condition as well as a more capacious, and indeed adequate, conception of science itself.

From Mythical to Historical Consciousness

Even though it is surely possible to speak (cautiously) of *the* human condition across time and place and even though this condition is, arguably, intimately tied to narrative, there is no question but that the specific form the human condition assumes—and, in turn, the specific form narrative assumes—varies widely (Freeman, 1998; Geertz, 1983; Shweder & Bourne, 1984; Taylor, 1989). There are, for instance, cultures where human personhood is framed less in terms of an individual identity, with its unique and unrepeatable story of coming-to-be, than in terms of its social place, its role in a cultural pattern that may be deemed timeless. Narrative remains a relevant category in such cultures but may be considered more a matter of public, rather than private, property. *Uniqueness* and *unrepeatability* may be alien terms of the human condition; sameness and repetition, the placement of lives within an eternal cosmic template, may instead be the order of the day. What's more, *living*, insofar as it entails a *living out* of a mythical story that transcends the boundaries of "my life," may be virtually inseparable from telling. As for autobiographical understanding—at least insofar as it involves the evaluative looking back over the terrain of the personal past from the vantage point of the present—it may be virtually nonexistent.

A qualification is in order in this context. The mode of autobiographical understanding just described is itself but one mode, and those (such as Gusdorf) who locate autobiographical understanding mainly in the West and mainly in the "looking-back-over-the-personal-past" form have sometimes been criticized for an overly restrictive, even imperialistic, view. This criticism is a valid one; surely, there are other modes of autobiographical understanding—and of autobiography itself—entirely. For present purposes, however, I will be concentrating my attention on the one at hand, partly for the sake of delimiting the scope of my inquiry and thereby interrogating this mode in greater depth and partly because this mode remains dominant in that sector of narrative inquiry that is oriented toward gathering life histories through interviews and other such "big story" methodological venues (Freeman, 2006). This qualification notwithstanding, what I wish to underscore here is the idea that, over the course of Western history, "my life" gradually becomes a more focal concern for many and marks a significant break with prevailing traditions of understanding. Gusdorf thus emphasizes that

> the man who takes delight in thus drawing his own image believes himself worthy of a special interest. . . . I count, my existence is significant to the world, and my death will leave the world incomplete. In narrating my life, I give witness of myself even from beyond my death and so can preserve this precious capital that ought not disappear. (p. 29)

The result is "my story," worthy in its own right—particularly for those more privileged, generally male, selves whose lives were seen to matter most (Conway, 1998; Heilbrun, 1988)—and in some instances worthy enough for others to learn about as well. In this story, there will be painful moments of decision but also twists and turns, accidents and unanticipated consequences, and, not least, considerations of the difference between life as it had been lived, in all its uncertainty and unknowingness, and life as it appears now, through the eyes of the present. In a distinct sense, the phenomenon of autobiographical understanding, as it is being explored herein, presupposes this very difference. It also presupposes the existence of historical consciousness, which may be understood as that specific form of narrative consciousness that entails an interpretive engagement with the ostensibly unrepeatable past. We want to know not how things *happen*—how they always occur, given the eternal order of things—but how they *happened*, the operative presumption being that we can tell a cogent, believable, perhaps even *true* story of how the present came to be by looking backward and situating the movement of events within a more or less coherent narrative form. Let us explore in greater detail how this quite distinctive view of personal understanding came to be, focusing especially on the transition from mythical to historical consciousness.

In *The Myth of the Eternal Return*, Mircea Eliade (1954) calls attention to "archaic" people's "revolt against concrete, historical time" (p. ix). In terms of conscious behavior, Eliade writes,

The "primitive," the archaic man, acknowledges no act which has not previously been posited and lived by someone else, some other being who was not a man. What he does has been done before. His life is the ceaseless repetition of gestures initiated by others. (p. 5)

Archaic man—and woman—thus existed in the order of what Eliade calls "mythical time," a time "when the foundation of the world occurred" (p. 20), and it was through myth that this world could be made present ever again. The aim of myth, therefore, Kearney (2002) explains, "was not so much to invent something that never happened"—which we have come to associate with the idea of fiction, "or to record something that did happen"—which we have come to associate with the idea of history

but to retell a story that had been told many times before. Primordial narratives were thus essentially recreative. And myth, the most common form of early narrative, was a traditional plot or storyline which could be transmitted from one generation to the next [and] generally had a sacred ritual function, being recited for a community in order to recall their holy origins and ancestors (p. 8).

Gusdorf does well to describe the view of personhood that is generally associated with the mythical worldview:

Throughout most of human history, the individual does not oppose himself to all others; he does not feel himself to exist outside of others, and still less against others, but very much *with* others in an interdependent existence that asserts its rhythms everywhere in the community. No one is rightful possessor of his life or his death; lives are so thoroughly entangled that each of them has its center everywhere and its circumference nowhere. The important unit is thus never the isolated being—or, rather, isolation is impossible in such a scheme of total cohesiveness as this. Community life unfolds like a great drama, with its climactic moments originally fixed by the gods being repeated from age to age. Each man thus appears as the possessor of a role, already performed by the ancestors and to be performed again by descendants. The number of roles is limited, and this is expressed by a limited number of names. Newborn children receive the names of the deceased whose roles, in a sense, they perform again, and so the community maintains a continuous self-identity in spite of the constant renewal of individuals who constitute it. (pp. 29–30)

The world to which Eliade, Kearney, and Gusdorf are referring is thus distinctly *pre*-autobiographical. The reason is straightforward enough, according to Gusdorf: "Autobiography is not possible in a cultural landscape where consciousness of self does not, properly speaking, exist" (p. 30). This "unconsciousness of personality," as he puts it, is characteristic not only of those "primitive" or "archaic" societies that Eliade and others have described but also in those more "advanced" societies that continue to adhere to an essentially mythical worldview governed by the principle of repetition, eternal recurrence.

Gusdorf opens himself up to a number of possible criticisms in this context. It can be argued, for instance, that the "isolated being" that emerges out of the socially cohesive, interdependent web of human relations itself bespeaks a mode of existence problematically disconnected from others. It can be argued further that his conception of self "properly speaking" is a parochial one. At the same time, the broad picture he wishes to paint is not without foundation. Consider in this context the situation of ancient Greece. Despite often being considered the wellspring of Western culture, the notion of the individual, and individuated, person was not to be found in Greek antiquity. Nor was the genre of autobiography. Rather than fashioning narratives that were personal and private, the primary concern of the person was to become integrated into the community; thinking about one's existence, therefore, was inseparable from thinking about the communal world (Freeman & Brockmeier, 2001; Vernant, 1995). The Greek sense of self was thus deeply embedded in a cultural whole; only later would there exist the possibility of this self "standing out" from its broader social context of being. And only later would it become appropriate for a person to seize on his or her personal memories, or "life stories," and communicate them to others.

In Gusdorf's account, autobiographical understanding, as well as autobiography itself, could only emerge when humanity had moved from the mythical domain, with its fundamentally "sociocentric" conception of personhood (Shweder & Bourne, 1984), into what he refers to as "the perilous domain of history":

> The man who takes the trouble to tell of himself knows that the present differs from the past and that it will not be repeated in the future; he has become more aware of differences than of similarities; given the constant change, given the uncertainty of events and of men, he believes it a useful and valuable thing to fix his own image so that he can be certain it will not disappear like all things in this world. History would then be the memory of a humanity heading toward unforeseeable goals, struggling against the breakdown of forms and beings. Each man matters to the world, each life and each death; the witnessing of each about himself enriches the common cultural heritage. (pp. 30–31)

By all indications, therefore, there emerges a complete revolution in both self-understanding and self-representation:

> At the moment it enters history, humanity . . . finds itself engaged in an autonomous adventure" and "man knows himself as a responsible agent. . . . The historic personage now appears, and biography, taking its place alongside monuments, inscriptions, statues, is one manifestation of his desire to endure in man's memory. (p. 31)

It is difficult to know how far to take this account. In the opening pages of *The Republic* (Plato, 2003), for instance, there is an exchange between Cephalus and Socrates in which there is talk of anxieties in the face of death, the process "reckoning up" the personal past, and, by virtue of what the process brings, "terror" and "foreboding" or "cheerfulness" and "hope." On some level, therefore, it would seem that autobiographical understanding was already on the scene in Plato's time—if not well before. We can also presume, however, that it was constituted in a manner entirely different from the kind of understanding we have come to know in modern times, being intimately tied to those mythical "stories about another world" through which personal existence was defined. The good life, one might say, was not yet *my* life per se; and self-reckoning had less to do with the vicissitudes of internally generated conscience than it did with transcendent images of virtue. Taylor's (1989) comments are useful in this context: For Plato, he notes,

> the moral sources we accede to by reason are not within us. They can be seen as outside us, in the Good; or perhaps our acceding to a higher condition ought to be seen as something which takes place in the 'space' between us and this order of the good. (p. 123)

The form of autobiographical understanding we find in the exchange between Cephalus and Socrates is therefore not to be mistaken for the form we find today for the "inner" and "outer" have yet to be split apart in the modern style.

Along with the transition from the mythical domain into the domain of history, there is the emergence of autobiographical understanding "proper"—or, more subtly put, that particular mode of autobiographical understanding that came to involve a process of looking back over the terrain of the personal past and discerning new meanings, ones that were unavailable in the flux of the immediate. Meaning thus becomes "unhinged," as it were, mobile, as much a function of "now" as "then." There has emerged a dimension of difference, of *deferral*, such that henceforth, the project of *knowing*, particularly *self*-knowing, becomes inextricably bound to historical understanding. It also becomes bound to the idea of *accountability* (Freeman & Brockmeier, 2001). It might be noted in this context that accounting for one's actions in court was one of the few occasions in Greek culture in which an individual might have told a first-person narrative (Most, 1989). This should serve to remind us that such accounts were in fact possible far earlier than is often assumed. By all indications, however, it is not until the time of St. Augustine's *Confessions* (397/1980) that we find accountability assuming the form of autobiographical reflection. Indeed, it is this great work that is generally taken to represent the inauguration of that sort of looking-back process that may be linked to the reflective work of autobiographical understanding (Freeman, 1993). On one level, the Augustinian position is quite continuous with the Platonic one. But there are two significant differences that ought to be recognized. The first is that, for Augustine, Plato's "Good" is essentially replaced by God. The second difference, more important for present purposes, is that Augustine's vision, though driven by God, has become more thoroughly internalized. As Taylor (1989) puts the matter,

> God is not just what we long to see, but what powers the eye which sees. So the light of God is not just "out there," illuminating the order of being, as it is for Plato; it is also an "inner" light. (p. 129)

Augustine, therefore,

> shifts the focus from the field of objects known to the activity itself of knowing. . . . [I]n contrast to the domain of objects, which is public and common, the activity of knowing is particularized. . . . To look towards this activity is to look to the self, to take up a reflexive stance. (p. 130)

Pursuing this idea still further, Taylor writes of the "radical reflexivity" that bursts on the scene with *Confessions* and "brings to the fore a kind of presence to oneself which is inseparable from one's being the agent of experience," that is, "creatures with a first-person standpoint" (p. 131). This first-person standpoint is constituted in and through autobiographical reflection, issuing in what is, arguably, the first instance of autobiographical narrative.

A qualification is in order here as well. Although I have just used the term "autobiographical reflection" to refer to Augustine's endeavor in *Confessions*, the form it assumes remains a far cry from the forms we find as we move closer to modernity. This is because the process of self-examination and self-reckoning in which he engages is addressed to God, the presumption being that whatever has transpired in this difficult life has, finally, been under God's ever-vigilant direction. Indeed, "it is in this paradigmatically first-person activity, where I strive to make myself more present to myself, . . . that I come most tellingly and convincingly to the awareness that God stands above me" (Taylor, 1989, p. 135). As pivotal as *Confessions* was in the emergence of autobiographical understanding as well as the autobiographic genre itself, the Augustinian project of self-reflection has therefore been seen by some as a "premature" form of the process. Weintraub (1978), for instance, insists that while the Augustinian project unquestionably represents "a historicizing of human realities which the classical mentality . . . could not have achieved, it is still only a step toward that historicist view of the self-concept on which the notion of individuality depends" (p. 47). "Only a step"—Augustine's mode of self-understanding, operating via a newfound and indeed revolutionary reliance on memory, is, according to Weintraub, not yet "there." It remains pre-historicist, pre-individual, pre-*us*. The transition from mythical to historical consciousness thus remains incomplete.

Autobiographical Understanding and the Modern Self

Putting aside for the moment the teleologically driven, progressivist thrust of Weintraub's emancipatory story—the story of Western Man extricating himself, finally, from the primitive morass of his pre-individual days—there is another significant transition being documented.

"In a medieval cosmic play," Dupré (1993) has noted, "the human person clearly had the lead, but an all-knowing, unchanging God directed the play. The outcome remained predictable and hardly varied from one period to another" (p. 145). Herein lies what is, arguably, the most central mark of distinction between autobiographical understanding in the Augustinian era on up through the Middle Ages and that which emerges in the modern era: The story being told, inward though its gaze may be, remains the story not of the *self* but the *soul*; it is bound up with the idea of the *transcendent*, the idea that the movement of a life is inseparable from God's watchful gaze and takes place against the backdrop of eternal realities. By all indications, this was so of men's and women's autobiographies alike. As Conway (1998) has pointed out, the tradition of Western European women's autobiography emerged in the context of religious life, in narratives about one's relationship to God. Indeed, women's stories of their mystical experiences "set the pattern for describing a woman's life in a way that shaped women's subsequent narratives as definitively as the odyssey gave the underlying form to male autobiography" (p. 13). It might also be noted that the idea of *sin* loomed large in many of these accounts as well, the supposition that the process of self-examination was inseparable from the process of reckoning with one's inevitable moral depravity. Whether one's attention was directed toward the spirit or the flesh, autobiographical understanding had thus remained inextricably bound to the divine order, the designs of the personal past being more God's than one's own.

All this was to change with the modern age, for "Once the temporal actor with limited foresight became director, . . . the outcome ceased to be certain and the passage of time took on a far more dramatic character," essentially tragic, "insofar as humans must shape their own future, however inadequately equipped and poorly enlightened they may be" (Dupré, 1993, p. 145). The space within which autobiographical understanding might operate thus widens. Enlightenment no longer bears the mark of God's guarantee; one must look more thoroughly within—or, more specifically, *backward*—to achieve whatever modicum of enlightenment there may be. "Paradoxically," therefore, "the modern orientation toward the future"—toward the new rather than the old, innovation rather than tradition, difference rather than sameness—"created a more acute awareness of the past" (p. 146). As Dupré is quick to remind us, systematic reflection on the past began well before the advent of the modern age; one only needs to consider the work of Thucydides and Herodotus. Nor, again, did the cyclical view of time prevent Greek and Roman historians from addressing the unique significance of certain events. Only in modernity, however, was the accent laid on the *modo*—the "now" of life—such that "the modern future appeared as the endlessly postponed terminus of a continuing history" (p. 156). And, this "one-directional move toward the future required a constant reinterpretation of the past" (p. 157). Dupré goes on to speak in this context of the loss of necessity, the loss of the operative presumption that there is, in history, an immanent logic and order. The loss of necessity is tantamount to the birth of contingency. And it is exactly this situation of contingency that calls for the retrospective gaze of autobiographical understanding.

There are many significant players in this story, particularly Montaigne, Rousseau, and Goethe, each of whom inaugurates new, and still more internalized, dimensions of autobiographical understanding. "Montaigne," especially, Gusdorf offers, "discovers in himself a new world, a man of nature, naked and artless, whose confessions he gives us in his *Essays*, but without penitence." The *Essays* would become "one of the gospels of modern spirituality. Freed of all doctrinal allegiance, in a world well on its way to becoming secularized, the autobiographer assumes the task of bringing out the most hidden aspects of his individual being." Greater value is placed on personal freedom, individuality, and sincerity, "the heroism of understanding and telling all. . . . Complexities, contradictions, and aberrations do not cause hesitation or repugnance but a kind of wonderment" (p. 34). In the case of Rousseau, there is also emphasis on the need for telling the unvarnished *truth* in the face of such complexities, contradictions, and aberrations, the assumption being that it is, in fact, possible to provide a more or less objective account of one's past. There are challenges and difficulties in doing so, to be sure, having to do with the distortions of memory, personal biases, and, not least, the coloring of the past through the eyes of the present. But these are not considered to be insurmountable.

In the case of Goethe's (1994) autobiography, *From My Life: Poetry and Truth*, the situation is somewhat different. There is the recognition that in trying to understand and write about oneself one cannot attain the same degree—or, perhaps more appropriately, the same *kind*—of objectivity as is possible in history or in biography. Precisely because there cannot be a full disentangling of "I" and "me," of subject and object, the resultant story is bound to be permeated by one's own irrevocably personal view. Weintraub's (1975) comments on definitional issues related to autobiography may be useful in this context:

> The essential subject matter of all autobiographic writing is concretely *experienced* reality and not the realm of brute external fact. External reality is embedded in experience, but it is viewed from within the modification of inward life forming our experience; external fact attains a degree of symptomatic value derived from inward absorption and reflection. . . . Autobiography [therefore] presupposes a writer intent upon reflection on this inward realm of experience, someone for whom this inner world of experience is important. (pp. 822–823)

From this perspective, we can perhaps understand more clearly Goethe's insistence on linking up "truth" and "poetry": The inner world is a world like no other, and coming to terms with it, through autobiographical reflection and writing, cannot be the sort of more dispassionate process one sometimes has recourse to in encountering the external world.

As an important aside, it should be emphasized that this issue presents quite remarkable challenges for narrative inquiry. What the narrative researcher often deals with, in essence, are *auto*biographical (i.e., first-person) data that he or she must render in *bio*graphical (i.e., third-person) terms. Even if he or she aspires toward achieving some measure of objectivity vis-à-vis these data, there nevertheless remains the stubborn fact that these same data will be shot through with subjectivity, interpretation, and imagination. Put in the simplest of terms, in auto-biographical understanding there is no object, no "text," outside the self; even though the autobiographer may draw on certain personal documents and the like during the course of fashioning his or her story, the phenomenon that is ultimately of concern—namely one's personal past—must itself be fashioned through *poiesis*, that is, through the interpretive and imaginative labor of meaning making (Freeman, 1999a, 1999b). The autobiographer thus interprets what he or she has already constructed through imagination, after which time the narrative researcher must try somehow to turn these rather unwieldy data into the kind of account that others might read and, perhaps, learn from. Subsequently, he or she will engage in another series of poetic processes during the course of interpreting these unwieldy data and then writing about them in a way that will not only be informative but, ideally (from my perspective), *artful*, such that the persons in question can live on the page. As traditionally conceived, all this is to take place in the name of *science*. How is it possible? We will address this set of issues in greater detail later on. For now, suffice it to say that autobiographical understanding, as it moves into the modern era, becomes not only more inward looking but also more epistemologi-cally questionable. Full-blown suspicion will be deferred until (what is sometimes called) the post-modern era, when it becomes less and less clear, to some at any rate, whether in fact there is any sure foundation at all to the entire venture.

Returning to the issue of autobiographical understanding as it relates to the emergence of the modern self, the defining feature involves the fact that, for many, God is no longer seen as the driving force behind the process. In Augustine's case, it may be recalled, God was at the very center of the process: The path inward was the path upward. In modern times, it is often said, the path upward has largely been closed off or considered a dead end. For better or for worse, the story generally con-tinues, we are left with ourselves, our only hope being that the depths we are thought to possess will suffice to bring us some measure of meaning.

The responses to this ostensible state of affairs vary. For Taylor (1989), there is, in part, a sense of loss: The process of interiorization becomes more self-sufficient but also more self-enclosed. With Descartes, for instance, there emerges "an ideal of self-responsibility, with the new definitions of freedom and reason which accom-pany it, and the connected sense of dignity" (p. 177). But with this very ideal, there also emerges a shutting off, or shutting out, of those transcendent sources that had earlier been deemed so central to the movement of self-understanding. Weintraub (1978) tells a quite different story. For him, again, there is a sense in which the Augustinian project of self-reflection is seen as a kind of preliminary stage on the way to the actualization of both autobiographical understanding and the autobio-graphic genre, which "took on its full dimension and richness when Western Man acquired a thoroughly historical understanding of his existence" (p. 821). For Weintraub, therefore, this development, rather than entailing loss, entails signifi-cant gain, the "full dimension and richness" that is made possible by the full his-toricization of human reality. While Taylor's and Weintraub's accounts differ, there is nevertheless agreement that something radical happened sometime following the Augustinian revolution: God, or Good, the supposition of a transcendent order giving form and meaning to personal existence, is seen to have diminished in import, leaving individuals to their own, largely internal, devices. Autobiographical understanding, in turn, becomes a matter of wrestling with one's own inner demons, of discerning how one has fared in relation to one's own personal standards and ideals. Pride, gratitude, and a sense of integrity may emerge when, on looking backward over the landscape of my life, I see what I have done and been, what I have made of my unique attributes. Conversely, there can also be shame, resentment, and despair on viewing my life's wreckage, to think that I have fallen so sorely short of my own potential.

Here, though, we might ask, To what extent have we, modern and post-modern selves, abandoned a reliance on transcendent sources? What does it mean to say that I am "grateful" for my life or that I am "disappointed" in it, that I have realized, or not realized, my own potential? There is unquestionably a reference to an inner landscape. It is also true that, for many, there is no God supporting the process; the ardent atheist can surely wrestle with his or her demons without invoking anything larger than the very self so embroiled. Even in this instance, however, there may remain the felt conviction that there is *some* order, or principle, or value that exists beyond me and that conditions the self-judgments and self-appraisals I make. There is, in any case, no mistaking the marked shift that takes place in the passage to modernity. While many autobiographies are those of public figures and are oriented toward celebrating deeds, "providing a sort of posthumous propaganda for posterity that otherwise is in danger of forgetting them or of failing to esteem them properly" (Gusdorf, 1980, p. 36), there also emerge those autobiographies that look more fully inward, not for the sake of setting the record straight or leaving a tidy, self-aggrandizing myth for posterity but for exploring the inner world. As Gusdorf writes,

> Rousseau, Goethe, Mill are not content to offer the reader a sort of *curriculum vitae* retracing the steps of an official career that, for importance, was hardly more than mediocre. In this case it is a question of another truth. The act of memory is carried out for itself, and recalling of the past satisfies a more or less anguished disquiet of the mind anxious to recover and redeem lost time in fixing it forever.... Furthermore, autobiography properly speaking assumes the task of reconstructing the unity of a life across time. This lived unity of attitude and act is not received from the outside; certainly events influence us; they sometimes determine us, and they always limit us. But the essential themes, the structural designs that impose themselves on the complex material of external facts are the constituent elements of the personality. (p. 37)

We therefore find in this account of the matter the modernist rendition of autobiographical understanding par excellence: In virtue of the "more or less anguished disquiet of the mind, anxious to recover and redeem lost time," there is a search for "unity," the resultant product being an expression of the innermost dimensions of self. The idea and ideal of authenticity loom large, the challenge at hand being nothing less than giving adequate form to the vicissitudes of Being itself. For men, personal agency is emphasized. For women, on the other hand, there emerges a tradition of writing that "conceals agency, concentrating on inner life," but leaving them largely "disembodied" (Conway, 1998, p. 43), owing especially to norms relating to sexual propriety. In both cases, nonetheless, the focus on the interior life remains paramount.

From Modern to Post-Modern

In post-modern conceptions of personhood and autobiographical understanding, all this changes yet again: With the ostensible "death of the author" (Barthes, 1977; Foucault, 1973, 1977), Gusdorf's "constituent elements of the personality" are themselves cast radically into question, particularly if they are imagined to be origins. Indeed, there is a certain sense in which the direction of influence becomes reversed: Autobiography, rather than being seen as an *expression* of the self, is more appropriately seen as its source, such that the self becomes a kind of creative *invention*, the possible unity attained essentially being an artifact of writing (Bruner, 1992). But let us return for a moment to the modernist project of autobiographical understanding; by doing so, perhaps the trajectory at hand will be made clearer. At base, there exists the supposition that the human person, "far from being subject to readymade, completed situations given from the outside and without him, is the essential agent in bringing about the situations in which he finds himself placed" (Gusdorf, 1980, p. 37). There also exists the supposition that this "essential agent" is capable of some measure of self-knowledge and that autobiographical understanding is the privileged route toward attaining it. Gusdorf presents a compelling reason for why this is so:

> An examination of consciousness limited to the present moment will give me only a fragmentary cutting from my personal being. . . . In the immediate moment, the agitation of things ordinarily surrounds me too much for me to be able to see it in its entirety. Memory gives me a certain remove and allows me to take into consideration all the ins and outs of the matter, its context in time and space. As an aerial view sometimes reveals to an archeologist the direction of a road or a fortification or the map of a city invisible to someone on the ground, so the reconstruction in spirit of my destiny bares the major lines that I have failed to notice, the demands of the deepest values I hold that, without my being clearly aware of it, have determined my most decisive choices. (p. 38)

Gusdorf even goes so far as to say that this autobiographical understanding, as a "second reading of experience," is to be considered "truer than the first because it adds to experience itself consciousness of it. . . . The past that is recalled has lost its flesh and bone solidity," it is true, "but it has won a new and more intimate relationship to the individual life that can thus, after being long dispersed and sought again throughout the course of time, be rediscovered and drawn together again beyond time" (pp. 38–39).

This is a daring, and most significant, move on Gusdorf's part. As against those who would deem the "aerial view" of memory little more than a vehicle for distorting the past "as it was," Gusdorf opens up a positive possibility: It may very well be, he essentially suggests, that the truest rendition of experience comes not from the immediate reality of the moment, flesh-and-bone solid though it may be, but from reflection, memory, *narrative* (Freeman, 2002a, 2003a). As I have suggested in some recent work, human existence may be characterized as involving a delay, or "postponement," of insight into its affairs (Freeman, 2003b). Realizations, narrative connections, are made after the fact, when the dust has settled. The result is that we are frequently *late* in our own understanding of things. This is particularly so in the moral domain, where there is a tendency to act first and think later. Autobiographical understanding can play a vitally important role in tending to this state of affairs by serving a kind of "rescue" function: By taking up what couldn't be seen, or known, in the moment, it can rescue us from the "forgetfulness" that so often characterizes the human condition. Autobiographical understanding thus emerges as a fundamental tool for ethical and moral *re-collection*, taken here in the classical sense of gathering together that which would otherwise be irretrievably lost.

Even if God's role in the project of autobiographical understanding is on the wane as we move toward the modern era, there still remains a prominent place for the idea and ideal of truth as well as for ethical, moral, and spiritual purposes. Undoubtedly, there already exists the recognition that the autobiographer is likely engaged in a process of justifying himself or herself somehow and that the resultant portrait is bound to entail a measure of artifice, but this is not necessarily seen as a liability, much less a danger, for the aim of autobiography is not simply to depict the past as it was but precisely to understand it, to make sense of it, to fashion meanings that were not, and could not be, available in the flux of immediate experience. According to Gusdorf, the "deepest intentions" of autobiography "are directed toward a kind of apologetics or theodicy of the individual being" (p. 39). This is particularly so, it would seem, in the modern era. Interestingly enough, however, it is but a short—albeit decisive—step from the modern to the post-modern era of thinking about autobiographical understanding.

Although Gusdorf himself, writing his essay in 1956, cannot possibly speak of this post-modern era (and although, in addition, it is problematic to link the idea of the post-modern to a discrete era), there is a distinct sense in which he could see, even then, the changes to come. Already aware of the "recent revolution in historical methodology," whereby "the idol of an objective and critical history worshipped by the positivists of the nineteenth century has crumbled," the "historian of himself," as Gusdorf puts it, faces much the same situation: The past cannot be resurrected, only told, from the standpoint of the present; and thus, the very positive possibility of autobiographical understanding referred to above paves the way to a rather more suspicious and doubtful rendition of the dynamics of the process at hand.

The narrative is conscious, and since the narrator's consciousness directs the narrative, it seems to him incontestable that it has also directed his life. In other words, the act of reflecting that is essential to conscious awareness is transferred, by a kind of unavoidable optical illusion, back to the stage of the event itself. . . . [A]utobiography is [thus] condemned to substitute endlessly the completely formed for that which is in the process of being formed. (p. 41)

As Gusdorf goes on to suggest—somewhat paradoxically, perhaps, given his earlier comments about the possibility of autobiographical understanding yielding a "truer" reading than immediate experience itself,

the difficulty is insurmountable: no trick of presentation even when assisted by genius can prevent the narrator from always knowing the outcome of the story he tells—he commences, in a manner of speaking, with the problem already solved. Moreover, the illusion begins from the moment that the narrative *confers a meaning* on the event which, when it actually occurred, no doubt had several meanings or perhaps none. This postulating of a meaning dictates the choice of the facts to be retained and of the details to bring out or to dismiss according to the demands of the preconceived intelligibility. It is here that the failures, the gaps, and the deformations of memory find their origin; they are not due to purely physical cause nor to chance, but on the contrary they are the result of an option of the writer who remembers and wants to gain acceptance for this or that revised and corrected version of his past, his private reality. (p. 42)

The account is a strange one: Beginning with the language of truth, Gusdorf has quickly moved to the language of illusion, failures, gaps, and deformations, all of which are tied to exactly that condition of "remove," of temporal distance, that created the possibility of there emerging a deeper truth in the first place. This language, which clearly bears within it a kind of negativity, is surely a function of Gusdorf's own modernist commitments.

Those with post-modernist commitments, on the other hand, are likely to use decidedly more positive, even celebratory, language. To speak of illusion, they might argue, is to rely, whether explicitly or implicitly, on a postulate of truth; and once one does away with this postulate, as many post-modernists are inclined to do, illusion drops out of the picture as well. In the end, it might be said, there are simply different modes of telling about the world, including the world of the person. None, from this perspective, are to be regarded as privileged, as truer, than any other for this would require a foundation that is plainly not to be had. "So," Lauren Slater (2000) says in her "metaphorical memoir" *Lying*,

I suppose you want to know how much is true, how much untrue, and then we can do some sort of statistical analysis and come up with a precise percentage and figure out where the weight is. That, however, would go against my purpose, which is, among a lot of other things, to ponder the blurry line between novels and memoirs. (p. 160)

It is clear enough, Slater goes on to note, that many memoirs make use of fictional elements. It is also clear that many works of fiction make use of autobiographical elements. "So how do we decide what's what, and does it even matter?" (p. 160). Perhaps not. Perhaps the aim of the autobiographer or memoirist is simply to write, as interestingly and as artfully as possible. This would not only spare one the (illusory) burden of somehow discovering and disclosing the (real, authentic) self; it would allow for the possibility of creating, through writing, a new self altogether.

Autobiographical Understanding and the Question of Truth

Liberating though the perspective just considered may seem, at least to those who are largely unconcerned about foundational matters, it can lead to some significant difficulties for those wishing to see in narrative inquiry a legitimate and defensible alternative to more mainstream social scientific approaches. If in fact autobiographical narratives are seen to bear no relationship whatsoever to such cherished notions as "reality" and "truth," how can they possibly be of value to students of the human condition? One might therefore ask at this point, Are there other ways of framing the issues at hand so as to open up a more defensible and constructive space for narrative inquiry?

Here, I want to turn to Gusdorf once more, focusing on another move that, on the face of it, is as paradoxical as the one we last explored but that also opens up just this desired space. In view of the aforementioned revolution in both historical and, by extension, autobiographical understanding, there is the need to "give up the pretence of objectivity, abandoning a sort of false scientific attitude that would judge a work by the precision of its detail." This false scientific attitude, I would suggest, is one that continues to hold sway in much contemporary social scientific methodology—which, in turn, is why narrative inquiry is often deemed to be *un*scientific or, at the least, insufficiently scientific. The argument is simple enough: Insofar as science sees "the real" as that which can be objectified and measured, narratives are bound to seem far removed from the scientific enterprise. And yet, a curious fact remains: Narratives often seem able to give us understandings of people in a way that more "objective" methodologies cannot. This is because they often emerge from a *true*, rather than a false, scientific attitude, one that practices fidelity *not* to that which can be objectified and measured but to the whole person, the whole human life, in all of its ambiguous, messy, beautiful detail (Freeman, 1997, 2005). Narrative inquiry, in its aim of practicing fidelity to the human experience, thus seeks, in a way, to be *more* scientific—more *authentically* scientific—than those more systematic, precise, quantitatively grounded empirical enterprises that have traditionally been enshrined.

The significance of autobiography should therefore be sought beyond truth and falsity, as those are conceived by simple common sense. It is unquestionably a document about a life, and the historian has a perfect right to check out its testimony and verify its accuracy. But it is also a work of art, and the literary devotee, for his part, will be aware of its stylistic harmony and the beauty of its images. (Gusdorf, 1980, p. 43)

So far so good: We need to move beyond truth and falsity, *as they are ordinarily understood*, and we need to recognize and appreciate the aesthetic dimension of autobiography. This basic idea holds, I believe, not only for those autobiographies we may wish to study as narrative researchers, whether they are those of our informants or those we find in bookstores, but for our own representations of them, in the research stories we wish to tell. The truth we seek to tell cannot be equated with fidelity to "the facts" alone; and, insofar as our own aim is truly to be faithful to the living, breathing reality of those we study, it will be imperative to summon all the artfulness we possibly can. But Gusdorf goes even farther than this:

> It is . . . of little consequence that the *Mémoires d'outretombe* should be full of errors, omissions, and lies, and of little consequence also that Chateaubriand made up most of his *Voyage en Amérique*: the recollection of landscapes that he never saw and the description of the traveller's moods nevertheless remain excellent. We may call it fiction or fraud, but its artistic value is real: there is a truth affirmed beyond the fraudulent itinerary and chronology, a truth of the man, images of himself and of the world, reveries of a man of genius, who, for his own enchantment and that of his readers, realizes himself in the unreal. (p. 43)

Bearing this in mind, Gusdorf's conclusion is that "the literary, artistic function is thus of greater importance than the historic and objective function in spite of the claims made by positivist criticism both previously and today" (p. 43).

This sort of "voyage," however, brings us into treacherous waters indeed. If our only evaluative criteria are aesthetic enjoyment or "lifelikeness," then what Gusdorf has to say in this context is hardly objectionable. But in the case of autobiographies, and of narrative data more generally, can it really be of "little consequence" if the texts before us are full of errors, omissions, and lies? And can it really be irrelevant whether the landscapes being depicted were ones for which there was no firsthand encounter at all? Consider the case of Binjamin Wilkomirski's (1996) *Fragments: Memories of a Wartime Childhood*, a "memoir" of concentration camp life that turned out to be patently, if unintentionally, false: Lifelike and artfully rendered though Wilkomirski's account was, the life depicted turned out not to have been his own but rather one that he had fashioned through his imagination. Does this matter? If, again, the only relevant criteria are aesthetic enjoyment or lifelikeness, then no; and, in fact, there were some critics who, on discovering the falsity of Wilkomirski's story, essentially argued that nothing substantial had changed: The book still remained a great, even informative, read. For others, however, the story had been irreparably tarnished—partly because, even if unwittingly, the "autobiographical pact" (Lejeune, 1989) had been broken but also because the very meaning of what had been read had been altered dramatically. Although Wirkomirski's descriptions could still be considered "excellent" (to use Gusdorf's term), they had suddenly lost a significant portion of their evidential, as well as emotional, value. One could sympathize with the dire childhood that had apparently provoked Wilkomirski to represent himself as a survivor, but that sympathy would, of necessity, be of a quite different order from that which we might feel in reading the words of an *actual* survivor. The controversy over James Frey's (2003) *A Million Little Pieces* has brought forth similar issues. There is no doubt that Frey's life had been messy and difficult. But the fact that he had shamelessly embellished his own suffering and had gone so far as to concoct horrific scenarios largely for dramatic effect has left readers with decidedly less sympathy than they might otherwise have had.

None of what is being said here should be taken to imply that the "literary, artistic function" of autobiography, along with our own narrative-based accounts, is unimportant or merely ornamental. On the contrary, just as the autobiographer must employ artistic form in a way that truly serves the content of his or her life, the narrative researcher must do much the same thing. In both cases, the challenge at hand is a *poetic* one, the foremost aim being not to reproduce reality but to actualize and explicate it, to bring meaning into being in such a way that the world is made visible. The difficulties we have been considering notwithstanding, Gusdorf gets this portion of his account quite right: "The truth is not a hidden treasure, already there, that one can bring out by simply reproducing it as it is. Confession of the past realizes itself as a work in the present: it effects a true creation of the self by the self" (p. 44). Neither expression (of a "hidden treasure") nor invention (of a wholly new self), neither strictly "found" nor strictly "made," it is an imaginative articulation "of the self by the self." This in turn "suggests a new and more profound sense of truth as an expression of inmost being, a likeness no longer of things"—of "objects," able neatly to be entrapped and encapsulated—"but of the person. . . . [T]his truth, which is too often neglected, nevertheless constitutes one of the necessary references for understanding the human realm" (p. 44). It is also, I suggest, a key vehicle for moving beyond dualistic thinking.

There is a tendency in narrative inquiry to view the truth about which Gusdorf speaks as a "narrative truth" (Gazzaniga, 1998; Ludwig, 1997; Spence, 1982), of the sort found in works of art rather than works of history or science. But this is problematic in its own right. For what it does, in the end, is split truth in two, one being objective, the other being subjective. "Biography," like history, "is fiction," Gazzaniga (1998) has argued. "Autobiography is hopelessly inventive" (p. 2). In the course of "trying to keep our personal story together," in fact, he continues, "we have to learn to lie to ourselves. . . . We need something that expands the actual facts of our experience into an ongoing narrative, the self-image we have been building in our mind for years" (pp. 26–27). Gazzaniga finds no need for lamentation in this context either: "Sure, life is a fiction, but it's our fiction and it feels good and we are in charge of it" (p. 172). Persons, in turn, are those fictions of order and coherence we are provoked to create in the face of what would otherwise be the mere flux of experiential states.

The perspective offered by Gazzaniga (1998) and others—let us call it the "narrative-as-fictive-imposition" perspective—has its attractions, not the least of which includes this last idea, that "we are in charge" of our own autobiographical fictions, able to shape them as we wish. Indeed, by rewriting the past according to our wishes and designs, we can shore up our ever-sagging selves and thereby bask in the light of our own betterment, illusory though it may be. But, as Gazzaniga himself avows, this perspective sees in the operation of autobiographical understanding little more than *lies*—or, less severely, purely subjective truths—that are likely to fly in the face of the *real* (i.e., objective) truths of our lives. There's "what really happened," in other words, the past "as it was," and then there are the imaginative stories that get told about it, in a way it is hoped that "rings true," that works, aesthetically or pragmatically. And so, the subject-object split returns, with autobiographical understanding its latest victim.

One of the foremost aims of narrative inquiry, I want to argue, is to think beyond this subject-object split and thereby to move in the direction of that "new and more profound sense of truth" toward which Gusdorf had earlier pointed. More specifically, what I want to suggest is that it may be useful to think about this set of issues in a way that is actually *opposite* to the view just considered. It could be that "what really happened" can only be predicated via autobiographical understanding itself. We often *do not know* what is happening when it is happening. Instead, and again, we are often late, sometimes too late, and all that can be done is to tell the story: Appearances aside, *this* is what happened (Freeman, 2003b). I do not wish to be overly objectivistic in framing the issues this way. "What really happened" is often highly contestable and is inevitably a function of the interpretive prejudices one brings to the task of narrating the past. Nor do I wish to suggest that the story is definitively over when someone has told his or her version of what really happened. There is an essential openness to the historical past, and there always exists the possibility that the story of what happened will be rewritten, again and again. Nor, finally, do I wish to suggest that the truth of narrative can be neatly encapsulated in some specific form. It is perhaps preferable in this context to speak of a *region* of truth (Freeman, 2002a) rather than a discretely bounded one. These qualifications notwithstanding, the challenge of telling what really happened remains. This telling, rather than being a reproduction of the past "as it was," is more appropriately understood as a "creative redescription" of the past (Hacking, 1995; Kearney, 2002) and is part and parcel of the narrative dimension that is intrinsic to any and all forms of autobiographical understanding. And it is this narrative dimension that can open the way toward not only a more capacious conceptualization of truth but a more adequate and humane framework for exploring the human realm.

The Narrative Dimension and the Project of Narrative Inquiry

Finally, however, we need to ask, What exactly is this narrative dimension? And how can our consideration of autobiographical understanding inform narrative inquiry? The narrative dimension of autobiographical understanding may be said to entail a quite remarkable series of dialectical relationships. First, as we have already seen, the interpretation and writing of the personal past, far from being a dispassionate process of reproducing what was, is instead a product of the present and the interests, needs, and wishes that attend it. This present, however—along with the self whose present it is—is itself transformed in and through the process at hand. Indeed, in a distinct sense, a new self is fashioned via this very process; dimensions of being are disclosed that literally would not have existed, would not have reached articulated form, had the autobiographical process not taken place (Bruner, 1992; Freeman, 1993). What this suggests is that there exists a dialectical relationship not only between past and present but between past, present, and future: Even in the midst of my present engagement with the past, I am moving into the future, giving form and meaning to the self-to-be.

> Autobiography is therefore never the finished image or the fixing forever of an individual life: the human being is always a making, a doing; memoirs look to an essence beyond existence, and in manifesting it they serve to create it. (Gusdorf, 1980, p. 47)

Or, as Kearney (2002) puts the matter, "the recounted life prises open perspectives inaccessible to ordinary perception," and in so doing, "marks a poetic extrapolation of possible worlds which supplement and refashion our referential relations to the life-world existing prior to the act of recounting" (p. 132).

There is thus a double *poiesis* at work in this process, such that the heterogeneous elements of a life are synthesized, drawn together via the narrative imagination, and the self in turn is reconstructed, *remade*, in its image (Ricoeur, 1991, 1992). The narrative dimension, it should be reiterated, is tied to the moral dimension as well for this process of remaking one's past and in turn one's self inevitably takes place against the backdrop of "strong qualitative distinctions" (Taylor, 1989) regarding how one ought to live. Indeed, if Taylor is right,

> in order to make minimal sense of our lives, in order to have an identity, we need an orientation to the good, . . . and this sense of the good has to be woven into my understanding of my life as an unfolding story. (p. 47; see also Freeman, 2003b, and Lambek, 1996)

Exploring the process of autobiographical understanding serves to underscore the idea that both the personal past and the self whose past it is are indeed constructions, issuing from the narrative imagination. This is emphatically not to say, however, that these constructions are fictions or illusions or lies: The imagined is not to be equated with the wholly imaginary, and *poiesis*, the act of making meaning, is not to be understood as one in which something is made *ex nihilo*, out of nothing. What Octavio Paz (1973) calls "the poetic experience" is rather to be understood as "a revelation of our original condition." This revelation is "always resolved into a creation: the creation of our selves." Along with Gusdorf, Paz insists that this revelation "does not uncover something external, which was there, alien, but rather the act of uncovering involves the creation of that which is going to be uncovered: our own being" (p. 137). We might therefore think of the self as a kind of *work*, an unfinished and unfinishable poetic project issuing from the narrative imagination as it is manifested in the process of autobiographical understanding (Freeman, 2001).

If we are to use the language of poetry in reflecting on the nature of autobiographical understanding, it is imperative that we recognize some of the challenges the poet of the personal past faces in seeking to tell the truth about the world. "It is not only that . . . words distort even as they reveal, that what is lived can never be the same as what is told," Hazel Barnes (1997) has written. "Questions of sincerity, the reliability of memory, and concern for others' feelings turn out to be far more complex than I had imagined." Moreover, Barnes adds, "The problem of selectivity, which in other contexts may be purely literary, becomes more urgent; to single out *these* factors as most important in shaping a self is to mold the self presented." And so, she offers, "The most I can claim, and this I do affirm, is that the fictional character portrayed here"—namely, *herself*—"is, at least in my eyes, a true reflection of what I reflectively see" (p. xix).

There are numerous additional challenges as well. As Brockmeier (1997) has pointed out, the "autobiographical agent" is to be understood as involved in a wide variety of "discursive interactions," his or her story thus being very much a function of the specific *situation*, or situations, in which the story is told. In a related vein, there is also the issue of *to whom* the story is told—whether, for instance, it is the interviewer, or the therapist, the research community, or the broader audience of readers of autobiography. In addition, Bruner (1991) has noted, the self disclosed through autobiography

> seems also to be intersubjective or "distributed" in the same way that one's "knowledge" is distributed beyond one's head to include the friends and colleagues to whom one has access, the notes one has filed, the books one has on one's shelves. (p. 76)

Just as Brockmeier wishes to think beyond the "monological I," Bruner urges us to recognize that it is a mistake to regard the self "as solo, as locked up inside one person's subjectivity, as hermetically sealed off" (p. 76). Moving still further into this territory, I have referred in some recent work to the idea of the "narrative unconscious" (Freeman, 2002b), which refers broadly to those culturally rooted aspects of one's history—particularly those issuing from such "secondhand" sources as books, movies, and other media—that are at once highly influential in shaping the process of autobiographical understanding but of which one may remain largely unaware. From this perspective, I have suggested, autobiography is not simply a matter of representing one's life from birth until death but rather a matter of discerning the multiple sources—firsthand and secondhand, personal and extrapersonal, near and far—that give rise to the self. As Hampl (1999) has stated in this context,

> We embody, if unwittingly and partially, our history, even our prehistory. The past courses through our veins. The self is the instrument which allows us not

only to live this truth but to contemplate it, and thereby to be comforted by meaning—which is simply the awareness of relationship. (p. 97)

In view of this more intersubjective, relational view of autobiographical understanding, the project of narrative inquiry widens considerably.

The act of autobiographical understanding, Hampl (1999) goes on to say, by virtue of it being "the work of the imagination," is more akin to poetry than to fiction. In both the lyric poem and the memoir, or autobiography, "a self speaks, renders the world, or is recast in its image," the "real subject" being

consciousness in the light of history. The ability to transmit the impulses of the age, the immediacy of a human life moving through the changing world, is common to both genres. To be personal and impersonal all at once is the goal of both. (p. 224)

According to Hampl, therefore, the "chaotic lyric impulse," rather than the "smooth drive of plot," is the "engine" of memory, as it functions in autobiographical understanding. "These are the details of memoir," she insists, "details that refuse to stay buried, that demand habitation. Their spark of meaning spreads into a wildfire of narrative," and while they may be "domesticated into a story, . . . the passion that begot them as images belongs to the wild night of poetry" (p. 224).

It is precisely here, in the context of this "wild night," that we come face to face with what may be considered the foremost challenge inherent in the project of autobiographical understanding and, more generally, of narrative inquiry. Ideally, we, narrative researchers, want people to move beyond telling us schematic stories, of the sort we have heard many times before, and instead tell us fresh and vital ones that somehow carry their own individual imprint and reality. But this is no easy task. "If one looks closely at the average adult's memory of the periods of his life after childhood," Schachtel (1959) has written,

Such memory, it is true, usually shows no great temporal gaps. . . . But its formal continuity in time is offset by barrenness in content, by an incapacity to reproduce anything that resembles a really rich, full, rounded, and alive experience. Even the most "exciting" events are remembered as milestones rather than as moments filled with the concrete abundance of life. (p. 287)

As a general rule, therefore, "The processes of memory thus substitute the conventional cliché for the actual experience" (p. 291).

On some level, of course, this "substitution" is inevitable and hardly to be lamented: Autobiographical memory, insofar as it makes use of language, of culturally-available genres of telling, culturally sanctioned plotlines, and so on, is irrevocably bound to convention. What's more, as we have seen repeatedly throughout the present chapter, there is no question but that such memory does not, and cannot, resurrect the "actual experience"—or, as I would prefer to frame it, the "past present" experience. For the most part, that is not the *purpose* of autobiographical memory; the purpose is rather to understand, to make sense of the past in the light of the present. Schachtel is nevertheless on to something important here, and it has to do with the fact that it is perilously easy for autobiographers to fall prey to overly schematized renditions of the past—ones that perhaps reveal more about extant ways of remembering and telling than about the particularities of the life in question. "At every step a word beckons, it seems so convenient, so suitable, one has heard or read it so often in a similar context, it sounds so well, it makes the phrase flow so smoothly." By following this temptation, the writer will perhaps describe something familiar and recognizable to many. In doing so, however, he or she "will have missed the nuance that distinguishes his [or her] experience from others" (p. 259).

The challenge at hand, therefore—and it is one that applies to both the autobiographer or research informant and the narrative researcher himself or herself—is to find a language that moves beyond these highly schematized, conventionalized, even clichéd portraits. The writer thus "has to fight constantly against the easy flow of words that offer themselves." Indeed, "It is this awareness and the struggle and the ability to narrow the gap between experience and words which make the writer and the poet" (p. 296). This awareness and struggle extend to any and all forms of autobiographical understanding as well as any and all attempts, on the part of narrative researchers, to tell others' stories. Whether narrative inquiry looks toward actual autobiographies and memoirs or whether it looks instead toward more standard forms of autobiographical data, as are derived from interviews and the like, it would do well to remain cognizant of this challenge along with the quite extraordinary potential that inheres in it, for what it suggests is that autobiographical understanding is at the very heart of the narrative enterprise, lying at the intersection of art and science, blurring their boundaries through its work.

There are numerous ways in which autobiographies and autobiographical data more generally might be employed in narrative inquiry. Most obviously, they might be employed to generate social scientific theory, for instance about memory or gender or identity. In keeping with the blurring-of-boundaries idea, however, what I want to suggest in closing is that these rich and humanly significant forms of data may also be in the service of a somewhat different aim. Insofar as such data are ultimately about what might be termed the "literature of experience" (Freeman, 2004), it follows that a portion of narrative inquiry might itself be more literary in its approach—which is to say more directed toward the poetically resonant and evocative than is often the case in more standard forms of social scientific inquiry. I offer this not in the name of some sort of antiscientific fervor but in the name of literature itself. The fact is, literature, autobiographical and otherwise, often does extremely well to embody that which we colloquially call *life* in its full measure: By being attentive to the concrete particularities of lives, by seeking ways of allowing these lives to live on the page, works of literature often seem to get nearer to the deep human stuff that many readers look for. This doesn't mean that narrative researchers and scholars ought to be creating works of literature per se; most aren't prepared to do this, and the very idea of narrative *inquiry* entails a conceptual "aboutness," one might say, that points beyond a purely literary approach. It means instead that a portion of narrative inquiry ought to be directed toward writing about human lives in such a way that their own inherent poetry can be made more visible.

I have referred in this context to the idea of "poetic science," a form of critical narrative inquiry that would lie at the intersection of art and science and that would support not only the *epistemological* aim of increasing knowledge and understanding of the human realm but also the *ethical* aim of increasing sympathy and compassion (Freeman, 2005). Perhaps in the name of scientific legitimacy, there remains a tendency in narrative inquiry to minimize the artful dimension and to maximize the dimension of scientificity, thereby leaving the aforementioned "deep human stuff" to poets and philosophers. But the social scientist, broadly conceived and imagined, can and should enter into the endeavor and, when the situation calls for it, do so as imaginatively and artfully as possible through creating work that not only purveys knowledge of this or that area but that uses writing, that uses *form*, in a way that truly serves the content, and the *people*, in question. This is a challenge—a poetic challenge—for autobiography and narrative inquiry alike, and it is well worth pursuing.

Consulting Editors: Jens Brockmeier and Anna Neumann

Notes

1. The Gusdorf quotes that appear in this chapter are taken from Olney, James, *Autobiograpy.* Copyright © 1980 Princeton University Press. Reprinted by permission of Princeton University Press.

2. These include James Olney's edited volume, *Autobiography: Essays Theoretical and Critical* (1980), which includes the Gusdorf essay, as well as his *Metaphors of Self: The Meaning of Autobiography* (1972) and, more recently, *Memory & Narrative: The Weave of Life-Writing* (1998); Weintraub's extended treatment of the emergence of historical consciousness via autobiography in *The Value of the Individual: Self and Circumstance in Autobiography* (1978); and a wide variety of other works, including Brodski and Schenck's (edited) *Life/Lines: Theorizing Women's Autobiography* (1988); Cavarero's *Relating Narratives: Storytelling and Selfhood* (2000); Conway's *When Memory Speaks: Reflections on Autobiography* (1998); Eakin's *Fictions in Autobiography: Studies in the Art of Self-Invention* (1985), his *How Our Lives Become Stories: Making Selves* (1999), and his (edited) *The Ethics of Life Writing* (2004); Folkenflik's (edited) *The Culture of Autobiography: Constructions of Self-Representation* (1992); Gunn's *Autobiography: Toward a Poetics of Experience* (1982); Hampl's *I Could Tell You Stories: Sojourns in the Land of Memory* (1999); Lejeune's *On Autobiography* (1989); Pascal's *Design and Truth in Autobiography* (1960); Spengemann's *The Forms of Autobiography: Episodes in the History of a Literary Genre* (1980); Smith and Watson's (edited) *Women, Autobiography, Theory: A Reader* (1998) and their *Reading Autobiography: A Guide for Interpreting Life Narratives* (2001); Stanton's (edited) *The Female Autograph* (1984); Steedman's *Past Tenses: Essays on Writing, Autobiography and History* (1992); and Zinsser's (edited) *Inventing the Truth: The Art and Craft of Memoir* (1987). Alongside these volumes, readers might also wish to consult Jolly's (edited) *Encyclopedia of Life Writing: Autobiographical and Biographical Forms* (2001) as well as the journals *Auto/Biography* and *Biography*, all of which are valuable venues for exploring autobiography.

References

Augustine, St. (1980). *Confessions.* New York: Penguin. (Original work published 397)

Barnes, H. E. (1997). *The story I tell myself.* Chicago: University of Chicago Press.

Barthes, R. (1977). *Image, music, text.* New York: Hill & Wang.

Benstock, S. (Ed.). (1988). *The private self: Theory and practice of women's autobiographical writings.* London: Routledge.

Brockmeier, J. (1997). Autobiography, narrative, and the Freudian concept of life history. *Philosophy, Psychiatry, & Psychology, 4,* 175–199.

Brodski, B., & Schenck, C. (Eds.). (1988). *Life/lines: Theorizing women's autobiography.* Ithaca, NY: Cornell University Press.

Bruner, J. (1991). Self-making and world-making. *Journal of Aesthetic Education, 25,* 67–78.

Bruner, J. (1992). The autobiographical process. In R. Folkenflik (Ed.), *The culture of autobiography* (pp. 38–56). Stanford, CA: Stanford University Press.

Cavarero, A. (2000). *Relating narratives: Storytelling and selfhood.* London: Routledge.

Conway, J. K. (1998). *When memory speaks: Reflections on autobiography.* New York: Alfred A. Knopf.

Dupré, L. (1993). *Passage to modernity: An essay in the hermeneutics of nature and culture.* New Haven, CT: Yale University Press.

Eakin, P. J. (1985). *Fictions in autobiography: Studies in the art of self-invention.* Princeton, NJ: Princeton University Press.

Eakin, P. J. (1999). *How our lives become stories: Making lives.* Ithaca, NY: Cornell University Press.

Eakin, P. J. (Ed.). (2004). *The ethics of life writing.* Ithaca, NY: Cornell University Press.

Eliade, M. (1954). *The myth of the eternal return: Or, cosmos and history.* Princeton, NJ: Princeton University Press.

Folkenflik, R. (Ed.). (1992). *The culture of autobiography.* Stanford, CA: Stanford University Press.

Foucault, M. (1973). *The order of things: An archeology of the human sciences.* New York: Vintage Books.

Foucault, M. (1977). *Language, counter-memory, practice.* Ithaca, NY: Cornell University Press.

Freeman, M. (1993). *Rewriting the self: History, memory, narrative.* London: Routledge.

Freeman, M. (1997). Why narrative? Hermeneutics, historical understanding, and the significance of stories. *Journal of Narrative and Life History, 7,* 169–176.

Freeman, M. (1998). Mythical time, historical time, and the narrative fabric of the self. *Narrative Inquiry, 8,* 27–50.

Freeman, M. (1999a). Life narratives, the poetics of selfhood, and the redefinition of psychological theory. In W. Maiers, B. Bayer, B. Esgalhado, R. Jorna, & E. Schraube (Eds.), *Challenges to theoretical psychology* (pp. 245–250). North York, Ontario, Canada: Captus.

Freeman, M. (1999b). Culture, narrative, and the poetic construction of selfhood. *Journal of Constructivist Psychology, 12,* 99–116.

Freeman, M. (2001). Worded images, imaged words: Helen Keller and the poetics of self-representation. *Interfaces, 18,* 135–146.

Freeman, M. (2002a). The burden of truth: Psychoanalytic *poiesis* and narrative understanding. In W. Patterson (Ed.), *Strategic narrative: New perspectives on the power of personal and cultural stories* (pp. 9–27). Lanham, MD: Lexington Books.

Freeman, M. (2002b). Charting the narrative unconscious: Cultural memory and the challenge of autobiography. *Narrative Inquiry, 12,* 193–211.

Freeman, M. (2003a). Rethinking the fictive, reclaiming the real: Autobiography, narrative time, and the burden of truth. In G. Fireman, T. McVay, & O. Flanagan (Eds.), *Narrative and consciousness: Literature, psychology, and the brain* (pp. 115–128). Oxford, UK: Oxford University Press.

Freeman, M. (2003b). Too late: The temporality of memory and the challenge of moral life. *Journal fur Psychologie, 11,* 54–74.

Freeman, M. (2004). Data are everywhere: Narrative criticism in the literature of experience. In C. Daiute & C. Lightfoot (Eds.), *Narrative analysis: Studying the development of individuals in society* (pp. 63–81). Thousand Oaks, CA: Sage.

Freeman, M. (2005). *Science and story.* Unpublished manuscript, Methods in Dialogue Conference, Centre for Narrative Research, University of East London.

Freeman, M. (2006). Life "on holiday"? In defense of big stories. *Narrative Inquiry, 16,* 139–146.

Freeman, M., & Brockmeier, J. (2001). Narrative integrity: Narrative, identity, and the reconstruction of the self. In J. Brockmeier & D. Carbaugh (Eds.), *Narrative and identity: Studies in autobiography, self and culture* (pp. 75–99). Amsterdam: John Benjamins.

Frey, J. (2003). *A million little pieces.* New York: Doubleday.

Gazzaniga, M. (1998). *The mind's past.* Berkeley: University of California Press.

Geertz, C. (1983). *Local knowledge: Further essays in interpretive anthropology.* New York: Basic Books.

Goethe, J. W. (1994). *From my life: Poetry and truth* (Parts 1–3). Princeton, NJ: Princeton University Press.

Gunn, J. V. (1982). *Autobiography: Toward a poetics of experience.* Philadelphia: University of Pennsylvania Press.

Gusdorf, G. (1980). Conditions and limits of autobiography. In J. Olney (Ed.), *Autobiography: Essays theoretical and critical* (pp. 28–48). Princeton, NJ: Princeton University Press. (Original work published 1956)

Hacking, I. (1995). Rewriting the soul: Multiple personality and the sciences of memory. Princeton, NJ: Princeton University Press.

Hampl, P. (1999). *I could tell you stories: Sojourns in the land of memory.* New York: W. W. Norton.

Heilbrun, C. G. (1988). *Writing a woman's life.* New York: W. W. Norton.

Jolly, M. (Ed.). (2001). *Encyclopedia of life writing: Autobiographical and biographical forms* (Vols. 1–2). London: Fitzroy Dearborn.

Kearney, R. (2002). *On stories.* London: Routledge.

Lambek, M. (1996). The past imperfect: Remembering as a moral practice. In P. Antze & M. Lambek (Eds.), *Tense past: Cultural essays in trauma and memory* (pp. 235–254). New York: Routledge.

Lejeune, P. (1989). *On autobiography.* Minneapolis: University of Minnesota Press.

Ludwig, A. (1997). *How do we know who we are? A biography of the self.* Oxford, UK: Oxford University Press.

Most, G. W. (1989). The stranger's stratagem: Self-disclosure and self-sufficiency in Greek culture. *Journal of Hellenic Studies, CIX,* 114–133.

Olney, J. (1972). *Metaphors of self: The meaning of autobiography.* Princeton, NJ: Princeton University Press.

Olney, J. (Ed.). (1980). *Autobiography: Essays theoretical and critical.* Princeton, NJ: Princeton University Press.

Olney, J. (1998). *Memory and narrative: The weave of life-writing.* Chicago: University of Chicago Press.

Pascal, R. (1960). *Design and truth in autobiography.* London: Routledge & Kegan Paul.

Paz, O. (1973). *The bow and the lyre.* New York: McGraw-Hill.

Plato. (2003). *The republic.* New York: Penguin.

Ricoeur, P. (1991). Life: A story in search of a narrator. In M. J. Valdés (Ed.), *Reflection and imagination* (pp. 425–437). Toronto, Canada: University of Toronto Press.

Ricoeur, P. (1992). *Oneself as another.* Chicago: University of Chicago Press.

Schachtel, E. (1959). *Metamorphosis.* New York: Basic Books.

Shweder, R., & Bourne, E. (1984). Does the concept of the person vary cross-culturally? In R. Shweder & R. LeVine (Eds.), *Culture theory: Essays on mind, self, and emotion* (pp. 158–199). Cambridge, UK: Cambridge University Press.

Slater, L. (2000). *Lying: A metaphorical memoir.* New York: Penguin Books.

Smith, S., & Watson, J. (Eds.). (1992). *De/colonizing the subject: The politics of gender in women's autobiography.* Minneapolis: University of Minnesota Press.

Smith, S., & Watson, J. (1998). *Women, autobiography, theory: A reader.* Madison: University of Wisconsin Press.

Smith, S., & Watson, J. (Eds.). (2001). *Reading autobiography: A guide for interpreting life narratives.* Minneapolis: University of Minnesota Press.

Spence, D. P. (1982). *Narrative truth and historical truth.* New York: W. W. Norton.

Spengemann, W. (1980). *The forms of autobiography: Episodes in the history of a literary genre.* New Haven, CT: Yale University Press.

Stanton, D. (Ed.). (1984). *The female autograph.* Chicago: University of Chicago Press.

Steedman, C. (1992). *Past tenses: Essays on writing, autobiography and history.* London: Rivers Oram Press.

Taylor, C. (1989). *Sources of the self: The making of modern identity.* Cambridge, MA: Harvard University Press.

Vernant, J.-P. (Ed.). (1995). *The Greeks.* Chicago: University of Chicago Press.

Weintraub, K. (1975). Autobiography and historical consciousness. *Critical Inquiry, 1,* 821–848.

Weintraub, K. (1978). *The value of the individual: Self and circumstance in autobiography.* Chicago: University of Chicago Press.

Wilkomirski, B. (1996). *Fragments: Memories of a wartime childhood.* New York: Schocken.

Zinsser, W. (Ed.). (1987). *Inventing the truth: The art and craft of memoir.* Boston: Houghton Mifflin.

CHAPTER 6

Talking to Learn

The Critical Role of Conversation in Narrative Inquiry

Sandra Hollingsworth and Mary Dybdahl

> [Conversation is] at its best when the participants are not impatient to conclude their business, but wish instead to spend their time together in order to deepen and enrich their understanding of an idea.
>
> —Nash (as cited in Florio-Ruane, 2001, p. 56)

The Beginning: A Contextual Story of Talking to Learn

Approximately once a month, for the past 18 years, Mary and Sandra—or "Sam"—have met in Berkeley, California, with Karen Teel, Anthony Cody, Jennifer Davis Smallwood, and Leslie Minarik (elementary and middle-school teachers and teacher educators) for dinner and conversation about learning to teach. Initially, the Berkeley Group was involved in a larger longitudinal study on learning to teach literacy that began with our preservice teacher education program in graduate school (Hollingsworth, 1989). Frustrated with the prescriptive nature of teaching and learning in our teacher education coursework, the questions unanswered, and the imposed silences, we discovered we could meaningfully learn about teaching through extended conversation with trusted colleagues. As a group, we also decided to investigate our talk in the form of narrative inquiry: both phenomenon (the experience studied) and method (inquiry tools) (Connelly & Clandinin, 1990, p. 2).

At graduation, all these middle-class teachers took jobs in the lower-class environments of urban schools. We moved beyond the *rhetoric of diversity, equity, and excellence* heard in our preservice programs and began to live difficult personal and political stories of trying to make a difference for disenfranchised students. We welcomed the chance to continue our group meetings, exchange ideas, and get feedback on our efforts.

Across the years, our group has struggled with differences in our positions: genders, races, sexualities, theoretical perspectives, the perceived need to publish our narrative inquiries, and the like. In fact, we've argued elsewhere (Hollingsworth, 1989) that such differences, in the context of trusted relationships, actually contribute to our learning. It's difficult to learn in total agreement. Our narratives reveal that we've gone through all the phases of a committed relationship with friends and colleagues. We've loved and respected each other, both deeply and not deeply enough. Our egos and our differently lived experiences outside of the group often got in the way of communication. At some point, all of us have felt silenced. We've struggled with issues of power and voice in reconciling how to describe our narratives. We've been hurt by each other's comments—misunderstood and misquoted. Yet most of the time, we feel that we can present what we've learned from our narrative inquiries so that each of us contributes to the overall story with a particular voice. How? We're committed to the continued inquiry into our stories for both personal and professional learning.

Eighteen years later, we have become administrators, professional developers, grant writers, teacher educators, and authors, as well as veteran classroom teachers in urban schools. Along with the professional stories those experiences bring, we also take stories of ourselves in relationship to the group. We've been wives and husbands, domestic partners, mothers and fathers, and aunts and grandmothers. We still find the braided narratives that unfold from our conversations supporting, challenging, and increasing our understanding of both learning to teach and learning to live.

What we've learned from these conversations has been presented and published in many different venues: in publications (Hollingsworth, 1992; Hollingsworth et al., 1994; Hollingsworth & Dybdahl, 1995; Hollingsworth & Minarik, 1992; Hollingsworth, Teel, & Minarik, 1990), at invited presentations (Hollingsworth & Minarik, 1992), at academic conferences (Hollingsworth, 1990), and at research colloquia (Hollingsworth, Teel, & Minarik, 1992). Initially, we had difficulty getting our narrative inquiries published in traditional U.S. journals. We were better understood in international contexts already involved in narrative inquiry. Here's a story originally published in a Canadian journal, *Curriculum Inquiry* (Hollingsworth, Dybdahl, & Minarik, 1993).[1]

At one of our meetings in the fourth year of our group, Mary narrated a classroom conversation with one of her second-grade students' African American grandmother. As required by her school, Mary had sent home results of standardized tests for parents to sign and return. Instead, this "parent" (the grandmother) came to the classroom with the test showing her granddaughter had failed in her hand. Mary continued to narrate,

[The] grandmother brought the point home to me. She took righteous exception to the "failing marks" I reported for her granddaughter. She said, "What does this say about my child—that she's a moron, she's stupid and slow? Does it say that I read to her every night? Does it say that her mother's in jail and her daddy died just last year? Does it tell you that she's getting her life together, slowly? Does it say that she's learning songs for Sunday school? Does it say she wants to be a doctor? What does this piece of paper say about my baby? I don't want it near her. She needs good things. She's had enough in her life telling her that she's no good. She doesn't need this and I won't have it. I refuse to sign a piece of paper that says my child is no good."

Mary shared her reflections on the grandmother's comments by saying,

"I wanted to give this wonderful loving grandmother a standing ovation. She spoke from her heart and her very sound mind. She expressed for me the misgivings I have about how we support the children in our schools."

The subsequent conversations that Mary's narrative evoked in our group eventually led all of us to understand evaluation of students' learning, "parental involvement," and relationships in schools from a new direction: listening to and valuing parents' alternative standards instead of simply demanding compliance with those of the school. As a result, Mary let go of standard performance and grade expectations and began to develop more personally responsive strategies and measures that helped her understand how better to improve her students' standardized test scores (see Hollingsworth & Dybdahl, 1995, for more on this issue).

In this chapter, we'll explore more narrative inquiries that demonstrate learning from conversation. To do so, we've organized the chapter into three parts. Part 1 addresses various theories and methods of studying conversations that yield narratives, either as data themselves or as descriptions of actions and events to generate stories (Polkinghorne, 1995). Part 2 examines narrative inquiries themselves, organized by recurring methodological themes and issues: (1) clarity of method; (2) issues of relationship, identity, and power; (3) the problem of structure; (4) studying conversational learning; and (5) implications of the narrative inquiries on practice and policy. As Part 2 is written, we'll return to the Berkeley Group for feedback and comment and to provide the coda as Part 3. By the end of this chapter, we will have reviewed examples of and reflections on narrative inquiries that

1. describe how narrative inquiries have been designed and studied across various professional disciplines in international contexts,

2. make explicit the importance of epistemologically and theoretically locating the methodology for purposes of data collection and interpretation, and

3. argue for the critical importance of conversation as a method in narrative inquiry.

Part 1: Theory and Method in the Study of Discourse

The Berkeley Group's studies, like all narrative inquiries, fall into the general paradigm of qualitative research methodology. Within that framework, there are many ontological (different positions on the nature of reality) and epistemological (the relationship between the knower and the known) stances that influence the study design. Most narrative inquiries involve some sort of conversation—from structured interviews to unstructured conversation—and some form of systematic analysis. Unfortunately, too many reports of narrative inquiries fail to make their methodological approaches transparent enough to help their audiences know explicitly how they reached their conclusions. Novice researchers are left without guidance about what to do after the conversations are transcribed (McCormack, 2004; Riessman, 1993). Furthermore, new researchers are often unaware of how their own epistemological stances and their theoretical frameworks inform their methods of study because they lack clear examples in published studies.

We'll begin this part of the chapter with a description of the Berkeley Group's narrative inquiry process, growing out of a bricolage—or interrelated collection—of critical epistemologies and theoretical perspectives. Our conception of narrative was grounded in Vygotsky's (1978) theory of learning, which suggests that personally meaningful knowledge is socially constructed through shared understandings; in Bahktin's (1981) notion of dialogic discourse, in which speakers are always addressing previous and future utterances across time and space; in cultural feminisms that emphasize historical, holistic, and collective orientations to experience (Gilman, 1988); in feminist epistemologies that value considered experience as knowledge (Belenky, Clinchy, Goldberger, & Tarule, 1986); in feminist therapeutic psychologies that embrace emotion as a means of learning about self and relationships (Schaef, 1981); and in the critical and contextually relevant nature of the social use of knowledge (Lorde, 1984; Zeichner & Gore, 1989).

To put the Berkeley Group's learning into the larger methodological traditions of studying discourse (broad, socially constructed systems of language), we'll now briefly review the theoretical groundings and methods that shape narrative inquiries.

There are many kinds of intersecting theories, ways of knowing, and questions that frame the methods narrative researchers use to study talk. (Written narratives as data are not addressed in this chapter, although they are routinely used in narrative inquiry.) To make the explanation more accessible, we'll borrow from Ann Rogan and Dorthea de Kock's (2005) approach of clustering methods into three analytical areas for discussion: the performative cluster, the structural cluster, and the literacy cluster. We combined those three into two categories: (1) performative/generative methods of eliciting conversational narratives and (2) structural/analytical methods of making sense of the transcribed conversations.

Performative/Generative Methods

Performative or generative methods in narrative inquiry, such as dialogues (two voices in turn or one voice in a self-reflective dialogue) or conversations (multiple voices, sometimes overlapping), produce narratives as data (Florio-Ruane, 2001). Depending on the researcher's epistemological stances on the relationship between the narrators and themselves (Lyons, 1990) and the theories used, specific methods will fall into different camps (see Table 6.1). From a post-positivist perspective (we can't really determine what is true in studies of human beings; Phillips & Burbules, 2000), the researcher is objectively separate from the narrators and controls the direction of the narration. She or he will use research designs that support that perspective. Methods include structured interviews and word-level analyses.

Table 6.1   Intersections of Epistemology, Theory, and Methods in Narrative Inquiry

Epistemological Perspective	Theoretical Position on Power, Relationship, and Identity	Methods
I. Post-Positivist: semistable truth in context	1. Researcher directly controls content 2. Identity of researcher is never considered in research design 3. Brief relationships 4. Power remains with researcher	a. Narrators are selected who represent the population b. Structured interviews or solicited narratives c. Structured observations and field notes d. Structured analyses; narrators give no feedback
II. Constructivist: unstable truth in context	1. Co-constructed to maintain intentions of narrators 2. Identity of researcher is considered in research design if warranted 3. Varying relationship time with narrators, depending on design 4. Power is shared between researchers and narrators	a. Narrators are selected who reflect the theoretical frame b. Semistructured interviews and conversations c. Semistructured observations and field notes d. Structured and open-ended analyses; narrators give feedback
III. Critical: no stable truth; temporal understandings situated in history and political relations	1. Direction of narrative shifts between narrators and researchers 2. Identity of researcher is always considered in research design 3. Usually long relationships 4. Power tensions are made explicit	a. Usually, narrators are those who meet and talk for regular life events b. Open-ended conversations c. Open-ended observations and field notes d. Critical whole-text analyses by researchers and narrators; semistructured analyses; narrators always give feedback

From a constructivist perspective (knowledge is co-constructed in specific social interactions: Gadamer, 1996; Vygotsky, 1978), there is much less separation between the researcher and the narrator, as the narratives are socially constructed from semistructured interviews or conversational interactions, reflecting the theory that participants' intentions and interpretations are as important as the researcher's (Connelly & Clandinin, 1990), although the researcher most often has more power in determining the narrative topics.

From a critical perspective (the sociopolitical, historical nature of knowledge production: Foucault, 1980; Smith, 1991), there is no separation between the researcher and the narrator, and the narrative is a temporal coproduct of all the narrators. In other words, the narratives from a critical perspective result from a bricolage of the narrators' self-conceptions in the temporal moment, place, or historical context in which the narrative is told, the depth of relationship between the narrators, and the purpose of their conversation. Again, the methods to support those views would be used for the analyses.

In negotiating conversations, the Berkeley Group now tries to adhere to a critical perspective. It was not, however, always the case. In the beginning of our relationship, Sam played much more of the "researcher" from a constructivist position. Sam proposed a topic (often a reading instruction—because of grant requirements supporting our work), with the intent that our conversation would focus on various aspects of her topic. What actually happened is that the other narrators, as novice teachers, had many other things on their minds such as classroom management, faculty relations, and the hierarchical nature of power and voice in schools. Even though Sam kept trying to bring the conversation back to it, the reading instruction was not actually discussed until the third year, when it became important to everyone. Sam finally realized that our conversational narratives were about where each of us was (experientially, theoretically, reflexively) at the time of the meeting. Our epistemological stances that influenced our narrative rarely fell into the post-positive camp but vacillated from a right-leaning constructivism to a left-leaning critical position, depending on what the "burning topics" were at the moment or what products we needed to produce.

As this chapter was under construction, Sam brought drafts to the group for discussion and feedback. She began with a constructivist question about what the group had learned from our narrative conversations. Sam hoped that there would be some clear reflections on their learning that she could incorporate into this chapter. Here's what happened:

Sam: So what did you learn from our group—from the conversation?

Mary: Pretty much everything!!

Karen: You can put that in the title [of this chapter]!!

Mary: You know what conversation is? . . . A whole hell of a lot of it is listening. Sometimes I hear people say something I don't believe here . . . but I have to trust that it might be of value to me. I need to understand it. . . . I need to keep listening and asking questions until I do.

Here, narrative topic shifted to the nature of the conversation and the importance of listening for others' meanings when they spoke. That prompts Karen to shift the topic to the process of learning from conversation.

Karen: I think that learning from conversation has everything to do with making a connection with somebody else. . . . Professionally, it works with some people and not others. . . . I think you have to believe that there's some value in conversation, that there's something to be learned. I think a lot of teachers don't see it . . . because . . . they haven't gotten anything out of them. . . . You have to be comfortable to learn from conversation. . . . If you feel like somebody thinks you're kind of a fool or that you're "not right" in the way you interpret the world, then the conversation's not going to go anywhere. You also need to know that you have things to learn. Some people think they know it all, that they have all the answers.

Karen's last comment caused Anthony to tell a story about the problem of admitting there is something else to learn.

Anthony: I think it's hard for professionals to acknowledge that they don't know something. If you're admitting out loud that you're struggling with something, you know, you're announcing your vulnerability and we're kind of trained not to do that. If you admitted that in school, someone with power would take advantage of that and tell you what to do.

Mary, responding as a first year principal, continued the story.

Mary: And I'd like to add that, if you are the person who is supposed to be the leader, and you make yourself vulnerable that way, it really makes teachers uncomfortable. It's very rare that I can be that [vulnerable] person, and it's been really hard. I always have to be guarded. I never know what's going to be taken out of a meeting, what will be said and what will be left unsaid. It's tough.

Leslie: Well, my experience is that when a principal is honest and vulnerable, it really prompts good relationships . . . but you can't do that in the first year of your leadership.

Jennifer: Not in the first five years!!!

Sam: What would happen?

Mary: Then I have people trying to tell ME what to do!!

Anthony: Then you have mayhem!!

So the conversation that began with a question to elicit narratives about "What did you learn here?" quickly shifted to stories about daily experiences of learning from conversation, to the political ramifications of speaking openly in schools. But simply reading the transcript of our conversation is not a narrative inquiry. Now we have to make sense of the talk.

Structural/Analytical Methods

The meaning of the narratives comes from analyses or interpretations of the conversation. How would the Berkeley Group have analyzed the passage just presented? Sam didn't ask the group about this, but from her perspective it would depend on our empirical and theoretical positions on learning from conversation. From a post-positivist position (see Table 6.1), we might stay focused on Sam's initial topic and conduct a frequency count of what helps and hinders learning from conversation or conduct a linguistic analysis of turn taking (Labov, 1972). We would support our analysis using methodological theories that support post-positive analyses. From a constructivist epistemological/theoretical perspective, we might look for themes that emerge from the intertwining conversation (e.g., the relationship between the narrator and the listeners). Those themes might also include literary analyses of narrative plot, characterization, and/or metaphor. From a critical perspective, we might highlight the themes representing the politics of conversation. In the end, our analyses would reflect a bricolage of the different stances and theories with one in the foreground, dependent on our purpose and audience.

Part 2: Recurrent Themes and Issues in Conversational Narrative Inquiry

Now that we've set the stage on the importance of the theoretical and epistemological perspectives in designing and studying narrative inquiries, we'll turn our attention to the literature on conversation in narrative inquiry across different disciplines and different geographical perspectives. Our primary criteria for choosing studies for review was that they study talk to construct, deconstruct, and reconstruct narratives. We wanted wide international representation in fields from education to medicine to business to law from a range of epistemological and theoretical perspectives. We also chose some reports that were not empirical but offered clear insights into the methodology of narrative inquiry.

Thus, we selected studies and essays on learning from conversation that (1) used or illuminated conversational approaches, (2) were explicit in articulating either the performative/generative or the structural/analytical methodologies from a variety of epistemological and theoretical positions, and (3) showed how using conversation as data in narrative inquiries enhanced its substantive and methodological power. In all, we reviewed 5 studies in law, 4 in political science, 1 in history, 3 in clinical psychology, 9 in medicine, 4 in social work, 10 in business, and 25 in education. Twenty-six of those reviewed were conducted outside the United States.

We annotated the studies for stance, content, and method and then identified recurrent themes and methods across all studies. We eventually organized the inquiries under five topics: (1) clarity of method; (2) issues of relationship, identity, and power; (3) the problem of structure; (4) study of conversational learning; and (5) implications of narrative inquiries on practice and policy. Of course, most of the narrative inquiries crossed categorical lines. We artificially placed them in one group for clarity of discussion.

The Need for Clarity of Method in Narrative Inquiry

One recurring problem mentioned in the introduction continued to surface as we looked for informative texts to include in this chapter: The methods used were not addressed at all, were addressed too generally, or didn't address the theoretical and epistemological stances that shaped their methods. Here, we'll review three that speak explicitly to the overall research design.

Michael Cortazzi (1993) and Catherine Riessman (1993) both wrote handbooks that included finding narratives in conversation by the structural method of recognizable story boundaries: the beginning (an orientation of who, when, what, and where) and the end (a coda bringing the story to a close). In between, there are evaluations (the important points; why the story is told), an abstract summarizing the story, and chronological events (Labov, 1972).

The Australian researcher Coralie McCormack (2004) used feminist and postmodern theories to create an analysis procedure called "storying stories" (p. 219). After her conversational interviews were transcribed, she looked at them through multiple lenses (active listening, narrative processes, language, contexts, and moments) to "highlight both the individuality and the complexity of a life" (p. 219). She then used the highlighted views to write the interpretive story and looked across those stories to create the final personal experience narrative. That process is reproduced in Table 6.2.

Ann Rogan and Dorothea de Kock (2005) were also very clear in describing their narrative methods. They unpacked the narrative inquiry processes in conversational interviewing, from choosing the narrators to determining the interview style to selecting the methods of analysis. They studied two South African preservice teachers' experiences while enrolled in a Postgraduate Certification in Education program (PGCE). Initially, they used a post-positivist approach of structured interviews for their transparent and "objective reality" (Lincoln & Guba, 1985, p. 82). Realizing that the interviews were not giving them the data they really wanted, they shifted to a more "constructivist" approach (Lincoln & Guba, 1985, p. 82), where they used a nondirective listening stance (Rogers, 1980) and a conversational style to elicit narratives. They used these and other techniques to elicit stories:

- Motivating information sharing by emphasizing the professional significance of their participation
- Sharing professional stories
- Defining the researcher as a person with similar interests
- Ensuring confidentiality
- Negotiating meaning with spontaneous questions

Table 6.2   Coralie McCormack's Process of Storying Stories

Stage	Steps	Tasks
Stage 1: Construct an interpretive story	Step 1: Compose the story middle	a. Reconnect with the conversation through active listening b. Locate the narrative process in the transcript c. Return enriched and constructed stories to participant for comment and feedback d. Respond to the participant's comments e. Form the first draft of the interpretive story middle: list agreed story titles; temporal ordering of story titles; add the text of each story f. Redraft story middle: view the transcript through multiple lenses: language, contexts, and moments; take into account the views highlighted through these lenses
	Step 2: Complete the story—add a beginning and an ending	a. Compose an orientation and choose the title b. Add a coda c. Use visual form and textual strategies to enhance the presentation d. Share the story with the participant e. Reflect on the story in the light of the participant's comments f. Compose an epilogue
Stage 2: Compose a personal experience narrative	Step 1: Construct a personal experience narrative	a. Temporally order the interpretive stories in a single document; this document forms the personal experience narrative b. Share the personal experience narrative with the participant c. Respond to the participant's comments
	Step 2: Construct an epilogue to close the narrative	a. Reflect on the personal experience narrative in the light of the research questions b. Add an epilogue to summarize these reflections and close the narrative

SOURCE: From "Storying stories: a narrative approach to in-depth interview conversations" by McCormick, C., in *International Journal of Social Research Methodology,* v. 7(3), copyright © 2004. Reprinted with permission of Taylor & Francis.

- Supplying linking statements to clarify meanings
- Making supportive comments
- Discussing word meanings in multiple languages (Rogan & de Kock, 2005, p. 633)

They triangulated their analysis procedures as follows:

- Choosing a structured global whole-text analysis approach consistent with a constructivist view of a multilayered reality to find themes or "universal statements" (Van Manen, 1998, p. 107)
- Then conducting a structural word-level analysis of a more positivist stance (situated meaning, syntax, semantics, and grammar) to support the global interpretations
- Then applying a literary criticism analysis using both word-level findings, such as figurative language, and whole text analysis, such as plot and theme

Rogan and de Kock (2005) concluded with a "reality check" (Lincoln & Guba, 1985, p. 211) with the narrators to confirm or amend the analysis. They concluded that what they had learned in the study was trustworthy because of the methods used, yet they cautioned that "the duration of the beliefs expressed in this set of themes is uncertain" (Rogan & de Kock, 2005, p. 646) and could be considered to be only "true for now" (Bruner, 1986, p. 25). They were also careful to point out how their changing relationships with the narrators affected the temporal stories.

Issues of Relationship, Identity, and Power in Narrative Inquiry

In any research study on human behavior, the relationship between the researcher and the participants is a primary influence on the study design, as we've seen. The researcher's epistemological perspective and methodological tradition depend on her or his stance on the relationship between the knower and the known. In narrative inquiries, researchers usually draw on constructivist or critical epistemologies rather than post-positive. Sometimes, as we saw in Rogan and de Kock's (2005) study, there is a shift within the study. Here are some varied examples.

Issues of Relationship

Engle Chan (2005) conducted a narrative inquiry with her Canadian college nurse educators about the impact of changes in health care and nursing education on their teaching lives. Drawing on Clandinin and Connelly's concepts about collaborative relationships (1988) as well as their insights on how place or context shapes the telling and retelling of stories (2000), she first thought collaboration meant sharing her interpretations of the stories with her narrators. She soon found the process to be "merely a theoretically driven, contrived exercise" (Chan, 2005, p. 47). The process of building a collaborative working relationship involved not only "negotiation of writings and interpretations" (p. 47) but also negotiation of relationship. It required extended conversations in real time (telephone conversations at home, meetings in homes and coffee shops) and living with the ambiguity of their co-interpreted stories.

Extensive relationships are one characteristic that distinguishes narrative inquiry from the methodology of ethnography. Ethnographies require at least 1 year of data collection. Most narrative inquiries, however, emphasize the ethnographic nature of their studies—that is, staying together as participant-observers (Denzin & Lincoln, 2005) long enough to develop trust and intimacy to get the "real stories" (Hollingsworth, Dybdahl, & Minarik, 1993; Lyons, 1993; Nias, 1984; Noddings, 1991). The contribution of feminist theory to research methodology (e.g., Fine & Macpherson, 1993; Lather, 1991; Oakley, 1981; Reinharz, 1992; Roberts, 1981; Stanley & Weis, 1983) has been to stress the importance of making the social relations between the researcher and the researched transparent: whose questions are we studying and whose interpretations have more validity. Add to that mix Michel Foucault's (1980) skeptical view about the power relations between the researcher and the researched, and we have a perspective on relationship in narrative inquiry that has almost become the "sacred story" (Crites, as cited in Connelly & Clandinin, 1990) or the "right" and only relationship model to use in narrative inquiry. Fortunately, narrative inquiries are so context reliant that they cannot be confined to one model. That makes for interesting studies, interesting reading, and the opportunity to build theory and shape policy and practice.

Fred Ramirez's (2003) narrative study of immigrant parents of schoolchildren, for example, sheds light on conversational interviews when the researcher and the narrators don't have an established relationship. He gathered their stories in groups of parents who knew each other well.

Pamela Hardin's (2003) study of 12 young women diagnosed with anorexia nervosa used a critical post-structural orientation to examine stories arising from different kinds of data (interview, autobiography, and Internet postings). Dr. Hardin reminded us that as a linguistic practice, "the interview is a social performance for both interviewee and interviewer, who are simultaneously the authors, characters and audiences of the stories being constructed" (p. 540). She was interested in how the interview, as a social practice, frames the production of the story. In particular, she examined "conversational moves" (p. 549) in the interview. Sometimes, for example, certain research questions moved the conversation to the "preferred response" (p. 540). Following Mishler (1995), Hardin (2003) also pointed out that "conversational moves are a circuitous process, as the interviewee also positions the researcher in ways that both constrain and enable conversation" (p. 541). Hardin concluded, "Stories have different functions and outcomes, depending on the purpose of the telling" (p. 536).

Lyn Yates (2001) gave us a twist on the "best model" of extensive relationships in a longitudinal research study of secondary-school students. Yates, a seasoned Australian feminist researcher, was explicit in saying that "dropping in twice a year and asking a series of fairly ordinary questions" (p. 189) would not have satisfied feminist criteria for appropriate research relationships. Yates pointed out that brevity of relationship was preferred in this study because the purpose was to minimize the effect of the project in students' lives and because of a methodological need to do all the interviewing and interpretation (i.e., not involve graduate researchers). Finally, she pointed out another influence on brevity of the research relationship: Yates and her colleagues were constrained by the political climate of what kinds of studies should be well financed and which should not. The latter position also shaped their inquiry.

Power-in-relationship is a recurring issue in conversational studies resulting in stories. Michelle Fine's (1991) classic ethnography of dropouts contained stories that suggested that the person who holds power in the classroom (i.e., the teacher) both controls the conversations and determines what is *not* spoken. As she wrote in a follow-up paper, students quickly learn the "dangers of talk, the codes of participating and not, and . . . which conversations are never to be had" (Fine, 1995, p. 124). Similarly, Olson and Craig (2001) found that in teacher-student relationships, some students' narratives are given more credence or narrative authority— seen as superior to others—and may lead to tensions and silencing of other narratives. Issues of narrative authority arose when we were discussing this chapter in our Berkeley Group. (We'll speak explicitly on the issue of power in our group later in the chapter.)

Karen: Well, I just want to add there are conversations and then there are conversations. [Looks at Leslie.] You talk a lot, right? And others, like me, don't talk a lot, and [Looks at Sam.] you don't talk a lot either. [So] all the voices are not being heard. I think that's problematic. It leads to silencing. The only way that conversations can be really valuable for everybody is if there's some control—some facilitation.

Sam: Say more.

Karen: It has to be an equitable conversation. Leslie, you know you and I are so different . . . why are you [Leslie] so comfortable talking in a group? And I'm very jealous of that. . . . I've struggled with that all my life, because I've always been very reluctant . . . to . . . speak up.

Leslie: Well, that's interesting, because the topics we talk about are really important to you.

Karen: Uh huh!!

Leslie: So I think it's interesting that you don't talk a lot.

Karen: Because I'm not really sure that what I have to say is all that important, or that I won't articulate it quite the way I want to. When I'm just relating with another person, it's OK, but I don't feel that way in a group.

Anthony: So what can be done about that?

Karen: I think you should go around the room and ask everyone to speak. I learn from every single person. If one person dominates, I get mad, and then that anger interferes with my learning. . . . When I can plan ahead what I'm going to say, then I'm comfortable. There's ways of doing that as a teacher, like having people write first or talk to somebody else before they talk. Some people can come up with what they want to say about a topic very quickly and articulately, but that's not me; it's not easy for me. It takes me a long time to really decide what I think and why and what I want to say. . . . To me, our conversations are so complex that it's hard to pinpoint where I come down on something. I'm mulling it all over and listening to everybody else.

What Karen's honest and vulnerable comment showed is that in every conversational narrative inquiry, there are varied relationships to the act of conversation itself, and those variations should be noted in the analyses. Furthermore, Karen's analysis of the different comfort levels in our conversation gave all of us an opportunity to examine our shifting identities in different conversational settings.

Issues of Identity

Many narrative inquiry studies and essays show how conversations in relationship with others influence identity construction. Here are a few examples. Concerned that South African students' social and educational identities are still shaped by dimensions of power long after Nelson Mandela was released from prison, Melanie Walker (2005) looked at intersections of history, biography, and society in her analyses. Her primary data sources were 2-hour narrative interviews with 12 black and white undergraduate students about their lives growing up and studying in South Africa. Looking at the students' narratives by using pertinent social and historical contexts, she found moments of transformation when new identities were made possible. The narrators also revealed that some of them rejected opportunities to reconstruct their identities. She concluded that both individual and educational "'default identities' (Kitzinger & Wilkinson, 1993) often erase or obscure the power relations of race and hence enable racism to persist" (p. 129).

Christine Leland and Jerome Harste (2005) reported results from a 2-year study of critical literacy in preservice education. Theoretically framed by Luke and Freebody's (1997) notion of literacy as social practice, they argued that engaging students in ongoing critical conversations about difficult social issues might help shape their identities as teachers so that they would choose to take social action by teaching in urban schools. A promising finding was that combining text readings with critical conversations about text topics allowed preservice teachers to "interrogate their own assumptions" (Leland & Harste, 2005, p. 65).

The Canadian professor Carola Conle (2001) reminded us about the importance of Habermas's (1981) standpoint on power positions in research relationships. To equalize the development of the story, he argued that conversational partners should concern themselves with understanding each other's stories rather than trying to position the story from their point of view. Researchers across traditions sometimes forget that. McLeod and Yates (1997) offer a joke to support Conle's claims.

Q: What does the postmodern ethnographer say to the interviewee?

A: Enough about you! Now let's talk about me! (p. 188)

Issues of Power

Power differences between researchers and the narrators they "study" is an issue that appears in many narrative inquiries, such as Walker's (2003) and Conle's (2001). In another excellent study, Mary McVee (2005) struggled with both her powerful position as a teacher educator gathering narratives from students and the cultural differences between herself and her students. To guard against wrongly analyzed findings, she had outside reviewers give her feedback and criticism of the preliminary findings.

In a conversation to elicit feedback on this chapter in press, the Berkeley Group also spoke of the issue of power. Sam brought up the topic and was interested to see where it would go.

Sam: Let's talk about power relations in our group.

Karen: The way our group works, I don't feel any power dynamics at all. And that's unusual for any group. I don't feel any kind of hierarchical positioning from people here, and no push and no fear that something you've said is going to be used against you.

Jennifer: But sometimes it happens. Sometimes we have major, strong disagreements. I mean, we were all over you about your book (Obidah & Teel, 2000) on race and teaching. (Some of us were angry about the way Karen seemed to be portrayed in her book—doing everything wrong as a White teacher in a predominantly African American classroom.)

Karen: Well, disagreeing isn't about power.

Jennifer: But I think it's important to acknowledge that you can't just say anything you want and people will always agree with you.

Karen: That's not what I meant. I didn't mean there was no struggle and conflict. Here we can say what is ever on our minds and no one is going to ding you for it.

Jennifer: Or tell you you're wrong and that you have to sit down and get quiet.

Mary: Or, if they do, it's not because of having power over you, it's because they feel passionately about something . . . and if that passion was not coming from an honest place, you can call them on it.

Jennifer: That's why we can have the kind of conversations we have. But I don't think that's the way of common conversations. Especially in faculty meetings. There *is* a hierarchy and it tempers what gets into the conversation and what is silenced.

Leslie: Here there are no power dynamics going on, and yet there are unspoken
standard[s] and structures . . . in terms of being thoughtful honest and
sincere . . . and everybody adheres to that.

The Problem of Structure in Narrative Inquiry

Capturing and making sense of conversation is a slippery thing. If researchers
can form appropriate relationships with narrators to get compelling stories, use
appropriate responses to get rich explications, and carefully critique the analyses,
then capturing them on a tape recorder is not a problem. Because of these difficulties and others, many researchers use structured interview questions (Labov, 1972).
In studies that seek to influence policy, narrative researchers tend to use more traditionally structured techniques that appeal to policy makers.

Catherine Riessman and Lee Quinney (2005) argued that narrative inquiry in
social work suffers in the United States because the National Institutes of Health's
(NIH) view of fundable scientific research excludes "the perspectives and assumptions" (p. 407) of narrative research. Even though "the norm of a detached, disinterested, and disengaged observer is applied inappropriately to human studies"
(p. 407), that view limits the development of narrative social work in the United
States . . . but not yet so much in Europe.

Researchers wanting to use narrative inquiries for policy studies have to cast
them in semi-post-positivist methods to be funded. For example, in a provocative
narrative inquiry into adolescents' transition from experimental to regular smoking, Baillie, Lavato, Johnson, and Kalaw (2005) showed how tobacco-use prevention programs, developed by adults without the use of adolescent narratives, are
way off the mark. Funded by the cigarette industry, they used a purposeful sampling method (former experimenters, limited, and daily smokers, etc.) to choose
35 participants whose smoking stories were elicited through 45- to 60-minute
structured interviews. Data were examined using Muller's (1999) four-step
process: identifying categories, identifying themes, then looking for negative
cases, and representing an account of the stories. In opposition to smoking abatement programs that treat the cause of smoking as peer pressure, the authors
found that smoking was used as a tool to negotiate the social world. It makes the
adolescents look "cool." "It provides [adolescents] with a script with which to
enter in social situations and begin the process of communication" (p. 102). The
authors argue for a change in prevention and abatement program design: "We fail
adolescents by clinging tenaciously to an intervention paradigm that typically
represents teen smoking as a foolhardy activity brought about through peer
pressure" (p. 106).

Researchers writing for purposes other than influencing policy (e.g., contributing to the knowledge base) tend to be less structured. Free to use constructive/
critical methods, they often challenge traditional models and create new methods.
Here are some examples.

Troy Glover (2004) argues for broadening methodological approaches in narrative inquiry. In studying the birth and development of a grassroots association, he

distinguishes between explanatory narrative inquiry (used to find out how and why events came about) and descriptive narrative inquiries (the expressions of self, other, and collective identity through stories). Glover hopes to foster "an appreciation for narrative inquiry as a 'new' method with which to study grassroots associations" (p. 47).

In a long, conversational study of student teachers' experiences, Xin Li (2005) explored a cross-cultural narrative inquiry theorized with an intersubjective ontology in the Taoist philosophy (Lao Tzu, 1990), a position echoed by Buber's (1970/1996) classic *I and Thou*. Using a self/other frame, she structured her study by getting students with opposing cultural views in conversation together, making sure that each had an equal opportunity to speak. She illustrated the resulting narrative through a series of Chinese knot drawings.

The Swedish academics Linnart Fredriksson and Unni Lindstrom (2002) drew on Ricoeur's (1991) hermeneutic circle to engage eight psychiatric patients and three nurses in conversation about suffering and shame. After 20 tape-recorded conversations were "gathered" (Fredriksson and Lindstrom, p. 398) or transcribed, they read the data through naively to gain a pre-understanding of the embedded narratives. They then followed with two structural analyses to explain the text, finally analyzing the stories by confronting various interpretations from the structural analysis and the pre-understanding to create a contextually situated whole understanding.

Julianne Moss (2002) produced a multivoiced text through teacher narratives, visual images, policy documents, and conversations. Drawing from a post-structuralist methodology and narrative theory, she *wove* visual and literary *data sources* to create a narrative of inclusive education in Tasmania. Her goal in creating the multivoiced text was to "enter into conversations with the reader rather than tell the story" (p. 231).

Drawing on Polanyi's (1985) method and Polkinghorne's (1991) theory of emplotment or transforming "a list or sequence of disconnected events into a unified story" (p. 141), Mary McVee (2005) looked closely at story retellings (Tannen, 1989) and how narrators reposition themselves through "re-emplotting" the narratives. In other words, rather than gather once-told stories (such as the intact "Grandmother Story" Mary told the Berkeley Group), McVee captured six retellings of Ellie's and others' story to create case studies. McVee asked Ellie, a Euro-American student teacher in a semester-long teacher education course, to describe her first encounter in a predominantly African American school. She told a story about awakening to issues of race. McVee then used theories of internalized racism (McIntyre, 1997) to explain how Ellie's conception of race was re-emplotted over time. Like other researchers (Bogdan & Biklen, 2002; Janesick, 2000), she rejected the simplistic view of triangulation of using three different types of data to establish trustworthiness. Therefore, she used six narrative retellings of an assignment on cultural border crossing (Ellie's journal, large- and small-group conversations, written narratives, oral discussion of the final narrative, and a postcourse interview). Furthermore, she did not stop the analysis with locating story kernels but looked at "evaluative sequences, flash sequences, resolutions, self-directed questions" (McVee, 2005, p. 189) for changes in the relationship between "events and their plot, through evaluation and interpretation of narratives, and ultimately, through the shift in how Ellie positions herself" (McVee, 2005, p. 189). Though Ellie didn't actually change much in her re-emplotments of her racial narrative, it is clear that McVee learned a great deal about the power of retellings.

Using theories of political discourses (Chilton & Schäffner, 2002), Shaul Shenhav (2005) located political narratives using the traditional narrative "beginning, middle and end" (Mink, 1987, p. 197). He then analyzed narratives from planned political events to informal conversations about politics from several interesting perspectives. The one that appealed most to Sam was his theoretical analysis of political narratives using the concept of space, applying Bahktin's (1981) notion of "chronotope" or time space. Shenhav (2005) saw the spatial aspect of narrative taking the form of geographical references to specific neighborhoods, towns, countries, and the like. Using this approach, he analyzed a political speech by Ariel Sharon, showing how Sharon's narrative constructed a geopolitical map where Israel had "one foot in the Middle East and the other in the 'free world'" (p. 94).

In Hardin's (2003) study on anorexia nervosa described earlier, she challenges the time-honored tradition of looking for themes across data.

> From an analysis of the data it became evident that although there were similarities across accounts, so too were their noticeable and significant differences. Attempting to compress the data into thematic categories would have reduced the complexity of analysis, notably erasing the social aspects of how the data were constructed: what was being produced, for whom, and in what social context. (p. 537)

So rather than illuminate themes, Harden used a post-structuralist theoretical approach foregrounding the independent relationship between narrative production and context. To support this approach as well as make it more concrete, she used conversational data from the study to illustrate the methodological arguments.

Learning From Conversation

As we have seen, different epistemological/theoretical structures frame what we can learn from conversational narratives. Sometimes conversations can be less than educative because of the tendency to interpret and judge dissonant conversational approaches according to one's own conventions of speaking (Gumperz, Jupp, & Roberts, 1979) or to harden one's own position and end the conversation (Florio-Ruane, 2001).

From the vast number of studies as essays on preservice and inservice teachers' development, however, there's no doubt that practitioners value conversation as a medium for learning. Although we found many articles to support that claim, we're limited (spatially) to reviewing six examples and some reflective comments.

In a year-and-a-half-long teacher inquiry group, Luna et al. (2004) used teaching journals, classroom videotapes, and transcripts of conversations about pedagogical implications of critical literacies or used texts with the purpose of "disrupting the commonplace, interrogating multiple viewpoints, focusing on sociopolitical issues and promoting social justice" (Lewison, Seely Flint, & Van Shuys, 2002, p. 202). Although they worried that their narrative authority as classroom teachers would be devalued in the scholarly world, their experiential narratives showed powerful professional development.

Jocelyn Glazier's (2003) study of students learning about race looked at "gaps" in conversation when the topic of race surfaced in course discussions. Ten white women enrolled in one of Florio-Ruane's semester-long courses and read and discussed Maya Angelou's novels using a semistructured format. The instructor established a topic for the discussion, and the students wrote responses and then moved into small groups for hour-long discussions, followed by a whole-class synthesis. As Glazier listened to transcripts of their conversation, she noted moments before and after "trouble spots" arose—moments filled with pauses, changes in tone or pace, topic shifts, or nervous laughter. Often, a passage clearly needing discussion of race was derailed to "get the facts straight" (p. 83). The "silence" surrounding the topic of race was an audible indicator of their resistance to reflecting on or learning about the topic.

At the end of the semester, the students continued to meet and read Angelou but no longer followed the structured format. Their overlapping conversation, rather than polite turn taking, showed that some students did shift their assumptions about race.

The Berkeley Group similarly struggled with discussions of race. Composed of two heterosexual white women, one African American lesbian, two white lesbians, and one white heterosexual male, it took us years to have deep, focused conversations on race. It's still difficult for us. Exposing our own racism and how we interpret each other's remarks about race is complex, emotional, and sometimes frightening. Intellectually, we know the importance of questioning our assumptions about race in learning and living. We also know that until we can unpack the issues of race in our conversations, our narratives will lack the richness they could have. So we keep working at it.

How to foster conversation in the classroom for student learning is another important area of research. Claude Goldenberg (1992) has been one of the leaders in this field. He has shown that narrative understandings of classroom discussions promote reading comprehension, interpretation, and thinking.

In a sense, learning from conversation in classrooms are mini narrative inquiries. Goldenberg described the 10 elements required for an instructional conversation (a conversation facilitated by a teacher as a pedagogical technique): (1) a challenging but nonthreatening atmosphere, (2) a high level of teacher responsivity to students' contributions, (3) open-ended questions, (4) connected discourse, (5) broad participation, (6) a thematic focus, (7) the elicitation of students' background knowledge, (8) direct teaching when necessary, (9) the promotion and use of complex language, and (10) the use of text and experience as a basis for statements and elaborations. He also pointed out that it is important to make explicit what students learn from the conversation. Goldenberg's work spawned many other research studies to test the feasibility of learning through instructional conversations (see O'Bryan, 1999; Pomerantz, 1998; Roskos, Boehlen, & Walker, 2000).

In the worlds of business, medicine, and social work, principles for learning to converse are varied yet have some common features. Baker (2004) suggested that a "receptive conversational space" (p. 695) is required for conversation around "undiscussables" (Argyris, 1994, p. 271). That space includes psychological safety for disagreeing and taking risks, a spirit of inquiry rather than advocacy, and emphasizing the importance of listening to learn or "intentionally asking questions without knowing what the answers might be" (Baker, 2004, p. 697). Zurawski (2004) concurred with those points and added that organizations can show they sincerely care about investing in human relationships and learning by providing time to talk. Sims (2004) reminded us that business ethics students rarely get an opportunity to sit and converse with others who hold opposing views. Given today's increasingly global world, it is imperative that students learn to converse and collaborate. Sims argues that business students need conversational experiences listening to each other's ethical and moral experiences to learn how to become effective managers.

Sam: So, how do we learn from conversation?

Mary: The question would be, do you come into the conversation ready to learn from it? Do you bring with you the value of "relational knowing" (Hollingsworth, Dybdahl, & Minarik, 1993) or the value of family or with a socialistic perspective where you have to depend on people around you so you'd best be in conversation?

Sam: For me, it's been in conversations like this where I've really learned what it means for people with your social justice values to teach in urban settings. So I took our process to my classrooms. I teach conversationally. All my students work in small groups and talk, talk, talk about what they're reading, experiencing, and discovering. The readings are helpful to start the conversation, give them an initial focus, but the real learning together comes through talking.

Mary: And how did you learn that?

Sam: By seeing it happen here. Now I can really see and hear students learn through conversation and it's tremendously exciting! And, of course, I do have students who don't learn from conversation—even in doctoral programs. My hunch is that they don't read critically, they're not thoughtful outside of the class so they don't bring much to their group. They sort of agree with what their peers have to say, or just enter the conversation using their own loosely-examined experience . . . it's easy to tell they are going to leave the class only with what they came in with.

What can narrative inquirers and educators across disciplines learn from the studies reviewed here? We found eight key principles:

1. Develop trust. Listen nonjudgmentally.

2. Initially, scaffold or structure conversations and set norms, if necessary.

3. Encourage talk about topics that are controversial and difficult.

4. Allow emergent purposes for the conversation to develop.

5. Value different discourse styles.

6. Specifically articulate the learning that occurs in conversation.

7. Examine assumptions.

8. Pay attention to issues of power-in-relationship.

Implications for Policy and Practice

Many narrative inquirers across disciplines hope to influence policy and organizational changes that affect practice. Here, we'll review some narrative inquiries that inform school reform policies and practices in the fields of education, medicine, social work, business, and law.

Conversations About Education

Jean Clandinin and Michael Connelly (1998) construct an argument for school reform by describing their personal narratives in work on teachers' "personal practical knowledge" (p. 150). Arguing that school reform is an epistemological matter that involves practitioner stories and narratives, the article concludes as follows:

> School reform becomes a question of the possibility of school participants reimagining their professional lives. This imagined middle ground shifts the terms for reform from initiative, control, and urgent problem solving . . . to new terms such as stories to live by, negotiation, improvisation, imagination, and possibility. (p. 162)

Sam and her university colleagues Margaret Gallego and David Whitenack (2001) have also used narrative inquiry to challenge current national reform movements. Watching reform happen in one elementary school for more than 3 years, they critique national reforms as being too harsh and immediate and as bypassing essential conversations in relationship.

Borrowing from Clandinin and Connelly's theories (2000) in a recent study of 11 teacher education program graduates, Vickie LaBoskey (2006) reported one teacher's narrative of policy barriers to teaching equitably in an urban school. LaBoskey argues that teachers' narratives put a human face on the effects of high-stakes testing and serve as a "reality check" (p. 121) on enacted policy. She sees a collection of teachers' lived narratives as a way to "influence policy-makers so that their decisions will be more supportive of the goals of equity and social justice" (p. 121).

Narrative inquiries show promise for changing school-level policy as well. In an essay intended to affect discipline policy and practice in Maori schools, Wendy Drewery (2004) argues against punishing disciplinary practices focused on punishment and advocated conversational alternatives akin to the restorative justice conversations in law (Morris & Maxwell, 2001). She argues for "restorative conferencing" (Drewery, 2004, p. 335), gathering all interested parties surrounding the student's misbehavior to have a conversation about the problem, rebuild relationships, and pool ideas for the next steps to make things right. In effect, the group would re-emplot the initial story that brought them together. She justifies her argument not only from a successful trial program by the Ministry of Education (Winslade, Drewery, & Hooper, 2000) but through reporting on psychological studies of the importance of conversation in learning. Such conversations restore people "from a state of disorientation to a state of being in community" (Drewery, 2004, p. 339).

Conversation in Medicine and Social Work

Citing an increasingly divergent client population, Angelelli and Geist-Martin (2005) speak of the complex layers of meaning that accompany conversations about health, illness, and medicine. Because of various orientations in linguistic, cultural, socioeconomic, and epistemological ways of being in the world, conversations between providers and patients have to include these complexities or risk miscommunication and noncompliance. The authors concluded that medical schools have to change their modes of instruction to include conversational narrative inquiries that will mirror the world where many graduates will practice.

Donald Fausel (2004) sees the field of social work changing from therapists as experts and therapy as diagnosis and treatment (the medical model) to clients and therapists as collaborative narrative inquiries. The client is viewed as an expert on his or her pain, and the therapist involves the client in conversations about appropriate treatment.

Joan Biever and Katherine McKenzie (1995) argue for the therapeutic narrative approach to therapy (Hoffman, 1991; Parry, 1991) for work with adolescents. They give advice on facilitating conversations: "1) maintain a 'not knowing' stance (Anderson & Goolishian, 1988); 2) be open and generate alternatives; 3) think in terms of both/and rather than either/or; 4) assume the adolescent has strengths and resources; 5) be aware of your own values and beliefs. This kind of narrative inquiry tends to elicit cooperation and investment by the adolescent and to circumvent the power struggles which may occur" (p. 371).

Some researchers have conducted narrative inquiries to learn how policies change through narrative inquiries. For example, in an inquiry into a Parliament Committee conversation in Israel, Daphna Birenbaum-Carmeli (2004) uncovers three narratives that shaped Israel's exceptional in vitro fertilization policy.

Conversation in Business

Some authors in the business world have suggested that organizational cultures have learned to value learning from conversational exchanges between managers and employers rather than top-down, power-heavy directives (Baker, 2004; Ford & Ford, 1995; Sims, 2004; Zurawski, 2004). Sims, like Angelelli and Geist-Martin (2005) in medicine, explained that global economics have made conversational learning in business essential since employees have differing ethical backgrounds, experiences, and worldviews. Conversational approaches also help foster ethical responsibility in business students. Drawing on Kolb's (1984) theory of experiential learning, Ann Baker (2004) argued that business ethics faculty should learn how to create "receptive conversational spaces" (p. 695), or classrooms that are psychologically safe, free of instructor control over interactions, and emphasize listening to learn. The instructors should prepare themselves to promote inquiry into conversational narratives about "undiscussables" (Argyris, 1994) and their underlying assumptions.

Conversation in Law

In a recent legal essay, Alexandra Natapoff (2005) argues that criminals are being denied conversation that might support their own self-defense and the emplotment of their stories. Although a million defendants pass through the criminal justice system every year, most remain silent or are barely given voice through their lawyers, if at all. Moreover, the criminal justice system is "fundamentally shaped" by the denial of speech to criminal defendants (p. 3). From Miranda warnings, through trial procedures, plea bargainings, and client-counsel relationships, criminal defendants are consistently asked to be quiet, particularly with personal stories, and let their lawyers speak for them. This particularly silences the poor, the undereducated, the unemployed, and racial minorities. Natapoff sees such silencing as "part of a larger, well-documented struggle over narrative social power" (p. 9).

David Hyman (2000) argues for the power of narrative to establish policy in law. He wrote,

> First person narrative accounts have always been a staple of policy debates. Reform advocates understand that policy wonks and academics may be persuaded by regression analyses, but the general public and legislators are more likely to be moved by a compelling story. (p. 1149)

The debate over the kind of conversation that is most beneficial to learning could lead to organizational change in law schools as well. Gregory Kalscheur (1996), a Jesuit scholar and law professor, argues that law should be reconceptualized as a meaning-making conversation to return legal education to a process approach to dialogue, trust, and learning. Borrowing from Lonergan's (1973) call for law school to be recast as a "culture of argument and conversation" (Kalscheur,

1996, p. 334), he evokes Ricoeur's (1991) notion of conversation as a process where humans confront their own versions of the good life, narratively re-emplotted while refining them through questioning, arguing, and consulting others. (See also Georgakopoulou, 2003, on contested plots.)

Hawkins-Leon (1998) and Rhode (2001) also argue for law schools to change their instructional methods to the experiential or problem-based learning—a model that incorporates both in-class and out-of-class conversational narrative inquiry. They both acknowledge, however, that such models are time intensive and would be an expensive change.

In response to this theme, Leslie starts a conversation about the influence of narrative inquiry in organizational and policy change in education.

Leslie: As an outgrowth of this group I started a conversational group after school, letting the conversation go where it needed to go, not mandated by one person's agenda. "Over the back fence" conversations were marginalized by the administration. . . . But the teachers kept pushing. Finally the district agreed to allow it to happen, if we would turn in a written document outlining our agenda, what we talked about, and what was accomplished. . . . After two years, our principal "decided to trust us" and the documentation was no longer required.

Part 3: Coda

Influenced by McVee's (2005) study of conversational retellings, Mary and Sam decided to close this chapter by hearing Mary talk about how she would re-emplot the grandmother story from the perspective of an elementary principal. These are Mary's words:

Some of the details of the grandmother story are beginning to fade but its importance will always stay with me. At the time I originally told it to our group, I took the grandmother's harsh comments as a condemnation of the educational system. She aimed her anger at the test scores, not at me. While she was very personal about her feelings and the experiences of her granddaughter, in retrospect she let me off the hook. I have no idea if she did this purposefully. I don't know how she viewed my relationship to her, or if she even thought that a relationship existed. My sense was not that I had the upper hand or a position of power by being able to "test" her granddaughter. As a matter of fact, it seemed to me that her granddaughter and I, as a beginning teacher, were victims of a terrible educational system that de-humanized us all. Yet I didn't engage in conversation to get to learn more about the grandmother or her granddaughter. I was simply silent.

Through 18 years of dinner meetings with the Berkeley Group, I learned the importance of conversation in relationships to make meaning. At the time of the grandmother story, I was in my second year of teaching. I was nowhere near the point of having a meaningful conversation with a parent, particularly around the issue of standardized testing. I had not clarified my identity as a teacher, and I had no perspective on how positions of power, either as a teacher or as a grandparent, played a part in our conversation. I look back at the grandmother story and am amazed at her vulnerability in the face of no reciprocal response. If I were to guess, from her point of view I was just another teacher in a long line of teachers that this woman had to endure. She never learned that her story shaped my story as a teacher.

For the next 12 years, my classroom practice centered on learning to teach in relationship to my students, their parents, and my colleagues. The Berkeley Group supported my development by listening, sharing their stories, and demanding from me a reflective approach to my lived stories of teaching and learning. When I was at my best, the instructional decisions I made came from careful consideration of relationships. What do I know about this child and how do I know it? How am I accommodating this parent's concerns or that teacher's special interests? Am I taking short cuts or am I being honest? Does my identity as "teacher" support or diminish others who have a stake in the education of students in my classroom?

As a beginning administrator, the grandmother story now takes on new and nested levels of meaning. But for years the story remained static, frozen in print, a touchstone that kept me questioning the educational system and my role in it. Now the story has become more problematic and complex. Rethinking it as a principal with responsibilities to support teachers, students, and parents, I'd tell it differently. I'd have to weave in my obligation to help beginning teachers know the value of building parent-teacher relationships before they send assessment data home, before the grandmother comes to call. I'd want them to see how power positions affect conversation and what's learned from it. I'd want them to respond to the grandmother, engage her in conversation, so that a new story would emerge from the engagement.

Earlier in the chapter, I shared my belief that conversation is primarily an act of listening. As I think about re-emplotting the grandmother story, I'm not so certain about that. As an elementary principal, I do a great deal of listening, but that does not mean that I'm in conversation. Nor does it mean that I can produce a meaningful narrative from the conversation. To develop living narratives to guide my work, I have to engage in conversations fully aware of the factors that shape the stories: the issues of relationship, identity, and power as we are constructing conversation; how to structure the narrative so that all characters' ways of seeing the world are included; and how to leverage the story to affect policy and practice. Although the structures and values of schools leave little time for this kind of reflection, the need is immediate. Policy makers across disciplines should encourage conversation narratives. The narrators learn from each other's stories to make positive changes in their practices. The grandmother story did that for me and the others in the Berkeley Group.

Over the years, I have experienced many more grandmother stories. What they bring adds to my understanding of children's lives: their families, their strengths and needs, their histories. Regrettably, my new role as a school administrator gives me even less time to build those relationships, even less time to reflect on the role of power and identity in conversation and how those issues will shape both the living and the telling (Clandinin & Connelly, 2000) of those stories. How can I tell those stories loudly enough to influence changes in the school structures to give teachers, parents, students, and me time to create, analyze, and learn from narratives of school? Until that happens, I look forward to examining these and other narrative inquiries with my friends in the Berkeley Group.

Consulting Editors: Mary McVee and Maximina Freire

Note

1.   The interview with the Berkeley Group—Karen Teel, Anthony Cody, Jennifer Davis Smallwood, and Leslie Minarik—is reprinted with permission.

References

Angelelli, A., & Geist-Martin, P. (2005). Enhancing culturally competent health communication: Constructing understanding between providers and culturally diverse patients. In E. Berlin-Ray (Ed.), *Health communication in practice: A case study* (pp. 271–284). Mahwah, NJ: Lawrence Erlbaum.

Argyris, C. (1994). Good communication that blocks learning. *Harvard Business Review, 72*(4), 77–85.

Bahktin, M. M. (1981). *The dialogic imagination: Four essays by M. M. Bahktin* (C. Emerson & M. Holquist, Trans.; M. Holquist, Ed.). Austin: University of Texas Press.

Baillie, L., Lavato, C. Y., Johnson, J. L., & Kalaw, C. (2005). Smoking decisions from a teen perspective: A narrative study. *American Journal of Health Behavior, 29*(2), 99–106.

Baker, A. (2004). Seizing the moment: Talking about the "undiscussables." *Journal of Management Education, 28*(6), 693–706.

Belenky, M. F., Clinchy, B. M., Goldberger, N. R., & Tarule, J. M. (1986). *Women's ways of knowing: The development of self, voice and mind.* New York: Basic Books.

Biever, J. L., & McKenzie, K. (1995). Stories and solutions in psychotherapy with adolescents. *Adolescence, 30*, 491–499.

Birenbaum-Carmeli, D. (2004). "Cheaper than a newcomer": On the social production of IVF policy in Israel. *Sociology of Health and Illness, 26*(7), 897–924.

Bogdan, R. C., & Biklen, S. K. (2002). *Qualitative research for education* (4th ed.). Boston: Allyn & Bacon.

Bruner, J. (1986). *Actual minds, possible worlds.* Cambridge, MA: Harvard University Press.

Buber, M. (1996). *I and thou.* New York: Touchstone. (Original work published 1970)

Chan, E. A. (2005). The narrative research trail: Values of ambiguity and relationships. *Nurse Researcher, 13*(1), 43–56.

Chilton, P., & Schäffner, C. (2002). Introduction: Themes and principles in the analysis of political discourse. In P. Chilton & C. Schäffner (Eds.), *Politics as text and talk* (pp. 1–41). Amsterdam: John Benjamins.

Clandinin, D. J., & Connelly, F. M. (1988). Studying teachers' knowledge of classrooms: Collaborative research, ethics and the negotiation of narrative. *Journal of Educational Thought, 22*(2), 269–282.

Clandinin, D. J., & Connelly, F. M. (1998). Stories to live by: Narrative understandings of school reform. *Curriculum Inquiry, 28*(2), 149–161.

Clandinin, D. J., & Connelly, M. (2000). *Narrative inquiry: Experience and story in qualitative research.* San Francisco: Jossey-Bass.

Conle, C. (2001). The rationality of narrative inquiry in research and professional development. *European Journal of Teacher Education, 24*(1), 21–33.

Connelly, F. M., & Clandinin, D. J. (1990). Stories of experience and narrative inquiry. *Educational Researcher, 19*(5), 2–14.

Cortazzi, M. (1993). *Narrative analysis.* London: Falmer Press.

Denzin, N., & Lincoln, Y. S. (2005). *Handbook of qualitative research.* Thousand Oaks, CA: Sage.

Drewery, W. (2004). Conferencing in schools: Punishment, restorative justice, and the productive importance of the process of conversation. *Journal of Community and Applied Social Psychology, 14*, 332–334.

Fausel, D. (2004). Collaborative conversations for change: A solution-focused approach to family-centered practice. *Family Preservation Journal, 3*(1), 59–74.

Fine, M. (1991). *Framing dropouts: Notes on the politics of an urban public high school.* Albany: State University of New York Press.

Fine, M. (1995). *Disruptive voices: The possibilities of feminist research.* Ann Arbor: University of Michigan Press.

Fine, M., & Macpherson, P. (1993). Over dinner: Feminism and adolescent female bodies. In S. Biklen, S. Knopp, & D. Pollard (Eds.), *92nd Yearbook of the National Society for the Study of Education* (pp. 126–154). Chicago: University of Chicago Press.

Florio-Ruane, S. (2001). *Teacher education and the cultural imagination: Autobiography, conversation, and narrative.* Mahwah, NJ: Erlbaum.

Ford, J., & Ford, L. (1995). The role of conversation in producing change in organizations. *The Academy of Management Review, 20*(3), 541–570.

Foucault, M. (1980). *Power/knowledge.* New York: Pantheon Books.

Fredriksson, L., & Lindstrom, U. A. (2002). Caring conversations: Psychiatric patients' narratives about suffering. *Journal of Advanced Nursing, 40*(4), 396–404.

Gadamer, H. G. (1996). *Truth and method.* New York: Continuum.

Gallego, M., Hollingsworth, S., & Whitenack, D. (2001). Relational knowing in the reform of educational cultures. *Teachers College Record, 103*(2), 240–266.

Georgakopoulou, A. (2003). Plotting the "right place" and the "right time": Place and time as interactional resources in narrative. *Narrative Inquiry, 13*(2), 413–432.

Gilman, C. P. (1988). The home (1903). In J. Donovan (Ed.), *Feminist theory: The intellectual traditions of American feminism.* New York: Continuum.

Glazier, J. A. (2003). Moving closer to speaking the unspeakable: White teachers talking about race. *Teacher Education Quarterly, 30*(1), 73–94.

Glover, T. D. (2004). Narrative inquiry and the study of grassroots associations. *International Journal of Voluntary and Nonprofit Organizations, 15*(1), 47–69.

Goldenberg, C. (1992). Instructional conversations: Promoting comprehension through discussion. *The Reading Teacher, 46*(4), 316–327.

Gumperz, J., Jupp, T. C., & Roberts, C. (1979). *Cross talk: A study of cross cultural communication.* Southall, UK: National Centre for Industrial Language Training, Havelock Centre.

Habermas, J. (1981). *Theory of communicative action.* Frankfurt am Main, Germany: Suhrkamp.

Hardin, P. K. (2003). Constructing experience in individual interviews, autobiographies and on-line accounts: A poststructuralist approach. *Journal of Advanced Nursing, 41*(6), 536–544.

Hawkins-Leon, C. G. (1998). The Socratic method-problem method dichotomy. *Brigham Young University Education and Law Journal, 8*(1), 1–18.

Hoffman, L. (1991). A reflexive stance for family therapy. *Journal of Strategic and Systematic Therapies, 10,* 4–17.

Hollingsworth, S. (1989). Prior beliefs and cognitive change in learning to teach. *American Educational Research Journal, 26*(2), 169–189.

Hollingsworth, S. (1990, April). *Learning to teach the culturally diverse through collaborative conversation: A feminist pedagogy.* Paper presented at the American Educational Research Association, Boston.

Hollingsworth, S. (1992). Learning to teach through collaborative conversation: A feminist approach. *American Educational Research Journal, 29*(2), 373–404.

Hollingsworth, S., Cody, A., Dybdahl, M., Minarik, L. T., Smallwood, J., & Teel, K. M. (1994). *Teacher research and urban literacy education: Lessons and conversations in a feminist key.* New York: Teachers College Press.

Hollingsworth, S., & Dybdahl, M. (1995). The power of friendship groups: Teacher research as a critical literacy project for urban students. In J. E. Brophy (Ed.), *Advances in research on teaching* (Vol. 5, pp. 167–193). Greenwich, CT: JAI Press.

Hollingsworth, S., Dybdahl, M., & Minarik, L. (1993). By chart and chance and passion: Learning to teach through relational knowing. *Curriculum Inquiry, 23*(1), 5–36.

Hollingsworth, S., & Minarik, L. M. (1992, November). *The role of collaboration in educational reform.* Paper presented at the College of Teachers Teacher Education Forum, British Columbia, Canada.

Hollingsworth, S., Teel, K., & Minarik, L. (1990). *A teacher's story about modifying a literature-based approach to literacy to accommodate a young male's voice* (Institute for Research on Teaching Research Series No. 206). East Lansing: Michigan State University, Institute for Research on Teaching, Center for the Learning and Teaching of Elementary Subjects.

Hollingsworth, S., Teel, K., & Minarik, L. (1992). Listening for Aaron: A beginning teacher's story about literacy instruction in an urban classroom. *Journal of Teacher Education, 43*(2), 116–127.

Hyman, D. (2000). Do good stores make for good policy? *Journal of Health Politics, Policy & Law, 25*(66), 1149–1156.

Janesick, V. J. (2000). The choreography of qualitative research design: Minutes, improvisation and crystallization. In N. K. Denzin & Y. S. Lincoln (Eds.), *Handbook of qualitative research* (pp. 379–400). Thousand Oaks, CA: Sage.

Kalscheur, G. (1996). Law school as a culture of conversation: Re-Imagining legal education as a process of conversation to the demands of authentic conversation. *Loyola University Chicago Law School, 28,* 333–371.

Kolb, D. A. (1984). *Experiential learning: Experience as the source of learning and development.* Englewood Cliffs, NJ: Prentice Hall.

LaBoskey, V. K. (2006). "Reality check": Teachers lives as policy critique. *Teachers and Teaching: Theory and Practice, 12*(2), 111–122.

Labov, W. (1972). *Language in the inner city: Studies in the black English vernacular.* Philadelphia: University of Philadelphia Press.

Lather, P. (1991). *Getting smart: Feminist research and pedagogy within the postmodern.* New York: Routledge.

Leland, C., & Harste, J. (2005). Doing what we want to become: Preparing urban teachers. *Urban Education, 40*(1), 60–77.

Lewison, M., Seely Flint, A., & Van Shuys, K. (2002). Taking on critical literacy: The journey of new comers and novices. *Language Arts, 79*(5), 381–392.

Li, X. (2005). A Tao of narrative: Dynamic splicing of teacher stories. *Curriculum Inquiry, 35*(3), 339–365.

Lincoln, Y., & Guba, E. (1985). *Naturalistic inquiry.* Beverly Hills, CA: Sage.

Lonergan, B. J. F. (1973). *Insight: A study of human understanding.* London: Darton, Longman & Todd.

Lorde, A. (1984). *Sister outsider.* Freedom, CA: Crossing Press.

Luke, A., & Freebody, P. (1997). Shaping the social practices of reading. In S. Muspratt, A. Luke, & P. Freebody (Eds.), *Constructing critical literacies* (pp. 185–225). Cresskill, NJ: Hampton.

Luna, C., Bothelho, M. J., Fontaine, D., French, K., Iverson, K., & Matos, N. (2004). Making the road by walking and talking: Critical literacy and/as professional development in a teacher inquiry group. *Teacher Education Quarterly, 31*(1), 67–80.

Lyons, N. (1990). Dilemmas of knowing: Ethical and epistemological dimensions of teachers' work and development. *Harvard Educational Review, 60,* 159–180.

Lyons, N. (1993). Constructing narratives for understanding: Using portfolio interviews to structure teachers' professional development. *Yearbook (Claremont Reading Conference), 3,* 1–17.

McCormack, C. (2004). Storying stories: A narrative approach to in-depth interview conversations. *International Journal of Social Research Methodology, 7*(3), 219–236.

McIntyre, A. (1997). *Making meaning of whiteness.* New York: State University of New York Press.

McLeod, J., & Yates, L. (1997). Can we find out about boys and girls today, or must we just settle for talking about ourselves? Dilemmas of a feminist, qualitative longitudinal research project. *Australian Education Researcher, 24*(3), 23–42.

McVee, M. B. (2005). Revisiting the black Jesus: Re-emplotting a narrative through multiple retellings. *Narrative Inquiry, 15*(1), 161–195.

Mink, L. O. (1987). Narrative form as cognitive instrument. In B. Fay, E. O. Golob, & R. T. Vann (Eds.), *Historical understanding* (pp. 182–203). Ithaca, NY: Cornell University Press.

Mishler, E. G. (1995). Models of narrative analysis: A topology. *Journal of Narrative and Life History, 5,* 87–123.

Morris, A., & Maxwell, G. (Eds.). (2001). *Restorative justice for juveniles: Conferencing, mediation and circles.* Oxford, UK: Hart.

Moss, J. (2002). Inclusive schooling: Representation and textual practice. *International Journal of Inclusive Education, 6*(3), 231–249.

Muller, J. (1999). Narrative approaches to qualitative research in primary care. In B. Crabtree & W. Miller (Eds.), *Doing qualitative research* (2nd ed., pp. 221–238). Thousand Oaks, CA: Sage.

Natapoff, A. (2005, April). *Speechless: The silencing of criminal defendants* (Legal Studies Paper No. 2005–12). Berkeley: University of California Press.

Nias, J. (1984). The definition and maintenance of self in primary teaching. *British Journal of Sociology of Education, 5*(3), 267–280.

Noddings, N. (1991). Stories in dialogue: Caring and interpersonal reasoning. In C. Witherell & N. Noddings (Eds.), *Stories lives tell: Narrative and dialogue in education* (pp. 32–69). New York: Teachers College Press.

Oakley, A. (1981). Interviewing women: A contradiction in terms. In H. Roberts (Ed.), *Doing feminist research* (pp. 30–61). London: Routledge.

Obidah, J., & Teel, K. M. (2000). Because of the kids: Facing racial and cultural differences in urban schools. New York: Teachers College Press.

O'Bryan, B. (1999). The development of one teacher's skills at instructional conversation. *Reading Horizons, 34*(4), 257–278.

Olson, M., & Craig, C. (2001). Opportunities and challenges in the development of teachers' knowledge: The development of narrative authority through knowledge communities. *Teaching and Teacher Education, 17*(6), 667–684.

Parry, A. (1991). A universe of stories. *Family Process, 30,* 37–54.

Phillips, D. C., & Burbules, N. C. (2000). *Postpositivism and educational research.* Lanham, MD: Rowman & Littlefield.

Polanyi, I. (1985). *Telling the American story: A structural and cultural analysis of conversational storytelling.* Norwood, NJ: Ablex.

Polkinghorne, D. E. (1991). Narrative and self-concept. *Journal of Narrative and Life History, 1*(2, 3), 135–153.

Polkinghorne, D. E. (1995). Narrative configuration in qualitative analysis. Narrative configuration in qualitative analysis. *Qualitative Studies in Education, 8*(1), 5–23.

Pomerantz, F. (1998, December). *What do students learn from classroom discussions? The effects of instructional conversations on college students' learning.* Paper presented at the annual meeting of the American Educational Research Association, Austin, TX.

Ramirez, A. Y. F. (2003). Dismay and disappointment: Parental involvement of Latino immigrant parents. *The Urban Review, 35*(2), 93–110.

Reinharz, S. (1992). *Feminist methods in social research.* New York: Oxford Press.

Rhode, D. (2001). *Balanced lives: Changing the culture of legal practice.* Chicago: American Bar Association, Commission on Women in the Profession.

Ricoeur, P. (1991). *From text to action: Essays in hermeneutics II.* London: Athlone Press.

Riessman, C. K. (1993). *Narrative analysis.* Newbury Park, CA: Sage.

Riessman, C. K., & Quinney, L. (2005). Narrative in social work: A critical review. *Qualitative Social Work, 4*(4), 391–412.

Roberts, H. (1981). *Doing feminist research.* London: Routledge.

Rogan, A. I., & de Kock, D. M. (2005). Chronicles from the classroom: Making sense of the methodology and methods of narrative analysis. *Qualitative Inquiry, 11*(4), 628–649.

Rogers, C. (1980). *A way of being.* Boston: Houghton Mifflin.

Roskos, K. A., Boehlen, S., & Walker, B. J. (2000). Learning the art of instructional conversation: The influence of self-assessment on teachers' instructional discourse in a reading clinic. *Elementary School Journal, 100*(3), 229–252.

Schaef, A. W. (1981). *Women's reality: An emerging female system in a white male society.* San Francisco: Harper & Row.

Shenhav, S. R. (2005). Thin and thick narrative analysis: On the question of defining and analyzing political narratives. *Narrative Inquiry, 15*(1), 75–99.

Sims, R. (2004). Business ethics teaching: Using conversational learning to build an effective classroom learning environment. *Journal of Business Ethics, 49*(1), 201–211.

Smith, D. E. (1991). *The everyday world as problematic: A feminist sociology.* Toronto, Canada: University of Toronto Press.

Stanley, L., & Weis, S. (1983). *Breaking out: Feminist consciousness and feminist research.* London: Routledge.

Tannen, D. (1989). *Talking voices: Repetition, dialogue and imagery in conversational discourse.* New York: Cambridge University Press.

Tzu, L. (1990). *Tao teaching* (V. H. Mair, Trans.). New York: Bantam Books.

Van Manen, M. (1998). *Researching lived experience.* Toronto, Canada: Althouse Press.

Vygotsky, Leo. (1978). *Thought and language.* Cambridge: MIT Press.

Walker, M. (2003, March). *The democratic potential of narrative in educational research and pedagogy: The case of Antjie Krog's country of my skull.* Paper presented at the University of Pretoria Education Faculty Monthly Seminar, Pretoria, South Africa.

Walker, M. (2005). Rainbow nation or new racism? Theorizing race and identify formation in South African higher education. *Race, Ethnicity, and Education, 8*(2), 129–146.

Winslade, J., Drewery, W., & Hooper, S. (2000). *Restorative conferencing in schools: Draft manual.* Wellington, South Africa: Ministry of Education.

Yates, L. (2001). Negotiating methodological dilemmas in a range of chilly climates: A story of pressures, principles and problems. *Asia Pacific Journal of Teacher Education, 29*(2), 187–196.

Zeichner, K., & Gore, J. (1989). Teacher socialization. In W. R. Houston, M. Haberman, & J. Sikula (Eds.), *Handbook of research on teacher education* (pp. 345–379). New York: Macmillan.

Zurawski, C. (2004). Talk is NOT cheap. *The Canadian Manager, 29*(2), 20–24.

CHAPTER 7

Charting the Life Story's Path

Narrative Identity Across the Life Span

Jenna Baddeley and Jefferson A. Singer

Erik Erikson (1959, 1963, 1968, 1982), more than any of the great pioneers in personality psychology, understood that the construction of a coherent and purposeful self-concept, or what he called *identity,* is a *psychosocial* process. The individual, a conflux of psychological and biological processes, is embedded in a sociocultural context. Only through the process of "triple bookkeeping" (Erikson, 1963, p. 46), an analysis of biological, psychological, and social dimensions of the individual, might we come to a comprehensive and meaningful understanding of a given person's identity. According to Erikson (1963), we gain access to this understanding by studying how individuals move through "crises" that accompany eight distinct phases of the human life cycle from birth to death. Despite certain dated assumptions about sexuality and gender roles (Josselson, 1996), the enduring legacy of Erikson's work is his emphasis on the psychosocial struggle for self-understanding and self-development in a life over time.

In the 1980s, building on recent developments in the study of narrative as both a mode of thought and a method of psychological investigation (Bruner, 1986; Polkinghorne, 1988; Sarbin, 1986; Spence, 1982; Tomkins, 1979), Dan McAdams offered a major extension of Erikson's work on identity. McAdams's (1987, 1988, 1990) life story theory of identity argued that the coherent, albeit often complex, narrative that we forge of our life experiences is in fact our identity. This life story is not simply an expression of the underlying construct of identity, but it is *the* fundamental way in which we know ourselves and to a large extent are known by others. In keeping with Erikson's psychosocial emphasis, McAdams argued that the stories we create of our lives are forged from the available repertoire of cultural myths, images, symbols, settings, and plotlines that we learn from family, community, literature, art, and media.

Singer (2004b) noted a variety of research in personality, clinical, and cognitive psychology that bears the influence of McAdams's life story theory of identity. He suggested that a new generation of researchers was converging around the concept of *narrative identity*. These narrative identity researchers share certain common principles, including an emphasis on cognitive models of autobiographical memory, a commitment to the study of sociocultural factors in identity, the adoption of a life span developmental perspective, and an openness to multimethod forms of investigation.

This chapter reviews the innovative methods employed by these narrative researchers in the service of understanding how identity develops and changes over the life course. By documenting the psychosocial construction of narratives at different developmental junctures, the chapter also demonstrates how narrative research is an ideal vehicle for illustrating the inherent tension between self and society that Erikson and later McAdams understood to be the essence of identity. Narrative research is examined from the following periods of the life cycle: birth, childhood, adolescence, young adulthood, middle adulthood, and older adulthood. Across these life span periods, social influences on narrative range from the most intimate interpersonal influences to community, institutional, and political pressures.

From birth to death, individuals struggle to define a unique self while simultaneously drawing on social influences that provide much of its raw material and often play a sculpting hand in its expression. Narrative research documents how parents, peers, and intimate partners in combination with societal scripts and templates guide individuals' life stories in certain normative directions. At the same time, individuals give familiar cultural tales a fresh voice filtered through their idiosyncratic life experience and personal memory. Despite this strong current of individuation, personal stories are inevitably relinquished at death and become legacies, merged with other similar stories, which belong to surviving generations and a larger historical record. As this chapter reviews narrative methods that help to chart the progress of the life story across the life span, we specifically highlight these social and developmental factors that influence narrative formation and expression.

The development of a healthy narrative identity leads individuals, as Erikson noted in the eighth and final stage of his theory, to a capacity for reflection and review. As individuals continually revise their life stories over the life span, they are not simply narrators but critics who apply an interpretive knowledge and accumulated wisdom about the narratives that they share. One other important theme of the application of narrative methods to the study of identity over the life span is to look for evidence of what Bluck and Habermas (2001) call *autobiographical reasoning*—the capacity of individuals to step back and draw inferences and lessons from the stories they tell of their lives.

Birth

The tension between self and other in narrative identity is present at our origins. The moment the umbilical cord is cut, we assume our separate identity in the world. Yet while our life story begins with our birth, our birth story does not begin as our own. We hear our birth story, perhaps multiple times over the years, before we can tell it as our own story. Accordingly, our literal first moments of existence as separate entities in the world are invariably defined through stories told by others.

To examine how these inherited birth stories might contribute to later narrative identity, Hayden, Singer, and Chrisler (in press) studied the sharing of birth stories between mothers and daughters and the relationship of this sharing to the daughters' self-esteem and attachment to their mothers. Sixty-one female college students gave written narratives of their own birth stories, indicating whether they had heard the story many times, a few times, or never. Thirty-three of these students' mothers agreed to participate as well. Each gave a narrative account of her daughter's birth and indicated the frequency with which she had shared this story with her daughter.

An innovation in this study was the use of raters, blind to the identity of mothers and daughters, who attempted to match the mothers' stories with their daughters' stories. Daughters whose stories were judged most similar to their mothers' stories of the same event and daughters who had heard their birth stories more times demonstrated higher self-esteem and indicated closer relationships with their mothers.

Furthermore, a high level of positive affect and detail in the mothers' and the daughters' stories was also linked to high self-esteem in daughters and to strong mother-daughter attachment. Although this study could not assess causal relationships between mothers' positively toned stories and daughters' positively toned stories and daughters' positive self-image, the results illustrated that these birth stories, despite their secondhand origins, had been incorporated into these young adults' self-concept. These findings highlight the idea that as individuals slowly assemble the narrative components that will become their comprehensive life story, their story commences with a self-conception that was initially mediated by the consciousness and language of others. With the emergence of their own words, toddlers begin to develop a coherent private consciousness along with the means to narrate the thoughts, feelings, and activities of their nascent self. When this process begins, narrative identity is no longer constructed in the "third person" but becomes a "first-person" account of individuals' unique autobiographical memories. Shifting gradually from reliance on parents as their amanuensis, individuals learn to tell their own stories (Nelson & Fivush, 2004).

Childhood

Much of the early development of autobiographical memory occurs within parent-child conversations about the shared personal past, also known as joint reminiscing (Fivush & Hudson, as cited in Nelson & Fivush, 2000). Joint reminiscing begins as soon as children begin to talk, at around 12 to 18 months of age (Haden, 2003).

It is not until the age of 3 or 4 that a child begins to initiate reminiscence talk and make independent contributions. By the age of 5 or 6, a child has begun to influence her mother's reminiscing style, even as the mother influences the child's reminiscing style (Reese & Farrant, 2003). Although the ability to produce single-episode autobiographical memories emerges in childhood, the ability to integrate autobiographical memories into an extended life story does not fully emerge until adolescence (Habermas & Bluck, 2000).

Research into the development of children's narrative skills in the context of joint reminiscing is frequently done longitudinally, so that researchers can determine predictive factors that influence the emerging story. Farrant and Reese (2000) observed the interactions of mother-child pairs at four different points in time (19, 25, 32, and 40 months) over a 1-year period. At all points, the mothers talked about selected past events with their children. These conversations took place in the participants' homes and were audiotaped, videotaped, and transcribed verbatim. The tapes and transcripts were coded for three types of behaviors: mothers' memory elaboration questions, children's memory elaborations (new information provided by the child), and children's placeholders (child taking a turn in the conversation but not offering new content).

This research found that starting at about 25 months of age children begin to influence their mothers' engagement in reminiscing conversations. Children contribute to joint reminiscing in small ways, either through articulating events and details that they remember (children's memory elaborations) or just through indicating interest and engagement in the conversation without contributing anything of substance (placeholders). However, none of these contributions has as much predictive weight as the guiding maternal contribution (mothers' memory elaboration questions) (Farrant & Reese, 2000; McCabe & Peterson, 1991; Reese & Fivush, 1993).

The "elaborativeness" of a mother's reminiscing style in conversations with her young child is a major determinant of that child's future capability for generating detailed autobiographical memories (Peterson, Jesso, & McCabe, 1999). Elaborative mothers provide detailed questions to elicit their children's recollections of the event under discussion, and they are responsive to new and unexpected input from the child. In the course of a conversation between an elaborative mother and her child, the pair talks about an event in depth and detail. Here is an example in which an elaborative mother discusses a treasure hunt with her 3-year-old:

Mother: There was [sic] a whole lot of people at the beach, and everyone was doing something in the sand.

Child: What was it?

Mother: Can't you remember what we did in the sand? We were looking for something.

Child: Umm, I don't know.

Mother: We went digging in the sand.

Child: Umm, and that was when um the yellow spade broke.

Mother: Good girl, I'd forgotten that. Yes, the yellow spade broke, and what happened?

Child: Um, we had to um dig with the other end of the yellow one.

Mother: That's right. We used the broken bit, didn't we?

Child: Yeah. (Fivush & Reese, 2002, pp. 111–112)

In joint reminiscing, parents model for their children how to tell stories of events in the personal past—what elements to include, delete, and emphasize. The nature and implicit aims of joint reminiscing are significantly shaped by cultural values. Gender roles prescribe male-female differences, and parents begin to construct those differences in joint reminiscing. Mothers and fathers alike discuss the personal past more elaborately with daughters than with sons. Girls report more detailed memories than boys from as young as 3 years of age, a gender difference that persists into adulthood (Farrant & Reese, 2000; Reese & Fivush, 1993). In joint reminiscing, parents are preparing their children to be the bearers of their culture's and their family's stories.

Joint reminiscing differs in significant ways across cultures. European American parents tend to use a child-centered and highly elaborative style of reminiscing, thereby teaching children how to be the kinds of individual and unique selves valued in this society (Leichtman, Wang, & Pillemer, 2003; Wang, 2004). Chinese parents, in contrast, use a didactic, hierarchically organized and low-elaborative approach to reminiscing with their children, promoting in children an understanding that the self's place is within a larger social order (Wang, 2004).

The audiotaping, transcription, and coding of parent-child conversations about narrative memory highlight how narrative methodology can indeed capture the subtle negotiation process between self and social influence that Erikson saw as the crucible of identity. The addition of longitudinal and cross-cultural samples provides further evidence for the multiple contributions of social factors to individuals' emerging narrative identity.

Even as children provide more independent autobiographical memories, parents and the surrounding society by and large shape the memory structure and content that forms the initial groundwork of these recollections. Because the capacity of children to narrate their lives is dependent on their parents' style of eliciting these narratives from them in joint reminiscing, children cannot yet be considered independent narrators.

One might employ the following analogy: In the kinds of theatrical dramas that were presented before Shakespeare's development of protagonists with interior psychological lives, characterization relied on convention, simple moral lessons, and rigidly defined parts. In a similar way, children are initially guided to construct stories that correspond to societal molds. Although they have become clearly identified characters with their own lines, they are not in the fullest sense speaking their own minds. However, as they continue to gain cognitive sophistication and accumulate idiosyncratic experiences with the world, children grow into adolescents who increasingly learn to tell a unique narrative that draws on an interior world and expands on as well as conforms to conventional molds.

Adolescence

The social and cognitive changes that occur in adolescence herald an opportunity for adolescents to begin to narrate the story of their own lives. By the end of childhood, individuals have learned how to tell stories, but it is not until adolescence that they learn how to organize memories and other self-relevant information coherently into a life story (Habermas & Bluck, 2000). It is through the creation of a life story that adolescents begin to tackle what Erikson (1968) considered the major psychosocial task of their life stage: the exploration and formation of a mature identity (Bluck & Habermas, 2001). Established in adolescence, this narrative identity evolves over the course of adulthood, reflecting the person's changing concerns, roles, priorities, and self-conceptions (Singer, 2004b).

The basic form of the life story is shaped by the powerful cultural influences that define the normative course of an autobiography. Autobiographical reasoning, the process by which the life story is constructed and applied, relies on the ability to understand and to produce coherent narratives. Habermas and Bluck (2000) identified four types of story coherence. Two of these types of coherence, *temporal coherence* and the *cultural concept of biography,* are social conventions for organizing narrative information. Temporal coherence is the ability to chronologically organize events that have occurred over an extended period of time (Habermas & Bluck, 2000). In one study (Friedman, 1992, as cited in Habermas & Bluck, 2000), 4-, 6-, and 8-year-olds could all accurately remember in which order the events of yesterday, last weekend, and last summer happened; however, only 8-year-olds could accurately recall the order of four annually occurring events such as Christmases or birthdays.

An understanding of the cultural concept of biography entails a grasp not only of the normative sequence of life phases or events (e.g., starting school comes before one's first job, which comes before retirement) but also of the kind of information that is and is not appropriate to include in the life story (Habermas & Bluck, 2000). In one study (Strube et al., 1985, as cited in Habermas & Bluck, 2000), preadolescent (11 years old), adolescent (19 years old), and adult (35–40 years old) participants selected normative life events from a possible array and organized these events into a probable chronological sequence. The preadolescents' ordering of the events deviated slightly from a strictly normative course; the adolescents' sequences of events adhered tightly to a normative course; and the adults' sequences of events again showed some variation from the expected sequence. These findings suggest that adolescents hold a stereotyped concept of the normative life course, whereas adults have more flexible concepts of how life unfolds. On the other hand, it is a testament to the power of cultural scripts that none of the groups' sequences varied widely from the normative life script.

Cultural scripts influence not just the ways we live our lives but also the ways that we remember and feel about our pasts. For example, Rubin and Berntsen (2003), in a study of the phenomenon known as the *reminiscence bump,* found that individuals recall the majority of their positive memories as having happened in their adolescent and young adult years. Berntsen and Rubin (2004) demonstrated that life scripts provide a compelling explanation for this phenomenon. They asked some of their participants to estimate the ages at which the happiest, saddest, most important, and most traumatic events would occur for the typical person and the ages at which the typical person would feel most in love and most afraid. The same bump was present in people's accounts of the distribution of negative and positive memories in the typical life and in people's accounts of negative and positive events in their own lives. An explanation for this bump in the scripts and in people's lives is that many events that are considered significant and positive in our culture occur in young adulthood or late adolescence, for example, falling in love for the first time, finishing one's education, getting a first job, getting married, having a first child. Negative events, in contrast, do not fit so clearly into cultural scripts.

The life story does not attain all its coherence from adherence to culturally pre-scribed event sequences. Social expectations for a story to be coherent do, however, prescribe that an individual must recognize and explain moments of discontinuity in her life story. Disparate events can be held together by *causal coherence* and *thematic coherence.* Causal coherence explains individual episodes in the life story by drawing links between these episodes or by connecting episodes to personal beliefs, traits, and preferences. For example, an adolescent might offer as an explanation of her fear of dogs an account of a time when she, as a young child, had been bitten by a dog, or she might link her victory at her school's swim meet to the love of swimming she developed as a child or to memories of being recognized for earlier athletic achievements.

Thematic coherence pulls together multiple episodes of the life story under the auspices of an overarching value or principle. This is perhaps the most sophisticated form of coherence—it requires the ability to summarize and interpret and synthe-size multiple episodes from one's life story. Themes that might run through a per-son's life include valuing and manifesting kindness to others, adhering to the principles of one's religion, and facing the continual disappointment of one's hopes.

Adolescents not only have the sociocognitive skills to form a life story, they also have the motivation to create one. Friends, family, and institutions expect adolescents to give coherent accounts of themselves to explain themselves in terms of their past and to anticipate their future (Habermas & Bluck, 2000). For example, adolescents are asked to write personal statements for college admission or to give accounts of their interests and activities during job interviews. School assignments may ask them to write about the family traditions, religious ceremonies, and cultural practices that have been meaningful in their lives and to express their personal reflections on their own experiences in relation to the academic material they are learning.

Elkind (1967) also posited a central role for social influences in the develop-ment of the adolescent's narrative identity. For Elkind, though, instead of promoting the construction of a new life story out of existing autobiographical memories, social pressures encourage the adolescent to modify an existing narrative of the self, the "personal fable" or private, internal story about the adolescent and his special qualities, into a more realistic form. The egocentric personal fable is, according to Elkind (1967), developed for an "imaginary audience," an audience who finds everything about the adolescent important, special, and unique and for whom the adolescent can spin anticipatory tales of glorious struggles and accomplishments. The sharing of personal stories within the context of intimate relationships begins the process wherein the imaginary audience is modified in the direction of the real audience and the personal story begins to resemble more closely the ways in which others perceive the adolescent.

Thorne (2000) emphasized the pivotal role of friends and family members to whom the adolescent tells his personal stories in the shaping of his life story. She argued that self-telling happens more often in adolescence and early adulthood than at other times in the life cycle, as do the kinds of highly emotional events that are most likely to be recounted. Thorne, Cutting, and Skaw (1998) found that the basic *plotlines* of personal stories tend to remain constant over time. On the other hand, the *meanings* of personal stories shift over time. In conversations with others, the meanings of personal stories are negotiated and reconstructed.

Having outlined the sociocognitive developments in adolescence that prepare individuals to craft an initial life story of identity, let us turn to the narrative methods researchers employ to track this emerging narrative capacity. Several studies have examined adolescents' identity development through looking at adolescents' representations of parental voices within autobiographical narratives (Arnold, Pratt, & Hicks, 2004). During an interview, each participant was asked to tell a story on one of the following topics: a value lesson learned from their parents, a difficult decision made with parental help, an influential experience. Raters coded each narrative as a whole on a five-point scale for the degree to which the parental voice is "assimilated within" versus "detached from" the adolescent's voice. On the low end of the scale, the parental voice is absent or summarily dismissed; on the high end, the parent's voice has been assimilated and rearticulated in the adolescent's own terms. Adolescent participants also completed measures of self-esteem, dispositional optimism, depression, and loneliness.

Adolescents who had assimilated and internalized parental teachings had higher concurrent self-esteem and optimism and were less lonely and depressed. Longitudinal studies showed that over the 4-year time span from age 16 to 20, adolescents who had assimilated parental voices in their narratives at age 16 had increased in self-esteem and decreased in loneliness by age 20. The 16-year-olds who had assimilated the parental voice also displayed a greater sense of social responsibility at age 20 (Arnold et al., 2004).

The most common way in which adolescent and young adult narrative memories have been studied is through the collection of "self-defining memories" (Blagov & Singer, 2004; McLean, 2005; McLean & Thorne, 2003; Moffitt & Singer, 1994; Singer & Moffitt, 1991–1992; Singer & Salovey, 1993; Sutin & Robins, 2005; Thorne & McLean, 2002; Thorne, McLean, & Lawrence, 2004; Wood & Conway, 2006). Self-defining memories are a particular type of autobiographical memory. They are highly significant personal memor[ies] that . . . evoke strong emotion, [are] vivid in the mind's eye, and to which we return repeatedly . . . [they] revolve around the most important concerns and conflicts in our lives: unrequited loves, sibling rivalries, our greatest successes and failures, our moments of insight, and our severest disillusionments. (Singer, 2004a, p. 195)

In these studies, individuals receive a request to write down narrative memories that fit these emotional and thematic criteria. Generally participants are asked to write down anywhere from 3 to 10 memories. After recording the memories, participants rate the memories for their current emotional responses, as well as the memories' vividness and importance. Reliable and validated scoring manuals (Singer & Blagov, 2002; Thorne & McLean, 2001) have been developed for coding the memories for narrative structure, meaning making, and thematic content. The memories can also be coded for motivational themes, such as agency and communion (McAdams, 2002).

Studies of self-defining memories have demonstrated that adolescents and young adults do indeed accumulate autobiographical memories that pertain to their most important ongoing goals (Moffitt & Singer, 1994) and that reflect relatively stable features of their personality (Sutin & Robins, 2005). In addition, these memories are recruited in efforts at meaning making that highlight the role of narrative memory in self-understanding and healthy adjustment (Blagov & Singer, 2004; McLean, 2005; Thorne et al., 2004).

As adolescents and young adults fashion their incipient life stories from the raw material of self-defining memories, they are simultaneously telling these memories to audiences of family, friends, and newly made acquaintances. Pasupathi (2003) investigated the effects of telling others about emotional experiences on one's own feelings about these events. Specifically, she looked at whether and under what circumstances telling an emotional experience helps a person feel better. Participants in her study wrote two narratives: (1) a narrative of the original experience and (2) a narrative of a time they told another person about the event. They rated each account on the extent to which it elicited each of 8 positive emotions (happiness, joy, contentment, excitement, pride, accomplishment, interest, and amusement) and 11 negative emotions (anger, sadness, fear, disgust, guilt, embarrassment, shame, anxiety, irritation, frustration, and boredom). Participants also selected the two motivations that were most important to them from a list of possible motivations for retelling the story and answered questions about their listener's responsiveness and the extent to which the listener agreed with the teller's version of events. A motivation to feel better was associated with decreases in negative emotion over time, and a high level of listener agreement was associated with an increase in positive emotions and a decrease in negative emotions over time (Pasupathi, 2003). That one's feelings about a remembered event are shaped by others' responses highlights the importance of social influences in the continual formation of our internalized life story. Clearly, adolescents and young adults engaged in the fragile enterprise of defining an independent narrative identity are likely to be particularly prone to these interpersonal influences on the memories they share.

Not only do others influence the stories we tell, the stories we tell also power-fully shape others' impressions of us. If we care how others perceive us, we are likely to be motivated to control what our stories convey. One way in which people can control the meanings that others hear in their stories is through "positioning" themselves in socially acceptable ways vis-à-vis their narratives. In a study of late adolescents' self-defining memories of life-threatening events, Thorne and McLean (2003) found that the bulk of their participants fit into one of just three positions in telling these emotionally charged narratives: the "Florence Nightingale" position of displaying empathy and concern for others; the "John Wayne" position of courage or bravery in the face of adverse events; and the "vulnerability" position of preoccupation with one's own fear or sadness. Of these three positions, the first two were more often accepted than rejected by listeners. The vulnerability position, on the other hand, met with rejection more than half the time. This suggests that there are a handful of dominant, broadly acceptable scripts or "master narratives" for how to relate traumatic events (e.g., the Florence Nightingale or John Wayne script) and that if one is motivated to secure listener approval, one will likely adopt one of these more widely acceptable positions.

In considering the social factors that coalesce to influence the adolescent's emerging narrative identity, one should not lose sight of the developmental jour-ney that is only beginning with this initial effort at a life story. During adolescence or at any point during adulthood, we may reconfigure the narrative trajectory on which we had launched ourselves. Josselson (1996) studied college-age women during the first leg of a longitudinal study of women's identity development from college to midlife. When she first interviewed these women in their late adoles-cence, she used two different interview protocols. The first was an interview proto-col that elicited the participants' and their parents' views and practices within four domains: occupation, religion, politics, and sexual values and standards. She also used a "personal history interview," with questions that allowed the participants to articulate the kinds of ideas, dreams, and values that were most salient to them rather than to give their views on an issue that the experimenter had chosen.

Josselson's (1996) participants were having a new kind of experience—they were the first generation of women to have had the broad range of opportunities from which women have benefited since the feminist revolution. Their lives did not fol-low the patterns of the male lives that had served as the basis for Erikson's identity theory and other related identity frameworks. She grouped the late adolescents into four categories, according to whether they had searched for an identity and whether they had chosen one. The "guardians" had settled on an established iden-tity already, usually the one that their parents had envisioned for them. The "path-makers" had searched for and found an identity and a set of values different from those with which they had grown up. The "searchers" were still earnestly exploring different possible life paths. The "drifters" had not settled on an identity nor were they actively searching for one.

Josselson (1996) explored how these women's identity making process in late adolescence affected their stories at midlife. Those women who had been perfec-tionistic and tightly self-controlled at the end of college began to be able to admit their imperfections and become more open to their own feelings and experiences. For example, one woman who had been very career oriented since college launched into a period of exploration of herself and her sexuality in midlife, when her husband of many years (he had been her college boyfriend) divorced her. Women who had been less certain of their identities and direction at the end of college ended up in midlife seeking and often finding structures with which to anchor their lives.

For Josselson (1996), these women's stories were shaped by their desires, inchoate as they often were, to "be someone" or to "do something" with their lives. The articulation and realization of this desire in women's lives may be on a timetable different from that in men's lives and may take different forms at different times. Ultimately, many of the changes in women's identity over the life course are not so much about introducing new elements into identity as discovering old ones that had been overlooked. Josselson (1996) wrote, "Like slowly turning kaleidoscopes, the shifts in a woman's identity involve rearrangement of pieces, now accenting one aspect and muting another, now altering the arrangement once more" (p. 243). Although the fundamental pieces may be identified in adolescence, they are unlikely to maintain the same configuration over the ensuing decades.

Young Adulthood

In Erikson's model, as late adolescents grow into adults in their midtwenties and thirties, they have forged a working identity and are ready to pursue mature intimacy, a step that begins a new chapter in the life story. Self-disclosing discussions in which two people share and respond to each other's highly detailed and emotional memories foster and maintain intimacy (Alea & Bluck, 2003). In some sense, this intensive exchange of stories facilitates the process by which the partners begin to negotiate a shared identity. As Bridges (1980, as cited in Randall, 2001) put it, "to become a couple is to agree implicitly to live in terms of another person's story" (p. 71). Thus, a shared identity is also a shared and co-constructed narrative. Within established relationships such as marriages, partners continue to build, revise, and reinforce a mutually understood set of values and meaning systems "as [they] carry on the endless conversation that feeds on nearly all they individually or jointly experience" (Berger & Kellner, 1964, pp. 13–14). Increasingly, narrative researchers are realizing that an emphasis on individuals' personal life stories may overlook these shared stories and understandings, which reflect the interdependent dimension of adult identity.

Couples' stories of intimacy are unique on the one hand and on the other hand heavily shaped by cultural scripts. In our culture, the choice of an intimate partner is deeply reflective of the individual personality: we often choose partners who balance out our personalities, mesh with our styles of interacting, and who form the complementary part of our story (Belove, 1980). On the other hand, we have been learning since we were children about the expected plotline of romance. Cultural scripts for romance appear all over—in nursery rhymes and popular ditties, in books, and on television programs. When both the authors were growing up, they used to hear (and sing) the following rhyme: "____ and ____, sitting in a tree, k-i-s-s-i-n-g. First comes love, then comes marriage, then comes the baby in the baby carriage." This rhyme encapsulates the bare bones of our culture's dominant relationship script, which consists of three consecutive elements: (1) heterosexual love, (2) marriage, and (3) children.

Gergen and Gergen (1995) have explored this romantic script as it has evolved historically in our culture. They have identified two opposing discourses of love that inform our enactment and narration of courtship: romantic love and modernist love. Romantic love is an intense, spiritual passion that reason cannot touch, that emanates from the lover's innermost depths, and whose ultimate goal is unity with the beloved. Modernist love is practical and skeptical, rational and self-analytical. It emphasizes the exchange value and performative qualities of relationships. Compatible with a culture of consumerism, romantic relationships are one form of life choice or self-expression that we can select or reject. The cultural relativism of our post-modern era makes these and other discourses available for us to sample, albeit with an ironic attitude, as we enact emotional scenarios within our relationships.

Despite this putative freedom to choose, we remain actors in romances that have been played out over and over again, with variations, by many people in our culture (Scheibe, 2000). Popular culture certainly reinforces traditional romantic plots. Wedding ceremonies and high school proms are among the most elaborately scripted events in our culture. Popular music is dominated by the clichés of love songs, and St. Valentine's Day holds a familiar niche in the national calendar of holidays.

More to the point of our concern with narrative identity, individuals' courtships and relationships not only follow cultural scripts, but the stories that they internalize are linked to cultural formulae about how to develop and maintain intimacy. Storytelling for this purpose becomes more frequent in young adulthood and beyond (Alea & Bluck, 2003). Memories that foster intimacy development and maintenance tend to be rich in detail and emotion (Tannen, 1990, as cited in Alea & Bluck, 2003). Women generally produce more of these types of memories (Alea & Bluck, 2003), and they reminisce more often than men for the purpose of maintaining intimacy in relationships.

Responsiveness affects how much intimacy is achieved when detailed, emotional autobiographical memories are told in conversation. Laurenceau, Barrett, and Pietromonaco (1998) asked participants to log their interactions for 7 days, during which they completed the Rochester Interaction Record after each of their daily interactions lasting more than 10 minutes, while rating the interaction for self-disclosure, partner disclosure, partner responsiveness, and intimacy. Participants who rated their partners higher in responsiveness experienced stronger intimacy in their interactions.

Wamboldt (1999) studied the process of couples' interactions in the co-construction of relationship narratives. Couples were interviewed jointly about their current relationship and the influence of their family of origin on the current relationship. Each interview was videotaped and then coded for several aspects of the couple's interaction. Couples who were more coordinated in their efforts at constructing their narrative were more satisfied with their current relationship; women who actively confirmed what their partner was saying were more satisfied with their relationship; and disconfirmation of one's partner's opinions was related to relationship instability. Thus, a couple's interaction pattern during the process of narrative co-construction is a valuable indicator of the quality of the relationship.

Interaction patterns within a romantic relationship are, in part, derived from the correspondence between the partners' implicit stories about the relationship. Sternberg (1998) takes the view that we all enter into romantic relationships hoping to live out our own unique preconscious ideal love story, which is influenced by life experience and cultural discourse. Romantic partners' long-term compatibility is largely based on the extent to which they have a shared understanding of the "story" they are enacting together. Sternberg, Hojjat, and Barnes (2001) proposed a list of 25 different story types based on analysis of love stories in literature, psychological research, and informally gathered case material. These stories range from the "horror story," in which one partner enjoys being taken charge of and terrorized by the other partner, while the other partner in turn likes to take charge and terrorize; to the "business story," in which the partners aspire for their relationship to operate like a well-run business, with each partner expected to perform his or her designated responsibilities; to the popular, romantic "fantasy story," in which one finds a perfect match and lives happily ever after.

Sternberg et al. (2001) developed a love story scale comprising several statements pertaining to each story type. Respondents read each statement and indicated on a Likert scale the extent to which the statement applied to their own view of and experience in romantic relationships. Couples who had been together for at least 1 year were recruited, and each partner completed a set of questionnaires, including a brief version of the love story scale along with a measure of relationship satisfaction. The results indicated that a higher degree of similarity between two partners' story types was associated with greater relationship satisfaction. Story type was related to relationship satisfaction, but only for maladaptive stories (e.g., the horror story), which were related to lower levels of relationship satisfaction. Thus, although adaptive stories may not ensure a good relationship, maladaptive stories may ensure a bad one (Sternberg et al., 2001).

In narrative couples therapy, the therapist helps clients to change their shared story by identifying the elements of personal and cultural stories that underlie the current, maladaptive story and to build a new story of the relationship that grows in strength as both members of the couple recruit previously overlooked memories from their past to support it (Zimmerman & Dickerson, 1993). Sometimes, a shared self-defining memory can symbolize the dominant story that is causing conflict within a couple's relationship and can be leveraged to "re-story" the relationship and resolve the conflict (Singer, 2004a).

In one example, a husband and wife remembered a car ride home from a facility at which the husband had been treated for alcohol abuse, a long-standing source of tension between his wife and him. After a lengthy treatment, the husband had felt ready to leave, but the wife had initially agreed with the psychiatrist's judgment that he should stay longer. During their car ride home, the wife (who was not usually expressive) reached out her hand to the husband and he pulled away. She then pulled away too and did not reach out again. In this series of gestures, they were each playing out separate, painful inner stories. For her, reaching out to him made her vulnerable, and his rebuff reawakened the familiar message that she had internalized from the loss of her father, who had died when she was 13: "Losses never heal and this gap will not close" (Singer, 2004a, p. 200). He, on the other hand, had pulled away out of fear. His sense of free will was vulnerable, and his wife's initial agreement with the authority (the psychiatrist) had dealt a blow to his autonomy, against which his most familiar defense was silence. Aside from drinking, mute withdrawal had been his previous primary weapon against oppressive and rigid authorities all his life (Singer, 2004a).

Both partners identified this moment and returned to it repeatedly as the starting point of a 17-year period in which they were never again physically intimate and remained emotionally distant from each other. The memory of this moment was indeed self-defining, symbolizing the rift between them. Toward the end of the husband's life, the couple sought psychotherapy and was able to revisit the memory through conversation and role playing. As they revisited the scene, they were gradually able to rewrite their story of disconnection as one of reconnection and affection.

Aside from the shared, couple-defining moments over the length of the relationship, couples usually have a shared story of their first encounter, which Belove (1980) called FECK (first encounters of the close kind) narratives. In most cases, according to Belove (1980), the members of a couple remember the same incident even when asked separately. Their tellings of the incident reflect their understanding of their complementary roles in the relationship, roles that they continue to play in their current relationship.

As mentioned earlier, women tend to remember and describe relationship events more clearly and vividly than their male partners do. Ross and Holmberg (1990) set up a study in which men and women would reminisce, either together or separately, about a preselected event from their relationship (a first date, for example), and then they each answered self-report questions about the clarity and vividness of their memory of the chosen event as well as their own and their spouse's ability to remember details of past events. The women were consistently rated higher on the clarity, vividness, and detail aspects of memory. Additionally, men were more likely to report forgetting aspects of the selected event when they recalled events in the presence of their female partners than when they recalled them alone, whereas women's recall was not significantly influenced by the presence of their partners. The evidence suggests that men tend to rely on their female partners to be the keepers of their shared interpersonal history (Ross & Holmberg, 1990).

So far we have focused our discussion of intimacy narratives on studies of heterosexual relationships. Western culture is still in the process of accepting homosexual relationships, let alone bringing stories of these relationships into mainstream culture (the recent phenomenon of the film *Brokeback Mountain*, which depicts two cowboys' tortured love for each other, is a case in point). However, narrative researchers have begun to explore and identify the varying ways in which homosexual men and women narrate their relationship stories. There even exists a cultural scheme for the expected elements of the gay or lesbian life story, including the order and the timing of these elements (Cohler & Galatzer-Levy, 2000). Cohler and Galatzer-Levy (2000) have also emphasized the impact of cohort effects, such as the unavailability of role models for gay men and lesbians during most of the last century, and sociohistorical events, such as the AIDS pandemic. These pervasive influences on gay lives shift their cultural scripts of intimacy. The use of gay participants' stories of relationships and self-discovery to illustrate these cohort effects once again demonstrates how narratives are a powerful methodological tool for tracking social contributions to individual identity. Stories of intimacy, whether heterosexual or homosexual, help to remind us of the relational dimension that defines most adults' self-understanding in their twenties and thirties. Analysis of these stories shows how each romantic relationship recombines existing cultural scripts in a way that is both derivative and unique.

Middle Adulthood

As individuals reach middle adulthood, they are likely to turn their focus to raising children or making meaningful professional and creative contributions or both. These generative actions and achievements lend a sense of purpose and meaning to adults' lives and are a means of forging a legacy of the self. Through generative tasks such as raising a family, identity also changes and grows. As Erikson (1982) proposed, generativity includes "a kind of self-generation concerned with further identity development" (p. 67).

Kotre (1999) identified four categories of generative behavior. One is biological, that is, bearing one's offspring. Another is parental, that is, raising children; another is technical, which refers to the teaching of skills and procedures; and the last is cultural, which has to do with creating, renovating, or maintaining—and ultimately passing on—a meaning system. The creation and passing on of life stories may be an integral part of generative activity in all these domains. Parents of young children frequently tell stories of their own childhood, serving the simultaneous functions of transmitting lessons about family and societal values to the children and developing and reconstructing the adults' own identities from the perspective of current parenting roles (Fiese, Hooker, Kotary, Schwagler, & Rimmer, 1995).

Psychobiography, the intensive study of individual lives and the developmental and psychological themes that run through them, has been a major method in the narrative study of generativity. Psychobiographical approaches range from intensive studies of one person whose life exemplifies generative accomplishment to studies of multiple people; data for psychobiographical research can include interviews with the subject, the subject's public or private creative output (art, music, writing), and biographies written by others about the subject (de St. Aubin, 1998).

Alexander (1990) contended that often psychobiographical studies were performed to demonstrate the way that a life fits either the Freudian or neo-Freudian (Eriksonian) theoretical framework. Two psychobiographical studies that investigate lives with reference to an Eriksonian framework, and in particular the Eriksonian construct of generativity, are discussed below.

De St. Aubin's (1998) study of American modernist architect Frank Lloyd Wright (1869–1959) was motivated by what Alexander (1990) considered a typical goal of psychobiographical inquiry: an attempt to "explain through appeal to psychological means the controversial or unexplained aspects of a subject's life experience" (p. 52). De St. Aubin (1998) explored Frank Lloyd Wright's generativity in different domains (fatherhood, mentorship, and architecture) and the development of his generativity over time, with special attention to the extremes of generativity that Frank Lloyd Wright embodied. On the one hand, Wright was a prolific and brilliant architect who transformed his discipline, and on the other hand he was a negligent and destructive father and teacher. De St. Aubin took as his sources of data biographies of Wright, including one written by a son and one by a former apprentice; Wright's autobiography; Wright's letters; tabloid reports; and Wright's architectural work.

Although de St. Aubin (1998) did not precisely articulate his research method, he did articulate the theoretical foundations of his conceptual process, the difficulties inherent in psychobiographical work, and some of his ways of dealing with these difficulties. Specifically, he mentioned the need to avoid pathologizing or idealizing, villainizing or deifying the subject; the need to try to encounter the subject as impartially as possible; and finally, the difficulty of using source materials (other biographies) that are subjective. He acknowledged that some of these difficulties, especially the third one, are insurmountable obstacles to full objectivity, which amounts to a disclosure that his product too will be somewhat subjective, although guided by reasoned, theoretically informed efforts at objectivity.

Peterson and Stewart (1990) employed psychobiographic methods to study longitudinally the psychosocial development of a single subject, Vera Brittain (1893–1970), from when she was 29 to when she was 54 years of age. Both World War I and World War II had directly affected Brittain's life, and the psychosocial themes reflected in her writings are strongly shaped by her sociopolitical context. Brittain became a pacifist on witnessing the devastation wrought by World War I, in which her fiancé, her brother, and two friends were killed, while she had served as a nurse to wounded soldiers. She passed on a generative legacy of pacifism in her novels and diaries, and these writings were Peterson and Stewart's (1990) data source.

Peterson and Stewart (1990) used the Stewart, Franz, and Layton (1984) coding manual (as cited in Peterson & Stewart, 1990) to analyze sections of Brittain's diaries and novels for psychosocial themes of identity, intimacy, and generativity. They analyzed randomly selected passages from each diary and novel. In all, they analyzed about 20 percent of each novel (29,753 words on average) and 10,000 words per year from the diaries. They coded the written material with meaningful phrases as the coding units. Analyses of the diaries and novels revealed an increase in generative concerns and a decrease in identity and intimacy themes over time. In this way, Brittain's psychosocial development was consistent with Erikson's idea that generativity increases over the course of adulthood.

However, analyses did not reveal a unitary concern with one generative agenda but a fluctuation over the adult years in her generative concerns: During the years in which she was gaining recognition for her writing, she largely expressed productivity themes; during the years of World War II, when she focused more on her children, she largely expressed themes of generative caring.

Surprisingly, identity concerns remained more prevalent throughout Brittain's adult years than either generativity or intimacy concerns. Peterson and Stewart (1990) offered several speculative explanations for this finding: Brittain's concern with identity may have been a function of her occupation, of her feminist awareness of her gender as a marginalizing factor, or of the social and political disruption she and others in her birth cohort faced as adolescents during World War I. In short, analyses of Brittain's written works revealed that her psychosocial development roughly followed Erikson's psychosocial stage theory, and yet it departed from the theory as well. In all phases of her life, her writings reflected not simply her personal voice but influences of sociopolitical and cultural forces that made her narrative emblematic of cultural trends as well as a highly distinctive life story.

Other researchers have used narrative methods to form a better picture of the elements that distinguish generative adults from less generative adults. McAdams, Hart, and Maruna (1998) discussed several studies that relied on intensive interviews conducted by McAdams and his colleagues with 40 generative and 30 less-generative adults. Members of the generative group were school teachers or community volunteers. The less-generative group was matched demographically with members of the generative group, but none of them taught or volunteered in the community. The generative group had higher scores compared with the less-generative group on the Loyola Generativity Scale (a measure of generativity concern) and the Generative Behavior Checklist (a measure of generative action).

Researchers conducted a 2-hour interview with each participant using McAdams's life story protocol, which elicits from participants an outline of the major chapters in their life stories and detailed descriptions of eight scenes in their life stories, including a high point, a low point, a turning point, and the earliest memory. Participants also described important people, values, beliefs, and the major theme from their lives. These interviews were tape-recorded, transcribed, and reliably coded for themes of agency (self-mastery, achievement, status, and empowerment) and communion (love, friendship, dialogue, communication, caring for others, feelings of community). Generative adults' stories contained more themes of communion than did less-generative adults' stories; however, the two groups did not differ in their inclusion of themes of agency.

Most interestingly, generative and less-generative adults did not differ in terms of the range or type of emotion expressed in their stories but did so in terms of the basic emotional sequences that the events in their stories tended to follow (i.e., good to bad or bad to good). Compared with the stories of less-generative adults, the stories of highly generative adults contained more "redemption sequences," in which a bad event is followed by a good outcome. For example, a person goes through a painful divorce (bad event) but is able to maintain a close relationship with his or her children (good outcome). Conversely, compared with the stories of highly generative adults, the stories of less-generative adults contained more "contamination sequences," in which a good event is followed by a bad outcome. For example, a person starts a great new job (good event) only to find that she or he does not get along with her or his boss (bad outcome) (McAdams et al., 1998).

Additionally, McAdams, Diamond, de St. Aubin, and Mansfield (1997) identified a storyline that was common in the life stories of highly generative adults. The "commitment story," as it is called, was as follows: The protagonist benefits from early advantage, becomes attuned early in life to the suffering of others, feels called on to care for others, and is guided by a clear, compelling, and steadfast ideology or purpose. The life stories of generative adults vary in terms of the degree to which they emphasize each of the pieces of the prototypical commitment story. Indeed, although this prototypical story seems to support generative strivings, some generative adults had entirely different life stories.

As the case of Vera Brittain illustrated, historical and political upheavals exert powerful effects on individuals' life stories and their capacity for integrating generativity into their narrative identity. Cohler and Galatzer-Levy (2000) described the effects of a watershed moment in the gay liberation movement, the resistance to the police raid on a New York City gay bar, the Stonewall Inn, on the possibilities for gays and lesbians to tell their life stories. Inspired by the larger civil rights movement and the resistances and struggles it comprised, this act of resistance signaled the emergence of the gay liberation movement and constituted an act of cultural generativity on the part of the resisters. Whereas the stories of gay men and lesbians who had come of age before Stonewall told of isolation, shame, and desperation, Cohler and Galatzer-Levy (2000) wrote that

> for the cohort of youth coming of age in the 1970s aware of same-gender desire, gay liberation made it possible to find others facing similar struggles. There were places to go and opportunities to read and talk about the gay experience. (p. 92)

Those who fought for gay liberation were providing for those growing up gay and lesbian in future generations the opportunity for life stories less fraught with secrecy and pain. Not only do the stories of midlife adults in our culture reflect the extent and nature of their contributions to society, these stories are in some cases generative contributions in and of themselves.

Older Adulthood

Although researchers on aging and clinicians who work with older adults have explored the role of reminiscence and life review in later life for many decades (e.g., Butler, 1963), narrative identity researchers have only recently taken more systematic steps to incorporate older adults' narrative memories into their models of adult identity. Much of this initial work has focused on reminiscence and the functions it serves for older adults. On the basis of interviews with 460 seniors between 65 and 95 years of age, Watt and Wong (1991) developed a taxonomy of reminiscence types. This taxonomy was theoretically derived but was ultimately shaped and validated empirically (Watt & Wong, 1991). The taxonomy identified six distinct functions of reminiscence: *integrative reminiscence,* whose main purpose is the achievement of a sense of coherence, meaning, and reconciliation with one's past; *instrumental reminiscence,* in which one draws on one's past experiences to help solve a current problem; *transmissive reminiscence,* which involves teaching others a lesson one has derived from one's own life experience; *narrative reminiscence,* the telling of descriptive accounts of the past to convey biographical information or simply for pleasure; *escapist reminiscence,* which involves exaggerating the happiness and success one had in the past and devaluing one's present situation; and *obsessive reminiscence,* which involves preoccupation with problematic or disturbing past experiences and the negative feelings associated with those experiences.

Using this taxonomy, Wong and Watt (1991) content-analyzed data from interviews with 65- to 95-year-olds, some of whom were aging successfully and some of whom were aging less successfully. Successful aging was operationally defined as higher than average ratings in mental and physical health and adjustment. All respondents were asked to talk about an important or influential event in their past. Interviews were audiotaped, transcribed, and coded. Transcripts were content-analyzed, with paragraphs as the unit of analysis.

Those participants who were aging successfully engaged more frequently in integrative and instrumental reminiscing but less frequently in obsessive reminiscing than their less successfully aging counterparts (Wong & Watt, 1991). These types of reminiscence can be taught in therapy, resulting in significant improvements in symptoms of depression. In a treatment study using both integrative reminiscence therapy and instrumental reminiscence therapy for older adults with moderate to severe depression, follow-up studies showed significant improvements in the majority of participants in both reminiscence therapy conditions (Watt & Cappeliez, 2000). These results, suggesting that integrative reminiscence is beneficial, lend support to Erikson, Erikson, and Kivnick's (1986) contention that reviewing the personal past to come to terms with it enhances psychosocial development and well-being in the elderly.

Webster (1993) developed the Reminiscence Functions Scale (RFS), a psychometrically sound self-report inventory that assesses the frequency and functions of reminiscence in which a person engages. Developed in pilot studies with adults of a broad age range (18–76 years), the scale has been used to determine the differences in the functions of reminiscence in older and younger adults. Older individuals are more likely to use their memory narratives for purposes of death preparation, the sharing of life lessons, and remembering a lost loved one, whereas younger individuals are more likely to use narrative memories for boredom reduction, problem solving, and establishing an identity (Webster, 1999).

That older adults have been found to reminisce less for the purpose of bitterness revival is consistent with other empirical and theoretical work suggesting that older adults tend to have happier memories than younger adults do. In a study of older adults' and college students' self-defining memories, Singer, Rexhaj, and Baddeley (2006) found that older adults' memories were not only more integrative but also more affectively positive than college students' memories. Erikson et al. (1986) noted that many of the elders they interviewed expressed an overall satisfaction with their lives despite having lived through periods of hardship. Erikson et al. (1986) offered the following explanation for these elders' satisfaction with their lives: "Perhaps . . . these omissions reflect a lifelong process of reintegration and recasting, whereby events and circumstances that were once experienced as painful have, over the years, taken on new meanings as part of the whole life cycle" (p. 71).

It is consistent with the cultural stereotype of the older person as a wise story-teller that elders tend to tell their stories to teach and inform people of younger generations. In old age, the life story spans many decades. Elderly people's stories embody cultural and family history, and to tell these stories is to pass on this history. Elders' stories are often rich in content, but they need not be considered finished. On the contrary, they are still evolving as these elders take on new roles and shed old ones. In response to the new challenges of aging, the elderly may model their own stories of aging on the stories of friends or relatives whose grace-ful aging they admired (Erikson et al., 1986). Yet at the same time, their stories are often not primarily stories of being old but of being themselves in old age (Kaufman, 1986).

Becker (2001) pointed out that growing old is assumed in our culture to follow a narrative path of decline. There are multiple declines and losses associated with old age: the loss of physical strength, sensory acuity, and energy; the loss of friends and age-mates; the realization that time is running out (Erikson et al., 1986). Becker (2001) pointed out that many elderly people consider pain an "ordinary" part of aging but to do so may in some sense submit people to a maladaptive dom-inant narrative. Having collected the narratives of 17 people who live with pain, she presented two narratives that manifest their narrators' struggle between, on the one hand, normalizing their pain by accepting it as an "ordinary" part of aging and, on the other hand, evocatively and poetically telling their lived experiences of pain in ways that resist the dominant discourse of decline (Becker, 2001).

Growing older is certainly not only a story of dealing with decline. Indeed, elders gain great satisfaction from taking on new roles, including, and especially, roles as grandparents. Grandchildren are a source of pride and delight and are a major part of the life stories of their grandparents (Erikson et al., 1986; Norris, Kuiack, & Pratt, 2004). As the children of their children, grandchildren are, in a sense, a validation of elders' generativity (Erikson et al., 1986). In addition to being a part of elders' life stories, grandchildren are an audience for elders' stories. In telling their stories to grandchildren, grandparents enhance familial bonds, contribute to their own and the grandchild's self-understanding, and further the grandchild's understand-ing of historical events (Ryan, Pearce, Anas, & Norris, 2004).

Narrative identity researchers, by collecting the stories of older adults and study-ing the functions served by these narratives, have once again helped to delineate the dynamic psychosocial tensions within individual identity. Older adults tell stories that are embedded in historical contexts and therefore transmit knowledge of past worlds as well as personal events. As their reminiscences knit together previous eras and draw on landmark events as memorial touchstones, their stories transcend their personal identities and become social records that define a given culture. If the birth stories that began this review showcased the role of others' voices in the creation of narrative identity, then older adults' narratives demonstrate how individuals' own voices can shape our perception and understanding of common culture.

Finally though, older adults entrust these life stories to the care of younger generations. With illness or death, their stories belong only to those who choose to perpetuate them in oral or written form. Despite all the lifelong efforts to gain purchase on a unique narrative identity, individuals ultimately return their handiwork to the larger society from whence they came.

Conclusion

This review has showcased the powerful ability of narrative methods to demarcate the shifting contributions of self and society while charting identity across the human life span. Erikson's original formulation of identity required this complex understanding of psychosocial dynamics. McAdams's reconceptualization of Erikson's ideas into a theory of narrative identity provided a bridge for operationalizing these dynamic processes. Within each period of the life span, narrative identity researchers have applied narrative techniques that track the emergence of a reciprocal relationship between individuals' distinct voices and the voices of their parents, peers, partners, and social institutions. Parent-child conversations, self-defining memories, life story interviews, collections of couples' memories, analyses of autobiographical and biographical documents, and the study of life review and reminiscence have all yielded invaluable information about the role of different facets of identity in self-understanding, meaning making, social communication, and generativity.

Future research needs to present narratives of self and identity as embedded in interpersonal contexts that are sensitive to both cultural and developmental influences. As social-cognitive and developmental research begin to evolve new models of narrative memory (Alea & Bluck, 2003; Nelson & Fivush, 2004), narrative researchers can begin to look at the microprocesses of narrative development and exchange that reflect social functions, including the building of intimacy, transmission of life lessons, and explanation of self to others.

For example, Baddeley and Singer (2006), drawing on Alea and Bluck's (2003) model of the social functions of autobiographical memory, conducted two studies to look at the intrapersonal and interpersonal functions of bereavement narratives. Alea and Bluck's (2003) model posits that the characteristics of a narrator and a listener, and the quality of their interpersonal interaction, will affect what kind of narrative is told and what functions that narrative serves. Baddeley and Singer's (2006) first study found significant relationships between narrators' personality traits and the characteristics and functions of their narratives. Narrators higher in Conscientiousness tended to tell briefer and less self-focused narratives, whereas individuals higher in Neuroticism tended to tell more self-focused narratives. People high in Extraversion and Openness were more likely to tell their stories for interpersonal reasons such as explaining themselves to other people and getting closer to other people. People high in Neuroticism were more likely, and people high in Conscientiousness were less likely, to tell their stories for intrapersonal reasons such as validating their feelings and gaining a better understanding of the memory.

Baddeley and Singer's second study showed that a narrative's characteristics influence how listeners receive it and its teller and, therefore, how well it serves social functions. In this study, a new group of participants read 12 of the narratives collected in Study 1. Six of these narratives were contamination sequences and 6 were redemption sequences. Compared with redemption sequences, contamination sequences garnered more sympathy and concern for the narrator's well-being but generated less acceptance and more social discomfort in participants. Additionally, participants reported feeling less close to, familiar with, and similar to contamination narrators than redemption narrators.

This research provides one example of the ways in which narrative methods in the study of identity can begin to integrate the personal and social functions of narratives told in interpersonal contexts. As the rest of this review has documented, narratives at each phase of the life cycle reflect a narrator's unique personal concerns but never in isolation from interpersonal and sociocultural contexts.

At the start of our lives, we inherit a story given to us by our culture through our parents. Our life is in some sense an effort to forge our unique version of this inherited story. We fill it in and embellish it with our lived experiences as we understand them. Because we and our stories are embedded in a social matrix, we are motivated to develop our stories in coherent forms that are understandable to ourselves and can be understood by others in our culture (Singer & Rexhaj, 2006). The presence of other people as coauthors is constant throughout life. Prototypically, children coauthor their stories with their parents; adolescents coauthor their stories with their friends; young adults coauthor their stories with their partners. In middle adulthood and beyond, our life story is adopted as part of others' stories: those of our children and others for whom we have cared or those with whom we have shared pursuits to which we have dedicated our life.

By the time we are ready to leave this world, we have returned our story, now made in our own image and filled with unique variations, back to the culture from which it began. We return it not only to our children but also to a larger community through our relations to institutions, such as churches, mosques, or synagogues and organizations, both social and political. We began life with a story that was not our own and slowly crafted it to be our unique possession, but in the end, we return it to the vast library of shared stories that constitute our culture.

Consulting Editors: Avril Thorne and Jennifer Pals

References

Alea, N., & Bluck, S. (2003). Why are you telling me that? A conceptual model of the social function of autobiographical memory. *Memory, 11,* 165–178.

Alexander, I. (1990). *Personology: Method and content in personality assessment and psychobiography.* Durham, NC: Duke University Press.

Arnold, M. L., Pratt, M. W., & Hicks, C. (2004). Adolescents' representations of parents' voices in family stories: Value lessons, personal adjustment, and identity development. In M. W. Pratt & B. H. Fiese (Eds.), *Family stories and the life course* (pp. 163–186). Mahwah, NJ: Lawrence Erlbaum.

Baddeley, J. L., & Singer, J. A. (2006). *Sorry for your loss: Functions, characteristics and personality correlates of bereavement narratives.* Unpublished manuscript, Department of Psychology, Connecticut College, New London.

Becker, B. (2001). Challenging "ordinary" pain: Narratives of older people who live with pain. In G. Kenyon, P. Clark, and B. de Vries (Eds.), *Narrative gerontology* (pp. 91–112). New York: Springer.

Belove, L. (1980). First encounters of the close kind (FECK): The use of the story of the first interaction as an early recollection of a marriage. *Individual Psychologist, 36,* 191–208.

Berger, P. L., & Kellner, H. (1964). Marriage and the construction of reality: An exercise in the microsociology of knowledge. *Diogenes, 46,* 1–24.

Berntsen, D., & Rubin, D. C. (2004). Cultural life scripts structure recall from autobiographical memory. *Memory and Cognition, 32,* 427–442.

Blagov, P., & Singer, J. A. (2004). Four dimensions of self-defining memories (specificity, meaning, content and affect) and their relationships to self-restraint, distress, and repressive defensiveness. *Journal of Personality, 72*(3), 481–512.

Bluck, S., & Habermas, T. (2001). Extending the study of autobiographical memory: Thinking back about life across the life span. *Review of General Psychology, 5*(2), 135–147.

Bruner, J. S. (1986). *Actual minds, possible worlds.* Cambridge, MA: Harvard University Press.

Butler, R. N. (1963). The life review: An interpretation of reminiscence in the aged. *Psychiatry, 26,* 65–76.

Cohler, B. J., & Galatzer-Levy, R. M. (2000). *The course of gay and lesbian lives: Social and psychoanalytic perspectives.* Chicago: University of Chicago Press.

de St. Aubin, E. (1998). Truth against the world: A psychobiographical exploration of generativity in the life of Frank Lloyd Wright. In D. P. McAdams & E. de St. Aubin (Eds.), *Generativity and adult development: How and why we care for the next generation* (pp. 391–427). Washington, DC: American Psychological Association.

Elkind, D. (1967). Egocentrism in adolescence. *Child Development, 38,* 1025–1034.

Erikson, E. H. (1959). Identity and the life cycle: Selected paper. *Psychological Issues, 1*(1), 5–165.

Erikson, E. H. (1963). *Childhood and society* (2nd ed.). New York: W. W. Norton.

Erikson, E. H. (1968). *Identity: Youth and crisis.* New York: W. W. Norton.

Erikson, E. H. (1982). *The life cycle completed.* New York: W. W. Norton.

Erikson, E. H., Erikson, J. M., & Kivnick, H. Q. (1986). *Vital involvement in old age.* New York: W. W. Norton.

Farrant, K., & Reese, E. (2000). Maternal style and children's participation in reminiscing: Stepping stones in children's autobiographical memory development. *Journal of Cognition and Development, 1,* 193–225.

Fiese, B. H., Hooker, K. A., Kotary, L., Schwagler, J., & Rimmer, M. (1995). Family stories in the early stages of parenthood. *Journal of Marriage and the Family, 57,* 763–770.

Fivush, R., & Reese, E. (2002). Reminiscing and relating: The development of parent-child talk about the past. In J. D. Webster & B. K. Haight (Eds.), *Critical advances in reminiscence work: From theory to application* (pp. 109–122). New York: Springer.

Gergen, M. M., & Gergen, K. J. (1995). What is this thing called love? Emotional scenarios in historical perspective. *Journal of Narrative and Life History, 5*, 221–237.

Habermas, T., & Bluck, S. (2000). Getting a life: The emergence of the life story in adolescence. *Psychological Bulletin, 126*, 748–769.

Haden, C. A. (2003). Joint encoding and joint reminiscing: Implications for young children's understanding and remembering of personal experiences. In R. Fivush & C. A. Haden (Eds.), *Autobiographical memory and the construction of a narrative self: Developmental and cultural perspectives* (pp. 49–69). Mahwah, NJ: Lawrence Erlbaum.

Hayden, J., Singer, J. A., & Chrisler, J. C. (in press). The transmission of birth stories from mother to daughter: Self-esteem and mother-daughter attachment. *Sex Roles.*

Josselson, R. (1996). *Revising herself.* New York: Oxford University Press.

Kaufman, S. R. (1986). *The ageless self.* Madison: University of Wisconsin Press.

Kotre, J. (1999). *Make it count.* New York: Free Press.

Laurenceau, J., Barrett, L. F., & Pietromonaco, P. R. (1998). Intimacy as an interpersonal process: The importance of self-disclosure, partner disclosure, and perceived partner responsiveness in interpersonal exchanges. *Journal of Personality and Social Psychology, 74*, 1238–1251.

Leichtman, M. D., Wang, Q., & Pillemer, D. B. (2003). Cultural variations in interdependence and autobiographical memory: Lessons from Korea, China, India and the United States. In R. Fivush & C. A. Haden (Eds.), *Autobiography and the construction of a narrative self: Developmental and cultural perspectives* (pp. 73–98). Mahwah, NJ: Lawrence Erlbaum.

McAdams, D. P. (1987). A life-story model of identity. In R. Hogan & W. H. Jones (Eds.), *Perspectives in personality* (Vol. 2, pp. 15–50). Greenwich, CT: JAI Press.

McAdams, D. P. (1988). Biography, narrative, and lives: An introduction. *Journal of Personality, 56*, 1–18.

McAdams, D. P. (1990). *The person: An introduction to personality psychology.* San Diego, CA: Harcourt, Brace, Jovanovich.

McAdams, D. P. (2002). *Coding autobiographical episodes for themes of agency and communion.* Retrieved May 15, 2006, from www.sesp.northwestern.edu/foley

McAdams, D. P., Diamond, A., de St. Aubin, E., & Mansfield, E. (1997). Stories of commitment: The psychosocial construction of generative lives. *Journal of Personality and Social Psychology, 72*, 678–694.

McAdams, D. P., Hart, H. M., & Maruna, S. (1998). The anatomy of generativity. In D. P. McAdams & E. de St. Aubin (Eds.), *Generativity and adult development.* Washington, DC: American Psychological Association.

McCabe, A., & Peterson, C. (1991). Getting the story: A longitudinal study of parental styles in eliciting narratives and developing narrative skill. In A. McCabe & C. Peterson (Eds.), *Developing narrative structure* (pp. 217–253). Hillsdale, NJ: Lawrence Erlbaum.

McLean, K. C. (2005). Late adolescent identity development: Narrative meaning making and memory telling. *Developmental Psychology, 41*(4), 683–691.

McLean, K. C., & Thorne, A. (2003). Late adolescents' self-defining memories about relationships. *Developmental Psychology, 39*(4), 635–645.

Moffitt, K. H., & Singer, J. A. (1994). Continuity in the life story: Self-defining memories, affect, and approach/avoidance personal strivings. *Journal of Personality, 62*(1), 21–43.

Nelson, K., & Fivush, R. (2000). Socialization of memory. In E. Tulving & F. I. M. Craik (Eds.), *The Oxford handbook of memory* (pp. 283–296). New York: Oxford University Press.

Nelson, K., & Fivush, R. (2004). The emergence of autobiographical memory: A social cultural developmental theory. *Psychological Review, 111,* 486–511.

Norris, J. E., Kuiack, S., & Pratt, M. W. (2004). "As long as they go back down the driveway at the end of the day": Stories of the satisfactions and challenges of grandparenthood. In M. W. Pratt & B. H. Fiese (Eds.), *Family stories and the life course* (pp. 353–374). Mahwah, NJ: Lawrence Erlbaum.

Pasupathi, M. (2003). Emotion regulation during social remembering: Differences between emotions elicited during an event and emotions elicited when talking about it. *Memory, 11,* 151–163.

Peterson, B. E., & Stewart, A. J. (1990). Using personal and fictional documents to assess psychosocial development: A case study of Vera Brittain's generativity. *Psychology and Aging, 5,* 400–411.

Peterson, C., Jesso, B., & McCabe, A. (1999). Encouraging narratives in preschoolers: An intervention study. *Journal of Child Language, 26*(1), 49–67.

Polkinghorne, D. (1988). *Narrative knowing and the human sciences.* Albany: State University of New York Press.

Randall, W. L. (2001). Narrative perspective on aging. In G. Kenyon, P. Clark, & B. de Vries (Eds.), *Narrative gerontology* (pp. 31–62). New York: Springer.

Reese, E., & Farrant, K. (2003). Social origins of reminiscing. In R. Fivush & C. A. Haden (Eds.), *Autobiographical memory and the construction of a narrative self: Developmental and cultural perspectives* (pp. 29–48). Mahwah, NJ: Lawrence Erlbaum.

Reese, E., & Fivush, R. (1993). Parental styles of talking about the past. *Developmental Psychology, 29,* 596–606.

Ross, M., & Holmberg, D. (1990). Recounting the past: Gender differences in the recall of events in the history of a close relationship. In J. M. Olson & M. P. Zanna (Eds.), *Self-inference processes: The Ontario symposium* (Vol. 6, pp. 135–152). Hillsdale, NJ: Lawrence Erlbaum.

Rubin, D. C., & Berntsen, D. (2003). Life scripts help to maintain autobiographical memories of highly positive, but not highly negative, events. *Memory & Cognition, 31,* 1–14.

Ryan, E. B., Pearce, K. A., Anas, A. P., & Norris, J. E. (2004). Writing a connection: Intergenerational communication through stories. In M. W. Pratt & B. H. Fiese (Eds.), *Family stories and the life course* (pp. 375–400). Mahwah, NJ: Lawrence Erlbaum.

Sarbin, T. R. (1986). The narrative as a root metaphor for psychology. In T. R. Sarbin (Ed.), *Narrative psychology: The storied nature of human conduct* (pp. 3–21). New York: Praeger.

Scheibe, K. E. (2000). *The drama of everyday life.* Cambridge, MA: Harvard University Press.

Singer, J. A. (2004a). A love story: Self-defining memories in couples therapy. In A. Lieblich, D. P. McAdams, & R. Josselson (Eds.), *Healing plots: The narrative basis of psychotherapy* (pp. 189–208). Washington, DC: American Psychological Association.

Singer, J. A. (2004b). Narrative identity and meaning making across the adult lifespan: An introduction. *Journal of Personality, 72*(3), 437–460.

Singer, J. A., & Blagov, P. (2002). *Classification system and scoring manual for self-defining autobiographical memories.* Unpublished manuscript, Department of Psychology, Connecticut College, New London.

Singer, J. A., & Moffitt, K. H. (1991–1992). An experimental investigation of specificity and generality in memory narratives. *Imagination, Cognition and Personality, 11*(3), 233–257.

Singer, J. A., & Rexhaj, B. (2006). Narrative coherence and psychotherapy: A commentary. *Journal of Constructivist Psychotherapy, 19,* 209–217.

Singer, J. A., Rexhaj, B., & Baddeley, J. L. (2006). *Comparing the self-defining memories of older adults and college students.* Unpublished manuscript, Department of Psychology, Connecticut College, New London.

Singer, J. A., & Salovey, P. (1993). *The remembered self: Emotion and memory in personality.* New York: Free Press.

Spence, D. P. (1982). *Narrative truth and historical truth: Meaning and interpretation in psychoanalysis.* New York: W. W. Norton.

Sternberg, R. J. (1998). *Love is a story: A new theory of relationships.* New York: Oxford University Press.

Sternberg, R. J., Hojjat, M., & Barnes, M. L. (2001). Empirical tests of aspects of a theory of love as a story. *European Journal of Personality, 15*(3), 199–218.

Sutin, A. R., & Robins, R. W. (2005). Continuity and correlates of emotions and motives in self-defining memories. *Journal of Personality, 73*(3), 793–824.

Thorne, A. (2000). Personal memory telling and personality development. *Personality and Social Psychology Review, 4,* 45–56.

Thorne, A., Cutting, L., & Skaw, D. (1998). Young adults' relationship memories and the life story: Examples or essential landmarks? *Narrative Inquiry, 8,* 237–268.

Thorne, A., & McLean, K. (2001). *Manual for coding events in self-defining memories.* Unpublished manuscript, Department of Psychology, University of California at Santa Cruz.

Thorne, A., & McLean, K. (2002). Gendered reminiscence practices and self-definition in late adolescence. *Sex Roles, 46*(9–10), 267–277.

Thorne, A., & McLean, K. (2003). Telling traumatic events in adolescence. In R. Fivush & C. A. Haden (Eds.), *Autobiographical memory and the construction of a narrative self* (pp. 169–185). Mahwah, NJ: Lawrence Erlbaum.

Thorne, A., McLean, K. C., & Lawrence, A. M. (2004). When remembering is not enough: Reflecting on self-defining memories in late adolescence. *Journal of Personality, 72*(3), 513–541.

Tomkins, S. S. (1979). Script theory. In H. E. Howe, Jr., & R. A. Dienstbier (Eds.), *Nebraska symposium on motivation* (Vol. 26, pp. 201–236). Lincoln: University of Nebraska Press.

Wamboldt, F. S. (1999). Co-constructing a marriage: Analyses of young couples' relationship narratives. *Monographs of the Society for Research in Child Development, 64,* 37–51.

Wang, Q. (2004). The cultural context of parent-child reminiscing: A functional analysis. In M. W. Pratt & B. H. Fiese (Eds.), *Family stories and the life course: Across time and generations* (pp. 279–301). Mahwah, NJ: Lawrence Erlbaum.

Watt, L. M., & Cappeliez, P. (2000). Integrative and instrumental reminiscence therapies for depression in older adults: Intervention strategies and treatment effectiveness. *Aging & Mental Health, 4,* 166–177.

Watt, L. M., & Wong, P. T. (1991). A taxonomy of reminiscence and therapeutic implications. *Journal of Gerontological Social Work, 16,* 37–57.

Webster, J. D. (1993). Construction and validation of the reminiscence functions scale. *Journals of Gerontology, 48,* 256–262.

Webster, J. D. (1999). Reminiscence functions across adulthood: A replication and extension. *Journal of Adult Development, 6,* 73–85.

Wong, P. T., & Watt, L. M. (1991). What types of reminiscence are associated with successful aging? *Psychology and Aging, 6,* 272–279.

Wood, W., & Conway, M. (2006). Subjective impact, meaning-making, and current and recalled emotions for self-defining memories. *Journal of Personality, 74,* 811–846.

Zimmerman, J. L., & Dickerson, V. C. (1993). Separating couples from restraining patterns and the relationship discourse that supports them. *Journal of Marital and Family Therapy, 19,* 403–413.

CHAPTER 8

The Language of Arts in a Narrative Inquiry Landscape

Dilma Maria de Mello

Beginning a chapter is always a difficult task. As we spend so much time in the midst of our storied lives, it is difficult not only to know where to begin but also to frame the plotline that the chapter's story might follow. For example, I could let art seduce me and go straight to an aesthetic plotline. I know, however, that this is not the academic way of writing, and knowing that the readers of this chapter could include both those familiar with narrative inquiry as arts-based/informed research and those less familiar, I decided not to narrow my vision and to follow a plotline that incorporates both aesthetic and the more traditional academic formats. In this way, I could construct an open text, which could be an invitation to many readers.

Considering that "narrative inquiry researchers need to deliberately imagine themselves as part of the inquiry" (Connelly & Clandinin, 2004, p. 13), the first part of this chapter represents my experience of engaging in arts-based/informed narrative inquiry. In the second and third parts, I attempt to develop a working definition of what I mean by art in narrative inquiry and then place arts-based/informed narrative inquiry within the narrative inquiry landscape. The fourth part suggests arts-based and arts-informed studies can be seen as distinct modes of working with art in narrative inquiry. The fifth part highlights what arts-based/informed narrative inquirers do. Finally, I examine this kind of research as a way of understanding its tensions and boundaries as well as to throw light on the history of qualitative research.

My Experience of Engaging in Arts-Informed Narrative Inquiry

I was beginning to travel through the experiences of being a teacher and also a researcher when I first encountered the concepts of narrative inquiry and arts-based research. I first treated them as separate terms: arts-based research and narrative inquiry. In my master's research (Mello, 1999), I was trying to understand how a teacher's personal "I" is expressed in classroom and class preparation. In part, I was trying to understand how each teacher was aware of the influence of personal experiences within the professional landscape. At first, I chose a narrative inquiry road. I believed that conceptualizing experience narratively was a powerful way to provoke reflection and transformation. As Dewey (1938) says, life experience is or could be the basis for education. He says, "One learns about education from thinking about life, and one learns about life from thinking about education" (p. 89).

Knowing I learned by bringing my personal stories to my teaching and by using my teaching experiences to reflect on the everyday situations I faced, narrative inquiry seemed to offer a way to think about what I was trying to do. Narrative inquiry could be a tasteful (Alves, 1995) way to teach, to learn, and also to think about how teacher knowledge is constructed. According to Alves (1995), "the aim of knowing is to increase our possibilities of tasting life" (p. 124). Discussing a similar topic, Eisner (2002) talks about the intrinsic satisfaction of knowing. Using narrative inquiry to study my own teaching created space for me to imagine how to live this intrinsic satisfaction and to express emotions, feelings, and images.

Expressing myself, however, has not been easy. When I was an undergraduate student, for example, I was told there are some things that cannot be defined or stated. Barthes (1989) points out these things are *unsayable/unspeakable*. Yet according to Eisner (2002), "meaning is not limited to what words can express" (p. 230). For him, "some meanings are 'readable,' and expressible through literal language; other meanings require literary forms of language; still others demand other forms through which meanings can be represented and shared" (p. 230). In narrative inquiry (Clandinin & Connelly, 2000), the form informs and the arts seem to be a powerful form to inform (Eisner, 1991) the experiences told and reconstructed. Trying to find another form to express meaning, I created the poem below as my first experience with the arts in my research.

The Teacher I Want to Become

I don't know

What sort of teacher I want to become

I want to be a different one

But I think

There are so many things to become

that I'd rather continue being an alive one

Maybe I'd like to be the teacher I am (at that future moment)

Again thinking about

The teacher I hope to become (Mello, as cited in Diamond & Mullen, 1999, pp. 76–77)

This piece was written during a course on arts-based research during my master's studies. Diamond was the teacher in charge of creating space for us to reflect on our practices as teachers through arts activities. By thinking on the teacher I wanted to become, the poem helped me become aware of myself as teacher and also as researcher. I realized what I wanted for my teaching experience. I realized that I could be a researcher and that knowledge could be constructed with satisfaction through my stories of experiences and through arts.

Since then, art has been part of my research analysis process. I used the literary form, particularly metaphors, in my writing because it gives the text a poetic tone. That is, art in my narrative inquiry work has been through literary writing. Literary writing is the artistic tool I use to live and to express the meanings I make of my stories. At least, this is a tool I think I can handle. It is, however, not the only way to work on arts-informed research. Throughout my master's and doctoral studies I discovered other ways of developing arts-based/informed research.

Art has been introduced to academic fields in different ways and in fields such as medicine (McNiff, 1988, 1998), education (Eisner, 1976; Eisner & Barone, 1997; Greene, 2001; Norris, 2000), and curriculum (Bach, 1998; Grumet, 1978). Some scientific works are constructed using photographs, drama, theater, poetry, paintings, video biographies, images, graffiti movements, dance, music, literature, movies, poetics, sculpture, fiction, and so on. Some scholars use art as a representational way of discussing the object studied or the investigation process lived; others use art as the beginning of a research process; and there are still others for whom art is the object studied. Many works using arts do not necessarily evolve from narrative inquiry, and there are narrative inquiries being developed without using art. Thus, it seems necessary to emphasize that not all arts-informed research is narrative inquiry and vice versa.

In this chapter, I want to focus specifically on the work of narrative inquiry, which can be considered arts-based/informed research. There are two main points I consider important in narrative inquiry and arts: (1) art as the beginning of a narrative inquiry process and as part of the data-gathering process and (2) art as a representational form and as part of the analysis process. First, I consider a definition of art.

Experiencing Art: A Working Definition

Since beginning this chapter, I have wondered if it was necessary to discuss what I mean by the concept of art. I was afraid, I must confess, someone would accuse me of not understanding enough of what art is. While I did not want to establish criteria to evaluate what could or could not be considered as art, it is relevant to offer a definition of what I assume art to be in this chapter. Thus, before diving deeper into the possibilities of using art in narrative inquiry, I swim on the surface and comment on a discussion of art in the movie *Mona Lisa Smile.*

In this movie, a teacher tries to convince her students that a photograph of her mother could be considered a work of art. As her students were only used to considering art as famous masterpieces such as those of Monet and Renoir, the teacher decided to discuss with them issues related to what could be considered art. She also wanted to discuss criteria for establishing who is able to decide what can be considered as a work of art. In the end, the teacher told her students that an ordinary photograph, such as the one she showed them, could be considered art. In so doing, she intended to show that art is not something static but very dynamic and that there may be different ways of having an aesthetic experience.

This idea has also been discussed in relevant academic studies. Steinberg and Kincheloe (as cited in Diamond and Mullen, 1999) note that the definition of art has changed radically. They note great difficulty in defining what art is exactly because, as Davidson (1997) points out, "whether something is art depends on whether someone thinks it is" (p. 125). While I agree with them, I feel the need to continue searching for a working definition to focus the discussion in this chapter.

Three terms—art, aesthetics, and work of art—are commonly used. In a general sense, art can be understood as the products of human creativity; the creation of beautiful or significant things; a superior skill; and modes or representations such as photographs, paintings, and poetry. Some authors prefer to use the term *work of art* because they believe that art cannot be something, an object. As declared by Coomaraswamy (1956), "Art is nothing tangible. We cannot call a painting 'art' as the words 'artifact' and 'artificial' imply. The thing made is a work of art made by art, but is not itself art. The art remains in the artist and is the knowledge by which things are made" (p. 18). While some use the term *art* and *work of art* interchangeably, most use an interpretation similar to that of Coomaraswamy. The term *aesthetics*, however, implies the provocative experience(s) a work of art can promote in a human being. According to Greene (2001), "aesthetics is an adjective used to describe or single out the mode of experience brought into being by encounters with works of art" (p. 5). The more perspectives it can be viewed and understood from, the more aesthetic a work of art is (Greene, 2001).

Having said that, my poem shared earlier seems to be based on the ideas expressed by the terms *work of art* and *aesthetics* as posed by Greene (2000). But I believe that there is more, and I intend to open up more perspectives in this chapter. I want to consider multiple modes of experiencing art. Thus, I see art not only as a product, a mode of representation, or even a superior skill but also as a way of living, a way of looking at the world and the life and education in it. Searching for multiple perspectives, I bring forward different authors' concepts of art.

In the eyes of Proust (as cited in Campbell & Ogden, 1999), art is an instrument, a means through which "instead of seeing a single world, our own, we see it multiply until we have before us as many worlds as there are original artists" (p. 205). In the *Artlex Art Dictionary* (www.artlex.com), Delahunt (2006) says that according to Picasso, art could be considered "an instrument that washes away from the soul the dust of everyday life." Rothko (Jacob, 2003) looks at art as a way of living and says, "Art is an adventure into an unknown world, which can only be explored by those willing to take the risks" (p. 37). Sontag (1966) claims that "art today is a new kind of instrument, an instrument for modifying consciousness and organizing new modes of sensibility" (p. 297). Greene (2000) comments that art is related to imagination and can enable us "to see more in our experience, to hear more on normally unheard frequencies, to become conscious of what daily routine have obscured, what habit and convention have suppressed" (p. 123).

I view art as these authors do, and I also understand it as an instrument to promote reflection and make us, as human beings, go deep inside our own conflicts and our emotional selves (Eisner, 2002). It can also be understood as an object of beauty and pleasure through which one can see and understand life, taste life, and understand the world. Through art I see how learning would be related to satisfaction (Eisner, 2002) and knowledge would be tasteful (Alves, 1995).

I turn now to considerations pertaining to art, aesthetics, science, and narrative inquiry.

In the beginning of this chapter, I said that not all narrative inquiry is arts-based research. Aiken (as cited in Delahunt, 2006) refers to art as an "intrinsic part of human behavior and that human beings could be called Homo aestheticus instead of only Homo sapiens." Greene (2001) says, "There are privileged aesthetic objects and natural things perceived aesthetically" (p. 24). She also says that "it is possible to live an aesthetic experience in the world around" (p. 53). Considering what Greene and Aiken say, I might state that all human work is a work of art. The use of art in narrative inquiry discussed in this chapter, however, is the one deliberately done "for the sake of aesthetic experiences" (Greene, 2001, p. 53).

Another consideration to be made is related to art as a means to live and narrate experiences in narrative inquiry. According to Dewey (1934), art could be a way to study educational experiences since art expresses meaning instead of stating meaning like science does. Based on Dewey, Eisner (1991) says that "symbols used in science are representational while those used in art are presentational" (p. 31). Thus, while science uses representational symbols that take us to their referents, art would take us straight to the referents without playing the mediator role. Based on these ideas, I believe that art is closer to experience—that is, it is possible to see, taste, and touch experience through art and, more than this, art constitutes itself as an experience because according to Dewey (1934), art "does something different from leading to an experience. It constitutes one." (p. 84). I also believe that this is one of the contributions of art to narrative inquiry. Considering that narrative inquiry is a kind of experience-based research (Clandinin, personal communication, 2004), it seems that art can help narrative inquirers create space where the experience can be vicariously lived (Barone, 1995). An example of this use of art is my poem. As Diamond and Mullen (1999) noted, by writing about the teacher I am, the teacher I want to become, I could also live the experience of moving backward and forward, inward and outward (Clandinin & Connelly, 2000; Connelly & Clandinin, 2004). In the next section, I place art in a narrative inquiry landscape.

Art in a Narrative Inquiry Landscape

To describe ways in which art has been brought to narrative inquiry, I present the studies of Bach (1998), Duarte (1996), Telles (1997, 2004, 2005), Mickelson (1995), and Murphy (2004). I start with Bach (1998):

> As a researcher and student of curriculum, I think about my limited position in the institution. I question what frames my knowing and who I am in this search. I am mindful to having my eyes turned in that studying myself has meant learning to turn my eyes in by turning the lens on myself. Looking back is difficult. These reflections layer my frames of knowing as I listen and understand what the girls show me in their camera-work. Turning the lens on self is a way to seriously play, imagine and trouble self-reflexivity. When I see photographs, I see what matters and learn to see anew. I learn to tell my stories in different ways. (p. 14)

After presenting her own stories of experience, Bach (1998) starts her work by looking narratively at her research experience. In her research on curriculum, she was trying to understand the stories left outside of girls' experiences of school. She engaged in a visual narrative inquiry. She asked four girls to make and take photographs of themselves. The photographs were used as a tool to start the story telling and its meaning-making process. In this way, the girls could talk about themselves and their personal stories related to their bodies and their images as teenagers at school and at home with their families. During moments of conversation they expressed stories that lived behind the photographs as well as the stories yet to come from them. The photographs and the conversations were the tools to construct both the field texts and the research texts. As another aspect of the research text, there are also poems that Bach composed, such as the one in which she reflects on the ethical issue concerned in making public the private lives of the girls studied.

Making the Private Public

The girls produced photographs

Mirrored within private/public production

Stories of the body

Basically private, intimate experiences

But also made public

For other

Knowledge

other people's stories

What re/presents knowledge

Both realized and evaded

How can

I

Grow without losing

Or becoming

Alien. (Bach, 1998, p. 55[1])

In this narrative approach to the study of the girls' experiences and following Bach's aesthetic plotline, it is possible to see knowledge constructed in her visual narrative inquiry. By using photographs, Bach (1998) not only created comfortable spaces for the girls to live the experience of telling their stories and learn from them but also promoted spaces for sharing these experiences and reflections with the readers. This approach, which sounds like an invitation, could open up possibilities for the readers to learn from the girls' narratives and make their own conclusions. Perhaps it is an example of the experiential continuum referred to by Dewey (1938). In this case, this continuum is specifically promoted and emphasized by the art of photography and the literary language used by Bach (1998).

By living the experience with the visual narrative inquiry constructed with the girls, Bach (1998) chose an approach I emphasize here. Instead of having photographed the girls and analyzed their stories as a researcher, having in mind some theories concerning the theme she aimed at studying, she gave the girls cameras so that they could construct their own visual narratives. In this way, they constructed personal knowledge by composing their narratives from their own perspectives, since photography was a language the girls could easily use. In terms of the academic landscape, Bach's approach was inclusive—that is, it included not only the research participants but also those who read her dissertation. In this way, it is not a writing for only some scholars and erudite people. The aesthetic narrative research developed invited not only research participants but also readers to take part in it.

Duarte (1996) chose the short story as an artistic tool in her study. Comparing her situation with the one lived by a boy in *Through the Tunnel* by Lessing (1955), Duarte (1996) studied her own experience of learning English. During her stay in England, she decided to investigate her own learning process, considering her anxieties and difficulties as a nonnative speaker of English. In Lessing's short story, a boy had to face the challenge of crossing an underwater tunnel, an activity imposed by boys who considered themselves gatekeepers in charge of deciding who would be accepted as part of their group. The only way to be accepted was to undergo that tunnel experience. Duarte uses this story as an analogy to reflect on her own difficulties in learning English and being accepted as a good speaker of this language. The novel was an artistic tool through which Duarte developed her research by moving inward and outward on her own reflective movement.

Another example of art in narrative inquiry can be seen in the work of Telles (2005), who focused on alternative modes of critical reflection and of knowledge representations of teachers by means of the arts. He aimed at answering three questions: (1) How do the objects of art (photography and theater performance) function as a device for triggering shared reflection among teachers? (2) What conversational features emerge from the shared reflections among teachers by means of photography and theater performance? (3) What representations of the teaching profession do teachers use during shared reflection? He analyzed the transcriptions of shared reflections among teachers when they were exposed to photographs of school life and to a theater play about teachers' and students' lives. Telles (2005) used some photos by Doisneau and Cavanna (2002) in order to collect oral field texts during reflective dialogue sessions with five groups of teachers working on a photography workshop.

  Instead of working with art at the beginning of her research journey, like Bach (1998), Duarte (1996), and Telles (2005) did, Mickelson (1995) used art as a tool to make sense of the stories told by mothers of boys with behavioral disabilities as well as to construct her research text. Her dissertation, written in letter format, consists of narratives such as the one called "These Are My Beginnings," which begins as follows:

> November/December 1993 Dear Mothers, Louisa, Lena, Caroline and Joan, You are familiar with the story that follows. I read it to you soon after we first met because I wanted you to know what led me to you. And I wanted you to know more than the bare bones of "Joy-Ruth Mickelson, student, interested in knowing about your lives as mothers of labeled sons." I needed to share with you my eagerness to hear and understand your stories and experiences, to twine them with my own, and then to write a narrative that would seek audience with those who care about children and their families. (Mickelson, 1995, p. 1[2])

As this example shows, Mickelson (1995) addressed the letters to her research participants. When the dissertation was published in a book format, she added a kind of introduction addressed to readers, keeping the letter format. It is called reader's guide.

> Dear Reader,
>
> In these pages I tell stories of four mothers, and you will meet the four mothers who, over a 12-month period, shared their stories with me. Their sons were labeled "Severely Behavior Disordered." I asked the mothers to tell me of their lives and their experiences. In letters to them I present their voices as they reflected on their words, actions, and feelings. As we journeyed through our dialogic relationship, I wove in my own reflections and experiences. In the Prologue I tell of my early teaching and learning. I start with the story of my very first teaching position: "Shout It Louder." I continue to describe experiences with students which affected me deeply and which led me to "The Road to This Inquiry." (Mickelson, 2000, p. xi)

In this letter she informs us of her research journey, emphasizing the dialogic relationship with her research participants, which was constructed over several meetings. Their conversations were taped and transcribed and became the researcher's field texts. Based on them, Mickelson (2000) constructed her research text, choosing the letter format as a way to keep the dialogic tone reflective of her relationship with the four mothers, Caroline, Lena, Louisa, and Joan, her research participants. She also created space for the mothers' voices. Through their stories, we learn about the difficulties of receiving a behavior-disordered (BD) diagnosis and also the oppression mothers facing this kind of label are exposed to. In this way, the problems BD children and their families experience when they go to school are illuminated, and themes such as diversity, inclusion, measurement at school, and pharmacotherapy are discussed. The following piece shows the way stories, theory, and research were connected. It also shows the way Mickelson said goodbye to the mothers at the end of her work.

> Holmquist and Clark (1984) have unwrapped Bakhtin for me and, using their words and his, I have been able to delve into "the relations between people and between persons and things that cuts across religious, political and aesthetic boundaries" (p. 348). I hope to be able to continue to delve deeper and want to acknowledge them both . . .
>
>   Thank you for your generous sharing of your lives with your sons. May your homecoming festival be in your horizons.
>
> Sincerely,
> Joy-Ruth. (p. 157)

Interweaving theory, research, and stories, Mickelson (2000) keeps a poetic tone throughout her work. As Oyler (2000) writes in a review of Mickelson's work, "It is an invitation into literature, history, philosophy and art" (back page). Besides its poetic tone and novel characteristic, Mickelson's work was also developed through fictionalized field texts. In her own words,

> To introduce the mothers and theirs sons, I wrote the first four letters as though they were written by administrators and sent to, or from, those in schools. The four letters are fictionalized; they were not actually sent to, or by, administrators about these mothers' sons. The letters do, however, include actual observation, assessments, and interpretations made by school or community professionals about these boys. (Mickelson, 2000, p. xi)

According to the author, "the fictionalization is made to protect identities but the letters reflect, in spirit, the assessments that were administered to the boys" (Mickelson, 2000, p. xii).

Fictionalization was also chosen by Murphy (2004). Trying to understand children's knowledge, Murphy develops a narrative inquiry into children's school experiences, using the language of fictionalization as a way to make meaning of his field texts and also of his own experience as a researcher. In his words,

> I was trying to get at my understanding of experience through the work of writing and in this, writing fiction, something different from rewriting field texts. Writing fictional interim texts allowed me to step back from field texts.

This helped me see my research in a new way. I became intrigued by the ways the fictionalised pieces made me aware of elements in the field texts and research experience I do not think I would have recognized if I had not engaged in this writing process. I also became interested, as I created the fictionalized pieces, in the process of creating fiction in a research framework and what that meant in the process of moving from field texts to research texts. It became an exploration of moving in and out of worlds, the worlds of the children in the inquiry, the fictionalized world, and the world I inhabited as narrative inquirer. (p. 44)

Murphy (2004) taped the conversations[3] he had with five children at school, where he also observed some of their classes. These conversation transcripts and field notes were the basis for writing fiction, which became the beginnings of his work of making sense of these field texts. The piece below is an example of his fictional writing:

Then [Sloughboy] begins to look for Travis. . . . Travis is rabbit-twitchy. He knows I am looking for him but he does not know where I am. Hide and seek is a both-ways game thinks Sloughboy. Travis is hiding but he is also at the same time seeking. Sloughboy watches Travis from close. Travis in his not looking has let Sloughboy get close. Sloughboy waits a moment like he has seen Coyote do. . . . He realizes this is fun . . . this hide and seek both-ways game . . .
   Travis yells.
   The yell makes Sloughboy jump back and fall down.
   The Travis yell makes Sloughboy yell.
   Then in the silence after Travis starts to laugh and Sloughboy starts to laugh. They recognized each other. This laughter is a way of talking—just like it is a way of talking with Coyote. I like this play thinks Sloughboy.
   You scared me.
   You scared me back
   Now you go and hide. (p. 58)

Murphy's (2004) fiction writing, part of his research text, shows the quality of his relationship with Travis, a research participant. It was made of laughing and sharing of humor, a sense of being "kind of the same" and a sense of hiding and seeking, since the researcher had to search for the boy's stories, which he seemed to be hiding during their talking. Hiding was also a way Travis used to search for the researcher's stories. That is why Murphy uses the expression "hide and seek both-ways game." He says:

One of the qualities of my relationship with Travis was the searching for his thoughts about the ideas we were discussing, a conversational hide and seek. In the transcripts there are many times when I shared a story of my boyhood to elicit a conversational response on his part. A comment that appears more than once in the transcripts is Travis telling me how we are "kind of the same." Another part of this research relationship was the laughing and sharing of humour. I used the idea of hide and seek to capture the sense of the seeking I did when we talked and the playful nature of the relationship. (p. 58)

Writing fiction is one of the ways in which Murphy uses art in his narrative inquiry. In addition to writing fiction pieces, he also gave his research participants names such as *Ghost-girl-who-knows, Boy-who-would-be-seen, One-who-stands-among*, and *Certain-girl-shifting*. Working with the children at school, he also used art as a way to compose field texts. For example, he asked the students to reflect on their experiences by creating poems based on their report cards.

I do not know if these authors would all describe their own work as examples of arts-based/informed narrative inquiry. Some such as Telles (2005) do; others call their work visual narrative inquiry (Bach, 1998); Mickelson (1995, 2000) and Murphy (2004) call their work narrative inquiry. So one could wonder how I could dare locate these works within the landscape of arts-based/informed narrative inquiry.

Considering Greene's (2001) notion of art deliberately made for the sake of aesthetic experience and having in mind photography, poems, novels, and fiction as well-known languages of the arts, as stated by Eisner (2002), the aesthetic approach chosen by Bach (1998), Mickelson (1995, 2000), Telles (2005), Murphy (2004), and Duarte (1996) can, in my view, be considered arts-based/informed narrative inquiry. By using photography, Bach and Telles promoted aesthetic experience not only for their research participants but also for their readers. Mickelson's choice of writing using a letter format, which gave it a novel-like quality, gave her study an aesthetic tone. Duarte's use of a short story as the basis for her investigation of her learning process and Murphy's fiction writing promoted aesthetic plotlines.

I now turn to the distinction I make when using the terms *arts-based* and *arts-informed* in referring to narrative inquiry.

Arts-Based Narrative Inquiry and Arts-Informed Narrative Inquiry

I have been reflecting on the use of the terms arts-based and arts-informed research since I first worked with narrative inquiry (Mello, 1999). It was still considered a major concern in Mello (2005). Diamond and Mullen (1999) refer to arts-based inquiries; Telles (2005) describes his work as arts informed and also as arts based. At first, I applied both terms interchangeably, but it became a tension, a puzzle I could not get rid of. Although I used both terms in Mello (2005), I realized that there were some differences in the kind of work developed by Bach (1998), Mickelson (1995, 2000), Duarte (1996), Telles (2005), Murphy (2004), and me. Although they were all working artfully in a narrative inquiry landscape, the ways this was done seemed to be somehow different. I decided to face this difficulty by investigating the meaning of these terms.

The *Longman Dictionary of Contemporary English* (1987) states that the word *base* is "the lowest part of something, esp. the part on which something stands" (p. 73). It is also seen as "something that provides the conditions which are necessary for a particular activity or situation" (p. 73). Although they are slightly different, these definitions imply the idea of a starting point, the beginning of something. Considering this perspective, the term *arts-based research* sounds as if art is at the beginning of a study.

In the same dictionary, the word *inform* is defined as "to give information or knowledge to"; the word *informed* as "having or showing knowledge; having information"; and the word *information* as "knowledge in the form of facts, news, etc." (p. 538). These definitions seem to rely on the idea of a mediating point—that is, it seems information is built on something already constructed so that something else can be constructed. Considering this perspective, the term *arts-informed research* suggests that art has been the way chosen to inform the analysis and the meaning made of the field text already existing.

My point is that when art is applied in narrative inquiry as part of the method, as a way of composing and gathering field texts, it is considered to be the base of the whole research process. In this case, art is the beginning of everything. That is why I call it arts-based narrative inquiry. The works of Bach (1998), Duarte (1996), and Telles (2005) are good examples of this possibility of working with art in narrative inquiry. But when art is used as part of the analysis, during the transition from field texts to research texts, as a way of informing the meaning made, it can be considered as arts-informed narrative inquiry. Mickelson (1995, 2000) and Murphy (2004) are examples of this use of art.

Perhaps it is important to note whether it is arts-based or arts-informed research; both can be part of narrative inquiry. It can be in the telling or in the living (Connelly & Clandinin, 2004). These two possible modes of doing narrative inquiry are described by Connelly and Clandinin (2004): "The inquirer may begin an inquiry with the "living' or with the 'telling' . . . the main version of narrative inquiry based on 'telling' is storytelling. Thus, Kramp (2004) says narrative inquiry is both process in which the narrator tells and it is a product, the story told" (p. 5). For inquiries that begin in the "living" mode, researcher and participants live the experience that is being studied.

Another distinction present in the narrative inquiry landscape is concerned with the way Clandinin and Connelly (2000; Connelly & Clandinin, 2004) refer to data gathering and data presentation. For them, a narrative inquiry researcher composes and gathers field texts and composes and presents research texts. Taking this perspective into account and considering the distinction proposed, it is perhaps important to emphasize that arts-based narrative inquiry has to do with field text gathering, while arts-informed narrative inquiry is related to research text presentation. There is no need, however, to follow an either/or path. Bach (1998) and Telles (2005), for example, did both. Thus, their work can be considered arts-based and arts-informed narrative inquiry.

There is still another consideration to be made. Aesthetic experiences seem to be addressed to different people by the researcher. I mean, when working on arts-based narrative inquiry, the researcher creates space for the participants to live an aesthetic experience. On the other hand, arts-informed narrative inquiry creates conditions for the readers to live an aesthetic experience. Although there is the possibility for the readers to experience aesthetics through arts-based narrative inquiry, it might have been experienced more strongly by the research participants, who lived the field text gathered. On the other hand, in arts-informed narrative inquiry, it might be possible that the field texts were gathered and composed through interviews without having the research participants living any kind of aesthetic experience. In this case, aesthetics can be lived just when the research text is composed.

Having made this reflection, I believe that we could partially face the tension related to the boundaries of arts-based and arts-informed narrative inquiry landscapes. I now return to Bach (1998), Duarte (1996), Telles (2005), Mickelson (1995, 2000), and Murphy (2004) to work on some general characteristics noted in arts-based and arts-informed narrative inquiries.

Through the analysis of these authors' studies, it is possible to illustrate what arts-based/informed narrative inquiry may be like. It has to do with creative field text gathering, creative research text presentation, empowering one's coresearchers/participants, inviting readers to make their own conclusions, supporting construction of personal knowledge, and honoring multiple perspectives.

Creative Field Text Gathering and Creative Research Text Presentation

I have shown earlier examples of arts-based and arts-informed narrative inquiries. It is possible to see creative field text gathering in the works of Bach (1998) and Telles (2005) as clearly as it is possible to note creative research text presentation in Mickelson (1995, 2000) and Murphy (2004). Other examples follow.

Concerning field text gathering, aesthetic experiences are provoked by the use of photographs and visual images as done in Bach (1998), Telles (2005), Diamond and Mullen (1999), and Collier and Collier (1986). The language of theater/drama has also been applied during field text gathering as in Telles (2004) and Mello (2005). Diamond and Mullen (1999) also propose many other ways of gathering field text by using music, painting, graphic drawing, poem writing, self-portrait painting, and so on. I will comment on some of these approaches.

To gather field text, Telles (2004, 2005) used the language of photography and the language of theater. Working with 20 undergraduate students of Modern Languages, a play of 45 minutes about specific policies of the Brazilian educational system was created and performed by undergraduate students from a public Brazilian university. They performed the play at five Brazilian universities. Right after the performances, a collaborative reflective session took place with students, teachers, and researchers. The play was the instrument to promote an aesthetic experience so as to gather field texts.

Mello (2005) also gathered field texts through drama presentation. To analyze the way students constructed knowledge, they were asked to create a play. Similar work has been developed by Duarte (1998), who carried out a research project called *Living Drama in the Classroom* at the Catholic University of São Paulo, Brazil. From a humanist perspective, she was (and still is) interested in affective issues that permeate the language-learning process.

I agree with Telles (2004) that we are still in the early stages of arts-based narrative inquiry. Mostly, we have arts-informed narrative inquiry. Like Mickelson (1995, 2000) and Murphy (2004), most narrative inquirers working on art use it when writing their research texts. And many of them use literary and visual forms as a way of making meaning of field texts and constructing their research text.

Besides letters, Mickelson (1995, 2000) also wrote poems, like the following one, in which she expressed the stress experienced by the four mothers in her study.

Cycle comes goes comes goes comes

again the nightmare starts; again pulsing

Our lives a whole new book the pages ripped.

Anger rises, climbs quickly daily, back to a beginning that won't or will be better;

is that voice screaming, my hand raising? I shake and I am shaking

my plate is full and spills the pills I can't erase the stain. No job no cash

I am betrayed.

my ear, my ear, my ear. In black night pain screams worse. My scream in pain back in my gut my mind my soul my purse (empty of bills and bits)

my heart

of blood.

My plastic cards erased. Even the dreaded Tylenol cannot be bought or brought. Empty drones the voice

Account Closed.

my ear my ear my ear my ear.

No cans, no bread, no milk. All to buy with bouncing cheque that bounced and then to top it all he bounced the bed and punched the wall. By police

removed

the echo stays

the room empties his smell of rigged distance.

bugging bugging bugging bugging bugging bugging bugging. Uuuuugh!

buttons pushing, in out in out in out push push push. Pushed . . .

Aaaah!

Screams of vulgar custodian, she who calls the shots

evicts. Who will lift the baggage baggage baggage I carry with me? my

shoulders sag, my guilt sinks me. I cover all the bases like a wizard Blue Jay

but why is there so little pleasure? those nice things rarely happen and really

I was afraid they would say he was awright and I was awrong.

Do I have to feel guilt when I don't like you

too much times? too many hates: And many nothings.

my son my son show me . . . my love is hard when kicked show me the

signs of son I sometimes see and others say

I love;

son we want my sons I do I do I love you. (Mickelson, 2000, pp. 115–116[1])

Examples of the fiction writing by Murphy (2004) have already been shown.

Aiming at understanding myself and my personal and professional landscapes (Mello, 1999), I chose to use literary forms in my research text. My poem, presented earlier, is an example.

After telling her personal stories during a course in narrative inquiry, Damianovic (1999) decided to use images as an aesthetic tool to illustrate the way she lived her reflective experience. She thought windows could be a good way to inform how she saw herself in the beginning, in the middle, and at the end of the telling stories process she experienced. (See Figure 8.1.)

Based on the movements of narrative inquiry (Connelly & Clandinin, 2004), first Damianovic (1999) opened the window inward so as to understand and make meaning of her own stories of experiences. Then, she felt she was able to open the windows outward to see her action considering the landscape she was placed in.

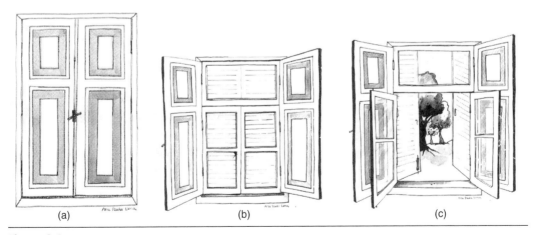

(a)   (b)   (c)

Figure 8.1

SOURCE: Images by Ana Paula Lima in Damianovic (1999, pp. 9, 55, 100). Reprinted with permission of Ana Paula Lima.

Also using images in the construction of research texts, Telles (1997) worked on a video biography with Rose, a teacher who taught Portuguese in Brazil. They were working on the value of words within the teaching-learning process. The video documentary (video biography) produced was the research text created to inform the final moment of a narrative inquiry process lived in a public school located in the city of São Paulo, Brazil.

There are other works on arts-informed narrative inquiry (Mwebi, 2005; Pires, 1998). The ones described are, however, representative of what arts-informed narrative inquiry can be. As pointed out before, not all arts-based/informed research can be considered narrative inquiry. Furthermore, qualities of narrative inquiry such as the empowerment of coresearchers and participants, the invitation to readers to reach their own conclusions, and the support for personal knowledge construction are present in all narrative inquiry work. We also see these characteristics in the arts-based/informed work of Bach (1998), Mickelson (1995, 2000), Telles (2005), Murphy (2004), and Duarte (1998). I now turn to a characteristic of arts-based/ informed narrative inquiry that holds promise and emphasis—that is, the honoring of multiple aesthetic perspectives.

Honoring Multiple (Aesthetic) Perspectives

Looking back at the works of Bach (1998), Mickelson (1995, 2000), Duarte (1996), Telles (2004, 2005), and Murphy (2004) I note that they honor multiple aesthetic perspectives in the development of their studies. Photography was the main tool used by Bach (1998) in collecting field texts. She also, however, composed poems in her research texts. Mickelson (1995, 2000) chose to use letters and poems to compose her research text. Duarte (1996, 1998) used drama and short stories to construct her research text. In different works, Telles (1997, 2004, 2005) applied the language of theater, of photography, and also of movies in composing a video biography of a teacher. Fiction writing was the main way Murphy (2004) composed his research text, but he also created a place for poems during the living of experiences with children. The landscape of arts-based/informed narrative inquiry seems engaged with the idea of honoring multiple aesthetic perspectives.

I see the consequences of using arts-based/informed narrative inquiries for researchers, participants, audience, and society. I draw on the work of Diamond and Mullen (1999), Greene (2000, 2001), and Eisner (2002).

Eisner (2002) points out that the opening up of multiple perspectives is a central point when working with art. In his words,

There is, in the arts, more than one interpretation to a musical score, more than one way to describe a painting or a sculpture, more than one appropriate form for a dance performance, more than one meaning for a poetic rendering of a person or a situation. In the arts diversity and variability are made central. (p. 197)

For Eisner (2002), honoring multiple perspectives is important because it can help schools, teachers, and students understand that there is not only one correct or appropriate answer to problems faced in everyday life. He writes, "One lesson the arts teach is that there can be more than one answer to a question and more than one solution to a problem; variability of outcome is okay" (p. 196).

Greene (2000, 2001) also talks about the need for releasing the imagination through arts as a way of changing our educational landscape and our society. For her, opening up a space for imagination is an important step for organizing a community in which pluralism and diversity exist and multiple voices are heard. According to Greene (2000), art is a way of achieving a pluralist path to expand community.

The idea of multiple aesthetic perspectives can be seen in Diamond and Mullen (1999) as they refer to different types of languages. Searching for examples of arts-based inquiries, they talk about romance, music, graphic arts, puppet performances, and poems as possible forms.

Based on these authors I believe that it is possible to conclude that the multiple aesthetic perspectives provided by arts-based/informed narrative inquiries can promote space for empowerment, construction of knowledge, and inclusion. The multiple languages in this mode of study can enable new and different discourses and contexts (Ely, Vinz, Downing, & Anzul, 2001). By considering the existence of different discourses, it opens up doors through which we realize that there are other contexts to be studied or at least other ways of looking at the world. We can construct knowledge in and about different landscapes. Taking into account the endless possibilities of composing art and promoting aesthetic experiences, we can note the number of perspectives that are still to be seen and lived. Being aware of the possibilities can empower people to take new roads. This sense of new and different perspectives of knowledge construction and research landscapes creates space for pushing boundaries.

Pushing Boundaries in the Qualitative Research Landscape

Arts-based/informed narrative inquiry is pushing the boundaries of the qualitative research landscape. First, narrative inquiry does not rely on searching for truth or broad generalization. Second, by honoring art and multiple aesthetic perspectives, narrative inquiry has provoked changes in the academic discourse. This change has happened through different ways of gathering data and different ways of presenting research texts.

Zamboni (2001) states that when paradigms are to be changed, some norms need to become flexible. He also comments that changes bring risks of marginalization. His idea makes me think of my concerns described in the beginning of this chapter. On the one hand, I was seduced to go straight to an aesthetic plotline, but on the other I recognized that it was not the accustomed academic way of writing and so I decided I would try to follow a middle road. Tensions like this challenge those interested in arts-based and arts-informed narrative inquiry. Narrative inquirers, however, have been pushing the boundaries for some years, and some changes have already occurred. Some issues posed here have already been considered and accepted by some communities within the academic landscape. Nevertheless, not everybody in the academic plotline considers this possibility.

But the boundaries to be pushed are not only evolving out of a narrative inquiry landscape. Telles (2005) and Diamond and Mullen (1999), for example, write of a lack of ability to use the artistic form. Many times when composing this chapter, for example, I felt like creating aesthetic forms to write this text. But my lack of ability to draw or write using literary forms as a nonnative speaker of English did not allow me to take this road. The lack of skills to work with images and other kinds of visual aids, however, can be faced. Diamond and Mullen (1999), Telles (2004), and Damianovic (1999) solved this problem by having technicians help them produce the images they were trying to compose. But then another tension emerges: Is it necessary to be an artist to produce art in narrative inquiry?

As we can see, there are some boundaries to be pushed even among those already involved. I hope this chapter can help open doors to a better understanding of what arts-based and arts-informed narrative inquiry is and the possible roads to be taken in this mode of narrative inquiry. I conclude as follows.

It seems that serendipity has been around me since I started writing this chapter. I read a poem by Stevens (1982) in many of the materials I studied. Often I thought I could transcribe it in this chapter, but I decided not to. At the end of my journey, however, this idea returned. I was almost done when I opened up some books and there the poem was. I realized something of it had to be here. According to Stevens, rationalists wear square hats and think in square rooms, and in his point of view it would be relevant if they could wear sombreros instead. This idea inspires me to close this chapter by summarizing what I've discussed in a different format. This way I take "the road not taken" in the beginning of this chapter.

> The language of arts in a narrative inquiry landscape
>
> art as a tool to promote reflection
>
> art for the sake of aesthetic experience
>
> photography images poems fiction novels films drama theater music dance whatever
>
> arts-based narrative inquiry,
>
> creative aesthetic field text gathering
>
> arts-informed narrative inquiry,
>
> creative aesthetic research text presentation
>
> multiple aesthetic perspectives
>
> empowerment inclusion construction of knowledge
>
> changing the qualitative research landscape
>
> pushing boundaries . . .

taking risks . . .

Does it mean wear sombreros?

Author's Note: I thank Professor Maria Antonieta Alba Celani, Professor Jean Clandinin, and Professor Pam Steeves for helping me with this chapter.

Consulting Editors: Hedy Bach and Margot Ely

Notes

1. Bach poem (1998) is used with permission of QualPress.
2. Quotations from Joy-Ruth Mickelson's dissertation (1995) and poem (2000) are reprinted with permission of Joy-Ruth Mickelson.
3. Murphy's taped conversations are reprinted with permission of Shaun Murphy.

References

Alves, R. (1995). *Conversas com quem gosta de ensinar* [Talking to those who like to teach]. São Paulo, Brazil: Artes Poética.

Bach, H. (1998). *A visual narrative concerning curriculum, girls, photography, etc.* Edmonton, Alberta, Canada: Qual Institute Press.

Barone, T. (1995). The purpose of arts-based educational research. *International Journal of Educational Research, 32*(2), 169–180.

Barthes, R. (1989). *Aula* (L. P. Moisés, Trans.). São Paulo, Brazil: Cultrix.

Campbell, C. S., & Ogden, M. H. (Eds.). (1999). *Constructed wetlands in the sustainable landscape.* New York: Wiley.

Chan, E. (2003). Ethnic identity in transition: Chinese new year through the years. *Journal of Curriculum Studies, 35*(4), 409–423.

Clandinin, D. J., & Connelly, M. (2000). *Narrative inquiry: Experience and story in narrative research.* San Francisco: Jossey-Bass.

Collier, J., & Collier, M. (Eds.). (1986). *Visual anthropology: Photography as a research method.* Albuquerque: University of New Mexico Press.

Connelly, M., & Clandinin, J. D. (2004). *Narrative inquiry. Complementary methods for research in education* (3rd ed.). Washington, DC: American Educational Research Association.

Coomaraswamy, A. K. (1956). *Christian and Oriental philosophy of art.* New York: Dover.

Damianovic, M. C. C. C. L. (1999). *Caminhando, buscando e tecendo significados de vida e educação* [Walking, seeking, and weaving meanings of life and education]. Unpublished master's thesis, Catholic University, São Paulo, Brazil.

Davidson, I. (1997). The power of pictures. In M. Conkey, O. Soffrer, D. Stratmann, & D. Jahonski (Eds.), *Beyond art: Pleistocene image and symbol* (pp. 125–160). Memoirs of the California Academy of Sciences, 23. San Francisco: California Academy of Sciences.

Delahunt, M. R. (2006). *Artlex art dictionary.* Retrieved April 8, 2006, from http://www.artlex.com

Dewey, J. (1934). *Art as experience.* Toms River, NJ: Capricorn Books.

Dewey, J. (1938). *Experience and education.* New York: Collier Books.

Diamond, C. T. P., & Mullen, C. A. (Eds.). (1999). *The postmodern educator: Arts-based inquiries and teacher development.* New York: Peter Lang.

Doisneau, R., & Cavanna, F. (2002). *Les doigts pleins d'encre* [Fingers full of ink]. Paris: Hoëbeke.

Duarte, V. B. C. (1996). *Aprendendo a aprender, experienciar, refletir e transformar: Um processo sem fim* [Learning how to learn, to experience, to reflect, and to transform: An endless process]. Unpublished doctoral dissertation, Catholic University, São Paulo, Brazil.

Duarte, V. B. C. (1998). *Living drama in the classroom: Uma proposta de abertura e aprendizagem significativa.* Research project, Catholic University, São Paulo, Brazil.

Eisner, E. W. (Ed.). (1976). *The arts, human development and education.* Berkeley, CA: McCutchan.

Eisner, E. W. (1991). *The enlightened eye: Qualitative inquiry and the enhancement of educational practice.* New York: Macmillan.

Eisner, E. W. (2002). *The arts and the creation of mind.* Harrisonburg, VA: Yale University Press.

Eisner, E. W., & Barone, T. (1997). Art-based educational research. In R. M. Jaeger (Ed.), *Complementary methods for research in education* (pp. 73–79). Washington, DC: AERA.

Ellis, V. (2002). Walking around the curriculum tree: An analysis of a third/fourth-grade mathematics lesson. *Journal of Curriculum Studies, 35*(4), 1–18.

Ely, M., Vinz, R., Downing, M., & Anzul, M. (2001). *On writing qualitative research: Living by words.* London: Writers and Readers Publishing Cooperative Society.

Geertz, C. (1995). *After the fact: Two countries, four decades, one anthropologist.* Cambridge, MA: Harvard University Press.

Greene, M. (2000). *Releasing the imagination: Essays on education, the arts, and social change.* New York: Teachers College Press.

Greene, M. (2001). *Variations on a blue guitar: The Lincoln Center Institute lectures on aesthetic education.* New York: Teachers College Press.

Grumet, M. (1978). Voice: The search for a feminist rhetoric for educational studies. *Cambridge Journal of Education, 20*(2), 277–282.

Jacob, T. B. (2003). *Rothko.* Berlin, Germany: Taschen.

Lessing, D. (1955). *Through the tunnel.* New York: New Yorker.

Longman Dictionary of Contemporary English (New ed.). (1987). Harlow, UK: Longman.

McNiff, S. (1988). *Fundamentals of art therapy.* Springfield, IL: Charles C Thomas.

McNiff, S. (1998). *Art-based research.* London: Jessica Kingsley.

Mello, D. M. (1999). *Viajando pelo interior de um ser chamado professor* [Traveling through the interior of a being called teacher]. Unpublished master's thesis, Catholic University, São Paulo, Brazil.

Mello, D. M. (2005). Histórias de *subversão do currículo, conflitos e resistências: Buscando espaço para formação de professores na aula de língua inglesa do curso de Letras* [Stories of subverting curriculum, conflicts, and resistance: Searching for a place for teacher education in English classes of the Modern Languages undergraduate course]. Unpublished doctoral dissertation, Catholic University, São Paulo, Brazil.

Mickelson, J. R. (1995). *Our sons are labeled behaviour disordered: Here are the stories of our lives.* Unpublished doctoral dissertation, University of Alberta, Edmonton, Canada.

Mickelson, J. R. (2000). *Our sons were labeled behavior disordered: Here are the stories of our lives.* New York: Educator's International Press.

Murphy, S. (2004). *Understanding children's knowledge: A narrative inquiry into school experiences.* Unpublished doctoral dissertation, University of Alberta, Edmonton, Canada.

Mwebi, B. M. (2005). *A narrative inquiry into the experiences of a teacher and eight students learning about HIV/AIDS through a child-to-child curriculum approach.* Unpublished doctoral thesis, University of Alberta, Edmonton, Canada.

Norris, J. (2000). Drama as research: Realizing the potential of drama in education as a research methodology. *Youth Theatre Journal, 14,* 40–51.

Oyler. (2000). Review. In J. R. Mickelson, *Our sons were labeled behaviour disordered: Here are the stories of our lives* (back page). New York: Educator's International Press.

Pires, E. A. (1998). *De mapas e posturas críticas: Histórias de reflexões entre uma professora e sua coordenadora* [From maps to critical stances: Stories of reflection lived by a teacher and her coordinator]. Unpublished master's thesis, Catholic University, São Paulo, Brazil.

Sontag, S. (1966). *Against interpretation.* New York: Noonday.

Stevens, W. (1982). *The collected poems of Wallace Stevens.* New York: Knopf.

Telles, J. A. (1997). *Brincando com Rosa: Uma professora busca o valor da palavra* [Playing with Rose: A teacher searching for the value of the word] [Videonarrativa]. São Paulo, Brazil: Videoteca da Secretaria do Estado da Educação do Município de São Paulo.

Telles, J. A. (2004). Ways of representation: The theatre as a tool for reflection and teacher development representation. In M. H. V. Abrahão (Ed.), *Prática de ensino de língua estrangeira: Experiências e reflexões* [Foreign language teaching practice: Experience and reflections] (pp. 61–106). Campinas, São Paulo, Brazil: Pontes Editores.

Telles, J. A. (2005). *Pesquisa educacional com base nas artes e reflexão compartilhada: Por formas alternativas de representação da docência e do conhecimento dos professores* [Arts-based educational research and shared reflection: Through alternative ways of representing teaching and teacher knowledge]. Unpublished postdoctoral work, UNESP, São Paulo, Brazil.

Tesch, R. (1990). *Qualitative research: Analysis types and software tools.* London: Falmer Press.

Zamboni, S. (2001). *A pesquisa em arte: Um paralelo entre arte e ciência* [Researching in art: Combining art and science]. Campinas, São Paulo, Brazil: Autores Associados.

CHAPTER 9

The Life Story Interview as a Bridge in Narrative Inquiry

Robert Atkinson

W e are the storytelling species. Storytelling is in our blood. We think in story form, speak in story form, and bring meaning to our lives through story. Our life stories connect us to our roots, give us direction, validate our own experience, and restore value to our lives. Life stories can fulfill important functions for us, and, as we recognize now more than ever, everyone has a story to tell about his or her life, and they are indeed important stories (Atkinson, 1995, 1998; Gubrium & Holstein, 1998; Kenyon & Randall, 1997; Randall, 1995).

The life story interview (Atkinson, 1998) provides a practical and holistic methodological approach for the sensitive collection of personal narratives that reveal how a specific human life is constructed and reconstructed in representing that life as a story. The life story interview has a multifaceted role as a narrative inquiry methodology, first and foremost in seeking to bring forth the voice and spirit within a life-as-a-whole personal narrative. This approach is built on a respect for individual storytellers and a regard for the subjective meaning carried within their stories. The life story offers a way, perhaps more than any other, for another to step inside the personal world of the storyteller and discover larger worlds.

The life story interview produces a first-person text, in the words of the storyteller, that can stand on its own, as any other text, or that can be examined through the lens of any theory or research question applied to it. This methodology has broad applications across disciplines: A researcher from any discipline can choose to apply this methodology to get at the particular research or disciplinary questions in hand, within the context of a life story, or a researcher from any field can turn to an existing life story text to examine it for the questions at hand. The life story approach has come into being through varied applications in a variety of disciplines.

The Historical and Disciplinary Context of the Life Story Interview

The life story interview is a qualitative, ethnographic, and field research method for gathering information on the subjective essence of one person's entire life experience. As a way of looking at life as a whole and of carrying out an in-depth study of individual lives, the life story may stand alone. It has become a central element of the burgeoning subfield of the narrative study of lives (Cohler, 1988; Josselson & Lieblich, 1993) for understanding single lives in detail and how the individual plays various roles in society (Cohler, 1993; Gergen & Gergen, 1993).

Because of its various applications across disciplines, there exist two very different and distinct ways of using a life story: for *ideographic* (individual or personal) or for *nomothetic* (universal, collective, or social) purposes. A life story can be analyzed or interpreted, from either an individual or collective perspective, and the content of a life story can also be gathered for either personal or social purposes or for both purposes at the same time. Within each of these ways of using a life story, there can also be differences of theoretical approach or research purposes.

Another important difference in the uses of life stories is whether the story stays in the words and voice of the storyteller (a first-person narrative) or whether the story is shifted to the words of the interviewer or researcher (a third-person narrative), or some combination of the two voices. No matter what the intended use of a life story, there is a significant difference depending on whose voice someone's story is ultimately told to others in after it passes beyond the interviewer or researcher.

Having evolved from many disciplinary and theoretical perspectives, what has become the life story interview can be traced back across time and disciplines through such terms as *life narratives, the study of lives, personal documents, personal history, life history, oral history,* and *the narrative study of lives* though each term, or categorization, is not synonymous with *life story* and has its own unique approach, perspective, and uses. The life story interview (Atkinson, 1995, 1998) is designed to help the storyteller, the listener, the reader, and the scholar to understand better how life stories serve the four functions of bringing us more into accord with ourselves (psychological), others (sociological), the mystery of life (spiritual), and the universe around us (philosophical). These four functions of life stories are briefly referred to here but are presented in more detail in my two books (Atkinson, 1995, chap. 1; 1998, pp. 9–16).

The Research Uses of Life Stories

Psychology

The ideographic use of life narratives for serious academic study is considered to have begun in psychology with Sigmund Freud's (1910/1957, 1911/1958) psychoanalytic interpretation of individual case studies although these were based on secondary documents. His usage of these narratives was primarily in applying his psychoanalytic theory to individual lives. Henry Murray (1938, 1955) was one of the first to study individual lives using life narratives primarily to understand personality development. Gordon Allport (1942) used personal documents to study personality development in individuals, focusing on primary documents, including narratives, while also considering the problems of reliability and validity of interpretation using such materials. Distinguishing between the ideographic and the nomothetic approaches, he raised the important question of "why not ask the person first if that is who you want to know something about."

The use of personal documents reached its maturation in Erik Erikson's studies of Luther (Erikson, 1958) and Gandhi (Erikson, 1969). Erikson (1975) also used the life history to explore how the historical moment influenced lives. This approach further led to a pursuit of psychobiography, or biography informed by psychological theory, a method used to understand the inner workings of the mind of individuals of historical significance (Runyan, 1982).

Another related approach was that of Robert Coles (1989), who, after having learned the value of stories from his parents who read to him as a child, listened to the stories of his patients, his students, and others and continued to learn yet more important lessons about life. For him, it was as much about the relationship involved in the telling and the listening—or as he put it, "We owe it to each other to respect our stories and learn from them" (p. 30).

The recent interest in story among personality psychologists, other social scientists, and scholars in diverse disciplines reflects the broader interest in narrative because it serves to illuminate the lives of persons in society. Theodore Sarbin (1986) uses narrative as the *root metaphor* and places it at the core of self-formation, for understanding human experience, while Jerome Bruner (1986) uses narrative as an important means for discovering how we *construct* our lives.

Dan McAdams (1985, 1993) uses the life story approach to understand better the formation of identity and the role of generativity in individual lives, two of Erikson's (1963) key developmental constructs. The narrative study of lives series furthers the theoretical understanding of individual life narratives through in-depth studies, methodological examinations, and theoretical explorations (Josselson, 1996; Josselson and Lieblich, 1993, 1995, 2000; Josselson, Lieblich, and McAdams, 2003; Lieblich and Josselson, 1994, 1997; Lieblich, McAdams, and Josselson, 2004; McAdams, Josselson, and Lieblich, 2002, 2006).

First-person narratives are an effective means for gaining an understanding of how the self evolves over time. Through the self-narrative process, researchers can secure useful information and come to the desired understanding of the self as a meaning-maker with a place in society, culture, and history (Freeman, 1992). These narratives may also be used as case studies to determine a subjective sense of identity formation and in particular how foreclosures or moratoriums may have limited or expanded life contexts (Erikson, 1963; Kroger, 1993; Marcia, 1966).

Gerontology

Personal stories are central to human development, the interaction between generations, and integrity in late life. It is commonly recognized in gerontology that a primary developmental task for the elder is the review of one's life (Butler, 1963). This is the process of remembering and expressing the experiences, struggles, lessons, and wisdom of a lifetime. Long before Butler described the "life review" process and referred to it as the "elder function," it was the traditional role of elders to pass on their values and wisdom through their stories. This is a time of life for remembering, clarifying, and even writing down one's "ultimate concerns" (Erikson, 1964; Tillich, 1957) before it is too late. "Narrative gerontology" is an emerging subfield focusing on the possibilities of the life as story metaphor in the field of aging and the ways narrative approaches, such as "guided autobiography" and life review, can be incorporated into practice to bring many benefits to the participants, including clarity, a deeper understanding of one's life themes, connection with others, and a new perspective on and meaning in one's life (Birren & Cochran, 2001; Birren, Kenyon, Ruth, Schroots, & Svensson, 1996; Kenyon, Clark, & de Vries, 2001).

Sociology

The nomothetic approach to life stories can be linked to the early narrative turn in sociology or to the Chicago School of sociology, represented by Thomas and Thomas (1928) and characteristically described in the words of Shaw (1929): "So far as we have been able to determine as yet, the best way to investigate the inner world of the person is through a study of himself through a life history" (p. 6). These groundbreaking works were followed up in sociology by Blumer (1969) and Becker (1976), and later by other sociologists using life histories to understand a social reality existing outside the story but described by the story, to define relationships and roles in a community, to explain an individual's understanding of social events, or to simply invite stories rather than reports during interviews (Bertaux, 1981; Chase, 1995; Linde, 1993; Mkhonza, 1995; Rosenthal, 1993).

Anthropology

The life history has long been a methodology of anthropological field work. L. L. Langness (1965) sees the life history as primarily biographical, not autobiographical, because of the way it is used to learn more about culture than the individuals in it themselves. He further defines the real nature of the life history as "seldom the product of the informant's clearly articulated, expressive, chronological account of his life" (p. 48). The life history is therefore an edited creation of the interviewer. As

James Spradley (1979) points out, some life histories are heavily edited by the ethnographer (often only 60% of the description is actually in the insider's own words or language), while others may be presented in the same form in which the recording occurred. Because of its broad use across disciplines, as well as the particular approach of each interviewer or researcher, the final form of a personal narrative can vary greatly. On the one hand, it can read as mostly the researcher's own description of what was said, done, or intimated. On the other, it can be a 100% first-person narrative in the words of the person interviewed. Anthropologists use the life history as the preferred unit of study for their measures of cultural similarities and variations (Abu-Lughod, 1993; Langness & Frank, 1981).

Folklore

The term *life story* has more of a home in folklore (Ives, 1986; Titon, 1980), defined simply as a person's story of his or her life or of what he or she thinks is a significant part of that life. Titon (1980) takes the distinction between terms an important step further, making it clearer how to distinguish *life story* from *biography* (the history of a life), *oral history*, and the *personal history* or *life history*. He notes that history is ultimately *found out* in the sense of discovery of knowledge, while a story, charged with the power of lived experience, is *made* not as in fiction or a lie but in the creative or imaginative sense. The life *history* typically removes, at least in part, the voice of the storyteller, putting the narrative more in the voice of the researcher, while a life story more often retains the voice of the storyteller, often in its entirety. A language that arises from deeply felt, personal experience is the language of the life story.

History

The oral history approach has long been used as an important source for enhancing local history (Allen & Montell, 1981). Memory and narrative are intricately linked in the *incomprehensibility* of the events of the Holocaust and the many testimonies resulting from this and other needs to remember on the part of survivors (Funkenstein, 1993; Langer, 1991).

Education

An interest in a narrative approach can be seen in the pioneering work of John Dewey (1938), whose focus on *experience* identified both the personal and the social along with the importance of the continuity of experience within both realms. Recently, other educators have used life stories and personal narratives as new ways of knowing in teaching and learning (Connelly & Clandinin, 1999; Witherell & Noddings, 1991). The life stories of educators can tell researchers how those individuals have found their own center through their chosen work; they can illustrate the primacy, in individual lives and in educational practice, of the quest for meaning and the importance of caring for persons.

Literature

Literary scholars use autobiography as texts through which to theoretically and critically explore questions such as design, style, content, literary themes, and personal truth (Olney, 1980). Autobiographies also hold much potential for other research endeavors such as reconstructing ways of knowing in women's lives (Helle, 1991) or charting cultural memory (Freeman, 2002).

Religion

A way of understanding the spiritual-religious-mystical function of stories and gaining insight into what people's greatest struggles and triumphs are, where their deepest values lie, what their quest has been, where they might have been broken, and where they were made whole again would be to examine religious autobiographies. These, as well as life stories, can portray religion and spirituality as a lived experience. Researchers can ask specific questions of the story. What beliefs, or worldview, are expressed in the story? Is the transcendent expressed? Did a spiritual community play a role in the life lived deeply? How does this spiritual autobiography compare with the lives of the classic spiritual leaders (Comstock, 1995)? Addressing questions of beliefs, values, customs, sacred traditions, and meaning in life has also long been the domain of anthropologists using life histories (Geertz, 1973; Langness & Frank, 1981). Folklorists know that life stories are the repositories of traditional beliefs, customs, and religious practices (Ives, 1986; Titon, 1980).

Philosophy

Personal stories can be examined to see how they bring us more into accord with the universe around us and to experience how subjective accounts of one's life often contain a personal worldview, a personal philosophy, a personal value system, a personal ideology, and a view of what is morally, if not politically, correct—in other words, how life is to be lived. A philosophical approach to how people make sense of the world we now live in or the personal vision or interpretation of what life and reality are about for the person could lead to important insights (Brockelman, 1985). Hermeneutic perspectives on narrative and life history have been taken to explore the relation between life and story—life as a process of narrative interpretation and stories as interpretations of life (Widdershoven, 1993).

Beyond disciplinary boundaries, some narrative researchers conceive of life narratives as a circumstantially mediated, constructive collaboration between the interviewer and interviewee. This approach stresses the situated emergence of the story told as opposed to the subjectively faithful, experientially oriented account. In this constructionist perspective, stories are evaluated not so much for how well they accord with the life experiences in question but more for how the accounts of lives are used by others for various descriptive purposes (Holstein & Gubrium, 2000a, 2000b).

Life narratives are needed especially of individuals from groups underrepresented in research studies to at least balance out the databases that have been relied on for so long in generating theory. More narratives in the voice of women would help to eventually achieve a synthesis of knowledge that would benefit both genders (Gergen & Gergen, 1993). A wide range of uses and applications of narrative knowing in relation to gender issues already exist (Helle, 1991; Lieblich & Josselson, 1994). For similar reasons, since how we tell our stories is mediated by our culture (Josselson & Lieblich, 1995), we need to hear the stories of individuals from culturally unheard from groups. Life stories of gay men and lesbians would also contribute to a more complete understanding of the issues related to change in people's lives (Ben-Ari, 1995; Boxer & Cohler, 1989).

The research applications of the life story interview are limitless. In any field, the life story itself could serve as the centerpiece for published research, or segments could be used as data to illustrate any number of research needs. The life story interview allows for more data than you may actually use, which is both good practice and provides a broad foundation of information to draw on. The life story approach can be used as a narrative inquiry methodology as well as for examining many substantive issues within the disciplines already mentioned.

Josselson and Lieblich (1993) make the connections between these approaches much clearer when they state,

> Life story is the interface between life as lived and the social times; like Erikson's concept of identity, life narrative interweaves individual experience with historical reality and thus interfaces with approaches in sociology, anthropology, and the burgeoning field of oral history. (p. xiii)

The Life Story Interview as a Methodological Bridge

The life story interview can be seen as a natural bridge (a) between the disciplines using narrative inquiry methodologies; (b) between the methodologies themselves and within this between ideographic and nomothetic approaches; (c) between the telling and the living of a narrative (or between the lived experience of life and living life); and (d) between the whole and the parts of the life being narrated.

My own evolution toward the life story interview, its ideographic approach, and wanting to view a life as a whole began as an undergraduate philosophy major when I was introduced to the work of Wilhelm Dilthey by my professor, William Kluback (1956), who was one of his translators. In the 19th century, Dilthey's work in what he called *geisteswissenshaften* (the scientific study of the whole person, or the human sciences) laid a foundation for an appreciation of the actual *lived experience* of individual persons and in particular recognized that describing lived experience is fundamentally an act of narrative interpretation. Whether it is on the part of the person living the life or another (a researcher) eliciting it from the one living it, the interpretation is the result of understanding from inside the meaning of the experience through a *psychological reenactment*, an imaginative reconstruction, or narration of the experience.

Dilthey's concept of *life* (*das Leben*) referred to something very real and significant, life as we experience it in our daily lives (Schwandt, 2001, p. 273). This represents a classical grounding for both narrative and interpretive approaches that look at human beings as whole persons. Dilthey understood that the individual's experience of life is something not to be discounted by the desire to achieve scientific knowledge since each individual life experience is simultaneously in some ways like no one else's (unique), in some ways like some others', and in some ways like everyone else's (universal). The life story interview brings each of these perspectives of lived experience into clear focus.

In 1968, as my thesis project for a master's degree in American Folk Culture, I undertook my first life story interview, sitting with Harry Siemsen, a Catskill mountain farmer-singer, at his kitchen table, recording his life and songs for many wonderful weekends, moved by his willingness to share his life with someone he hadn't known before and learning how a deep connection can be forged between people through this exchange.

It was during this graduate work that I also began to look at the bigger picture of stories and their role in traditional communities. Stories traditionally served as a primary guide in the lives of the people. Stories told from generation to generation carried timeless elements, enduring values, and lessons about life lived deeply. Traditional stories, myths, and folktales followed a pattern that has been represented as separation, transition, incorporation (van Gennep, 1960); birth, death, rebirth (Eliade, 1954); or departure, initiation, return (Campbell, 1968). This pattern is like a blueprint that communicates a balance between opposing forces and offers a structure forming the basis for the plot of a story.

The stories we tell of our own lives today are still guided by the same pattern and contain the same enduring elements—universal themes and ageless motifs and archetypes. We discover meaning within the stories we tell of our lives through the recognizable structure of *beginning, muddle,* and *resolution.* Our lives consist of many repetitions of this pattern, a series of events and circumstances drawn from a well of archetypal experiences that are common to all other human beings (Atkinson, 1995; Campbell, 1968). It is within this ageless and universal context that we can best begin to understand the importance and power of the life story and how it is fundamental to our very nature.

During my second master's degree, in counseling, I began to see the power not only in telling but in retelling, or composing and recomposing, recasting and reframing one's story and especially in getting to one's deeper or inner story. In my doctoral work, focusing on cross-cultural human development, I further expanded this interest by using the life story interview to explore how cultural values and traditions influenced development across the life cycle. My postdoctoral research work allowed me to explore further Henry Murray's (1938) study of the lives approach and the connections between this, Bert Cohler's (1982) life history interests, and Dilthey's human studies (Rickman, 1979).

All along, I have felt that it is important, in trying to understand another's experience in life or their relation to others, to let their voice be heard, to let them speak for and about themselves first, and to look for the wholeness in their life. If we want to know the unique perspective of an individual, there is no better way to see this, and how the parts do fit together, than in their voice in their life story. It is, after all, this subjective perspective that tells us what we are looking for in all our research efforts and what constitutes their reality of their world. The storyteller is the first interpreter of the story they tell. What is new about *the new ethnography* Holstein and Gubrium (1995) describe is first allowing the storytellers' construction of their own reality and then, as researchers, learning what we can from this about who they are.

Since creating the Center for the Study of Lives at the University of Southern Maine in 1988, I have tried to merge all these interests not only in building bridges across disciplines but also in building a growing archive of life stories, currently numbering more than 500, to offer researchers with various purposes and interests a unique database. Most of the life stories in the archive were gathered by my graduate students for class projects designed for them to learn as much as possible about how one person views his or her development over time and across the life cycle. The life stories in the archives are available to all researchers for secondary usage and can be searched by topics or categories on the cover sheet. These will soon be searchable online as well.

The 1990s saw a rapid growth in the understanding and use of life stories and other narrative approaches. The movement toward life stories, where we tell our own story in our own words, is a movement toward acknowledging the importance of personal truth from the subjective point of view. This movement is championed by Bruner (1986, 1987, 1990, 1991), the cognitive psychologist who has illustrated that personal meaning (and reality) is actually constructed during the making and telling of one's narrative, that our own experiences take the form of the narratives we use to tell about them, and that stories are our way of organizing, interpreting, and creating meaning from our experiences while maintaining a sense of continuity through it all. James Birren (Birren & Birren, 1996), the gerontologist, has also long been using guided autobiography (a variation of form on the life story—the story of a life written by the one who has experienced it) as a source of personal insight and clarity as well as psychological and social science research material. I believe that there is much in each life story to identify the unique value and worth of each life and that there are many common elements, motifs, and issues that all life stories express, indeed that we all share as human beings, along with some differences that exist.

Defining a Life Story

With the various disciplinary applications of the life story, and other narrative inquiry approaches providing many definitions to consider, I will just offer the one I have used previously:

> A life story is the story a person chooses to tell about the life he or she has lived, told as completely and honestly as possible, what is remembered of it, and what the teller wants others to know of it, usually as a result of a guided interview by another. . . . A life story is a fairly complete narrating of one's entire experience of life as a whole, highlighting the most important aspects. (Atkinson, 1998, p. 8)

To this original definition of the life story, from Dilthey's framework, can be added the following: putting one's life as a whole, one's entire lived experience, into story form.

A person's life story, the one he or she chooses to tell others, is what is most real, most important to him or her and is what gives us, the casual reader as well as the researcher, the clearest sense of the person's subjective understanding of his or her lived experience, his or her life as a whole. The key to the life story is keeping the story in the words and voice of the one telling it. The life story narrative that results from the life story interview, after it is transcribed, with the interviewer's questions left out, and the storyteller's words put into sentence and paragraph form, becomes the essence of what has happened to a person. It presents an insider's perspective on, and understanding of, a life lived.

A life story interview is not a procedure for collecting and documenting a category of data as a qualitative counterpart to demographic statistics. It is not intended to be data collected with specific theoretically embedded research questions that would guide data collection as well as interpretation, although it is possible a researcher might want to apply the methodology of the life story interview in carrying out such a project. The research question of a life story interview may only be, What is the story this person wants others to hear and what meaning does this story convey? More will be said about this in the next section.

A life story is an ideographic, subjective approach to expressing the parts of one's life as a whole and conveying the meaning taken from them. A life story gives us the vantage point of seeing how one person experiences and understands her or his life over time. It enables us to see and identify threads that connect one stage or component of one's life to another.

A recorded life story can take a factual form, a metaphorical form, a poetic form, or any other creatively expressive form. What is important is that the life story be told in the form, shape, and style most comfortable to the person telling the story. It can cover the time from birth to the present, or before and beyond. It includes the important events, experiences, and feelings of a lifetime and is a way of understanding better the past and the present and a way of leaving a personal legacy for the future. The point of the life story interview is to give the person the opportunity to tell his or her story, the way he or she chooses to tell it, so we can learn from their voice, their words, and their subjective meaning of their experience of life.

An important distinction between the life story and an oral history is made by Titon (1980):

> In oral history the balance of power between the informants and historian is in the historian's favor, for he asks the questions, sorts through the accounts for the relevant information, and edits his way toward a coherent whole . . . . But in the life story the balance tips the other way, to the storyteller, while the listener is sympathetic and his responses are encouraging and nondirective. If the conversation is printed, it should ideally be printed verbatim. (p. 283)

It is this sense of encouragement in guiding the telling, the sympathetic listening for the subjective meaning of one's life story, or the subjective interpretation of one's lived experience as told to others (usually at least implicit in the story itself), along with the mutually equitable approach and outcome, that is most characteristic of the life story. The life story seeks the identity one has shaped, a glimpse of the personality one has developed, the important interpersonal and social relationships one has formed, and a sense of one's values, beliefs, and worldview in the storyteller's own words. This is how the life story carries subjective psychological, sociological, spiritual, and philosophical functions for the storyteller all in one ideographic text.

A Question of Theory

The life story interview, as used here, avoids debates of theoretical approaches because it is first and foremost concerned with getting the entire subjective story of the life lived in the words of the person who has lived it rather than with primarily addressing a particular research agenda. The need for specific research questions is sometimes expected, but this is not an essential, inherent part of the methodology.

The life story itself, as told to an interviewer, is atheoretical in that people do not tell their own story based on a preconceived theory. As individuals, we experience the world not as scientists, through a theoretical lens, but as persons who are trying to give meaning to our own unique or universal lived experiences. We do not approach understanding our own lives with the rigor of a scientific experiment or research project, but we do, however, bring our own subjective understanding or interpretation to our lived experience based on an inner sense of what our experience means to us. Individual lives do carry meaning of their own (at least personal meaning), and it is the purpose of the life story interview to help bring forth this meaning. The life story interview is therefore not typically guided by specific theoretical or research questions, other than the questions that would be used to help elicit the story itself.

The subjective, first-person, atheoretical life story text can also be seen as pretheoretical—a narrative gathered initially as much for the service provided to the storyteller in guiding his or her process as for its potential research use in a variety of ways. A researcher can, however, add, apply, or assign his or her theoretical stance or understanding to it, just as a literary scholar could add a theoretical perspective to an autobiography. It is also possible, under any methodological circumstances, for a researcher to undertake a life story interview with specific research questions embedded into the interview itself along with those designed to elicit the entire life story. What the life story interview approach shows is that people do not tell their story based on a theoretical framework, yet there can be much meaning expressed in the story, and any theory that fits can be applied to it.

The inquiry in the narrative approach of a life story interview is in assisting, if necessary, the storyteller to become more aware of the meaning within his or her experience as he or she tells and crafts it into story form. Inquiry, in the life story interview approach, is a two-part process: First, in the telling it focuses on helping the storyteller develop his or her subjective meaning of the story through using open-ended, reflective questions as much as possible that help bring this out. Second in the reading of the text of their story it can focus on objectively identifying themes, issues, or connections across the story that may be inherent to the lived experience of the story itself or based on an existing or preferred theory of inquiry, interpretation, or analysis that may also be based on the research questions used, if any. It is only when the researcher comes to the life story later, as a text to be interpreted, with a theoretical framework in hand to read it with, that the life story takes on a specific theoretical perspective. This becomes the objective theory applied to the text of the life story, which can then stand alongside the storyteller's unique subjective meaning given to his or her lived experience and expressed within the text and carried in the story itself.

Benefits of the Life Story Interview

It is impossible to anticipate what a life story interview will be like, not so much for how to do it but for the power of the experience itself. I find this to be the case over and over with students who report how meaningful it was for them to have done the interview, especially when it was with someone they were already close to, like a parent or spouse. Just witnessing—really hearing, understanding, and accepting, without judgment—another's life story can be transforming.

A woman who had completed a life story interview with her father said, "There was no way I could have prepared for the emotional impact this experience had on me." She was overwhelmed by what she had learned about her father—from his having been raised during the Depression by a single mother as one of four children in poverty and with constant uprooting—to having witnessed the frontline horrors of WW II and struggling to enter the postwar working world with a grade school education.

There may be no equal to the life story interview for revealing more about the inner life of a person. Historical reconstruction may not be the primary concern in a life story; what is, is how people see themselves at this point in their lives and want others to see them. A life story offers a sometimes hidden glimpse of the human qualities and characteristics that make us all so fascinating *and* fun to listen to.

I have found that the vast majority of people really want to share their life story. All that most people usually need is someone to listen or someone to show a sincere interest in their story and they will welcome the interview. For those who may be reluctant for reasons of being intimidated, embarrassed, or shamed or simply be unsure about it or uncomfortable with it, here are a few of the many valuable benefits that can come with sharing a life story for those who are willing and able to reflect on the process and the content of their story:

1. A clearer perspective on personal experiences and feelings is gained, which brings greater meaning to one's life.

2. Greater self-knowledge and a stronger self-image and self-esteem are gained.

3. Cherished experiences *and* insights are shared with others.

4. Joy, satisfaction, and inner peace are gained in sharing one's story with others.

5. Sharing one's story is a way of purging, or releasing, certain burdens and validating personal experience—it is in fact central to the recovery process.

6. Sharing one's story helps create community and may show that we have more in common with others than we thought.

7. Life stories can help other people see their lives more clearly or differently and perhaps be an inspiration to help them change something in their life.

8. Others will get to know and understand us better, in a way that they hadn't before.

9. A better sense of how we want our story to end, or how we could give it the "good" ending we want, might be gained. By understanding our past and present, we also gain a clearer perspective of our goals for the future.

Not everyone will experience the life story interview in the same way. Some may look back on certain parts of their lives with regret, and for some it could even be a painful process. But even this kind of reaction to the interview could have its eventual positive outcomes.

The Life Story Interview as Process

Doing a life story interview is both an art and a science. Although a fairly uniform research methodology can be used to gain much important data, there is also much left to individual variation in the depth of reflection and reporting involved in telling one's life story. The life story interview is essentially a template that will be applied differently in different situations, circumstances, or settings.

For example, there are more than 200 questions suggested in *The Life Story Interview* (Atkinson, 1998) that can be asked to obtain a life story. These are suggested questions only, with only the most appropriate few to be used for each person interviewed. There are times when a handful of the questions might actually be used and other times when two or three dozen might be used, and in each case, very likely a different set of questions are chosen. The key to getting the best interview is being flexible and being able to adapt to specific circumstances.

In my view, the life story interview can be *approached* scientifically, but it is best *carried out* as an art. Though there may be a structure (a set of questions) that can be used, just as there are good and better artists, there are good and better interviewers. The execution of the interview, whether structured or not, will vary from one interviewer to another.

A life story interview involves the three following steps: (1) *planning* (preinterview)—preparing for the interview, including understanding why a life story can be beneficial; (2) *doing the interview itself* (interviewing)—guiding a person through the telling of his or her life story while recording it on either audio or video tape; and (3) finally, *transcribing the interview* (postinterview)—leaving questions and comments by the interviewer, and other repetitions, out (only the words of the person telling his or her story remain, so that it then becomes a flowing, connected narrative in the person's own words). One might then give the transcribed life story to the person to review and check over for any changes he or she might want to make in it. Once the final draft of the life story has been read and approved by the storyteller, then the interviewer or researcher can respond to the life story in the form of a personal reaction, substantive interpretation, or theoretical analysis.

The length of a life story interview can vary considerably. Ideally, it is best to let the interview take its course naturally to cover all that the life storyteller wants to cover of his or her life. What may be typical is anything from a 1-hour interview to two or three interviews of 1 hour each with the person to record his or her entire life story. In some cases, this may be considered a brief life story interview, but much can be learned about the person's life in a two- or three-part interview that extends over 3 hours.

Some life story interviews could even go on for 2 or 3 dozen hours. This length of interview would be more like a full-length assisted autobiography. I have done a life story interview of more than 40 hours that was later published as the autobiography of Babatunde Olatunji, the African drummer (Olatunji & Atkinson, 2005). The interviews took place as we were able to fit them into our respective schedules, and with time needed for transcriptions, editing, and the publication process, the entire project took 12 years to complete.

The Life Story Interview as Product

What we will end up with is a flowing life story narrative in the words of the person telling the story, essentially a verbatim transcription, leaving out only repetitions, other completely extraneous information that has nothing to do with the life story itself, and the interviewer's questions. Some reordering of content to make it chronological may or may not be necessary to add to the clarity or readability of the story. A great advantage to the life story approach is that the person whose story it is can be consulted and given the final say in what the life story will look like in its final form. He or she can also answer any questions or concerns that may come up after transcription. The person telling his or her life story should always have the last word in how his or her story is presented in written form before it gets passed on to others or is published.

The Life Story Interview in the Continua of Narrative Approaches

In looking at the life story as a bridge, we can also see a series of continua generated by its use. First, between the disciplines using narrative inquiry methodologies, the life story interview represents a bridge in the unique-to-universal continuum. Research methodologies in most disciplines look for either data that are specific to a case study or data that are generalizable from many sources. The life story interview is a methodology that yields data that are both unique-to-the-individual and universal-for-the-individual (as in the common motifs and archetypes experienced). Second, between the narrative inquiry methodologies themselves, there is a continuum that exists between ideographic and nomothetic approaches. This continuum would look something like this: Starting on the ideographic side would be autobiography and personal documents, with life story representing a bridge between this and the nomothetic side, which would continue on with life history, oral history, and biography.

Third, between the telling and the living of a narrative (or between the lived experience of life and living life), the life story interview represents a natural bridge between the process of telling a life story and the experience of living a life story. The life story interview methodology may be more clearly understood as, and characterized by, the process of one person assisting another in the *telling* of his or her life story. Yet this is only part of what is happening. The life story interview is also, as importantly, the telling of lived stories or the conveying of meaningful experiences from the past, the present, or even the future that are still *living* within the teller of the story in a familiar and recognizable story form.

Even though the working method of the life story is interview, which guides the telling of stories (process), it is the experience of having lived the stories of one's life that makes the product possible. And even in an ethnographic setting, when the interviewer lives in relation with the participants, the telling of the story is usually not entirely in the present or unfolding as they are in relationship. Although the beginning point may be this living in relation with others to get the living of stories, this more often than not includes the telling of stories once lived as well.

Both the telling and living of stories happen in the life story interview, too. Though the beginning point of a life story interview may more often be the past or the telling of stories lived, the life story not only moves up to the present, not only gets closer and closer to the living of stories, but by its very nature it keeps alive or brings to life again stories that are living in the mind, heart, and soul of the teller.

The telling of stories affords us a subjective perspective on one's life as it *has* unfolded while at the same time giving us a glimpse into the ongoing role of how those stories *continue to live for and within* the teller. There may not be as much difference or as clear a distinction between *telling* and *living* stories as we might imagine. In the context of a life story, this difference may not even exist. The life story is both story that is told and story that is lived. Sometimes the telling can involve living, and sometimes the living can involve telling.

Fourth, between the parts and the whole of the life being narrated, the life story interview represents a bridge from seeing an individual life in its parts to seeing it as a whole. The life story is told in parts, chronologically or thematically, and these stand out as key parts to a life but are also able to be seen as parts that fit together as a whole life. At the same time, the life-as-a-whole perspective is not lost when particular life story questions or focused research questions illuminate or highlight a part of the life. These more specific parts of a life gotten at by in-depth questions of any sort would still be best understood in the context of the whole life.

This situating the life story interview within the continua of narrative approaches makes the life story a powerful and innovative multidisciplinary narrative inquiry methodology. The life story interview is a unique bridge between narrative inquiry methods; it is a forward-looking, open-ended, inclusive methodology that represents for many disciplines a significant shift in design, focus, and intent, perhaps even a new *paradigm* in gathering *data* for holistic purposes that looks for, takes the lead of, and fully respects the viewpoint of the one from whom the data is being gathered. The life story interview is one of the best ways of giving full voice to those who would not normally be heard, to those who might be at the margins of any number of communities, and those whose valuable insights and reflections would not otherwise come to light.

Ethical and Interpretive Issues

We are asking real people to tell us their personal stories and taking their story to a larger audience. We, therefore, have to ask ourselves and be able to answer satisfactorily several questions, starting with, What is ethically prudent of us to make this exchange mutually beneficial to our interviewee and to our research agenda? How do we make sure that we maintain a consistency between our original intention and the final product and that this is clear all the way through? These are important questions, especially if we ask people for their stories and then write only *about* them, not using their own words to tell their story (Josselson, 1996; see also Chapter 21 in this volume).

Such questions are tied to the ultimate aim of narrative inquiry, which is the interpretation of experience (Josselson & Lieblich, 1995). Qualitative, or narrative, approaches and the review of each narrative text or life story bring forth their own categories of analysis and interpretive needs, rather than these being set from the beginning, as in quantitative studies (McCracken, 1988). In life storytelling, we are really seeking the *insider's* viewpoint on the life being lived.

A fundamental interpretive guideline is that the storyteller should be considered both the expert and the authority on his or her life, thus having the final say in what gets told. This would create a multiplicity of interpretive perspectives, just as a portrait painted from the side or from the front is still a faithful portrait (Frank, 1980; Runyan, 1982). A personal narrative is not meant to be read as an exact record of everything or even what actually happened in the person's life (Riessman, 1993). Historical truth is not the main issue in narrative. What matters is if the life story is deemed trustworthy, more than "true." We are, after all, seeking the subjective reality.

One view holds that the stories that convey the subjective quest of the person, even though they might be evasive, are their *own truth* (Frank, 1995). Some people may be as factual as is possible, some may invent pieces to satisfy some need, and some may be creative.

An example of these possibilities is B. B. King, the great blues singer, who states in his autobiography (King & Ritz, 1996), "Some may accuse me of remembering wrong. That's okay, because I'm not writing a cold-blooded history. I'm writing a memory of my heart. That's the truth I'm after—following my feelings, no matter where they lead" (p. 2). He wants to remember the best he can and tells a story of the heart. This may be all we can ask of someone telling his or her story who doesn't have a photographic memory.

There are, by definition, limits to all life stories, all autobiographies, all interviews. Since people aren't under oath when telling their life story, interviewers should be aware that what they are getting may not be the whole truth. We can be sure, though, that what we are getting is the story they want to tell us. That in itself tells us much about what we really want to know. As Arras (1997) points out, such narratives ought to be favored because we can't do any better.

Future Directions

Any consideration of future directions will, to some degree, be built on speculation while also taking into account current trends. If future research directions reflect other trends in society, we might want to consider the movement in social, cultural, and economic realms toward recognizing the interconnectedness between the parts and the whole. We might want to ask if the world we live in is being seen as more and more interconnected, how this might affect the interviewer-interviewee relationship. Will this change in any way the relationship between a person being interviewed and the one doing the interviewing? If a greater connection between human beings conducting research and generating data were felt, could this mean a greater openness to really explore various research questions, a greater desire to want to learn more or maybe even different kinds of things, both objectively and subjectively, about each other? Could it ultimately lead to an even deeper understanding of how, why, and in what ways we, as human beings, are connected?

This possibility is already somewhat built into the life story interview methodology. The life story interview is more than a methodology. It is a way of being in relationship with another that is rarely found in today's harried world. The opportunity for a deep connection between the teller and the listener in a life story interview is unparalleled. When I had the honor of listening to and recording Baba Olatunji's entire life story for his autobiography, from his traditional Yoruba upbringing to his becoming a cultural ambassador for Africa to his role in the civil rights movement to his vision for Voices of Africa, I was literally hearing a story that no one else in this world today could tell (Olatunji & Atkinson, 2005). This experience brought me closer to not only Baba the person but to his culture and his world. Yet this is as it could be for any life story interviewer. The experience becomes a rare and unique opportunity to fully enter another's life, culture, and world. This then becomes part of one's own life, culture, and world. The life story interview—and other narrative inquiry methodologies—could play a role in the greater realization of our understanding of the world as a network of multiple and diverse, yet interrelated, relationships.

If the notion of interviewer as separate from the interviewee shifted with the trends of our time to a notion of interconnectedness, we might also come closer to what Erikson (1987) spoke of as a "wider identity," which he described as "a future all-human, all-inclusive identity" (p. 497), one that would acknowledge what we already are—one species. He says identity is an issue reaching much deeper than the conscious choice of roles; moving toward a wider identity, our narrower identities loosen and we gradually identify with mankind. If identity in the future becomes as bound up with others as it now is with one's self, how might the research relationship change and how would this affect narrative inquiry?

These possible changes would not necessarily threaten research as an endeavor but could even enhance and enrich our efforts. An individual consciousness usually comes with clear boundaries that separate us from others and our environment. A consciousness of the whole and of our identities as interpenetrating each other, however, would overcome boundaries and could enable us to still be as eager and committed to learn as much about others as possible as we ever were. Such a shift could also affect the existing power differentiation between researcher and interviewee.

Conclusion

A life story is not a history that is discovered, it is a story that arises from lived experience. It is a retelling of one's life as a whole in the voice of the teller, as it is remembered and in a language that is deeply felt. Life stories serve as an excellent means for understanding how people see their own experiences, their own lives, and their interactions with others. They allow us to learn more than almost any other methodology about human lives and society from one person's perspective.

Life stories told seriously and consciously are timeless; settings, circumstances, and sometimes meanings change, but motifs remain constant across lives and time. Life stories make connections, shed light on the possible paths through life, and lead us to our deepest feelings, the values we live by, and the commonalities of life.

More life stories need to be brought forth that respect and honor the personal meanings the life storytellers give to their stories. There is an exciting future for life stories, the narrative study of lives, and narrative inquiry. The more we share our own stories, the closer we all become.

Consulting Editors: Catherine Kohler Riessman and Geert Kelchtermans

References

Abu-Lughod, L. (1993). *Writing women's worlds: Bedouin stories.* Berkeley: University of California Press.

Allen, B., & Montell, L. (1981). *From memory to history: Using oral sources in local historical research.* Nashville, TN: American Association for State and Local History.

Allport, G. (1942). *The use of personal documents in psychological science.* New York: Social Science Research Council.

Arras, J. D. (1997). Nice story, but so what? Narrative and justification in ethics. In H. L. Nelson (Ed.), *Stories and their limits: Narrative approaches to bioethics.* New York: Routledge.

Atkinson, R. (1995). *The gift of stories: Practical and spiritual applications of autobiography, life stories, and personal mythmaking.* Westport, CT: Bergin & Garvey.

Atkinson, R. (1998). *The life story interview.* Qualitative Research Methods Series, No. 44. Thousand Oaks, CA: Sage.

Becker, H. (1976). The career of the Chicago public school teacher. In M. Hammersley & P. Woods (Eds.), *The process of schooling: A sociological reader* (pp. 75–80). London: Routledge & Kegan/Open University Press.

Ben-Ari, A. (1995). It's the telling that makes the difference. In R. Josselson & A. Lieblich (Eds.), *The narrative study of lives: Vol. 3. Interpreting experience* (pp. 153–172). Thousand Oaks, CA: Sage.

Bertaux, D. (1981). *Biography and society.* Beverly Hills, CA: Sage.

Birren, J. E., & Birren, B. A. (1996). Autobiography: Exploring the self and encouraging development. In J. E. Birren, G. M. Kenyon, J. E. Ruth, J. J. F. Schroots, & T. Svensson (Eds.), *Aging and biography: Explorations in adult development* (pp. 283–299). New York: Springer.

Birren, J. E., & Cochran, K. N. (2001). *Telling the stories of life through guided autobiography groups.* Baltimore: Johns Hopkins University Press.

Birren, J. E., Kenyon, G. M., Ruth, J. E., Schroots, J. J. F., & Svensson, T. (Eds.). (1996). *Aging and biography: Explorations in adult development.* New York: Springer.

Blumer, H. (1969). *Symbolic interactionism: Perspective and method.* Englewood Cliffs, NJ: Prentice Hall.

Boxer, A. M., & Cohler, B. (1989). The life course of gay and lesbian youth: An immodest proposal for the study of lives. *Journal of Homosexuality, 17,* 315–355.

Brockelman, P. (1985). *Time and self.* New York: Crossroads.

Bruner, J. (1986). *Actual minds, possible worlds.* Cambridge, MA: Harvard University.

Bruner, J. (1987). Life as narrative. *Social Research, 54,* 1, 11–32.

Bruner, J. (1990). *Acts of meaning.* Cambridge, MA: Harvard University Press.

Bruner, J. (1991). The narrative construction of reality. *Critical Inquiry, 18,* 1–21.

Butler, R. (1963). The life review: An interpretation of reminiscence in the aged. *Psychiatry, 26,* 65–67.

Campbell, J. (1968). *The hero with a thousand faces.* New York: Meridian Books.

Chase, S. E. (1995). *Ambiguous empowerment: The work narratives of women school superintendents.* Amherst: University of Massachusetts Press.

Cohler, B. (1982). Personal narrative and the life course. In P. B. Baltes & O. G. Brim (Eds.), *Life span development and behavior* (Vol. 4). New York: Academic Press.

Cohler, B. (1988). The human studies and life history. *Social Service Review, 62*(4), 552–575.

Cohler, B. (1993). Aging, morale, and meaning: The nexus of narrative. In T. R. Cole, W. A. Achenbaum, P. L. Jakobi, & R. Kastenbaum (Eds.), *Voices and visions of aging* (pp. 107–133). New York: Springer.

Coles, R. (1989). *The call of stories: Teaching and the moral imagination.* Boston: Houghton Mifflin.

Comstock, G. L. (1995). *Religious autobiographies.* Belmont, CA: Wadsworth.

Connelly, R. M., & Clandinin, D. J. (1999). *Shaping a professional identity: Stories of educational practice.* New York: Teachers College Press.

Dewey, J. (1938). *Experience and education.* New York: Collier.

Eliade, M. (1954). *The myth of the eternal return*. Princeton, NJ: Princeton University Press.

Erikson, E. (1958). *Young man Luther: A study in psychoanalysis and history*. New York: W. W. Norton.

Erikson, E. (1963). *Childhood and society*. New York: W. W. Norton.

Erikson, E. (1964). *Insight and responsibility*. New York: W. W. Norton.

Erikson, E. (1969). *Gandhi's truth: On the origins of militant nonviolence*. New York: W. W. Norton.

Erikson, E. (1975). *Life history and the historical moment*. New York: W. W. Norton.

Erikson, E. (1987). *A way of looking at things: Selected papers*. New York: W. W. Norton.

Frank, A. (1995). *The wounded storyteller*. Chicago: University of Chicago Press.

Frank, G. (1980). Life histories in gerontology: The subjective side to aging. In C. L. Fry & J. Kieth (Eds.), *New methods for old age research: Anthropological alternatives*. Chicago: Loyola University of Chicago.

Freeman, M. (1992). Self as narrative: The place of life history in studying the life span. In T. M. Brinthaupt & R. P. Lipka (Eds.), *The self: Definitional and methodological issues*. Albany: State University of New York Press.

Freeman, M. (2002). Charting the narrative unconscious: Cultural memory and the challenge of autobiography. *Narrative Inquiry, 12,* 193–211.

Freud, S. (1957). Leonardo da Vinci and a memory of his childhood. In J. Strachey (Ed. & Trans.), *The standard edition of the complete psychological works of Sigmund Freud* (Vol. 11, pp. 59–137). London: Hogarth. (Original work published 1910)

Freud, S. (1958). Psycho-analytic notes on an autobiographical account of a case of paranoia. In J. Strachey (Ed. & Trans.), *The standard edition of the complete psychological works of Sigmund Freud* (Vol. 12, pp. 3–82). London: Hogarth. (Original work published 1911)

Funkenstein, A. (1993). The incomprehensible catastrophe: Memory and narrative. In R. Josselson & A. Lieblich (Eds.), *The narrative study of lives*. Newbury Park, CA: Sage.

Geertz, C. (1973). *The interpretation of culture: Selected essays*. New York: Basic Books.

Gergen, M. M., & Gergen, K. J. (1993). Narratives of the gendered body in popular autobiography. In R. Josselson & A. Lieblich (Eds.), *The narrative study of lives* (Vol. 1, pp. 191–218). Newbury Park, CA: Sage.

Gubrium, J. F., & J. A. Holstein. (1998). Narrative practice and the coherence of personal stories. *Sociological Quarterly, 39,* 163–187.

Helle, A. P. (1991). Reading women's autobiographies: A map of reconstructed knowing. In C. Witherell & N. Noddings (Eds.), *Stories lives tell: Narrative and dialogue in education* (pp. 48–66). New York: Teachers College Press.

Holstein, J. A., & Gubrium, J. F. (1995). *The active interview*. Qualitative Research Methods Series, No. 37. Thousand Oaks, CA: Sage.

Holstein, J. A., & Gubrium, J. F. (2000a). *Constructing the life course* (2nd ed.). Dix Hills, NY: General Hall.

Holstein, J. A., & Gubrium, J. F. (2000b). *The self we live by: Narrative identity in a postmodern world*. New York: Oxford University Press.

Ives, E. (Ed.). (1986). Symposium on the life story. *Folklife Annual,* 154–176.

Josselson, R. (Ed.). (1996). *The narrative study of lives: Ethics and process in the study of lives* (Vol. 4). Thousand Oaks, CA: Sage.

Josselson, R., & Lieblich, A. (Eds.). (1993). *The narrative study of lives* (Vol. 1). Newbury Park, CA: Sage.

Josselson, R., & Lieblich, A. (Eds.). (1995). *Interpreting experience: The narrative study of lives* (Vol. 3). Thousand Oaks, CA: Sage.

Josselson, R., & Lieblich, A. (Eds.). (2000). *Making meaning of narratives in the narrative study of lives* (Vol. 6). Thousand Oaks, CA: Sage.

Josselson, R., Lieblich, A., & McAdams, D. (2003). *Up close and personal: The teaching and learning of narrative research.* Washington, DC: American Psychological Association.

Kenyon, G., Clark, P., & de Vries, B. (Eds.). (2001). *Narrative gerontology: Theory, research, and practice.* New York: Springer.

Kenyon, G., & Randall, W. (1997). *Restorying our lives: Personal growth through autobiographical reflection.* Westport, CT: Praeger.

King, B. B., & Ritz, D. (1996). *Blues all around me: The autobiography of B. B. King.* New York: Avon.

Kluback, W. (1956). *Wilhelm Dilthey's philosophy of history.* New York: Columbia University Press.

Kroger, J. (1993). Identity and context: How identity statuses choose their match. In R. Josselson & A. Lieblich (Eds.), *The narrative study of lives* (Vol. 1, pp. 130–162). Newbury Park, CA: Sage.

Langer, L. L. (1991). *Holocaust testimonies: The ruins of memory.* New Haven, CT: Yale.

Langness, L. L. (1965). *The life history in anthropological science.* New York: Holt, Rinehart, & Winston.

Langness, L. L., & Frank, G. (1981). *Lives: An anthropological approach to biography.* Novato, CA: Chandler & Sharp.

Lieblich, A., & Josselson, R. (Eds.). (1994). *Exploring identity and gender: The narrative study of lives* (Vol. 2). Thousand Oaks, CA: Sage.

Lieblich, A., & Josselson, R. (Eds.). (1997). *The narrative study of lives* (Vol. 5). Thousand Oaks, CA: Sage.

Lieblich, A., McAdams, D., & Josselson, R. (2004). *Healing plots: The narrative basis of psychotherapy.* Washington, DC: American Psychological Association.

Linde, C. (1993). *Life stories: The creation of coherence.* New York: Oxford.

Marcia, J. E. (1966). Development and validation of ego identity status. *Journal of Personality and Social Psychology, 3,* 551–558.

McAdams, D. (1985). *Power, intimacy and the life story: Personological inquiries into identity.* New York: Guilford.

McAdams, D. (1993). *Stories we live by: Personal myths and the making of the self.* New York: William Morrow.

McAdams, D., Josselson, R., & Lieblich, A. (2002). *Turns in the road: Narrative studies of lives in transition.* Washington, DC: American Psychological Association.

McAdams, D., Josselson, R., & Lieblich, A. (2006). *Identity and story: Creating self in narrative.* Washington, DC: American Psychological Association.

McCracken, G. (1988). *The long interview.* Qualitative Research Methods Series, No. 13. Newbury Park, CA: Sage.

Mkhonza, S. (1995). Life histories as social texts of personal experiences in sociolinguistic studies: A look at the lives of domestic workers in Swaziland. In R. Josselson & A. Lieblich (Eds.), *Interpreting experience: The narrative study of lives* (Vol. 3, pp. 173–204). Thousand Oaks, CA: Sage.

Murray, H. A. (1938). *Explorations in personality.* New York: Oxford University Press.

Murray, H. A. (1955). American Icarus. In A. Burton & R. E. Harris (Eds.), *Clinical studies in personality* (Vol. 3, pp. 615–641). New York: Harper & Row.

Olatunji, B., & Atkinson, R. (2005). *The beat of my drum: An autobiography.* Philadelphia: Temple University Press.

Olney, J. (Ed.). (1980). *Autobiography: Essays theoretical and critical.* Princeton, NJ: Princeton University Press.

Randall, W. (1995). *The stories we are.* Toronto, Canada: University of Toronto Press.

Rickman, H. P. (1979). *Wilhelm Dilthey: Pioneer of the human studies.* London: Paul Elek.

Riessman, C. K. (1993). Narrative analysis. In *Qualitative research methods series* (Vol. 30). Newbury Park, CA: Sage.

Rosenthal, G. (1993). Reconstruction of life stories: Principles of selection in generating stories for narrative biographical interviews. In R. Josselson & A. Lieblich (Eds.), *The narrative study of lives* (Vol. 1, pp. 59–91). Newbury Park, CA: Sage.

Runyan, W. M. (1982). *Life histories and psychobiography: Explorations in theory and method.* New York: Oxford University Press.

Sarbin, T. R. (1986). The narrative as root metaphor for psychology. In T. R. Sarbin (Ed.), *Narrative psychology: The storied nature of human conduct.* (pp. 3–21). New York: Praeger.

Schwandt, T. A. (2001). *Dictionary of qualitative inquiry* (2nd ed.). Thousand Oaks, CA: Sage.

Shaw, C. (1929). *Delinquency areas.* Chicago: University of Chicago Press.

Spradley, J. (1979). *The ethnographic interview.* New York: Holt, Rinehart & Winston.

Thomas, W. I., & Thomas, D. S. (1928). *The child in America: Behavioral problems and programs.* New York: Knopf.

Tillich, P. (1957). *Dynamics of faith.* New York: Harper & Row.

Titon, J. (1980). The life story. *Journal of American Folklore, 93*(369), 276–292.

van Gennep, A. (1960). *The rites of passage.* Chicago: University of Chicago Press.

Widdershoven, G. A. M. (1993). The story of life: Hermeneutic perspectives on the relationship between narrative and life history. In R. Josselson & A. Lieblich (Eds.), *The narrative study of lives* (Vol. 1, pp. 1–20). Newbury Park, CA: Sage.

Witherell, C., & Noddings, N. (1991). *Stories lives tell: Narrative and dialogue in education.* New York: Teachers College Press.

PART III

Starting With Living Stories

Narrative inquiry in the field is a form of living, a way of life.

—Clandinin and Connelly (2000, p. 78)

Many narrative inquirers become so enamored with stories and the study of stories—things to be "picked up," listened to, categorized, written down—that they lose track of the fact that narratives began as living things created in the moment-to-moment action and interaction of particular people in a particular place, at a particular time, engaged in particular events. We shape stories to create them with beginnings, middles, and ends, but in the living the boundaries are less clear, more organic. This section attempts to explore the issues that emerge when narrative inquirers engage in making sense of narratives as they are lived or as living entities. Each chapter opens for our consideration different ambiguities that materialize when narrative inquirers live alongside the events, the lives, and the ideas they are attempting to understand.

Each of these chapters begins by placing us as readers in the midst of the three-dimensional narrative space. Each of the authors clearly understands that once any knowing comes into existence as a present situation, idea, practice, or event, it is already a past. They try to help us understand the experience of narrative inquiry conducted in the moment but in the space before the present moment, which, already in awareness, is no longer present but past. This being in the midst is a commonality of those who attempt to explore human relationships and human practices: nursing, teaching, organization, therapy, learning, etc. Each of these chapters provides us with tools for making meaning in the midst of attempting to understand, explore, and act in human interaction and practice.

Images and impressions are a valuable tool for understanding in the midst; however, Hedy Bach quickly opens for us the vulnerability of image—the visual—in holding meaning steady. This vulnerability becomes evident as soon as we begin to explore visual narratives and their role in understanding living alongside as a narrative inquirer. She helps us appreciate the value, ambiguity, and irreducibility of frames. Still photographs, no matter how clear, are always ambiguous. They capture a story, but even in the capturing, the stilling, the multiplicity of frames, and the issues of ownership, the absent and the present raise a cacophony of meaning. Thus, this stillest of forms escapes and lives in new stories about the event captured, the meaning of the event, the story of taking the photo, the feelings that led to the shot, the feelings the photo elicits, the relationships caught at that moment in time in tension with the relationships remembered or inferred.

As Bach poignantly reminds us, visual narratives are the most elusive of metaphors. Their meaning pulsates in the three-dimensional narrative space for as every dimension becomes layered as we hold a photograph in our hand and speak about it—time collapses. The backward-forward movements reverberate since the photo captures the moment it was taken. But we hold it in this moment and speak, not only of the moment it was taken but possibly the other moments in which we have viewed it, the others we have viewed it with, and the moments that led to the moment of taking. The photograph itself represents the inward and outward movement, and the movement from the personal and interpersonal to the social and intrapersonal of the three-dimensional narrative space, present in the photo but now revisited in the inward and outward in this moment of the viewing or retelling or exploration of meaning. The dimension of place explodes as we stand in this place, holding a representation of another space. Dangling in narrative from the photo are the other spaces of its discussion and creation, and all fit here in this moment in time.

Think of the living quality not then of just this single photo and its multiple tellings and retellings, but think of the photos in relation to others taken and untaken, told and untold, present and absent. Thus, coming to understand making meaning in a visual narrative inquiry captures the complexity of making meaning in living alongside and supporting the living and meaning making of others.

David Boje reminds us of the quality of narrative as living story. His accounts of the emergence of his grandmother from competing sources of fragments of family story, corroboration of historic facts, and understandings from personal living and memory capture well the struggle for meaning making that living alongside always entails. Living story exists in a space between dead and alive/forgotten and interpellating. He reminds us of the ways in which histories are reduced texts told by elites to elites and ignore the ability of storytellers to slant stories. His analytic tool, the use of critical antenarrative, helps us to see the ways in which narrative inquirers, who understand the role of fragmentation and trajectory in the creation of living story, are able to add texture and density to their inquiries. Stories are never full-blown, either in living or telling. He reminds us that as we both listen to and experience story, there is much that is left to the imagination, to inference. Listeners fill pauses, blanks, and silences with stories of their own. *Trajectory* as a term captures the condition of the emergence of coherence out of incoherence through the passageway of antenarrative or "prenarrative." Trajectory as a tool for understanding living story reminds us that stories pick up and shed meaning along the three dimensions of the narrative inquiry space: time, place, and relationship. This interaction of trajectory and fragmentation leads to assemblage and reassemblage of living story as we live alongside them.

Jean McNiff explores the difficult questions of validity that often dog the steps of those who engage in narrative inquiries from the perspective of living alongside. How do researchers make claims about meaning when conducting inquiries in living alongside and interacting with others in the construction of meaning about human interaction and understanding? Speaking from a perspective of action research and self-study, which focuses on improving the accuracy with which our practice and living reflect our values, Jean McNiff reminds us that as a result of the living quality of our inquiry, the form of the narrative mirrors the form of the inquiry. She helps us understand issues of making judgments about living and written texts of human lives. She argues that validity is intimately linked with ideas about goodness—good practice and good research accounts are valid and meaningful. Doing good means trying to live one's values and communicating what one is doing in honesty, sincerity, and truthfulness and in a form that is appropriate to the context. She reminds us that, even though we are always in the midst of such work, we experience ourselves across these living narratives as a unity, and in this unity we ground our meaning making. When we engage in these kinds of living processes of inquiry, we make a commitment to each moment since we recognize that each moment holds all possible futures. Narrative inquirers' accounts of living alongside do more than create examples—they create realities.

Relationship is the heart of living alongside in narrative inquiry—indeed, relationships form the nexus of this kind of inquiry space. Craig and Huber explore the complexity of living alongside. Through their own narratives of research projects, they help us understand the relational reverberations of these kinds of inquiries. In exploring the complications and layered learning that emerge in living alongside, they articulate ideas that improve understanding from such inquiries and provide edges and boundaries for mining meaning. They offer ideas such as identity threads, learning through wakefulness to relationships, the tensions and disease of living alongside and knowing "things," self in relationship, a fluid held in a vessel of many strands, and layered ways of learning. They raise questions such as the following: What do tensions help us understand? What is the aftermath in children's lives of plotlines for good research? How do we account for agency—our own and those with whom we are in relation? They introduce us to cover stories; participant observation as a way of being, rather than a research tool; and reimagining human subject agreements through relational ethics. They speak to us of a particular kind of Truth-telling where the truth told is not absolute but communal, where inquirers seek to understand but not critique, and where, in making relationships the foreground, we are more able to maintain research rigor.

Looking across these chapters, we are reminded that in living alongside we engage narratively with individuals, creating lives with stories that are alive, and use tools that somehow prompt living rather than stilling of narrative. Through these accounts, we understand the need for narrative researchers working with data that live to not only hold themselves within the three-dimensional narrative space defined by Clandinin and Connelly but to stand with integrity and honor relationships within that space.

—*Stefinee Pinnegar*

CHAPTER 10

Relational Reverberations

Shaping and Reshaping Narrative Inquiries in the Midst of Storied Lives and Contexts

Cheryl J. Craig and Janice Huber

> *As researchers, we come to each new inquiry field living our stories. Our participants also enter the inquiry field in the midst of living their stories. Their lives do not begin the day we arrive nor do they end as we leave. Their lives continue. Furthermore, the places in which . . . [participants] live and work, their classrooms, their schools, and their communities are also in the midst when we researchers arrive. Their institutions and their communities, their landscapes in the broadest sense, are also in the midst of stories.*
>
> —Clandinin and Connelly (2000, pp. 63–64)

The invitation to coauthor this chapter of the handbook provided the impetus for us to ponder how we came to relationally live alongside one another in the past and how that conjoined narrative history contributes to our present exploration of the interpersonal aspects of narrative inquiry. In these beginning conversations we shared many stories of our lives. Some of our stories took us backward in time and place to memories of the early 1990s, when we first came to know and work alongside one another. Sometimes our stories took us inward as we told of relationships negotiated alongside diverse participants and their shaping influences on who we are becoming as narrative inquirers. Other times, our stories spoke about how our situatedness in particular places across Canada and the United States shaped our choices of narrative inquiries. Often, our stories took us outward to thoughts of how the works of other narrative inquirers and people who write about experience as narratively and relationally composed supported, sharpened, and stretched our narrative thinking. Many of our stories nudged us toward wonders around future ways in which narrative inquiries negotiated in the midst of storied lives and contexts might transform educational research.

As our chapter unfolds, we invite you into a conversation that continues to move in these directions. In many ways, our conversation builds on conversations begun long ago, conversations about the temporal and contextual meeting of peoples' lives in contexts (Buber, 1958), conversations attentive to negotiating multivocalic spaces (Greene, 1995) shaped and reshaped by the necessarily entangled experiences of diverse peoples. By attending to some of the interconnected awakenings, transformations, resonances (Chan & Boone, 2001; Conle, 1996), tensions, dilemmas, and possibilities inherent in the meeting of diverse lives in contexts, our chapter seeks to keep inexhaustible the story of what it might mean to "walk in a good way" (Young, 2005, p. 179) as we negotiate relationships and narrative inquiries with participants.

> The story depends upon every one of us to come into being. It needs us all, needs our remembering, understanding, and creating what we have heard together to keep on coming into being. The story of a people. Of us, peoples. (Trinh, 1989, p. 119)

Awakening to Narrative Knowing and Inquiry

Our coming to know one another began in the early 1990s, when Cheryl was a doctoral student and Janice was a master's student at the Centre for Research for Teacher Education and Development (CRTED) at the University of Alberta. When we think back to this time and place, our memories are, in part, filled with thoughts of experiences around the large CRTED table. Steeves (2004) characterizes this table as a kind of "kitchen table," which continues to draw "people together . . . providing a rich inquiry space for researchers to work collaboratively for the purpose of furthering knowledge with a central focus on the educational experiences of children, teachers, parents, student teachers and administrators" (p. 16).

In the fall of 1990 we each began to participate in Research Issues, one of the "rich inquiry spaces" Steeves (2004) highlighted. These Tuesday lunchtime conversations drew local, national, and international graduate students, faculty, and, at times, visiting professors into sustained conversation about our lives as researchers. Mickelson's (1996) poetic text, which we excerpt as follows, provides a sense of how an often uncertain, question-filled space of inquiry shaped Research Issues conversations:

Everyone welcome. . . . I don't want to silence participants . . . how much of our own vantage point do we bring into our inquiries? . . . was there any tension in that collaborative process? . . . let's talk about alternative forms of data representation . . . what is an evaded curriculum? . . . can we negotiate a space within our research that allows for opening up and not shutting down? (p. 1)

Being invited into this evolving process of storying and restorying the experiences we and others shared each week at Research Issues created spaces where we began to gradually awaken to and learn from our narrative knowing.

These understandings continued to reverberate within us as we engaged in other kinds of inquiry spaces that came into being at the CRTED table. Guests, as mentioned, were always encouraged to pull up a chair. Thus, during our shared time at the CRTED (1990–1992), not only did students from numerous departments across the university find themselves welcomed to the CRTED table but so too did visiting professors, people such as Miriam Ben-Peretz (1995), Christopher Clark (1995), Eleanor Duckworth (1996), Sandra Hollingsworth (1994), Yvonna Lincoln (Denzin & Lincoln, 2000), Nona Lyons (1990), and Bob Yinger (1990). As these scholars each shared stories of their research lives, they opened up additional inquiry spaces where we were called to think hard about the kinds of educational research Noddings (1986) imagined as "research *for* teaching" (p. 506).

What we now remember as significant about these CRTED table inquiry spaces are ways in which we felt invited into a process "of knowing through relationship, or relational knowing" (Hollingsworth, 1994, p. 77). For us, this process was deeply experiential (Dewey, 1938), narrative in form (Bruner, 1990; Gudmundsdottir, 1996; Mishler, 1986; Polkinghorne, 1986; White, 1987), held in bodies and minds (Estola & Elbaz-Luwisch, 2003; Lakoff & Johnson, 1999), given expression in our narratives of experience (Crites, 1971; MacIntyre, 1981; Witherell & Noddings, 1991), and shaped and reshaped by the contexts and people with whom we interacted (Belenky, Clinchy, Goldberger, & Tarule, 1986; Carr, 1986; Geertz, 1973; Hoffman, 1989; hooks, 1996; Ladson-Billings, 2001; Marmon Silko, 1996; Oyler, 1996).

In part, this learning supported our becoming more attentive to what we were coming to know from our experiences as graduate students. For example, not only had the two of us experienced dilemmas stemming from the stories we lived in the school settings of which we previously were a part, but we both signed up for a change course in the Educational Administration Department to fulfill our respective degree requirements. As it turned out, we were the only students in the class not involved in educational leadership. For each of us, the course was a startling revelation of how some administrators talk about teachers and their work. Frequently referred to as "my teachers" and distantly as "they," the images portrayed of teachers and teaching were not the same ones we held and expressed as teachers fresh from the field and enrolled in a different course of study. We winced when we found ourselves—by virtue of the broad generalizations—portrayed as naïve, less intelligent, and needy of being led. Furthermore, the "power over" stance particularly hit us hard since both of us knew from our school-based experiences prior to embarking in our respective graduate programs that teachers' personal stories rub against administrators' stories. While neither of us voiced it to others at the time, our one class in educational administration—along with the disparaging remarks about "deficit teachers" (Carter, 1993, p. 9) that we routinely encountered in the literature (which arose from what Eisner [1988] appropriately titled "commando raids" [p. 19] in schools)—confirmed for us why we needed to engage in collaborative inquiries attentive to the teacher perspective and representative of reality expressed in teachers' terms (Jackson, 1968; Schwab, 1971).

It was, as well, in the courses where Jean Clandinin served as our instructor and our weekly meetings with her in which she responded to our writing in progress that we continued to experience spaces where narrative knowledge was valued and explored. Rather than being expected to set aside those matters that were of greatest concern and interest to us as educators as we observed other graduate students doing, these phenomena were embraced as we and colleagues—people such as Hedy Bach (1993), Laurie Bowers (1993), Katy Campbell (1994), Nophanet Dhamborvorn (1994), Merle Kennedy (1992), Jan Knutson (1994), Haya Lachman (1993), Joy Ruth Mickelson (2000), Margaret Olson (1995), Marni Pearce (1995), Heather Raymond (1995), Ian Sewall (1994), Pam Steeves (1993), and Kathy Webb (1995)—vigorously pursued them as active topics of inquiry. Fortunate for us, our fundamentally human wonders and ponders did not become sacrificed "for the sake of research precision" (Clandinin & Connelly, 2000, p. xxii).

Being in the Midst of Our and Participants' Storied Lives and Contexts

While the CRTED milieu shaped multiple inquiry spaces where we were able to learn from and about narrative knowledge and inquiry, it also nurtured relationships that indelibly shaped the inquiries we each undertook. This relational backdrop to our work continued when we were each invited to situate our graduate student narrative inquiries within a broader research study focused on teacher's "personal practical knowledge" (Connelly & Clandinin, 1988, p. 25) and their professional contexts. This project was funded by a research grant held by Michael Connelly and Jean Clandinin that drew Jean and us into sustained conversations with other teacher inquirers (Annie Davies, Pat Hogan, and Karen Keats Whelan in Edmonton), and doctoral students Rosalie Young and Ming Fang He, who were undertaking the same inquiry at the Centre for Teacher Development table with Michael in Toronto. Prior to that, Jean worked closely with Pat, Annie, and Barbara Kennard (see Clandinin, Davies, Hogan, & Kennard, 1993). And immediately after that, the members of the research group shifted again as Annie Davies (1996), Karen Keats Whelan (2000), Janice Huber (2000), and Chuck Rose (1997) pursued doctoral studies in Edmonton with Jean, while Ming Fang He (2003), Jo Ann Phillion (2002), Sally Quan (Quan, Phillion, & He, 1999), Norman Beach (He, Phillion, & Beach, 1999), Florence Samson (1999), and Sheila Dermer Applebaum and Juijiang Du (1999) worked with Michael as part of the same research enterprise in Toronto. Meanwhile, Cheryl traversed the two sites of inquiry when she began her postdoctoral work, coadvised by Jean and Michael.

As readers can see, webs of relationships shaped our beginnings as narrative inquirers, forming deep roots within, between, and among us. From others' perspectives, these relationships might be viewed as research contamination or criticized for the researcher studying people just like her. How close the researcher is to participants and what becomes written within the context of relationship form a major challenge to this mode of inquiry (Behar, 1996; Carter, 1993; Rager, 2005; Wolcott, 2002). Yet, from a relational standpoint, connections such as these offer richness and depth and allow insights that would otherwise not be possible. We have learned that nested within this relational background, the issue is not so much about negating subjectivities because that would result in "empty-headedness" (Eisner, 1990, p. 50). Rather, the matter has to do with "managing subjectivities" (Peshkin, 1986)—that is, coming to terms with the values we bring to bear on situations. As Clandinin and Connelly (2000) affirm, relationships form the nexus of what narrative inquirers do:

> Narrative inquiry is the study of experience, and experience, as John Dewey taught, is a matter of people in relation contextually and temporally. Participants are in relation, and we as researchers are in relation to participants. Narrative inquiry is an experience of the experience. It is people in relation studying with people in relation. (p. 189)

Although in the early 1990s we were less aware than we are today about this commingling of the life and inquiry stories we and others were living, telling, reliving, and recomposing as our lives met at the CRTED and within and across multiple research projects, as we look back from our more present vantage points we see how this thread of "people in relation studying with people in relation" has imprinted our becoming as narrative inquirers. It is an identity thread that reverberates in moments lived through and recorded in our field texts and that was picked up and pulled forward in some of our research texts; it is a thread that reverberates in our present narrative inquiries and as our lives continue to unfurl in diverse contexts and relationships.

In the following sections, we attend to these relational reverberations, drawing more sharply into focus their often complex and uneasy yet vital place in our learning as narrative inquirers. The narrative inquiry Janice foregrounds transpired over one school year and was negotiated with a teacher, children, and families. The narrative inquiry Cheryl brings to the fore began nearly a decade ago and continues to unfold alongside multiple teachers and administrators in one school context immersed in a number of reform agendas.

Negotiating a Narrative Inquiry Alongside a Teacher, Children, and Families at City Heights School

During the 1999 to 2000 school year, Janice engaged in a year-long narrative inquiry at City Heights School, a multicultural elementary school situated in a western Canadian city centre. This opportunity was shaped by a history of relationships which connected Emily, [1] a teacher at City Heights, with Janice and with Jean and Michael, who coheld a national research grant focused on understanding the experiences of diverse teachers, children, and families as their lives met in schools.

Entering Into Lives in Contexts and Into Relationships

The previous year Emily taught children in Year 2–3 and was now excited to continue to work with many of the same children as they moved into their third and fourth years in school. As Emily welcomed back 25 returning children and 3 children new to City Heights School and to Canada, she also welcomed Jean and Janice, friends and former colleagues, to spend the year alongside her, children, and families in the Year 3–4 classroom. Janice and Jean participated in classroom life as researcher teachers, working alongside Emily and children on a daily basis in all the ways that teachers do, participating in and, at times, helping to plan and facilitate learning activities. They also wrote field notes of their participation in the classroom, school, and community. Janice was in the classroom on a 0.5 basis and Jean on a 0.1 basis. As their relationships with children and families developed, Emily, Jean, and Janice engaged in tape-recorded and transcribed research conversations with eight children and four mothers.

As Janice and Jean lived as narrative inquirers in the midst of this meeting of their, Emily's, children's, and family members' lives in the classroom, school, and community, much was going on. Trying to stay wakeful to all that was happening around and within them as they lived in this midst was not easy. Working with field texts and previously published research texts, in what follows Janice traces ways in which wakefulness to relationships shaped both their living and telling of their narrative inquiry at City Heights School.

Learning Through Wakefulness to Relationships

Emily and Jean, after you read this, can we please talk? I initially wrote the following field note only saying that Ella talked about the complexities of her life at home but when I reread it I thought it smoothed over so much of Ella's experience. . . . I do, however, have really mixed feelings about whether or not this field note [which now includes a much more detailed account of my experiences alongside Ella] should stay as it is.

This message of mine to Emily and Jean, typed in bold font at the start of my field notes for September 8, is my earliest written record of tensions I felt as I lived alongside children in the Year 3–4 classroom. Although in my message I did not explicitly state that my feelings of tension were connected with knowing stories of Ella's life that she described as "secret," in my field notes I wrote the following:

After recess when we returned to publishing the children's "Who Am I" pieces [of writing], I worked a lot with Ella. . . . As I sat beside her while she worked she leaned over and whispered that she had a secret. She said it was a "secret between her and her mom." Then, she told me the secret. . . . I had a really hard time focusing on the last few minutes of the day after I heard Ella's story.

My initial feelings of tension occurred as I lived through an experience with Ella, an experience in which she shared secret stories of her life. Later, as I wrote field notes, I first hid my felt tensions about knowing these stories of Ella's life by "only saying that Ella talked about the complexities of her life at home." In this version of my field notes I did not include an account of Ella's told stories because I felt uncomfortable recording them. Yet, still later, as I reread my initial field note and decided to rewrite it inclusive of the stories Ella shared, my continuing dis-ease about recording her told stories shaped the message I wrote to Emily and Jean.

Not long after Ella shared these secret stories with me, she left City Heights School. However, Ella's leaving did not stop Jean or me from continuing to feel tensions as we lived alongside children in the Year 3–4 classroom. We later saw that these tensions around who we were in our relationships with children were threaded across many of our field notes. After the school year ended, and as Jean and I read through our field notes, we became more thoughtful about the many moments where we recorded feelings of tensions about our interactions with or alongside Emily, children, and family members.

In part, we began to inquire into what these tensions might help us to understand about our moral and ethical responsibilities as narrative inquirers with children. For example, the following two field notes, the first written in March and the second in April, shaped a space where we could step back from the intensity of living in the midst of our and the children's storied lives and inquire into "how the children saw us as coresearchers, how they saw themselves as coresearchers, and how we saw ourselves as coresearchers with them" (Huber & Clandinin, 2002, p. 788).

After lunch I had an interview with Azim. I'm calling it an interview because I didn't feel like our talk was back and forth, like a conversation at all. I want to think a lot more about the process of talking with children because Azim shared some stories with me that, while he was sharing them, I felt his mom might not want him to tell me. I say this because if I had children, I'm not sure I would want them telling someone the kinds of things Azim told me. I need to think more about why I feel this way.

It was time to go back . . . [inside] then. Emily called the children and started to walk with them back across the street. Barbara and I stayed behind to walk with children who were still playing. . . . While we were walking Barbara said she had been "really embarrassed" when Azim told her that [in our research conversation] he told me about . . . [an experience they lived through during a recent visit with family on the reservation where Barbara was raised]. . . . I reached out and touched Barbara's arm and told her I worried she might feel this way. I told Barbara that the point of this research is not to judge people's lives and I said that Jean, Emily and I also have stories of difficult times, difficult situations in our lives and that we would never write anything based on my conversation with Azim unless both Azim and her were comfortable with it. She laughed and said that when Azim trusts someone he is very open and I said I knew that. She said she has talked with Azim before about not sharing those kinds of stories. She said she really worries about Azim because he is a very trusting person.

As Jean and I revisited these two field texts and puzzled through our wonders about who we and children were becoming in our narrative inquiry, we were drawn toward questions such as the following:

> Was our dis-ease in hearing Azim's stories the result of moving from the in-classroom to an out-of-classroom place? Was our dis-ease the result of shifting in our stories of ourselves as teacher researchers to researcher teachers? Was our dis-ease the result of the permanent record created by the tape recorder? Was our dis-ease the result of falling into an assumption that children do not have the narrative authority to tell their stories? (p. 791)

These were not easy questions to ask of ourselves nor were they questions to which we felt we held answers. Yet, by trying to puzzle through them, we began to understand something more about our need to attend not only to the stories children and families were living and telling of their lives but to ways in which children's and families' lives could be understood through dominant cultural and institutional narratives. By choosing to engage in a narrative inquiry with children as coresearchers, we realized,

> We have a heightened need to attend to where stories are told, and knowing that when stories are taken from their relational contexts, they can be understood, particularly for children whose lives are at the edges of dominant plotlines, from within more common social and cultural narratives, narratives that are miseducative for the children involved. (Huber & Clandinin, 2002, p. 800)

In this way we began to see that as we lived in the midst of moments with Emily, children, and families as the year at City Heights unfolded, our felt tensions were, at least in part, shaped by knowing that the dominant plotlines for "good" researchers "do not often attend to the aftermath for children's lives as their first concern" (Huber & Clandinin, 2002, p. 801). We realized that our negotiation of morally and ethically responsible relationships within inquiries with them was a "relational responsibility" (Clandinin & Connelly, 2000, p. 177) that called us to be thoughtful about children's lives not only as we lived alongside them but as they continued to story and restory who they were becoming as their lives unfolded into the future.

Understanding our relational responsibilities with children as coresearchers in these ways drew us toward new understandings about the centrality of trying to understand the bumping places between and among lives and contexts. We—Jean,

Janice, Emily, children, and families—were people in relation inquiring into the lives we were composing and recomposing in the midst of classroom, school, and community contexts. It was this sense of being and inquiring in relation that enabled us to attend to the reverberations of experiences in multiple people's lives. Staying wakeful to and trying to understand these reverberations was never easy. Yet, it was these complex, uncertain, and often tension-filled narrative understandings that we imagined as contributing, in educative ways, to the ongoing storying and restorying of teachers, children's, family members', and narrative inquirers' lives.

Negotiating Narrative Inquiry: Living Alongside Teachers and Administrators Amid Multiple Stories of Reform at T. P. Yaeger Middle School

As readers can see, Janice's research dwells on the relational questions that bubbled to the surface as she and Jean engaged in a narrative inquiry with a teacher, children, and families as their lives met in a classroom, school, and community context in a western Canadian city. Cheryl's research below highlights different relational considerations that surfaced when she entered an existing maze of relationships among teachers and administrators in one middle school context in a major urban centre in the midsouthern United States despite the fact that only a few of the educators served as primary research participants in her study. Cheryl's narrative inquiry on the influence of school reform on teachers' knowledge began at T. P. Yaeger Middle School in 1997. Initially a school segregated by race and then desegregated through the partial introduction of a gifted-and-talented plotline, Yaeger continues to be a school in socioeconomic, racial, and educational transition, as Cheryl's first-hand account shows.[2]

Entering the Inquiry

When I first negotiated entry into Yaeger, then-principal Brianne Larson and the initial teacher participants with whom I worked were very welcoming. Nevertheless, it was a struggle to become accepted in a school peopled by 1,500 students and a faculty of 85 teachers and 25 support staff, particularly since the campus was in turmoil because three stories of school reform (Craig, 2001) were simultaneously under way. As foreshadowed, I stepped into the midst of a number of reform agendas and found my relationships with the Yaeger educators significantly shaped by them. Here, I hone in on one experience that unearthed many of the exigencies of the multiple stories of reform (Craig, 2003) seeded on the campus and the entailments they brought to bear on human relationships.

Finding Oneself in the Midst

At the time I entered the Yaeger scene, then-principal Brianne Larson had just finished participating in a study group associated with the second reform movement chronologically introduced to the school. Desirous of extending growth opportunities to Yaeger's faculty, Larson arranged to have a similar study group start that fall. Larson's plan was to ask teachers to volunteer to participate in the activity, which would be led by two assistant principals. However, the national reform movement—in its quest to bring school reform to scale—made two quick decisions. It allowed Yaeger to create two teacher groups instead of one and collapsed the timeline within which the groups would be established. These changes denied the Yaeger teachers the possibility of choosing whether they would participate. This added to the ongoing discomfort the teachers felt about their 20 teaching colleagues who had been told not to return to their teaching positions, a direct result of Yaeger's new school district charter, the campus's third reform plotline.

In a sense, the scene evolved in a similar manner for me. I also was expected to participate in the groups. The administrators hoped my presence would reduce the uneasiness they felt about their new roles as facilitators. Focused on developing relationships with the teachers and them, I did not realize that neither the assistant principals nor the teachers had volunteered to be involved. I also was unaware that most of the teachers did not know of my participation.

Two concurrent happenings on the broader school landscape paved the way to how my introduction to the groups played out, but I did not see them as being related at the time. One hint came from one of my study participants, who told me,

> There are a group of teachers, very good teachers.... "Are you not one of the 20?" they question. Most of the members of the study groups [associated with the second reform movement] are also part of the [first] reform initiative. The teachers appear elite, separate, better-than-the-rest. And it hurts.

This teacher suggested that teachers not included in the group were just as concerned by their exclusion as teachers inside the group were puzzled by their inclusion. Second, another teacher, a study group member, approached me, urging me to find a location other than the school district office to meet. I did so. Only after the meeting did I realize she knew I was involved and others did not.

The day before the combined study group meeting I received an e-mail from one of the administrators explaining that one or two teachers were "somewhat uncomfortable" with my attendance. Knowing the importance of comfort and safety, I insisted that my presence not be forced on the teachers. The administrators, however, reiterated their desire to have me attend the meeting. Not wanting to insult one another, we sought a middle ground solution. They would discuss the matter with the teachers in the morning, and I would time my arrival at noon.

I arrived at the meeting as planned. The teachers posed tough questions of me that I candidly answered. I explained the following:

> I enter a school landscape as a participant-observer and seek to understand school life and the stories people live. I do not critique people but attempt to contextualize situations and try to figure out what prompts people to act in the ways they do. The view I take of educators ... creates amazing double jeopardy situations for me. Some academic critics occasionally critique my

research for its practitioner focus, while some practitioner critics fear I will act like some of the academic critics of which I speak.

In the discussion, I listened intently to the teachers. I felt genuinely heard by them, even though a full spectrum of response was evident in their body language. For example, one female, African American teacher never made eye contact with me. Also, a white, male teacher, an individual whose support I did not expect, gave me his fullest attention. On the whole, though,

I felt the confidence of the majority of the people. . . . I underscored the fact that I was not attached to any reform initiative. My focus was on how reform initiatives influence students' lives, teachers' lives, and school contexts.

Coming to Know Through Relationship

Once the professional development day ended, though, I found myself filled with a great sense of "So what was that all about?" Realizing that I had experienced an up-close view of the school context, I wondered what meaning the meeting held for the teachers involved. Using my understanding of teachers' knowledge communities (Craig, 1995) and my sense of how to enter them, I seized the uncomfortable situation as a "commonplace of experience" (Lane, 1988, p. 188) around which to form relationships with the educators and through which to restory our shared experience and develop their narrative authority (Olson, 1995).

As it turned out, some teachers approached me, others I approached, and for still others, it was debatable who made the first move. In our close interactions, I became introduced to multiple ways of knowing Yaeger's complicated school situation and the complex web of social, historical, and professional relationships that contributed to it. The ongoing conversations helped me to more fully understand the subtle nuances of Yaeger Middle School as a relational place in which teachers' past and present experiences reverberated amid multiple stories of school reform.

For example, one teacher with whom I already was in relationship, explained her African American colleague's behavior by saying,

You have to understand our history. We [black people] have to be suspicious of everyone. . . . She [the teacher who would not give you eye contact] will be fine once [it is apparent] that people like me trust you.

Her comment tactfully reminded me that I represented an additional white, adult face in a student population that had been racially balanced through legal intervention, a phenomenon totally outside the borders of my experience as a Canadian. Then, a second African American teacher connected the situation to the school's gifted and talented program. "The root source of the problem," he explained, "is mistrust. . . . The fascinating thing is what causes this mistrust. . . . The magnet concept thrives on making distinctions between people. It highlights differences, not similarities." This teacher then added that my doctorate and university position further added dimensions of mistrust to school relationships because my presence challenged the hierarchy of position already in place, not only administratively but also from a gifted-and-talented-teacher perspective. Meanwhile, a third study group participant boldly declared that "teachers . . . have been flat suspicious of researchers for the past 20 years." I learned that the pervasive quantitative approach to research and evaluation, with its associated emphasis on deficit and blame—along with the work of armchair critical theorists (who only served to stir the pot)—offered scant support to these urban teachers in their face-to-face work with students. Furthermore, the ongoing theory-practice split, which casts researchers of all methodological and ideological persuasion on the high ground of knowing and all teachers on the low ground of having to be told what to do (Schön, 1983), did precious little to support my acceptance at Yaeger. A fourth teacher picked up on the same narrative thread but developed it differently. To her, the naming of the administrators as facilitators, along with my inclusion as a researcher, represented new forms of "regulation." She wondered when teachers' professionalism would be recognized. In the meantime, other teachers felt it was the hierarchy of power and the use of influence that fuelled what happened. While some detected awkwardness on the part of the facilitators, others focused on particular group members who "like to add poison to the school stew." Still others, males of two races, quickly observed that the one or two individuals expressing concern were females. This gendered reading of the situation represented a further way of understanding human relationships on Yaeger's school landscape. The most common theme expounded, however, traced its way back to one outstanding and one emergent matter. The outstanding issue was that the teachers were uncomfortable with and uninformed as to why they had been organized in study groups led by the assistant principals in the aftermath of a number of faculty members being told they could not continue to teach at the school. The educators were understandably worried that teachers had become interchangeable parts in stories of reform that could be arbitrarily assigned to activities or removed from duty. As for the emergent problem, a concern was raised that a few teachers had access to information not universally available. This latter issue surprisingly had nothing directly to do with me. Rather, prior knowledge of my participation in the groups served to publicly disclose a few teachers' privileged status on the school faculty, which, in turn, was problematic to others.

This unpacking of my rocky introduction to the T. P. Yaeger school landscape reveals some of the personal, interpersonal, temporal, situational, and institutional influences that shaped the educators' knowing—and subsequently, my knowledge and how I made sense of situations and formed relationships at Yaeger, which necessarily involved those who were participants—and nonparticipants—in my study. It shows how I laid my vulnerabilities on the table and how I, in turn, encouraged the teachers to lay their vulnerabilities alongside mine. Mostly, the experience illustrates that how emergent research situations are grappled with is largely dependent on relationships—theirs, mine, and ours—developed over time and within the particularities of context.

Expanding the Conversation: Learning Through the Relational Lives and Inquiries of Others

While our two foregoing descriptions of narrative inquiries we have undertaken are quite different from one another contextually and temporally, the similarity that dwells in the space between them is relationships. In other words, in both narrative exemplars (Lyons & LaBoskey, 2002), the relational deeply informs our reflections, conversations, and actions as researchers. We now turn from our discussion of learning from the relational reverberations in our narrative inquiries to highlighting the groundbreaking contributions made by Vivian Gussin Paley, in early childhood education, Robert Coles, in psychiatry and social ethics, and Mary Catherine Bateson, in cultural anthropology, who have greatly enriched our thinking. We then focus attention on the legacies of Jean Clandinin and Michael Connelly because they have not only illuminated pathways concerning what it means to be narrative inquirers attending to relationships, but they have also shown us how narrative inquirers can work fruitfully together across the seasons of life and career and with multiple graduate students, frequently at the same time. Each of these five individuals—in their unique ways—deepened our knowing, challenged our thinking, and urged us to keep working toward ways in which we might more visibly show the relational as integral to expanding our and others' horizons of knowing and as essential to widening the possibilities of what personal experience research is able to make known.

Vivian Gussin Paley: Becoming Curious

The decisive factor for me was curiosity. When my intention was limited to announcing my own point of view, communication came to a halt. My voice drowned out the children's. However, when . . . [children] said things that surprised me, exposing ideas I did not imagine they held, my excitement mounted. . . . I kept the children talking, savoring the uniqueness of responses so singularly different from mine. The rules of teaching had changed; I now wanted to hear the answers I could not myself invent. . . . Indeed the inventions tumbled out as if they simply had been waiting for me to stop talking and begin listening. (Paley, 1986, p. 125)

We weave Vivian Gussin Paley's knowing into our conversation by beginning, through this quote, in the midst of her life and writings as a teacher researcher. A teacher for 37 years, Vivian's inquiries chronicle her living and learning alongside children in nursery and kindergarten classrooms. As revealed previously, Vivian was not always curious about the knowing children carried into the classroom. In fact, she stories her early teaching years as times during which she "paid scant attention to the [children's] play and did not hear . . . [their] stories" (Paley, 1990, p. 5).

In Vivian's tracing of her becoming curious, she temporally situates her gradual transformation as beginning in the early 1970s, when six African American parents joined a faculty meeting to express their concerns about the "prejudice and unfairness" (Paley, 2002, p. xiii) experienced by their children. The parents' concerns drew Vivian into a process of "watching herself" through which she realized that she "never imagined . . . we did so much talking in the kindergarten or that there were so many things to think about in what we said to one another" (p. xiv). In these beginnings as an inquirer, Vivian came to understand that her inattention to the lives and differences of African American and non-African American children was shaped by the denial and invisibility she felt as a Jewish child in public schools, experiences through which she became caught into a plotline of "pretend[ing] . . . to be like everyone else. Those of us who became teachers adopted the conventional wisdom that teacher knows best and fashioned our classrooms in the manner of those who went before us" (p. xv). By sharing her awakenings about the vital place of trying to stay curious about experience as inquiries unfold, Paley simultaneously showed us how she was opened up to new questions about the lives of children with whom she was working. In this way we saw Vivian turning toward the "imperative of *story*" (Paley, 1986, p. 124) as a way of understanding children. By listening to the stories children lived and told of their lives as they engaged in spaces shaped through the sharing of literature or through their interactions with one another in the doll corner, the art table, or the sand box, Vivian taught us,

> The key is curiosity, and it is curiosity, not answers, that we model. As we seek to learn more about a child, we demonstrate the acts of observing, listening, questioning, and wondering. When we are curious about a child's words and our responses to those words, the child feels respected. The child *is* respected. (p. 127)

Robert Coles: Honoring Narrative Authority

The second relational inquirer whose scholarship we spotlight is Robert Coles, whose work demonstrates for us the role of narrative authority in a researcher's life and in the lives of research participants. When Coles was a teen, experiencing the storminess associated with young adulthood, his mother did not confront him about his behavior but encouraged him to relate to particular characters in books and to inquire as to how those individuals made sense of their wonders and ponders, issues and concerns. Not only that, Coles's parents regularly read literature to one another and to their children, and the family frequently engaged in robust conversations about the texts read, experiences had, and meanings made. It is not surprising, then, that years later we find Robert Coles as a practicing professor of psychiatry and social ethics not only taking up "the call of stories" (Coles, 1989) but cultivating his narrative authority (Olson, 1995) while developing and honoring the narrative authority of patients he serves—whether they be adults or children.

Coles's awakening to the primacy of narrative authority in the act of human meaning making teaches us much about the fundamental nature of relational aspects of
inquiry and how it most fruitfully can be conducted.

As a medical resident, Coles worked with psychiatric patients and discussed
their symptoms with his university professors. One of his professors was theoretical and diagnostic in his approach and "[gave Coles] words to grasp; he was 'treating' the floundering 'doctor' so that the doctor could in turn 'treat' the patient"
(Coles, 1989, p. 4). In stark contrast, his second professor held this view:

> The people who come to see us bring us their stories. They hope they tell them
> well enough so that we understand the truth of their lives. They hope we know
> how to interpret their stories correctly. We have to remember that what we
> hear is *their story.* (p. 7)

In the first instance, we see Coles's induction to the authority of the discipline
of psychiatry and all the scientific certainty, abstractions, and absolute truth that it
affords. But in the second instance, Coles is invited to consider a different kind of
authority, the narrative authority that stems from relationally making sense of
another person's pain and the narrative truth (Spence, 1986) associated with the
telling and retelling, living and reliving, of it.

When Coles was introduced to these differing philosophies and practices, he was
simultaneously working with a patient. While the paper trail he laid adequately
diagnosed the case, he fell dreadfully short of entering the female patient's reality.
In desperation, Coles set aside the urge to "consign . . . [her and himself] to territory populated by many" (Coles, 1989, p. 17) and began to "concentrate on understanding her, not on trying to change her behaviour" (p. 9). And when Coles
refocused his attention, she claimed some of her narrative authority, and certain
stories of experience began to spill out. As a result, critical understandings were
forged between the two, and a pathway for possible change—on both their parts—
was opened up. Thus, Coles was able to learn in a layered way from his experiences
with his patient and his professors. He additionally came to know that his professors, like his parents, interpreted situations and texts differently, yet shared goals
and sustained productive relationships across differences (Coles, 1993, p. xvi)
through acknowledging and respecting one another's narrative authority. Coles
additionally shares how he both called forth and shaped the manner in which his
patients told their stories and also what the central purpose of storytelling is to his
way of thinking. In Coles's (1997) words,

> the point of personal stories . . . is not self-accusation. . . . The point is to
> summon one's frail side so as to enable a more forthright sharing of experi-
> ences on the part of all of us: that guy has stumbled, and he's not making too
> much of it, but he *is* putting it on the table, and thereby I'm enabled to put
> some of myself, my remembrances, my story, on the table, whether explicitly,
> by speaking up or, in the way many of us do, by also remembering—another's
> memories trigger our own. (pp. 11–12)

Mary Catherine Bateson: Weaving Lives in Context

Weaving "the wholeness of lives" (Bateson, 2000, p. 11) within the contexts in which they unfold forms, in our view, one of the major contributions of cultural anthropologist Mary Catherine Bateson to what we know about the relational aspects of inquiry. Over a period of decades, she has explored, from the perspective of individuals, self (as a female, daughter, mother, spouse, person), others (women's lives, her parents' lives, her daughter's life), and the nature of human learning (personal learning, intergenerational learning, cultural learning, change). The daughter of prominent ecologist Gregory Bateson and world-renowned anthropologist Margaret Mead, Mary Catherine Bateson demonstrates for us how an epistemological stance anchored in observation and the reporting of personal experience finds its rigor in "asserting, claiming, acknowledging" (Bateson, 1984, pp. xi–xii). In the process, Bateson advances "a definition of relationship as knowledge, achieved and exchanged through information exchange—through conversation and communion . . . as if we were parts of a single whole" (pp. 292–293). As narrative inquirers, we learn from Bateson (1994) that the self in relationship is "fluid, held in a vessel of many strands" (p. 63). At the same time, we see that the strands of self are situated in context "like the baskets closely woven by some Native American tribes, caulked tightly enough to hold water" (p. 63).

Bateson's scholarship, to our way of thinking, is replete with concepts and metaphors that are enormously instructive to making sense of experience, life, and human development from an individual perspective. Expressions such as *life compositions, continuities, discontinuities, spirals, rhythms, multiplicities of vision,* and *improvisation* distinguish her prose. In *Composing a Life* (Bateson, 1989), for example, we witness Bateson probing the female life span by "weav[ing] something new from many different threads" (p. 16) and "lining [colleagues' life compositions] up for comparison" (p. 39). Bateson also notes the "symmetry in . . . mutual recognition" but recognizes asymmetry as well because, as she states, "I am the one who goes off and weaves our separate skeins of memory into a single fabric" (p. 100). At the same time, she acknowledges that the "single fabric" she composed would change over time. Bateson's narrative of one of her research participants, Alice, forms a case in point. At one time, Bateson would have anchored Alice's story in her need to practice forgiveness. At another time, she would have centered the research text on the necessity of Alice working through anger. And more recently—in the aftermath of her parents' deaths—she would focus that narrative on how people stitch the painful and joyful parts of their lives together as if they were all of one piece (p. 229).

In *Full Circles, Overlapping Lives,* Bateson (2000) offers further insights as to why she approaches relational aspects of inquiry in the manner she does:

> Stories of individuals and their relationships through time offer another way of looking, but we need ways to tell stories that are interwoven and recursive, that escape from the linearity of print to incite new metaphors. I believe that the choices we face today are so complex that they must be rehearsed and woven together in narrative. (p. 247)

Hence, Bateson (1994) views participant observation not as a research tool but as "a way of being, especially suited to a world of change" (p. 8). It constitutes an approach that allows her—and us—to attend to the individual; that is, to be present, "sometimes with companionship, sometimes with patience," demonstrating care through observation and contemplation and a "deeper noticing of the world" (p. 109). In addition, Bateson's personal writing "affirms relationships," with the texts she weaves being "contingent on being understood and responded to" (p. 78). In a multitude of ways, Mary Catherine Bateson, to our way of thinking, follows family tradition by carving a path distinctively her own and breaking fresh ground where relationships in inquiry are concerned.

D. Jean Clandinin and F. Michael Connelly: Foregrounding Relationships

Early in their shared program of research focused on experiential understandings of curriculum studies, teacher knowledge, and school reform, Michael Connelly and Jean Clandinin were drawn to attend to the collaborative processes they engaged in as they lived in schools and alongside teachers in classrooms. As their and teachers' lives met in inquiry spaces, Jean and Michael sensed that what was at work was much deeper than a procedural application of principles in negotiating entry and exit from a research site. Drawing on their earlier conceptualization of "narrative unity" as an experiential, narrative, temporal, and contextual way of understanding teachers' knowledge, they saw that "the negotiation of two people's narrative unities" (Clandinin & Connelly, 1988, p. 281) offered a new way of understanding how collaboration, ethical participation, and negotiation were intertwined in the living through of inquiry. Because they and participants each carried their individual experiential histories into the inquiry, the relationships they negotiated with one another both shaped and became shaped by the joining of their experiential histories:

> Collaborative research constitutes a relationship. In everyday life, the idea of friendship implies a sharing, an interpenetration of two or more persons' spheres of experience. Mere contact is acquaintanceship, not friendship. The same may be said for collaborative research which requires a close relationship akin to friendship. Relationships are joined, as McIntyre implies, by the narrative unities of our lives. (p. 281)

Carrying this narrative, experiential understanding of the relationships among researchers and participants as continuously composed and recomposed in the "negotiation of a shared narrative unity" (Connelly & Clandinin, 1990, p. 3) into their unfolding work, Michael and Jean showed us that while relationships shaped how they and participants became positioned in the living through of the inquiry, relationships also shaped how they and participants became positioned in the telling of the inquiry in research texts:

We found that merely listening, recording, and fostering participant story telling was both impossible (we are, all of us, continually telling stories of our experience, whether or not we speak and write them) and unsatisfying. We learned that we, too, needed to tell our stories. Scribes we were not; story-tellers and story livers we were. And in our storytelling, the stories of our participants merged with our own to create new stories, ones that we have labelled *collaborative stories*. The thing finally written on paper (or, perhaps on film, tape, or canvas), the research paper or book, is a collaborative document: a mutually constructed story created out of the lives of both researcher and participant. (p. 12)

Staying wakeful to tensions they and others experienced in negotiating both the living and telling of narrative inquiries sharpened Jean's and Michael's focus on the ongoing negotiation of relationships. Tracing the temporal, and often complex, uncertain, and nonlinear, unfolding of their and graduate students' narrative inquiries by attending to transitions from being in the field and composing field texts to working with field texts in writing research texts, Michael and Jean helped us awaken to how narrative inquirers' tensions are often shaped as they bump against plotlines for research that either ignore experience or values taking apart or reducing experience. Jean's and Michael's slowing down of the moments of living and of telling narrative inquiries and their attention to the bumping places between narrative inquiry and other forms of research positioned "relationship[s] . . . at the heart of thinking narratively. Relationship is key to what it is that narrative inquirers do" (Clandinin & Connelly, 2000, p. 189).

In their continuous returnings to the ongoing negotiation of relationships in narrative inquiry, what Michael and Jean called us to hold on to is that while narrative names both the "phenomenon and method" (Connelly & Clandinin, 1990, p. 2) of narrative inquiries, it can, as well, be understood as a way of living, as a way of composing a life in which relationships matter.

Lingering With Present and Future Complexities of Narrative Inquiries Negotiated in the Midst of Lives in Contexts

We began this chapter by inviting readers into a conversation where we moved backward and forward, inward and outward, as we engaged in reflective back talk (Schön, 1987) with the relational aspects of narrative inquiry as we have come to know them in our graduate studies, in our work in the field with teachers, principals, children, and families, and in our readings of the literature and how they inform our personal and professional knowing and becoming. As we and the fellow researchers and writers with whom we entered into this conversation have shown, narrative inquiries negotiated in the midst of lives and contexts, and through which relationships are formed and transformed, are filled with inevitable complexities. Yet, it is through attending to these complexities that we continue to learn what it means to live and inquire into lives as they are temporally and situationally composed and recomposed.

It is in this spirit that we now pull forward three issues that have lingered throughout our conversation and that we imagine as continuing to influence the horizons of narrative inquiry as we and others stay at the work of learning through relationships negotiated with diverse participants. We highlight these present and future complexities and possibilities so that we and other narrative inquirers can continue to reimagine how best to live through and tell of narrative inquiries negotiated in the midst of storied lives and contexts.

Reimagining Human Subjects' Agreements Through Relational Ethics

One of the issues that sits in the background and foreground of our conversations is ways in which narrative inquirers rub up against the human subject agreements upheld by universities. Because narrative inquiry is a fluid form of research, it is highly subject to change, mostly due to the intimate involvement of individual persons as holders, users, and creators of knowledge. Thus, narrative inquiry cannot be predicted or defined in the ways that stable forms of inquiry can. In fact, narrative inquiry cannot be reduced to a research design—a "rhetoric of conclusions" (Schwab, 1962, p. 64) per se, although it most certainly takes a perspective and involves a number of "tools" that researchers and participants use as they collaboratively make sense of their unfolding experiences. Yet, human subject agreements typically demand a form of "research precision," as Clandinin and Connelly (2000, p. xxii) suggested earlier, that creates enormous tensions for narrative inquirers. It is not that we do not want to comply with institutional regulations or that our intent is to engage in research practices that are disrespectful of participants' fundamental human rights. Rather, it is because of our relational attentiveness to participants that we experience turmoil when we are called to institutionally "confine them to territory populated by many"—as Coles (1989, p. 17) phrased it—as a way of advancing our research agendas. Even simple requirements befuddle us: How many "subjects" will participate? How will they be identified? How will the rights of those not involved in the study be protected? Where will posters soliciting participation be hung? Which interview questions will be asked? When? Perhaps an interviewer should be hired? Perhaps an independent observer should be employed? Should a psychologist be present when child subjects are interviewed? How many "subjects" will be added? How will they be chosen? Where will research products be disseminated? As can be seen, much about current human subject agreements, built around a medical model research, does not work well for those of us who privilege relationships and value relational knowing in our research enterprises. Furthermore, tensions heighten when committees respond to our applications. While we tend to view their comments as being representative of their lack of understanding our form of inquiry, they tend to associate our perceived shortcomings as being reflective of our research ineptitude. In a sense, both interpretations are correct. Clearly, relational forms of inquiry call for different agreements: understandings deeply grounded in ethical beliefs about relationship as Noddings (1986) proposed rather than in formalistic approaches and legalistic requirements. Nevertheless, those of us who presently conduct narrative inquiries in which relationships are crucial frequently find ourselves living cover stories (Crites, 1979). Outwardly, we comply with the sacred story (Crites, 1971) of scientific research upheld by the academy, but inwardly and in our living and telling we hold to a relational ideal (Clandinin & Connelly, 2000). We suppose that the possibility of researcher participant agreements that honor the relationships among narrative inquirers and participants sits on the horizon. For the time being, however, we call forth the works of researchers from diverse backgrounds as we move toward this imagined future.

We are drawn, for example, toward Piquemal's (2001) thoughts that informed consent needs to be continuously negotiated in cross-cultural research between aboriginal and nonaboriginal peoples: "Recurrent confirmation is needed to ensure that consent is continually informed. Negotiating free and informed consent in a circular way decenters the researcher's authority and ensures that each participant's voice is represented" (p. 77). In her more recent research with children of Ojibway ancestry, Piquemal (2005) additionally explores ways of negotiating research ethics in which the children can maintain their "cultural loyalty" (p. 523).

The work of Charon and Montello (2002) also draws us toward the possibilities of more relational research ethics. As they develop the idea of "narrative ethics" in medicine, they encourage us to think about an "ethics of life" (p. xi) that attends, firstly, to the lives of patients and their families. Within this same field, Morris (2002) draws on Basso's (1996) research with people of Western Apache ancestry to show how stories can help us think through ethics:

One Apache male describes how such [narratives], when retold in the context of moral misconduct, have a way of almost literally getting under your skin: "That story is working on you now. You keep thinking about it. That story is changing you now, making you want to live right. That story is making you want to replace yourself. . . . " The stunning concept of stories that make you want to replace yourself might be said to underwrite an entire ethics of narrative. Stories from this perspective are not detached fictions or casual entertainment but . . . incur an obligation on the listener. Such stories exert a kind of "call." (p. 197)

Echoing Schön's emphasis on reflective back talk, Young's (2005) description of "talking back and forth" with stories as a way "to connect . . . [her life with the lives of two young people of Anishinabe ancestry] in a respectful and special manner, in a circular way" (p. 144), also calls us to imagine research ethics in respectful, relational, and transformative ways. As an Anishinabe person and researcher, Young highlights the relational and narrative ways in which she, Niin, and Aanung shaped a transformative space where they storied and restoried who they were becoming as aboriginal peoples shaped by an intergenerational history of colonization.

We have travelled many places; we have re-lived our stories, re-collected our experiences; we laughed and spilled many tears. By doing that we have rejuvenated ourselves. By sharing our lives, our stories and our experiences and everything we have done together, I hope someone will recognize herself/himself and begin to heal. Like you said *Aanung,* "pimatisiwin, that is what it is all about." For you *Niin,* it is about being "a good person" and I respond by saying, "I am going to try to learn to walk in a good way." Both of you taught me that, and if we achieve that one small step towards all of us walking in a good way, both Anishinabe and non-Anishinabe, then we have accomplished something we didn't see at the beginning of our journey nor could we have even imagined. (p. 179)

With Niin and Aanung, Young urges us to live out our narrative inquiries in ways in which the relationships we compose and recompose in the meeting of our and participants' lives in contexts might have a place in healing past wrongs, thereby contributing to a future in which diverse peoples might meet face to face, laying their experiences side by side and, in mutually satisfying and equally productive ways, learn to walk together in good ways.

Truth Telling in Relational Forms of Inquiry

The notion of narrative inquirers learning to walk together in good ways not only relates to ethical aspects but also forms a dimension of the research texts composed by narrative inquirers. In Janice's exemplar introduced earlier, she situates her tensions around knowing a story told by Azim as the place for inquiry. Even though Janice discussed her knowing of Azim's story with his mom, who made sense of the situation both through her knowing of Azim and through her knowing of Emily, Janice, and Jean, Jean's and Janice's subsequent inquiry is infused by questions of who they are in relation with Azim and his mom. Similarly, Cheryl chose to focus on her uncertain negotiation of entry into T. P. Yaeger Middle School rather than write about a student suicide that happened a few years ago or what more recently occurred in the aftermath of Hurricane Rita. The latter happenings, while they are fresher experiences, are sensitive ones with which she and her research participants continue to wrestle. Time and continuing relationships have been part of the healing process, particularly since it is through research relationships that the teachers have found spaces to make sense of their pain and uncertainty. Also, serious dangers lurk in these territories. What if Cheryl were to narrate a tale of a school and faculty acting in ways perceived to be contrary to school district policy? What if Janice crafted a text that contributed to a child's removal from his or her home? That Janice and Cheryl unabashedly acknowledge these and a plethora of other uncomfortable truths is one matter. That they mindfully chose not to narratively delve further into them—at least, at this particular point in time—is quite a different matter.

All researchers make conscious decisions about what they will show and tell in their research texts. Leaving out details that could harm participants or result in job loss is one of the decision points around which narrative inquirers frequently have to think hard. Even when participants agree that tough details can be made public, we, as researchers, may hang back, thinking of their long-term consequences on persons and effects on relationships as we project our research participants and ourselves into the future. Also, because of the relational reverberations that shape our narrative inquiries and who we are becoming as narrative inquirers, we frequently are able to work our way through challenges by not drawing on field texts that might create present or future trouble for participants or ourselves or be potentially litigious.

We imagine that as we and others continue to grapple with issues of truth telling in relational forms of inquiry, writers such as Marmon Silko (1996), who draws on her Laguna Pueblo ancestry to describe truth not as absolute but as communal, will help us to keep our focus on understanding rather than judging the lives participants and we are composing over time and in contexts. As earlier reflected in Paley's work, Ross (2003) shows her living out of a plotline of understanding lives as she reflects on her belief that "as a narrative inquirer, I must strive to put away attitudes of judgement, and allow an openness to others to guide the work" (p. 584). Carger (2005) also encourages a kind of truth telling that includes the "emotion inherent in a caring relationship . . . without removing it from the realm of respectable research" (p. 232).

Imbuing Research Texts With Relational Forms of Knowing

A third issue we see hovering over our unfolding conversation about the centrality of relationships in negotiating narrative is how to imbue our research texts with the relational knowing that produced them while simultaneously maintaining fidelity to research participants as Janice brought forward in her exemplar and avoiding the sentimentality that Cheryl alluded to in her discussion of her research practices with teacher participants. Frequently, others do not comprehend that narrative inquiry seeks to understand, not to critique. The notion of the centrality of the child's, the teacher's, the parent's, or the administrator's experience, rather than privileging theory or a particular form of inquiry, is an often foreign idea. However, as Pinnegar (2006) has described, once a story is introduced in a narrative research text, readers are invited to engage in "wonderings" that "invite and enable readers to reimagine the story being lived, connect the story to their own lived experience in schools or as researchers, and rethink research, schools, and lives" (pp. 178–179).

Another closely related matter is finding a narrative way of presenting our research so that it foregrounds relationships while maintaining research rigor with which others can identify. How to achieve the appropriate tone-pitch-ambience is very critical. One way we see narrative inquirers honoring the relational aspects of their inquiries is by consciously inviting participants to live as coresearchers. In some instances, these coresearcher relationships have led to narrative inquirers and participants co-composing field texts. For example, in their narrative inquiries,

Bach (1998), Caine (2002), and Mwebi (2005) invited participants to take photographs showing aspects of their lives that they later connected with stories of their experiences. In his narrative inquiry with a teacher and children, Murphy (2004) invited children to write found poems from the teachers' comments on their report cards as a way of understanding how children's experiences with report cards shapes their knowledge and identities. Furthermore, as Murray Orr (2005) lived alongside children in a classroom and in weekly lunchtime book conversations, she drew on what she knew of each child's stories of their lives to select literature to share with them. In this way, the literature chosen became a kind of co-composed field text shaped from the life stories shared between and among Murray Orr and each child.

As a way of showing the relational knowing they negotiated with participants, Davies (1996), Mickelson (2000), Pushor (2001), and Raymond (2002) each created interim research texts that drew forth participants' experiences as lived or given voice to through photographs, autobiographical interviews, or transcripts of research conversations to compose letters in which they shared back narrative accounts with participants. We understand these interim research texts as a kind of co-composition because they focused explicitly on participants' lived and told stories shaped in relation with each narrative inquiry. Steeves (2000) and her participants created an "improvisatory story cloth installation" (p. 3) from fabric scraps that drew on their lived and told stories as they negotiated relationships with one another throughout the inquiry.

Other narrative inquirers have invited coresearchers to coauthor research texts (e.g., Ollerenshaw & Lyons, 2002; Sweetland, Huber, & Keats Whelan, 2004; Webb, 1995). Still others have experimented with alternate forms of representing research texts that have allowed participant voice and research relationships to shine through. Here we are particularly thinking of Paokong and Rosiek's (2003) sonata form; Butler-Kisber's (2002) found poetry; Clandinin et al.'s (2006) word images; Diamond and Mullen's (1999) arts-based methods; and Craig's (1997) telling stories and parallel stories (Craig, 1999) approaches.

Imagining Forward

This chapter has taken us on a circular journey in that we began with reflections on the experiences we lived as graduate students around the CRTED table and the knowing and relationships nurtured in that milieu. We then showed that the horizons of our knowing as narrative inquirers have and continue to be inextricably transformed through relationships with participants with whom we have engaged in narrative inquiries and through the works of other narrative inquirers and writers. For some months now, and across the many revisions of this chapter, we have clung to Bateson's (2000) following words because she speaks so eloquently to us about the international community of narrative inquirers and researchers who, in multiple and diverse ways, sometimes also at rich inquiry tables and sometimes in moments or through extended relationships shaped in multiple contexts, are reaching out to people with whom they work or the participants with whom they engage in inquiry, as well as to one another, as a way of forging new understandings of the relational potential of narrative knowing and inquires shaped and reshaped in the midst of storied lives and contexts.

> We . . . created a circle, not just by sitting around a table but by watching one another and attending with respect, sharing something passed from hand to hand. We had each become a part of something larger than ourselves, unknown and unpredictable. There is no more powerful symbol of unity than a circle, and no more powerful symbol of the stages of life, cycling from generation to generation. "Let the circle be unbroken" in the words of the spiritual, so that no one is lost or excluded. (p. 46)

Authors' Note: The authors deeply appreciate Jean Clandinin, who, together with Michael Connelly, awakened them to the relational aspects of narrative inquiry. They also wish to collectively thank their many research participants, who over time and across place have broadened their horizons of knowing. Where this chapter is concerned, Cheryl Craig wishes to recognize Dixie Keyes, who served as her lead research assistant, and Kyongmoon Park, Mark Seaman, and Blake Bickham, who provided additional research support. Janice Huber wishes to recognize Eleanora Huber, Celine Fernando, and Mabel Corkum for the child care they provided. Together, we thank Carol Mullen and Jerry Rosiek, whose reviews strengthened our chapter.

Consulting Editors: Carol Mullen and Jerry Rosiek

Notes

1. Emily is the pseudonym the classroom teacher chose for herself.
2. Cheryl Craig's first-hand account contains some of the original material, summary statements that survey the original material, and some new interpretation from "Characterizing the human experience of reform in an urban middle school context" by Cheryl Craig (2003), in *Journal of Curriculum Studies*, vol. 35:4, pp. 1–22. Reprinted with permission of Taylor & Francis, http://www.tandf.co.uk

References

Applebaum, S. D., & Du, J. (1999). Learning to dance in administration: A two-step in professional development. In F. M. Connelly & D. J. Clandinin (Eds.), *Shaping a professional identity: Stories of educational practice* (pp. 141–149). New York: Teachers College Press.

Bach, H. (1993). *Listening to girls' voices: Narratives of experience.* Unpublished master's thesis, University of Alberta, Edmonton, Canada.

Bach, H. (1998). *A visual narrative concerning curriculum, girls, photography, etc.* Edmonton, Alberta, Canada: Qual Institute Press.

Basso, K. (1996). *Wisdom sits in places: Landscape and language among the Western Apache.* Albuquerque: University of New Mexico Press.

Bateson, M. C. (1984). *With a daughter's eye: A memoir of Margaret Mead and Gregory Bateson.* New York: W. Morrow.

Bateson, M. C. (1989). *Composing a life.* New York: HarperCollins.

Bateson, M. C. (1994). *Peripheral visions: Learning along the way.* New York: HarperCollins.

Bateson, M. C. (2000). *Full circles, overlapping lives: Culture and generation in transition.* New York: Ballantine.

Behar, R. (1996). *The vulnerable observer: Anthropology that breaks your heart.* Boston: Beacon Press.

Belenky, M. F., Clinchy, B. M., Goldberger, N. R., & Tarule, J. M. (1986). *Women's ways of knowing: The development of self, voice, and mind.* New York: Basic Books.

Ben-Peretz, M. (1995). *Learning from experience: Memory and the teacher's account of teaching.* Albany: State University of New York Press.

Bowers, L. (1993). *Mothers in teaching: The career stories of three women.* Unpublished master's thesis, University of Alberta, Edmonton, Canada.

Bruner, J. (1990). *Acts of meaning.* Cambridge, MA: Harvard University Press.

Buber, M. (1958). *I and thou* (2nd ed.). (R. G. Smith, Trans.). New York: Scribner.

Butler-Kisber, L. (2002) Artful portrayals in qualitative inquiry: The road to found poetry and beyond. *Alberta Journal of Educational Research, 48*(3), 229–239.

Caine, V. F. J. (2002). *Storied moments: A visual narrative inquiry of aboriginal women living with HIV.* Unpublished master's thesis, University of Alberta, Edmonton, Canada.

Campbell, K. (1994). *Collaborative instructional design: A transformative social activity.* Unpublished doctoral dissertation, University of Alberta, Edmonton, Canada.

Carger, C. L. (2005). The art of narrative inquiry: Embracing emotion and seeing transformation. In J. Phillion, M. F. He, & F. M. Connelly (Eds.), *Narrative and experience in multicultural education* (pp. 231–245). London: Sage.

Carr, D. (1986). *Time, narrative, and history.* Bloomington: Indiana University Press.

Carter, K. (1993). The place of story in the study of teaching and teacher education. *Educational Researcher, 22*(1), 5–12.

Chan, E., & Boone, M. (2001). Addressing multicultural issues through teacher stories. *Journal of Critical Inquiry Into Curriculum and Instruction, 3*(2), 36–41.

Charon, R., & Montello, M. (2002). Memory and anticipation: The practice of narrative ethics. In R. Charon & M. Montello (Eds.), *Stories matter: The role of narrative in medical ethics* (pp. viiii–xii). New York: Routledge.

Clandinin, D. J., & Connelly, F. M. (1988). Studying teachers' knowledge of classrooms: Collaborative research, ethics, and the negotiation of narrative. *Journal of Educational Thought, 22*(2A), 269–282.

Clandinin, D. J., & Connelly, F. M. (2000). *Narrative inquiry: Experience and story in qualitative research.* San Francisco: Jossey-Bass.

Clandinin, D. J., Davies, A., Hogan, P., & Kennard, B. (Eds.). (1993). *Learning to teach, teaching to learn: Stories of collaboration in teacher education.* New York: Teachers College Press.

Clandinin, D. J., Huber, J., Huber, M, Murphy, S., Murray Orr, A., Pearce, M., & Steeves, P. (2006). *Composing diverse identities: Narrative inquiries into the interwoven lives of children and teachers.* New York: Routledge.

Clark, C. M. (1995). *Thoughtful teaching.* New York: Teachers College Press.

Coles, R. (1989). *The call of stories: Teaching and the moral imagination.* Boston: Houghton Mifflin.

Coles, R. (1993). *The call to service: A witness to idealism.* Boston: Houghton Mifflin.

Coles, R. (1997). *The moral intelligence of children: How to raise a moral child.* New York: Random House.

Conle, C. (1996). Resonance in preservice teacher inquiry. *American Educational Research Journal, 33*(2), 137–152.

Connelly, F. M., & Clandinin, D. J. (1988). *Teachers as curriculum planners: Narratives of experience.* New York: Teachers College Press.

Connelly, F. M., & Clandinin, D. J. (1990). Stories of experience and narrative inquiry. *Educational Researcher, 19*(5), 2–14.

Craig, C. (1995). Knowledge communities: A way of making sense of how beginning teachers come to know. *Curriculum Inquiry, 25*(2), 151–172.

Craig, C. (1997). Telling stories: Accessing beginning teacher knowledge. *Teaching Education Journal, 9*(1), 61–68.

Craig, C. J. (1999). Parallel stories: A way of contextualizing teacher stories. *Teaching and Teacher Education, 15*(4), 397–412.

Craig, C. (2001). The relationships between and among teachers' narrative knowledge, communities of knowing, and school reform: A case of "The Monkey's Paw." *Curriculum Inquiry, 31*(3), 303–330.

Craig, C. (2003). Characterizing the human experience of reform in an urban middle school context. *Journal of Curriculum Studies, 35*(4), 1–22.

Crites, S. (1971). The narrative quality of experience. *Journal of American Academy of Religion, 39*(3), 291–311.

Crites, S. (1979). The aesthetics of self-deception. *Soundings, 62,* 107–129.

Davies, A. (1996). *Team teaching relationships: Teachers' stories and stories of school on the professional knowledge landscape.* Unpublished doctoral dissertation, University of Alberta, Edmonton, Canada.

Denzin, Y. S., & Lincoln, N. K. (2000). *The handbook of qualitative research.* Thousand Oaks, CA: Sage.

Dewey, J. (1938). *Experience and education.* New York: Collier Books.

Dhamborvorn, N. (1994). *Reflecting on teachers' stories: Finding ways to live with dilemmas.* Unpublished doctoral dissertation, University of Alberta, Edmonton, Canada.

Diamond, C. T. P., & Mullen, C. A. (1999). *The postmodern educator: Arts-based inquiries and teacher development.* New York: Peter Lang.

Duckworth, E. (1996). *The having of wonderful ideas & other essays on teaching & learning.* New York: Teachers College Press.

Eisner, E. W. (1988). The primacy of experience and the politics of method. *Educational Researcher, 17*(5), 15–20.

Eisner, E. W. (1990). *The enlightened eye: Qualitative inquiry and the enhancement of educational practice.* New York: Macmillan.

Estola, E., & Elbaz-Luwisch, F. (2003). Teaching bodies at work. *Journal of Curriculum Studies, 35*(6), 1–23.

Geertz, C. (1973). *The interpretation of cultures.* New York: Basic Books.

Greene, M. (1995). *Releasing the imagination: Essays on education, the arts, and social change.* San Francisco: Jossey-Bass.

Gudmundsdottir, S. (1996). The teller, the tale, and the one being told: The narrative nature of the research interview. *Curriculum Inquiry, 26*(3), 293–306.

He, M. F. (2003). *A river forever flowing: Cross-cultural lives and identities in the multicultural landscape.* Greenwich, CT: Information Age.

He, M. F., Phillion, J., & Beach, N. (1999). An ESL instructor's teaching stories in a shifting landscape. In F. Michael Connelly & D. Jean Clandinin (Eds.), *Shaping a professional identity: Stories of educational practice* (pp. 73–79). New York: Teachers College Press.

Hoffman, E. (1989). *Lost in translation: A life in a new language.* New York: Penguin Books.

Hollingsworth, S. (1994). *Teacher research & urban literacy education: Lessons & conversations in a feminist key.* New York: Teachers College Press.

hooks, b. (1996). *Bone black: Memories of girlhood.* New York: Henry Holt.

Huber, J. (with Keats Whelan, K.). (2000). *Stories within and between selves: Identities in relation on the professional knowledge landscape.* Paper-formatted doctoral dissertation, University of Alberta, Edmonton, Canada.

Huber, J., & Clandinin, J. (2002). Ethical dilemmas in relational narrative inquiry with children. *Qualitative Inquiry, 8*(6), 785–803.

Jackson, P. W. (1968). *Life in classrooms.* New York: Holt, Rinehart & Winston.

Keats Whelan, K. (with Huber, J.). (2000). *Stories of self and other: Identities in relation on the professional knowledge landscape.* Paper-formatted doctoral dissertation, University of Alberta, Edmonton, Canada.

Kennedy, M. (1992). *Narrative journeys: A mother/teacher's story.* Unpublished master's thesis, University of Alberta, Edmonton, Canada.

Knutson, J. (1994). *Resistance: Authoring my own teacher education.* Unpublished master's thesis, University of Alberta, Edmonton, Canada.

Lachman, H. (1993). *Learning to teach with computers: Teachers' perspectives from the inside.* Unpublished master's thesis, University of Alberta, Edmonton, Canada.

Ladson-Billings, G. (2001). *Crossing over to Canaan: The journey of new teachers in diverse classrooms.* San Francisco: Jossey-Bass.

Lakoff, G., & Johnson, M. (1999). *Philosophy in the flesh: The embodied mind and its challenge to Western thought.* New York: HarperCollins.

Lane, B. (1988). *Landscapes of the sacred: Geography and narrative in American spirituality.* New York: Paulist Press.

Lyons, N. (1990). Dilemmas of knowing: Ethical and epistemological dimensions of teachers' work and development. *Harvard Educational Review, 60,* 159–180.

Lyons, N., & LaBoskey, V. (2002). *Narrative inquiry in practice: Advancing the knowledge of teaching.* New York: Teachers College Press.

MacIntyre, A. (1981). *After virtue: A study of moral theory.* Notre Dame, IN: University of Notre Dame Press.

Marmon Silko, L. (1996). *Yellow woman and a beauty of the spirit: Essays on Native American life today.* New York: Touchstone.

Mickelson, J. R. (1996). *Research issues.* Unpublished poem, Centre for Research for Teacher Education and Development, University of Alberta, Edmonton, Canada.

Mickelson, J. R. (2000). *Our sons are labelled behaviour disordered: Here are the stories of our lives.* Troy, NY: Educators International Press.

Mishler, E. G. (1986). *Research interviewing: Context and narrative.* Cambridge, MA: Harvard University Press.

Morris, D. B. (2002). Narrative, ethics, and pain: Thinking with stories. In R. Charon & M. Montello (Eds.), S*tories matter: The role of narrative in medical ethics* (pp. 196–218). New York: Routledge.

Murphy, S. (2004). *Understanding children's knowledge: A narrative inquiry into school experiences.* Unpublished doctoral dissertation, University of Alberta, Edmonton, Canada.

Murray Orr, A. (2005). *Stories to live by: Book conversations as spaces for attending to children's lives in school.* Unpublished doctoral dissertation, University of Alberta, Edmonton, Canada.

Mwebi, B. (2005). *A narrative inquiry into the experiences of a teacher and eight students about HIV/AIDS through a child-to-child curriculum approach.* Unpublished doctoral dissertation, University of Alberta, Edmonton, Canada.

Noddings, N. (1986). Fidelity in teaching, teacher education, and research for teaching. *Harvard Educational Review, 56*(4), 496–510.

Ollerenshaw, J., & Lyons, D. (2002, April). *"Make that relationship": A professor and a pre-service teacher's story about relationship building and culturally responsive teaching.* Paper presented at the annual meeting of the American Educational Research Association, New Orleans, LA.

Olson, M. (1995). Conceptualizing narrative authority: Implications for teacher education. *Teaching and Teacher Education, 11*(2), 119–135.

Oyler, C. (1996). *Making room for students: Sharing teacher authority in room 104.* New York: Teachers College Press.

Paley, V. G. (1986). On listening to what the children say. *Harvard Educational Review, 56*(2), 122–131.

Paley, V. G. (1990). *The boy who would be a helicopter.* Cambridge, MA: Harvard University Press.

Paley, V. G. (2002). *White teacher.* Cambridge, MA: Harvard University Press. (Original work published 1979)

Paokong, J. C., & Rosiek, J. (2003). Anti-colonialist antinomies in a biology lesson: A sonata-form case study of cultural conflict in a science classroom. *Curriculum Inquiry, 33*(3), 251–290.

Pearce, M. (1995). *A year in conversation: Negotiating relationships.* Unpublished master's thesis, University of Alberta, Edmonton, Canada.

Peshkin, A. (1986). In search of subjectivity: One's own. *Educational Researcher, 17*(7), 17–21.

Phillion, J. (2002). *Narrative inquiry in a multicultural landscape: Multicultural teaching and learning.* Westport, CT: Ablex.

Pinnegar, S. (2006). Afterword: Renarrating and indwelling. In D. J. Clandinin, J. Huber, M. Huber, S. Murphy, A. Murray Orr, M. Pearce, & P. Steeves, *Composing diverse identities: Narrative inquiries into the interwoven lives of children and teachers* (pp. 176–181). New York: Routledge.

Piquemal, N. (2001). Free and informed consent in research involving Native American communities. *American Indian Culture and Research Journal, 25*(1), 65–79.

Piquemal, N. (2005). Cultural loyalty: Aboriginal students take an ethical stance. *Reflective Practice, 6*(4), 523–538.

Polkinghorne, D. (1986). *Narrative knowing and the human sciences.* New York: State University of New York Press.

Pushor, D. (2001). *A storied photo album of parents' positioning and the landscape of schools.* Unpublished doctoral dissertation, University of Alberta, Edmonton, Canada.

Quan, S., Phillion, J., & He, M. F. (1999). Nancy's conflicting story of teaching in her professional knowledge landscape. In F. M. Connelly & D. J. Clandinin (Eds.), *Shaping a professional identity: Stories of educational practice* (pp. 32–41). New York: Teachers College Press.

Rager, K. (2005). Self-care and the qualitative researcher: When collecting data can break your heart. *Educational Researcher, 34*(4), 23–27.

Raymond, H. (1995). *Voices from the inside: School experiences of people with developmental disabilities.* Unpublished master's thesis, University of Alberta, Edmonton, Canada.

Raymond, H. (2002). *A narrative inquiry into mothers' experiences of securing inclusive education.* Unpublished doctoral dissertation, University of Alberta, Edmonton, Canada.

Rose, C. (1997). *Stories of teacher practice: Exploring the professional knowledge landscape.* Unpublished doctoral dissertation, University of Alberta, Edmonton, Canada.

Ross, V. (2003). Walking around the curriculum tree: An analysis of a third/fourth-grade mathematics lesson. *Journal of Curriculum Studies, 35*(5), 567–584.

Samson, F. (1999). A first-year vice-principal's position on the landscape: In- and out-of-classroom splits. In F. Michael Connelly & D. Jean Clandinin (Eds.), *Shaping a professional identity: Stories of educational practice* (pp. 135–140). New York: Teachers College Press.

Schön, D. A. (1983). *The reflective practitioner: How professionals think in action.* New York: Basic Books.

Schön, D. A. (1987). *Educating the reflective practitioner.* New York: Jossey-Bass.

Schwab, J. J. (1962). *The teaching of science: Teaching of science as enquiry.* Cambridge, MA: Harvard University Press.

Schwab, J. J. (1971). The practical: Arts of the eclectic. *School Review, 79*(4), 493–542.

Sewall, I. (1994). *The folkloral voice.* Unpublished doctoral dissertation, University of Alberta, Edmonton, Canada.

Spence, D. (1986). *Narrative truth and historical truth.* New York: W. W. Norton.

Steeves, P. (1993). *An exploration of voice in the research process in a primary classroom.* Unpublished master's thesis, University of Alberta, Edmonton, Canada.

Steeves, P. (2000). *Crazy quilt: Continuity, identity and a storied school landscape in transition: A teacher's and a principal's works in progress.* Unpublished doctoral dissertation, University of Alberta, Edmonton, Canada.

Steeves, P. (2004). A place of possibility: The Centre for Research for Teacher Education and Development. *Alberta Teachers' Association Magazine, 84*(4), 16–17.

Sweetland, W., Huber, J., & Keats Whelan, K. (2004). Narrative inter-lapping: Recognising difference across tension. *Reflective Practice, 5*(1), 45–74.

Trinh, T. M.-H. (1989). *Woman, native, other.* Indianapolis: Indiana University Press.

Webb, K. (1995). *Teacher knowledge: Narratives of relationship in curriculum making and teacher development.* Paper-formatted doctoral dissertation, University of Alberta, Edmonton, Canada.

White, H. (1987). The value of narrativity in the representation of reality. In H. White (Ed.), *The content of the form: Narrative discourse & historical representation.* Baltimore: Johns Hopkins University Press.

Witherell, C., & Noddings, N. (1991). *Stories lives tell: Narrative and dialogue in education.* New York: Teachers College Press.

Wolcott, H. F. (2002). *Sneaky kid and its aftermath: Ethics and intimacy.* Walnut Creek, CA: AltaMira Press.

Yinger, R. (1990). The conversation of practice. In R. Clift, W. R. Houston, & M. Pugach (Eds.), *Emerging reflective practice in education* (pp. 73–94). New York: Teachers College Press.

Young, M. (2005). *Pimatisiwin: Walking in a good way: A narrative inquiry into language as identity.* Winnipeg, Manitoba, Canada: Pemmican.

CHAPTER 11

Composing a Visual Narrative Inquiry

Hedy Bach

Figure 11.1   Field Texts in My Picture Window

SOURCE: Reprinted with permission of Hedy Bach.

NOTE: This image is the first cameraworks from a participant in the Mother Earth Children's Charter School inquiry as I begin to write photographic field texts.

Narrative Beginnings

Alice was beginning to get very tired of sitting by her sister on the bank, and having nothing to do: once or twice she had peeped into the book her sister was reading, but it had no pictures and conversations in it, "and what is the use of a book," thought Alice, "without pictures or conversations?"

—Carroll, 1955, p. 3

What use is a book without pictures and conversations, what use is research without image and story? Being a visual narrative inquirer is not so much about what I *do*. For me, it is a way of "being" in my world: being—living a life, not just doing a life. Seeing is a way of being in relation with people, nature, and self. Being a visual narrative inquirer involves an active process of photographing my life and is a natural way for me to hold an experience. As a visual learner with deep roots, I love the mystery of narrative inquiry—the mystery of simultaneously inquiring while living a life narratively, a being that engages fully with the senses of the body and the mind. Being truly mindful has meant seeing my heart as "a living museum" (Ackerman, 1994, p. 336), and in each of its galleries, there are both open and closed doors and doors that need to be opened to fully understand an experience. In this chapter, I attempt to be "fully present" and, with "warm heart" and "still emptiness," to hear and see possibilities not yet lived. I recognize that nothing in life is any more permanent or secure than an ocean wave. I am always riding the crest of a wave. To try to hold on to anything is to pursue an impossible illusion of security. When I accept the truth of this impermanence, I realize that all boundaries are human constructs imposed on the unpredictable, and therefore uncontrollable, process of reality. In my experience, visual narrative inquiry begins in mystery.

A Definition of Bringing the Visual to Narrative Inquiry

In coming to a definition of visual narrative inquiry, I draw on my experiences, my personal practical knowledge (Connelly & Clandinin, 1988) informed by both my lived and told stories and by the theories of other scholars. My knowing of what it means to learn, to construct knowledge, is that the visual is important. Following from this, visual narrative inquiry is an intentional, reflective, active human process in which researchers and participants explore and make meaning of experience both visually and narratively. I see experience as an undivided continuous transaction or interaction between human beings and their environments that includes not only thought but also feeling, doing, suffering, handling, and perceiving (Dewey, 1938). As I turn to consider what I mean by researchers and participants making meaning of their experiences visually in visual narrative inquiry, I draw on the work of Clandinin and Connelly (2000), who note that "experience happens narratively" (p. 19). By narrative inquiry, they note that arguments for the development and use of narrative inquiry come out of a view of human experience in which humans, individually and socially, lead storied lives. People shape their daily lives by stories of who they and others are and as they interpret their past in terms of these stories. Story, in the current idiom, is a portal through which a person enters the world and by which their experience of the world is interpreted and made personally meaningful. Looked at this way narrative is the phenomenon studied in inquiry. Narrative inquiry, the study of experience as story, then, is first and foremost a way of thinking about experience. Narrative inquiry as a methodology entails a view of the phenomenon. To use narrative inquiry methodology is to adopt a particular view of experience as phenomenon under study. (Connelly & Clandinin, 2006, p. 375)

Following this, narrative inquiry is a form of narrative experience. My work is also informed by theorists such as Bateson (1990, 1994) for learning along the way; Heilbrun (1988), Dillard (1982, 1989), and Sarton (1959) for writing a life; Freeman and Brockmeier (2001) and Freeman (2002) for identity and selfhood via autobiographical narrative; Haug (1987) and Morrison (1987) for memory work; Jaggar (1994) and Jaggar and Bordo (1989) for recognition of the body; Ackerman (1990, 1994) for sensory knowing; and feminist theorists such as Irigaray (1985), Cixous (1994), and Le Dœuff (1989, 1991) for desires involved in the aesthetic.

Visual narrative inquiry allows another layer of meaning to narrative inquiry. Experience as a whole includes all that is experienced as well as the experiencer and the way he or she experiences. Experience differs from person to person; each undergoes and acts and reacts differently. Each has a different "angle of vision" that touches on a common world. This angle of vision is an important component of visual narrative inquiry. There are no static categories of understanding or static forms of perception—one perception leads to another perception.

While at one level experience is an individual process, on another level experiences overlap. Our experiences are always our own, but they are shaped by the social, cultural, and institutional narratives in which individuals are embedded. We compose our own experiences, but others shape our experiences and so there is much that is shared. What individuals have in common is the basis of shared meaning. As individuals compose their lives, they tell stories of those experiences, and one of the ways in which individuals tell their stories is through the photographs that they take and through the photographs that others take of them. As photographs and stories are shared, resonance across stories becomes apparent, and what might be seen as old common ground is revealed, even as new common ground among persons is created. Photographs, whether those of common places, of common events, or of unique events, are a way of sharing experiences—the everydayness of lived experience.

I begin my narrative inquiries with my passion and understanding of the influence of the place of still photography within narrative inquiry. I have seen the possibility for narrative inquirers and participants to take pictures of their lived experiences over months and many conversations. Just as Dewey (1934) intends to "recover the continuity of esthetic experience with normal processes of living"

(p. 16), I believe the photographs participants take have an "everyday ordinariness" to showing how they are composing their storied lives and stories of those lives.

As I worked through my stories of experience that involve the "active process" of composing a life in and through photography, I learned that visual narrative inquiry allows me, as autobiographical narrative inquirer and as narrative inquirer in relation with others, to add layers of meaning to stories lived and told. Photographs positioned within the process of visual narrative inquiry become more than photographs or stories. They add one to the other. Working within a relational method of narrative inquiry I became aware of the intentionality, the negotiated, and the recursive nature of how visuality enriches the "three-dimensional narrative inquiry space" (Clandinin & Connelly, 2000, p. 50). Visuality refers to the socialization of vision: "this socialization is a network of cultural meanings generated from various discourses that shape the social practices of vision" (Walker, 2005, p. 24). Within this space I move backward and forward with words and with images and visualize how and where those words and photographs are located. According to Clandinin and Connelly (2000) these dimensions are directions or avenues to be pursued in narrative inquiry.

The Temporal Dimension

Working within the three-dimensional space of narrative inquiry as a researcher means that I have met myself in the past, the present, and the future as I tell remembered stories as well as current stories. As I lived alongside participants in various narrative inquiries, I came to see that telling stories of who we each are, and who we are becoming, offers possible plotlines for the futures as we tell and retell stories (Clandinin & Connelly, 2000). Building on my experience, I was drawn to the work of Weiser, a psychologist whose practice includes working with phototherapy techniques. Along with Weiser (1975, 1988, 1993), I was introduced to the work of Spence (1986, 1995), Spence and Holland (1991), and Ziller (1990) as ways of exploring visuality within narrative inquiry. Through a workshop with Weiser, I began to learn how phototherapy techniques might inform my work as a visual narrative inquirer. I saw and felt firsthand how Weiser's techniques with still photography evoked feelings and emotions quickly. As I adapted Weiser's work with still photography to my research work, I learned that people enjoy composing their lives through photography and that people have stories to tell and retell about the images they create. Drawing on the notion of temporality, we are not only concerned with life as it is experienced in the here and now but also with life as it is experienced on a continuum—people's lives, institutional lives, lives of things (Clandinin & Connelly, 2000, p. 19).

The Sociality and Place Dimensions

Experience is the organic intertwining of living human beings and their natural and built environment. For Dewey (1934), human beings are not "subjects" or "isolated individuals" who have to build bridges to go over to other human beings or the things of nature; human beings are originally and continually tied to their environment, organically related to it, changing it even as it changes them. Human beings are fundamentally attached to what surrounds them. In this way I attend to the place dimension. Working within the three-dimensional narrative inquiry space and attentive to the sociality dimension, I learned to negotiate relationships, negotiate purpose, and negotiate transitions. I see these dimensions as directions to be continued in my inquiries. As a researcher, I come to each new inquiry living my stories alongside my participants. The stories I bring as a researcher are nested within the institutional confines of my work and the larger social narratives within which I live.

Living Out Visual Narrative Inquiries: Intentional Relational Moves

The active process of composing a life in photography, an aesthetic experience, is the "experience in which the full creature is alive and most alive" (Dewey, 1934, p. 33). Within the active process of composing a life in photography, *photography* is a verb. Participants tell stories of feeling alive as they photograph what matters to them. For most participants, this is the first time anyone has provided them a camera with which to photograph and an opportunity to talk—that is, to tell stories one-to-one about their images. As I listen to the stories and look at and work with the photographs, I also feel my senses liven as I look, wonder, write, and listen to what participants tell.

As a visual narrative inquirer, I want to make meaning of participants' experiences visually. One intention of my visual narrative research is to work with participants who are active in their subcultures and to find out what matters to them through the photographs they compose about their lives. Narrative inquiry is always composed around a particular wonder, a research puzzle. Visual narrative inquiry, through the use of cameraworks, carries a sense of a search, a "re-search," a searching again. A second intention of visual narrative inquiry is to have participants work through a series of four cameraworks (modified from Weiser's, 1993, work) and numerous research conversations about their camerawork. As part of visual narrative inquiry, the relational aspect sustained over time and place is critical. For a description of the four camera works, see *A Visual Narrative Concerning Curriculum, Girls, Photography, Etc.* (Bach, 1998). Engaging in visual narrative inquiry is work that extends across time—time is layered, layer upon layer. As Clandinin and Connelly (2000) write, "narrative inquiry carries more of a sense of continual reformulation of an inquiry than it does a sense of problem definition and solution" (p. 124). I think about the phenomena, my wonders, and parts of the puzzle in my visual narrative inquiries as I necessarily trouble questions such as "What is my visual narrative inquiry about?" "What is the experience of interest to me as a narrative inquirer?" and "How do these connect to my understanding of visuality?"

Beginning the process of composing a life in photography, I meet with participants individually and speak about the ethical issues of working with cameras. We discuss the possibilities of composing photographs, collecting photographs, and conversing with/through/about photographs. I obtain informed consent from parents for youth under the age of consent and an assent agreement from the underage children to work with their photographs and taped conversations. Being a visual narrative inquirer means staying open to the inquiry, knowing that there are shifts and changes, so I am always negotiating relationships, reevaluating purposes, negotiating transitions before and after narrative inquiries, and maintaining flexibility and openness to an ever-changing landscape.

A third intention of visual narrative inquiry is the recursive nature of engaging with participants to have them take photographs and tell stories of those photographs over time. The inquiry space and the ambiguity implied remind me to be aware of where my participants and I are placed at any particular moment—temporally, spatially, in terms of the personal and the social. Our awareness carries over to our *field texts* (the term used to describe the photographs, the conversations, and the stories about those photographs and the journals and field notes that the participants and I write), where texts are always situated on a personal-social continuum. As I live out this third intention with my research participants, I begin by inviting participants to take photographs of their lives over a short time span of a week or two. The camerawork experiences are related to the diverse relationships possible among people, cameras, and images—and in practice, the tasks of these separate cameraworks overlap. Living within the ambiguity of the three-dimensional narrative inquiry space created through the cameraworks becomes most complex when temporality is considered. As Clandinin and Connelly (2000) remind us, "one's experience becomes tinged with time, making it sometimes difficult to sort out where exactly one is located in time" (p. 89).

As a visual narrative inquirer, I am mindful of my intentions, knowing that they will shift and that they are negotiated within the narrative inquiry space, depending on what my position is on the landscape and who I am in relation to the participant, the program, and the audience.

The Techniques of Visual Narrative Inquiry

I begin with photographing my own storied life as a way of portraying the particularities of an autobiographical narrative point of view. In any story told, multiple selves speak, and these selves are temporal productions residing in both the present and a reconstructed past.

To this extent, past, present, and future, as contained in stories, can be seen as productions or creations that may intersect and overlap in nonlinear organic ways. Just as living a life is unbounded, visual narrative inquiry is also open to possibilities and imaginings.

At the beginning of research relationships, I provide participants with cameras and camerawork tasks. Once the participant has taken the photographs, I collect the camera and have the film developed with two sets of prints—one for myself as a researcher and another for the participant. Before meeting with each participant, I study his or her photographs. Alone and in silence, I study each of the photographs, which I hang in my picture window for observation. I then construct a "field text" of possible meanings. In these field texts I wonder about what stories each participant will tell around their photographs and what conversations will emerge and be sustained over time. When I meet with each participant, at a time and place of his or her choosing, I listen to the stories that person tells. I invite the participant to speak about the photographs of his or her choice. From my experience, participants are intentional in composing their photographs—they have a story to tell, and they want to be heard. I say little during the research conversation. I listen. When I review the transcriptions of their tellings, I spend time looking and relooking at their images and hearing what they are telling and retelling about their photographs. In my mind's eye, I try to think about the connections between the stories they tell and the theories I have read.

We work through this process together several times. I think deeply about the images participants create as they retell their stories over the four cameraworks (Bach, 1998, 2000, 2003). I compose "field texts to help fill in the richness, the nuance, the complexity of the exchange, providing a richer, more complex, and puzzling landscape that memory alone is not likely to construct" (Clandinin & Connelly, 2000, p. 83). Visual narrative inquiry field texts are always "interpretive, always composed by an individual at a certain moment in time just as a photograph is one telling, one shot, one image" (Clandinin & Connelly, 2000, p. 84).

As I think about what is important for visual narrative inquirers in composing field texts, I am reminded of what Clandinin and Connelly (2000) say about working within the three-dimensional narrative inquiry space. As I think about the field texts, I think about the importance of positioning my field texts within that space. Knowing how field texts are positioned means visual narrative inquirers are "aware of their position and consequences for the epistemological status of their texts and, ultimately, of the research text that draws from them" (p. 118). Being attentive to the complexity generated by thinking of field texts in terms of the three-dimensional space makes clear the extent to which the texts are contextual reconstructions of events. Without this careful positioning of field texts, "the research texts ultimately constructed from them are endlessly open to questions and criticisms about knowledge claims being made and meanings generated" (p. 118).

Using my diverse field texts composed over multiple research conversations, I negotiate the possibility of many meanings from the participants' perspectives in a process Clandinin and Connelly (2000) call "back and forthing" (p. 138). What photographs do the participants want public? What photographs do they want to remain as private? What stories do they want to tell? As we co-construct research texts, we re-represent the participants' stories visually beside their words. My desire is to place the person, the image, and the story at the forefront. As a researcher, I also want to inform the reader of the theoretical connections I make with the participants' experiences.

One of my intentions in visual narrative inquiry is to trouble and be awake to my position as a researcher. By providing cameras with film to the participants,

I hope that what matters to them will surface and that my place as researcher remains initially submerged. For Dewey (1938), "taking in" any vital experience is more than placing something on top of that already known—it involves reconstruction and back and forthing.

In my definition of visual narrative inquiry, I have referred to theorists who have added to my understandings. My definition also includes qualities of the boundaries of visual narrative inquiry, reminding researchers of the fluidity of its boundaries and the recursive nature of its process. In the next section, I describe other visual theoretical sources.

Narrative Inquiry Theoretical Sources

Hanna Arendt, a theorist of ruptures, reversals, and distinctions, makes me think about what I am "being" as I gather narrative theoretical sources that influence my life story. In *The Human Condition*, Arendt (1958) outlines three human activities—labor, work, and action—that are each grounded in *conditions* of human existence: life, worldliness, and plurality. Arendt sees these human conditions as ruptures within the history of the West, as reversals of human activities and their location, and as categorical distinctions necessary for their conceptual illumination (Norris, 2004). Playing deeply with ruptures, reversals, and distinctions within a post-modern theoretical backdrop means that I support an assumption that reality is ultimately unknowable.

In post-modernism, all things are relevant, meaning that pop culture and high culture acquire equal status. Working with and hearing participants' stories of experience of their subcultures, I listen carefully when they tell me what they watch, what they listen to, what they read—all their extracurricular activities matter. By learning about what matters for my participants, I stay open to notions of multiplicity, plurality, fragmentation, and indeterminacy.

Greene (1997a) presents visions of the learner developing through concentrated observation, intense reflection, and a willingness to break from traditional subjectivities to move beyond what she has been. The process of learning, of moving beyond, calls for an inherent focus for the learner: "Ordering the materials of his own life-world when dislocations occur, what was once familiar abruptly appears strange" (p. 142). Each person deals continuously with the transience of his or her life-world, of the manner in which he or she relates to people, ideas, art, and values.

I borrow from the work of Clandinin and Connelly (1994, 2000). As a visual narrative inquirer, I include the particulars of experience, and I avoid studying experience through a set of skills, techniques, or tactics. As a visual narrative inquirer, storytelling around photography places me as centrally involved in the study of experience and, at the same time, recognizing there is no one truth. I believe experience is both temporal and storied and follow Carr's (1986) thinking that when individuals note something of their experience, either to themselves or to others, they do so in story form. Stories about participants' photographs may be the closest we can come to experience as we tell and retell our stories in the narrative inquiry space.

Participants' visual narrative field texts (their photographs) have a sense of being full and of coming out of a personal and a social history—that matters to them (Bach, 1995, 1996a, 2001b, 2003). As Carr (1986) argued, individual and social actions are lived stories—photographing a life is individual social action. I use Clandinin and Connelly's (1994) standpoint that story is neither raw sensation nor cultural form, it is both and neither. Experiences structure expressions, but expressions also structure experiences (Bruner, 1986). "Canonical events," or scripts (Bruner, 1990, p. 67), are predictive frames by which a culture interprets particular instances of behavior associated with that script. Scripts can be used as a basis for understanding new, unexpected elements. Scripts do not require an evaluative component. I want to retain a sense of openness.

As a researcher, I can play with ruptures, reversals, and distinctions in the narrative inquiry space. My point of reference is imagining what experience is and how it might best be studied and represented by participants' multistoried field texts. An intention in visual narrative inquiry for using photography is that visuality has the ability to elaborate on the meaning of, or connection between, participants' photographs and their interpretations. In representing those multistoried field texts, there are numerous ways in which story and image can be presented as research texts. This creates new possibilities for their re/imagining living their lives.

I have seen photographs that show past experiences that give significance to current experiences. In visual narrative inquiry, the recursive cameraworks permit participants to photograph past, present, and future events, which allow us to build on or create new stories and, perhaps, relive them in new ways. The active process of photographing a life enables participants to assign importance to events, people, and things in their individual experience. Inquiring about life at the boundaries allows for and structures the notion of intentionality, both implicitly containing a sense of temporality or movement within and over time. The theoretical frame for identifying tension at the boundary comes from Dewey's (1938, pp. 29–33) two criteria of experience—that is, from continuity and interaction. These tensions at the boundaries are not independent but rather interconnected.

The Research of Other Visual Narrative Inquirers

Although narrative inquiry is used repeatedly as a methodology for investigating teaching, professional, and personal lives and identities, bringing the photograph into the narrative inquiry has been understudied. For me, as a visual researcher it is not simply a question of adding photography to a grab bag of available techniques but rather a way of bringing into play visual media as we thread the margins between social science and cultural study (Bach, 1996b, 1996d, 1997c, 1997d, 2001a). Visual narrative inquiry suggests a need for conversation about the use of photographs throughout the inquiry, knowing that is not restricted to questions of method but rather begins with the distinction between the public and the private use of photographs—those stories that matter, those intentional photographs composed by the participants with time.

There are narrative inquiry studies into teacher identity that include drawing as well as speech and writing to document teachers' lives (see Johnson, 2004; Pole, 2004; Weber & Mitchell, 1995). These works typically work with one image, a single source with supportive written text. Johnson (2004) works with data contained in a *picture book* to encourage teachers to use a visual and verbal approach to storytelling as a method of critical reflection. Harrison (2002) examines the ways in which *photographic images* can be used in narrative inquiry and examines the ways in which researchers have utilized the camera or photographic images in forms of narrative inquiry such as biography and autobiography, photographic journals, video diaries, and photo-voice. She concludes that photographs can be used as a resource for narrative inquiry. One intention of visual narrative inquiry is to uncover the visuality around the evaded (Bach, 1996c, 1996e, 1997b, 1998, 1999, 2003) by reference to photographs of everyday stories typically not seen or heard by those outside the community.

There are researchers who work with photography as a way of inquiring into experience that overlaps other photographic narratives. Bell (1999) examines documentary film and still photographic accounts of the narratives of lives of women affected by the drug DES. She asks "How do these images matter? What are the benefits to a social science understanding of women's lives by taking visual narratives seriously?" (p. 348). What can images do and not do for narrative inquiry—knowing images do not have the same format as writing and film? Radley (2002, 2004) and Radley and Taylor (2003) use what they call a photo narrative to examine *illness narratives* through the use of still photography to elicit life experiences in the contexts of hospitalization and homelessness. Walkerdine (1990) explores gender and class through the analysis and use of *video diaries* in her studies of class and gender. Rich and Chalfen (1999) and Rich, Patashnick, and Chalfen's (2002) *Video Intervention/Prevention Assessment* (VIA) gathered the visual illness narratives and analyzed them with software. Illness narratives are logged, structured, and coded as a way of learning more about improving related behaviors and medical plans. Frohmann (2005) uses photography as a *therapeutic tool* in a collaborative, community action-education research project that is built on the use of participant-generated photographs and photo-elicitation interviews as methods for exploring with women, in support group settings, the meanings of violence in their lives and their approaches to creating safer spaces.

There is a growing body of narrative inquiry dissertations that use photographs within a narrative inquiry framework. Caine (2002) uses "photography as narrative" in her inquiry *Storied Moments: A Visual Narrative Inquiry of Aboriginal Women Living With HIV.* Pushor (2001) uses the metaphor of "photo albums" in her narrative inquiry in *A Storied Photo Album of Parents' Positioning and the Landscape of Schools.* Her use of photographs follows a tradition that implies preservation and permanence. The inclusion of photographs complements the text, adding permanence to moments. In both studies, visual narrative inquiry combines the use of storytelling with photography to express life experiences.

Genres of Photographs Used in Visual Narrative Inquiry

In my visual narrative inquiries, photographs are a form of field text. Photographic field texts may be already existing photographs, photographs taken by participants, or photographs taken by researchers. As participants work within the narrative inquiry process we/they create hundreds of photographs.

Still photography is used for various purposes, various contexts, and various phenomena in each individual visual narrative inquiry. Understanding the historical place of the photography facilitates an understanding of the details of using photography that unfold over time during the narrative inquiry process. It also keeps the researcher mindful to the changing nature of working with photography. I use photographs created by the participants at every stage of the inquiry as a way of getting inside participants' experiences of a subculture, a program, a context, and a life.

As a relational method, having conversations with photographs may bridge psychological and physical realities for participants and researchers. I have found that the photograph assists in building trust and rapport for self as a researcher working with participants. This makes the relationship between self and participants central in the creating of photographic field texts, shaping what is told as well as the meaning of what is told (Clandinin & Connelly, 2000).

In my work with children, youth, and adults, I used already existing photographs (past or temporal) as photographic field texts in the visual narrative inquiry process. These photographs include (a) those taken by participants; (b) those of participants; and (c) family photographs. In my visual narrative inquiries with youth and children, they worked through a series of cameraworks, and we worked with these photographs as field texts.

Photographs taken by researchers are used as field texts. In autobiographical narrative inquiries, I photographed my lived experiences through a narrative series on the body (Bach, 1999; Bach, Kennedy, & Mickelson, 1999); the place of the horse in a community (Bach, 2000, 2001b, 2003); skaterboys; and my classroom experiences as an art educator, photographing two-dimensional and three-dimensional art works of future elementary and secondary education students (Bach, 2001c).

Narrative Inquiry Into Photographs: A Collaborative Process

"To collect photographs is to collect the world" (Sontag, 1977, p. 3). As a visual narrative inquirer, I collect my world with autobiographical photographs as well as the photographs of research participants. This raises questions around my research practice within this collaborative process of creating photographs, collecting photographs, conversing with photographs, and constructing visual narrative composites. Inquiring into photographs begins with knowing that I am always negotiating relationships, reevaluating purposes, and negotiating transitions as I live alongside my participants' experiences.

Creating Photographs

Discussing the ethics of using photography and the ethics of seeing with my participants is imperative. I want participants to experience the joy of being image-makers and know the ethical considerations of being photographed and being photographers. I am mindful of what sense participants make in relation to photographing their life experiences. I show them examples in books, publications, and earlier work of what might be possible. I talk about being an imagemaker and playing with cameraworks as a way to photographing a life within the narrative inquiry process. After this conversation, each participant is in control of the camera. They make decisions about being the photographer and being photographed as they work through the cameraworks experience. As a researcher, I trust and allow for uncertainty to be present. The next time each participant and I meet, he or she will have completed one camerawork as we begin to nurture our research relationship. I ask them questions about who they photographed and how others felt about being photographed. Each time the participant begins a new film, I confirm he or she has been sensitive in working with the camera.

Collecting Photographs

The participants in my narrative inquiries have taken 2 to 3 weeks to complete a film—if it takes longer, I gently nudge them as either a reminder or a way out of the inquiry. It is important for me that all participants know there is a way out of the inquiry. Visual narrative inquiry requires participants to be active in the process of collecting field texts, and so if their desires wane I want them to be comfortable in choosing to no longer participate. Typically, I plan a date at the participants' convenience to collect their film and have two sets of prints developed: one set for the participant and the other a working set—for photographic field texts. In the past, I have negotiated the safe keeping of the negatives. Now, with the changing technology, I keep a record of their images on CD. With exponential software changes, visual narrative inquirers will need to stay abreast of issues in media.

As I study their photographs, I begin composing a field text with their photographs, imagining what stories participants may or may not tell about the photographs they have taken. A post-modern critique of photography begins with the idea that the meaning of the photograph is constructed by the maker and the viewer, both of whom carry their social positions and interests to the photographic act (Tagg, 1988). This critique reminds me that the meaning of the photograph changes in different viewing contexts. I live with my participants' photographs, they hang on my picture windows, and I look and revisit them often over weeks at a time. Reflecting on the photographs, I am curious—open to what might be. The mystery remains. With time, these photographic field texts are fleshed out deeper after each conversation, thickened with information and theories I read and gather along the way. Each time I begin our research conversations, I bring along the photographic field texts and any other artifacts that fit within the inquiry space. I share what I see and read with my participants as I learn along the way.

Conversing With Photographs

While conversing with participants about their photographs, I recognize issues and dilemmas that participants face in their daily lives. With the recursive nature of working through the series of cameraworks and playing with multiple cameras and film, I am able to hear stories that matter to them. Dialogue can arise from storytelling in a shared research space, and as Greene (1997b) writes, "out of dialogue and conjecture can come the making of projects also shared." Time and space allow the participants to connect threads of their lived experiences and discover new ones. Our conversations are taped and then transcribed. I read and reread the transcripts, often able to recite text by heart and visualize text on the page. I listen and hear participants' voices of the stories they choose to tell. I hear how human beings make sense of experience by constructing stories and listening to their constructions. Embedded within our conversations with the photographs are intimations of emotion and a sense of connecting through sensory knowing. With the photographs in front of us, our shared conversation moves back and forth between both the photograph and the story. I am mindful that the stories I bring as a researcher are set within the institutions in which I work, the social narratives of which I am a part, the landscape on which I live (Clandinin & Connelly, 2000). I use the stories of the photographs for the photographic field texts as well as for my reflections that are woven into and through experience and theory. These shared stories are told and retold with time over numerous camerawork experiences.

Listening to the participants, I am aware that there may be a cathartic release when they speak about photographs in their cameraworks. Most times I sense that the children and youth responded viscerally, without the mediation of their intellect. Participants are always provided the option to bypass a photograph. I am listening, not agreeing with or simply confirming what I already think. I wonder, Am I open to hearing something new? What is the nature of such a "mattering" conversation with photographs between participants and researchers? I observe my reactions as I talk—I listen to the sounds of my voice and my participants' voices. Picking up sounds other than the sound of my own voice—my own reactions to what I hear—I listen for vibrations, possible feelings of tension or uncertainty. It is not always easy to listen, especially when emotions are present. Even when I am not emotional, it is not easy to listen, knowing that we are always listening from our position. Chase (2003) concurs with the need for "listening well" during research conversations and discusses the ways in which knowledge of the processes of narrative analysis recursively shapes the capacity to listen: "When we listen carefully to the stories people tell, we learn how people as individuals and as groups make sense of their experiences and construct meanings and selves" (p. 80). People's narratives reflect not only their own meaning making but the scripts of society or culture in which they live. Participants see the iterative nature of their stories as a photograph is repeated and as they retell those stories.

Listening is hard work. Being available, being "present," having an open heart to the participants matters. I follow their leads, their interests, and as I write photographic field texts I look for photographs that tell a variety of stories. Is there more than one? Are the divisions artificial or real? What is still being discovered? This is when I have learned it takes time and that participants need several cameras and film and research conversations to uncover the unknown. At times I get lost in additional narratives, the site, the participants' plotlines, the actions, the body language, or being overexcited. Sometimes I hear the minutiae of sighing; I see the nodding and eye glazing, which is a cue for me that the participant has had enough. I am awake to any surface tension, I want to keep a sparkle, to retain the undercurrent—so it flows and segues into the next moment.

Constructing Visual Narrative Composites

Photographic Field Texts

I write notes on what I see. I scribble notes, jot questions, cut out newspaper articles, look widely at the subcultures of which participants are a part. Constructing visual narrative composites, my interpretive texts, includes sensory knowing, body language, and ongoing questions. My photographic field texts are images and notes that I gather along the way to unlearn and learn, to listen, to hear fully, and to confirm what I see and hear. As I study the participants' photographs, I think and write field texts that may differ from what the participants tell me about their photographs. I honor their stories. I allow for the mystery of lived experience to unfold for them. I question: What is the content of the photograph? What does the photograph communicate? What is missing? What are they trying to tell? Who needs to know this? And why?

Writing within the three-dimensional narrative inquiry space, I feel as though I am in the middle or muddle of things. As a researcher, I am also living my life narratively in relation to and alongside the inquiry. I have learned that no middle lasts forever and that the inquiry moves on. For me, this space has been a delicate transition—conjuring up feelings and emotions of "Who am I?" in this inquiry. And who am I? I see myself in the midst—located somewhere along the dimensions of time, place, the personal, and the social (Clandinin & Connelly, 2000). I see myself in "the midst in another sense as well; that is, we see ourselves as in the middle of a nested set of stories—ours and theirs" (p. 63). Negotiating this transition, for me, requires silence—long walks with my dogs and much-needed time outdoors, as well as a research community. Writing on the body of my participants creates a tension for me, a tension that implies holding/containing/fixing the participants' visual narrative composites in time and place. How will these narrative inquiry research texts be read over time? How will participants feel over time? What is gained in making these visual narrative composites public? These questions emerge again and again and are negotiated differently by different research communities dependent on their frameworks and positions. A collaborative research community assists in making sense of what I am constructing and thinking. I look for reciprocity of other likeminded researchers and the continued engagement of participants to work "back and forthing," knowing that human lives are woven stories. Individuals construct their identities through their own and others' stories (Clandinin & Connelly, 2000). Studying and exploring participants' photographs overlaps with stories of my lived experience. Images of friends, families, pets, and everyday life echo experiences of my identity.

Once I have the photographs and the tapes are transcribed, I continue with the meaning making of the photographic field texts, going over the dozens of photographs and the numerous conversations. As I listen and relisten to the tapes and look and relook at the participants' photographs, I turn inward. I prepare for the sharper edges—a need to reflect, meditate, and live with silence from the protective viewing of the participants' photographs. How will I or we show our understandings of our experience? What is the level of analysis? What is our purpose? How will I or we select photographs? What do my photographic field texts say? What do the conversations about the photographs say?

Photographic Research Texts

How people respond to photographs and how they choose to photograph can tell us much about individuals. I have looked at my field notes and transcripts, and the photographs are hung on my window and I look for a recurring rhythm, a story that has been told more than once, a photograph taken and retaken, a narrative series, a clue, the details, that hunch, that presses me to get out of the muddle and into the writing of the photographic research text. Reading the photographs is like learning to "read" an artifact, needing to apply careful descriptions. Photographs can connect us with other stories, and we can bridge the gap of time by applying our senses, intellect, and emotions to experience as a human commonality and express our connection in a narrative form.

Through our multiple conversations with photographs over a year or more in writing and rewriting around the photographic field texts, I create a photographic research text—the visual narrative composite—by juxtaposing historical, philosophical, and theoretical positions concerned with the reading of participants' photographs and stories within history, memory, culture, geography, language, and identity. The narrative form I have been working with has been writing the visual narrative composite in columns. I start with an agreed on image, followed by the participant's story, and, in a third column, my story as a researcher and a reader of theories runs alongside.

Thinking about writing a visual narrative research text allows me to conceptualize the inquiry experience as a visual story on many levels. Following Dewey, my hope from these experiences is the growth and transformation in the life story that we as researchers and our participants author. I concur with Clandinin and Connelly (2000) that, as difficult as it may be to tell a story, the more difficult but important task is the retelling of stories that allow for growth and change. "We imagine, therefore, that in the construction of narratives of experience, there is a reflexive relationship between living a life story, telling a life story, retelling a life story, and living a life story" (p. 71).

Pervasive Ethics

Eleven years ago, I presented a part of my doctoral work at the 1995 AERA annual meeting—it was the first time I had made the girls' visual narratives public. I learned firsthand about response to research texts and the ethical dilemmas of "using" the girls' photographs in public. "Photographs furnish evidence" (Sontag, 1977, p. 5), and Thya, one of the high school girls, had documented an underage weekend party where a group of her friends were smoking pot, drinking beer, listening to music, and talking about boys. When a female educator-scholar looked at the visual narrative composites, she began telling me, "that girl will never get into graduate school if people saw those photographs." (Since then Thya has completed a master's degree.) I was troubled. Her response left me feeling naïve, thinking "you've got to be *real*." I am not a scholar of ethics, but I read, work visually, and have ideals. I am not convinced we live in a time in history that allows security for a visual researcher. How can I as a researcher protect, guarantee safety, and question an ethic of seeing? Herein lies an ethical dilemma of being a narrative inquirer as I learn to respond while making the private public. What is that? What is never? What are they doing? What is seen? Creating photographic research texts means troubling my responsibility of being a researcher. When I see participants' photographs, I understand from the onset of my inquiries that one of my intentions has been to uncover or reveal aspects of the evaded curriculum. I wonder whether the evaded is also illegal or the illegal is very often evaded? Making the private public has been a contentious issue for me from the beginning of all my inquiries. I was faced with the irony of reencapsulating the evaded by realizing that knowing the coded indexical nature of reading photographs, there are some I did not wish to show. The further irony is that by maintaining that position, I call into question the intentionality of my research. In discussions with the participants, we negotiate if we are prepared to take the risk and make the private public. In *The Open Door*, Helen Keller's (1957) words convey some of my feelings about the ethics of working visually:

> Security is mostly a superstition. It does not exist in nature. . . . Avoiding danger is no safer in the long run than outright exposure. The fearful are caught as often as the bold. Faith alone defends. Life is either a daring adventure or nothing. (p. 17)

Visual narrative inquiry is living life at the boundaries—knowing that providing participants with cameras and film can uncover "secrets" (Rich, 1979), similar to lifting a heavy stone and uncovering a myriad of organic living. "A photograph is a secret about a secret. The more it tells you the less you know" (Arbus, 1972, p. 64). The research question for me is which stones to lift. How many to lift? Which remain uncovered? There is risk in our visual work. Is visual narrative inquiry "a daring adventure or nothing?" Prosser (2005) writes there is limited agreement on theoretical positions and accepted ethical practices on which to base ethical everyday judgments in visually oriented research, relative to word and numbers research.

Over the past 15 years of exhibiting participants' photographs, I have encountered viewers' responses that place me within the ethical position of needing to acknowledge those responses. How can I respond to ignorant, romantic, and even naïve or moralistic commentaries about these photographs? How can there be conversation around the silence? The illegal? The private? What becomes public? I have learned that photographs alter and enlarge our notions of what is worth looking at and what we have a right to observe (Sontag, 2004). They are a grammar and, even more important, what Sontag (1977) once called "an ethics of seeing" (p. 3).

Figure 11.2   Evading the Evaded

SOURCE: With permission of Kelsey D. Hilsen.

NOTE: This image is one in a series of narratives on the encroachment of urban life from a participant in the *Children as imagemakers with horses.*

As a visual narrative inquirer, I employ a quality of "sensitivity" (Bach, 1997a, 1997d, 2000, 2001a, 2003, 2006; Becker, 1974, 1988, 1995; Harper, 1987; Weiser, 1993) that lies at the center of my relation with participants. Sensitivity requires that I work diligently against "othering" by attempting to understand participants' lives so that they may determine which individuals and activities to photograph and how resulting images ought to be used. I see sensitivity rooted in the reciprocal nature of the inquiry and of the caring relationships among those engaged in visual all-narrative inquiry. I continue to be mindful to a "covenantal ethic" (May, 1980, p. 362) as a way of negotiating relations between those who tell and visually show life stories and share personal experiences. Although the relationship is fluid and unfixed, "we cannot escape our relational condition," says Noddings (1989, p. 237), "but we can reflect on it, evaluate it, move it in a direction we find good." I am mindful of my responsibility as a researcher of how photographs taken by and of youth are made public. I ask myself, What are my ethical intentions as a visual researcher creating field texts and research texts? What are each participant's intentions? What "good" will come of this? These are ethical questions of which I am constantly mindful.

I take seriously the words of May (1977), who advocates the covenant as a way of being between researcher and participants because "the covenantal relationship is primary; it involves neither subjects nor objects, but human beings" (p. 69). I see the participants writing their lives, authoring stories and creating images of their daily lives. As Bateson (1994) describes this process within the study of cultures, so must we craft our vision of the caring relationship in the visual narrative inquiry process:

> Arriving in a new place, you start from an acknowledgement of strangeness, a disciplined use of discomfort and surprise. Later, as observations accumulate, the awareness of contrast dwindles and must be replaced with a growing understanding of how observations fit together within a system unique to the other culture. (p. 27)

Knowing who I am in relation to the participants and knowing that I have written field texts from their cameraworks, I attend to May's (1980) definition of a covenantal ethic:

> At the heart of a covenant is an exchange of promises, an agreement that shapes the future between two parties. This promise grows . . . and acknowledges the other. . . . It emphasizes gratitude, fidelity, even devotion, and care. (p. 367)

I am also mindful of how I position myself and how I negotiate relations between participants who tell stories and share personal experiences about their photographs. As a visual narrative researcher, caring, sensitivity, and covenantal ethics are related. I cannot be engaged in the reciprocal relationship required by the covenant without engaging myself in and hearing and understanding the participants' lived experiences, beliefs, values, and views of their worlds. The covenantal ethic cues me to deliberate the participants' needs in my researching and publishing.

Images can be obtained overtly or covertly. The introduction of a camera to participants can take place on the first day as a "can opener" (Collier & Collier, 1986, p. 10) or over a period of time using a "softly softly" approach (Prosser, 1992, p. 398). I am attentive to the unique dilemmas that arise from employing visual methods—without becoming paralyzed by the many gatekeepers. I continue to believe that the application of sensitivity grounded in covenantal ethics and an ethic of seeing will provide insight and understanding made available using photography within visual narrative inquiry without harming participants or myself. Working within a framework of care enhances the research relationship by encouraging me to stay aware of the participants' understandings of what is included in the visual narrative inquiry process. However, no code, outlook, or technique ensures that ethical problems will be resolved. "Covenant ethics is responsive in character" (May, 1977, p. 69), and consequently, I remain ready to alter or abandon the use of visual re/presentation if I have good reason to believe that the participants are being adversely affected (May, 1977, 1980; Weiser, personal communication, February 20–23, 1994).

To date, perhaps the strongest discussion of ethical issues related to photography appears in *Image Ethics: The Moral Rights of Subjects in Photographs, Film and Television* (Gross, Katz, & Ruby, 1988a) and *Image Ethics in the Digital Age* (Gross, Katz, & Ruby, 2003).

Gross, Katz, and Ruby (1988b) suggest that the following aspects be considered at all times: (a) intrusion, (b) embarrassment, (c) false light, and (d) appropriation. Accordingly, the following questions will be negotiated within the narrative inquiry process for both the researcher and the participant:

- What point of intrusion into people's lives is acceptable? Are points different in private and public places?
- What is our intention in making a photograph public? Or keeping it private?
- Will the photograph embarrass or humiliate a person today or in the near future if it were to be made public?
- Does the photograph show the person in a false light? What is their "truth" of the image? Does a righteous social purpose diminish some of these concerns?
- What exactly does consent mean? What does assent mean? Is consent to take a picture the same as consent to use it?

As Prosser (1998) points out, there is a delicate division between being sly, deceitful, and furtive, and being sensitive and judicious. Establishing participant confidence means assuring participants that they will not be damaged, misrepresented, or prejudiced in any way; in terms of researchers, confidence means agreeing to ethical procedures that protect respondents yet ensure trustworthiness of discoveries. How and who will make the final decisions of ethical practice for visual research: the researcher herself or himself? The research community? The institutional gatekeepers?

Ideally, a photograph is an untouched, unmanipulated transcript of what was there. Except, says Gross (Gross et al., 2003), everybody knows there are elements of built-in selection. As he notes, cropping and the angle of the photograph are two common means of altering content. As Sontag writes (1977),

> Photographs, which fiddle with the scale of the world, themselves get reduced, blown up, cropped, retouched, doctored, tricked out. They age, plagued by the usual ills of paper objects; they disappear; they become valuable, and get bought and sold; they are reproduced. Photographs, which package the world, seem to invite packaging. They are stuck in albums, framed and set on tables, tacked on walls, projected as slides. Newspapers and magazines feature them; cops alphabetize them; museums exhibit them; publishers compile them. (p. 4)

In my visual narrative inquiries, I practice sensitivity within an ethic of seeing, knowing that I remain open to questions of working with images and asking if visual narrative inquiry is "a daring adventure or nothing" whether the visual narrative inquirer is held to an ethical standard different from that of a photojournalist. Or is the subject similar? Will visual researchers all use the same standards? How will visual researchers employ the same standards? And who will construct the criteria of those standards?

A Case of My Visual Narrative Inquiry

My doctoral work began and ended with a narrative autobiographical story, as a way to hold an experience. The idea of boxing an experience can be troubling: How do I write those ruptures, reversals, and distinctions as a visual narrative inquirer as I continue to live my life? I write stories of experience because I learn to live stories in new ways and have a desire to create knowledge. I have an alternative way of seeing—segueing into the mystery.

Figure 11.3   "From skateboarding we gain new perspective. I see something new every time I step on my skateboard and therefore I learn something new every time I ride." —Jordan

SOURCE: With permission of Jordan Perrault.

NOTE: This image and words are from one participants' Cameraworks II series in *Skaterboys.*

My work with girls in the 1990s began from a passion—strong feelings of equity, fairness, with imaginings of possibilities and openings. I followed the body of work on girls' experiences, those stories of silence (Fine, 1991, 1992; Fine & Weis, 2003), those stories of the evaded (Bach, 1997c, 1998, 2003), those stories of being shortchanged. I read the papers, watch the news, see the popular magazines, and witness the place of women and girls. I read the headlines of the human condition, those stories of war, abuse, murder, rape; stories of mutilation on the body that stain our global culture. Sweeping reports, inquiries, court cases of victims and villains fill the news channels. I also see the television shows, such as *The O.C.*, *Falcon Beach*, and *One Tree Hill*, that youth culture watches that perpetuate those scripted characters similar to the Archie comics of the 1960s and 1970s. As I read the research of boys who are reluctant readers and those who will not write, I now read of how schools shortchange boys.

As an autobiographical researcher, I study my professional story positioned on the landscape as a contract academic—as a "wanna-be" teacher educator. I am mindful of how these lived experiences shape my stories and identity as a researcher and as a teacher educator. Some ruptures have been fashionable, but they are not about gender or the reversals of girls' and boys' experiences at/in/through school; they are about the need to ask questions, questions about knowledge. What does knowledge look like? What does knowledge feel like? What counts as knowledge? Who gets to decide what matters?

Our daughter, Chloe, loved magpies in Grade 3. Now, in Grade 12, she loves boys. I watch and listen to romance stories and those of her friends. I see them entering the "sleeping beauty phase," a time of losing themselves to cultural scripts, dreams and desires of needing to be coupled, needing to be thin, needing to be fashionable, needing to be smart, sadly needing to be "perfect." An ideal of "being good enough" that is held out for girls and boys—is so real and so unreal. As a teacher educator in elementary and secondary education, I work mainly with women. In my hands-on art classes, I work with zines as a way for my students to show alternative ways of knowing, through the use of graphic design and typology. For many women, their bodies are the subject, and after reading many zines over many years, I have seen the images and read the stories of my students' self-loathing. Positioned differently, I see how these stories echo and mirror past, present, and future stories of how women and men's bodies continue to be re-rep-resented in the media and popular culture. Although I live these stories out differently, teach them differently, hear them differently, my wonders have changed. What keeps this story of disconnection to the body in place? What does it mean to be an educated person, an educated girl, an educated boy? And what is gained in research for public knowledge?

I have learned to uncover and lift stones through being an autobiographical narrative researcher as well as a visual narrative inquirer. Over the past 10 years, I've connected with all my girls from my initial visual narrative inquiry in person, by telephone, in letters and email, and through conversations over tea. I have continued to hear their stories and see their photographs of marriage, and I learn of divorce, of the joys of working as a photographer, of struggles in postsecondary education, and of success in a musical career. As a visual narrative inquirer, I have experienced and am grateful for our caring relationships. This matters for me. Eleven years later, I asked Quinn, a participant, about her experiences of photographing her life as a girl in high school. Here is what she wrote:[1]

Hedy,

You asked what the photography process does for me . . . photography benefits me because I am a visual, hands-on learner . . . it's how I process information. The conversations I have with myself in my head when I'm trying to better understand life, emotions and the world in general are primarily represented by shapes and colors. It's done unconsciously, but I've become self-aware enough to know that every experience, every body, every place I've had, met, or been to is filed somewhere in my brain and catalogued by a color scheme or visual essence. Participating in the art of photography, somehow, represents the art of my mind. I feel closely related to and well-represented by the camera. As all human beings crave at some point or another, I long to be deeply understood. The thing I've come to realize lately is that it's less about others but instead the truth is I want to understand myself. The medium of photography, as well as the good ol' pen and paper, have helped me in the infinite journey of doing just that. To this day, most of my artwork pertains to the architecture of nature and the fascinating formula of how we interpret light and colors . . . because that's how I identify my own experiences.

Psycho babble aside though, photography simply helps me remember things in detail where I otherwise might not. I have a small fear that one day I may lose my ability to remember, not wanting to give that fear any strength to manifest itself, I chalk it up to some past life issue that doesn't have a place in the here and now . . . still, I continue to document my life in photographs, my memory works in snap-shots.

It's a bit odd, yet in true Q fashion, very intriguing to be asked what photography does for me. Quite honestly I just like the feel of it, it's natural for me. When I was younger, during the visual narrative I did with you and the other girls, I was so eager to share my insides, everything about my life. Hedy, you gave me a platform in which I could control the way I was viewed by others (even though ultimately the author/editor has control) and I could tell my story as it made sense to me. Certainly, at that age, I'm not sure anything made sense, but in my effort to be an adult and get a grasp on the world outside of myself, the visual narrative was a healthy and safe outlet for being candid and expressive when it felt like no one else (outside my family) was listening. I have to give credit where it's due, had it been anyone besides yourself, the experience could have been a disaster. The adolescent trust each of us automatically had with you was reciprocated with an honest reflection of our lives in the end product. You did not allow our stories to be skewed or altered for the adult world, which is what makes re-reading the book so much more fascinating. That it involved photography as a tool was just my good fortune, I'm not sure I would have found the visual narrative near as therapeutic had it been something like painting or drawing. (Quinn)

Each of the girls noted my sensitivity in how I held or contained their stories together. Hearing this has meant I have a sense of safekeeping while working visually with participants.

Knowing that I position and reposition myself within a three-dimensional narrative inquiry space, in 1998, building on my experiences of being in a research relationship, I started to work with girls and boys in a visual narrative inquiry titled *Children as Imagemakers With Horses.* The beginning feelings of uncertainty and ambiguity in this visual narrative inquiry were the same yet different in that I understood more clearly the positive influence that photographing a life has on a person. Ambiguity makes for new experiences, new understandings, new ways of being, and new kinds of relations with each other by keeping the meaning incomplete. The ambiguity of the world keeps the meaning in a constant state of flux and openness (Bateson, 1994). I experienced the girls' affirmations of them telling and retelling stories of experiences and the possibility of living a life by appreciating just being—knowing that their stories mattered and that I listened. Visual narrative inquiry allows space to combine visual and verbal language with the recursive nature of working through the camerawork series, several research conversations photographs, and the writing of research texts.

The recursive nature of using multiple cameras and film provides an element of resonance to improve reflection. As Dewey (1938) reminds us, reflection or knowledge is but a small part of experience. Beneath the surface of dividing the world up into separate objects, of classifying and analyzing and thinking about things, there is a continuum, a unitary experience of feeling, having, suffering, undergoing, doing, etc. Beneath intellectual compartmentalization and "objectifying" is our felt unity with the world. Knowledge only seems to "break up" reality, to detach objects from subjects and objects from objects. Greene's (1997a) observations acknowledge that a human being may feel strange, disengaged, frustrated, or helpless in the face of ever-changing realities and that a willingness to acknowledge the strangeness, the uncertainty, is part of learning.

Meeting the girls who played in the arts, the girls and boys with horses, and the boys who skateboard touched my heart. Working with young children and youth, I found that the use of cameras and photography promoted longer, more detailed conversations—there is a fluidity to the conversation, and to the surprise of many parents, they tell me they have never heard their sons or daughters talk so much. Talking one-to-one with "other" people's children is an honor. My narrative inquiries have centered on the relation between the participants' photographs and the stories they live by, their identities, and the landscape of their subcultures. I am inspired by Nhat Hanh (1991, 1996, 1997) to gain wisdom inside, manifesting service and compassion outside, as I work alongside of my participants' experiences. I have been intentional in my inquiry and interpretation of bringing the photograph into the narrative inquiry. I have listened to and learned from stories participants told about their photographs as their positions shifted on the institutional landscape to off the institutional landscape. In my most recent (Bach & Baydala, 2006) collaborative visual narrative inquiries, *A Visual Narrative Inquiry: Mother Earth's Children's Charter School* and *A Visual Narrative Into the Experiences of Two*

Children Living With Obesity with Misericordia Community Pediatric Research Group Child Health Clinic, we explore the photographic form as a core technique to enhance collaborative/community research and needs assessments.

Listening to and learning from stories participants tell assists in making sense of how plotlines of their stories to live by and their identities shift in response to their ever-changing positions. Through my first inquiry, I came to understand the intimate connection between identity and the subculture of the arts. For me, a deeper understanding is gained of both the photograph and the story when stories to live by are laid side by side and overlap. The laying of stories side by side illuminates qualities of the subculture to which participants belong and reveals the contribution these qualities make to change the stories we live by. I believe that visual narrative inquiries begin in mystery and end in mystery.

Autor's Note: I am grateful to Jean Clandinin for her support and for her belief in seeing new possibilities in narrative inquiry. I give my collective thanks to my research participants for awakening me to adventures I had never imagined. I acknowledge Steve and Chloé Bach, and Merle Kennedy, for their unrelenting support and devotion. I am forever thankful to Joy Ruth Mickelson for her caring friendship and for her attentive reviews of my chapter.

Consulting Editors: Joy Ruth Mickelson, Vera Caine, and Debbie Pushor

Note

1. Interview is reprinted with permission of Quinn Covington.

References

Ackerman, D. (1990). *A natural history of the senses.* New York: Random House.

Ackerman, D. (1994). *A natural history of love.* New York: Random House.

Arbus, D. (1972). *Diane Arbus: An Aperture monograph.* New York: Aperture Foundation.

Arendt, H. (1958). *The human condition.* Chicago: University of Chicago Press.

Bach, H. (1995). Listening to girls' voices: If not now, when? *Teaching Education, 7*(1), 109–116.

Bach, H. (1996a, June). *Schoolgirls: Visual narratives of the evaded curriculum.* Poster presented at the annual meeting of the Canadian Society for the Study of Education, Brock University, St. Catherines, Ontario, Canada.

Bach, H. (1996b, April). *Troubling photography.* A roundtable session presented at the annual meeting of the American Educational Research Association Invisible College, New York.

Bach, H. (1996c, April). *Visual narratives: Girls dancing with the evaded curriculum.* A roundtable session presented at the annual meeting of the American Educational Research Association, New York.

Bach, H. (1996d, April). *Visual narratives: Not a basic photograph.* Poster presented at the annual meeting of the American Educational Research Association, New York.

Bach, H. (1996e, January). *Visual narratives: Viewing the evaded curriculum.* Multimedia paper presented at the annual meeting of the Conference on Qualitative Research in Education, University of Georgia, Athens.

Bach, H. (1997a, April). *Photographic re/presentation: Visual narratives.* Paper presented at the presented at the annual meeting of the American Educational Research Association, Chicago.

Bach, H. (1997b). Seen any good movies? Creating space to talk about popular culture. *Canadian Social Studies, 31*(2), 87–89.

Bach, H. (1997c, March). *Visual narratives: Contests of meaning.* Paper presented at the annual meeting of the International Conference on Teacher Research, National-Louis University, Evanston, IL.

Bach, H. (1997d, March). *Visual narratives: Photography as research.* Invited address presented at the annual meeting of the American Educational Research Association, Chicago.

Bach, H. (1998). *A visual narrative concerning girls, curriculum, photography etc.* Edmonton, Alberta, Canada: QUAL Institute Press.

Bach, H. (1999, April). *Breast wishes: A visual narrative.* Poster/paper presented at the annual meeting of the American Educational Research Association, Montreal, Quebec, Canada.

Bach, H. (2000, April). *Children as imagemakers with horses.* Poster/paper presented at the annual meeting of the American Educational Research Association, New Orleans, LA.

Bach, H. (2001a). The place of the photograph in visual narrative research. *Afterimage, 29*(3), 7.

Bach, H. (2001b, April). *A visual narrative: A look at animal assisted research work in curriculum.* Multimedia paper presented at the annual meeting of the American Educational Research Association, Seattle, WA.

Bach, H. (2001c). Zines: Teaching for openings in visual education. *Canadian Art Teacher, 1*(1), 21–36.

Bach, H. (2003, June). *A visual narrative: Children as imagemakers with horses.* Paper/poster presented at the annual meeting of the Canadian Society of Studies in Education, Halifax, Nova Scotia, Canada.

Bach, H., & Baydala, L. (2006, January). *The place of visual narrative inquiry in evaluative research.* Paper presented at the annual meeting of the Caritas Research Day of Integrating Research into Clinical Practice, Edmonton, Alberta, Canada.

Bach, H., Kennedy, M., & Mickelson, J. R. (1999). Bodies at work: Sensory knowing. *Teaching Education, 10*(2), 24–36.

Bateson, M. C. (1990). *Composing a life.* New York: Plume/Penguin.

Bateson, M. C. (1994). *Peripheral visions: Learning along the way.* New York: HarperCollins.

Becker, H. (1974). Photography and sociology. *Studies in the Anthropology of Visual Communication, 1,* 3–26.

Becker, H. (1988). Visual sociology, documentary photography, and photojournalism: It's (almost) all a matter of context. In J. Prosser (Ed.), *Image-based research: A sourcebook for qualitative researchers* (pp. 84–96). London: Falmer Press.

Becker, H. (1995). Visual sociology, documentary photography, and photojournalism: It's (almost) all a matter of context. *Visual Sociology, 10*(1/2), 5–14.

Bell, S. E. (1999). Narratives and lives: Women's health politics and the diagnosis of cancer for DES daughters. *Narrative Inquiry, 9*(2), 347–389.

Bruner, E. M. (1986). Experience and its expressions. In V. W. Turner & E. M. Turner (Eds.), *The anthropology of experience.* Urbana: University of Illinois Press.

Bruner, J. (1990). *Acts of meaning.* Cambridge, MA: Harvard University Press.

Caine, V. (2002). *Storied moments: A visual narrative inquiry of aboriginal women living with HIV (immune deficiency).* Unpublished master's thesis, University of Alberta, Edmonton, Canada.

Carr, D. (1986). *Time, narrative, and history.* Bloomington: University of Indiana Press.

Carroll, L. (1955). *Alice in wonderland.* New York: Random House.

Chase, S. E. (2003). Learning to listen: Narrative principles in a qualitative research methods course. In R. Josselson, A. Lieblich, & D. P. McAdams (Eds.), *Up close and personal: The teaching and learning of narrative research: The narrative study of lives* (pp. 79–99). Washington, DC: American Psychological Association.

Cixous, H. (1994). *The Cixous reader* (S. Sellers, Ed.). London: Routledge.

Clandinin, D. J., & Connelly, F. M. (1994). Personal experience methods. In N. K. Denzin & Y. S. Lincoln (Eds.), *Handbook of qualitative research* (pp. 413–427). London: Sage.

Clandinin, D. J., & Connelly, F. M. (2000). *Narrative inquiry: Experience and story in qualitative research.* San Francisco: Jossey-Bass.

Collier, J., & Collier, M. (1986). *Visual anthropology: Photography as a research method.* Albuquerque: University of New Mexico Press.

Connelly, F. M., & Clandinin, D. J. (1988). *Teachers as curriculum planners.* Toronto, Canada: O. I. S. E. Press.

Connelly, F. M., & Clandinin, D. J. (2006). Narrative inquiry. In J. Green, G. Camilli, & P. Elmore (Eds.), *Handbook of complementary methods in education research* (pp. 375–385). Mahwah, NJ: Lawrence Erlbaum.

Dewey, J. (1934). *Art as experience.* New York: Perigee Books.

Dewey, J. (1938). *Experience and education.* New York: Collier Books.

Dillard, A. (1982). *Living by fiction.* New York: Harper & Row.

Dillard, A. (1989). *The writing life.* New York: Harper & Row.

Fine, M. (1991). *Framing dropouts: Notes on the politics of an urban high school.* Albany: State University of New York Press.

Fine, M. (1992). Passions, politics, and power: Feminist research possibilities. In M. Fine (Ed.), *Disruptive voices: The possibilities of feminist research* (pp. 205–231). Ann Arbor: University of Michigan Press.

Fine, M., & Weis, L. (2003). *Silenced voices and extraordinary conversations: Re-imagining schools.* New York: Teachers College Press.

Freeman, M. (2002). Charting the narrative unconscious: Cultural memory and the challenge of autobiography. *Narrative Inquiry, 12,* 193–211.

Freeman, M., & Brockmeier, J. (2001). Narrative integrity: Autobiographical identity and the meaning of the "good life." In J. Brockmeier & D. Carbaugh (Eds.), *Narrative and identity* (pp. 75–99). Amsterdam: John Benjamins.

Frohmann, L. (2005). The framing safety project: Photographs and narratives by battered women. *Violence Against Women, 11*(11), 1396–1419.

Greene, M. (1997a). Curriculum and consciousness. In D. J. Flinders & S. J. Thornton (Eds.), *The curriculum studies reader* (pp. 137–149). New York: Routledge.

Greene, M. (1997b). Teaching as possibility: A light in dark times. *Journal of Pedagogy, Pluralism & Practice, 1*(1). Retrieved from www.lesley.edu/journals/jppp/1/jppp_issue_1.toc.html

Gross, L., Katz, J. S., & Ruby, J. (Eds.). (1988a). *Image ethics: The moral rights of subjects in photographs, film and television.* New York: Oxford University Press.

Gross, L., Katz, J. S., & Ruby, J. (1988b). Introduction: A moral pause. In L. Gross, J. S. Katz, & J. Ruby (Eds.), *Image ethics: The moral rights of subjects in photographs, film and television* (pp. 1–34). New York: Oxford University Press.

Gross, L., Katz, J. S., & Ruby, J. (Eds.). (2003). *Image ethics in the digital age.* Minneapolis: University of Minnesota Press.

Harper, D. (1987). Visual sociology: Expanding sociological vision. *The American Sociologist, 19*(1), 54–70.

Harrison, B. (2002). Photographic visions and narrative inquiry. *Narrative Inquiry, 12*(1), 87–111.

Haug, F. (1987). *Female sexualization.* London: Verso.

Heilbrun, C. (1988). *Writing a woman's life.* New York: Ballantine.

Irigaray, L. (1985). *This sex which is not one* (C. Porter, Trans.). Ithaca, NY: Cornell University Press.

Jaggar, A. M. (1994). *Living with contradictions: Controversies in feminist social ethics.* Boulder, CO: Westview Press.

Jaggar, A. M., & Bordo, S. (1989). *Gender/body/knowledge: Feminist reconstructions of being and knowing.* New Brunswick, NJ: Rutgers University Press.

Johnson, G. (2004). Reconceptualising the visual in narrative inquiry into teaching. *Teaching and Teacher Education, 20*(5), 423–434.

Keller, H. (1957). *The open door.* Garden City, NY: Doubleday.

Le Dœuff, M. (1989). *The philosophical imaginary* (C. Gordon, Trans.). Stanford, CA: Stanford University Press.

Le Dœuff, M. (1991). *Hipparchia's choice: An essay concerning women, philosophy, etc.* Oxford, UK: Blackwell.

May, W. (1977). Code and covenant or philanthropy and contract? In J. Stanley, A. J. Dyck, & W. Curran (Eds.), *Ethics in medicine: Historical perspective and contemporary concerns* (pp. 65–76). Cambridge: MIT Press.

May, W. (1980). Doing ethics: The bearing of ethical theories on fieldwork. *Social Problems, 27*(3), 358–370.

Morrison, T. (1987). The site of memory. In W. Zinsser (Ed.), *Inventing the truth* (pp. 101–124). Boston: Houghton Mifflin.

Nhat Hanh, T. (1991). *Peace is every step: The path of mindfulness in everyday life.* New York: Bantam Books.

Nhat Hanh, T. (1996). *The miracle of mindfulness: A manual on meditation.* Boston: Beacon Press.

Nhat Hanh, T. (1997). *Teachings on love.* Berkeley, CA: Parallax Press.

Noddings, N. (1989). *Women and evil.* Berkeley: University of California Press.

Norris, T. (2004). Hannah Arendt and modernity. *The Encyclopedia of Informal Education.* Retrieved November 22, 2005, from www.infed.org/thinkers/arendt.htm

Pole, C. (2004). *Seeing is believing? Approaches to visual research.* Oxford, UK: Elsevier.

Prosser, J. (1992). Personal reflections on the use of photography in an ethnographic case study. *British Educational Research Journal, 18*(4), 397–411.

Prosser, J. (1998). The status of image-based research. In J. Prosser (Ed.), *Image-based research: A sourcebook for qualitative researchers* (pp. 97–114). London: Falmer Press.

Prosser, J. (2005, October). *Visual ethics seminar.* Paper presented at the University of Alberta, Edmonton, Canada.

Pushor, D. (2001). *A storied photo album of parents' positioning and the landscape of schools.* Unpublished doctoral dissertation, University of Alberta, Edmonton, Canada.

Radley, A. (2002). Portrayals of suffering: On looking away, looking at, and the comprehension of illness experience. *Body & Society, 8*(3), 1–23.

Radley, A. (2004). Pity, modernity and the spectacle of suffering. *Journal of Palliative Care, 20*(3), 179–184.

Radley, A., & Taylor, D. (2003). Images of recovery: A photo-elicitation study on the hospital ward. *Qualitative Health Research, 13*(1), 77–99.

Rich, A. (1979). *On lies, secrets, and silence: Selected prose 1966–1978.* New York: W. W. Norton.

Rich, M., & Chalfen, R. (1999). Showing and telling asthma: Children teaching physicians with visual narrative. *Visual Sociology, 14,* 51–71.

Rich, M., Patashnick, J., & Chalfen, R. (2002). Visual illness narratives of asthma: Explanatory models and health-related behavior. *American Journal of Health Behavior, 26*(6), 442–443.

Sarton, M. (1959). *I knew a phoenix: Sketches for an autobiography.* New York: W. W. Norton.

Sontag, S. (1977). *On photography.* New York: Delta.

Sontag, S. (2004, May 23). Regarding the torture of others. *New York Times Magazine.* Retrieved May 23, 2004, from www.nytimes.com

Spence, J. (1986). *Putting myself in the picture: A political, personal and photographic autobiography.* London: Camden Press.

Spence, J. (1995). *Cultural sniping: The art of transgression.* London: Routledge.

Spence, J., & Holland, P. (Eds.). (1991). *Family snaps: The meanings of domestic photography.* London: Virago.

Tagg, J. (1988). *The burden of representation: Essays on photographies and histories.* Basingstoke, UK: Macmillan.

Walker, S. (2005). Artmaking in an age of visual culture: Vision and visuality. *Visual Arts Research, 59,* 23–37.

Walkerdine, V. (1990). Video replay: Families, films and fantasy. In M. A. & J. O. Thompson (Eds.), *The media reader* (pp. 339–357). London: BFI.

Weber, S., & Mitchell, C. (1995). *That's funny, you don't look like a teacher.* London: Falmer Press.

Weiser, J. (1975). PhotoTherapy: Photography as a verb. *B. C. Photographer, 2,* 33–36.

Weiser, J. (1988). PhotoTherapy: Using snapshots and photo-interactions in therapy with youth. In C. Schaefer (Ed.), *Innovative interventions in child and adolescent therapy* (pp. 339–376). New York: Wiley.

Weiser, J. (1993). *Phototherapy techniques: Exploring the secrets of personal snapshots and family albums.* Vancouver, BC, Canada: PhotoTherapy Centre Press.

Ziller, R. (1990). *Photographing the self: Methods for observing personal orientations.* Newbury Park, CA: Sage.

CHAPTER 12

My Story Is My Living Educational Theory

Jean McNiff

This chapter aims to show the links between narrative inquiry (Clandinin & Connelly, 2000) and action research, a form of research that enables practitioner researchers to tell their stories of how they have taken action to improve their situations by improving their learning. They explain how reflecting on their action can lead to new learning, which can inform future learning and action. Their stories comprise their descriptions and explanations of practice, which constitute their own living educational theories of practice (Whitehead, 1989). By offering these theories of practice, they are able to show how they hold themselves accountable for what they are doing and why they are doing it.

Telling stories and getting them listened to are, however, complex processes that involve several considerations. First, there is the business of what kind of story to tell and how to tell it. Telling a story as straight narrative is different from telling a story as a research narrative. A research narrative contains a descriptive account of the systematic nature of doing the research (Stenhouse, cited in Skilbeck, 1983), as well as an explanatory account of the reasons for the research and what the researcher hoped to achieve. Unless people are told about the research, they will not appreciate its reasons or potential significance. In his *Induction and Intuition in Scientific Thought,* Medawar (1969) says that a scientific inquiry begins with a story about a possible world that we invent, criticize, and modify as we live, so it ends by being a story of real life. On this view, research can be seen as disciplined narrative inquiry. Second, there is the business of getting people to listen to the story. This means telling a story that is acceptable in terms of normative conventions, what people expect to hear as part of the orthodox canon. Difficulties, however, now set in, because often research stories, especially practitioners' stories about the generation of their living theories of practice, tend to step outside the orthodox canon and fall into a category of unauthorized knowledge (Apple, 1993). This can amount to an act of cultural transgression because what counts as authorized knowledge is held in place by an elaborate cultural infrastructure, also containing an editorial infrastructure, to decide which stories qualify for entry into the public domain and which are excluded. Getting a story accepted, therefore, means engaging in cultural politics as well as editorial politics. Consequently, ensuring that their work is listened to means that practitioner researchers need to raise their awareness of and engage with the issues. They need to strengthen their capacity to produce robust research stories that will withstand the strictures of cultural and editorial politics. Their stories can then be used as mediating representations that enable them to exercise their educational influence in the public sphere.

These are some of the substantive issues in this chapter. I explain how practitioners need to engage with cultural and editorial politics as they produce their accounts of practice, especially in relation to demonstrating the validity of their research. I also raise contextual questions about how validity is intimately linked with the idea of goodness, especially in terms of what counts as *good practice* and *good research accounts*. I ask whether my work and my account may be judged as good, as I question whether my responsibility is to do good in the world or tell a good story (see Coetzee, 2004). I deal with these issues in turn. First, and as part of my own research practice, I explain how and why I have structured the chapter in its present form.

I position myself as an educational action researcher, part of whose work is to tell stories of educational action research. The stories I tell are those of myself in company with others who are also telling their stories. My main theme is about how I offer explanations for my educational practices, my personal theories of practice. I show how and why I do what I do and justify my practice as good practice, including the form and content of my research report as an integral part of that practice. I maintain that an account of practice should demonstrate its own validity and the validity of the practice, in terms of whether they both show explicitly how and why they should be considered valuable or good. I link the ideas of validity and goodness. I also explain that the validity claim needs to be tested against specific personal and social criteria. I ask what, therefore, counts as a good story? If practitioners claim that their practice is good, how do they ensure that their stories demonstrate the kind of validity that will appropriately communicate the validity of their work? This is especially important in contexts of national assessment, when, for example, the U.K. Research Assessment Exercise states that work claiming to be top quality should be judged as internationally relevant in terms of its originality, rigor, and significance.

To explore these issues, I tell my own research story. The form my narrative takes mirrors the form of my inquiry, as I address these questions to understand and explain what I am doing:

- What is my concern?
- Why am I concerned?

- What kind of experiences can I describe to show the reasons for my concerns?
- What can I do about it? What will I do about it?
- How do I evaluate the educational influence of my actions?
- How do I demonstrate the validity of the account of my educational influence in learning?
- How do I modify my concerns, ideas, and actions in the light of my evaluation? (see McNiff & Whitehead, 2005, 2006)

My story is, however, a story of stories. My own story is about how I have exercised my educational influence so that people can exercise their originality and critical engagement and have their stories about the generation of their living educational theories accepted in the public domain. These stories tend not to abide by the conventions of the mainstream canon. I explain how my inquiry itself becomes part of a politics of narratives, of narrativized differences. Ultimately, it becomes a politics of ethics, because making decisions about which stories are permissible and who is permitted to tell them becomes a domain of political ethics within a wider framework of what counts as good and how it should be judged. For me, whether my story should be accepted is not a case of whether it abides by the conventions of the orthodox canon but whether the validity I am claiming for it can be justified in terms of rational inquiry.

I now set out to do this. Using the questions above as a guide to my narrative, I ask whether by asking these kinds of critical questions, I can show how I have worked systematically toward realizing my educational values and have offered sufficient evidential grounds for my story to be validated and legitimized in the public domain.

What Is My Concern?

I am currently concerned about two interrelated issues.

First, I am concerned about the dominant stories in the literature, that educational research should continue to be conceptualized from the relatively narrow perspectives of traditional social science in spite of a major body of literature, comprising practitioners' stories of practice, that shows educational research also as a process of making sense of our own personal and professional lives through personal inquiry as we try to realize our values in our practices. While I recognize the major contributions of the social sciences to the field of human inquiry, I am concerned about their excluding and hegemonizing power. For example, the dominant stories from the British Educational Research Association (see Whitty, 2005) explain how educational research should continue to be the province of specialized social science researchers. A special emphasis is laid in these stories about how the criteria and standards of judgment for assessing the quality of the research, often to do with the statistical analysis of results to show the potentials of the research for generalizability and replicability, are firmly established and are used to demonstrate the validity of the account and, thus, legitimize the status of the research and the researcher. I am concerned about how these stories can act as a force of centralized control, shutting out less powerful voices and forming a grand narrative that excludes local narratives.

Second, I am concerned about the way action research itself has been colonized and reconfigured in some quarters to fit into the dominant social sciences framework, a situation that denies the values of social justice and democratic forms of life that underpin action research and distorts its potentials for social change. The stories that communicate this kind of instrumental action research adopt the same criteria and standards of judgment as the traditional social sciences. They assume an air of the legitimate force of instruction so that the more personalized narrative form through which practitioners' educational theories tend to be communicated is frequently delegitimized and threatened. The hegemonizing power of the stories of performance management fit well within political contexts such as the United States, whose dominant policy research stories are about the implementation of actions to ensure specific end results, with substantial funding for those who conform and penalty points for those who do not.

I am expressing concern about how the legitimacy of the form of research is subject to the censoring power of those already legitimated within the field as knowledgeable experts, how their stories become a normative body of knowledge by whose standards other stories are judged, and how structural regimes of power are sustained by power-constituted strategies. I am concerned about how and why the underpinning assumptions of these stories go virtually unquestioned.

Yet because I systematically interrogate my own practice in relation to any thorny issues I raise, a new concern emerges about the ethics of my own practice. As well as positioning myself as a practitioner researcher, I am also frequently positioned as a judge. Like others in higher education, I am called on to examine higher-degree submissions or review articles submitted for publication, so I potentially become an editor-censor. This is a powerful position because I decide whether someone's voice is heard or silenced. The position also carries responsibility for ethical conduct. I have to clarify for myself and others, especially the researcher whose work is under consideration, which standards of judgment I am using and whether they can be justified as rational standards of validity and not as my own irrational prejudices. Developing such understandings is crucial if editorial practices are to maintain educational validity. Donmoyer (1996) expresses similar concerns when he asks *what a journal editor has to do* in order to act responsibly in an era of paradigm proliferation.

So I am addressing multiple dilemmas and concerns: how to combat the hegemonizing power of dominant stories that extends their continuing normativization and so potentially prevents other stories from being legitimized; how to combat trends in the field of educational action research that embed it within the dominant institutional and literary canon; how to develop new narrative forms, grounded in learning, so that the stories of practitioner action researchers can also gain legitimacy on their own terms; and when practitioners turn judges and editors, how they can demonstrate accountability for their practices by articulating the standards of judgment they use in making their assessments.

To clarify, let me tell you a story.

I was recently sent an article for review by an action research journal. The article was well written and engaging. I was so taken with the quality of the writing that initially I could not understand my unease about the content.

The article, by a North American teacher-researcher, spoke of an intervention he had implemented in his class of second-grade students, some of whom had difficulty in word recognition. Having decided to use a reading program, he targeted five students as respondents (in this case, data sources) to see whether the intervention worked. It evidently did, and the students' scores improved on posttests.

It took time to identify the reasons for my discomfort. I gradually realized that the story was too neat. It worked on the assumption that the researcher did this so that that happened, a traditional positivist assumption of cause and effect: The research aims to show causal relationships through the input of a stimulus to ensure a specific outcome. My understanding, however, is that action research is about learning, not about controlling practices. It is about problematizing practice so that practice does not become the implementation of rules to fit action into a predetermined model. It is about asking interesting questions about whether we are exercising our influence in a way that we hope is educational, for the good. I wrote as much in my recommendations.

I was aware, as I wrote my report (and I said this to the journal editors), that I was possibly doing a disservice to the researcher because, as noted, there are distinct trends in North America and elsewhere to regard action research as just this kind of linear programming, input-output, the implementation of prepackaged action plans to ensure a neat, predetermined outcome. Because research funders, however, often require this kind of framework, to fulfill policy mandates that demand results in classrooms and the accumulation of results into a body of knowledge to act as the basis of future policy and practice, some researchers produce textbooks about using action research to achieve a specific end result. This approach can have destructive consequences. I regularly receive e-mails from action researchers around the world in terms of "I began my action research with high hopes, and now I am in despair because I am not achieving what I expected." This can be devastating when anticipated results are linked to funding and professional status.

I now appear to be contradicting myself, in relation to what I am saying in the chapter, about how some stories are censored in terms of editors' standards of judgment, and in relation to my story, about how I censor work in terms of my own standards of judgment. I could be seen as positioning myself as a living contradiction (Whitehead, 1989) and invalidating my claim to be practicing in the direction of the good because I am critiquing others for practices that I engage in myself. In my example, I explained that I was judging the quality of a story of instruction. Yet I, too, produce books that advise people how to achieve their educational visions. There are differences here, however. There is a distinct difference between what I do as an action researcher and what social scientists dressed as action researchers do. Social scientists produce explanations that are frequently underpinned by a logic of domination (Marcuse, 1964). Their explanations appear as sets of propositional statements that show, by the internal relationship of the statements, how they have eliminated contradictions. The explanations carry the force of instructions, telling people how to implement action steps. I work differently. I invite people to ask questions about what they are doing and decide for themselves what action to take. There is a distinct difference between the two approaches, one of which is premised on a logic that aims for closure through providing general answers to particular questions and the other on a logic that aims for open-ended inquiry through problematic questioning. There are also differences in their philosophical underpinnings. The practice of issuing instructions for implementation is grounded in Aristotelian logic, which assumes a cause-and-effect relationship with no room for contradiction. This view is perpetuated by philosophers such as Popper, who said that a logic that accepted contradiction was based on "a loose and woolly way of thinking" and that a "theory which involves a contradiction is therefore useless *as a theory*" (Popper, 1963/2002, p. 429), and by philosophers such as Peters (1966) and Hirst (1983), who wrote that research and training should be carried out under the aegis of the different disciplines of education. It also informs dominant institutional stories, underpinned by specific institutional epistemologies (Schön, 1995), about how knowledge should be seen as packages of information delivered to allegedly unknowing practitioners.

I do not subscribe to these philosophies, and I do not tell such stories. I tell stories about how I avoid telling people what to do, on my understanding that people are fully competent to make their own decisions, including whether what I have to say is right for them. I assess the quality of my educational influence in terms of whether I encourage people to make judgments that are right for them in relation to the values they espouse. I ground my practice in the philosophies of Polanyi (1958), who speaks of the vast store of tacit knowledge that people possess; Plato (see his *Phaedrus*), who speaks of the capacity of knowers to hold the one and the many together at the same time; and Chomsky (1986), who speaks of the innate capacity of individuals to create language, an idea that I develop as the innate capacity of individuals to come to know in their own original way and to generate an infinitude of knowledge. My practice is informed by the kind of ontological and epistemological values that influence the life-affirming flow of humanity in all its forms (Whitehead, 2004c). In my philosophy, deciding which values to live by is a deeply moral activity that reflects our capacities as humans to make choices and decide which are morally binding choices.

I now relate these ideas to the main thrust of this chapter, about how judgments are made about the living and written texts of human lives and about the legitimation processes involved in deciding which stories should enter the mainstream and which should not. If I am claiming to act as an action researcher with educational intent, and so practicing in the direction of what I consider to be the good, I need to look into the mirror and interrogate my practice in terms of whether I fulfill my rhetoric. I have to justify my claim to the authority of my present best thinking, which, although open to further modification and critique, has to act as the grounds for my future intentional action. I address these questions, first, by articulating the reasons for my concerns.

Why Am I Concerned?

Several interrelated stories are running through this chapter about how to contribute to the legitimization of the stories of practitioner action researchers within the hegemonizing context of the legitimacy of dominant social science stories, a story that itself is embedded within a framing story about the legitimacy of those who make judgments about which stories should enter the public domain and so contribute to a valid educational research literary canon and how this links with the idea of moral practice. Many elements of these stories constitute concerns, in terms of violating my ontological and epistemological values, as I now explain.

I do not believe that people need to be told what to do. They can be advised or guided but not told. We can all think for ourselves. In the same way that we are born with the capacities to walk and talk as part of our human genetic inheritance, we are born with the capacity to think, to make choices, and to reflect critically on our actions. We are moral creatures, fully equipped to exercise our agency by acting on our decisions. In professional life, practitioners are already fully equipped to make their own decisions about practice and show how they hold themselves accountable for the consequences of those decisions. I work from a sense of self—my own and others'—that is consistent with the following:

> What exactly do people mean when they speak of the self? Its defining characteristics are fourfold. First of all, continuity. You've a sense of time, a sense of past, a sense of future. There seems to be a thread running through your personality, through your mind. Second, closely related is the idea of unity or coherence of self. In spite of the diversity of sensory experience, memories, beliefs and thoughts, you experience yourself as one person, as a unity.
>
> So there's continuity, there's unity. And then there's a sense of embodiment or ownership—yourself as anchored to your body. And fourth is a sense of agency, what we call free will, your sense of being in charge of your own destiny. (Vilayanur, 2003, p. 1)

So it is with a sense of alarm that I read the dominant stories about policy formation and implementation and how the different social formations involved in decision making in education are perceived. It is popularly understood (see Thomas & Pring, 2004) that policy makers, researchers, and practitioners are different groups with separate roles and responsibilities, and each positions the others in relation to its perceptions of the public positioning of themselves. Each takes on its own, separate role as characters in a story told by invisible narrators. The characters do not tell their own stories but read the scripts provided by the absent storytellers. Thus, policy makers make policy; external researchers do research whose findings will inform policy; and practitioners, whose practices become the grounds for the researchers' research, implement the researchers' theories. The stories themselves communicate an underpinning assumption that all participants agree with and contribute to these discourses, which are then systematically communicated through the culture (Williams, 1961). Furthermore, according to books such as

Gibbons et al. (1994), each grouping grounds its expertise, and presumably its professional identity, in different epistemological foundations. Furlong and Oancea (2005) sum it up as follows:

> Traditionally it has been assumed that there is a clear distinction between the worlds of research and the worlds of policy and practice, that there are "two communities." On the one hand there is the world of research, based on explicit, systematic work aimed at the growth of theoretical knowledge. Practice and policy on the other hand are seen as taking place in the "real world," a world based on different forms of knowledge—for example, on tacit knowledge and practical wisdom. (p. 10)

So practitioners' knowledge, generated from their own research, counts as "Mode 2" knowledge, whereas academic-led research becomes "Mode 1" knowledge (Gibbons et al., 1994).

This situation is an utter denial of my educational and epistemological values. It denies the view of personhood outlined earlier above and positions people as objects of data within other people's stories rather than real people with real identities who are telling their own stories. I have already stated my views around the capacity of all to make informed decisions. These views are rooted in deeper ontological values regarding the precious uniqueness of each individual, an idea close to Arendt's (1958) concept of natality. People are not born as already categorized, although many are born into social systems that automatically categorize them in terms of ethnicity, class, gender, physical ability, or any other alterity that comes to mind. These false categorizations are perpetuated by the stories that are understood as the prevailing truth. For me, to discriminate against a person because of physical *differences* is bad enough. To discriminate against them because of their intellectual capacity is, on Arendt's and my terms, one of the most egregious forms of personal violence, and to set up a regime whereby knowledge itself is used as a marker of symbolic power is one of the most flagrant violations of the concepts of social justice.

What stories do I tell? My stories say that we are all equal as persons, and practitioners, on the understanding that those who act with deliberate social intent are involved in a practice. Furthermore, if our commitment is to social improvement, we can say we are involved in a praxis. In Groome's terms (as cited in Glavey, 2005), we become participants in communities of praxis.

This gives me the explanatory frameworks for my inquiry—how and why I present it in narrative form. How do I demonstrate the realization of my values around the uniqueness of each individual and one's capacity to come to know in one's own way? How do I challenge and transform the dominant underpinning logics that perceive people as *naturally* belonging to categories that are themselves socially constructed fictions? How do I show the validity and legitimacy of the narrative form through which I communicate my inquiry, which is full of contradictions, within a dominant form of logic that rejects narrative forms of theorizing and metaphorical forms of expression that are grounded in contradictions and ambiguity? How do I show the validity of my work?

Let me give some examples of the power of the dominant form and also some examples of what can happen when this form and its underpinning power are challenged by forms that are grounded in a different kind of power.

What Kind of Experiences Can I Describe That Show Why I Am Concerned?

One does not have to travel far to see the reasons for my concerns. The most cursory glance at the mainstream educational research literature will show that the majority are written in a propositional form and abide by the conventions of the traditional social sciences. Seldom does one encounter the word *I*. Yet it is widely acknowledged that world sustainability is premised on the personal commitment of citizens finding ways, in free agreement, of taking responsibility for their own futures through negotiated collaboration (Sen, 1999).

It is also not difficult to see the hegemony of the current orthodoxy by moving into the academy, especially in relation to higher-degree assessment. Many universities, including some with which I have worked, insist on excluding the personal pronoun from dissertation and thesis titles. Questions of the form "How do I . . . ?" (Whitehead, 1989) are rejected in favor of bland titles that are appropriate to forms of abstract theory not grounded in the researcher's personal knowledge.

Closer to home, here are three examples of how practitioner researchers' accounts have been suppressed by the imposition of dominant forms.

The two PhD theses of Jack Whitehead, who has exercised world influence in the dissemination of practitioners' accounts of their living educational theories, were rejected in the 1980s on grounds that included a judgment that they contained nothing of publishable worth. His theses, which constituted his own living theories of practice, were unacceptable to the examiners, who were prepared neither to engage with the issues being explored or the standards of judgment used to validate his theories nor to accept the narrativized form, which placed *I* at the heart of the inquiry. The university regulations refused him permission to question his examiners' judgments under any circumstances. Ironically, doctorates since legitimated in Jack's university have included ideas from the rejected theses. Whitehead's (1993) story in *The Growth of Educational Knowledge* can be accessed from www.bath.ac.uk/~edsajw/bk93/geki.htm. He was finally awarded his doctorate from the University of Bath in 1999.

Geoff Suderman-Gladwell was prohibited from pursuing his classroom research by a university's research ethics committee. He, therefore, undertook an inquiry into how he studied his own learning from the experience (Suderman-Gladwell, 2001). He wrote about his own reflections on his learning and how his learning informed new actions.

Similarly, a PhD faculty member whose studies I was supporting had his action research blocked by his university's ethics committee. He wanted to study how he was exercising his educational influence in his own learning in relation to the learning of his colleagues, so his colleagues would become participants in his research.

The ethics committee believed this would jeopardize the well-being of his colleagues, and he was refused permission. He did not continue his research.

As well as these stories of potential ruin (Lather, 1994), many victory stories also are available about how practitioner researchers have overcome obstacles to realize their educational values and celebrate their *I* questions as they generate their living educational theories. Many of these reports are on www.actionresearch.net and www.jeanmcniff.com. Examples from www.actionresearch.net:

Eames, K. (1995). *How do I, as a teacher and educational action-researcher, describe and explain the nature of my professional knowledge?* PhD thesis dissertation, University of Bath, Bath, UK. Retrieved December 12, 2005, from www.actionresearch.net/kevin.shtml

Laidlaw, M. (1996). *How can I create my own living educational theory as I offer you an account of my educational development?* PhD thesis, University of Bath, Bath, UK. Retrieved December 12, 2005, from www.actionresearch.net/moira2.shtml

Examples from www.jeanmcniff.com:

Burke, T. (1998). *How can I improve my practice as a learning support teacher?* MA dissertation, University of the West of England, Bristol, UK. Retrieved December 12, 2005, from www.jeanmcniff.com/tereseabstract.html

Ní Mhurchú, S. (2000). *How can I improve my practice as a teacher in the area of assessment through the use of portfolios?* MA dissertation, University of the West of England, Bristol, UK. Retrieved December 12, 2005, from www.jeanmcniff.com/siobhan.htm

These accounts contain some significant features:

- They are storied accounts about how practitioners can undertake their action inquiries from the grounds that their values are being denied in their practice. Each researcher imagines how to overcome the denial and systematically finds ways of doing so.
- Practitioners take as their guideline the question, "How do I improve what I am doing?"
- Practitioners develop new forms of practice inspired by educational values. They explain how they are also contributing to new theory by showing how learning from practice and systematic reflection on the learning can inform new practices.
- Practitioners come from a range of educational constituencies. Their stories are located in schools, workplaces, and higher-education settings.
- The stories explain how practitioners can become part of networked learning communities and so test their claims to improved practice and knowledge against the critical feedback of informed others.

These contradictory experiences show the reasons for my concern. The passionate inquiries (Dadds, 1994) of practitioner researchers, however, are still not fully accepted within a normative mainstream context of absent researchers' dispassionate stories. So now, following my explanatory framework, I need to say what I am doing to realize my values in practice.

I work as a professional educator, supporting practitioners' higher-degree studies. The library of the University of the West of England contains 65 validated master's dissertations completed under my supervision. I am aware, however, that I need to improve my supervisory practices, especially in relation to doctoral work, by encouraging the explicit articulation of the standards of judgment that researchers use to assess their work—that is, how they have tested the validity of their work to have that validation process legitimated in the public domain. How I can improve my practice, therefore, becomes the focus of the next section.

What Can I Do About It?
What Will I Do About It?

First, I outline the relationship between stories, intentions, truth, and validity.

When we tell a story, we imply that the story has a relationship with truth. The myths and legends of a culture represent deep truths about that culture (Frazer, 1963). Fairy stories contain truths about the nature and underpinning values of human relationships. Habermas (2003) draws on Husserl's (1982) insights that any act of knowing, once begun, has "an immanent relation to truth" (Habermas, 2003, p. 22). This immanent relation of intentional action to truth implies that people know what they are doing when they seek to influence the creation of themselves in company with one another. Said (1995) also develops this theme, explaining that each intentional beginning becomes its own methodology, a realization of its underlying intent. From these works, I understand how intentional action can be shown to have an immanent relation to truth by demonstrating its validity. By telling their stories, practitioners can show how their action has an immanent relation to truth by articulating explicitly how they give meaning to their lives in terms of what they consider valuable or good. They show the validity of their value-informed practices by establishing the validity of the story.

These ideas are new territory for me, and possibly also for the wider community of action researchers. Existing stories of practice in the public domain tend to be descriptions of actions without articulating their grounding in explanations for the actions. This kind of explanatory grounding is, however, essential if the procedures used to test the validity of the research are to be explicated. Furthermore, procedures for establishing the validity of the research story itself need to be explicated. All this involves consideration of two distinct though interrelated issues:

Showing the Internal Validity of the Research

The research needs to be shown as meaningful—that is, fulfilling its original intent, in Habermas's (1987) terms, of enabling participants to create meaningful relationships for mutual benefit, in terms of what they understand as of value or good. Creating meaning is not simply about taking action but also involves focusing on the learning that enters into the action so that the action is understood as informed purposeful practice. The relationship between learning and action needs to be articulated in stories, and the relationships between practitioners' stories need to be articulated when the practitioners say they are influencing their own learning and one another's learning.

Showing the Internal Validity of the Research Story

Telling a research story is an integral part of research practice. A story does not appear out of nowhere. It is written by a researcher who brings his or her own values to the writing process. Consequently, the story can be understood as the articulation of the values of the writer, which communicates these values through its content and form. In action research reports, the content is about accounting for oneself through a process of showing the validity of the work as it links, in Husserl's (1982) terms, with realizing the researcher's guiding values.

Therefore, practitioner researchers have two responsibilities: (1) to show the validity of their research through (2) showing the validity of their research report. These issues have to be made explicit, which is essential if practitioner researchers wish to be seen as competent theorists rather than skilled implementers. Furlong (2000) said this in his evaluation of the Best Practice Research Scholarship initiative, reporting that teachers tend to see their action research as a form of professional development leading to school improvement but do not appreciate the need to raise their own capacity to do research and engage in quality theorizing.

I am currently attending to this issue in my own practice. In my PhD thesis (McNiff, 1989), I evidently understood the need to articulate the criteria and standards of judgment I wished to be used to assess the quality of my account. I wrote,

> So when you come to judge the thesis as a submission for an academic award, please remember that you are focusing on one central issue, one unit of appraisal; and that is my claim to educational knowledge. Am I justified in saying that I understand my own educational development? Do I defend my claim adequately by showing the processes by which I came to my present knowledge? I regard the developmental form of my thesis as part of that claim, in demonstrating in action the processes involved in my present form of life (my claim). Do you agree? (p. 4)

I had not, however, made explicit the link between values and standards of judgment, a focus that has been developed by Jack Whitehead (2004a, 2004b). From him, I have learned the significance of articulating criteria and standards of judgment in assessing research accounts. Furthermore, traditional technical rational criteria such as generalizability and replicability, inappropriate for practitioners' living inquiries, can be replaced by new criteria such as the experienced realization of one's values. Values can transform into the living critical criteria and standards of judgment whereby practice may be assessed through the critical scrutiny of others. The validity of research can be established by explaining how the researchers have realized their values and how this realization has given meaning to their lives (see Whitehead & McNiff, 2006). Research stories need to show explicitly how values have transformed into living standards of practice.

It is, however, not sufficient only to make explicit the immanent relationship between the significance of the values that informed the work and the significance of how the values were transformed into living critical standards of judgment. The claim to validity itself has to be tested against critical feedback. This can take two forms: first, by subjecting the account to the test of commensurability with one's own internal commitment and, second, by subjecting it to external public critique to establish the commensurability of the research claim with publicly agreed norms of validity. The first test is grounded in Polanyi's (1958) idea of having faith in the rightness of one's capacity for personal knowledge, bearing in mind that one's personal knowledge may be mistaken—for example, it may be rooted in self-delusion. The second test is grounded in the researcher's willingness to engage with criteria such as those suggested by Habermas (1987, 2003), that the claim be made in honesty, sincerity, and truthfulness and with an awareness that it is made within a normative context. These ideas have to be relevant to practitioners if they wish to re-create their professional identities as practical theorists and not only as practitioners acting as data that external researchers can use.

These insights inform new actions, as I now explain.

How Do I Evaluate the Educational Influence of My Actions?

I am explaining how I try to do what I suggest others should do. I, and others, need to evaluate the influence of our actions, to check whether we are living the values that inform our lives. Realizing our values enables us to show the validity of our work, how we understand our work as good practice. This raises for me the question of how I understand good, to explain how and why I wish my practice to be evaluated.

Like Raz (2001), I believe that abstract values become meaningful when we live them in practice. I understand good in terms of what I and others do, how we realize the values that communicate a life-affirming energy for the future sustainability of humanity (Whitehead, 2004c). The values, I hope, I demonstrate in my practice include those of freedom, creativity, critical judgment, justice, care, inquiry, love, compassion, and accounting for myself. These values also inform the writing of this story. The realization of values, for me, constitutes good practice, and the communicative adequacy of the story constitutes a good story. I wish my work to be judged in terms of whether I tell a good (valid, meaningful) story of good (valid, meaningful) practice. I draw on another story to help me clarify the idea.

Coetzee's (2004) novel *Elizabeth Costello* tells of a woman novelist whose reputation rests on one early outstanding book. Since then, her originality has declined and lost its sparkle. The story tells how, having read a novel by Paul West about the shocking realities of the execution of Hitler's would-be assassins, she tries to prevent West from speaking about his work in a public lecture on the grounds that he will intensify people's distress. It is best that some things are kept silent, she feels. She experiences herself, in Whitehead's (1989) terms, as a living contradiction when she is torn between the values of doing good and the values of telling a story.

> The answer, as far as she can see, is that she no longer believes that storytelling is good in itself, whereas for West . . . the question does not seem to arise. If she, as she is nowadays, had to choose between telling a story and doing good, she would rather, she thinks, do good. West, she thinks, would rather tell a story. (Coetzee, 2004, p. 167)

I once thought like Elizabeth Costello. I used to believe that I should do good— substantive good. I no longer think so. Life, and many good books, and conversations with friends who also struggle to give meaning to their lives have taught me that good is not substantive and cannot be imposed. From Berlin's (2002) *Freedom and Its Betrayal* I have learned that the imposition of freedom means no freedom for those on whom it is imposed, and equally, the practice of doing good can be harmful in terms of imposing one's own values, one's own understanding of the good, on others. Over time, I have come to realize that doing good means trying to live one's values and communicating what one is doing in honesty, sincerity, and truthfulness and in a form that is appropriate to the context (Habermas, 1987). For me, doing good is showing how one is living in the direction of one's values, being honest about the degree to which one is doing so, so that the quality of work can be assessed rationally. This means I have to articulate how I account for myself, which brings me to how I judge my practice and how I understand the *good* in good practice.

I understand my practice as good if I can show that I have encouraged others to exercise their originality and creativity and explicate my own processes of critical judgment, justice, care, inquiry, love, compassion, and accounting for myself so that others can tell their stories of practice in a way that is right for them. I understand that I do good work if I encourage others to account for themselves through developing appropriate conditions and relationships as the living realizations of my ontological values. Unlike Elizabeth Costello, I judge my work in terms of whether I tell a good story of good practice. Unlike her, I resist thinking in the binary divides of either/or. I understand my practice as integrated, and I link the idea of doing with the idea of communicating. Do I tell a good story that communicates how I have tried to realize my values?

To help me further in evaluating whether I have influenced others in an educational way, I draw on work already in the public domain, from practitioners whose studies have been supported by Jack Whitehead, who communicate how they have transformed their values into their living critical standards of judgment. Church (2004), Hartog (2004), and Holley (1997) use an action research methodology to clarify the meaning of love as an explanatory principle and standard of judgment in their living educational theories of their own learning. For example, Church writes,

> I show how my approach to [my] work is rooted in the values of compassion, and fairness, and inspired by art. I hold myself to account in relation to these values, as living standards by which I judge myself and my action in the world. This finds expression in research that helps us to design more appropriate criteria for the evaluation of international and social change networks. Through this process I inquire with others into the nature of networks, and their potential for supporting us in lightly-held communities which liberate us to be dynamic, diverse and creative individuals working together for common purpose. I tentatively conclude that networks have the potential to increase my and our capacity for love. (Church, 2004, p. 1)

This theme is developed by Marian Naidoo (2005), who explains how she clarifies the meaning of her loving relationships as her living critical standards of judgment in her living theory of her own learning.

> I am a story teller and the focus of this narrative is on my learning and the development of my living educational theory as I have engaged with others in a creative and critical practice over a sustained period of time. This narrative self-study demonstrates how I have encouraged people to work creatively and critically in order to improve the way we relate and communicate in a multi-professional and multi-agency healthcare setting in order to improve both the quality of care provided and the well being of the system. (p. i)

I have learned, and I am developing the same practices in my work, as follows.

I support the doctoral inquiries of five practitioner researchers at the University of Limerick. Each articulates her values as her living critical standards of judgment. For example, Bernie Sullivan (2006) explains how the experience of living her values of justice has transformed into her living theory of justice. She writes in her dissertation,

> I examine the influence and relevance of my practice in relation to my claim to have influenced in a positive way the educational opportunities for a marginalized group, namely Traveller children. I demonstrate how this improvement at the micro-political level has had repercussions at the macro level in terms of the achievement of social transformation. I draw on my embodied values of social justice and equality to provide the standards of judgement against which to test the validity of my claim to have improved my educational practice as well as the circumstances of my pupils. Finally, I show how, through engagement with more emancipatory pedagogies, I was able to promote a more

equitable situation within the educational system for a minority group, and in so doing, generate my own living theory of justice. (p. 46)

I support the master's and doctoral inquiries of 14 practitioner researchers at St Mary's University College, London, as part of a systematic academic staff development program. I encourage all participants to produce their living theories of practice and explain how they ground the validity of their stories within their values base. In parallel, I am developing a master's program with teachers in disadvantaged contexts in South Africa, validated by St Mary's College, encouraging them to produce accounts that show how values can be clarified and validated in the academy as living critical standards of judgment.

I write. I consistently make a case, as here, that practitioners need to rigorously evaluate their work by explaining how they transform their values into their living critical standards of judgment. To support my claim that my writing is having some influence, I produce three pieces of evidence from international initiatives.

My first piece of evidence is the story of Jacqueline Delong, whose PhD was supervised by Jack Whitehead. She explains how she exercises her educational influence as she asks, *How can I improve my practice as a superintendent of schools and create my living educational theory?* (Delong, 2002). She has influenced the growth of a culture of inquiry in her school board by encouraging practitioners to study their own practices and submit their living educational theories for higher-degree accreditation. Jacqueline and colleagues Heather Knill-Griesser and Cheryl Black have produced five volumes of teachers' accounts as they study their own practice (see Delong & Black, 2002; Delong, Black, & Knill-Griesser, 2003).

My second piece of evidence is the story of Moira Laidlaw, a volunteer in China with Voluntary Services Overseas. Based in Ningxia Teachers University in Ningxia Province (one of the most disadvantaged regions in China) and working with Dean Tian Fengjun, she has helped create China's Experimental Centre for Educational Action Research in Foreign Languages Teaching. Her ideas have been taken up in other institutions in other regions. In 2004, she was awarded the prestigious State Friendship Award by the Chinese Government. In 2005, her work was recognized in the national press as "Action Research Revolutionises the Classroom" (Perrement, 2005). Moira has published the stories of the teachers she supports online (from www.actionresearch.net/moira.shtml). Some are also reproduced in my joint publications with Jack Whitehead (see McNiff & Whitehead, 2005, 2006; Whitehead & McNiff, 2006).

My third piece of evidence is from two important scholarly events in 2004. The first was a symposium at the American Educational Research Association (AERA, 2004) titled *The Transformative Potentials of Individuals' Collaborative Self-Studies for Sustainable Global Educational Networks of Communication*, which Jack and I convened (see www.bath.ac.uk/~edsajw//multimedia/aera04sym.htm). The proposal for the symposium was as follows:

This session aims to demonstrate the transformative potentials of individuals' collaborative self-studies for the development of sustainable global educational networks of communication. For this potential to be realised we see certain practices as necessary. Here we explain some of those practices and how we believe we are achieving and justifying them by making our evidence base and the outcomes visible through multi media representations of our learning.

We are a group of teachers, professional educators, and education administrators, working across the levels of education systems. Each of us asks, "How do I improve what I am doing for personal and social good?" Each of us aims to generate our personal educational theories to show how we are doing so through our contributions to the education of social formations in our own settings. (p. 2)

The second significant scholarly event was a similar symposium presented at the British Educational Research Association (BERA) annual meeting (see www.bath.ac.uk/~edsajw//bera04/frontbera.htm).

The fact that these symposia took place perhaps counts as evidence of the educational influence of my own and others' collaborative learning. The fact that the symposia were attended to capacity and received warm praise from participants and critical discussants supports my present claim that by working collaboratively with others, I am exercising educational influence.

At this point, I would like to comment on the far-reaching contributions of Jack Whitehead. As well as coauthoring our books, he has systematically produced influential papers that constitute a reconceptualizing of educational theory, including contributions to the *International Handbook of Self-Study of Teaching and Teacher Education Practices* (Whitehead, 2004a) and articles for conventional refereed journals (e.g., Whitehead, 1999) and new electronic journals (Whitehead, 2004b). He consistently addresses the concerns of the British (and other) educational research communities (see Furlong & Oancea, 2005), about demonstrating the quality of practitioner research by defining quality in educational research in terms of how a researcher's underpinning ontological values can be transformed into living and communicable epistemological standards of judgment (Whitehead, 2004c). An especially valuable aspect of the electronic forms of technology with which he works is that interrelationships, which communicate the inclusional and relational nature of practitioners' underpinning logics and values, may be more adequately expressed in visual narratives than in a solely linguistic form. An archive of the visual narratives of practitioners, which communicate the meanings of inclusional, ontological, epistemological, methodological, and postcolonial living standards of judgment (Whitehead, 2005), can be accessed from www.bath.ac.uk/~edsajw/.

One of my own aims is to produce texts that encourage people to develop their capacity for research and theory generation. Textbooks are available for practitioners, many written collaboratively with Jack, about the principles and practices of living action research (McNiff, Lomax, & Whitehead, 2003; McNiff & Whitehead, 2000, 2002, 2005, 2006; Whitehead & McNiff, 2006). All contain practical advice, grounded in the living case studies of practitioners.

I now turn to how I judge the validity of the story of my learning and educational influence.

How Do I Demonstrate the Validity of the Account of My Educational Influence in Learning?

I need to consider whether this account itself constitutes a good story in terms of showing the validity of the work through the communicative adequacy of the content and form of the story. To explain this idea of communicative adequacy, I tell another story.

During the 1980s, I rejected a traditional disciplines approach to learning and instead explored a generative transformational approach that sees all things in an ongoing process of emergence (Chomsky, 1965). I link these ideas with a generative narrative form, as explained by Todorov (1990), who speaks of two principles of narrative. The first is the principle of propositional form. A text can be a "sequence of propositions that is easily recognized as a narrative" (p. 27). The second has transformational quality, where each episode contains the potential to generate the next, which, as Lyotard (1984) says, is the nature of narrative as a work of art that continuously re-creates itself through the process of communication.

Living educational theory stories self-consciously demonstrate this generative transformational potential, commenting throughout on the living process of inquiry and the underpinning living form of logic, a reflection of the researcher's conscious commitment to each moment as holding all possible futures already within itself. Narrative forms can transform value-based commitments into their lived articulation in the form of practitioner researchers' networks, thus eradicating the artificial divides of *them* and *us*, as mentioned earlier, or Mode 1 and Mode 2 forms of knowledge. Practitioners in higher education and in schools can communicate in face-to-face and virtual contexts and, through their printed and electronically transmitted storied accounts, show how they are learning collaboratively to exercise their educational influence in their own and one another's learning. Examples can be found at www.actionresearch.net, where the accounts of the 2004 AERA and BERA symposia can also be found, and at www.jeanmcniff.com, where the accounts of three similar symposia presented at the Universities of Limerick (2003), Cork (2005), and Cyprus (2005) can be found. At these events, practitioners in higher-education and school settings came together to share their research stories. Their published accounts, which can be accessed from the Web sites, explain how participation in the symposia and networks and the giving and receiving of critical support has enabled them to produce their own living educational theories of practice and so reconceptualize the nature of educational theory for themselves and their wider communities.

Furthermore, I can show, through my own narrative, how I am realizing Habermas's (2003) idea that "the student who has learned a rule has become a potential teacher. For owing to her generative ability, she can herself now create examples: not only new examples, but even fictitious ones" (p. 55). I believe I have done this, although I would not use the word "student." I learn as much from those formally positioned as my "students" as they learn from me. We are all participants. Furthermore, they do more than create examples; they create realities.

How Will I Modify My Concerns, Ideas, and Actions in the Light of My Evaluation?

I return to Elizabeth Costello and bring in Steven Spielberg, who, in an interview with *Time* (2005), speaks about his new movie *Munich.*

Interviewer: Do you think this film will do any good?

Spielberg: I've never, ever made a movie where I said I'm making this picture because the message can do some good for the world—even when I made *Schindler's List.* I was terrified that it was going to do the opposite of good. I thought perhaps it might bring shame to the memory of those who didn't survive the Holocaust—and even worse to those who did. I made the picture out of just pure wanting to get that story told. . . . I certainly feel that if filmmakers have the courage to talk about these issues— whether they're fictional representations or pure documentaries—as long as we're willing to talk about the real tough, hard subjects unsparingly, I think it's a good thing to get out in the ether. (Schickel, 2005, p. 71)

At the end of the story, Elizabeth Costello is kept waiting at the Gates until she can offer an explanatory account for her life's work. What will happen to me, especially in these contemporary days of editorial gatekeeping? What kind of explanations do I offer for my life's work? My story is that I use my educational influence to encourage others to tell their stories of practice, explain how they give meaning to their work as thoughtful and caring people, and show how they hold themselves accountable for their own stories of educational intent.

Have I done this? Have I told a good story that shows how I try to live my values and transform them into my living standards of judgment? I hope so. I hope that you, my reader, will agree that my story is of value, that it contains material from which others can learn, and that I am justified in offering my action research story as my living educational theory.

Consulting Editors: Mary Beattie, Naama Sabar, and Michal Zellermeyer

References

American Educational Research Association (AERA). (2004, April). *The transformative potentials of individuals' collaborative self-studies for sustainable global educational networks of communication.* Symposium conducted at AERA, San Diego, CA. Retrieved from www.bath.ac.uk/~edsajw//multimedia/aera04sym.htm

Apple, M. (1993). *Official knowledge.* New York: Routledge.

Arendt, H. (1958). *The human condition.* Chicago: University of Chicago Press.

Berlin, I. (2002). *Freedom and its betrayal.* London: Chatto & Windus.

British Educational Research Association. (2004). *Have we created a new epistemology for the new scholarship of educational enquiry through practitioner research? Developing sustainable global educational networks of communication.* Symposium presented at the annual meeting. Retrieved from www.bath.ac.uk/~edsajw//bera04/frontbera.htm

Chomsky, N. (1965). *Aspects of the theory of syntax.* Cambridge: MIT Press.

Chomsky, N. (1986). *Knowledge of language: Its nature, origin and use.* New York: Praeger.

Church, M. (2004).*Creating an uncompromised place to belong: Why do I find myself in networks?* PhD submission, University of Bath, Bath, UK. Retrieved January 24, 2005, from www.bath.ac.uk/~edsajw/church.shtml

Clandinin, D. J., & Connelly, F. M. (2000). *Narrative inquiry.* San Francisco: Jossey-Bass.

Coetzee, J. M. (2004). *Elizabeth Costello.* London: Vintage.

Dadds, M. (1994). *Passionate enquiry and school development: A story about teacher action research.* London: Falmer.

Delong, J. (2002). *How can I improve my practice as a superintendent of schools and create my own living educational theory?* PhD thesis, University of Bath. Retrieved November 26, 2004, from http://www.actionresearch.net/delong.shtml

Delong, J., & Black, C. (Eds.). (2002). *Passion in professional practice* (Vol. 2). Ontario, Canada: Grand Erie Board of Education. Retrieved January 21, 2005, from www .schools.gedsb.net/ar/passion/pppii/index.html

Delong, J., Black, C., & Knill-Griesser, H. (Eds.). (2003). *Passion in professional practice* (Vol. 3). Ontario, Canada: Grand Erie Board of Education. Retrieved January 21, 2005, from www.schools.gedsb.net/ar/passion/pppiii/index.html

Donmoyer, R. (1996). Educational research in an era of paradigm proliferation: What's a journal editor to do? *Educational Researcher, 25*(2), 19–25.

Frazer, J. (1963). *The golden bough.* London: Macmillan.

Furlong, J. (2000). *Higher education and the new professionalism for teachers: Realising the potential of partnership.* London: CVCP/SCOP. Retrieved November 26, 2004, from www.edstud.ox.ac.uk/people/furlong.html

Furlong, J., & Oancea, A. (2005). *Assessing quality in applied and practice-based educational research: A framework for discussion.* Retrieved May 29, 2005, from http://www.bera .ac.uk/pdfs/Qualitycriteria.pdf

Gibbons, M., Limoges, C., Nowotny, H., Schwartzman, S., Scott, P., & Trow, M. (1994). *The new production of knowledge: The dynamics of science and research in contemporary societies.* London: Sage.

Glavey, C. (2005). [Transfer paper MPhil to PhD (Dublin)]. University of Glamorgan, Pontypridd, Wales, UK.

Habermas, J. (1987). The theory of communicative action. Vol. 2: *The critique of functionalist reason.* Oxford, UK: Polity.

Habermas, J. (2003). *On the pragmatics of social interaction.* Oxford, UK: Polity.

Hartog, M. (2004). *A self-study of a higher education tutor: How can I improve my practice?* PhD thesis, University of Bath, Bath, UK. Retrieved November 26, 2004, from www .bath.ac.uk/~edsajw/hartog.shtml

Hirst, P. (Ed.). (1983). *Educational theory and its foundation disciplines.* London: Routledge & Kegan Paul.

Holley, E. (1997). *How do I as a teacher-researcher, contribute to the development of a living educational theory through an exploration of my values in my professional practice?* MPhil thesis, University of Bath, Bath, UK. Retrieved December 20, 2005, from www.actionresearch .net/erica.shtml

Husserl, E. (1982). *Ideas pertaining to a pure phenomenology and to a phenomenological philosophy, Book I.* The Hague, Netherlands: Martinus Nijhoff.

Lather, P. (1994, April). *Textuality as praxis.* Paper presented at the annual meeting of the American Educational Research Association, New Orleans, LA.

Lyotard, J.-F. (1984). *The postmodern condition: A report on knowledge.* Manchester, UK: Manchester University Press.

Marcuse, H. (1964). *One-dimensional man.* Boston: Beacon Press.

McNiff, J. (1989). *An explanation for an individual's educational development through the dialectic of action research.* PhD thesis, University of Bath, Bath, UK.

McNiff, J., Lomax, P., & Whitehead, J. (2003). *You and your action research project* (2nd ed.). London: Routledge.

McNiff, J., & Whitehead, J. (2000). *Action research in organisations.* London: Routledge.

McNiff, J., & Whitehead, J. (2002). *Action research: Principles and practice* (2nd ed.). London: Routledge.

McNiff, J., & Whitehead, J. (2005). *Action research for teachers.* London: David Fulton.

McNiff, J., & Whitehead, J. (2006). *All you need to know about action research.* London: Sage.

Medawar, P. (1969). *Induction and intuition in scientific thinking.* London: Methuen.

Naidoo, M. (2005). *I am because we are (a never ending story). The emergence of a living theory of inclusional and responsive practice.* PhD thesis, University of Bath, Bath, UK. Retrieved December 20, 2005, from www.bath.ac.uk/~edsajw/naidoo.shtml

Perrement, M. (2005, May 10). *Action research revolutionises the classroom* (China Development Brief). Retrieved August 3, 2005, from www.jackwhitehead.com/china/cdbmay05

Peters, R. (1966). *Ethics and education.* London: Allen & Unwin.

Polanyi, M. (1958). *Personal knowledge.* London: Routledge & Kegan Paul.

Popper, K. (2002). *Conjectures and refutations.* London: Routledge. (Original work published 1963)

Raz, J. (2001). *Value, respect and attachment.* Cambridge, UK: Cambridge University Press.

Said, E. (1995). *Beginnings: Intention and method.* London: Granta.

Schickel, R. (2005, December 12). His "prayer for peace." *Time,* p. 71.

Schön, D. (1995, November–December). Knowing-in-action: The new scholarship requires a new epistemology. *Change,* pp. 27–34.

Sen, A. (1999). *Development as freedom.* Oxford, UK: Oxford University Press.

Skilbeck, M. (1983). Lawrence Stenhouse: Research methodology. *British Educational Research Journal, 9*(1), 11–20.

Suderman-Gladwell, G. (2001). *The ethics of personal, narrative, subjective research.* MA thesis, Brock University, St. Catharines, Ontario, Canada. Retrieved November 28, 2005, from www.bath.ac.uk/~edsajw/values/gsgma.pdf

Sullivan, B. (2006). *Towards a living theory of a practice of social justice.* PhD thesis, University of Limerick, Limerick, Ireland.

Thomas, G., & Pring, R. (2004). *Evidence-based practice in education.* Maidenhead, UK: Open University Press.

Todorov, T. (1990). *Genres in discourse.* Cambridge, UK: Cambridge University Press.

Vilayanur, S. R. (2003). *Lecture 5: Neuroscience: The new philosophy. The Reith lectures 2003.* Retrieved May 28, 2005, from http://www.bbc.co.uk/radio4/reith2003/lecture5.shtml

Whitehead, J. (1989). Creating a living educational theory from questions of the kind, "How do I improve my practice?" *Cambridge Journal of Education, 19*(1), 137–153. Retrieved November 26, 2004, from www.bath.ac.uk/~edsajw/writings/livtheory.html

Whitehead, J. (1993). *The growth of educational knowledge: Creating your own living educational theories.* Bournemouth, UK: Hyde. Retrieved January 21, 2005, from www.bath.ac.uk/~edsajw/bk93/geki.htm

Whitehead, J. (1999). Educative relations in a new era. *Pedagogy, Culture & Society, 7*(1), 73–90.

Whitehead, J. (2004a). What counts as evidence in the self-studies of teacher education practices? In J. J. Loughran, M. L. Hamilton, V. K. LaBoskey, & T. Russell (Eds.), *International handbook of self-study of teaching and teacher education practices.* Dordrecht, Netherlands: Kluwer Academic.

Whitehead, J. (2004b). *Action research expeditions: Do action researchers' expeditions carry hope for the future of humanity? How do we know? An enquiry into reconstructing educational theory and educating social formations.* Retrieved November 26, 2004, from www.arexpeditions.montana.edu/articleviewer.php?AID=80

Whitehead, J. (2004c, September 16). *Do the values and living logics I express in my educational relationships carry the hope of Ubuntu for the future of humanity?* Paper presented at the BERA 04 Symposium, Manchester, UK. Retrieved May 30, 2005, from www.jackwhitehead.com/jwbera04d.pdf

Whitehead, J. (2005). *Do these standards of judgement, used in validating explanations of educational influences from a living educational theory perspective, express a loyalty to humanity?* Draft paper, University of Bath, Bath, UK.

Whitehead, J., & McNiff, J. (2006). *Action research living theory.* London: Sage.

Whitty, G. (2005, September). *Education(al) research and policy making: Is conflict inevitable?* Presidential address to the annual conference of the British Educational Research Association, University of Glamorgan, Pontypridd, Wales, UK.

Williams, R. (1961). *The long revolution.* London: Chatto & Windus.

CHAPTER 13

From Wilda to Disney

Living Stories in Family and Organization Research

David M. Boje

The purpose of this chapter is to introduce "living story theory" and a "critical antenarratological" methodology. The key elements of living story theory are systemicity constraints: simultaneity, fragmentation, trajectory, and morphing. The result is a "story fabric," a weave of living story threads between times and places. A critical antenarratology is a combination of "critical theory" and "antenarrative" study. An antenarrative is a "prestory" and a "bet" that fragmented, tersely told stories, missing the usual coherence of a beginning, middle, and end, can be transformative to a social systematicity. *Systemicity* gives more attention to unmergedness and unfinalizedness than do traditional models of *system*, which tend to be univocal and monologic. The chapter gives examples of living story research about my grandmother Wilda and Disney Corporation.

Introduction

In this chapter, I propose a middle ground called *living story* between narrativists, folklorists, and antenarrativists. I begin by defining *living story*, proceed to develop my thesis, and then introduce a method to study living stories that I call *critical antenarratology*. I follow with family research into living story, into Wilda, my grandmother on my mother's side. Then, I get into Disney research, which I have been doing for over a decade. What connects the two pieces of research is what Derrida (1994) calls "hauntology" (p. 10). What is hauntology? Hauntology is a pun on *ontology* and refers to the specter (ghost), which is neither being nor nonbeing. Derrida plays on the fact that ontology and hauntology, in French, sound exactly the same. *Living story* is neither being nor nonbeing: it is a form of haunting. The living story is between dead and alive, between forgotten fragments and revitalizing those into one's own life. Story or narrative research can be an interpellating, a way of objectifying and tidying up oral records into a deadening text (Boje, Alvarez, & Schooling, 2001). The past of Walt Disney cannot be separated from his haunting presence in contemporary Disney. Reconstructing Wilda's living story cannot separate her past from my living present. Hauntology is what connects the two living story examples I will explore.

Kaylynn TwoTrees (1997), a Lakota storyteller, taught me elements of living story. "What is the Lakota penalty for changing a story, telling a story wrong or without permission?" I asked. "It is death," TwoTrees replied, "because the story in an oral culture is the entire living history of the community." She stresses three aspects: First, living stories not only have relativistic temporality (i.e., bridging past and present), there are times when a story can be told (e.g., seasons). Second, living stories have a place, and places have their own story to tell. Finally, living stories have owners, and one needs permission to tell another's story of a time or a place. This is similar to what the Navaho say about story—living embodiments of Navaho reality, living dramas, language that creates reality, not the reverse (Toelken, 1996). Not getting the story straight has its consequences; stories that were told badly by Toelken, and perhaps without permission, in the wrong place and time, were affecting his "mental and physical imbalance" (p. 55). There is a crucial point here, the idea that story is more than interpretation, and a living story transforms the "real."

Defining Living Story

Living story transforms that which it stories, in moments of living performance. Living story picks up and sheds context and characters, twisting, turning, and morphing along various social trajectories until versions die (perhaps to be reborn, who knows when). Living story has many authors and as a collective force has a life of its own. We live in living stories. Living story is a collective social process and has no existence apart from, and is indeed inseparable from, the event during which the story is performed (Boje, 1991; Georges, 1980). That is not to say that *living story* is only oral performance, it can be written, photographic, or videographic; it resides between many modes of expression. Each of us has living stories we do not quite comprehend that unfold; we are born into family and thrown together in various organizations; we become part of one another's living stories in societies, and we cocreate a *systemicity* of living stories. I use the term *systemicity* (short for *systematicalness*) instead of *system*, following Bakhtin (1973, 1981), to acknowledge the unfinalizedness and unmergedness of chaotic parts of the social (Boje, Enríquez, González, & Macías, 2005).[1]

I frame the research problem of living story as the opposition of coherence (narrativity) and incoherence (antenarrative) and of being in between. Antenarrative is defined as a "prestory" and a "bet" that terse fragments of not yet coherent story can be transformative to a social systemicity (Boje, 2001). We can look at the dance of story-incoherence and narrative-coherence as part of what is living storytelling. For ease of presentation, I refer to this basic opposition of coherence and incoherence, narrative and antenarrative as living story. There seems to be a hegemonic tendency to tell the cohesive story, in family and in organization research (Barry, 1997), in ways that make antenarration invisible. The trajectory of a living story from ante-narrative emergence to final dissolution reverberates through a social systemicity, according to particular collective dynamics (these are explored in the following, after my thesis is developed and the critical antenarratology method is introduced).

My thesis is that living story is part of a systemicity bigger than what previous studies and theories of storytelling have explored. I believe the reason for this is that our story definitions are constraining researchers and practitioners to see only a minuscule portion of the actual living story fabric of a social systemicity. In organization narratology and folkloristics, "proper" story is defined quite narrowly: (a) following Aristotle (350 BCE/1954), as having a beginning, middle, and end (Gabriel, 2000), with a linear (developmental) plotline that assumes "a solution to a problem" (Czarniawska, 1997, 1998) and (b) in traditional views of system (von Bertalanffy, 1956, 1962) that share full-blown stories from person-to-person, as one might share a book or e-mail attachment.[2] Living story theory contributes a different direction in story or narrative research by going beyond the story-as-dead-text collection approaches focused on plot or motif-index-classification (Thompson, 1946). The theory explains how living story keeps changing and rearranging context. Living story theory is defined here as the emergence, trajectory, and morphing of living story from antenarrative-conception to the death of decomposition and forgetting to tell anymore.

Strands of narrative and antenarrative are interwoven, raveling and unraveling, weaving and unweaving in families and storytelling organizations and in societal discourse. *Storytelling organization* is defined as "collective storytelling system[icity] in which the performance of stories is a key part of members' sensemaking and a means to allow them to supplement individual memories with institutional memory" (Boje, 1991, p. 106). I think it is the relation between proper and improper story that makes it living story and unleashes transformative complexity dynamics in storytelling organizations (Boje, 2005). It is the storytelling organization struggle to control and to amplify that keeps story living, changing, and rearranging. It is collective ongoing, simultaneous, fragmented, and distributive restorying by all the storytellers reshaping, rehistoricizing, and contemporalizing. In Bakhtin's (1973, 1981) conception, it is dialogized heteroglossia, the opposing centripetal (proper control) and centrifugal (improper amplification) forces. The living story fabric of a social system (be it family, organization, or society) is a complex collective-weave of many storytellers and listeners who together are co-constructing (along with researchers) the dynamics that reduce living story opposed by antenarrative forces of more amplifying-transformation.

I am interested in the relationship of living story to its living story fabric, to the emergence of less coherent antenarratives, constraining monologic-linear-narratives, and more dialogized stories, and the hegemony of the living story fabric. The next section introduces critical antenarratology as a method of studying living story.

Critical Antenarratology Method

I propose critical antenarratology as a method of tracing and pre-deconstructing an ongoing interweaving antenarrating that is always composing and self-deconstructing. In a study of Enron, we refined our definition: "Antenarratives are bets that a pre-story can be told and theatrically performed that will enroll stake-holders in 'intertextual' ways transforming the world of action into theatrics" (Boje, Rosile, Durant, & Luhman, 2004, p. 756). There has been increasing interest in antenarrative theory and research (Barge, 2004; Boje, 2001, 2002, in press-a; Boje et al., 2004; Collins & Rainwater, 2005; Vickers, 2005).

A critical antenarratology is rooted in the *critical theory* work of Marcuse, Adorno, Horkheimer, Fromm, and critical theorists who have followed them, such as Clegg, Willmott, Knight, Parker, Jones, Hussard, Oswick, Alvesson, Grimes, and Nord. There is quite a long list of folks ("critters") attending conferences such as Critical Management Studies, Critical Discourse conferences, and the Standing Conference for Management and Organization Inquiry (sc'MOI).

The differences between narratology's *story-as-text* focus and critical antenarra-tology's living story allow important insights into collective storytelling processes. First, in story-as-text research, the text is not being treated as a social production. In the text approach, one merely apprehends a text, without attending to the authors, beholders (readers), characters, and directors of living story production, distribution, and consumption. Second, in critical antenarratology, the analysis does not stop once a text is apprehended; analysis continues by sorting out the ways living stories of various persons are brought together in times and places. Third, there is a tendency in story-as-text research to develop a story more coherently into narrative reduction. In critical antenarratology, in contrast, telling and listening are socially constructed in situ in a systemicity context that is more ephemeral, emer-gent, theatric, multistylistic, and dialogic. Fourth, with a critical antenarratology approach, we can study the interplay of living story, cajoled narrative, and history. History produces story-as-text, reducing collective storytelling processes to a few stories told by elites, about elites. In some history studies, the power of the story-tellers to spin or slant a story is ignored. The old cliché that those with the sword write history has merit. History is written from the point of view of the victors, not those who are vanquished (White, 1973, 1978, 1987). The story-as-text approach, while pointing us to intertextuality, falls short; it is about one point of view. Fifth, critical antenarratology focuses attention on hegemonic processes of collective sto-rytelling practice that privilege some tellings over others and create a heroic façade. Antenarration and narration can serve the elite as well as the marginalized, the oppressors and the oppressed. To be more precise, critical antenarratology expresses a cynical view of family and organizational storytelling; narratology without antenarratology limits focus to the positive stories of elite storytellers, while marginalizing stories of the less powerful and less fortunate.

From a critical antenarratology perspective, managerialist organizational story-telling is biased to one positive (or appreciative) story of an elite point of view. It is what Marcuse (1964) calls *one dimensional,* a product of what Horkheimer and Adorno (1972) term *culture industry.* Story becomes dead narrative or epic history, constituted in spectacles of mass illusion by the culture industry, now triumphant over reality. Finally, rather than study antenarratives instead of narratives, I explore interactions of story-as-text *and* living story apprehensions of the collective story-telling process that is heteroglossic (centripetal and centrifugal).

Having defined critical antenarratology, next we can examine the dimensions of the story fabric in family and organization contexts.

Four Qualities of Story Fabric

Story fabric is the systemicity of living stories unfolding simultaneously in families and in organizations. Story fabric is defined by four qualities along the landscape and time dimensions: first, the landscape of *simultaneous fragmented* antenarrative performances as well as full-blown or partial living stories; second, the *morphing* story along *trajectories* across temporalities (past or future into present) in living stories.

Simultaneity

First is the constraint on living story systemicity of simultaneity; many stories are being told simultaneously across the landscape of here-and-now. *Tamara* is the name of a play by John Kriznac that takes place in a mansion with several floors, with a story performance in each room; *Tamara* explores how storytelling is simultaneous in about a dozen rooms, and a member of the audience, rather than being stationary, observing a single stage, must choose which room to enter. Depending on that choice and the order of rooms entered, one will walk away with understandings of who did what to whom that are different from those of someone making different choices (Boje, 1995). People do not visit every room; people are not able to be everywhere in the landscape to experience all the simultaneous action; in short, one cannot be everywhere at once. If there are a dozen stages and a dozen storytellers, the number of storylines an audience could trace as it chases the wandering discourses of *Tamara* is 12 factorial or 479,001,600. *Tamara* is a simultaneous landscape of multiple storytellers and listeners co-constructing living stories that co-construct meaning, depending on one's choice of which rooms to visit during the play. The key implication is that *Tamara*, with its simultaneity and choice constraints on meaning, is much more like real life than a story performed on a single stage, with everyone in a stationary audience, unable to move about.

Fragmentation

In the simultaneous story performance and choice-making landscape, there is a good deal of fragmentation. People do not tell full-blown stories from the beginning to the end; tellers leave most of the story to the imagination of the listeners, who fill in blanks, pauses, and silences with stories of their own. Oftentimes, listeners tune out a teller getting carried away with telling a story to themselves (Stein, 1935). The other aspect of fragmentation is the distributed nature of storytelling in *Tamara*. This aspect of fragmentation refers to seeing or hearing only a part of the unfolding story because not only spectators but also actors rove from room to room, and these actors reveal new aspects of their character that, if missed, lead and mislead interpretations.

Trajectory

Given the simultaneity and fragmentation in a storytelling system, the collective dynamics give rise to what I am calling *trajectory*. It is not the trajectory of a coherent, whole story with a beginning, middle, and end. Rather, it is more of an antenarrative trajectory, a condition of emergence of coherence out of incoherence in storytelling systemicity. The trajectory is the passageways of an emergent antenarrative as it picks up and sheds meaning along different places and across different temporalities. We did a preliminary study of the antenarrative trajectories of Enron as the corporation went from an exemplar of the "New Economy" of free market energy trading to a debacle of bankruptcy and executives being led off to jail in handcuffs in a theatric spectacle staged to make it appear that the State was in control of the corporation (Boje & Rosile, 2003; Boje et al., 2004).

Morphing

There is a morphing of living story elements (choice of incidents, characterizations, implications) that change from one performance site in the landscape to the next. Morphing the story is part of what spin is all about: changing a story that is problematic to some stakeholders into a more legitimating account for self and others. Morphing is also what happens when each new occurrence in the present prompts storytellers to restory reminiscences of the past to highlight values, persons, or episodes differently (Rosile, 1998). There is a drifting of content as new elements are emphasized and some are jettisoned or skipped over. Morphing is part of the constant ebb and flux of rehistoricizing. It is what makes living story transformative to context.

Simultaneity, fragmentation, trajectory, and morphing are qualities of living story fabric that are centrifugal and opposed to more narrative forces that reduce story to a linearly developed beginning, middle, and end. Next, I present living examples of the critical antenarratology study of the story fabric in family tales about my grandmother Wilda and organization tales of Disney.

Wilda Shelton

It was August 8, 2003; I was 55 when my mother, for the very first time, told me anything about the early life of my grandmother (Boje, 2005).[3] I did not even know her name until that day; she was just "grandma" to me. "What is her name?" I asked. "Wilda" my mother replied. "Wow, what a fantastic name, like Wild with an 'a.' Why did you never tell me about her?" There was a very long pause. "You visited her a few times, you were very young" replied my mother. I was 9 when we moved away, and I did not see her again until age 18, for just a moment, the very last time. Her fragment, and my reminiscence were interrupted suddenly. My mother began telling me about a person I never knew. In 2005, she told a version a bit different from the August 8, 2003, version: "Wilda could do anything. She could fell a grouse with a rock, live for months in the wilderness on berries and fish. Wilda was a trick rider in the rodeo, at a time when women did not do that" (Boje, 2005, p. 345). Another long pause, and I began to fill in the silence, wondering what Wilda was like, wondering how she had gone against the grain of society and become so wild.

My mother did not tell me about Wilda, the wild roping, hardworking woman of the wilderness. She said it was because her memories of the Depression were so hurtful. She did not want to recall living in tents, cabins, and caves, doing stoop work on the vegetable farms, that her dad was a bootlegger and a sheepherder, or that her mother lived off the land. My mother was embarrassed by the wild life and preferred to live in the city, watching television and pretending to live the middle-class life in her double-wide.

The June 2005 interview included my mother (Lorane), sister (Karen), one of two brothers (only Kevin, because the other brother, Steve, is a heroin addict who sends us e-mail every year from Manhattan but never replies to our messages), and my cousin (Renee Flansburg). Together, we have been consulting photo albums; studying documents copied from hospitals, county, and other records; and visiting grave sites. In addition, I have been reading the history of the times when Wilda was a young rodeo star, marrying at 16, and heading off into the wilderness of Washington and Idaho.

I paid particular attention to Native American history. Although Wilda was not Native American, her brother Gerald married Stella LaClaire (actually, we can find no record of the marriage), a Native American (we cannot find which tribe), and had a child named Georgina. The fragments of my living story, of Wilda, are widely distributed. Yet there is an antenarrative cluster and trajectory when it comes to family ties to Native Americans. Wilda remarried to Percy Brown, who we suspect had Native American blood because his mother abandoned "Brownie" (as we call him) to be raised by Indians; we suspect it is the Yakima tribe (but we do not know for sure). As with many people's family stories, there are a great many black holes, family secrets, and people written out of the family history. And there is morphing in the telling—it is now socially acceptable to be Native; in Wilda's time, the genocide was still terrorizing tellings.

For example, on my dad's side of the family tree, there was a brother to his dad named Edward Boje who married a woman of the Puyallup tribe (we do not know her name, nor is there a marriage record), and Edward and his bride were ostracized. Edward's name was lined out of the family bible and was never spoken of again, not even in whispers. It was just a few years ago that I learned of Wilda and of Edward and Gerald's wife, Stella LaClaire, their daughter Georgie, and all the unspoken Native American influence in my family ancestry.

In June 2005, I returned to my mother's home, and she agreed to tell me more about Wilda than I was disclosed in the August 2003 visit. My sister Karen and my cousin Renee Flansburg were in Yelm, Washington; I went up to Seattle to visit my brother Kevin, who told me more fragments. Slowly, we co-constructed our living story of Wilda as a young woman; it took more shape as we read her poems, studied the photographs and the birth, death, and other available records. I also read histories and novels of the period and began to re-create the younger Wilda, the one who existed before I was born. Her poems are fluffy romantic fantasy, yet they display a love for Brownie, the great outdoors, and for her children, her grandchildren, and her dog.

This poem is titled by Wilda *Listening 1956*:

> Listening, I hear the quiet stillness of everything; no whirr of wings, or chirp of bird. Nor sound to break this holy moment as our creator pauses for a breath to permeate the atmosphere, of his Being.
>
> All creatures know, within, of his presence; each leaf and plant or growing thing.
>
> The rush of wind, rustle of branch . . .
>
> The lap of water on the sand; resume the steady course of time.
>
> To all who know the rhythm; be still, be still and listen.[4]

Wilda did not have the abhorrent view of wilderness or poverty; my mother wanted no part of either; I am drawn to nature and can feel its rhythm pulling me.

Wilda's living story is a piece of research in progress. It takes a good bit of forensic detective and archaeological digging to get Wilda story fragments, to reclaim little people's history from elite history.

Wilda's living story is part of an ever-changing and rearranging tapestry, a story fabric that is collectively woven and unwoven. It morphs as each new tidbit is discovered. Yet the family social systemicity interwoven into the fabric of living stories is an unmerged, unfinalized tapestry, with all kinds of black holes in it. Wilda's story, to me, is interesting not only because I get to discover my relationship to a great lady but because her story fabric is in tatters, much already so forgotten and unrecorded that I can only glimpse disappearing fragments.

I confess something haunts me: The living stories of how much prejudice and hatred between immigrants and natives spews in the Americana "melting pot." In what I will share with you, the reader, I am putting Wilda's living story into the context of prohibition (her first husband was a bootlegger) and the Great Depression (my grandmother and mother lived in shacks and tents, some with dirt floors). I have been interviewing horse people to find out about trick riders, and blacksmiths to find out about what life was like for Wilda's father (he opened a blacksmith and livery stable business after failing to make it as a wheat farmer) and reading texts about life on the Oregon Trail and about people resettling from Iowa to Washington.

I began by telling you Wilda's living story in a rather straightforward fashion but did not reshape it into some kind of coherent storyline. To be candid, I know a few pieces, some fragments, and have lots of speculations of various family members but only a few facts. We are still piecing it all together. In terms of method, my mother and cousin got to swapping stories (June 2005), my sister inserted dates based on archival research, and I typed the co-construction into my laptop. This is the result:

Wilda Shelton was born on January 28, 1902, after her parents crossed the Rocky Mountains in a covered wagon on the Oregon Trail, from Iowa to Washington State. It was hard times and a perilous journey; Wilda's older brother, Henry Wayne Shelton, was born on the Oregon Trail (January 16, 1897) and died within a month (February 1897) before the family reached Goldendale, Washington.

Wilda's younger brother, Gerard Shelton (born June 13, 1904; died August 18, 1937), was married (or had a common law marriage) to a Native American, Stella LaClaire; they had a child named Georgie (maybe short for Georgia).

Wilda's parents were William Henry Shelton (born July 26, 1863, in Brownstown, Indiana; died August 18, 1946, in Toppenish, Washington, buried at Tacoma Cemetery in Yakima, Washington) and Virginia Tuttle (born March 13, 1863, in Wayne County, Iowa, and died October 11, 1944, in Toppenish and was buried in Yakima, Washington; my sister went to the grave site). Growing up, we Boje children were told that a Tuttle (ancestor of Allerton lineage) crossed over on the Mayflower in 1620. I did more research (Society of Mayflower Descendants, 2005): It appears that an ancestor (Francis Eaton) to Wilda's first husband, Raymond Eaton, could have been on the Mayflower (this has to be confirmed).

At age 16, Wilda lived common law with Raymond Eaton (born April 17, 1894; died in the 1970s, no exact date known—we have not found a grave). Another version of the tale is that she married Raymond, the marriage supposedly having occurred on or about January 1, 1920, at a Baptist Parsonage in Goldendale, Washington. The date of the supposed marriage is just 19 days before the Prohibition Amendment took effect throughout America; it was already law on January 1, 1916, in Washington State. In fact, Initiative No. 3, passed on November 1, 1914, Election Day, by the citizens of Washington State by a margin of 52%, just did not take effect until January 1916. The Prohibition Amendment (the 18th amendment to the U.S. Constitution) was effective from January 20, 1920; prohibition was repealed on April 15, 1933. Wilda and Ray were poor. I make this aside to tell you prohibition was an industry employing poor folk.

As my mother tells it, "Ray was gone for entire seasons, not spending any money, living off the chuck wagon, saving it all, to bring back to his family. It was the depression [1920–1933] and times were hard." Ray lost an eye to dynamite in a mining accident; he became a bootlegger during the depression, hopping a freight train to head off to bootlegging territory. At other times, Ray was just another hobo looking for work. My mother says "he was gone months at a time." Wilda and her daughter Lorane lived off the land, waiting for him to return, or were holed up in a tent city during the picking season. Wilda worked alongside the men. Other seasons, Wilda was out in the woods and would have to kill a pheasant (other versions say squirrel, rabbit, or grouse) or catch a fish to exist; this kept on for about 4 years. When Wilda was 20, their child (my mother Lorane) was born (November 4, 1925), during the Great Depression.

Wilda and Ray split up about 1927, a couple of years after Lorane was born; the stock market crash was on Black Tuesday, October 29, 1929, but they had no stock. And these were the depression years before the New Deal (1933–1938). Wilda moved from the wilds to the town and became a telephone operator. That is when Wilda met Percy Brown and left Raymond Eaton for ever.

Percy Brown was born on March 17, 1894, in Ellensburg, Washington, and died on March 20, 1970. His mother's family name was Stutsman; we do not know her first name, and we do not know who the father is.

Why Wilda left Ray Eaton for Percy Brown (Brownie, as he was called) is a mystery. Brownie had many sides to him: Some hated him, most feared him, some liked him. My mother says Brownie was a monster. Wilda, my mother says, "could have left Ray out of sheer loneliness of living months on end in the wilderness, and the camps, while Ray was off bootlegging, or with the sheep, or prospecting, and dreaming of striking it rich." My mother speaks of Brownie in bitter tones, repeating the phrase *sadistic bastard*; "he made a pass at me." "Do you want me to type that in," I checked. "Yeah, it's okay," she replied in whispered tones. My cousin Renee (my aunt Val's daughter) does not remember Percy being a monster. He never made a pass at her. She often went fishing and hunting with him and Wilda and loved every minute of it.

My sister Karen and I have another theory as to why Wilda left Ray for Brownie; we think that Wilda went off with Brownie because of his Native American upbringing and his wilderness savvy. We don't know for sure if Brownie had native blood; his mother might just have decided she was too young and poor to raise her infant. We learn a little from studying the family photos, records of births and deaths, and getting my mother to talk. We speculate that Wilda's brother may have married a Native American woman named Stella LaClaire. There is a picture of Stella with her child wrapped in a papoose: Her name is Georgie (short for Georgia, we think; there are no records of them anywhere, erased from history). In talking to my relatives, the best guess is that Brownie's mother abandoned him shortly after he was born in Ellensburg, Washington, on the closest Indian reservation, which would be the Yakima. As my cousin tells it, he was older; "Grandpa [Brownie] was dropped off at the Indian reservation when he was 3 years old and did not see his mother again until he was 16 and bought him a motorcycle. That is why he learned to fish and hunt like he did." My mother says, "No, it was when he was born." Cousin Rene continues, "Mama (Val) said he always said *Ikkes Cuppa Whappachee* and drove her crazy trying to figure out what it meant."

Brownie's mother married a rich man, and they had a son named Claude, who grew up in a life of wealth and privilege; Claude became an executive at Shell Oil. Percy's story is fit for a movie, a story of two brothers, Percy raised on the reservation, and Claude raised in wealth and privilege. Percy would go to work for Claude, at Shell Oil, but was soon let go. When Percy was older, his uncles taught him to run steam shovels and build and grade roads; he also worked as a constable in a state forest and then for the railroad.

When Percy met Wilda, he was working as a forest ranger, in the deep wilderness of Washington. In an old shoebox, we found pictures of Percy and Wilda riding horses in the deep forest. Percy and Wilda lived common law from about 1927 until they finally got married on May 22, 1953. This is a story my mother and Renee knew but my sister, brother, and I had never heard:

> While Wilda and Percy lived in the Washington State forest [mother and cousin debated the forest's name but could not agree], they found a deer, whose mother had been shot by hunters. They built a pen for the young doe. A hunter came along one day, finding the baby deer, caged in a pen, just raised his rifle and shot it dead; he left the carcass lying there. "It's like killing Bambi," I interjected [nods all around]. Percy and Wilda tracked him down, and after a fight, Percy took the man's rifle away from him, and kicked the hunter out of forest. He was ready to kill the man.

My mother always shies away from talking about her past; she particularly does not want to talk about Brownie. I know he ran over her tricycle on purpose, and after Wilda and Brownie conceived Val (short for Valamina, born August 1, 1928), Brownie got meaner. Lorane and Val had an intense sibling rivalry that lasted all their lives; yet during Val's last 15 years, they lived in trailers, not 30 feet away from each other, still feuding, some months not talking to each other, but sharing the same piece of property. Last time I saw Val she was getting relief from cancer, puffing on a marijuana joint: That was just before she passed away.

What little love Brownie had, my mother (Lorane) says it was dispensed to Val. "He gave her privileges I did not have." I asked mom if it was alright to tell you that Val and Brownie often went off fishing and hunting together; how Brownie seemed to treat her right but would lock my mother in the woodshed hours on end to punish her for trivial infractions such as not sitting perfectly still or not finishing some food that she hated. He would never let her out of the yard. Another fragment she said I could divulge here: Brownie made passes at her when she got to be a teenager. Mom looked and dressed just like Veronica Lake (you should see the photos). Brownie, she says, was sort of schizophrenic—not bad all the time. She says, "He would make the children beg to take them to the dime movies; three shoes for 10 cents. But first they had to be very good, and if they did not do exactly as he said, it was always, 'you are not going.'" I recalled such incidents from my visits with Brownie.

My sister Karen and I believe that Wilda practiced Native American spirituality until she got older (around 71) and was converted by missionaries to Mormonism. Renee says Brownie would send the missionaries running until he passed away; we think it was then that Wilda converted from Native American spiritual practices to Mormon ways.

Wilda's first husband, Ray, stayed in touch with his daughter Lorane, about every other year when she was in the States. In the year 1961, after my dad and mom split up, mom returned to Washington from Paris with the four kids. I recall Ray visiting his only child, Lorane, and his grandchildren, of whom I am one (I was 14). Ray had a glass eye or wore an eye patch. At that visit, Ray was a hermit and sheepherder when he was not off gold and silver prospecting in Idaho. My cousin says, "The thing I remember is I said [to Ray], 'what you mean you have a glass eye; what are you talking about?' He reached up, popped it out, and rolled it across the table at me. I was afraid to pick it up. I was real young when that happened. It was on [35 North] Proctor" (north end of Tacoma, Washington).

Ray would keep visiting Wilda and my mother and us kids. My little brother (Steve) and I used to steal into his room when he visited our mother (Lorane, his daughter) and us the grandkids. We found him snoring and heisted the glass eye out of his water glass. By stealth, we crawled back to our room and did play marbles with the eye. We thought we would never be found out because of all the precautions we took. We polished the malevolent eye and inspected it carefully for nicks and chips, and finding none, we put it back in the water glass and poured the water to the finger mark we had left. He spotted our game on the second visit, and this would be his very last visit ever to us. He ranted and raved; we thought he was going to explode. He told us how he hated towns and all civilization and put the black patch over his vacant eye and left forever. We felt quite bad—how many of us have a grandfather who has a patch over his glass eye, lives in the mountains of Idaho in the caves, and herds sheep to buy the provisions he needs to survive all alone?

Piecing more story fragments together, one can get some sense of what Wilda's life was like. We are co-constructing a young woman out of reminiscences, some stories we heard growing up, and other stories pieced together with bits of records, poems, and photos.

My mother (Lorane Joyce Eaton, daughter of Wilda and first husband, Ray Eaton) told me this story (June 2005), a slightly expanded version of what she told me before (August 8, 2003, see Boje, 2005, pp. 344–345). I want to focus now on a pause. "Wilda," says my mother, "could ride a horse better than any man." [Mom's voice rose at the end of the sentence, when it usually trails off to a whisper.] There was a long pause, a pregnant pause (4 seconds), and she continued, "She did trick riding at the Rodeo with her brother Gerald, and that was when that kind of thing was just not allowed. She could kill a rabbit at 50 paces by hitting it between the eyes with a stone. Her parents were away for months at a time but never worried because Wilda would take care of them. Wilda could live in the wilderness, knew how to catch a fish with some string and bent wire, and knew the names of all the trees and bushes and all the herbal remedies for things." In that telling, my mother had become wild (during that pregnant pause), she was once again the "Blond Bomber," her nickname when she played basketball in high school, and would fight anyone who got in the "paint" (that area in front of the net). She says, "some girls had razor blades in their hair, but I just charged em anyhow." My cousin adds another fragment, "Wilda would prop her leg up on the saddle and roll up a cigarette with one hand. When they [Wilda and second husband, Percy] worked in the forest, they did not have a telephone but could shinny up the pole and make a phone call using a clip on phone thing; she was a switchboard operator at one time." We recalled visiting Wilda and the "wilderness salads" she made, "picking what we thought were weeds from a field, lots of wild flowers and dandelions tossed together." My sister continues, "Wilda knew the names of plants and what each one was good for."

Wilda Brown died about 1972, and I was not told about it. So far I cannot find a record of just when and where she died. Living stories are like that—lots of loose ends, and each new discovery presents more loose ends. I met her when she was older, a silver-haired grandmother with leathery skin, hugging me and giving me cigarettes before I knew how to smoke, and then telling me about a native spirituality I did not comprehend.

Wilda's story is interesting because it goes against the grain of colonization. The Wilda living stories name the juxtaposed history of family ancestry with societal narrative, in our case the white culture's rejection of Native American culture during colonization. Wilda left the comforts of white culture to live in the wilderness with her parents, then with Raymond, and for decades with Percy. Wilda was a wilderness woman, a trick rider in the rodeo, and lived off the land. Gerard Shelton and his Native bride (at least we think they married), Stella LaClaire (and daughter Georgie), could not find peace in Washington. These are not the only stories of this sort. On my dad's side, my grandfather's brother, Edward Boje, fell in love with a Puyallup Indian woman (again, we do not know her name), and they moved onto the reservation and had children, Glen, Ida, Alex, and Fred, with the last name of Boje. We know that there were Native American Boje descendents living on a Cheyenne reservation in Wyoming, but they too have forgotten her name. The Boje family wrote them out of family history, refusing to utter their names.

These living stories thread the past into the present and can, in my case, allow a critical antenarrative reading of family story's relation to national and tribal history. Living stories of our ancestry juxtapose and fractionate with societal hegemony and our contemporary living stories. As Clair (1997, p. 323) puts it, "no story stands alone." This research changes my living story; my ethnic and racial identities are unfolding. Living story research is a way of dealing with the organizing of silence about secretive ancestral identities, identities marginalized in the melting pot. In living story, "those silenced voices can be organized in ways to be heard" (Clair, 1997, p. 323). For example, my sister Karen pursues Native American healing practices, wears her beads, and does her drumming. In the case of Edward Boje and Gerald Shelton, their voices were muzzled; their living story was put to death. Reconstructing these living stories gives me a passion for finding out the names of birds, plants, and trees and learning about the history of the Apaches in the Organ Mountains of New Mexico, which I can see from this window above this very keyboard.

In this way, Wilda's stories are a kind of hauntology, a specter-ghost "becoming-body" (Derrida, 1994, p. 6). They raise my critical concern about why there was so much secrecy and hatred around Native American relatives. In the case of Gerald, he was literally beaten to death, and his wife and child went off with my grandmother, Wilda, into the wilds. The story told is that Gerald had left the rodeo circuit to become the town drunk. As my mother tells it, "the sheriff got tired of arresting him, and one night, he and a deputy beat him to death." In the case of

Edward and his nameless bride (and children), it was death by shunning, the hegemony of silence that Clair (1997) writes about as part of the nested stories of family, tribal life, and colonization in the great "melting pot." Clair's (1993, 1994, 1996, and especially 1997) work resituates personal narrative. Her work nests ancestral, gender, political economy, and societal narratives. In my telling, we get to glimpse the interaction of antenarrative fragments, some simultaneous, some morphing, making trajectories about lost Native American roots in a society bent on forgetting such a heritage.

Finally, these Wilda stories, for me, juxtapose Native American history with European colonization during the dawn of the Great Depression. Colonization is generally celebrated in the United States. Yet the other side of the story is about repopulating Native lands with Europeans while extracting resources from native ecosystems to ship back to Europe. As Native resistance increased, the colonists cleared the land of Natives in acts of genocide. Colonies were like chess pieces on the New Europe game-board. "Pieces changed hands. New Amsterdam for the Dutch became New York for the English. King Georgia was winning" (Amble, 2005).

White and Epston (1990) point out that each story of a family is an ideological representation and is embedded in the family system. The story fabric of my family living stories has been torn asunder by murders (that of Gerald and a murder of my aunt Dorothy, on my dad's side) and a long succession of divorces. The divorces begin with Wilda's and continued with my parents' and those of three of my siblings, and then there are my own. To restory Wilda is a way of healing some family memories, to find in Wilda a wild passion for living, a forgotten sense of nature spirit, a way of vitalizing me.

For Clair (1997), nested stories (family, tribe, society) focus on the importance of naming acts of oppression and on how the oppressors have named those same acts. The oppression I have in mind relates to how a society (and its academic disciplines) enforces ways of narrating a story that are hegemonic. I can locate the oppression of Gerard, Percy, Stella, Georgie, and Edward (and his children) in the grander narration of U.S. history and the treatment (name it genocide) of Native Americans. Living stories of oppression have a material existence in discursive practices of families, tribes, organizations, and nations—at least that which has not been Disneyfied.

Disney

Why turn to Disney after telling Wilda stories? I want to make a link to the way in which family ties relate to organization storytelling. Spins and counterspins set up the *story fabric* of organization as well as family storytelling. Disney is also both family storytelling enterprise and organizational storytelling.

I continue the theme of hauntology (Derrida, 1994). Walt's ghost still walks the Magic Kingdom; and as employees would whisper whenever Walt approached, "man is in the forest" (a line from the Bambi movie). Why? Because, unlike the official stories about Walt, there are many marginalized accounts by former employees and a few executives that depict a maniacal Walt, one who ruled his kingdom with an iron, paternalistic fist.

In the official lore, Disney began as a partnership between Walt Disney and Ub Iwerks (later written out of the official history, reduced to an artisan, a drawer of cartoons, not a partner). Walt is characterized as the iconic hero of the American Dream. Walt's is the grand narrative of rags to riches. He came from the Midwest town and moved to the big West City to become wealthy and powerful by being the entrepreneur. Walt did not invent cartooning or animation, and Taylorism of the animation industry was well under way when Walt and Ub formed their partnership.

There is something unique about Walt; Walt was the manager of other people's talent, and he used story as a way to control others. Walt's way of controlling Disney was to keep it flat, with few layers in the hierarchy, and to storyboard every kind of project from cartoon to movie to theme park. Ron Miller (a relative by marriage) took over after Walt's death but was, unlike Walt, not much of a storyteller. Ron was an accounting type and had such a meek personality that people kept making decisions the way they imagined that Walt would have done. At every meeting, someone would say, "What would Walt have done." This is one example of how resilient a storytelling system is to changing its story fabric, even after the demise of its leader. Ron Miller (Walt's son in law) could not shake the "hauntology" of Walt (Derrida, 1994); Michael Eisner fares no better. Living story is a hauntology because a story, like a ghost, is between dead and alive. And living story just keeps changing and rearranging.

The following excerpt from a transcript of a stockholders' meeting shows Eisner invoking the Disney hauntology in a way that brings in voices other than that of the dead Walt (Boje, 1995):

> In 1923, Walt arrived in Hollywood with drawing materials under his arm, $40 in his pocket, and a dream. Waiting for him at Union Station was his brother Roy, who would dedicate his life to making Walt's dream come true. Together with their wives, Lilly and Edna, working alongside them at night around the kitchen table, they struggled to keep a tiny studio alive. (p. 1020)

Eisner restoried Walt stories, fighting the specter of Walt, giving impetus to new organizing processes such as the move away from Walt's storyboards in favor of scripts, the kind that Eisner was familiar with at Paramount (Boje, 2005). Eisner discusses how there were no scripts at Disney for animated films before he took over:

> I couldn't follow it. I'd go down there and they'd go through the storyboards. And you go through one storyboard and they'd bring in another storyboard. And I'd sit there for hours and I couldn't remember what was in the first storyboard. And it was a hard process for me to deal with. I'd been used to working in the script area. . . .
>
> And every time I'd say: "How was it done in the past?" And I'd hear about Walt. He'd just be there and he'd jump up and down and he'd go back and

forth between things and so forth. And Roy Disney (Jr.) told me a story about how he (Walt) sat on his bed when he had the flu or the mumps or something and told the entire story of *Pinocchio* in the bed. And I finally discovered they did have a script.

And the script was in Walt Disney's head. We didn't have Walt Disney. And therefore we didn't have a single mind, tracking the entire movie. We had (a) committee of minds. And that was the problem. And now we do scripts. (p. 1023)

Eisner is telling his story in a way that deconstructs Walt's hauntology. He is pulling on one of the strings of the story's fabric and, in the process, unraveling the legend of dead Walt.

Walt's hauntology lived on despite Eisner's other ways of telling. Walt stories continue to take hold of collective storytelling practices at Disney. Roy Disney clashes with Eisner's new ways of storying "what Walt might have done" (Boje, 2005, p. 1020). Roy Disney's (2003) Letter of Resignation became part of the story fabric of organization overcoming family life at Disney. It mentions another hauntology, the death of Frank Wells (Disney, 2003).

Initially, Eisner put together a competent team of executives, but then Frank Wells died, and Katzenberg and many others had their falling out with Eisner. In official Disney storytelling, Eisner does no wrong, but in unofficial works such as Stewart (2005), Eisner is storied as just as iron fisted, autocratic, and micromanaging as Walt. Hauntology is being noticed; some suggest "Katzenberg felt that the spirit of Walt Disney was guiding him," while Eisner thought himself to be "the reincarnation of Walt Disney" (Elle, Verrier, & Bates, 2005). Roy Disney had been leading the call to get Eisner replaced and had finally succeeded. Eisner's honeymoon with Disney was all but over.

Fast forwarding to contemporary Disney, inside the Magic Kingdom, there are living stories of a struggle for power between Roy Disney (Walt Disney's nephew) and Michael Eisner. Eisner's almost 21-year reign is almost over (1984–2005); Roy was allegedly squeezed off the board by Eisner and then resigned; and Bob Iger took over as CEO on September 30, 2005; Eisner retains a seat on the board (Disney Press Release, 2005). Iger took over a company with more than $30 billion in revenues and a net income of $2.3 billion. Roy Disney and Stanley Gold, two former board members, are still opposed to Iger, a longtime friend and confidant of Eisner.

Disney and Gold released a statement saying, "We find it incomprehensible that the board of directors of Disney failed to find a single external candidate interested in the job and thus handed Bob Iger the job by default," they said. "The need for the Walt Disney Company to have a clean break from the prior regime and to change the leadership culture has been glaringly obvious to everyone except this board" (Kurtzberg, 2005).

Roy E. Disney and Stanley Gold filed a lawsuit (May 9, 2005) seeking to invalidate February's board election and March's selection of Iger. There is even a Web site called SaveDisney.com that Roy has put up (Elle et al., 2005).[5] Disney and Gold (2005) have also been putting articles in the *Los Angeles Times*:

Of course, we've since learned that the search involved only one real candidate—Eisner's handpicked heir apparent, Disney President Robert Iger. By caving in to Eisner's demand that he be allowed to sit in on interviews of potential successors, by not even attempting to interview a single outside candidate until after its annual meeting in February, by refusing to insist that Eisner commit to leaving the company as soon as the new CEO was named, and by not objecting to the aggressive public relations campaign Eisner had his minions wage on Iger's behalf, the board effectively endorsed the notion that "the fix was in" and virtually guaranteed that no serious outside executive would be willing to be considered for the job.[6]

A new book, *DisneyWar*, by Pulitzer Prize–winning journalist James Stewart (2005) alleges Iger's judgment was poor and he had a tendency to kowtow to CEO Michael Eisner. An article in *Fortune* amplifies some of Stewart's charges:

Eisner was so consumed with top-tier dysfunction, he practically ignored Iger. When he did take notice, it wasn't with a ringing endorsement. Early on in Iger's tenure, Eisner wrote the board about Iger's prospects for becoming CEO someday: "He is not an enlighten [sic] or brilliantly creative man, but with a strong board, he absolutely could do the job." Eisner claims he has overcome his doubts: "I bought into the cliché of Bob—that because he didn't get on top of the table and rant and rave and act like a fool, he wasn't a creative, passionate person." (Sellers, 2005)

Disney is also an enormously more complex global organization with a higher diversity of theme parks in various countries bending a global mold to fit local tastes in food and story. In Walt's day, it was one studio and one theme park; now there are multiple TV networks, a fifth theme park opening, a cruise line, merchandising in the malls and airports, publishing houses, real estate, including hotel resorts, and more.

There is a dynamic relation of Disney's official story and the living counterstories. Disney's annual reports and official biographies are a study in spin, in presenting one way of telling while ignoring the other ways of telling stories about the Magic Kingdom. Their official stories are centripetal, tugging at the centrifugal ways of telling to calm the whirlwind of reporters, activists, and special interest groups that swirl around Disney, forever unraveling the official ways of telling, juxtaposing these with the counterstories (Boje, 2000).

After Roy was out, Eisner put his spin on it—that by replacing Roy and longtime insider Stanley Gold with two new board members (Aylwin Lewis and John Chen), Eisner was making an effort to make the Disney board more independent of the Disney family, and served to add outsiders' voices to the boardroom. Of course, there are counterstories that just the reverse had happened, that there are now fewer independent voices and fewer calls for Eisner to plan his succession (Gross, 2004).

The Disney storytelling machine has its work cut out—to restory Iger into a leaderly CEO, one who can lead the empire especially after Stewart's (2005) exposé. The spin is on, and the new image is being cast.

Where Eisner is a micromanager, Iger is regarded as team-oriented. If Eisner favors funny Disney ties and drives a yellow Volkswagen Beetle, Iger is a fashion plate who favors a sleek Porsche. Smooth and cautious, he is known as a man who chooses his words and actions carefully. (McCarthy & Levin, 2005)

Stewart's (2005) book was released just as the Disney board was deliberating on making Iger their choice for CEO. Iger is being presented by Disney as a team leader, not at all what Stewart portrays. In short, there is simultaneous story action, fragmentation everywhere, trajectories that are clashing, and attempts by Disney and its critics to morph their versions.

As Disney opens its Hong Kong theme park in August 2005, the workers are learning that Disney workers are called "cast members." They don't go to work, they "put on a show," and when they are out in the park, they're "on stage" (Disney's Hong Kong Workers, 2005). When the Taipei workers return from their training in Disney Florida, Wynnie Poon, 29, who is being trained as a greeter at the Epcot park, is not sure it will work. "Chinese culture is more conservative and they're not that expressive about feelings," said Poon. She is imagining the response she'll get back home when she tells Disney visitors, "Have a magical day!" "People will say 'Oh you're insane! You're crazy!'" (Disney's Hong Kong Workers, 2005). This is Disneyfication, making the Chinese employee into what Van Maanen (1991) calls a "smiling robot" in the "smile culture" of Disney (cited in Boje, 1995, p. 1020).

With a change in CEO, the Disney corporate empire is restorying its living story fabric to claim its new CEO as hero. Even before the new CEO took office, the "central strategic planning committee" of Disney disbanded (Stewart, 2005). The story being constructed is that Eisner overdid the centripetal force, whereas the new CEO will give all divisions more autonomy, and the system overall will be more centrifugal than under either Walt or Eisner. Time will tell if the prestory (an antenarrative) will continue its transformative trajectory. Or will this be yet another example of a story that is centripetal, out to control, to set out a spin, that cast members are supposed to accept as the latest script change?

Discussion and Conclusion

I want to discuss the theory embedded in my presentation of Wilda and Disney fragments. Wilda and Disney are theorized to be living stories: in the moment, raveling and unraveling simultaneously, distributed, fragments, and morphing in spin and counterspin.

Wilda and Disney are story fabrics where what is patched and covered over keeps coming undone. I think it is important to study many sides of the story. Storytelling is a collective process, tellings by many tellers. A critical antenarratology addresses ways in which one way of telling is counter to another way of telling. Antenarrative trajectory, the interplay of centripetal and centrifugal forces, lets us explore what is dynamic in the interrelationship of living story of family, organizations, and society. It is a method of exploring the landscape, of looking at the opposition of official and marginal ways of telling, and of looking at how coherent narratives are opposed by more unraveling stories. Living story is theorized as the interplay of narrative coherence, antenarrative (prestory) trajectory, and more dialogized stories (with a multiplicity of styles, logics, and voices).

The ways of telling and not telling are very telling. The ways of telling emerging in the present are changing from the ways of telling in the past. There is less "answerability" for what one tells and how to listen ethically to a telling (Bakhtin, 1990). Answerability is the plurality of ways of telling in one time and another (even anticipated times) and ways of telling in one part of the landscape versus another. Dialogicality is not the same as dialogue. Dialogue is people in a common time and place. Being dialogic can be across times and places.

A problematic research implication is that what is being taken as a "proper narrative" (or story confined to narrative coherence) in the vast majority of research projects excludes all the many diverse fragmented, morphing, distributed, simultaneous living story forms. In short, the story fabric is only being partially imagined or investigated. The implication of the living story theory, with its focus on simultaneity, fragmentation, trajectory, and morphing is that a story is much more ephemeral than is plotted in Aristotelian poetic narrative approaches or in motif indexes of folkloristics.

Living story is embedded in systemicity and an environment that is intertextual, nested, and dynamic because it is unmerged, unfinished, and partial. Coherence is overgeneralized. There is a relation between living story and systemicity that needs to be explored. It is not a choice of mechanistic, organic, or open systemicity of some kind. Rather, it is a multilanguaged, multilayered systemicity at the higher reaches of Boulding's (1956) scales of system complexity. In this higher-order systemicity-complexity (Pondy, 1976, 1978; Pondy & Mitroff, 1979), I think it is possible to explore Bakhtin's (1981, 1990) concern with heteroglossia (the opposition of centripetal and centrifugal forces of language that are dialogic). I have stressed here that there is ongoing degeneration and the whirlwind centrifugal forces are opposed by the forces of coherence, which are more centripetal. It is a theory that allows us to see how narrative and story forces are different yet implicated in our families, organizations, and societies.

In current work, I am attempting to relate four types of dialogism to the fields of system theory and strategy (Boje, in press-b). And each of the four dialogisms is beyond Boulding's Level-4 open system theory. First, there is polyphonic dialogism, the full-embodied voices expressing different logics and ideologies. Second, there is stylistic dialogism, where instead of voices what is dialogic is a multiplicity of different styles (*skaz* of everyday speech made into corporate speech, such as *Just Do It* or *I'm Lovin It*; letters to shareholders, photos, science-sounding charts and numbers, etc.). There is an orchestration of multiple styles, including in décor, in gestures that express story without words at all. Third is chronotopic dialogism. A *chronotope* is defined by Bakhtin (1981) as a relativity of time and space after Einstein. Bakhtin identified some 10 chronotopes in more dialogized novels, where a variety of chronotopes become dialogic to one another. In Wilda and Disney, there is a juxtaposition of different chronotopes (biographies, autobiographies, romantic adventure, everyday adventure, and various folkloric chronotopes). One chronotope in a narrative is not dialogic, but put several into intertextual relation, with either other narratives, with stories, or with both, and the result can be dialogic. I say *can* because it is not their being multiple or being juxtaposed but the manner in which they answer and challenge one another that makes them dialogic. Fourth is the architectonic dialogism. This was the first in the series of dialogisms that Bakhtin theorized in his career but was translated into English only more recently (Bakhtin, 1990). This is at the societal level of discourse. It is an extension of Kant's work on cognitive architectonics, by looking at how cognitive discourse interanimates with ethical and aesthetic discourses. I am interested in how the interanimation of multiple discourses is related to complexity dynamics. Story and narratives are domains of discourse. At the societal level, discourses affect the organization. Within the organization, the multiple discourses are affected by and affect the embedded environment of societal discourse.

What is exciting is how the four dialogisms begin to interact or interanimate. How is it that polyphonically dialogized tellings interanimate with stylistic, chronotopic, and archetechnoic dialogisms? For it is at this level of multidialogic complexity that we begin, I believe, to explore Boulding's more complex orders of systemicity, which are beyond open systems. Indeed, if the third level (control) is first cybernetics of deviation-counteraction (or the centripetal), and the open system fourth level is deviation-amplifying (or centrifugal), that is a crude approximation of heteroglossia but still does not get us to higher orders of complexity. We (Boje & Baskin, 2005) called for a "third cybernetic revolution" in system thinking. We see possibilities of looking at what Boulding saw as image, symbol, social, and transcendental orders of complexity (Levels 6–9). I think polyphonic dialogism takes us beyond an open system, as well as mechanistic and organic frameworks, too deeply rooted in simplifying narratives. To get to image storytelling (Level 6) brings us into an examination of multistylistics. Chronotopicities or what Boulding saw as a need to look at history, symbolism, and self-reflexivity (Level 7) is another necessary move. Since Boulding saw social networks at the societal level as an even higher order of complexity (Level 8), it seems that architectonic dialogism can help us explore this level. Finally, Boulding imagined transcendental, a relation between what is knowable and what is unknowable. In my exploration of Wilda living stories, I was consciously looking at spiritualities, at what I think is a dialogism of the four dialogisms that Bakhtin imagined. I named this dialogism of dialogism the *polypi* (Boje, 2005).

The critical antenarratological method is about the dialogic manner of the living story, it is multidialogicality, the interplay of not only polyphonic voices but the entire polypi of dialogisms. One-dimensional narratological methods take one way of telling a dialogically living story, such as a managerialist account, or some official way of telling. Marcuse's (1964) *One-Dimensional Man* was a reaction to ways of telling that were biased in academia to telling only the positive story. Today, that argument is very much alive. For example, in organizational development work, "appreciative inquiry" commends itself for being one-dimensional, for sticking to the positive story, labeling any critical inquiry as negative science (Srivastva & Cooperrider, 1990).

In *Tamara*, people cannot be everywhere at once, the telling morphs as we chase the living story from room to room, from place to place. A family or an organization is not a story performance on a singular stage with a stationary audience, respecting the boundary of the invisible fourth wall of the theatre. Living story fabric is thoroughly dialogized. There are many stages of distributed simultaneous story action; one must decide which rooms to enter, which doors to unlock, and which skeletons to bring out of the closet or leave in their grave. There is no such thing as common experience, no such thing as common sense; the sense is fragmented, the stories are not mostly coherent, they are mostly disputed and morphing before the ink is dry.

Dead stories are the subject of most research. These stories are dead the moment they are ripped from their performative context, repackaged into coherent tales that are put into collections, themed, or indexed. The meaning of living story is embedded in socioeconomic context. The accepted "way" of telling a living story is also contextually embedded. While academic disciplines have their definitions of what is and is not a story, the socioeconomic system has its own rules about story, who can tell a story, how a story is restoried. Each academic discipline has its own ways of researching and telling living stories. I have chosen a "critical antenarratological" approach, a mix of critical theory and my antenarrative work, a mix of several dialogisms I called *polypi complexity*.

The context of living story is more than a social network of storytellers and listeners; context is also the answerability of multiple authors, many beholders, diverse characters, and the many directors that make up the dialogically complex systemicity of the living story fabric. Wilda haunts me, just as Walt haunts Disney.

―――――――――

Consulting Editors: Claudia Mitchell and Bill Maynes

Notes

1. Bakhtin (1981, p. 152) uses the term *systematicalness* to denote unmerged parts and unfinalized wholeness—I abbreviated this to *systemicity*. Bakhtin (1973, pp. 4, 6, 12) develops unmergedness and unfinalizedness.

2. Czarniawska (2004) has relaxed her earlier traditional narrative restriction of "telling a story from beginning to end in front of an enchanted and attentive audience" (p. 38) looking at terse telling.

3. Boje (2005) is a set of interviews about Wilda conducted on August 8, 2003; the current chapter expands the analysis with interviews transcribed on June 2005.

4. The poem by Wilda Shelton is reprinted with permission of David M. Boje.

5. Roy Disney's Web page SaveDisney.com, as of April 17, 2006, is no longer on the Web.

6. Excerpt from Kurtzburg (2005) is reprinted with permission of ElitesTV.com.

References

Aristotle. (1954). *Rhetoric and poetics: Introduction by Friedrich Solmsen* (W. R. Roberts, Trans., Rhetoric; I. Bywater, Trans., Poetics). New York: Random House. (Original work published 350 BCE)

Bakhtin, M. (1973). *Problems of Dostoevsky's poetics* (C. Emerson, Ed. & Trans.). Manchester, UK: Manchester University Press.

Bakhtin, M. M. (1981). *The dialogic imagination: Four essays by M. M. Bakhtin* (M. Holquist, Ed.). Austin: University of Texas Press.

Bakhtin, M. M. (1990). *Art and answerability* (M. Holquist & V. Liapunov, Eds.; V. Liapunov, Trans.; Notes: K. Brostrom, Suppl. Trans.). Austin: University of Texas Press.

Barge, K. J. (2004, Spring). Antenarrative and managerial practice. *Communication Studies.*

Barry, D. (1997). Telling changes: From narrative family therapy to organizational change and development. *Journal of Organizational Change Management, 10*(1), 30–46.

Berg, P. (2005). *Amble toward contingent congress.* Retrieved June 24, 2005, from www.planet drum.org/amble.htm

Boje, D. M. (1991). The storytelling organization: A study of storytelling performance in an office supply firm. *Administrative Science Quarterly, 36,* 106–126.

Boje, D. M. (1995). Stories of the storytelling organization: A postmodern analysis of Disney as "Tamara-land." *Academy of Management Journal, 38*(4), 997–1035.

Boje, D. M. (2000). Phenomenal complexity theory and change at Disney. *Journal of Organizational Change Management, 13*(6), 558–566.

Boje, D. M. (2001). Narrative methods for organizational and communication research. London: Sage.

Boje, D. M. (2002). *Critical dramaturgical analysis of Enron antenarratives and metatheatre.* Plenary keynote presented at the 5th International Conference on Organizational Discourse: From Micro-Utterances to Macro-Inferences, July 24–26, 2002, London.

Boje, D. M. (2005). Wilda. *Journal of Management Spirituality & Religion, 2*(3), 342–364, 399–405. (With accompanying commentaries by Eduardo Barrera, Heather Höpfl, Hans Hansen, David Barry, Gerald Biberman, Robin Matthews, & John W. Bakke, pp. 365–398)

Boje, D. M. (in press-a). The antenarrative cultural turn in narrative studies. In M. Zachry & C. Thralls (Eds.), *The cultural turn: Communicative practices in workplaces and the professions.* Amityville, NY: Baywood.

Boje, D. M. (in press-b). *Storytelling organization.* London: Sage. Online version retrieved April 17, 2006, from http://business.nmsu.edu/~dboje/690/book

Boje, D. M., Alvarez, R. C., & Schooling, B. (2001). Reclaiming story in organization: Narratologies and action sciences. In R. Westwood & S. Linstead (Eds.), *The language of organization* (pp. 132–175). London: Sage.

Boje, D. M., & Baskin, K. (2005). Emergence of third cybernetics. *Emergence: Complexity and Organization Journal, 7*(3–4), v–viii.

Boje, D. M., Enríquez, E., González, M. T., & Macías, E. (2005). Architectonics of McDonald's cohabitation with Wal-Mart: An exploratory study of ethnocentricity. *Critical Perspectives on International Business Journal, 1*(4), 241–262.

Boje, D. M., & Rosile, G. A. (2003). Life imitates art: Enron's epic and tragic narration. *Management Communication Quarterly, 17*(1), 85–125.

Boje, D. M., Rosile, G. A., Durant, R. A., & Luhman, J. T. (2004). Enron spectacles: A critical dramaturgical analysis. *Organization Studies, 25*(5), 1–24. (Special issue on Theatre and Organizations edited by Georg Schreyögg and Heather Höpfl)

Boulding, K. E. (1956). General systems theory: The skeleton of science. *Management Science, 2*(3), 197–208.

Clair, R. P. (1993). The use of framing devices to sequester organizational narratives: Hegemony and harassment. *Communication Monographs, 60,* 113–136.

Clair, R. P. (1994). Resistance and oppression as a self-contained opposite: An organizational communication analysis of one man's story of sexual harassment. *Western Journal of Communication, 58,* 235–262.

Clair, R. P. (1996). Discourse and disenfranchisement: Targets, victims, and survivors of sexual harassment. In E. Berlin Ray (Ed.), *Communication and the disenfranchised: Social health issues and implications* (pp. 313–327). Hillsdale, NJ: Lawrence Erlbaum.

Clair, R. P. (1997). Organizing silence: Silence as voice and voice as silence in the narrative exploration of the treaty of New Echota. *Western Journal of Communication, 61*(3), 315–337.

Collins, D., & Rainwater, K. (2005). Managing change at Sears: A sideways look at a tale of corporate transformation. *Journal of Organizational Change Management, 18*(1), 16–30.

Czarniawska, B. (1997). *Narrating the organization: Dramas of institutional identity.* Chicago: University of Chicago Press.

Czarniawska, B. (1998). *A narrative approach to organization studies.* Qualitative Research Methods, No. 43. Thousand Oaks, CA: Sage.

Czarniawska, B. (2004). *Narratives in social science research.* London: Sage.

Derrida, J. (1994). *Specters of Marx* (P. Kamuf, Trans.; Introduction by B. Magnus & S. Cullenberg). New York: Routledge.

Disney, R. (2003, January 12). Text of Roy Disney's resignation letter. *USA Today.* Retrieved June 24, 2005, from www.usatoday.com/money/media/2003-12-01-disney-letter_x.htm

Disney, R. E., & Gold, S. P. (2005). The mice on Disney's board. *Los Angeles Times.* Retrieved April 17, 2006, from www.shamrock.com/pages/media/media_press_ 03_17_05.asp

Disney Press Release. (2005, March 13). *Robert A. Iger named chief executive officer of the Walt Disney Company.* Retrieved July 29, 2005, from http://corporate.disney.go.com/news/corporate/2005/2005_0313_iger_ceo.html

Disney's Hong Kong workers learning to "have a magical day." (2005). *Tai Pei Times.* Retrieved June 28, 2005, from www.taipeitimes.com/News/biz/archives/2005/04/17/2003250847 (Reprinted and AP released April 17)

Elle, C., Verrier, R., & Bates, J. (2005, February 8). *Tempers flare over "DisneyWar."* Retrieved July 30, 2005, from http://msnbc.msn.com/id/6934818

Gabriel, Y. (2000). *Storytelling in organizations: Facts, fictions, and fantasies.* London: Oxford University Press.

Georges, R. (1980). A folklorist's view of storytelling. *Humanities in Society, 3*(4), 317–326.

Gross, D. (2004, February 4). *The haunted mansion: How Michael Eisner continues to hang on at Disney.* Retrieved June 24, 2005, from http://slate.msn.com/id/2094923

Horkheimer, M., & Adorno, T. W. (1972). *Dialectic of enlightenment* (J. Cumming, Trans.). New York: Herder & Herder. (Original work published 1944)

Kurtzberg, B. (2005). *Disney ousts Eisner, Robert Iger to take over October 1. ElitesTV.* Retrieved July 29, 2005, from www.elitestv.com/pub/2005/Mar/EEN423516d4d7653.html

Marcuse, H. 1964. *One-dimensional man: Studies in the ideology of advanced industrial society.* Boston: Beacon Press.

McCarthy, M., & Levin, G. (2005, March 13). For Iger, no easy task at Disney. *USA Today.* Retrieved July 29, 2005, from www.usatoday.com/money/media/2005-03-13-iger-inside_x.htm

Pondy, L. R. (1976). *Beyond open system models of organization* (Working paper). Champaign-Urbana: University of Illinois.

Pondy L. R. (1978). Leadership as a language game. In M. W. McCall & M. M. Lombardo (Eds.), *Leadership: Where else can we go?* (pp. 87–99). Durham, NC: Duke University Press.

Pondy, L. R., & Mitroff, I. (1979). Beyond open system models of organization. In B. Staw (Ed.), *Research in organizational behavior* (Vol. 1., pp. 3–39). Greenwich, CT: JAI Press.

Rosile, G. A. (1998, April). *Restorying for strategic organizational planning and development: The case of the sc-fi organization.* Paper presented to the International Academy of Business Disciplines, Postmodern Organization Theory Track, San Francisco.

Sellers, P. (2005, March 7). The two faces of Bob Iger. *Fortune.* Retrieved July 29, 2005, from www.mutualofamerica.com/articles/Fortune/March2005/Fortune.asp

Society of Mayflower Descendants in the Commonwealth of Pennsylvania. (2005). *Mayflower passenger list.* Retrieved July 10, 2005, from www.sail1620.org/joinus_passenger_list.shtml

Srivastva, S., & Cooperrider, D. L. (Eds.). (1990). *Appreciative management and leadership.* San Francisco: Jossey-Bass.

Stein, G. (1935). *Narration: Four lectures* (Introduction by Thornton Wilder). Chicago: University of Chicago Press.

Stewart, J. (2005). *Disney war.* New York: Simon & Schuster.

Thompson, S. (1946). *The folktale.* New York: Dryden Press.

Toelken, B. (1996). The icebergs of folktale: Misconception, misuse, abuse. In C. L. Birch & M. A. Heckler (Eds.), *Who says? Essays on pivotal issues in contemporary storytelling* (pp. 35–63). Little Rock, AR: August House.

TwoTrees, K. (1997). *Stories with mind.* Session presented at the International Academy of Business Disciplines Conference, Postmodern Organization Theory Track, April 1997. Available from http://scmoi.org

Van Maanen, J. (1991). The smile factory: Work at Disneyland. In P. J. Frost, L. F. Moore, M. R. Louis, C. C. Lundberg, & J. Martin (Eds.), *Reframing organizational culture* (pp. 58–76). Newbury Park, CA: Sage.

Vickers, M. H. (2005). Illness, work and organization: Postmodern perspectives, antenarratives and chaos narratives for the reinstatement of voice. *Tamara: Journal of Critical Postmodern Organization Science.* Available from http://findarticles.com.

von Bertalanffy, L. (1956). General systems theory, general systems. *Yearbook of the Society for the Advancement of General System Theory, 1,* 1–10.

von Bertalanffy, L. (1962). General system theory: A critical review. *General Systems, 7,* 1–20.

White, H. (1973). Metahistory*: The historical imagination in nineteenth-century Europe.* Baltimore: Johns Hopkins University Press.

White, H. (1978). *Topics of discourse: Essays in cultural criticism.* Baltimore: Johns Hopkins University Press.

White, H. (1987). *The content of the form: Narrative discourse and historical representation.* Baltimore: Johns Hopkins University Press.

White, M., & Epston, D. (1990). *Narrative means to therapeutic ends.* New York: W. W. Norton.

PART IV

Narrative Inquiry in the Professions

The following chapters make visible the promise of narrative inquiry in the professions. We view professions as they are enacted, spoken, and expressed and are invited to see each profession not as a disembodied activity but as a part of the world of those who participate in it. Narrative inquiry allows access to professional craft and experiential knowledge otherwise invisible to those outside the occupation, allowing for the complexities of life in these professions to be preserved in the research product.

Such research focuses on the particular, not just on generalizations, facilitating knowing about these professions without sifting all the information through a single filter. The researchers in these chapters are part of the inquiry, so we are presented with interactive stories instead of being shown "data" collected by an unseen author, with stark lines between the interpreter and the interpreted.

Freema Elbaz-Luwisch provides an overview of 25 years of narrative inquiry into the lives and practice of K–12 teachers. She tells the story of narrative inquiry from its beginning, through various plot twists, and provides a map for these journeys of understandings. Elbaz-Luwisch points to potential pitfalls and trouble spots as well as the reward of designing research projects that overcome such pitfalls. Finally, she reminds us that "narrative inquiry remains unfinished and unfinishable business," and calls attention to the importance of reflecting on our practices as researchers as well as the practices of the teachers with whom we study.

Barbara Czarniawski describes the evolution of narrative inquiry in business and organizational studies from its beginnings in the early 1970s, when similarity was sought through stories "plotted along the same lines," to its current concern with the complexities involved. She offers insight into ways in which narrative inquiry allows access to "the drama of organizational power and resistance" and "the emotional life of organizations" and provides the interpretive frames necessary for understanding such complexities.

Cheryl Mattingly offers an overview of narrative inquiry into the lives and practices of health professionals, reminding us of the relationship between narrative and experience, which "serves as a moral aesthetic underlying clinical action." Drawing on literature from anthropology and philosophy, she describes "healing as a locally situated, socially complex, and embodied narrative act" and provides, as an example, the narrative of a single session of occupational therapy enacted by Tania, a 5-year-old diagnosed with brain cancer, her mother, Celeste, and their occupational therapist, Leslie.

Catherine Kohler Riessman and Jane Speedy explore narrative inquiry in three fields: social work, counseling, and psychotherapy. They remind us of important questions that the narrative inquirer should address. "For whom was this story constructed, how was it made, and for what purpose? What cultural discourses does it draw on—take for granted? What does it accomplish?" The authors argue that narrative inquiry differs from other forms of discourse in its emphasis on "sequence and consequence . . . *how* and *why* events are storied, not simply the content to which language refers."

These chapters allow us entry into the lives, practices, and knowledge of the professions studied and provide models for those wishing to understand other professions and the lives, experience, and knowledge of those who live the narratives of those professions.

—*Barbara Morgan-Fleming*

CHAPTER 14

Studying Teachers' Lives and Experience

Narrative Inquiry Into K–12 Teaching

Freema Elbaz-Luwisch

Over the past 25 years, a significant body of narrative inquiry has been produced studying the lives of teachers and the practice of teaching in K–12 settings around the world. These studies are diverse in their choice of the particular narrative methods used, in their substantive focus, and in the conceptualizations that guide the inquiry; a comprehensive review of this extensive body of work would be a daunting task. The present chapter sets itself a more modest, but possibly also more useful, project: that of drawing one map to guide the reader through this complex and changing territory. The development of narrative ways of studying what goes on in classrooms and with the teachers who spend their lives there has been, for many researchers, a challenging and unique research journey. The present chapter will retrace this journey, beginning with an examination of the precursors of narrative inquiry in classrooms and early studies using narrative methods to examine teaching, continuing with a look at how the field has established itself through selected examples of narrative studies with diverse foci, and concluding with a critical examination of some of the questions to be confronted by narrative researchers of teaching in the future. Thus, the chapter will sketch out the journey with scenes from the past, present, and possible futures of narrative inquiry in classrooms from kindergarten through elementary, junior, and high school.

Before the Story Begins

The development of a narrative understanding of teaching follows directly from the realization that teachers are central to the development of curriculum and pedagogy. This understanding, so clear today in the light of research on teaching from a narrative perspective, was not self-evident in the history of the study of teaching and developed over time through insights gleaned from a diverse range of studies. Early research on teaching in the 1960s and 1970s examined the psychology of teaching using the conceptual lenses of that discipline; researchers asked about the personality of the "good" teacher, about the reasons for entering teaching or leaving it, about which teachers had difficulties with classroom discipline and why. One of the main goals of such research was to enable policy makers to select the most appropriate candidates for the profession, those whom personality tests deemed "most likely to succeed" as teachers. These aspirations were not realized, however, and it is not difficult to dismiss this type of research as contributing little to our current understanding of teaching. However, some early studies did look at aspects of teaching that have been taken up from a narrative perspective on teaching. For example, Jersild (1955/1970) asked questions about the personal difficulties and dilemmas faced by teachers; his themes of anxiety, fear, helplessness, loneliness, meaninglessness, and hostility were invoked by Cole (1997) and found to be most apt for looking at how teachers in her graduate course experienced their work in the profession and why the development of reflection in teaching was not fostered in the schools. An early study by Ada Abraham (1972) also looked at the inner lives of teachers, in this case from a psychodynamic perspective; however, Abraham wrote in French and in Hebrew, and her work was not known among English-speaking researchers on teaching.

Although this early work on teaching might have had something to say about how to begin to study the ways in which teachers lived their lives in classrooms, such research was criticized for being vague and "soft" and for contributing little to the improvement of teaching. These critiques helped to fuel the next development, the "scientific study of the art of teaching" (Gage, 1978) in what came to be termed the process-product mode. It is easy to view the process-product research on teaching in a negative light, stressing that it too failed to take teachers and their work seriously and this limited its usefulness in contributing to work in classrooms (Bolster, 1983). Indeed, much of the research on classroom teaching processes and the resulting outcomes in terms of student achievement only served to validate common-sense understandings of teaching. However, this research can be seen to highlight the importance of zeroing in on well-chosen episodes of classroom interaction, and in this respect, it prefigures some of the narrative work that was to come later.

During the heyday of the scientifically oriented study of teaching, Schwab was also developing his conceptualization of education and, more particularly, of curriculum as practical endeavors. With the concept of "practical deliberation" (Schwab, 1978), drawing on Aristotle and Dewey, he envisioned a dialogic view of curriculum development in which teachers would take part as practitioners fully knowledgeable about their students and about life and work in classrooms. Schwab's objection to the classic conception of educational research had already been elaborated in an early paper that exposed "the corruption of education by psychology" (Schwab, 1958). Through these writings, Schwab was probably the first educational theorist to call for close attention to the lived experience of children and teachers in classrooms. He also conceived the scientific text as, in effect, a type of narrative, formulating a distinction between texts that provided a rhetoric of conclusions and those that, less commonly, offered a narrative of discovery. Somewhat later on, narrative research began to develop in psychology, as Bruner (1986) and other psychologists (Lieblich 1978, 1981; Polkinghorne, 1988; Sarbin, 1986; Spence, 1982) took the narrative turn, indirectly contributing to the warrant for narrative research in education.

Beginnings: Early Studies of Teachers' Knowledge, Lives, and Life Stories

Understanding teaching requires that we pay attention to teachers both as individuals and as a group, listening to their voices and the stories they tell about their work and their lives. Narrative research on teaching has proceeded from the assumption that teachers' knowledge itself has a storied form (Carter, 1993; Elbaz, 1991; Gudmundsdottir, 1991) and is developed out of teachers' stories about their work and their dialogues with one another, with pupils, with teaching materials, and with themselves. Because of the concern for lived experience, narrative inquiry typically begins with a focus on individual teachers and their personal understandings. However, the understanding of the individual cannot be fully realized without a simultaneous consideration of context: Not only the place of the individual biography within a wider historical story but also the embeddedness of the teacher in a school and school system and its mandated curricula, ideologies, pedagogical trends, and reform processes need to be taken into account. This attention to teachers' understandings of their work began to develop in the 1970s in studies that, while not strictly narrative in character, provided a foretaste of the possibilities of understanding teaching from the inside: The work of Bussis, Chittenden, and Amarel (1976) was an interview study of American teachers' understandings of curriculum, while Marland (see MacKay & Marland, 1978) carried out a study of teachers' interactive teaching.

Responding to this new interest in teaching as teachers themselves saw and experienced it, Elbaz (1981) conducted a case study of a single teacher with a view to developing a conceptualization of the practical knowledge held and used by the teacher in her ongoing work. This study described itself as a case study with ties to the ethnography of classrooms, to grounded theory, and to the phenomenology of Schutz (Schutz & Luckmann, 1983), which had used the term *practical knowledge*, albeit in a narrow sense, to describe people's knowledge of ongoing matters in everyday life. The study examined the stories of a single teacher, Sarah, her experience in the classroom, and the knowledge that underpinned her work. The study suggested that this teacher's knowledge appeared to be organized on three different levels: (1) at its most specific level in terms of rules of practice, (2) at a midlevel of organization in terms of practical principles, and (3) holistically in terms of imagery. Although this study did not conceptualize the research on teaching in strictly narrative terms, it developed some of the methodology and ideas that would come into play in narrative research on teaching: the use of open-ended qualitative interviews, close and attentive listening to the voices of teachers, the development of grounded understanding from the texts of the interviews themselves, and attention to teachers' practical knowledge and to the ways they use imagery and metaphor to express that knowledge and make sense of their work.

Clandinin's (1985) study of two teachers in the context of an inner-city school in Toronto established a unique pattern for the developing methodology of narrative inquiry and contributed important new elements to the narrative study of teaching. First, understanding thought and action not as two clearly distinct phenomena or events that make up the work of teaching but as interconnected and complementary sides to the unified experience of the teacher, Clandinin's study blended participant observation in the classroom with ongoing conversations with the two teachers and letters written to them to raise issues that came up for the researcher as she took part in the lives of the teachers and their students in the classroom. Second, based on a respect for teachers as professionals who did not necessarily have an interest in admitting researchers into their classrooms, this study began the development of an ethic of participatory narrative inquiry: the study held that researchers should have something of value to contribute to the school and to the teachers whose classrooms they enter. In her study, Clandinin functioned as an adjunct teacher in the classrooms of Stephanie and Aileen, inevitably becoming a part of the developing story that was being told about the classrooms. Clandinin's work highlighted the teachers' images as central to an understanding of their knowledge and further emphasized the personal nature of that knowledge; her analysis followed the threads of the developing narrative that were being woven throughout the teachers' accounts of their work, of classroom events, and of happenings in their personal lives.

Another early narrative account of teaching that I have found particularly helpful in demonstrating (especially to students who are new to narrative inquiry) the power of close attention to the everyday realities and happenings of the classroom for developing an understanding of teaching is provided in Connelly and Clandinin (1986). This text offers a narrative account of the work of two seventh-grade science teachers. In observing the work of one of the teachers, Bruce, a number of occurrences were noted in Bruce's teaching that, from the perspective of science teaching, would hardly appear to be best practice: Bruce sometimes dictated notes to the students, which they copied into their notebooks; on various occasions, he told students not to bother with technical terms that came up in the course of the biology lesson. Connelly and Clandinin point out that one could easily view Bruce's teaching as conveying a conception of science as given and static knowledge and a sense of his students as having limited potential and therefore not needing a sophisticated and accurate knowledge of science. They show how a complex narrative understanding of Bruce's teaching can be constructed, grounded in many discussions with him about these and other practices, about the students and the setting of the school. On the narrative view, Bruce's concern for the future of his students, growing up in a troubled inner-city environment, is paramount: He is concerned with helping them acquire academic skills (such as note taking) that will serve them in the future and enable them to remain in school. If they do so, they will revisit biology in higher grades and have opportunities to learn the "fancy technical terms" that were passed over in Bruce's seventh-grade classroom. Bruce also draws on his own working-class origins and uses his knowledge of the neighborhood dialect to build a relationship with his students. The narrative account of Bruce's teaching connects all these diverse elements: the mandated curriculum for junior high school; Bruce's own background; his understanding of his students' needs, their lives, and their possible futures; and his sense of possibilities and limitations of time and resources. It is a complex and nuanced account, which moves quickly away from the misunderstandings that a superficial look at Bruce's classroom would have generated, and in so doing still teaches a great deal about how (and why) to study teaching as experienced.

The attention to the way in which teaching is structured as a narrative unfolding through time is further developed in Clandinin and Connelly (1986), which elaborates the notion of rhythm in teaching. An overall conceptualization of narrative inquiry is presented in Connelly and Clandinin (1990), where the authors sketch out a two-part agenda for narrative inquiries into teaching: "We need to listen closely to teachers and other learners and to the stories of their lives in and out of classrooms. We also need to tell our own stories as we live our own collaborative researcher/teacher lives" (p. 12). Around this time, Witherell and Noddings (1991) brought together a range of work on narrative ways of knowing, telling, and enacting caring relationships in education. With Carter's (1993) statement of the place of narrative methods in the study of teaching and in the practice of teacher education (first delivered as a vice-presidential address at the American Educational Research Association annual meeting), it was clear that narrative inquiry had created a place for itself in the study of teaching.

The Plot Thickens: Diverse Directions for Narrative Studies of Teaching

Narrative studies of teaching have burgeoned since the early work sketched above (see, e.g., Clandinin & Connelly, 1995; Gudmundsdottir, 1997, 2001; Jalongo & Isenberg, 1995; Lyons & Laboskey, 2002). It is not easy to categorize this body of work as it is characterized by considerable diversity, both thematic and methodological. The understanding of narrative and its contribution to educational research has evolved over the years, and there has been a profusion of writing on the methodology of narrative inquiry in education, as evidenced by the work collected in volumes by Hatch and Wisniewski (1995) and Tierney and Lincoln (1997) and the work of Bloom (1998) and Conle (1999), among others. Clandinin and

Connelly (2000) provided a definitive account of the methodology of narrative inquiry, drawing on their experience and that of many graduate student researchers studying teaching in classroom settings; this text is unique in developing a methodology for carrying out narrative research specifically in the school context.

Thematically, narrative studies of teaching have explored a wide, and often overlapping, array of themes and concepts. Studies have examined teacher identity (e.g., Connelly & Clandinin, 1999; Nias, 1985, 1993); teacher professional development as revealed through autobiographical writing (e.g., Butt & Raymond, 1989; Heikkinen, 1998; Raymond, Butt, & Townsend, 1992); life stories (e.g., Goodson, 1997; Kelchtermans, 1993) and narrative inquiry (Johnson & Golombek, 2002) as teacher research; the education and development of new and beginning teachers (Clandinin, Davies, Hogan, & Kennard, 1993; Conle, 1996; Craig, 1995; Doecke, Brown, & Loughran, 2000; Estola, 2003; Kelchtermans & Ballet, 2002; Knowles & Cole, 1994; Olson, 1995; Makela & Laine, 1998); teachers' curriculum stories and the application of narrative thinking to curriculum (e.g., Clandinin & Connelly, 1992); the concepts of voice, discourse, and multivoicedness in teaching (e.g., Britzman, 1991; Elbaz-Luwisch, Moen, & Gudmundsdottir, 2002; Marsh, 2002); teachers' stories from the perspective of diversity and multiculturalism (e.g., Phillion, He, & Connelly, 2005); and stories of teachers' knowledge and work in the school context, particularly their involvement in school reform and its impact on teachers' lives (e.g., Clandinin & Connelly, 1998).

The studies mentioned here might be characterized—by their authors or others in the field—under diverse labels: Researchers may choose to call their work autobiographical, biographical, life story, life-history research, or feminist inquiry, among other labels. I include them here because I begin thinking about the nature of a study by focusing on research activities and practical outcomes rather than on abstract labels. The studies mentioned above are among those that have contributed to the vital and ongoing task of placing the lives and stories of teachers at the forefront of inquiry into teaching and schooling; they have made the voices of teachers and their ways of speaking central to the discourse on research on teaching (see Elbaz, 1991). Each of the themes mentioned above merits detailed and in-depth attention; in lieu of that, I will discuss selected studies related to five themes: (1) curriculum stories, (2) teachers' lives and identity, (3) studies of the interaction of knowledge and context, (4) stories of change, and (5) stories of diversity in teaching. These five themes (and the particular examples selected for each) cannot of course represent all the work done by many talented researchers, but I hope they provide a sense of the scope and richness of that work.

Curriculum Stories

The narrative perspective on teaching gave rise early on to an understanding of the teacher as a maker of curriculum (Clandinin & Connelly, 1992). Johnston (1990), for example, talked to teachers about their involvement in curriculum work and suggested images that not only captured the nature of their work but implicitly influenced their development work as well as the curricular outcomes. Once we view curriculum as developed and shaped by teachers' narratives, it becomes possible to ask questions about the conditions and constraints under which teachers tell their stories. Clandinin and Connelly's (1995) work showed that cultural sacred stories play a powerful role in schooling, leading teachers to formulate and tell secret and cover stories in settings where their understandings of their work do not seem to be legitimate. This gives rise to a sense of multiple stories, interacting and sometimes conflicting; Olson (2000) conceptualized curriculum as a multistoried process.

One important elaboration of the focus on curriculum stories was provided by the work of Gudmundsdottir (1991), who studied the classroom practice of two experienced teachers of high school history through intensive observation and interview. This study was carried out within the tradition of pedagogical content knowledge studies, under the mentorship of Lee Shulman at Stanford University (a tradition that probably influenced many other narrative studies that focused on teachers' stories of curriculum in particular subject matter contexts as well). Gudmundsdottir found that the teachers' work was organized and shaped in distinctively narrative terms. Both teachers, Harry and David, felt that they needed to supplement the mandated textbooks for their subject with additional materials they had gathered from a variety of sources. Furthermore, they found that this expanded subject matter needed to be organized for teaching. Both teachers arranged and sequenced their material, prepared to teach, and indeed taught in a way that Gudmundsdottir characterized in terms of curriculum stories and "short stories."

Using Jakobson's (1956) theory of the poetic function of language as an organizing framework to conceptualize the teachers' practice, Gudmundsdottir (1991) saw the curriculum story as functioning along a "horizontal axis, providing continuity and structure to content throughout the school year," while the shorter stories that teachers tell as "explanations, illustrations or examples function like the vertical axis" (p. 208). Teaching American history, both Harry and David had drawn on story schemas as organizational devices "to transform an inadequate story into a more complete, compelling, and convincing one" (p. 212). For example, David organized his curriculum chronologically, in line with the mandated curriculum, but developed four stories, each of which took the whole school year to unfold: Women, Reform, Supreme Court Cases, and Wars. Importantly, these stories not only help to organize the curriculum in a more coherent fashion, but they also provide a "stage" for the presentation of the many interesting short stories that each teacher has gathered to help make important points and to convey matters of human and moral weight. Thus, "many of the explanations and illustrations David includes in the curriculum stories, especially his Wars story, are characterized by a distinct moral point of view, a perspective that highlights the horrors of war" (pp. 215–216). David's story of Wars is also motivated, not surprisingly, by his personal history as a peace activist. But the way in which David's experience influences his developing curriculum story is complex: Gudmundsdottir found that both David and Harry engage in the taking of multiple perspectives in their teaching, looking at "the many layers of meaning that are embedded in the interpretation of past events" (p. 216). She concludes, "There are no simple explanations and no simple solutions to historical problems in David's and Harry's classrooms. That is perhaps one of the many reasons why their stories are good" (p. 216). Another reason, no doubt, for the "goodness" of these curriculum stories is that they are anchored—albeit invisibly so—in the personal, drawing on the lived experience of the two teachers; in this particular study, the biographies of the teachers are not stressed, but it is certainly clear that their teaching is grounded in their personal resources, values, and life experience.

In later work, Gudmundsdottir gave more attention to the life stories of the teachers with whom she worked but combined this with an interest in the public story. She drew on the work of Vygotsky and activity theory to make sense of the social underpinnings to classroom organization and structure and on the work of Bakhtin to understand how teachers listen to and appropriate many voices in developing their personal understandings of teaching (Gudmundsdottir, 1995; Elbaz-Luwisch et al., 2002). On this understanding, the strength of narrative research lay in its ability to represent teachers' diverse voices, "through which the language of practice ventriloquates, a voice that does not reproduce the gendered, hierarchical, and patriarchal structure of our culture" (Elbaz-Luwisch et al., 2002, p. 216). In effect, although Gudmundsdottir did not use this formulation, one of the tasks of narrative inquiry is to enable teachers' secret stories to be heard.

Studies of Teacher Lives, Voice, and Identity

Several different lines of research have focused direct and careful attention on teachers' lives, life stories, and life histories. Within this area, the examination of teacher identity began with the work of Nias (1985, 1993), who listened with a sociologist's ear to the narrative accounts of British teachers, paying attention to themes and concerns in their stories that seemed to characterize teachers as a group as well as emerging themes that reflected changes in the profession over time. Goodson's work (1992, 1997) has had a double focus, on the one hand, advocating the importance of hearing the teacher's unique voice and, on the other, stressing the importance of historical setting and context in coming to a critical understanding of teachers' lives, transforming life story into life history. Connelly and Clandinin (1999) understand teacher identity as a storied identity, paying attention not only to how teachers tell the stories of their work but also to when, where, and to whom the stories are told.

I will focus here on the work of Estola, Erkkilä, and Syrjälä (2003) because it seems to bring together many of the concerns elaborated by other researchers: voice, storied identity, and the influence of life history on the work and careers of teachers. Their work began from a research project headed by Syrjälä, in which life stories were collected from over 100 Finnish teachers, many of whom had submitted their independently produced narratives to a public competition. The research group studied the biographies from a number of different perspectives, looking at some of the individual life stories in terms of their unique contributions (e.g., Estola & Syrjälä, 2002a) and also asking questions about the historical period in which these teachers had worked and how their life stories reflected their experience of the various reforms that the Finnish school system had undergone during that time (Estola

& Syrjälä, 2002b). Reading and rereading the life stories, the researchers were surprised to notice the theme of vocation recurring; this notion seemed to them rather old-fashioned, with religious connotations. They decided to examine closely the stories of three Finnish teachers, different in terms of age, background, and the settings in which they taught. Each of the researchers worked closely with one of the three teachers and came to know her well; the intimacy of their relationships is clearly reflected in the study. At the same time, this enabled them to come to a nuanced understanding of the concept of vocation in its historical context.

The oldest teacher, Kaija, grew up in northern Finland in the 1930s in a home where, unusually for the time, she was educated to respect and be interested in different cultures, religions, and life styles.

> When I was 12, and I had three elder brothers, we used to study the world's religions. . . . I was always there to listen when they read about Buddhism and Hinduism and African religions. That's where my tolerance comes from . . . my mother was a person who couldn't bear to see anybody persecuted. (Estola et al., 2003, p. 243)

Kaija's mother was a teacher, and she commented,

> My family is full of teachers, and at first I thought I would never want to become a teacher myself. But that's what I ended up doing after all, and I felt that teaching little children has so much more scope than being a subject teacher, for instance. (Estola et al., 2003, pp. 242–243)

Given Kaija's background and the times in which she grew up, it is perhaps not surprising to find her speaking about vocation, and the same might be said for the second teacher, Inkkeri, who grew up in the postwar period. For the third teacher, Tiina, however, the story is different: "I decided to become a teacher after some eventful episodes . . . this idea to become a teacher was really not a youthful dream" (Estola et al., 2003, p. 245). Tiina grew up in a small northern town, reared by her grandmother. When she was at school in the 1970s, comprehensive schooling came into effect in Finland, and for Tiina, "education was no longer an opportunity, but rather an obligation. Although she got good marks, she began to be absent from school with increasing regularity" (Estola et al., 2003, p. 246). Tiina later studied at a trade school and became a hairdresser. It was only when her son encountered learning problems that Tiina began to contemplate becoming a teacher.

> After his first year at school, my son still couldn't read. He wanted to, and we bought lots of books, but he just couldn't, and I wasn't able to help him. During the summer that followed, my son and I did a lot of exercises that the teacher had given him. We worked for a full hour every day. Just think about it, an eight-year-old boy doing those exercises all summer long . . . in the fall, he handed in all the exercises he had done to his teacher. And the teacher didn't even check them. She just gave them back the following day. And I know

that she didn't look at them, because there were many mistakes in the papers. (Estola et al., 2003, p. 246)

Shocked by this experience, Tiina too has come to speak in the language of vocation (a concept that is, by implication, absent from the story of her son's teacher):

The more I think about it and the more time I spend at school, the more I feel that this will be my vocation. It must be the greatest change that has ever happened in me—the feeling that I am heading in the right direction. (Estola et al., 2003, pp. 245–246)

Estola et al.'s (2003) account brings three unique teachers into view and allows us to hear their distinctive ways of telling their stories. We also learn about Finnish society and the history of the educational system as it influenced the life stories of these women and the elaboration of their identities as teachers. However, the issue of vocation is a broader issue that has relevance for the study of teaching around the world. The discourse on vocation can still be heard in the stories of many teachers, but it is often in conflict with other discourses—those on professionalism, standards, high-stakes testing. In the narratives presented by the authors, the sense of vocation is strong and can be seen in terms of a moral horizon that orients the work of all three teachers. Their study focuses on the moral voice of the three teachers and on how the concept of vocation interacts with the notion of moral voice; as such, it has important implications for teacher education and teacher development. It would also be interesting to look for those places in teacher narratives where the discourse on vocation may be in conflict with the competing discourse on professionalism and to see how a teacher's life story can be told when it is torn by conflicting allegiances and appears on a rockier moral horizon, shaped by discourses that do not agree.

Studies of the Interaction of Knowledge and Context

Like all qualitative inquiry, narrative method is necessarily sensitive to context. In narrative studies of teaching, however, the attention to context has been given a unique and critical focus by the metaphor of professional knowledge landscape, introduced into the literature by Clandinin and Connelly (1995, 1996). This metaphor reflects the understanding of teaching as a profession grounded in knowledge, which has been a feature of the narrative study of teaching from its beginnings and has helped to shape our understanding of teaching as a profession. The metaphor of landscape broadens this understanding of teachers' knowledge by calling attention to the wider contexts—social, cultural, political, and historical— within which the knowledge of teaching originates, is shaped, and is brought to use (see Greene, 1995, for a profound rendering of the complexities of the intellectual landscape of teaching). As Clandinin and Connelly emphasize, the term landscape invites a consideration of place, time, and relationships among various agents, of interactions that play out over time on the landscape. The notion of a knowledge landscape reminds us that teaching is a minded practice, an intellectual activity shaped by the various discourses at work in society in a given period; equally, it is a moral practice concerned with realizing the values and ends-in-view of the teacher for the benefit of students.

Clandinin and Connelly (1995, 1996) pioneered the development of a language that enables discussion of the complexity of the professional knowledge landscape of teaching, showing how it is shaped by sacred stories passed down in the culture at large and the school system more directly about what constitutes knowledge, what learning and teaching should look like, and how schools should conduct their business. In response to these sacred stories, teachers learn to censor their own stories and tell cover stories; thus, teachers come to talk about their practice in the public forum in ways that accord with the official perspective, while inside their classrooms or in relationships of trust with researchers, they tell their stories in ways that express their personal understandings of the experiences and relationships lived out in their classrooms. Within this conceptual framework, Craig (1995) began an exploration of the way in which knowledge communities develop in schools, enabling teachers to learn and grow professionally as they tell and retell their stories of practice with colleagues. Olson (1995) highlights the narrative authority that teachers develop when they are able to discuss their work with like-minded colleagues willing to sustain a conversation. Working together, Olson and Craig (2001) draw out the almost necessary connections between the concepts of knowledge community and narrative authority, showing how teachers' narrative authority inevitably develops in the context of a community. The concepts of the professional knowledge landscape, knowledge community, and narrative authority have particular significance for teachers and schools in the context of reform efforts, as the next section shows.

Stories of Change

The understanding of school change and how it can be brought about has been pursued most fruitfully through narrative inquiry. Conle (1997) invokes a range of images of change drawn from fields such as art and architecture, as well as from nature. The slowly changing natural landscape and the gradual processes of change and aging in the human body both have something to teach us about changes in schooling. These images are characterized by ongoing and gradual development, by complexity, by embeddedness in context, and by layering of different levels of change. Conle piles images one upon another like an artist building up an effect in a painting or collage, suggesting that no one image alone is adequate to capture everything that needs to be said about educational change or school reform. She holds with MacIntyre (1984) that change itself has a narrative quality, coming about "when practitioners are on a quest to find the goods inherent in a practice, as well as in lives and traditions" (Conle, 1997, p. 216).

Looking narratively at teachers' experiences of reform has produced a range of illuminating accounts. For example, Casey (1992) studied the stories of women teachers from different backgrounds working for social change, to try to understand what enabled them to continue and what caused them to give up. Walsh, Baturka, Smith, and Colter (1991) illustrate through a single case how teaching identities are always much broader than what is implicated in any given reform. Craig's (2003) work, in particular, highlights the way in which the complexities of the professional knowledge landscape have an impact on teachers' experiences of reform. Kelchtermans (2005) draws together several strands when considering teachers' participation in educational reform, particularly with respect to emotion: Teachers' self-understandings and the vulnerability of their positions within schools, especially under conditions of reform, have to be taken into account, and these aspects are uniquely accessible through teachers' narratives and biographies. In the Israeli context, a life-story study of Muslim women teaching in the Arab sector who had been involved in leading innovative projects in their schools was carried out by Hertz-Lazarowitz and Shapira (2005), highlighting the particular cultural circumstances that mediate the possibilities of innovation for these teachers.

Building on this work, I examined the life stories of two teachers involved in school change processes (Elbaz-Luwisch, 2005; Elbaz-Luwisch et al., 2002) to learn from their stories about the limits and possibilities of reform in the Israeli school system and beyond. Here, I focus on the story of Yael. In her thirties, Yael grew up in a family with a tradition of volunteering and social involvement, had been active in a socialist youth organization, and eventually joined a kibbutz. Yael taught in a kibbutz elementary school, where she initiated a program for gender equality. In the interview, Yael first reviewed the different phases of her life quickly; while talking about her work, she sometimes backtracked to reminisce and elaborate on events from childhood. The form portrays Yael in the midst, sometimes sketching the main lines of the story, sometimes filling in details.

She tells how she heard about a project on gender equality run by the Ministry of Education and the Women's Lobby:

> I said O.K., we will join that. . . . I went ahead to a meeting, and when I had to introduce myself, I told them who I was and said "I'm going to force you to do this project in our school." That's how I introduced myself, the height of nerve ("hutzpah") . . . but the fact is, things started rolling. (Elbaz-Luwisch, 2005, p. 154)

Yael seems to quickly and confidently invite others to enter into a knowledge community with her, where other teachers might continue in more conventional forms of teacher communication (Craig, 2004). When a decision was made not to involve parents more in the project, Yael did not agree: "I think our community is ready for this, and even if two or three parents complained, there would have been a debate and that is legitimate, it's meaningful" (Elbaz-Luwisch, 2005, pp. 155–156). On Yael's professional knowledge landscape, one should note the kibbutz movement tradition of open discussion whereby difficulties are examined and problems solved communally. Yael sees debate, and even conflict, as valuable and legitimate and doesn't want everyone to simply do as she says.

While the importance of enacting a curriculum that is relevant to her pupils is self-evident for Yael, her story embodies dialogue on diverse curriculum issues, with teachers, parents, and pupils:

Anything that gets the children's attention, I easily go in that direction—if a child comes with something from the news, something about values, that belongs to everyday living, or if there's a problem in class, it attracts me much more than teaching another unit in arithmetic. (Elbaz-Luwisch, 2005, p. 158)

Yael's work in the gender equality program also reflects an ongoing curricular dialogue that mediates changes in the school's programs:

The idea of "Mothers' Day" always bothered me, and I wouldn't do it in my class, I had "Family Day" and I remember that people were very angry with me because I was the only one who refused to invite the mothers . . . today no one would even think of celebrating only "Mothers' day." (Elbaz-Luwisch, 2005, p. 154)

Among the many changes taking place in the school related to gender equality, Yael mentions discussions during Bible lessons: "This year they taught the Creation differently than every other year, about the creation of woman. They taught about two stories of creation" (Elbaz-Luwisch, 2005, p. 154).

Yael's personal and professional lives are also in dialogue, as she interweaves stories of family and career. She is sensitive to the difficulties posed by the equality program for teachers:

For some people it's threatening . . . to see that I am making mistakes, it's scary . . . how am I raising my children with respect to this? It's very personal . . . afterwards the teachers go home and live together on the kibbutz and sometimes one chairs a committee that deals with the other one's child or husband . . . so they're very sensitive to that. (Elbaz-Luwisch, 2005, p. 155)

Yael's views on the issue of gender equality developed gradually. Early on, she thought that *one should choose on the basis of ability and not male/female.* Later, she came to the understanding that if women were not supported in their political and other aspirations, they would not be represented.

I noticed the women were not there, in politics. I had a friend who ran for a position with the Youth Wing of the party, and it really bothered me when people asked her, How can you do it when you have a baby daughter? Running against her was a man who also had a baby, and no one even raised the question. (Elbaz-Luwisch, 2005, p. 153)

Yael steadily became more involved in working for equality of opportunity for women and came to a broader view of the issues:

It's more correct to talk about equality of opportunity . . . in the State of Israel, in the whole world, everyone should have an equal chance to develop and get to wherever they want . . . you can't say, I want equality between the sexes but not between races, or between Ashkenazim and Sephardim, or Arabs and Jews. (Elbaz-Luwisch, 2005, pp. 153–154)

Despite her assertive, sometimes spontaneous, and perhaps "irrational" use of power, Yael seems to hold and enact an underlying "theory of change." She says that it takes someone who is a little crazy ("*meshugaat ladavar*") to take on a change project and also believes that timing is important: The change needs to arrive at a propitious moment, when the school is searching for something.

It is apparent that Yael is deeply involved in the philosophy and worldview of socialist and kibbutz ideology, which ground and organize her thinking. This philosophy, combined with her temperament, leads Yael to work hard and be involved rather than watching from the sidelines; she believes in her ideas and wants to influence others. The fact that she has a clear and compelling set of beliefs to guide her educational work makes her stand out in comparison with many teachers who find themselves torn between the conflicting alternatives that characterize postmodern times. Despite her single-mindedness, diverse voices can be heard in Yael's story, even voices usually associated with teacher resistance, but these appear only occasionally. Speaking the same language as her colleagues may boost Yael's credibility—she is not seen as "holier than thou." However, she is also aware that she "will not be a teacher forever . . . it seems to me too difficult, and one's patience wears thin after a while" (Elbaz-Luwisch, 2005, p. 153). A year or so after the interviews, Yael began working as a teacher-advisor for the Gender Equality program.

Bakhtin's (1981) distinction between authoritative discourses and internally persuasive discourses helps to make sense of Yael's story. Authoritative discourse "demands that we acknowledge it, that we make it our own; it binds us, quite independent of any power it might have to persuade us internally . . . its authority was already acknowledged in the past" (p. 342). Internally persuasive discourse, however, "is denied all privilege, backed up by no authority at all, and is frequently not even acknowledged in society" (p. 342) yet "is of decisive significance in the evolution of an individual consciousness" (p. 342). In these terms, Yael can be seen as living and working within the confines of an authoritative discourse, yet it is a discourse that is also highly internally persuasive for her. Thus, she gains power and confidence from accepting the dictates of an authoritative discourse, but her story also elaborates a debate with received knowledge, and challenging aspects of the authoritative discourse is energizing for her. This perhaps begins to explain why Yael does not seem to experience the kind of conflict between her own stories and those of the school system that appear elsewhere in the literature, which portrays the professional knowledge landscape of teaching as marked by wide gaps and inevitable tensions between the sacred stories of schooling and the stories told and valued by teachers in their classrooms and communities.

The dialogic, multivocal nature of Yael's story and the way it lives out a coherent (if partial) theory of change suggest important considerations to be taken into account by those working on school change. Furthermore, it speaks to Conle's

(1997) point that change occurs "when practitioners are on a quest to find the goods inherent in a practice, as well as in lives and traditions" (p. 216). Yael's case resonates with the work on knowledge communities and narrative authority (Olson & Craig, 2001), and like other narrative studies of reform (e.g., Craig, 2001, 2003), it illustrates the potential of a single case for illuminating wider issues.

The ultimate purpose of narrative inquiry into schooling is the restorying of practice on both the individual and the school levels. Thus, many narrative researchers see their task as one of working in close collaboration with practitioners to bring forth, elaborate, and reflect together on stories of schools and classrooms, both stories told by teachers themselves and those told by others in the school and its milieu (Clandinin & Connelly, 1996, 1998). Working closely with practitioners to understand their experience of reform highlights the importance of the professional knowledge landscape on which teachers work and interact and that necessarily has an impact on how reform processes are played out (Craig, 2003). This is what can make narrative inquiry a form of intervention and an influence in making schools better places—places where teachers can communicate their ideas openly, reflect and learn together, and cooperate to write new stories of teaching. Narrative inquiry does not prescribe in advance the directions or substantive content of change, but in envisioning this kind of change, it is clearly not neutral or indifferent to what happens in schools.

Stories of Diversity in Teaching

In an early critique of studies of teaching from an insider's perspective, Clark (1986) expressed the concern that researchers had a tendency to study teachers who were too much like themselves. He suggested that researchers were inclined to work with successful and articulate teachers, who were predisposed to be thoughtful and reflective about their work. This tendency to study what one already knows is not surprising given that narrative research depends heavily on the establishment of good rapport and trust between researcher and participants—trust that may, we imagine, be easier to establish with participants who are like oneself, who come from the same social and cultural context as the researcher. However, while this tendency may have characterized narrative studies early on, researchers have since discovered the intrinsic interest as well as the challenges and rewards of working across social, cultural, and other boundaries.

My personal awakening to the value and importance of stories of diversity in teaching came from reading Oberg and Blades (1990), who present the story of Tom, a Canadian teacher whose story traced the development of his career in what appears at first to be a "culture-free" context. Tom was a reflective and thoughtful teacher who initially followed the curricular prescriptions laid down by the authorities; paying close attention to experience, he gradually asked more and more questions. Toward the end of his story, Tom is a principal in a small rural school attended by diverse students. He has a critical encounter with a student from a First Nations background, a boy who has just lost the grandfather who had been his parent, mentor, and friend. Tom, who we understand has not experienced this kind of relationship in his own life and cultural context, has to stretch to understand the boy's feelings but in doing so attains new insights into his own values as an educator.

Rereading this story today, I recall the feeling of excitement I experienced vicariously as Tom's mind was opened up by the encounter with a child from a culture different from his own. In studies of diversity in classrooms, the narrative approach is particularly powerful. Studies of the narratives of immigrant teachers, for example, hold significant potential for understanding schooling and teaching for all students and teachers through a process that sets in motion the interaction of the strange with the familiar. Seeing how immigrant teachers tell their stories of becoming teachers in a new environment teaches us about schooling in the "host" culture and allows new questions to be asked about that culture and its arrangements for learning and teaching. Phillion's (2002) study of multicultural education through the narrative of a teacher who is an immigrant to Canada illustrates vividly how the encounter with this teacher, Pam, forces Phillion to question her own preconceptions about good multicultural education. A study of the life stories of immigrant teachers in Israel (Elbaz-Luwisch, 2004) similarly brought to the fore many questions about the meaning of being a teacher and of belonging in Israel. Craig (2004) discusses the case of two African American teachers who engage in discussion of a painful episode during the desegregation of schools in their district. This case highlights some of the ways in which members of a particular teacher community tell and understand the stories of their experience, ways that can be understood by a listener (such as Craig herself) who listens carefully from inside a knowledge community context but may not be understood at all by other teachers who have not been part of the process of negotiating knowledge through ongoing participation in telling and listening to shared stories.

In these studies, the researcher's reflective involvement in the study is crucial (whether or not the researcher is an immigrant). It is apparent that Feuerverger's (2001) experience as an immigrant to Canada animates her inquiry into a Jewish-Palestinian village in Israel; her own childhood longing for a sense of place and belonging help her, and us, to reach a deeper understanding of the setting she studies. The same is true for the work of He (2003), who tells her own story as one of three interwoven stories of Chinese women teachers in Canada. He (2005) eventually comes to see her own experience as being in between in a complex, nuanced way: She describes it as a "cross-cultural movement between landscapes that are themselves moving" (p. 1) as she negotiates her place in between China and North America, in between diverse intellectual traditions and historical moments. This "in-betweenness" puts her in a unique place as a researcher learning about the lives of her participants, Chinese immigrant students and their families who are also living lives in between.

In the context of teacher education in situations of cultural diversity, working with narrative provides unique possibilities. Listening to the life stories of fellow students enables a process of resonance to take place as prospective teachers respond to one another's stories (Conle, 1996; Conle, Li, & Tan, 2002; Elbaz-Luwisch, 2001). This may allow prospective teachers to undergo what Nieto (1999) conceptualizes as "a process of personal transformation based on their own identities and experiences . . . [and to] engage in a collaborative and imaginative encounter to transform their own practices and their schools" (pp. 175–176).

Sleeter (2001) points to the usefulness of narrative research in studying multicultural teacher education because it "situates teacher education experiences in the life of a teacher educator, a teacher, or a student. It enables teacher educators to connect strategies or observations with examined life experiences and to communicate emotions" (p. 238). Narrative in this case is both a powerful pedagogical approach and a particularly appropriate mode of studying the process of becoming a teacher.

Narrative studies of schooling have also focused on children from diverse backgrounds, enabling a rich and contextualized understanding of their experience that makes it possible to adapt teaching practice to the needs of the children. Barone's (1989) study of the school experience of a boy named Billy Charles Barnett is both a memorable account of a unique individual and a narrative that poses hard questions about the purposes of schooling in a competitive technological culture that leaves little room for other modes of living. Carger (1996) studies the education of Mexican immigrants in the United States; drawing on her different voices as teacher, ethnographer, and friend of the family, she makes it possible for the reader to experience vicariously the struggles of one family and their son, Alejandro, thereby coming to a better understanding of a group. Moen (2005) studied the work of a Norwegian teacher named Ann and two of her pupils who can be described as having special needs. Kyratzis and Green (1997) looked closely at an elementary-school classroom, focusing on the joint construction of narratives by teacher and students. These studies have good stories to tell about children in classrooms, but more important perhaps, they point the way to taking children seriously and taking seriously the small events of their lives, which often have momentous importance for the future; they also allow us to see and become sensitive to diversity in settings we might otherwise have regarded as mainstream.

Toward Stories of Transformation: Possibilities and Difficulties Facing Narrative Inquiry in the Future

Narrative inquiry into classroom teaching is now well established and does not lack for topics and sites to be studied further. However, a number of critical questions face narrative inquiry and will have to be confronted by researchers in the future. These questions concern the process of narrative inquiry as a collaborative, ongoing process carried out in school settings; the invention and legitimization of new forms for representing teaching and of presenting research texts, in particular to understand and represent teaching as embodied; and the ever-present political issues that attend narrative inquiry.

Process, Roles, and Relationships

One of the central questions that arises when one considers the development of narrative inquiry in K–12 settings concerns the possibility of establishing narrative inquiry in schools as part of the ongoing development work of the school and as a format for the continuing professional development of teachers. The work carried out by Clandinin and Connelly (1986, 1992, 1995, 1996, 1998) and graduate-student researchers at Bay Street School is a singular example of a productive and ongoing collaboration over many years between a school, its staff and community, and an academic community of researchers. This work is at one end of a continuum of collaborative efforts, an example in which the school found ways to make time and place for the research process even as the academic researchers learned to find a satisfactory place for themselves within the ongoing life of the school. In the literature, however, this kind of full-fledged cooperative work is relatively rare. For many narrative researchers the extent of collaboration with teachers and schools is more limited—ideally, confined to doing no harm. The researcher strives to be sensitive to the needs and concerns of teacher participants, invites their comments on the texts of interviews, and perhaps even opens the way for their participation in interpretation of the texts. Often, however, the researcher finds that teachers are satisfied with minimal involvement in the research process, perhaps even uninterested in the eventual product. A typical example is the account by Bloom (1998), whose participants—female educational administrators—took the research process seriously, viewed the interviews as part of their own work, and included them in their schedules but still did not understand the researcher's interest in a long-term cooperative venture. As Gudmundsdottir (2001) reminds us, teachers lead busy and complex lives, they care about their students and their careers, and it is not self-evident that participation in narrative research projects can contribute to the diverse purposes they have formulated for themselves.

Narrative researchers acknowledge all this and strive to take it into account in formulating our research intentions. We should not ignore the fact that researchers also lead complex lives, organized around their own sets of priorities and timelines. Teaching and departmental responsibilities, the pressures of publication, promotion and tenure reviews, all create constraints that militate against full participation in teachers' lives (assuming we are genuinely invited to do so), and against conducting collaborative inquiry. We should also guard against the "stage-managing" of a Hollywood-style collaborative inquiry in which teachers may have an interest in playing a role for a short time. I would argue that collaborative inquiry is an important goal and ideal to be held up, but that each particular inquiry may fall short in different ways depending on the unique situation; this is not necessarily a fault of the inquiry but rather a feature of the complicated reality of academics and school people trying to work together. And as Gudmundsdottir (2001) suggests, perhaps it is incumbent on researchers to exercise their interpretive authority: Once the phase of participation in the school life, interviewing, and gathering of data is completed, the next phase (even if there is an overlap)—analysis and interpretation of the texts of interviews, observation reports, and other documents and the writing process—is the researcher's job, not the teacher's.

Inventing New Forms for Narrative Inquiry

Like other genres of qualitative inquiry, narrative studies confront a range of problems resulting from the difficulty of presenting a complex, layered, and dynamic reality within the limited framework of a journal article or other academic publication. The field has progressed significantly since the days when stringent limits on the length of published articles made publication of narrative studies difficult. But there are still many challenges to the process of adequately representing what has been learned from a narrative inquiry.

First, narrative inquiry remains an unfinished and unfinishable business: Even if a project is relatively long-term, researchers step in and out of school settings, coming away with stories that are always incomplete and partial. This can be frustrating for the researcher, who has to tell a story that lacks a satisfying ending; it can also be damaging to the research relationships, as the researcher leaves, moving on to other projects and interests, while school participants continue grappling with their problems (Nespor & Barber, 1995). However, the reality of life in schools is that it is both ongoing and constantly interrupted: Classes, exams, interesting discussions, and even episodes of misbehavior and loss of control are inevitably interrupted by the bell. Teachers in most schools get to know their pupils for only a year, while many teachers in higher grades hardly get to know their students at all as they move from class to class. Educational processes are fundamentally nonlinear, unpredictable, and even mysterious; this may be difficult for researchers to accept, but teachers are often comfortable with this characteristic of their work, as Lydia, an Israeli teacher of English near retirement says. Lydia sometimes receives letters from former students or meets them in the street: "You look at his face and you see a man, you've forgotten the boy but he reminds you and tells you certain things, incidents that happened. These kinds of things give us a good feeling" (Elbaz-Luwisch, 2005, p. 63). This suggests that the task for narrative researchers is to find ways of telling open-ended narratives in a manner that is compelling and illuminating. Narrative researchers can learn from post-modern fiction and journalism in this regard.

Second, narrative inquirers are increasingly becoming aware of the multi-voiced nature of teaching, as well as the multisensual nature of teaching and learning (Erikson, 1985). These qualities are what make for the excitement of studying teaching and learning from a narrative perspective. Yet they pose particular challenges for narrative inquiry. Johnson (1989) called attention to the embodied nature of teacher knowledge, yet too little has been done to represent this aspect of teaching. For this to happen, it is necessary to "feel one's way into schooling"—in other words, the researcher must first allow himself or herself to experience the research topic with all the senses, for only then can the topic be fully understood. In Estola and Elbaz-Luwisch (2003) the researchers tried to draw on their own bodily experience as researchers and teacher educators to better understand the stories of Finnish and Israeli teachers about their bodily understandings of teaching. Zembylas (2003) explores emotion as one of the resources used in the crafting of teacher identity and suggests taking a post-modern perspective on the emotions and how they come into play in the ways that "teachers are emotionally engaged in forming their identities" (p. 215) in social, cultural, and historical contexts and in light of power relations (see also Kelchtermans, 1996). Taking into consideration a complex view of teaching that privileges body, feeling, and emotion as well as thinking, planning, and acting, it is incumbent on the researcher to find new ways to express and represent more adequately what has been learned (Denzin, 1995); the use of dialogues and read-ers' theater, poetry, photo essays, and other visual and graphic materials can serve in this task. Phillion's (2002) evocative account of her personal experience with Japanese and West Indian music is one example: an account of a researcher tak-ing a risk to portray her process of coming to an understanding of the culture and background of her research participant in an innovative and moving way. Sweetland, Huber, and Keats Whelan (2004) use an innovative format of parallel texts, responding to and interrogating one another to display and, in effect, to constitute the narrative interlappings of a collaborative research process charac-terized by tensions around difference—the different emotions, life experiences, and concerns that each of the three researchers/graduate students brought to their joint work. Chang and Rosiek (2003) draw on a sonata form to tell the com-plex and nuanced story of a Hmong teacher's encounter with the traditional beliefs of a student in his English as a second language (ESL) science class; the story skillfully weaves together the literature on education and colonialism, his-torical background, classroom events, and personal experience to create a seam-less and compelling narrative that traces the teacher's deep engagement with the issues raised by an encounter with one of his students. These new formats are sometimes challenging for the reader, perhaps because of their main strength: These complex texts resist closure, refuse simple or univocal readings, and insist on holding conflicts and complexities up for examination.

The Personal and the Political in Narratives of Teaching and Schooling

Teacher knowledge is deeply personal, so research that studies teaching from a narrative perspective has no choice but to go in close. In upsetting the tradi-tional separation between researcher and research subject, this challenges the persisting gap between the private and the public. Focusing on the personal has been a problematic undertaking in research in education and teaching (Elbaz-Luwisch, 1997); in so many cases, "the biography of the researcher and the influence this has on the text tends to have been neglected" (Packwood & Sikes, 1996, p. 341).

Taubman (2002) discusses the importance for educators engaged in multicul-tural and antiracist education of examining their personal investments in their work. Among reasons for an avoidance of the personal, he points out that "to look at the personal, to begin to face the provisionality and contingency of identity, is to surrender the security of stable identities" (p. 99). Further, it is difficult to examine the personal because "we have yet to develop a public language to describe the personal that does not dissipate into psychologisms or unexamined narratives, or reduce our experience to some sociopolitical script" (p. 99). In the current climate of yet another return to basics, with a focus on standards and high-stakes testing and calls for the development of *evidence-based practice,* the need for a convincing public language in which to speak about the lived personal experience of people in schools is particularly acute. Narrative inquiry has already made a significant contribution to the development of such a public language, but much more work is needed, and the task is a long-term one.

One reflection of the general unease with the personal is the criticism that has been leveled against narrative work as glorifying given practices and being insufficiently critical (Hargreaves, 1996). The criticism touches on a genuine dilemma in narrative research—listening to research participants with respect precludes one-sided judgment of their work—and calls on researchers to examine closely their own assumptions and biases. One finds examples of this in He (2003), Phillion (2002), Feuerverger (2001), and Carger (1996), among many others. One hopes that in a situation of cooperation and trust, the research participants will also be led to examine their assumptions and biases, but this may not happen. If the researcher is committed to not overriding the participant's story with an academic story that is more politically correct, the only option may be to invent a multivocal narrative that gives free play to all the voices, including those that are unexamined and uncritical. As suggested by Gudmundsdottir (2001), "We may not be able to dismantle our culture's patriarchy, but we have an opportunity to rid interpretative research of its narrative coercion" (pp. 236–237).

Coda

This chapter has traced the development of narrative research on teaching in K–12 classrooms, providing an account that inevitably leaves out many interesting avenues of inquiry and spotlights others. It is hoped that the account serves to highlight the pleasure and intellectual excitement that come from looking closely at classrooms and at the lives led by the teachers and students inside them. The main challenges to be confronted in the future stem from the nature of narrative inquiry as personal, engaged inquiry that seeks to share the experience of life in classrooms, learn from it directly, and represent it in ways that are respectful of participants, faithful to the nature of their experience, and useful to practitioners in furthering the good of their students. Based on the achievements of the diverse forms of narrative inquiry to date, much remains to be discovered in the years to come.

Consulting Editors: Michael Samuel and Cheryl Craig

References

Abraham, A. (1972). *Le monde intérieure des enseignants.* Paris: Epi Editeurs.

Bakhtin. (1981). *The dialogical imagination: Four essays by M. M. Bakhtin* (M. Holquist, Ed.). Austin: University of Texas Press.

Barone, T. (1989). Ways of being at risk: The case of Billy Charles Barnett. *Phi Delta Kappan, 71*(2), 147–151.

Bloom, L. (1998). *Under the sign of hope: Feminist methodology and narrative interpretation.* Albany: State University of New York Press.

Bolster, R. (1983). Towards a more effective model of research on teaching. *Harvard Educational Review, 53,* 239–265.

Britzman, D. P. (1991). *Practice makes practice: A critical study of learning to teach.* Albany: State University of New York Press.

Bruner, J. (1986). *Actual minds, possible worlds.* Cambridge, MA: Harvard University Press.

Bussis, A. M., Chittenden, E., & Amarel, M. (1976). *Beyond surface curriculum: An interview study of teachers' understandings.* Boulder, CO: Westview Press.

Butt, R., & Raymond, D. (1989). Studying the nature and development of teachers' knowledge using collaborative autobiography. *International Journal of Educational Research, 13*(4), 403–419.

Carger, C. L. (1996). *Of borders and dreams: A Mexican-American experience of urban education.* New York: Teachers College Press.

Carter, K. (1993). The place of story in research on teaching and teacher education. *Educational Researcher, 22*(1), 5–12.

Casey, K. (1992). Why do progressive women activists leave teaching? Theory, methodology and politics in life-history research. In I. G. Goodson (Ed.), *Studying teachers' lives* (pp. 187–208). London: Routledge.

Chang, P. J., & Rosiek, J. (2003). Anti-colonialist antinomies in a biology lesson: A sonata-form case study of cultural conflict in a science classroom. *Curriculum Inquiry, 33*(3), 251–290.

Clandinin, D. J. (1985). Personal practical knowledge: A study of teachers' classroom images. *Curriculum Inquiry, 15*(4), 361–385.

Clandinin, D. J., & Connelly, F. M. (1986). Rhythms of teaching: The narrative study of teachers' personal practical knowledge of classrooms. *Teaching and Teacher Education, 2*(4), 377–387.

Clandinin, D. J., & Connelly, F. M. (1992). The teacher as curriculum maker. In P. W. Jackson (Ed.), *Handbook of research on curriculum: A project of the American Educational Research Association* (pp. 363–401). New York: Macmillan.

Clandinin, D. J., & Connelly, F. M. (1995). *Teachers' professional knowledge landscapes.* New York: Teachers College Press.

Clandinin, D. J., & Connelly, F. M. (1996). Teachers' professional knowledge landscapes: Teacher stories—stories of teachers—school stories—stories of school. *Educational Researcher, 19*(5), 2–14.

Clandinin, D. J., & Connelly, F. M. (1998). Stories to live by: Narrative understandings of school reform. *Curriculum Inquiry, 28*(2), 149–164.

Clandinin, D. J., & Connelly, F. M. (2000). *Narrative inquiry: Experience and story in qualitative research.* San Francisco: Jossey-Bass.

Clandinin, D. J., Davies, A., Hogan, P., & Kennard, P. (Eds.). (1993). *Learning to teach, teaching to learn: Stories of collaboration in teacher education.* New York: Teachers College Press.

Clark, C. (1986). Ten years of conceptual development in research on teacher thinking. In M. Ben Peretz, R. Bromme, & R. Halkes (Eds.), *Advances of research on teacher thinking* (pp. 7–20). Lisse, Netherlands: Swets & Zeitlinger.

Cole, A. (1997). Impediments to reflective practice: Toward a new agenda for research on teaching. *Teachers and Teaching: Theory and Practice, 3*(1), 7–27.

Conle, C. (1996). Resonance in preservice teacher inquiry. *American Educational Research Journal, 33*(2), 297–325.

Conle, C. (1997). Images of change in narrative inquiry. *Teachers and Teaching: Theory and Practice, 3*(2), 205–219.

Conle, C. (1999). Why narrative? Which narrative? Struggling with time and place in life and research. *Curriculum Inquiry, 29*(1), 7–32.

Conle, C., Li, X., & Tan, J. (2002). Connecting vicarious experience to practice. *Curriculum Inquiry, 32*(4), 429–452.

Connelly, F. M., & Clandinin, D. J. (1986). On narrative method, personal philosophy and narrative unities in the study of teaching. *Journal of Research in Science Teaching, 23*(3), 15–32.

Connelly, F. M., & Clandinin, D. J. (1990). Stories of experience and narrative inquiry. *Educational Researcher, 19*(5), 2–14.

Connelly, F. M., & Clandinin, D. J. (Eds.). (1999). *Shaping a professional identity: Stories of educational practice.* New York: Teachers College Press.

Craig, C. J. (1995). Knowledge communities: A way of making sense of how beginning teachers come to know. *Curriculum Inquiry, 25*(2), 151–175.

Craig, C. J. (2001). The relationships between and among teachers' narrative knowledge, communities of knowing, and school reform: A case of "the monkey's paw." *Curriculum Inquiry, 31*(3), 303–331.

Craig, C. J. (2003). Characterizing the human experience of reform in an urban middle school context. *Journal of Curriculum Studies, 35*(5), 627–648.

Craig, C. J. (2004). Shifting boundaries on the professional knowledge landscape: When teacher communications become less safe. *Curriculum Inquiry, 34*(4), 395–424.

Denzin, N. (1995). The experiential text and the limits of visual understanding. *Educational Theory, 45*(1), 7–18.

Doecke, B., Brown, J., & Loughran, J. (2000). Teacher talk: The role of story and anecdote in constructing professional knowledge for beginning teachers. *Teaching and Teacher Education, 16*(3), 335–348.

Elbaz, F. (1981). The teacher's practical knowledge: Report of a case study. *Curriculum Inquiry, 11*(1), 43–71.

Elbaz, F. (1991). Research on teachers' knowledge: The evolution of a discourse. *Journal of Curriculum Studies, 23*(1), 1–19.

Elbaz-Luwisch, F. (1997). Narrative research: Political issues and implications. *Teaching and Teacher Education, 13*(1), 75–83.

Elbaz-Luwisch, F. (2001). Personal story as passport: Storytelling in border pedagogy. *Teaching Education, 12*(1), 81–101.

Elbaz-Luwisch, F. (2004). Immigrant teachers: Stories of self and place. *International Journal of Qualitative Studies in Education, 17*(3), 387–414.

Elbaz-Luwisch, F. (2005). *Teachers' voices: Storytelling and possibility.* Greenwich, CT: Information Age.

Elbaz-Luwisch, F., Moen, T., & Gudmundsdottir, S. (2002). The multivoicedness of classrooms: Bakhtin and narratives of teaching. In H. Heikkinen, R. Huttunen, & L. Syrjälä (Eds.), *Biographical research and narrativity* (pp. 197–218). Jyväskylä, Finland: SoPhi Press.

Erikson, J. M. (1985). Vital senses: Sources of lifelong learning. *Boston University Journal of Education, 167*(3), 85–96.

Estola, E. (2003). Hope as work: Student teachers constructing their narrative identities. *Scandinavian Journal of Educational Research, 47*(2), 181–203.

Estola, E., & Elbaz-Luwisch, F. (2003). Teaching bodies at work. *Journal of Curriculum Studies, 35,* 1–23.

Estola, E., Erkkilä, R., & Syrjälä, L. (2003). A moral voice of vocation in teachers' narratives. *Teachers and Teaching: Theory and Practice, 9*(3), 239–256.

Estola, E., & Syrjälä, L. (2002a). Love, body and change: A teacher's narrative reflections. *Reflective Practice, 3*(1), 53–69.

Estola, E., & Syrjälä, L. (2002b). Whose reform? Teachers' voices from silence. In R. Huttunen, H. Heikkinen, & L. Syrjälä (Eds.), *Narrative research: Voices of teachers and philosophers* (pp. 177–195). Jyväskylä, Finland: SoPhi Press.

Feuerverger, G. (2001). *Oasis of dreams: Teaching and learning peace in a Jewish-Palestinian village in Israel.* New York: RoutledgeFalmer.

Gage, N. L. (1978). *The scientific basis of the art of teaching.* New York: Teachers College Press.

Goodson, I. F. (1992). Sponsoring the teacher's voice: Teachers' lives and teacher development. In A. Hargreaves & M. Fullan (Eds.), *Understanding teacher development* (pp. 110–121). London: Cassell/New York: Teachers College Press.

Goodson, I. F. (1997). The life and work of teachers. In B. J. Biddle, T. K. Good, & I. F. Goodson (Eds.), *International handbook of teachers and teaching* (pp. 135–152). Dordrecht, Netherlands: Kluwer.

Greene, M. (1995). *Releasing the imagination: Essays on education, the arts, and social change.* San Francisco: Jossey-Bass.

Gudmundsdottir, S. (1991). Story-maker, story-teller: Narrative structures in curriculum. *Journal of Curriculum Studies, 23*(3), 207–218.

Gudmundsdottir, S. (1995). The narrative nature of pedagogical content knowledge. In H. McEwan & K. Egan (Eds.), *Perspectives on narrative and teaching* (pp. 24–38). New York: Teachers College Press. Retrieved from www.svt.ntnu.no/ped/sigrun/publikasjoner/PCKNARR.html

Gudmundsdottir, S. (1997). Introduction to the theme issue on "Narrative Perspectives on Research on Teaching and Teacher Education." *Teaching and Teacher Education, 13*(1), 1–3.

Gudmundsdottir, S. (2001). Narrative research on school practice. In V. Richardson (Ed.), *Fourth handbook for research on teaching* (pp. 226–240). New York: Macmillan.

Hargreaves, A. (1996). Revisiting voice. *Educational Researcher 25*(1), 12–19.

Hatch, A. J. H., & Wisniewski, R. (Eds.). (1995). *Life history and narrative.* London: Falmer Press.

He, M. F. (2003). *A river forever flowing: Cross-cultural lives and identities in the multicultural landscape.* Greenwich, CT: Information Age.

He, M. F. (2005 April). *In-between China and North America.* Paper presented at a symposium on Narratives of Chinese Immigrant Students' and Teachers' Cross-Cultural Experience, AERA Annual Meeting, Montreal, Quebec, Canada.

Heikkinen, H. (1998). Becoming yourself through narrative: Autobiographical approach in teacher education. In R. Erkkilä, A. Willman, & L. Syrjälä (Eds.), *Promoting teachers' personal and professional growth* (pp. 111–131). Oulu, Finland: Oulu University Press.

Hertz-Lazarowitz, R., & Shapira, T. (2005). Muslim women's life stories: Building leadership. *Anthropology and Education Quarterly 36*(2), 51–67.

Jakobson, R. (1956). *Fundamentals of language* (Janua Linguarium, Series Minor, I). The Hague, Netherlands: Mouton.

Jalongo, M. R., & Isenberg, J. P. (1995). *Teachers' stories: From personal narrative to professional insight.* San Francisco: Jossey-Bass.

Jersild, A. T. (1970). *When teachers face themselves.* New York: Teachers College Press. (Original work published 1955)

Johnson, K. E., & Golombek, P. R. (Eds.). (2002). *Narrative inquiry as professional development.* New York: Cambridge University Press.

Johnson, M. (1989). Embodied knowledge. Personal practical knowledge series. *Curriculum Inquiry, 19*(4), 361–377.

Johnston, S. (1990). Understanding curriculum decision-making through teacher images. *Journal of Curriculum Studies, 22*(5), 463–471.

Kelchtermans, G. (1993). Getting the story, understanding the lives: From career stories to teachers' professional development. *Teaching and Teacher Education, 9*(5/6), 443–456.

Kelchtermans, G. (1996). Teacher vulnerability: Understanding its moral and political roots. *Cambridge Journal of Education, 26,* 307–324.

Kelchtermans, G. (2005). Teachers' emotions in educational reforms: Self-understanding, vulnerable commitment and micro-political literacy. *Teaching and Teacher Education, 21*(8), 995–1006.

Kelchtermans, G., & Ballet, K. (2002). Micropolitics in teacher induction: A narrative-biographical study on teacher development. *Teaching & Teacher Education, 18*(1), 105–120.

Knowles, J. G., & Cole, A. L. (1994). Through preservice teachers' eyes: Exploring field experiences through narrative and inquiry. New York: Macmillan.

Kyratzis, A., & Green, J. (1997). Jointly constructed narratives in classrooms: Co-construction of friendship and community through language. *Teaching and Teacher Education, 13*(1), 17–37.

Lieblich, A. (1978). *Tin soldiers on Jerusalem beach.* New York: Pantheon Books.

Lieblich, A. (1981). *Kibbutz Makom: Report from an Israeli kibbutz.* New York: Pantheon Books.

Lyons, N., & Laboskey, V. K. (Eds.). (2002). *Narrative inquiry in practice: Advancing the knowledge of teaching.* New York: Teachers College Press.

MacIntyre, A. (1984). *After virtue.* Notre Dame, IN: University of Notre Dame Press.

MacKay, D., & Marland, P. W. (1978, April). *Thought processes of teachers.* Paper presented at the annual meeting of the American Educational Research Association, Toronto, Canada.

Makela, M., & Laine, T. (1998). Student teachers' personal and professional development from a biographical perspective. In R. Erkkila, A. Willman, & L. Syrjälä (Eds.), *Promoting teachers' personal and professional growth* (pp. 132–147). Oulu, Finland: Oulu University Press.

Marsh, M. M. (2002). The shaping of Ms. Nicholi: The discursive fashioning of teacher identities. *Qualitative Studies in Education, 15*(3), 333–347.

Moen, T. (2005). Activity genre, a theoretical construct in the studying of inclusive teaching practice. *Teachers and Teaching: Theory and Practice, 11*(3), 257–272.

Nespor, J., & Barber, L. (1995). Audience and the politics of narrative. In J. A. Hatch & R. Wisniewski (Eds.), *Life history and narrative* (pp. 49–62). London: Falmer Press.

Nias, J. (1985). Reference groups in primary teaching: Talking, listening and identity. In S. Ball & I. F. Goodson (Eds.), *Teachers' lives and careers.* Lewes, UK: Falmer Press.

Nias, J. (1993). Changing times, changing identities: Grieving for a lost self. In R. G. Burgess (Ed.), *Educational research and evaluation* (pp. 139–156). London: Falmer Press.

Nieto, S. (1999). *The light in their eyes: Creating multicultural learning communities.* New York: Teachers College Press.

Oberg, A., & Blades, C. (1990). The spoken and the unspoken: The story of an educator. *Phenomenology and Pedagogy, 8,* 161–180.

Olson, M. (1995). Conceptualizing narrative authority: Implications for teacher education. *Teaching and Teacher Education, 11*(2), 119–135.

Olson, M. (2000). Curriculum as a multistoried process. *Canadian Journal of Education, 25*(2), 169–187.

Olson, M. R., & Craig, C. J. (2001). Opportunities and challenges in the development of teachers' knowledge: The development of narrative authority through knowledge communities. *Teaching & Teacher Education, 17*(6), 667–684.

Packwood, A., & Sikes, P. (1996). Adopting a postmodern approach to research. *International Journal of Qualitative Studies in Education, 9*(3), 335–345.

Phillion, J. (2002). Narrative multiculturalism. *Journal of Curriculum Studies, 34*(3), 265–279.

Phillion, J., He, M. F., & Connelly, F. M. (2005). *Multicultural education: Narrative and experiential approaches.* Thousand Oaks, CA: Sage.

Polkinghorne, D. (1988). *Narrative knowing and the human sciences.* Albany: State University of New York Press.

Raymond, D., Butt, R., & Townsend, D. (1992). Contexts for teacher development: Insights from teachers stories. In A. Hargreaves & M. Fullan (Eds.), *Understanding teacher development.* London: Cassell/New York: Teachers College Press.

Sarbin, T. (Ed.). (1986). *Narrative psychology: The storied nature of human conduct.* New York: Praeger.

Schutz, A., & Luckmann, T. (1983). *The structures of the life-world.* (R. Zaner & H. T. Engelhardt, Jr., Trans.). Evanston, IL: Northwestern University Press.

Schwab, J. J. (1958). On the corruption of education by psychology. *School Review, 66,* 169–184.

Schwab, J. J. (1978). The practical: Arts of eclectic. In I. Westbury & N. J. Wilkof (Eds.), *Science, curriculum, and liberal education: Selected essays* (pp. 322–364). Chicago: University of Chicago Press.

Sleeter, C. (2001). Epistemological diversity in research on preservice teacher preparation for historically underserved children. *Review of Research in Education, 25,* 209–250.

Spence, D. (1982). *Narrative truth and historical truth: Meaning and interpretation in psychoanalysis.* New York: W. W. Norton.

Sweetland, W., Huber, J., & Keats Whelan, K. (2004). Narrative inter-lappings: Recognizing difference across tension. *Reflective Practice, 5*(1), 47–77.

Taubman, P. (2002). Facing the terror within: Exploring the personal in multicultural education. In C. Korn & A. Bursztyn (Eds.), *Rethinking multicultural education: Case studies in cultural transition* (pp. 97–129). Westport, CT: Bergin & Garvey.

Tierney, W. G., & Lincoln, Y. S. (Eds.). (1997), *Representation and the text: Re-framing the narrative voice.* Albany: State University of New York Press.

Walsh, D. J., Baturka, N. L., Smith, M. E., & Colter, N. (1991). Changing one's mind—maintaining one's identity: A first-grade teacher's story. *Teachers College Record, 93*(1), 73–86.

Witherell, C., & Noddings, N. (1991). *Stories lives tell: Narrative and dialogue in education.* New York: Teachers College Press.

Zembylas, M. (2003). Emotions and teacher identity: A poststructural perspective. *Teachers and Teaching: Theory and Practice, 9*(3), 213–238.

CHAPTER 15

Narrative Inquiry in and About Organizations

Barbara Czarniawska

Before demonstrating to the readers the variety of uses of the narrative approach in organization studies, I will shortly sketch the route by which this approach reached organization scholars. Sometime in the early 1970s, the interest in narrative spread beyond literary theory to the humanities and social sciences. William Labov and Joshua Waletzky (1967) espoused and improved on Vladimir Propp's formalist analysis of Russian folk tales, suggesting that sociolinguistics should analyze simple narratives, which will eventually provide a key to understanding the structure and function of complex narratives. Hayden White shocked his fellow historians by claiming that there can be no discipline of history, only of historiography, as the historians emplot the events into histories, instead of *finding* them (White, 1973). The sociologist Richard Harvey Brown (1977), in a peculiar act of parallel invention, spoke of *a poetics for sociology*, unaware that Mikhail Bakhtin had postulated it before him (Bakhtin & Medvedev, 1928/1985).

By the end of the 1980s, the trickle became a stream. The political scientist Walter R. Fisher (1984, 1987) pointed out the central role of narrative in politics and of narrative analysis in his discipline. Donald E. Polkinghorne (1987) did the same for the humanities, especially psychology, where Jerome Bruner (1986, 1990) initiated a strong narrative interest. Deirdre McCloskey (1990) scrutinized the narrative of economic expertise.

In organization studies, it is usual to evoke Burton R. Clark's (1972) study of three U.S. colleges, although Clark is not an organization scholar himself. In all these places (Reed, Antioch, and Swarthmore), he discovered a story in circulation that was rooted in history, claimed unique accomplishment, and was held in warm regard by the group that was recalling it. He called these stories organizational sagas.

All three sagas fulfilled the same (symbolic) function, but they differed in plot. The Reed College saga told the story of creative acts performed by a pioneer-like leader in an (educational) desert. The Antioch College saga was the story of an established organization in deep crisis, saved by a utopian reformer. The Swarthmore College saga was a story of a successful organization that was in danger of succumbing to complacency until rescued by a leader sensitive to the winds of change. The sagas were used as a means of self-management, as it were, strengthening the collegial feeling among the employees.

Ian I. Mitroff and Ralph H. Killman (1975) gave their article a title that sounded provocative at the time: "Stories Managers Tell: A New Tool for Organizational Problem Solving." By the 2000s, their prediction has become a matter-of-fact description: The Danish hi-fi producer Bang and Olufsen used for a long time a self-description "a story-telling company" on their homepage, and consultant Stephen Denning (2005) best-sold his *The Leader's Guide to Storytelling: Mastering the Art and Discipline of Business Narrative.* The managerial fashion of using narratives as a management tool awaits its chronicler, but it might be too early to depict its spreading and its local variations.

Organizational stories have become a legitimate topic of management and organization studies[1] in the 1980s, as exemplified by a well-known article "The Uniqueness Paradox in Organizational Stories" by Joanne Martin, Martha S. Feldman, Mary Jo Hatch, and Sim B. Sitkin (1983). This text makes it obvious that organization studies have passed through the "Ma, look, there is a story!" period (Solow, 1988); the authors systematically analyze organizational stories as a cultural manifestation. Inspired by Clark's study, they demonstrate how such stories, intended to depict the unique character of a company, are in fact plotted along the same lines. This point prefigured a focus on organizational storytelling that will characterize organization studies in the late 1990s, to which I will return later. Here, it is enough to say that in the last two decades the narrative approach to organization studies has flourished and became varied to a point where some categorization is necessary.

It is possible to see various uses of narrative and its analysis in organization studies as extending from the field of practice—the field of management and organizing that we study—to the field of theory, that is, our own practice. Following the chronology of a research project, a list of such uses might look as follows (adapted from Czarniawska, 1999, p. 22):

Studying a field of practice (management and organizing):

Watching how the stories are being made

Collecting the stories

Provoking story telling

Working with the field material:

  Interpreting the stories (what do they say?)

  Analyzing the stories (how do they say it?)

  Deconstructing the stories (unmake them)

Constructing organization theory:

  Putting together one's own story

  Setting it against/together with other stories

In what follows, I shall provide examples of all these. While some—for example, close readings of novels—existed before the narrative turn took place in social sciences, others, such as deconstruction, have clearly appeared because of it. All in all, one could say that organization practitioners and scholars found themselves in a Molièresque situation: Like Mr. Jourdain in *The Miser*, who always talked prose without knowing it, they always heard and told stories without noticing it. The narrative turn in social sciences focused their attention on what was badly seen because it was taken for granted.

Field of Practice as a Site of a Narrative Production, Circulation, and Consumption

How Stories Are Being Made

David Boje (1991) took inspiration from studies of Harvey Sacks (1992) and his followers, who investigated the occurrence of stories in conversations.[2] One context especially rich for the story-carrying conversation was, he observed, a work organization:

> In organizations, storytelling is the preferred sensemaking currency of human relationships among internal and external stakeholders. People engage in a dynamic process of incremental refinement of their stories of new events as well as on-going interpretations of culturally sacred story lines. When a decision is at hand, the old stories are recounted and compared to an unfolding story line to keep the organizations from repeating historically bad choices and to invite the repetition of past successes. In a turbulent environment, the organization halls and offices pulsate with a story life of the here and now that is richer and more vibrant than the firm's environments.
>
> Even in stable times, the story is highly variable and sometimes political, in that part of the collective processing involves telling different versions of stories to different audiences. . . . Each performance is never the completed story; it is

an unraveling process of confirming new data and new interpretations as these become part of an unfolding story line. (Boje, 1991, p. 106)

Boje thus set out to record everyday conversations in a large office-supply firm that he was studying to capture spontaneous storytelling episodes. His findings concerned two aspects of storytelling: (1) how they occur in conversations and (2) in what way they are used. As far as the first aspect is concerned, Boje discovered that storytelling in contemporary organizations hardly follows the traditional pattern of a narrator telling a story from the beginning to the end in front of an enchanted and attentive audience. Narrators told their stories in bits and pieces and were often interrupted, sometimes for the purpose of complementing the story and sometimes for aborting the storytelling. As for the uses to which stories were put, Boje classified them into pattern finding, pattern elaboration, and pattern fitting. This classification exemplifies well Karl Weick's (1995) insights concerning sense-making. A story is a frame—a frame that emerges and is tried out, a frame that is developed and elaborated, or a frame that can easily absorb the new event.

Boje's studies (1991, 2001) show that the line between "story making" and "story collecting," topics of two separate sections in this chapter, is very thin, if it exists at all. Also, although Boje's and other studies that I will present here were done in workplaces, storytelling is not limited to such sites. Family is an obvious site for telling stories, as are playgroups and various associations. Stories can also be told after work, as is the case in Julian E. Orr's (1996) ethnography of the work of technicians who repair copying machines. Although employed by a big corporation, the technicians practically ignored the company. They conceived their job as a work practice rather than a relation of employment and hierarchy and, consequently, as an individual, challenging task, made possible by a supportive community. The community was a context where work stories were swapped and where the collective knowledge was produced, maintained, and distributed. Orr (1996) concluded that

the skilled practice of field service work [is] necessarily improvised . . . , and centered on the creation and maintenance of control and understanding. Control and understanding are achieved through a coherent account of the situation, requiring both diagnostic and narrative skills. Understanding is maintained through circulation of this knowledge by retelling the narratives to other members of the community, and this preservation of understanding contributes to the maintenance of control. (p. 161)

Orr (1996) was very clear on one point: The stories are not about work; they are the work of the technicians, even though they may create other outcomes:

When technicians gather, their conversation is full of talk about machines. This talk shows their understanding of the world of service; in another sense, the talk creates that world and even creates the identities of the technicians themselves. But neither talk nor identity is the goal of technicians' practice. The goal is getting the job done, keeping the customers happy, and keeping the machines running. (p. 161)

The technicians' stories were not *organizational stories*—that is, stories that tell about organizing events that already came to a completion; they were stories that organize (Czarniawska & Gagliardi, 2003)—that is, stories that are a part of the organizing effort. Most likely, the storytelling registered by Boje (1991) fulfilled similar functions, although he focused more on its formal role in the sensemaking process. What makes the difference between storytelling as reported by Boje and Orr and that described by Yiannis Gabriel (in the next section) is that stories that organize are often of a doubtful aesthetic or political value, usually elliptic and difficult to understand for a bystander. Organizational stories, on the other hand, seem to be meant for a general audience and—although no doubt fulfilling multiple functions—can hardly be of practical use for a problem at hand. Yet it is undoubtedly so that as organizing proceeds, stories become more complete too (for the analogy between action and text, see Ricoeur, 1981). How then, do stories that organize become organizational stories?

Hayden White's studies of historiography taught me how to recognize a story in the making. In contrast to Boje and Orr, I find narratologists' distinction between a narrative and a story (see Todorov, 1978/1990; White, 1987) very useful. A narrative is a set of events or actions put chronologically together; the story is emplotted—that is, a logical (in a wide sense of logic) connection is introduced. Like the Europeans who in writing down their history, went from simple annals to chronicles to an emplotted history, people in organization use the minutiae of everyday events as material—first for reports, as organizational chronicles are usually called, and then for stories, sometimes of heroic dimensions.

There was a clear analogy between these three forms of historiography and the story making that I was able to watch during my study of the city of Stockholm (Czarniawska, 2004a). The register of my direct observation resembled annals, even if contemporary metrology permits a more detailed measure of time. Field notes, like annals, simply register what is happening at any given time. Many of these seemingly disconnected events and actions, however, were related by a common theme: the reform of city administration. Interviews with people engaged in carrying the reform through resembled chronicles: They reported the chronological and causal chains of events but did not have a point or a plot. After some time, however, complete stories of reform began to emerge, as the actors and the observers connected separate events and actions into a plot leading to a point. In doing so, they replaced chronological time with kairotic time (i.e., time punctuated by meaningful events; Czarniawska, 2004b) or, as Cunliffe, Luhman, and Boje (2004) suggest, introduced a *narrative temporality*.

I have observed this process many a time in my fieldwork. It confirms that sensemaking (Weick, 1995) is a retrospective process, requiring time, but the question remains, *how* is the narrative actually woven from disparate events? This is difficult to evince because of the inevitable conflict of "the prospective orientation of life with the retrospective orientation of narrative" (Ryan, 1993, p. 138). It is impossible to monitor the actors to capture the moments during which they elaborate their life experience into a story. Yet Marie-Laure Ryan (1993) succeeded in locating what she calls "a factory of plot" (p. 150): live radio broadcasts of sports events. There, "the real life situation promotes a narrative tempo in which the delay between the time of occurrence of the narrated events and the time of their verbal representation strives toward zero, and the duration of the narration approximates the duration of the narrated" (p. 138). A broadcast is constructed around three dimensions: *the chronicle* (what is happening), *the mimesis* (how it looks, a dimension that allows the listener to construct a virtual picture of the events), and the *emplotment* (introducing logical structure that allows making sense of the events).

It is obviously the chronicle that is central to a sports broadcast; nevertheless, the broadcasts become emplotted as well. The broadcasters perform it using three basic operations: (1) *constructing characters*—that is, introducing legible differences between the actors (a hero and an opponent); (2) *attributing a function* to single events; and (3) *finding an interpretive theme* that subsumes the events and links them in a meaningful sequence ("near success," "near failure," etc.; Ryan, 1993, p. 141).

The close analogy between sports events and organizational performance in contemporary societies has been extensively commented on by Hervé Corvellec (1997), who studied the notion of organizational "performance" from a narratological perspective. The spectators (e.g., the shareholders) insist on seeing the chronicle of the events ("annual report"), not the least because they want to have an opportunity to make their own emplotment. Although the real interest concerns the plot ("why do you have losses?"), the loosely espoused principles of logico-scientific knowledge[3] that characterize the genre of annual reports turn the attention away from the operation of emplotment. Plots are given (in the form of scientific laws of economics), so the only activity required is to recognize their pattern in the chronicle.

Collecting Stories

Each workplace has a contemporary and historical repertoire of stories, sometimes divided into *internal stories* and *external stories*, sometimes stories spread abroad with a hope of their return in a more legitimate form, for example, via mass media (Kunda, 1992). Any researcher who cares to spend some time in an organization, listening to what is told and reading some of its textual production, will encounter such narratives.

Sabine Helmers and Regina Buhr (1994) carried out a field study in a large German company producing typewriters. They spent three weeks in the company, conducting interviews and observing. During their stay, several interlocutors, all men, told them the following story:

The Tactful Typewriter Mechanic
The new secretary had called in the mechanic many times because her electric typewriter kept making spaces where they didn't belong. After trying unsuccessfully to find the cause, the mechanic decided to observe the secretary at work for a while. He soon discovered the problem. The girl, generously endowed with feminine attractions, kept hitting the space key involuntarily every time she bent forward. The mechanic showed that he was capable of dealing with this rather delicate situation. He found the excuse to send her out of the office and raised her swivel-chair four centimeters. Since then she had

no problems with her machine and has nothing but praise for the excellent mechanic. (p. 176)

At first, say Helmers and Buhr, they did not pay much attention to the story, but its repetitions made them curious. The story was told as if the event took place the day before, but the attempt to trace it led them to an Austrian in-house publication for a typewriter dealer dated June 2, 1963 (the excerpt is quoted from that source). Thus, a practically ancient story was kept alive by retelling it and was given relevance by situating it contemporarily and in the narrators' own company. The tale had its "sisters" in other companies, industries, countries, and times. Helmers and Buhr were able to show that such stereotyping women as "dumb blondes" actually hampered the technological developments in the typewriter industry. Stories of the kind they encountered redefined many technically solvable machine errors as "users' problems."

Yiannis Gabriel (1995, 2000) has collected stories related to the use of computers and information technology (in the study conducted in 10 organizations, 130 interviews gave rise to 404 stories). Here is an example of a story that is worth repeating for its entertainment value:

There was a chap driving a lorry and he hit a cat so he got out of the lorry and saw this cat on the side of the road and thought I'd better finish it off . . . smashed it over the head, got back in and drove off. A lady or a chap phoned the police and said I've just seen a Board lorry driver get out and kill my cat. So they chased after the van and found it and asked the driver whether he had killed the cat so he said he had run over it and couldn't leave it like that . . . it's cruel so I finished it off. So they said can we examine your van and he said yes by all means so they examined the van and found a dead cat under the wheel arch. So it was the wrong cat [he had killed] sleeping at the side of the road. (Gabriel, 2000, p. 23)

Gabriel points out that it does not make sense to check the veracity of the story and treats it as an example of organizational folklore. I would like to point out that like the story of the tactful mechanic, it contains many a message about the Board company. It is not the plot (a comic road story involving a case of mistaken identity) but the mimesis that carries the message: We learn that Board drivers are people sensitive to the suffering of animals and that the British police force reacts promptly to even extremely exotic complaints with exceptional thoroughness and alacrity.

Somewhat surprisingly, Gabriel (2000) does not seem to believe that story-based research has a future in organization studies:

Unlike the café and the pub, the village square and the family table, organizations do not appear to be a natural habitat of storytelling—after all most people in organizations are too busy appearing to be busy to be able to engage in storytelling. Nor is trust, respect, and love among members of organizations such as to encourage free and uninhibited narration. Moreover, stories in organizations compete against other narrativities, especially against information and data, but also against clichés, platitudes, acronyms, artefacts small and large, arguments, opinions, and so forth. In such an environment, amidst the noisy din of facts, numbers and images, the delicate, time-consuming discourse of storytelling is easily ignored or silenced. Few organizations are spontaneous storytelling cultures. (p. 240)

The ample collection of stories that he found seem to contradict his statement, and the analysis that follows elucidates several extremely important and often otherwise hidden aspects of social life. One such aspect is the role stories play in the drama of organizational power and resistance. Another is that stories permit access to the emotional life of organizations. This topic has been taken up by other writers (see a collection edited by Fineman, 1993), but Gabriel addresses a highly original aspect: stories as revealing the nostalgia present in organizations. A third aspect, closely related, is the religious side of organizing: Gabriel (2000) offers a compelling interpretation of the longevity of the leader-as-a-hero kind of plot; the leader is a kind of surrogate god in organizations. "By highlighting the untypical, the critical, the extraordinary, stories give us access to what lies beyond the normal and the mundane" (p. 240). Gabriel speaks here in tune with Jerome Bruner (1990), who pointed out that "the function of the narrative is to find an intentional state that mitigates, or at least makes comprehensible, a deviation from a canonical cultural pattern" (pp. 49–50). Thus, stories might not tell all about work worlds, but they do tell a lot.

Boland and Tankasi (1995) took a critical view of "collecting" organizational narratives, treating them as if they were artifacts forever petrified in organizational reality waiting to be "discovered" by a researcher. Yet every narrative becomes new with each retelling, and the "petrification" of narratives is not the result of the myopia of the researcher but of intensive stabilizing work by the narrators. Long-lived narratives are sediments of norms and practices and as such deserve careful attention.

How to Prompt for Narratives

"Telling stories is far from unusual in everyday conversation and it is apparently no more unusual for interviewees to respond to questions with narratives if they are given some room to speak" (Mishler, 1986, p. 69). An interview situation can easily become a microsite for production of narratives or just an opportunity to circulate them, where a researcher is allowed to partake in narratives previously produced. In many cases, answers given in an interview are spontaneously formed into narratives. This is usually the case of interviews aiming at life histories or, in an organizational context, at career descriptions, where a narrative is explicitly asked for and delivered. This is also the case of interviews aiming at a historical description of a certain process. When the topic of an interview is a reform or reorganization—that is, a chain of events that unfold in time, there is nothing unusual in formulating a question that prompts a narrative. "Could you tell me the story of the budget reform as you experienced it?" "Can you recall when you first started to talk about the necessity of reorganizing your department? And what happened next?"

This does not mean that research interviews always evoke narratives. Unlike spontaneous conversation, they may incite a conscious avoidance of narratives insofar as they are constructed as arenas where only logico-scientific knowledge can be legitimately produced. Both sides have to combat the shared conviction that *true knowledge* is not made of narratives (Czarniawska, 2002). "What were the factors that made a reorganization necessary?" will be perceived as a more "scientific" question, prompting analytic answers. It is thus a task of the interviewer to "activate narrative production" (Holstein & Gubrium, 1997, p. 123).

One way of doing it is just to ask for stories. Gabriel asked for accounts concerning the use of computers in companies, and I asked students of management, psychology, and sociology in different countries to describe in writing an incident involving organizational power that they had recently observed. This instruction resulted in a whole collection of very interesting stories (Czarniawska-Joerges, 1994). Scheytt, Soin, and Metz (2003) applied the same instruction in a study of the notion of "control" in different cultures. Monika Kostera is using a similar technique in variations. For example, the respondents (scholars, students, practitioners) are asked to complete a story of which they are given the first line ("'You are free to go,' said the Managing Director."). She also asked managers and management scholars to write short poems (Kostera, 2005). She suggests a *narrative experimentation* resulting in a *narrative collage* as ways of enriching both fieldwork methods and forms of writing. Before I turn to the latter topic, however, a vast field of interpretive and analytical approaches to narrative needs to be mapped out.

How to Read a Narrative

The first unsystematic approaches to stories and narratives in organizations looked in a more or less straightforward fashion at their contents, following the correspondence theory of truth (Rorty, 1980) and assuming that the narratives reveal (or hide) what has happened "in reality." The symbolic approaches (e.g., Martin, Feldman, Hatch, & Sitkin, 1983) moved the attention to the form; growing interest fostered growing sophistication. Certain themes and topics remain interesting (as a current example, I have chosen identity construction via narratives), but the rapprochement with the literary theory and discourse analysis produced several schools of reading organizational texts, which I present briefly. I begin with the analysis of life stories, continue with rhetorical analyses, structural analysis, and deconstruction. At the end of the section, I also include close readings of "professional stories"—looking for organizational insights in novels.

Looking for Identity Narratives: Life Stories, Career Stories, Organizational Biographies

While it may not be surprising that organizational narratives offer a conventional stock of characters, they also offer material for constructing subjectivity, or personal identities (Gabriel, 1995). This focus of narrative analysis has the longest tradition in the social sciences, far exceeding the ample field of management studies.

In the organizational context, life stories acquire two variations: (1) career stories and (2) organizational identity narratives. Career stories are most often analyzed within the framework of Foucauldian discourse analysis, situating the process of identity construction within, or against, the dominant discourse (Fournier, 1998; Peltonen, 1999). Organizational identity narratives are not only official historical documents but all kinds of collective storytelling that attempt to create a quasi-subject, the Organization (Czarniawska, 1997).

Lately, the topic of organizational identity (including its special case, corporate identity) is becoming central in management studies. Examples can be found in three recent collections, Schultz, Hatch, and Larsen (2000), Holger and Holmberg (2002), and Hatch and Schultz (2004), where narrative approaches to identity play an important role. They tend to take up two issues, sometimes related to one another: (1) the construction of a corporate identity, especially well illustrated by branding (see, e.g., Christensen & Cheney, 2000; Salzer-Mörling, 2002), and (2) the construction of personal identities by organizations (Alvesson & Willmott, 2004) or in relation to organizations (e.g., consumers, Du Gay, 2000; freelancers, Metz, 2003).

Rhetorical Analyses

Rhetorical analysis is the most traditional way of analyzing the form of the narrative, but it has not been used often in management studies. The situation has begun to change, as exemplified by the special issue of *Studies in Cultures, Organizations and Societies* (1995, 1(2); see especially Höpfl, 1995; Linstead, 1995; Prasad, 1995).

One of the recent examples of fruitful application of traditional rhetorical analysis to organizational stories can be found in Feldman and Sköldberg (2002). They point out that organizational stories often capitalize on the use of enthymeme—the most persuasively effective of rhetorical figures, according to Aristotle—that is, inviting the audience to fill in one of the major premises of the argument, or of the story point.

> At the minimum, the reader must be willing to complete the story, but also is often required to complete the story. In the extreme, a convincing story is constructed in such a way that the audience can fill in much of what they need to be convinced. (p. 275)

The narrators play on the audience's need (and habit) of closure: Without accepting the hidden premise the story will not make sense. Annual reports are good examples of frequent use of the enthymeme.

Hervé Corvellec (2001) has chosen to follow the inspiration of Perelman's new rhetoric to examine a long-lasting debate about the "third track" of the railway in the center of Stockholm. New rhetoric is a study of the discursive techniques that aim at causing or increasing the acceptance of ideas that are presented for approval. It is close to classical rhetoric in that it focuses on the process of persuasion, but unlike classical rhetoric it includes both oral and written presentation of arguments, takes into consideration all kinds of audience (including talking to oneself), and stresses the importance of the social conditions of acceptance. Corvellec's analysis shows that it is the public debate that makes and unmakes the project; the rational plans produced by organizational actors are just a contribution to the debate. It should be pointed out that the new rhetorical analysis is close to discourse analysis, another strong trend in recent management studies.

Structural Analysis

One traditional way of analyzing a narrative is that of a structural analysis, an enterprise close to semiology and formalism (Propp, 1968; Barthes, 1977). Organization studies show, however, a preference for the work of Algirdas Greimas, most likely because it has become popular via actor-network theory (for a recent collection of such studies, see Czarniawska & Hernes, 2005).

Anne-Marie Søderberg (2003) chose the narrative approach to analyze the interviews she conducted in a longitudinal study of international acquisitions. Thus, collected narratives were seen by her as retrospective interpretations of change processes in the acquired company, made by the involved people to make sense of organizational actions and events. She used Greimas's *actantial model* to systematize the different plots, which can be seen as results of both individual and collective processes of sensemaking. This narratological analysis revealed that different work views and worldviews, which separated people within an acquired company from the one making acquisition, led to different ways of emplotting the same course of events. Everybody she interviewed agreed about what had happened but not what it meant. Therefore, it might be more a problem than a solution if top management insists on propagating one "corporate story," unless it has been produced in a negotiation between the different versions that circulate around.

Deconstruction

Almost before structuralism acquired legitimacy in the social sciences, it was swept away by post-structuralism. One could claim that the move from structuralism to post-structuralism meant abandoning the depth for the surface: If "deep structures" are demonstrable, they are observable. Structures can no longer be "found," as they are obviously put into the text, by those who read the text, including the author (after all, reading is writing anew). This meant abandoning the ideas of the universal structure of language, or of mind, and accepting the idea of a common repertoire of textual strategies (Harari, 1979), which are recognizable to both the writer and the reader.

An extension of post-structuralism is deconstruction, a technique and a philosophy of reading characterized by a preoccupation with desire and power. Used by Derrida (1976) for reading philosophical texts, it became a kind of philosophy itself (Rorty, 1989). Used by gender scholars, it became a tool of subversion (Johnson, 1980). Used by organization researchers, it became a technique of reading by estrangement (Feldman, 1995). It is worth pointing out that, perhaps surprisingly, deconstruction met with more interest from organization scholars than other methods of textual analysis. I quote extensively an example of such use to show the critical potential of the reader's deconstruction in an organizational context.

Joanne Martin (1990) attended a conference, sponsored by a major U.S. university, on the ways in which individuals and businesses might help solve societal problems. One of the participants, the CEO of a large transnational, told the conference participants the following story:

> We have a young woman who is extraordinarily important to the launching of a major new (product). We will be talking about it next Tuesday in its first worldwide introduction. She has arranged to have her Caesarian yesterday in order to be prepared for this event, so you—We have insisted that she stay home and this is going to be televised in a closed circuit television, so we're having this done by TV for her, and she is staying home three months and we are finding ways of filling in to create this void for us because we think it's an important thing for her to do. (p. 339)

Martin (1990) decided to deconstruct and reconstruct the story from a feminist standpoint (the alternative standpoints were, e.g., the political leftist or the rationalist). Let me give short examples:

1. *Public/private dichotomy*: "We have a young woman" (rather than a young woman works for us). The text itself shows the company's awareness that this division cannot be maintained, revealing at the same time that "woman is to private as man is to public," and that actions intended as improvement in the private sphere turn out to be serving the public sphere; in other words, the public sphere invades the private under the aegis of "helping."

2. *Silenced voices*: "We insisted that she stay home." One voice that is never heard is the physician's voice, although it could be expected in this context. The woman is given a voice ("She arranged to have her Caesarean yesterday"), but it is not clear whether she did it on suggestion from the company or spontaneously. The final word is the company's: "We insisted."

3. *Disruptions*: "We are finding ways of filling in to create this void for us." This incoherence, points out Martin, happens at the point where the costs of the arrangement are taken up in the text, thus revealing the speaker's ambivalence regarding the benefits of the situation.

4. *The element most alien*: Pregnancy, says Martin, is an alien element in a male-dominated organization. The visibility of pregnancy calls attention to a whole series of organizational taboos: emotional expression and nurturance, sexual intercourse.

5. *Metaphors*: Child as a product, product as a child ("Why a product can be launched and a baby cannot" [p. 351]).

6. *Double entendres*: "We have a young woman."

7. *Reconstruction*: Martin creates several, and I am quoting only one that I found most poignant, achieved by changing the gender of the protagonist—and consequently, a type of operation:

> We have a young man who is extraordinarily important to the launching of a major new [product]. We will be talking about it next Tuesday in its first world wide introduction. He has arranged to have his coronary bypass operation yesterday in order to be prepared for this event, so you—We have insisted that he stay home and this is going to be televised in a closed circuit television, so we're having this done by TV for him, and he is staying home three months and we are finding ways of filling in to create this void for us because we think it's an important thing for him to do. (p. 346)

The absurdity of this reconstructed text corroborates what the deconstruction revealed: evidence of a suppressed gender conflict in work organizations, blind spots of management practice, and theory that fueled the conflict and kept it out of view.

Blurring Genres, or How Wide Is the Field?

All the above examples concerned narratives produced in the field of practice or in the encounter between the researchers and the field of practice. It has been pointed out, however, that there exist a great variety of narratives about various fields of practice in fiction (Phillips, 1995). Reading the text created by fiction writers, both in a research mode and in a teaching mode (Cohen, 1998), offers a variety of insights not always easily accessible in field studies. Thus, organization scholars have closely read 19th-century European novels (Czarniawska-Joerges & Guillet de Monthoux, 1994), Greek mythology (Gabriel, 2004), Jorge Luis Borges (De Cock, 2000), and science fiction (see the special issue of *Organization*, edited by Parker, Higgins, Lightfoot, & Smith, 1999), to name a few among the growing number of examples.

One novel seems to have been especially often read by organization researchers: David Lodge's *Nice Work*. To me, it was an epitomic example of anthropological work in an organizational context (Czarniawska-Joerges, 1992). Robyn, a postfeminist, post-structuralist academic, lives in a two-dimensional world: composed of symbols and politics. Because of the vagaries of the U.K. university system, she is forced to enter—as an observer—another world, that of the industry. Her counterpart in that world, Managing Director Vic, lives similarly in two dimensions: political and practical. Symbols do not exist for Vic; practical things do not exist for Robyn.

Robyn is determined to colonize the other world, taking for granted that her world contains all the concepts and the tools needed to dismantle the other. For Vic, her visit is an intrusion that has to be tolerated, but he has no fear of being colonized. Vic, too, takes his world to be the only correct one. The encounter proves to be a shock to both of them, especially when Vic, like some other "natives," decides to pay a visit to the university to observe Robyn at her work. They both experience first, the estrangement, then the understanding of the completeness of the other world, then curiosity, and finally respect for one another and their worlds—in short, a guide to fieldwork for management researchers.

To Richard Boland (1994), the center of interest resided in Vic's Jaguar, which Boland compared with the racing horse of Silas Lapham, the hero of the first realist novel on U.S. business, by William Dean Howell. As a condition for accepting his position as a new managing director, Vic (Victor Wilcox) insisted on a Jaguar, convinced that it is superior to all the other cars on the road. For him, as for many other managers, driving a fast car to and from work was a powerful moment. The Jaguar, like Lapham's horse, allowed a vivid experience of power,

> unleashed, yet controlled. . . . In the uniquely personal space provided by their rides to and from work, Silas Lapham and Victor Wilcox can, for a brief time, find a mastery over nature and others that eludes them both at home and in the office. (Boland, 1994, p. 124)

Knights and Willmott (1999) read *Nice Work* to illustrate several issues central to their *Management Lives: Power and Identity in Work Organizations*. I choose one example, especially pertinent: the two protagonists as exemplifying two different conceptions of inequality, polarized and pluralistic.

Robyn perceives workers in Vic's factory as subjected to labor exploitation and repression typical of capitalist production—the polarized view of inequality, according to Knights and Willmott's classification. She, however, has also espoused the post-modernist views and therefore ought to be closer to the pluralistic perspective. Although Knights and Willmott do not say so, Lodge pokes fun at Robyn's eager espousal of post-modernism, so that the fact that she does not seem to notice the discrepancy is not really surprising.

Vic is a "working-class-lad-made-good," so he subscribes to the pluralistic model and is highly critical of those who do not work hard or who exploit their positions of power. His worldview is as inconsistent as that of Robyn because his firm belief in "real business" prevents him from understanding that the business of industry is giving way to the business of services, where there is perhaps no room for a "hardworking businessman" like himself.

Thus, novels are not so much sources of information about management practice as sources of meaning. They are texts to be taken into account while other texts are produced—models not for imitation but for inspiration. They are versions of the world, and insofar as these are relevant and valid, it is not by virtue of correspondence with "the world" but by the virtue of containing right ("entrenched") categories and of being acceptable (Goodman, 1984). Such versions of worlds gain acceptability, not in spite of but because of their aesthetic features. It is the power of creative insight and not documentary precision that makes novels both a potential competitor and a dialogue partner for organization theory. Organization studies will not, in all likelihood, lead to a production of good novels but might learn quite a lot from the ways fictive texts are written, and I turn to this issue in the last section of this chapter.

Narrative Approach to Writing

Stories From the Field

Stories from the field were at first treated as material to be interpreted by field researchers. Recently, however, they are increasingly retold in a slightly stylized way in the belief that they can teach young students the practices of the field much more successfully than texts written in a scientific mode. Well-known examples are Frost, Mitchell, and Nord (1978 and subsequent editions); Sims, Gabriel, and Fineman (1993 and subsequent editions[4]); Fineman and Gabriel (1996); and Frost, Krefting, and Nord (2004). As all these focus on Anglo-Saxon organizations, a new trend is to situate such collections in a local context (for a Swedish example, see Corvellec & Holmberg, 2004).

There exists organizational research that is written in a fictive fashion, for example, Goodall's (1994) *Casing a Promised Land: The Autobiography of an Organizational Detective as Cultural Ethnographer* or autobiographical short stories by Grafton Small (2003) and Sharifi (2003). Harju (1999) and Westwood (1999) tried out post-modern experimental writing techniques. Writing straightforward fiction is not, however, seen as a legitimate social science endeavor: Writing like fiction might be another matter.

Reporting From the Field in a Narrative Form

What might appear like an obvious move—that of retelling the story of the events that took place in a field of practice in the form of a well-constructed narrative—is often treated with suspicion by authors familiar with narrative analysis who want to know how a text has been constructed. The choice is between analyzing one's own narrative, a procedure that might be tedious for the readers from outside of academia, or hiding the work put into the construction of the text, a procedure that might be criticized by colleagues in academia. Creative ways are searched for, and found, to circumvent this difficulty. John Van Maanen (1988) and Tony Watson (1995) have both early on reflected on the craft of writing organizational ethnographies. My *Writing Management* (1999) and Carl Rhodes' *Writing Organization* (2001) both address the challenges posed by an ambition of writing about polyphonic and heteroglossic organizations in ways that do not diminish the weight of the original voices from the field yet give an author the opportunity to create some added meaning.

One narrative solution has been applied by Ellen O'Connor (1997), who told the story of a U.S. employee who mobilized an opposition against the company policy that pushed people toward involuntary retirement. She presented the event as a sequence of narratives (letters, documents, and also excerpts from interviews and media comments), showing how various people conformed or rebelled against the common repertoire of characters, functions, and plots, in their roles of both storytellers and the interpreting audience. In organizational life, unlike in literature, she concludes, "One may intervene directly in the text to determine the limits and possibilities of intertext" (p. 414).

Ellen O'Connor applied "decision making" as her emplotment device point, and this might explain why she has attributed so much freedom in shaping of the narrative, and the intertext, to her characters. Kaj Sköldberg (1994, 2002) used genre analysis[5] in his reading of change programs in Swedish municipalities and saw the local actors carried away by the dramatic genres they employed rather than empowered by them. Two competing genres—a tragedy and a romantic comedy—resulted in a mixture that presented itself to the audience, including the researcher, as closest to satire, an effect unintended by either the directors or the actors of the drama.

Yet another way of avoiding the accusation of an unreflective narrative construction in research is to incorporate the analysis into the narrative itself, to exploit "the content of the form," in White's (1987) formulation. Sköldberg's way of treating his field material is halfway to this solution; a complete step often involves a dramatization of the narrative. Such an operation makes at least a part of the construction work visible to the reader, and the choice of a device is a major choice in the analysis, as in the examples that follow.

Dramatizing Narratives

The title of Michael Rosen's article "Breakfast at Spiro's: Dramaturgy and Dominance" (1985, 2002) summarizes it well. Rosen picked up his observation of a business breakfast at an advertising agency and decided to present it as a social drama, which was also a convention decided on by the organizers of the event themselves. The text has, therefore, the form of an annotated screenplay. As the events unfold, Rosen offers a dramaturgical critique, a connection to the events outside the time and the place of the drama, and a commentary on the reactions of the audience.

Bengt Jacobsson went even further, forming the results of the study of municipal decision making into a script for a *commedia dell'arte*:

Firm Principles (A Play in Three Acts)
Dramatis Personae:

Columbine: Minister of Industry and Energy; a servant of her Country, as represented by its Government; she is attractive and much courted.
Brighella: First Servant of the Ministry; Columbine's assistant; he is indefatigable when it comes to duping and deceiving, and is shrewd and cynical.
Capitano Energetico: Managing Director of a large company; he is vain and often falls into fantasies of heroic exploits and measureless glory . . .

First Act (Scene One: Brighella's Office)
Capitano Energetico comes in from the street, wearing a dazzling dark suit and carrying his company's accounts under his arm. He is received by Brighella,

and tells Brighella of the recent years of great successes and high profits, with new products that already exist and new markets opening up in the U.S. of A, in Eastern Europe, and wherever the demand for energy exists. (Czarniawska-Joerges & Jacobsson, 1995, pp. 383–384)

The choice of this form summarizes the final results of his analysis, revealing the theatricality and ritualism of the political organization, its skillful production of the improvisation effect based on routines and rehearsals, and its standard stock of characters.

In a similar vain, Ken Starkey (1999) represented scenes from an imaginary MBA class's reaction to the showing of the movie *Wall Street.* George Cairns and Nic Beech (2003) presented their study of "Ersilia" (a government agency) as an interplay of scripted and structured improvisations, thus not only dramatizing their presentation of the field material but also creating an opportunity for dramaturgical[6] and narrative analysis.

My last example of the uses of narrative analysis concerns its application to the narratives from the writer's own field of practice—that is, the field of theory.

Applying Narrative Analysis to Organization Theory

The narratives from one's own practice are analyzed like all others, possibly with more bravado (after all, the analyst is on safe ground, at least epistemologically if not always politically) but also with special care due to the fact that the narrators cannot be anonymized. As in previous examples, different options are open. Thus, I have analyzed March and Simon's *Organizations* as an example of my thesis that research writings often contain a plot without a narrative (Czarniawska, 1999). Martin Kilduff (1993) deconstructed the same text, coming to the conclusion that it contains a simultaneous rejection and acceptance of the traditions the authors sought to surpass. Kilduff ended his deconstruction with yet another narrative—a confessional tale that analyzed his motives in undertaking such an enterprise.

The tone of the analyses varies from critical to eulogical. Thus, Calás and Smircich's (1991) famous application of Foucault's genealogy, Derrida's deconstruction, and feminist post-structuralism to four classics of organization theory produced a harsh critique and a lively debate (especially from the still living classics); my depiction of "the styles and the stylists of organization theory" (Czarniawska, 2003) was aimed at demonstrating exemplary writings.

Coda

Organizational narratives, as the main mode of knowing and communicating in organizations, have become an important focus for organization scholars. Their construction and reproduction is being documented and their contents interpreted.

Narrative forms of reporting enrich organization theory, complementing, illustrating, and scrutinizing logico-scientific forms of reporting. By relinquishing some aspirations to power through the claim of factuality and one-to-one correspondence of theory and the world, organization studies attempt to open their texts for negotiations and enter into a dialogical relationship with practitioners of organizing.

Consulting Editors: Yiannis Gabriel and John Luhman

Notes

1. In this text, management is understood as a kind of organizing.

2. The reader might wonder how David Boje in 1991 was able to partake of the insights of Sack's book published in 1992. Sack's complete *Lectures on Conversation* were first published in 1992, 17 years after his tragic death, but circulated as paper copies of the transcriptions made by Gail Jefferson, and some of them were published separately before 1992.

3. As contrasted with narrative knowledge (see Jerome Bruner, 1986).

4. The order of editors' names rotates from one edition to the other: Sims is the first in the 1993 edition, Gabriel in the 2000 edition, and Fineman in the 2005 edition).

5. Sköldberg's use of genre analysis has been inspired by Hayden White (1973).

6. There is a vast and growing tradition of dramatist and dramaturgical analyses in organization studies, which are, however, beyond the scope of this chapter. For a review, see the special issue of *Organization Studies*, edited by Georg Schreyögg and Heather Höpfl (2004).

References

Alvesson, M., & Willmott, H. (2004). Identity regulation as organizational control. In M. J. Hatch & M. Schultz (Eds.), *Organizational identity* (pp. 436–465). Oxford, UK: Oxford University Press.

Bakhtin, M. M., & Medvedev, P. N. (1985). *The formal method in literary scholarship. A critical introduction to sociological poetics.* Cambridge, MA: Harvard University Press. (Original work published 1928)

Barthes, R. (1977). Introduction to the structural analysis of narratives. In R. Barthes (Ed.) & S. Heath (Trans.), *Image-music-text* (pp. 79–124). Glasgow, UK: William Collins. (Original work published 1966)

Boje, D. (1991). The story-telling organization: A study of story performance in an office-supply firm. *Administrative Science Quarterly, 36,* 106–126.

Boje, D. (2001). *Narrative methods for organizational and communication research.* London: Sage.

Boland, R. J. (1994). Identity, economy and morality in "The Rise of Silas Lapham." In B. Czarniawska-Joerges & P. Guillet de Monthoux (Eds.), *Good novels, better management* (pp. 115–137). Reading, UK: Harwood Academic.

Boland, R. J., Jr., & Tankasi, R. V. (1995). Perspective making and perspective taking in communities of knowing. *Organization Science, 6*(3), 350–372.

Brown, R. H. (1977). *A poetic for sociology: Toward a logic of discovery for the human sciences.* New York: Cambridge University Press.

Bruner, J. (1986). *Actual minds, possible worlds.* Cambridge, MA: Harvard University Press.

Bruner, J. (1990). *Acts of meaning.* Cambridge, MA: Harvard University Press.

Cairns, G., & Beech, N. (2003). Un-entwining monological narratives of change through dramaturgical and narrative analyses. *Culture and Organization, 9*(3), 177–194.

Calás, M., & Smircich, L. (1991). Voicing seduction to silence leadership. *Organization Studies, 12*(4), 567–601.

Christensen, L. T., & Cheney, G. (2000). Self-absorption and self-seduction in the corporate identity game. In M. Schultz, M. J. Hatch, & M. H. Larsen (Eds.), *The expressive organization. Linking identity, reputation, and the corporate brand* (pp. 246–270). Oxford, UK: Oxford University Press.

Clark, B. R. (1972). The organizational saga in higher education. *Administrative Science Quarterly, 17,* 178–184.

Cohen, C. (1998). Using narrative fiction within management education. *Management Learning, 29*(2), 165–182.

Corvellec, H. (1997). *Stories of achievement. Narrative features of organizational performance.* New Brunswick, NJ: Transaction.

Corvellec, H. (2001). The new rhetoric of infrastructure projects. In B. Czarniawska & R. Solli (Eds.), *Organizing metropolitan space and discourse* (pp. 192–209). Malmö, Sweden: Liber.

Corvellec, H., & Holmberg, L. (2004). *Organisationers vardag—sett underifrån.* Malmö, Sweden: Liber.

Cunliffe, A. L., Luhman, J. T., & Boje, D. M. (2004). Narrative temporality theory: Implications for organization study. *Organization Studies, 25*(2), 261–286.

Czarniawska, B. (1997). *Narrating the organization. Dramas of institutional identity.* Chicago: University of Chicago Press.

Czarniawska, B. (1999). *Writing management. Organization theory as a genre.* Oxford, UK: Oxford University Press.

Czarniawska, B. (2002). Narrative, interviews and organizations. In J. F. Gubrium & J. A. Holstein (Eds.), *Handbook of interview research* (pp. 733–750). Thousand Oaks, CA: Sage.

Czarniawska, B. (2003). The styles and the stylists of organization theory. In H. Tsoukas & C. Knudsen (Eds.), *The Oxford handbook of organization theory* (pp. 237–261). Oxford, UK: Oxford University Press.

Czarniawska, B. (2004a). *Narratives in social science research.* London: Sage.

Czarniawska, B. (2004b). On time, space and action nets. *Organization, 11*(6), 777–795.

Czarniawska, B., & Gagliardi, P. (Eds.). (2003). *Narratives we organize by.* Amsterdam: John Benjamins.

Czarniawska, B., & Hernes, T. (Eds.). (2005). *Actor-network theory and organizing.* Malmö, Sweden: Liber.

Czarniawska-Joerges, B. (1992). Nice work in strange worlds: Anthropological inspiration for organization theory. In T. Polesie & I.-L. Johansson (Eds.), *Responsibility and accounting. The organizational regulation of boundary conditions* (pp. 59–78). Lund, Sweden: Studentlitteratur.

Czarniawska-Joerges, B. (1994). Gender, power, organizations: An interruptive interpretation. In J. Hassard & M. Parker (Eds.), *Towards a new theory of organizations* (pp. 227–247). London: Routledge.

Czarniawska-Joerges, B., & Guillet de Monthoux, P. (Eds.). (1994). *Good novels, better management.* Reading, UK: Harwood Academic.

Czarniawska-Joerges, B., & Jacobsson, B. (1995). Politics as *commedia dell'arte*. *Organization Studies, 16*(3), 375–394.

De Cock, C. (2000). Fiction, representation and organization studies. *Organization Studies, 21*(3), 589–609.

Denning, S. (2005). *The leader's guide to storytelling: Mastering the art and discipline of business narrative*. San Francisco: Jossey-Bass.

Derrida, J. (1976). *Of grammatology*. Baltimore: Johns Hopkins University Press.

Du Gay, P. (2000). Markets and meanings: Re-imagining organizational life. In M. Schultz, M. J. Hatch, & M. H. Larsen (Eds.), *The expressive organization. Linking identity, reputation, and the corporate brand* (pp. 66–74). Oxford, UK: Oxford University Press.

Feldman, M. (1995). *Strategies for interpreting qualitative data*. Thousand Oaks, CA: Sage.

Feldman, M., & Sköldberg, K. (2002). Stories and the rhetoric of contrariety: Subtexts of organizing (change). *Culture and Organization, 8*(4), 275–292.

Fineman, S. (Ed.). (1993). *Emotions in organizations*. London: Sage.

Fineman, S., & Gabriel, Y. (1996). *Experiencing organizations*. London: Sage.

Fisher, W. R. (1984). Narration as a human communication paradigm: The case of public moral argument. *Communication Monographs, 51*, 1–22.

Fisher, W. R. (1987). *Human communication as narration: Toward a philosophy of reason, value, and action*. Columbia: University of South Carolina Press.

Fournier, V. (1998). Stories of development and exploitation: Militant voices in an enterprise culture. *Organization, 5*(1), 55–80.

Frost, P., Krefting, L., & Nord, W. R. (2004). *Managerial and organizational reality: Stories of life and work*. Toronto, Canada: Prentice Hall.

Frost, P., Mitchell, V., & Nord, W. R. (1978). *Organizational reality: Reports from the firing line*. Toronto, Canada: Longman.

Gabriel, Y. (1995). The unmanaged organization: Stories, fantasies and subjectivity. *Organization Studies, 16*(3), 477–502.

Gabriel, Y. (2000). *Storytelling in organizations*. Oxford, UK: Oxford University Press.

Gabriel, Y. (Ed.). (2004). *Myths, stories, and organizations. Postmodern narratives for our times*. Oxford, UK: Oxford University Press.

Goodall, H. L., Jr. (1994). *Casing a promised land. The autobiography of an organizational detective as cultural ethnographer*. Carbondale: Southern Illinois University Press.

Goodman, N. (1984). *Of mind and other matters*. Cambridge, MA: Harvard University Press.

Grafton Small, R. (2003). Fluid tales: A preservation of self in everyday life. In B. Czarniawska & P. Gagliardi (Eds.), *Narratives we organize by* (pp. 237–245). Amsterdam: John Benjamins.

Harari, J. V. (1979). Critical factions/critical fictions. In J. V. Harari (Ed.), *Textual strategies: Perspectives in post-structuralist criticism* (pp. 17–72). Ithaca, NY: Methuen.

Harju, K. (1999). Protext: The morphose of identity, heterogeneity and synolon. *Studies in Cultures, Organizations and Societies, 5*(1), 131–150.

Hatch, M. J., & Schultz, M. (Eds.). (2004). *Organizational identity*. Oxford, UK: Oxford University Press.

Helmers, S., & Buhr, R. (1994). Corporate story-telling: The buxomly secretary, a Pyrrhic victory of the male mind. *Scandinavian Journal of Management, 10*(2), 175–192.

Holger, L., & Holmberg, I. (Eds.). (2002). *Identity: Trademarks, logotypes and symbols*. Stockholm: National Museum & Raster.

Holstein, J. A., & Gubrium, J. F. (1997). Active interviewing. In D. Silverman (Ed.), *Qualitative research: Theory, method and practice* (pp. 113–129). London: Sage.

Höpfl, H. (1995). Organisational rhetoric and the threat of ambivalence. *Studies in Cultures, Organizations and Societies, 1*(2), 175–188.

Johnson, B. (1980). *The critical difference: Essays in the contemporary rhetoric of reading.* Baltimore: Johns Hopkins University Press.

Kilduff, M. (1993). Deconstructing organizations. *American Management Review, 18*(1), 13–31.

Knights, D., & Willmott, H. (1999). *Management lives! Power and identity in work organizations.* London: Sage.

Kostera, M. (2005). *The quest for the self-actualizing organization.* Copenhagen, Denmark: Copenhagen Business School Press.

Kunda, G. (1992). *Engineering culture: Control and commitment in a high-tech organization.* Philadelphia: Temple University Press.

Labov, W., & Waletzky, J. (1967). Narrative analysis: Oral versions of personal experience. In J. Helms (Ed.), *Essays on the verbal and visual arts* (pp. 12–44). Seattle: University of Washington Press.

Linstead, S. (1995). After the autumn harvest: Rhetoric and representation in an Asian industrial dispute. *Studies in Cultures, Organizations and Societies, 1*(2), 1231–1252.

Martin, J. (1990). Deconstructing organizational taboos: The suppression of gender conflict in organizations. *Organization Science, 1*(4), 339–359.

Martin, J., Feldman, M. S., Hatch, M. J., & Sitkin, S. B. (1983). The uniqueness paradox in organizational stories. *Administrative Science Quarterly, 28,* 438–453.

McCloskey, D. N. (1990). *If you're so smart. The narrative of economic expertise.* Chicago: University of Chicago Press.

Metz, D. (2003). From naked emperor to count zero. Tracking *knights, nerds* and *cyberpunks* in identity narratives of freelancers in the IT-field. In B. Czarniawska & P. Gagliardi (Eds.), *Narratives we organize by* (pp. 173–191). Amsterdam: John Benjamins.

Mishler, E. G. (1986). *Research interviewing. Context and narrative.* Cambridge, MA: Harvard University Press.

Mitroff, I. I., & Killman, R. (1975). Stories managers tell: A new tool for organizational problem solving. *Management Review, July,* 18–28.

O'Connor, E. S. (1997). Discourse at our disposal. Stories in and around the garbage can. *Management Communication Quarterly, 10*(4), 395–432.

Orr, J. E. (1996). *Talking about machines. An ethnography of a modern job.* Ithaca, NY: Cornell University Press.

Parker, M., Higgins, M., Lightfoot, G., & Smith, W. (1999). Amazing tales: Organization studies as science fiction. *Organization, 6*(4), 579–590.

Peltonen, T. (1999). Finnish engineers becoming expatriates: Biographical narratives and subjectivity. *Studies in Cultures, Organizations and Societies, 5*(2), 265–295.

Phillips, N. (1995). Telling organizational tales: On the role of narrative fiction in the study of organizations. *Organization Studies, 16*(4), 625–649.

Polkinghorne, D. E. (1987). *Narrative knowing and the human sciences.* Albany: State University of New York Press.

Prasad, P. (1995). Working with the "smart" machine: Computerization and the discourse of anthropomorphism in organizations. *Studies in Cultures, Organizations and Societies, 1*(2), 253–266.

Propp, V. (1968). *Morphology of the folktale.* Austin: University of Texas Press.

Rhodes, C. (2001). *Writing organization. (Re)presentation and control in narratives at work.* Amsterdam: John Benjamins.

Ricoeur, P. (1981). The model of the text: Meaningful action considered as text. In J. B. Thompson (Ed. & Trans.), *Hermeneutics and the human sciences* (pp. 197–221). Cambridge, UK: Cambridge University Press.

Rorty, R. (1980). *Philosophy and the mirror of nature.* Oxford, UK: Basil Blackwell.

Rorty, R. (1989). *Contingency, irony and solidarity.* Cambridge, UK: Cambridge University Press.

Rosen, M. (1985). Breakfast at Spiro's: Dramaturgy and dominance. *Journal of Management, 11*(2), 31–48.

Rosen, M. (2002). *Turning words, spinning worlds: Chapters in organizational ethnography.* London: Routledge.

Ryan, M.-L. (1993). Narrative in real time: Chronicle, mimesis and plot in baseball broadcast. *Narrative, 1*(2), 138–155.

Sacks, H. (1992). *Lectures on conversation.* Oxford, UK: Blackwell.

Salzer-Mörling, M. (2002). In pursuit of the modern—A story of the Swedish Post Office. In L. Holger & I. Holmberg (Eds.), *Identity: Trademarks, logotypes and symbols* (pp. 201–212). Stockholm: National museum & Raster.

Scheytt, T., Soin, K., & Metz, T. (2003). Exploring notions of control across cultures: A narrative approach. *European Accounting Review, 12*, 515–547.

Schreyögg, G., & Höpfl, H. (2004). Theatre and organization: Editorial introduction. *Organization Studies, 25*(5), 691–704.

Schultz, M., Hatch, M. J., & Larsen, M. H. (Eds.). (2000). *The expressive organization. Linking identity, reputation, and the corporate brand.* Oxford, UK: Oxford University Press.

Sharifi, S. (2003). Ticking time and side cupboard: The journey of a patient. In B. Czarniawska & P. Gagliardi (Eds.), *Narratives we organize by* (pp. 215–236). Amsterdam: John Benjamins.

Sims, D., Gabriel, Y., & Fineman, S. (1993). *Organizing and organization.* London: Sage.

Sköldberg, K. (1994). Tales of change: Public administration reform and narrative mode. *Organization Science, 5*(2), 219–238.

Sköldberg, K. (2002). *The poetic logic of administration. Styles and changes of style in the art of organizing.* London: Routledge.

Søderberg, A.-M. (2003). Sensegiving and sensemaking in an integration process: A narrative approach to the study of an international acquisition. In B. Czarniawska & P. Gagliardi (Eds.), *Narratives we organize by* (pp. 3–36). Amsterdam: John Benjamins.

Solow, R. M. (1988). Comments from inside economics. In A. Klamer, D. N. McCloskey, & R. M. Solow (Eds.), *The consequences of economic rhetoric* (pp. 31–37). Cambridge, UK: Cambridge University Press.

Starkey, K. (1999). Eleven characters in search of an ethic, or the spirit of capitalism revisited. *Studies in Cultures, Organizations and Societies, 5*(1), 179–194.

Todorov, T. (1990). *Genres in discourse.* Cambridge, UK: Cambridge University Press. (Original work published 1978)

Van Maanen, J. (1988). *Tales of the field.* Chicago: University of Chicago Press.

Watson, T. (1995). Shaping the story: Rhetoric, persuasion and creative writing in organisational ethnography. *Studies in Cultures, Organizations and Societies, 1*(2), 301–311.

Weick, K. E. (1995). *Sensemaking in organizations.* Thousands Oaks, CA: Sage.

Westwood, R. (1999). A "sampled" account of organisation: Being a de-authored, reflexive parody of organisation/writing. *Studies in Cultures, Organizations and Societies, 5*(1), 195–233.

White, H. (1973). *Metahistory. The historical imagination in nineteenth century Europe.* Baltimore: Johns Hopkins University Press.

White, H. (1987). *The content of the form. Narrative discourse and historical representation.* Baltimore: Johns Hopkins University Press.

CHAPTER 16

Acted Narratives

From Storytelling to Emergent Dramas

Cheryl F. Mattingly

For a long time, I have thought about the importance of stories for professionals when trying to make sense of situations in which they are expected to intervene. For more than 20 years, I have been studying practitioners and have been intrigued by how much their efforts were directed not simply to solving problems but to discovering and "framing" what problems should be solved. Practitioners were routinely engaged in *setting the problem*, as Donald Schon (1983, 1987) used to say. I began to notice that often this problem setting relied on storytelling (Mattingly, 1991a, 1991b, 1998a). Professionals were especially likely to tell stories when struggling to sort out difficult relationships with clients or other key actors. Such stories were likely to involve a puzzling about motives. What were their clients up to? Why did they want (or not want) certain things? Why were they "noncompliant?" Why did they have "unrealistic" hopes? Why didn't they show up for appointments, as scheduled? These sorts of troubling questions tended to beget rounds of storytelling, often with understanding colleagues, and while such stories might crop up during official meetings, they often occurred during informal moments of the work day—at lunch, in an elevator, at a work party. While the professionals themselves have tended to characterize such narrativizing in trivial terms—letting off steam, gossiping, recruiting allies for "their side," getting a little sympathy—I became fascinated with what appeared to be an essential, if unacknowledged, aspect of practical work, fundamental to professional decision making.

The importance of stories in professional decision making first became apparent to me in the early 1980s, when I undertook an ethnographic study of World Bank project officers (mostly economists, financial analysts, and engineers) engaged in helping to develop urban loans projects for Calcutta and a number of cities in Kenya

(Mattingly, 1991a). However, the surprising centrality of stories in professional work came home with special force when I turned my attention to clinical practices. I began carrying out ethnographic studies of clinicians in urban hospitals within the United States. Initially, I focused on occupational therapists but in subsequent research expanded my study to include a broad range of other health professionals who treated children with severe illnesses and disabilities. This has included, for example, physical and speech therapists, rehabilitation aides, oncologists, surgeons, hematologists, nurses, social workers, psychologists, and nutritionists.

But it was my earlier study of occupational therapists that led me, in a very basic way, to reconsider the place of narrative in professional work and, more fundamentally, to reconsider the relationship between narrative and experience. Although clearly *storytelling* plays a critical (if largely unnoticed) role in the problem-setting aspects of clinical work and clinical reasoning, there is more to the connection between narrative and experience than this. In my work, and in this chapter, I argue that narrative not only functions as a form of talk but also serves as a moral aesthetic underlying clinical action. That is, therapists and patients not only tell stories but sometimes create storylike structures through their interactions. Furthermore, this effort at story making, which I will refer to as *therapeutic emplotment*, is integral to the healing power of this practice. Thus, I consider the narrative structure of action and experience.

Clinical action itself can be thought of, at least in some moments, as an "untold story." The heart of this argument concerns a difficult claim that we can think of (at least some) clinical interactions as narratively shaped. Clinical interactions sometimes take the shape of emergent stories, "proto-narratives," in Ricoeur's terms. Ricoeur (1984, 1985, 1987) contends that action is in quest of a narrative. Whether or not this holds generally true, it has been very compelling in my research that many occupational therapists and a number of other health professionals want therapy to be experienced by their patients as significant. They are in quest of dramatic plots that will transform the painfulness, irrelevance, or sheer tedium of therapeutic activities into important events, ones that figure for the patient as critical episodes in their healing experience. Therapists want, as they often say, "something to happen" in therapy, by which they often mean something memorable, something they and their patients can recall later, can recognize as a milestone, even a transformative moment, along a path from illness to rehabilitation.

Before proceeding to a discussion of the analysis of clinical work as acted or performed narrative (a *healing drama*), I briefly review the connection of my own line of narrative research to the rapidly growing "narrative turn" in studies of illness and healing. I pay particular attention to work within cultural (and specifically medical) anthropology, my home discipline.

Healing and Narrative in Anthropology and Beyond

In the mid- and late 1980s, anthropologists began to examine narrative and its relationship to illness and healing in the context of biomedical care. They have not been alone; this exploration has been an interdisciplinary effort and has included increasing interest by clinicians themselves. In this fertile area of research, scholars have relied on and developed a broad range of analytic strategies. Narrative studies are extremely interdisciplinary; anthropologists have depended on a number of theoretical frameworks and research traditions. Interpretive lenses may be strictly cognitive or purely phenomenological; sensemaking may be focused on face-to-face interactions, on cultural activities of entire social groups, or on the interface between personal experience and cultural models of thought and action. Narrative theory has been imported from other disciplines (sociology, linguistics, psychology, literary theory, philosophy) as well as other subfields within anthropology. Some of the most interesting work on illness and healing narratives published in anthropological journals has been carried out by scholars who are not medical anthropologists. Despite wide variations in method, subject matter, and analytic frame, narrative-centered renderings of illness share common threads.

Broadly speaking, what draws these studies together is a focus on the meaning-making aspects of illness and healing. They tend to fall into what has come to be known as an interpretive or meaning-centered paradigm of medical anthropology (Csordas, 1994; Gaines, 1991, 1992; B. Good, 1994; M. J. Good, 1995; Kleinman, 1980, 1988; Kleinman, Eisenberg, & Good, 1978). Scholars interested in narrative have, by and large, emphasized activities through which healers, patients, and their kin construct and negotiate interpretations of their experiences and use those interpretative frames to guide future actions. Often, though not always, there is an interest in the dramas that surround illness, in the temporal contexts in which illness occurs, and in illness and healing as dynamic processes in which meaning is not a given but something actors struggle to discover.

Why has narrative become so attractive, especially in connection with chronic or disabling clinical conditions? When illness is protracted, when there is no chance of return to the person one once was, or when there is no hope of being "normal," a person's very sense of self is lived in a special way through the body. Personal identity becomes intimately tied to the pain, uncertainty, and stigma that come with an afflicted body. What might it mean to be healed when a cure is only a distant possibility or no possibility at all? The inevitable poverty of biomedical responses to this question has a great deal to do with why narrative is so irresistible. Stories reveal a world. They can help transform identity, interpret the meaning of the past, and even provide images of possible futures.

Stories can render experience meaningful by placing events into a culturally and personally understandable plot. It is often contended that narratives provide coherence to the chaos introduced by illness. This can be heard in anthropologist (and psychiatrist) Arthur Kleinman (1988) in his influential discussion of illness narratives:[1]

"The illness narrative," he writes, "is a story the patient tells, and significant others retell, to give coherence to the distinctive events and long-term course of suffering. The plot lines, core metaphors, and rhetorical devices that structure the illness narrative are drawn from cultural and personal models for arranging experiences in meaningful ways and for effectively communicating those meanings." (p. 49)

Telling stories can offer a way to make meaning of what is otherwise unthinkable, uninterpretable. It allows the sufferer to assimilate the illness experience into his or her life. Gay Becker (1997), in her study of how people deal with disrupted lives created by illness and other unexpected tragedies, notes that creating a coherent plot out of these unexpected and disruptive events constitutes a "crucial imaginative task" (p. 27). The sociologist Arthur Frank (1995) argues along similar lines: "Serious illness is a loss of the 'destination and map' that had previously guided the ill person's life: ill people have to learn 'to think differently'" (p. 1). He is speaking in general but also autobiographically, mining his own personal narrative of illness. For him, this different thinking provoked by serious illness engenders a certain kind of storytelling. The ill "learn by hearing themselves tell their stories, absorbing others' reactions, and experiencing their stories being shared" (p. 1).

Medically and cognitively oriented anthropologists interested in the relationship between culture and mind have examined stories in terms of socially shared "explanatory models" of illness and healing that they explicate and draw on. This work has resulted in studies of narratively structured explanatory models across a broad range of cultural communities (Cain, 1991; Garro, 1992, 1994, 2000; Holland, Lachicotte, Skinner, & Cain, 1998; Mathews, Lannin, & Mitchell, 1994; Price, 1987). Some have also turned to recent work in autobiographical memory, investigating culturally shared memories as resources for individual storytellers in constructing meaning out of illness experiences. Memories of the past shape future action, including actions individuals take in seeking to recover from illness. Linda Garro (2000) writes: "In response to a disruptive life event like illness, the reconstruction of the past in accounting for an illness, and dealing with the illness in the present and future, are often closely connected" (p. 70). Cognitive and cultural psychology, particularly the enormously influential work of Jerome Bruner (1986, 1990, 1996, 2002), has helped focus anthropological attention on stories of illness and healing. Bruner has argued that narrative offers one of two key ways that we make sense of the world. His arguments have been invoked and elaborated in narrative sensemaking of both sufferers and healers (Garro, 2003; Garro & Mattingly, 2000; Good & Good, 1994; Mattingly, 1998b; Mattingly, Lawlor, & Jacobs-Huey, 2002).

Healing Dramas

In my own work, I have examined the relationship between narrative and healing with particular attention to healing dramas—stories that are acted rather than told (Mattingly, 1991b, 1994, 1998a, 2000). In speaking about acted narratives, I am not referring to the habitual enactment of pregiven cultural scripts but rather to a more emergent, improvised, and socially orchestrated emplotment of action. The cultural stock of stories actors bring to any situation is an essential resource for this kind of improvisational emplotment but, in the situations I have in mind, such stories do not provide automatic recipes for routine behavior. I connect the creation of healing dramas to the actors' concerns that actions unfold in hopeful directions—that is, good stories develop and bad ones are avoided. But, more important, I connect them to the social creation of *significant experiences,* to the transformation of routine time into dramatic time. Through the last 20 years of research in North American clinical settings, I have come to discover the complexity of what "recovery" can mean for those living in bodies relentlessly, perilously present as well as those that have grown largely "silent," to call on Robert Murphy's (1987) eloquent image. I have grown to respect and even to wonder at the power of small moments, recovery located in a walk to the bathroom, a checkers game, a successful trip to the hospital gift shop in the new wheelchair.[2] As Oliver Sacks (1987) has said, "recovery is events . . . advents, which are births and rebirths" (p. 154).

As with any good story, healing dramas reveal life in the breach, in this case a breach that suggests healing possibilities. In these dramatic moments, time itself takes on narrative shape, is imbued with those qualities we take to be the markers of a good story: suspense, riskiness, trouble, enemies, desire, transformation, and plot (Mattingly, 1994, 1998a). By plot, I mean an emergent temporal configuring in which particular actions become meaningful as part of a larger, unfolding drama (see Ricoeur's [1984, 1985, 1987, 1992] extensive treatment of plot and its relationship to historicity). There are times when even an ordinary clinical encounter shifts into this dramatic form, offering the patient images of a possible future worth living.

My own analysis of healing dramas draws largely from hermeneutic and phenomenological traditions of philosophy, as well as literary criticism and anthropological theories of ritual. Phenomenological discussions of *human time* and the temporality of action and experience in philosophy (Carr, 1986; Dilthey, 1989; Gadamer, 1975; Heidegger, 1927/1962; Olafson, 1971, 1979; Ricoeur, 1984, 1985, 1987) have been especially significant. In various ways, phenomenological and anthropological theorists offer us a picture of the unevenness of lived time, the way that some experiences are more meaningful, more significant, and more dramatic than others. I gradually came to recognize how important this distinction was for the efficacy of much clinical work. Thus, the narrative analysis I offer here is an analysis of action and it depends on the notion of *dramatic or narrative time.* Before turning to a concrete case of an occupational therapist working with a young child, I will say a bit more about what I mean by dramatic time.

Dramatic time is a time when we would say something significant is happening. This kind of time is most clearly contrasted with those moments in life when we might say that nothing much seems to be going on. Times when, if someone asked us what we were doing or what happened, we might reply "oh nothing really." Dramatic time is also time that is more than linear, more than mere "clock time," one moment following another in simple chronological fashion. It is not, as we sometimes say, just "one damn thing after another." Rather, it is time that takes on unity and shape of a "something," a "particularity."[3]

In speaking of dramatic or narrative time, I am saying something more than that we are always living in history—though this is an important and necessary precursor to the potential for time to emerge as, in some particularly heightened and significant way, narrative. As historical beings, we locate ourselves in a stream of history—in fact, we find ourselves participating in, and living out, multiple histories at the same time. For example, a person might be identified (and find himself) as, at once, a New Yorker in a post–9/11 world, a father of young children, a brother of difficult siblings, a grower of roses, and a middle-aged college professor hoping for promotion to full professor. These identities are not so much static categories as social and personal histories (and anticipations) in the making. As the philosopher Alisdaire MacIntyre (1981) has argued, meaning itself is a narrative matter precisely because it always involves locating ourselves and others within such histories, just as a matter of making sense of action.

The narrative quality of human time is more than passively experienced; we actively try to make certain sorts of stories come true and avoid others. We attempt to anticipate and control the future, and this is an essential aspect of what it means to be historical beings. That is, we understand our situations not only by reference to the past but also by reference to the possible, to a subjunctive world of "what ifs." Such efforts are necessarily vulnerable; it is not that we can control or even fully anticipate the future, only that we often try to. It is within this historical or fundamentally narrative picture of action and meaning making that I locate dramatic time. For there are moments when participants (or, at least, some of them) are especially invested in what transpires, especially attentive to "reading" and trying to shape the story that is unfolding before them. This is time that matters, where something is "at stake" in a marked way.

The hermeneutic tradition in philosophy has historically informed dramatic and aesthetic notions of social action in anthropology, including Turner's concept of social dramas and Geertz's notion of action as text. It has also influenced some strains of literary theory, particularly reader response theory (Iser, 1974, 1978). The hermeneutic tradition since Dilthey (1989) has explored the aesthetic structure of action and the phenomenology of aesthetic experience. The works of Gadamer (1975) and Ricoeur (1984, 1985, 1987) give the fullest contemporary expression to this line of thinking.

Anthropology's classic investigation of non-Western healing rituals has a great deal to contribute to this line of investigation. Ethnographies drawing on Victor Turner's social dramas as well as phenomenological investigations of the healing process are of particular relevance here. The sheer *eventfulness* of recovery, so often suppressed in biomedicine, is highlighted in a variety of nonbiomedical healing practices. Because anthropology has such a long and important history of analyzing healing from dramatistic perspectives, this tradition can illuminate healing as a locally situated, socially complex, and embodied narrative act.

The performative aspects of healing have been explored in some very interesting ways in anthropology, ways that have helped to introduce certain streams of phenomenology to anthropology. But, in an effort to distance themselves from earlier structuralist treatments of ritual, many scholars elaborating a phenomenological approach to the study of healing distinguish their approach from a narrative one. They frequently view narrative as offering only a disembodied semiotics of healing. This is unfortunate. What is needed is not a sharp distinction between a structuralist, narrative approach to healing, on the one hand, and a phenomenologically sensitive reading of the healing process, on the other. Rather, as in hermeneutic phenomenology (Carr, 1986; Dilthey, 1989; Gadamer, 1975; Ricoeur,

1984, 1987), narrative ways of knowing and doing need to be connected to embodied, extralinguistic modes of experience. This link cannot be made without reformulating narrative itself as a construct such that it can be seen as connected, in complex ways, to the very shaping of embodied experience.

Healing rituals across a wide array of cultures have been noted for features that also characterize many clinical healing dramas. These include (a) multiple communicative channels that carry the meaning of events, creating a "fusion of experience"; (b) a rich array of aesthetic, sensuous, and extralinguistic features typical of dramatic interactions; (c) heightened attention to the moment, the sense that something important is at stake; (d) the socially shared nature of experience that is further intensified through mutual bodily engagement with others; (e) symbolic density, creating images that refer backward and forward in time so that the "patient" and perhaps others as well are located symbolically in history; (f) efficacy linked to potential transformations of an individual patient and sometimes a larger social community as well (Briggs, 1997; Csordas, 1994, 1996; Danforth, 1989; Desjarlais, 1996; Hughes-Freeland, 1998; Jackson, 1989; Kapferer, 1983, 1986; Laderman, 1996; Schechner, 1993; Schieffelin, 1996; Stoller, 1989, 1996, 1997; Tambiah, 1985; E. Turner, 1992; V. Turner, 1969, 1986a, 1986b).[4]

At first glance, biomedicine seems an unlikely spot to discover healing dramas, and indeed, it is important that they are often well hidden from view. Sometimes only the patients seem to be aware of them or find themselves in something they view as a drama while the health professional sees it as routine. Professionals are often quick to describe dramatic moments in the language of biomedicine so that they appear to be doing professional clinical work, not "playing" or "wasting time," "just being friends" with their patients or, perhaps most dangerous, going "outside their turf" by directing attention to matters that are supposed to be the province of psychological specialists such as social workers, psychiatrists, or clinical psychologists. Sometimes, healing practitioners themselves seem to be unaware when they have helped to create a powerful healing moment, one that speaks to the patient in a deeply personal way. Rehabilitation therapists speak reluctantly, with some embarrassment, of how they tailor their interventions to draw in a patient, sometimes defending themselves (in case they are perceived as not sufficiently scientific or objective) by saying that they need to "motivate" patients to get them to participate in treatment. Certainly the espoused theories of biomedical treatment do not advocate the creation of powerful dramatic moments as necessary to healing (Mattingly, 1998a; Mattingly & Lawlor, 2001).

I offer an example of one such healing drama, drawing from research conducted over the past 10 years in Los Angeles and Chicago among African American families who have children with serious disabilities or chronic illnesses and the health professionals who serve them. The following case is based on one of the 30 families that my colleagues and I have been following for the past 8 years—a 5-year-old girl, Tania, diagnosed with brain cancer, and her mother, Celeste. I examine a single session of occupational therapy to explicate a notion of narratives as something that can be acted as well as told and to explore some of the dramatic features that transform it into an acted narrative that generates healing. It is important that healing is not the same as curing and that such dramatic and acted narratives may contribute to a picture of healing that can even be coupled with a grim prognosis.

In offering a picture of how a single clinical session can contribute to a picture of hope, I not only describe and analyze the session and its dramatic form but also nest this session within a larger temporal frame, the broader illness and healing story that Tania and her mother are living out. This larger narrative frame includes both the initial struggle of Tania's mother to get good clinical care for her child and some other key events that have occurred in Tania's life while suffering through this illness. When placed within a larger context of her unfolding life story, particularly the many losses that Tania has suffered, it becomes clear how much the meaning and dramatic power of the clinical session is due not only to what happens within the session but also to the place of this session within a life.

Dinosaur Stew

For nearly a year, Celeste took Tania to emergency rooms all over the city, seeking some kind of diagnosis for her increasingly ill child. Time and time again, she was told to go home, that nothing was really wrong. Finally, after Celeste's very strong protests that she would not leave until someone looked at her daughter because she knew something was very wrong, a doctor examined her and recognized that there was a serious problem. Within 2 days, Tania was diagnosed with a brain tumor that had grown unchecked for a year and was, by the time of diagnosis, the "size of an egg." Prognosis was not good; no more than 60% chance of recovery, the doctors told Celeste. Tania had surgery and radiation, followed by chemotherapy.

After surgery, Celeste and Tania spent at least 2 days a week at the hospital for the next year and a half. Tuesdays were "chemo." Thursdays were outpatient physical and occupational therapy. Her oncologist was someone Celeste gradually came to trust, and there was a physical therapist, Jane, whom Tania was particularly fond of. Celeste credited this physical therapist with teaching Tania to walk again after surgery, a healing drama of momentous proportions when one hopes for a child to recover. And Tania loved her therapy days because (a) she did not get a shot and (b) she had a chance to play with some new people who, sometimes at least, knew how to have fun.

In what follows, I describe a moment when a narrative is created in a treatment session with one of her occupational therapists.[5]

Here is the scene. A little room with a small table and child-sized chairs. Tania is busy heading to all the possible toys of interest. She particularly loves the closets, which might have interesting toys in them. (She seems to think of therapy time as a trip to a giant play store.) Celeste and I sit in child-sized chairs by the door, away from Leslie (the therapist) and Tania. Leslie finally settles Tania at the small table, poking into a little box of theraputty (bright yellow, the consistency of the silly putty I played with as a child) that has some marbles in it.

Leslie:	Did you find the marble? Where did it go? *(Tania is pressing her fingers into the putty.)*
Leslie (in typical therapist sing-song accompaniment):	Smoosh, smoosh, smoosh.
Tania (Gets up and wanders around. Then she comes back, peers into the box.):	Where da marble?

Leslie doesn't say anything but takes Tania's hand and tries to get her to dig through the putty to find the marble. Tania soon begins to squirm, looking around the room. Leslie asks her to wash her hands and Tania jumps up, moving quickly to the sink at one end of the little room, Leslie trailing behind. Tania happily washes her hands and then begins to wash out a bowl left in the sink.

Leslie:	OK Tania, I really want you to use this hand. *(Tania is neglecting her left hand.)* Try some of this soap. You need some soap. Here, let me put some soap on you. *(Leslie helps her so that they are both doing this hand washing together.)*
Leslie:	Do you know zippers? Are you good with those? *(Tania continues to wash the bowl she found, not using her left hand and basically ignoring Leslie.)*
Leslie:	I'm going to count to 10 and then we'll finish those up, OK? *(Leslie begins to count.)*

Tania speaks but her speech is low and slurred.

Leslie:	You are going to have to speak louder. I don't know what you are saying.
Celeste (Across the room, Celeste leans over and whispers to me):	She needs speech therapy. Her speech is goin'. I can't hardly understand her no more.

Leslie and Tania move back to the putty.

Leslie:	How's this hand been feeling?
Tania:	OK.
Leslie:	*(Leslie wants Tania to take out the marble and other objects that have gotten stuck in the putty.)* Let's take this stuff out.

Tania:	No.
Leslie:	No? How about let's take half of it out. *(Leslie produces a cookie cutter and shows Tania how to make a cookie shape in the play dough.)* Do you want to make a cookie?
Tania:	Yeah. *(Tania watches Leslie and begins to slow down and focus.)*
Leslie:	There's one cookie! *(Leslie takes her cookie and puts it on a "baking pan"—actually the lid of the metal tin the theraputty is kept in.)*
Tania (joyfully):	There's one cookie!
Leslie:	Let's try another. *(Gives the cutter to Tania and helps her to press it in the dough.)* You have to push and then twist it to come up. *(Tania tries and Leslie helps her, putting her hand on top of Tania's part of the time to guide her.)*
Leslie:	Push, push, push! Twist, twist, twist!

Tania accidentally drops the theraputty on the floor.

Leslie (singing out cheerfully):	Uh oh uh oh spaghettio.

Tania laughs. Cuts another piece with the cutter and gets it out to put in the "baking pan." Does one or two more.

Leslie:	Good job! Look at this. *(Leslie suddenly takes out a small wooden stick, like a little baseball bat, and vigorously begins to flatten one of the cookies.)*
Tania (in horrified fascination):	No! Don't smash the cookie!
Leslie:	Yeah, watch this. Here, you try it.

Tania enthusiastically takes the wooden stick proffered and starts pounding her cookies so that they become flatter and flatter. They make more cookies and immediately smash them.

Leslie:	What happened? *(The cookie won't come off the cutter.)* How are we going to get that out?
Tania:	Let's get it out. *(Tania mumbles something about a nasty boy.)*
Leslie:	A nasty boy? Who's a nasty boy?
Tania (with relish):	Nasty boy.
Leslie:	So Tania, do you have a brother or a sister?
Tania:	Yeah.

Leslie tries to find out more, but Tania's speech is difficult to understand so she doesn't get far. Several times, I think Celeste is going to interrupt and correct, since Tania does not have a brother but a nephew her age she is very close to. But Celeste doesn't say anything. I wonder if she is trying to figure out whether she should have anything to do in the session but Leslie keeps her attention focused on Tania the whole time. She doesn't look toward either of us.

Leslie and Tania have been putting their smashed cookies back into the metal box which has turned into a kind of big stew pot, full of mixed in cookie cutters, marbles, and other strange things, all swirled in the play dough.

Leslie:	Are you going to make dinner?
Tania:	Yeah.
Leslie (looking thoughtful):	Something with *(pause)* dinosaur in it? *(There is now a little plastic dinosaur mixed into the putty, sitting mostly on top. Leslie is still trying to get Tania to use her left hand.)*
Leslie (addressing the room at large):	One of the reasons we're doing therapy is to get that hand stronger. *(Tania begins to use her left hand a bit. Leslie finds a scarf which she ties around Tania's wrist. Celeste and I laugh. Tania stirs her stew vigorously, paying no attention to us.)*
Leslie:	You need an apron when you cook. Are you cooking dinosaur? How are you going to prepare it? Bake it? Or fry it? *(Tania continues to stir the putty, saying nothing.)* What does it taste like?
Tania:	It bites.
Leslie:	But what does it taste like?
Tania:	Like an orange.
Leslie (puzzled):	Like an orange. Oh. *(Leslie tries to show her how to use both hands to push the dinosaur into the putty, as part of cooking it.)*

Tania brushes Leslie away. She suddenly plucks the dinosaur out of the stew, bringing him close to her face.

Tania:	OK. *(She tells him sternly)* Now, *you* eat it.
Leslie:	Oh, I see. You're baking *for* the dinosaur.

Having finally discerned what Tania is up to, that she wants to cook for the dinosaur rather than eat it, Leslie and Tania look about for something suitable to put in their stew that a brontosaurus might like. They settle on a plastic lamb.

Leslie:	He looks hungry!
Tania:	He's hungry but. . . .
Leslie (peering at their stew):	So whaddya think, do ya think?
Tania (affirms):	He wants to eat it.

How to Make Dinosaur Stew: Dramatic Time and the Narrative Emplotment of a Therapy Session

As a means of more carefully analyzing the narrative properties of this acted drama, I have proposed six elements of narrative time: plot, motive, desire, transformation, trouble, and suspense (Mattingly, 1994, 1998a). These elements, culled primarily from literary analysis, are typically identified as essential ingredients of narrative form (especially but not exclusively within western literary traditions). While these are familiar elements of narrative as a *mode of discourse,* I draw on them here as critical elements of acted narratives, of *dramatic time.* In what follows, I briefly describe these elements and examine how they function in a narrative analysis of this clinical encounter.

I begin with the notion of *plot.* A plot links disparate actions (and events) into a meaningful whole. Within a plot, discrete actions come to take on a unity, a figure sketched in time. Each event takes its meaning as part of a larger, temporal whole. It, as we say, "contributes to the plot." As such, an emplotted story offers a "sense of an ending." One thing after another becomes, in narrative logic, one thing because of another.

The interlude just recounted marks a shift from a therapy time the therapist designates as "scattered" to a focused and dramatic moment, narrative time governed by a desire, suspense, drama, and a sense of the whole. Putty becomes cookie dough becomes stew fit for a hungry dinosaur. Few words are spoken but this is a story all the same, one imbued with symbolic density, a story that signifies.

I turn now to *motive.* In dramatic time, the meaning of what happens depends very much on the motives of actors. Particular actions are understandable and interpretable as connected to who acts and what motivates their actions. Narratives, in other words, link motives to actions to consequences. Taking this into the world of clinical practice, dramatic or narrative time differs from biomedical time because it is actor centered rather than disease centered. While from a purely physical or biomedical perspective the "main character" in illness is the pathology, from a narrative perspective the main character is the person with the pathology (Sacks, 1987). Because stories foreground the role of intending, purposeful agents in explaining why things have come about in a certain way, emplotted time is a time of social doings, shaped by actions of oneself and others.

From a biomedical perspective, this clinical session could be described as addressing Tania's faltering fine motor coordination and strength as well as cognitive deficits that have been engendered by both the disease process of a growing brain tumor and the toxic consequences of the cancer treatments (surgery, radiation, chemotherapy). From a narrative perspective, this clinical session becomes a place for making dinosaur stew, the temporary creation of a world in which unexpected and interesting guests appear and must be fed. The importance of motive as part of creating this shared, acted story is perhaps nowhere so apparent as when things break down, as when the therapist mistakenly believes that they are in a story in which they will be eating dinosaur stew instead of feeding a hungry dinosaur. Tania corrects this misapprehension on the therapist's part in a key episode. This is the moment when Tania refuses to cooperate with the therapist's attempts to get her to push the plastic dinosaur deeper into the theraputty (good for hand strengthening). Instead, Tania suddenly lifts the dinosaur out of the "stew" and tells her sternly, "Now *you* eat it." The therapist suddenly realizes her mistake (her misreading of Tania's intentions) and replies, "Oh I see. You're baking *for* the dinosaur." This correction not only allows the therapist to reinterpret Tania's behavior it also reframes the story they are in, allowing her to contribute to a shared narrative.

Desire is critical to any compelling narrative. The actions that form the central core, the causal nexus, of a narrative are not motivated in some trivial sense, as when we are moved to make a cup of coffee or pick up the morning paper. They are driven forward by desire. A story is governed, the folklorist Vladimir Propp (1968/1986) tells us, by a "lack" or a need that must be addressed. This lack may be caused by some kind of "insufficiency" (p. 34) or created in response to the action of a villain who "disturb[s] the peace" (p. 27). In either case, it is set in motion either by the protagonist's desire to attain something she does not have or to right some wrong. The presence of desire brings with it a readiness to suffer. Our desire causes us to take risks (or pay a price when we fail to take risks) and this in itself causes suffering. Often our object will not be attained, or when attained it will not give us what we hoped for, and these things also cause pain. Our desire for something we do not yet have strongly organizes the meaning of the present and makes us vulnerable to a disjuncture between what we wish for and what actually unfolds. It creates a *narrative gap*.

There are multiple protagonists in the clinical drama I have presented and each comes with her particular desires. But something more than this fact is at stake when I speak of desire as a key element of an acted story. For desire is also something that can, and often needs to be, socially created within the action itself. And, in fact, from the therapist's perspective, this presents a fundamental practical problem. If she cannot create any desire in Tania to participate in the session, she will not be able to do any exercises with her at all. This is a tricky business because Tania, in fact, is perfectly content to wander about the therapy room—in fact, she finds too many things of interest as she opens cabinet drawers to see what toys might be found. Leslie's task is to find a way to channel Tania's energy into a set of focused tasks that will allow her to work on the designated therapeutic tasks but enfold them into activities that compel Tania's attention. Leslie makes a few aborted tries, trying to get her to search for marbles in a box of theraputty, or to work a zipper, but something such as narrative time only begins when Leslie has the idea of "making cookies." Tania is interested in this. Leslie further seduces Tania into a "baking story" by violating the usual cooking rules. She introduces a breach that compels Tania's full attention when she suddenly takes a wooden stick and begins smashing the "cookies" they have been making. "No!" Tania protests, utterly fascinated at this unexpected turn of events. "Don't smash the cookie!" At this moment, the "plot" has thickened and it is clear that this is not an expected cooking session. It is not marked by predictable time (one cookie after another) but dramatic time, where it is not clear what will happen next.

This turning point marks a key *transformation* in the session. Transformation is critical to the plot structure of narrative. In a story, time is structured by a movement from one state of affairs (a beginning) to a transformed state of affairs (an ending). In story time, things are different in the end. Thus, narrative time is marked by change, or by the attempt at change, or the surprise of change. In this session, a series of transformations or turning points occur, such that there is a sense of movement. It is not simply that scattered time is transformed into an imaginative dinner event in which a dinosaur (evidently a rather uncooperative one) is expected to eat. There is also a more potent transformation. The little girl who initially appears unsocial, even oblivious of others, scattered, difficult to understand—in short, a little girl presenting some clear cognitive deficits—is transformed into a highly social and engaged girl who has the power to shape a plot she cares about. Even the quality of her speech changes. Where at first she talks in a blurry, low voice, her words become stronger, clearer.

No good story can do without *trouble*. Even the happy story, the one which ends well, takes us through a drama of plight—a lack or need that sets the story in motion and propels the protagonist in a quest to obtain his goal through the overcoming of a series of obstacles. The process of overcoming, however happy the result, almost inevitably engenders periods of suffering for the story's heroes. This is such a pervasive feature of the structure of narrative that Propp (1968/1986) made it central to his analysis of folktales, and later narrativists expanded it to include many other kinds of narratives. Nothing is guaranteed in the realm of human action. We do what we can but—in the narrative at least—there are always impediments.

The importance of trouble and suffering in the narrative is due to the sort of actions narratives recount, actions in which desire is strong but where there is also a significant gap between where the protagonists start out and where they want to be. In compelling stories, there are always enemies and adversaries—and these can come in many forms, sometimes human, sometimes not. The strength of our desire comes in part from the length of the reach required to attain what we want. Most stories we choose to tell feature difficult passages toward precarious destinations, journeys fraught with enemies who may defeat us at any moment.

In attempting to set a therapeutic story in motion, as Leslie does in this case (or, as she would put it, the attempt to motivate her client to carry out some therapeutic activities), Leslie introduces trouble in a classic way, through her "breach" of a cooking ritual—cookie baking that suddenly becomes cooking smashing. She herself becomes Trouble, to Tania's delight, suddenly shifting from responsible adult to bad child, enthusiastically breaking the rules and encouraging Tania to do the same. This playful Trouble is used to attack the real deep Trouble that both are presented with—Tania is living with a body that is becoming weaker and weaker, despite efforts of clinicians and family to build back her strength to where it was before her illness. The therapist does not, of course, try to invent this sort of trouble for her patient. This comes with chronic disability.

Dramatic time is *suspenseful*. The presence of powerful enemies, and of dangers and obstacles, means that dramatic time is a time of uncertainty. Our desire for an ending may be strong, but if our enemies are equally strong, or danger is prevalent, there is no telling what will finally unfold. Narrative time is inevitably marked by doubt, by what Jerome Bruner (1986) and Byron Good (1994; Good & Good, 1994) speak of as "subjunctivity." If lived experience positions us in a fluid space between a past and a future, then what we experience is strongly marked by the possible. Meaning itself, from this perspective, is always in suspense. If the meaning of the present, and even of the past, is contingent on what unfolds in the future, then what is happening and what has happened is not a matter of facts but of interpretive possibilities that are vulnerable to an unknown future. Life in time is a place of possibility; it is this structure that narrative imitates. For narrative does not tell us that what happened was necessary but that it was possible, displaying a reality in which things might have been otherwise (Barthes, 1975a, 1975b). Endings, in action and in story, are not logically necessary but possible, and seen from the end and looking backward, plausible. Ricoeur (1984) writes,

> To follow a story, is to move forward in the midst of contingencies and peripeteia under the guidance of an expectation that finds its fulfillment in the "conclusion" of the story. This conclusion is not logically implied by some previous premises. It gives the story an "end point," which, in turn, furnishes the point of view from which the story can be perceived as forming a whole. To understand the story is to understand how and why the successive episodes led to this conclusion, which, far from being foreseeable, must finally be acceptable, as congruent with the episodes brought together by the story. (pp. 66–67)

Dramatic time is not, at least in any simple or linear sense, about progress. It is not about building one thing onto another in some steady movement toward a defined goal. Time is characterized by suspense—both the suspense of not knowing whether a desired ending will come about, and the suspense of wondering whether the ending one pictures is the one that will still be desired or possible as the story unfolds.

The emergent and social character of this little acted story provides suspense. What will one do after smashing cookies? What does one feed a dinosaur, after all? But the dramatic qualities of this narrative are not confined to the small surprises that move this plot along. All of the narrative elements I have just reviewed take their deepest dramatic meaning when this clinical session is placed within the unfolding and uncertain drama of Tania's (and her mother Celeste's) unfolding life.

The depth of its signifying power is never guessed at by the therapist who so beautifully orchestrates it. Understanding why this therapeutic moment holds power for Tania and her mother depends on knowing more about Tania's life than this therapist does. However, the therapist is fully aware that she and Tania have effected a transformation in this part of the session. They have managed to shift from clinical time, which is scattered, where she cannot get minimal cooperation from Tania and where, if she is unlucky and this persists, she may have to force Tania to perform a set of tasks directed to discrete problems (weakness of her left side and especially her left hand, attention deficits caused either by the original tumor or brain damage from the surgery). She knows that out of an inauspicious beginning, they move into imaginative play where treatment of pathology is embedded within such cooking adventures as smashing cookies and fixing dinner for a brontosaurus.

The drama relies on their ability to move into a cultural script they share, one surrounding the everyday business of making and eating meals. They bake, they make stews, they feed others. For this purpose, metal lids of boxes become baking pans, theraputty turns into cookie dough, plastic lambs and marbles the tasty ingredients for a good, thick soup. But they do more than enact a familiar cultural script. They also improvise a story that carries dramatic weight, especially in the context of Tania's unfolding illness and her life events more generally. This clinical session emerges as a dramatic moment, a short story, within this unfolding life story.

The therapist's ability to follow the *pacing* of Tania and to build opportunistically on what intrigues her allows all of us—as actors or audience—to enter the "same story"—to create a healing story—for the space of a therapy session. But it is only when placed in context of Tania's (and Celeste's) unfolding life that the real drama is revealed. This session connects Tania to everyday life in the sense that it plays out a familiar canonical scene. (Tania, like other children her age, loves nothing more than playing at being grown-up and cooking is a quintessential everyday activity reserved for those older than herself.) But its dramatic potency is due to the way it disconnects; it creates a breach from the life Tania has been living since her illness. Leslie and Tania make an upside-down story of her life.

Dinosaur Stew as a Short Story in Tania's Life Story

This little performed narrative connects clinic life to a hopeful plot Celeste is fiercely trying to live out, despite the devastating losses that have recently occurred. This story is one where Tania has a joyful childhood, where she lives to the fullest. This hopeful plot requires such nurturing because it runs counter to the life story that has been unfolding. It is an upside-down story in light of the many losses of her recent life. Here is a brief catalog of the most important ones: (a) she leaves preschool, which she loves, and stays home all the time, away from her friends; (b) her father moves out and her parents are now divorcing; (c) she and her mother move from a small rental house to an apartment because her mother has been fired (missing too many days due to Tania's illness) and can no longer pay the rent on the house; (d) since they are now cramped for space, her 23-year-old sister, who had been living at home, moves out, taking her son who is Tania's age and is very close to Tania; (e) Tania loses her old neighborhood and now lives in a place with no yard; (f) Tania's grandmother is diagnosed with stomach cancer and has become quite ill, and cannot visit Tania as much as she once did; (g) Tania eats so little, has grown so thin from the illness and the chemotherapy, that her mother now gives her a baby bottle because she will eat more that way. Tania seems to be hurtling backward in developmental time.

Tania cries sometimes at the loss of school playmates, father, and nephew, and is frequently mutinous at her mother's constant entreaties that she eat. Eating has become something of a battle between the two of them. How much nicer to feed someone else, to be the Mommy and boss them around in the process, than to have to eat oneself!

And what about the therapists? Leslie is well attuned to Tania, but she is not at all aware of how her work fits into the larger lifeworld of this child. She, and the other therapists who work with Tania, would be further astonished to discover the way this mother has incorporated the work of therapists like her into home life, recreating the outpatient therapy clinic in her cramped living room by moving out the couch and putting in affordable versions of slides, swings, and child-sized tables perfect for working on "fine motor skills," as they say in therapy talk.

Conclusion

In this chapter, I have considered narrative as something that can be acted as well as told. And I have offered a particular interpretive structure for analyzing acted stories. The genre of acted story I have discussed here, in some detail, and have written about elsewhere, is the *healing drama*. I have offered an example of a rather ordinary clinical moment in pediatric therapy; I have tried to illustrate the way a narrative approach can usefully be expanded to include acted stories.

I have also pointed toward what is revealed when a small moment, a single clinical encounter, is placed within broader narrative contexts, such as the illness story that a patient, or a family, is living out. A clinical encounter is dramatic not merely because of its internal aesthetic structure but because of what it points to, what it suggests about the possibilities for a life. Its power and meaning are derived, in significant part, from its position as a short story, an episode, within larger life stories that are still unfolding. These broader narrative contexts also bring other key actors into the scene. For example, the session I have described has two key protagonists— a therapist and a child. While a mother is there, she is a shadowy, off-stage figure that sits, quite literally, at the outskirts of the drama. And yet, once this clinical drama is nested within the life story of Tania, her mother emerges as a central figure in the narrative.

While such a narrative approach might be applicable to many domains of practical life, it has a special kind of salience in the clinical world, and when examining the sensemaking of those facing serious illnesses and disabilities. Stories, acted or told, call on our imagination, our imaginative ability to identify with characters and their plights. As Aristotle himself says, in stories "events are depicted as 'the sort of thing that might happen' to ourselves or our loved ones" (as cited in Nussbaum, 2001, p. 166).

Stories, whether acted or told, explore and create possible worlds. When healing means living with chronic illness or disability, it cannot be reduced to matters such as taking away the pain, restoring life, or curing disease. Instead, it involves an active exploration of how life can be lived, how there can still be a way to act, to desire, to participate in the world, even with this body and under these circumstances. The practical reasoning involved in recovery becomes a complex problem, practically and morally. What can one hope for? How should one make one's life now? How can one imagine possibilities when every door seems closed?

Author's Note: I would like to thank members (past and present) of the "Boundary Crossing" research team: Erica Angert, Nancy Bagatell, Jeanine Blanchard, Jeannie Gaines, Lanita Jacobs-Huey, Teresa Kuan, Stephanie Mielke, Ann Neville-Jan, Melissa Park, Carolyn Rouse, Katy Sanders, and Kim Wilkinson. In particular, heartfelt thanks goes to my long-time research partner, Mary Lawlor. Thanks also to Linda Garro and Atwood Gaines for comments on earlier drafts of this chapter. I gratefully acknowledge support by the National Center for Medical Rehabilitation Research, The National Institute of Child Health and Human Development, and National Institutes of Health (No. 1RO1HD38878).

Consulting Editors: Linda Garro and Atwood Gaines

Notes

1. See also Gaines (1991) for a discussion of the relationship between the illness story and societal models of illness and Rittenberg and Simons (1985) for an earlier discussion of the place of story in psychiatric diagnosis.

2. Geertz's (1973) classic treatment of religious experience and the concern among many phenomenologists to emphasize the "mundane, quotidian world" has also pointed toward a position that attends to the small moments of everyday life (A. Gaines, personal communication, September 26, 2005).

3. While I speak here in general terms, it is important to point out that this picture of agents actively attempting to shape their destiny is not an unproblematic universal condition but one that is culturally specific. My depiction has special salience within lifeworlds where there is a strong emphasis on living in history and where history is viewed as transformative and shifting, even if not necessarily progressive.

4. This list is abbreviated from an earlier paper written with Mary Lawlor, "The Fragility of Healing."

5. The interview with Tania, Celeste, and Leslie is reprinted with permission of Cheryl Mattingly.

References

Barthes, R. (1975a). An introduction to the structural analysis of narrative. *New Literary History, 6,* 237–272.

Barthes, R. (1975b). *The pleasure of the text.* New York: Hill & Wang.

Becker, G. (1997). *Disrupted lives: How people create meaning in a chaotic world.* Berkeley: University of California Press.

Briggs, C. (Ed.). (1997). *Disorderly discourse: Narrative, conflict, and inequality.* New York: Oxford University Press.

Bruner, J. (1986). *Actual minds, possible worlds.* Cambridge, MA: Harvard University Press.

Bruner, J. (1990). *Acts of meaning.* Cambridge, MA: Harvard University Press.

Bruner, J. (1996). *The culture of education.* Cambridge, MA: Harvard University Press.

Bruner, J. (2002). *Making stories: Law, literature and life.* New York: Farrar, Straus and Giroux.

Cain, C. (1991). Personal stories: Identity acquisition and self-understanding in alcoholics anonymous. *Ethos, 19,* 210–253.

Carr, D. (1986). *Time, narrative, and history.* Bloomington: Indiana University Press.

Csordas, T. (Ed.). (1994). *Embodiment and experience: The existential ground of culture and self.* Cambridge, MA: Harvard University Press.

Csordas, T. (1996). Imaginal performance and memory in ritual healing. In C. Laderman & M. Roseman (Eds.), *The performance of healing* (pp. 91–113). London: Routledge.

Danforth, L. (1989). *Firewalking and religious healing: The Ana Stenari of Greece and the American firewalking movement.* Princeton, NJ: Princeton University Press.

Desjarlais, R. (1996). Presence. In C. Laderman & M. Roseman (Eds.), *The performance of healing* (pp. 143–164). London: Routledge.

Dilthey, W. (1989). *Introduction to the human sciences: Vol. 1. Selected works* (R. A. Makkreel & F. Rodi, Eds.). Princeton, NJ: Princeton University Press.

Frank, A. (1995). *The wounded storyteller: Body, illness, and ethics.* Chicago: University of Chicago Press.

Gadamer, H. G. (1975). *Truth and method.* New York: Seabury Press.

Gaines, A. D. (1991). Cultural constructivism: Sickness histories and the understanding of ethnomedicines beyond critical medical anthropologies. In B. Pfleidere & G. Bibeaux (Eds.), *Anthropologies of medicine: A colloquium on West European and North American perspectives* (pp. 221–258). Wiesbaden, Germany: Vieweg und Sohn Verlag.

Gaines, A. D. (1992). Ethnopsychiatry: The cultural construction of psychiatries. In A. D. Gaines (Ed.), *Ethnopsychiatry: The cultural construction of professional and folk psychiatries* (pp. 3–49). Albany: State University of New York Press.

Garro, L. (1992). Chronic illness and the construction of narratives. In M. J. Delvecchio Good, P. E. Brodwin, B. J. Good, & A. Kleinman (Eds.), *Pain as human experience* (pp. 100–137). Berkeley: University of California Press.

Garro, L. (1994). Narrative representations of chronic illness experience: Cultural models of illness, mind, and body in stories concerning the temporomandibular joint (TMJ). *Social Science & Medicine, 38*(6), 775–788.

Garro, L. (2000). Cultural knowledge as resource in illness narratives: Remembering through accounts of illness. In C. Mattingly & L. Garro (Eds.), *Narrative and the cultural construction of illness and healing* (pp. 70–87). Berkeley: University of California Press.

Garro, L. (2003). Narrating troubling experiences. *Transcultural Psychiatry, 40,* 5–44.

Garro, L., & Mattingly, C. (2000). Narrative as construct and construction. In C. Mattingly & L. Garro (Eds.), *Narrative and the cultural construction of illness and healing* (pp. 1–49). Berkeley: University of California Press.

Geertz, C. (1973). Religion as a cultural system. In C. Geertz (Ed.), *The interpretation of cultures* (pp. 87–125). New York: Basic Books.

Good, B. (1994). *Medicine, rationality, and experience: An anthropological perspective.* New York: Cambridge University Press.

Good, B., & Good, M. J. (1994). In the subjunctive mode: Epilepsy narratives in Turkey. *Social Science & Medicine, 36*(6), 835–842.

Good, M. J. (1995). *American medicine: The quest for competence.* Berkeley: University of California Press.

Heidegger, M. (1962). *Being and time* (E. Robinson & J. Macquarrie, Trans.). New York: Harper & Row. (Original work published 1927)

Holland, D., Lachicotte, W., Skinner, D., & Cain, C. (1998). *Identity and agency in cultural worlds.* Cambridge, MA: Harvard University Press.

Hughes-Freeland, F. (1998). Introduction. In F. Hughes-Freeland (Ed.), *Ritual, performance, media* (pp. 1–28). New York: Routledge.

Iser, W. (1974). *The implied reader: Patterns of communication in prose fiction from Bunyan to Beckett.* Baltimore: Johns Hopkins University Press.

Iser, W. (1978). *The act of reading: A theory of aesthetic response.* Baltimore: Johns Hopkins University Press.

Jackson, M. (1989). *Paths toward a clearing: Radical empiricism and ethnographic inquiry.* Bloomington: Indiana University Press.

Kapferer, B. (1983). *A celebration of demons: Exorcism and the aesthetics of healing in Sri Lanka.* Bloomington: Indiana University Press.

Kapferer, B. (1986). Performance and the structure of meaning and experience. In V. Turner & E. Bruner (Eds.), *The anthropology of experience* (pp. 188–202). Urbana: University of Illinois Press.

Kleinman, A. (1980). *Patients and healers in the context of culture: An exploration of the borderland between anthropology, medicine, and psychiatry.* Berkeley: University of California Press.

Kleinman, A. (1988). *The illness narratives: Suffering, healing, and the human condition.* New York: Basic Books.

Kleinman, A., Eisenberg, L., & Good, B. (1978). Culture, illness and care: Clinical lessons from anthropological and cross-cultural research. *Annals of Internal Medicine, 88,* 251–258.

Laderman, C. (1996). Poetics of healing in Malay Shamanistic performances. In C. Laderman & M. Roseman (Eds.), *The performance of healing* (pp. 115–141). New York: Routledge.

MacIntyre, A. (1981). *After virtue: A study in moral theory.* South Bend, IN: University of Notre Dame Press.

Mathews, H., Lannin, D. R., & Mitchell, J. P. (1994). Coming to terms with advanced breast cancer: Black women's narratives from Eastern North Carolina. *Social Science & Medicine, 38,* 789–800.

Mattingly, C. (1991a). Narrative reflections on practical action: Two learning experiments in reflective storytelling. In D. Schön (Ed.), *The reflective turn: Case studies in and on educational practice* (pp. 235–257). New York: Teachers College Press.

Mattingly, C. (1991b). The narrative nature of clinical reasoning. *American Journal of Occupational Therapy, 45,* 998–1005.

Mattingly, C. (1994). The concept of therapeutic emplotment. *Social Science & Medicine, 38*(6), 811–822.

Mattingly, C. (1998a). *Healing dramas and clinical plots: The narrative structure of experience.* Cambridge, UK: Cambridge University Press.

Mattingly, C. (1998b). In search of the good: Narrative reasoning in clinical practice. *Medical Anthropology Quarterly, 12*(3), 273–297.

Mattingly, C. (2000). Emergent narratives. In C. Mattingly & L. Garro (Eds.), *Narrative and the cultural construction of illness and healing* (pp. 181–211). Berkeley: University of California Press.

Mattingly, C., & Lawlor, M. (2001). The fragility of healing. *Ethos, 29*(1), 30–57.

Mattingly, C., Lawlor, M., & Jacobs-Huey, L. (2002). Narrating September 11: Race, gender and the play of cultural identities. *American Anthropologist, 104*(3), 743–753.

Murphy, R. (1987). *The body silent.* New York: Henry Holt.

Nussbaum, M. (2001). *Upheavals of thought: The intelligence of emotions.* Cambridge, UK: Cambridge University Press.

Olafson, F. (1971). Narrative history and the concept of action. *History & Theory, 9,* 265–289.

Olafson, F. (1979). *The dialectic of action: Philosophical interpretation of history and the humanities.* Chicago: University of Chicago Press.

Price, L. (1987). Ecuadorian illness stories: Cultural knowledge in natural discourse. In D. Holland & N. Quinn (Eds.), *Cultural models in language and thought* (pp. 313–342). Cambridge, UK: Cambridge University Press.

Propp, V. (1986). *Morphology of the folk tale* (L. Scott, Trans.). Austin: University of Texas Press. (Original work published 1968)

Ricoeur, P. (1984). *Time and narrative* (Vol. 1; K. McLaughlin & D. Pellauer, Trans.). Chicago: University of Chicago Press. (Original work published 1983)

Ricoeur, P. (1985). *Time and narrative* (Vol. 2; K. McLaughlin & D. Pellauer, Trans.). Chicago: University of Chicago Press.

Ricoeur, P. (1987). *Time and narrative* (Vol. 3; K. Blamey & D. Pellauer, Trans.). Chicago: University of Chicago Press.

Ricoeur, P. (1992). *Oneself as another.* Chicago: University of Chicago Press.

Rittenberg, W., & Simons, R. C. (1985). Gentle interrogation: Inquiry and interaction in brief initial psychiatric evaluations. In R. A. Hahn & A. D. Gaines (Eds.), *Physicians of western medicine: Anthropological approaches to theory and practice.* Dordrecht, Netherlands: D. Reidel.

Sacks, O. (1987). *The man who mistook his wife for a hat and other clinical tales.* New York: Perennial Library.

Schechner, R. (1993). *The future of ritual: Writings on culture and performance.* New York: Routledge.

Schieffelin, E. (1996). On failure and performance: Throwing the medium out of the séance. In C. Laderman & M. Roseman (Eds.), *The performance of healing* (pp. 59–89). London: Routledge.

Schon, D. (1983). *The reflective practitioner: How professionals think in action.* New York: Basic Books.

Schon, D. (1987). *Educating the reflective practitioner.* San Francisco: Jossey-Bass.

Stoller, P. (1989). *The taste of ethnographic things: The senses of anthropology.* Philadelphia: University of Pennsylvania Press.

Stoller, P. (1996). Sounds and things: Pulsations of power in Songhay. In C. Laderman & M. Roseman (Eds.), *The performance of healing* (pp. 165–184). London: Routledge.

Stoller, P. (1997). *Sensuous scholarship.* Philadelphia: University of Pennsylvania Press.

Tambiah, S. (1985). *Culture, thought, and social action: An anthropological perspective.* Cambridge, UK: Cambridge University Press.

Turner, E. (1992). *Experiencing ritual: A new interpretation of African healing.* Philadelphia: University of Pennsylvania Press.

Turner, V. (1969). *The ritual process: Structure and anti-structure.* Chicago: Aldine.

Turner, V. (1986a). *The anthropology of performance.* New York: PAJ.

Turner, V. (1986b). Dewey, Dilthey, and drama: An essay in the anthropology of experience. In V. Turner & J. Bruner (Eds.), *The anthropology of experience* (pp. 33–44). Chicago: University of Illinois Press.

CHAPTER 17

Narrative Inquiry in the Psychotherapy Professions

A Critical Review

Catherine Kohler Riessman and Jane Speedy

We examine how the concept of narrative has entered several psychotherapy professions in the United Kingdom and the United States over the past 15 years, with special emphasis on research applications. Approaching our task from distinctive standpoints and locations, the chapter reviews definitions of narrative, criteria for "good enough" narrative research, and patterns in the literatures of social work, counseling, and psychotherapy. Our evaluation uncovered fewer studies in the United States than in English language journals in Europe and Canada and fewer studies in social work in contrast to the volume of narrative research in counseling[1] and psychotherapy. Four exemplars of narrative inquiry—"model" research completed by social workers, counselors, and psychotherapists—show the knowledge for practice that can be produced with careful application of narrative methods, in all their diversity. Drawing on our respective locations and experiences, we cautiously suggest some reasons for the paucity of quality research in the United States and greater representation in English language journals in Europe and for differences between the interlinked overlapping professions of counseling, psychotherapy, and social work.

Context for Our Review

Beginning in the late 1960s and continuing at a hectic pace, the idea of narrative has penetrated almost every discipline and profession. No longer the sole province of literary scholarship, narrative study is now cross-disciplinary, not fitting within the boundaries of any single scholarly field. The "narrative turn" has entered history, anthropology and folklore, psychology, sociolinguistics and communication studies, cultural studies, and sociology. The professions, too, have embraced the concept, along with investigators who study particular professions: law, medicine, nursing, education, and occupational therapy.[2] The narrative turn is part of a larger "turn to language" in the human sciences, evidence of a blurring of genres between the humanities and sciences (Denzin & Lincoln, 2005, pp. 1–32). Although narrative may have some roots in phenomenology (Ricouer, 1991), applications now extend beyond lived experience and worlds "behind" the author. A central area of narrative study is human interaction in relationships—the daily stuff of social work, counseling, and psychotherapy.

Our purpose is to examine the status of narrative in the three interlinked fields, with particular attention to research applications in journals, and to critically interrogate the results of the review. Limiting our search to journals in some ways disadvantages the newer fields of counseling and psychotherapy, which are less well established than social work within academies, but in the interests of equity and expediency, this was the parameter we set. There is narrative scholarship by social workers, counselors, and psychotherapists in books and book chapters (see Angus & McLeod, 2004a, 2004b; Etherington, 2000; Hall, 1997; Hermans & Hermans-Jansen, 1995; Laird, 1993; Levitt & Rennie, 2004; McLeod, 1997; Riessman, 1994; Shaw & Gould, 2001; Toukmanion & Rennie, 1992; White & Epston, 1990; White, 2000, 2004). In counseling and psychotherapy, much remains unpublished within master's and doctoral theses (see Grafanaki, 1997; Leftwich, 1998). Academic and professional journals remain a significant outlet for publication, particularly within the more professionally established social work field. How has narrative shaped social work and counseling and psychotherapy scholarship? More specifically, has there been systematic application of narrative methods (however diverse) in research? All three fields of practice are based on talk and interaction, and we expected to find many investigators taking up narrative approaches to study interactions with clients, and talk about clients with other professionals. We were surprised by the small corpus of systematic research but pleased to uncover several exemplars.

First, a couple of caveats: one about our use of the terms *counseling* and *psychotherapy* and another about our mode of presentation, before turning to complexities of definition, evaluation of the literature, and speculation about possible reasons for the paucity of narrative research in some fields. The terms *counseling* and *psychotherapy*, although contested, are used fairly interchangeably and flexibly in the United Kingdom and to a certain extent also across Australia and New Zealand. The North American usage is somewhat different, with *counseling* more firmly established within counseling psychology or education contexts; *psychotherapy* is a widely used term that crosses disciplinary boundaries. Wherever possible, we will use the terms *counseling* and *psychotherapy* conjointly in our text, unless citing a source that explicitly defines the terms in different ways.

The chapter includes several voices because we occupy distinct social locations and bring different perspectives and experiences to the evaluation, and we had different roles in the project. Riessman is a senior narrative researcher, North American sociologist, and former faculty member in several U.S. schools of social work, far removed from practice but with extensive knowledge about the diversity of narrative inquiry in the social sciences. Speedy is a narrative researcher with a post-structuralist/feminist and arts-based genealogy, working within a British school of education. She is a practitioner-researcher within the counseling and psychotherapy domains and practices as a narrative therapist (a genre that crosses the borders of counseling, psychotherapy, and family therapy). She adds a critique, the literatures from her field, and the voice of a practitioner to the chapter. We approached our topic from particular standpoints, as all investigators do, and these generated differences in our writing styles. Readers will notice shifts in pronouns and differences in writing style and that at points in our text, one or other of our names identifies a particular set of ideas. Although awkward, the device preserves our respective voices—a hallmark of narrative—and allows us to present a "story" of our research endeavor. An implicit dialogue between us should be evident to readers as they notice different ways of knowing buried in our text (evident in narrative studies generally): narratives as expressions of meaning-in-context and narratives as sites for constituting meaning. Both of us have preferred positions in relation to these issues, and we have both shifted, constructing our positions in light of the other's arguments. A more complex, dialogic text has emerged that neither of us could have produced separately. Our process parallels the construction of all stories—multiple voices and identities come into play.

What Is Narrative?

The term *narrative* carries many meanings and is used in a variety of ways by different disciplines, often synonymously with *story*. We caution readers not to expect a simple, clear definition of narrative here that can cover all applications, but we will review some definitions in use and identify essential ingredients. Narrative inquiry in the human sciences is a 20th century development; the field has "realist," "post-modern," and constructionist strands, and scholars and practitioners disagree on origins and precise definition (see Chase, 2005; Langellier, 2001; McLeod, 1997; Polkinghorne, 1988; Riessman, 1993, in press; Speedy, in press).

Riessman (1997) has written elsewhere about the tyranny of narrative, and her concerns continue: The term currently has a level of popularity few would have predicted when some of us began working with stories that developed in research interviews and medical consultations 20 years ago. To put it simply, the term has come to mean anything and everything; when someone speaks or writes spontaneously, the outcome is now called *narrative* by news anchors and qualitative investigators alike. Politicians speak of the need for "new narratives" to steer them through election periods, and jazz musicians are composing narrative pieces.[3] It is not appropriate to police language, but specificity has been lost with popularization. All talk and text is not narrative. Developing a detailed plotline, character, and the complexities of a setting are not needed in many communicative and written exchanges. Storytelling is only one genre, which humans employ to accomplish certain effects (detailed below). Other forms of discourse besides narrative include chronicles, reports, arguments, question and answer exchanges, to name a few (Polkinghorne, 1995; Riessman, 1993, in press).

In everyday use, however, narrative has become little more than metaphor—everyone has his or her story—a trend linked to the use of the term in popular culture: telling one's story on television or at a self-help group meeting. Missing for the narrative scholar is analytic attention to how the facts got assembled *that* way. For whom was *this* story constructed, how was it made, and for what purpose? What cultural discourses does it draw on—take for granted? What does it accomplish? Are there gaps and inconsistencies that might suggest alternative or preferred narratives? In popular usage, a *story* seems to speak for itself, not requiring excavation or interpretation—an indefensible position for serious scholarship or rigorous professional practice.

Although personal stories are certainly prevalent in contemporary life cognate with the current cult of the self as project (Giddens, 1991), narrative has a robust life beyond the self. Narrative has energized an array of fields in the social sciences: studies of social movements, organizations, politics, and other macrolevel processes. As individuals construct stories of experience, so too do identity groups, communities, nations, governments, and organizations construct preferred narratives about themselves. Perhaps a push toward narrative comes from contemporary preoccupations with identity in times of rapidly shifting populations, national, international, and neighborhood borders (see Bauman, 2004). Identities are no longer given and "natural," individuals must now construct who they are and how they want to be known, just as groups, organizations, and nations do. In post-modern times, identities can be assembled and disassembled, accepted and contested (Holstein & Gubrium, 2000; McAdams, 1993), and, indeed, performed (Langellier & Peterson, 2004).

Among scholars working with personal accounts for research purposes, there is a range of definitions of narrative, often linked to discipline, and significant overlap between narrative as an overarching paradigm or world view (Toukmanion & Rennie, 1992) and narrative as an object of investigation (Riessman, 1993, in press). In social history and anthropology, narrative can refer to an entire life story, woven from threads of interviews, observations, and documents. Barbara Myerhoff's ethnography of Aliyah Senior Citizens in Venice, California, is a classic example of the inroads made by narrative inquiry into other qualitative research traditions.[4] From taped conversations of Living History classes, combined with observations of the life of the Center, poems and stories written by members, and reflections on her biography, she composed compelling narratives of the lives of elderly Jews living out their days—performing their lives (Myerhoff, 1978, 1992). This work also became hugely influential in informing and sustaining the development of narrative therapy practice.

At the other end of the continuum lies a very restrictive definition. Here a story refers to a discrete unit of discourse: an answer to a single question, topically centered and temporally organized. The classic example is from social linguistics

(Labov, 1982; Labov & Waletzky, 1967). Resting in the middle on a continuum of definitions is work in psychology and sociology. Here, personal narrative encompasses long sections of talk—extended accounts of lives in context that develop over the course of single or multiple interviews (or therapeutic conversations). The discrete story that is the unit of analysis in Labov's definition gives way to an evolving series of stories that are framed in and through interaction. An example here is Mishler's (1999) study of the trajectories of identity development among a group of artists/craftspersons, constructed through extended interviews with them.

The diversity of working definitions of narrative in these brief examples of research shows the absence of a clear-cut definition. Do varying definitions have anything in common? What distinguishes narrative from other forms of discourse? Our answer is *sequence* and *consequence:* Events are selected, organized, connected, and evaluated as meaningful for a particular audience (Hinchman & Hinchman, 1997; Morgan, 2000; Riessman, 2004). Analysis in narrative studies interrogates language—*how* and *why* events are storied, not simply the content to which language refers (McLeod, 1997; Riessman, 1993, in press).

Storytelling can disrupt research and practice protocols when brief answers to discrete questions are expected. Instead, narrators take long turns to create plots from disordered experience,[5] giving reality "a unity that neither nature nor the past possesses so clearly" (Cronon, 1992, p. 1349). Typically, narrators structure their tales temporally and spatially; "they look back on and recount lives that are located in particular times and places" (Laslett, 1999, p. 392). Temporal ordering of a plot is most familiar (and responds to a Western listener's preoccupation with forward marching time—"and then what happened?"), but narratives can also be organized thematically and episodically (Boothe, 1999; Cazden, 2001; Gee, 1991; Heath, 1983; Meier & Boivin, 2000; Michaels, 1981; Riessman, 1987). In conversation, storytelling typically involves a longer turn at talk than is customary. Narrative research explores the extended account rather than fragmenting it into discursive meaning-laden moments or thematic categories, as is customary in other qualitative approaches. In practice, researchers in counseling/psychotherapy often combine narrative/thematic analyses (Grafanaki & McLeod, 2002) or discourse/narrative analyses (Reeves, Bowl, Wheeler, & Guthrie, 2004) in a bricolage of methods.

The act of telling can serve many purposes—to inform, embrace or reassess and retell (White, 2000), remember, argue, justify, persuade, engage, entertain, and even mislead an audience (Bamberg & McCabe, 1998). The persuasive function of narrative is especially relevant for the practicing professions. Some clients narrate their experience in ways that engage and convince, while other tellings can leave the audience skeptical. In case conferences, one speaker can persuade others of a particular clinical formulation, while another fails to convince—a process that can be studied by close analysis of the rhetorical devices each employs to "story" the case. The processes of remembering and retelling are key elements in counseling and psychotherapy conversations. Clients consulting therapists may experience aspects of their life stories as fragmented, chaotic, unbearable, hopeful, dreamlike, and/or scarcely visible (Bird, 2000, 2004; Dimaggio & Semerari, 2004; Frank, 1995; Hermans, 1999; Hermans & Hermans-Jansen, 1995; White, 2000). These brief examples suggest some points of entry for research investigation.

Approaching texts as narrative, whether written or conversational, has a great deal to offer the practicing professions, showing how knowledge is constructed in everyday worlds through ordinary communicative action. Social workers, counselors, and psychotherapists deal with narrative all the time: when they hear clients' stories about their lives and situations and when they try to persuade colleagues and governmental bodies in written reports. Narrative frameworks can honor professional values and ethics by valuing time with and diversity among people. Participatory practice that is empowering for clients depends on developing relationships in creative spaces between speakers. Angus and McLeod (2004b) write that the concept of narrative is so fundamental to human psychological and social life, carries with it such a rich set of meanings, that it provides a genuine meeting point between theoretical schools of therapy that have previously stood apart from each other.

Our Methods for Examining the Narrative Turn in Several Psychotherapy Professions

How have social workers, counselors, and psychotherapists employed the concept of narrative in professional writings? How have they differed from each other? Our review is based on a literature search of social work, counseling, and psychotherapy journals published in English-speaking countries, including those that occasionally publish work by social workers and therapy practitioners (such as the journal *Narrative Inquiry*). A list of English language journals was created as a starting point and then expanded after consultation with experienced academics, librarians, Internet resources, and databases (e.g., Applied Social Sciences Index and Abstracts, PsycINFO, Psychological and Sociological Abstracts). Colleagues familiar with narrative methods suggested citations. We limited the review to articles published between 1990 and 2002 and later updated the search by reexamining major journals through early 2005. Undoubtedly, we missed some work. Few relevant pieces were published before the mid-1990s, and the rate has increased since.

The social work literature was recently reviewed and critiqued by Riessman and Quinney (2005) and is included in this chapter. The search of the counseling and psychotherapy literatures (possibly less exhaustive) was conducted later by Speedy and colleagues.[6] The therapy field differed from social work in that a small group of high-profile narrative researchers within the United Kingdom and Canada have spearheaded and maintained an interest in narrative practice (see Angus & McLeod, 2004a; McLeod, 1997, for overviews). The output from narrative therapy practitioners has been prolific over the last 15 years, particularly from the Dulwich Centre in Adelaide, South Australia, which has its own publishing house and produces the *International Journal of Narrative Therapy and Community Work*.

Articles could be caught in our net if they used *narrative* in the title, abstract, or as a key word and they appeared in journals identified with social work, counseling, psychotherapy, or closely associated areas, such as family therapy, community work, mental health, addiction, health, or children and families. Reading through the collection of potentially relevant work—extremely diverse in purpose, theoretical perspective, and substantive topic—several additional questions were asked: Did authors align themselves with social work, counseling, or psychotherapy through a direct statement or an affiliation with a training program? We attempted, through a gradual winnowing process, to cull from more than 350 potentially relevant works those written by members of the three fields. Finally, we classified the articles into four broad groups based on purpose: improving practice, educating social work and psychotherapy students, reflections on the professional field, or empirical research. We then looked within each group for patterns and points of contrast. The groupings (and professional identity claims) were overlapping with fuzzy boundaries—an issue discussed below.

Patterns in the Literature

The vast majority of papers were practice oriented, specifically clinical, reflecting a privileging of conversation and relationships. Within social work, the practice articles appeared in U.S. publications (e.g., *Clinical Social Work Journal*) but increasingly in English language European ones as well, whereas in counseling and psychotherapy (the newer field with a smaller population of scholarly journals), the vast majority were in English language European, Australian, and Canadian publications (e.g., *Counselling and Psychotherapy Journal*). In some, the purpose was theoretical: a postpsychological critique of dominant paradigms in clinical practice, with an argument for attention to meanings and contexts because clinical theory is historically contingent and culture bound (Drewery, 2005; Gonçalves & Machado, 2000; Polombo, 1992). Publications were often organized around case examples: the therapeutic use of storytelling, for example, to facilitate discovery of competencies and resilience. Within the domains of traditional approaches to counseling/ and psychotherapy (including psychodynamic, cognitive behavioral, and humanistic approaches), there was a significant flowering of narrative models of assessing and analyzing psychotherapy process that, quite apart from borrowing aspects of the more widely known narrative therapy approach, included the core conflictual relationship theme (Luborsky, Barber, & Diguer, 1992) and the structured analysis of narrative performance known as JAKOB, an acronym for actions and objects (see Boothe, Von Wyl, & Wepfer, 1999). The self-narratives of individuals in therapeutic contexts and/or in social care were the focus of practice-oriented, case-centered papers (about struggles of adoptees, trauma survivors, the chemically dependent, individuals going through bereavement). Writers describe helping clients restory their situations, emphasizing positive effects of deconstruction and reconstruction of life stories. At times, particularly within the U.S. social work literature, narrative theory was in short supply—an add-on that allowed for reflection on a particular case. In contrast, in Australian and U.K. journals (e.g., *European Journal of Psychotherapy, Counselling and Health*), many authors discussed cases by drawing on and critiquing narratology and drawing on narrative therapy principles (an influential branch of the postpsychological, discursive therapies, originating within family therapy; see Morgan, 2000, 2002; Russell & Carey, 2004, for overviews of narrative therapy approaches).

Within a narrative therapy frame, for instance, thinly described dominant stories constructed by families about a "trouble-making" child were thickened with multiple other versions of the events, including preferred (and in this case transforming) stories for the child and family (e.g., Betchley & Falconer, 2002). There were few recent papers describing group work based on narrative principles, only classic articles (Dean 1995, 1998). There was an increase, both inside and outside the family therapy field, of the reflecting team and outsider witness group practices advocated by narrative therapists (see Behan, 1999).

The second, far smaller group was oriented to issues of pedagogy and professional development (most social work papers appeared in the *Journal of Social Work Education* or *Journal of Teaching in Social Work* but increasingly in others; in counseling and psychotherapy they tended to appear in special issues (*International Journal of Narrative Therapy and Community Work*, 2004, Volume 4). Although the pedagogical papers overlapped with practice-focused pieces that stressed theoretical critique and reflective practice, the thrust was toward curricular change to include "post-modern" and discursive approaches to practice and research, such as narrative (Speedy, 2000). The narrative therapy perspective was increasingly cited. A model paper describes using social work students' written narratives about their work with clients to forge reflexivity, linking past, present, and future actions. The field setting became a site for helping students use writing to develop critical reflexivity; the authors and field supervisors subsequently dialogued with the students' written narratives about clients, creating a multivoiced conversation (Crawford, Dickinson, & Leitman, 2002). Another paper explores the storying of professional identity among trainee counselors as a way of sustaining the training of narrative therapists (Winslade, 2003).

A third and related group of papers was composed of first-person autobiographical accounts. They typically appeared in highly specialized journals, such as *Reflections* and *Reflective Practice and Auto/biography*, where experimental writing (creative nonfiction) is encouraged, but we also found recent examples in mainstream U.S. and European journals (*Social Work, Counselling and Psychotherapy, The British Journal of Psychotherapy Integration*). Authors were faculty members in social work and psychotherapy programs, administrators in agencies, a range of practitioners, very occasionally, policy makers, and, even more rarely, clients and service users (e.g., Sands, 2000). Storytelling about an experience allowed the narrator to appeal directly to the reader. Social work and psychotherapy practitioners, it seems, are finding academic outlets in which to use narrative forms to make meaning of difficult events in their personal and professional lives, just as clients do in therapeutic conversations (see White & Hales, 1997).

The fourth group of papers used narrative concepts and methods for research purposes (some narrative therapy practitioners further blurred the boundaries and regimes of truth between therapy and research, as we show below). The diverse group of research-oriented papers appeared in general and specialty journals read by practitioners (e.g., *Social Work, Child and Adolescent Social Work Journal, Child and Family Social Work, British Journal of Guidance and Counselling, Counselling Psychology Quarterly, Gecko: A Journal of Deconstruction and Narrative Ideas in*

Therapeutic Practice, Family Therapy Networker, Families in Society, Health and Social Work, International Journal of Narrative Therapy and Community Work, Journal of Psychotherapy Integration, Psychotherapy, Psychotherapy Research) and in journals publishing research in the human services generally (*Qualitative Social Work, Qualitative Health Research, International Journal of Critical Psychology*). There were a few pieces written by social work and counseling practitioners in social science, feminist, and qualitative journals, such as *Qualitative Inquiry,* and the specialty publication *Narrative Inquiry.*

We were disappointed with the size of the research corpus, particularly in relation to social work. Counseling and psychotherapy is a newer, smaller professional domain in the United Kingdom, with a developing research trajectory that, perhaps to its advantage, parallels the recent surge of interest in qualitative research methods. We would get excited when reading an abstract that contained the words *narrative analysis* and *data,* only to discover the author of a compelling case study (the talk of a person with dementia, or ethnography of a learning disabilities classroom or of clients contemplating suicide) was from experimental psychology, nursing, or education—not social work, counseling, or psychotherapy. In other instances, authors said they applied "narrative analysis," but on closer inspection, findings were constructed by inductive thematic coding ("we looked for themes"). Snippets of talk (mostly non-narrative, stripped of sequence and consequence) were presented to illustrate common thematic elements across interviews. Appropriating the terminology of narrative by social work and psychotherapy investigators appears to be on the rise among those doing forms of discourse analysis and/or grounded theory research.

In an earlier paper, Riessman asked a number of specific questions of research in social work related to standards for "good enough" narrative inquiry (Riessman & Quinney, 2005); they served as guidelines for this chapter also. Was the work empirical, that is, based on systematic observations? Did analysis attend to sequence and consequence? Was there some attention to language, and were transcriptions made and interrogated? Did analysis attend to contexts of production (research and/or therapy relationships and macroinstitutional contexts)? Were epistemological and methodological issues treated seriously, that is, viewed critically, seen as decisions to be made, rather than "given"—unacknowledged? During the process of inquiry, previous divisions blurred: What about autoethnography and/or intensive case studies of particular interactions with clients using critical reflexivity? Boundaries between clinical inquiry, reflective practice, and research on clinical process are not always clear, a blurring of genres compounded by claims (evident below) that narrative therapy practice is a form of "live" coresearch.

Research that claimed to be narrative was extremely diverse in topic, approach, and quality. We uncovered some exemplary work but lots that was not. In one unfortunate set of papers, methods relied on story completion techniques, investigator ratings of narrative characteristics (e.g., coherence of stories, event structure analysis), or content analysis (frequency of particular words in an extended text). With few exceptions, direct quotation of interview discourse of any length was nowhere to be found. Audiotape recording and videotape recording were rare in social work, making any systematic examination of transcripts of interviews or group meetings impossible. Videotape or audiotape recording is much more common in psychotherapy, particularly in family therapy, with tapes often used in supervision and training. Nonetheless, researchers from all fields routinely summarized the content of speech, mediating the engagement of reader and narrative text. It is difficult under these circumstances to independently evaluate evidence for an author's argument or to interrogate the process of research that generated particular findings.

Frankly, we were surprised to see such limited use of the storehouse of narrative theory and methods now widely available in the qualitative research literature (Andrews, Sclater, Squire, Tamboukou, 2004; Andrews, Sclater, Squire, & Treacher, 2000; Bhabha, 1994; Chase, 2005; Clandinin & Connelly, 2000; Clough, 2002; Cortazzi, 2001; Fraser, 2004; Gergen & Gergen, 1984; Greenhalgh & Hurwitz, 1998; Hollway & Jefferson, 2001; Hurwitz, Greenhalgh, & Skultans, 2004; Josselson, Lieblich, & McAdams, 2003; Lieblich, McAdams, & Josselson, 2004; Lieblich, Tuval-Mashiach, & Zilber, 1998; McAdams, 1993; Mishler, 1986, 1995; Murray, 2003; Plummer, 2001; Poindexter, 2002; Riessman, 1993, 2004; Speedy, in press; White, 2000, 2004; White & Epston, 1990). Instead, many investigators adopted reductionistic techniques, in what became a kind of *statistics* of qualitative research: Lengthy accounts of lives were abstracted from their contexts of production, stripped of language, and transformed into brief summaries.

Data reduction is a task that confronts all qualitative investigators: Journals do not allow us to present the "whole story"; narrative accounts are typically long, and some selection is absolutely necessary. The challenge for narrative research is to work with the detail and particularity that is a hallmark of narrative, rather than mimicking positivist science in modes of data reduction.

Four Exemplars of Narrative Research

We now turn to research in counseling, psychotherapy, and social work that offers positive models—a counterweight to reductionism. Each of four exemplars, briefly presented here, meets several standards for "good" narrative research (outlined above); together, they offer models of diverse ways of approaching texts that take narrative form. We urge readers to consult the full articles and associated bodies of work for rich and lengthy description of methods and findings. The choice of exemplars reflects Riessman's preferences, learned from Mishler (1986, 1999): reliance on detailed transcripts; focus on language and contexts of production; some attention to the structural features of discourse; acknowledgment of the dialogic nature of narrative; and (where appropriate) a comparative approach—interpretation of similarities and differences among participants' stories. Regarding the dialogic criterion, Phil Salmon's (in press) words are instructive:

> All narratives are, in a fundamental sense, co-constructed. The audience, whether physically present or not, exerts a crucial influence on what can and cannot be said, how things should be expressed, what can be taken for granted, what needs explaining, and so on. We now recognize that the personal account, in research interviews, which has traditionally been seen as the expression of a single subjectivity, is in fact always a co-construction.

Despite many similarities, the four exemplars are extremely diverse. They explore very different questions, deal with different kinds of narrative texts, and employ contrasting forms of excavation and analysis. The first explores the constructs and values leading to aspirations for "the good life" within a client's experiential counseling relationship; the second explores the use of counternarratives with clients, when up against the dominant discourse of anorexia nervosa. The third examines written self-narratives of young clients as they leave foster care; and the fourth analyzes narratives about clients developed by professionals in team meetings. Our sequencing of the exemplars is purposeful: from the micro toward the macro—we start with an individual case and end with the construction of cases by professionals in organizational settings. The first two exemplars from counseling and psychotherapy illustrate the work of research teams, each reflecting a different way of combining psychotherapy process and outcome research.

Stories of the Good Life

Two British counseling researchers, McLeod and Lynch (2000), examine the first few minutes of an initial counseling session, when a client's core stories are told (and later elaborated). The authors' analysis of the initial texts is contextualized with materials from subsequent sessions, which they summarize. The client and counselor were both Canadian women, and the case was deemed, at the outset, an example of successful client-centered therapy. The researchers focus on philosophical concepts of the good life, particularly how client and counselor embed their conversation in respective conceptions of what it means to live a good life. The authors ask, How do client and counselor convey moral understandings and values, and how might they change over time in a therapeutic relationship?

These issues have been neglected in studies of therapeutic interaction. The authors draw on moral philosophers, as Taylor (1989) observes: "the sense of the good life has to be woven into my life as an unfolding story" (p. 470; also see MacIntyre, 1981). Taylor makes a distinction between *weak* and *strong* moral evaluations: choices between multiple possibilities, on the one hand, and, on the other, virtues that people are in awe of—would perhaps die for—that set the tone of a life.

McLeod and Lynch (2000) are clear about their standpoint and the particularity of their case study—they have not applied the moral framework to other cases (and strongly encourage others to do so):

> It is important to acknowledge that other plausible interpretations of this case are possible. Hermeneutic inquiry of this kind can never achieve a "factual" or "objective" explanation of a phenomenon. Its goal, instead, is to construct a representation of a slice of social reality that promotes a sense of an enhanced understanding, and contributes to new ways of seeing that reality. (p. 403)

The authors present a *slice* of narrative text that they analyze in relation to the client's (Margaret's) stated problems: marital difficulties, a daughter's forthcoming wedding, and her discomfort with her son's girlfriend. They adapted the approaches of Gee (1991), Mishler (1986), and Riessman (1993), creating a poetic representation of a therapy exchange. They use a three-stage method of interpretation: successive readings and rereadings of the transcripts by multiple readers, selection of segments for microanalysis (the first few moments of the first session) by the principal researchers, and an interpretive account of the whole therapy in relation to the part.

Margaret's initial account is presented in stanza form; the subsequent 11 sessions are summarized.

Margaret provides context for her depressed feelings in the initial session:

> and we based our whole life on our children
> you know
> we have to
> and you know
> we had
> it was always family holidays
> and that type of thing like we never left our children
> *and this was an agreement that*
> *this is our life*
> *you know*
> *and we were very happy with it*
> *but I always had sort of*
> *the feeling*
> *that*
> *when the children grew up*
> *and were independent*
> *we would become a couple again*
>> and of course the timing of all this just
>> just
>> that's just not what happened
>> and I think
> *I just felt so let down* (McLeod & Lynch, 2000, p. 396[7])

The authors do not include the therapist's interventions within the text (for reasons that are not clear) but do examine them later when reviewing contributions in subsequent therapy sessions.

In the excerpt, Margaret is evaluating her life and emotional well-being in relation to several noncommensurate principles of the good life, such as having an intimate relationship (with her husband) and fulfilling duties to others (children). When her children left, and they failed "becoming a couple again," Margaret experienced a *narrative fracture*, resulting in depression; she sought the help of a counselor.

The therapist held humanistic constructions of the good life, centering on emotional authenticity and awareness of a *deep interior* self that needs expression. These were communicated in the therapist's responses to Margaret: "And yet it sounded like at some point you were saying that what's really going on for you is hard for you to express" (McLeod & Lynch, 2000, p. 400).

The researchers build support for their theoretical argument with references back and forth between the excerpted text in stanza form and summaries of later sessions. The focus, however, is larger than the microprocess of the unfolding therapeutic relationship. In descriptions of explicit and implicit conceptions of the good life, they argue that successful therapy in this case was dependent on the counselor and client responding to the evaluative aspect of storytelling, that is, co-constructing Margaret's stories in relation to collective and historically specific discourses (Calvinist, dutiful; Romantic, intimate; Humanistic, self-aware) that underpins the client's understanding of her conflict.

As other exemplars (see following) do, McLeod and Lynch's (2000) work challenges the climate of evidence-based practice that is seeping across counseling and psychotherapy in the United Kingdom from elsewhere within the health and welfare disciplines (see Rowland & Goss, 2000). The research provides a theoretical framework and ways of presenting data that others can use to evaluate counseling sessions in narrative terms. Their emphasis on moral stories that shape practice extends beyond narrow approaches (on "inner worlds" of clients). The study meets several of the criteria identified earlier as hallmarks of "good" narrative research: A detailed transcribed excerpt is presented. There is attention to "macro" contexts of production, that is, available cultural discourses that therapist and client draw on. There is less attention to methodological issues, sequence and consequence, and the specifics of the client's (and the therapist's) language choices. The relationship between the counselor and client from one country, and research team in another, remains opaque; no comparisons are made with other dyads, but future researchers could adapt the approach.

Our second exemplar from counseling and psychotherapy troubles the edges between research and practice, and was included only after intense discussion between us. Some readers may continue to contest its inclusion in an overview of narrative "research." The particular study shows how narrative therapists, having listened intently to a client's stories, use their archive of knowledge about the co-construction of narratives and the social construction of possible identities to produce a counternarrative—different ground for the client to stand on. It represents, Speedy would argue, an example of a "live" performance of narrative coresearch.

These claims for narrative therapy practice as a form of collaborative, "living" research are more extensively presented elsewhere (see Crockett, 2004; Epston, 2001; Speedy, 2004, in press). They are, predominantly, sustained in two ways: firstly by descriptions of the *position* of the narrative therapist (Morgan, 2002), who is explicitly positioned as a coresearcher (in the archeological or anthropological sense) within the shared endeavor of scrutinizing, excavating, and exoticising[8] the particularities of aspects of their client's life story. Secondly, narrative therapists overtly attend to the sequence and consequences of the client's life stories in relation to discourse, context, relations of power (see White, 2004), landscapes of identity and meaning (see Bruner, 1990, 1991), personal agency, and absent but implicit possibilities (see Derrida, 2001). Thus, within the therapeutic exchange, narrative therapists are engaging in a collaborative practice of that which is described by others as narrative analysis or narrative inquiry. This is a *living practice of narrative coresearch-in-action*, even if it is frequently followed up with further scholarly reflections (see Crockett, Drewery, McKenzie, Smith, & Winslade, 2004).

Sustaining Counternarratives in the Face of "Discursive Parasites"

Like McLeod and Lynch's research, the exemplar represents a tale of a life re-authored but one that originates from a different school of narrative therapy (the process is described as coresearch, rather than therapy). The case study explores one client's stories, embedded within comparable narratives from a range of people, all of whom are engaged with countering "that which is called Anorexia"[9] (Lock, Epston, & Maisel, 2004).

The authors begin with a deconstruction of the historical and cultural discourses of that which is called anorexia; they trace a lineage from 12th-century saintly aestheticism, through witchcraft, to the contemporary construct of eating disorders (Hepworth, 1999). The authors educate readers about the purposes and collaborative coresearch practices of their particular narrative therapy approach. For example, they draw on conceptions of human nature in which the self is a discursive cultural construction, steering away from essentialist representations of problems people bring to therapy (e.g., "I am anorexic"). They turn, instead, toward socially and contextually situated understandings (e.g., "the position that anorexia has come to take up in a life"). The task of therapists, the authors suggest, is to help clients tell the stories/histories of their lives within the context of evaluative and fluctuating relationships with problems, rather than as problem lives. They also seek to generate alternative and/or preferable stories that might support changes in their clients' situations (see Morgan, 2000; Payne, 2000; Russell & Carey, 2004 for more on externalizing problem stories and re-authoring practices).

Lock et al. (2004) explore in some detail the tactic of externalizing problem stories as "driving a wedge between the person and the problem" (p. 282). They include short illustrative transcripts of therapeutic conversations between one of the authors (Epston) and several of his clients to demonstrate the pervasive and "parasitic" characteristics of anorexia as a category. The already compelling "voices" of anorexia have been compounded by medical narratives, which frequently describe people (mostly, though not exclusively, young women) as anorexics. Foucault (2001) argues that powerful dominant discourses often produce resistance against themselves. Lock and colleagues (2004) suggest that "that which calls itself Anorexia" attacks and indeed "co-opts" people who, almost by definition, do not have the resources to resist but rather find themselves drawn toward "excelling" at anorexia.

The authors (Lock et al., 2004) present Epston's conversations with two young women. Here he constructs *radical* externalizing counternarratives to the voice of anorexia. The therapist takes a clear position: "How immoral it is for Anorexia to try to talk you out of your life, a life it wants to terminate even before it has almost begun" (pp. 283–284). The excerpt illustrates how a counternarrative might begin to be performed.[10]

The journal article provides readers with two "unashamedly lengthy" excerpts of conversations (between Epston and a young client named Caroline and between Epston, Caroline, and Paula, another therapist[11]). The extracts represent a dramatic departure from what is typical in many narrative inquiries, especially those concerned with therapy and counseling. First, although it is now commonplace for narrative researchers to acknowledge that the narratives generated in research (or therapy) interviews are co-constructed, investigators typically give only perfunctory reference to the interviewer's or researcher's contributions; the focus is almost invariably on the other (client or interviewee). Second, the study treats the therapeutic conversation *as* collaborative research. The deconstruction of the multiplicity of available stories is shown as a live process that engages clients and therapists alike. This account of *narrative-analysis-in-the moment* later becomes the subject of further scholarly reflection as two other researchers, Lock and Maisel (see Lock et al., 2004, p. 275), describe their subsequent contribution to the study, embedding the therapeutic conversations within the literatures of the field.

A form of *living analysis* is illustrated with short excerpts from conversations between Epston and a different client (Chloe): Epston invites her to speculate about the different positions that "treaters" of anorexia might have taken at times of life-threatening crisis, asking her to speculate about the differences that these positions would make to the stories she tells about herself. Chloe's replies warrant greater scrutiny than space allows here,[12] but one comment indicates her general response: "Simply by using different language such as 'forbidding anorexia to murder me' rather than 'saving my life,' I'm sure that would have had an impact" (see Lock et al., 2004, p. 283).

Other extracts focus on therapists' (rather than client's) narratives and, as such, make an important and unusual contribution to therapy research. In one, Epston speaks from the position of anorexia (inviting another client to construct some kind of counternarrative). In another, Epston continues as anorexia, and another therapist (Paula) responds with counternarratives in the voice of anti-anorexia. The conversations did not develop out of the blue but emerge from their engagement with, and deconstruction of, the extensive experience the client (Caroline) has been describing. She speaks little at the beginning of the extract (below), but it is clear from her one line response that she is listening intently, taking up her own position:

E (as anorexia):   Well, who is Caroline going to believe, me or you? I have got a lot going for me. If she would only be perfect, I would give her everything.

P (as anti-anorexia): What would you give her?

E: Perfect happiness . . . and every dream she had would come true. Every dream she has ever had in her life, I would make come true.

P: That's a lot to believe.

E: Look at all the other people I've helped.

P:	Like whom?
Caroline:	Can Karen Carpenter[13] be Number 1?
E:	Yes! Karen Carpenter! Without me, she wouldn't have been such a great singer.
P:	Without you, we would still be listening to Karen Carpenter. . . .

Counternarratives provide "gentle defiance and resistance" (Andrews, 2002). With the excerpt, the authors "live" narrative analysis of therapeutic discourse; when actively offering extreme narratives and counternarratives, therapists can invite those consulting them to take up their own positions.[14] Not advocating the routine adoption or generalizability of their tactics, the authors explore the process, in context, as "it is fitted to the person, the history of the therapeutic relation, and, in this instance, the dire circumstances" (p. 289).

Lock et al. (2004; see also Maisel, Epston, & Borden, 2004) challenge the politics and conventions of therapy research by going beyond retrospective narrative analyses (that-which-occurs-in-therapy-that-might-inform-subsequent-improvements-in-practice). Instead, they model how therapists and clients can work as narrative coresearchers in the moment, rigorously excavating[15] the narratives available to re-author troubled lives. In extreme situations (such as self-starvation), therapists can construct narratives that

> provide resources that resonate through the fog of the previous resources the client has had to work with. Revealed in this way, the insidious logic of the dominant discourse can be deflected by counter-narratives such as these anti-anorexic ones from their otherwise inevitable dead-end. (p. 298)

The research fits with a number, although not all, of our stated criteria for good narrative research. Transcriptions of therapy conversation are presented alongside theoretical discussions that draw on narrative theory. The coresearch process with clients is presented in "live" excerpts; more extensive transcripts are made available to readers on request. The texts, when coupled with theoretical interpretation, illustrate a dialogic form of narrative analysis (e.g., interpretation of talk between therapist and client and, subsequently, an entire therapeutic team with the client). The exemplar does not attend to methodology—decisions made about what to present and how—that could guide future researchers.

We turn next to research in social work. Although many work with individuals in therapeutic relationships, neither exemplar focuses on individual cases.

Writing Narratives With Youth: Experimenting With a Method

Fay Martin (1998), a Canadian social worker who completed her dissertation in Britain, developed a technique in practice that she calls *direct scribing* to amplify muted voices of young people in child protection. She describes the narrative approach invented for practice and then adapted for her dissertation—participatory/critical research on the complex transition to independence for youngsters coming out of child protection. Martin's past experience indicated that many young people "felt strongly that child welfare files misrepresented their reality" (p. 2). Consequently, she invited them to dictate their self-narratives to her; she typed on the computer as they talked and watched the screen. Conversations about the stories followed—these were also transcribed. In collaboration with another adult guide, the life stories were eventually published in a book (Fay, 1989), where they spoke out, "saying their word to change the world, in the spirit of Freire" (Martin, 1998, p. 2).

The explicitly political research project involved 30 young people, randomly selected from a group who were coming out of care in a child welfare agency; all had lived in group or foster homes or institutions for some part of their lives. Because of their histories, they were "very sophisticated interviewees" who had "well-honed awareness of the power differential inherent in interview situations . . . enhanced understanding of the differential power of the spoken vs. the written word, and of the politics of ownership of the word" (Martin, 1998, p. 2). Many had spent hours facing workers who took notes and went away to write reports that became the "facts" of their cases, providing grounds for crucial decisions. Clients, of course, have not had easy access to their files to check them against their versions of events, nor can they change "facts" once entered in the file. The written word is privileged: "the person who chooses the word is more powerful than the person who the word purports to be about" (p. 3).

Given awareness of the politics of language, Martin decided to approach the problem by asking the youths to generate written self-narratives with her and later discuss them over the course of several meetings. She engaged participants in thinking about the adolescent transition—"when you were the responsibility of someone else [to] when you are responsible for yourself" (Martin, 1998, p. 5). She creatively instructed the writers in narrative concepts:

> The job of the Narrator is to choose among all the things that *could* be included in the story, what things *will* be included, and *how* they will be included. The Narrator is the boss: s/he has absolute authority about how to build the story. Because you know that there are many ways to tell the same story so that each, although different, is still true . . . just differently true. So the Narrator's job—that's you—is to figure out what of all the things you *could* put into the story you *will* put in, and how you'll string them together to make what points. As much as possible, I'd like you to tell the story as if you were talking to yourself as an audience. . . . I'm going to directly scribe the story, type, whatever you say. You should watch the screen and correct me if I make a mistake, or tell me if you wanted to take back or change something you said. (pp. 5–6)

Martin made provisions for different levels of literacy, but all participants became competent partners over time. Youngsters asked her questions, and she queried them about what they included or left out and why. Each participant left with a hard copy—of the story, and the dialogue with Martin about the story.

At the next meeting, participants interrogated what they had produced guided by the researcher:

> We approached the narrative as a piece of written text and analyzed it in various ways to ensure that it represented as accurately, as thoroughly as possible what they meant to say about their transitional experience, before the story was launched, independent of its author, into the world. (Martin, 1998, p. 6)[16]

More teaching about narrative form—beginnings, middles, ends—took place, including how to highlight turning points toward independence, a personal epiphany perhaps (although one participant emphatically declared that "she was not independent and would not be for some time," [Martin, 1998, p. 7]). The outcome was a set of written self-narratives—different trajectories out of adolescence and toward adulthood—accomplished collaboratively between investigator and participants.

Martin's project offers an example of participatory/critical research that is empowering: she took past inequalities into account in her research design, and created an alternative research context where muted voices could be heard. Her narrative method required participants "to preside over the transformation of the oral word into written text" (Martin, 1998, p. 9)—a process usually accomplished by investigator alone. Martin retained the right to query the story. Her insights from the research process are instructive for all narrative scholars:

> To speak is one thing, to be heard is another, to be confirmed as being heard is yet another. I believe the narrative interview operates at the third level. . . . The [written] assignment requires the participant to self-reflect on both the parts and the whole of his/her story. My experience of what the participants did with the assignment suggests that this engaged them at a fourth level, a step beyond being confirmed as heard. . . . The narrativists say that one creates and recreates oneself and positions oneself socially through narrative choices. My sense was that many of these participants, reflecting on themselves in the middle of the developmental task that was the focus of investigation, found themselves in the telling, experiencing themselves as creating themselves and as recovering themselves from the stories that had been told about them. (pp. 9–10)

The research benefited the youth—rare in research: Their marginalized voices found an outlet. With eventual dissemination of the book produced from the self-writings, alliances for social change in child welfare practices could be formed.

As an exemplar of good narrative research, Martin's study meets several criteria noted earlier. She created and then worked from detailed transcripts (though they are not included in the published paper) rather than simply memories of what may have been said at meetings. She describes in detail the conditions of production of the "final" life stories and how they were subject to change at varying points in the research process. She attends to structural features of narrative in the instructions she gives participants about beginnings, middles, and ends and turning points. Finally, the dialogic nature of the life stories is central to the project.

The fourth and last example carries issues of power, specifically in professional language about clients, into a pediatric setting.

Professional Storytelling at Team Meetings

Susan White (2002), a British social work academic, examines how cases are constructed through interprofessional talk at team meetings in a child health centre. How is the attribution of causality accomplished? Specifically, how do clinicians (pediatricians) tell cases in ways that persuade listeners (social workers and other professionals) of a particular formulation? Her ethnographic approach relies on detailed transcription of team meetings and presentation of lengthy excerpts that illustrate the narrative practices professionals employ.

The attribution of causation can be particularly complex in child health settings. The boundary between biological and psychosocial etiology is fuzzy but deemed necessary in medical contexts to accomplish diagnosis and formulate a treatment plan. How do professionals do it? Storytelling, White observes, is the major way cases get made, with the clinician ordering and sequencing clinical facts and social observations into versions that are recognizable to other team members, and can be processed. Storytelling enables professionals to render their formulations recognizable and accountable to colleagues on the team.

White (2002) displays the *ordering work* pediatricians do with fragments of material. They narratively construct an unproblematic "medical" case, on the one hand—where etiology is biological—and a psychosocial one on the other—a "not just medical" case. At least in part, the case is constituted through its telling; other possible readings of the material are closed off. White looks at the rhetorical and linguistic devices tellers adopt to narrate their formulations about patients, which signal particular readings of the material that can persuade colleagues. Her method draws on approaches originally developed in conversation analysis that she adapts to examine lengthy exchanges at team meetings. From transcriptions that sometimes approach 20 pages, she presents and analyzes excerpts, including ones that illustrate a particular narrator's strategies of argumentation in potentially contestable formulations—not just medical cases:

These formulations involve particularly complex story-telling, since the presence of an "intrinsic" disorder requires that any psychosocial component be worked up in the talk. Narratives about these cases have the flavour of detective stories with anomalous physical findings, such as failure to gain weight, set alongside characterisations of carers [typically mothers]. Cases may begin as "medical" and evolve gradually to a "not just medical," or psychosocial formulation through formal and informal case-talk between professionals. Once they have shifted in this way, they rarely return to a purely medical reading, since the relevances for storytelling and observation are extended to the child's relationships and social circumstances, which once exposed are almost always found wanting. (p. 418)

The outcome in such instances is often referral to the social services department or a child welfare agency.

White (2002) presents a series of extracts from team meetings about a child she calls Sarah, each of which she meticulously unpacks. She notes the alternative ways the case might have been told, with less deleterious consequences for the family—a child protection plan. Instead, the telling "silenced a potential alternative reading of Sarah's mother as a distressed or depressed parent who was struggling to care for her child and needed help, but was not herself morally culpable for the predicament" (p. 433). White reveals how the team meeting becomes a backstage space "where professionals can shore up and contest their formulations of cases and often rehearse their next [frontstage] encounters with patients and their families" (p. 425).

The research is important for the professions in a time of evidence-based practice. Professional sensemaking about complex cases is best revealed by ethnographic investigations, White (2002) argues, because it can uncover the "backstage" work clinicians do to collectively work up particular versions of a child and/or family. Parents get classified as "troublesome" or "negligent," and hence in need of social work intervention, as part of a complex reasoning process that defies analytic scrutiny using traditional methods of research. Technologies based on bureaucratic rationality, she argues, provide a particularly poor fit for the complexity and uncertainty found in many social care settings.

As an exemplar of narrative research, the work meets many of the criteria outlined earlier for good narrative inquiry: White presents detailed transcripts of excerpts of team meetings and analyzes language and narrative form, noting structural features of the professional narratives—precisely how they are rhetorically crafted to persuade. Because the investigator is working from transcribed tapes of professional meetings, her dialogic relationships with informants and the data are not included but could be in future studies of team meetings.

Conclusion

We began with the observation that the idea of narrative has touched almost every discipline and practicing profession and, in many, generated extensive research and practice programs (e.g., in nursing, medicine, occupational therapy, law, and education). We conclude from our review that social work has embraced narrative concepts for reflective practice and teaching but only to a very limited degree in research. Counseling and psychotherapy have established some very significant centers for the promotion of narrative practice and research in Canada, Spain, the United Kingdom, New Zealand, and Australia[17] (and to a lesser extent the United States) although much of the output from these centers still remains in the form of unpublished work by graduate students.[18]

The four exemplars show the kinds of relevant knowledge for social work, counseling, and psychotherapy that can be produced with diverse narrative approaches. The findings pinpoint key issues of process essential to professional practice: how attention to the *morality tales* of both clients and therapists can foster congruent practice (McLeod & Lynch, 2000); how radical constructions of counternarratives can undermine the pervasive and life-threatening discourse of anorexia (Lock et al., 2004); how adolescents' self-writings can foster discovery and client empowerment (Martin, 1998); and how professionals' talk about patients serves to construct particular case formulations, marginalizing other ways of thinking (White, 2002). The narrative methods each author/research team used—and they were very different—allowed process to come to the fore, rather than narrow outcomes alone.

We uncovered other solid research that could have served as exemplars (Botella & Herrero, 2000; Hydén, 1995; Hydén & Overlien, 2005; Lillrank, 2002, 2003; Markey, 2001; McLeod & Balamoutsou, 1996; Overlien & Hydén, 2003; Perry, 1999; Poindexter, 2002, 2003a, 2003b; Rennie, 2004a, 2004b; Urek, 2005; White & Featherstone, 2005). We undoubtedly missed a few studies in our search. But given that 30 years have passed since the "narrative turn" began to reshape the social sciences, and given contemporary preoccupations with identity construction, why is there so little research reflecting these trends in social work? Why is detailed attention to transcripts underpublished within counseling and psychotherapy? Are these professions, in their preoccupation with status and legitimacy, wary of narrative research because of a continuing infatuation with "hard" science, the experimental model, and "evidence-based" outcome studies?

The vast majority of the research we did find was published in British and European (English language) journals, joint British/U.S. ones, or interdisciplinary specialty journals. Given the sheer size of the U.S. social work and counseling/ psychotherapy market, the minimal amount of narrative research in major U.S. publications is puzzling. To initiate a dialogue about the anomaly, we offer some thoughts about possible reasons for the geographic divide, fully aware of the danger of generalizing across contexts. We present observations from distinct standpoints and refer readers to the contribution of Rennie (2004a, 2000b), whose speculations concur with our own.

Riessman's observations are informed by years of teaching narrative research methods in the United States and, in the last 10 years, in the United Kingdom, several Scandinavian countries, and Western Australia. She has been impressed by the extent of interest outside the United States in narrative methods. Speedy's reflections are informed by more than a decade spent practicing, researching, and teaching into the space between narrative inquiry and the narrative therapies across Europe and in South Africa, New Zealand, and Australia. We offer some tentative thoughts on how research cultures in the United States and E.U. countries may explain, in part, the geographic distribution of research articles uncovered in the literature review.

Health authorities in the United Kingdom are struggling to recruit and retain social workers. There is the appeal to an opportunity to build relationships and understand clients in depth—an opening for postgraduate students in research programs to undertake narrative inquiry that involves listening and interpreting. The United Kingdom has a strong socialist history and far more libertarian tradition of liberalism (which, in turn, has been of some influence within Australia and New Zealand). Within the United Kingdom (part of the European Union), universal and free social welfare services and commitments to social justice (including access to health care) remain. The demands of the market and consumerism are not, as yet, as cruel or as taken for granted as in the United States, perhaps. At the same time, there is an increasing push in both public and private sectors for "evidence," not ethnography, and a conservative agenda is increasing in influence in the United Kingdom and elsewhere. These trends are being felt in the funding of research, which may, in time, affect the questions social work postgraduates choose to explore and methods they select in dissertations.

Counseling and psychotherapy within the United Kingdom have developed outside the constraints of mainstream psychology and predominantly outside statutory provisions (such as the NHS). Practitioners have emerged from diverse and divergent disciplinary programs, including the arts, humanities, anthropology, sociology, and theology as well as psychology (McLeod, 2001; Speedy, 2005). These diverse training contexts enable practitioners/researchers to embrace literary and post-positivist paradigms more easily compared with their colleagues within North America, who tend to be trained in mainstream psychology and education contexts.

Narrative study is cross-disciplinary, drawing on diverse epistemologies, theories, and methods. Detailed analysis takes time and immersion; there are ethical issues that stretch customary practices in areas such as informed consent (Riessman, 2005; Riessman & Mattingly, 2005; Speedy, 2004). These realities create exciting opportunities for creative collaborative research but also problems for social work, counseling, and psychotherapy. Put simply, there is a great deal to read, and it typically lies outside the professional canon and toward the literatures of anthropology, philosophy, and literary theory. All professional groups tend to think and read in their own fields of specialization: We tend to be "blinkered" by our disciplines.[19] The structure of many universities further contributes to isolation, with different faculties and departmental division of knowledge. Young scholars in the United States are evaluated by colleagues in social work and/or counseling psychology, further isolating them.

In Europe, more than in the United States, there are counterforces to disciplinary narrowness. Some university programs in Sweden, Spain, and the United Kingdom, for example, are structured around broad areas of inquiry (children and families, policy studies, health) or broad groupings of disciplines (the social sciences). This is even more the case in Australian and New Zealand academies. These structures promote interdisciplinarity, perhaps contributing to the greater representation of European, Australian, and Canadian practitioners and researchers, compared with U.S. ones, in our review. Interdisciplinary programs foster competence in social theory, philosophy, biography, anthropology, creative writing, and other fields of knowledge relevant to narrative studies. In particular, therapy practitioners in New Zealand and Australia, where narrative approaches first emerged, were a long way away from the constraining forces of established therapeutic approaches; they had more license to develop their own forms of practice alongside the emergent narrative and post-modern turns within the social sciences (Bird, 2000; McLeod, 2003).

The structure of social work (and many counselor) education programs in North America is different from those in the rest of the world and, at the master's level, subject to strict accreditation procedures that leave little space for innovation or interdisciplinarity. The concern in master's programs is often about producing competent practitioners, but the large number and size of these programs in the United States have an effect on resources available for doctoral education, where researchers get trained. Research methods courses in U.S. and Canadian schools of social work and counseling psychology programs at all levels teach research designs appropriate for quantitative research and statistical analysis, with only cursory attention to forms of qualitative inquiry. Professional journals and texts reflect these biases in practitioner education. Practice journals provide a place for the broad spectrum of models for clinical work and increasingly, a place for narrative reflection. The problem is that practice journals do not necessarily foster the theoretical and/or empirical generalization that is possible with social research. Profound insights about a particular client, a particular interaction, or a therapeutic group process do not translate easily into broader insights about a phenomenon. In addition, practitioners who might want to develop research publications can feel disabled before they begin—by the very language of research they have been taught, reflected also in the journals they read. The majority of research published in professional journals in the United States is quantitative, mirroring the pattern in social work and counselor education. Some qualitative research is now getting into print, but rarely narrative studies (in the sense we have described them here), it seems. Research based on grounded theory and other qualitative traditions using analytic induction can be defined by editors and reviewers as "scientific," while some ethnographic work has had difficulty getting through the review process (and ethnographic methods are decades old). All these factors, and no doubt others, are shaping contemporary scholarship in journals and other publications within the United States. Practice knowledge from narrative therapy is far ahead of research applications right across the spectrum, a trend reflected in our review.

We offer a final comparison related to research funding, supported by Jean Gilgun's (2002) trenchant analysis of a document produced by the National Institutes of Health (NIH). She suggests that the NIH (which is the major supporter of social research in the United States) appears to hold a particular definition of science, embedded in language, that excludes the perspectives and assumptions of many forms of qualitative research. We could not agree more. The model and language of the natural sciences has migrated and is now used routinely to define acceptable procedures for research about the social world. The norm of a detached, disinterested, and disengaged observer is still being applied, often inappropriately, to human studies. Concepts of reliability and validity developed for quantitative work are misapplied as evaluative criteria; qualitative research has evolved different standards and different sets of ethical principles.[20] Faculties in U.S. universities are increasingly dependent on funding from the NIH, which further structures the kind of research that gets produced and how doctoral students are trained. The research agenda embedded in the No Child Left Behind Act is generating constraints that are seeping into education and psychotherapy research as well (see Lincoln & Cannella, 2004).

Funding streams and research priorities in European countries are different from U.S. ones, and social research may be less constrained by conservative political agendas (although this is changing with increased research governance within the United Kingdom[21]). The Economic and Social Research Council (ESRC)—the major source of funding there—has supported numerous projects using qualitative approaches. Some ESRC directives we have read would astonish U.S. colleagues by their breadth, reach, and interdisciplinarity. Indeed, one of the most successful ESRC-funded investigations of counseling/psychotherapy provision within the United Kingdom was spearheaded by a school of geosciences (Bondi, Fewell, & Kirkwood, 2002).

In sum, traditions and structures of education differ substantially between the two regions, shaping the amount and kind of research published. Counseling and psychotherapy practice within Europe is a relatively new field, which has only recently begun researching itself. Thus far, it has not attracted major funding, and research has tended to remain piecemeal, small scale, and underpublished (McLeod, 2001). Paradoxically, these factors may have enabled a more creative and diverse field to emerge.

We offer our respective speculations about possible reasons for the patterning of narrative scholarship in the hope of initiating a creative and constructive dialogue among students, educators, journal editors, reviewers, and funders within these domains. Dialogue is needed if narrative inquiry—in all its diversity—is to find a firmer foothold within counseling, psychotherapy, and social work scholarship.

Consulting Editors: Elliott Mishler and Denise Larsen

Notes

1. Publisher's note: Sage Publications prefers the spellings *counseling* and *counselor*, which will be used in this chapter except where *counselling* and *counsellor* are used in journal title and titles of published works.

2. For citations of theoretical and empirical work in each of these disciplines, see Angus and McLeod (2004a) and Riessman (2001, in press).

3. See Rawnsley (2002) for "new Labour" narratives in the United Kingdom, and Marsalis (2004) for jazz narratives.

4. Rennie (2004b), for example, illustrates the ways in which narrative constructs have begun to shape and influence the work of Canadian-grounded theorists conducting counseling and psychotherapy research.

5. There is lively philosophical debate about whether primary experience is "disordered"—that is, whether narrators create order out of chaos. This discussion is particularly pertinent to therapists working with client groups with chronically disordered lives. See Hinchman and Hinchman (1997, pp. xix–xx) and Dimaggio and Semerari (2004).

6. Speedy and colleagues from the Centre for Narratives and Transformative Learning, University of Bristol, United Kingdom, contributed collectively to this review. They were supported in this endeavor by Meier's (2004) critical review of narrative in psychotherapy, although the terms of Meier's evaluation were somewhat looser.

7. Margaret's poem "This is our life" is taken from McLeod and Lynch (2000), *European Journal of Psychotherapy, Counselling and Health, 3*(3), 389, Routledge (Taylor & Francis) and is reprinted with permission.

8. A term coined by the sociologist, Bourdieu (1988) to describe his work on "exoticising the domestic" and later borrowed by Michael White (2004) to shed light on the process within narrative therapy whereby attention to the particularities of "ordinary" life stories (to the extent of an intense scrutiny of taken for granted stories) renders people's lives both extraordinary and rich in unexcavated plots and possibilities.

9. Anorexia nervosa is now a widely recognized medical condition. The authors of this exemplar, however, seek to position anorexia nervosa as a recently constructed historical and social phenomenon. They introduce the possibility of using terms that carry more meaning or seem closer to the lived and felt experiences of their clients.

10. The authors point out that their work does not offer any generalizable "blueprints" since anorexia will manifest itself and operate differently within different lives. They illustrate the persistent tactics of anorexia in disciplining people's lives and describe the "radical territories" that therapists may be required to inhabit to offer their clients opportunities to find moments in their lives that are not dominated by anorexia. It is within these spaces, they argue, that points of entry to other stories of people's lives might emerge.

11. Conversations between Epston and his clients are reprinted with permission of David Epston.

12. Extensive extracts from Epston and Chloe's investigations into anorexia's constructions can be found at www.narrativeapproaches.com.

13. Karen Carpenter of "The Carpenters," a well-known pop group, died in 1983 of heart failure caused by chronic anorexia.

14. The researchers' practice of narrative therapy is informed by Vygotsky's (1962) ideas about the internalization of constructions of self.

15. Archeological metaphors are frequently used by post-structuralist/post-psychological therapists to inform and sustain their practice; see Monk, Winslade, Crockett, and Epston (1997).

16. A reviewer noted complexities hidden in Martin's instruction here: the suggestion to represent "as accurately and thoroughly as possible." Most analysts agree that any narrative representation involves a *version* of events and experiences, shaped by audience and other contexts—a perspective Martin obviously shares, evidenced in previously quoted material.

17. The Psychotherapy Research Group, Toronto, Ontario, Canada; Ramon Llull University, Barcelona, Spain; the counseling program at the University of Abertay Dundee, United Kingdom; the Centre for Narratives and Transformative Learning, University of Bristol, United Kingdom; the Family Centre, Auckland, New Zealand; the counseling programs at the University of Waikato, New Zealand; the Dulwich Centre, Adelaide, South Australia; the Evanston Therapy Center, Evanston, Illinois.

18. Many of these unpublished papers and theses can be accessed online at www.narrativeaproaches.com.

19. Riessman thanks Kim Etherington for this formulation.

20. On the evolving issue of criteria for qualitative research in its various forms, see Maxwell (1992), Mishler (1990), Seale (2002), Sparkes (2002), and Speedy (in press).

21. See Bond (2004) on the rise of U.S. styles of "governance" in the United Kingdom.

References

Andrews, M. (2002). Memories of mother: Narrative reconstructions of early maternal influence. *Narrative Inquiry, 12,* 7–27.

Andrews, M., Sclater, S. D., Squire, C., & Treacher, A. (Eds.). (2000). *Lines of narrative: Psychosocial perspectives.* New York: Routledge.

Andrews, M., Sclater, S. D., Squire, C., & Tamboukou, M. (2004). Narrative research. In C. Seale, G. Gobo, J. Gubrium, & D. Silverman (Eds.), *Qualitative research practice* (pp. 109–124). Thousand Oaks, CA: Sage.

Angus, L., & McLeod, J. (2004a). *The handbook of narrative and psychotherapy.* Thousand Oaks, CA: Sage.

Angus, L., & McLeod, J. (2004b). Toward an integrative framework for understanding the role of narrative in the psychotherapy process. In L. Angus & J. McLeod (Eds.), *The handbook of narrative and psychotherapy practice, theory and research* (pp. 367–374). London: Sage.

Bamberg, M. G. W., & McCabe, A. (1998). Editorial. *Narrative Inquiry, 8*(1), iii–v.

Bauman, Z. (2004). *Identity.* Cambridge, UK: Polity Press.

Behan, C. (1999). Linking lives around shared themes: Narrative group therapy with gay men. *Gecko: A Journal of Deconstruction and Narrative Ideas in Therapeutic Practice, 2,* 18–35.

Betchley, D., & Falconer, W. (2002). Giving Colin a voice: The challenge of narrative therapy with a client who has an intellectual disability and communication difficulties. *Australian Social Work, 55*(1), 3–12.

Bhabha, H. (1994). DissemiNation: Time, narrative and the margins of the modern nation. In H. Bhabha (Ed.), *The location of culture* (pp. 175–199). London: Routledge.

Bird, J. (2000). *The heart's narrative: Therapy and navigating life's contradictions.* Auckland, New Zealand: Edge Press.

Bird, J. (2004). *Talk that sings: Therapy in a new linguistic key.* Auckland, New Zealand: Edge Press.

Bond, T. (2004). Ethical guidelines for researching counselling and psychotherapy. *Counselling and Psychotherapy Research, 4*(2), 4–20.

Bondi, L., Fewell, J., & Kirkwood, C. (2002). *Counselling and society: A case study of voluntary sector provision in Scotland.* End of award report to ESRC, No R000239059.

Boothe, B. (1999). Narrative episodes and the dynamics of psychic conflict. *Journal for Gestalt Theory and Its Applications, 21,* 6–24.

Boothe, B., Von Wyl, A., & Wepfer, R. (1999). Narrative dynamics and psychodynamics. *Psychotherapy Research, 9,* 258–273.

Botella, L., & Herrero, O. (2000). A relational constructivist approach to narrative therapy. *European Journal of Psychotherapy, Counselling and Health, 3*(1), 407–418.

Bourdieu, P. (1988). *Homo academicus.* Stanford, CA: Stanford University Press.

Bruner, J. (1990). *Acts of meaning.* Cambridge, MA: Harvard University Press.

Bruner, J. (1991). The narrative construction of reality. *Critical Inquiry, 18,* 1–21.

Cazden, C. B. (2001). *Classroom discourse: The language of teaching and learning* (2nd ed.). Portsmouth, NH: Heinemann.

Chase, S. E. (2005). Narrative inquiry: Multiple lenses, approaches, voices. In N. K. Denzin & Y. S. Lincoln (Eds.), *Handbook of qualitative research* (3rd ed., pp. 651–679). Thousand Oaks, CA: Sage.

Clandinin, J., & Connelly, F. M. (2000). *Narrative inquiry: Experience and story in qualitative research.* San Francisco: Jossey-Bass.

Clough, P. (2002). *Narratives and fictions in educational research.* Buckingham, UK: Open University.

Cortazzi, M. (2001). Narrative analysis in ethnography. In P. Atkinson, A. Coffey, S. Delamont, J. Lofland, & L. Lofland (Eds.), *Handbook of ethnography* (pp. 384–394). Thousand Oaks, CA: Sage.

Crawford, F., Dickinson, J., & Leitman, S. (2002). Mirroring meaning making: Narrative ways of reflecting on practice for action. *Qualitative Social Work, 1*(2), 170–190.

Crockett, K. (2004). From narrative practice in counselling to narrative practice in research: A professional identity story. *International Journal of Narrative Therapy and Community Work, 2*, 63–68.

Crockett, K., Drewery, W., McKenzie, W., Smith, L., & Winslade, J. (2004). Working for ethical research in practice. *International Journal of Narrative Therapy and Community Work, 3*, 61–67.

Cronon, W. (1992). A place for stories: Nature, history, and narrative. *Journal of American History, 78*(4), 1347–1376.

Dean, R. G. (1995). Stories of AIDS: The use of narrative as an approach to understanding in an AIDS support group. *Clinical Social Work Journal, 23*(3), 287–304.

Dean, R. G. (1998). A narrative approach to groups. *Clinical Social Work Journal, 26*(1), 23–37.

Denzin, N., & Lincoln, Y. (2005). Introduction. In N. Denzin & Y. Lincoln (Eds.), *The Sage handbook of qualitative research* (pp. 1–29). Thousand Oaks, CA: Sage.

Derrida, J. (2001). *Writing and difference.* London: Routledge. (Original work published 1978)

Dimaggio, G., & Semerari, A. (2004). Disorganised narratives: The psychological condition and its treatment. In L. Angus & J. McLeod (Eds.), *The handbook of narrative and psychotherapy* (pp. 263–282). London: Sage.

Drewery, W. (2005). Why we should watch what we say: Position calls, everyday speech and the production of relational subjectivity. *Theory and Psychology, 15*(3), 305–324.

Epston, D. (2001). Anthropology, archives, co-research and narrative therapy: An interview with David Epston. In D. Denborough (Ed.), *Family therapy: Exploring the field's past, present and possible futures* (pp. 177–182). Adelaide, South Australia: Dulwich Centre.

Etherington, K. (2000). *Narrative approaches to working with adult male survivors of child sexual abuse: The client's, the counsellor's and the researcher's story.* London: Jessica Kingsley.

Fay, M. (Ed.). (1989). *Speak out: An anthology of stories by youth in care.* Toronto, Canada: Page Adolescent Resource Centre.

Foucault, M. (2001). Truth and power. In J. Faubion (Ed.), *Michel Foucault: Power. Essential works of Foucault, 1954-1984, volume three.* London: Allen Lane, Penguin Press.

Frank, A. (1995). *The wounded storyteller: Body, illness, and ethics,* Chicago: University of Chicago Press.

Fraser, H. (2004). Doing narrative research: Analyzing personal stories line by line. *Qualitative Social Work, 3*(2), 179–201.

Gee, J. P. (1991). A linguistic approach to narrative. *Journal of Narrative and Life History/Narrative Inquiry, 1*, 15–39.

Gergen, M., & Gergen, K. (1984). The social construction of narrative accounts. In M. Gergen & K. Gergen (Eds.), *Historical social psychology.* Mahwah, NJ: Erlbaum.

Giddens, A. (1991). *Modernity and self-identity, self and society in the late modern age.* Cambridge, UK: Polity Press.

Gilgun, J. F. (2002). Conjectures and refutations: Governmental funding and qualitative research. *Qualitative Social Work, 1*(3), 359–375.

Gonçalves, O., & Machado, P. (2000). Emotions, narrative and change. *European Journal of Psychotherapy, Counselling and Health, 3*(3), 376–388.

Grafanaki, S. (1997). *Client and counsellor experiences of therapy interaction during moments of congruence and incongruence: Analysis of significant events in counselling/psychotherapy.* Unpublished doctoral dissertation, University of Keele, Keele, UK.

Grafanaki, S., & McLeod, J. (2002). Experiential congruence: A qualitative analysis of client and counsellor narrative accounts of significant events in time-limited personal therapy. *Counselling and Psychotherapy Research, 2*(1), 20–33.

Greenhalgh, T., & Hurwitz, B. (1998). *Narrative-based medicine: Dialogue and discourse in clinical practice.* London: BMJ Books.

Hall, C. J. (1997). *Social work as narrative: Storytelling and persuasion in professional texts.* Oxford, UK: Ashgate.

Heath, S. B. (1983). *Ways with words: Language, life and work in communities and classrooms.* New York: Cambridge University Press.

Hepworth, J. (1999). *The social construction of anorexia nervosa.* London: Sage.

Hermans, H. (1999). Self-narrative as meaning construction: The dynamics of self investigation. *Journal of Clinical Psychology, 55,* 1193–1211.

Hermans, H., & Hermans-Jansen, E. (1995). *Self narratives: The construction of meaning in psychotherapy.* New York: Guilford.

Hinchman, L. P., & Hinchman, S. K. (Eds.). (1997). *Memory, identity, community: The idea of narrative in the human sciences.* Albany: State University of New York Press.

Hollway, W., & Jefferson, T. (2001). *Doing qualitative research differently: Free association, narrative and the interview method.* London: Sage.

Holstein, J. A., & Gubrium, J. F. (2000). *The self we live by: Narrative identity in a postmodern world.* New York: Oxford University Press.

Hurwitz, B., Greenhalgh, T., & Skultans, V. (Eds.). (2004). *Narrative research in health and illness.* Oxford, UK: Blackwell/BMJ Books.

Hydén, M. (1995). Verbal aggression as prehistory of woman battering. *Journal of Family Violence, 10*(1), 55–71.

Hydén, M., & Overlien, C. (2005). Applying narrative analysis to the process of confirming or disregarding cases of suspected child abuse. *Child and Family Social Work, 10*(1), 57–65.

Josselson, R., Lieblich, A., & McAdams, D. P. (Eds.). (2003). *Up close and personal: The teaching and learning of narrative research.* Washington, DC: American Psychological Association.

Labov, W. (1982). Speech actions and reactions in personal narrative. In D. Tannen (Ed.), *Analyzing discourse: Text and talk* (pp. 219–247). Washington, DC: Georgetown University Press.

Labov, W., & Waletzky, J. (1967). Narrative analysis: Oral versions of personal experience. In J. Helm (Ed.), *Essays on the verbal and visual arts* (pp. 12–44). Seattle, WA: American Ethnological Society.

Laird, J. (Ed.). (1993). *Revisioning social work education: A social constructionist approach.* New York: Haworth.

Langellier, K. M. (2001). Personal narrative. In M. Jolly (Ed.), *Encyclopedia of life writing: Autobiographical and biographical forms* (pp. 699–701). London: Fitzroy Dearborn.

Langellier, K., & Peterson, E. (2004). *Storytelling in everyday life.* London: Routledge.

Laslett, B. (1999). Personal narrative as sociology. *Contemporary Sociology, 28,* 391–401.

Leftwich, A. (1998). *But I must also feel it as a man: The experience of male bereavement.* Unpublished master's thesis, University of Bristol, UK.

Levitt, H., & Rennie, D. (2004). Narrative activity: Clients' and therapists' intentions in the process of narration. In L. Angus & J. McLeod (Eds.), *The handbook of narrative and psychotherapy* (pp. 299–314). London: Sage.

Lieblich, A., McAdams, D., & Josselson, R. (2004). *Healing plots: The narrative basis of psychotherapy,* Washington, DC: American Psychological Association.

Lieblich, A., Tuval-Mashiach, R., & Zilber, T. (1998). *Narrative research: Reading, analysis, and interpretation.* Thousand Oaks, CA: Sage.

Lillrank, A. (2002). The tension between overt talk and covert emotions in illness narratives: Transition from clinician to researcher. *Culture, Medicine and Psychiatry, 26,* 111–127.

Lillrank, A. (2003). Back pain and the resolution of diagnostic uncertainty in illness narratives. *Social Science & Medicine, 57,* 1045–1054.

Lincoln, Y., & Cannella, G. (2004). Dangerous discourses: Methodological conservatism and governmental regimes of truth. *Qualitative Inquiry, 10*(1), 5–15.

Lock, A., Epston, D., & Maisel, R. (2004). Countering that which is called anorexia. *Narrative Inquiry, 14*(2), 275–301.

Luborsky, L., Barber, J., & Diguer, L. (1992). The meanings of narratives told during psychotherapy: The fruits of a new observational unit. *Psychotherapy Research, 2,* 277–290.

MacIntyre, A. (1981). *After virtue: A study in moral theory,* London: Duckworth.

Maisel, R., Epston, D., & Borden, A. (2004). *Biting the hand that starves you: Inspiring resistance to anorexia/bulimia.* New York: W. W. Norton.

Markey, C. (2001). It was not the words that hit mum: Working with the effects of domestic violence. *Gecko: A Journal of Deconstruction and Narrative Ideas in Therapeutic Practice, 2,* 3–29.

Marsalis, W. (2004). *Wynton Marsalis to perform jazz narrative: "Suite for human nature."* Retrieved December 2, 2004, from www.wyntonmarsalis.net

Martin, F. E. (1998). Tales of transition: Self-narrative and direct scribing in exploring careleaving. *Child and Family Social Work, 3*(1), 1–12.

Maxwell, J. A. (1992). Understanding and validity in qualitative research. *Harvard Educational Review, 62,* 279–300.

McAdams, D. (1993). *The stories we live by: Personal myths and the making of the self.* New York: Guilford Press.

McLeod, J. (1997). *Narrative and psychotherapy,* London: Sage.

McLeod, J. (2001). Developing a research tradition consistent with the practices and values of counselling and psychotherapy: Why counselling and psychotherapy research is necessary. *Counselling and Psychotherapy Research, 1*(1), 3–12.

McLeod, J. (2003). *An introduction to counselling.* London: Sage.

McLeod, J., & Balamoutsou, S. (1996). Representing narrative process in therapy: Qualitative analysis of a single case. *Counselling Psychology Quarterly, 9,* 61–76.

McLeod, J., & Lynch, G. (2000). This is our life: Strong evaluation in psychotherapy narrative. *European Journal of Psychotherapy, Counselling and Health, 3*(3), 389–407.

Meier, A. (2004). Narrative in psychotherapy theory, practice, and research: A critical review. *Counselling and psychotherapy research, 2*(4), 239–254.

Meier, A., & Boivin, M. (2000). The achievement of greater selfhood: The application of theme analysis to case study. *Psychotherapy Research, 10,* 57–77.

Michaels, S. (1981). "Sharing time": Children's narrative styles and differential access to literacy. *Language and Society, 10,* 423–442.

Mishler, E. G. (1986). *Research interviewing: Context and narrative.* Cambridge, MA: Harvard University Press.

Mishler, E. G. (1990). Validation in inquiry-guided research: The role of exemplars in narrative studies. *Harvard Educational Review, 60,* 415–442.

Mishler, E. G. (1995). Models of narrative analysis: A typology. *Journal of Narrative and Life History, 5*(2), 87–123.

Mishler, E. G. (1999). *Storylines: Craftartists' narratives of identity.* Cambridge, MA: Harvard University Press.

Monk, G., Winslade, J., Crockett, K., & Epston, D. (Eds.). (1997). *Narrative therapy in practice: The archaeology of hope.* San Francisco: Jossey-Bass.

Morgan, A. (2000). *What is narrative therapy?* Adelaide, South Australia: Dulwich Centre.

Morgan, A. (2002). Beginning to use a narrative approach in therapy. *International Journal of Narrative Therapy and Community Work, 1,* 85–90.

Murray, M. (2003). Narrative psychology and narrative analysis. In P. M. Camic, J. E. Rhodes, & L. Yardley (Eds.), *Qualitative research in psychology* (pp. 95–112). Washington, DC: American Psychological Association.

Myerhoff, B. (1978). *Number our days.* New York: Simon & Schuster.

Myerhoff, B. (with Metzger, D., Ruby, J., & Tufte, V.) (Eds.). (1992). *Remembered lives.* Ann Arbor: University of Michigan Press.

Overlien, C., & Hydén, M. (2003). Work identity at stake: The power of sexual abuse stories in the world of youth compulsory care. *Narrative Inquiry, 13,* 217–242.

Payne, M. (2000). *Narrative therapy: An introduction for counsellors.* London: Sage.

Perry, L. (1999). There's a garden—somewhere. In A. Morgan (Ed.), *Narrative therapy with children and their families* (pp. 47–53). Adelaide, South Australia: Dulwich Centre.

Plummer, K. (2001). *Documents of life 2: An invitation to critical humanism.* London: Sage.

Poindexter, C. (2002). Meaning from methods: Re-presenting stories of an HIV-affected caregiver. *Qualitative Social Work, 1*(1), 59–78.

Poindexter, C. (2003a). Sex, drugs, and love in middle age: A case study of a sero-discordant heterosexual couple coping with HIV. *Journal of Social Work Practice in the Addictions, 3*(2), 57–83.

Poindexter, C. (2003b). The ubiquity of ambiguity in research interviewing: A case study. *Qualitative Social Work, 2*(4), 383–409.

Polkinghorne, D. (1988). *Narrative knowing and the human sciences.* New York: State University of New York Press.

Polkinghorne, D. (1995). Narrative configuration in qualitative analysis. *Qualitative Studies in Education, 8*(1), 5–23.

Polombo, J. (1992). Narratives, self-cohesion, and the patient's search for meaning. *Clinical Social Work Journal, 20*(3), 249–270.

Rawnsley, A. (2002, April 21). New Labour grows up. *The Observer.* Retrieved December 2, 2004, from http://observer.guardian.co.uk/comment/story/0,,687946,00.html

Reeves, A., Bowl, R., Wheeler, S., & Guthrie, E. (2004). The hardest words: Exploring the dialogue of suicide in counselling: A discourse analysis. *Counselling and Psychotherapy Research, 4*(1), 62–72.

Rennie, D. (2004a). Anglo-North American qualitative counseling and psychotherapy research. *Psychotherapy Research, 14*(1), 37–55.

Rennie, D. (2004b). Storytelling in psychotherapy: The client's subjective experience. *Psychotherapy: Theory, Research, Practice, Training, 31*(2), 234–243.

Ricoeur, P. (1991). Life in quest of narrative. In D. Wood (Ed.), *On Paul Ricoeur: Narrative and interpretation* (pp. 20–33). London: Routledge.

Riessman, C. K. (1987). When gender is not enough: Women interviewing women. *Gender & Society, 1*(2), 172–207.

Riessman, C. K. (1993). *Narrative analysis.* Newbury Park, CA: Sage.

Riessman, C. K. (Ed.). (1994). *Qualitative studies in social work research.* Thousand Oaks, CA: Sage.

Riessman, C. K. (1997). A short story about long stories. *Journal of Narrative and Life History, 7*(1–4), 155–159.

Riessman, C. K. (2001). Personal troubles as social issues: A narrative of infertility in context. In I. Shaw & N. Gould (Eds.), *Qualitative research in social work: Method and context* (pp. 73–82). Thousand Oaks, CA: Sage.

Riessman, C. K. (2004). Narrative analysis. In M. S. Lewis-Beck, A. Bryman, & T. Futing Liao (Eds.), *The SAGE encyclopedia of social science research methods* (pp. 705–709). Thousand Oaks, CA: Sage.

Riessman, C. K. (2005). Exporting ethics: A narrative about narrative research in South India. *Health: An Interdisciplinary Journal for the Social Study of Health, Illness and Medicine, 9*(4), 473–490.

Riessman, C. K. (in press). *Narrative methods for the human sciences.* Thousand Oaks, CA: Sage.

Riessman, C. K., & Mattingly, C. (2005). Introduction: Toward a context-based ethics for social research in health. *Health: An Interdisciplinary Journal for the Study of Health, Illness and Medicine, 9,* 427–429.

Riessman, C. K., & Quinney, L. (2005). Narrative in social work: A critical review. *Qualitative Social Work, 4*(4), 383–404.

Rowland, N., & Goss, S. (2000). *Evidence-based counselling and psychological therapies: Research and applications.* London: Routledge.

Russell, S., & Carey, M. (2004). *Narrative therapy: Responding to your questions.* Adelaide, South Australia, Australia: Dulwich Centre.

Salmon, P. (in press). Some thoughts on narrative research. In M. Andrews, S. Squire, & M. Tamboukou (Eds.), *Doing narrative research in the social sciences.* London: Sage.

Sands, A. (2000). Falling for therapy. *Counselling and Psychotherapy Journal, 11*(100), 614–616.

Seale, C. (2002). Quality issues in qualitative inquiry. *Qualitative Social Work, 1*(1), 97–110.

Shaw, I., & Gould, N. (Eds.). (2001). *Qualitative research in social work: Method and context.* Thousand Oaks, CA: Sage.

Sparkes, A. C. (2002). Autoethnography: Self-indulgence or something more? In A. P. Bochner & C. Ellis (Eds.), *Ethnographically speaking* (pp. 209–232). Walnut Creek, CA: AltaMira.

Speedy, J. (2000). The storied helper. *European Journal of Psychotherapy, Counselling and Health, 3*(3), 361–375.

Speedy, J. (2004). Living a more peopled life: Definitional ceremony as inquiry into psychotherapy "outcomes." *International Journal of Narrative Therapy and Community Work, 3,* 43–53.

Speedy, J. (2005). Failing to come to terms with things: A multi-storied conversation about poststructuralist ideas and narrative practices in response to some of life's failures. *Counselling and Psychotherapy Research, 5*(1), 65–73.

Speedy, J. (in press). *Narrative inquiry and psychotherapy.* Houndsmill, UK: Palgrave Macmillan.

Taylor, C. (1989). *Sources of the self: The making of the modern identity.* Cambridge, UK: Cambridge University Press.

Toukmanion, S., & Rennie, D. (Eds.). (1992). *Psychotherapy process research, paradigmatic and narrative approaches.* Newbury Park, CA: Sage.

Urek, M. (2005). Making a case in social work: The construction of an unsuitable mother. *Qualitative Social Work, 4,* 451–467.

Vygotsky, L. (1962). *Thought and language.* Boston: MIT Press.

White, C., & Hales, J. (1997). *The personal is professional,* Adelaide, South Australia: Dulwich Centre.

White, M. (2000). *Reflections on narrative practice: Essays and interviews.* Adelaide, South Australia: Dulwich Centre.

White, M. (2004). *Narrative practice and exotic lives: Resurrecting diversity in everyday life.* Adelaide, South Australia: Dulwich Centre.

White, M., & Epston, D. (1990). *Narrative means to therapeutic ends.* New York: W. W. Norton.

White, S. (2002). Accomplishing the case in paediatrics and child health: Medicine and morality in inter-professional talk. *Sociology of Health and Illness, 24*(4), 409–435.

White, S., & Featherstone, B. (2005). Communicating misunderstandings: Multi-agency work as social practice. *Child and Family Social Work, 10,* 207–216.

Winslade, J. (2003). Storying professional identity. *International Journal of Narrative Therapy and Community Work, 4,* 33–35. Retrieved December 2, 2004, from www.dulwich centre.com.au

PART V

Complexities in Narrative Inquiry

No authors in this handbook claim that narrative research is simple. Indeed, as the layers of conducting narrative research—being in the field, writing field texts, constructing research texts—are unfolded, engagement as a narrative inquirer becomes increasingly complicated. Yet this part has been strategically named Complexities in Narrative Inquiry. What can make narrative inquiry more complex than a multilayered recognition of what it means to conduct research as a human with humans collecting stories or living alongside and trying to understand being and acting in a particular place, at a particular time?

In considering the complicating nature of power differentials and boundary crossing, these authors explore the dimensions, tools, tensions, and ethics of conducting research with children and indigenous populations and across cultural boundaries. They lead us to focus on themes of sovereignty (control), ownership, representation, and understanding.

In exploring the theme of sovereignty, Maenette K. P. Benham raises the questions of "who tells and retells, how, for whom, and for what purpose" in terms of the "prickly issues of authorial privilege and rights." These questions reverberate when we care more deeply about who speaks or has spoken for indigenous peoples, who did not speak, what native populations were consulted, who was listening, who was hearing, how and what was reported by whom and to whom, and how reports were read and understood. These questions and the rich discourse provided by Benham explore deeply the issues of authorial rights and privileges. She reminds us that *indigenous* refers to something "innate" that belongs to the very "soil of the place." She articulates concerns with the sacred in every aspect of engaging in narrative inquiry with indigenous populations. She makes us see again and again the issues of power and control in such research.

Yet sovereignty also raises issues when we consider the narratives of children. Min-Ling Tsai's study was of how she came to listen to and hopefully "hear" An-zou's narratives told in Life Report in their kindergarten classroom. If we think of adults in relationship to, and learning from, children, we cannot help but be concerned with issues of dominion, power, rule, independence, autonomy, control, and subjugation. Min-Ling Tsai's own question reverberates in such research. She asks, "Why couldn't I hear children's narratives?"

Molly Andrews also asks questions of sovereignty as she studies the life stories of those engaged across their lives in social activism in England, with citizens formerly of East Germany and South Africa. She wonders, "How is it that we access, interpret, analyze stories which, at their heart, are distant from experiences that we ourselves may have encountered?" As she explores the stories of activists during the Gulf War during a period of time when she returned to her country of origin (the United States), she further questions our ability to gather, interpret, and represent stories "of others that are a part of our own narrative repertoire." Others in the handbook would soothe us about issues of sovereignty by proposing that stories, as they are collected, are co-constructed by researcher and research participant but that in the interpreting and representing they become the stories of the researcher constructed for the research audience. Somehow, after reading these chapters, we probably will remain unconvinced and worry further about how we might respond.

Such explanations call forth questions of ownership. Benham's exploration of how a particular narrative of Koʻolau, a Kauaʻi man afflicted by leprosy, captured in a short story by Jack London, is restoried and indigenized through a newer narrative by Dennis Kawaharda. This provides an example of how indigenous populations can respond in reasserting ownership of stories. Molly Andrews explores with us the ownership complications of South Africans whose life stories and experiences of atrocities were posted to the World Wide Web and allowed to be appropriated by researchers and others across the globe. Min-Ling Tsai's account of how a teacher responded to students' pictures resonated with us as researchers because in her account we so clearly saw our own action in collecting, interpreting, and representing narratives as narrative inquirers. In the moment of our reading her account, we saw ourselves and were forced to reconsider our narrative inquiry scholarship. Here is her report of a Taiwanese teacher's and her students' consideration of stories they had written through illustration:

T: Is this Yun's picture? Yun said, "My mom and I went outside."

Yun nodded.

T: It rained yesterday and they held an umbrella.

         OK. Next. Whose picture is this? Oh, Po-Gia. Po-Gia said "In the festival, I played bowling." Now, did you get any present for that?

Po-Gia: Yes.

T: What is it?

Po-Gia: Milk bar.

T: Milk bar! Oh, congratulations! Too bad I wasn't there.

           Next. Dong, what have you drawn?

As we read Tsai's work, we wondered about our own research practices—that is, the appropriation of a representation (narrative, photograph, event), the provision of an interpretation in the language of the participant, and then a request for reconfirmation of our interpretation (for validation). We were confronted with deep issues of ownership.

After being uneasy about the complexity of sovereignty and ownership, we further questioned understanding—by this we mean what we learn and report from narrative inquiries or what we think we come to know and understand in our research. The complexity of understanding is highlighted across these three chapters. Through her introduction of the tool of indigenization, Maenette Benham makes us aware of what it might require to claim understanding in such settings. Benham's process of indigenizing narratives in these kinds of narrative inquiries shows promise for deepening narrative inquiry results in other settings as well.

Min-Ling Tsai's use of multiple tools of interpretation and sensitivity to those whose cognitive and social development and their status as children helped us learn about additional strategies for building understanding. Her exploration of An-zou and her concern with truly hearing An-zou was insightful as well. If, however, we still dismiss the complexities of understanding participant's worlds because our research resides within our own cultural boundaries or engages adults rather than children, we need only consider Molly Andrews's work exploring the meaning of patriotism with activists in the United States. She articulates the problems of non-narratability when we engage people in exploring experiences "which lie most deeply within the self." But more important, she argues thus:

> The possibility, and the limits of possibility, of conversing with others, through speech and through silence, needn't only be explored on journeys to distant, "other" cultures. There are potentially new partners for dialogue within one's own neighborhood, perhaps even within one's family. When we acknowledge that there may be much we do not know even about those with whom we are most intimate, the possibility of listening, and of being able to hear something new, becomes more promising. All the while, we accept that our "interpretations are provisional" and that our own life experiences "both enable and inhibit particular kinds of insights." (Rosaldo, 1989, p. 8. as quoted in Andrews)

What we come to understand about responding to the complexities of narrative inquiry is the need to attend more intently and authentically so as to honor and respect our participants. Narrative research is a human and relational endeavor. We learn from these pieces not only that we must attend but also potential ideas about how to honor people, places, and heritages in narrative inquiry. In the same vein, we learn further what it might look like to truly respect the people, places, and heritages of those with whom we inquire about the human. We are called to think harder about collecting, analyzing, and living alongside as narrative inquirers. We require of ourselves that we respond more ethically, being in the field, writing field texts, and constructing research texts.

—Janice Huber and Stefinee Pinnegar

CHAPTER 18

Understanding Young Children's Personal Narratives

What I Have Learned From Young Children's Sharing Time Narratives in a Taiwanese Kindergarten Classroom

Min-Ling Tsai

From Narrating Research to Researching Narratives

I tend to think and express almost everything narratively. This way of expression seems to be so natural to me that I seldom cast doubts on its appropriateness, even when I was in graduate school and when I became a professor in a teachers college in Taiwan. Ironically, while I regarded narratives as a very common way of thinking, children's narratives seemed to have evaded me completely in my years of observing kindergarten children's classroom lives. It was not until the sixth year of my research life in Taiwan that I started to listen attentively to children's personal narratives in sharing time. Why was it so? Weren't there supposed to be abundant narratives in school and everywhere? Why couldn't I hear children's narratives?

One reason is that in my original research from 1993 to 1998, the focus had been on classroom interaction. What caught most of my attention had been the social organization of classroom talk and the power relations manifested in classroom interaction. I observed how talking turns were allocated, paid attention to the function of each turn, and coded accordingly to discern possible patterns in the process of classroom interaction (Tsai & Garcia, 2000). After doing research in this way for a few years, I looked at the slots of coded talk on my computer screen and felt that the observed classroom life seemed to have been cut into pieces and the taste of those experiences lost.

Had I never heard children's narratives when studying classroom interaction? Rarely indeed. Assuming that the power relation manifests itself most clearly in whole group time in which the formal curriculum is the focus of discussion, I had always chosen it to do more fine-grained analyses among other data collected in a school day. On those occasions, children's long, personal narratives were rarely heard or, if heard, not recognized. In 1999, during a routine meeting of a learning group, focusing on group discussion in kindergarten classrooms, a senior kindergarten teacher, Miss Wang,[1] shared her dissatisfaction with the scant and incomplete personal narratives in sharing time with me and four other kindergarten teachers. In an attempt to help her, I came to her classroom to find out what had been happening. To my surprise, I heard some long narratives from young children in her classroom. However, I found that her frequent "And then?" questions interrupted some children's sharing and sometimes even stopped their sharing. That might be the major reason why she could not hear children's long narratives. This unexpected visit kindled my interest in sharing-time narratives.

The rare chance to hear children's narratives in school said something about the status of personal experiences in kindergartens in Taipei. In a more recent study, I heard the following conversation:

T: Is this Yun's picture? Yun said, "My mom and I went outside."

Yun nodded.

T: It rained yesterday and they held an umbrella.

OK. Next. Whose picture is this? Oh, Po-Gia. Po-Gia said "In the festival, I played bowling." Now, did you get any present for that?

Po-Gia: Yes.

T: What is it?

Po-Gia: Milk bar.

T: Milk bar! Oh, congratulations! Too bad I wasn't there.

Next. Dong, what have you drawn? (May 18, 2004; transcript from video-taped observation)

Children were invited to reconfirm the teacher's reading of their representation of personal experiences rather than given a chance to share their experiences independently. There seemed to be no opportunities for the children to further explore their experiences outside school.

My visits to more than 30 kindergartens in Taipei city in the past 4 years, either for evaluation work or practicum courses, confirmed the need to inquire more into children's personal narratives in school. Many kindergarten teachers do not regard providing space for children's personal narratives as a significant pedagogical act. Sharing personal experiences or picture diaries is a common activity in kindergartens in Taipei. However, some of them only treated sharing time as a whole group activity through which children could tune themselves back into school after vacations. Some would do the same thing as the teacher in the example above; they did the sharing on behalf of the children and only asked for their confirmation.

As Cazden (1988) pointed out, sharing time is "the only opportunity during official classroom air time for children to create their own oral texts" (p. 8). Given what had been observed in kindergartens in Taipei, I conducted a study[2] on kindergarten children's sharing-time narratives to explore what could be learned from listening attentively to children's oral texts when the teacher respected and provided such a space. This was the first aim of the study.

The second aim of the study is about how to analyze children's narratives. In the past 5 years, there has been a rapid increase in the amount of narrative research in the field of education in Taiwan. Personal experiences were narrated lavishly in these studies. However, I had a hard time reading some theses or papers in which it was not stated or made clear to the reader how the narratives were analyzed. Narratives were collected and narrated again by the researcher. Some authors simply kept on narrating but remained silent on how they understood others' narratives (Tsai, 2004). As for children's narratives, among the small number of studies in Taiwan, most of them used prescribed categories to quantify the elicited narratives. Being dissatisfied with these approaches, I explored ways of analyzing children's narratives and tried to apply Gee's (2000) system of discourse analysis and found it helpful.

The report of my first attempt at understanding children's narratives in this chapter has three goals: first, to share how and what I learned from young children's personal narratives in a kindergarten; second, to invite an examination of the theoretical and practical values of the approach; and third, to discuss the complexities of inquiring into children's narratives in school.

Before presenting how and what I learned from these Taiwanese children's narratives, I will state my definition and assumptions of *narrative* in this study. Following that, I will discuss some approaches in understanding children's narratives. After sharing the preliminary understanding of these children's narratives, I will talk about how the analysis of the narrative texts shed light on my interpretation of one girl's narrative. Finally, I will discuss the complexities of understanding children's narratives and point out further work to be done on this journey.

A Working Definition and Assumptions of Narrative

In this study, children's personal narratives were collected in a recurring activity called Life Report time. In this context, a child who volunteered to share was expected to talk about what she or he did on weekends or holidays. The teacher might help out when the sharer paused and appeared not to know what to say. In such a context, *narrative* in this study is defined as an oral representation of one or more events organized in a certain order, which is assumed to show the sharer's understanding of what happened. This definition was inspired and informed by Mishler's (1995) discussion of the typology of narrative analysis he developed. In describing the various approaches in the first category of the typology, Mishler cited *Webster's Collegiate Dictionary* definition of narration as "discourse, or an example of it, designed to represent a connected succession of happenings" (p. 90). He drew our attention to "two ambiguities" of this definition to show the major aspects various approaches of narrative analysis differ in. One is whether the analysis focuses on "the actual 'succession of happenings' or its textual representation" and the other is how "connected succession" (p. 90) is defined in a study. In this study, the focus is on the textual representation of the children's lives. The certain order discerned may be temporal, causal, or thematic. The assumption is children make sense of what happens to them by the way they represent their lives in personal narratives.

Since sharing-time narrative is a specific kind of discourse, such a working definition relates to my assumptions on the relationship between language and realities, which have practical implications for the aspects I attended to when analyzing children's narratives.

My assumption of the relation between language use and social realities remains the same as the assumption that influenced my studies on classroom interaction—that is, language use and realities are mutually constituted. Children's oral representation of their lives therefore is not seen as a direct reflection of their experiences. As Riessman (1993) also stressed, "A personal narrative is not meant to be read as an exact record of what happened nor is it a mirror of a world 'out there'" (p. 64). A child's personal narrative is regarded as a construction within social contexts and is something that mediates self and culture.

In the chapter "The narrative creation of self," Bruner (2002) states succinctly that self-narrating is "from outside in as well as from inside out" (p. 84). The inside refers to "memory, feelings, ideas, beliefs, [and] subjectivity" (p. 65). The outside concerns "the unspoken, implicit cultural models of what selfhood should be, might be—and, of course, shouldn't be" (p. 65). Narrative is a process of self-construction and at the same time a product of cultural shaping. In narrating self, we construct and reconstruct self—one self or many selves in different cultural contexts. Such views on the three-way construction among self, narrative, and culture serve as the basic assumption in this study.

Bruner (2002) talked about how self-narrating was under the influence both from inside and outside. Gee (2000) used the term *reflexivity* to explain the "reciprocity between language and 'reality'" (p. 82). While using language,

> We simultaneously construct or build six things or six areas of "reality," [which are] the meaning and values of aspects of the material world, . . . activities, . . . identities and relationships, . . . politics, . . . connections, . . . [and] semiotics. (p. 12)

How does such reciprocity proceed? On one hand, "cues and clues in the language we use . . . help assemble or trigger specific situated meanings through which the six building tasks are accomplished" (p. 86). On the other hand, "these situated meanings activate certain cultural models" (p. 86) and inform us how to use language in accordance with the recognized ways of being. Under such assumptions, discourse analysis is also a reciprocal process in which the analyst "shuttle[s] back and forth between the structure . . . of a piece of language and the situated meanings it is attempting to build about the world, identities, and relationships" (p. 99). The way Gee defined the structure of discourse is adopted in this study and will be discussed more in the next section.

Let me go back to explain more of the definition of narrative in this study since it is different from some established definitions of narrative. I agree with Engel's (1995) point that "every utterance is not necessarily a narrative" (p. 65). What should a narrative include? According to Labov and Waletzky (1967/1997), the normal form of narrative contains orientation, complication, evaluation, resolution, and coda. Among these parts, they stressed the evaluative function of narratives, stating that a narrative without an evaluation section is one that "lacks significance, [one that] has no point" (p. 28). Miller (1994) discussed the socializing potential of mundane accounts of personal experiences and based her argument on the four affinities between narrative and self. They include "the temporal affinity, . . . the affinity for representing human action, . . . the evaluative affinity, . . . [and] the conversational affinity" (pp. 160–161). In my working definition of narrative, the evaluative element was not explicitly stressed because the aim of my analysis was to understand how the children organized their experiences and showed their perception of the social world. Among the narrative texts of the study, some contained a list of events without an explicit evaluative perspective. Were such utterances not counted as narrative then? Also, the degree to which these children's personal narratives resemble adults' full-fledged narratives was not the aim of my analysis. I believe the views on what kind of talk counts as narrative is culturally defined. As an initial attempt to understand children's narratives, the working definition here leaves more space for me to find out how these kindergarten children represented their worlds.

Approaches in Understanding Children's Narratives

Researchers who are interested in children's narratives in classrooms have different ways of expressing their curiosity and care for children. The differences might in part result from their distance—both mentally and physically—to young children. Also, the difference might be a result of the different ways in which researchers "deal with the problematic relation between the telling and the told" (Mishler, 1995, p. 100). Third, researchers have different aims and methods in analyzing children's narratives. The following approaches differ in the extent researchers take contexts into consideration in their producing, reading, and analyzing narrative texts. At one end of the continuum, teachers such as Vivian Paley constructed life contexts by, through, and in narratives. At the other end, researchers paid exclusive attention to the narrative texts that were collected with minimum interaction. In any case, these approaches were either inspiring or provocative to the current study.

Paley (1986) urged those who lived with children to listen to what they say "with curiosity and care" (p. 131). She listened to children with a tape recorder, wrote down the stories children told, and acted them out together with children. Instead of giving answers, she wrote, "I wanted to hear the answers I could not myself invent" (p. 125). Her stories with children so vividly depicted in her books provide eloquent and heartwarming examples of how narratives mediate self and culture. It was through the ongoing and emerging narratives that Paley and her children found who they were and invented ways of connecting to one another. When Paley no longer had a class of her own, she kept visiting other classrooms and again, through weaving personal narratives of her own, of her mother, and of those she met, witnessed the "victory of goodness, for connectedness to other people"[3] (Paley, 1999, p. 28). As she said, "Like a child, without a story I cannot explain myself" (p. 4). The key of her sound understanding of children's narratives might be what she herself observed, "I have taken on the young child's perspective" (Paley, 1986, p. 128).

Paley's (1986) approach serves as an ideal model for me regarding how to live truly close to children in kindergarten classrooms. She listened to children's narratives with curiosity, became one of the characters in their stories, and found a place and purpose in the ever-expanding narratives. Her way of weaving her own and children's narratives and living them out is similar to Clandinin and Connelly's (2000) approach in doing narrative inquiry. Their inquiries were initiated from personal experiences, proceeded in experiences, and were accomplished by telling stories about "people living storied lives on storied landscapes" (p. 145). To them, "context makes all the difference" (p. 26). By listening to, telling, and writing about their own and others' stories in a certain place, they connect the internal and the existential, as well as the past, the present, and the future. Their narrative texts and the contexts they gathered and constructed narratively shape each other in "a three-dimensional narrative inquiry space" (p. 51).

Michaels (1981) listened to children's sharing-time narratives in an ethnically mixed first-grade classroom. She contended that the child's narratives "could not be analyzed in isolation" (p. 427). Therefore, besides doing fine-grained analysis of children's narrative styles, she explored the teacher's sharing schema and the interactive consequence of different sharing styles. She identified two narrative styles: topic centered and topic associating. In recognizing these two styles, the aspects of narratives Michaels attended to included the sharing intonation, the narrative structures, the references of temporal shifts or spatial perspective, lexical cohesion, and thematic development. The teacher and the white children who used a topic-centered style "have a shared sense of what the topic is and are able to collaborate in rhythmically synchronized exchanges" (p. 431). In contrast, the teacher had difficulty discerning the topic of the black children's topic-associating sharing and often raised questions that were "thematically inappropriate and seemed to throw the child off balance" (p. 434). Such unintentional differential treatment, Michaels inferred, "may ultimately affect the children's progress in the acquisition of literacy skills" (p. 440).

Labov and Waletzky[4] (1967/1997) made important efforts regarding how to analyze a narrative text. According to Mishler (1995), their work on narrative analysis "is the first attempt to apply a linguistic approach to oral narratives of personal experiences" (p. 92). They assumed that "the fundamental structures [of narrative] are to be found in oral versions of personal experiences" (p. 3) and that narratives function to "recapitulate" (p. 4) experience. Therefore, the aim of their analysis was to "relate the sequence of clauses in the narrative to the sequence of events inferred from the narrative" (p. 12).

Labov and Waletzky's (1967/1997) assumption that narrative functions to recapitulate experience as well as their presupposed normal form of narrative structure have both been challenged. For example, Riessman (1993) pointed out that "many narratives do not lend themselves to Labov's framework" (p. 59). However, as Riessman also commented, "the model often provides a useful starting point" (p. 59). The presupposed functional parts of narratives proposed by Labov and Waletzky were very helpful for me to think about the relative relationship of the subportions of a narrative text.

Rather than assuming any piece of narrative contains presupposed sections, Gee (2000) constructed parts of a narrative inductively. His way of dissecting discourse and assembling parts of it to identify the narrative structure revealed his assumption on how people's minds worked in using language. He pointed out that speech is "produced in small spurts" (p. 99). When a spurt contains one piece of salient new information, it is called a line, the basic unit of his analysis. By discerning how lines are structured in a text, we could understand how the focus of the speaker's consciousness was formed and shifted. A group of lines "devoted to a single topic, event, image, perspective or theme [constitutes] a stanza. . . . When the time, place, character, event, or perspective changes," (p. 109) a new stanza emerges. Following this logic, a group of stanzas will constitute "higher-level organizations" (p. 110). He called this "larger 'body part' of the story . . . macrostructure" (p. 110). In his analysis of a story by a 7-year-old girl, the macrostructure included setting, catalyst, crisis, evaluation, resolution, and coda. Even though these larger parts of the story were defined inductively, their names clearly revealed the influence from Labov and Waletzky's (1967/1997) work.

From this emerging narrative structure, Gee (2000) then inferred the situated meanings of the narratives, the activated cultural models, and the values. This is the approach used in the current study to find narrative structures. How I analyzed children's narrative texts and the interactive process will be discussed in the next section.

Sharing-Time Narratives in a Kindergarten Classroom in Taipei

The Background of the Study

In March 2003, two assistants and I began to listen to children's personal narratives in sharing time in a kindergarten classroom.[5] In April, after gaining consent from the children and their parents, we started to record these sharing-time narratives with a digital video camcorder. In the meantime, three kindergarten teachers (including the teacher whose classroom we worked in) and I continued meeting once or twice a month to talk about what I had learned in the two classrooms. I usually pulled out portions of the videotaped sharing-time scenes, invited comments from the three kindergarten teachers, and then shared my observations. Initially, the discussion focused on the interaction pattern. From November 2003 on, when I gradually had some grasp of how to analyze the narrative texts, we narrowed our discussion to my analysis of children's personal narratives. In July 2004, I completed the initial analysis of the narratives and the interaction process. In the following 6 months, I analyzed these narrative texts in a more systematic way.

The speech event that is called sharing time in American primary schools is called Life Report in this classroom. Most of the time, this event occurred around 10:30 every Monday morning. Sometimes it happened on the day after a vacation. Calling it Life Report was the idea of a teacher, Miss Lee. She felt the word *report* carried a connotation of "being more formal" (telephone conversation, August 2004). Usually, the sharer would stand right beside the teacher and talk to the whole class with a microphone in hand. With such an arrangement, Miss Lee expected the formal sense created by the name of the event would remind the children that everyone should respect the sharer and listen to her/him carefully.

Miss Lee had been teaching kindergarten for 17 years when we worked in her classroom. Life Report was a routine activity for her in the first few years of teaching. Starting 7 or 8 years ago, according to her, when classroom life received more attention and she had more contact with academics, she started to be aware of some issues in the classroom, such as how to run a group time. She gave more thought to how to be a teacher and how to create a space where children can talk about their experiences and learn to interact with peers. To her, the goal of this sharing activity would be accomplished if a child, after sharing, wanted to share during the next week. By listening to how children interacted with each other, she had more opportunities to learn about children's thinking (telephone conversation, April 23, 2003).

Life Report could be subdivided into three portions. First, the class negotiated and confirmed who was to share that day. Children wrote down their number on a calendar hung in the reading corner to show their willingness to share on a certain week. Since there were usually more children who wanted to share than time would allow, the negotiation process happened all the time and sometimes took a long time. Second, the sharer stood beside the teacher and shared a personal narrative. Lastly, the other children posed questions based on what had been shared or reported.

How I Analyzed the Interaction Process and the Personal Narratives

The Interaction Process

In the first analysis of the interaction process, I attended to the rules governing the negotiation session, the sharing session, and the following question and answer (Q & A) session. In the second analysis, I focused on the Q & A session. I examined every speaking turn, categorized these turns into questions, comments, and the sharing of related personal experiences, and counted their numbers respectively. Questions and comments were further categorized into those posed based on what had been shared and those posed regarding the sharer's response or the comments of the audience. Finally, questions were reviewed the third time and sorted into different types according to their major focus: facts, competence, confirmation, evaluation, and reason.

The Analysis of the 36 Narrative Texts

The 36 narrative texts were collected in six Life Report events in this classroom. These texts were constructed by 18 children—2 children shared four times, 3 children shared three times, 6 children shared two times, and 7 children shared once only. In analyzing the 36 narrative texts, I attended to the following five aspects:

1. Independent narration or co-construction

2. The length of every narrative

3. The contents of what had been shared

4. The presentation of narrative awareness (language repairs, how the child started and closed a narrative)

5. Narrative structure

The first three aspects are self-evident. Let me explain more about narrative awareness and narrative structure.

My attention to children's presentation of narrative awareness was influenced by Cazden's (1988) comments on repairs. Cazden thought the corrections made by the narrator in the midst of the narration were based on the narrator's judgment that some parts of the narratives might be unclear or unintelligible to the audience. In doing so, the narrator gauges whether what had been shared is clear enough from the point of view of the audience. Such correction might be presented in two ways, according to Cazden. One is "lexical replacements [and the other is] bracketing" (p. 20). *Lexical replacements* means replacing words in narration, such as "from an inaccurate noun to a more accurate nominalization, . . . from an ambiguous anaphoric pronoun to an unambiguous noun, . . . from indirect to direct discourse" (p. 20). *Bracketing* is a device used often in the children's narratives collected in this study. It refers to "the insertion of explanatory material . . . in the middle of an otherwise intact sentence" (p. 20). See the following example:

And then, my father,

(He has one, one of his feet was hurt.)

But, he was, was the last to get to the mountain. (Zi-hao, May 19, 2003)

Before reporting his father was the last among all family members to get to the mountain, Zi-hao inserted a sentence to explain his father's physical situation, marked by parentheses. To discern the way children made repairs is important in understanding the narrative texts in this study. Miss Lee had not set the rule that children could say only one thing at a time, as had the teacher in Michaels's (1981) study. Most of the children talked about more than one event, and their narration was not necessarily in accordance with a temporal order. While narrating more than one event, these children's bracketing often diverted from the ongoing plot-line. With these deviations, the narrative was sometimes hard to understand. Identifying various kinds of repairs helped me understand the narratives better. Also, attending to what was chosen for explanation and how this occurred helped me grasp the theme better.

Besides attending to the repairs, I also looked at the ways these children started and ended their narrative, which also demonstrated different degrees of narrative awareness. For example, one child started her narrative by saying "Yesterday I went, I went to that . . . the place . . . (inaudible) . . . took us to. Some place you have never been before" (An-zou, June 16, 2003). The pronoun *you* indicates the narrator was clearly aware of the existence of the audience, indicating she was not only thinking retrospectively but telling her experiences to others. The same child ended her narrative with "Well, this is how things are" (An-zou, June 16, 2003). This way of ending a narrative shows more narrative awareness than those who stood silently beside the teacher after they finished saying the last thing he/she did that day, such as "I then brushed my teeth and went to bed" (Lee-Ching, April 14, 2003). Some children seemed to be more able to sense the distance between the narrated context and the immediate context. As Labov and Waletzky (1967/1997) commented, "the coda is a functional device for returning the verbal perspective to the present moment" (p. 35).

Allow me to explain how I discerned the narrative structures of these texts. Since the texts were constructed orally at first, it would be hard to detect when the structure took shape. It is equally difficult to say whether the children had a structure in mind before the narrative was shared. In any case, my analysis of narrative structures aimed to see the relative status of each narrated event, the relation of these narrated events, and the patterns or variations of the discerned structures. To do so, every narrative text was read at least three times.

In the first reading, I allowed my instinct to find out what structure had been given by the narratives. In the second reading, I used Gee's (2000) system to recognize lines, stanza, and macrostructures of narratives and represented the narratives in such a way that its found structures could be clearly seen. In identifying a line, I only looked at the semantic aspects of words to decide whether a piece of new information was given. The intonational contour, pitch movement, or stress patterns discussed by Gee were not attended to in this study for two reasons. In speaking Mandarin, the stress is also important in signaling salient information. But I am not sure if other constructs apply. Second, attending to those aspects could be very time consuming, requiring more time than I could afford.

Depending on the local context of the text, a line could be a phrase or a clause. A group of lines about one happening or focusing on a theme form a stanza. In the same manner, some stanzas constitute a larger part of the narrative. As can be seen from the following example, some names of the parts were similar to those in Labov and Waletzky's (1967/1997) framework, and other names emerged from the analysis.[6]

Abstract
  Thursday I played cars with my brother at home

Background
  Then my younger sister and elder sister were sleeping at home

Catalyst
  Then, I built a house with my brother
  Then put the car inside
  And see who ran faster[7]
    (Then, my brother's car was bigger than mine
    His was red
    And mine was blue
    My brother, his tire was bigger than mine)

Complicating Actions
  And then, my brother he controlled
  Controlled till there
  Then he hit me
  Then my car was turned over

Ending
  Then my brother he, he went to the end
  (Then my car had been turned over)
  So I was the second getting to the end (Zi-hao, June, 2, 2003, number 22 in Table 18.1)

In the third reading, I used the patterns and possible meanings constructed from the previous reading as a background to read every individual text again. In this way, some texts were interpreted in a new way.

What Was Learned From the Analysis

The Length, Contents, and Structures of the Narratives

Table 18.1 presents a summary of the age of the sharer, the length and contents of the children's personal narratives.

Table 18.1   An Abstract of Children's Personal Narratives

Number	Date	Narrator	Age of Narrator	Duration of Narration	Major Contents of the Narrative
1	April 7, 2003	(1)Gee-xian (boy)	6.3	1 sec 2 min, 7 sec	First part: Watching TV, playing computer games Second part: The story of a transformed king
2		(2)Pin-xuan (girl)	5.8	1 min, 30 sec	Visiting a grave, playing computer games, watching TV, making paper flowers
3		(3)Yi-ru (girl)	6.7	1 min, 16 sec	Going to grandma's on Saturday
4		(4)Hao-song (boy)	5.11	1 min, 21 sec	Mom took me to feed the squirrel, and the fish. Watching TV (the story of a transformed king)
5	April 14, 2003	(1)Po-xiun (boy)	5.8	1 min, 56 sec	Playing computer game at my uncle's
6		(2)Lee-ching (girl)	5.8	40 sec	Going to my aunt's/playing in the park
7		(3)An-zou (girl)	5.11	2 min, 26 sec	Going to church, catching the butterfly at night
8		(4)Wei-jie (boy)	6.4	51 sec	Playing badminton and the sticky ball
9	April 21, 2003	(1)Ya-gue (boy)	6.2	2 min, 45 sec	Catching the turtles with my dad at mountains
10		(2)Chang xin (girl)	5.7	1 min, 5 sec	My dad took my grandma to a place by car
11		(3)Yee-cheng (boy)	5.10	2 min, 19 sec	The whole family playing in the neighborhood Playing games at home
12	May 19, 2003	(1)Wei-un (girl)	6.5	33 sec/40 sec	Going to Sogo with my family (the same experience was narrated twice)
13		(2)An-zou	6.0	48 sec	An aunt took me to the church
14		(3)Wei-yun	6.2	1 min, 13 sec	What I did in a day
15		(4)Gee-xian	6.4	4 sec 1 min, 14 sec 1 min, 15 sec	Playing computer games at home A portion of a story from the computer game Another portion of the story
16		(5)Chang xin	5.8	1 min, 25 sec	Playing with my younger brother at home; going to A-ma's on Saturday; going to A-ma's before going to grandma's on Sunday
17		(6)Zi-hao (boy)	6.8	57 sec	Climbing a mountain

Table 18.1 (Continued)

Number	Date	Narrator	Age of Narrator	Duration of Narration	Major Contents of the Narrative
18		(7)Yee-cheng	5.11	3 min, 57 sec	Playing computer games at home/ a story from the computer games
19		(8)Yi-zu	6.8	1 min, 26 sec	Going to A-ma's
20		(9)Wei-jie	6.5	36 sec	Playing computer games at home
21	June 2, 2003	(1)Yu-ting (girl)	5.2	2 min, 20 sec	Climbing Yang-ming mountain
22		(2)Zi-hao	6.9	42 sec	Playing cars with my brother at home
23		(3)Yee-xin (girl)	6.8	9 sec 1 min, 19 sec	Going to Ta-an park on Sunday Encountering a classmate
24		(4)Hao-song	6.1	32 sec	My brother and I went to classes on Sunday
25		(5)Pin-xiun	5.10	5 min, 38 sec	Going out with my family on Sunday
26	June 9, 2003	(1)Wei-yun	6.3	Life report: 1 min, 4 sec Sharing the picture diary: 1 min, 3 sec	Teaching my sister how to draw on Friday evening/playing pottery on Sunday A scene of me teaching my sister how to draw
27		(2)Ya-geu	6.4	3 min, 26 sec	Going barbecuing with my dad The sound of *pong, pong, pong* when playing computer games
28		(3)Pin-xiun	5.10	5 min, 11 sec	Going to the park, watching TV at home, riding the bike, watching TV at home
29		(4)Yi-zu	6.9	1 min, 22 sec	Going to A-ma's, my sister was scolded at night
30		(5)Yee-cheng	6.0	3 min, 50 sec	My brother, my sister and I went playing there, my dad drove us home
31	June 16, 2003	(1)Wen-seng	6.6	30 sec	Watching TV at home, playing computer games
32		(2)Gia-xiang (boy)	6.3	1 min, 2 sec	Having lunch at McDonalds on Sunday, going swimming, playing marble games
33		(3)Pin-xiun	5.10	4 min, 10 sec	Going to San-Yee on Sunday
34		(4)An-zou	6.1	1 min, 31 sec	Playing at the dollhouse with my sister, catching the butterflies
35		(5)Hao-song	6.1	36 sec	My brother and I went to classes on Sunday
36		(6)Yi-zu		1 min, 25 sec	A-ma took me to the park on Saturday I did not have breakfast on Sunday

Concerning the contents, as can be seen from Table 18.1, most of the sharing was about going to relatives or places together with their family. A lot of them were about watching TV or playing computer games at home. What merits our attention is that playing computer games was the only and major content in seven narrative texts, such as Gee-xian's narrative in number 1. There were five more texts in which watching TV or playing computer games was mentioned as part of the contents, such as Pin-xuan's narrative in number 2. That is, one third of these narrative texts included watching TV or playing computer games as part of the sharing. This finding might be a result based on the location of the kindergarten. It is located in the central part of Taipei, the biggest city in Taiwan. To what extent did these children's narratives reflect their daily lives? Are TV and computer games the dominant contents of children's narratives elsewhere? These issues need to be addressed by further studies.

As to the duration of the narratives, there was great variation. They ranged from the shortest, 9 seconds, to the longest, 5 minutes and 38 seconds. How can we explain such variation? The duration of narration and the length of the narrative texts were not necessarily correlated because of the speed of narrating. Also, there seemed to be no correspondent relations between the age of the narrator, the duration of the narration, and the length of the narrative. However, for those children from whom we collected more than three narrative texts, it appeared their narratives tended to have similar duration and length. See Table 18.2.

In Table 18.2, except for An-zou, the other children's narratives tended to be of similar duration. Moreover, these children structured their narratives in similar ways.

Table 18.2   A Pattern of the Duration of Some Children's Personal Narratives

Number in Table 18.1	Date	Narrator	Age of Narrator	Duration of Narration
2	April 7, 2003	Pin-xuan	5.8	1 min, 30 sec
25	June 2, 2003	Pin-xiun	5.10	5 min, 38 sec
28	June 9, 2003	Pin-xiun	5.10	5 min, 11 sec
33	June 16, 2003	Pin-xiun	5.10	4 min, 10 sec
3	April 7, 2003	Yi-ru	6.7	1 min, 16 sec
19	May 19, 2003	Yi-zu	6.8	1 min, 26 sec
29	June 9, 2003	Yi-zu	6.9	1 min, 22 sec
36	June 16, 2003	Yi-zu	6.9	1 min, 25 sec
7	April 14, 2003	An-zou	5.11	2 min, 26 sec
13	May 19, 2003	An-zou	6.0	48 sec
34	June 16, 2003	An-zou	6.1	1 min, 31 sec
4	April 17, 2003	Hao-song	5.11	1 min, 21 sec
24	June 02, 2003	Hao-song	6.1	32 sec
35	June 16, 2003	Hao-song	6.1	36 sec
11	April 21, 2003	Yee-cheng	5.10	2 min, 19 sec
18	May 19, 2003	Yee-cheng	5.11	3 min, 57 sec
30	June 9, 2003	Yee-cheng	6.0	3 min, 50 sec

Six different narrative structures were identified from the 36 texts. They include (1) using only one sentence to talk about one event, (2) reporting a list of events according to the temporal order and no macrostructures recognized, (3) short sub-sections within the narratives with different functions or macrostructures, (4) presenting contrasting roles or plots, (5) giving outlines and then going into details, (6) long narration with complex structures and abundant details.

The narrative structure was helpful, especially in reading long narratives with many deviating bracketed statements. The identified structure showed the relative status of different events or parts of the events and revealed children's perspectives in narrating their experiences. Second, even with such limited amount of narrative texts, it demonstrated children tended to use similar structures in different narrations. The consistent narrative structures were related to the consistent duration of these children's narratives. For example, the narrative structures of Pin-xuan's and Yee-cheng's narratives were both categorized as type 6 and their narratives were long. Hao-song's and Yi-zu's narrative structure were categorized as type 4 and their narratives were shorter than those categorized as type 6.

However, there were exceptions. For example, Ya-gue (number 9 in Table 18.1) completed his simple and short narrative with the teacher's assistance whereas he had a fascinating and complex narrative on his own on a different day (number 27 in Table 18.1). Besides narrative structures, the local interactive context was influential on the duration and therefore, the contents of children's narratives.

The Local Interactive Context and the Narratives

In the 36 narrative texts, only three of them were constructed with the assistance of the teacher. See the following example.

T:	OK, Ya-geu is going to report now.
Ya-geu:	Hi, everyone. I am Chen, Ya-geu[8] *(pause for five seconds)* I forgot where I went.
T:	You forgot where you went? You can talk about what you did.
Ya-geu:	I went playing in a place.
T:	And then?
Ya-geu (pause for 1 second):	To the mountain, to catch turtles.
T:	To catch what?
Some children:	Turtles.
T:	Turtles, ok.
Ya-geu:	And then my father said, the name of the turtle is Ha-Ba-Xi.
. . . . . .	
Ya-geu:	Then, my father said he, he walked slowly, but, my father, um, I forgot what my father said. I forgot. (Ya-geu, April 21, 2003, number 9 in Table 18.1)

Ya-geu went blank twice when his narrative came to important details of the experience. Miss Lee's "And then?" and other questions encouraged Ya-geu to continue. However, earlier in the chapter, we saw Miss Wang's frequent "And then?" stopped children's narration. This contrast might have something to do with how children perceived the teacher's expectations. Miss Lee seldom commented on what children shared. According to her, it was more important for a child to feel comfortable sharing rather than what was actually shared. Sometimes a child would tell her that she/he had been home during the weekend and had nothing to share. She would make it clear the things to report did not have to be something extraordinary. She urged the children to talk about things they did at home (recorded conversation in group meeting, April 9, 2003). On the other hand, Miss Wang's quick response to what the children shared might have discouraged their intention to continue sharing.

Similarly, quick responses from the peers in this classroom could bring the narration to an abrupt end. For example, after Yu-ting (number 21 in Table 18.1) said only one sentence "Sunday, I went, went, climbing Yang-ming mountain," four children said they already knew the mountain and Yu-ting stopped sharing. Yu-ting resumed the narration after the teacher expressed her interest to learn more. After that, Yu-ting's voice was barely audible and the teacher had to repeat a sentence or a word of what was said. Her narrative became fragmented. On other occasions, I had heard Yu-ting tell her personal experiences to a student teacher, and the complex narrative lasted for more than 15 minutes.

However, most of the time, peer interaction was vigorous in this class. The large number of questions raised after a child shared her/his experiences indicated Life Report time was treated as a process of co-construction rather than a solo performance. The number of questions after a narration ranged from 2 to 19. All together, there were 271 questions, 24 comments or suggestions, and 5 sharings of related experiences from the audience. Seventy-six percent of the questions were directed toward what had just been shared, and 23% of them were based on the sharer's response to those questions. It showed the class attended not only to the shared personal narratives but also to the following questions and responses.

However, what makes a narrative interesting enough to provoke questions? These children certainly did not share the same criteria with me in this matter. The narratives that seemed simply a list of happenings to me aroused more questions than the one I regarded as the most complex and vigorous. For example, after Pin-xuan's long narrative (Number 25 in Table 18.1), there were only 3 questions, whereas Li-ching's short narrative (Number 6 in Table 18.1) aroused 15 questions. As to the type of questions, unsurprisingly, the narratives without many details were followed by questions about factual information, whereas with the narratives containing abundant details and complex plots, the audience tended to ask *why* questions—the type of questions that one would pose only after gaining a sense of the narrative as a whole.

The Major Themes Implicit in These Thirty-Six Texts

As these children represented their personal experiences in Life Report time, they actively reorganized these experiences and reconstructed their meanings. The choices these children made regarding which events to share, as well as the way they arranged these events or portions of events, informed me of their perceptions, feelings, and understanding of their daily lives. What follows are some common themes synthesized by looking closely at what the children shared as well as how they shared.

Family as an Axis in Framing Time and Space of Life

Be the structure simple or complex, the whole narrative long or short, 31 out of the 36 texts had *home* as a referential point in narrating life experiences. After the setting was introduced, the major plotline developed with the characters' relative distance to home. Most of the events narrated were either what happened at home or away from that home. In narratives with more complex structures, the description of being at home and that of being away alternate with each other. Almost all the narratives ended with "going back home and going to bed."

A related aspect is the role of parents in these narratives. To be away was always initiated by parents, and to be home could not be accomplished without parents. Family and parents meant a lot in these children's narratives, and to be together with the family was a default circumstance in most of the narratives.

A Struggle Between Doing What Was Required and What Was Intended: Dependence/Independence, Observance/Autonomy

Even though parents played a critical role in these children's narratives, they seemed to become opposing characters in the imagined or practical process of these children's self-construction. It is interesting to note that in these narratives, children usually talked about what their parents wanted them to do first and put what they themselves wanted to do as a complementary remark, which violated the temporal order. For example, Wei-un talked about different places his mother took him and the things they did. The narration went all the way to "going home and had dinner" but after that Wei-un inserted a sentence saying "And then, before going back home, we had been to a place to play" (Wei-un, May 19, 2003, Number 12 in Table 18.1). Wei-un actually shared twice that day because his peers complained that his voice was not loud enough. Interestingly, when sharing his weekend life the second time, he still put the "playing" episode at the end of the narrative as something added.

In the next example, Lee-ching narrated what the adults wanted her to do and what she was possibly more inclined to do in turn.

Yesterday, I went to my aunts,
To see the baby,
After finishing the seeing, I went to the park near our house.

Then, eating dinner.
Then (pause for 1 second) playing with the doll,
Then my mother asked me to go to sleep,
I then brushed my teeth and went to bed. (Lee-ching, April 14, 2003, Number 6 in Table 18.1)

At first sight, this narrative was a simple list of happenings. However, it can also be seen as an interlacing plot of what the adults wanted her to do and what she wanted to do. It would be hard to judge whether this kind of opposing structure is a deliberate or unintentional arrangement. If making personal narratives can be seen as a way of making sense of life, in thinking back to what happened, the way life was told revealed how children observed and experienced that portion of life.

Explanations and the Confrontation of Boredom

Besides the way these children structured their personal narratives, their perception of parents' expectation could also be seen from the things they chose to explain. In the excerpt, Gia-xiang described what he played and inserted an explanation of how he played in a Pa-Ching-Ko in a bracket. He made it clear that he did not waste any money there since he only played with the marbles he picked up.

Event 3
After swimming, we went to my sister's
And then, I went to
(Mine and my sister's, very close to my sister's)
There was a Pa-Ching-Ko,
(I, We did not waste any money
We only picked them up
The marbles dropped and I picked them up) (Gia-xiang, June 6, 2003, Number 31 in Table 18.1)

In the following excerpt, Po-xiun also explained within brackets why he kept on playing computers:

Background
My mother took me and my sister to my uncle's, to, to, to that uncle's,
To take a break,
Cause mother had a lot of things to be busy with

Catalyst
Then we,
My sister and I just, just playing with toys, just playing with toys first.

Crisis
Then, I was the only one playing the computer games.
(But, I always lose when playing computer games,
But I might possibly succeed and gain lots of points.)

Resolution
So So I kept on playing playing playing playing playing, playing till, playing till evening. (Po-xiun, April 14, 2003, Number 5 in Table 18.1)

Po-xiun's explanation of why he kept playing the computer games made it clear he did it for two good reasons. One, he had to confront the boredom caused by being left at his uncle's by his mother. Second, it might be a good chance to increase his competence (*but I might possibly succeed and gain lots of points*). When the situation in which the children were left alone by their parents was described as boring, boredom became something the children had to deal with. In this case, even if what was done was not in accordance with parents' guidance or expectations, they could be justified, as shown by such explanations in the foregoing and in the following examples:

Background: The adults all went to visit the grave.
(. . . . . omitted)
They all went to visit the grave.

Resolution
As a result, that, my aunt and I went to the supermarket to buy some cookies to eat, (My sisters, they ate the cookies, too.
My sisters, they ate the cookies, too). (Yi-zu, April 7, 2003, Number 3 in Table 18.1)

Yi-zu's use of "As a result" shows the situation of adults being away was the context of her going "to the supermarket to buy some cookies to eat." Her repeated mentioning of her sisters eating the cookies revealed her concerns about how her parents might have reacted to their actions. Interestingly, even though these children talked about how they were able to confront boredom, they seemed to desire their parents' assistance to get them out of a situation where they could not be fully autonomous.

Children and parents, to be home and to be away, autonomy and dependence, observance and breaking the rules, these pairs of themes appeared again and again in the 36 texts but were entangled in different ways and with different proportions—that is, some children simply mentioned where their parents took them; some interwove what their parents wanted and what they themselves intended; some were aware of the boring situation when the adults were away, and some used this context to justify their actions. Some children were more eager to create a space where a more competent self could be presented, even when doing what the adults required.

A Concern About How Self-Competence Is Presented
Let's look at the following excerpt:

Scene II
Then we went to feed the fish.

Crisis
That my brother almost fell into the water.

Resolution
Then I pulled him up,
Up and then,
(As a result, he was too heavy.
Because he was in second grade, too heavy,
He was two years older than I).
T (smiling): um, too heavy for you to pull?
I can pull him up.
Then that, then that, throwing him down onto the ground. (Hao-song, April 7, 2003, Number 4 in Table 18.1)

Hao-song's narratives were usually very short. In two of the three narrative texts collected from him, Hao-song's narrations cast his brother as the protagonist, and the plotline developed according to what his brother did. The above text shows a reversed depiction. In this narrative, he saved his brother, who was older and heavier than he. Hao-song presented a more competent self in this part of his narrative that day. Before and after this part, the narrative was about what he and his brother did under his mother's guidance.

How might the above themes help us? What follows is a narrative text and some excerpts from An-zou. I will use these texts as an example to show how the foregoing analysis served as an important context, against which the significance of An-zou's narratives was recognized.

A Possible Interpretation of An-zou's Narratives

The self most of the children constructed in their personal narratives was one that was always with family members. Against such a context, An-zou's narratives appeared very different. With the above themes in mind, the sharp contrast between An-zou's narratives and those of other children regarding the definition of *home* led me to read through her texts again. I found that An-zou's texts were also different regarding the other three themes. In her narratives, the struggles she experienced were not those between doing what her parents wanted and doing what she wanted. What she chose to explain was not something that might defy parents' expectation. She presented a needy self rather than a competent one. It was against these common themes that I reread An-zou's texts and saw a very different experience depicted in her narratives.

The three narrative texts from An-zou all mentioned home. However, being together with her family members was not a default situation in her depictions. Rather, her three personal narratives were all about what she did when her family members were not around. See the following example:

Abstract
What I did at home yesterday

Background
My aunt said, my aunt said
while she was doing something
I had to do things by myself

Crisis: Being Alone
Then, then, my grandma just, said, my grandma went to the market.

Resolution
Then, at that time, the phone rang.
That was from an aunt.[9]
Then, my aunt came to pick me up.
(There is one more person, they, two brothers)

Complicating Actions
Then, then that, an, an aunt took us to the church, to,
Then, to play together happily at church,
Then, then, the teacher let us play together.

Coda
OK, the things were all told. (An-zou, May 19, 2003, Number 13 in Table 18.1)

Another obvious difference is the narrative awareness shown in these three texts. As can be seen in this example, her way of starting and closing the narrative clearly revealed her awareness of being a narrator. Her narrative awareness was also shown in her use of the third-person narrative tone as in the sentence "At that time, the phone rang." She said it as if she herself was one of the spectators of what she remembered and chose to say.

At the very beginning, An-zou told us she was going to report "what she did at home yesterday," but what she said was mainly what she did away from home. Such internal conflict made me wonder, Was "being at home" the situation An-zou desired to say and to be? Or was An-zou's definition of *home* different from that of the other children in this study? An-zou might not have detected the sharp contrast between what she claimed to say and what she actually said. Another kind of contrast can be seen in the following excerpt:

Playing in the Park
Then I went to play by myself.
Then, that little brother,[10] his mother cooked something for him.
Then, then that, when done, when. . . . .
The teacher told us that mine was fake,
The teacher said "You can't eat that, you can't eat. . . . ."
I then said "OK, we won't eat that."
Then someone, he sneakily put that. . . . .,
then. . . . . (An-zou, April 14, 2003, Number 7 in Table 18.1)

"I played by myself" and "The little brother's mother cooked something for him" are two contrasting situations. What might this contrast mean? "The teacher told us that mine was fake," but the little brother was eating something his mother cooked for him, something real. Following this line of thought, playing house was "fake," and it was a real home An-zou desired. This concern seemed to be a major struggle appearing in her texts.

Such inference would be shaky without being informed of things outside the narrative text—that is, what happened in An-zou's life. After making this analysis, I called Miss Lee to know more about An-zou. Miss Lee told me An-zou's mother had left home with no reason and her father told An-zou her mother was dead. This information helped me appreciate An-zou's longing to be with her mother, of being really at home. To be told the reason for her mother's sudden disappearance was important for me as a researcher and for An-zou as a 5-year-old girl. I read her narrative again and found one stanza in which she narrated her grandma's temporary absence from her:

Grandma's Leaving
Then, right that, then, after finishing playing,
Grandma said "I am leaving now."
Then, "Grandma, you are leaving?"
Then grandma said "You be good in church."
Then I stayed in church and played.
Then grandma went home to take some rest.

Play Resumed
Then that brother said. . . . .,
Then playing this way, playing this way, up until in the evening.
. . . . . . (An-zou, April 14, Number 7 in Table 18.1)

An-zou gave such details to depict the scene of her grandma's leaving. One possible interpretation could be she needed to be clearly told why her grandma had to leave. After knowing the reason, she could play heartily even when no family member was around. To be told why someone had to leave seemed to be important both in her text and in her life.

In these three texts, to be alone at home was something she had to deal with. Other children described such situations as being boring, whereas she felt alone. In all of them, aunts, brothers, or sisters would come and take her to church to be with others. In two of her narrative texts, An-zou mentioned a butterfly-catching event. Look at the following two excerpts:

Catching the Butterflies
Then we went to catch the butterflies at night, with . . . , and that . . .
Catching for a long time and letting it go.
Because that, that was animal, very pitiful,
we let it go.
. . . (An-zou, April 14, 2003, Number 7 in Table 18.1)

Catching the Butterflies
After finishing lunch, we went to catch the butterflies again.
A sister caught, a very, very big butterfly,
Then sister let it go,
Then let me go catching it.

But I cannot get hold of it.
He flied up too high.
Then, then sister, each of us, each carried a net to catch the butterfly,
But I cannot get hold of it. (An-zou, June 16, Number 34 in Table 18.1)

As can be noted, the second text was constructed 2 months from the time the first text was narrated. I do not have any clue why the butterfly-catching event was told again. However, the repeated sentence "But I cannot get hold of it" made me think of how often I observed An-zou playing alone in the classroom. In whole group times, she usually paid little attention to what was going on and rambled around. In and through narratives, An-zou, the child with much clearer narrative awareness, seemed to be clarifying the sudden change in her life, trying to get hold of something that was beyond her comprehension. As Gee (2000) commented, "narrative is the way we make deep sense of problems that bother us" (p. 113). Even though I did not have sufficient narrative texts to explore this issue further, my interpretation of An-zou's narratives showed me such a possibility.

In a context where children had plenty of opportunities to raise questions, An-zou seldom did so. In these 36 rounds of sharing, An-zou only asked three questions. One of them was not related to what was shared—"Why, she, does her mother treat Wei-yun well?" (May 19, 2003). After finishing the analysis of her texts, this question struck me again. Indeed, this question has little to do with what was shared, but it has something to do with the puzzles and concerns in her mind.

In sum, An-zou's narratives and questions took on different meanings after a process of going back and forth between what I had learned from the analysis of the 36 texts, from her 3 texts, from what Miss Lee told me about her family, and from my observations of her actions in the classroom.

Discussion: The Complexities of Doing Narrative Inquiry

An-zou's narration would have been just a text to be analyzed, rather than a story to be understood if I focused on and analyzed the narrative text only. However, treating children's narratives as a sample and ignoring what happened in the context from which children's narratives are gathered or elicited is an approach taken by many researchers working on children's narratives in Taiwan. In the limited amount of studies on children's narratives in Taiwan, not many researchers positioned themselves where children live to listen to what they narrate in ordinary contexts.

Chang and Chang (2002) explored the narrative competence of 15 children when they were 3 and 7 years of age, respectively. The researchers went to these children's homes to interview the children. Chang and Chang applied the prompt strategies developed by Peterson and McCabe (1983) to elicit narratives from children. Whether the prompt and the interactive process influenced these children's narratives was not discussed by the researchers. Likewise, in a study on how Chinese mothers[11] elicit narratives from their young children across time, Chang (2003) had her research assistant visit 16 children's (3 years and 6 months of age) homes four times in a year and ask their mothers "to get one rich, elaborate account of past experience from the child and to interact with her child in as natural a way as possible" (p. 102). In Chang, one of the research questions was "What is the relationship between the mother's interactive strategies and children's narrative skills concurrently and later in development?" (p. 102). It seemed Chang was aware of the possible impact the mother, as a conversational partner, might have on what children narrate. With such awareness, the lack of discussion on the impact of the prompt on the elicited narratives in Chang and Chang (2002) becomes difficult to understand.

As seen, the local interactive context of Life Report time had a great influence on the children's perception of this event as well as their willingness to share. Would not the prompt tell the children how their narratives were considered and therefore influence their intention to go on or stop?

At first, I thought the disregard of the influences from this interaction or deliberately noninteractive process might be a result of these researchers' attempts to collect large amounts of narratives to have them quantified. However, it seemed not to be the case. In a study that aimed to compare Japanese and Canadian family narrative patterns, the comparison was made based on the conversations of eight pairs of mothers and their 5-year-olds in each culture. In Minami and McCabe's (1991) study, only 17 Japanese children were interviewed. In Chang's (2003) study, 16 pairs of Taiwanese mother-child dyads were interviewed.

As Mishler (1986) showed us by his experiences in conducting interviews, "terms take on specific and contextually grounded meanings within and through the discourse as it develops and is shaped by speakers" (p. 64). The internal history of the developing discourse" (p. 53) merits more attention in our attempt to understand children through their narratives if the narratives were gathered in a context of interaction.

Actually, as much as I would like to have explored more about the contexts of the narrative texts, it was often not possible. When I walked into Miss Lee's classroom, I planned to talk to children to learn more about them based on what I heard in Life Report time. However, the other teacher in the classroom[12] required children to remain silent at snack time or lunch time. My assistant and I then sat beside the children and tried not to initiate any kind of talk. However, when we were listening to children's talk at snack time or lunch time, this teacher would walk around and scold the children for being too loud. Sometimes she even threatened to punish the children who took too long to finish the meal. To avoid placing more burdens on the children and teacher, we left after Life Report time and missed the moments to inquire more about what the children had just shared.

Children in this classroom seemed to be very willing to tell me what they had in mind. I remembered what Wei-yun told me the day I explained our work to the children. On the outdoor playground, Wei-yun walked to me and showed me a small sword she had made out of a snack wrapper. Then she said, "I like a tall boy." "Which one?" I asked. Her gaze showed me where to look. "The one in orange pants." Our conversation continued, focusing on how she thought about the boy (written retrospective notes, April 29, 2003). I was surprised with Wei-yun's readiness to share her personal experience with a person she barely knew. With these children's willingness to share, how might the preliminary understanding of their narratives be helpful for them or other researchers inquiring into children's narratives?

Since my analysis proceeded slowly and lasted for a long time, by the time I completed the analysis, An-zou was a first-grade student in an elementary school. I missed the appropriate time to share my interpretation of her narratives with Miss Lee. The aim of understanding these children's narratives was nothing clinical. However, what would be the value of understanding if it is only kept in a research paper? The understanding of the local interactive context and the themes recognized from the 36 narrative texts informed me about a possible way of interpreting one particular child's narratives. To do something to help the child was a need that emerged in the inquiring process. I think the aim of understanding kindergarten children's personal narratives does not necessarily have to dismiss such a need. What help was this understanding if I could not assist a child right in front of me? This remains one of the limitations and puzzles of this study.

One of the other new puzzles growing from the study concerns the narrative styles of young children in Taiwan. The identified narrative structures were helpful for me in this study, but I was not sure how valuable the typology of six narrative structures might be. Though it was still very preliminary, one of my graduate students found it helpful for her to understand children's long narratives. She also found some children used consistent structures to narrate their experiences in a day care (Chung, 2006). Whether Taiwanese children developed certain narrative styles as early as at 4 or 5 years of age needs to be explored more in further studies.

There are other issues to be further explored. As mentioned, this study was conducted in Taipei city. If self, culture, and narrative are so mutually constructed, it would be beneficial to conduct research in other kindergarten classrooms and listen to the narratives of children of different cultures. I might be able to establish a better base and have more clues with which to judge how basic the four themes are in children's representations of their personal experiences. For example, will boredom appear as frequently in children's narratives who live in places other than Taipei city? Another issue to be followed is the cultural models revealed in these narratives. As found, there were not many texts in which *crisis* was an appropriate name for a portion. Is there a better name than *crisis* to describe the situation in which a child has to deal with boredom? Is it possible that Taiwanese people have a different definition of *crisis* from that of American scholars?

Another piece of contextual information I was not able to provide in this study is the general cultural values placed on young children's narratives in Taiwan. It is a difficult issue even for a Taiwanese such as me. This study was a response to the limited space given for children's personal experiences in kindergarten classrooms based on what I have learned from years of fieldwork in kindergartens in Taipei county and Taipei city. To know more about the general or different cultural values placed on young children's personal narratives in Taiwan will require more empirical work and more thorough readings of related literatures.

Coda

Bruner (2002) states that "we are so adept at narrative that it seems almost as natural as language itself" (p. 3). However, my journey of understanding Taiwanese children's personal narratives in a kindergarten classroom has told me the space given for children's narratives in school is not so natural as Bruner assumes. Various narrative structures and themes sorted from the 36 personal narrative texts have helped me see how these Taiwanese children struggled between a desire to "create a conviction of autonomy [and a need] to relate the self to a world of others" (p. 78). At the same time, I had some insights about how cultural values might have shaped these desires and needs. What I learned from An-zou's narrative, on the other hand, led me to realize that I knew too little about her and did not provide necessary help based on what I had heard. As Rosen so wisely put, when encountering "the remitting flow of events, [we must] invent, yes, invent, beginnings and ends [to] give order to this otherwise unmanageable flux" (cited in Cazden, 1988, p. 24). My first attempt at understanding children's narratives served as a beginning for me, and the end is yet to come. To treat children's narratives as an expression of who they are and where they are, I need to learn more about the contexts where such an expression was made possible. In this regard, I have much to learn from kindergarten teachers, many of whom respond to children's narratives by telling stories for them and with them. I hope this way of understanding children's narratives as shared in this chapter will be of some help to kindergarten teachers, who live very closely with young children and have many opportunities to listen to them. Learning together with kindergarten children and teachers has been an ongoing part of my life as a researcher and has continued throughout the writing of this chapter. I am still on my way to learning how to listen to children's narratives.

Author's Note: I would like to express my deep gratitude to Dr. Jean Clandinin, who encouraged me to think about the complexities of narrative inquiry and provided very insightful comments to an earlier draft of this chapter; Dr. Daniel Walsh, who read the draft carefully, posed significant questions, and provided helpful criticism; and Dr. Shaun Murphy, who had a wonderful review of the draft, edited it meticulously, and helped move the work along. Also, I would like to thank Miss Lee and her students for making this study possible.

Consulting Editors: Daniel Walsh and M. Shaun Murphy

Notes

1. The last names of the teachers and the names of all the children who appear in this chapter are pseudonyms.

2. The study was sponsored by National Science Council in Taiwan. NSC 91-2413-H-152-004.

3. The words were from Jerry, a high school teacher described in Paley's (1999) book.

4. This work was first published in 1967. In 1997, the *Journal of Narrative and Life History* had a special issue focusing on the discussion of this work.

5. We actually worked in two classrooms at the beginning of the study. Due to the chaotic interaction in one classroom and therefore the poor acoustic quality of the recorded narratives, I decided to focus my analysis to the narratives collected in the other classroom only.

6. In all of the examples given in this chapter, children's narration will be presented in italics, the bracketing statement will be put in parentheses and the topic or macrostructure will be labeled in bold capitals.

7. The grammatical error here was a choice of translation. In Mandarin, the child's words here were grammatically inappropriate. This choice is applied to other examples in this chapter.

8. Miss Lee audiotaped children's narratives so she could listen to them after work. That was why she asked the children to say their names before sharing.

9. Children in Taiwan call those women who are of or around the same age as their mothers "aunt."

10. Little brother refers to young boys in Mandarin.

11. These mothers are Taiwanese women actually.

12. The kindergarten in this study is affiliated to a public elementary school. In such public kindergartens in Taiwan, there are two teachers in a class.

References

Bruner, J. (2002). *Making stories: Law, literature, life.* New York: Farrar, Straus and Giroux.

Cazden, C. B. (1988). *Classroom discourse: The language of teaching and learning.* Portsmouth, NH: Heinemann.

Chang, C. (2003). Talking about the past: How do Chinese mothers elicit narratives from their young children across time. *Narrative Inquiry, 13*(1), 99–126.

Chang, C., & Chang, G. (2002, November). *The development of young children's narrative competence: A longitudinal study.* Paper presented in 2002 annual conference of Teachers College in Taiwan. Gia-yee: National Gia-yee University.

Chung, W. C. (2006). *The contexts and narrative structures of young children's narratives in a day-care center* (in Chinese). Unpublished master's thesis, National Taipei University of Education, Taipei, Taiwan.

Clandinin, D. J., & Connelly, F. M. (2000). *Narrative inquiry: Experience and story in qualitative research.* San Francisco: Jossey-Bass.

Engel, S. (1995). *The stories children tell.* New York: W. H. Freeman.

Gee, J. P. (2000). *Discourse analysis: Theory and method.* New York: Routledge.

Labov, W., & Waletzky, J. (1997). Narrative analysis: Oral versions of personal experience. *Journal of Narrative and Life History, 7*(1–4), 3–38. (Original work published 1967)

Michaels, S. (1981). "Sharing time": Children's narrative styles and differential access to literacy. *Language Society, 10,* 423–442.

Miller, P. G. (1994). Narrative practices: Their role in socialization and self-construction. In U. Neisser & R. Fivush (Eds.), *The remembering self: Construction and accuracy in the self-narrative* (pp. 158–179). New York: Cambridge University Press.

Minami, M., & McCabe, A. (1991). Haiku as a discourse regulation device: A stanza analysis of Japanese children's personal narratives. *Language in Society, 20,* 577–599.

Mishler, E. G. (1986). *Researching interviewing: Context and narrative.* Cambridge, MA: Harvard University Press.

Mishler, E. G. (1995). Models of narrative analysis: A typology. *Journal of Narrative and Life History, 5*(2), 87–123.

Paley, V. G. (1986). On listening to what the children say. *Harvard Educational Review, 56*(2), 122–131.

Paley, V. G. (1999). *The kindness of children.* Cambridge, MA: Harvard University Press.

Peterson, C., & McCabe, A. (1983). *Developmental psycholinguistics: Three ways of looking at a child's narrative.* New York: Plenum.

Riessman, C. K. (1993). *Narrative analysis.* Newbury Park, CA: Sage.

Tsai, M. (2004). Some problems and difficulties in the sense-making process of educational qualitative research: Issues on experiencing, analyzing and recontexualization (in Chinese). *Journal of National Taipei Teachers College, 17,* 233–260.

Tsai, M., & Garcia, G. (2000). Who's the boss: How communicative competence is defined in a multilingual preschool classroom. *Anthropology & Education Quarterly, 31*(2), 230–252.

CHAPTER 19

Exploring Cross-Cultural Boundaries

Molly Andrews

Erika Apfelbaum (2001) writes that "the issue of communicating across cultural boundaries is a major challenge to the very foundations of our dominant theoretical frameworks" (p. 32). While Apfelbaum's focus is on cultural boundaries associated with articulating, and listening to, traumatic narratives, the issues that she raises have a wider applicability. We are, all of us, individuals who have come to be as we are not as isolated beings but as social animals who live, breathe, and survive in particular historical, social, and political contexts. None of this is new, but the implications of Apfelbaum's statement for cross-cultural narrative work are profound. How is it that we access, interpret, and analyze stories that, at their heart, are distant from experiences that we ourselves may have encountered not only in our own lives but in the accounts of others, which are part of our own narrative repertoire? How do we prepare ourselves for the very demanding task that listening must be if it is to be anything? And how is our own sense of identity affected by opening ourselves to the very different realities that are encountered by others? Is it desirable or even possible to remain unchanged when we come to know, however indirectly, the worlds that exist beyond the radar of what has always been familiar to us?

In this chapter, I will discuss my own experience of conducting narrative research in a range of different cultural contexts. I wish to argue that cross-cultural narrative research is predicated on narrative imagination (Brockmeier, in press); put simply, if we wish to access the frameworks of meaning for others, we must be willing and able to imagine a world other than the one we know. I will argue that narrative imagination, which Donoghue describes as "the seeing of difference" (1998, p. 16), lies at the heart of cross-cultural research. The argument that I will make here is not new; indeed, Marcus Aurelius, in the second century AD, claimed that "to become world citizens we must cultivate in ourselves a capacity for sympathetic imagination" (as cited in Nussbaum, 1997, p. 85). In this chapter, I will explore what comprises that imagination and through a discussion of some of my own research, discuss what happens when our imaginations fail us, as inevitably they do from time to time.

Let me begin with a brief overview of my entry into this discussion. I was born and educated in the United States. In the mid-1980s, I came to England to register for a PhD, and I have remained in England for most of the time since then. When people hear me speak, they often ask about my accent, unable to place it neatly onto either side of the Atlantic. The one-line response that I have developed over the years offers the explanation that I was dropped in the middle of the Atlantic Ocean, somewhere between the east coast of the United States and England. My cultural placement lies in this vast body of water, which encompasses both the country of my origin and that of my current life, as well as all my journeys in between and beyond. Bhabha (1994) describes a process of cultural hybridization that entails "the migrant's double vision," whereby an individual moves with "psychic uncertainty across boundaries of cultural difference" (as cited in Selby, 2004, p. 148). What is particularly appealing about Bhabha's description, and Selby's use of his work, is that the product of the hybridization is a new entity, one that is not reducible to its component parts. It is, rather, an integration of two or more worlds that are integrated one into the other. This wandering between cultural borderlands, thus, affords a ripening of creativity.

Over the past two decades, I have been involved in narrative research, which has brought me not only to England and the United States but also to East Germany and South Africa as well. In England, I examined the phenomenon of lifelong socialist activism as displayed in the lives of 15 British women and men who had been politically active on the left for 50 years or longer. In the United States, my research shifted to an exploration of the meaning of patriotism, as expressed in the political activism of a small group of antiwar protesters. Three years after the fall of the Berlin Wall, I spent 6 months in the German Democratic Republic (GDR), speaking with 40 women and men about their views of what had happened to their country and how this affected their own sense of self. This research, which included a series of interviews with one of the architects of East Germany's truth commission, led to another project: Using the transcripts of South Africa's Truth and Reconciliation, I explored negotiations of forgiveness in highly public and politicized contexts.

The four projects outlined above, although all very different, did nonetheless have some common ground between them. First, and fundamentally, they were all conducted by me and as such were guided in some sense by the same, or at least similar, meaning-making framework. In producing the narrative about my own narrative research, the connection between the projects is highlighted; there is a clear relationship between my interests and I can, in hindsight, identify the subsequent imprint of one project upon another. Second, the central focus for each of these projects is the study of individual lives in highly politicized contexts. I have always been interested in the ways in which people make sense of the historical times in which they live and have taken C. Wright Mills's (1959) injunction very seriously in my work:

> Continually work out and revise your views of the problems of history, the problems of biography, and the problems of social structure in which biography and history intersect. Keep your eyes open to the varieties of individuality, and to the modes of epochal change. (p. 225)

This is the problem I have returned to, and will always return to, in my research. How does this individual with whom I am speaking reflect wider social and historical changes that form the context of his or her life? I am convinced that if I can listen closely enough, there is much to learn from every story that one might gather. For society really is comprised of human lives, and if we can begin to understand the framework that lends meaning to these lives, then we have taken the important first step to being able to access the wider framework of meaning that is the binding agent of a culture.

The anthropologist Clifford Geertz, in his classic *The Interpretation of Cultures* (1973), argues that culture cannot be separated from meaning.

> Culture . . . is public, like a burlesqued wink or a mock sheep raid. . . . The thing to ask about a burlesqued wink or a mock sheep raid is . . . what their import is: what it is, ridicule or challenge, irony or anger, snobbery or pride, that, in their occurrence and through their agency, is getting said. (p. 10)

For Geertz (1973), culture and meaning are accessed not through the universal and generalizable but through exploration of fine detail. "We must," Geertz advises us, "descend into detail" (p. 53), for "Seeing heaven in a grain of sand is not a trick only poets can accomplish" (p. 44). Apfelbaum (2000), too, makes a similar claim: "The singularity of experience offers one of the possible ways to confront the universal" (p. 173). Geertz (1973) argues that good interpretation "takes us into the heart of that of which it is an interpretation" (p. 18).

My research has always been guided by a similar outlook, and this journey "into the heart" has most often taken the form of in-depth life history interviews. Paraphrasing Robert Jay Lifton's (1986) explanation of the methodology he used in his research on Nazi doctors, "My assumption from the beginning, in keeping with my 25 years of research [in my case slightly shorter] was that the best way to learn about [a group of people] was to talk to them" (p. 6). Geertz (1973) describes the goal of his research in the following way:

> We are not . . . seeking either to become natives . . . or to mimic them. Only romantics or spies would seem to find point in that. We are seeking, in the widened sense of the term in which it encompasses very much more than talk, to converse with them, a matter a great deal more difficult, and not only with strangers, than is commonly recognized. (p. 13)

I have spent many hours, over many years, conversing with a small group of people about their lives. The framework of my research projects has invariably changed in the course of the research as I encounter new systems of meaning and of making sense of the world. Rosaldo (1989) describes this "interpretive approach," associated with Geertz, in the following way:

> Ethnographers begin research with a set of questions, revise them throughout the course of inquiry, and in the end emerge with different questions than they started with. One's surprise at the answer to a question, in other words, requires one to revise the question until lessening surprises or diminishing returns indicate a stopping point. (p. 7)

This approach contrasts with more traditional methodology that has been employed to learn about other cultures. Ember and Ember (2001), for instance, produce a seven-point set of guidelines that are meant to assist researchers in cross-cultural research. The first of these reads, "Ask a clear *one-sentence* research question" (p. 136). Steps 2 and 3 consist of "Formulate at least one hypothesis to test" and "Operationalize each variable in the hypothesis" (p. 136). In contrast to Geertz, the focus of these authors is on that which can be generalized across cultures. For me personally, such an approach does not help transport me to where I want to go: someplace that I have not been before and where I may well not know what questions might be relevant until I am well on my journey.

And so my route has been a different one to that prescribed by Ember and Ember; mine has been an attempt to converse, in the deep sense identified by Geertz earlier, with women and men from different cultures. Some of these conversations have been very concentrated, typified by my encounter with Sebastian Kleinschmidt, an East German philosopher and literary critic, who was the editor of the well-known journal *Sinn und Form*. I had been given his name and contact details by someone who knew the area of my research project. Kleinschmidt agreed to be interviewed, and my translator and I arrived at his home early one afternoon. Once I turned on the tape, he did not stop talking—not for more than 5 hours. It was as if I was standing at the base of Niagara Falls, capturing on tape the flood of thought and emotion that spilled forth from Sebastian Kleinschmidt as he described in much detail the life he had led in his country, which was no longer, and the implications of the momentous changes that had happened in his own life. Here, surely, was a transforming self in a transforming society. But as intensive and engaging as this meeting was, we were never to meet again. He had said what he had to say. We had his life history, and ultimately, this would become part of a much larger data set, his individual story only one small part in the fabric of this community's collective memory.

But my relationships with those I have interviewed have not always been so transitory. Indeed, at the time of writing this chapter, I continue to be in conversation with some of the women and men who participated in my study of lifetime British socialist activists, which I began 20 years ago this month. I have written elsewhere about the importance of these ongoing conversations in my life (Andrews,

2003a). The question of what constitutes data becomes rather blurred when researchers develop ongoing relationships with those who participate in their projects. Using the icon of the tape recorder as an ultimate arbitrator of this murky area, however, my interviews were almost always conducted one-on-one. That is, regardless of the social context that often formed the backdrop of my visits (including sometimes staying in their homes, visiting friends with them, and often becoming integrated into the larger family gatherings), I was guided in my life history work by the sense that people's abilities to think and talk about the events, as well as the overall meaning, in their lives are most developed when they are on their own—or rather on their own with me, the researcher.

Life Histories and Cultural Practice

Although I can still see some reasons for conducting life history research in this fashion, I now see that this very method is itself indicative of my own cultural lens. Why is it that we assume that social animals such as human beings make the most coherent or most meaningful sense of their lives when they are virtually stranded on their own with a stranger and a recording machine? Qi Wang and Jens Brockmeier describe autobiographical remembering as a form of cultural practice (Wang & Brockmeier, 2002).

Wang & Brockmeier (2002) argue that the very notion of autobiographical memory is itself a cultural product. They cite the work of Greenwald (1980), who states that individuals who are socialized in the West "remember their past as if it were a drama in which the self is the leading player; moreover, in the drama of one's personal history the self acts in an all-determining, 'totalitarian' fashion" (p. 46). This way of thinking about autobiographical memory emphasizes "individuality, autonomy and power in explicating and evaluating human lives" (p. 47). Wang and Brockmeier argue that

> the Western notion of autobiographical remembering as intimately connected to the development of an autonomous self is only one possible form in which individuals remember their pasts. There also exist other cultural genres of remembering, such as genres that are connected to a process of increasing social interrelatedness. (p. 47)

In the West, there is a strong undercurrent of asking individuals to account for themselves as selves, to display ways in which they stand out from the rest of the crowd. We orient ourselves toward that which is unique about each individual while often ignoring the social fabric that forms the framework of a person's life. Effectively, life history methodology enhances the salience of the distinctive boundaries between this self, the interviewee, and all others.

My choice of the one-to-one life history method, with its emphasis on the unique life story, can be interpreted as a cultural signifier of my own socialization. There were several occasions during my research on lifetime socialist activists when it became clear that some respondents felt somewhat ill at ease spending so much time talking about themselves. While the descriptions of the events of their lives that they offered me challenged the notion of an isolated self (and indeed one can read these interviews as evidence for the social interrelatedness of individual identity), most of them, most of the time, nonetheless did what I asked them to do, which was to talk to me about their lives and to do so on their own.

Eileen, one of the respondents in this study, writes to me after reading transcripts from our first interview:

> I found it rather shocking because I felt it was very self-indulgent. I think that's what hit me and I think after our discussion I had felt the same . . . my reactions were "Oh dear, we do try to get away from our egos—how do you break out of the circle of your ego—and here I am locked into it."

But it was the very methodology I had chosen that had caused her to be so "self-indulgent." Ironically, once she had agreed to the interview, she was strategically positioned to provide an individualized account of a life that had been guided by acting, as part of a collective, in the social good. Other respondents in the study remarked on my use of the word identity. "I don't really think of myself as having an identity," Mary told me. "Perhaps you as the younger generation think more in that kind of way. I wouldn't think many people go on consciously thinking about themselves really." But that is precisely what the life history asks of those who participate in our research.

Interestingly, my respondents had their own creative ways of circumventing this overly individualistic orientation that underlay my chosen methodology. First, they gave me feedback such as that quoted above, communicating their discomfort with this narrow lens. On occasion, they would invite a spouse or a family member to sit with us while we spoke. Their accounts were almost always peppered with "ghostly audiences" (Langellier, 2000): all those people, and political movements, who had been critical to the selves they had become. And finally, nearly all of them expressed much curiosity about the others in my study: How did they respond to this question or that? What did they feel about a certain current event? How had they balanced responsibilities to their political work and to their families? The questions persisted for such a long time that I decided that I owed it to all of them to arrange a meeting for those who were able and/or wished to attend. Many of them made the journey across England to come for afternoon tea in the home where I rented a room. There we sat and talked, and talked, and talked. They behaved as if they knew one another intimately, though this was their first meeting, and expressed a desire to keep in touch. They joked that if they did not see each other on this side of the heavenly divide, they would meet in the not-too-distant future on the other.

The individualistic focus of the method was less apparent in other settings, perhaps due to the content of the research projects. It is not wholly surprising that people who have devoted their lives to social movements would experience some discomfort with the individual accounting I was asking of them. All the interviews

I conducted in East Germany were with at least three people present (the interviewee, my translator, and me). The addition of the translator had a number of effects on the conversations that we had (Andrews, 1995), including enhancing the sense that we were participating in a social gathering. The multiple directions of communication—between me and the translator, the translator and the interviewee, and even at times the attempts at direct communication between the interviewee and myself—added to the semblance that we constituted a microcommunity, an example of the "three or more" basis of group life. My primary translator was also my close friend, who had generously offered me space to sleep on her floor for several months. In the midst of conducting our interviews, I celebrated my birthday, and through her instigation, we invited a number of the interviewees to my party in her loft. It is unlikely that I would have made such a gesture had I conducted the interviews on my own.

My research in East Germany included interviews with three women—Irene Kukutz, Barbel Bohley, and Katja Havemann—whose group, Women for Peace, had been a very effective voice for political change in the years leading up to 1989. In the summer of 1989, as thousands began to pour out of East Germany through the Hungarian border, these three friends sat together in the garden and promised one another that the following year they would travel together to Italy, a place that for them represented all that had been previously forbidden to them. Indeed, the following summer they did go, together. Kukutz describes the experience as follows:

> When we were crossing the Alps, I had the same feeling as when the border was opened. Total collapse. I was thinking, by what right, with what justification did they imprison us for years and why couldn't I see that [the view from the Alps] earlier. . . . One somehow felt cheated over a chunk of one's life.

They had been through much together in the years, and it was important to them to make this trip together. Two years later, in 1992, the files of the East German secret service (the Ministerium fur Staatsicherheit [MfS]—more commonly known as the "Stasi") were made public (see Andrews, 1998). On the second day that the records were opened, these three friends went to see what their files contained. Although it had been stipulated by the Gauck Commission (the body responsible for administering the Stasi records) that the files must be read only by individuals, these women disregarded this and insisted on viewing their files together. Irene Kukutz, in our interview together, explains the reasoning behind their determination: "We are all in the files together, and we are going to look at them together!" I had versions of this same story told to me by each of the three women, but ironically, the context in which they were giving me their accounts was, once again, as isolated individuals. Logistically, it may have been rather difficult to coordinate an interview including the three of them. Nonetheless, it is quite possible that in opting for the methodology that I used, I inadvertently stripped away an important framework of meaning that they not only shared but that had been nurtured by their close friendships with one another.

Ethics and Cultural Positioning

We as researchers are influenced by our culture not only in our expectations of the conditions under which people might feel most inclined to give an account of their lives but also in ways in which we are taught to go about gathering this information. Specifically, our professional training teaches us that there are certain universal ethical standards that we must adhere to when conducting our research. Like a number of other researchers engaged in multicultural projects, I have found that what might be considered ethical in one context may be something very different in another. Riessman (2005), candidly discussing some of the challenges she faced in conducting research on nonfertile women in South India, offers a powerful critique of "the inherent and practical risks associated with ethical universalism—applying 'universal' moral principles that have been constructed (that is, derived) in one cultural context and exporting them, without modifications, to another" (p. 473). This point seems, at one level, so trivial that it should hardly need expression. And yet, as Riessman and others have argued, it is not something that has been taken on by institutional review boards in the United States and the United Kingdom. Again, I will use examples from my own research.

When I began my interviews in East Germany, it was made clear to me immediately that the ideas that are implicit in an informed consent form are entirely inappropriate in the East German context. Invariably, the effect of showing this form to interviewees was to call attention to myself as a foreigner. Not only had no one ever heard of such a thing, but when I began to explain its function and why it might be beneficial to them to sign it, the situation only worsened. They explained to me, with varying degrees of incredulity and patience, that in their culture no one felt that they "owned" someone's words. Not only were they not at all worried about what I might do with the transcripts of our conversations, but the very exchange between us on this topic made them somewhat suspicious of me, personally.

At first, I wondered if this rejection of the consent form was particular to the first person from whom I encountered this reaction, and so I persisted in the next few interviews. Each time, I found that this piece of paper produced the same tension between us. I knew then that I must either abandon the consent form or keep it and accept the cost that it might have on future publications. I decided on the former. Moreover, interviewees wanted me to use their real names. These were their words, about their lives: Why, they asked me, should they not have their names identified? Fine, I would use their names and not require consent forms; in fact, this felt like the only option open to me that would sit comfortably with what these men and women felt about the representation of their lives.

Mostly, this choice was without consequences for me. Several years later, however, an article that I had written using some of these data had been accepted by an international, refereed journal. Just before the article was due to go to press, the editor of the journal contacted me querying my use of names. I explained the situation to him: Yes, they were their real names, and no, I did not have consent forms. He nearly pulled the article out of the journal but instead made what he considered a significant concession: He would publish the piece if I would withdraw the real names. Although I was uncomfortable changing names when it had been the clear preference of my interviewees to be accurately identified, I decided to concede this point as this particular publication depended on it. When I offered the revised article, with altered names, it too was rejected, however. Ultimately, the only version that was acceptable to the editor was the one in which there were no names at all but only initials and those with no correspondence to real names. Who did these ethical guidelines serve? While they may have been appropriate in a litigious society such as the United States, they were contrary to the preferences of those whom they were meant to protect. The rigidity of the guidelines—indeed, in this case they proved not to be guidelines at all but rather prerequisites for publication—seemed to me to be an indication of an inability to imagine that others may perceive the world in a different way than we do; one manifestation of this may be that they wish to tell us about their lives differently than the way we think they should. The inflexible imposition of a "universal" set of ethical guidelines is evidence of cultural hegemony combined with a lack of narrative imagination.

In another context, that of working with the transcripts of the Truth and Reconciliation Commission (TRC) of South Africa, I felt that the guidelines were not sufficiently sensitive to the needs of those who had given personal testimony to the TRC. Women and men who agreed to tell their very painful stories in the presence of the truth commission did so for a wide range of reasons (see Andrews, in press). They were advised, at the time, that in participating in this process, they were agreeing to share their stories with the general public. There were also a number of incentives (some imagined, some real) for them to offer their stories. What is not clear is whether people who came before this national body and recounted the horrors which had befallen them and their loved ones actually understood what "public access" to their transcripts actually would entail: Their testimonies would be available online literally to anyone in the world who has Internet access (see Gready, in press). Of course, for those of us who work with personal narratives, this data set is at one level an extraordinary resource. But when one begins to read what is actually being said, and to allow oneself to contemplate the intensity of the anguish experienced by many of those who gave testimony, one begins to question if one's perusal of this material for research purposes is sufficiently respectful of the women and men whose words are displayed on the Internet, as one scrolls through screen after screen after screen. I grappled with this issue for some time and finally decided that although using this material was considered to be ethical by Western academic bodies, my own comfort zone told me something different. These stories were not meant for my eyes. I was never part of the imagined audience for these speakers as they broke down and told of their last embrace with their children. Here, our accepted ethical guidelines are inadequate to address the potential of academic voyeurism.

Yazir Henri (2003), a former anti-apartheid activist and a former officer in Umkhonto We Sizwe, the military wing of the African National Congress, describes his experience of giving testimony to the TRC: "It took me almost a complete year to recover psychologically from my testimony and the form it took publicly after having testified" (p. 264). He then elaborates on the source of the pain that followed from his public testimony:

At the time of my testimony I had no idea what the consequences of "public" could have meant in the context of public hearings. The fact that my testimony could be appropriated, interpreted, re-interpreted, re-told and sold was not what I expected. . . . Serious thought needs to be given to the ethics of appropriating testimony for poetic license, media freedom, academic commentary and discourse analysis. Arguing these lines and "It's on the public record" are too easy positions to take since they do not address the rights of self-authorship and the intention of the speaker, the reclamation of one's voice and one's agency. (p. 266)

The argument being made here is not strictly one of cultural specificity, however—that is, Henri's thoughts on this subject are not a product of his cultural upbringing, or at least not only a product of this. Rather, I think they are a very understandable reaction to seeing one's words used for purposes wholly outside of their original intention and having to encounter this misrepresentation of oneself time and again in a range of public forums. I have had direct experience of having a personal interview made accessible online, and it is a chilling feeling to encounter one's own personal history, problems, joys, and challenges on display for anyone who can be bothered to read it. The experiences that I have had in my life are not comparable with those of Yazir Henri; nonetheless, the feeling of exposure and vulnerability that engulfed me when I inadvertently came upon this interview was most illuminating for me. I never contemplated that relinquishing copyright to this interview would involve such public vulnerability.

Jane Selby (2004) discusses the complexity of conducting responsible research in an indigenous setting. Echoing the work of Jouve (1991), she argues that "writing is never innocent" (Selby, 2004, p. 144). Her research, involving children in a remote indigenous community in Australia, explores candidly some of the intractable challenges that are incurred when working across divides of disadvantage. Observing that "we use traditional methods and practices to help avoid experiencing the difficulties of working with others. But in such 'hiding' from uncomfortable experiences we do our work less well" (p. 143); she argues that cultural difference "can be brought into play as an interpretive resource" (p. 147). While working "fairly with disadvantage" may be "an ideal [that] is impossible, a fantasy of good research/teaching or good politics" (p. 144), there is, nonetheless, much to be learned in exploring what lies beyond one's cultural boundaries. "Cultural uncertainty affords creativity" (p. 148).

While most of my research was not across divides of overt disadvantage (other than that incurred by the power imbalance inherent in the structure of research interviews), Selby's argument is relevant to the point I wish to make here: Most cross-cultural research is guided by a set of ethical considerations that are irrelevant, unrealistic, and/or possibly inappropriate and insufficient to address the complexity of such encounters. We are better researchers when we push ourselves to confront those aspects of our work that cause us discomfort.

Narrative and National Identity

It is not wholly surprising that my work, which has been based in several countries, and sometimes simultaneously so, has led me to think about how people position themselves vis-à-vis the country of their birth and/or the country of their residence. I have spent hundreds of hours listening to people tell me stories about themselves and their countries. Sometimes these conversations have taken the form of history lessons—teaching me about events that it was assumed that I, somehow constituted as "other" either through nationality or through age, would have little knowledge of. But more often, the stories of the nation were interwoven as part of the fabric of the individual life. Historical events, as it were, would form the backdrop for personal biography. People would explain to me, for instance, the effect that living under certain social-historical conditions had exercised on the choices that they made in their lives.

In preparation for the data-gathering phase of all of my research projects, I have spent considerable time familiarizing myself with the social history of the community that I was exploring. In conducting my project on British lifetime socialists, for instance, I spent more than a year sitting in the library reading books on the social history of Britain between the world wars, a fertile environment for the radicalization of significant portions of the population. I would not have been able to understand much of what was said to me if I had been ignorant of the political ferment that accompanied the vast unemployment of the 1920s in Britain. By December 1921, 18% of insured workers were unemployed (Branson, 1975). Only 1 year earlier, the Communist Party of Great Britain (CPGB) had been formed, and the devastating effects of massive unemployment, combined with the international rise of fascism, meant that this political group attracted a great number of sympathizers.

One such sympathizer was Walter Gregory, a participant in my lifetime socialist project, who was laid off from his job as an office worker as a young man. He joined the National Unemployed Workers Union and participated in the Hunger March to London in 1934. Walter developed a political understanding of the circumstances that had led to massive unemployment, of which his own job loss was but one statistic. He explained the effect of this lesson: "The things I learned in 1934 on the Hunger March. . . . I hold fast to this day. . . . I was never the same after that Hunger March. I could never go back to being just the same person." Indeed, Walter returned from the march, only to volunteer several years later with the British Battalion of International Brigade, fighting for the Republican cause in the Spanish Civil War, where he became a lieutenant.

Time and again in my interviews, it was clear that personal biographies could only be understood in the wider context of these harsh living conditions. As Aldous Huxley once commented, experience is not what happens to you but how you understand what happens to you (as cited in Kegan, 1982, p. 11). Not everyone who lived in this society at this time emerged with a similar, left-wing political explanation of it; and all those who were dedicated to the left did not necessarily encounter these conditions in the same way—indeed, class was not a predictor for political radicalization. But the social conditions were ripe for a particular political narrative, and the comprehensive explanation offered by the CPGB did appeal to many. Christopher Cornford, one of the respondents in my study, explained the situation to me in the following way:

> You can see it, can't you, how unemployment, fascism, war preparations, political reaction . . . one knew that all the right-wing conservatives were really anti-Semitic and pro-Hitler in their heart of hearts, and they really wanted Hitler to attack Russia . . . one saw in Russia this wonderful, creative, just, egalitarian society with infinite potential, and everything seemed to add up, and everything seemed to cut the same way.

Christopher describes the dramatic effect of his political conversion:

> You suddenly see the world in a different perspective, the world becomes much more luminous and exciting and comprehensible and involving and significant and you feel that you have a sort of function in the world, as distinct from being a little dry leaf that is blown around in the world.

One can hear in Christopher's words the pronounced shift in his sense of agency; this political understanding is not merely something abstract but rather for him a blueprint for action and one that will stay with him all his years. For Christopher, his political radicalization was part of a growing sense of belonging to a community that would fight for social justice and change, even or perhaps especially in conditions of such social disparity as that which characterized Britain in the interwar years. Looking back on nearly 8 decades of his life, Christopher tells me that he feels he has found "a path with heart."

For Walter and Christopher, as with all of the respondents in my study, their identity is anchored in being part of a larger community, which refuses to accept the government of the day as the ultimate arbitrator of national interest. They seek to help those whose needs have been neglected, and they feel that this emanates partly from their responsibilities as citizens. (One is reminded here of Marcus Aurelius's comment, cited earlier: To be world citizens, we must have the capacity for sympathetic imagination.) Walter and Christopher come from vastly different social backgrounds. Walter's family was working class, and they experienced "chronic economic hardship." Christopher, in contrast, was a direct descendent of both Charles Darwin and the Wedgewoods, and the environment in which he was raised was very privileged. Yet these two men, with very different sets of personal circumstances, arrived at a common political narrative, which was to stay with them all their years. The stories they told me are much more than just their personal stories; they are also national stories, which cast light on the condition of life in Britain in the 20th century.

My research in East Germany was very different in a number of ways from that which I had carried out in Britain. When I arrived in East Berlin in February 1992, East Germany no longer existed. During my 6 months there, however, it occurred to me that it may be easier to wipe off nations from the globe than it is to wipe a sense of national identity from individual consciousness. It is ironic that as some researchers have observed, times of political upheaval are particularly ripe conditions for collective narrative reconstruction (Roßteutscher, 2000). The political demise of East Germany created the possibility for the revitalization of national identity, of the collective story of what it meant to be East German. Benedict Anderson (1983) has famously described the nation as an imagined community. There is evidence to suggest that the imagined community of East Germany held a far deeper attachment for many than the actual state; the disappearance of the latter created a possibility for the enhancement of the former. One can see in this example the power of narrative imagination as it applies to the internalization of national identity. Brockmeier (2001) examines the cultural fabric of national identity, arguing that the latter is

> one of the strongest threads to bind the individual into the cultural whole of a social community. Miraculously enough, there is a sense of national belonging that turns Kang and Margy, Gyorgy and Ana, Tadashi and Hanife, you and me into a Spaniard and a Basque, a North and a South Korean, a Canadian and a Quebecer, a member of a ruling elite and a resistance fighter. (p. 216)

For Brockmeier (2001), then, national identity is "a symbolic construction . . . a process of continuous cultural interpretation and reinterpretation" (p. 215). National identity, according to this view, is something that is never finally arrived at but is part of an ongoing process that binds the individual and his or her community across time and space.

Nowhere was the imaginative and transformational potential of national identity more dramatically symbolized than in the chants of *Autumn 1989*, "We are the people." Prior to this time, the East German government had an unusually concerted program inducting its population in civic education. Young people were effectively required to join groups (first, the Young Pioneers, then the Free German Youth) in which they received instruction relevant to their national identity. Failure to participate in such groups came with a serious price—for instance, the foreclosure of schooling opportunities. Because of this very rigid and formal tuition, many East Germans complied with the activities required of them while failing to internalize any compelling sense of national belonging. It was something that was required of them and, as such, a site of psychological, if not physical, resistance.

In the years immediately following 1989, all this changed rather dramatically. In 1990, 66% of East Germans identified themselves as more German than East German, whereas by 1995, this figure had dropped to only 34%. Correspondingly, in 1990, 28% identified themselves as more East German than German, while in 1995, this figure had climbed to 60% (Yoder, 1999, pp. 204–205). The effect of the demise of the country was an increase in the sense of national belonging. Jennifer Yoder (1999) explains the causes for this phenomenon:

> Eastern identity has been rediscovered as a response to the encroachment of west German norms and rules for behaviour and the devaluation of eastern

culture and identity. This rediscovery can also be interpreted as a positive/ proactive development . . . a process of self-assertion, an expression of pride and autonomy, and a recognition that the east was and is different from the west. (p. 209)

In my own research, I asked respondents how they would answer the question "When you are asked where are you from, what do you say?" The reactions that this question triggered were often emotional and sometimes dramatic. In my article "Continuity and Discontinuity of East German Identity Following the Fall of the Berlin Wall: A Case Study" (Andrews, 2003b), I summarize the answers I received:

Most interview participants paused over their response, but eventually gave some form of the answer "the GDR," in the present tense, with comments such as "throughout my life I will remain a citizen of the GDR." (Variations on this included one respondent describing himself as "coming from the east of Germany" and another saying she was from "the other Germany.") Several respondents said they did not feel German at all, but rather European. Virtually no one responded that they felt they were from "Germany." (p. 114)

In this article, I argue that in the 10 years following the fall of the Berlin Wall, East German identity is not as wholly changed as some have suggested. Rather,

East Germans living in a unified Germany experience neither a total transformation of their former existence, nor an identity which is unaffected by the profound changes of the context in which they live their lives. Rather, such research reveals a continuity of self co-existing with a profound sense of personal and political change. . . . Undeniably, the events of the German autumn have precipitated profound psychological change for East Germans, but importantly, this change has occurred within a relative constancy of identity. As MP Ingrid Koppe comments to me " . . . the past . . . is not as past as we assume. We are the result of the past and the past is in us." (Andrews, 2003b, pp. 120–122)

The enduring and evolving East German identity has taken a number of forms. In recent years, a new industry has emerged around consumer items imbued with national identity, such as the Trabbant (the car long associated with East Germany), and new board games that rely on cultural knowledge of life before 1989. For some, this is regarded as a rose-tinted nostalgia, but others write of the "multiple meanings of *Ostalgie*," claiming that it stems not from an identification with the former GDR state "but rather an identification with different forms of oppositional solidarity and collective memory" (Berdahl, 1999, p. 203). It is an expression of belonging to a community that experiences itself as under threat.

The stories that I heard were framed around an existence that was lived within the physical and psychological confines of the Berlin Wall. At the time of my interviews, very little of the actual wall still remained (apart from a small segment that had been retained as a form of memorialization and that had been designated as an outdoor gallery). But the wall had not disappeared from the psyche of those who had lived with it for so many years. Many people spoke to me about the significance of the wall, both its presence and now its absence. This wall inside the head was also an enduring legacy of what it meant to be from East Germany. It was far easier to expunge it from the landscape than from the soul.

The women and men whom I interviewed communicated to me stories about their national identity in a number of ways. Sometimes, they directly addressed the feelings they had for their country and what its demise had meant to them personally. Sometimes, the significance of the physical landscape permeated the narrative (as in the omnipresence of the Berlin Wall). Still another way of communicating national identity was in the overt integration of personal biography and social history.

My research in East Germany, for instance, clearly demanded that I familiarize myself with the critical events of the social history of the country's 40 years of existence. One such event that assumed massive importance in the lives of the people with whom I spoke was the expulsion of Wolf Biermann from East Germany in 1976, in what became known as the "Biermann-*Ausbürgerung.*" Biermann, East Germany's answer to Bob Dylan, was a political folksinger, who enjoyed a wide base of popularity both in East Germany and beyond. Like Dylan, he was considered by many to be "the conscience and the voice of the people." In November 1976, Biermann was granted a temporary exit visa to perform a series of concerts in West Germany. While he was out of the country, the East German leadership officially expelled him, based on the critical content of his performances. (These performances were viewed by millions of East Germans via television satellite.) This expulsion marked a significant turning point in the tensions between the state and the critical intelligentsia. Signatures were collected in East Germany protesting the decision of the party to dispel Biermann, but those who added their names did so at high personal and professional risk to themselves and their families. People anonymously left wreaths at places across the country that featured in Biermann's songs.

Before beginning my research in East Germany, I had never heard Biermann's name (despite his widespread popularity across Europe). In my interviews, however, I encountered time and again stories that revealed the importance of this moment in history in the biographies of those with whom I spoke. One example of this was my interview with Werner Fischer, a leading opposition figure in the decade before the opening of the wall and the man who ultimately became responsible for the disbanding of the Stasi. When I asked Fischer about the awakening of his political consciousness, he responded by speaking of the Biermann affair:

> This was for me as well as for many others a test case, the expulsion of Wolf Biermann . . . the first time when I publicly . . . protested. There were naturally repercussions. . . . I was summoned, there was an interrogation by the Stasi, they threatened sanctions and dismissal. . . . I knew I had to make a decision whether I wanted to be a normal law abiding GDR citizen. It was also

important for me insofar as I realized then that my opposition could not just rest with my refusal to acknowledge the system but that once having made a commitment, I had to attempt to delve further into this system and find its causes.

Fischer is recounting for me a moment of deep personal significance, a turning point in his own life, when he knew that he must decide where he stood in relation to the state and how far he was willing to go to act in accordance with his beliefs. I hear his story as both a personal and a political narrative. Fischer clearly does not place himself alone in his experiences; he describes the Biermann affair as something that was "for me, as well as for many others, a test case." It is, thus, an East German story par excellence. In this example, I think we can see the strength of Geertz's argument that accessing a culture is more than an ontological exercise. To understand a culture, one must explore the meaning(s) embedded in its rituals, its history, and its institutions. The very deep and enduring disaffection that resulted from the Biermann affair of November 1976 can thus shed much light on the underlying causes of the bloodless revolution 13 years later.

The third and final example that I will use to explore narratives of national identity is the research I conducted in the United States. As mentioned earlier, I returned to the United States, after living abroad for 4 years, only days after Iraq had invaded Kuwait in the late summer of 1992. My "homecoming" thus coincided with the months leading up to "Operation Desert Storm," better known as the Gulf War. My new home was to be in Colorado Springs, Colorado, where at that time, 55% of the total economy was involved in the defense industry. Here, I interviewed a small group of antiwar activists who kept a 24/7 outdoor vigil to express their opposition to the war, as well as two leaders of the community who helped organize the citywide event "One Hour for America." I was led to this research by my curiosity, which was raised by the display of the American flag at the antiwar vigil. What did this flag, my flag, have to do with the message of these people who chose to live outdoors in the bitter winter months to express their opposition to the war?

William Carlos Williams has written that "there are no ideas but in things" (1946, p. 6). Janet Hoskins (1998), in her book *Biographical Objects: How Things Tell the Stories of People's Lives*, argues that objects play an important role in the personal narratives we tell and hear and that histories of objects and life histories of persons cannot be separated: "People and the things they valued were so complexly intertwined they could not be disentangled" (p. 2). Hoskins is an anthropologist whose work focuses on the Kodi people of the Eastern Indonesian island of Sumba. Hoskins argues that stories of individuals and their societies can be recounted through the exploration of the meaning of certain objects, such as the betel bag, "a sack for souls and stories" (p. 25). Betel bags are "the most portable of Kodi items . . . almost inseparable from its owner. The deep, pleated inner pouches of the betel bag are a place of secrets and can stand for certain forms of hidden knowledge" (p. 25). My research in Colorado Springs could be described as an exploration of the meaning of a particular object, the American flag. What did this symbol, these 13 red and white stripes with the 50 stars on the blue background, mean to those who displayed it? Part of this exploration was a journey inward: What did this flag mean to me? Is it important that people who display the same symbol share their understanding of its meaning, or is meaning to be negotiated by individuals according to their own needs, aspirations, and limitations?

The antiwar activists used the language of love, responsibility, and civic duty when they spoke about the motivations for their actions. They had the flag at their vigil because, they said, they loved their country. They knew that they were regarded by many in the community as being anti-American; questioning their country's decision to go to war was, for their critics, a straightforward expression of disloyalty. "Go back to Baghdad," passersby shouted at them. Those who stayed at the vigil, which was located on a median in the middle of the city, had to contend with being the target of sustained physical harassment:

> The people of Colorado Springs . . . pelted us with snowballs, bottles, beer cans, tennis balls, you name it . . . they spat on us . . . tried to run us over. . . . There were a couple of times in which people with huge American flags tried to hit us over the head with the actual flagpoles and sort of drape the flags over our heads. . . . There was another time when this pickup truck with some rednecks stopped next to the vigil and they harassed us for a while and then they ran around us with their flag in a circle.

Clearly the protesters' attempt to tell a different kind of story of what it meant to be a good, responsible citizen created in others a response that was difficult to contain. One of the organizers of the vigil explained to me the source of the anger that their protest provoked.

> We were clearly "un-American," right? And our attempts to prove that that wasn't the case, having an American flag there for instance, served to make them, if anything, more angry. . . . How could we hold up the American flag? We were "bad Americans."

In terms of learning about other cultures, my research in Colorado Springs was among the most educational for me of any I have ever conducted. It is interesting that here I was "returning home" but to a culture I could not recognize as my own. If national identity is, as Brockmeier (2001) suggests, a cultural sense of belonging, what could I say about my national identity in the cultural context of a place like Colorado Springs? We were, all of us, Americans: the protestors, their tormentors, and me. But what did we have in common? One thing that we did not have in common was a shared understanding of what this national identity meant. If culture is, as Geertz suggests, inextricably bound to questions of meaning, then in a very profound sense, those who physically threatened the antiwar protestors were operating within a different cultural framework from mine, a framework that alienated and saddened me in equal measure. It was a contest over the meaning of national identity—my national identity—more than anything else, which was being physically fought over with the weapon of the U.S. flag.

My interviews with two of the key people who organized the event "One Hour for America" (approximately 25,000 people who gathered together for 1 hour to show their support for the U.S. troops) were very illuminating for me. One of them, in particular, framed the current conflict in the Gulf War in terms of what it should not be. Specifically, the specter of Vietnam, and what he felt was the lack of support shown to the U.S. military at that time, loomed large for him. I was intrigued by the way the public perception of one historical event helped frame subsequent events. Not only was this explicit correlation exhibited by my respondent, but it was also taken up by the antiwar movement itself, which made public pleas to "support the troops by bringing them home," an inversion of the alienation expressed toward the "baby killer" soldiers who fought in Vietnam. Indeed, everyone, from the president to civilians, appeared to be in agreement that the United States did not want to have "another Vietnam," although the lessons to be gleaned from that conflict in Southeast Asia two decades earlier were still a point of significant debate.

What has this to do with accessing and understanding cross-cultural narratives? It is not because I was American that I could understand what my respondents were saying to me regarding their wish to "avoid another Vietnam." But if one is conducting research outside of one's own community (however large or small that is to be defined), it is imperative to obtain a sense of what the larger narratives are that guide the self-understanding, and therefore the self-presentation, of that group. Being American, having grown up in Washington, D.C., during the late 1960s, and having been brought by my parents to antiwar protests on the mall were all part of myself as I tried to listen to what was being said to me. While my personal background may have assisted me in accessing the relevant national narrative (e.g., the importance of Vietnam to the public discourse surrounding the Iraq war), it is also probable that this contributed significantly to the way in which I processed meaning in my research in Colorado Springs.

Welch and Piekkari (in press) refer to another researcher's self-report, in which the latter "explained that because she could not take anything for granted in the foreign country, she is consequently 'a better listener' there than in her home country." Perhaps the same could be said of me. In all likelihood, my "insider knowledge" probably assisted me in my interviews with the protestors. While it is possible that they may have wished to articulate positions that were in subtle but important ways different from my own, generally we shared a political viewpoint, and they were aware of this when we spoke together. In my conversations with the two respondents who had organized "One Hour for America," however, it was difficult for me to listen nonjudgmentally to what they were saying to me, as I have long-standing and deeply felt beliefs about the militarism of the United States. In East Germany, I had been very open to being educated about events of which I had no knowledge—for instance, the expulsion of Wolf Biermann and its importance to the dissident movement in East Germany. This is not true of my work in the United States, and it is ironic to me that in some sense I felt more of a stranger in the land of my birth than I did in the other countries where I conducted my research.

Cross-Cultural Research and the Construction of the "Other"

I began this chapter by citing Erika Apfelbaum's (2001) statement: "The issue of communicating across cultural boundaries is a major challenge to the very foundations of our dominant theoretical frameworks" (p. 32). The language of boundaries invites questions of who is allowed in and who must remain outside, questions that are of concern to both individuals and states. In some sense, these boundaries can be seen as defining features of identity—for who am I, if there is no not-I? Our sense of self (both individual and social) is built on the premise of the existence of an "other," and it this critical construction of boundary that lies between them.

If this is so, then the veracity of Apfelbaum's statement becomes apparent: Our dominant theoretical frameworks are the ones that emphasize the importance of boundaries, which function to distinguish between "us" and "them." Our socialization leads us to be deeply invested in the meanings attached to these boundaries, and we come to believe in the moral superiority of the position from which we emanate. The discourse of autonomy and individuality, a defining feature of our culture, is built on the assumption that such boundaries are and should be impermeable. To cross boundaries is to risk the self.

Cross-cultural research is, at its heart, a deeply risky venture.

When I began thinking about writing this chapter, I conducted a review of the existing literature on living and being in cultures other than one's own. Although I had myself been doing this for approximately 20 years, I had never really encountered this large "self-help" genre of writing, aimed at those who find themselves having to live abroad. The review made me aware of others' basic assumptions regarding the nature of living in another culture: (1) it is assumed that this experience will be traumatic, and as such the literature is full of suggested mechanisms for minimizing shock, and (2) writers, and presumably consumers, of such books and manuals regard the "home community" as one that is primarily homogeneous, a group with shared values, understandings, and communication styles, not to mention tastes in food and dress. What seemed to characterize most of the articles and books that I read (e.g., Shames, 1997; Storti, 1994, 2001) is a shared assumption that encountering "others" is problematic, and the aim of these materials was to put coping mechanisms in place.

Not only have I never shared these two basic assumptions (regarding the traumatic nature of cross-cultural encounters and the homogeneity of the home community), but they are in conflict with my own models of understanding. How do we define our home community, and what is it that binds us together? What is the stuff of cultural belonging? Where we derive our most profound sense of belonging, that community that helps us define for ourselves who we are, is a place in flux, not only across our lifetimes but even across our days. I believe that the construction of a static "home" community, marked by shared values, is just that, a construction, albeit one of deep personal and social significance, which resides in the imagination of individuals. Many of us experience our home, and the meaning of home, in conflicting and sometimes even incoherent ways. The reality of who we are, and where we belong, is rarely as simple as the picture of static homogeneity would suggest.

If we accept that home is a more fluid category, which might be the location of a range of contradictory social practices, then our understanding of the other is also made more porous. For part of accessing the world of an other is the critical realization that the way we see and understand life is a function of our own narrative imagination, something that is itself profoundly affected by cultural location and practices. In Margaret Mitchell's (1936) *Gone With the Wind*, Scarlett O'Hara finds ultimate solace in the brown earth of the grounds of Tara, the plantation on which she grew up. But while home is or can be a physical place, it is more often than not something that resides within us, a composite picture of where we have come from, which lends strength to us as we set out to explore other new places.

When, in 1990, I first knew that I would be moving back to the United States, after living abroad for several years, I constructed this as going "home." In fact, the reality was far more complicated than that. I had been forever transformed, the embodiment of Bhabha's (1994) "cultural hybridization," by the experiences I had had while living away from my "homeland." I had very little in common with many of the residents of Colorado Springs, my new "home." I could not understand how they could assault their fellow citizens, our fellow citizens, physically harming them with broken glass bottles or attacking them with a flag pole, simply because they had a different idea of what it meant to be a responsible American. Home for me was both smaller and larger than the country of my birth.

The self-help literature on how to survive exposure to, and possible immersion in, other cultures was perplexing for me in its depiction of such experiences as essentially traumatic. Why should this be so? Genuinely opening up oneself to listening to any other person, and even on occasion to oneself, is a raw experience. Ryen (2002) notes the recent growth in cross-cultural research, much of which emphasizes the "methodological difficulties of transporting experiential data across cultures (Ryen, 2002, p. 335). Ryen herself documents some of the "communicative hurdles" (p. 336) that she has encountered, but not all of these seem unique to cross-cultural research. For instance, problems associated with "erotic experiences in the field" (p. 338) have been written about by other researchers operating within their "home culture" (e.g., Kong, Mahoney, & Plummer, 2002). One key challenge, that Ryen identifies, however, is to "get hold of the data in the form they are stored in the interviewee's cultural reservoir" (2002, p. 226). This can be particularly problematic, for as researchers, we have been trained to orient ourselves toward obtaining findings that must fit within the framework of understanding that we have constructed in advance. But this very process limits the possibilities of immersing oneself in wholly new ways of thinking, which is the essence of engagement with the other. If we are unable to release ourselves from the frameworks of meaning with which we are already acquainted, then we stand little possibility of learning something new.

Equally, in this journey to understand "the other," we must accept that what we learn, and what we "uncover" about their experiences, as mediated through our own interpretive lens, will always and can only be a partial knowledge. Sometimes those experiences that lie most deeply within the self "defy narrative expression because they are not completely known, grasped, nor understood" (Apfelbaum, 2001, p. 2). This "non-narratability" can be especially common in cases of severe trauma: "The analysis of the difficulties of communication across traumatic boundaries is equally relevant when people attempt to communicate across cultural boundaries" (Apfelbaum, 2001, p. 31). Once we begin to explore the potential of our imaginations to expose us to new and different realities, we soon encounter "the limits of each person's access to every other. . . . The habits of wonder . . . define the other person as spacious and deep, with qualitative differences from oneself and hidden places worthy of respect" (Nussbaum, 1997, pp. 89–90). It is then incumbent on researchers to attend not only to what is said but also to what is not said, "the silence and the 'unspoken'('le non-dit')" (Apfelbaum, 2000, p. 172). We must be comfortable knowing that we do not, and can never, know all about another; equally, we must resist the temptation to overinterpret those empty spaces that lie within our conversations.

The possibility, and the limits of the possibility, of conversing with others, through speech and through silence, needn't be explored only on journeys to distant, "other" cultures. There are potentially new partners for dialogue within one's own neighborhood, perhaps even within one's family. When we acknowledge that there may be much we do not know even about those with whom we are most intimate, the possibility of listening, and of being able to hear something new, becomes more promising. All the while, we accept that our "interpretations are provisional" and that our own life experiences "both enable and inhibit particular kinds of insights" (Rosaldo, 1989, p. 8).

This chapter is written from the viewpoint of one who has lived outside of her native homeland for 15 of the last 20 years. Although I was asked to write about cross-cultural narrative research, this has expanded to a larger discussion of living between cultural boundaries. Interestingly, when I first moved abroad to conduct my doctoral research, my intention was to return "home" after 3 years. But my understanding of myself and of my home were themselves transformed by my experiences in those 3 years. I believe that anyone who is genuinely touched by dialogues with others will be forever changed by that experience. The book *The Art of Coming Home* (Storti, 2001) begins by describing the "complicated and usually difficult experience" of reentry to the home culture. The phenomenon now known as "reverse culture shock" is reputably "more difficult than adjusting overseas ever was" (p. xiv). The introduction to the book opens with a quote from Somerset Maugham's *The Gentleman in the Parlour*: "When I go back I know I shall be out of it; we fellows who've spent our lives out here always are" (p. xiii). Maybe those of us who live and work between cultural boundaries are forever destined to be "out of it" or, perhaps more accurately, simultaneously occupy the contradictory positions of insider and outsider. Our narrative research—in terms of what we choose to explore and how we make sense of the phenomenon we observe—is at least partially a product of our narrative identity, which is itself located at the intersection of different cultures.

Our narrative imagination is our most valuable tool in our exploration of others' worlds, for it assists us in seeing beyond the immediately visible. It is our ability to imagine other "possible lives"—our own and others—that creates our bond with "diverse social and historical worlds" (Brockmeier, in press). Without this imagination, we are forever restricted to the world as we know it, which is a very limited place to be.

Consulting Editors: Pam Steeves and Angela Baydala

References

Anderson, B. (1983). *Imagined communities: Reflections on the origin and spread of nationalism.* London: Verso.

Andrews, M. (1995). Against good advice: Reflections on conducting research in a country where you don't speak the language. *Oral History Review, 20*(1), 75–86.

Andrews, M. (1998). One hundred miles of lives: The Stasi files as a people's history of East Germany. *Oral History, 26*(1), 24–31.

Andrews, M. (2003a). Conversations through the years: Reflections on age and meaning. In *Proceedings of the 4th International Symposium on Cultural Gerontology*, Tampere, Finland.

Andrews, M. (2003b). Continuity and discontinuity of East German identity following the fall of the Berlin Wall: A case study. In P. Gready (Ed.), *Cultures of political transition: Memory, identity and voice* (pp. 107–126). London: Pluto Press.

Andrews, M. (in press). *Constructing and interpreting political narratives.* Cambridge, UK: Cambridge University Press.

Apfelbaum, E. (2000). The impact of culture in the face of genocide: Struggling between a silenced home culture and a foreign host culture. In C. Squire (Ed.), *Culture in psychology* (pp. 163–174). London: Routledge.

Apfelbaum, E. (2001). The dread: An essay on communication across cultural boundaries. *The International Journal of Critical Psychology, 4,* 19–35.

Berdahl, D. (1999). '(N)Ostalgie' for the present: Memory, longing, and East German things. *Ethnos, 64*(2), 192–211.

Bhabha, H. K. (1994). *The location of culture.* London: Routledge.

Branson, N. (1975). *Britain in the nineteen twenties.* London: Wiedenfield and Nicolson.

Brockmeier, J. (2001). Texts and other symbolic spaces. *Mind, Culture and Activity, 8*(3), 215–230.

Brockmeier, J. (in press). Reaching for meaning: Human agency and the narrative imagination. *Theory & Psychology: Special Issue on Holzkamp.*

Donoghue, D. (1998). *The practice of reading.* New Haven, CT: Yale University Press.

Ember, C., & Ember, M. (2001). *Cross-cultural research methods.* Lanham, MD: AltaMira Press.

Geertz, C. (1973). *The interpretation of cultures: Selected essays.* New York: Basic Books.

Gready, P. (in press). The public life of narratives: Ethics, politics, methods. In C. Squire, M. Tamboukou, & M. Andrews (Eds.), *Doing narrative research in the social sciences.* London: Sage.

Henri, Y. (2003). Reconciling reconciliation: A personal and public journey of testifying before the South African Truth and Reconciliation Commission. In P. Gready (Ed.), *Cultures of political transition: Memory, identity and voice* (pp. 262–275). London: Pluto Press.

Hoskins, J. (1998). *Biographical objects: How things tell the stories of people's lives.* London: Routledge.

Jouve, N. W. (1991). *White woman speaks with forked tongue: Criticism as autobiography.* London: Routledge.

Kegan, R. (1982). *The evolving self: Problem and process in human development.* Cambridge, MA: Harvard University Press.

Kong, T., Mahoney, D., & Plummer, K. (2002). Queering the interview. In J. Gubrium & J. Holstein (Eds.), *Handbook of interview research: Context and method* (pp. 239–258). Thousand Oaks, CA: Sage.

Langellier, K. M. (2000). "You're marked": Breast cancer, tattoo and the narrative performance of identity. In J. Brockmeier & D. Carbaugh (Eds.), *Narrative and identity: Studies in autobiography, self and culture* (pp. 145–184). Amsterdam: John Benjamins.

Lifton, R. J. (1986). *The Nazi doctors: Medical killing and the psychology of genocide.* New York: Basic Books.

Mills, C. W. (1959). *The sociological imagination.* New York: Grove Press.

Mitchell, M. (1936). *Gone with the wind.* New York: Macmillan.

Nussbaum, M. (1997). *Cultivating humanity: A classical defense of reform in education.* Cambridge, MA: Harvard University Press.

Riessman, C. K. (2005). Exporting ethics: A narrative about narrative research in South India. *Health, 9*(4), 473–490.

Roßteutscher, S. (2000). Competing narratives and the social construction of reality: The GDR in transition. *German Politics, 9*(1), 61–82.

Rosaldo, R. (1989). *Culture and truth: The remaking of social analysis.* London: Routledge.

Ryen, A. (2002). Cross-cultural interviewing. In J. Gubrium & J. Holstein (Eds.), *Handbook of interview research: Context and method* (pp. 335–354). Thousand Oaks, CA: Sage.

Selby, J. M. (2004). Disruptions of identity: Dynamics of working across indigenous differences. *Qualitative Studies in Education, 17*(1), 143–156.

Shames, G. (1997). *Transcultural odysseys: The evolving global consciousness.* Yarmouth, ME: Intercultural Press.

Storti, C. (1994). *Cross-cultural dialogues: Seventy-four brief encounters with cultural difference.* Yarmouth, ME: Intercultural Press.

Storti, C. (2001). *The art of coming home.* Yarmouth, ME: Intercultural Press.

Wang, Q., & Brockmeier, J. (2002). Autobiographical remembering as cultural practice: Understanding the interplay between memory, self and culture. *Culture and Psychology, 8*(1), 45–64.

Welch, C., & Piekkari, R. (in press). Crossing language boundaries: Qualitative interviewing in international business. *Management International Review.*

Williams, W. C. (1946/1992). *Paterson Manchester: Carcanet.* New York: New Directions.

Yoder, J. (1999). *From East Germans to Germans? The new post-communist elites.* Durham, NC: Duke University Press.

CHAPTER 20

Mo'ō lelo

On Culturally Relevant Story Making From an Indigenous Perspective

Maenette K. P. Benham

'A'ohe pau ka 'ike i ka hālau ho'okāhi.
[One can learn from many sources.]

—Pukui (1997, p. 24)

The writing of this chapter recounts a journey that began in the laps of my *nākūpuna* (grandparents), has danced joyfully in the voices of teachers and mentors, and now rests, as Leslie Marmon Silko (1988) poetically writes in the poem *Ceremony*, in the belly of our living. Stories have the power to explore people's relationships, both public and private, with their environment and with one another. In this way, stories illuminate knowledge in such a way that it connects us to the roots of who we are as individuals and as a community. For native/ indigenous[1] people, narratives are evocative accounts of sovereignty and loss, as well as identity and home. They are detailed and contextual, recognizing the importance of community and place.

My own journey begins with the stories told to me by my grandparents and elders. These stories, as all good personal and cultural stories do, have shaped how I have come to know my *mana* (personal power) and *kuleana* (responsibility). From the lap of my *'ōhana* (family), the value of stories as a pathway to knowledge generation was encouraged by many teachers, but none as passionate as my qualitative research mentor in graduate school. To be in the belly of her class as the value and power of narrative unfolded was revealing and empowering. I learned that narrative, within the world of scholarship, would not homogenize rich indigenous knowledge so it fit a Western view—that, in fact, because narrative recognizes the value of indigenous knowledge and its connection with other forms of knowledge (e.g., scientific), it has a place in research and policy arenas. For example, my first published narratives, coauthored with my mentor, revealed the race and gender bias of school systems toward ethnically diverse women school leaders (see Benham & Cooper, 1998). All my writing since then, mostly narrative in nature, reflects the challenge I have chosen as a *Kanaka Maoli* (Native Hawaiian) scholar and researcher—that is, to interrogate and explore the complexities of diverse social realities around the themes of leading, learning, and teaching so that I can best describe specific instances as well as general principles that answer important questions regarding social justice. I present this story of my work only to situate a conundrum that those native and nonnative scholars who employ narrative methodologies must address.

This puzzle has many multipronged pieces, but three require attention in this chapter. They include the following queries: (a) What is indigenous/native perspective? (b) Is this work mythmaking or advocacy or inquiry? (c) How does one explore, interrogate, and retain the sacred of indigenous knowledge? Defining the penultimate meaning of what is indigenous far exceeds the scope of this chapter and, indeed, requires input from a larger sociological terrain. To better situate the message of this chapter within the broader indigenous scholarship, however, I define indigenous perspective as having qualities of both the physical and the abstract (the metaphysical or spiritual), which have been disrupted by the power of colonialism. So the source of indigeneity is located in the physical environment and in one's genealogy, which is connected to that place, one's homeland. In this sense, one can argue that everyone is indigenous to some place—that is, claiming deep cognitive and historical roots to a particular physical place. The indigenous perspective is, however, distinct as it defines an ontology and epistemology[2] of a cultural group's way of theorizing knowledge that is rooted in historical contexts. While these practices and protocols predate the intrusion of colonization, they have been (to some degree) diminished or decimated by the encroachment of a colonial power; hence, they have undergone redefinition over time by an indigenous collective (i.e., family, kin group, etc.).

As indigenous scholars who share the stories of our colonized communities, we are subject to a cluster of knotty challenges. First is the accusation that the mythical nature of some of our narratives appears to lack scholarly "rigor." Indeed, the mystical nature of the indigenous narrative appears to draw more criticism than recognition of its ability to relate (albeit in a lyrical manner) the complex history of a native community caught in a collision of political change, racial tensions, and spiritual controversy. In addition, because native scholars employ narratives to subject mainstream institutions and policies to interrogation through the eyes of people who historically have been oppressed, we are labeled advocates and not scholars. Whatever the criticism, the power of narrative is that, because it deeply explores the tensions of power by illuminating its collisions (e.g., differences of knowledge and practices), it reveals interesting questions that mobilize processes and resources that benefit native people and their communities. Indeed, the political impact of narrative cannot be dismissed.

To complicate the puzzle further, the native researcher must be respectful of the tradition, and especially the ritual and ceremony, of narratives in the native communities (e.g., some stories are never written, some stories are told only on certain occasions, etc.). And the researcher must be cautious that what is indigenous narrative originates from a particular place, belonging to and designed by the natives of a specific region. In the end, the scholar must not fall victim to Western appropriation of indigenous knowledge through the narrative. Instead, the researcher must be respectful of indigenous wisdom and the intellectual and cultural rights of native communities while at the same time adhering to the rigor of the narrative discipline. This is a puzzle full of twists and turns and with no prescriptive answer. What I attempt to do in this chapter, therefore, is to present one native scholar's synthesis and understanding of indigenous narrative—that is, *na pua, na lei, na mamo*, where we have been, where we are, and where we need to go.

Na Pua: The Stories That Begin

As one might have noticed, it is difficult for many native scholars to talk about a topic without telling stories.[3] Across many indigenous groups, oral storytelling is the primary manner through which life's lessons are taught. In Hawai'i , we "talk story." That is, we sit together, we are present with each other, and we share our stories, which range from day-to-day activities to our hopes and dreams. And we talk story with our young people, sharing stories about Hawai'i, about people and places, about relationships, about possibilities. For example, in Hawai'i we have *'ōlelo no'eau*, wise sayings that give insight into how one thinks and behaves. An example is *Nānā ka maka; ho'olohe ka pepeiao; pa'a ka waha*: Observe with the eyes; listen with the ears; shut the mouth. Thus, one learns (Pukui, 1997, p. 248). This is a view of indigenous educational philosophy. In old Hawai'i , children and youths were in apprenticeship with skilled *nā kumu* (teachers) who presented learning opportunities across many different settings, locating situations that presented provocative experiences that led to deep thinking and growth. For young people, learning is an important process that requires expertise and compassion in the *kumu* and discipline in the student.

Similar to people of other indigenous cultures, Native Hawaiians have stories, told over and over, that teach values and worldviews. We also have *mele* (songs) and *hula* (dances) that tell stories about our history, people, and land. An example of this voice is revealed in the song *Mele 'Ai Pōhaku*, written by Mrs. Ellen Wright Prendergast in opposition to the annexation of Hawai'i by the United States of America.

Kaulana nā pua a'o Hawai'i	Famous are the children of Hawai'i
Kupa'a ma hope o ka 'āina	Ever loyal to the land

Hiki mai ka ʻelele o ka loko ʻino	When the evil-hearted messenger comes
Palapala ʻanunu me ka pākaha.	With his greedy document of extortion.
Pane mai Hawaiʻi moku o Keawe.	Hawaiʻi , land of Keawe answers.
Kōkua nā Hono aʻo Pīʻilani.	Piʻilaniʻs bays help.
Kākoʻo mai Kauaʻi o Mano,	Manoʻs Kauai lends support
Paʻapū me ke one Kakuhihewa.	And so do the sands of Kakuhihewa.
ʻAʻole ʻaʻe kauʻi ka pūlima	No one will fix a signature
Ma luna o ka pepa o ka ʻenemi,	To the paper of the enemy
Hoʻohui ʻāina kuʻai hewa,	With its sin of annexation
I ka pono sivila aʻo ke kanaka.	And sale of native civil rights.
ʻAʻole mākou aʻe minamina	We do not value
I ka puʻukālā a ke aupuni.	The government's sums of money.
Ua lawa mākou i ka pōhaku,	We are satisfied with the stones,
I ka ʻai kamahaʻo o ka ʻāina.	Astonishing food of the land.
Ma hope mākou o Liliʻulani	We back Liliʻulani
A loaʻa ʻe ka pono a ka ʻāina.	Who has won the rights of the land.
(A kau hou ʻia e ke kalaunu)	(She will be crowned again)
Haʻina ʻia mai ana ka puana	Tell the story
Ka poʻe i aloha i ka ʻāina.	Of the people who love their land.

(Elbert & Mahoe, 1976, pp. 63–64)

What we find in indigenous narrative is a temporal element that affects the nature and meaning of events within particular moments. In addition, the narrative is a part of cumulative moments over time; it is deeply embedded in and emerges from multiple, interrelated, and at times contradictory contexts to include the ecological (place based), cultural, political, and historical arenas.[4] Captured in the oral and written text of indigenous narrative are natural taxonomies that organize and interpret unique perspectives. These are particularly salient points, especially if we are to understand the lyrical narratives of the past. For example, the short story about Koʻolau, a Kauaʻi man afflicted by leprosy in 1893, is taught in many elementary schools throughout Hawaiʻi (as Hawaiian literature or in Hawaiian history). The version of the story that often is used was written by Jack London (1909/1912)[5] and attributes Western values of individualism and freedom to the main character to explain his refusal to be exiled to Molokaʻi. This dismisses, as Dennis Kawaharada (1999) points out, the Native Hawaiian version of the story, which emphasizes the values of *ʻōhana* (family), keeping the family intact, and

Ko'olau's responsibility to *mālama* (care for) the afflicted on his *'āina* (land). At the end of London's version of the story, Ko'olau reflects on the superiority of his captors, venerating the White way. As Kawaharada writes, London's version is a classic example of a work by a writer from a colonizing culture visiting a colony and usurping the voice of the indigenous people by telling their stories, imputing to the native the worldview of the colonizers, and portraying the natives as accepting the fate of colonization (pp. 86–87).

A recent rendering of the Ko'olau story, however, written by M. S. Merwin (1998), *The Folding Cliffs*, reveals the resurgence of the native voice (and indigenous values) through an epic poem reminiscent of an ancient Hawaiian *oli* (chant). Merwin, a resident of Hawai'i for 25 years, retells the story through the eyes of Ko'olau's wife by drawing on the lyricism of imagery to recount the struggle of Ko'olau within the context of *'āina* (historical place/land) and *'ohana* (family). The *kaona* (hidden meaning) of the story presented by Merwin retells the calamitous history of Hawai'i at the turn of the century, a history filled with missionaries and colonialists, as well as the decimation and disempowerment of Kanaka Maoli. Different from London's (1909) narrative, Merwin's narrative (1998) captures the communal and family values of the Hawaiian culture, as well as the complexities of the social and political tensions of the time.

To view indigenous narrative in a comparative manner across time is useful, as the example of the short story about Ko'olau demonstrates. That is, a comparative analysis aids in uncovering social conditions by revealing the historical, cultural, and political contexts that shape narratives over time. The distinctive qualities and nuances recounting daily life and its complicated relationships with social and political forces provide an opportunity for the scholar to broaden social and cultural knowledge as well as correct benevolent versions of stories that support a colonial state. Although comparative analysis of narrative within a particular society (e.g., Kanaka Maoli, Dine, Inuit, Maori) is important to deepen understanding, comparative work across diverse indigenous narratives is useful in the process of bringing cultural diversity to the surface, acknowledging differences, and creating cross-cultural or cross-indigenous narrative. Suspending time and geographic boundaries might lead to knowing the humanness of people and place and serve to foster communities of care, respect, hope, and justice.

Na Lei: The Stories That Tell of Now

Most published work has come from the perspective and/or the interests of the outsider, without indigenization—that is, the outsider (not native to the community/culture group) studies particular problems that are of interest to the outsider through outsider theories. As Lave, Duguid, Fernandez, and Axel (1992) point out, the dynamics of context, action, and relationships are key elements of identity that are often captured in narrative. I use the word "captured" here on purpose, as this form of outsider narrative has often been marked by its colonizing attitude toward the native community (see my previous reference to Kawaharada's work). Because the narrative offers a relational and cultural site for learning, it becomes a powerful tool. That is, identity formation, problem solving, intellectual inquiry, and skill acquisition can be defined by the messages embedded in the narrative. To counter these oppressive narratives of the past, there is a growing body of work from the perspective of the insider—the indigenous perspective in narrative—which addresses the needs identified by those who are native to that cultural community. Additionally, it is essential to note that the topics of study are also defined by indigenous epistemological and methodological foundations that guide how the topic is studied.

So, depending on the intention of the researcher, narrative can lead to illumination—activity that makes a just difference in the lives of people—or it can lead to parochialism. The challenge is to develop complementary approaches to indigenous narrative so that it is neither exclusive nor insular but instead inclusive and dynamic. The goal, then, of indigenous narrative is to invite participation of native people and their communities in the narrative process. This participation engages the researcher/scholar and native/indigenous people in building relationships that bring to the surface stories of experienced phenomena—concrete evidence—around pressing issues (e.g., historic hurt and pain). Making visible and loud what has been silent and invisible—transcending the concrete—has the power to promote a generative learning process (see Lave & Wenger, 1991) that might lead to community transformation. On a more theoretical level, this process breaks down the dualism of empirical/objective reality and transcendental/subjective reality into a both/and, as advocated by Vygotsky, Foucault, Bourdieu, and Latour (among others).

Although a review of current indigenous narratives in education (and across related disciplines) goes well beyond the scope of this chapter, I hope to provide the reader with a sense of methodological queries within the context of three themes, clear issues confronting contemporary native communities that might benefit from further exploration. The themes emerged from a careful reading of native/indigenous narratives from education, anthropology, sociology, and law over the last 20 years and include (a) sovereignty: indigenization of the narrative, (b) knowledge: illuminating unique worldviews, and (c) analysis and application: pedagogical practice and policy.

Sovereignty: Indigenization of the Narrative

The question of *who* tells and retells, *how*, for *whom*, and for *what* purpose raises the prickly issue of authorial privilege and rights. There is a good deal of discussion in native/indigenous scholarly circles about who is and is not speaking, who should study the native/indigenous way, and who is hearing and how. For many native/indigenous communities, the telling of stories, historical memories, is part of a sacred whole. That is, stories, whether they are myth/legend or recollections of daily activities or events, are told and retold to ensure that the ontology (what is known of the world), the life of native/indigenous people, does not diminish; hence, the story is sacred. From the Maori perspective, Bishop (1996) writes,

Simply telling stories as subjective voices is not adequate [either] because it ignores the impact that the stories of the other research participants have on our stories. Instead [as researchers] we need to acknowledge our participatory connectedness with the other research participants and promote a means of knowing in a way that denies distance and separation and promotes commitment and engagement. Narrative inquiry is an approach that addresses Maori people's concerns about research into their lives. (pp. 23–24)

A fundamental challenge of native/indigenous scholars/researchers engaged in indigenous narrative is to indigenize the narrative. What does this mean? By definition, *indigenous* refers to something that is innate or belongs to the soil of a place (Guralnik, 1984, p. 716). When something is said to be indigenized, it is authentically from that place. Earlier, I defined the indigenous perspective as distinct in its association to the issue of colonization (imperialism). So the sticky situation for many native/indigenous communities and scholars is that over time their ontologies and epistemologies have been misappropriated and repackaged by modern (Western) scientific orientations (often mechanistic and materialistic), hence becoming a knowing that now meets a nonindigenous (colonial) standard, which sweeps away the rich native/indigenous knowledge contained in traditional sacred texts (or this knowledge exists but under the radar screen). We see this, for example, in the assimilation polices of schools, which replaced the mother tongue as the medium of learning and governance, introduced curriculum and teaching tools that devalued metaphor and spirituality as key elements of indigenous-medium knowledge, and disrupted the intergenerational transmission of knowledge (see Aluli-Meyer, 2003; Benham & Heck, 1998; Smith, 1999). The focus, then, of native/indigenous scholars/researchers is to relate the narratives of indigenous people and communities that describe the social, cultural, political, and organizational patterns that reveal ontological and epistemological dilemmas through authentic indigenous perspectives.

This effort to indigenize narrative is becoming visible today through the works of authors such as Aluli-Meyer (2003) in *Ho'oulu: Our Time of Becoming.* The author grounds her work in the ontology and epistemology of Hawai'i —that is, the nature or wisdom of the Kanaka Maoli metaphysical world and how it is expressed in knowledge (also, see her chapter "Indigenous and Authentic: Hawaiian Epistemology and the Triangulation of Meaning" in Denzin, Lincoln, & Smith's [in press] *Handbook of Critical and Indigenous Methodologies*). As Aluli-Meyer asserts, transforming the root of our work challenges the way we think and do narrative inquiry to describe cultural and social phenomena and to explain sophisticated and relevant relationships in native/indigenous contexts. It moves us to the telling of stories "in" the field as opposed to Van Maanen's (1988) stories "of" the field.

So *who* should tell? The answer is that native/indigenous scholars, storytellers, cultural experts, and communities should be the first tellers and the owners of the telling. This conversation, however, about transforming the *who* and the *how*, within academic circles, includes both indigenous and nonindigenous researchers in a careful exchange that does not belabor the insider/outsider and indigenous/nonindigenous tension. I argue that in this conversation, the dichotomies of native/insider and nonnative/outsider are too simplistic a starting point, for both are not homogeneous but diverse (see Minh-Ha, 1989, 1991, 1999). In essence, we need to acknowledge the value of multiplicitous realities, where the role of the researcher, whether indigenous or nonindigenous, is as *kumu* (teacher). That is to say that the *kumu* explicitly and intentionally presents a set of critical accounts that creates space for multiple audiences, convenes conversations that critique the approach within local and global contexts, and directs learning and inquiry toward community empowerment. Hence, conversation regarding the ontology and epistemology of a cultural group brings to the surface multiple realities, defined over time, in a manner that benefits (does no harm to) the indigenous community. The methodology (the logic behind the research/inquiry approach) should not be seen as an end in itself (this often leads to artificiality) but must engage scholars in an ongoing discussion to ensure that there is no one-size-fits-all solution but a broader, more dynamic position of possibilities that encourages diverse representation and voice.

Additionally, Aluli-Meyer (2003) ponders the questions of how, who, and why while taking up relevant social and political issues. In fact, this movement to indigenize narrative requires native/indigenous scholars to take up issues that address vital and relevant contemporary topics, such as sovereignty, social justice, and equity. Bakhtin (1986) speaks of the power of narrative to open up a space for voice, where power, authority, and representation can be heard, in particular the voice and voices of those most vulnerable, those most often not heard. Here, then, is the riddle raised by this point of indigenization, that although the narrative provides the space for the indigenous voice to take up pressing social issues, *who is listening and how?*

The tension that must be held by native/indigenous scholars is selecting a topic(s) that is of import to the realities of the indigenous community (within) or selecting a topic(s) that may be of interest to a policy (scientific) or broader audience (without). As native/indigenous researchers, positioning ourselves somewhere within and between the contrasting worldviews of the indigenous and the discipline is an itchy proposition. That is, casting off the prevailing disciplinary ethos (narrow view) for one that is more reflexive (viewing both/all sides at all times; for more on this topic, see Smith, 1999) is imperative to maintaining cultural truth and pushing toward deeper critical analysis. Extending the boundaries of narrative to embrace native/indigenous scholars who are writing from their particular native/indigenous knowledge base has resulted in critical design approaches that are more problem oriented (micro or local)and geared to knowing (scholarly pursuit) as well as forging (application) interventions that address social, cultural, and economic concerns (macro or cross-cultural). Examples of narratives will be presented throughout this chapter.

In *The Elephant's Child*, Rudyard Kipling (1902) writes as follows:

> I keep six honest serving men
> (They taught me all I knew);
> Their names are What and Why and When
> And How and Where and Who. (pp. 6–7)

These six key thoughts are essential elements to understanding the importance of indigenization of narrative. Indigenous narrative must be honest. It must emerge from the voices of native/indigenous people through a culturally appropriate native/indigenous ontology. Why? Because the power of narrative to define what is real can be either a means to illuminate or an instrument to destroy. In light of this, the native/indigenous scholar must ensure that indigenous narrative not perpetuate the nonindigenous as the standard referent. In his article "'Two People': An American Indian Narrative of Bicultural Identity," Michael Tlanusta Garrett (1996) provides a model of indigenized narrative. Here is an example of how a scholar illuminates the tensions of bicultural (often multicultural) identity development as a process of enculturation within a contemporary context of Western policies.

In his work to view acculturation and enculturation through the lived experiences and traditional wisdom of his native community, Garrett addresses honestly the six elements of what, why, when, how, where, and who. He also questions a priori conclusions about native/indigenous identity (e.g., biases created by an exclusion of native presence). Indigenizing narrative, then, can provide information that corrects previous work that could only speculate on what was native and package it in a palatable form (for broad consumption). For example, in Leslie Leyland's (1997) book *Alaska's Commercial Fishing Women Tell Their Lives*, we are treated to an account of the role of women in the native fishing industry of Alaska through vivid portrayals of the personal and professional tensions of commercial fishing interwoven with humor and an awareness of the female, native voice. In Chinn's (2002) article "Asian and Pacific Islander Women Scientists and Engineers: A Narrative Exploration of Model Minority, Gender, and Racial Stereotypes," our a priori conclusions and biases about gender, culture, and what it means to be a scientist are tested.

A careful review of indigenous narratives reveals the delicate tensions that are held by the author(s) working to indigenize narrative. Another concern regards presenting the indigenous narrative as a dialectical, communal process that is individual as well as collective as well as temporal representation. Fundamentally different from Western academic knowledge, most indigenous ways of knowing define power to bring about change not as individual power but as a sacred power that is passed on through story and ceremony. The point is that indigenous narrative is not solely personal but is deeply communal. How do we write the indigenous narrative, which is often shared in fragments by different people and in different forms (oral stories, ceremony, dance, etc.) over time, honoring the style and structure of the native/indigenous way? How do we do this while knowing that the textual presentation will push against traditional Western ways (publishable) of writing narratives?

A native/indigenous scholar must stretch her or his use of narrative strategies to systemically observe and document indigenous social worlds. A dimension of participation is inherent in this process, which begins with the story that is situated in a particular place/context. In addition, there is a fundamental knowing that because native stories are embedded with multiple meanings, they will be told by many respondents. The storyteller/recorder, therefore, must employ a variety of strategies to elicit conversation among the respondents and cultural experts (usually elders) in order to guide the process of meaning making. In the end, the storyteller/researcher creates a frame that anchors the messages of the narrative in a manner that can be accessed by a broad readership. This she or he does at the same time as she or he holds respectfully the sacredness, mother tongue, and history of the respondents. In the end, the narrative text is explicit/obvious as well as implicit/subtext. For example, in their article, Langer and Furman (2004) explore indigenous identity in a dialogic format by first presenting interview data embedded in the researcher's comments. This is followed by the voice of the respondent presented in a poem ending with a reflexive writing by both author and respondent about the meaning of the sovereign voice and assimilation.

Approaching narrative in a communal manner and employing different literary tools that highlight respondents' views can minimize the number of narratives that misrepresent native communities. Certainly, stylistically presenting one's work by employing both creative literary devices and academic markers (e.g., headings and subheadings, APA formatting) may seem inappropriate (indeed pedantic) to some readers, but these markers are needed to avoid falling into the romantic-tale trap, keeping the reader mindful of the intellectual purposefulness of indigenous narrative and ensuring the honesty of the story. That is, indigenous narratives should not be a nice story but ought to present cogent theories of the complexities of the sociopolitical organization of native communities, thereby increasing understanding of the rich historical and contemporary life of indigenous people.

Indigenization of the narrative is an important responsibility of native/indigenous scholars because there is a sacredness that connects the telling and retelling to the traditional wisdom and lifeways of a native community. I recognize that holding the tension between what is culturally traditional and what is intellectually useful, at this time, is a challenge. Hence, it is useful to remember that in indigenous story, theory is embedded in metaphor and story. Because of this, there is a protocol for sharing that holds the storyteller/researcher accountable to more than the discipline and peer scholars. In the end, as is the case in many native/indigenous communities, we are accountable to our elders and to our children/youth (see Benham, 2005). Indigenous narrative, then, must include an explicit accounting of this process. Matthews and Jenkins (1999) provide a brilliant example of this framing in their article "Whose Country Is It Anyway?: The Construction of a New Identity Through Schooling for Maori in Aotearoa/New Zealand":

> It is important to explain that the primary documentary sources used in our research are regarded as *taonga* (treasure) and that there is *kawa* (protocol) associated with taking taonga offshore and half-way round the world. First, as researchers we are accountable to those who are the guardians of the taonga. We have to arrive at certain undertakings about what is being done/talked about. It has to be checked out by both sides. It has to be talked about in a Maori way. Questions are asked, such as: Where are you taking this? Where do they come from? Who are they? Do we have any connections to them? Can we trust them with this knowledge? (p. 339)

Positioning them and acknowledging the communal and reciprocal processes of indigenous narrative enables the authors to talk back to Western ways of organizing education through a Maori ontology, *kaupapa Maori*. Theorizing and methodologies must lead to principles of knowing and practice that honor the wisdom of cultural lineage and at the same time meet the global needs of our indigenous youth.

Indigenizing the narrative clearly supports a sovereign voice that is deeply embedded in native/indigenous ontology and is constructed and presented in a manner that both honors sacred texts (native taxonomies) and approaches the narrative as a site to explore important issues of ecological, social, cultural, political, and educative concern. Having said this, it is also important to mention that indigenizing the narrative is not a pathway to exploit the exotic or similar to the fecundity of King Arthur tales, conjuring images of romantic primitivism (it is not myth making). The challenge of indigenizing the narrative is to maintain and sustain the language and context of the indigenous without falling prey to the mysticism of enlightenment.

Knowledge: Illuminating Unique Worldviews

The quest for what is native/indigenous knowledge follows a thorny path. Many of the narratives written about indigenous communities have been woeful misrepresentations. For example, recent criticism of Margaret Mead's (1928/2001) work in Samoa reveals the collision between Western scientific thought and native/indigenous thoughtways. For instance, the data-collection approach that Mead employed can be characterized by its isomorphic relationship between respondent and researcher, instead of a more communal data-collection process. As we know from earlier discussion, the notion that a key informant(s), representative of a community, can be the gateway to understanding the substance of a distinct community leads to an oversimplified, hence artificial, portrayal of a distinct lifeway (and it does not meet the rigor of qualitative inquiry).

Nevertheless, past narratives written about indigenous communities have contained the native/indigenous ethos (lifeway) and eidos (thoughtway) in text, thereby reducing what is native knowledge to a commodity. Indeed, the display of these texts has led to the fetishization of indigenous memory (e.g., coffee table books of native life sayings, motifs of native leadership, sacred native healing ceremonies reduced to how-to videos), which has been appropriated to rejuvenate Western knowledge (the cultural tourist). See also Minh-Ha, 1999, for an insightful discussion on how indigenous communities have been marginalized by Western scholars through cinema. To counter this trend, indigenous narrative must employ the natural taxonomies that are rooted in cultural, historical, ecological, and political contexts to tell stories that describe, explain, and compare how indigenous people and institutions interact in multiple contexts (e.g., ecological, political, philosophical).

So we begin our scholarly work with an emphasis on the use of indigenous, natural taxonomies as theoretical lenses through which to design, analyze, present, and apply our inquiry/indigenous narrative (see, e.g., Aluli-Meyer, 2003; Bishop, 1996;

Matthews & Jenkins, 1999; Smith, 1999). This affirms the need for each unique indigenous community to reclaim its own indigenous ethos and eidos and draws attention to the problem that indigenous narrative often struggles against hegemonic disbelief (Western disbelief). That is, stories about indigenous history and cultural beliefs often are difficult for some people (both native and nonnative) to believe. For example, among Australian Aborigines it is known that the *dreaming* that created their land can listen and smell and feel. Similarly, these symbols of human expressions, for example, the *pōhaku* (stone) having power and insight, are deeply embedded in Native Hawaiian narrative and are essential to *kaona* (hidden meaning). While there are Western scholars who employ this tool (see, e.g., Jean Baudrillard's, 1996, *The System of Objects*), mainstream Western thought would consider anthropomorphism—the giving of human qualities to inanimate objects or ideas—as irrational!

Indeed, indigenous frameworks do not fit easily into Western natural or objective fact, nor should they be made to fit. Furthermore, authors should not have to commit most of their text to persuading and/or informing readers of the principles and value of their traditional knowledge base, thereby relegating important questions regarding pedagogy, policy, and practice to an endnote. At the same time, authors should (as recommended earlier in this chapter) be clear about their authorial voice and the unique tenets of their distinctive knowledge, the conceptual wisdom that shapes the lives of native/indigenous people. The critical work of indigenous narrative inquiry is deeply embedded in this wisdom. In her seminal work *Decolonizing Methodologies: Research and Indigenous People*, Smith (1999) questions the place of Western theory and methods in Maori research, advocating for a native theory (ontology) that guides how research is constructed (see also Aluli-Meyer, 2003). Examples of how to frame indigenous research through a traditional native lens include Scott Rushforth's (1994) work with the Bearlake Indians (Sahtúot'įne) in the Northwest Territories of Canada; Alene Stair's (1994b) work with the indigenous people of Canada, in which she examines the school-going experiences of young people; and Lipka, Mohatt, and the Ciulistet Group's (1998) work with the Yup'ik Eskimo.

What we see in recent indigenous narrative is that indigenous knowledge is used as a framework to present the narrative and that the author often works hard to explicitly contextualize the respondents' texts. A seminal example of this is Henrietta Mann's (1997) book *Cheyenne-Arapaho Education 1871–1982: A Drama of Human Dimensions About Individuals, Families, Tribes, and the Federal Government*. This critical history of education within a context of sociopolitical and economic dominance is retold in Mann's narrative, which is drawn from the oral histories of several generations and the stories told by Mann's great-grandmother, White Buffalo Woman. Other examples include Norman Denzin's (2002) autoethnography, memoir, and essay "Cowboys and Indians" and the compelling collective piece by Morrill, Yalda, Adelman, Musheno, and Bejarano (2000), which shares experiential stories written by native youths about the violence in their lives. In Chadwick Allen's (2002) *Blood Narrative: Indigenous Identity in American Indian and Maori Literary and Activist Texts*, we explore through comparative analysis of indigenous narratives the political and social tensions within and in light of oppressive contexts. This work is one that features a native theoretical base and is of both scholarly import and social-justice advocacy.

Indigenous narrative, theorized from a native/indigenous foundation, must raise critical questions that might emerge as a result of this storytelling and recognize the narrative's potential ethical and cultural implications. That is, the narrative, by its very nature, explores power tensions embedded in knowledge. Revealing the ethos and eidos of a particular native community, this can result in collisions with other native and nonnative knowledge bases and practices. A little skepticism here is good. Engaging the narrative also means challenging the story—that is, probing sideways or asking questions about its meaning at different times and in different contexts, asking for linkages to other events and other stories, and asking for supportive evidence. There is, after all, not just one indigenous worldview. The more I read and learn about my own and other indigenous communities, the more I realize how little I know. Nevertheless, making these collisions explicit and concrete, which I will talk more about later in this chapter, can lead to interesting questions of policy and practice that require rethinking the processes and resources that have been and should in the future be mobilized to benefit indigenous children, youths, and communities.

The point regarding authorial rights, ownership, and intellectual and cultural rights to knowledge is one that cannot be glossed over. Through narratives of Australian Aborigines, Whittaker (1994) asserts that much of what is believed to be indigenous/aboriginal knowledge has been written by nonindigenous authors/researchers, in a Western way (without aboriginal references), and for a Western audience. What is lacking in the narrative about an indigenous group or event is the sacred ontology that gives fundamental meaning to a place, a practice, a long history of knowing. We are reminded by the quotation from Rudyard Kipling cited earlier that the *for whom* is just as important as the *who* tells/retells. Because the *for whom* is often a broad academic/scholarly audience, it is essential that the native/indigenous author takes care to present only that which she or he is authorized to share.

This tension of what is sacred in the story and what from indigenous story can be shared in widely distributed texts needs to be held graciously by native/indigenous scholars. What does this mean, held graciously? Take, for example, the Gwich'in tale of *Two Old Women*, an important story that defines values of generosity, responsibility, respect for age, cooperation, and humility, which had been passed on orally from generation to generation. This tale was translated from its oral text to the written form by a Gwich'in author (Wallis, 1993) and became a bestseller and an award-winning book. On the one hand, this provided the community with some recognition, but on the other, it raised the question of who owns the story—the author, the indigenous community, or the readers who purchased the story? This question was especially relevant because the two women were seen by the broad readership as similar to the characters *Thelma and Louise* (Scott, 1991)!

In a situation like this where the meaning is distorted, Paula Gunn Allen (see Babb, 1997) recommends that it becomes the responsibility of the scholar/ researcher to present an analysis of the indigenous narrative from alternative perspectives, through indigenous theorizing, to better bring to the surface the intended meanings. This process of employing diverse approaches that reveal multiple cultural perspectives, for example, can uncover the dualism in a community, describing a part that is Westernized and another that remains culturally traditional, yet both operating parallel to one another. The existence of this dualism and parallelism creates tensions (e.g., differences in interpretations) that indigenous narrative must uncover. The beauty of the narrative method is that the story has the capacity to explore these collisions.

Deciding what is appropriate to share is a prickly dilemma that must be carefully resolved by the indigenous scholar/researcher in dialogue with cultural elders and experts. For example, I am somewhat hesitant in my presentation of only a handful of native/indigenous views in this section. This is due primarily to the fact that there are many lifeways and thoughtways and many that are fundamentally different from each other. I also want to point out that ownership is extremely important, although in most cases, "ownership" is not a native/indigenous value. In his speech "Protecting Our Thoughts," Jonathan Osorio (1993) argues that indigenous people must assert sovereignty over their cultural practices and knowledge:

> In our nearly 2000-year history, Hawaiians have regarded knowledge not as public property but as deeply personal and spiritual understanding. We receive our instruction as signs from our ʻaumakua (personal gods) and from moʻōlelo (stories) via our kūpuna (elders). . . . Native people must recognize that a paradox exists between how we view knowledge and how the western professional sees it. We may not like to think of knowledge as property (just as we did not think of land as property a century ago) but we must be willing to adjust our thinking if we do wish not to be victimized again. (pp. 1–2)

Analysis and Application: Pedagogical Practice and Policy

Thoughtfully crafted indigenous narrative brings to light traditional native/indigenous knowledge, as well as tensions created as a result of the cultural diversity within a particular society. For example, among Native Hawaiians there are differences due to diverse definitions of what is traditional, what are traditional-contemporary meanings, what is Hawaiian and what is non-Hawaiian in light of one's mixed heritage (part-Hawaiian), where one lives (e.g., different islands, on the continental United States), and so on. There are multiple perspectives within a society that are not often shared. A deep understanding of these cultural collisions presented in counternarratives can only support the development of culturally relevant pedagogy and policy.

The work of the scholar/researcher, then, is to discover those stories that give further dimension to grand themes that might emerge (e.g., experiential learning, individual collectivism). A salient issue here is how both traditional indigenous narrative and counternarrative are interpreted or explained through an indigenous lens. That is, how does an indigenous scholar meaningfully analyze and present narrative so that it is respectful of traditional cultural factors and has the strength to influence change in policy and pedagogical practice? A perusal of published indigenous narratives reveals an emergent cluster of well-framed studies. For example, Theresa Mague Sonnleitner's (1995) insightfully written article (and her dissertation) "Yaqui Voices: Public Schooling Experiences of Urban American Indian Students" presents first-hand accounts of school experiences through the oral life histories of Yaqui students from the southwestern United States. By clearly identifying the conflicts between Yaqui traditions and their urban public schools, Sonnleitner is able to explore the need for policies and practices that encourage language immersion and advocate for them. Here is an example of Sonnleitner's use of voice to bring to the surface the differences in cultural knowledge, in particular the notion of success as promoted by the dominant culture differing from the view held by participants' families, which support involvement in and continuance of cultural beliefs and practices. RT, a participant in Sonnleitner's study (1995), explains,

> I felt successful at home, but I didn't know how there could be a demand for success in the other [world]. It didn't make sense to me. I didn't know what the definition was. I heard monetary, I heard those kinds of things, but when I looked around me, I didn't see any of those things. The demand on the other side was, "You do this because you are going to have to succeed in life" and I thought what I was already feeling was success. But the indoctrination I got must have not been right because I was living in a poor community. I was living in a situation where, now they call it dysfunctional, where people were very huddled together, very isolated from the larger community. And what I was hearing in school was that I wasn't successful yet, so I must be off and I must not be right in my success. (p. 331)

So how does the scholar/researcher present indigenous narrative so that it captures the process of learning and illuminates both conceptual and applied dimensions? Although some of the answer was taken up in the previous discussion regarding indigenizing narrative, I would like to further suggest using a heuristic framework, a working model if you will, that fundamentally accepts the idea that native/indigenous ethos and eidos have existed and evolved over time in a place-based environment. The analytical work of the scholar/researcher, then, is to explore ecological features (i.e., the physical and organic place), sociocultural features (i.e., family, culture, politics, economics, education, and spirituality), institutional features (i.e., school system, communication systems, political and judicial systems), and the relationships across all three.

An example of indigenous narrative that reflects on the ecological, social, and institutional, and is written in a dialogic and reflexive manner, is "Voices in a Reservation School: a Sonata-Form Narrative From a Professor and a Dakota Pre-Service Teacher About Their Professional and Practical Knowledge Teaching Science in Culturally Responsive Ways, Unfolds the Relationship Between a Non-Indian Professor and an Indian Pre-Service Teacher" (Ollerenshaw & Lyons, 2002). The professor is immediately confronted with the importance of grounding pedagogy in the Umo"ho" culture and language. Encounters with native learners engage both the professor and the preservice teacher in a process of unlearning Western educative institutions and relearning in the native way. This reveals the differences between the two worlds in light of sociocultural and institutional dimensions and leads the authors to compelling questions regarding pedagogy and policy.

Another powerful indigenous narrative work is Stephen Gilbert Brown's (2000) *Words in the Wilderness: Critical Literacy in the Borderlands.* Brown grounds his work in the ecology of the Athabascan Indian reservation in Alaska. In light of encounters with native learners he writes in the introduction, "The work is thus as hybridized as the bicultural milieu that comprises the setting of it: a compendium of autobiography, Native American resistance struggle, postcolonial discourse, radical composition theory, case study, and ethnography" (p. 2). Brown's critical study of pedagogy embedded in place and founded on traditional sociocultural elements is a solid effort to transform the pedagogical practices of teachers.

The value of this analytical approach is that it offers an opportunity for multilevel analysis and deeper, broader understanding. That is, the process helps the scholar/researcher to (a) define and articulate cogently important concepts that are idiosyncratic to a particular society and to reveal counternarratives that add both temporal and cultural dimensions, (b) reveal and examine relationships between institutions within the society as well as the links between people across institutions, and (c) place the individual and family as a central focus of the conversation as the scholar/researcher works to understand the implication of shifting structures for their well-being. Indigenous narratives that offer a robust analysis that leads to shifts in policy, epistemology, and pedagogy are beginning to emerge across disciplines and geography; for example, we can find it in the "ancient narratives" of Korea, which are used to address the spread of HIV/AIDS (Cheng, 2005); it is used to tackle the prescriptiveness and ambiguity of nursing from a First People's (Canada) perspective (Barton, 2004); it is employed to better understand the knowledge and practices of mental health workers in Guatemala (Miller, 1996); and we find it describing the deeply contentious tensions regarding environment in Australia (Robertson, Nichols, Horwitz, Bradby, & MacKintosh, 2000). In the end, analysis of indigenous narrative has the ability to reveal the historic influence of policy on lives and to advocate for particular action that creates and sustains change.

Furthermore, indigenous narrative that seeks to illuminate and transform educational policy and practice also has a more global reach as we can now find its use in the exploration of myth in education in South Africa (Lillejord & Mkabela, 2004) and science education in Kenya (Thomson, 2003). Arnoson, McDonald, Maeers, and Weston's (2001) study employs indigenous narrative to understand cultural nuances that can be appropriately integrated into math instruction and curriculum. In addition, Stephen Graymorning's (1999) personal Arapaho teacher's narrative recounts the work of introducing a language immersion program and illuminates the pragmatic and political tensions as well as the structure and content of such a program. There is indigenous narrative work that seeks to unveil the influence of policies that create institutional inequity, such as T. S. Tsutsumoto's (1998) master's thesis, titled *Higher Education Perspective: Through the Narratives of Samoan College Students.* In addition, there is a growing body of indigenous narrative that supports the development of more culturally relevant learning experiences (see Greenfield, 2001). And in a special issue of the *Canadian Journal of Education,* edited by Arlene Stair (1994a, Spring), scholars present conceptual and applied work that employs narrative to examine teaching, learning, evaluation, and policy implications.[6]

In essence, the purpose of this section of the chapter has been to propose a pathway to claim authorial ownership and ensure the cultural authenticity of indigenous narrative. I propose an analytical model—a work in progress—that can be used to understand both idiosyncratic and more universal sociocultural and institutional networks that may reveal relational connections and disconnections that lead to robust meaning making. The value, then, of indigenizing the narrative, illuminating unique worldviews, and applying what is learned to create culturally relevant/appropriate pedagogical policies and practices is threefold. First, it requires native/indigenous (as well as nonnative/indigenous) scholars/researchers to cast off Western ways of describing native/indigenous ethos and eidos, thereby correcting long-held (perpetuated) stereotypes and the mythologizing of the native. Second, it promotes the use of alternative research design approaches, creative presentation formats, and the mother-tongue to present the communal nature of indigenous narrative, authentically presenting the respondents' subjective and sacred sense on important topics. Third, it takes control (ownership) of the sociological, cultural, psychological, and educative roots of traditional native/indigenous ontology and epistemology and, in so doing, adds unique lifeways and thoughtways to the field of narrative inquiry.

Na Mamo: Where We Will Journey

It is important that native/indigenous scholars take the lead in framing indigenous narrative. The telling of memory can be difficult; indeed, it can be painful. Therefore, it takes work to access and to release these stories. Because of their lineage, native/indigenous scholars must take responsibility to be held accountable by their ancestors and elders, to build bridges essential to the native spirit, which becomes the lifeline that flows from the sacred bones of the generations that walk the earth to their past and to their future generations. As I write this chapter, however, I am struck by the reality that there is little in the way of formal (both academic and culture based) training to prepare critical native/indigenous scholars working in the field of narrative inquiry. A challenge, then, would be to construct learning opportunities and institutional support mechanisms that provide research and practicum within the indigenous setting.

As I have maintained throughout this chapter, indigenous narrative is important because it has the capacity to tell the truth about history—that is, the sociopolitical and cultural nuances and nature of a community and its relationships across time through the eyes and voices of the indigenous community members. As I have emphasized in this chapter (see the reference to the story of Koʻōlau), the indigenous perspective requires that the storyteller acknowledge that she or he is telling a narrative of a community embedded in place (land) and space (time/history and metaphysical metaphor). Hence, there will be many decisions regarding how (i.e., the content and attitude) the storyteller represents the life force of an indigenous community. The truth of the narrative resides in the ability of the storyteller(s) to engage the community (e.g., cultural experts, elders, and so on) in a participative process that seeks to probe sideways and head-on the various viewpoints of a particular event and/or phenomenon.

Indeed, we might say that indigenous narrative recovers a collective memory that raises social consciousness. That is, for Native Hawaiians the memory retold in stories recounts their loss of land and self-governance, for Australian Aborigines the collective memory speaks of their lost stories of the dreaming due to early contact with Whites, and for American Indians the stories recall the deep wounds created by boarding schools. Indigenous narrative, therefore, is a crucial means for the telling of memories for at least three reasons. First, recognizing a collective memory that is different from dominant texts requires that history be reconstructed. Hence, the indigenous narrative presents a political discourse that asserts alternative realities and advocates for native/indigenous sovereignty, indigenization of the narrative. Second, indigenous narrative is about personal/family and societal healing—that is, illuminating native knowledge and wisdom, collective memory, which makes possible recovery from the effects of generations of oppression and systemic racism. Third, native/indigenous narratives of native resistance and cultural resurgence can have powerful pedagogical and policy implications.

The journey forward for indigenous narrative does require a reconceptualization of what is traditionally cultural and intellectual within a contemporary indigenous environment. I have argued that this approach might demonstrate dual or, in many cases, multiple literacies (ways of knowing) because, to live within a sovereign system of reciprocity and stewardship, holding the tension of what is native and what is nonnative (e.g., disciplinary), the indigenous scholar/researcher must employ both culturally traditional discourses and 21st-century discourses that engage critical key issues. Thus, indigenous scholar/researchers must become more skilled at both pivoting between and building bridges across native and nonnative discourse systems.

This journey must start by honoring the sacredness of the process of telling. Henrietta Mann (1997) writes that protocol is observed in the telling of indigenous narrative: "Long ago, when storytellers, the keepers of history and culture, were to repeat the oral traditions of their people, they observed a certain ceremony" (p. 185). She goes on to share a sacred ceremony with which storytellers prefaced each telling, which reminded both the teller and the listener that the story connected all life and was being watched over by the Creator. Indigenous narratives unfold; they are rarely told in a single, bounded story but are often told and constructed over a lifetime of a people. If we actively engage in listening to these stories, knowing how they are told, to whom, and why, we can learn much about who we are and where we might journey. The voice of my *kūpuna*, Sarah Keahi (2000), closes this chapter:

Ehele wawae kākou, e like me ko kākou kūpuna me ke kapukapu a me ka ha'aheo. [Let us walk like our ancestors with dignity and pride.] (p. 60)

Author's Note: I am grateful to Elizabeth Murakami-Ramalho, who worked with me to gather and review many indigenous narratives across several disciplines. I am also thankful for the insightful guidance of two *kūpuna* (Sarah Keahi and Henrietta Mann) who spent long hours with me, telling me stories that carved the pathway for this chapter. And I am deeply appreciative of the graciousness and gentle guidance of two friends and colleagues, Joanne Cooper and Robert Rhoads, who provided insightful comments on earlier drafts of the chapter.

Consulting Editors: Joanne Cooper and Robert Rhoads

Notes

1. In this chapter, I use *native* and *indigenous* interchangeably. I recognize that the terms are imbued with social and political rigidities and pressures; however, I use the terms in this chapter to best identify aboriginal populations, in particular (but not exclusively) Northern American, Pacific Islanders (Native Hawaiians and Maori), and Australian Aborigines (with whom I am most familiar). In fact, native/indigenous people constitute complex and distinctly different communities, among whom there are thousands of different languages and stories/memories.

2. For the purposes of this work, I define ontology as the nature of philosophy of a culture group's metaphysical world. I define epistemology as how this knowing (which emerges from ontology/ontologies) generates knowledge.

3. I would like to acknowledge the support of two elder mentors (both requested not to be identified). Before beginning this chapter, I had long conversations with two elder mentors, both indigenous scholars and cultural experts. They told me stories about native narratives and storytellers and about how the native experience had been portrayed (both good and bad). Although they never told me what to write or how to write this chapter, their message was clear. First, I needed to write from my heart, remembering that the Creator and the elders speak from the heart. Second, native/indigenous narrative is fluid—that is, a good story connects the past, present, and future, offering lessons from which both an individual and a community (society) can grow. And third, and perhaps most important, native/indigenous narrative is just that, "indigenous." It describes the engagement of indigenous people in the world since the beginning of time; therefore, these stories belong to them.

4. For more discussion regarding the importance of social, cultural, and political context in narrative, please see Ivor Goodson (1995).

5. The short story "Koʻolau the Leper" first appeared in *The Pacific Monthly* in December 1909. It was then included in a volume of Jack London's short stories in 1912.

6. Please see the following articles in this special issue: McAlpine and Herodier, "Language and Content"; Robinson, "Teaching Process and Evaluation"; Douglas, "Community Values and Roles"; Sarrasin, "Cultural and Linguistic Evolution"; and Leavitt, "Identity and Literacy."

References

Allen, C. (2002). *Blood narrative: Indigenous identity in American Indian and Maori literary and activist texts.* Durham, NC: Duke University Press.

Aluli-Meyer, M. (2003). *Hoʻoulu: Our time of becoming. Hawaiian epistemology and early writings.* Honolulu, HI: ʻAi Pōhaku Press.

Arnoson, K., McDonald, J., Maeers, M., & Weston, J. H. (2001). *Interweaving mathematics and indigenous cultures.* Paper presented at the International Conference on New Ideas in Mathematics Education, Palm Cove, Queensland, Australia, August 19–24. (ERIC Document Reproduction Service No. ED472097)

Babb, G. (1997). Paula Gunn Allen's grandmother: Toward a responsive feminist-tribal reading of two old women. *American Indian Quarterly, 21*(2), 299–320.

Bakhtin, M. M. (1986). *Speech genres and other late essays.* Austin: University of Texas Press.

Barton, S. (2004). Narrative inquiry: Locating aboriginal epistemology in a relational methodology. *Journal of Advanced Nursing, 45*(5), 519–526.

Baudrillard, J. (1996). *The system of objects.* London: Verso.

Benham, M. (2005). Leading in full vision of the kiha: A Native Hawaiian woman's perspective of leadership and spirituality. In C. Shields, M. Edwards, & A. Sayani (Eds.), *Inspiring practice: Spirituality and educational leadership* (pp. 117–128). Lancaster, PA: Pro>Active.

Benham, M., & Cooper, J. (1998). *Let my spirit soar! Narratives of diverse women in school leadership.* Thousand Oaks, CA: Corwin Press.

Benham, M., & Heck, R. (1998). *Culture and educational policy in Hawaiʻi : The silencing of native voices.* Mahwah, NJ: Lawrence Erlbaum.

Bishop, R. (1996). *Collaborative research stories: Whakawhanaungatanga.* Palmerston North, New Zealand: Dunmore Press.

Brown, S. G. (2000). *Words in the wilderness: Critical literacy in the borderlands.* Albany: State University of New York.

Cheng, S. (2005). Popularising purity: Gender, sexuality and nationalism in HIV/AIDS prevention for South Korean youths. *Asia Pacific Viewpoint, 46*(1), 7–20.

Chinn, P. W. U. (2002). Asian and Pacific Islander women scientists and engineers: A narrative exploration of model minority, gender, and racial stereotypes. *Journal of Research in Science Teaching, 39*(4), 302–323.

Denzin, N. (2002). Cowboys and Indians: Symbolic interaction. *Social Science Module, 25*(2), 251–261.

Denzin, N., Lincoln, Y., & Smith, L. T. (Eds.). (in press). *Handbook of critical and indigenous methodologies.* Thousand Oaks, CA: Sage.

Elbert, S. H., & Mahoe, N. (1976). *Na mele o Hawaiʻi nei: 101 Hawaiian songs.* Honolulu: University of Hawaiʻi Press.

Garrett, M. T. (1996). "Two people": An American Indian narrative of bicultural identity. *Journal of American Indian Education, 36*(1), 1–21.

Goodson, I. (1995). The story so far: Personal knowledge and the political. *Qualitative Studies in Education, 8*(1), 89–98.

Graymorning, S. (1999). *Running the gauntlet of an indigenous language program. In Revitalizing indigenous languages.* Paper presented at the Annual Stabilizing Indigenous Languages Symposium, Louisville, Kentucky, May 15–16. (ERIC Document Reproduction Service No. ED428924)

Greenfield, P. J. (2001). Escape from Albuquerque: An Apache Memorate. *American Indian Culture and Research Journal, 25*(3), 47–71.

Guralnik, D. B. (Ed.). (1984). *Webster's new world dictionary of the American language* (2nd college ed.). New York: Simon & Schuster.

Kawaharada, D. (1999). *Storied landscapes: Hawaiian literature and place.* Honolulu, HI: Kalamakū Press.

Keahi, S. (2000). Advocating for a stimulating and language-based education: "If you don't learn your language where can you go home to?" In M. Benham & J. Cooper (Eds.), *Indigenous educational models for contemporary practice: In our mother's voice* (pp. 55–60). Mahwah, NJ: Lawrence Erlbaum.

Kipling, R. (1902). *The elephant's child.* Retrieved February 28, 2006, from www.boop .org/jan/justso/elephant.htm

Langer, C. L., & Furman, R. (2004). Exploring identity and assimilation: Research and interpretive poems [Electronic version]. *Forum: Qualitative Social Research, 5*(2), Article 5. Retrieved February 28, 2006, from www.qualitative-research.net/fqs

Lave, J., Duguid, P., Fernandez, N., & Axel, E. (1992). Coming of age in Birmingham: Cultural studies and conceptions of subjectivity. *Annual Reviews in Anthropology, 21,* 257–282.

Lave, J., & Wenger, E. (1991). *Situated learning: Legitimate peripheral participation.* New York: Cambridge University Press.

Leyland, L. (1997). *Alaska's commercial fishing women tell their lives.* Champaign: University of Illinois Press.

Lillejord, S., & Mkabela, N. (2004). Indigenous and popular narratives: The educational use of myths in a comparative perspective. *South African Journal of Higher Education, 18*(3), 257–268.

Lipka, J., Mohatt, G. V., & the Ciulistet Group. (1998). *Transforming the culture of schools: Yup'ik Eskimo examples.* Mahwah, NJ: Lawrence Erlbaum.

London, J. (1912). Ko'olau the leper. In *The house of pride and other tales of Hawai'i.* New York: Macmillan. (Original work published 1909)

Mann, H. (1997). *Cheyenne-Arapaho Education 1871–1982: A drama of human dimensions about individuals, families, tribes, and the federal government.* Niwot: University Press of Colorado.

Marmon Silko, L. (1988). *Ceremony.* New York: Penguin.

Matthews, K. M., & Jenkins, K. (1999). Whose country is it anyway? The construction of a new identity through schooling for Maori in Aotearoa/New Zealand. *History of Education, 28*(3), 339–350.

Mead, M. (2001). *Coming of age in Samoa: A psychological study of primitive youth for Western civilisation.* New York: HarperCollins. (Original work published 1928)

Merwin, W. S. (1998). *The folding cliffs: A narrative of 19th-century Hawai'i.* New York: Knopf.

Miller, K. (1996). The effects of state terrorism and exile on indigenous Guatemalan refugee children: A mental health assessment and an analysis of children's narratives. *Child Development, 67*(1), 89–106.

Minh-Ha, T. T. (1989). *Women, native, other: Writing postcoloniality and feminism.* Bloomington: Indiana University Press.

Minh-Ha, T. T. (1991). *When the moon waxed red: Representation, gender, and cultural politics.* New York: Routledge.

Minh-Ha, T. T. (1999). *Cinema interval.* New York: Routledge.

Morrill, C., Yalda, C., Adelman, M., Musheno, M., & Bejarano, C. (2000). Telling tales in school: Youth culture and conflict narratives. *Law and Society Review, 34*(3), 521–565.

Ollerenshaw, J., & Lyons, D. (2002). Voices in a reservation school: A sonata-form narrative from a professor and a Dakota pre-service teacher about their professional and practical knowledge teaching science in culturally responsive ways, unfolds the relationship between a non-Indian professor and an Indian pre-service teacher. In *Proceedings of the Annual International Conference of the Association for the Education of Teachers in Science*, Charlotte, NC, January 10–13. Retrieved February 28, 2006, from www.ed.psu.edu/ci/journals/2002aets/02file1.asp

Osorio, J. K. K. (1993). *Protecting our thoughts.* Paper presented at the Voices of the Earth Conference, Amsterdam, Netherlands, November. Retrieved February 28, 2006, from www.hawaii.edu/chs/osorio.html

Pukui, M. K. (1997). *ʻŌlelo Noʻeau Hawaiian Proverbs & Poetical Sayings.* Honolulu, HI: Bishop Museum Press.

Robertson, M., Nichols, P., Horwitz, P., Bradby, K., & MacKintosh, D. (2000). Environmental narratives and the need for multiple perspectives to restore degraded landscapes in Australia. *Ecosystem Health, 6*(2), 119–133.

Rushforth, S. (1994). Political resistance in a contemporary hunter-gatherer society: More about Bearlake Athapaskan knowledge and authority. *American Ethnologist, 21*(2), 335–352.

Scott, R. (Director). (1991). *Thelma & Louise* [Motion picture]. United States: Metro-Goldwyn-Meyer.

Smith, L. T. (1999). *Decolonizing methodologies: Research and indigenous people.* Auckland, New Zealand: University of Auckland Press.

Sonnleitner, T. M. (1995). Yaqui voices: Public schooling experiences of urban American Indian students. *Bilingual Research Journal, 19*(2), 317–336.

Stair, A. (Ed.). (1994a). Aboriginal settings, concerns, and insights [Special issue]. *Canadian Journal of Education, 19*(2).

Stair, A. (1994b). Indigenous ways to go to school: Exploring many visions. *Journal of Multilingual and Multicultural Development, 15*(1), 63–76.

Thomson, N. (2003). Science education researchers as orthographers: Documenting Keiyo (Kenya) knowledge, learning and narratives about snakes. *International Journal of Science Education, 25*(1), 89–115.

Tsutsumoto, T. S. (1998). *Higher education perspective: Through the narratives of Samoan college students.* Unpublished master's thesis, University of California, Los Angeles.

Van Maanen, J. (1988). *Tales of the field: On writing ethnography.* Chicago: University of Chicago Press.

Wallis, V. (1993). *Two old women.* New York: Harper Perennial.

Whittaker, E. (1994). Public discourse in sacredness: The transfer of Ayers Rock to aboriginal ownership. *American Ethnologist, 21*(2), 310–334.

PART VI

Narrating Persisting Issues in Narrative Inquiry

I n these chapters, two questions that frequently occur in narrative inquiry are discussed. Ruthellen Josselson discusses ethical issues related to conducting and publishing works of narrative inquiry, and Margot Ely offers insight into possible narrative forms for presenting narratives to readers outside the original narrative context.

Josselson draws on extensive experience and knowledge to discuss ethical practices in narrative inquiry, describing "an ethical conundrum (that) derives from the fact that the narrative researcher is in a dual role—in an intimate relationship with the participant . . . and in a professionally responsible role in the scholarly community." The existence of this conundrum makes it impossible for her to provide a list of rules and practices that will apply to all instances of narrative inquiry. Instead, she "define[s] an ethical attitude toward narrative research, a stance that involves thinking through these matters and deciding how best to honor and protect those who participate in one's studies while still maintaining standards for responsible scholarship."

Ely is concerned with the reader of narrative inquiry. Her focus is the product of narrative inquiry as well as its process, and she offers examples of a variety of rhetorical forms, including first-person story, poetry, and pastiche. Rhetorical form is important because "no matter how excellent the gathering of information in the final instance people must want to read what we wrote, must want to stay. Toward that aim our reports must glow with life." To do this, the narrative inquirer must work to create "forms that come closest to the essence of our understandings and present them in trustworthy ways . . . [engaging in] a crucial, ongoing, interactive dance."

Both authors remind us that as researchers conducting narrative inquiry, we must communicate and create relationships with those with whom we are involved in inquiry, but we must go a step further and also communicate and create relationship with communities of scholars and readers. Just as we must create and re-create principles and practices of methods for research, we must also be concerned with creating principles and practices that allow us to meaningfully re-present narratives to those reading our work. Their ideas and examples help provoke the discussion that is necessary for all of us to succeed in this task.

—*Barbara Morgan-Fleming*

CHAPTER 21

The Ethical Attitude in Narrative Research

Principles and Practicalities

Ruthellen Josselson

> *The gap between engaging others where they are and representing them*
> *where they aren't, always immense but not much noticed, has suddenly*
> *become extremely visible. What once had seemed only technically difficult,*
> *getting "their" lives into "our" works, has turned, morally, politically, even*
> *epistemologically delicate.*
>
> —Geertz (1988, pp. 130–131)

Narrative research consists of obtaining and then reflecting on people's lived experience and, unlike objectifying and aggregating forms of research, is inherently a relational endeavor. Every aspect of the work is touched by the ethics of the research relationship. It is self-evident that narrative researchers have an ethical duty to protect the privacy and dignity of those whose lives we study to contribute to knowledge in our scholarly fields. But, in the particularities of practice, this self-evident principle is fraught with dilemmas of choice that attend ethics in all relationships.

In essence, ethical practice and ethical codes rest on the principles of assuring the free consent of participants to participate, guarding the confidentiality of the material, and protecting participants from any harm that may ensue from their participation (Kvale, 1996; Sieber, 1992; Smythe & Murray, 2000; Stark, 1998). But these principles have no self-evident implementation. As I have wrestled with writing this chapter, I realize that the issues are too complex for me to be able to craft a cookbook chapter saying "here is exactly what you have to *do* to do this work ethically." Instead, I mean here to define an *ethical attitude* toward narrative research, a stance that involves thinking through these matters and deciding how best to honor and protect those who participate in one's studies while still maintaining standards for responsible scholarship. Like issues of ethics in life, often there are contradictory goods, and an ethical stance involves taking responsibility for choosing among them, minimizing harm.

The ethics of narrative research is in a state of evolution, deriving both from an adaptation of principles espoused for biomedical interventions, enforced by institutional review boards, and arising inductively from accumulating experience of narrative researchers. In this chapter, I want to examine the complexities of the ethical reasoning that underlies a "best practices" decision-making stance as well as the situational "real practices" that require narrative researchers to make ethical choices *in situ*. Where possible, I offer some suggestions about the concrete, practice implications of the ethical attitude I try to describe. I recognize that narrative researchers engage in different ways with their participants. My discussion will draw primarily on my experiences with interview-based narrative research (because this is what I know best and struggle to help my students learn), but the principles and reasoning could apply to other narrative research designs as well.

Narrative researchers do their work by (politely) intruding on people in the course of living real lives and asking them to help us learn something. We do this in hopes that what we learn will be of some benefit to others or will contribute to basic knowledge about aspects of human experience. Those people who agree to talk to us about their lives and/or allow us to observe them become our "participants." The naive view might be that it is only a matter of obtaining "informed consent" from our participants and then disguising names and places in published accounts to be able to sleep soundly. After reviewing what others have written over the last 20 years about ethics in narrative research, I am struck by how thorny these dilemmas are. Indeed, nearly all writers say in one way or another, after arguing the various positions one may take, that there is simply no good general set of rules or guidelines that would ensure moral behavior in working with narrations about other people's lives (Apter, 1996; Aron, 2000; Bar-On, 1996; Clandinin & Connelly, 2000; Ellis, 2004; Estroff, 1995; Kvale, 1996; McLeod, 1996; Miles & Huberman, 1994; Patai, 1991; Punch, 1994). Ethics in narrative research, as many of these writers point out, is not a matter of abstractly correct behavior but of responsibility in human relationship. The actual ethical dilemmas of practice, however, the failures and regrets, are seldom written about (Price, 1996; Punch, 1994).[1]

The essence of the ethical conundrum in narrative research derives from the fact that the narrative researcher is in a dual role—in an intimate relationship with the participant (normally initiated by the researcher) and in a professionally responsible role in the scholarly community. Interpersonal ethics demand responsibility to the dignity, privacy, and well-being of those who are studied, and these often conflict with the scholarly obligation to accuracy, authenticity, and interpretation.

Fulfilling the duties and obligations of both of these roles simultaneously is what makes for the slippery slopes. Perhaps the only solution is for the narrative researcher to demonstrate a clear recognition of the inherent dilemmas. In reflecting on the ethics of journalism, which shares predicaments with narrative research, Janet Malcolm (1990) says, "The wisest know that the best they can do . . . is not good enough. The not so wise, in their accustomed manner, choose to believe there is no problem and that they have solved it" (p. 162).

In full recognition, then, both of the existence of the problem and that I cannot solve it, I intend to outline its contours by sequentially considering the ethics of the relationship, the ethics of the report, the ethics of the design, and the role of ethics guidelines and institutional review boards (IRBs).

Ethics of the Relationship

The Contract: Explicit and Implicit

The essence of the narrative research approach, what gives it its meaning and value, is that the researcher endeavors to obtain "data" from a deeply human, genuine, empathic, and respectful relationship to the participant about significant and meaningful aspects of the participant's life. This involves both an implicit and explicit contract. The explicit contract states the role relationships between researcher and participant (e.g., "This is who I am. This is the purpose of my study. You are free to participate or not. The interview will be tape-recorded. You may withdraw at any time.") and is often fairly straightforward.[2] The development of the individual, personal, intimate relationship between researcher and participant rests on and contains an implicit contract, the terms of which are difficult to foresee or make explicit and the arena for differing assumptions, expectations, and contingencies. (See Lieblich, 2006, for an excellent, detailed exposition of the dynamics of the contracting phase.)

In that narrative research is founded in an encounter embedded in a relationship, the nature of the material disclosed is influenced not by the explicit contract but by the trust and rapport the researcher/interviewer is able to build with the participant. Thus, the participant is reading, not what has been made explicit, but rather the subtle interpersonal cues that reflect the researcher's capacity to be empathic, nonjudgmental, concerned, tolerant, and emotionally responsive as well as her/his ability to contain affect-laden material. The "data" that result reflect the degree of openness and self-disclosure the participant felt was warranted and appropriate under the *relational* circumstances she/he experienced. Researchers try to build a research relationship in which personal memories and experiences may be recounted in full, rich, emotional detail and their significance elaborated. The greater the degree of rapport and trust, the greater the degree of self-revealing and, with this, the greater degree of trust that the researcher will treat the material thus obtained with respect and compassion. What constitutes respect and compassion in the minds of this researcher/participant pair is the nature of the implicit contract between them.

Elsewhere I have written that I think that there is something oxymoronic about the idea of "informed consent" in narrative research (Josselson, 1996a). I don't think we can fully inform a participant at the outset about what he or she is in fact consenting to since much of what will take place is unforeseeable. Thus, consent has to be construed as an aspect of a relational process, deriving from an ethics of care rather than rights (Gilligan, 1982).

Dilemmas of the Informed Consent Form

Most textbooks on narrative and qualitative research suggest that an ethical approach requires full disclosure of the nature and purpose of the research. In general terms, this seems straightforward enough, but like so much in narrative research, translation into specificities is what unearths the fissures and uncertainties in this minefield.

For most narrative studies, the ethical requirement to set out the general nature and purpose of the study must be balanced against the need not to unduly direct the participant's attention to a particular phenomenon that the researcher wishes to study (Holloway & Jefferson, 2000). If one wants to know how a particular experience is interwoven in a participant's life, narrative research technique often mandates asking about the life rather than the experience. In these cases, one must tell the participant what one is generally doing without being too specific. For example, Amia Lieblich (2006) wanted to investigate the long-term effects of being in a particular special high school program. She was interviewing midlife adults. As a matter of research design, she believed it was better to ask her interviewees about their life stories and then see on analysis how they included their high school experience rather than to make explicit that she was focusing on this particular program, which may have induced the interviewees to take an evaluative stance toward the program rather than allow her to observe the more subtle effects in which she was interested. When I was interviewing Ethiopian immigrants to Israel, I framed the study as being focused on relationships within non-Western cultures so as not to offend the Ethiopian sensitivity to being singled out as "different." These choices, then, place the study in a larger context than is the more limited focus of the research. The statement of purpose is not untrue although it is a partial truth.

As a matter of practice, I think that the "scholarly good" of framing the study to the participant in a way that makes possible the kind of narration the researcher needs outweighs the "moral" good of telling the participant the exact nature of the study. But the statement of the purpose of the study should be as close to the researcher's focus as possible. As a matter of good methodology, the researcher has to be transparent about his/her interests in order to make a research alliance with the participant. In other words, good narrative practice requires intense collaboration about the topic such that the participant can inform the researcher about the area of the participant's life or experience that is of interest to the researcher. That the researcher is interested in a more narrow aspect of the participant's experience than the initial statement of purpose states seems to me to be not unethical, although it is ethically important to discuss with the participants at the end of the meeting the more focused areas of particular interest the researcher began with so that participants will not feel surprised or deceived later on if or when they may read the published report. One also has to bear in mind that the nature of the researcher's interest in the material may change as the study proceeds. Therefore, more general statements may be advisable in order to encompass the potential for discovery of avenues of exploration of the data unforeseen at the time of the interview or observation.

Some requirements of the explicit contract, embodied in the consent form, are unproblematic, and most of these are actually negotiated before the meeting. Usually, consent forms say that the participant is willing to take part in the study and is free to withdraw participation at any time. In the case of interviews, the consent form notes that the participant is willing to have the interview tape-recorded. The duration of participation should be determined before the formal consent form is signed—that is, in contracting with the participant, usually over the phone, one must specify what will happen, where the meeting will be held, and how much time is required. One must also tell the participant ahead of time if and how material will be recorded; I think it unethical to surprise participants with recording devices as this may constitute undue pressure to consent to something unexpected.

Most participants sign that they are willing to participate (otherwise why are they there?), but the thoughtful (ethical) researcher will also be alert to signs of subtle coercion (even if the participant endorses his/her willingness to participate). In particular, people who are institutionalized or vulnerable may be participating—but not exactly freely. As a matter of good research practice, as well as ethics, researchers must always be thinking about what motives lead a person to participate in our studies (Corbin & Morse, 2003). And even when people consent, the researcher must be aware of vulnerabilities and consequences that participants may not recognize (Ely, 1991; Estroff, 1995).

Some have pointed out that signing an informed consent form actually compromises anonymity, especially because research material has no legal privilege (Lipson, 1994; Price, 1996; Warren, 2001). In cases where participants are illegal immigrants, for example, or members of legally marginal populations, a tape-recorded verbal consent would preserve anonymity better. Then, no names need ever be used.

Ethical Practicalities of Consent Forms

The principle of assurance of confidentiality and privacy to participants is central to the very possibility of doing narrative research. Unless our participants trust that we will insure their anonymity, they would not tell us what they tell us. Therefore, we must do everything we can to safeguard their privacy. In an effort to be "procedural" about this, institutions are engendering rules for consent forms and thereby dictating practices that are often harmful to the research project and do not in any meaningful way protect the participant.

Most consent forms nowadays, under pressure from review boards, specify what will be done with the data—who else will listen to the tapes, when names will be changed, who else will read the transcripts, how the data will be stored, etc. The principle here is that we have to do everything possible to disguise and safeguard material so that participants will not be recognized by others. Exactly how we do that will vary, depending on the structure of the research project. I think we need to tell participants that we will do all that is humanly possible to keep material confidential. I don't think we need to tell them that we will keep their material in a locked file cabinet or promise them not to send data over the Internet, except through a secure line.[3] (We may, though, specify to IRBs our safeguards in detail.)

Some people ask their participants to make up names for themselves—and some have even gone so far as to address them by this false name. The former practice strikes me as a conflation of roles and the latter as a hindrance to the relationship, but these are not a matter of ethics.

As a practical matter, when keeping narrative interviews, field notes, or research journals, it is necessary to change *all* the names in these texts. Sometimes people just change the name of the participant. But since participants generally refer to family members, friends, or close associates by name, or they refer to places where they lived or companies where they worked, they could still be identified by someone who came across or read, for example, the interview text, unless every proper name in the interview is changed.[4] This is why a codebook is necessary—so that the researcher, if necessary, can reconstruct the original data, and the researcher should double check the method of disguises before publication. Most breaches of the ethics of disguise come through clerical (or unconscious) errors. I remember one time when I was writing about a participant who, according to the transcript, lived in Los Angeles. I, therefore, in my write-up, placed her as living in San Diego. Only when I went to re-interview her years later did I realize she actually did live in San Diego. I had evidently changed the place name on the transcript and then forgotten I had made this change. (It is important to keep the codebook very separate from the transcripts. Do not store it on the same computer as the transcripts—keep a notebook instead. Organize it so only *you* could reconstruct it.)

In terms of who else will work with the material, it is, in general, good practice to make these parameters as wide as possible—"material will only be shared with people involved in working with me on the research project and then only with all names, places, and identifying information removed or disguised." Too often, people write on the consent form, to impress the IRB, a very restricted definition of who can listen to the tapes, only to find that they want to have a research consultation with someone else but are now contractually bound not to. (Then what do you do? Call the participant 4 years later and say, Is it all right with you if I play your tape for someone I didn't even know at the time of the interview? This may be ethical, but it makes us look foolish as researchers.)

Institutional review boards are often asking researchers to state that the material will be destroyed after 5 years. This seems to me to be an indefensible requirement as one never knows when one might like to do follow-up or longitudinal studies, and I do not understand how it benefits the participant. (If anything, the longer the data are kept, the less likely the participant is to feel attached to that particular version of self.) As long as data are stored so that the participants could not be identified on the transcripts and so that they are under the control of the researcher, I see no problem in keeping the material. (It is important, though, to keep in a separate place a codebook that allows the researcher to identify who was who.)

The freedom to withdraw participation at any time seems to me to be absolute. This sometimes strikes terror into researchers because it means just what it says— that even at the time of publication of the completed work, a participant can ask that his or her material be deleted. This is frightening, but I see no ethical way around it. If a participant no longer wishes to be part of our study, at any time, that person must be free to say so and to have us obliterate any public use of his or her material.

Consent forms also say that the material given by the participant will be suitably disguised to be used in published reports. This is such a big topic and so mired in enigmas that I will return to it later.

The Potential for Harm

Increasingly, I have seen IRBs ask that consent forms talk about potential harmful effects of the interview, usually insisting that the researcher include some caution that people may become upset talking about their own experiences and, if this should happen, will be referred for psychotherapy. These are standards that come from medically based consent forms (Corbin & Morse, 2003) and conflate harm and distress (Holloway & Jefferson, 2000). Within the narrative research arena, statements like this in consent forms set a relational frame for suspicion and, through the power of suggestion, are more likely to make the interview both an unpleasant experience for the interviewee and an unproductive one for the researcher. In general, people will only tell researchers what they want to tell, and it seems to me that there is no need to warn them that they might become upset. I believe it infantilizes and thereby denigrates participants to tell them that they might become upset while talking or that they may have some distress days later following the interview. Interviewees control what they share, and experiencing painful feelings in an interview, while distressing, may for them be in the service of integration and growth.

Affective expression is usually a sign of enough comfort in the relationship with the interviewer that the interviewee can relax her or his controls and defenses, and this level of self-disclosure can also lead to growth-promoting self-reflection for the interviewee (Birch & Miller, 2000; Corbin & Morse, 2003; Miller, 1996; Ortiz, 2001; Riessman, 1990). IRBs often make the questionable assumption that not to talk about painful experiences is preferable to talking about them with an empathic listener (Corbin & Morse, 2003). The challenge is for the interviewer to be able to maintain equilibrium, go on listening, and contain (i.e., calmly bear) the emotional experiences being recounted or expressed. In all my years of interviewing and supervising students, I have never seen anyone fall apart as a result of a research interview.[5] Nor have I found any published reports of such an experience.[6]

What is not stated on consent forms but is central to the implicit contract is that the interviewer be qualified to listen to and contain a wide range of human experience and that if, on some rare occasion an interviewee should become distressed to the point that he or she cannot resume his or her habitual level of functioning at the close of the interview, the researcher is prepared with a procedure for making a referral. I think it much more unethical for an inexperienced, anxious researcher to advise someone who cried during the interview to see a psychotherapist than *not* to warn an interviewee that they may feel some pain as a result of choosing to narrate difficult experiences in their lives.

Prior warning about harm that could come from the interview therefore seems to me to derive from institutional anxiety rather than to promote the interests of narrative researchers or to protect the participant.

Fine, Weiss, Weseen, and Wong (2000) discuss the ways the very *introduction* of the informed consent form may impinge on the trust and collaboration possible in the relationship in that it serves to remind the participant (as well as the researcher), early on in the relationship, of the power differential between them. The researcher must present himself/herself as part of an institutional framework to a participant often weary of the impersonality of bureaucratic forms. Thus, the act of obtaining informed consent itself becomes an aspect of the interaction with the participant, an interaction to be analyzed and considered as part of the context of all the material that is forthcoming in the interview.

In my own view, it makes sense to have two "informed consent" forms—one at the beginning of the interview agreeing to participate, to be taped, and acknowledging that the participant has a right to withdraw at any time. The second form would be presented at the end of the interview with agreements about how the material will be managed from that point on.[7] If this occurs at the end of the interview, at least the interviewee knows what has been recorded and has the opportunity to specify certain sections of the material that he or she would not want shown to others or published. Even without a formal second consent form, consent has to be regarded as a continuing process, and the participants must be accorded the human right to bestow or withdraw the use of their material.

Ending the Interview

Ethical considerations are just as important at the end of the interview as at the beginning. Good interviewing practice means returning to less emotionally saturated ground than may have been present earlier in the interview (Corbin & Morse, 2003) and trying to end on a positive note. This is often a time of vulnerability for interviewees who have just exposed important aspects of their lives and may feel intimately connected to the interviewer, who they now realize they will likely never see again. Thus, the end of the interview in some ways encapsulates a termination process in psychotherapy, where it becomes important for both people to voice how they felt about the experience and to note its meaningfulness.

Interview studies should always end with a question such as "How was it for you to be talking to me in this way?" This is the equivalent of debriefing, inviting the participant's reflections on the experience as a way of beginning the process of saying goodbye. At this point, the researcher should stay alert to any signs of hesitation or discomfort on the side of the participant and be ready to empathically process or clarify any ways in which the participant may have felt distressed by the interview[8] (or interviewer). Then the researcher should invite the participant to ask whatever questions he or she may have of the researcher. ("What questions do you have for me as we end our time together?") In this phase, interviewers must say something human about their experience in the interview but should reemphasize their role as a researcher: "I appreciate your openness and willingness to share your experiences with me. I feel that I have learned a lot from you that will help me in my work."

Another ethical dilemma the researcher must be prepared for is the participant who wishes to continue the relationship. Especially when working with lonely or vulnerable people, the special attention offered by the interviewer may be so gratifying that the participant wishes for its continuation (Booth, 1999). In such circumstances, the researcher must gently but clearly restate his or her role as having just a certain period to devote to each participant. With such participants, it is probably better to schedule an interview in a single sitting. Multiple interviews over time are more likely to encourage the fantasy of a continuing relationship.

Where prolonged contact with a community is necessitated by the research, the researcher may be called on to continue the relationship in unforeseen ways. These become delicate matters of withdrawing gradually and gracefully in a way that leaves the participants feeling honored and not exploited (see Lieblich, 1996). There is, however, nothing unethical about the researcher who wishes to continue a relationship with the participant if this wish is mutual.

Reflexivity and the Ethics of the Relationship in Research Interviews

The nature of the relationship that develops in narrative studies is emergent and cannot be predicted at the outset, and here lie some of the murkiest and most subtle of ethical matters, realities that cannot be made explicit. People can give informed consent to participate in the *research* project, but they cannot give prior consent to participate in an open-ended *relationship* that is yet to be established.

The researcher's self, with its fantasies, biases, and horizons of understanding, is the primary tool of inquiry. Therefore, self-knowledge and self-reflection become necessary to the project to tease out what aspects of what is "observed" derive from the researcher, what from the object of observation (the participant), and what from the interaction between them. A full understanding of this is, of course, only an ideal, but an ethical stance in narrative research requires that such an exploration be undertaken as completely as possible. This is true in fieldwork situations as well as interviews (Hunt, 1989), but there are some dynamics that, because of the potentially broad and deep penetration into the experiential world of the participant, may be especially in need of attention in the interview situation. That will be my focus in this section, and I leave it to the reader to apply its principles to other research designs.

All interviews are interventions. Unlike the therapy situation, where the task of the intervention is to effect change in the participant, the research situation treats the interviewee as the expert, with the task being to effect change in the researcher's understanding of the phenomena of interest. In other words, the therapeutic situation is constructed for the *patient* to learn something; the research interview is oriented to the *researcher* learning something. Nevertheless, the perceived power differential in the narrative research interview generally favors the researcher, who is often believed by the participant to be expert in something. Particularly if one introduces oneself as a psychologist or mental health professional, the fantasy (whether conscious or unconscious) on the part of the participant is that the interviewer "knows" the good of living one's life—whether this is cast in terms of morality or mental health. Or the participant assumes that the interviewer already has a narrative position or expectation that forms a template against which their own narrative is constructed. Thus, the encounter itself inevitably has an impact on the interviewee's life in the sense that it will lead to some rethinking or added meaning making as the interviewee, after the interview, reflects on her/his own words.

If we are good interviewers and the interview is intensive and extensive, people will often take the opportunity to articulate the most sensitive areas of their lives, the matters about which they are doubtful or ashamed. It is not uncommon for people to tell us things they have never told anyone else, and they are then exquisitely attuned to our emotional response.

Above all, this interpersonal dynamic requires that we be good containers, that we can listen empathically but nonjudgmentally, feeling from within the participant's emotional space ("That must have been very confusing for you" or "How painful that must have been") rather than from the locus of our own idiosyncratic reactions. Sometimes the participant will seem to demand a personal response ("What do you think of what I did?") At such times, I often respond by generalizing and normalizing, saying something such as "So many people, more than you imagine, have experienced something similar" or "You know, as a psychologist I know that there is no right way to handle this." One of my interviewees recently disclosed to me that she had been sexually abused as a child by her (now deceased) grandfather, that her therapist urged her to confront him with this, but that she refused and left therapy. She then began debating with herself about whether she had done the right thing, clearly inviting me into this debate. This was, I thought, one of those times where telling her (feelingly) that I believe that there is not a "right" way, that all choices have their benefits and costs, was the best response I could make, and it did seem to reassure her enough that she could continue with her narration.

Interviewers must be sufficiently in control of their own inner processes such that impossible binds are not created in the interview situation. The narrative interviewer has to be comfortable dealing with complex and painful emotions. My experience is that the student who reports that the participant "didn't want" to talk about something is usually reporting what he/she was unable to hear. Most participants will talk about whatever they think can be heard. We listen people into speech. I think that one of the most profound ethical problems in this work lies in inviting someone to talk and then subtly indicating that what they wish to share is too much for the interviewer to bear—or that it is boring or irrelevant. On the other hand, an accepting and sympathetic response to participants' disclosures may lead participants to find their experiences less disconcerting or worrisome (Holloway & Jefferson, 2000).

The interviewer must refrain from overt and subtle judgment about the participant's life. Students often think this is obvious but miss the myriad of ways they are doing just this in their interview. Interviewers who would never say "I think it is terrible that you behaved that way" think it is perfectly appropriately to commend and praise: Variants of "I think its wonderful that you did that" are also judgments that set up the question about why other actions reported by the participant do not merit the same response. Saying "that's good" during an interview is just as judgmental as saying "that's bad."

I believe it unethical to provocatively use confrontation to elicit more data. I once supervised a group of narrative researchers in a workshop where one researcher, interviewing women who had been abused by their husbands, challenged them about why they remained in the relationship by saying things such as "Why would you be so self-destructive as to return to him?" Her thought was that she would learn a lot from the participant's response to this question. I agreed that the participant's response would indeed tell her something about how the participant would defend herself in this situation but that this form of question was, on its face, unethical. Researchers must eschew trying to enlist, overtly *or* covertly, participants to embody some political agenda they may carry into the project (see also Patai, 1991).

Sometimes researchers might share something of their own world and experience with the participant, and there is nothing unethical about this. Self-disclosure, as long as it does not embarrass the participant, may encourage a sense of collaboration and build rapport. Its influence on the relationship and the material that emerges become issues of analysis.

Researchers must become sufficiently acquainted with the social and cultural world of their participants to be able to engage appropriately in interaction with them. This means knowing enough about their mores and expectations so as not to appear rude, insensitive, or intrusive—but knowing little enough to be able to inquire deeply about those aspects of the world of the participant one wishes to learn about.

We cannot foresee all the eventualities within the relationship that will unfold. Therefore, I think we have an ethical obligation to be aware of the implicit aspects of participants' consent—all those unstated expectations they may have of us—and to manage these in the dynamics of the relationship we form with each participant, both during the personal contact and in our handling of the material thus obtained.

Ethics of the Report

In considering the ethics of the relationship, we have explored one side of the narrative researcher's dual role—the role of being in appropriately respectful relationship to the participant. Having gathered the material, whether through interview or observation, the researcher now resumes the role that instigated the research project, that of the scholar reporting to the academic community about what he or she has learned and how it advances knowledge in the field.

Assuming that all material has been suitably disguised, the researcher is now left to grapple with the problems ensuing from analyzing a narrative that has changed ownership. What was once the participant's story now becomes a co-constructed text, the analysis of which falls within the framework of the interpretive authority of the researcher (Chase, 1996; Smythe & Murray, 2000). New dilemmas arise when the researcher turns to the task of making a report of what has been learned.

The written word, at least in Western society, has a power far beyond that of words that are spoken. Thus, access to print and the authority to indelibly inscribe a point of view in regard to participants gives the narrative researcher special (even if unwanted) powers that must be acknowledged and ethically managed in a published report.

Interpretive Authority: Beyond Disguise

The interpretive process depends on the aims of the research. "Who should control the interpretive process in any particular case depends in large part on the aim or purpose of the research and thus what kind of material needs to be collected and what kind of interpretation best suits that material" (Chase, 1996, p. 51). There are differences among narrative researchers in terms of whether their research goal is "giving voice" to their participants or "decoding" the texts of their interviews at some other level of understanding (Josselson, 2004). Those whose research is designed to "give voice" struggle with the problems of faithful representation of the experiences of their participants and the constrictions of linear forms of presentation to fully re-present what has been told. Those whose research designs involve making use of narrative texts to analyze unconscious or socially constructed processes, issues latent in the text, struggle with the ethical problems of interpretive authority—the dilemmas that arise from participants *not* finding their manifest meanings represented in what is written about them.

When the narrative researcher construes the project as "giving voice" to underrepresented participants, the researcher conceives the role as being a collaborator and a conduit rather than an interpreter: The participant is the authority on the meaning in the text (Etter-Lewis, 1996). These researchers ground the ethics of the report in their participants being, in one way or another, coproducers of the published text (Ely, 1991; Mishler, 1986; Wengraf, 2001) and tend to collaborate with their participants in fashioning the published outcome.

Much narrative research, however, in its goal of advancing knowledge, involves some interpretive efforts at a conceptual level, excavating the intention and meaning behind appearances (Holloway & Jefferson, 2000; Hoskins, 2000; Moustakas, 1994). Researchers report "what the text says to us" (Gadamer, 1975, p. xviii). This mode of narrative research involves the task of understanding a narrator differently than he/she understands himself/herself. Researchers who work from this point of view tend not to involve participants in the interpretation/publication phase of the project.[9]

Of course, many researchers work from both points of view, wishing to be both collaborative and interpretive. There is a wide range of (often heated) opinion about whether participants should be given transcripts for verification and/or final reports to comment on the interpretations.[10] Some believe that participant concurrence with interpretation is an inappropriate principle on which to base either ethics or research practice (Chase, 1996; Holloway & Jefferson, 2000). Some, at the other extreme, go so far as to advocate that participants be encouraged to change what has been written (Ramcharan & Cutcliffe, 2001).

My position is that the primary ethical attitude in the report rests in the researcher's authority, stressing that the report is the researcher's understanding or interpretation of the text. The inherent ethics of narrative research lies in the resolute honesty of the researcher's reflexivity, which states clearly the biases, aims, and positioning of the knower and the circumstances under which the knowledge was created, with the researcher taking full responsibility for what is written. From this point of view, the report is not "about" the participants but "about" the researcher's meaning making.

The task of the narrative researcher is to relate the meanings of an individual's story to larger, theoretically significant categories in social science, a task distinct from the individuals' specific interest in their own personal story (Smythe & Murray, 2000). While the task of the researcher in the data-gathering phase is to clarify and explore the *personal* meanings of the participant's experience, the task in the report phase is to analyze the conceptual implications of these meanings to the academy. Thus, at the level of the report, the researcher and the participant are at cross-purposes, and I think that even those who construe their work as "giving voice" and imagine the participants to be fully collaborative with them in the research endeavor are in part deluding themselves.[11] The researchers are interested in the research questions (and their careers). The participants are interested in themselves. Thus, there is a division between the personal narrative told by the participant and the "typal" narrative, a narrative that exemplifies something of theoretical interest, created by the researcher.[12] From the moment of arranging to meet, through the interview or observation, through the transcription, through the analysis, the researcher's interpretation is omnipresent.

If there were some kind of impenetrable wall between the social world and the academy at this point, all would be well enough. The problem here arises when those who have participated in our studies may read what we have written.[13] As I have phrased it elsewhere (Josselson, 1996a), we are then in a position of openly talking about them behind their back. What, then, to do with the ethical dilemma of the person who recognizes himself/herself—and may not like what we say about him or her? By writing about people, we stir up a welter of narcissistic tensions—in them and in us (Josselson, 1996a).

The question of the people themselves—people we once interviewed or observed but who are now our *dramatis personae*—reading our report has puzzled all who have taken it up (Chase, 1996; Ellis, 2004; Stacey, 1988). It is more complex than it appears. The self is multiple and evolving. The aspects of persons we write about are contingent and selective. Thus, the participant-self who is "reading" our report is related to, a part of, but not identical with, the participant we write about.[14] Some of our participants are more cognizant of this than others, who may expect to find in our writings an exact mirror of the self they thought they presented to us or the self they feel they are at the time of reading. In addition, we may write about aspects of our participants unknown to them, unconscious aspects of their experience, structural aspects of their narrative, or socially constructed or linguistic elements of their discourse. Participants are unlikely to disagree with our presentation of the "facts," suitably disguised, of their experiences, which is why "member checking" (i.e., verifying the transcript with the participants) doesn't solve the problem. If they find our writing troubling, it is usually our interpretations they object to.[15]

Certainly, we must take care in our written reports to maintain our respect for the dignity of our participants as individuals, recognizing that what we are treating as an exemplar that illustrates a conceptual or theoretical point is a very personal narrative to the person whose story it is. If we choose to write about short vignettes, this is less problematic than when we use long case examples with extensive interpretation. It is when we make use of lengthy and detailed case material that we must confront the question of What if the participant does not agree with our interpretation?—or, worse, What if he or she feels narcissistically injured (i.e., insulted) by it?

Every aspect of our report may have unforeseen idiosyncratic meaning to the individual we are writing about, no matter how careful we are. *Not* writing about someone we have interviewed can be wounding, as I discovered in my study of "ordinary" women, some of whom searched my book in vain to find themselves.

After the meeting(s) with the participants, the text belongs to the researcher, and what we write is our interpretation of it. We take full interpretive authority for our understanding of it (Chase, 1996). I think it is foolhardy to foist our writings on our participants, although we should make them available. I think the best principle is that the more public the published work is to be, the more participant consent should be sought at each stage of the publication (see Lieblich, 2006)—that is, the ethics of publication consent are differently shaded when the material will appear in a trade book as opposed to a scholarly journal or a dissertation. (Most researchers have the experience that their participants are not that interested in reading journal articles in which their material appears or are unlikely to try to decipher the theorizing [Holloway & Jefferson, 2000]).

If we do send our work to them, we need to caution the participants that our interest in writing was about the topic for which we made use of their material but that they are unlikely to find a faithful representation of themselves since that was not our purpose. As an ethical position at this point, we must be prepared to stay in relationship with the participant, to explain our purposes as fully as we can, to make transparent our choices in as kind a way as possible, and to be prepared to contain whatever responses the participant may have. We can reassure ourselves that we are unlikely to permanently or seriously damage anyone although we do run a risk of hurting their feelings, surprising them, or influencing them (for better or worse). But here we enter the moral dilemmas of what harm is and what potential benefits outweigh the risks of harm.

Many critics of narrative research, it seems to me, write about their worries about how people *may* respond. We need to base our ethical practices, however, on our accumulating understanding of how people *do* respond and under what circumstances. Some researchers report that their participants treasure published reports about them and may use the distance of the researcher's interpretation of their lives to view themselves from an insight-producing new angle (Josselson, 1996a; Lieblich, 2006). Others report about participants who had disagreements or misgivings about what was written. Dan Bar-On (1996) reports that one participant in his longitudinal study of children of Nazi perpetrators was "hurt" by what he wrote and did not want to continue meeting with him.[16] Terri Apter (1996) quotes one of her teenage participants as saying "I see how you got what you said. I'm not saying it's wrong, but when you read about yourself. . . . Well, it's me, but not me. It's really weird" (p. 31). Much more sophisticated about these matters than Apter's teenager, one of Carolyn Ellis's graduate students, an insider to writing about others, echoed the teenager's experience when she told Ellis on reading what she wrote about her, "Reading about myself through your eyes was a bit surreal" (Ellis, 2004, p. 315). The evidence at this point suggests that reading about oneself written through another's viewpoint and prose is unsettling, even more so than, but akin to, seeing a photo of oneself or hearing one's voice on tape. Written speech differs from spoken speech. A linear portrayal of a person is always flattened and thereby inaccurate—and it requires a certain distance from the self as depicted to understand that in being written about, one has become an illustrative character in the researcher's text.

In general, I think that it is difficult to represent the potential consequences of reading about oneself written about by another in a balanced way. Certainly, reading what someone has said about oneself has impact, but I see no evidence that there is significant harm or long-term impact except perhaps in the rarest of cases.[17] There have, however, not been enough published reports about the actual responses of participants—most of our knowledge here is through oral accounts. We need a more extensive narrative ethics, the actual experiences of participants and researchers, to better understand the particularities of our moral duties (Nelson, 2001; Widdershoven, 1996).

Every narrative contains multiple truths. All selves are multiply voiced. Therefore, whatever narrative emerges in the final report is a construction of the interpreter, and the writer needs to make this plain in the presentation of results. But this is unlikely to fully assuage those who find objectionable some aspect of how their material has been portrayed or understood.

A number of writers have tried to suggest ways out of this dilemma. Smythe and Murray (2000) and others have urged narrative researchers to clarify the issues of narrative authority at the time of the consent process. But this has potentially lethal effects on the interview relationship if what is communicated is some form of "I want you to tell me about yourself but you may not like what I say about you when I write this up." Smythe and Murray's suggestion to have an interval of time between the consent process and the interview so that the issues of multiplicity of meanings and differing intent don't unduly influence the content of the interview doesn't seem to solve this problem. If anything, having a discussion with the interviewee at the end of the interview about the overall focus of the project may help the interviewee understand that the researcher is ultimately interested in the research question, of which the interviewee is but an instance. Such a discussion may help participants understand that the final report will not be a simple mirror of *them*.

Some have suggested showing participants what is to be published and asking for their permission, but this has its own set of ethical quagmires. Here, the dynamics of persuasiveness, personality, and power cast their shadow on what might be hoped to be an authentic conversation. The researcher is writing as a psychologist, sociologist, anthropologist, educator, nurse, or other brand of scholar. The participant cannot possibly be expected to engage in the merits of the scholarly argument. The participant will, however, understand that it is of some professional importance for the researcher to publish whatever it is he or she wishes to publish and the participant's consent will in part reflect the wish to please. Moreover, once what is written is shown to the participant, then whatever it says will have its impact, whether it is published or not.[18] In other words, the participant who is going to feel offended or misunderstood by what the researcher has written will feel this way as much in response to the draft as to the published version. Therefore, the goal of sparing the participant's feelings will not be accomplished, and the damage, if any, will already have been done.

I have been wrestling with this dilemma for many years, and I have come to believe, at least at this point, that the most ethical approach is to explain to the participant at the close of the interview that what I will write about his or her interview will depend on the general conclusions I make about the whole group. I tell them that what I will write will probably not feel to them as though it is fully about them since I usually highlight certain themes in the text to make whatever point about the whole topic seems to me to be important to make. I caution them, though, that although I can disguise them enough so that anyone who does not know that they are in the study would never recognize them, I cannot disguise enough so that those who know them well *and* know they are in the study would not recognize them. Therefore, I suggest that they be cautious about letting others know of their participation. I offer to send them a summary of my general findings from the study if they would like to see what I have learned from doing the project. I then try to write about each person with great sensitivity to how they might feel if they were to read it,[19] but I take some comfort in knowing that, for most participants, it is highly unlikely that they will ever read what I publish. If the published work will be more widely available, in a book of interest to a wider public rather than a scholarly journal, for example, then I offer, at the time of publication, to send the work to each participant. I remind them that if someone close to them knows of their participation in the study, they could be recognized despite my efforts at disguise, and I therefore suggest that they give me a private address where receiving the work will not compromise their anonymity in the study. I then send the work with a letter explaining that of course I have taken liberties with the textual material to make general points and that I hope they understand that I have taken literary license with the texts I produced from their interviews and that my representation of them is an interpretation that is not intended to be any kind of literal truth about *them* as *they* are in their actual lives.

We write from a post-modern position, knowing the relativity of all "truths," and I think that we cannot then approach our participants in a modernist frame and try to negotiate with them a shared single truth. It is better, I think, to take responsibility for our interpretations, even with our participants.

One of my participants, when I asked her 10 years later about her reaction to my previous book, said, "I remember I didn't like what you said about me. I don't remember now what it was. I didn't let it bother me. I just decided to ignore it." She went on then to tell me about her current life and how it has evolved. She understood her life in her terms, not mine. Participants have their own ways of dealing with the experience of being written about,[20] and in most cases the worry about potential harm is the stuff of researcher nightmares more than actual participant experience. But the nightmares keep us vigilant, and this is preferable to a complacency that might lead us to be inattentive to the potential for harm.

Another suggestion made to solve the dilemma of the ethical bind when participants read about themselves is to create composites out of several participants (Bakan, 1996). This, however, runs the danger of fictionalizing data. If narrative research lies in the close observation of people in the highly specific details of their lives, then cutting and pasting between lives destroys the integrity of the data. Thus, to stay in a pristine relationship with the participant, the researcher runs the risk of being in an unethical relationship to the scholarly field.

There is, of course, also good that may come personally to those who read what we write about them. For some, the narcissistic gratification of feeling important enough to be the object of someone's close scrutiny and presentation can be empowering. For others, the opportunity to view their lives from a different vantage point can be enlightening and growth promoting (Apter, 1996; Atkinson, 2001; Josselson, 1996a; Lieblich, 2006). Some of my participants proudly showed what I had written about them to their children, partly in hopes of being better understood (see also Lieblich, 2006).

An ethical attitude requires that we write about other people with great respect and appropriate tentativeness and that we recognize that what we write may be read by the person we are writing about. The ethical thin ice is that we cannot predict or control all the reactions our participants who read our reports may have. Most people, as they go through life, are accustomed to others having a view of them that they do not share. They develop defenses against this through a recognition of the contingency of perception—adult versions of the "Says you" of the playground. On the one hand, we have enormous power and authority with our access to print, but we can also be easily dismissed as incomprehensible academics engaged in arcane and meaningless ivory tower pursuits. If we underestimate our power, we may harm; if we overestimate it, we risk paralysis or the cessation of narrative research. Finding this balance is the challenge.

Anonymity Revisited in the Report

We must also protect the integrity of participants' ongoing relationships with those who figure in their stories. Sometimes the dangers of publication outweigh the potential benefits precisely because when we study people who know one another, people could be harmed by what others have said about them. Recently, I had an opportunity to interview the daughter of a woman I have been following for 33 years, a daughter the same age her mother was when I first interviewed her. This was a rare opportunity in social science and afforded me the opportunity to observe the parallels in identity formation processes between mother and daughter. Both gave me permission to interview the other and to write about the material. But the content of the daughter's interview was such that I believe that it would be unduly painful for the mother to learn about. I decided, therefore, that despite the fascinating nature of the material, I would not publish it. I don't, however, preclude the possibility that in another 10 years, as their relationship and their lives evolve, it will become less sensitive to both and that I may feel that, with their consent, which I would again obtain, I could write about it. Or perhaps I may just use what I have learned and find a way of bringing this knowledge into my writing without discussing them specifically.

Issues of privacy and confidentiality may recur at the level of the report when the research is conducted in small communities (see Lieblich, 1996) or on members of the same family (Mauthner, 2000). Where other people might be recognized (especially when participants tell others that they were in a specific study that may have gotten wide attention), the ethical problem is to protect those who are unwitting characters in others' narratives (Hadjistravropoulos & Smythe, 2001). We are ethically bound to consider how publication of the material might affect the person's reputation in the community were their identity to be revealed. Similar concerns emerge when participants are drawn from the same subcommunity (and could therefore be recognized by other members of that subcommunity, no matter how well we "disguise" them) or "snowballing" techniques of finding participants are used such that participants know the identity of the other participants (Chase, 1996). Amia Lieblich, who has done a good deal of such research, advises researchers in these instances to take great care to collaborate with participants about what will be published and to be ready to rescind any material the participant feels might be injurious to others or to their relationships with others.[21] If we suspect at the outset that there is no way of doing the research such that the participants or the important others in their lives can be sufficiently disguised so as to be unrecognizable to others, then one simply cannot publish the research unless all those significantly mentioned read what is to be published and agree to its dissemination. This is, however, highly problematic in student dissertations and theses where publication of the research is mandatory.

Ethics of the Design: The Wider Social Context of the Research

Increasingly, qualitative researchers have been trying to articulate an ethics of design in terms of who benefits from the research. This involves the larger questions about the role of the academy within society and the relationship between basic and applied research (Christians, 2000; Fine et al., 2000; Greenwood & Levin, 2000; Punch, 1994). In line with this is also a consideration of the politics of representation. Here issues of research design, politics, and ethics interweave.

One pragmatic ethical question that arises focuses on a debate about whether it is ethical to gather people's life experiences for the sole purpose of understanding better what it is to be human and whether we need to define specific potential gain to a group of people. In recruiting participants for a narrative research project, we say either explicitly or implicitly that our work offers the potential of benefiting the population the participants represent. We take care, though, not to promise that participation in the research will help them personally (Chase, 1996). Usually, researchers claim that the experience of people who compose the group of which they are a part is underrepresented in the professional literature and the researcher's aim is to give voice to these experiences. What, then, is the ethical obligation to see that some benefit accrues to this group? These concerns may be more in the foreground in fieldwork where whole communities are involved, but they are also at issue in more individualized narrative research as well.[22]

Those who argue for explicit benefits to participants are working in a social justice framework, hoping that their work will lead to empowerment of the participants and/or the group they represent and also engender better societal treatment of those whom they study. Those working from a basic science stance implicitly assume that greater knowledge of human experience will lead to a more humane society. George Rosenwald (1996) argues that a narrative psychology, based on the study of situated human beings, subverts the increasingly fragmented and mechanistic approach to the person within psychology and thus contributes to creating a viable social image of "wholeness" in the person. This, in his view, is the overarching ethical concern: What kind of human being is our science portraying?

To define a pragmatic ethical attitude of design, one must work from the conviction that the research carried out is, at least, not exploitative—that is, we study people to better understand them or the society in which they live; it is unethical to study people out of curiosity about what seems to be different or exotic with the intention of voyeuristic engagement.

An ethical attitude toward design involves deep contemplation about what it means to encounter and represent "otherness." This mandates that the researcher question personal assumptions about the normal, healthy, or desirable. Unexamined biases and prejudices may be injurious to participants both at the site of the data gathering, when attitudes are easily transmitted nonverbally in the form of disdain, contempt, or disgust, or at the time of the write-up, when, now physically distant from the participant, the researcher's values saturate the presentation.

An ethics of design necessitates sensitivity to the (sub)cultural values and frame-work of the participants and reflection on what it may mean to protect the com-munity of which the participants are a part (Johnson, 2001). The researcher must be aware of the potential to stereotype or subtly denigrate others and the ways in which his/her own attitudes have been shaped by his/her own social positioning. (Thus, given that most of us have been socialized into a racist, sexist, ageist, homo-phobic society, an ethical attitude requires that one be aware of how one experi-ences and expresses these prejudices. I am never persuaded by anyone who declares that they are *not* racist, sexist, etc. If anything, I am more worried about their potential to abuse.) Examination of one's own social and personal horizons of understanding is of paramount importance and also particularly problematic for researchers working on politically sensitive topics.

Many writers who have focused on ethics have stressed the power dynamics inherent in the study and representation of the other and have pointed out that any representation has political implications (Christians, 2000; Fine, 1998; Punch, 1994).[23] The society is impacted by representations that might lead or add to social stereotyping, and one purpose of narrative research is often to present a counter-story that subverts an oppressive master narrative (Nelson, 2001). Indeed, any thoughtful analysis of these matters leads to questions about the political implica-tions of scholarship itself (Denzin, 2000; Patai, 1991).

For decades now, anthropologists have been criticizing their forebears for pater-nalistic, imperialistic, or just plain insensitive portrayals of those they studied. But the objectionable viewpoints are themselves products of the cultural milieu in which the ethnographic work was written rather than matters of ethical oversight. Advances in the narrative understanding of human experience can only come through a good deal of error as the field endeavors to find the balance between observer and observed and discovers how otherness can be captured with appro-priate empathy and minimal distortion, subject to the inevitability of our horizons of understanding.

Archived Material

So far, I have been considering narrative research where the researcher (or a research team) gathers the data. As narrative research, which is expensive in time and cost, proliferates, people are increasingly archiving their materials so that other researchers can investigate them further or differently (see Richardson & Godfrey, 2003, for a fuller discussion). This raises other ethical concerns. Should the partic-ipants be informed at the time of the data collection that their material may be archived? If they have not been, must their consent be obtained before archiving? Are there different standards of disguise since the material will now be available to other researchers who do not know the particularities of each participant's life circumstances?

I think that participant permission should be obtained before archiving and that participants should be given the opportunity to review whatever will be archived.

I think they should also have the right to ask that their material be deleted from the archive at any point they wish. In this sense, I believe that the text belongs to the participant at every stage (although the interpretive authority belongs to the researcher).

Ethics Guidelines and Institutional Review Boards

The role of institutional review boards (IRBs) has become increasingly problematic for narrative research (Lincoln & Tierney, 2004). Wolcott (1994) identifies a confusion of rules and moral principles, noting that "'Genuine ethics' . . . are at risk of giving way completely to meeting the letter of the countless regulations promulgated by institutional review boards" (p. 403).

The dominant discourse that guides these boards is rooted in health/medical research and is often at odds with the discourse of social science research (Ramcharan & Cutcliffe, 2001). Unlike, for example, drug trials, narrative research investigates no specifiable effect nor is it likely to change a person's life irremediably (and certainly not physically). Research rooted in experiment requires certain safeguards that protect participants by fully informing them of the potential risks and benefits of participation in the research. In narrative research, neither risks nor benefits can be fully articulated.

In some hypothesis-testing social science research, issues of deception move to the center of the ethics concern. Some research must be done covertly, and here ethics boards strive to balance the potential risks and benefits and try to solve the dilemmas by "debriefing" the participants afterward. In narrative research, initial purposes may be stated explicitly, but outcomes, being unforeseeable, cannot be specified in advance. What the researcher finds of interest and importance in a narrative study may be far afield from what was expected at the outset, and thus the analytic focus on the material may differ from what was initially stated to the participant.

Most narrative studies are only loosely designed at the outset because narrative understanding is emergent. Thus, for example, interview questions and approaches may change in light of emerging analyses of the data. Good narrative research is conducted inductively, modifying procedure in light of growing understanding, shifting strategies as themes develop (Ouellette, 2003). McLeod (1994) argues that ethics in narrative research should be more reflexive than procedural. As with the methodology, the work proceeds according to general principles, interpreted under local conditions, rather than fixed rules. This creates havoc for ethics boards accustomed to fixed designs, to wanting to know exactly what will be asked of and told to participants. Narrative research, with its contingencies and explorations, cannot be controlled at the outset by outside observers in the same way as hypothesis-testing studies.

Thus, ethics in narrative research requires commitment to certain ethical values rather than a priori behaviors and may be difficult for ethics boards to monitor. The imposition of clearly bounded rules, applied across the board, is what leads to the outraged protest of narrative researchers who find their studies subjected to constraints that are either irrelevant to the research or may actually interfere with it.

Some ethics and review boards work with values and principles rather than rules because it is impossible to anticipate every contingency a researcher might find (Stark, 1998). Ethics review involves, among other things, a determination that the researcher has obtained the necessary training to conduct an empathic, nonjudgmental and respectful interview (or other intervention),[24] has thought through and given reasonable consideration to the possible effects the inquiry may have on the participants, and is prepared to deal with consequences in an ethically sound way. Thus, a review board may well raise concerns about a researcher with no clinical training interviewing survivors of trauma and expect that researcher to demonstrate her/his competence in dealing with flashbacks or traumatized affect. The focus here is on the interviewer's capacity to contain and manage what might emerge. Or, a review board may raise questions about cultural sensitivity if a researcher from one subcultural group sets out to participate in and observe another.

In narrative research, there is always the potential for impact on the family and social networks of the person who participates. Ethical practice involves the need to respect the dignity and welfare of others, and this must be interpreted broadly by ethics boards. The focus must be on the *principle* of "awareness of and sensitivity to issues relating to power and vulnerability" (Stark, 1998, p. 203) rather than on specific rules that may themselves have paradoxically injurious consequences—to both the participants and the research itself. Clandinin and Connelly (2000) propose that we ought to be thinking, throughout the research, in terms of *relational responsibility*. Such a framework is more likely to protect participants than abstract (or worse, concrete) ethical principles.

Institutional review boards (whose primary task is often to protect their institutions rather than either the participant or the research) that wish to implement a procedure to insure that they are not culpable for the possibility of emotional harm to participants might require that the researcher inform *the ethics board* that she/he is prepared with referrals, should such become necessary. An ethical attitude mandates, for example, that the researcher tell participants that they may call the researcher if they have further reactions to the interview they wish to discuss and then for the researcher to be prepared to refer if necessary or to request supervision if uncertain about how the interview may have affected the participant. Thus, the IRBs may require that the researcher include on the consent form a phrase inviting such postinterview reactions with appropriate contact information.

The agreed-on principles that ethics review boards should enforce include the following: that participants not be coerced in any way into participation and that they have the right to withdraw participation at any time; that participants and researcher not be in dual relationships that might imply coercion (e.g., teachers interviewing their own students); that the researcher is adequately trained; and that the researcher will take unassailable steps to maintain the privacy and anonymity of the participants. Researchers are also obliged to satisfy ethics review boards that they are familiar with local laws that mandate reporting of instances of sexual or child abuse[25] and that they would be prepared to deal with someone who indicates potential suicidality. These matters, in my view, should be managed between the researcher and the board and not between the researcher and the participant by way of the consent form.

Ethics boards tend to operate in the most conservative ways, maximizing the principle of eschewing any kind of risk. If some member of the board is able to imagine any circumstance where a participant might be harmed ("what if"), the anxiety introduced into the group will usually be sufficient to instigate an insistence on some kind of action to try to prevent the possible (regardless of how unlikely) event.[26] Institutional review boards are generally composed of researchers who have never actually carried out a narrative research study and have only fantasies of what is involved (i.e., how they personally might feel about having their "secrets" written about). I think it important that boards that review narrative research have at least significant representation from narrative researchers.

Narrative researchers endeavor to conduct research *with* other people rather than *on* them. Especially where communities are the focus of the research, good ethical practice may involve consultation before the research is carried out on the interests of the community in the research. Assessment of benefit from the ethics board may thus involve demonstration of who is likely to benefit from the research, but even these benefits may be emergent, given the contingent nature of narrative research.

Reflections and Conclusion

Many, if not most, perhaps all, narrative researchers end their studies with some questions about the absolute ethicality of what they have carried out, although only a few have said so in print (Apter, 1996; Bar-On, 1996; Estroff, 1995; Josselson, 1996a; Lieblich, 1996). This seems to me to be the most ethical position of all. It indicates that the researcher is internally responsive to the tensions and dilemmas of this kind of work and is conversant with the ultimate complexity of moral choice when confronted with the situational particularities (MacIntyre, 1984; Nussbaum, 1986). Because we are dealing with the real lives of real people, we can never know *for sure* at the outset that we will not have an impact on them that could be in some way painful. We can never know that what we publish will not be in some way distressing to them. We have a lot of evidence that most people find our interviews with them healing, integrative, useful, and meaningful, but this does not guarantee that nobody will ever have a less sanguine experience. We have little evidence about the effects on people of what we write about them, but what we have seems to suggest that most people are not very interested in what we have to say and will be highly unlikely to read our scholarly articles and books. We researchers are preoccupied with our studies; our participants go on with their lives. Because of the time it takes to do a narrative study and publish it, those participants who *do* read what we write do so at a point in their lives different from the moment represented by the text we have analyzed. They may recognize some aspect of themselves in what we say but will be aware that although we have "got" something right about them, we also got them wrong. Most people will not be very bothered by this or not for very long.

I can imagine that there are some ethicists who might protest and say, "Well, but even if one person feels wounded and wronged by the interpretation you make of them, doesn't that make the whole enterprise morally suspect?" Ethics is always most difficult when there are competing goods. I believe that the benefit science can derive from studying whole human beings in context[27] outweighs the highly unlikely possibility that someone might become severely distressed as a direct result of participation. If such an eventuality should come about, I would think it morally necessary that the researcher offer that person consultation (even pay for his or her psychotherapy) to try to contextualize whatever felt insulting or wounding and help that person recognize that all truths are partial and situated and that researchers distort unintentionally or misunderstand.

As social scientists, our primary task is the better understanding of human experience in society and in time, and we believe that this knowledge will ultimately and along the way lead to a betterment of human life. We cannot fulfill this task unless we can study humans as they are engaged in living their lives, and we cannot do this without incurring some potential for risk. There are few worthwhile endeavors that are completely risk-free.

Above all, an ethical attitude requires that we consider the dilemmas and contingencies rampant in this work. We can never be smug about our ethics since the ice is always thin, and there is no ethically unassailable position. We must interact with our participants humbly, trying to learn from them. We must protect their privacy. What we think might do harm we cannot publish. We cannot put our career advancement over the good of our participants. There will always be dilemmas because virtue in this work stems from contextual ethics that are best specified in each situation through discussion with informed colleagues.[28] I believe that if we work from these fundamental principles, we can do this work ethically enough.

Consulting Editors: Amia Lieblich and Susan Chase

Notes

1. See Sue Estroff (1995), who writes poignantly about the ethical dilemmas of research with the chronically mentally ill.

2. See Smythe and Murray (2000) for a review of the basis and fundamentals of the ethics codes.

3. Consent forms themselves, because they have participants' signatures, should be locked away somewhere and *never* be shown to anyone (such as publishers or granting institutions) who may ask for them.

4. This practice, though, makes it difficult for other researchers to contextualize the data (Poland, 2001)—for example, when working collaboratively with other researchers. Here again, the researcher must balance the needs for participant anonymity and privacy with the research purpose.

5. The only time in my years of doing narrative research interviews that I even raised the question of psychotherapy was with a person who wanted to keep exploring something that came up during the interview and would not allow me to end it. I simply said that it seemed like the interview had unearthed some unexamined and unresolved feelings that he was only dimly aware of and that, understandably, he wanted to pursue examining them. I told him that this was outside the frame of the work I was engaged in but that there were people, therapists, who were available to help him continue thinking about what all this meant to him. I said I would be happy to offer some names of people who he could consult with and pursue these meaningful issues. I suggested he think about it for a day or two and then get in touch with me for some names if he wished. He never did, but I assume he used whatever self-understanding he gained in his further development—and I was able to end the interview.

6. Corbin and Morse (2003) say that in their 50 years of combined experience doing narrative research interviews, they have never had an incident of grave concern. Holloway and Jefferson (2000) report a case of a woman who decided to pursue counseling, which she had anyway been considering, as a result of her interview. They presumed that this was a result of her positive experience of feeling listened to in a nonjudgmental way.

7. Richardson and Godfrey (2003) and Thompson (2003) have made similar suggestions.

8. This is one reason why people who are to conduct in-depth interviews need to have specific training in the relational process and to receive feedback on what they bring relationally to the interview situation.

9. Much published research does not report that participants have been involved after the interview phase, which leads me to assume that they have not seen the report prior to publication.

10. Rita Charon (2001), writing from the perspective of narrative medicine, believes that patients should be shown what has been written about them and should have the right to decline publication. Lieblich (2006), Ellis (2004), Ely (1991), and many others also hold to the principle of obtaining agreement from participants about what will be written about them.

11. Judith Stacey (1988) makes a strong argument for the position that the appearance of equality with research subjects can be a mask for exploitation. She questions whether it is possible to have an approach to research that is authentic, reciprocal, and fully intersubjective—and still be research. Similarly, Daphne Patai (1991) offers an impassioned statement about the ethical conundrums in trying to take a feminist approach to research on people who are less powerful than the researcher by virtue of class, race, or ethnicity. She wonders if it is possible to research the oppressed without becoming an oppressor and largely concludes that it is not. These are extreme positions that raise questions worth thinking about. Sue Estroff (1995) concludes her wrenchingly honest analysis of her work with chronically mentally ill people by saying "I do not think it is possible to work in complete collaboration, in actual equality or in total accord or consensus with our informants. Nor am I certain that these are unassailably good goals" (p. 97). What we may have to give up is the fiction that narrative research can be fully collaborative and still be research.

12. Smythe and Murray (2000) suggest that, in contrast to personal or archetypal narratives, typal narratives are constructed by social scientists in an effort to subsume individual experience to broader typologies of theoretical interest.

13. My comments about written reports apply as well to public presentations.

14. Estroff (1995) begins her article with the rage of one of her participants who, 10 years after the interview, was humiliated to read about how she was when in a psychotic state. See Graves (1996) for a discussion of this issue with regard to psychoanalytic case reports.

15. For example, I classified one woman in my study of identity development (Josselson, 1996b) as diffuse in identity according to criteria specified by the identity status research tradition (Marcia, 1993). Later, on reading the publication, she objected to being placed in this category because it did not match how she *felt*. Some researchers have published responses from participants who disagree with their interpretations in order to open for scrutiny the terms of the differing stances (Osherson, 1980; Stacey, 1990). Other researchers who have tried to do this, however, find that the respondents' objections are often not germane to the research focus but refer to idiosyncratic matters of consequence to the participant, but not to the point of the research (Tova Halbertal, personal communication, 2005).

16. Bar-On (1996) reports one German woman who did not expect her full account to appear in the (English) book, and Bar-On promised her to delete this chapter from the German version.

17. Hadjistravropoulos and Smythe (2001) take up one of my own examples to argue that impact can be severe. The example involved a psychoanalyst whom I had used as an example of idealizing processes in relationships (Josselson, 1992). In "On Writing Other People's Lives" (Josselson, 1996b), I reported that he said that for some time after the publication of my book he thought about himself as "an idealizer" and used my categorization of him as something he had to respond to in his understanding of himself. Hadjistravropoulos and Smythe (2001) say, in effect, that if even a psychoanalyst has such a reaction, imagine how less psychologically reflective people may respond. I would make a different argument, however. I think that precisely because we are in the same field and speak the same language, my participant took my interpretation more seriously and added it to the range of ideas that he used in his ongoing self-explorations. He did not say this was harmful to him, only that it had impact. Less psychologically minded people would, I think, be *less* likely to try to apply unfamiliar scholarly language to themselves and would, like so many of my other research participants, simply ignore my interpretation as something foreign to their lives—as long as they did not feel demeaned or criticized by what I wrote. This, at least, has been my impression of the response of most of the participants in my longitudinal study of women.

Estroff (1995) reports an instance of (and her intense guilt about) one participant who years later felt harmed by reading her words in print since the report preserved a state of being she was deeply ashamed of and had overcome. I know of one other instance of a person who read and gave permission for the publication of a clinical case study about her but then felt mortified (and enraged) for quite some time after it appeared. Both these are related to reports about mental disorders. If there are other occurrences of harm from a published report, I couldn't find them. As social scientists, we need to think about how many cases of negative reactions we are willing to tolerate; we will never be able to prevent them absolutely.

18. If the dilemma here, as Kvale (1996) states it, is that our research may confront participants with new understandings of themselves they have not asked for, then it follows that taking those interpretations to them directly only exacerbates the problem by directing their attention to something that they may not have otherwise known about.

19. Bar-On (personal communication, May 25, 2005) reports an instance of an interview in which he believed that there were many indirect references to incestuous relations which he could not clarify. He decided not to write about this because he knew she might read the text but felt that his presentation omitted what he thought were some of its major features. In this instance, as an ethical position, responsibility to the participant transcends responsibility to the scholarship.

20. Studying women in their longitudinal sample, Gail Agronick and Ravenna Helson (1996) found that women who were most likely to say they had been influenced by the published results of the study were those who were more intellectual, open to new ideas,

emotionally expressive, independent, assertive, and self-confident. Those who were more guarded and controlled in their lives were less likely to say they were influenced by the study.

21. Chase (1996) suggests that often what participants find most sensitive in their texts is not what they say about themselves but what they say about others.

22. In addition, ethical questions arise about who owns the final product, and these can be complex when matters of financial reward to the researcher are present.

23. Susan Chase (personal communication, 2005) points out that those who are, outside of the research relationship, more powerful than us are also subject to our prejudicial "othering."

24. See the discussion between Smythe and Murray (2000, 2001) and Gottlieb and Lasser (2001) in *Ethics and Behavior.*

25. June Price (1996), studying child-abusing mothers, was required to warn her participants not to disclose to her any incident of abuse not yet known to the authorities.

26. Hadjistravropoulos and Smythe (2001), in their paper on elements of risk in qualitative research, similarly "imagine" circumstances of risk in the absence of actual cases of harm.

27. Rosenwald (1996) makes the case that this "making whole" is central to the ethics of the human sciences.

28. Institutional review boards could best serve narrative research by serving as informed colleagues rather than purveyors of rigid rules.

References

Agronick, G., & Helson, R. (1996). Who benefits from an examined life? Correlates of influence attributed to participation in a longitudinal study. In R. Josselson (Ed.), *Ethics and process in the narrative study of lives* (pp. 80–93). Thousand Oaks, CA: Sage.

Apter, T. (1996). Expert witness: Who controls the psychologist's narrative? In R. Josselson (Ed.), *Ethics and process in the narrative study of lives* (pp. 22–44). Thousand Oaks, CA: Sage.

Aron, L. (2000). Ethical considerations in the writing of psychoanalytic case histories. *Psychoanalytic Dialogues, 10,* 231–245.

Atkinson, R. (2001). The life story interview. In J. F. Gubrium & J. A. Holstein (Eds.), *Handbook of interview research: Context and method* (pp. 121–140). Thousand Oaks, CA: Sage.

Bakan, D. (1996). Some reflections about narrative research and hurt and harm. In R. Josselson (Ed.), *Ethics and process in the narrative study of lives* (pp. 3–8). Thousand Oaks, CA: Sage.

Bar-On, D. (1996). Ethical issues in biographical interviews and analysis. In R. Josselson (Ed.), *Ethics and process in the narrative study of lives* (pp. 9–21). Thousand Oaks, CA: Sage.

Birch, M., & Miller, T. (2000). Inviting intimacy: The interview as therapeutic opportunity. *International Journal of Social Research Methodology, 3*(3), 189–202.

Booth, W. (1999). Doing research with lonely people. *British Journal of Learning Disabilities, 26,* 132–134.

Charon, R. (2001). Narrative medicine: Form, function, and ethics. *Annals of Internal Medicine, 134*(1), 83–87.

Chase, S. (1996). Personal vulnerability and interpretive authority in narrative research. In R. Josselson (Ed.), *Ethics and process in the narrative study of lives* (pp. 22–44). Thousand Oaks, CA: Sage.

Christians, C. G. (2000). Ethics and politics of qualitative research. In N. Denzin & Y. Lincoln (Eds.), *Handbook of qualitative research* (2nd ed., pp. 133–155). Thousand Oaks, CA: Sage.

Clandinin, D. J., & Connelly, F. M. (2000). *Narrative inquiry: Experience and story in qualitative research.* San Francisco: Jossey-Bass.

Corbin, J., & Morse, J. M. (2003). The unstructured interactive interview: Issues of reciprocity and risks when dealing with sensitive topics. *Qualitative Inquiry, 9*(3), 335–354.

Denzin, N. K. (2000). The practices and politics of interpretation. In N. K. Denzin & Y. S. Lincoln (Eds.), *Handbook of qualitative research* (2nd ed., pp. 897–922). Thousand Oaks, CA: Sage.

Ellis, C. (2004). *The ethnographic I.* Walnut Creek, CA: AltaMira Press.

Ely, M. (1991). *Doing qualitative research: Circles within circles.* London: Falmer Press.

Estroff, S. E. (1995). Whose story is it anyway? Authority, voice and responsibility in narratives of chronic illness. In S. K. Toombs, D. Barnard, & R. A. Carson (Eds.), *Chronic illness: From experience to policy* (pp.77–104). Bloomington: Indiana University Press.

Etter-Lewis, G. (1996). Telling from behind her hand: African American women and the process of documenting concealed lives. In R. Josselson (Ed.), *Ethics and process in the narrative study of lives* (pp. 97–113). Thousand Oaks, CA: Sage.

Fine, M. (1998). Working the hyphens: Reinventing self and other in qualitative research. In N. K. Denzin & Y. S. Lincoln (Eds.), *Handbook of qualitative research* (pp. 70–82). Thousand Oaks, CA: Sage.

Fine, M., Weis, L., Weseen, S., & Wong, L. (2000). For whom? Qualitative research, representations, and social responsibilities. In N. Denzin & Y. Lincoln (Eds.), *Handbook of qualitative research* (2nd ed., pp. 107–132). Thousand Oaks, CA: Sage.

Gadamer, H. (1975). *Truth and method.* New York: Seabury Press.

Geertz, C. (1988). *Works and lives: The anthropologist as author.* Palo Alto, CA: Stanford University Press.

Gilligan, C. (1982). *In a different voice.* Cambridge, MA: Harvard University Press.

Gottlieb, M. C., & Lasser, J. (2001). Competing values: A respectful critique of narrative research. *Ethics & Behavior, 11,* 191–194.

Graves, P. (1996). Narrating a psychoanalytic case study. In R. Josselson (Ed.), *Ethics and process in the narrative study of lives* (pp. 72–80). Thousand Oaks, CA: Sage.

Greenwood, D. J., & Levin, M. (2000). Reconstructing the relationships between universities and society through action research. In N. Denzin & Y. Lincoln (Eds.), *Handbook of qualitative research* (2nd ed., pp. 85–106). Thousand Oaks, CA: Sage.

Hadjistravropoulos, T., & Smythe, W. E. (2001). Elements of risk in qualitative research. *Ethics and Behavior, 11*(2), 163–174.

Holloway, W., & Jefferson, T. (2000). *Doing qualitative research differently.* London: Sage.

Hoskins, M. J. (2000). Living research: The experience of researching self, other and discourse. *Journal of Constructivist Psychology, 13,* 47–66.

Hunt, J. C. (1989). *Psychoanalytic aspects of fieldwork.* Newbury Park, CA: Sage.

Johnson, J. (2001). In-depth interviewing. In J. F. Gubrium & J. A. Holstein (Eds.), *Handbook of interview research: Context and method* (pp. 103–120). Thousand Oaks, CA: Sage.

Josselson, R. (1992). *The space between us.* San Francisco: Jossey-Bass.

Josselson, R. (1996a). On writing other people's lives. In R. Josselson (Ed.), *Ethics and process in the narrative study of lives* (pp. 60–71). Thousand Oaks, CA: Sage.

Josselson, R. (1996b). *Revising herself: The study of women's identity from college to midlife.* New York: Oxford University Press.

Josselson, R. (2004). The hermeneutics of faith and the hermeneutics of suspicion. *Narrative Inquiry, 14*(1), 1–29.

Kvale, S. (1996). *Inter-views: An introduction to qualitative research interviewing.* Thousand Oaks, CA: Sage.

Lieblich, A. (1996). Some unforeseen outcomes of conducting research with people of one's own culture. In R. Josselson (Ed.), *Ethics and process in the narrative study of lives* (pp. 172–186). Thousand Oaks, CA: Sage.

Lieblich, A. (2006). Vicissitudes: A study, a book, a play: Lessons from the work of a narrative scholar. *Qualitative Inquiry, 20*(10), 1–21.

Lincoln, Y. S., & Tierney, W. G. (2004). Qualitative research and institutional review boards. *Qualitative Inquiry, 10*(2), 219–234.

Lipson, J. G. (1994). Ethical issues in ethnography. In J. M. Morse (Ed.), *Critical issues in qualitative research methods* (pp. 333–355). Thousand Oaks, CA: Sage.

MacIntyre, A. (1984). *After virtue.* Notre Dame, IN: University of Notre Dame Press.

Malcolm, J. (1990). *The journalist and the murderer.* New York: Alfred A. Knopf.

Marcia, J. (1993).The ego identity status approach to ego identity. In J. E. Marcia, A. S. Waterman, D. R. Matteson, S. L. Archer, & J. L. Orlofsky (Eds.), *Ego identity: A handbook for psychosocial research* (pp. 22–41). New York: Springer-Verlag.

Mauthner, M. (2000). Snippets and silences: Ethics and reflexivity in narratives of sistering. *International Journal of Social Research Methodology, 3*(4), 287–306.

McLeod, J. (1994). *Doing counselling research.* London: Sage.

McLeod, J. (1996). Qualitative approaches to research in counselling and psychotherapy: Issues and challenges. *British Journal of Guidance & Counselling, 24,* 309–317.

Miles, M. B., & Huberman, A. M. (1994). *Qualitative data analysis* (2nd ed.). Thousand Oaks, CA: Sage.

Miller, M. E. (1996). Ethics and understanding. I and Thou in dialogue. In R. Josselson (Ed.), *Ethics and process in the narrative study of lives* (pp. 114–128). Thousand Oaks, CA: Sage.

Mishler, E. (1986). *Research interviewing: Context and narrative.* Cambridge, MA: Harvard University Press.

Moustakas, C. (1994). *Phenomenological research methods.* Thousand Oaks, CA: Sage.

Nelson, H. L. (2001). *Damaged identities: Narrative repairs.* Ithaca, NY: Cornell University Press.

Nussbaum, M. (1986). *The fragility of goodness.* New York: Cambridge University Press.

Ortiz, S. M. (2001). How interviewing wives became therapy for wives of professional athletes: Learning from a serendipitous experience. *Qualitative Inquiry, 7,* 192–220.

Osherson, S. (1980). *Holding on or letting go.* New York: Free Press.

Ouellette, S. (2003). Painting lessons. In R. Josselson, A. Lieblich, & D. McAdams (Eds.), *Up close and personal: The teaching and learning of narrative research* (pp. 13–28). Washington, DC: APA Books.

Patai, D. (1991). U.S. academics and third world women: Is ethical research possible? In S. Gluck & D. Patai (Eds.), *Women's words: The feminist practice of oral history* (pp. 137–153). New York: Routledge.

Poland, B. (2001). Transcription quality. In J. F. Gubrium & J. A. Holstein (Eds.), *Handbook of interview research: Context and method* (pp. 629–651). Thousand Oaks, CA: Sage.

Price, J. (1996). Snakes in the swamp: Ethical issues in qualitative research. In R. Josselson (Ed.), *Ethics and process in the narrative study of lives* (pp. 207–215). Thousand Oaks, CA: Sage.

Punch, M. (1994). Politics and ethics in qualitative research. In N. Denzin & Y. Lincoln (Eds.), *Handbook of qualitative research* (pp. 83–98). Thousand Oaks, CA: Sage.

Ramcharan, P., & Cutcliffe, J. R. (2001). Judging the ethics of qualitative research: Considering the "ethics as process" model. *Health and Social Care in the Community, 9*(6), 358–366.

Richardson, J. C., & Godfrey, B. S. (2003). Towards ethical practice in the use of archived transcripted interviews. *International Journal of Social Research Methodology, 6,* 347–355.

Riessman, C. K. (1990). *Divorce talk.* New Brunswick, NJ: Rutgers University Press.

Rosenwald, G. (1996). Making whole: Method and ethics in mainstream and narrative psychology. In R. Josselson (Ed.), *Ethics and process in the narrative study of lives* (pp. 245–274). Thousand Oaks, CA: Sage.

Sieber, J. E. (1992). *Planning ethically responsible research.* Newbury Park, CA: Sage.

Smythe, W. E., & Murray, M. J. (2000). Owning the story: Ethical considerations in narrative research. *Ethics & Behavior, 10*(4), 311–336.

Smythe, W. E., & Murray, M. J. (2001). A respectful reply to Gottlieb and Lasser. *Ethics & Behavior, 11*(2), 195–200.

Stacey, J. (1990). *Brave new families. Stories of domestic upheaval in late twentieth century America.* New York: Basic Books.

Stacey, J. (1988). Can there be a feminist ethnography? *Women's Studies International Forum, 11,* 21–27.

Stark, C. (1998). Ethics in the research context: Misinterpretations and misplaced misgivings. *Canadian Psychology, 39*(3), 202–211.

Thompson, P. (2003). Towards ethical practice in the use of archived transcripted interviews: A response. *International Journal of Social Research Methodology, 6,* 357–360.

Warren, C. A. B. (2001). Qualitative interviewing. In J. F. Gubrium & J. A. Holstein (Eds.), *Handbook of interview research: Context and method* (pp. 83–102). Thousand Oaks, CA: Sage.

Wengraf, T. (2001). *Qualitative research interviewing.* London: Sage.

Widdershoven, G. (1996). Ethics and narratives. In R. Josselson (Ed.), *Ethics and process in the narrative study of lives* (pp. 275–289). Thousand Oaks, CA: Sage.

Wolcott, H. (1994). *Transforming qualitative data.* Thousand Oaks, CA: Sage.

CHAPTER 22

In-Forming
Re-Presentations

Margot Ely

How does this title strike you? Double entendre? Quadruple? More? A title isn't everything. But it is something perhaps undervalued in crafting a narrative. Consider some of the titles that have urged you, impelled you to enter; here are a few examples that have winked seductively at me:

Teaching With Your Mouth Shut (Finkel, 2000)

Troubling Angels (Lather & Smithies, 1997)

The Professional Stranger (Agar, 1980)

Bird by Bird (Lamott, 1994)

Small Victories (Freedman, 1990)

Punished by Rewards (Kohn, 1993)

Consider some titles so deadly, pompous, and gray that they repel your attempts to enter the text or, at least, make it more difficult to do so. No examples needed.

Titles are gatekeepers. They signify the author's intent, stance, and style. At their best they hint at what's to come. This is often abetted by tacking on a colon and another explanatory phrase:

Punished by Rewards: The Trouble With Gold Stars, Incentive Plans, A's, Praise and Other Bribes

Bird by Bird: Some Instruction on Writing and Life

And yes, titles are narrative representations.

It was a thorny task for me to settle on a title for this chapter. Often, in and around my writing process, possible titles unfold like a kaleidoscope, and I want to use them all. So, my first subversive act is to share them with you in this pastiche.

A QUESTION OF TITLES

PROOF OF THE PUDDING

CRITICAL CONSTRUCTIONS

Shaping up

In-Forming

Forming

Re-Forming

Presents

Reformations

Litmus Tests

Product Line

Form to Function

Function in Form

Seeking Essence

Finals

EVOCATIONS

Voicing

More later about pastiche.

This chapter highlights representation in narrative research writing. To me, representation has at least a double-edged meaning: (1) the rhetorical forms we use in our efforts (2) to re-present, evoke, and discuss what we have lived and learned in doing narrative research. This business of creating forms that come closest to the essence of our understandings and presenting them in trustworthy ways is a crucial, ongoing, interactive dance.

In the pages that follow, I describe a variety of rhetorical forms and discuss their functions in final narrative research reports, be they dissertations, films, operas, dramas, articles, books, chapters, online presentations, lectures, or other reporting venues I have not as yet imagined. I do so out of the conviction that while the use of a variety of representational forms is accepted and supported by a vast group of colleagues—both close acquaintances and people I have never met—it is strange or not palatable to a host of other people who often influence what and how narrative research reports are written, published, and funded. I have no illusions that this chapter will magically do away with all the false "rules" and dogmatic stances about if, when, and where to use such forms and how these forms relate to "truth." This would necessitate a shift in worldview. But it seems essential to wade in to the fray, seek those who might listen and, more, who might find here additional support they need.

The clear objective is to present and sustain the view that, no matter how excellent the gathering of information, in the final instance people must want to read what we wrote, must want to stay. Toward that aim, our reports must glow with life. This not only to honor our stories but, more important, to support the ethic that undergirds them: Much, if not most, narrative research centers on information people have provided us. Whether in liberatory mode or not, narrative researchers are obligated to present the stories of those people in ways that cleave as closely as possible to the essence of what and how they shared. Rhetorical forms are key (Ely, 2003). In this chapter, I depend deeply on work done with my friend and colleague Ruth Vinz in league with our coauthors Margaret Anzul and Maryann Downing in our book *On Writing Qualitative Research: Living by Words* (Ely, Vinz, Anzul, & Downing, 1997).

These pages do not boast to be a compendium of ideas and strategies of writing, writ large. Other people have done that job well. Also sometimes not so well. However, I want to touch on several ideas about writing that seem critical to crafting representational forms. And here is as good a place as any to emphasize that while I focus on specific forms in this essay, all writing that comprises a research report contributes to a series of forms. Every word, every phrase, every citation, as well as the researcher's narrative that binds other forms together, helps make them meaningful and clarifies both the process of research as well as the findings. Thus, a research report can be, must be, conceptualized as a seamless integration of writing forms intentionally crafted to make the case, whatever the case may be.

On Research Writing and Form

Research writing is birthed from data collection writing. But it is far different. It has been transformed out of the hundreds, often thousands, of log pages, transcripts, and collected social evidences—from the raw, scribbled, unburnished, messy writing that is often characteristic of data collection—that first and essential narrative research phase, already shaped by the researcher. There the drive was to "get it down," do recursive cycles of primary analysis for in-process direction, work with a support group, and "get it down" some more. Never mind great readability, beauty, or focus on wider communication. Research writing, on the other hand, minds readability, beauty, and wider communication. The difference between data collection writing and research writing (Clandinin & Connelly, 1994) is often most poignantly experienced at the point when less experienced narrative researchers have come to what they consider to be the end of their data collection. The thought that even more, and even more important, writing is to come is often overwhelming, a surprise; the responsibility seems awesome. This is where research writing—In-Forming Re-Presentations—comes in. When I use the term *writing* in this chapter, I am talking about research writing.

Writing is often wrenchingly difficult, lonely, and upsetting. Imagine me, my behind firmly planted on a chair, struggling to write this—over and against the fact that today I am literally frozen-still as a result of reading some essays on writing and form that are more beautiful and brave than those I can ever attain. Or is this another case of the famous cop-out many writers experience as they set themselves the task? One more aspect of writing to consider.

So. Writing demands more than some of us think we possess—a propelling energy, commitment, courage, stick-to-itiveness, and a deep acceptance, one that powers the stance in this chapter, that writing is inquiry (Britton, 1982; Mayher, 1990; Richardson, 1994). Flannery O'Connor (1985) says, "I have to write to discover what I am doing. I don't know as well what I think until I see what I say; then I have to say it all over again" (p. ix). There is no getting around it. We write to know. We write to learn. We write to discover:

> I consider writing a method of inquiry, a way of finding out about yourself and your topic . . . a method of discovery and analysis. By writing in different ways, we discover new aspects of our topic and our relationship to it. Form and content are inseparable. (Richardson, 1994, p. 516)

Given most of our histories with writing, particularly in schools, it is often not easy to view writing in this light. After all, wasn't writing—hasn't it always been— boring, repetitive, uncreative, depersonalizing, someone else's talent? Yes. Perhaps. Except, of course, at those times when we ourselves deeply wished to write something meaningful. A love letter! A personal diary!

Aren't some people natural writers, and don't the rest of us fall into another category? Certainly some people have been fluid, meaningful writers all along. Those fortunates probably wonder what all the fuss is about. For the rest of us, it is exactly our history with writing and the emotions it generated and generates now that we must conquer and rise above to write with sufficient courage and joy. This "rise" I am talking about demands actively seeking to embrace what we have avoided: the power of writing drafts upon drafts, the need for constructive feedback, the trust in our tacit knowledge, the tolerance for mess and unfinished bits of thought, the battle to vanquish insecurities and anger—just an iota—so that we can move forward yet again, the need for play, the productive loneliness.

For a whole lot of us, it is crucial to accept another shift. And that is a shift in our deepest beliefs about what is worthwhile to write and what is acceptable as narrative research writing. Toward that shift, we have a great deal of support. There is now a huge body of literature on narrative inquiry methodologies (see the bibliographies in this handbook), research writing, and representation, and a host of research reports that exemplify different methodological developments.

Well, not so different actually. Take the case of Freud, as only one example. In 1893, Sigmund Freud (1893–1895) grappled with the question of form in this way:

> I have not always been a psychotherapist. Like other neuropathologists, I was trained to employ local diagnoses and electro-prognosis, and it still strikes me as strange that the case histories I write should read like short stories, and that, as one might say, they lack the serious stamp of science. I must console myself with the reflection that the nature of the subject is evidently responsible for this,

rather than any preference of my own. The fact is that local diagnosis and electrical reactions lead nowhere in the study of hysteria, whereas a detailed description of mental processes such as we are accustomed to find in the works of imaginative writers enables me, with the use of a few psychological formulas, to obtain at least some kinds of insight into the course of that affliction. Case histories of this kind are . . . an intimate connection to and between the story of the patient's sufferings and the symptoms of his illness—a connection for which we still search in vain in the biographies of their psychoses. (pp. 160–161)

Imagine how Freud might have ventured forward from suggesting the importance of story in his "case" to what he might have produced as story now. As early as 1913, Freud observed that in the future his book *Traumdeutung* (*The Meaning of Dreams*) should be revised "to include selections from the rich material of poetry, myth, usage of language [idiom], and folklore" (Langer, 1953, p. 239).

The 20th century witnessed a growing trend of such textual experimentation. In this key, Atkinson (1992) describes the literary analytical creations of specific anthropologists, ethnographers, psychologists, and sociologists of science in their quest to produce increasingly readable texts. The essence of the message about many contemporary research approaches is that they are founded on

a radical questioning of the certainty of the scholarly text; a rejection of the search for "truth" and reason as absolutes; a rejection of the moral and intellectual distance between the academic and his or her human "subjects"; a suspicion of the "big" narratives of totalizing theory. (p. 38)

When this statement is spun out to embrace narrative research writing, the following tenets seem reasonable:

1. There are many ways of coming to know something, and even then such knowing is partial.
2. There are numerous ways for us to report.
3. All our messages have agendas—personal, political, gendered, racial, ethnic.
4. Our language creates reality.
5. As researchers, we are deeply interrelated with what and who is being studied. Research is context-culture bound. So is writing.
6. Affect and cognition are inextricably united.
7. What we understand and report as social reality is multifaceted, sometimes clashing, and often in flux.
8. We cannot say that narrative reflects "the" reality. We can say that with the help of the reader, narrative creates a version of reality. (Ely et al., 1997)

The search, then, is to strive for narrative research writing that is consonant with these stances. Laurel Richardson (2000) describes the character of writing engendered by this search:

> Increasingly ethnographers desire to write ethnography which is both scientific—in the sense of being true to a world known through the empirical senses—and literary—in the sense of expressing what one has learned through evocative writing techniques and form. More and more ways of representing ethnographic works emerge. (p. 253)

Although Arthur Bochran and Carolyn Ellis (1996) are speaking about ethnographic representation, surely they are addressing all narrative research writers when they state that forms and modes of writing become part and parcel of ethnographic "method." The goal is not only to know but to feel ethnographic "truth" and thus to become more fully immersed—morally, aesthetically, emotionally and intellectually (p. 4).

This chapter considers these forms and modes of writing.

I do not intend here to set up a dichotomy of "conventional" versus "unconventional" writing, of "old" versus "new." Such dichotomies do more to stop the conversation than to nurture it. In my experience, I have met up with fascinating "conventional" research writing and deadly "unconventional" research writing. The variety of presentational forms and their functions described here, as well as others created by researchers every day, are useful because they allow for a communication of different meanings and emphases via their different conventions. They help us to tell the stories of our research. A shower of possibilities. In what follows, I want to share how some particular devices—ways of in-forming re-presentations—have worked; what they have brought to the research and to the researcher; what they have left unfinished or unanswered. Assigning such uses and effects is a slippery, always-shifting business, but I rest contentedly on the knowledge that you, as reader, will make your own meanings in any case. This will happen as you compare your experiences and ways with what is written on these pages. In a sense, here is a smorgasbord. Maybe you'll dig in right away. If not, try a bite!

The I of the Storm: First-Person Stories

I placed this section up front because in the past 5 years or so it has become increasingly clear to me that I have missed saying something in the public arena about first-person stories and the use of first person altogether.

Please read pieces of Paulette Henderson's (2005)[1] two versions about Mei Ling, an adult English as a second language (ESL) student. Both these versions stemmed from Paulette's complex analysis of her field log, qualitative research interview audiotapes, and transcripts. Consider how you see the voice and the presentation of each:

Paulette's Version 1

The reading class appears to have presented the greatest challenge to her because of her inability to understand the professor at first. ESL students usually attend writing classes that are for ESL students only.

Mei Ling tackles her reading class by concentrating on repeated readings of the text: "Sometimes I read it, but I don't understand it, so I have to read it again and again so I can get the idea." She says: "I can read the text and I can understand what the professor said, so I catch up and I get a good grade." The confidence she gains from getting good grades serves to propel her forward. She is exempted from a reading class on her first try. "So it raised my confidence since then and I continue to take other courses, and I have some perfect scores."

Paulette's Version 2

My reading class was the most difficult for me at first because I could not understand the professor. Yah! Also in this class were many people who were born here, but who still needed to improve their reading. So maybe the professor didn't think he need to speak slowly like our writing professor did. I didn't have anybody to help me at home because my husband was not living with us. But I didn't have anybody to help me in China either. So I was used to struggling by myself . . . struggling.

I always try to do everything well. I think I know how to study well and get top grades. It's very important. It gives me confidence to go ahead. And so let me tell you what I did to improve my reading. Sometimes I read it but I don't understand it. So I have to read it again and again until I can get the idea. So I catch up and I get a good grade. Yah! Doing well, getting a good grade, this raised my confidence and then I continue to take other courses and I have some perfect scores.

In Version 1, Paulette tells us her conclusion, poses some possible reasons for what she considers Mei Ling's greatest challenge, directs her readers to share her analytical insights, and uses some of Mei Ling's edited quotes to bolster her reasoning. The researcher is very much at center. Paulette created Version 2 entirely in Mei Ling's voice, also edited, woven together from transcript pieces. She shaped it to communicate what she understood to be the essence of Mei Ling's report. The participant is very much at center. In my view, the second version is more respectful of Mei Ling and more powerful in the reading. Paulette reports it was also smoother to write.

Three related issues come to mind here. First, Mei Ling is an immigrant to the United States whose first language is Chinese. The aim of some research is a complex linguistic analysis of chunks of her actual language. However, that is not the aim of narrative research and its presentation. In narrative work, Mei Ling's voice must be communicated with just enough of her own color, cadence, and usage to "show" her to the readers, all the while taking great care so that her voice cannot be used to stereotype and/or denigrate her. Atkinson (1992) puts it this way:

The reflective ethnographer will need to be sensitive to the ways in which his or her representation of speech establishes the speaking subjects as "Others" in a dialogue of difference, or assimilates them to a complicity of identity with ethnographer and reader. (p. 29)

Paulette explains:

> I deleted most pauses and repetitions, and markers like "uh, mmm, yah," all of which appeared in the transcripts where I had tried to record speech as accurately as possible. Some colloquialisms such as "gonna" and "wanna" were changed to Standard English. Not all. But I did not find it necessary to change participants' speech in order to impart a veneer of eloquence to their words. All four of them freely gave moving accounts, told with great conviction. I strove to communicate the essence of their stories without embellishment, and I believe they speak to others like themselves as well as to researchers in the field and the world beyond.

The second issue bears on how Paulette placed herself in the preceding paragraph. Heretofore in speaking of herself in the text, Paulette had explained, guided, summarized, and referred to herself as "the researcher." It is in this paragraph that Paulette finds her voice, lets us hear her own sense of the impact of her presentation strategy. Clandinin and Connelly (1994) call this "the development of voice after silence" (p. 423). Speaking up in our research texts is often difficult for a variety of reasons. Some have to do with what we have learned and continue to learn is acceptable writing in academia and publishing. Some have to do with how we see ourselves as writers. Some have to do with how we see ourselves as female or male writers. Some have to do with our own sensitivities and reticence to speak when we feel we shouldn't. After all, the aim of much of our narrative research is to provide a sense of how other people experience life. So our silence counts as we strive to give people voice or as we invite our readers to make sense rather than telling them what to think. No matter. A researcher's voice must be heard. When, how, where, what, and why are the crucial questions. If these are not asked and answered and asked again, there is no research writing.

The third issue centers on the word *creating* in my phrase "creating first-person stories." Creating is exactly what we are doing. What is on paper as an entire, unbroken story is not a verbatim replica of how it was spoken with all of its bumps, hesitations, silences, repetitions, loops, and wanderings. In the majority of cases, it is indeed a story that was crafted painstakingly from all the data with great attention to faithfully representing participants' points of view. The story is the heart of the matter. At best this story has been shared and checked with the person(s) who provided it in the first place. Paulette writes this about her participant check:

> Last Tuesday I went to see Mei Ling with both versions. After reading the third person one, she told me I did a good job and asked for a copy. After reading the first person one, she was visibly moved to tears, and without any prompting on my part, told me she liked that one best.

Before you barrage me with sighs, let me state this quickly: I am not advocating that all narrative representations must be in one form. Indeed, this chapter presents a variety of forms that may not sit easily in an "I Story": pastiche, poetry, layered stories, drama, and so on. Forms that can have great impact and utility. What I am advocating is for more attention to the power of first-person stories both for giving voice—to our participant as well as to ourselves—and for breaching as best we can the We/Other divide with its elitist noncollaborative messages.

The attempt to avoid the personal may be one of the final echoes of a dying stance; the belief that researchers must be removed, impersonal, neutral, and, at the same time, all-knowing in their texts. Most academic culture has for so long supported the distanced, dry, third-person, "neutral" research writings done by a distanced dry "neutral researcher" that opening up to the different possibilities—even probabilities—endorsed by this very book is seen by some almost like personal attack or at the least as a shock. The tide has turned. But not for all. However, there are signs of spring in the most unexpected places. For example, see these quotations from the venerable *Publication Manual of the American Psychological Association* (2001), long a standard-bearer for what is traditionally acceptable in much academic research: "Verbs are vigorous, direct communicators. Use the active rather than the passive voice, and select tense or mood carefully" (p. 41) and "Use I if you are the sole author of the paper" (p. 39). Writing "The experimenters instructed the participants" when "the experimenters" refers to yourself is ambiguous and may give the impression that you did not take part in your own study. Instead, use a personal pronoun (pp. 37–38).

The selection of voice must be a purposeful act. Emphasis on *purposeful*. It is as blind to overwrite in first person as it is narrow to stick obsessively with third. Both have their uses. However, when it is clear to the author that a text is distanced, authoritarian, and impersonal, when it is plain boring, then the danger whistles must blow, the lights must flash, and something needs to be done.

Pieces of Virtual Life: Poetry

The poet's business is to create the appearance of "experience," the semblance of events lived and felt, and to organize them so they constitute a purely and completely experienced reality, a piece of virtual life. (Langer, 1953, p. 212)

And isn't this our quest as we create narrative representations? Poetry allows for maximum input in and between the lines. Poems streamline, encapsulate, and define, usually with brevity but always with the intent to plumb the heart of the matter; to bring the reader to live the emotions, the tone, the physicality, the voiced and not-voiced moments. Poems spotlight particular events in ways that lift them out of the often overwhelming flood of life so that they can be understood as part of that. Complex business.

After years of slogging through my students' and my own interview transcripts, fighting for clarity in their diffuse rambling and knowing there must be better ways, I came upon the work of Daphne Patai (1993). Doors opened.

Patai interviewed Brazilian women to compose their life stories. She too struggled with her first transcripts, dry and cleaned up versions, until she came upon the idea of "dramatic poetry." This concept is based on Dennis Tedlock's (1983) suggestions that to get away from "the distortion that occurs when oral narratives are translated to prose" and to retain the flavor and cadences "narratives be transcribed following the pauses and inflections in the speakers speech in the form of free verse" (p. 115). Thus, Patai presented the life stories of her interviewees in such free verse. Line breaks came when the woman paused, and "groping" was symbolized by three dots. Others have added nuances to this presentation scheme, but in general, this was it.

Here is Michele Bellavita's poem from her study "Good Enough Fathers: Fathers of Toddlers Tell Their Stories"; please read it in the spirit of Patai. Let the line breaks be pauses:

Suddenly there was this Person—
on experiencing the birth of his son

We never expected three days of labor
The caesarian came as a relief by that time

And there you were—on the operating table
Awake and conscious
Behind a sheet like a curtain

And the doctor said—
"I'll tell you when it's coming out
You can get up and look."

And the midwife came in—just to be with us

So she said—so she said—
So she pulled down the curtain

And I said, "I can't—
I don't think I can watch this."

I didn't—I couldn't
Imagine what it was like

I mean—I wasn't at all squeamish
About a natural birth

But a c-section—
I was a little—
I didn't know what was coming

So the midwife—so well—
She put it back up

So she said,
"When he's out, I'll tell you
You can look."

So the doctor said—"Here he co—omes."

So I stood up
And I peeked over

And I saw him—I actually saw him
Coming out

It was just like a dream
I couldn't believe it

There was this **person**
Suddenly, there was this **person**
Suddenly—
He was just **there**

And the staff—they all started carrying on—
"It's a boy! It's a boy!"
All really excited

And it was just—it was just
Just a magical moment

I mean—he was there
He was there
I didn't know what to do

So the midwife—she said
"Well touch him—he's **yours**!"

And so I leaned over
And I put my finger
And I touched his hand

And he tipped his head back
And he looked right up at me

It was just—it was just

Wondrous!

And I'll never forget, I'll never forget
I'll never forget that moment[2]

These lines came exactly from the transcribed interview. Breaks occurred when this man paused. Michele did add a few touches; bold type when his voice became louder—more emphatic, dashes for longer silences, double spaces between stanzas that signal even longer silences. The sparseness of the presentation that encompasses such a complex and lengthy event attest to the power of what my students and colleagues now lovingly call "doing a Patai." It bears noting that Michele removed herself entirely from the poem, even though she was the interviewer and did some speaking in that role. The important person here is the father. "To situate the researcher at the center of the universe is a mistake. By doing so we are again overvaluing our role as individuals in charge" (Patai, 1993, p. 10).

Diane Austin (2004), however, had a different purpose in mind when she created the following layered poem. One voice is her participant's, a man who describes himself as a recovering alcoholic. The other voice is hers, the researcher's:

Parallel Process

"No judgment" he says.
Yeah, I think—don't we all long for that.
"Somebody to understand" he says.
Yeah, I think—don't we all long for that.
"Watching people grow and recover."
I *know* just what he means.
"Keep it simple, saved my life."
and I think about my complicated life.
"I've got to tend my garden," he says.
and I think about the weeds in mine.[3]

In this sparse presentation, Diane allows us some insight about her participant, but to me the highlight is in how much she shares about herself. There is now great emphasis on transparency in qualitative research. That is, we are to write not as unknown, all-knowing forces but as people who share our stances, methods, feelings, biases, reasoning, successes, and failures. Diane did this in five lines. Her writing breaks with an assumption of "scientific objectivity" and thus works to level the field of power relations between researchers and audience.

Brooke Smith responded directly to the issue that Patai (1993) highlights as ". . . the further distortion of conveying in English what was spoken in Brazilian Portuguese—moreover Portuguese with different regional and class characteristics" (p. 148). Brooke presents her Patai in two versions, Spanish, the language of choice of the interviewee, Maria, and English, so that those of us who do not speak Spanish can read the translation. What follows are the first three of five stanzas:[4]

Maria's Migration Story

And so I came here with her because
I think that if I came alone I wouldn't be able to handle it
I cried every day, the first days, ohh!! I cried and cried, ay! "I don't want to be here"

because
you know about what I've told you that life here is really different, well is
really different from life in my country
In my country everything is slower
here everything is . . .

And more than that I spend an hour coming here in the train
That's two hours that I lose every day in my life in the train [laughs]
So, I get to my house
I put some music on to listen to, read, ah, ah, to learn to play chess
or read a book
or play with the dog or with my birds . . .

Maria: El Cuento de la Emigración

Y yo me vine con ella porque
Yo creo que si yo vine sola yo no aguantaba bien
Yo lloraba todo los días, los primeros días ohh! ¡Lloraba y lloraba, ay! "yo
no quiero estar aquí"

porque
Tú sabes es lo que te dije la vida aquí es muy diferente, o sea es muy
diferente de la vida en mi país
en mi país todo es mas lento
Aquí todo es . . .

O sea además de eso yo digo una hora venir aquí en tren
Son dos horas que pierdo de mi vida a diario en el tren [laughs]
Entonces llego a mi casa
Y me pongo a escuchar música, a leer, ah, ah, aprender ajedrez
o a leer un libro
o jugar con el perro o con mis pajaritos . . .

When Brooke read the English version to her research writing support group, she felt it fell flat:

They ask that I read it again, in Spanish. All of a sudden I have Maria back! "Yo lloraba todo los días, los primeros días ohh! ¡Lloraba y lloraba, ay! 'yo no quiero estar aquí" she says without a breath, without a pause. And it is her. Her voice becomes alive as I read her words. I stop and look up. Everyone agrees; even though my support group members don't understand exactly what she is saying, providing her words exactly as she spoke, in her language, with the long breathless phrases and pregnant pauses, makes them more real, more meaningful. While it is true that providing the text in the original language and then the translated language does require more physical space, it gives authenticity to the words of the speaker and allows readers of that language the opportunity to read the words as they were said. Reading Patai's verse rendition of Maria's life story in Spanish is powerful because her words jump off the page.

Lisa Martin (2004) discovered that James Gee's (1999) system for narrative analysis adds a few more possibilities to hearing words on paper in order to highlight both linguistic details and situated meanings, a move in rounds from specifics to context. Attention is beamed on what participants say, how the researcher transacts, and how aspects of the environment relate to what was and was not said. Here is the first stanza of a longer piece:

Interviewer: *What's it like for you to take medication for your asthma?*

Stanza 1: Introduction

1	At first, I couldn't STAND taking medication//
2	I'm the type, I really <u>don't</u> like <u>medication</u>//
3	Cause I don't even like to take <u>pills</u>//
4	So it was <u>hard</u> for me . . . at first
5	See that's why I was <u>saying</u>
6	that Beth <u>knew</u> when I <u>didn't take it</u>//
7	It was HARD to take medication <u>for me</u>
8	cause I didn't <u>like</u> taking it.

Gee's notations are built to help in meaning making, drawing a reader's attention to loudness, emphasis, and pitch. And talking of pitch, in his book *Talk and Social Theory,* Frederick Erickson (2004) presents two chapters in which musical scores are used to signify the pitch and timing of transcripted interactions. It is impossible for my chapter to do justice to the mountain of existing analytical schemes for narrative presentation. And I doubt this is necessary. Most of these systems can be used, in their own ways, to represent an increasingly clearer picture of how things were said and meant. Toward this, the impetus has not always come from seasoned researchers. Budding researchers are amazingly inventive. They have created all sorts of helpful communication devices: various spacings, bold and gentler types, uppercase and lowercase, music notations, dance notation, different fonts, live drawings, road signs, particular punctuation, side-by-side placements, pictures, form combinations. Every one of these is meant to invite their readers to share what was witnessed and what was considered. Obviously deep desires to understand and to communicate are keys to this sort of industry.

Poetry is a special and particular device. The poems that have been shared in this section have resided in all sections of narrative research reports: acknowledgments, introductions, reviews of literature, method, findings, metadiscussions, and appendices. At times the same poem has been part of multiple sections. Poems have functioned to foreshadow, encapsulate, introduce, bolster, feel, summarize, argue, contradict, cause doubt, provide thinking space, assess, explain, lift, involve readers in analysis—and in other ways that I am sure to have omitted. This is not a call for the liberal and cavalier peppering of poems throughout the writing. It is a call for thoughtful, meaningful creation of poems and their sensitive placement so that they serve in particular ways.

Rashômon-on-the-Page: Layered Stories

In 1952, the great Japanese movie director Akira Kurosawa elated many of us with his film *Rashômon,* a story in four parts, each from the eyes of a different person about the same event: a rape and killing in the forest. Surely, other artists created layered stories before then, but for many, for me, the work was a thrilling awakening. Of course, the ideas that one event can have many meanings and that there is no such thing as an objective truth are key to narrative research. Thus, they become key to narrative research writing in the layered mode.

We never knew if the term *layered stories* had been coined before. But we made it ours as our group of colleague writers began to use it in the 1980s. This naming made sense in the search to create meaningful, consonant forms. Since then, the ranges of layered stories, or layering, in research writing has expanded happily to embrace even more rhetorical possibilities than those presented by *Rashômon.* Much of this is due to the inventiveness and courage of people new to research.

Zachary Moore does a present-day version of the *Rashômon* form by presenting his view of how three people lived the same event.[5] Zach studied life in a shelter that provided meals for people labeled *homeless*:

Please Pass the Water

Evan—A Client

> Man, I was sitting in that line forever. I must have been waiting a half an hour. All I wanted to do was come in, eat my meal and be left alone. I don't understand why we have to get here so early and wait so long to get some food. I'm starving. I just hate this place. They treat us like we are kids. . . .
>
> I hate being bothered while I eat my dinner. So, I was just sitting there, minding my own business, not bothering anybody, when this guy asks me to pass the water. He had arms. It's not like the water was far away from him. I just wanted to mind my own business and be left alone. . . . He told me that he didn't want to reach over me. Well what disturbs my meal more, him reaching over to get the water himself, or him making me stop eating so that I could get the water for his lazy ass?
>
> I'm just tired of people bothering me for what they want, but never giving a damn about what I want. So I decided to start then and there with letting every body know that I will be heard! That's why I yelled it to the whole cafeteria. They needed to know that they can't treat us like kids or make us wait in line forever just to get this crappy food. I don't care if they didn't want to listen, I was going to make them, and I did. Maybe next time I'll get a little more respect from them. Hell, they're not any better than I am. We all breathe the same air and all of our shit stinks!

Jeremy—A Client

I don't know what happened. I was just sitting there enjoying my meal. It had been a while since I have had a hot meal. I was just eating; I wasn't bothering anybody. . . . This place is ok. I can just come here, get some food, and head out again. It's nice. The food is usually pretty good too. I've never had any troubles with anyone here before.

That guy was just strange. From the moment he sat down he was grumbling something under his breath. He just seemed to be in a pissed off mood so I just didn't say anything to him. I don't know why he was so mad. He had just gotten some hot food for free. What was there to be pissed off about?

So all I did was ask him to pass the water. It was to his left and I didn't want to reach over the guy. I was thirsty, I thought I was being polite, but apparently he didn't. Have you ever seen someone get so upset over being asked to pass the water? It was really strange.

He got up to leave soon after and just started yelling things. I don't know what he was talking about. He just kept saying, "I will be heard." What the hell does that mean? The one problem with coming to a place like this is that there are a few people who are just a little crazy. When they're crazy and pissed about something they can sometimes go off. This was no big deal; he just needs to relax.

Vinnie—A Staff Member

That guy? Yea, I don't know what he was talking about as he walked out. "I will be heard." What does that mean? I mainly just watched him to make sure he wasn't gonna hit anybody. Since he was leaving I didn't say anything to him about his yelling. I'll watch out for him and keep an eye on him if he comes here again. It's no big deal. Stuff like that happens here a lot. I don't know why I'm even talking about it.

The juxtapositions, the layering, offer a rich picture for consideration. All these versions did spring from one person, Zachary. But it was a Zachary who purposely put himself into the shoes of three different people. Not such an easy task at times, especially if some characters are not as lovable to the writer as others. However, it is a task worth undertaking, worth practicing, and not only to create powerful layered stories. The attempt to understand our participants deeply, to be fair, no matter our personal opinions about them, is at the crux of narrative research. It is as dangerous to allow ourselves to be swayed by negative feelings as it is by enchantments about some of our participants. Involving oneself in writing layered stories and reflecting on them is one way of providing sufficient distance for better understanding.

Aimee Bergonia titled her layered story "Leader-Hero-Human: The Fire Department Captain."[6] Different from the "several people–one incident" form, her layers consist of three facets of the same person in communication with one another:

Sensemaker: Guys, looks like we have a fully engulfed 23-story tenement-old house. Let's do what we do—seek and rescue. Take the lead on that nozzle Lou. Alright, you . . .

Adrenaline: Alright. You know that tingling thrill that starts in your stomach? That feeling you get right before you get on that roller coaster? That spectacular rush? It's that same feeling that I get each time I know it's a real fire. You know, like when you jump in that front seat of the Coney Island Cyclone and I hear . . .

Fear: I hear my son telling me, "Dad, I don't want you to get hurt anymore." My son . . . my son telling me that he doesn't want me to get hurt. He is a good kid, smarter than I was at his age, you know, not such a cocky risk-taker like I was. Ha . . . what a kid. I love my kid, and it worries me, ahhh I need you to . . .

Sensemaker: I need you guys to take a step in with me. . . . You see how the smoke is blowing directly in your face? That's it boys, stay with me. Take another step with me. Stay low, feel the difference in the heat. Listen to the sounds around you. Keep moving toward . . .

Adrenaline: Keep moving toward the front of the line. Ahhh, the thought of the Cyclone rising slowly up, up, up, and reaching the top, right before WHOOSH . . . you know the drop? . . . The force of gravity rushes us down and I get that shot of energy, like when I walk into that burning building, filled with smoke and . . . well, the unknown. I still get it . . . I still remember . . .

Fear: I still remember my boy when he was born. I was afraid to hold him in these hands of mine, thought he might break. Ha . . . what a look he gave to me, looked right at me as if to say, hey Dad, yeah you're my Dad. I thought I was gonna cry. I want my kid to know how much I love him. I watch him at his hockey games and when he scores that goal he circles around high fivin' the guys and then he looks up into the crowd to find me. When he catches me cheerin' for him, well . . . well, you know my heart just fills up, and I think, that's my son. I want him to know that I am here for him.

Sensemaker: I want you to know that we are here for you. Can you hear me sweetheart? What's your name? Shannon? Shannon? . . . Well Shannon, me and my boys are here to get you out of this place. . . . We're gonna get you out now sweetheart.

Adrenaline: This rush for the ride that always thrills me. I need that feelin,' you know, it's a part of me. A part of my life that I do not want to . . .

Fear: A part of my life that I do not want to miss. That's what my son means to me. I don't want to miss things that are important—his hockey games, his baseball games, his first girlfriend. The weekends where we go up to that swimmin' hole and every time we get there I think I am not gonna jump in because that water is way too cold. But my son always says, "Dad, we came all this way, you gotta do it!" And then, I think to myself, "It's worth taking that long drive." To have a day with my son, I would never regret that.

> *Sensemaker:* No Sir, Chief. I would never regret crawling through that hallway. That's what I had to do.
>
> *Sensemaker:* I love the job.
>
> *Adrenaline:* I love the rush.
>
> *Fear:* I love my son.

Aimee reports that this layered story echoes her understanding of the Captain's complex mix and that the rhetorical use of repeated segues was, at first, a happy accident.

Bellwethers: Anecdotes and Vignettes

Anecdotes

Inevitably, in the process of research, some incidents, some stories, stand out like beacons. They may be brief or long, happy or unhappy. They may center on oneself as researcher, or participants, or context. They may nudge our awareness until we pay attention, or they may scream for it. What they all have in common, however, is that they carry a nugget of meaning—often crucial to insight. They are stories and more. They are called anecdotes. Max Van Manen (1990) puts it this way: "Anecdotes can be understood as methodological devices in human science that make comprehensible some notion that easily eludes us" (p. 166). It is this making comprehensible that powers the process of analysis. The following anecdote stems from a study of life in a Montessori early childhood classroom. The teacher, Janet Santos, is speaking:

> I am working with three-year-old Sergio on a math material presentation. Three-year-old Pedro hovers nearby, seemingly attending to other events in this multi-age classroom. Sergio finishes his work, and I turn to Pedro, "Let's do it Pedro! It's your turn now." Pedro replies with great indignation, "I know it already! I learned when you were with Sergio. What do you think!!!" (Ely & Matías, 2004, p. 1)

Few lines. Complex messages. This anecdote threw a bright beam on the energizing force of independent learning. For Janet, it was both a vindication of Maria Montessori's philosophy and a call to focus on and to enable more such self-motivating experiences for the children in her classroom. For us, the researchers, it shifted and intensified our observations and interviews.

Gayle Newshan's (1996) heart-wrenching anecdote was written early in the process of her research:

> I found a resident who was charting at the nurses' station and introduced myself and my task—to interview an AIDS patient who was experiencing pain. I asked if he knew any likely candidates. The resident barely looked up at me

and shrugged. But a nurse overheard me and said, "What about Jay?" The doctor said, "Sure, you could see him, but he's not really in pain. He just wants drugs. You know, he's a junkie." I said, "Well, let me talk to him anyway." I got his full name and went to his room which was down the hall.

Jay shared a room with one other patient who was not in the room at the time. After hearing about my study, he agreed to be interviewed. Jay was Black, about 5'10", slightly taller than me, of medium build. He was clean-shaven, with close-cropped hair. He wore hospital pajamas and his bedside table was bare—no flowers, no cards and no snacks piling up. He walked slightly bent over as he went to the bathroom before we began and eased himself gingerly into the bed. His face seemed somewhat older than his 32 years.

Jay told me he'd experienced severe abdominal pain for about a month. He had lost 20 pounds during that time and was feeling more and more fatigued. Although he had an alcohol and cocaine habit for ten years, he hadn't been using anything in the last two months because alcohol made him vomit. He spoke in a monotone, as if he had given up. "No one will listen to me—they think I'm faking. But my belly hurts; something's wrong!" he spoke simply, as if it were matter of fact. When we were finished, he agreed I could come back. He said he was homeless and was waiting to be placed in a single-room occupancy hotel.

When I returned a week later, Jay's face was gray and his temples and cheeks looked sunken. He was too weak to talk much. Before I left, the intern stopped by and said to him, "Jay, you could get up if you wanted. You gotta try." Turning to me, he said, "You know, there's nothing wrong with him!" I expressed my concern that he appeared to have deteriorated quite a bit since I last saw him, but the intern shrugged and walked off.

I found out later that Jay died that week. An autopsy showed a large tumor occupying more than half of his liver. (Ely et al., 1997, pp. 65–66)

Gayle's decision to flesh out her anecdote was spurred by her living its last two lines. They called out to her that the incident needed deep understanding. Prior to this, her research focus had been on hospital patients' experiences of pain. However, when she and her research support group mined the anecdote, its inherent ethical and human relations issues meshed into an urgent metaphor. While Gayle never left her first focus on pain, it now became far more contextually located. Gayle broadened out as other questions made themselves heard about hospital bureaucracy, interns' and nurses' experiences, and the possible roles of race, poverty, and disease in caring and less-than-caring interactions. I return to the possible broader impact of this anecdote in the section "Elevations: The Lift."

Vignettes

While vignettes seem quite similar to anecdotes, they are somewhat different in content and function. An anecdote is an encapsulated crucial event—often unforgettable—that provides a variety of possibilities for research direction. A vignette is a brief portrayal that captures an important slice of what has been learned.

Vignette: Bob

Bob cannot raise his hand by himself. When the boys ask the class for questions he starts his spasmodic movements. The boys are sensitive to observe this in spite of the others raising their hands. They look at him and ask, "Bob, any questions?" He is about to ask, pauses and says, "Never mind." The boys say, "Bob, ask it, we will wait. Take your time, don't worry about us. . . ." We all wait a long and silent 50 seconds. Bob starts gathering his strength and with his spasmodic movement blurts out, "Did you enjoy doing your topic? Why or why not?" (Ana Balboa-Geunthner, as cited in Ely & Matías, 2004, p. 36)

This vignette is a meaningful story about Bob as well as the others who make up his surroundings. In its essence, it characterizes life in this classroom. The writer chose this incident to illustrate growth of respect in her class. Vignettes are economical devices.

Battling Linearity: Pastiche and Other Quiltings

Diane Duggan (1998) created the pastiche at the top of the next page about Tina, a teenager of indomitable spirit. Tina had completed high school, her father had been murdered, she became pregnant by a man who didn't stay, she had a daughter Danisha, and she found out that her mother had AIDS.

This pastiche is composed entirely of snippets from interview transcripts.[7] Diane built it purposefully to focus her readers on one theme in her data: Tina's feeling that she was left out of essential family communications. Diane juxtaposed the pieces in specific ways so that we might enter and consider deeply this aspect of Tina's experience. Diane reflects on Tina's voice in the pastiche:

While I wanted to convey the participants' distinct voices, I did not want to denigrate them through overuse of unconventional spellings and thereby fall into what Preston referred to as the "Li'l Abner Syndrome" (Atkinson, 1992, p. 28). This is a decision I made while transcribing the interviews from audiotape. Thus, conventional orthography predominates in the participants' stories. However, I did preserve heritage of the Nuyorican (New York Puerto Rican) and African-American communities of which these young people are a part. I feel that these are valid and expressive linguistic forms, and not "incorrect" English. I hope that my decision will not diminish the dignity of the participants in the eyes of some readers or detract from their ability to empathize with the young people. (Duggan, 1998, p. 50)

Pastiche is the product of textual experiments that seek to challenge linear, simplistic descriptions of meaning exactly because the nature of narrative research is antithetical to such linearity. Pastiche may be composed of various chunks of data, analytical insights, layouts, multiple genres—art, musical notation, drama, poetry, photographs, layered stories, diaries, parodies, picture strips, multivoice accounts, collage, in various configurations built to provide a meaningful whole. What is

DISCLOSURE

My mother didn't tell me that she was sick for a long time. She told my two sisters first. I don't know who I was living with then. I know I wasn't home. I didn't know until my aunt told me.

I DIDN'T KNOW NOTHING.

Tina's twelve year old sister Melissa is sitting on the living room couch watching TV. Her mother is sitting quietly on a chair nearby. Suddenly the mother stands up.

Mother: "No!"
Melissa: "Mom, what's the matter? Why'd you say that?"
Mother: "I got it"
Melissa: "You got what?"
Mother: "I got the virus. The AIDS virus."

Melissa begins to cry and walks over to her mother and hugs her.

Melissa: "Don't worry Mom, everything's gonna be ok. (pauses) We gotta tell Lashawn when she gets home. And what about Tina?"
Mother: "I don't know. I just don't know."

The two cry quietly, embracing in the middle of the living room.

It was a couple days before Christmas. My aunt said, "Tina, you know what your mother got?" And I was like, "What?" And she was like, "She got what I got." And I said, "What you mean?" But when she said that, I automatically knew, cause my mother told me about her.

We had brung it up somehow, I don't remember. My mother said, "Auntie is sick. She got the AIDS virus." My heart just dropped. I didn't even know how to act when my aunt walked back in the house, cause she was staying with us for a couple of days. My mother said, "Don't say nothing. Let her tell you. Cause she might not want you to know." And I was like, "Ok, I'm not gonna say nothing."

I took it calmly, cause I didn't want to look suspicious. I waited til my aunt told me she had the virus. Then I said I didn't know. She said, "You didn't know I had it?" I didn't want to say yeah, cause my mother said don't say nothing. So I said, "No, I didn't know." She said, "I thought they told you." I said, "Auntie, when it comes down, you know nobody tells me nothing."

I DIDN'T KNOW NOTHING.

So, I knew about my mother, but I didn't bring it up until I was pregnant with Danisha. She never said anything to me about herself, cause she didn't know how to tell me. My mother and me, we didn't talk. But when I was pregnant with Danisha I felt like, it's better for me to try to get the tightness with my mother now.

Me and my sisters was in the kitchen, and my mother was coming back from somewhere. As she was walking in the door, I said to my sister, "Do you know about Mommy? Do you know about our mother got AIDS?" She say yea. And my mother say yea. I didn't talk to her until she told me first. And then I told her that I didn't know. Again. Like I told my aunt.

I DIDN'T KNOW NOTHING.

And then we talked about, am I gonna be alright when she leaves. I told her yeah.

more, these "wholes" always communicate more than the pieces of which they are composed.

I began this chapter with a pastiche of some possible chapter titles that were whirling around my brain. That pastiche is about me, the author. It is presented also to draw my readers into the conundrum of title making that I believe we all experience at one time or another. Diane's pastiche is about Tina, her participant. Of course, by the way she constructed it, it is also about Diane. Diane used a three-column format in which the reader can move horizontally as well as vertically. I chose to form my pastiche into a question mark. Thus, the very shape of the entire pastiche sends messages. Furthermore, its shape, as well as its contents, creates a texture that opens up the possibility of lifting to yet more insights, more meanings than were inherent at first glance in its pieces or its shape. Pastiches invite readers to make their own.

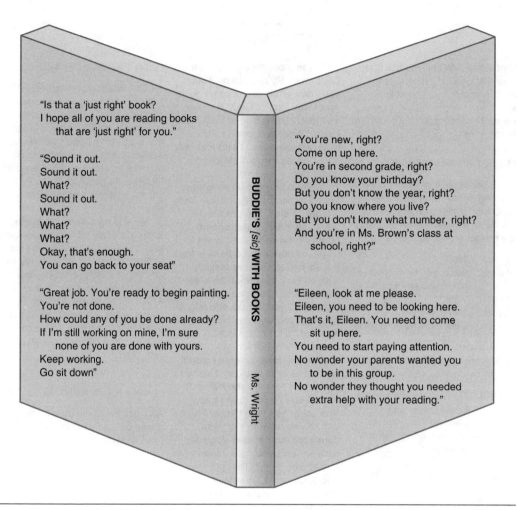

Figure 22.1   *Buddie's* [sic] *With Books:* A Text by Ms. Wright

Eliza Ross's pastiche centers on her study of life in a community center that provides urban children of poverty with after-school programs. Please enter. What do you understand? What do you feel?

Eliza's piece is a character study of one teacher, bounded in time and context. It becomes clear almost immediately that the title of the pastiche belies its contents. In juxtaposition, the title and the contents of the pastiche open up the possibility of perhaps sarcastic, perhaps sad, perhaps angry, perhaps multimeanings. Eliza created her pastiche from field observation entries[8] (see Figure 22.1). She writes this:

> Ms. Wright made it too easy, really. I went back to my field notes from the first day I observed the Buddies with Books program [or, as her handwritten sign referred to the reading program she led for the first through third graders, "Buddie's with Books"].

Of course, it is fairly simple to paint a negative picture of nearly anyone by including only the things they say or do that demonstrate those traits while neglecting the positive ones that conflict with the chosen characterization. For my pastiche to be useful as a form of analysis, rather than just an artistic endeavor, I needed to show the full picture, even if culling only the negative or nasty statements might have made for a more powerful pastiche.

And so, to avoid skewing the data for the sake of the art, I set out to include *all* of the feedback she offered the youth participants, both positive and negative. Do not let the nature of the text fool you: it is *all* here. The analysis writes itself. One line—"Great job. You're ready to begin painting"—covers the extent of positive feedback she offered in the entire hour during which I observed. The remaining text demonstrates the overarching attitude and tone she maintained throughout the class.

The pastiche offers an ideal analytic form for this situation. Without the distraction of the physical descriptions and bracketed editorial asides that dilute the strength of Ms. Wright's own words in my field log, the ratio of negative to positive responses becomes unavoidable when culled as poem.

As I fought with the word processing program to do the layout, I began to see the space I had created in the image as an opportunity to provide the necessary context to support the text and to do so in a way that matched its minimalism. The spine of a book, after all, holds the book's title and author. Ms. Wright, then, was not just the speaker but the titlist and author of this text, this poem, this story, this tragedy. The irony of the program's name—typified not only by the misspelling of a word but by the certain lack of partnership/buddyship—is highlighted. Her role as author—as the speaker of these words, as the one in *charge* of the *partnership*—is featured.

Here in the pastiche, there is nothing superfluous to obscure the language of a reading teacher who works with poor, urban youth. Thus Eliza's sparse pastiche functions both to involve readers in her research experience and to forcibly trigger their pedagogical stances and emotions.

Pastiche can re-create, push the boundaries of distance, time, voice, physicality, directionality, participation. All in severely economical ways. Oftentimes, pastiche can send messages and trigger thinking far more complex than implied by their brevity. One might think that their often complex demands on readers would make it difficult to enter and to play by the rules. Not so in my experience. Readers delight in the invitation:

I was intrigued by the presentation of analytic data in a format that displayed words within a visual context. I was impressed by The Destructive Path of Addiction. The visual depicting addiction as a tornado with its many victims bordering along its path touched my eyes, heart and soul. The picture drew me in, and I slowly and carefully read every word on the page—thinking about how awful it would be, feeling how awful it must be, to be one of the victims— a parent, a child or a spouse. What an amazing way to communicate data to readers! (Kathy Isoldi[9])

Students delight in the learning:

I found the exercise in constructing pastiche to be the most fruitful thus far. The nature of the endeavor—the effort to build around a theme to create a textual representation of my reflection on my log—prompted deep, meaningful contemplation of my log. I pored over it, hoping to recognize an emergent theme, set of themes, or map of the narrative that might shed new light on the experience, specifically the experience of the participants in my study. After a while, a leitmotiv emerged, one I hadn't previously focused on too intently. (Michael Guinan[9])

And seasoned researchers-writers delight in pushing the envelope:

Pastiche produces a texture—a weave of co-existing meanings. . . . Every piece of text harbors traces of other related texts. Julia Kristeva (1980), semiotician and psychoanalyst, named the blend of signs *intertextuality*. "Any text is constructed as a mosaic of quotations; any text is the absorption and transformation of another" into a new articulation of meaning (p. 66). Thus, arrangements of *text* impinge so that each text acts upon another until a *texture* results. The effect is kinetic, giving a dynamic quality and a sense of immediacy as the separate pieces deliver new meaning, at times complementary and at others contradictory. (Ruth Vinz, as cited in Ely et al., 1997, pp. 98–101)

Making the Future: Drama

Drama, though it implies past action (the situation), moves not toward the present, as narrative does, but toward something beyond: it deals essentially with commitments and consequences. Persons, too, in drama are purely agents—whether consciously or blindly, makers of the future. (Langer, 1953, p. 307)

Drama throws purposeful light on a mesh of actions, words, and surroundings of particular events in an effort to communicate their essence. For narrative research, dramas are most often read from the page. Drama always happens in the present even when it is located in the past or future. But it is more than a recounting of what is happening, has happened, or might happen. If the drama works, the substance of the temporal happening, the contextualization, offers readers layered, nuanced pictures that make sense of often puzzling, complex events—pictures meant to trigger understandings, feelings, and considerations about past, present and future.

Lynn Becker Haber's (Becker, 1995) *Playlet in Two Voices* was written out of her research in one kindergarten classroom. The following field log entries provide a context for her playlet:

On October 11, Lynn wrote this:

I decide to spend the next few minutes at the table where Walter has been playing with dominoes. When I return to that table, Walter is sitting next to another boy, and they are both working on puzzles. Walter is telling the other boy, William that he will be his friend and that William won't have to worry about not having any friends in the classroom. As Walter is saying this, William silently works on his puzzle. Sue, the teacher, comes over and separates the boys to different tables.

On November 8, Lynn wrote the following:

At one points, she (Sue) tells Walter, who is sitting on a chair, that he didn't put his jacket away properly and that he should go back and fix it. Walter says, "Oh yeah. That's right," and rushes back to his cubby to pick up his jacket. As he starts to walk back to his chair, he says, "May I" and Sue cuts him off and says, "No, you may not get a mat. Now sit down quietly." Walter has a pained expression on his face, and he looks as if he is about to cry. He sits down at a table and says, "I want to lie down for my nap."

And now, a piece of Lynn's *Playlet in Two Voices—Kindergarten.*[10] As you read it, please consider the varied roles of dialogue here. You may opt to read this playlet aloud with another person so that each of you takes the part of one of the two characters. You may opt to read it silently and hear the words in that way. Plays invite reader choice.

Playlet in Two Voices—Kindergarten

Walter: It's naptime, and I'm so glad Miss Harris let me have a mat today. Last week I was so tired, and all I wanted to do was lie down and rest before snack time.

Teacher: *I'm going to put on a record that I know all of you will really like. It's from Peter Pan.*

Walter: My favorite Peter Pan song. I can fly! I love this song. I have to sit up to hear this. I want so much to sing along with this.

Teacher: *Close your eyes and listen carefully. Relax every part of your bodies.*

Walter: I want so much to sing along with this. I have to sit up.

Teacher: *Keep your bodies still. Relax your toes, and your feet, and your legs.*

Walter: I can fly! I can fly!

Teacher: *Keep still now.*

Walter: I'm Superman!

Teacher: *Your mouths shouldn't be moving.*

Walter: I have to take my sweater off. I'm so warm now.

Teacher: *Relax your stomachs and your arms.*

Walter: I'll just hold it in my lap and she won't care.

Teacher: *You shouldn't be wearing that.*

Walter:	I wish I could really fly like Superman.
Teacher:	*Keep your bodies still and lie down while you listen to the music.*
Walter:	I can't sit still anymore. I want to fly out of this room.
Teacher:	*Put it on now. You just got over being sick.*
Walter:	Maybe I could turn my sweater into a great cape.
Teacher:	*Now, Walter!*

It seems perfectly obvious that Lynn created this play. The teacher's voice was constructed from Lynn's field note observations of Sue's verbal and nonverbal classroom behaviors. Walter's voice was inferred almost entirely from his nonverbal behaviors. In crafting the play, Lynn selected, shaped, arranged, juxtaposed, and rearranged to present this streamlined, heavily meaning-laden piece. Furthermore, its brevity speaks volumes—volumes that transport me to consider my own professional life. Lynn's play fuses emotions and understandings.

Essentially, for me, if narrative research drama does not help us to see future possibilities—what to do similarly, differently, what broader social actions to consider, what to avoid—then it is not worth writing. Lynn, too, indicated that were she to develop her playlet in the future, she would document and interweave more of the teacher's verbalized motives into the piece. Lynn reflected on her prime purpose for writing her play:

> I saw this particular piece of writing as more than an attempt to express classroom life from Walter's point of view. It was my attempt to understand how Walter thinks and to experience something of his struggle for a sense of power and voice in this environment. For me this kind of writing is not "frills" in qualitative research. It seems to be an important and necessary part. "Becoming the other" or using the first-person "I" helps me get beyond the limits of being in the "researcher" mode. This kind of writing seems to be more honest in some ways than writing that aims to be "objective."

Readers who wish to explore further the possibilities of the use and functions of drama in research writing may be interested in the work of Carole Di Tosti (1993). Carole's dramas comprised entire chapters of her dissertation, which reported on several whistle-blowers in education.

Drama presents a unique opportunity to create a close, sometimes seamless fit between what we have experienced and learned in one narrative inquiry and what we find essential to share. In its three-dimensionality-on-paper, drama can broaden understandings of themes, metathemes, contexts, social/political/cultural/economic surrounds, the players, the complex researcher, and the pulse of the story. Furthermore, the flow of time inherent in drama need not be linear but can dip back and forth between futures, pasts, and presents. In a deep sense, drama is a clarion call for a future that might yet be.

Elevations: The Lift

Lift!

Dig in, dig deeper.

Bin, sort, chunk,

Shape, winnow, layer, weave,

Lift!

Dig in, dig deeper.

Push into it, pull it apart,

Probe, and

Lift. (Joan Zaleski, as cited in Ely et al., 1997, p. 162[11])

As they work their way through the early stages of research writing, just when researchers cannot imagine yet one more task, I am known to stamp, plead, and demand "Lift! Lift!" As I see it, all analysis is basically sorting and lifting (Ely et al., 1997). Throughout their work, and particularly in this final phase, narrative researchers must inevitably seek to reach increasingly broader, more nuanced understandings of what they have studied and to write in forms that honor such complexities.

I want to be understood here. The term *lifting* is often seen in counterproductive ways. In the case of narrative research writing, lifting is never a matter of priority, of reaching the "highest, most important" findings. That view is both simplistic and dangerous. Indeed, all pieces of the presentation are equally important. If that were not so, the lifting would be baseless. Lifting is a matter of intent. It is the researcher's product from striving to make overarching meanings. It is created in order to reach out to a wider audience to share those meanings and to address broader social/professional issues. For this and related matters on judging the quality of research reports, please see the useful article by Lincoln and Guba (1990).

Joan Zaleski (Ely et al., 1997) was working on her qualitative pilot project when she wrote the poem that opens this section. In the accompanying analytic memo to her support group, she wrote that she had no idea how complex analysis and interpretation of qualitative data could become and that she now looked back on her first efforts at "sorting and lifting" as "flabby and shallow." It stands to reason that this could only have been realized in hindsight!

Metathemes are one powerful device that provides a basis for lifting an interpretive presentation. Whereas a theme statement is usually drawn from analysis of particular "bins" of data for one or several participants (Wolcott, 2001), a metatheme is more frequently drawn from the entire body of data or from a particularly powerful finding. It is an overarching thematic statement that may be discussed in the light of extant literature and experience. Metathemes also may have the "meta" quality of reflecting back on the research process as well as on the findings (see Ely et al., 1997, chaps. 4 and 5, for extensive discussion and examples).

In Juanita Mendez's (2004) study of the parenting experiences of long-term incarcerated men, one strong theme that ran through her interview narratives was the concern of these fathers that their children not follow in their footsteps, follow the call of the streets, and wind up in prison themselves. This led to the metatheme "The social conditions that provided a context for the inmates' early lives are still prevalent in the lives of a younger generation" (p. 211). Juanita then discussed this in light of a body of literature about street culture, which had been home for most of her participants as they grew up.

Here Jay Pecora shares his lift experience. Jay carried out and studied drama in education about the Holocaust with his high school students:

As you know, I have always had a little anxiety about my ability to go "meta." I create codes, and bins, but moving from local findings to metathemes is often troublesome for me. In this final writing of my dissertation it worried me a bit that I didn't have the lifts I need.

Then the other night I had a dream. The details have mostly left me now. I recall a large market and moving amongst the large crowd. There was also a child in there, mine, but not real, who died. Grief.

When I woke up I was so struck by the powerful images and feelings the dream evoked that I began to think about the implications it had for my life. The metatheme of "control" began to rattle around in my head. "Why is control so important?" I wondered. I could see some areas where I felt like I had little or no control. Lying there, in the dark with the traffic sounds filtering in from outside it hit me: "many of the themes in my data are about control!" [12]

I started to run through the themes. Student resistance, my use of humor and swearing, outside world barging in, and others all seemed to fit within this umbrella of control. So now, as I rewrite my method chapter and begin on findings, I have my first metatheme to work on. I still have to do some more exploration before I am certain there is a good fit, but I feel I am on the right track. So the moral of this story? Be open to everything when lifting!

I commend to you the power of dreams and of all the odd, seemingly unrelated moments in the day that produce "Aha" moments when you least expect them—moments that enrich research writing. Mine come during the night and early in the morning just before arising. Keep a pad and pencil ready.

Just as Jay found the metaphor of "control," researchers often identify a metaphor that embodies the essence of their metathematic interpretation. Laurie Knis-Matthews's (2004) metaphor of the "cyclone of addiction" was referred to by Kathy Isoldi on page 589. Laurie's research focus was on the reported parenting experiences of persons who were in a year-long substance abuse rehabilitation program. Based on her own experiences as a counselor in substance abuse programs of shorter duration, Laurie selected a setting that offered a long-term program with a parenting component. Over months of in-depth interviews with her participants, she documented the strength of the pull of drug addiction in their lives. For most of them this outweighed the pull of family ties or any personal ambition. The force of addiction was so strong that some of the staff and the director at this facility, who had been former users, were themselves drawn back into addiction while the study was in progress. Laurie opened the chapter devoted to metathematic analysis with a powerful graphic of a cyclone that pulled in and destroyed everything within its reach.

An anecdote in an earlier section described the experience of Gail Newshan (1996) as she observed over time the death of a patient in a hospital. Her original research focus had been on hospital patients' experiences of pain. The event described in her study acted as a revelation to her, pointing beyond the experience of physical pain to broader questions she had not yet considered. Physical pain became a metaphor for broader social issues—the pain in her profession that some patients' sufferings are taken more seriously than others, to the pain of social injustice in society.

Findings that are "moments of revelation," powerful enough to address larger professional and social issues, are also at times powerful enough to challenge conventional thinking or existing paradigms. When Allan Weidenbaum (2005) was in the midst of writing up his findings about his study of African American women with HIV/AIDS, he frequently and urgently said, "These women aren't victims. They're survivors." One of Allan's metathemes became "Chronic conditions can inspire people in marginalized populations to develop strengths and resources that permit them to exceed the expectations of society" (p. 158). In his discussion, Allan addressed an issue with which he was professionally familiar: that as health care professionals focus on the traumatic and devastating effects of chronic illness, they often fail to recognize potentially life-transforming experiences.

Not every narrative researcher presents major findings in the forms of themes and metathemes. Nor is this necessary. Not everyone discovers an overarching metaphor. But at some point in their writing, narrative researchers must communicate important, binding ideas and insights about what it all meant to them, what they learned, and what this might mean to others. The major ideas may be illuminated in a variety of rhetorical and nonrhetorical forms—some of which have been described in this chapter—they may be titled with one word or many or none. But they must be addressed.

When All Is Said and Done: Persona

I just love Toots Thielemans. His plaintiff, playful, magnificently melodic weavings almost—but just almost—put to lie that they flow from a tiny harmonica. I always know when Toots is playing. Whether backing or partnering Diane Krall, Luis Bonfa, Bill Evans, Stephane Grappelli, Ivan Lins, Billy Joel, Quincy Jones, Sonny Rollins, Frank Sinatra, The London Symphony, Kenny Rankin, whether faintly heard in the background as Carrie and Big ride through Central Park or as the Sesame Street citizens do their thing, I have no doubt that Toots is on hand. He plays like no one else: subtle, supportive, inventive, open, light, assured. For me he has persona.

When it comes to research writers, some authorities (Clandinin & Connelly, 1994; Geertz, 1988) speak of the phenomenon of writing with a distinct authorial presence as "signature." That makes sense. After all, each signature is quite uniquely personal. However, for me, the term *persona* allows for a more complex view: one that fuses a distinct, consistent authorial presence with a distinct, consistent professionalism and ethical stance. This ethic does not speak its name. It is inherent.

A few of the names on my "persona list": Mahatma Gandhi, Stephen Sondheim, Thelonius Monk, Georgia O'Keefe, Michael Jordan, David Mamet, Mabel Mercer, Brancusi, Norman H. Davila, Martin Luther King, Jr., Pedro Albizu Campos, Rosa Parks, Maradona, Kathe Kollwitz. While most of these people are not writers, they all meet the criteria for communicating persona in their particular spheres. Each makes a personal, identifiable statement; each does so with integrity. For narrative research writers, it is necessary but not sufficient to put a personal stamp on one's work. That work must also clearly stand for something. It must contribute.

The focus on persona is inextricably related to narrative in-forming re-presentations. When the research writing is complete, when all has been said and done—well, let us say all that is possible within the life space of the research tasks—that product stands on its own, is most often read on its own. At this point the issue of persona is paramount.

The presentation gives the author away. If it is dry, distanced, diffuse, elitist—that speaks worlds. The presentation speaks as an entity: by what is said and not said, by how the author shares voice of self and that of others, by how the reader is invited in, by the variety and impact of its rhetorical forms, by its verbal and non-verbal messages about people. Taken as a whole, the piece meshes into a tapestry that signifies the unique spirit and ethic of its author.

Persona can be, usually is, an almost unexamined, taken-for-granted presence because we write who we are. But this is not sufficient. Purposeful reflection on and attention to constructing the whole must power researchers to shape authorial persona. Thus, we come closer to being the writers we long to be.

It is true that this chapter deals with presentation forms. By themselves many of them don't look like narratives—stories—at all. However, their sole purpose is to strengthen the readability of the whole text so that readers may envision cohesive complex, meaningful stories about people's lived and relived experiences.

In the final say, it is not the fragments that move us but a wholeness that speaks to the mind and heart.

Author's Note: The author gratefully acknowledges the following colleague contributors: Michelle Bellavita, Margaret Anzul, Kathy Isoldi, Michael Guinan, Tina Curran, Judith McVarish, Brooke Smith, Zachary Moore, Eliza Ross, Joshua Schreier, Aimee Bergonia, Jody Polleck, Belen Matias, Joan Zaleski, Elizabeth Quintero, and Jay Pecora.

Consulting Editors: Amos Hatch and Becky Atkinson

Note

1. Citations in this chapter fall into three categories: (1) Citations from the literature are in standard APA format. (2) Citations from published writing by students/colleagues are first mentioned by author's full name and year of publication, for example, Paulette Henderson (2005). In ensuing discussion, I use first name. (3) Citations from unpublished writing by students/colleagues are first mentioned by author's full name, for example, Eliza Ross. In ensuing discussion, I use the first name.

   These excerpts are reprinted with permission of Paulette Henderson.
2. The poem is reprinted with permission of Michelle Bellavita.
3. The poem is reprinted with permission of Diane Austin.
4. The poem is reprinted with permission of Brooke Smith.
5. Reprinted with permission of Zachary Moore.
6. Reprinted with permission of Aimee S. Bergonia.
7. The pastiche is reprinted with permission of Diane Duggan.
8. The pastiche is reprinted with permission of Eliza Ross.
9. These comments are reprinted with permission of Kathy Isoldi and Michael Guinan.
10. The playlet is reprinted with permission of Lynn Becker Haber.
11. Reprinted with permission of Joan Zaleski.
12. Reprinted with permission of Jay Pecora.

References

Agar, M. H. (1980). *The professional stranger: An informal introduction to ethnography.* New York: Academic Press.

American Psychological Association. (2001). *Publication manual of the American Psychological Association* (5th ed.). Washington, DC: Author.

Atkinson, P. (1992). *Understanding ethnographic texts.* Newbury Park, CA: Sage.

Austin, D. (2004). *When words sing and music speaks: A qualitative study of in depth music psychotherapy with adults.* Unpublished doctoral dissertation, New York University.

Becker, L. (1995). *Autobiography and teacher education: A qualitative study of three student teachers.* Unpublished doctoral dissertation, New York University.

Bochran, A., & Ellis, C. (1996). Taking ethnography into the twenty-first century: introduction. *Journal of Contemporary Ethnography, 25*(1), 3–5.

Britton, J. (1982). *Prospect and retrospect: Selected essays of James Britton.* Montclair, NJ: Boynton/Cook.

Clandinin, D. J., & Connelly, F. M. (1994). Personal experience methods. In Y. Lincoln & N. Denzin (Eds.), *Handbook of qualitative research* (1st ed., pp. 413–427). Thousand Oaks, CA: Sage.

Di Tosti, C. (1993). *Whistleblowers: The experience of a superintendent and teacher who exposed corruption in their school system.* Unpublished doctoral dissertation, New York University.

Duggan, D. (1998). *Out here by ourselves: The stories of young people whose mothers have AIDS or have died of the disease.* Unpublished doctoral dissertation, New York University.

Ely, M. (2003). Braiding essence: Learning what I thought I knew about teaching qualitative research. In R. Josselson, A. Lieblich, & D. P. McAdams (Eds.), *Up close and personal* (pp. 215–238). Washington, DC: American Psychological Association.

Ely, M., & Matías, B. (2004). *Montessori voices from the field.* Chicago: American Montessori Society.

Ely, M., Vinz, R., Anzul, M., & Downing, M. (1997). *On writing qualitative research: Living by words.* London: Falmer Press.

Erickson, F. (2004). *Talk and social theory: Ecologies of speaking and listening in everyday life.* Cambridge, UK: Polity Press.

Finkel, D. L. (2000). *Teaching with your mouth shut.* Portsmouth, NH: Boynton/Cook.

Freedman, S. G. (1990). *Small victories: The real world of a teacher, her students, and their high school.* New York: Harper & Row.

Freud, S. (1893–1895). *Case history: Fräulein Evon R* (J. Strachey, Trans.). London: Hogarth Press.

Freud, S. (1913). *The interpretation of dreams* (A. A. Brill, Trans.). New York: Macmillan.

Gee, J. P. (1999). *An introduction to discourse analysis: Theory and method.* New York: Routledge.

Geertz, C. (1988). *Works and lives: The anthropologist as author.* Cambridge, UK: Polity Press.

Henderson, P. (2005). *Staying power: The experience of ESL students at an urban community college.* Unpublished doctoral dissertation, New York University.

Knis-Matthews, L. L. (2004). *The experiences of six parents who are substance dependent and in a year-long drug treatment program.* Unpublished doctoral dissertation, New York University.

Kohn, A. (1993). *Punished by rewards: The trouble with gold stars, incentive plans, A's, praise and other bribes.* New York: Houghton Mifflin.

Kurosawa, A. (Director). (1952). *Rashômon.* Tokyo, Japan: Daiei Co.

Lamott, A. (1994). *Bird by bird: Some instruction on writing and life.* New York: Pantheon Books.

Langer, S. (1953). *Feeling and form.* New York: Scribner.

Lather, P., & Smithies, C. (1997). *Troubling the angels: Women living with HIV/AIDS.* Boulder, CO: Westview Press.

Lincoln, Y., & Guba, E. (1990). Judging the quality of case study reports. *International Journal of Qualitative Studies in Education, 3*(1), 53–59.

Martin, L. (2004). *The wide river of chronic illness: The experience of four women with asthma in an inner-city clinic setting.* Unpublished doctoral dissertation, New York University.

Mayher, J. S. (1990). *Uncommon sense: Theoretical practice in language education.* Portsmouth, NH: Boynton/Cook.

Mendez, J. (2004). *Personal narratives of long-term incarcerated African American men on the meaning of fatherhood.* Doctoral dissertation, New York University, University Microfilms, Ann Arbor, UMI No. 3124955.

Newshan, G. (1996). *Is anybody listening? A phenomenological study of pain in hospitalized persons with AIDS.* Unpublished doctoral dissertation, New York University.

O'Connor, F. (1985). *Preface.* New York: Farrar, Straus and Giroux.

Patai, D. (1993). *Brazilian women speak: Contemporary life stories.* New Brunswick, NJ: Rutgers University Press.

Richardson, L. (1994). Writing: A method of inquiry. In N. Denzin & Y. Lincoln (Eds.), *Handbook of qualitative research* (pp. 516–529). Thousand Oaks, CA: Sage.

Richardson, L. (2000). Evaluating ethnography. *Qualitative Inquiry, 2*(6), 253–255.

Tedlock, D. (1983). *The spoken word and the work of interpretation.* Philadelphia: University of Pennsylvania Press.

Van Manen, J. (1990). *Researching lived experience: Human science for an action sensitive pedagogy.* London, Canada: University of Western Ontario.

Weidenbaum, A. (2005). *Reversing the script: Six African American women living with HIV/ AIDS who are winning a losing battle.* Unpublished doctoral dissertation, New York University.

Wolcott, H. F. (2001). *Writing up qualitative research* (2nd ed.). Thousand Oaks, CA: Sage.

PART VII

Future Possibilities

The final part of the handbook engages readers in considerations about the promise of narrative inquiry. Nona Lyons turns our attention to the realm of policy and practice and responds to the questions about how narrative inquiry as research methodology can respond to the pressing issues emerging around policy and practice. Lyons points out a paradox when she notes that in the United States there is a present-day narrowing of what counts as scientific research, a view that would not include narrative inquiry, at the same time when there is an unprecedented growth in the uses of, and interest in, exploring narrative inquiry as research methodology.

In the last chapter we hear the voices of significant figures in the field of narrative inquiry, individuals who have shaped the field and continue to provide leadership and direction to the field. They take on some of the pressing issues that the field faces within the discipline of narrative inquiry but also within the larger field of research methodology. Amia Lieblich, Don Polkinghorne, and Elliot Mishler offer their insights on what it means to engage in ethically responsible narrative inquiry, the challenges of learning to engage in narrative inquiry, and the larger questions around the place of narrative inquiry on the methodological landscape.

Finally, in contemplation of the promise of narrative inquiry, we looked back across the handbook through the creation of the introductions. As we considered the introductions to the different parts of the handbook, we saw that our introductions might begin another kind of conversation. They might help narrative inquirers in their search for ways in which to talk across boundaries and borderlands. As we begin a second conversation that weaves across the chapters, we see possibilities for engaging each other in ways that will push the work of narrative inquirers into new conversations, new possibilities. While we realize some of these conversations will be tension filled, we also sense those who work in the field are ready to engage in these difficult conversations.

—*D. Jean Clandinin*

CHAPTER 23

Narrative Inquiry

What Possible Future Influence on Policy or Practice?

Nona Lyons

To address today the likely influence of narrative inquiry and its methodologies on future policy and practice is to grapple with a daunting challenge and a paradox, a seeming contradiction having international implications. On the one hand is the remarkable, meteoric rise of narrative inquiry research, still dazzling as it races into new fields and disciplines—an aspect of a critical phenomenon of at least 30 years known as the "interpretive turn" (Mitchell, 1981; Rabinow & Sullivan, 1979/1987). In contrast is the present, precipitous narrowing of the definition of what counts as valid education research, especially for qualitative research, of which narrative is a part.[1] Scientifically based research (SBR), coming to be known as the *gold standard*, is now the single acceptable standard for education research, one that calls for the use of experimental designs with randomized trials. Advocated by the U.S. government's National Research Council (NRC) in its report *Scientific Research in Education* (NRC, 2002), it was enacted into the No Child Left Behind Act (NCLB, 2001), presumably to insure research that yields predictable outcomes of educational practices and thus effective government policies. This unprecedented action is expected to have a significant, if deleterious, impact, not only on American but international research because of its effect on research funding and the international nature of much of today's research.[2] Given this context, with its unique tensions between narrative's unparalleled growth and the potentially crippling impact of the new NRC research standard, what influence can/or might narrative inquiry research have on future policy and practice?

Introduction: A Brief Survey of Concepts and Aims

As a practitioner of narrative research for nearly 25 years, I have a decided interest in this discussion. But my aim here is to open alternative perspectives on the current controversy to assess the future possibilities for narrative inquiry and its research. In sum, I consider narrative inquiry to be a scientific endeavor in which narrative is simultaneously story, a way of knowing, and a mode, a method of inquiry.[3] It thus reveals how it shares in narrative's ancient roots, in meanings derived from the Latin *gnarus* ("knowing," "acquainted with," "expert," "skillful") and *narro* ("relate," "tell") from the Sanskrit root *gna* ("know") (White, 1981). But narrative *inquiry* is a term today covering a diverse range of approaches and of methods of analyzing narrative accounts (Mishler, 1995). In this chapter, I focus on the intersection of the *uses* of narrative inquiry and the current controversy, examining both how present government policy is influencing narrative inquiry and its practices and how narrative inquiry is itself informing new education practices that have policy implications.

At least two surprising but significant dimensions of the paradox shape this discussion. First, how debate over the government's claim as final arbiter of what counts as scientific research is resurfacing and reinvigorating the long contested history of the role of interpretation as a part of the human sciences. Second, in an emerging dimension, how the expanding use of narrative appears to be decidedly an educative one for several professions, tying the current controversy about the validity of education research directly to the future edge of narrative itself. In this chapter, I open with a brief context and take up these issues to do three things:

1. *To examine the current controversy surrounding what should count as "scientifically based research,"* especially identifying the terms of the controversy—that is, how the issues raised by the NRC report are delineated, how they are justified and responded to, and where narrative intersects this debate. The controversy—directed in particular to qualitative research in education—is examined primarily through current and ongoing discussions being published by one of the international standard-bearers of education research, the American Educational Research Association (AERA, 2003; see also Cochran-Smith & Zeichner, 2005), and through policies being advanced by influential organizations, such as the National Academy of Education (2004) and AERA. Locating the center of the controversy in the current government's desire for predictability of educational effects, and therefore in the idea of causality, I explicitly explore conflicting conceptions of causality as one significant issue of several. Here—with others—I suggest considering qualitative narrative research not in opposition to SBR but, rather, as a necessary equal. (Although the NRC claims that qualitative research has such a role, to date it is clearly assigned a second-class one.)

2. *To place the current conflict not only in the present but also in its historical context, briefly outlining both the development within the social sciences of an interpretive*

tradition and its convergence with the development of narrative. The present controversy will be examined explicitly as a coda to this history. Yet I ask, How do con-
tending conceptions of causality and issues of predictability and interpretation
underlie this history? How do they appear in today's conflict? Furthermore, when
the interpretive turn disrupted the hegemony of scientific science, what was the
projected future for the human sciences at that instance?

3. *To examine and describe aspects of the continuing explosion of narrative
inquiry research and its methodologies, asking why narrative remains so powerful,
how it is used, why it is valued, and what its proponents see as its potential future.*
A sampler of the uses of narrative inquiry in law, medicine, and education provide data to frame an important argument: that a fast emerging feature of narrative is as an educative tool for the refinement of the use of interpretation within
several professions, highlighting narrative inquiry research as, in part, education
research, linked to narrative's ancient interpretive history *and* to the contemporary controversy—itself a question of interpretation as well as power and
government control (see Cochran-Smith & Fries, 2005; Donmoyer, 2006; Feuer,
Towne, & Shavelson, 2002).

At least three questions undergird this discussion: Who constructs, warrants,
and evaluates knowledge claims, such as causality or valid scientific research?
By what authority? With what consequences? Ethical, political, and epistemological issues thus reside at the heart of this investigation and are intertwined in the
discussion.

In closing the chapter, I will project possible futures for narrative inquiry and
its methods. The need for "wakefulness" (Clandinin & Connelly, 2000) on the part
of researchers to current implications is clear. What efforts are or ought to be
addressed? How and by whom? What might be at risk or lost if narrative inquiry
were stifled? What might be gained if it were viewed as complementary, equal to
SBR? But I approach these projections with caution for, as Bruner (2002) warns,
"narrative in all its forms is a dialectic between what was expected and what came
to pass" (p. 15).

Context: The Ubiquity of Narrative

Any historical context, however brief, must usefully examine narrative inquiry in
two ways: both in its own development as well as in its role within the important
movement of the 1970s and 1980s with the flowering of the interpretive turn.
I begin with the historical context and will address the interpretive turn more fully
later in this chapter.

The power and pervasiveness of narrative is as old as human history. Roland
Barthes (1988), the literary theorist, considers that "narrative is simply there like
life itself international, trans-historical, and trans-cultural . . . [ceaselessly substi-
tuting] meaning for straightforward copy of the events recounted" (p. 95):

The narratives of the world are without number. In the first place the word "narrative" covers an enormous variety of genres which are themselves divided up between different subjects, as if any material was suitable for the composition of the narrative: the narrative may incorporate articulate language, spoken or written; pictures, still or moving; gestures and the ordered arrangement of all the ingredients; it is present in myth, legend, fable, short story, epic, history, tragedy, comedy, pantomime, painting, . . . stained glass windows, cinema, comic strips, journalism, conversation. In addition, under this almost infinite number of forms, the narrative is present at all times, in all places, in all societies; the history of narrative begins with the history of mankind; there does not exist, and never has existed, a people without narratives. (Barthes, as cited in Polkinghorne, 1988, p. 14)

In his "pocket history" overview of narrative scholarship, Jerome Bruner (2002, p. 109) contends that it begins seriously with Aristotle's *Poetics* and its concept of *peripeteia,* what Aristotle calls a sudden reversal in the course of events that constituted good or ill fortune, especially when coupled with some disclosure (Aristotle, as translated in Potts, 1968, p. 31). Narrative is not attended to in medieval literary scholarship and was pushed into the background by the burgeoning rationalism of the Renaissance and the Enlightenment. For many, the modern study of narrative begins with the work of Russian folklorist Vladimir Propp (1968). Propp recognized that "the structure of the story form not only was a matter of syntax but also reflected the human effort to cope with the untoward and unexpected in life" (Bruner, 2002, pp. 109–110), what Aristotle saw as the sudden reversal of the expected and Bruner terms *trouble*. Even though Propp was so preoccupied with the structural universals of folklore plights that he did not explore the uses of narrative beyond storytelling, Bruner says that Propp deserves full credit for having launched the modern study of narrative.

Bruner (2002) identifies the 1960s as the years of Chomsky's linguistics, of the cognitive revolution, of artificial intelligence, and of "not great years for narrative studies in the human sciences" (p. 110). Story and its forms were left to the literary community and to historians. But there were exceptions. For example, the linguist William Labov produced a touchstone article on the subject with Joshua Waletsky in 1967, "Narrative Analysis" (Labov & Waletsky, 1967). Labov, although primarily interested in the language of narrative, also wrote about its uses. Significantly, Labov's work provided important linguistic research tools for advancing narrative inquiries of all sorts. (See the 1997 special issue of *The Journal of Narrative and Life History* honoring Labov and Waletsky with commentaries on the impact of their work.)

Then in 1979, a symposium at the University of Chicago brought together some of the most important narrative thinkers who singularly "dramatized and clarified the fundamental debates about the value and nature of narrative as a means by which human beings represent and structure the world" (Mitchell, 1981, p. viii). Probably the most important sense of this historical conference was

the aura of intellectual excitement and discovery, the common feeling that the study of narrative, like the study of other significant human creations, has taken a quantum leap in the modern era. The study of narrative is no longer the province of literary specialists or folklorists borrowing their terms from psychology and linguistics but has now become a positive source of insight for all branches of the human and natural sciences. The idea of narrative seems . . . to be repossessing its archaic sense as *gnarus* and *gnosis,* a mode of knowledge emerging from action, a knowledge which is embedded not just in the stories we tell our children or to while away our leisure but in the orders by which we live our lives. (Mitchell, 1981, pp. ix–x)

Interest in narrative grew steadily in the years following, especially in the past two decades, in the power of narrative "to shape conceptions of reality and legitimacy." Indeed, a "narrative turn" took place, with historians leading the way. Bruner (2002) asks why the narrative turn affected many other fields as well, "Was it disenchantment with cut-and-dried, impersonal history, sociology, and anthropology that produced it? Or was it a response to the enormous personal suffering and dislocation of the most destructive century in human history?" (p. 111).

This dramatic development of narrative as a mode of insight and knowledge was clearly inspired in part by the larger disillusionment with positivism and its guiding postulates at mid-20th century and by the concomitant and impressive development of interpretation as a research tradition. At the heart of the emergence of the interpretive or hermeneutic approach was the recognition of the need for a human science. Knowledge was "not to be seen as a technical project but . . . in the human sciences, as inescapably practical and historically situated" (Rabinow & Sullivan, 1979/1987, p. 2). While interpretation gained an increasing currency during the 1970s and 1980s, and disciplinary barriers were called into question, so too did narrative advance, especially in its research methods.

Ten years ago, when Elliot Mishler (1995) reviewed the narrative research field, he offered a state-of-the-art perspective on narrative inquiry methods and theories. By then, narrative had experienced such growth that Mishler opens his review with this comment:

Depending on one's temperament, the current state of near anarchy in the field of narrative might be a cause for despair or exultation, for shaking one's head or clapping hands. Researchers have different answers for each question: What *is* a narrative? Does it have a distinctive structure? Are there different genres? When are stories told and for what purposes? Who has the right to tell them? What are their effects—cultural, psychological, social? (p. 87)

Mishler went on to define narrative not as a separate discipline, such as narratology, but as a *problem-centered area of inquiry,* a position this reviewer shares. Mishler believed narrative would always include a multiplicity and diversity of approaches. Believing, too, that researchers could learn from each other, Mishler proposed and set out a typology as a framework for comparing extant studies.

Mishler (1995) addressed his framework to issues of concern to researchers who specifically focus on the "production and functions of narratives in social contexts—conversations, rituals, professional encounters—and on the analytic use of narrative modes of interpretation in historical and scientific accounts" (p. 88). He found three general categories that corresponded closely to language functions that linguist Michael Halliday had proposed in his systematic grammar:

> *reference* (the correspondence between temporal sequence of actual events and their order of presentation in a text); *structure* (linguistic and narrative strategies through which different types and genres of stories are organized); and *function* (the cultural, social, and psychological contexts and functions of stories). (p. 88)

Mishler goes on to present an impressive array of reviews of his own and the work of others.

The models of narrative analysis that Mishler reviews demonstrate the depth, strength, and diversity of the narrative turn. They mark the widespread recognition of how we "story the world," making meaning of events and experiences through our tellings and retellings of stories for different purposes in various contexts. Mishler (1995) is clear that his typology is presented as a heuristic "to counter claims that there is one singular or best way to define and study 'narrative,' and to open the exploration of what we may learn from other approaches" (p. 121).

Mishler's work remains exemplary, a major contribution useful to researchers. But surprisingly, in his conclusion, Mishler alludes to a context remarkably similar to today's when he suggests this:

> Historically, studies of stories and their meanings were marginalized, excluded from the positivist hegemony in psychology and the social sciences. The large and diverse body of work reviewed here suggests how much can be learned from a narrative perspective on human action and experience. There are now strong grounds for its claims to legitimacy as a way of doing science. This does not mean it will be welcomed with open arms by those who excluded it. . . . But the domain of science is now contested territory. We have a firm foothold within it and can have confidence that the work will continue, gaining in depth and significance. (p. 121)

Ironically, today one can ask, Is the foothold loosening as the legitimacy of narrative inquiry and its methodologies as qualitative research are again being contested, this time potentially perniciously at the highest levels of government?

The Once and Future Controversy: Qualitative Research Versus or Plus Scientifically Based Research?

Contemporary arguments about qualitative and quantitative research methodologies—what Maxwell (2004) terms the *process/realist approach versus the regularity/variable oriented approach*—have most recently been dramatically accelerated by the efforts of the United States' federal policy makers and their requirements for evidence-based education research. The NRC's (2002) call for establishing "scientifically-based research" in education, that is, "rigorous, systematic and objective procedures to obtain valid knowledge," includes research that "is evaluated using experimental or quasi-experimental designs" (as cited in Maxwell, 2004, p. 3), preferably with random assignments. The mandate for funding "only" research using experimental methods is a move that has set off fear and trepidation in academia (Feuer et al., 2002; Shavelson, Phillips, Towne, & Feuer, 2003; see also Cochran-Smith & Zeichner, 2005). It is expected to have widespread implications for education research funding, including narrative inquiry methodologies and international research as well. Qualitative narrative research is a worldwide phenomenon reaching international audiences through organizations such as the AERA at their annual meetings. Here, I examine the controversy focusing on the central assumption of the NRC report—that is, that experimental methods are the preferred strategy for causal investigations. In this, I especially draw on Joseph Maxwell's cogent articulation of the causality issue, as well as Robert Slavin's and others' arguments for why "evidence-based" education policy could transform education practice.

Robert Slavin (2002), a proponent of evidence-based education policies, places the controversy regarding the NRCs new standard in its starkest terms—that is, those of a new potential of education research, to make reliable predictions useful to solving educational problems of practice. Slavin argues that at the dawn of the 21st century education research is "finally" entering the 20th century through the use of randomized experiments, ones he sees as having earlier transformed medicine, agriculture, and technology:

> Education, following a similar path, now stands on the brink of a scientific revolution through its new mandate to uphold rigorous experiments to evaluate replicable education programs and practices. To do so will build confidence in education research, generally so ill reputed because of its inability to make predictions. (p. 15)

Presumably, this research leads to valid predictions of what works or does not in America's classrooms.

Today's concerns about causality are bolstered by the long-standing dissatisfaction with education research precisely because of its lack of predictability. Eminent educators acknowledge that since its beginnings at the start of the 20th century, educational scholarship has had an "awful reputation" (Kaestle, 1993), been "regarded as something of a step-child, reluctantly tolerated at the margins of academe and rarely trusted by policy makers, practitioners, or members of the public at large" (Lagemann, 2000, p. x; see also Bruner, 1999; Feuer et al., 2002; Lagemann & Shulman, 1999). But these same critics often point to "the romance with quantification that has so profoundly influenced the behavioral sciences, including education, during the past century" (Lagemann, 2000, p. xi).

Maxwell (2004), recently addressing the current controversy, is similarly concerned with predictability. Writing in *Educational Researcher*, Maxwell focuses on the NRC's report, *Scientific Research in Education*, and its key assumption—that is, its regularity conception of causality. He argues that this conception, which also underlies other arguments for SBR, is "narrow and philosophically outdated, and leads to misrepresentation of the nature and value of qualitative research for causal explanation" (p. 3). He presents an alternative approach, a realist approach to causality that supports the legitimacy of using qualitative research for causal investigation, and reframes the arguments for experimental methods in educational research that "can support a more productive collaboration between qualitative and quantitative researchers" (p. 3).

Maxwell points to a critical flaw in the causality argument. He finds that the central manifestation of the regularity view of the NRC (2002) report is its presentation of causality as primarily pertaining to *whether* x caused y, rather than *how* it did so. Although addressing some mechanisms of cause, it uses cause—Is there a systematic effect?—mainly for the systematic relationship between variables rather than for causal processes. "Knowledge about causal relationships" is equated with "estimating the effects of programs" (p. 125), and the phrases "causal questions" and "causal studies" primarily refer to investigation *of causal effects rather than the search for causal mechanisms*" (Maxwell, 2004, p. 4).

Maxwell (2004) asserts that the most widely accepted alternative to this regularity approach to causality is "a realist approach that sees causality as fundamentally referring to the actual causal mechanisms and processes that are involved in particular events and situations" (p. 4). Maxwell cites Salmon as the most systematic developer of this view for the philosophy of science, who refers to it as the causal/mechanical view. Salmon argues thus:

> This approach makes explanatory knowledge into knowledge of the . . . mechanisms by which nature works. . . . It exhibits the ways in which the things we want to explain come about. This way of understanding the world differs fundamentally from that achieved by way of the unification approach. Whereas the unification approach is "top down," the causal mechanical approach is "bottom-up." (Salmon, 1989, pp. 182–183)

Salmon goes on to argue that the two approaches "may be taken as representing two different, but compatible, aspects of scientific explanation" (as cited in Maxwell, 2004, p. 4). However, he considers only the causal/mechanical view to be causal explanation. For others of this school,

> realism replaces the regularity model with one in which objects and social relations have causal powers which may or may not produce regularities, and which can be explained independently of them. In view of this, less weight is put on quantitative methods for discovering and assessing regularities and more on methods of establishing the qualitative nature of social objects and relations on which causal mechanism depend. (Sayer, as cited in Maxwell, 2004, p. 4)

In sum, Maxwell suggests that for the social sciences, the unification approach lacks the prerequisite knowledge to provide a powerful explanatory tool. This suggests that realist, process-oriented investigations deserve a more prominent place in educational research, including experimental research. Maxwell summarizes his point quoting Shadish, Cook, and Campbell who state,

> The unique strength of experimentation is in describing the consequences attributable to deliberately varying a treatment. We call this *causal description.* In contrast, experiments do less well in clarifying the mechanisms through which and the conditions under which that causal relationship holds—what we call *causal explanation.* (as cited in Maxwell, 2004, p. 9)

Maxwell suggests that in contrast to these balanced perspectives is variance theory. The NRC (2002) confirms the variance theory of causality and in addition affirms it as a "fundamental scientific concept in making causal claims" (p. 5). Yet, Maxwell (2004) argues, this is in contrast to process theory that deals with events and the processes that connect them and is based on the processes that caused them. "It is fundamentally different from variance theory as a way of thinking about scientific explanation. For realists the idea is that the mechanism is responsible for the relationship itself" (p. 5).

Maxwell argues that similar distinctions have been presented by many other writers and found in the natural sciences as well. For example, Stephen Jay Gould (1989) argues that there are two styles of science, one characteristic of physics and chemistry and the other of evolutionary biology and geology, that deal with unique situations and historical sequences:

> The stereotype of the "scientific method" has no place for irreducible history. Nature's laws are defined by their invariance in space and time. The techniques of controlled experiment, and reduction of natural complexity to a minimal set of general causes, presupposes that all times can be treated alike.
>
> But the restricted techniques of the "scientific method" cannot get to the heart of [a] single event involving creatures long dead on an earth with climates and continental positions markedly different from today's. The resolution of history must be rooted in the reconstruction of past events themselves—in their own terms—based on narrative evidence of their own unique phenomena.
>
> Historical evidence is not worse, more restricted, or less capable of achieving firm conclusions because experiment, prediction, and subsumption under invariant laws of nature do not represent its usual working methods. The sciences of history use a different mode of explanation, rooted in the comparative and observational richness of our data. (Gould, as cited in Maxwell, 2004, p. 5)

Like contexts, realist social scientists see meanings, beliefs, values, and intentions held by participants in a study as essential parts of the causal mechanisms operating in that setting, including mental phenomena. Again, these features are a part of the settings of research, not part of the phenomenon under investigation. Maxwell (2004) summarizes thus:

I have argued that the NRC (2002) report (and scientifically based research generally) assumes a regularity, variance oriented understanding of causation, and ignores an alternative, realist understanding. *This leads the authors to ignore or deny the possibility of identifying causality in particular cases, the importance of context as integral to causal processes, and the role of meaning and interpretive understanding in causal explanation—all issues for which qualitative research offers particular strengths* [italics added]. (Maxwell, 2004, p. 8)

Meaning/interpretation cannot be divorced from causality. And this is not the first time these arguments have been made. It seems that they fit well with what narrative researchers have argued in the past and with what some, such as psychologist John Cole, have called for more recently—that is, the need for a new science, cultural psychology.

A cultural psychology is an interpretive psychology. . . . It seeks out rules that human beings bring to bear in creating meanings in cultural contexts. These contexts are always contexts of practice: it is always necessary to ask what people are doing or trying to do in that context. (Bruner, 1990, p. 118)

The larger history of the interpretive turn reviewed next explicates and augments these arguments. I ask, Where are concepts of causality, issues of predictability or interpretation in this history? What was interpretation's projected future?

The Interpretive Revolution: What Is a Science of the Human Sciences?

Paul Rabinow and William Sullivan (1979/1987), who coined the term *interpretive turn* in their 1979 pathbreaking book, *Interpretive Social Science*, provide an insightful discussion of the history of this scholarship and include some 12 essays by the scholars who themselves defined the interpretive approach. Their observations are at times uncannily similar to today's conflicts surrounding SBR. They open their excellent review with a somewhat sobering assessment of the history of interpretation within a larger context—that is, within the search for a science for the social sciences. They assert, "Many contemporary researchers in the social sciences continue to see themselves, as did their predecessors, as the heralds of the new age of an at-last-established science. They remain, like their predecessors, disappointed" (p. 3; see also Bernstein, 1983; Hiley, Bohman, & Shusterman, 1991). Recounting the long-hoped-for expectation that a social science would turn "from its humanistic infancy to the maturity of hard science . . . through the liberating use of reason," Rabinow and Sullivan argue that "social investigators have never reached the extraordinary degree of basic agreement that characterizes modern natural science" (Rabinow & Sullivan, 1979/1987, pp. 2–3). According to Thomas Kuhn (1962/1970), such agreements among practicing investigators constitute the "paradigmatic" stage of science, that time of development, of extending the explanatory capacity of an agreed-upon paradigm (see pp. 176–179). While most fields are in this situation throughout their history, Rabinow and Sullivan (1979/1987) summarized the case for the social sciences on a far from sanguine note:

> The time seems ripe, even overdue, to announce that there is not going to be an age of paradigm in the social sciences. We contend that the failure to achieve paradigm takeoff is not merely the result of methodological immaturity, but reflects something fundamental about the human world. If we are correct, the crisis of social science concerns the nature of social investigation itself. The conception of the human sciences as somehow necessarily destined to follow the path of modern investigation of nature is at the root of this crisis. Preoccupation with that ruling expectation . . . has often driven investigators away from a serious concern with the human world into the sterility of purely formal argument and debate . . . the "about-to-arrive science" just won't do. (p. 5)

Rabinow and Sullivan (1979/1987) fashion a wider critique—that is, of the view of the knowing subject in a scientific model and its inadequacy for comprehending a human world. For comprehending the human world, there is needed

> the subject who knows himself through reflection upon his own actions in the world as a subject not simply of experience but of intentional action as well . . . practical understanding in context cannot be reduced to a system of categories defined only in terms of their relations to one another . . . or subsumed under law like operations. (pp. 4–5)

Needed is a different view of the human subject. Key to this alternative view is the critical idea of interpretation.

Interpretation begins, these researchers (Rabinow & Sullivan, 1978/1987) argue,

> from the postulate that the web of meaning constitutes human existence to such an extent that it cannot ever be meaningfully reduced to prior speech acts, dyadic relations, or any predefined elements. Intentionality and empathy are rather seen as dependent on the prior existence of the shared world of meaning within which the subjects of human discourse constitute themselves. It is in this literal sense that interpretive social science can be called a return to the objective world, seeing that world as in the first instance the circle of meaning, within which we find *ourselves and that we can never fully surpass* [italics added]. (pp. 6–7)

Language and Meaning

Some within the interpretive community offer a strong reading of the implications of these views, not always shared by others. For example, philosopher Charles Taylor (1979/1987) argues that the baseline realities for both the observer and the observed are practices, socially constituted actions, and these cannot be identified in abstraction from the languages we use to describe them. These practices are . . . the basis of community, argument, and discourse. Meanings or norms are not just in the minds of the actors but are out there in the practices themselves; practices which cannot be conceived as a set of individual actions, but which are essentially a mode of social relations, or mutual action. . . . From this it follows that the exactitude that is open to the human sciences is quite different from that available to the natural sciences. Our capacity to understand is rooted in our own self-definitions, hence in what we are. We are fundamentally self-interpreting and self-defining, living always in a cultural environment, inside a web of signification we ourselves have spun. There is no outside, detached standpoint from which we gather and present brute data. When we try to understand the cultural world, we are dealing with interpretations and interpretations of interpretations. Thus the mode of interpretation is hermeneutic. (p. 7)

Philosopher Paul Ricoeur does not share this view. Rather, for him, a method of mediating and judging between conflicting interpretations would look rather more like a "transformed version of textual criticism in the humanities." But even he acknowledges that at present "we have only the barest beginning of such a dialectic" (Ricoeur, cited in Rabinow & Sullivan, 1979/1987, p. 9). In summary, Rabinow and Sullivan see this is a formulation; one farther from positivist orthodoxy would be hard to find:

We propose a return to the human world with all its lack of clarity, its alienation, and its depth, rather than continuing the search for a formal deductive paradigm of the social sciences. The aim is not to uncover universals or laws but rather to explicate context and world. (p. 9)

Emphasis is on discourse as the basis for the human sciences. Hans-Georg Gadamer is credited with focusing an emphasis on discourse, on keeping open to what is other, to more universal points of view. Gadamer presents a case that human existence can only be adequately understood as inherently historical and inescapably embedded in tradition. However,

Gadamer understands tradition to be a struggle for meaning . . . of a constant re-appropriation of history. Social life then appears as an ongoing conversation in many voices about current reality, a process of interpretation, not a reiteration of permanently fixed truths or traditions. (Rabinow & Sullivan, 1979/1987, p. 23)

The Interpretive Turn:
Epistemological Concerns

Rabinow and Sullivan (1979/1987) contend that the interpretive turn is not simply a new methodology, or a set of research methods, but rather a challenge to the very idea that inquiry into the social world and the value of the understanding that results is to be determined by methodology . . . inquiry is necessarily engaged in understanding the human world from within a specific situation . . . it is always and at once historical, moral, and political. It provides not just the starting point of inquiry but the point and purpose for the task of understanding itself. But if this is so, interpretation is not simply a dimension of science. Rather, it means that science, like all human endeavors, is rooted in a context of meaning which is itself a social reality, a particular organization of human action defining a moral and practical world. (p. 14)

Cultural Psychology and Scientific Research in Education

Cultural psychology is an important development within the history of psychology and an interesting case study in the history of the interpretive turn, especially for considering the appropriateness of SBR in education. To trace this history, I focus on Michael Cole's (1996) brilliant, award-winning book, *Cultural Psychology*. As psychologist Sheldon White (1996) points out in his Foreword, since the 1960s, Cole has been engaged in a long, slow realization of cultural-historical psychology as a cooperative human enterprise. He has asked some fundamental questions: What does it mean to study a human's development scientifically? What kind of science do you arrive at? How broadly does it apply? What use can be made of it?

Although the history of psychology is, from its beginnings in the late 19th and early 20th centuries, the quest to follow the model of the natural sciences, its followers also hoped that such a science would yield data useful to provide "uncontroversial resolutions of the dilemmas, choices, and political confrontations of people living in institutions of modern society" (White, 1996, p. xi). The methods of the naturalistic science would reveal patterns of human perception, learning, and development and "the rhetoric of that program would assert that such patterns must be true of everyone everywhere. Michael Cole's point of entry into the problems of the twentieth-century was the discovery that part of that assertion was not true" (p. xi). In the 1960s, Cole took part in an effort to take the "new math" to Kpelle children living in a traditional society in Africa. But there he discovered that although tribal children classify, learn, remember, form concepts, and reason in everyday life, they do not perform in a sophisticated manner on experimental procedures designed for the study of age changes in those faculties. Western procedures are grounded in a world in which children go to school at 6 years of age and are surrounded by the life, language, and thought of a modern society. "Much of what we consider to be normal to child development is simply a recognition of what usually happens when children grow up in such a world" (pp. xi–xii).

As White (1996) suggests, it is not completely surprising that psychology produced findings that are only true within situational boundaries. . . . Before this century a number of distinguished philosophers argued that in order to fully understand how the human mind works we will require two psychologies of different orders. We will need a naturalistic psychology and . . . we will also need a less-familiar "second psychology" describing higher-level mental phenomena as entities given form by the language, myths, and social practices in which the individual lives. Such a second psychology would not be expected to yield universal findings. Since higher order mental processes are formed by culture, they differ from one society to another. (p. xii)

We still struggle today with the need for a second psychology. Michael Cole's work to develop a cultural psychology documents that long quest. But today the rise of a cultural psychology is clear. Others are joining that quest. *The Culture and Psychology Reader*, put together by Nancy Goldberger and Jody Veroff (1995), presents the work of 47 researchers, including that of Richard Shweder, a central figure and explicator of cultural psychology. He sees it as the study of intentional worlds, of how meanings and intentions are products of the inevitable interdependence of psychology and culture. Shweder (1995) notes: "Most of the work of cultural psychology is still ahead of us" (p. 71). Cultural researchers value the place of narrative within their work. Goldberger and Veroff (1995) point especially to personal narratives of individuals who are not part of the dominant power center of our society who "can speak to us from the margins (hooks, 1984) and can alert us, as Cherie Moranga calls it, to 'the specificity of oppression'" (p. 595).

Narrative Inquiry Research Creates a Narrative Turn

To consider the role of narrative within the interpretive research tradition, I return to the work of Jerome Bruner. In his discussion of "The Narrative Construal of Reality," Bruner (1996) asks,

Why, rather suddenly, did so many of us in psychology become so interested in the narrative construction of reality. Was it the new post-modernism that finally provoked psychologists into rejecting stimulus-response linkages as the "causes" of behavior? Probably not. For the malaise that led to the new interest in the narrative construal of reality long predates the rise of anti-foundational, perspectively oriented post-modernism. Sigmund Freud probably had more to do with it than Derrida or Foucault, if only by proposing a "psychic reality" that seemed more driven by dramatic necessities than by states of the objective world. . . . More recently, it was probably the rebellion against Piaget's generalized rationalism—that mental development consisted in logical leaps forward nurtured by general experience with the environment. Mental development turned out to be much more domain-specific than that: learning how a seesaw works, for example, does not by any means lead automatically to understanding what makes a balance beam work. . . . The new mantra was that the achievement of knowledge was always "situated," dependent upon materials, task, and how the learner understood things . . . intelligence [was not] simply "in the head" but as "distributed" in the person's world—including the toolkit of reckoning devices and heuristics and accessible friends that the person could call upon. (pp. 131–132)

But in 1984, at the annual meeting of the American Psychological Association, Bruner made a pronouncement that challenged the old positivism, with a startling assertion about narrative. Bruner cast narrative in an entirely new perspective. He asserted baldly that there were two modes of thought or cognitive functioning: the traditional logical-scientific mode and a narrative mode. Bruner contended that although the two modes are complementary, neither is reducible to the other. Each provides a distinctive way of ordering experience, of constructing reality and causality. The logical scientific (or paradigmatic) mode is centered on the narrow epistemological question of how to know the truth, and searches for universal truth conditions; the "narrative, looks for particular conditions and is centered around the broader and more inclusive question of the meaning of experience" (Bruner, 1986, pp. 11–13; see also Polkinghorne, 1988, p. 17). One seeks explications context free and universal, and the other context sensitive and particular.

Bruner's work paralleled the unprecedented shift of interest in narrative and interpretation in several social science disciplines. It especially caught the attention of educators and psychologists who were making use of narrative in their own research and practice. Narrative as story seemed especially useful to capture the situated complexities of teachers' work and classroom practice, often messy, uncertain, and unpredictable.

But narrative promises more than action vignettes. As Bruner contends, narrative operates by constructing two landscapes simultaneously, two planes, one of action and one of consciousness—that is, of "*what those acting know, think, or feel*" (quoted in APA, 1984; emphasis added). Philosopher Alasdair MacIntyre (1984) suggests that all human actions are enacted narratives. "It is because . . . we understand our own lives in terms of narratives that narrative is appropriate for understanding . . . others" (pp. 211–212).

Bruner's work brought claims and counterclaims for narrative knowing in the human sciences. It connected current arguments with ones most ancient: Explanation was not interpretation or meaning (Bruner, 1986; see also Bernstein, 1983; Hiley et al., 1991). The standards of positivism that had dominated the social sciences no longer remained unchallenged. There was not one framework but many. The result of Bruner's pronouncement was to accelerate discussions about narrative already begun across many disciplines—in literary criticism, history, psychology, philosophy, feminist theory, and the law.

In the 1970s and 1980s, feminist scholars especially advanced narrative inquiry. They made narrative research crucial to the idea of giving voice to those excluded from mainstream psychological research, acknowledging with Maxine Greene (1978) that "without articulation, without expression, the perceived world is in some way nullified" (p. 223). Such voices aided in identifying meaning and constructing new theoretical views. Research interviewing, autobiography, and case studies were part of the methodologies. They were used in theory-building efforts, for example, to name a few scholars, by Carol Gilligan (1982) and Nel Noddings (1984) in moral psychology; by Mary Belenky, Blythe Clinchy, Nancy Goldberger, and Jill Tarule (1986) in self psychology and epistemology, especially ways of knowing research; and by Jane Martin (1985) in philosophy. In science, Evelyn Fox Keller (1984) forged important achievements in documenting the story of naturalist Barbara McClintock. And the field is still emerging. Jean Clandinin and Michael Connelly (2000) and Ruthellen Josselson (Josselson, Lieblich, & McAdams, 2003) only recently published texts outlining how they and scholars such as Blythe Clinchy (2003) and others teach narrative inquiry research, a mixed genre enterprise, as Josselson and her colleagues write, marrying science and the humanities, integrating systematic study of phenomena with literary deconstruction of texts and hermeneutic analyses of meaning. But even as this work proceeds, new cautions about narrative, especially in the field of education and particularly about what is to count as knowledge, emerged as they appear today (see Lyons & LaBoskey, 2002)

In this section, I have presented the growth of the powerful ideas of meaning and interpretation in the several disciplines and in alternative psychologies. The idea has been there in the earliest developments of the disciplines. Yet it still struggles for recognition. Where does it fit in considering narrative practices today or in the future?

Narrative Practices Today: What Uses? What Influence? Some Selected Cases

Several provocative questions frame this section and the set of mini cases of contemporary uses of narrative that it contains: Why is narrative so powerful within a profession? Why is it valued? How is it used? Justified? What does its future look like to its practitioners? Here I examine in brief the uses of narrative in law, medicine, and education. These are clearly not the only choices. Much is being done in narrative inquiry in many other disciplines and professions and for specialized studies, for example, biology, history, literary criticism, sociology, anthropology, psychiatry, therapy, management, child studies, Holocaust studies, trauma studies, feminist studies, gender studies, critical race theorists, to name only some. A quick perusal of the Internet can nearly overwhelm with articles, conferences, programs, books on any subset of narrative. It is beyond the scope of this chapter to even attempt to document all this in full, and it is not possible here to begin to do justice to the rich array of projects and methodologies involved in these disciplines. Here, rather, by looking in a deeper way at the uses of narrative across a few disciplines and professions, we can see the outline of the specificity of values and elements at work in them to answer the question "Why is narrative so powerful within these disciplines?" Several important aspects of the uses of narrative in professional education emerge in this review:

- How narrative is embedded within professions, and how ubiquitous it is; but how often this is a discovery previously unknown to professionals who are unaware of it.
- How a focus on narrative can make a professional aware of different kinds of knowledge needed to practice effectively as a lawyer, doctor, teacher, by what some call making the familiar "strange."
- How practitioners are discovering important ways in which narrative provides an avenue of inquiry to deepen knowledge, for example, to uncover new ways of interpreting and understanding one's clients' ways of knowing and making meaning—otherwise hidden from view.
- How narrative introduces and heightens an awareness of the centrality of interpretation and meaning in one's own professional development as well as in one's discipline.

But how does this happen? I turn to examine these considerations in several professions.

The Law

No set of legal institutions or prescriptions exists apart from the narratives that locate it and give it meaning. For every constitution there is an epic, for each Decalogue a scripture. Once understood in the context of the narratives that give it meaning, law becomes not merely a system of rules to be observed, but a world in which to live. (Cover, as cited in Bruner, 2002, pp. 12–13)

To open this discussion, two different views and uses of narrative and the law are presented. I look first briefly at observations on the role of narrative within the teaching of law, then at how the field of the law and literature has been developing. Anthony Amsterdam and Jerome Bruner (2000), in their book, *Minding the Law: How Courts Rely on Storytelling and How Their Stories Change the Ways We Understand the Law—and Ourselves*, characterize narrative and the law from their practitioner role in analyzing and teaching constitutional law:

Law lives on narrative, for reasons both banal and deep. For one, the law is awash in storytelling. Clients tell stories to lawyers, who must figure out what to make of what they hear. As clients and lawyers talk, the client's story gets recast into plights and prospects, plots and pilgrimages into possible worlds. (What lawyers call "thinking through a course of action" is a narrative projection of the perils of embarking on one pilgrimage or another.) If circumstances warrant, the lawyers retell their clients' stories in the form of pleas and arguments to judges, and testimony to juries. . . . Next, judges and jurors retell the stories to themselves or to each other in the form of instructions, deliberations, a verdict, a set of findings, or an opinion. And then it is the turn of journalists, commentators, and critics. This endless telling and retelling, casting and recasting is essential to the conduct of the law. It is how the law's actors comprehend whatever series of events they make the subject of their legal actions. It is how they try to make their actions comprehensible again within some larger series of events they take to constitute the legal system and the culture that sustains it.

Increasingly we are coming to recognize that both the questions and the answers in matters of "fact" depend largely upon one's choice (considered or unconsidered) of some overall narrative as best describing *what happened or how the world works*. We now understand that stories are not just recipes for stringing together a set of "hard facts"; that, in some profound, often puzzling way, stories construct the facts that comprise them. For this reason, much of human reality and its "facts" are not merely recounted by narrative but *constituted* by it. To the extent that law is fact-contingent, it is inescapably rooted in narrative. (Amsterdam & Bruner, 2000, pp. 110–111)

Writing in the Preface for the second edition of his book, *Law and Literature,* Richard Posner (1988), Chief Judge, U.S. Court of Appeals for the Seventh Circuit and senior lecturer at the University of Chicago, offers a different view of the law: a review of the field of law and literature over the 10 years since the first edition of his book appeared. He documents a long list of markers for how the field has grown: The number of courses of law and literature in law schools alone has doubled. The first edition of Posner's book is the most frequently assigned or recommended nonfiction work in such courses. A number of monographs have appeared. And scholars of distinction such as Thomas Grey and Martha Nussbaum (1997) have become engaged in the movement and "attest to its vitality." There is a continuing spate of symposia, anthologies, and general works on law and literature. A first-class law and literature scholarship by practicing lawyers has emerged. And two new journals have been started, *Cardoza Studies in Law and Literature* and the *Yale Journal of Law and Literature.* Nourished by the law's continuing fascination for American writers, the field of law and literature is prospering, and its status of interdisciplinary legal scholarship seems secure (p. vii).

Turning to how things have developed, Posner (1988) sees that two things have changed in the field over the intervening 10 years:

Interest in the application of literary methods to the interpretation of statutes and constitution has diminished in the face of a growing sense that interpretation is relative to purpose and therefore unlikely to raise the same issues for different interpretanda (dreams, operas, labels, constitutions, sonnets), and is also one of those activities that is not much, if at all, improved by being pursued self-consciously. (p. viii)

But imaginative literature unrelated, or at least seemingly unrelated, to law is now being used by White, Nussbaum (1995), and others as the basis for a new model of legal scholarship:

The new model emphasizes narration and reminiscence rather than analysis, prefers judicial biography to the study of judicial opinions, promises fresh insights into the plight of people (blacks and women, for example) with whom American law has had troubled encounters, and in general seeks to promote compassion and empathy by enlarging the imagination of lawyers and judge. (Posner, 1998, p. viii)

Although Posner (1998) makes a claim for the ubiquity of the law as a theme in literature, the techniques and imagery of law have permeated Western culture from its earliest days. But as a field of organized study, law and literature did not exist—Posner observes—before the publication in 1973 of James Boyd White's textbook, *The Legal Imagination.* The fields of legal and literary scholarship were autonomous: "defined by specific, narrowly circumscribed, and nonoverlapping body of texts. . . . Recent [developments] . . . got legal scholars interested in parallel fields, including literature, while literary scholars . . . have become interested in nonliterary texts, including those of law" (p. 4).

Looking to the future, Posner (1998) states that

an increasing number of legal scholars, inspired in part by philosophers and literary scholars, . . . want to reclaim law as a humanity from economists and economics-minded lawyers, who view law as a social science. They want to do this both by giving lawyers a literary education and by shifting the emphasis in legal scholarship . . . from analysis to narrative and metaphor. Some want to bring works of imaginative literature into the legal classroom in order to present vivid pictures of the despised, the overlooked, and the downtrodden, and by fostering empathy for them to encourage legal reform along egalitarian or even revolutionary lines. This novel turning of the law and literature movement, one manifestation of which is an increased interest in biography and autobiography. . . . I am deeply skeptical about this branch of the law and literature movement. It has all the drawbacks of the didactic or moralistic school of literary criticism . . . there is just a chance that in the long run the movement will affect even more strongly ways of thinking about justice, interpretation, the judicial opinion, legal education, and legal scholarship, though this impact is bound to be more diffuse and only obliquely related to practice. (p. 6)

Amsterdam and Bruner (2000), who opened this discussion of narrative and the law, acknowledge that their purpose in undertaking their analysis of constitutional *law is to make the familiar strange again, to unearth concealed presuppositions, categorical pitfalls, narrative predilections, rhetorical constructions, cultural biases.* But they go on to say their book is not about "right" outcomes for the law but about commonplace hidden pitfalls and snares that infest every path that any lawyer or judge could follow.

Any constitutional theory, we argue, will benefit from a better sense of how the law is embedded in a culture's way of life and in the thinking processes of those who must administer and interpret and abide by the law. (p. 287)

Their objective, then, has been

> to increase awareness, to intensify consciousness, about what people are doing when they "do law." We have emphasized that the framing and adjudication of legal issues necessarily rest upon interpretation. Results cannot be arrived at entirely by deductive, analytic reasoning or by the rules of induction, although these have their place. There always remains the "wild card" of all interpretation— the consideration of context, that ineradicable element in meaning-making. And the deepest, most impenetrable feature of context lies in the minds and the culture of those involved in fashioning an interpretation. (p. 287)

Medicine: "Can Understanding Narrative Make You a Better Doctor?"

Melanie Thernstrom (2004), writing in the *New York Times Magazine*, poses the above question. She focuses on the work of Rita Charon, who introduced Narrative Medicine as a program at the College of Physicians and Surgeons of Columbia University, one of the first medical schools with a program in narrative competence.

Charon first coined the term *narrative medicine* in 2001 in an article she wrote for the *Annals of Internal Medicine*. She defines narrative medicine as "medicine practiced with the narrative competence to recognize, absorb, interpret and be moved by stories of illness" (as cited in Thernstrom, 2004, p. 44). Her own interest in the subject led her to go over to the English Department of Columbia to see if they could help her understand how stories are built and told and understood. She planned to take a course but wound up with a master's and then a doctoral degree. She found she believed literature made the medicine make more sense:

> I could listen to what my patients tell me with greater ability to follow the narrative thread of their story, to recognize the governing images and metaphors, to adopt the patients' or the family members' points of view, to identify the sub-texts present in all stories, to interpret one story in the light of others told by the same teller. Moreover, the better I was as a "reader" of what my patients told me, the more deeply moved I myself was by their predicament, making more of myself available to patients as I tried to help. (Charon, 2005)

Dr. Charon (2005) began to write up what her patients told her and later would show them what she had written and ask, "Did I get it straight?" She felt the patients believed she tried to understand them and could say, "I think we left something out." At the same time, she coached her medical students and her colleagues in writing reflectively about their practices. She then encouraged them to keep "Parallel Charts" on patients in their care as a way of capturing what could not be put into a hospital chart—the fears, anguish in caring for others, their fear of mistakes, mourning, and joy. Gradually, Dr. Charon realized

> that most all of medicine is deeply saturated with narrative practices, not only in creating therapeutic alliances with patients and instilling reflection in our

practices but also generating hypotheses in our science, learning our fabulous tradition of explanations about the human body, teaching students and colleagues what we know about sickness, acting with so-called professionalism toward one another and our patients, and entering into serious discourse with the public about what kind of medicine our culture wants.

Other doctors suggest that

the notion of interpretation—the discernment of meaning—is a central concern of philosophers and linguists, but it is a concept with which doctors and other scientists are often unfamiliar, and hence uncomfortable . . . clinical medicine shares its methods of knowing with history, law, economics, anthropology, and other human sciences less certain and more concerned with meaning than the physical sciences. But unlike those disciplines, it does not explicitly recognize its interpretive character or the rules it uses to negotiate meaning . . . medicine is better characterized as a "moral knowing, a narrative, interpretive, practical reasoning." (Greenhalgh & Hurwitz, 1999, p. 49)

Alan Bleakley (2005), writing in *Medical Education*, to make sense of narrative inquiry in clinical education, opens with Mark Haddon's 2003 novel, *The Curious Incident of the Dog in the Night-Time*, which offers an insight into the mind of a boy suffering from Asperger's syndrome, a condition on the autistic spectrum. The boy's world is numbers, not people: "He knows a very great deal about maths and very little about human beings" (Bleakley, 2005, p. 534). The central character, Christopher, shows a striking inability to empathize with the narrative accounts of others that carry messages about their desires:

An equivalent lack of narrative acumen can be seen to have been systematically cultivated in medicine, where the telling symptom is the characteristically flat, detached account of the medical case study, serving to conceal the reality that medical practice is entrenched in stories. Further, such stories afford rich sources for research. As a challenge emerges to medicine's self-imposed institutional autism that is a denial of the importance of story, clinical education researchers are beginning to draw on disciplines such as anthropology, psychology, and sociology that have honed their narrative inquiry methodologies, to address the maxim: "treat the patient, not the numbers." (p. 534)

Bleakley (2005) goes on to argue thus:

Analytic methods tend to lose the concrete story and its emotional impact to abstract categorizations, which may claim explanatory value but often remain descriptive. . . . Medical education can redress this imbalance through attention to "thinking with stories" to gain empathy for a patient's experience of illness. Such an approach can complement understanding of story as discourse—how narratives may be used rhetorically to manage both social interactions and identity. (p. 534)

Education: The Case Study Approach

To take up the uses of narrative within the field of education, I turn to the case study and offer a mini exploration of the use of cases in the education of professionals. In particular, I want to examine how the case study emerged as a critical part of the pedagogy of law, business, medicine, and most recently education. Here, I focus on that history and especially the use of cases within the professional schools of Harvard University because of its pioneering role in making the case study approach a critical part of professional education.

The case study is a pretty varied medium, as is revealed in the following historical account. The Law School in the beginning used actual appellate court decisions, Business School cases usually center on some firm and its managers' tough choices, and Education School cases may focus on actual teaching dilemmas. Cases are thus narratives themselves, and case pedagogies entail shaping a good story about what is going on or ought to be (Hansen, 1987).

The purpose of the use of a case study approach varies considerably across these professions. Yet as David Garvin (2003) argues in a recent review of the development of the case study approach at Harvard, the central task of professional education is how to prepare students for the world of practice, "especially how to diagnose, decide and act" (p. 56).

The Harvard Law School initiated the method in 1870, when Dean Langdell turned to a set of appellate court decisions for students to ponder and to extrapolate general principles from. Students were not only to know the facts of the cases but were to be able to offer their own interpretations and analyses and be ready to face tough questioning. In this approach, the mastery of principles was first, and hands-on experience less important. Fifty years later, the Business School adopted the method, in what was called the "problem method," but the cases were different from those for law. Now, the primary concern would be "with making and implementing decisions, often in the face of considerable uncertainty" (Garvin, 2003, p. 60). The student would be faced with actual cases and would be able to practice decision making and action. Much less time was to be spent on identifying principles or theories. It was the particular situation that was paramount to understand and to act in, often in the face of missing information. The purpose was to teach students to think in the presence of new situations, to help them to develop skills of persuasion, to "tell a compelling story, marshal evidence, and to craft persuasive arguments . . . and to develop distinctive ways of thinking—and acting" (p. 61).

In 1985, the Harvard Medical School began using cases when it initiated the "New Pathway" curriculum and a move away from lectures to active learning. Daniel Tosteson, dean, answering his own question "What do we want Harvard Medical School graduates to know how to do?" answered:

> Medicine is a kind of problem solving, and each medical encounter was unique in a personal, social, and biological sense. All these aspects of uniqueness impose on both physician and patient the need to learn about the always new situation, to find a plan of action that is most likely to improve the health of that particular patient at that particular time. (Garvin, 2003, p. 63)

In the new Pathways program, medical cases are stories of real patients, progressively disclosed over several weeks through which students themselves develop their own learning agendas. As one first-year student said, "I choose the topics I feel uncomfortable with, the topics I would not be able to discuss intelligently. I study what I don't understand" (Garvin, 2003, p. 64). The program, promoters believe, thus fosters a true spirit of inquiry.

Recently, the Harvard Education School announced, as part of a major rethinking of the school's curriculum, the adoption of a case method with its details yet to be announced, but it is clear that there will be unique differences. Yet the basic goals will demand new expertise for the high-stakes exercise of deciding what is important for educators to know.

This brief review of current professional schools' practices that forefront narrative clearly indicate why narrative is so powerful and continuously expanding. There is no doubt that narrative is a mode of knowing in the professions. It is believed by many to contribute in unique ways to learning, not simply of useful but fundamentally necessary perspectives on a discipline, its clients, and its practitioners. This is true across professions and is achieved through narratives, read, created, and enacted. Key to this is the significance of meaning and interpretation. No growth or development, professional or personal, is possible without interpretation.

Implications: What Future Influence for Narrative Inquiry Research on Policy and Practice?

In our Prologue, . . . we tried to give a sense of what it was about narrative that led us to turn to it in our own work. We might say that if we understand the world narratively, as we do, then it makes sense to study the world narratively. For us, life—as we come to it and as it comes to others—is filled with narrative fragments, enacted in storied moments of time and space, and reflected upon and understood in terms of narrative unities and discontinuities. . . . We saw our research problem as trying to think of the continuity and wholeness of an individual's life experience. . . . This brought us to narrative. . . . We then began to reflect on the whole of the social sciences and its concern with human experience. For social scientists, and consequently for us, experience is a key term . . . it is what we study and narrative thinking is a key form of experience and a key way of writing and thinking about it. (Clandinin & Connelly, 2000, p. 17)

I come now to the critical place in this chapter to address its compelling question: What is the future of narrative inquiry research? To answer the question, I return to two issues the chapter explores: the dispute over the role of scientific-based education research, and current advances in the uses of narrative, especially for the education of professionals. I want to juxtapose these two, to ask what each might portend for the future of narrative inquiry. Hovering in the background is the question of the connection of this discussion to larger issues of policy. That will be addressed as well.

I start by looking first at the response of researchers and the education community to the controversy. A brief survey reveals a somewhat diverse set of responses that will, I believe, affect the future of narrative inquiry research.

The Controversy and the Response: Predictability, Government Policy, Control, and the Reemergence of a Search for a Science of Education

"If we retain the word *rule* at all, we must say that scientific results furnish a rule for the conduct of *observations and inquiries,* not a rule for action" (Dewey, 1929, p. 30).

The NRC's (2002) report, *Scientific Research in Education,* instituted as government policy a gold standard of SBR for education mandating control groups in randomized trials for funded research. Sponsored by U.S. policy makers, the NRC standard is predicated on the government's desire to insure that education research can identify good teaching practices for American classrooms. To achieve the government goal of showing "what works" implies two things: the necessity to define causality in a given piece of research and/or practice and to demonstrate its generalizability. The NRC report outlines the foundations of this new education science. It defines what scientific research entails, identifies six major principles for research, and then suggests how a federal agency can be organized to foster the growth of this science. The six principles are the following: Pose significant questions that can be investigated empirically, link research to relevant theory, use methods that permit direct investigation of the questions, provide a coherent and explicit chain of reasoning, yield findings that replicate and generalize across studies, and disclose research data and methods to enable and encourage professional scrutiny and critique (Shavelson & Towne, as cited in NRC, 2002). How did the education community respond to these proposals and principles?

Responses From the Ed Community

The education community initially was quick to acknowledge government charges that the history of education research was dismal at best, perhaps itself "broken in our country" (Castle, as cited in NRC, 2002). In the wake of the NRC's report, the responses of educators have varied. Some are deeply troubled and predict alarming results, others accept the premises and urge the promotion of more methodological rigor for education research, and others attempt to show ancient objections. This sampling of comments is taken from AERA or other refereed journals:

Establish a Stronger Sense of a Research Community

The NCLB Act of 2001 requires federal grantees to use their funds on evidence-based strategies. The law includes definitions of research quality. . . . These initiatives pose a rare opportunity and formidable challenge to the field: What are the most effective means of stimulating more and better scientific educational research? . . . the authors argue that the primary emphasis should be on nurturing and reinforcing a scientific culture of educational research . . . the call for building a stronger sense of research community applies broadly.

The development of a scientific culture rests with individual researchers, supported by leadership in their professional associations and a federal educational research agency. (Feuer et al., 2002, p. 21)

Wanting to Know: What Works?

Every year, teachers, principals, superintendents, and other educators have to make hundreds of decisions of potentially great importance to students. What reading program is most likely to ensure high reading performance? Should "social promotion" be used or should retentions be increased? Should kindergarten be half day or full day? What are the most effective means of providing remediation to children who are falling behind? In a word: What works? (Slavin, 2004, p. 27)

Treatments Cannot Be Defined Objectively

Slavin's call for evidence-based research on the effectiveness of treatments is criticized for its unreflective concept of a "treatment." It is argued that treatments cannot be defined objectively but only relative to the beliefs, goals, and intentions of those supposedly affected by the treatments. (Olson, 2004, p. 24)

Research from Around the World Highlights Its Complexity

By using a variety of examples of research from around the world that highlights the need for complex historical, political, and cultural lenses to examine policy, research, knowledge and power constructions, Bloch suggests that the report represents only one truth among many, limiting further inquiry. By examining the relationship between knowledge and truth, the danger in a limited perspective is underlined. (Bloch, 2004, p. 96)

NRC's Flawed Idea of an Education Science: Nostalgia for a World That Never Was

National Research Council Committee's report, in part a response to congressional legislation, pursues an outline for the foundations of an education science necessary for policy making. This article focuses on these foundations and argues that they have little to do with science and its relation to policy and may not be as fruitful as the committee believes. The so-called bedrocks of science are based on, at best, weak premises and an unrigorous understanding of the sociology, history, and philosophy of science. There is a nostalgia for a simple and ordered universe of science that never was. (Popkewitz, 2004, p. 62)

The Federal Government Is Seeking to De-center the University as a Knowledge Center

> This paper examines paradigm proliferation in the context of ongoing efforts by the federal government in the US to regulate academic research. It argues that these efforts amount to an attempt to reposition and de-center universities as sites of knowledge production, not just about education but across domains. (Nespor, 2006, p. 115)

It is clear from this sampling of responses to the *Scientific Research in Education* report that there are different reactions and some deep divisions over it. The responses indicate, too, the resurgence of ancient arguments from the last century and indeed before (see Darling-Hammond & Youngs, 2002; Gardner, 2002; Lather, 2004; Oakes & Lipton, 2003). But current discussions such as these, and the level of government intervention into funding policies, if sustained, will no doubt have important effects on research funding now and into the future. Identifying the level of government funding of qualitative research today is difficult,[4] but there can be no doubt about the potential effect funding limits could have on narrative research. Yet the need for research on difficult educational problems remains. Some practitioners point to the need to take a more rigorous approach to narrative inquiry and all education research (Bruner, 1999; Lagemann, 2000; Lagemann & Shulman, 1999). That has not been the case to date but it is now urged by AERA and also by the National Academy of Education (see Cochran-Smith & Frees, 2005; Cochran-Smith & Zeichner, 2005; Darling-Hammond & Youngs, 2002; Oakes & Lipton, 2003).

The Vibrancy of Narrative Inquiry Research

The future of narrative inquiry research offers a more hopeful prospect. If one looks at recent publications of journals such as the *Journal of Narrative and Life History,* the international composition of the boards of such journals, and the range of research they report, there is a clear sense of the vibrancy of narrative work. Similarly, in the Narrative Special Interest Group of AERA, there is a sense of vitality. Today's efforts to create a science of education seem to recapitulate the search in the past for a scientific human science, and the continuing advance of narrative inquiry, especially in the professions, reveals its acknowledged value. It is addressing important aspects of human concern.

The Question of Policy: What Influence of Narrative Inquiry Is Possible on Future Policy?

The question of the potential influence of narrative inquiry on practice is more easily suggested, and positively, especially given its current vibrant growth, but the question of narrative inquiry's influence on policy is more difficult to perceive. Given its close alignment to qualitative research, it will clearly be influenced in funding situations. The strictures for research designs and models are clearly delineated in research guidelines being supplied by the Institute of Education Sciences. Simultaneously, there are a plethora of policy issues at large. A quick perusal of the researchers quoted above reveals the following questions, ones that will need to be asked and answered for any funding consideration: What is a science of education? How should such a science be carried out? By whom? What implications lie in the new guidelines for scientific research? For the necessity for hard evidence? What influences might be placed on given theories? It is not difficult to see how historical contexts and political agendas will need to be addressed. How might narrative inquiry influence these policy issues?

I would like to suggest that narrative inquiries may have an important role to play in these future policy deliberations. I believe this may be precisely through research agendas—that is, through narrative investigations into some of the complex issues of contexts, history, culture; of individual students as learners; of educational studies and their results that may be usefully addressed through narrative research (see Clandinin & Connelly, 2000; Josselson et al., 2003, for a range of narrative research projects and methods that might be used).

Ray Rist (1998), who has explored and identified possibilities for engaging in qualitative research for policy purposes, uses the three phases of the policy cycle as a framework—that is, policy formulation, implementation, and policy accountability. For policy implementation—the current stage of the NRC's (2002) implementation of the *Scientific Research in Education* report mandating quantitative research designs—Rist (1998) suggests a two-way focus: on the degree to which a program is reaching its intended goals and reexamining the problem condition that prompted the policy response in the first place. While Rist suggests excellent questions for possible research, for each policy phase, he is surprisingly pessimistic that this will ever get implemented. He argues as follows:

> These contributions are more in the realm of the potential than the actual . . . . The issue is . . . how to link those in the research and academic communities who are knowledgeable in conducting qualitative research studies to those in the policy arena who can commission the work and who will make use of the findings. . . . The issues of institutional cultures, academic reward systems, publication requirements, funding sources and methodological limitations are but five among many that will have to be addressed. (pp. 422–423)

Rist compellingly presents the ongoing possibilities and the defying dilemmas. These needs are not likely to diminish—in spite even of government mandates. They will challenge narrative researchers to discover and invent ways of addressing them. Narrative inquiry very likely will take on the challenge and, in doing so, will develop and expand.

My fundamental hunch is that, as Barthes (1988) declares, narrative is "simply there like life itself" (p. 95). It will, I believe, remain so, strong, compelling, life-giving.

Author's Note: I want to thank the three reviewers of this article, Jane Attanucci, Vicki LaBoskey, and Tom Barone, for their thoughtful critiques and suggestions. I thank Joan Moon for her several readings and editorial keenness. Carla Lillvik, of Harvard's Gutman Library, contributed useful research. I wish to acknowledge as well the long-standing mentorship of Maxine Greene, the inspiring work of Elliot Mishler, the insightful discussions with Nel Noddings and Blythe Clinchy, and the ongoing support of Jean Clandinin.

Consulting Editors: Jane Attanucci, Vicki LaBoskey, and Tom Barone

Notes

1. *Qualitative Research:* In this discussion, I use *qualitative* and *narrative* somewhat interchangeably, recognizing that narrative is a subset of qualitative research and that each has its own history. Qualitative research has grown spectacularly over the past 20 years, gaining in reputation for itself and for several of its variants, such as narrative inquiry. Qualitative research is usually distinguished from quantitative, experimental research by its use of words, not numbers. It involves multimethods and an interpretive, naturalistic approach to its subject matter. Researchers "study things in their natural settings, attempting to make sense of, or interpret, phenomena in terms of the meanings people bring to them" (Denzin & Lincoln, 1998, p. 3). These can make use of a variety of forms, such as case studies, interviews, life histories, and historical or visual texts. Narrative inquiries depend on the interactions of the individuals involved in some form of collaboration.

2. *International Research:* I consider that today it is increasingly likely that international researchers are and will be engaged together in many studies, and, as the world grows ever interconnected, this will continue, even grow, for narrative inquiry research. A brief review of the 2006 annual meeting of the AERA reveals that the conference program carries a special "Subject Index" heading for "International Education Studies" presentations. In addition, there are some eight Special Interest Groups (SIGs), permanent members of the organization who represent international interests, such as Global Child Advocacy, Dual Language International Research, etc. Of course, many international members are not identified as such.

3. *Narrative, Narrative Inquiry, and Narrative Inquiry Research:* In this chapter, I make certain distinctions among these terms. *Narrative* I consider both as story and its telling, what is constructed and then related. A narrative inquiry is an investigation into some puzzle or problem, in Dewey's sense (Dewey, 1933/1998, p. 12). Narrative can function as a method—an interview, a case study, etc.—and as a product. Narrative inquiry research is a way of knowing, a method of investigation involving an intentional, reflective process, the likely actions of several people interrogating some puzzle/problem of their practice and constructing and telling the story of its meaning and how it might be used in the future (Lyons & LaBoskey, 2002, p. 2).

4. *Funding of Qualitative Research:* The question of how qualitative narrative research is being affected by the new research mandates of National Research Council's report titled *Scientific Research in Education* is difficult to tease out. To date, data documenting the level or change in funding are not immediately available by category. Guidelines from the

Institute of Education Sciences available at its Web site emphasize quantitative research. Baseline data to determine changes would demand a research project in their own right. It was interesting, however, to discover a document from the National Institutes of Health (NIH) that gives guidelines for preparing proposals addressing how to meet the new requirements for NIH funding titled *Qualitative Methods in Health Research*.

References

American Educational Research Association. (2003). *Resolution on the essential elements of scientifically-based research.* Washington, DC: Author.

American Psychological Association. (1984, November). Narrative knowing. *Monitor.*

Amsterdam, A. G., & Bruner, J. (2000). *Minding the law (How courts rely on storytelling, and how the stories change the ways we understand the law and ourselves).* Cambridge, MA: Harvard University Press.

Barthes, R. (1988). Introduction to the structural analysis of narratives. In R. Harris (Trans.), *The semiotic challenge* (pp. 95–135). New York: Hill & Wang.

Belenky, M., Clinchy, B., Goldberger, N., & Tarule, J. (1986). *Women's ways of knowing.* New York: Basic Books.

Bernstein, R. (1983). *Beyond objectivism and relativism: Science, hermeneutics, and praxis.* Philadelphia: University of Pennsylvania Press.

Bleakley, A. (2005). Stories as data, data as stories: making sense of narrative inquiry in clinical education. *Medical Education, 39*(5), 534–540.

Bloch, M. (2004). A discourse that disciplines, governs, and regulates. *Qualitative Inquiry, 10*(1), 96–110.

Bruner, J. (1986). *Actual minds, possible worlds.* Cambridge, MA: Harvard University Press.

Bruner, J. (1990). *Acts of meaning.* Cambridge, MA: Harvard University Press.

Bruner, J. (1996). The narrative construal of reality. In J. Bruner (Ed.), *The culture of education* (pp. 130–149). Cambridge, MA: Harvard University Press.

Bruner, J. (1999). Postscript: some reflections on education research. In E. C. Lagemann & L. Shulman (Eds.), *Issues in education research: Problems and possibilities* (pp. 399–410). San Francisco: Jossey-Bass.

Bruner, J. (2002). *Making stories: Law, literature, life.* Cambridge, MA: Harvard University Press.

Charon, R. (2005). *Narrative medicine.* Retrieved June 3, 2005, from www.gp-training .net/training/consultation/narrative.htm

Clandinin, D. J., & Connelly, F. M. (2000). *Narrative inquiry: Experience and story in qualitative research.* San Francisco: Jossey-Bass.

Clinchy, B. (2003). An epistemological approach to the teaching of narrative research. In R. Josselson, A. Lieblich, & D. McAdams (Eds.), *Up close and personal: The teaching and learning of narrative research* (pp. 29–48). Washington, DC: American Psychological Association.

Cochran-Smith, M., & Fries, K. (2005). The AERA panel on research and teacher education: Context and goals. In M. Cochran-Smith & K. Zeichner (Eds.), *Studying teacher education: The report of the AERA panel on research and teacher education* (pp. 37–67). Mahwah, NJ: Erlbaum.

Cochran-Smith, M., & Zeichner, K. (2005). Executive summary. In M. Cochran-Smith & K. Zeichner (Eds.), *Studying teacher education: The report of the AERA panel on research and teacher education* (pp. 1–36). Mahwah, NJ: Erlbaum.

Cole, M. (1996). *Cultural psychology: A once and future discipline.* Cambridge, MA: Harvard University Press.

Darling-Hammond, L., & Youngs, P. (2002). Defining "highly qualified teachers": What does "scientifically-based research" actually tell us? *Educational Researcher, 31*(9), 13–25.

Denzin, N. K., & Lincoln, Y. S. (1998). *Collecting and interpreting qualitative materials.* Thousand Oaks, CA: Sage.

Dewey, J. (1929). *The sources of a science of education.* New York: Horace Liveright.

Dewey, J. (1933/1998). *How we think.* Boston: Houghton Mifflin.

Donmoyer, R. (2006). Take my paradigm . . . please! The legacy of Kuhn's construct in educational research. *International Journal of Qualitative Studies in Education, 19*(1), 11–34.

Feuer, M. J., Towne, L., & Shavelson, R. J. (2002). Scientific culture and educational research. *Educational Researcher, 32*(80), 21–24.

Gadamer, G. H. (1979/1987). The problem of historical consciousness. In P. Rabinow & W. Sullivan (Eds.), *Interpretive social science: A second look* (pp. 82–140). Berkeley: University of California Press.

Gardner, H. (2002). The quality and qualities of educational research. Retrieved on October 11, 2003, from www.edweek.org/ew/ewstory.cfm?slug=01gardner.h22

Garvin, D. (2003, September–October). Making the case: Professional education for the world of practice. *Harvard Magazine,* pp. 56–107.

Gilligan, C. (1982). *In a different voice.* Cambridge, MA: Harvard University Press.

Goldberger, N., & Veroff, J. B. (1995). *The cultural and psychology reader.* New York: New York University Press.

Gould, S. J. (1989). *Wonderful life: The Burgess shale and the nature of history.* New York: W. W. Norton.

Greene, M. (1978). *Landscapes of learning.* New York: Teachers College Press.

Greenhalgh, T., & Hurwitz, B. (1999). *Narrative based medicine: Why study narrative?* Retrieved June 3, 2005, from http://bmj.bmjjournals.com/cgi/content/full/318/7175/48

Hansen, A. (1987). Suggestions for seminar participants. In C. R. Christensen & A. J. Hansen (Eds.), *Teaching and the case method* (pp. 69–76). Boston: Harvard Business School Press.

Hiley, D. R., Bohnam, J., & Shusterman, R. (1991). *The interpretive turn: Philosophy, science, culture.* Ithaca, NY: Cornell University Press.

Josselson, R., Lieblich, A., & McAdams, D. P. (Eds.). (2003). *Up close and personal: The teaching and learning of narrative research.* Washington, DC: American Psychological Association.

Kaestle, C. F. (1993). The awful reputation of educational research. *Educational Researcher, 22*(1), 26–31.

Keller, E. F. (1984). *A feeling for the organism.* New York: W. H. Freeman.

Kuhn, T. (1962/1970). *The structure of scientific revolutions.* Chicago: University of Chicago Press.

Labov, W., & Waletsky, J. (1967). Narrative analysis: Oral versions of personal experience. In J. Helm (Ed.), *Essays on verbal and visual arts: Proceedings of the 1966 annual spring meeting of the American Ethnological Society* (pp. 12–44). Seattle: University of Washington.

Lagemann, E. C. (2000). *An elusive science: The troubling history of education research.* Chicago: University of Chicago Press.

Lagemann, E. C., & Shulman. L. (1999). *Issues in education research.* San Francisco: Jossey-Bass.

Lather, P. (2004). This IS your father's paradigm: Government intrusion and the case of qualitative research in education. *Qualitative Inquiry, 10*(1), 15–34.

Lyons, N., & LaBoskey, V. (2002). *Narrative inquiry in practice.* New York: Teachers College Press.

MacIntyre, A. (1984). *After virtue: A study in moral theory* (2nd ed.). Notre Dame, IN: University of Notre Dame Press.

Martin, J. (1985). *Reclaiming a conversation.* New Haven, CT: Yale University Press.

Maxwell, J. (2004). Causal explanation, qualitative research, and scientific inquiry in education. *Educational Researcher, 33*(2), 3–11.

Mishler, E. (1995). Models of narrative analysis: A typology. *Journal of Narrative and Life History, 5*(2), 87–103.

Mitchell, W. J. T. (1981). *On narrative.* Chicago: University of Chicago Press.

National Academy of Education. (2005). NAEd collaborates with National Research Council. *Academy Notes, 7*(2), 3.

National Research Council. (2002). *Scientific research in education.* Washington, DC: National Academies Press.

Nespor, J. C. (2006). Morphologies of inquiry. *International Journal of Qualitative Studies in Education, 19*(1), 115–128.

No Child Left Behind Act of 2001, Public Law No. 107–110 (2001).

Noddings, N. (1984). *Caring.* Berkeley: University of California Press.

Nussbaum, M. (1995). *Poetic justice: The literary imagination and public life.* Boston: Beacon Press.

Nussbaum, M. (1997). *Cultivating humanity: A classical defense of reform in liberal education.* Cambridge, MA: Harvard University Press.

Oakes, J. & Lipton, M. (2003). *Teaching to change the world.* Boston: McGraw-Hill.

Olson, D. (2004). The triumph of hope over experience in the search for "What Works?" a response. *Educational Researcher, 32*(1), 24–26.

Polkinghorne, D. (1988). *Narrative knowing and the human sciences.* Albany: State University of New York Press.

Popkewitz, T. S. (2004). Is the National Research Council's report on scientific research in education scientific? Or trusting the manifesto. *Qualitative Inquiry, 10*(1), 62–78.

Posner, R. A. (1998). *Law and literature.* Cambridge, MA: Harvard University Press.

Potts, L. J. (1968). *Aristotle on the art of fiction: An English translation of Aristotle's poetics.* London: Cambridge University Press.

Propp, V. (1968). *Morphology of the folktale* (2nd ed.). Austin: University of Texas Press.

Rabinow, P., & Sullivan, W. (1979/1987). *Interpretive social science: A second look.* Berkeley: University of California Press.

Ricoeur, P. (1981). Narrative time. In W. J. T. Mitchell (Ed.), *On narrative* (pp. 165–186). Chicago: University of Chicago Press.

Rist, R. (1998). Influencing the policy process with qualitative research. In N. K. Denzin & Y. S. Lincoln (Eds.), *Collecting and interpreting qualitative materials* (pp. 619–644). Thousand Oaks, CA: Sage.

Salmon, W. C. (1989). Four decades of scientific explanation. In P. Kitcher & W. C. Salmon (Eds.), *Scientific explanation* (pp. 3–219). Minneapolis: University of Minnesota Press.

Shavelson, R. J., Phillips, D. C., Towne, L., & Feuer, M. J. (2003). On the science of education design studies. *Educational Researcher, 32*(1), 25–28.

Shweder, R. A. (1995).Cultural psychology: What is it? In N. R. Goldberger & J. B. Veroff (Eds.), *The culture and psychology reader* (pp. 41–86). New York: New York University Press.

Slavin, R. E. (2002). Evidence-based education policies: Transforming educational practice and research. *Educational Researcher, 31*(7), 15–21.

Slavin, R. E. (2004). Education research can and must address "What Works?" Questions. *Educational Researcher, 33*(1), 27–28.

Taylor, C. (1979/1987). Interpretation and the sciences of man. In P. Rabinow & W. Sullivan (Eds.), *Interpretive social science: A second look* (pp. 32–81). Berkeley: University of California Press.

Thernstrom, M. (2004, April 18). Can narrative medicine make you a better doctor? *New York Times Magazine*, pp. 41–86.

White, H. (1981). The value of narrativity in the representation of reality. In W. J. T. Mitchell (Ed.), *On narrative* (pp. 1–24). Chicago: University of Chicago Press.

White, J. B. (1973). *The legal imagination: Studies in the nature of legal thought and expression.* Boston: Little, Brown.

White, S. (1996). Foreword. In M. Cole (Ed.), *Cultural psychology: A once and future discipline* (pp. 1–10). Cambridge, MA: Harvard University Press.

CHAPTER 24

Looking Ahead

Conversations With Elliot Mishler,
Don Polkinghorne, and Amia Lieblich

D. Jean Clandinin and M. Shaun Murphy

As we envisioned this last chapter, we wanted to take a look forward to the future of narrative inquiry, a framing of the chapter that would take an imaginative turn. As we engaged in our own views of what the possibilities and promises of narrative inquiry might be, we included the voices of Amia Lieblich, Elliot Mishler, and Don Polkinghorne,[1] who are widely acknowledged as people who contributed to the shaping of the field of narrative inquiry. Their works are so frequently quoted in most narrative inquiry works that it is almost impossible for new narrative inquirers not to be referred to their works.

Our overarching conversation topic was on what their advice might be to new narrative inquirers paying particular attention to tensions with other research traditions, the political contexts of research, and the ethics of narrative inquiries. While our conversations took different twists and turns, we did find common threads that linked us back to these questions. What we offer below are segments from the transcripts of the conversations with them. While we spoke to each of them individually, we represent the conversations by laying segments of different conversations side by side. We edited the transcripts slightly to make them more readable and grouped them around topical threads. As we threaded the transcripts together, we reflected on what we heard them saying and linked it to what we are thinking about the future of narrative inquiry.

Topical Thread One: The Importance of Distinguishing Narrative Inquiry From Other Forms of Qualitative Research

When Don Polkinghorne and Elliot Mishler spoke of narrative inquiry, they described it as philosophically different from other qualitative methodologies.

D. P.: I think in qualitative research there is a general push to provide taxonomies and conceptual systems and so on which sort of look for commonalities across interviews and other things. And my own point there is, I think that narrative is quite different, that it really deals with individual lives. . . . I come at narrative more than from a philosophical perspective in terms of it's—it's the way we understand human existence. And so I really push . . . for my students . . . to do individual case study narrative life stories and they can, if they want, usually have a final chapter of comment on it, on especially noticing the differences, how people have responded differently to similar events in their lives and how they've responded in some similar ways. But that when you use narrative as a kind of data which is sort of equivalent to any other kind of interview data and you analyze it and the way qualitative analysis normally looks at things I think it misses the significance of what narrative is about. That it can capture, you know, in this kind of temporal development of lives, of the unique histories of people.

S. M.: With those two different ones is there a tension with the ethics then about how you're doing it with narrative and your comparison with qualitative?

D. P.: I see it as a tension and that I have some real questions about . . . approaches that we've been doing. This renewal of qualitative research has been going on for about 30 years now, and we've got a lot of stuff out there. But there are two problems with it. One, it's not very good, and a lot of it has to do with people who aren't trained to do it, but the first thing they do is their dissertation and a lot of other things come out of that. And the second, it doesn't seem, it doesn't get integrated in any way, but it is looking for things that are common across people and so on. And I think what narrative is about and that it's a different kind of knowledge, it's a knowledge of the particular, the unique, the development rather than a kind of abstractive common concept. . . . My own history goes way back to existential philosophy which focuses on the uniqueness and personal history as the thing that makes up human beings and makes them different from other things. . . . In terms of my own work with students I haven't had any problems, and I'm, a lot of the qualitative research we do here is much more case study, case, in a particular way, but it's the individual lives or episodes in an individual life.

J. C.: And that's what you do in the narrative?

D. P.: Yes.

J. C.: As opposed to the qualitative where they're taking, trying to do semantic analysis and, and in some ways lose the particular and lose the people?

D. P.: Right.

J. C.: So we lose the uniqueness of the experience looking for the commonality of the experience?

D. P.: I wrote an article where I distinguish, and I have some problems with the terms I use now, but the difference between analysis of narratives which I felt was a qualitative approach. You have stories, and then you try to analyze them by coming up with common themes and so on, and I sort of thought that's what qualitative research is doing. And the difference was the narrative analysis which was looking at an individual life or portion of the life and the final result was a story. . . . It came from a lot of different sources, but what you tried to end up with was a description of the life movement of a particular person.

J. C.: Right. And that's an article that we talk a lot about here in the Centre where I do my work because I think that's a really helpful distinction, Don. Maybe you could talk about people who would call themselves narrative researchers or narrative inquirers who are still taking those narratives and analyzing them. Elliot Mishler talks about not policing the boundaries or the borders. Do you think we need to get a little clearer about what we mean when we say "narrative research"? Do you think we need to just keep encouraging anybody who says "I'm doing narrative" to name their work *narrative*?

D. P.: Well one of the difficulties I think is with the word *narrative* because it does have a general meaning of any kind of prose. So if you're filling out a form, there's a narrative place for why you want to go to the school or something like that, and that's called narrative. And I think, and in reading qualitative books and so on they're always talking about "we've got narrative data from interviews," but it's just that it's somebody's description of something that happened to them. It is not necessarily in story form. So I think some people talk about doing, they're doing narrative research when what they're doing is basically qualitative research and their data is narrative, but it is not storied. And how do, I mean whenever I present on this stuff, I always start off with trying to clarify that what makes my approach narrative research is that it is a particular kind of my grammar of language which describes changes through time experienced as it gets sedimented and affects other things. And that that's quite different and it really, it is a story form, and the story itself is very much related to the way we experience our own lives and so on, and the narrative research deals with that. Policing, I have some general problems with. I think clarifying whenever possible. I don't know how to go to people and say, "Well you're not really doing." But I would like to reserve the

term for just kind of philosophical meaning and, and in terms of story. . . .
But that language in a storied form presents a different kind of,
of well not, not reality, but it describes things in ways that can't be described
when you're talking about concepts and commonalities and so on.

J. C.: [Elliot we want to ask you about] the explosion of narrative going on everywhere. You've written, Elliot, about not wanting to police the boundaries.

E. M.: Well, that's because no one can. That doesn't mean that I like everything that
I see. But I think I probably do what other people do; there's some work that
I never refer to and I don't have to worry about people thinking, "My God
he's not reading everything." But it just doesn't fit with my ways of thinking
about what's useful to do in working with narratives or how to go about it.
But there are just a lot of different ways because people have come from different fields. I mean our concerns—that is, you in education and me, in
psychology—come out of the quantitative positivist traditions that we were
in one way or another breaking away from. . . . But anyway, so there is a lot
of work, and I think my own sense is we can each learn from, there is something to be learned from various alternative approaches. I think that it kind
of wastes time to get involved in squabbles about this. I mean I tend, my own
biases from my own work and by and large from many of the people that are
in my narrative study group, so . . . all together, I tend to . . . be particularly
interested in doing detailed analyses of the talk. I'm not trained in social linguistics, but . . . those are the resources I tend to use. And so I tend to focus
on selecting materials doing as close and detailed analysis as I can of particular stretches of talk and of narratives. A lot of people in the field don't do
that. I mean you know they work with themes so they do grounded theory
kinds of stuff or they take chunks of stuff and then comment or interpret
them. And mostly I don't . . . use that material very much in my own work,
I mean if giving a paper or talking within my narrative groups on a particular topic, you know, we will bring something from those traditions in, of
that work, but it's not stuff that I find draws me or that I learn very much
from. But that doesn't mean I think people shouldn't be doing it. I mean
that's how they go about it. If there's something in that work other people
will come to do it and there'll be a particular subcell of narrative research.
There's different research communities. And this will be one of them. But
that's true in a lot of the advanced sciences. . . . I tend to think of narrative
as a problem-centered area of inquiry. And that people address the kinds of
problems they're interested in and find that one or another form of narrative methodology is useful for doing it. So I rarely, and every once in a while
I get upset and will be critical of something, but mostly I try not to pay
attention. I don't pay attention; I don't have time.

As we read the transcripts from Don and Elliot, we were struck by the tensions
we saw between different ways of understanding narrative inquiry within the larger
field of qualitative methodologies. Don spoke of his distinction between narrative
analysis and analysis of narratives. For him, analysis of narratives can be seen as a

form of qualitative research more generally—that is, narratives are analyzed into themes and categories. Narrative analysis, however, fits within narrative inquiry, which understands lives as unfolding temporally, as particular events within a particular individual's life. The final result is a story. This distinguishes narrative inquiry, what he is calling narrative analysis, from analysis of narratives and qualitative research more generally. He hopes for more clarification on how researchers distinguish their work as narrative inquiry rather than qualitative research more generally.

Elliot notes that we cannot police the boundaries of narrative inquiry. For him, the field of narrative inquiry will be defined from within the different communities of narrative inquirers with researchers picking up on each others' work that helps them address issues salient to their own research problems. We can learn from various alternative approaches, picking up and applying what seems appropriate to what each of us is attending to.

E. M.: It's not something we can do by rules, and there are various kinds of difficulties. I mean I've always thought that doing this kind of work actually provides other investigators and readers with material that allows them to make their judgment, that as we're presenting the stories that we're analyzing. And somebody reading it can look at the story and look at our analyses and make some judgment as to whether that makes sense. That's my reservation about people who simply give you a fragment of text and then interpret it without analyzing the text. I find it difficult to think in terms of validating what they're doing. It's too broad a way. But others, clinicians who do that work all the time or therapists don't find that problematic. I find it problematic. But it's in that sense that we were always presenting our material so that a reader, other researchers, can make her or his own judgments about whether the interpretation makes sense, whether the analysis brings up something that's of interest. But the problem that has come up more and more in recent years at least in our discussion groups for which we don't have . . . a way to think this through yet because of the work we do, and though we're presenting some of the material, it's a very small hunk of the data that we have. And what we have not done I don't think . . . anywhere in the field because I don't know anybody who's really tried to attend to this in a serious way, is how to describe the process by which we selected that . . . story to present as representing our body of data. And we don't have any, I don't know that there could ever be formal rules about this, but we don't even have ways of, we don't require people when they publish things to provide some description of how they went about selecting what they've presented as their data. Or how they see it as representing the larger pool of data. . . . I think that my own predictions or that among the directions that we'll be likely be moved in, one is the business of visual. And that has lots of consequences because we will move even a little further away from our text-based ways of analysis . . . into something that includes visual material and gestures and movements and whatever. The other is that I think there's somewhat more attention to, to group stories. And I have people in my group who are studying family stories of people sitting around a dinner table and telling a story about what's happened in their family, where the story gets developed by several people together interacting.

One concern that Elliot highlighted, and that he feels we as narrative inquirers need to attend to, is about selection of the small bits of data that we include as representative of our large data set. He sees this problem of data selection as a problem of validation. Another concern is visual narrative inquiry, which shifts us from our historically text-based method of analysis. He highlights for us the technological influences in how we collect our data and how this shapes our work as narrative inquirers. We wonder, too, about the ways in which technology allows us to represent our narrative inquiries, and this, too, will further shape our work. His final point draws us to the place of community in his conceptions of narrative inquiry. Here, he wonders about the ways stories are co-constructed in groups. In his words, "The story gets developed by several people together interacting." While his wonder is about the generation of stories that become our data, we wonder, too, how our interpretations are shaped as we come together in groups to make sense of the stories lived and told.

Topical Thread Two: Narrative Inquiry on a Shifting Methodological Landscape

One thread of conversation was how the shifting landscape of methodology influenced narrative inquirers. We had not made this a specific question, but it was a strong thread in the conversations of both Amia Lieblich and Don Polkinghorne. Both Amia and Don work closely with graduate students and experience tensions alongside their students on the shifting landscape. Elliot Mishler explained that he did not work with graduate students but mostly with postdoctoral fellows and others in academic positions.

A. L.: Tremendous ambition to belong to the sciences, to the exact sciences or life sciences and with behaviorism having such a tremendous influence in the American academy and this is actually the pioneer for the whole field. So clinical psychology where a more humanistic holistic view of human beings was possible was eliminated from mainstream psychology in academia. And this was not considered research, it was case studies maybe and stories, but not research. So this is such a strong tradition, which is positivist, which is objective, and they find it very hard to accept what, let me say simply, what I do as scientific work. So I'd say maybe they, the problem is with how you define *science*. As Ken Gergen says that the traditional science is so old-fashioned, but still this is, to as much as I can see within the colleges, this is a dominant canonical way of how the curriculum is formed with all the educational aims that excellent departments put before the students. And they make it much easier for students who go, you know, along their objective, scientific quantitative experimental manner [than those who go] to this narrative. So we have an island in psychology of people like myself and Dan McAdams . . . and last May we had a conference here in Jerusalem and I, and we really shared our feelings among the more, more old timers. Mark Freeman was also here and, and [we realized we have] . . . the same feelings that we are somehow marginalized in psychology and as long as we can just keep it up and not give up and so on, then maybe the trend will change.

D. P.: Almost all the people who are in leading positions now were trained as quantitative researchers and in that belief system. We have a new doctoral EdD program and almost all the students in that program are doing qualitative dissertations. They're being supervised by people who basically don't really believe in them but are willing to go along with them but somehow, so I don't know what to tell students about that, but we allow them to do it. And, but I don't think they have sufficient background. You know still our requirements are six courses in statistics and research, traditional research design, and one course in general qualitative research. I had a study with one of my students on, in fact, APA counseling psych. programs and it's the same thing there that those, most of those programs do offer a qualitative course, but it's usually in addition to the basic research courses and often it's not a required course and something they have to do in the end, and it also comes after, at the end of their programs, if they take it. So it's too late in the sense of really giving them background to do a study. I'm just hoping that time heals some of that and people who were the students, present students will end up in these faculty positions and so on.

Amia Lieblich drew attention to the loneliness of the work of narrative inquirers, particularly in psychology, where she felt the loneliness of her work. She noted the importance of sharing her experiences with other narrative inquirers at conferences to push against the marginalizing forces of positivistic plotlines in the academy. She found encouragement alongside other narrative inquirers to persevere in order to change the methodological plotlines.

Don Polkinghorne, positioning himself within education and psychology, notes the difficulties of graduate students wanting to be narrative inquirers but confronting supervisors and programs oriented toward positivistic plotlines. He speaks of the low position of qualitative research methodologies in programs with one course tagged on at the end of a full program. For him, change on the methodological landscape may come as these current students assume faculty positions.

As we talked with Amia and Don, they both spoke of the place of mixed methods on the shifting landscape. They spoke of the place of mixed methods in remarkably different ways.

A. L.: It is a question that I didn't raise directly of doing a study which has a combination of quantitative and qualitative methods together. Can this be done? Can this be a way to answer the critiques that this is not a very academic work with all the serious requirements? OK, so I do part of my study with statistics, with significant tests and so on and so forth. And the dilemma is very serious from my point of view because I think that the philosophical basis of our work as narrative scholars is post-modern, and it is really in contradiction with many of the basic assumptions of quantitative research. So it's not just a matter of having a repertoire of the different methods that you could use because you have been trained in very highly, you know, sophisticated statistics and the computer world as well. It is a question of how you really philosophically combine this use of the human being which underlines the system of objective research as compared to the system of qualitative, constructive, post-modern, or whatever narrative research. I've mixed feelings about this. Sometimes for political reasons really to help in the careers of my students, I advise them to do a combination study. For example, I have now a PhD student who is doing a fantastic, I think, piece of research on "what does it mean for a new immigrant to construct" to, how would I tell it, "to conceive the immigration story as a good story, as a positive successful story or a story of failure." What are the differences that make people really conceive their immigration as success or failure? So, basically, what she wanted is to interview maybe you know 15 immigrants from . . . to Israel who have come 10 years ago and we know that they consider their transition to be very successful and compare it to people who would say that their transition was not successful or even a failure. But in order to be on the safe side with this kind of . . . she started by collecting from 300 new immigrants questionnaires about their quality of life now. And she has very, very interesting statistical material about these 300 immigrants, and she kept presenting me all kinds of high-quality journals that require statistical documentation, et cetera. Out of this sample of 300, she has really handpicked the most successful 15 people and the most, least successful 15 people, and she approached them very gently and asked them would they be willing to meet with her again and to have now a different approach to their experience by telling their life story. And she's now analyzing the qualitative part. I don't know yet what will come out of it. So this is an example where I think we've been able to defend this project also against the most ardent critics of the objective, you know, science community. And for this young woman it is a good strategy because she can show in her PhD that she is mastered in both the statistical approaches to doing good research as well the narrative approach. But as I said in my introduction to this idea, the basic assumptions which are underlying those two, those two approaches, they are not doing big harmony among. . . . And this is a little embarrassing. I don't think it will come up in her PhD, but I think like basically between us we know that it is not perfectly all right. You really have to make your choice, you know, and I'm sad to say that it's difficult.

J. C.:   Right. And I agree Amia. I mean there is, philosophically, a big divide. And what you're saying is that it's a way of starting to shift the field if we get students to do this more mixed-method kind of approach knowing that philosophically there's a conflict. But maybe that's the way we can move the field and certainly create some safety for our new researchers.

D. P.:   I think one of the areas that it is really making an impact though is in evaluation studies. And there, there seems to be more acceptance for the multiple methods. And there it's sort of added to, it gives depth to an understanding of what the statistics are talking about. But the evaluation studies are not trying to make generalized things of it, coming up with this particular therapy or this particular set of techniques will produce the results sort of within any context. There they're looking at a particular program and how people have experienced it and what kind of outcomes that program has had. And that's one of the areas. It's a different kind of research and, I think I don't know if you call it more basic but more sort of not looking to find out whether a program worked or not or what somebody's experience of a particular program was. But it's an area, I think, that there's more acceptance.

For Amia, the use of mixed methods allowed beginning narrative inquirers into the complex political landscape of academia. For Amia, and for us, this is not without tension given the different epistemological and ontological assumptions that can underlie different methodologies. For Don, the use of multiple methods has limited contexts to be successfully used. Evaluation studies are one place where he sees narrative inquiry as successfully blending with other methodologies.

Topical Thread Three: The Political Contexts of Narrative Inquiry

When we asked them to speak about the political context within which we work as narrative inquirers, each of them took up our question although in slightly different ways. We pull forward the most salient pieces of their transcripts in what follows.

A. L.:   As a psychologist I'm talking within the field of psychology. I would be very careful in advising people to go only in their narrative or qualitative way. I would make it very clear that with all the richness and the real complexity that one can touch with this matter, there are also many, many risks and dangers involved in pursuing this manner of research. Because in psychology, and this really relates to your political question, I have a feeling that we didn't make very much progress in being accepted in by the mainstream of this field, and I would be very hesitant in telling young people who plan to have academic careers to base their research on narrative or qualitative methods alone because I'm afraid they will have much difficulties in finding jobs or in getting promoted later, even in getting published in what are considered psychology's top-level journals. So with much regret, I would say to my students that one advice is to postpone maybe this kind of research for later in their careers when they are more mature, when they have established their reputation, when they have accepted jobs and maybe tenure, and they can then be more free to pursue this kind of work.

D. P.:   In the USA we still have people who are true believers in, that, if you do a between-group study, you've found truth. They actually give the answers on what one should do . . . and this seems to be the federal government position and also the Department of Education position in that the *No Child Left Behind* policy lists what is acceptable for evidence on what points of practice and so on and then down at the bottom of the list they have what's called anecdotal things, and I think they would include narrative there.

J. C.:   Probably.

D. P.:   I think there's more and more people who are interested, and it's a kind of reform movement in education and in the social sciences which accepts more of the language and the broader thing of qualitative research. And at the same time either it's a reaction to that or some sort of notion that we really have to find out and know in advance what things work and what to do in working with people. So I see there are real tensions . . . between student interests and more and more work being done in qualitative and narrative research and the sort of official positions.

E. M.:   But I think that one of the things that I think is possible is that with all of these restraints the areas of narrative inquiry, that broad areas of narrative inquiry have really grown enormously. I mean there's narrative research going on all over . . . in all sorts of disciplines I mean and you keep running across it. I only recently discovered some new work by sociologists who were doing legal research, work in the law, and I had been doing work on what I call "Narratives of Resistance" in the medical area and suddenly discovered that there are these people who have worked on narratives of resistance, calling it by the same name, drawing on some of the same sources that I drew on, but they're studying how people deal with the legal system. And . . . we can then link up. So there are people in different disciplines and all over the world. Now I mention that because I think for all of us it has been very critical to being able to sustain our work because . . . what has not happened is that within their own departments everybody still remains somewhat the loner doing narrative research. . . . And I've been surprised that we've now, in this past couple of months, been reviewing how our work has changed over the last twenty years in the field and in our own work. . . . But people are still reporting that they feel like outsiders in their department of psychology or sociology or whatever.

We noted that all three researchers took the long view as researchers composing lives over time when they spoke to the political context. Amia Lieblich drew attention to the risks that individual researchers took when they focused only on the narrative or even only on qualitative research methodologies. She highlighted the academic political context of tenure, promotion, and publications and cautioned young researchers on the need to make sure that their work was widely recognized. For her, that meant expertise in a wide range of research methodologies.

Don Polkinghorne drew our attention to the larger policy context that sets the requirements for research funding within a kind of hierarchy that positions narrative inquiry at the bottom. He highlights that beginning researchers often want to explore the complex issues that narrative inquiry enables but that this is in tension with official policy positions.

Elliot Mishler sees that narrative inquiry is expanding into multiple disciplinary fields and is being taken up with reference to similar problems and theoretical resources. He encourages narrative inquirers who feel isolated in their own departments or disciplines to look broadly in search of other researchers exploring similar problems in their particular contexts.

Topical Thread Four: Advice on Learning to Be a Narrative Inquirer

In the following pieces of transcript, Amia, Don, and Elliot spoke of the kinds of advice they would give to beginning narrative inquirers.

A. L.: This advice is not only politically correct in terms of the field as I see it but also maybe very young people are not highly equipped with the life experience to be able to do the kind of research that good narrative scholars are doing which really requires maturity and experience and sensitivity to people and to one's self, which takes years to develop. It is not easy to say this to young people like those . . . it's not very popular unless they respect the teacher or whoever is giving this advice. . . . Because often, really, very young people find it difficult to see all the levels of what can be really interpreted as the things people tell us when they tell their lives' stories or when we observe their behaviors. So I think it's not only politically good advice but also maybe from the point of view of how this research is carried out and how much personal involvement is really required which is not technical know-how, but it is some kind of steps and understanding and life experience. . . . We can help them I think, of course, because education can always help, but some processes say will take more time and some need really life experience. How can we help? One is by reading a lot. I think that reading and not only psychological research which is relevant or educational research but reading literature. Novels and poetry is a way to expose people to experiences of others and to make people more aware of their own inner world and how they view others and the way maybe they tend to construct others in their lives and so on. So literature and poetry and have people discuss in small groups, in peer groups, different interpretations to expose people to the multilevels of all these and to show them how each experience or each little story or big story can have so many meanings for different people. So I guess that if you have seminars or reading groups where people really [work] with the classics, with Shakespeare, with Tolstoy, I think this might be some sort of a replacement of real-life experience which we cannot just, you know, push people into. But also sending people out of academia into schools where they are exposed to different cultures, to different places when they face problems that they may have been sheltered from. The other things will open them up to what I see is necessary for people to, to really do their interpretation and understand what's going on in really writing about life, writing about the other people in the holistic fashion and not in an analytical fashion you know this piece and that piece and . . .

S. M.: Amia when you talk about doing this kind of work, you talk in, in some of your writing about it being a craft. Do you see this as part of that experience of working towards it as a craft?

A. L.: I didn't understand your question because the only thing was . . .

S. M.: Well you talk about the research as a kind of craft, craftsmanship. And I'm wondering if when you talk about having life experience and working with different kinds of methods if I understand you, are you talking about that as an idea of working with a craft or coming to know what you're doing?

A. L.: Yes. Like all skills, it takes training and supervision and the good teachers that will correct your work and will, you know, explain how to do it and so on. But I think it's more complex because there is no cookbook for doing this. There are no very clear and simple instructions. And it is so frustrating for people who want teachers that will tell them exactly how to do it. And there are a lot of things we can tell them but not exactly the step-by-step method of achieving the rich and the complex results that I believe is always there when you're studying human life or human life story . . . and another thing I was going to say when you asked me, "How can we help them?" the whole trend for autobiographical studies, and it is quite similar to the way people in training to become psychotherapists are required to go through samples, bits of therapy themselves. I think that this is also very helpful to get people really to study their own life and development and to consider, for example, I do with my students always as we begin a class on qualitative research, I dedicate at least two weeks to their own construction of their life story by chapters you know, they say, the famous way where you say this, your life story, your life can become a book. What will be your chapter, say give titles to the chapters, write one episode from each one on their own lives. And then they share in small groups what they did, what they wrote, what they thought about. Of course, there are some things which remain unrevealed, it is after all not therapy, and that's OK with me, but at least for themselves they get the sense that what we require of our interviewees is something that we should be able to look at in ourselves as well. So this is another line, after what I said about literature and poetry, I think that self-study and this kind of autobiographical work is extremely important.

D. P.: My major concern now is how you teach this stuff. And I don't think we know how to do that yet. And there's some notion that if you understand it, so if you have a course in it you can do it. And almost no appreciation for the skill required and how you teach skills of interviewing for instance. And the skill of analyzing or putting together this material in terms of a story that speaks to someone. And you can't do it in one course. . . . Should our students end up as first-class novices when they graduate, which means they have a set of rules they can follow. And I think that that doesn't really work in doing this kind of work, that they have to move beyond a novice level if they're going to actually do any of this research. And there are a lot of things that can be learned by doing interviewing, not necessarily as part of a research project but to learn how to interview. That most of the data we end up with is not very worthy of even doing an analysis of it. That to get the kind of information from someone requires an intensive interaction and an awareness of how to relate and let people take them into memories and deeper understandings and so on. And so I guess it would take more time than the curriculum makes available now to get students to a point where their dissertation was really going to produce something of significance in terms of a worthy outcome. . . . The students who come out of literature backgrounds and the students who come out of the clinical backgrounds where they have a lot of interviewing in terms of clinical interviewing are much further along. And then when you get a student who has a literary, a literature background as an undergraduate and a clinical background in graduate program, then in a sense they have the stuff and you can, they can move on.

E. M.: With people who were young as we all were at one time, young narrative researchers and what that process has been and my feelings you know about how important it's been for all of us in our work. And what I mean specifically has to do with and I talk about as the importance of developing and becoming part of a research community, that is a narrative research community. [In Elliot Mishler's own experience, he has been part of several groups.] So the group has been a supporting environment, but it's also been a place where we've learned from each other. You know because people doing work in different fields who have different approaches you know come to it with different history. So one recommendation, a major recommendation I would have for a young narrative researcher, it's for older ones as well, is to find friends. I mean it seriously.

J. C.: Oh, I so agree!

E. M.: Yeah and find in your local community whoever is doing this kind of work and develop some kind of way of being together and supporting each other in the work. . . . And I think it would be very good if people were able to have that kind of experience instead of being located so completely within their own disciplinary department. So I would encourage them to interdisciplinary research projects and . . . to interdisciplinary research communities and finding people in other fields because unfortunately there's not going to be that much support coming from one's home discipline. And I think young people need to have something which will sustain them so they don't feel as if they're crazy, you know, doing what they're doing. For that reason I tend to also emphasize a focus on the kinds of problems that people are addressing if they want to come to work with one or another form of narrative methodology rather than the disciplinary field itself. But you know that's the particular bias and I can have it because I haven't been locked into one of the particular academic disciplines. . . . One of the things that young people should do . . . is go to the conferences where these people are because there are conferences on narrative research in Canada, the U.K., Sweden, Germany, Italy. There's lots of places where they can find other people . . . doing work like that. Now that's not the same thing as how to make your way within your own academic department. But at least it helps to give younger people the sense that they're not crazy you know. . . . There's work going on and there are people who respond to the work and you kind of build it that way. I mean when we think of various kinds of deviant developments in our fields, they grew in this kind of way. . . . I mean think of behaviorism; in the early years, Skinner couldn't get his work published, and it took years until they developed their own journal because nobody would publish them in their journal. . . . You know the work that they were doing. And we now do have journals; I mean *Narrative Inquiry* and there are other narrative journals. . . . And there are places in, certainly in medicine and in anthropology where people are publishing, so there are places to get things out; it's not just the best scientific journals in psychology or whatever . . . And people have to start finding ways to do that. And I know that this, it's not easy, and if you're a young person trying to get promoted or get tenure you're kind of caught in this. But I think you have to look outside of your discipline to get the kind of support and response you know that would allow you to.

J. C.: And maybe even outside your local community for people who perhaps live in places that are a little more isolated, but that's always possible with the Internet and all kinds of ways of getting connected and sharing work.

E. M.: Well, it's like I said, the general point I'm making is find ways of, of establishing connections. You know you read an article by somebody that you find interesting who's doing narrative work and is in Australia. Send them an e-mail. And you know there are narrative Web sites and servers.

J. C.: Many of them now I'm discovering. As I work on this handbook I'm finding many kinds of narrative pockets that I didn't know existed and I've been doing this for a while now too and it's interesting to find those, and it's a way of trying to get connected to who is doing the work.

E. M.: Yeah and I guess I'm just sort of emphasizing that but . . . you can have the feeling if you're this young person and in a department of psychology or a school of education and you know some place where there's not very much else around you can feel as if you really are this odd person out. These are ways to be able to connect in that kind of way. And support people who respond to your work and whose work you can respond to.

Amia draws our attention most strongly to the importance of each narrative inquirer's own experience and to how a rich development of maturity and sensitivity to diverse people is central to a narrative inquirer's ability to engage in research. For her, this rich life experience is a kind of prerequisite for understanding the complexity of others' experiences. She does think we can do some things to educate narrative inquirers such as having them read literature, participate in response groups, move into cultures and contexts unfamiliar to them, and engage in autobiographical narrative inquiry. She sees that these activities can help educate but notes that it is not possible to provide a recipe that narrative inquirers can follow.

Don's words echo Amia's as he speaks of the complexity of being able to engage in narrative inquiry. He too says that you cannot teach how one should live as a narrative inquirer in a course, although you can teach some important skills. He also refers to the importance of reading literature in shaping the experiences of narrative inquirers. He feels that both a strong literature and a clinical background provide narrative inquirers with the ability to engage sensitively with lives. We wonder, along with Don, about novice narrative inquirers' ability to engage in sensitive, complex ways with both interviewing participants and making sense of interview data.

Elliot draws our attention to the importance of response communities in the development of narrative inquirers. He offers suggestions about how to create and maintain interdisciplinary, intergenerational response communities, what we would call works in progress communities. He writes about creating communities through attending conferences, through making contacts on the Internet, and by accessing journals and other publications that encourage narrative inquiry.

Topical Thread Five: Emerging Ethical Concerns

We asked each of our interviewees to comment on the ethical dimensions of narrative inquiry work. Ethical considerations permeate our own work and, we feel, are important considerations for beginning narrative inquirers.

A. L.:   Well I, I think that . . . by listening to a person's life story or even shorter, you know, stories about what they heard. More . . . their life or by observing people in their real life in the surrounding, we respect them a great deal. We honor them. We show them our interest and our concern and we legitimize them. We empower them. So from the policy side, I think that narrative research and qualitative research is very ethical because it respects the other. It's not just that. When I ask students, "What do you mean by doing ethical research," they immediately tell me "do no harm."

OK. This is the negative side. I start with the positive side. I think that this is an extremely positive enterprise to listen to each other, to allow space for each other, to respect. And this is half of the story already. So when I tell my students that they need to learn the attitude of listening, of empathic listening and of really containing the other and of not being judgmental . . . suspending their disbelief and so on, it is I think a highly ethical project for them. This is half of it. The other half is really "do no harm." And here I think we have to teach how to be careful with the privacy of people. How to be careful in the way we approach them and in the way we ask questions and when we stop, how we terminate our meeting and how we write about people and the whole issue of consent forms and what should be there and when they should be given their consent forms. Because when we start a conversation, we rarely know what will come up. And what we will do with it later and it might take two years until we have decided how to write about it so I go back to my interviewees. I went back to my interviewees maybe four times in my last research and I wrote about it. . . . I did the research by interviewing women who are, who don't have a, we call it "new family," they don't have a husband or male partner on a regular basis in their life, but they do have children. So I interviewed them, and of course, like before I had to get permission to come and talk to them and to record our conversations. But then I came back when I wrote the book with my chapters and I sought permission to publish it with all the, you know, concealing their identity and changing their other details and so on. I even let them pick their pseudonyms if they wanted. And then to my amazement somebody offered to do a play based on this book so, four of the women were selected by the playwright to have their stories depicted as a play. So I went back again and this was already two and a half years, three years after I met them the first time. And I said, "Would you be, would you be kind to allow us to develop this into a play?" And people told me I am legally entitled to do the play because now it's academic freedom or poetic freedom. It has been published already, one can use it for whatever. But I said, "No, I have my obligation to my participants." And I went back, and I can't say it's easy because every time I had this feeling that I'm requiring something from them, some favor from them. And I had to [tell] myself that I gave back something to them by really making their life a lesson to teach others. But this interaction goes on, and I think this is the ethics of narrative research. It is a relationship. It is an interaction with our participants. And we are still, to teach our students and the young scholars how it develops from one state to the other and there's always different requirements. And one has to be sensitive to all these levels and to all these requirements. And to always balance it with a positive side. But it seems like "not to harm" is just one half of the story.

J. C.:   [Don], I want to just come back to the ethics question just a bit more; when we do the intensive kind of relational work with one person when we're doing a narrative analysis and, we, in many ways spend a lot of time with an individual person, do you see any of the ethical kinds of issues, and how do you help your students think about the ethical issues of the more intensive relational kind of work that we end up doing in narrative?

D. P.: Well, I think there are different levels. The first thing I now ask my students is to always contract and pay the participant, the person they're working with. That it's their story, they own it. And we're taking their time. And I get opposition to this as [it] somehow makes it impure if you actually reward. . . . I think we're asking a tremendous amount from people, and we're asking for things that are theirs and are very personal and so on. So there's one level of the relationship and I just, I think we need to honor the people who are willing to become involved with us in terms of our research and not just in respect but within our society paying or giving a gift or something like that or letting them know that . . . what we want is their stuff. And then there are issues about confidentiality and respect in terms of the relationship and so on. The alternative notions "well the people get so much out of it by telling us their story, they feel so good and so on and so . . . their reward is enough just if we are interviewing" and I think that's not appropriate. I think they relate, the ethical issues in all of this kind of research now in terms of relationship between the researcher and the participant is a very important issue, one we, I think, have not treated well in that . . . the researcher gets all the glory and the promotions and everything. They are the ones who benefit from this research. And so that's, anyway that's what we do now. We always pay.

J. C.: OK. Do you have any troubles or concerns with the research boards, the IRBs [institutional review boards] in terms of how you help students think about working their proposals through the IRB?

D. P.: Yes. We have new IRB members come on. . . . And we get biologists who come on and they want to know why it is that we, they read stuff, "How come you're only, you're not interviewing somebody from all the different cultures and you're only interviewing people from two cultures" or something like that. Those kinds of things. We do, I think we've fought the battle now, but the IRB doesn't have any governance over the research design. We used to get that "well, you can't do that, that's not real research" and so on. They're mainly concerned that, at least with us, primarily that they don't get sued.

J. C.: Yes there's a lot of that here, too, I think.

D. P.: And so we have to put things in. One of the studies that I supervise, a student was interviewing adolescents who had committed, who had attempted, suicide. And they were very concerned, "Well what happens if . . . this brings up stuff," and so we had to have . . . "who's going to pay for a therapist? How is that going to happen?" So they get very worried about those things. We haven't had any in terms of you're going to make public intimate details or something about somebody's life. I mean that all has to be in terms of confidentiality. And how we approach that. But their concerns have been more of a legal concern than the kinds of things the IRB is supposed to be about. They always go to the lawyer, the university lawyers to have them read over the permissions that are signed and so on.

E. M.: It's a serious kind of issue . . . but I don't have wise advice on it, but it comes up more and more . . . we have found in my study groups over the last few years that it has come up more strongly and more frequently because people are now using visual data. . . . Starting about, oh, I don't know five or six years ago in my group suddenly people began showing up with videotapes instead of audiotapes, and there's a lot of work. . . . I don't know what IRBs are doing. I think it would be worthwhile having some sorts of conferences where people can talk about the ethical issues and what's involved in identification. I don't think there's any way you can conceal if you're working with individuals. In my story line book working with four or five craftspeople, they know who they are. . . . And that I circulated that to them in advance . . . to ask . . . what they thought about it or whether there was something they wanted me to change. I had the same experience other researchers had; they didn't care. I mean really, I mean you go back to your subjects and they kind of shrug. On the whole, they find what we're writing dull, you know. And not that interesting to them.

J. C.: Probably the more visible people are and the more identifiable they are depending on who they are in a community, they probably care more about how they are represented. . . . And, I think, what the handbook can perhaps do is start to raise some of these issues for people so they can start conversations about them. And there's not very much yet written around the ethics and institutional research boards and how we negotiate, how we might think about it. And it's a place for more narrative study groups to come together and explore and then make visible the conversations they're having around these topics.

For Amia, the complexity of ethics in narrative inquiry is both a negative and a positive dialogue. She draws our attention to how we attend to the tensions between doing no harm and doing something of benefit for our participants. Too often she feels the focus has been on "do no harm" without consideration of the positive enterprise of listening to others. She highlights the temporal dimension of negotiating an ongoing ethical relationship with participants.

Don, situated in a North American context, draws attention to the need for some kind of reciprocity and contract in the research relationship. While he acknowledges that IRBs are more attuned to the ethics of narrative inquiry—that is, they pay less attention to research design and more to questions of ethics, he raises the concern that the focus has become more legal.

Elliot turns our ethical eye toward technology and its burgeoning influence on narrative inquiry. Visual data raise particular ethical concerns regarding participant privacy and anonymity. He also raises questions about the value of going back to the participants to show them the research texts. He encourages narrative inquirers to come together in conferences and other settings to discuss these emerging ethical concerns.

Final Reflections

Our intention in inviting Amia, Don, and Elliot into conversation with us was to bring together the views and impressions of three of the most senior scholars in narrative inquiry. We locate this temporally in our initial question of what advice they would give to beginning narrative inquirers with a focus on ethics, the political contexts, and tensions with other methodologies. Drawing on their words, spoken in three separate conversations, we have woven a text that we hope both illuminates and troubles the field of narrative inquiry in ways that will move our work as narrative inquirers forward.

Note

1. These conversations are reprinted with permission of Elliot Mishler, Donald E. Polkinghorne, and Amia Lieblich.

Author Index

Abelson, R., 30
Abraham, A., 358
Abrams, P., 86
Abu-Lughod, L., 228
Ackerman, D., 281, 282
Adelman, M., 523
Adorno, T., 48, 334
Agar, M. H., 567
Alea, N., 187, 188, 197
Alexander, I., 191, 192
Alldred, P., 101
Allen, B., 228
Allen, C., 523
Allport, G., 226, 1000
Althusser, L., 84, 86
Aluli-Meyer, M., 518, 519, 522, 523
Alvarez, R. C., 331
Alves, R., 204, 207
Alvesson, M., 392
Amarel, M., 359
Amsterdam, A. G., 617, 618
Anas, A. P., 196
Anderson, H., 167
Anderson, B., 501
Andrews, M., 435, 441, 459, 492,
    495, 502
Angelelli, A., 167, 168
Angus, L., 427, 431
Anzaldúa, G., 58, 59
Anzul, M., 219, 569, 571, 585, 590, 593
Apfelbaum, E., 489, 491, 507, 509
Apple, M., 309
Applebaum, S. D., 254
Appleby, J., 26, 83
Apter, T., 538, 551, 553, 559
Arbus, D., 295
Arendt, H., 23, 287, 315
Argyris, C., 165, 168

Aries, P., 84, 85
Aristotle, 332, 358, 603
Arnold, M. L., 184
Arnoson, K., 527
Aron, L., 538
Arras, J. D., 240
Atkinson, B., 56
Atkinson, P., 571, 573
Atkinson, R., 224, 225, 231, 232, 236,
    237, 240, 553
Augoustinos, M., 48
Augustine, St., 125, 126
Austin, D., 578
Axel, E., 516

Babb, G., 524
Bach, H., 205, 208, 209, 210, 213, 214, 215,
    218, 254, 273, 280, 284, 286, 288, 289,
    290, 296, 300, 302
Baddeley, J. L., 195, 197
Bailie, L., 161
Bakan, D., 553
Baker, A., 165, 168
Bakhtin, M. M., 101, 149, 163, 331, 332,
    348, 349, 370, 383, 519
Bal, M., 20
Balamoutsou, S., 446
Ballet, K., 362
Bamberg, M. G. W., 430
Barber, J., 432
Barber, L., 375
Barge, K. J., 333
Barnes, H. E., 139
Barnes, M. L., 189
Bar-On, D., 538, 551, 559
Barone, T., 205, 207, 373
Barrett, L. F., 188
Barry, D., 332

Barthes, R., 131, 204, 393, 419, 602, 627
Baskin, K., 349
Basso, K., 70, 270
Bates, J., 345
Bateson, M. C., 13, 14, 266, 267, 273, 282, 302
Baturka, N. L., 368
Baudrillard, J., 523
Bauman, Z., 429
Baydala, L., 302
Beach, N., 254
Becker, B., 196
Becker, G., 408
Becker, H., 227, 296
Becker, L., 590
Beech, N., 399
Behan, C., 433
Behar, R., 255
Bejarano, C., 523
Belenky, M. F., 24, 58, 149, 253, 615
Bell, S. E., 289
Belove, L., 187, 190
Ben-Ari, A., 230
Benham, M., 513, 518, 521
Ben-Peretz, M., 253
Benstock, S., 121
Bereiter, C., 30
Berger, P. L., 187
Bergson, H., 39
Berlin, I., 321
Bernstein, R., 609, 614
Berntsen, D., 183
Bertaux, D., 227
Betchley, D., 433
Bhabha, H. K., 435, 490, 508
Bhaskar, R., 44
Biever, J. L., 167
Biklen, S. K., 162
Birch, M., 543
Bird, J., 430, 447
Birenbaum-Carmeli, D., 167
Birren, B. A., 232
Birren, J. E., 227, 232
Bishop, R., 517, 522
Bkavog, P., 184
Black, C., 323
Blades, C., 371
Blagov, P., 185
Bleakley, A., 620
Bloch, M., 624
Block, J., 100
Bloom, L., 361, 374
Bluck, S., 178, 180, 182, 183, 187, 188, 197

Blumer, H., 227
Bochran, A., 572
Boehlen, S., 165
Bogdan, R. C., 162
Bohman, J., 609, 614
Boivin, M., 430
Boje, D. M., 331, 332, 333, 335, 336, 341, 344, 345, 346, 347, 349, 385, 386, 387
Boland, R. J., Jr., 390, 396
Bolster, R., 358
Bond, L. A., 58
Bondi, L., 449
Boone, M., 252
Booth, W., 545
Boothe, B., 430, 432
Borden, A., 441
Bordo, S., 282
Borland, K., 67, 101
Botella, L., 446
Bothelho, M. J., 163
Boulding, K. E., 348
Bourne, E., 121, 124
Bowers, L., 254
Bowl, R., 430
Boxer, A. M., 230
Bradby, K., 527
Branson, N., 499
Braudel, F., 23, 87
Breuer, J., 100
Briggs, C., 411
Britton, J., 570
Britzman, D. P., 362
Brock, T. C., 5
Brockelman, P., 229
Brockmeier, J., 50, 124, 139, 282, 489, 493, 501, 505, 510
Brodski, B., 121
Brown, J., 362
Brown, R. H., 383
Brown, S. G., 527
Bruner, J., 5, 6, 7, 13, 18, 29, 36, 100, 131, 138, 139, 156, 177, 226, 232, 253, 288, 359, 383, 390, 408, 418, 438, 464, 486, 602, 603, 604, 606, 609, 613, 614, 616, 617, 618, 625
Buber, M., 252
Buhr, R., 388
Bullough, R. V., Jr., 15, 21
Burbules, N. C., 44, 150
Burguiere, A., 84, 86
Burke, T., 317
Burman, E., 101
Bussis, A. M., 359
Butler, R. N., 66, 194, 227

Butler-Kisber, L., 273
Butt, R., 362

Cain, C., 408
Caine, V., 273, 289
Cairns, G., 399
Calás, M., 399
Campbell, C. S., 206
Campbell, J., 231
Campbell, K., 254
Cannella, G., 448
Cappeliez, P., 195
Carey, M., 433, 439
Carger, C. L., 272, 373, 377
Carr, D., 82, 253, 287, 288, 409, 410
Carroll, L., 281
Carter, K., 254, 255, 359, 361
Casey, K., 367
Casey, M., 109
Cavanna, F., 210
Cazden, C. B., 430, 463, 469, 486
Chalfen, R., 289
Chambers, W., 23
Chan, E., 252
Chan, E. A., 156, 157
Chang, C., 483, 484
Chang, G., 483, 484
Chang, P. J., 50, 375
Charon, R., 36, 71, 270, 619
Chase, S. E., 227, 292, 428, 435,
        548, 549, 550, 554, 555
Cheney, G., 392
Cheng, S., 527
Chilton, P., 163
Chinn, P. W. U., 520
Chittenden, E., 359
Chomsky, N., 313, 325
Chrisler, J. C., 179
Christensen, L. T., 392
Christians, C. G., 555, 556
Chung, W. C., 485
Church, M., 322
Cixous, H., 282
Clair, R. P., 342, 343
Clandinin, D. J., xi, xv, 2, 4, 5, 6, 7, 12, 13,
        14, 20, 21, 25, 36, 37, 38, 40, 42, 43,
        45, 55, 57, 58, 60, 67, 69, 81, 82, 146,
        151, 156, 157, 166, 171, 203, 204, 207,
        214, 217, 228, 247, 251, 254, 255, 257,
        258, 267, 268, 269, 270, 273, 281, 282,
        283, 284, 285, 286, 287, 288, 290, 292,
        293, 294, 308, 360, 361, 362, 363, 364,
        366, 367, 371, 374, 435, 466, 538, 558,
        569, 574, 596, 602, 615, 622, 626

Clark, B. R., 383
Clark, C. M., 253, 371
Clark, K., 211
Clark, P., 227
Clifford, J., 11, 14, 28
Clinchy, B. M., 24, 149, 253, 615
Clough, P., 435
Cochran, K. N., 227
Cochran-Smith, M.,
        601, 602, 606, 625
Cody, A., 147
Coetzee, J. M., 309, 321
Cohen, C., 395
Cohler, B. J., 191, 194, 225,
        230, 231
Cole, A. L., 358, 362
Cole, M., 612
Coles, R., 14, 21, 226, 264, 265, 269
Collier, J., 215, 297
Collier, M., 215, 297
Collins, D., 333
Colter, N., 368
Comstock, G. L., 229
Conle, C., 159, 160, 252, 361,
        362, 367, 370, 372
Connelly, F. M., xi, xv, 4, 5, 6, 7, 12, 13, 14,
        20, 21, 25, 36, 37, 38, 40, 42, 43, 45,
        55, 57, 58, 60, 67, 69, 81, 82, 146, 151,
        156, 157, 166, 171, 203, 204, 207, 214,
        217, 228, 247, 251, 254, 255, 258, 267,
        268, 269, 270, 281, 282, 283, 284, 285,
        286, 287, 288, 290, 292, 293, 294, 308,
        360, 361, 362, 363, 364, 366, 367, 371,
        374, 435, 466, 538, 558, 569, 574, 596,
        602, 615, 622, 626
Conquergood, D., 66
Conway, J. K., 122, 127, 131
Conway, M., 184
Coomaraswamy, A. K., 206
Cooper, J., 513
Cooperrider, D. L., 349
Corbin, J., 541, 543, 544
Cortazzi, M., 154, 435
Corvellec, H., 388, 392, 397
Craig, C. J., 158, 259, 261, 273,
        362, 367, 368, 371, 372
Crawford, F., 433
Crites, S., 253, 270
Crockett, K., 438, 439
Cronon, W., 430
Csordas, T., 407, 411
Cunliffe, A. L., 387
Cutcliffe, J. R., 549, 557
Cutting, L., 184

Czarniawska, B., 332, 384, 387, 391, 392, 393, 399
Czarniawska-Joerges, B., 391, 395, 399

Dadds, M., 318
Damianovic, M. C. C. C. L., 217, 220
Danforth, L., 411
Darling-Hammond, L., 625
Davidson, I., 206
Davies, A., 6, 254, 273, 362
Dean, R. G., 433
De Cock, C., 395
de Kock, D. M., 149, 154, 156
Delahunt, M. R., 206, 207
de Lauretis, T., 50
Delgado, R., 61, 62
Delong, J., 323
Denning, S., 384
Denzin, N. K., xiv, 4, 14, 15, 25, 66, 157, 253, 376, 427, 556
De Rivera, J., 102
Derrida, J., 56, 330, 342, 343, 344, 393, 438
de St. Aubin, E., 191, 192, 194
de Saussure, F., 52, 107
Desjarlais, R., 411
de Sousa, D., 86
de Vries, B., 227
Dewey, J., 2, 38, 39, 41, 44, 50, 204, 207, 209, 228, 253, 255, 281, 282, 283, 284, 287, 288, 302, 358
Dhamborvorn, N., 254
Diamond, A., 194
Diamond, C. T. P., 205, 206, 207, 213, 215, 218, 219, 220, 273
Dickerson, V. C., 189
Dickinson, J., 433
Diguer, L., 432
Dillard, A., 282
Dilthey, W., 230, 231, 233, 409, 410
Dimaggio, G., 430
Disney, R. E., 345
Di Tosti, C., 592
Doecke, B., 362
Doisneau, R., 210
Dollard, J., 100
Donmoyer, R., 311, 602
Downing, M., 219, 569, 571, 585, 590, 593
Drewery, W., 167, 432, 439
Du, J., 254

Duarte, V. B. C., 208, 209, 210, 213, 214, 215, 216, 218
Duckworth, E., 253
Du Gay, P., 392
Duggan, D., 586
Duguid, P., 516
Dupré, L., 127
Durant, R. A., 333, 335
Durkheim, É., 26, 86
Dybdahl, M., 147, 148, 157, 165

Eames, K., 317
Eisenberg, L., 407
Eisner, E. W., 66, 204, 205, 207, 213, 218, 219, 254, 255
Ekert, J., 109
Elbaz, F., 359, 362
Elbaz-Luwisch, F., xiv, 253, 362, 364, 368, 369, 370, 372, 375, 376
Elbert, S. H., 515
Elder, G., 100
Eliade, M., 122, 123, 231
Elkind, D., 183, 184
Elle, C., 345
Ellis, C., 538, 550, 551, 572
Ely, M., 219, 541, 548, 569, 571, 584, 585, 586, 590, 593
Emerson, R. W., 81, 96
Engel, S., 465
Enríquez, E., 331
Epston, D., 22, 427, 435, 438, 439, 440, 441, 446
Erickson, F., 580
Erikson, E. H., 100, 177, 182, 187, 191, 195, 196, 226, 227, 241
Erikson, J. M., 195, 196, 375
Erkkilä, R., 364, 365, 366
Estola, E., 253, 362, 364, 365, 366
Estroff, S. E., 538, 541, 559
Etherington, K., 427
Evant, S., 24
Ezzy, D., 101

Falconer, W., 433
Farrant, K., 180, 181
Faulconer, J. E., 7
Fausel, D., 167
Fay, M., 442
Featherstone, B., 446
Feldman, M. S., 384, 392, 393
Fenstermacher, G. D., 15
Fernandez, N., 516
Feuer, M. J., 602, 606, 624

Feuerverger, G., 372, 377
Fewell, J., 449
Fiese, B. H., 191
Fine, M., 63, 100, 101, 157, 158,
    300, 544, 555, 556
Fineman, S., 390, 397
Finkel, D. L., 567
Fisher, W. R., 383
Fivush, R., 179, 180, 181, 197
Florio-Ruane, S., 146, 150, 163
Fontaine, D., 163
Ford, J., 168
Ford, L., 168
Foucault, M., 8, 17, 54, 131, 151, 157, 439
Fournier, V., 392
Frank, A., 239, 408, 430
Frank, G., 228, 229, 239
Franzosi, R., 17
Fraser, H., 435
Frazer, J., 318
Fredriksson, L., 162
Freebody, P., 159
Freedman, S. G., 567
Freeman, M., 121, 122, 124, 129, 132, 134,
    137, 138, 139, 141, 142, 226, 229, 282
French, K., 163
Freud, S., 26, 100, 107, 226, 570
Frey, J., 136
Fries, K., 602, 625
Frohmann, L., 289
Frost, P., 397
Funkenstein, A., 228
Furlong, J., 319, 324
Furman, R., 521

Gable, E., 28
Gabriel, Y., 332, 390, 391, 395, 397
Gadamer, H.-G., 151, 409, 410, 549
Gage, N. L., 358
Gagliardi, P., 387
Gaines, A. D., 407
Galatzer-Levy, R. M., 191, 194
Gallego, M., 166
Gallop, J., 117
Garcia, G., 462
Gardner, G. H., 625
Garrett, M. T., 520
Garro, L., 408
Garvin, D., 621, 622
Gavriel, Y., 389
Gazzaniga, M., 136, 137
Gee, J. P., xv, 430, 437, 463, 465,
    467, 470, 483, 579

Geertz, C., 6, 7, 8, 11, 14, 22, 30, 121,
    229, 253, 491, 492, 537, 596
Geist-Martin, P., 167, 168
Georgakopoulou, A., 169
Georges, R., 331
Gergen, K. J., 101, 188, 225, 230, 435
Gergen, M. M., 188, 225, 230, 435
Gibbons, M., 315
Giddens, A., 429
Gilgun, J. F., 448
Gilligan, C., 100, 540, 615
Gilman, C. P., 149
Glassie, H., 28
Glavey, C., 315
Glazier, J. A., 164
Glover, T. D., 161
Godfrey, B. S., 556
Goethe, J. W., 128
Gold, S. P., 345
Goldberger, N. R., 24, 149, 253, 613, 615
Goldenberg, C., 164
Golombek, P. R., 362
Gonçlaves, O., 432
González, M. T., 331
Good, B., 407, 408, 418
Good, M. J., 407, 408, 418
Goodall, H. L., Jr., 397
Goodman, N., 396
Goodson, L. F., 362, 364
Goolishian, H., 167
Gore, J., 149
Goss, S., 438
Gould, N., 427
Gould, S. J., 608
Grafanaki, S., 427, 430
Grafton Small, R., 397
Graymorning, S., 527
Green, J., 373
Green, M. C., 5
Greene, M., 205, 206, 207, 218,
    219, 252, 287, 292, 302, 366, 614
Greenfield, P. J., 528
Greenhalgh, T., 36, 435, 620
Greenwood, D. J., 555
Grey, T., 617
Gross, D., 346
Gross, L., 298
Gruber, H. E., 10
Grumet, M., 205
Guba, E. G., 12, 15, 20, 30, 154, 156, 593
Gubrium, J. F., 224, 229, 232, 391, 429
Gudmundsdottir, S., 253, 359, 361, 363,
    364, 368, 374, 377

Guilfoyle, K., 11
Guillet de Monthoux, P., 395
Gumperz, J., 163
Guralnik, D. B., 518
Gusdorf, G., 120, 123, 128, 130, 131, 132,
    133, 134, 135, 136, 138
Guthrie, E., 430

Habermas, J., 159, 318, 319, 320, 321, 325
Habermas, T., 178, 180, 182, 183
Hacking, I., 137
Hadden, J., 50
Haddon, M., 620
Haden, C. A., 179
Hadjistravropoulos, T., 554
Hales, J., 433
Hall, C. J., 427
Hall, L., 66
Hamilton, M. L., 11
Hampl, P., 139, 140
Handler, R., 28
Hansen, A., 621
Harari, J. V., 393
Harding, S., 28
Hardin, P. K., 157, 163
Hargreaves, A., 377
Harju, K., 397
Harper, D., 296
Harre, R., 101
Harrison, B., 289
Harste, J., 159
Hart, H. M., 193, 194
Hartog, M., 322
Harvey, O., 100
Hatch, A. J. H., 361
Hatch, M. J., 384, 392
Hauerwas, S., 27
Haug, F., 282
Hawkes, D., 47
Hawkins-Leon, C. G., 169
Hayden, J., 179
He, M. F., 254, 362, 372, 377
Heath, S. B., 430
Heck, R., 518
Heidegger, M., 409
Heikkinen, H., 362
Heilbrun, C. G., 122, 282
Helle, A. P., 229, 230
Helmers, S., 388
Henderson, P., 572
Henri, Y., 497
Henry, F., 50
Hepworth, J., 439

Hermans, H., 427, 430
Hermans-Jansen, E., 427, 430
Hernes, T., 393
Herrero, O., 446
Herts-Lazarowitz, R., 368
Hicks, C., 184
Higgins, M., 395
Higham, J., 26
Hiley, D. R., 609, 614
Hilsen, K. D., 296
Hinchman, L. P., 430
Hinchman, S. K., 430
Hirst, P., 313
Hoffman, E., 253
Hoffman, L., 167
Hogan, D., 102, 362
Hogan, P., 6, 254
Hojjat, M., 189
Holger, L., 392
Holland, D., 408
Holland, J., 109
Holland, P., 283
Holley, E., 322
Hollingsworth, S., 146, 147, 148,
    157, 165, 253
Holloway, W., 435, 540, 543,
    547, 549, 550
Holmberg, D., 190
Holmberg, I., 392
Holmberg, L., 397
Holmquist, M., 211
Holstein, J. A., 224, 229, 232,
    391, 429
Hood, W., 100
Hooker, K. A., 191
Hook, S., 50
hooks, b., 253, 613
Hooper, S., 167
Höpfl, H., 392
Horkheimer, M., 48
Horwitz, P., 527
Hoskins, J., 504
Hoskins, M. J., 549
Huber, J., 58, 254, 257, 258,
    273, 376
Huber, M., 273
Huberman, A. M., 12, 538
Hughes-Freeland, F., 411
Hunt, J. C., 545
Hunt, L., 26, 83, 84, 87
Hurwitz, B., 36, 435, 620
Husserl, E., 318, 319
Hutton, P., 84, 85

Hydén, M., 446
Hyman, D., 168
Hymes, D., 12

Irigaray, L., 282
Isdr, W., 410
Isenberg, J. P., 361
Iverson, K., 163
Ives, E., 228, 229

Jackson, M., 411
Jackson, P. W., 254
Jacob, M., 26, 83
Jacob, T. B., 207
Jacobs-Huey, L., 408
Jacobsson, B., 399
Jaggar, A. M., 282
Jakobson, R., 363
Jalongo, M. R., 361
James, W., 40, 46, 99
Jameson, F., 48
Janesick, V. J., 162
Jefferson, T., 435, 540, 543, 547, 549, 550
Jenkins, K., 521, 523
Jersild, A. T., 358
Jesso, B., 180
Johnson, B., 393
Johnson, G., 289
Johnson, J., 556
Johnson, J. L., 161
Johnson, K. E., 362
Johnson, M., 42, 253, 375
Johnson, S., 25
Johnston, S., 362
Josselson, R., 5, 6, 13, 69, 100, 177, 186,
        187, 225, 226, 230, 239, 435, 548,
        549, 551, 553, 559, 615, 626
Jouve, N. W., 498
Joyce, P., 84, 85
Jupp, T. C., 163

Kaestle, C. F., 606
Kalaw, C., 161
Kalscheur, G., 168
Kanpol, B., 61
Kapferer, B., 411
Katz, J. S., 298
Kaufman, S. R., 196
Kawaharada, D., 515
Keahi, S., 529
Kearney, R., 123, 137, 138
Keats Whelan, K., 58, 254, 273, 376
Kegan, R., 499

Kelchtermans, G., 362, 368, 376
Keller, E. F., 615
Keller, H., 295
Kellner, H., 187
Kennan, G., 23
Kennard, B., 6, 254, 362
Kennedy, M., 66, 254, 290
Kenyon, G. M., 224, 227
Kerr, D., 66
Kidder, L., 101
Kilduff, M., 399
Killman, R. H., 384
Kincheloe, J., 66
King, B. B., 240
King, T., 60
Kipling, R., 519
Kirk, J., 17, 21
Kirkwood, C., 449
Kitchen, J. D., 22
Kitzinger, C., 159
Kivnick, H. Q., 195, 196
Kleinman, A., 407
Kluback, W., 230
Knights, D., 396
Knill-Griesser, H., 323
Knis-Matthew, L. L., 594
Knowled, J. G., 362
Knutson, J., 254
Kohn, A., 567
Kolb, D. A., 168
Kong, T., 508
Kostera, M., 391
Kotary, L., 191
Kotre, J., 191
Kramp, M. K., xi, 214
Krefting, L., 397
Kristeva, J., 590
Kroger, R., 101, 227
Kuhn, T. S., 18, 29, 609
Kuiack, S., 196
Kunda, G., 388
Kvale, S., 537, 538
Kyratzis, A., 373

LaBoskey, V. K., 166, 263, 361, 615
Labov, W., xv, 153, 154, 161, 383,
        430, 465, 467, 470, 471, 603
Lacan, J., 106, 107, 108, 113
Lachicotte, W., 408
Lachman, H., 254
Laclau, E., 48
Laderman, C., 411
Ladson-Billings, G., 253

Lagermann, E. C., 606, 625
Laidlaw, M., 317
Laine, T., 362
Laird, J., 427
Lakoff, G., 253
Lambek, M., 138
Lamott, A., 567
Lane, B., 261
Langellier, K. M., 428, 429, 494
Langer, C. L., 521
Langer, L. L., 228
Langer, S., 571, 575, 590
Langness, L. L., 227, 228, 229
Lannin, D. R., 408
Larsen, M. H., 392
Laslett, B., 430
Lather, P., 65, 66, 157, 317, 567, 625
Latour, B., 27
Laubscher, L., 50
Laurenceau, J., 188
Lavato, C. Y., 161
Lave, J., 516, 517
Lawlor, M., 408, 411
Lawrence, A. M., 184, 185
Le Dœuff, M., 282
Leftwich, A., 427
Leichtman, M. D., 181
Leitman, S., 433
Lejeune, P., 135
Leland, C., 159
Lerner, D., 23
Lessing, D., 209
Levin, G., 347
Levin, M., 555
Levi-Strauss, C., 23
Levitt, H., 427
Lewin, K., 100
Lewison, M., 164
Leyland, L., 520
Li, X., 162, 372
Lieblich, A., xv, 5, 6, 36, 69, 225, 226, 230,
    239, 359, 435, 539, 540, 545, 550, 551,
    553, 554, 559, 615, 626
Lifton, R. J., 491
Lightfoot, G., 395
Lillejord, S., 527
Limoges, C., 315
Lincoln, Y. S., 4, 12, 14, 15, 20, 25, 30, 154,
    156, 157, 253, 361, 427, 448, 557, 593
Linde, C., 227
Lindstrom, U. A., 162
Linstead, S., 392
Lipka, J., 523

Lipson, J. G., 541
Lipton, M., 625
Lock, A., 439, 440, 441, 446
Lomax, P., 324
London, J., 515, 516
Lonergan, B. J. F., 168
Lorde, A., 149
Loughran, J., 362
Luborsky, L., 432
Luckmann, T., 359
Ludwig, A., 136
Lugones, M., 59
Luhman, J. T., 333, 335, 387
Lukacs, G., 48
Luke, A., 159
Luna, C., 163
Luttrell, W., 100
Lynch, G., 436, 437, 438, 445
Lyons, D., 273, 526
Lyons, N., 150, 157, 253, 263, 361, 615
Lyotard, F., 52, 54, 325

Maccoby, E., 17
Machado, P., 432
Macías, E., 331
MacIntyre, A., 26, 27, 253, 367,
    410, 436, 559, 614
MacKay, D., 359
MacKintosh, D., 527
Maeers, M., 527
Maher, F., 50
Mahoe, N., 515
Mahoney, D., 508
Maisel, R., 439, 440, 441, 446
Makela, M., 362
Malcolm, J., 539
Mann, H., 523, 529
Mansfield, E., 194
Marcia, J. E., 227
Marcuse, H., 48, 313, 334, 349
Marcus, G. E., 14, 28
Markey, C., 446
Marland, P. W., 359
Marmon Silko, L., 37, 253, 272, 512
Marsh, M. M., 362
Martin, F. E., 441, 442, 443, 446
Martin, J., 17, 384, 394, 615
Martin, L., 579
Martin, W., 5, 6, 9
Maruna, S., 193, 194
Marx, K., 23, 26, 47, 48, 49
Mathews, H., 408
Matías, B., 584, 586

Matos, N., 163
Matthews, K. M., 521, 523
Mattingly, C., 405, 406, 408, 409, 411, 416, 447
Maxwell, G., 167
Maxwell, J., 605, 606, 607, 608, 609
May, W., 296, 297, 298
Mayher, J. S., 570
McAdams, D., 1, 6, 7, 69, 100, 177, 178, 193, 194, 226, 429, 435, 615, 626
McCabe, A., 180, 430, 483, 484
McCarthy, M., 347
McClintock, B., 615
McCloskey, D., 383
McCormack, C., xv, 149, 154, 155
McCracken, G., 239
McDonald, J., 527
McGlaughlin, T., 25
McIntyre, A., 162
McKenzie, K., 167
McKenzie, W., 439
McLean, K. C., 184, 185, 186
McLeod, J., 160, 427, 428, 430, 431, 436, 437, 438, 445, 446, 447, 449, 538, 557
McNiff, J., 310, 319, 320, 323
McNiff, S., 205
Mcpherson, P., 157
McVee, M. B., 160, 162, 163, 169
Mead, M., 13, 522
Medawar, P., 308
Medvedev, R. N., 383
Meier, A., 430
Mello, D. M., 204, 205, 213, 215, 216, 217
Mendez, J., 593
Merleau-Ponty, M., 39
Merwin, M. S., 516
Metz, D., 392
Metz, T., 391
Michaels, S., 430, 466, 470
Mickelson, J. R., 208, 210, 211, 213, 214, 215, 216, 217, 218, 252, 254, 273, 290
Miles, M. B., 12, 538
Miller, K., 527
Miller, M. E., 543
Miller, M. L., 17, 21
Miller, P. G., 465
Miller, T., 543
Mills, C. W., 491
Minami, M., 484
Minarik, L. T., 147, 157, 165
Minh-Ha, T. T., 519, 522
Mink, L. O., 163

Mishler, E. G., 69, 100, 103, 157, 253, 390, 430, 435, 437, 464, 465, 467, 484, 548, 601, 604, 605
Mitchell, C., 289
Mitchell, J. P., 408
Mitchell, M., 508
Mitchell, V., 396
Mitchell, W. J. T., 600, 603, 604
Mitroff, I. I., 348, 384
Mkabela, N., 527
Mkhonza, S., 227
Moen, T., 362, 364, 368, 373
Moffit, K. H., 184, 185
Mohatt, G. V., 523
Montell, L., 228
Montello, M., 270
Moranga, C., 613
Morgan, A., 430, 433, 438, 439
Morrill, C., 523
Morris, A., 167
Morris, D. B., 270
Morrison, T., 282
Morrow, R. A., 84
Morse, J. M., 541, 543, 544
Moss, J., 162
Mouffe, C., 48
Moustakas, C., 549
Mullen, C. A., 205, 206, 207, 213, 215, 218, 219, 220, 273
Muller, J., 161
Murphy, R., 409
Murphy, S., 208, 211, 212, 213, 214, 215, 216, 217, 218, 273
Murray, H., 100, 226, 231
Murray, M., 435
Murray, M. J., 537, 548, 549, 551
Murray Orr, A., 273
Musheno, M., 523
Mwebi, B. M., 218, 273
Myerhoff, B., 429
Myrdal, G., 22

Naidoo, M., 322
Nakkula, V., 109
Natapoff, A., 168
Nelson, H. L., 551, 556
Nelson, K., 179, 197
Nespor, J. C., 375, 625
Newshan, G., 584, 595
Nhat Hanh, T., 302
Nias, J., 157, 362, 364
Nichols, P., 527
Nieto, S., 372

Ní Mhurchú, S., 317
Noddings, N., 6, 66, 157, 228, 253, 270,
      297, 361, 615
Nord, W. R., 397
Norris, C., 44
Norris, J. E., 196, 205
Norris, T., 287
Novick, P., 26
Nowotny, H., 315
Nussbaum, M., 421, 490, 509,
      559, 617

Oakes, J., 625
Oakley, A., 157
Oancea, A., 324
Oberg, A., 371
O'Bryan, B., 165
O'Connor, E., 397
O'Connor, F., 570
Ogden, M. H., 206
Olafson, F., 409
Olatunji, B., 237, 240
Ollerenshaw, J.,
      273, 526
Olney, J., 229
Olson, D., 624
Olson, M., 158, 254, 261, 264, 362,
      363, 367, 371
Orr, J. E., 386
Ortiz, S. M., 543
Osorio, J. K. K., 525
Ouellette, S., 557
Overlien, C., 446
Oyler, C., 211, 253

Packwood, A., 376
Paley, V. G., 263, 264, 466
Paokong, J. C., 273
Parker, M., 395
Parks, K., 91, 96
Parry, A., 167
Parsons, T., 84
Pastashnick, J., 289
Pasupathi, M., 5, 185
Patai, D., 538, 547, 556, 575,
      576, 577, 578
Patter, J., 100
Payne, M., 439
Paz, O., 138
Pearce, K. A., 196
Pearce, M., 254, 273
Peirce, C. S., 56
Peltonen, T., 392

Perrement, M., 323
Perry, L., 446
Peshkin, A., 255
Peters, R., 313
Peterson, B. E., 192, 193
Peterson, C., 180, 483
Peterson, E., 429
Phillion, J. A., 254, 362, 372, 376, 377
Phillips, D. C., 44, 150, 606
Phillips, N., 395
Piaget, J., 16, 100
Pietromonaco, P. R., 188
Piles, S., 37
Pillemer, D. B., 181
Pinnegar, S., 11, 15, 272
Piquemal, N., 270
Pires, E. A., 218
Placier, P., 11
Plato, 124
Plummer, K., 435, 508
Poindexter, C., 435, 446
Polanyi, L., 5, 162, 313, 320
Pole, C., 289
Polkinghorne, D. E., xv, 5, 6, 7, 12,
      15, 69, 148, 162, 177, 253, 359,
      383, 428, 429, 603, 614
Polombo, J., 432
Pomerantz, F., 165
Pondy, L. R., 348
Popkewitz, T. S., 624
Popper, K., 313
Posner, R. A., 617, 618
Potter, D., 22
Potts, L. J., 603
Powell, S., 50
Prasad, P., 392
Pratt, M. L., 8, 13, 26
Pratt, M. W., 184, 196
Price, J., 538, 541
Price, L., 408
Pring, R., 314
Propp, V., 393, 417, 418, 603
Prosser, J., 295, 297, 298
Pukui, M. K., 512, 514
Punch, M., 538, 555, 556
Pushor, D., 273, 289

Quan, S., 254
Quinney, L., 161, 431, 434

Rabinow, P., 600, 604, 609, 610, 611
Radley, A., 289
Rager, K., 255

Rainwater, K., 333
Ramcharan, P., 549, 557
Ramirez, A. Y. F., 157
Randall, W. L., 187, 224
Raymond, D., 362
Raymond, H., 254, 273
Raz, J., 320
Reese, E., 180, 181
Reeves, A., 430
Reinharz, S., 157
Rennie, D., 427, 429, 446
Revel, J., 83, 84, 87
Rexhaj, B., 195, 198
Rhodes, C., 397
Rich, A., 295
Rich, M., 289
Richardson, J. C., 556
Richardson, L., 570, 571
Rickman, H. P., 231
Ricoeur, P., 138, 162, 169, 387, 406, 409,
    410, 419, 427, 611
Riessman, C. K., 149, 154, 161, 239, 427,
    428, 429, 430, 431, 434, 435, 436, 447,
    464, 467, 496, 543
Rimmer, M., 191
Rist, R., 626
Ritz, D., 240
Roberts, C., 163
Roberts, H., 157
Robertson, M., 527
Robins, R. W., 184, 185
Rogan, A. L., 149, 156
Rogers, A., 105, 109
Rogers, C., 154
Rorty, R., 27, 391, 393
Rosaldo, R., 459, 492, 509
Rose, C., 254
Rosen, M., 398
Rosenthal, G., 227
Rosenwald, G., 555
Rosiek, J. L., 37, 50, 56, 65, 70, 273, 376
Rosile, G. A., 333, 335
Roskos, K. A., 165
Ross, M., 190
Ross, V., 272
Rossides, D. W., 86
Roßteutscher, S., 501
Rowland, N., 438
Rubin, D. C., 183
Ruby, J., 298
Runyan, M., 100
Runyan, W. M., 226, 239
Rushforth, S., 523

Russell, S., 433, 439
Ruth, J. E., 227
Ryan, E. B., 196
Ryan, M. -L., 387, 388
Rychlak, J. F., 13
Ryen, A., 508

Sacks, H., 385
Sacks, O., 409
Said, E., 318
Salmon, W. C., 607
Salovey, P., 184
Salzer-Mörling, M., 392
Samson, F., 254
Sands, A., 433
Sarbin, T. R., xv, 5, 6, 102, 177, 226, 359
Sarton, M., 282
Sarup, M., 7
Sayer, D., 106
Scardamalia, M., 30
Schaef, A. W., 149
Schäffner, C., 163
Schahtel, E., 140, 141
Schama, S., 26
Schank, R., 5, 30
Schechner, R., 411
Scheibe, K. E., 188
Schenck, C., 121
Scheytt, T., 391
Schickel, R., 326
Schieffelin, E., 411
Schön, D. A., 262, 268, 313, 405
Schooling, B., 331
Schroots, J. J. F., 227
Schultz, M., 392
Schutz, A., 39, 359
Schwab, J. J., 254, 269, 358, 359
Schwagler, J., 191
Schwandt, T. A., 231
Schwartzman, S., 315
Schweder, R., 121, 124
Sclater, S. D., 435
Sconiers, Z. D., 37, 50, 65
Scott, J., 84, 85
Scott, P., 315
Scott, R., 524
Searle, J., 101
Seely Flint, A., 164
Selby, J. M., 490, 498
Sellers, P., 346
Semerari, A., 430
Sen, A., 316
Sewall, I., 254

Shames, G., 507
Shapira, T., 368
Sharifi, S., 397
Shavelson, R. J., 602, 606, 624
Shaw, C., 227
Shaw, I., 427
Sheffield, S., 28
Sheinberg, N., 109
Shenhav, S. R., 163
Sherif, C., 100
Sherif, M., 100
Sherriff, 56
Shulman, L., 606, 625
Shusterman, R., 609, 614
Shweder, R. A., 613
Sieber, J. E., 537
Sikes, P., 376
Sims, D., 396
Sims, R., 165, 168
Singer, J. A., 178, 179, 182, 184,
    185, 189, 190, 195, 197, 198
Sitkin, S. B., 384
Skaw, D., 184
Skilbeck, M., 308
Skinner, D., 408
Sköldberg, K., 392, 398
Skultans, V., 36
Slamon, P., 435
Slater, L., 133
Slavin, R. E, 606, 624
Sleeter, C., 373
Slife, B. D., 10, 11
Smallwood, J., 147
Smircich, L., 399
Smith, D. E., 151
Smith, J. K., 9, 29
Smith, L., 439
Smith, L. T., 518, 519, 523
Smith, M. E., 368
Smith, S., 121
Smith, W., 395
Smithies, C., 567
Smythe, W. E., 537, 548, 549, 551, 554
Søderberg, A. -M., 393
Soin, K., 391
Solow, R. M., 384
Sonnleitner, T. M., 526
Sontag, S., 207, 290, 295, 296, 298
Sorrell, K., 35
Spanbauer, T., 35
Speedy, J., 343, 428, 435, 438, 447
Spence, D. P., 136, 177, 265, 283, 359
Spradley, J., 228

Squire, C., 435
Srivastva, S., 349
Stacey, J., 550
Stair, A., 523, 528
Stake, R., 66
Stanley, L., 157
Stark, C., 537, 558
Stark, R., 26
Starkey, K., 399
Steeves, P., 252, 254, 273
Stein, G., 335
Sternberg, R. J., 189
Stevens, W., 220
Stewart, A. J., 192, 193
Stewart, J., 345, 346, 347
Stoller, P., 411
Stone, L., 83
Stone-Mediatore, S., xiv, 51, 62, 63, 65, 66
Storti, C., 507, 509
Strange, J. J., 5
Streams, P., 101
Strube, 182
Suderman-Gladwell, G., 316
Sullivan, B., 322
Sullivan, S., 50
Sullivan, W., 600, 604, 609, 610, 611
Sutin, A. R., 184, 185
Svensson, T., 227
Sweetland, W., 273, 376
Syrjälä, L., 364, 365, 366

Tagg, J., 291
Tambiah, S., 411
Tamboukou, M., 435
Tan, J., 372
Tankasi, R. V., 390
Tannen, D., 162
Tarule, J. M., 24, 149, 253, 615
Tator, C., 50
Taubman, P., 376
Taylor, C., 121, 125, 126, 129,
    138, 436, 610
Taylor, D., 289
Tedlock, D., 575
Teel, K. M., 147
Telles, J. A., 208, 209, 210, 213,
    214, 215, 216, 218, 220
Thayer-Bacon, B. J., 7
Thernstrom, M., 619
Thomas, D. S., 227
Thomas, G., 314
Thomas, W. I., 227
Thompson, S., 332

Thomson, N., 527
Thorne, A., 184, 185, 186
Thrift, N. J., 37
Tierney, W. G., 361, 557
Tillich, P., 227
Titon, J., 228, 229, 233
Todorov, T., 325, 387
Toelken, B., 331
Tomkins, S. S., 177
Torres, C. A., 84
Tosh, J., 85
Toukmanion, S., 427, 429
Towne, L., 602, 606, 624
Townsend, D., 362
Treacher, A., 435
Trinh, T. M.-H., 252
Trow, M., 315
Tsai, M., 462
Tsutsumoto, T. S., 527
Turner, E., 411
Turner, P., 25
Turner, V., 411
Tuval-Mashiach, R., xv, 5, 36, 435
Two Trees, K., 331
Tzu, L., 162

Urek, M., 446
Uysal, A. E., 88

van Gennep, A., 231
Van Maanen, J., 347, 397, 518
Van Manen, M., 156, 584
Van Shuys, K., 164
Vaz, K., 36
Vernant, J. -P., 124
Veroff, J. B., 613
Verrier, R., 345
Vilayanur, S. R., 314
Vinz, R., 219, 569, 571, 585, 590, 593
von Bertalanffy, L., 332
Vonèche, J. J., 10
Von Wyl, A., 432
Vygotsky, L. S., 149, 151

Waletzky, J., 383, 430, 465, 467, 470, 471, 603
Walker, B. J., 165
Walker, B. K., 89
Walkerdine, V., 289
Walker, M., 159, 160
Walker, W. S., 88, 89
Wallis, V., 524

Walsh, D. J., 368
Wamboldt, F. S., 188
Wang, Q., 181, 493
Ward, J., 50
Warren, C. A. B., 541
Watson, J., 121
Watson, T., 397
Watt, L. M., 194, 195
Webb, K., 254, 273
Weber, M., 26
Weber, S., 289
Webster, J. D., 195
Weick, K. E., 386, 387
Weidenbaum, A., 595
Weinstock, J. S., 58
Weintraub, K., 29, 128, 129
Weis, L., 63, 300, 544, 555
Weis, S., 157
Weiser, J., 283, 296
Wenger, E., 517
Wengraf, T., 548
Wepfer, R., 432
Wertsch, J., 100, 101
Weseen, S., 544, 555
West, C., 50, 57
Weston, J. H., 527
Westwood, R., 397
Wetherell, M., 48, 100
Wheeler, S., 430
White, B., 100
White, C., 433
White, H., 28, 253, 333, 383, 387, 398
White, M., 22, 427, 430, 435, 438
White, R., 28, 100, 612
White, S., 444, 445, 446, 601
Whitehead, J., 308, 310, 312, 316, 320, 321, 323, 324
Whitenack, D., 166
Whittaker, E., 524
Widdershoven, G. A. M., 229, 551
Wilkinson, S., 159
Wilkomirski, B., 135
Williams, R., 314
Williams, R. N., 7
Williams, W., 23
Williams, W. C., 504
Willmott, H., 392, 396
Winslade, J., 433, 439
Winslade, L., 167
Wisniewski, R., 361
Witherell, C., 6, 228, 253, 361

Wittgenstein, L., 101
Wolcott, H. F., 255, 557, 593
Wong, L., 544, 555
Wong, P. T., 194, 195
Wood, L., 101
Wood, W., 184

Yalda, C., 523
Yates, L., 157, 160
Yinger, R., 253
Yoder, J., 501

Young, M., 252, 270
Youngs, P., 625

Zamboni, S., 219
Zeichner, K., 149, 601, 606, 625
Zembylas, M., 375
Zilber, T., xv, 5, 36, 435
Ziller, R., 283
Zimmerman, J. L., 189
Zizek, S., 48
Zurawski, C., 165, 168

Subject Index

Academic disciplines, 53–55
Accountability, 125–126, 312, 521
Actantial model, 393
Acted narratives, 405–406
   biomedical care, illness/healing
      narratives and, 406–408, 410, 411
   clinical interactions, proto-narratives
      and, 406
   cultural script and, 419–420
   desire in, 417
   dinosaur stew therapy case
      example, 412–415
   dramatic time/narrative emplotment
      in therapy, 416–420
   emplotment of action and, 408–409
   healing dramas and, 408–421
   healing dramas, characteristics of, 411
   hermeneutic tradition of philosophy
      and, 409, 410–411
   life story, clinic life/therapeutic
      activities and, 420–421
   meaning in experience and, 407–408
   motive of actors and, 416–417
   patient awareness of healing
      drama and, 411–412
   performative aspect of healing
      and, 410–411
   phenomenological tradition of
      philosophy and, 409, 410
   plot in, 416
   recovery experiences and, 409, 410
   socially shared explanatory models
      and, 408
   suspenseful uncertainties and, 418–419
   time, narrative quality/shape of,
      409–410
   transformation and, 417–418, 419
   trouble/suffering and, 418

Action, 4, 6, 9, 45
   emplotment of action, 408–409
   generative action/achievement, middle
      adulthood and, 191–194
   identity construction, individual
      action and, 85–86
   intentional action, 318
   language use and, 101
   See also Human interaction;
      National identity
Action research. *See* Educational
   action research
Actor-network theory, 393
Adolescent self-narrated stories, 182–187
Aesthetics, 135–136, 206, 215, 218–219, 284
Agency, 86, 87, 130–131, 139
Aliveness of narrative, 247–250
American Educational Research Association
   (AERA), 232, 601, 606, 623
Anecdotes, 584–585
Antenarratological methodology.
      See Critical antenarratological
      method; Living story theory
Anthropological research, 7–8, 11, 26,
      227–228, 406–408
Architectonic dialogism, 349
Archival work, 81
   digital archival research, 87–88
   Dunbar School, archival
      example, 91–95
   E. C. Struggs, interview
      transcript of, 92–93
   ethics considerations and, 556–557
   historical knowledge, particulars/
      specifics and, 83
   history, nature of, 81–82
   identity construction, individual
      action/agency and, 85–86, 87

individual self, modernity and, 83
institutional records, individual voices
and, 90–91
online sources and, 83
oral narrative forms and, 89
ordinary people, disparate voices of,
84–87, 90–91
positivist research vs. narrative inquiry
and, 82–83
post-modernism and, 84, 85–86
Southwest Collection, 89–91
structural functionalism and, 84, 85, 86
understanding stories of past and, 95–96
Uysal-Walker Archive of Turkish Oral
Narrative, 88–89
Vietnam Center/Virtual Vietnam
Archive, 89
William Powell, interview transcript
of, 93–95
Arts-based/informed narrative
inquiry, 203
art/aesthetic experience, definition of,
205–207, 215
arts-based vs. arts-informed inquiry,
213–215
boundaries of qualitative research
landscape and, 219–221
engagement in, case example, 204–205
field text, gathering of, 215–216
multiple aesthetic perspectives
and, 218–219
narrative inquiry landscape
and, 208–213
research text presentation and,
216–218, 217 (figure)
symbolic presentation and, 207
See also Autobiography; Visual narrative
inquiry
Authority:
lived experience, disempowerment
of, 50–51
researcher interpretive authority, 13–14,
68, 101–102, 264–265, 548–554
See also Researcher-researched
relationship
Autobiographical reasoning, 178, 182
Autobiography, 100, 120–121, 229
accountability, radical reflexivity
and, 125–126
aesthetic dimension of, 135–136
agency and, 130–131, 139
art-science enterprise, blurred
boundaries of, 141–142
author, death of, 131

autobiographical understanding,
uniqueness vs. sameness and,
121–122
contingency, retrospective
understanding and, 127–128
forgetfulness, ethical/moral re-collection
and, 132, 138
historical consciousness and, 124–126,
129–130, 140
interior life, focus on, 130–131
memory and, 131–132, 140–141,
408, 493
modern self and, 126–131
mythical worldview, unconsciousness
of personality and, 122–124, 127
narrative-as-fictive-imposition
perspective and, 136–137
narrative dimension/narrative inquiry
project and, 137–142
narrative unconscious and, 139–140
objectivity and, 128–129, 134, 136
poetic project, creation of selves and,
138–139, 140, 142
post-modern personhood and, 131–134
self-knowing, historical understanding
and, 125, 127, 131–132
transcendence/eternal realities and,
126, 127, 130
truth/illusion and, 132–137, 138
unity, search for, 130, 131
See also Life span narrative identity
Autoethnography, 434
Autonomous individuals, 83, 102, 106, 107

Bateson, Mary Catherine, 266–267
Bay School research, 14
Behaviorism, 12, 13, 30, 100
Berkeley Group, 146, 149, 151,
153, 160, 164, 170
Best Practice Research Scholarship
initiative, 319
Bias:
interpretive authority and,
68, 101–102
researcher-researched,
objectivity and, 10
Biomedical care, 406–408
Birth stories, 179, 198
Blurred knowing, 25, 61
culture of laboratories/research
specialties and, 28
decontextualized/encyclopedic knowing
and, 26–27
embodied narratives and, 27

multiple ways of knowing and, 25
narrative inquiry and, 25–28
neopragmatism and, 27
positivistic knowing, challenges
    to, 26–27
science as solidarity and, 27–28
social sciences, resurgence of
    narratives and, 26
validity and, 25, 30
See also Knowing; Narrative inquiry
    development; Narrative
    methodologies
Borderland spaces, 57–59, 68
conceptual cartography and, 37, 42–43
dichotomized human
    experiences and, 58
ethical responsibility and, 61
Marxism/critical theory and,
    47–51, 61–64
personal narratives of inquiry
    and, 58–59
post-positivism and, 43–47, 60–61
post-structuralism and, 51–57, 64–68
tensions/conflicted possibilities and,
    58–59, 60, 62–65, 67–68
See also Narrative methodologies
Boundary concept, 4
arts-based/informed narrative
    inquiry and, 219–221
autobiographical understanding
    and, 141
blurred areas/noise in data sets, 17
bounded researchers/researched and, 10
continuity of experience and, 41
cross-cultural research, language of
    boundaries and, 507–508
non-narratability, traumatic
    boundaries and, 509
pastiche construction and, 589–590
personal narratives of inquiry
    and, 58–59
phenomenon under study,
    definition of, 18
social science research and, 9–10
story boundary recognition
    method, 154
visual narrative inquiry and, 295–296
See also Borderland spaces;
    Cross-cultural narrative
    inquiry; Narrative methodologies
Bracketing device, 469–470
British Educational Research Association
    (BERA), 310, 324
Business conversation, 168

Capitalism, 23, 47
Case study approach:
education and, 621–622
to professional education, 621–622
Categorical content category, xv
Categorical form category, xv
Causal modeling, 17, 606
meaning/interpretation and, 608–609
realist approach to causality, 607
regularity conception of causality,
    606–607
variance theory of causality and, 608
Causation in social relations, 9
Center for the Study of Lives (University
    of Southern Maine), 232
Centre for Research for Teacher Education
    and Development (CRTED;
    University of Alberta),
    x, xviii, 252, 253
Chicago School of sociology, 227
Childhood narratives, 179–182
See also Children's personal narratives;
    Young muted voices
Children's personal narratives, 461
analytical process for, 463, 469–471
analytical results, 471–483
audience, narrator awareness of, 470
classroom interaction and, 461–463
co-construction process and, 476
corrections by narrator, lexical
    replacements/bracketing
    and, 469–470
divergent thematic material,
    interpretation of, 480–483
ethnic diversity and, 466–467
implicit themes in, 477–480
language-social reality reciprocity
    and, 464–465
length/contents of, 471–474,
    472–474 (tables)
Life Report time activity and,
    463–464, 468, 469
local interactive context and,
    475–476, 483–485
narrative, assumptions/definition
    of, 463–465
perspective of the child and, 466
recapitulation of experience, sequences
    of narrative/events and, 467
researcher approaches to, 465–466
sharing-time narratives and, 463, 464,
    466–467, 468–483
situated meanings of narratives
    and, 467

socializing potential of narratives
and, 465, 466
structures of narratives and,
467, 470–471, 474–475, 485
study background, 468
three-dimensional narrative inquiry
space and, 466
understanding children's narratives,
approaches to, 465–467
Child welfare representations, 442
Chronotopic dialogism, 348–349
City Heights School case, 255–259
Civil rights movement, 24
Clandinin, D. Jean, 267–268
Classroom studies. *See* Children's personal
narratives; Curriculum narratives;
Teachers' lives/experience
Co-constructed nature of narratives,
435, 438, 439–441, 476, 548
Coding process, 5
classroom observations, 461–462
numeric codes, experience/
relationship and, 15
See also Data
Cognition:
illness/healing narratives and, 408
language, expressed cognition
and, 12–13
narrative and, 5
Coles, Robert, 264–265
Collaborative living research, 438,
439–441, 476, 548
Colonialism, 36, 51, 59, 311, 342, 343
See also Indigenous perspective
Common sense, 350
Communist Party of Great Britain
(CPGB), 499, 500
Communities, 30, 314
communities of praxis, social
improvement goals and, 315
individualism, authenticated self and, 83
mediated experience, shared reality
and, 44
oral communities, stories and, 331
silenced communities, 50–51
sustainability and, 316, 320
Complexities of narrative inquiries,
268–269, 457–460
ethics issues, narrative inquirers/human
subject agreements and, 269–271
research texts, relational forms of
knowing and, 272–273
truth telling, relational forms of inquiry
and, 271–272

Conceptual cartography, 37, 42, 71
Confidentiality, 541–542, 554
Conjoined narrative history. *See* Storied
experience
Connelly, F. Michael, 267–268
Consciousness:
false consciousness, ideology and,
47–48, 50, 62–63
historical consciousness, 124–126
language use and, 109–110
mythical consciousness, 122–124
Consciousness-raising groups, 24
Constructivist perspective:
discourse analysis and,
150 (table), 151, 153
interviewing technique and, 154, 156
See also Identity construction; Social
constructionism
Context, Research, 443, 555–556
Contextualization, 10, 11
decontextuaized knowledge, 26
experience and, 45–46, 62–63, 70
living stories and, 332, 348, 350
sociality/place dimensions of
experience, 283–284
wholeness of lives in context, 266–267
See also Storied experience
Continuity of experience, 40–41, 69, 228
Contradictions, xiv, 62–63
Conversation, 146
business and, 168
clarity of method in inquiry
and, 154–156
collaborative working
relationships and, 157
constructivist approach to interviewing
and, 154, 156
conversational narrative inquiry,
themes/issues in, 153–166
discourse analysis, theory/method in,
149–153, 150 (table)
education policy and, 166–167
emplotted narratives and,
162–163, 169–171
identity construction issues
and, 159–160
law and, 168–169
learning from conversation, 163–166
medical practice and, 167
policy issues and, 161, 166–167
power-in-relationship issues and,
158–159, 160–161
researcher-researched relationship,
transparency in, 156–159

safety, receptive conversational spaces
    and, 165
social work practice and, 167
story boundary recognition method
    and, 154
story-carrying conversations, 385–386
storying stories procedure and,
    154, 155 (table)
structure in narrative inquiry
    and, 161–163
talking to learn, contextual story of,
    146–148
See also Narrative interviewing
Corporate story research, 343–347
Correspondence theory of truth, 391
Counseling. *See* Psychotherapy professions
Counternarrative production,
    438, 439–441
Critical antenarratological method,
    330, 333–334, 349
Critical realism, 44, 62–63
Critical theory, 5, 333
    discourse analysis and, 150 (table),
        151, 153
    Marxism and, 47–53
    personal narratives, borderland spaces
        and, 61–64
    See also Critical antenarratological
        method
Cross-cultural narrative inquiry,
    162, 489–490
    autobiographic memory and, 493
    biographical objects and, 504–505
    boundaries, language of, 507–508
    cultural/historical context, problems of,
        490–491, 499–506
    cultural hybridization, migrant's
        double vision and, 490, 508
    data, blurred definition of, 493
    ethical universalism, cultural
        positioning and, 496–498
    in-depth life history interviews and,
        491–492
    indigenous communities, divides of
        disadvantage and, 498
    informed consent issues and, 496–497
    interpretive lens in, 509–510
    life histories, cultural practices and,
        493–495
    narrative imagination and, 510
    national identity, politicized narrative
        content and, 499–506
    non-narratability, traumatic boundaries
        and, 509

one-to-one life history method and,
    493–494
other, construction of, 507–510
public access to testimonies, 497–498
self-understanding, larger narratives
    behind, 506
seven-point set of guidelines and, 492
social movements, anti-individualism
    and, 494–495
See also Indigenous perspective
Cultural concept of biography, 182–183
Cultural hybridization, 490, 508
Cultural psychology, 609, 612–613
Cultural studies, 14, 408
    See also Cross-cultural narrative
        inquiry; Indigenous perspective
Curriculum narratives, 362–364
    See also Teachers' lives/experience

Data:
    blurred areas/noise and, 17
    data reduction, 435
    interpretable data, researcher
        authority and, 13–14
    language, expression of cognition
        and, 12–13
    longitudinal data, 23
    numbers vs. word data, 15–21
    recursive knowledge effects and, 45
    standardized collection process, 16–17
    trustworthiness of, 20–21
    validity issues and, 17–18, 20, 637
    See also Coding process
Deconstruction, 393–395, 439
Decontextualized knowledge, 26–27
Deep understanding:
    numeric data and, 16–17, 20–21
    See also Understanding
Democratic forms of life, 311
Descriptive inquiry/research, xv, 16–17
Developmental narratives. *See* Life span
    narrative identity
Deweyan theory of experience,
    38–43, 50, 61
Dialogism, 348–350
Dichotomous thinking, 58
Digital archival research, 87–88
Direct scribing technique, 442–443
Discourse analysis, 101–102
    constructivist perspective and, 151
    critical perspective and, 151
    performative/generative methods,
        150–153, 150 (table)
    post-positivist perspective and, 150

structural/analytical methods, 153
theory/method in, 149–153
See also Conversation
Disempowerment process, 50–51
Disney corporate story, 343–347
Dominant culture. *See* Cross-cultural
    narrative inquiry; Educational action
    research; Indigenous perspective
Dramatic/narrative time, xv, 409–410,
    416–420
Dramatic poetry form, 575–580
Dramatizing narratives, 398–399, 590–593
    See also Acted narratives
Dramaturgy, 398
Dunbar School archive, 91–95

Economic and Social Research Council
    (ESRC), 449
Educational action research, 308
    colonization/reconfiguration of,
        dominant frameworks and,
        311–313
    dominant stories, narrow
        perspectives of, 310–311
    generative transformational
        potential and, 325
    influence, demonstrating validity of, 325
    influence of researcher actions,
        evaluation of, 320–324, 326
    power of the dominant form,
        challenges to, 316–318
    practitioner researchers,
        responsibilities of, 319
    praxis, social improvement goals and, 315
    story content/form, communicative
        adequacy of, 325
    story/knowing, relation to truth
        and, 318
    story selection, decisions/legitimizing
        processes and, 314–315
    storytelling, cultural/editorial politics
        and, 308–309, 310, 312
    validity of action research/research story
        and, 318–320
    validity of practice and, 309
    See also Education research
Education policy:
    case study approach to professional
        education and, 621–622
    conversation on, 166–167
    scientifically based research
        and, 606–609
    See also Educational action research;
        Education research

Education research, 228
    cultural psychology, scientific research
        in education and, 612–613
    education practice, evidence-based
        policy and, 606
    funding of, 606, 625
    narrative research, future
        of, 623–625
    predictability, regularity conception of
        causality and, 606–607
    realist approach to
        causality and, 607
    scientifically based research and, 600,
        601, 606–609, 612–613, 623
    variance theory of causality and, 608
    See also Educational action research;
        Teachers' lives/experience
Elders. *See* Gerontological research;
    Older adulthood life review
Embodiment, xvi
    embodied narratives, 27
    stories, living embodiment
        of reality, 331
Emergent dramas. *See* Acted narratives
Emplotted narratives, xvi, 162–163,
    408–409, 416–420
Encyclopedic knowledge, 26–27
Enlightenment philosophies, 25–27
Enthymeme, 392
Epistemological understanding,
    xiv, 611–612
Equality issues:
    liberation movements and, 23–24
    See also Gender
Ethics, xv-xvi, 46, 61, 537–538
    anonymity in the report and, 554
    archived material and, 556–557
    confidentiality, 541–543, 554
    consent forms, ethical practicalities
        of, 541–543, 544
    continuing relationships and, 545
    contracts, explicit/implicit types
        of, 539, 541, 544
    deception issues, 557
    emergent concerns in ethical
        practice, 646–649
    ethical universalism, cultural
        positioning and, 496–498
    harm potential and,
        543–544, 558
    informed consent and, 270, 496–497,
        540–541, 544, 551–552
    institutional review boards and, 538,
        542, 543, 557–559

interpretive authority, multiple truths/voices and, 548–554
life story interviews and, 239–240
narrative researchers, dual roles of, 538–539
participatory narrative inquiry and, 360
political ethics, 310
power dynamics in research and, 556
reflexivity, interview relationships and, 545–547
relational ethics, narrative inquirers/human subjects and, 269–271, 539–547
reporting on research and, 548–554
research design, social context of the research and, 555–557, 558
researcher qualifications/ expertise and, 544
tensions/dilemmas in research and, 559–560
termination of the interview, debriefing process and, 544–545, 552–553
visual narrative inquiry and, 295–299
vulnerabilities of participants and, 541, 545
Ethnographies, 157, 492
See also Autoethnography; Cross-cultural narrative inquiry; Indigenous perspective; Life story interviews
Evidence-based practice, 438
Evidence-based research. See Scientifically based research (SBR)
Experience. See Ethics; Lived experience; Particular experience; Theory of experience

Facts. See Social facts
False consciousness, 47–48, 50, 62–63
Falsehoods, 46–47
Family story research, 336–343
Feedback loops, 45
Feminist approach, 149, 157, 614–615
Field texts, 5, 215–216, 286, 290, 293–294, 387, 397–398
First Peoples. See Indigenous perspective
First-person stories, 572–575
Folklore, 228, 229
Foregrounding relationships, 267–268
Formalism, 393
Four-cell matrix in narrative inquiry, xv
Future trends. See Narrative inquiry; Narrative inquiry's future trends

Gauck Commission, 495
Gender:
salary inequity, 24
science, gendered nature of, 28
storytelling/narrative and, 24, 190
Generalizability, 5
longitudinal data and, 23
narrative inquiry and, 29–30
power of the particular and, 21–22
social science research and, 10, 11, 12, 15
Generativity, 191–194, 226, 325, 517
Gerontological research, 227
Good life stories, 436–439
Government policy. See Education policy; Policy formation
Grand theories, 16, 22
Grassroots movements, 24

Hauntology, 330–331, 342, 343, 344, 345
Healing dramas, 408–421
Healing narrative, 406–408
Hermeneutic circle technique, 162
Hermeneutic perspectives, 229, 409, 436
Historical consciousness, 124–126
Historical knowledge, 83
Historiographic methods, 5, 86
Homosexual relationship, 190–191
Human interaction:
experience, transactional nature of, 39–42, 69
homosexual relationships and, 190–191
language, expression of cognition and, 12–13
relationship narratives and, 187–191
See also Life span narrative identity; Life story interview; Self; Storied experience
Humanism, 27, 48
Human sciences, 6, 25–28, 601
blurred knowing, validity issues and, 25–28
cultural psychology, scientific research in education and, 612–613
epistemological concerns, interpretive turn and, 611–612
interpretive turn and, 609–610
language/meaning and, 610–611
narrative inquiry research, narrative turn and, 613–615
See also Social science research
Hybridization. See Cultural hybridization

Identity construction, 159–160
national identity and, 499–506
psychotherapeutic practice,
counternarratives and, 438–441
See also Life span narrative identity; Life
story interviews
Identity narratives of organizations,
391–392
Ideographic approach, 100, 225,
226, 230, 233
Ideology, xiv, 47–48, 50, 62–63
Illness narrative, 406–408
Images. *See* Visual narrative inquiry
Imaginary order of subject, 108–109, 115
Imagination, xvi, 50, 129
In-depth interviews, 491–492
Indigenous perspective, 459, 512–514
accountability ethic and, 521
analysis/application, culturally
relevant pedagogical practice
and policy, 525–528
authorial rights/ownership issues,
524–525
colonized communities, mythical
narrative label and, 513–514
comparative analysis of indigenous
narratives and, 516
cross-cultural narrative inquiry, divides
of disadvantage and, 498
cultural truth, problem-oriented critical
design approaches and, 519–520
dialectical/communal process of
indigenous narrative and, 520–522
indigenous narrative, natural
taxonomies of, 515–516, 522–523
insider/native/indigenous scholars,
framing narratives and, 528–530
knowledge, illumination of unique
worldviews and, 522–525
multiplicitous realities,
indigenous/nonindigenous
researchers and, 518–519, 529
oral storytelling, indigenous
traditions/values and, 514–516
outsider narrative, colonizing attitudes
and, 516
participatory indigenous narrative,
generative learning process
and, 517
sacred texts, 521, 522, 524, 529
sovereignty, indigenization of the
narrative and, 517–522
temporal element in, 515, 516

voices of the vulnerable and, 519, 526
Western appropriation of, 514, 515–516,
522, 524
See also Cross-cultural narrative inquiry
Individual experience, 48, 49–51
See also Autobiography; Life span
narrative identity; Life story
interviews; Personal
narratives/descriptions
Individualism. *See* Autonomous
individuals
Informed consent, 270, 496–497, 540–541,
544, 551–552
Institutional narratives, xvi, 90–91
Institutional review boards (IRBs),
xvi, 538, 542, 557–559
Intentional action, 318
Internet resources:
action research and, 317
archival research and, 87–88
Uysal-Walker Archive of Turkish Oral
Narrative, 88–89
Vietnam Center, 89
Interpersonal narratives. *See* Human
interaction; Storied experience
Interpretation, xv, 4, 9
autobiography, objectivity in, 128–129
causality and, 608–609
cultural psychology and, 609
human science, interpretive revolution
and, 609–615
interpretive authority, 13–14, 68,
101–102, 264–265, 548–554
interpretive poetics, listening to
unconscious, 109–110
life story interviews and, 239–240
metathemes, interpretive presentation
and, 593–595
narrative turn and, 613–614
national identity and, 499–506
objectivity/generalizability and,
11–12, 15
social science research and, 601–602
three-dimensional narrative
space and, 20, 21
three-stage method of, 437
trustworthiness of data
and, 20–21
Interpretive poetics, 109–110
Interventionist inquiry, xv, 65–66
Interviewing. *See* Life story interviews;
Narrative interviewing
Intimacy stories, 187–191

Kairotic time, 387
Knowing:
    local knowledge, 30
    narrative knowing and, 6, 7, 14, 18
    narrative modes of knowing
        framework, 100
    paradigmatic knowing, 18, 21–22, 29–30
    positivistic knowing,
        challenges to, 26–27
    relational forms of knowing, research
        texts and, 272–273
    researcher objective authority
        and, 13–14, 15
    self-knowing, historical understanding
        and, 125, 127
    truth and, 318
    See also Blurred knowing; Knowledge;
        Narrative methodologies
Knowledge:
    counternarrative production and, 438
    critical realism, 44
    decontextualized/encyclopedic
        knowledge, 26–27
    historical knowledge, particulars and, 83
    knowledge generation,
        temporality of, 39–40
    lived experience and, 41–42, 48, 49–50
    post-structuralism, narrative structure
        of knowledge and, 52
    power-knowledge relationship, 53–54
    pragmatic view of, 38–39
    professional knowledge landscape,
        366–367
    recursive knowledge effects, 44–45
    See also Knowing

Lacanian psychoanalysis, 105–109
Landscape of professional
    knowledge, 366–367
Language, xiv
    anthropological research and, 7–8
    cognition, expression of, 12–13
    conscious/unconscious aspects
        of, 109–110
    cross-cultural research, language
        of boundaries and, 507–508
    dialogic conception of, 101
    discursive psychology, reality
        construction and, 101–102
    human psychology and, 108
    human sciences, meaning making
        and, 610–611
    number vs. word data and, 15–21

post-structuralism and,
    52–53, 56, 102–103
signifier-signified relationship
    and, 52, 105–109
signifiers of the unconscious and,
    115–117
social realities and, 464–465
sociolinguistic analysis and, 5
unsayable and, 113–115
verbal accounts and, 16–17, 19
Law, 22, 26
    case study approach to professional
        education, 621
    conversation in, 168–169
    judicial biography vs. judicial opinion
        and, 617–618
    legal institutions, narratives and,
        616–619
    legal/literary scholarship and, 618–619
Layered stories, 581–584
Learning from talking. See Conversation
Learning research, 9
    See also Educational action research
Legal institutions, 616–619, 621
Lexical replacements, 469–470
Liberation movements, 23–24
Life narratives. See Autobiography; Life
    span narrative identity; Life story
    interviews
Life Report time activity, 463–464,
    468, 469
Life reviews, 194–197, 227
Life span narrative identity, 177–178
    adolescence, self-narrated
        stories and, 182–187
    autobiographical reasoning and,
        178, 182
    birth stories and, 179, 198
    childhood, joint reminiscing
        and, 179–182
    children's narrative skills and, 180
    cultural concept of biography
        and, 182–183
    disparate events, causal/thematic
        coherence and, 183
    egocentric personal fables, imaginary
        audience and, 184
    gender, narrative content and, 190
    homosexual relationship and,
        190–191
    middle adulthood, generative
        actions/achievements and, 191–194
    mothers' reminiscing style and, 180–181

narratives, characteristics/functions
of, 197–198
narrative trajectories, reconfiguration of,
186–187
older adulthood, reminiscence/life
review and, 194–197, 198
parental teachings, adolescents'
representations of, 184
psychobiographical studies and,
191–193
self-defining memories, 184–185
self-esteem and, 179, 184
self-telling, life story evolution and,
184, 185–186
social/self influence and, 181–182,
183–184, 191, 197, 198
temporal coherence in narratives, 182
young adulthood, intimacy stories
and, 187–191
See also Autobiography; Life story
interview
Life story interviews, 224–225, 491–492
anthropological research and, 227–228
artistic/scientific process of, 236–237
atheoretical nature of, 234–235
autobiographical texts and, 229
benefits of, 235, 237
education research and, 228
ethical/interpretive issues and, 239–240
folklore and, 228, 229
future directions in, 240–241
gerontological research and, 227
historical/disciplinary context
of, 225–230
life story, definition of, 232–234
lived experience and, 230–232
marginalized populations
and, 229–230
methodological bridge of, 230–239
narrative approaches, position
among, 237–239
oral history approach and, 228, 233
personal truth, subjective viewpoint
and, 232
philosophical interpretation and, 229
product of, 237
psychological research and, 226–227
religious functions of stories and, 229
research uses of life stories and, 226–230
sociological research and, 227
See also Narrative interviewing
Life story theory of identity, 177–178
Literary criticism, 6, 9
Literature-based research, 229

Lived experience, xiv, 69
experience, temporal/contextual
nature of, 45–46
impact of narratives on, 5
individual experience, knowledge
generation and, 48, 49–51
number vs. word data and, 15–21
sociolinguistic analysis and, 5
stories and, 4–5, 41–42
theory of experience and, 38–43
wholeness of lives in context and,
266–267
See also Autobiography; Imagination;
Life span narrative identity; Life
story interview; Living story
theory; Memory; Narrative
inquiry; Particular experience;
Storied experience
Living nature of narrative, 247–250
Living story theory, 330–331
common sense and, 350
corporate story research, 343–347
critical antenarratology method and,
333–334, 349
dialogism, types/applications of,
348–350
family story research, 336–343
fragmentation of story fabric and, 335
living stories, aspects of, 331
living stories, definition of, 331–333
morphing of story fabric and, 335, 349
narrativity/antenarrativity and, 331–332
simultaneity of story fabric and,
334, 350
stories, living embodiments
of reality, 331
story fabric and, 332–333, 334–335
systemicity/intertextual environments
and, 332, 348, 350
telling/not-telling, varieties of,
347–348, 350
trajectory of story fabric and, 335
See also Storied experience; Storytelling
Living theories of practice. See Educational
action research
Local knowledge, 30
See also Indigenous perspective
Love story scale, 189

Marginalized populations, 229–230,
442–443
Marxist social theory, 23, 47–51, 61–64
Meaning:
causality and, 609

cultural psychology and, 613
discourse analysis and, 101–102
human sciences, language/
    meaning and, 610–611
illness/healing, meaning-making
    and, 406–408
signifier-signified relationship and,
    108–109
See also Deep understanding;
    Understanding
Medical conversation, 167
See also Narrative medicine
Medical education, 621–622
Medical research, 36, 406–408
Memoir. *See* Autobiography
Memory, xvi, 106
    autobiographical understanding and,
        131–132, 140–141, 408, 493
    limits in, 110–111
    reliance on, 126
    self-defining memories, 184–185
    See also Life span narrative identity; Life
        story interviews
Metanarrative methods, 5
Metaphors:
    narrative inquirers and, 29
    numbers as words and, 19
    photo albums metaphor, 289
    professional knowledge
        landscape, 366–367
    stories and, 5
    wild metaphor, phenomenon
        of interest and, 18–19, 29
Metathemes in interpretive
    representation, 593–595
Middle adulthood generativity, 191–194
Migrant's double vision, 490, 508
Mindfulness, 281
Modernity, 83
Moral stories, 436–438
Mythical consciousness, 122–124, 513–514

Narrative-as-fictive imposition perspective,
    136–137
Narrative couples therapy, 189–190
Narrative forms, xiv, 4, 465
    dramatic poetry form, 575–580
    embodied narrative and, 27
    literary components, analytic tools of, 5
    See also Acted narratives; Representation
Narrative imagination, 50
Narrative inquiry, xiv, 4–5
    co-constructed nature of narratives and,
        435, 438, 439–441, 476, 548

contemporary practices,
    utility/influential power
    and, 615–622
dramatic/narrative time and, xv,
    416–420
education research and, 623–625
feminist scholarship and, 614–615
four-cell matrix and, xv
funding for, 448–449, 606
future influence of, policy/practice and,
    602, 622–626
human sciences, interpretive revolution
    and, 609–615
medical practice, narrative medicine
    and, 406–408, 410, 411, 619–620
narrative, definition of, 428–431,
    464, 604
narrative, method/phenomena of
    study and, 5
narrative, power/pervasiveness of,
    602–605
narrative turn and, 613–614
narrator corrections and, 469–470
natural science research models
    and, 9, 27–28, 448
policy formation and, 625–626
relational endeavor of, 459–460
scientifically based research and,
    600, 601, 606–609, 623
self-insulating habits of
    attention/analysis and, 51
vibrancy of, 625
See also Descriptive inquiry/research;
    Ethics; Interventionist inquiry;
    Narrative inquiry development;
    Narrative inquiry's future
    trends; Narrative methodologies;
    Three-dimensional narrative
    inquiry spaces
Narrative inquiry development, 3, 604–605
    anthropological research and, 7–8, 11, 26
    blurred knowing, validity in human
        sciences and, 25–28
    emergence of narrative inquiry, 5–6
    generalizability assumption and, 29–30
    historical accounts, emerging
        themes in, 6
    intersections of research
        strategies and, 4
    narrative inquiry, stories and, 4–5
    number vs. word data and, 15–21
    objectivity assumption and, 29
    paradigmatic knowing and,
        18, 21–22, 29–30

particular/specific, power
of, 21–24
power negotiation, water image and, 8
public realm and, 30
qualitative research tradition and, 4
reliability assumption and, 29
researcher-researched relationship
and, 9–15
turns toward narrative inquiry, 7–28
See also Narrative inquiry; Narrative
inquiry's future trends; Narrative
methodologies
Narrative inquiry's future trends, 632
emergent ethical practice concerns
and, 646–649
methodological landscape, shifts
in, 637–640
narrative inquiry vs. general qualitative
research and, 633–637
political contexts of narrative inquiry
and, 640–642
professional training for narrative
inquiry, advice on, 642–646
Narrative interviewing, 99
clinical case studies, psychoanalytical
insight and, 100
collaborative/respectful approach to,
100–101, 103–105
conscious/unconscious aspects of
language and, 109–110
discourse analysis, social
activity/meanings and,
101–102, 105
divided "I" and, 111–112
in-depth life history interviews, 491–492
memory, limits on, 110–111
narrative modes of knowing
framework and, 100
narrative psychology, practices of,
99–105
other/address of narrative
and, 112–113
post-modernism and, 102
post-structuralism and, 102–103, 105
repression, shaping of speech and, 110
researcher interpretive authority
and, 101–102
self as narrator and, 102–103, 104
signified-signifier relationship and,
105–109
signifiers of the unconscious and,
115–117
social constructivist stance and,
102, 104–105

story threads in, 110–117
unsayable, languages of, 113–115
See also Conversation; Life story
interview
Narrative knowing, 6, 7, 14, 18
Narrative medicine, 619–620
Narrative methodologies, 35–38
academic disciplines, social production
and, 53–55
blurred knowing and, 25–28, 61
border conditions, intersections of
theories and, 43–57
borderland spaces and, 57–68
commonplaces/shared
commitments in, 69–70
conceptual cartography and, 37, 42, 71
Deweyan theory of experience and,
38–43, 50, 61
divergent strands in, 37
experience, temporal/contextual nature
of, 45–46, 69–70
ideology, false consciousness and,
47–48, 50, 62–63
individual experience, knowledge
generation and, 48, 49–51
Marxism/critical theory and,
47–51, 61–64
post-positivism and, 43–47, 60–61
post-structuralism and, 51–57, 64–68
reconstruction of experience,
social/cultural influence and,
55–56, 66–67
recursive knowledge effects and, 44–45
self-insulating habits of
attention/analysis and, 51, 66
semiotic theories and, 56–57
storied experiences and, 37–38
tensions/conflicted possibilities and,
58–59, 60, 62–65, 67–68
transactional experience
and, 39, 42–43
universal narrative structures
and, 60–61
See also Narrative inquiry; Narrative
inquiry development; Narrative
inquiry's future trends
Narrative modes of knowing
framework, 100
Narrative psychology. *See* Narrative
interviewing
Narrative temporality, 182, 387
Narrative therapy, 22, 99–105
co-constructed nature of
narratives and, 435

collaborative living research, 438–439
couples therapy, 189–190
See also Narrative interviewing;
    Psychotherapy professions
Narrative unity, 130, 131, 267
Natality concept, 315
National Academy of Education, 601
National identity, 499–506
National Institutes of Health
    (NIH), 161, 448
National Research Council (NRC),
    600, 601, 606, 623, 624
Native scholars. *See* Indigenous perspective
Natural science research models,
    9, 27–28, 448, 608, 612
Neopositivism, 14
Neopragmatism, 27
No Child Left Behind (NCLB)
    Act of 2001, 600, 623–624
Nomothetic purpose, 225
Non-narratability problems, 459, 509
Numeric data, 15–16, 29
    blurred knowing, validity and, 25–28
    counting, limitations of, 18–19, 30
    limited/untrustworthy representation
       and, 20–21
    linguistic properties of, 19
    probability/norm curves and, 19
    sterility of numbers as discourse
       and, 17–19
    verbal accounts/personal descriptions
       and, 16–17, 19

Objectivity:
    autobiography and, 128–129, 134, 136
    humanists and, 27
    researcher-researched
       relationship and, 29
    social science research and, 9, 10,
       11–12, 15, 26–28
    See also Numeric data; Post-positivism;
       Quantitative research
Older adulthood life review, 194–197, 198
    See also Gerontological research; Life
       span narrative identity
One Hour for America event, 504, 505–506
One-to-one life history method, 493–494
Online archival sources, 83
Oppressive systems:
    ideology, false consciousness
       and, 47–48, 50
    institutionalized oppression, 63–64
    Marxist social theory and, 47–51
    speech, repressive shaping of, 110

storytelling, empowerment and, 61–62
    transformation of oppressors and, 62
Oral history approach, 228
Oral narrative forms, 89
Organization studies, 383–385
    blurred genre boundaries and, 395–396
    collection/circulation of narratives
       and, 388–390
    deconstruction/reconstruction
       and, 393–395
    dramatizing narratives and, 398–399
    field narratives and, 397–398
    field stories, fiction vs.
       fiction-like and, 397
    historiographic forms, story making
       and, 387
    identity narratives and, 391–392
    narrative analysis, organization
       theory and, 399
    organizational performance,
       narratological perspective and, 388
    petrification of narratives and, 390
    production of narratives, story-carrying
       conversation and, 385–388
    prompts for narratives and, 390–391
    reading of narratives and, 391–396
    rhetorical analysis and, 392–393
    sensemaking, retrospective
       process of, 387–388
    structural analysis and, 393
    writing, narrative approach to, 397–399
    See also Acted narratives; Corporate
       story research
Other, 86
    construction of, 507–510
    narrative receiver, 112–113
    See also Cross-cultural narrative
       inquiry; Indigenous perspective
Ownership of stories, 26, 30, 457–459,
    524–525, 548, 549–550

Paley, Vivian Gussin, 263–264
Paradigmatic knowing,
    18, 21–22, 29–30
Participants:
    co-constructed nature of narratives
       and, 435
    inquirer-subject agreements and,
       269–271
    researcher-researched relationship
       and, 9–15
    See also Ethics; Narrative inquiry;
       Researcher-researched relationship;
       Researchers

Particular experience, 21
fact-law relationship and, 22
generalizability, power of the particular
and, 21–22, 23, 29–30
grand theories and, 22
historical knowledge and, 83
local knowledge and, 30
social conditions/movements,
understanding of, 22–24
See also Autobiography
Pastiche construction, 586–590
Patriarchy, 36, 51, 59
Personal narratives/descriptions,
16–17, 19, 24, 61–62
See also Acted narratives;
Autobiography; Children's
personal narratives; Life span
narrative identity; Life story
interview; Lived experience; Living
story theory; Storied experience
Petrification of narratives, 390
Phenomenological approach,
39, 102, 409
Philosophical interpretation, 229
Photographic research texts. *See* Visual
narrative inquiry
Phototherapy techniques, 283, 289
Physical science research. *See* Natural
science research
Piaget, Jean, 16
Place:
as part of narrative inquiry
commonplaces, 69–70
three-dimensional narrative inquiry
space and, 20, 21, 283–284, 285,
286, 293, 302, 466
Poetic form in representation,
575–580
Poetic science, 142
Poetics. *See* Interpretive poetics
Poiesis, 129, 138
Policy formation, 314–315,
623, 625–626
narrative inquiry and, 625–626
scientifically based research and,
600, 601, 606–609, 623
See also Education research
Policy studies, 161, 166–167, 311
Political discourse theories, 163
Political narratives of teaching, 376–377
Politics of narratives, 309, 310, 314–315,
442, 640–642
See also Power

Polyphonic dialogism, 348
Positivistic perspective,
4, 6, 9, 15, 23, 43–44
blurred knowing, validity in human
sciences and, 25–28
challenges to, 26–27, 614
generalizability and, 29–30
liberation movements and, 23–24
validity/true beliefs and, 30
See also Narrative inquiry development;
Narrative methodologies;
Post-positivism
Post-modernism, 14
historical context and, 84, 85–86
personhood, perceptions of, 131–134
post-modern subject, 107
self, idea of, 102
Post-positivism, 4
borderland spaces and, 60–61
discourse analysis and,
150, 150 (table), 153
narrative inquiry and, 43–47
Post-structuralism, xiv, 14
borderland spaces and, 64–68
deconstruction and, 393–395
narrative inquiry and, 51–57
narrative interviewing and, 102–103
Power:
conversational studies, power in
relationship and, 158–159, 160–161
editorial politics, 309, 312
hegemonizing power of dominant
stories, 311–313
identity construction, individual agency
and, 85–86
knowledge-power relationship
and, 53–54
knowledge, symbolic power and, 315
oral history, balance of power and, 233
particular, power of, 21–24
power negotiation, 8
professional storytelling, formulations
about patients and, 444–445
See also Indigenous perspective;
Marginalized populations
Pragmatic view of knowledge, 38–39
Praxis, 315
Privacy issues, 541–542, 554
Professional education practices, 621–622
Professional knowledge
landscape, 366–367
Professional training in narrative
inquiry, 642–646

Proto-narratives, 406
Psychoanalysis. *See* Lacanian
    psychoanalysis; Narrative
    interviewing; Psychotherapy
    professions
Psychobiographical studies, 191–193, 226
Psychology research, 11, 26
    cultural psychology, interpretation
        and, 609
    cultural psychology, scientific research
        in education and, 612–613
    illness/healing narratives and, 408
    life story interviews and, 226–227
    See also Narrative interviewing;
        Psychotherapy professions
Psychotherapy professions,
    426–428, 446–447
    act of telling, purposes of, 430
    autobiographical accounts, 433
    case example literature, 432–433
    child welfare misrepresentations,
        442–443
    co-constructed nature of narratives
        and, 435
    counternarratives, collaborative living
        research and, 438, 439–441
    data reduction in research literature, 435
    direct scribing of muted voices, youth
        narratives and, 441–443
    evidence-based practice and, 438
    exemplars of narrative research,
        435–445
    externalization of problem stories, 439
    good life concepts/moral understanding,
        client-centered therapy, 436–439
    knowledge construction, communicative
        action and, 431
    literature review on, 431–435, 446
    narrative concepts/methods for research
        purposes, 433–434, 435
    narrative, definition of, 428–431
    narrative research, diversity in,
        434–435
    patterns in the literature, 432–435
    pedagogy/professional development
        literature, 433
    poetic representation of therapy
        exchange, 437
    professional storytelling, formulations
        about patients and, 444–445
    standards for good research,
        434, 435
    storytelling and, 430

three-stage method of
        interpretation in, 437
    training programs for, 447–448, 449
Public realm, 30

Qualitative research, 4
    arts-based/informed narrative research
        and, 219–221
    narrative inquiry, distinctive approach
        of, 633–637
    verbal accounts and, 16–17
    See also Discourse analysis; Quantitative
        research
Quantitative research, 4
    number vs. word data, 15–21
    See also Blurred knowing; Qualitative
        research

Race:
    conversation on, 164
    race-based inequity, 24, 59
    science, raced nature of, 28
    See also Cross-cultural narrative
        inquiry; Indigenous perspective
Radical reflexivity, 125–126
Rationalist perspective, 9, 27
Realist perspective, 9–10, 44
Reality:
    discourse analysis, constructed reality
        and, 101–102
    ideological processes, experience
        and, 62–63
    post-positivism and, 43–44
    redescriptions of the
        world, 54–55
    shared reality, 44
    See also Lived experience; Storied
        experience
Real order of subject, 109
Recursive knowledge effects, 44–45
Reflexivity:
    language-reality reciprocity and,
        464–465
    radical reflexivity, accountability
        and, 125–126
    research interview relationships,
        ethics of, 545–547
    See also Educational action research
Relational reverberations. *See* Storied
        experience
Relationship narratives, 187–191
Reliability, 29
Religious function of stories, 229

Reminiscence Functions Scale (RFS), 195
Reminiscences:
  childhood reminiscences, 179–182
  functions of, 195
  integrative/instrumental
      reminiscing and, 195
  legal scholarship and, 617–618
  mother's reminiscing style, 180–181
  older adulthood and, 194–197
  transmission of culture/historical
      meaning and, 196–197
Report writing. *See* Writing
Representation, 35, 567–568
  anecdotes and, 584–585
  appropriation of representation
      and, 458–459
  child welfare misrepresentations,
      442–443
  conceptual cartography and, 37
  creation/recreation of stories
      and, 574–575
  definition of, 568
  dramatic poetry form and, 575–580
  dramatizing narratives and, 590–593
  false representation of experience, 46–47
  first-person stories, 572–575
  language, descriptive function of, 101
  layered stories, multiple meanings
      and, 581–584
  linguistic details/situated meanings,
      system of analysis, 579–580
  metathemes, interpretive presentation
      and, 593–595
  other/difference, modifications
      of, 573–574
  pastiche, weave of co-existing
      meanings and, 586–590
  persona in, 595–596
  post-structuralism and, 52
  pragmatic view of knowledge, 39
  researcher/personal voice, research
      texts and, 574, 575
  research writing, forms/modes
      of, 569–572
  revelation, moments of, 595
  rhetorical forms and, 568–569
  selective representation of experience
      and, 39–40
  vignettes and, 585–586
  voice, purposeful selection of, 575
Researcher-researched
      relationship, 9, 69–70
  atemporality and, 10
  bounded researchers/researched and, 10

  decontextualized findings and, 11
  generalizability of findings and,
      10, 11, 12, 15, 29–30
  interpretive process and, 12
  language, expression of cognition
      and, 12–13
  narrative interviewing and,
      100–101, 156–159
  narratives, engagement with, 14
  object-like research subjects and,
      9–10, 29
  physical science methodology and, 9
  relational view of, 13, 14
  researcher authority, interpretable data
      and, 13–14
  researcher objectivity and, 11–12, 14, 15
  social facts and, 9
  static participants/interactions
      and, 10–11
  subjects' responses, researcher
      shaping of, 13
  transparency in, 156–159
  verbal accounts/personal descriptions
      and, 16–17
  See also Narrative inquiry development;
      Participants; Researchers
Researchers, 4, 5
  co-constructed nature of
      narratives and, 435
  interpretive authority and, 13–14, 68,
      101–102, 264–265, 548–554
  objectivity of, 11–12
  researcher-researched relationship
      and, 9–15
  turns toward narrative inquiry and, 7–28
  See also Ethics; Narrative inquiry;
      Participants
Research texts, 208, 212, 214, 271, 286, 288
  creative field text gathering and
      presentation of, 215–218
  photographic, 294–295
  relational forms of knowing and,
      272–273
Rhetorical analyses in management
      studies, 392–393
Rhetorical forms. *See* Representation
Romantic scripts, 188–191

Salary inequity, 24
Science. *See* Human sciences; Natural
      science research; Scientifically based
      research (SBR); Scientific law;
      Scientific method; Social science
      research

Scientifically based research (SBR),
    600, 601, 606–609, 612–613, 623
Scientific law, 26
Scientific method, 10, 608
Self:
    autonomous self, 83, 102, 106, 107
    divided "I" and, 111–112
    first-person narratives and, 226–227
    illusion of, 108
    narrative-self affinities and, 465
    objectification of self, 106
    self-defining memories, 184–185
    signifier-signified relationship, 105–109
    unity of self, 314
    See also Autobiography; Life span
        narrative identity; Narrative
        interviewing
Self-disclosing discussions, 187–191
Self-insulating habits of
    attention/analysis, 51, 66
Semiotic theories, 45, 56–57, 393
Seven-point set of guidelines, 492
Shared explanatory models, 408
Shared reality, 44, 408
Sharing-time narratives. *See* Children's
    personal narratives
Signifier-signified relationship, 52,
    105–109
Signifiers of the unconscious, 115–117
Social change, 50, 63, 315
Social constructionism, 102, 104–105, 149
    See also Constructivist perspective;
        Identity construction
Social facts, 9–10, 22
Sociality as narrative inquiry
    commonplace, 69–70
Socializing potential of narratives, 465
Social justice, xv, 63, 311, 315
Social laws, 9
Social movements, 23–24
Social production, 53–54
Social science research, 6, 9
    causality, meaning/interpretation and,
        608–609
    disenchantment with, 12–13
    findings, context boundedness and, 10
    generalizability and, 10, 11, 12,
        21–22, 29–30
    interpretive tradition and, 601–602
    liberation movements and, 23–24
    narrative ways of knowing and, 25–28
    neutral/atemporal/bounded
        research, 9–10
    objectivity and, 10, 11–12

positivist science and, 22–23, 29
public realm and, 30
solidarity in science and, 27–28
subjects, object-like existence of, 9
unification approach to, 607–608
validity issues and, 13
    See also Human sciences
Social work conversation, 167
Sociolinguistic analysis, 5
Sociological research, 227
Sociology, 26, 42
Solidarity in science, 27–28
Southwest Collection, 89–91
Sovereignty issue, 457–459
    See also Indigenous perspective
Specific. *See* Particular experience
Speech-act theory studies, 12–13
Statistical analysis, 5, 18–19, 29, 30, 310
    See also Numeric data; Quantitative
        research
Storied experience, xiv, 251–252
    being in the midst of, 254–262,
        259–261, 268–273
    City Heights School case and, 255–259
    complexities of narrative inquiries
        and, 268–273
    curiosity, Vivian Gussin Paley
        and, 263–264
    ethics issues, narrative inquirers/human
        subject agreements and,
        269–271
    foregrounding relationships, D. Jean
        Clandinin/F. Michael Connelly
        and, 267–268
    future inquiry trends and, 273–274
    knowing through relationship
        and, 261–262
    learning through wakefulness to
        relationship and, 256–259
    living nature of narrative and,
        247–250
    metaphor of story and, 5
    narrative analysis and, xiv, 4–5
    narrative authority, Robert Coles
        and, 264–265
    ownership of stories and, 26, 30
    relationships,
        reflections/conversations/actions
        and, 263–268
    research texts, relational forms of
        knowing and, 272–273
    social realities, reflection of, 41–42
    stories to live by, and narrative
        identity, 166, 303

storying/restorying experiences,
  evolving process of, 252–254
T. P. Yaeger Middle School case and,
  259–262
transactional experience and,
  39, 42–43
truth telling, relational forms
  of inquiry and, 271–272
wholeness of lives in context, Mary
  Catherine Bateson and, 266–267
  See also Imagination; Lived experience;
    Memory; Narrative methodologies;
    Representation; Theory of
    experience
Story boundary recognition, 154
Storying stories procedure, 154,
  155 (table)
Storytelling, xiv, 5, 24, 36, 100
  aliveness of the narrative and, 247–250
  empowerment and, 61–62
  generation of new stories and, 62
  narrative, definition of, 428–431
  oppressors, transformation of, 62
  professional storytelling, formulations
    about patients and, 444–445
  psychotherapy practice and, 430
  story-carrying conversations, 385–387
  See also Acted narratives; Conversation;
    Educational action research; Life
    story interviews; Living story
    theory; Narrative interviewing
Structural analysis, 393
Structural functionalism, 84, 85, 86
Stylistic dialogism, 348, 349
Subject, 108
  imaginary order and, 108–109, 115
  real order and, 109
  signifiers/signifying chain and, 109, 115
  signifiers of the unconscious
    and, 115–117
  subject-object split, 137
  symbolic order and, 108
  See also Signifier-signified relationship
Surveys, 5, 17
Sustainability, 316, 320
Symbolic order of subject, 108
Symbolic power, 315
Symbolic presentation, 207

Talking to learn. See Conversation
Teachers' lives/experience, 357
  complex understanding, everyday
    reality and, 360–361

continuing professional
  development/school development
  and, 373–374
curriculum narratives, 362–364
diversity in contemporary narrative
  inquiry on, 361–373
diversity in teaching, narratives
  of, 371–373
early narrative inquiry on, 359–361
ethical issues, participatory narrative
  inquiry, 360
evolving forms of narrative inquiry
  and, 375–376
multivocal/multisensual nature
  of, 375–376
narrative understanding of teaching
  and, 358–361
personal/political narratives and,
  376–377
practical deliberation, curriculum
  development and, 358–359
professional knowledge landscape,
  knowledge-context interaction
  and, 366–367
restorying of practice and, 371
rhythm in teaching and, 361
school change/reform narratives,
  367–371
teacher knowledge, organization of, 360
teacher life story/voice/identity and,
  364–366
thought/action,
  interconnected/complementary
  nature of, 360
transformation stories, future narrative
  inquiry and, 373–377
  See also Educational action research;
    Education research
Temporal coherence in narratives, 182, 387
Temporality of experience, 40–41, 45–46,
  69, 283, 409–410
Temporality of knowledge generation,
  39–40, 45
Tensions in understanding. See Narrative
  methodologies
Theories of practice. See Educational
  action research
Theory of emplotment, 162–163
Theory of experience, 38–39, 61
  continuity of experience and,
    40–41, 69
  selective representation of
    experience and, 39–40

storied experiences, reflection of
social realities and, 41–42
stretch of experience and, 41
temporality in knowledge
generation and, 40
transactional nature of
experience and, 39, 41
See also Narrative methodologies
Therapy. *See* Acted narratives; Narrative
therapy; Psychotherapy professions
Thing-in-itself concept, 39
Three-dimensional narrative inquiry
spaces, xv, 20, 21, 466
T. P. Yaeger Middle School case,
259–262
Transactional experience, 39–43, 69
Trends in inquiry. *See* Narrative inquiry;
Narrative inquiry's future trends
Truth:
autobiographical understanding
and, 132–137, 138
correspondence theory of, 391
intentional action and, 318
knowing, relation to truth and, 318
narrative truth, 136
personal experience and, 65
personal truth, subjective
viewpoint and, 232
positivistic research, true
beliefs and, 30
regions of truth, 137
relational forms of inquiry,
truth telling and, 271–272
universal truth, 16, 22, 30, 60
See also Representation
Truth and Reconciliation Commission
(TRC; South Africa), 497–498

Unconscious:
language use and, 109–110
mythical worldview, unconsciousness
of personality and, 122–124
narrative unconscious, 139–140
signifiers of, 115–117
Understanding, 4, 5, 9
blurred knowing, validity in human
sciences and, 25–28
children's narratives, 465–467
deep understanding, numeric data
and, 16–17, 20–21
generalizability and, 15
lived experience and, 41–42
personal stories and, 16–17, 19, 24

power of the particular and, 21–24, 30
research goal of, 15, 459
stories of the past and, 95–96
tensions in, xiv
See also Autobiography; Knowing;
Knowledge
Unity. *See* Narrative unity
Universal narrative structures, 60–61
Universal truth, 16, 22, 30, 60
Unsayables, 113–115, 204
Uysal-Walker Archive of Turkish Oral
Narrative (U-W ATON), 88–89

Validity, 17–18, 20
action research, internal validity
and, 318–320
blurred knowing and, 25, 30
intentional action and, 318
researcher/research status and, 310–311
validity of practice, 309
Variance theory of causality, 608
Verbal accounts, 16–17, 19
Video Intervention/Prevention
Assessment (VIA), 289
Vietnam Center (Texas Tech University), 89
Vignettes, 585–586
Virtual Vietnam Archive, 89
Visual narrative inquiry, 280
being in the midst of lived
space and, 293–294
boundary issue of, 295–296
collaborative process of, 290–294
collecting photographs and, 291
composites, construction of, 293–294
conversing with photographs and,
292–293
creating photographs and, 291
ethical issues in, 295–299
example of, 299–303
genres of photographs in, 290
living visual narrative, intentional
relational moves and, 284–285
narrative beginnings and, 281
other inquirers in, 288–289
photographic research texts and, 294
sociality/place dimensions and, 283–284
techniques of, 285–287
temporal dimension and, 283
theoretical sources of, 287–288
visual in narrative inquiry, definition
of, 281–287
See also Arts-based/informed
narrative inquiry

Whole content category, xv
Whole form category, xv
Wholeness of lives in
    context, 266–267
Wild metaphor,
    18–19, 29
Wilda living story, 336–343
Women for Peace, 495
Women's movement, 24
World Bank study, 405–406
Writing:
    ethical issues in, 548–554

organization studies writing, narrative
    approach to, 397–399
research writing, representational
    forms and, 569–572

Young adulthood intimacy stories,
    187–191
Young muted voices, 442–443
    See also Children's personal narratives;
        Young adulthood intimacy stories

Zone of proximal development, 149

About the Editor

D. Jean Clandinin is Professor and Director of the Centre for Research for Teacher Education and Development at the University of Alberta. She is a former teacher, counselor, and psychologist. She is coauthor with F. Michael Connelly of four books and many chapters and articles. Their book *Narrative Inquiry* was published in 2000. She also authored a book based on her doctoral research and coauthored a book based on research from an experimental teacher education program. Her most recent coauthored book, *Composing Diverse Identities: Narrative Inquiries Into the Interwoven Lives of Children and Teachers*, drew on several years of her research with children and teachers in urban schools. She is part of an ongoing inquiry into teacher knowledge and teachers' professional knowledge landscapes. She is past Vice President of Division B of the American Educational Research Association (AERA) and is the 1993 winner of AERA's Early Career Award. She is the 1999 winner of the Canadian Education Association Whitworth Award for educational research. She was awarded the Division B Lifetime Achievement Award in 2002 from AERA. She is a 2001 winner of the Kaplan Research Achievement Award, the University of Alberta's highest award for research, and a 2004 Killam Scholar at the University of Alberta.

About the Contributors

Molly Andrews is Reader in Sociology and Codirector of the Centre for Narrative Research (www.uel.ac.uk/cnr/index.htm) at the University of East London, London, England. Her research interests include the psychological basis of political commitment; the psychological challenges posed by societies in times of acute political change; the psychology of patriotism; the politics of remembering and its relationship to told and untold stories; gender and aging; and counternarratives. She is the author of *Lifetimes of Commitment: Aging, Politics, Psychology* (1991) and *Shaping History: Narratives of Political Change* (in press) and is coeditor of *Lines of Narrative* (2000), *Considering Counternarratives* (2005), and *Doing Narrative Research* (in press).

Robert Atkinson is Professor of Human Development and the Director of the Center for the Study of Lives at the University of Southern Maine, where, with the help of his graduate students, he has built up an archive of more than 500 life stories. He is the author or coauthor of six books, including *The Life Story Interview* (1998), *The Gift of Stories: Practical and Spiritual Applications of Autobiography, Life Stories, and Personal Mythmaking* (1995), and *The Teenage World: Adolescent Self-Image in Ten Countries* (1988), as well as more than two dozen articles. His primary research areas are life stories, autobiography, personal narratives, and adult psychospiritual development. He received his PhD in cross-cultural human development from the University of Pennsylvania; has a background in philosophy, folklore, and counseling; and was a postdoctoral research fellow at the University of Chicago.

Hedy Bach is a freelance scholar in curriculum studies and teacher education. She was a 1995–1997 Killiam Scholar at the University of Alberta. Her doctoral dissertation, *A Visual Narrative Concerning Curriculum, Girls, Photography, Etc.*, was published in 1998 by the International Institute for Qualitative Methodology. She was the Horowitz Teacher Education Research Scholar at the Centre for Research for Teacher Education and Development. In keeping with her research interests in photography, visual narrative inquiry, identity, and visuality, she continues to pay attention to evaded experiences in the lives of children and youth. She has researched and written widely on issues of gender, sensory knowing, visuality, and the evaded in curriculum and educational research. She received the William Hardy Alexander award for her excellence in sessional teaching at the University of Alberta and continues to provide workshops and teach visual studies curricula and visual research methods.

Jenna Baddeley is a doctoral candidate in clinical and social psychology at the University of Texas at Austin. She received her master's from Connecticut College, where her research focused on the telling and reception of narratives of bereavement.

Maenette K. P. Benham, a Native Hawaiian scholar and teacher, is Professor in the Department of Educational Administration at Michigan State University. As a scholar, mentor, and teacher, her inquiry centers on the nature of engaged and collective educational leadership, the wisdom of knowing and praxis of social justice envisioned and enacted by indigenous communities, and the effects of educational policy on native/indigenous people. She is the author of numerous articles and books on these topics, including *Culture and Educational Policy in Hawai'i: The Silencing of Native Voices; Let My Spirit Soar! The Narratives of Diverse Women in School Leadership* (Corwin Press); *Indigenous Educational Models for Contemporary Practice: In Our Mother's Voice; The Renaissance of American Indian Higher Education: Capturing the Dream;* and *Case Studies for School Administrators: Managing Change in Education.*

David M. Boje is Professor in the Management Department at New Mexico State University. His main research is the interplay of story, strategy, and systemic complexity. His books include *Managing in the Postmodern World* (with Dennehy), *Narrative Methods in Organization and Communication Research,* and the just released *Passion for Organizing* (with coeditors). His current book is *Storytelling Organizations* (Sage; see http://business.nmsu.edu/~dboje for online copy). He has published articles in *Administrative Science Quarterly, Management Science, Management Communication Quarterly, Organization Studies, Leadership Quarterly,* and other journals. He is President of Standing Conference for Management & Organization Inquiry (http://scmoi.org), editor of *Tamara Journal* (http://tamarajournal.com), and associate editor for *Qualitative Research in Organization & Management* (QROM). He serves on 13 other editorial boards.

Cheryl J. Craig is Professor in the College of Education at the University of Houston. Her narrative inquiries appear in journals such as *Curriculum Inquiry, Journal of Curriculum Studies, Teachers College Record,* and the *American Educational Research Journal.* She is the author of the book *Narrative Inquiries of School Reform: Storied Lives, Storied Landscapes, Storied Metaphors* (2003).

Barbara Czarniawska holds a Science Research Council/Malmsten Foundation Chair in Management Studies at Gothenburg Research Institute, School of Business, Economics and Law, Göteborg University, Göteborg Sweden. Her research takes a constructionist perspective on organizing, most recently in the field of big-city management and finance. She applies narratology to organization studies. Her latest books in English are *Writing Management* (1999), *A Tale of Three Cities*

(2002), and *Narratives in Social Science Research* (Sage, 2004). She has recently edited *Actor-Network Theory and Organizing* (with Tor Hernes, 2005), *Global Ideas* (with Guje Sevón, 2005), and *Management Education & Humanities* (with Pasquale Gagliardi, 2006). She has an MA in social and industrial psychology from Warsaw University (1970), a PhD in economic sciences from the Warsaw School of Economics (1976), and *doctor honoris causa* from the Stockholm School of Economics, Copenhagen Business School, and Helsinki School of Economics.

J. Gary Daynes is Associate Professor of History and Director of the Center for Civic Engagement at Westminster College in Salt Lake City, Utah. His teaching and research focus on the relationship between history, education, and democracy. He is the author of recent articles on the educational theory of Jane Addams and on the value of social networks in educating for democracy. He is currently working on a book titled *On Being Local*. He holds a PhD in American History from the University of Delaware.

Dilma Maria de Mello is Professor at the University of Uberlândia, Minas Gerais, Brazil, where she works in the area of applied linguistics. Her main concerns are with narrative inquiry, arts-based and arts-informed narrative research, language, teacher education, and curriculum. Under the supervision of Professor Antonieta Alba Celani, a well-known professor in Brazil, she completed her MA (1999) and PhD (2005) at the Catholic University of São Paulo. Sponsored by CAPES, part of her doctoral studies (2004) was done at the University of Alberta in the Centre for Research for Teacher Education and Development, supervised by Professor Jean Clandinin. While working on her MA, she had two of her poems about teacher education published in Canada.

Mary Dybdahl currently serves as Principal of the Beverly Hills Elementary School. She began her teaching career in Vallejo, California. She spent 10 years as a classroom teacher in Grades 2 through 5. During that time, she was engaged in many action research projects through the district's professional development center and in conjunction with UC Davis Cress Center. In 1998, she left the classroom to become a reading support teacher and categorical program coordinator. This broadened her perspective on school organization and funding and led to her returning to UC Berkeley to get her administrative credential in 2002. Since that time, she has worked as a site administrator in several Vallejo elementary schools. Throughout her career, she has been an active member of the Learning to Teach Collaborative, a nonprofit organization that promotes and supports classroom-based teacher research. Along with members of this collaborative, she has presented her work at national conferences. The collaborative shared their collected research in a book, *Teacher Research & Urban Literacy Education*, published in 1994. She received her teaching credential and her MA in education from UC Berkeley's Developmental Teaching Education program in 1988.

Freema Elbaz-Luwisch teaches in the preservice and graduate programs of the Faculty of Education at the University of Haifa. Her main research interests are in narrative research in multicultural contexts, the use of personal stories in teacher education, and the contribution of narrative in border pedagogy in situations of diversity and conflict.

Margot Ely is Professor at New York University, with particular interest in thinking about, doing, and supporting a number of ways of seeing and studying people's experiences—ways that she has come to understand fall under the qualitative research umbrella. She finds her greatest satisfaction in seeking and building collaborations that mesh her work into a mélange of research, writing, teaching, community involvement, and social action writ large. While her endless lot seems to be to strive for newer, more integrated, and just professional insights and strategies, she knows that her work rests on the productions of a host of others over the centuries and that much of their work needs conservation. She hopes to enter into some conversations with her readers.

Mark Freeman is Professor of Psychology at the College of the Holy Cross in Worcester, Massachusetts. He is the author of *Rewriting the Self: History, Memory, Narrative* (1993), *Finding the Muse: A Sociopsychological Inquiry Into the Conditions of Artistic Creativity* (1993), and numerous articles on memory, the self, autobiographical narrative, and the psychology of art and religion. He is currently at work on a book titled *Hindsight: The Promise and Peril of Narrative* and has recently sought to complement his long-standing interest in the self with an in-depth exploration of the category, and place, of the Other in psychological life.

Wesley Fryer is an educator, author, and digital storyteller. His blog, "Moving at the Speed of Creativity" (www.speedofcreativity.org), was selected as the 2006 Best Learning Theory Blog by eSchoolnews and Discovery Education. He secured $1.3 million in grant funding for West Texas schools participating in the Texas Technology Immersion Pilot Project in 2004–2008. He was named an Apple Distinguished Educator in 2005. He is completing his doctorate in curriculum and instruction in 2006–2007 at Texas Tech University. He has published numerous articles relating to education and technology integration in *Technology and Learning*, *Learning and Leading With Technology*, *Interactive Educator*, TCEA's magazine *TechEdge*, and the journal *Internet and Higher Education*. He has presented numerous times at national and international conferences and is a vocal advocate in the K-20 edublogosphere for learning as conversation, messy assessment, digital storytelling, and the use of primary sources to study the diverse voices of history.

Sandra (Sam) Hollingsworth is Visiting Professor at the University of California, Berkeley, and Professor of Teacher Education at San Jose State University. She is currently the coeditor of the *American Educational Research Journal (Social and Institutional Analysis)*. A former published historian and K–12 classroom teacher, she has studied teachers' understanding of the equity issues in minority students' literacy development since the beginning of her career. She and several classroom teachers published many articles and a full-length book, *Teacher Research and Urban Literacy Education* (1994). Her latest book, coauthored with Margaret Gallego and published in 2002, is titled *Personal, Community and School Literacies: Challenging a Single Standard*. In all, she has published 22 refereed journal articles,

4 books, 6 book chapters, and 13 monographs. She has given 119 presentations on her work and serves as associate editor on 12 journals. Her after-hours passions revolve around gardening, visual arts, and her five grandchildren.

Janice Huber is Associate Professor in the School of Education at St. Francis Xavier University. Since 1991, she has been privileged to engage in diverse narrative inquires, both as a research assistant on numerous grants coheld by Jean Clandinin and Michael Connelly and within which her MEd, PhD, and postdoctoral narrative inquiries alongside children, families, teachers, and principals were nested. Since her doctoral research, which was collaboratively undertaken with Karen Keats Whelan, understanding identity narratively has continued to shape her research interests. Within each narrative inquiry, relationships with participants, core-searchers, and friends whom she first met or whose work she first learned about at the Centre for Research for Teacher Education and Development at the University of Alberta continue to teach her about narrative inquiry.

Ruthellen Josselson, PhD, is a psychologist on the faculty of the Fielding Graduate University and was formerly a professor at the Hebrew University of Jerusalem and a visiting professor at Harvard University. She is the author of *Revising Herself: The Story of Women's Identity from College to Midlife* (1996), a longitudinal study of women's development based on intensive interviews, and *The Space Between Us: Exploring the Dimensions of Human Relationships* (1992), a phenomenological study of how people connect with each other over the life course. She is also the coeditor of the annual *The Narrative Study of Lives*. Most recently, she coauthored *Best Friends: The Pleasures and Perils of Girls' and Women's Friendships*. Recipient of the Henry A. Murray Award from the American Psychological Association and a Fulbright Fellowship, she is also a practicing psychotherapist. Her research interests focus on the use of narrative to understand life history in a number of populations.

Nona Lyons, Visiting Research Scholar at the National University of Ireland at Cork, has a long interest in narrative, precipitated largely from interviewing her teacher education students, primarily in the United States, to uncover the meanings they made of their experiences of learning to teach. Her work in Ireland has engaged her in a collegewide initiative working with university faculty from across disciplines on documenting their teaching as part of the Scholarship of Teaching program. Her current work focuses on the development of reflective engagement across professions, especially untangling the ethical, intellectual, and epistemolog-ical dimensions of professional growth and development. She is interested in how reflective engagement facilitates change in one's practice and what exactly people do change when they change their practice.

Cheryl F. Mattingly, PhD, holds a joint appointment as Professor in the depart-ments of anthropology and occupational therapy at the University of Southern California. The constant themes in her research are narrative reasoning and the phenomenology of lived experience. For the past 10 years, she has explored clinical practices in a variety of inner-city health care settings in the United States. She is currently conducting ethnographic research among African American children with severe disabilities in urban Los Angeles. She has published extensively on narrative, and she received the Victor Turner Prize in 2000 for *Healing Dramas and Clinical Plots* (1998). She also coedited *Narrative and the Cultural Construction of Illness and Healing* (2000).

Jean McNiff is Professor of Educational Research at St. Mary's University College, Visiting Professor at Ningxia Teachers University, and Adjunct Professor at the University of Limerick. She works nationally and internationally, supporting the enquiries of practitioners across educational sectors who ask, "How do I improve what I am doing?" She writes about how practitioners in all walks of life can produce their living educational theories to show how they hold themselves accountable for what they are doing; many resources are freely available from her Web site www.jeanmcniff.com. She lives in Dorset, on the beautiful south coast of England.

Barbara Morgan-Fleming is Associate Professor in the Department of Curriculum and Instruction at Texas Tech University. Her research interests include classroom performance of curriculum and informal aspects of teachers' knowledge. She has recent publications in *Curriculum Inquiry*, the *International Journal of Social Education*, *Social Studies*, and the *Educational Forum*.

M. Shaun Murphy is Assistant Professor at the University of Saskatchewan. He was an elementary classroom teacher for 20 years in the primary grades. He is interested in the diverse experiences of children and the ways they understand their lives in school. His current research interests focus on the ways children, parents, and school personnel compose curriculum in schools. He understands his research life in relationship with other members of his research community.

Stefinee Pinnegar is a teacher educator in the McKay School of Education at Brigham Young University. As Acting Dean of the Invisible College for Research on Teaching, she is concerned with developing arenas for conversations about teaching and learning research. Her research is informed by her teaching experience, both as a teacher and as a teacher educator. She has worked with linguistically, culturally, and learning diverse students. She is most interested in what and how teachers know as teachers and the research methodologies, such as self-study and narrative, that allow investigation in tacit memory and practical knowledge. She has published in the areas of teacher education, self-study research, and research methodology. She received her PhD in educational psychology from the University of Arizona.

Sandra Riegle is a PhD student in curriculum and instruction, at Texas Tech University. Prior to beginning her studies in education, she completed a master of arts in political science at Illinois State University. She received her BA in political science from Texas Tech University.

Catherine Kohler Riessman is Research Professor in the Department of Sociology at Boston College, where she teaches graduate courses titled Health, Gender, and the Body and Narrative Methods in the Social Sciences. She is Professor Emerita at Boston University School of Social Work and has taught at Smith College. She has authored four books, including *Narrative Methods for the Human Sciences* (Sage, in press), *Narrative Analysis* (Sage, 1993), and *Divorce Talk* (1990), as well as numerous book chapters and articles on narrative research. She completed fieldwork in South India supported by a Fulbright Indo-American Fellowship from 1993 to 1994 on the meaning and management of infertility among women and families. Her current research examines the performance of identity in narrative accounts of disruptive life events such as infertility, divorce, and chronic illness.

Annie G. Rogers is Associate Professor of Clinical Psychology at Hampshire College in Amherst, Massachusetts. Her research and writing traverse two fields: clinical psychology and English literature (poetry). The recipient of a Fulbright Fellowship to study children's experiences of trauma in Ireland and of a Radcliffe Fellowship to write about her research and clinical work, she is the author of *A Shining Affliction* (1995) and *The Unsayable: The Hidden Language of Trauma* (2006). A published poet and watercolor painter, she lives in Ireland with her partner during the summers. She is currently engaged in training as a Lacanian psychoanalyst.

Jerry Rosiek is Associate Professor of Education at the University of Oregon, where he teaches qualitative research methods and the cultural foundations of education. His articles have appeared in leading journals such as *Harvard Educational Review, Educational Researcher,* the *Journal of Teacher Education, Curriculum Theory,* and *Educational Theory.* His current research focuses on the nature and content of teachers' practical knowledge, specifically the knowledge that enables teachers to teach across cultural differences and in unjust institutional circumstances. He has a BS in physics and a BA in philosophy from Texas A&M University and a PhD in education from Stanford University.

Jefferson A. Singer is Professor of Psychology at Connecticut College in New London, Connecticut. He has spent the past two decades researching emotionally significant memories and their role in personality and psychotherapy. He is a recipient of the Fulbright Distinguished Scholar Award, which funded his research on self-defining memories at Durham University in Durham, England. He is the author of four books, *Memories that Matter; Personality and Psychotherapy: Treating the Whole Person; Message in a Bottle: Stories of Men and Addiction;* and *The Remembered Self: Emotion and Memory in Personality* (with Peter Salovey). He served as an associate editor for the journals *Contemporary Psychology* and *Journal of Personality* and is on the editorial board of the *Review of General Psychology.* He is a fellow of the American Psychological Association (APA) and the 2005 recipient of the Theodore R. Sarbin Award for Distinguished Contributions in Narrative Psychology, given by Division 24 (Society for Theoretical and Philosophical Psychology) of the APA.

Jane Speedy is Director of a research center in "narrative and transformative learning" at the University of Bristol, United Kingdom, where she also coordinates a doctoral program in narrative and life story research. She spent her earlier career in special education and has a more recent background as a counselor educator and narrative therapy practitioner. She continues to offer a small therapeutic and supervisory practice. Her current interest is in "troubling the edges" between therapy and research and in the development of new research methodologies, such as visually and arts-informed narrative inquiries, autoethnographies, collective biographies, and writing methodologies. She is widely published in these areas, and her book *Narrative Inquiries in Counselling and Psychotherapy* is to be published in 2007.

Min-Ling Tsai is Professor of Early Childhood Education at National Taipei University of Education, Taiwan. Her interests in classroom interaction and qualitative methodology have been recorded in a book, *Exploring the Rhythms and Variations of Whole Group Interaction in a First-Grade and a Kindergarten Classroom* (in Chinese), as well as in several articles (both in English and in Chinese). As a person who conceptualizes and writes almost everything narratively, she is now a learner and inquirer into Taiwanese children's narratives in various cultural contexts. She received her PhD from the University of Illinois at Urbana-Champaign in 1993.

Guming Zhao is a doctoral candidate with the Center for Research for Teacher Education and Development, University of Alberta. Her dissertation is a narrative inquiry into immigrant children's intergenerational experiences of schools. Her passion for narrative inquiry started when she was doing her master's project titled Thinking and Teaching for a Narrative Perspective. Before pursuing her graduate studies in North America, she taught English as a second language for 12 years in Nanchang Vocational and Technical Teachers' College, Jiangxi, China. She immigrated to Canada in 2003 and lives in Edmonton with her husband and daughter. She earned her bachelor's degree at Jiangxi Normal University, China. She was part of the working editorial group for this handbook.